MW00908261

Integrated Science

level RED

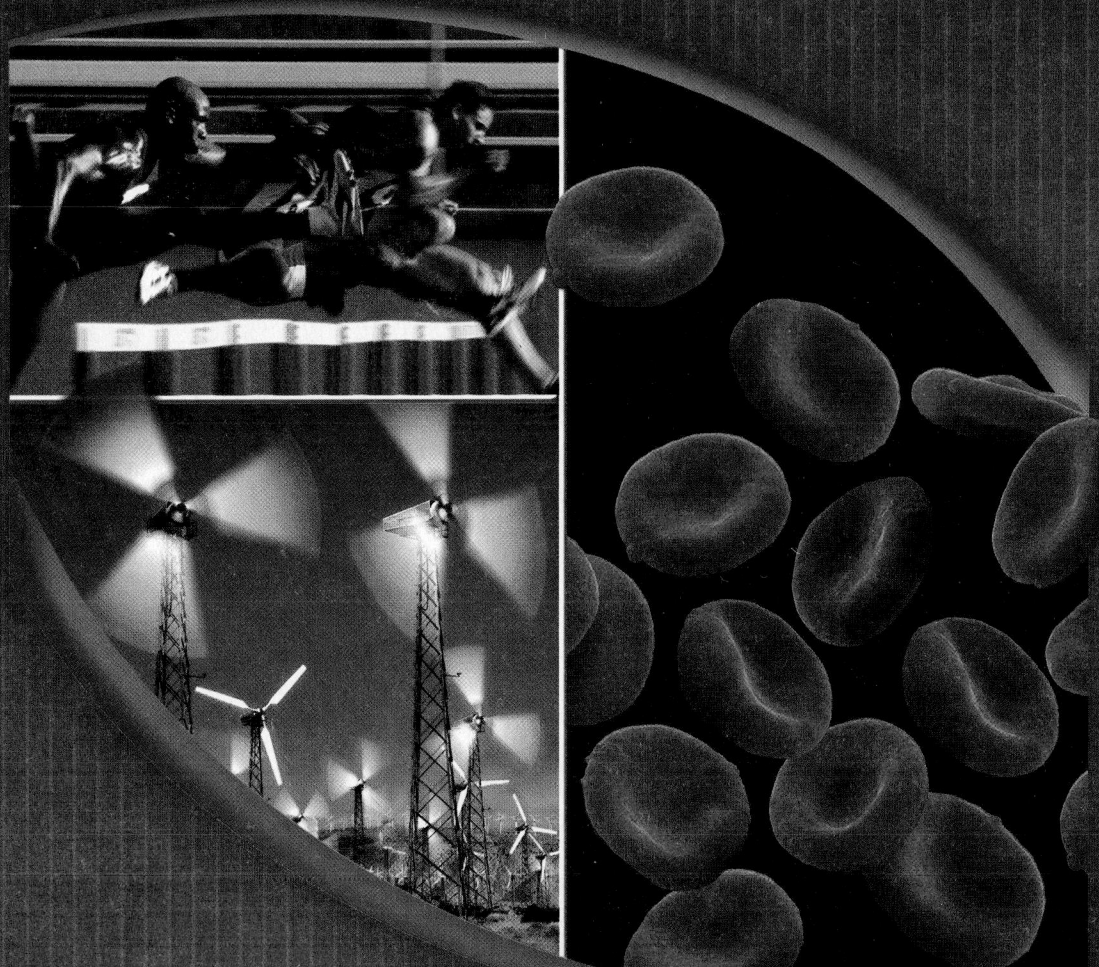

HOLT, RINEHART AND WINSTON
A Harcourt Education Company
Orlando • Austin • New York • San Diego • London

Acknowledgments

Contributing Authors

Katy Z. Allen
Science Writer
Wayland, Massachusetts

Linda Ruth Berg, Ph.D.
Adjunct Professor of Natural Sciences
St. Petersburg College
St. Petersburg, Florida

Kathleen Meehan Berry
Science Chairman
Canon-McMillan School District
Canonsburg, Pennsylvania

Christie Borgford, Ph.D.
Assistant Professor of Chemistry
Department of Chemistry
The University of Alabama
Birmingham, Alabama

Barbara Christopher
Science Writer and Editor
Austin, Texas

Mapi Cuevas, Ph.D.
Professor of Chemistry
Department of Natural Sciences
Santa Fe Community College
Gainesville, Florida

Robert H. Fronk, Ph.D.
Chair of Science and Mathematics Education
Florida Institute of Technology
West Melbourne, Florida

Joel S. Leventhal, Ph.D.
Emeritus Scientist, Geochemistry
U.S. Geological Survey
Denver, Colorado

Peter E. Malin, Ph.D.
Professor of Geology
Division of Earth and Ocean Sciences
Duke University
Durham, North Carolina

Mark F. Taylor, Ph.D.
Associate Professor of Biology
Biology Department
Baylor University
Waco, Texas

Sally Ann Vonderbrink, Ph.D.
Chemistry Teacher (retired)
Cincinnati, Ohio

Safety Reviewer

Jack Gerlovich, Ph.D.
Associate Professor
School of Education
Drake University
Des Moines, Iowa

Inclusion Specialist

Karen Clay
Inclusion Consultant
Boston, Massachusetts

Ellen McPeek Glisan
Special Needs Consultant
San Antonio, Texas

Academic Reviewers

Glenn Adelson, Ph.D.
Instructor
Department of Organismic and Evolutionary Biology
Harvard University
Cambridge, Massachusetts

Mead Allison, Ph.D.
Associate Professor
Department of Earth and Environmental Sciences
Tulane University
New Orleans, Louisiana

Katy Z. Allen
Science Writer
Wayland, Massachusetts

Linda Ruth Berg, Ph.D.
Adjunct Professor of Natural Sciences
St. Petersburg College
St. Petersburg, Florida

Acknowledgments
continued on page 813

Printed in the United States of America

ISBN-13: 978-0-03-095871-7
ISBN-10: 0-03-095871-7
8 9 0914 13 12 4500369301

Contents in Brief

Contents

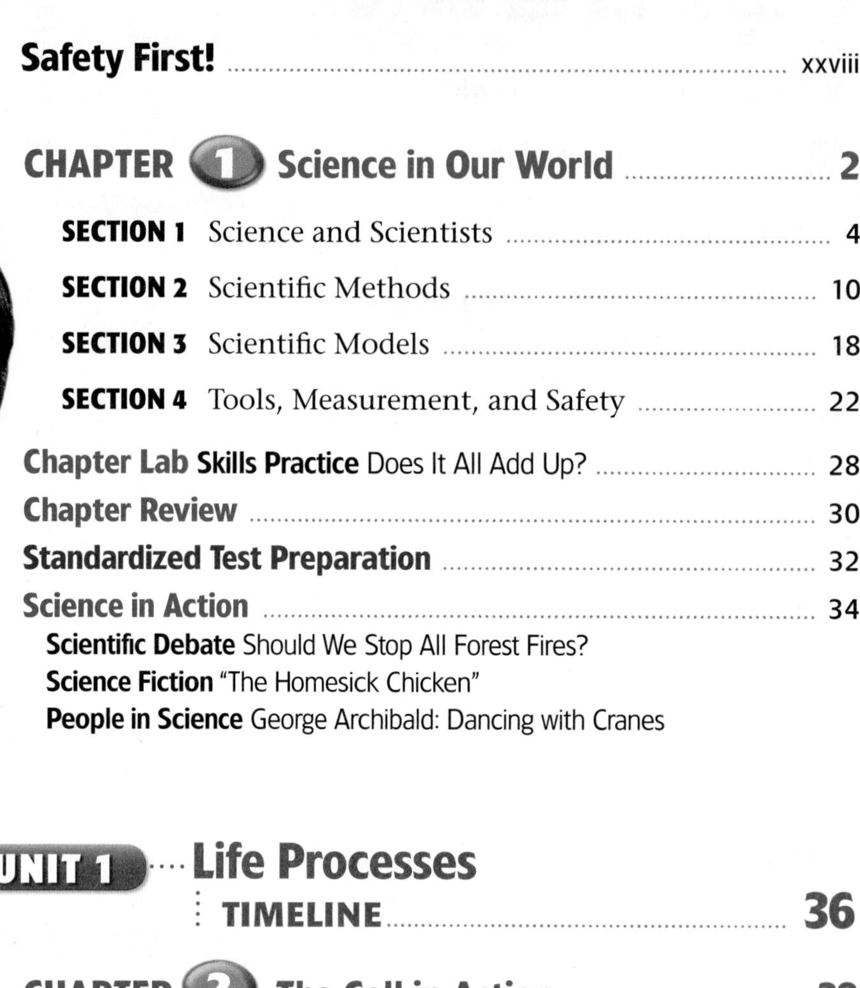

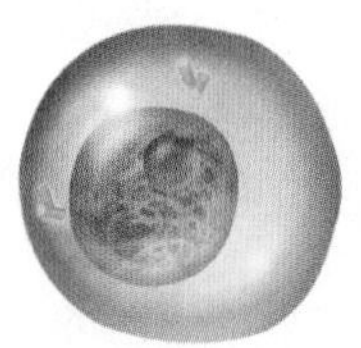
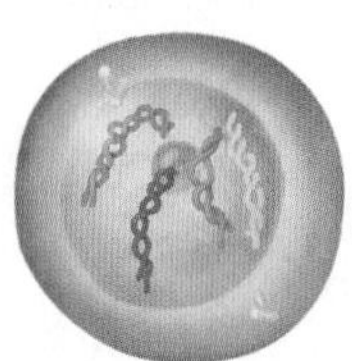

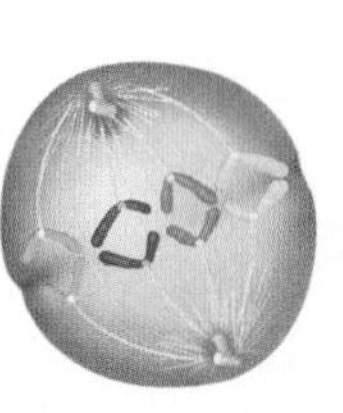
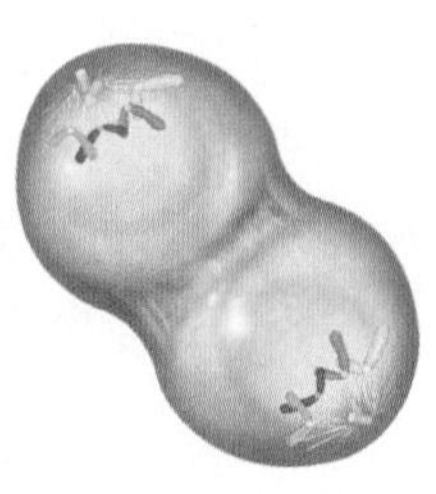

330
0
30
60
90
120
150
180
210
N
E
S
NW
NE
SE
SW

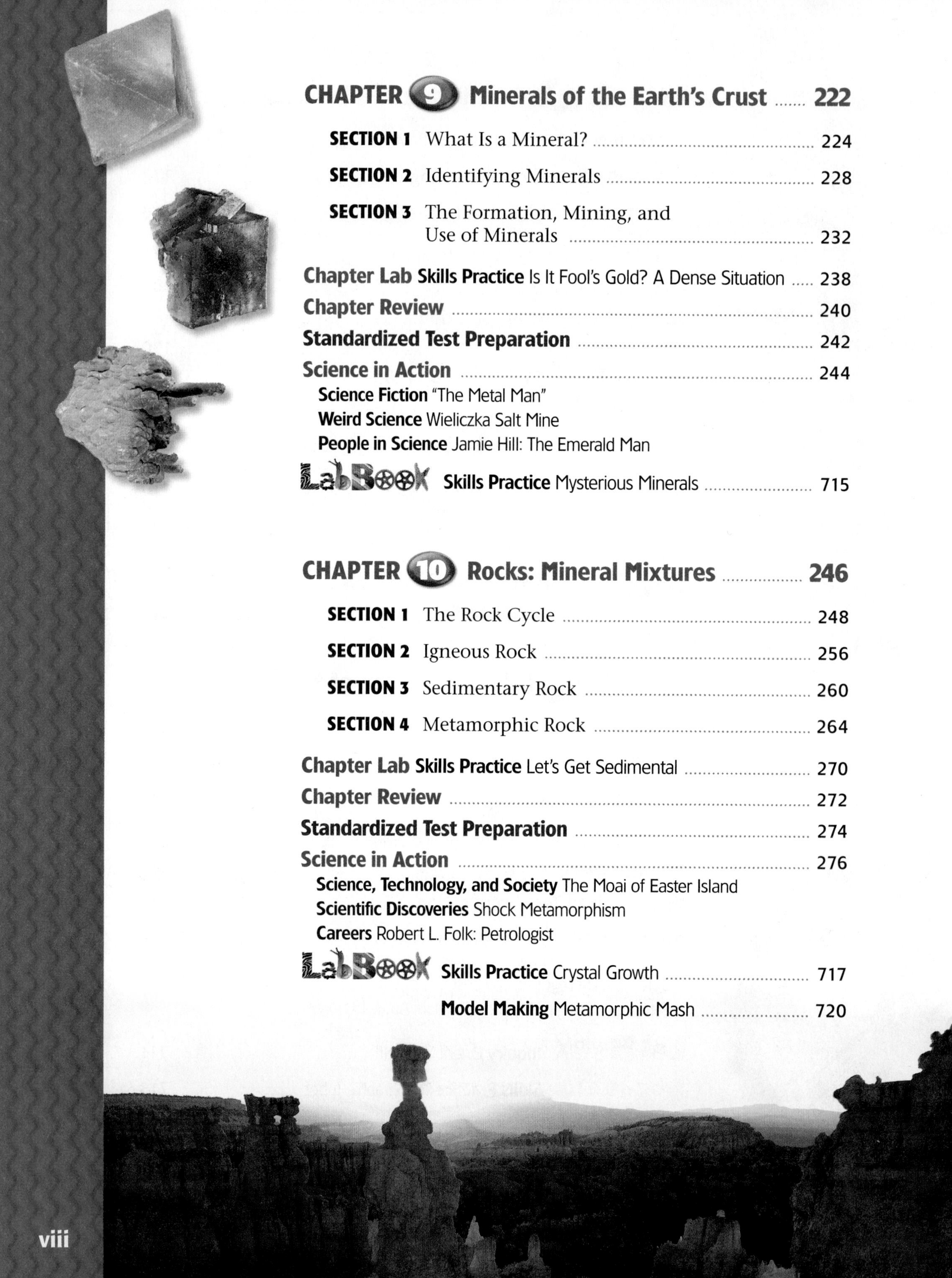

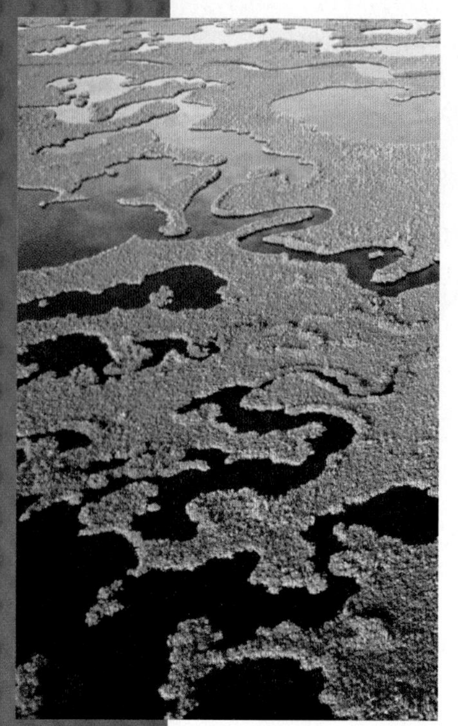

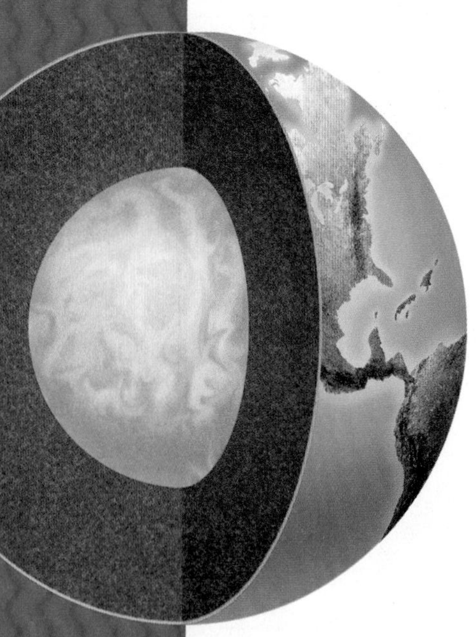

UNIT 5 Matter and Atoms

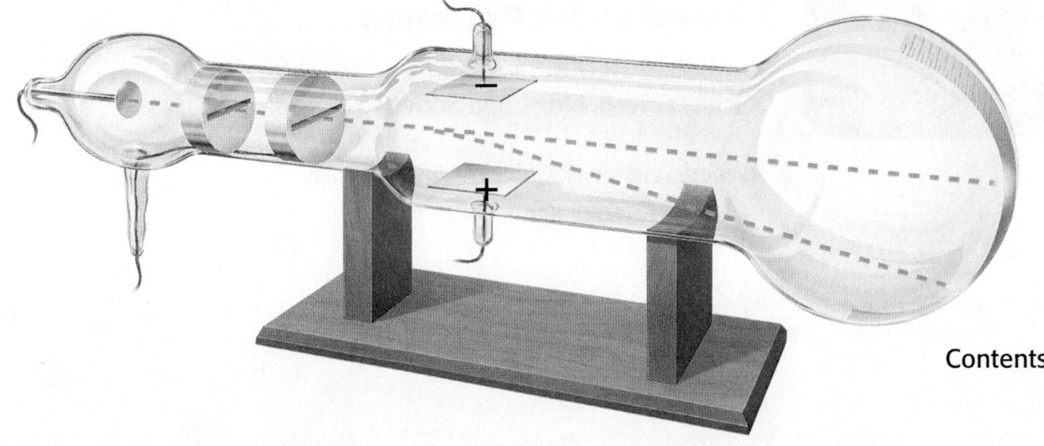

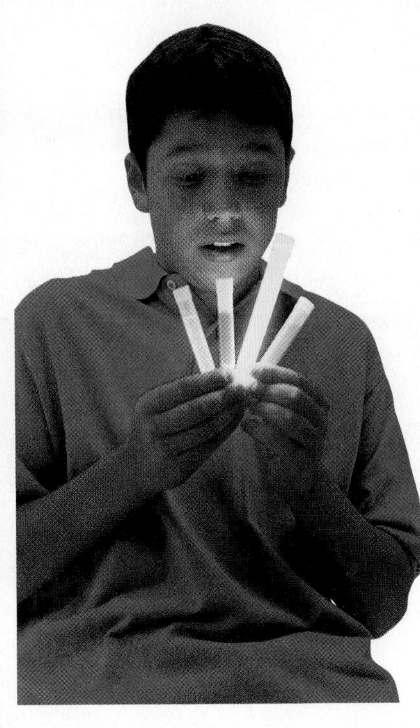

Chapter Labs

Make science a "hands-on" experience.

Each chapter ends with a chapter lab designed to help you experience science firsthand. But please don't forget to be safe. Read the **Safety First!** section before starting any of the labs.

LabBook Labs

The more labs, the better!

Additional labs appear within a special **LabBook** in the back of the textbook. Use these labs to help you extend your lab skills. Don't forget to read the **Safety First!** section before starting any of the labs.

Quick Labs

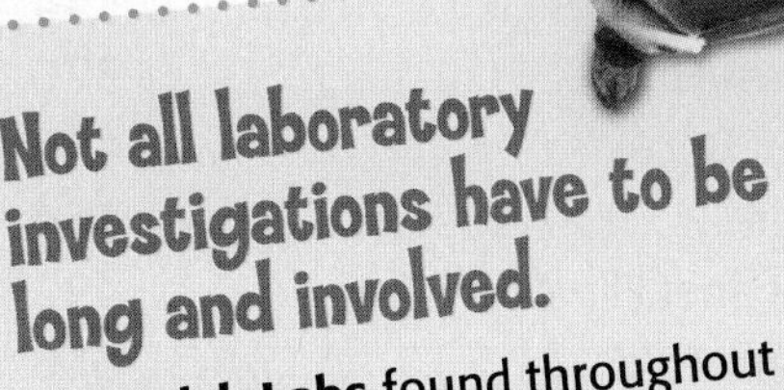

Not all laboratory investigations have to be long and involved.

The **Quick Labs** found throughout the chapters of this textbook require only a small amount of time and limited equipment. But just because they are quick, don't skimp on safety.

Activities

Pre-Reading Activities

FOLDNOTES

Start your engines with an activity!

Get motivated to learn by doing the two activities at the beginning of each chapter. The **Pre-Reading Activity** helps you organize information as you read the chapter. The **Start-Up Activity** helps you gain scientific understanding of the topic through hands-on experience.

Graphic Organizer

Start-Up Activities

Reading Strategies

Remembering what you read doesn't have to be hard!

A **Reading Strategy** at the beginning of every section provides tips to help you remember and/or organize the information covered in the section.

Internet Activities

Get caught in the Web!

Go to **go.hrw.com** for **Internet Activities** related to each chapter. To find the Internet Activity for a particular chapter, just type in the keyword listed below.

School to Home

Science brings you closer together!

Bring science into your home by doing **School-to-Home Activities** with a family member or another adult in your household.

Science and math go hand in hand.

Each **Math Practice** activity contains a word problem related to the topic at hand. **Math Focus** activities provide step-by-step instructions and practice questions designed to help you apply math directly to science.

Math Practice

Math Focus

Connection to...

One subject leads to another.

You may not realize it at first, but different subjects are related to each other in many ways. Each **Connection** explores a topic from the viewpoint of another discipline. In this way, all of the subjects you learn about in school merge to improve your understanding of the world around you.

Science In Action

Science moves beyond the classroom!
Read **Science in Action** articles to learn more about science in the real world. These articles will give you an idea of how interesting, strange, helpful, and action-packed science is. At the end of each chapter, you will find three short articles. And if your thirst is still not quenched, go to **go.hrw.com** for in-depth coverage.

How to Use Your Textbook

Your Roadmap for Success with Holt Science and Technology

What You Will Learn

At the beginning of every section you will find the section's objectives and vocabulary terms. The objectives tell you what you'll need to know after you finish reading the section.

Vocabulary terms are listed for each section. Learn the definitions of these terms because you will most likely be tested on them. Each term is highlighted in the text and is defined at point of use and in the margin. You can also use the glossary to locate definitions quickly.

STUDY TIP Reread the objectives and the definitions to the terms when studying for a test to be sure you know the material.

Get Organized

A Reading Strategy at the beginning of every section provides tips to help you organize and remember the information covered in the section. Keep a science notebook so that you are ready to take notes when your teacher reviews the material in class. Keep your assignments in this notebook so that you can review them when studying for the chapter test.

What You Will Learn

- Describe two ways rocks have been used by humans.
- Describe four processes that shape Earth's features.
- Describe how each type of rock changes into another type as it moves through the rock cycle.
- List two characteristics of rock that are used to help classify it.

Vocabulary

rock cycle, deposition, rock, composition, erosion, texture

READING STRATEGY

Reading Organizer As you read this section, make a flowchart of the steps of the rock cycle.

The Rock Cycle

You know that paper, plastic, and aluminum can be recycled. But did you know that the Earth also recycles? And one of the things that Earth recycles is rock.

Scientists define **rock** as a naturally occurring solid mixture of one or more minerals and organic matter. It may be hard to believe, but rocks are always changing. The continual process by which new rock forms from old rock material is called the **rock cycle.**

The Value of Rock

Rock has been an important natural resource as long as humans have existed. Early humans used rocks as hammers to make other tools. They discovered that they could make arrowheads, spear points, knives, and scrapers by carefully shaping rocks such as chert and obsidian.

Rock has also been used for centuries to make buildings, monuments, and roads. **Figure 1** shows how rock has been used as a construction material by both ancient and modern civilizations. Buildings have been made out of granite, limestone, marble, sandstone, slate, and other rocks. Modern buildings also contain concrete and plaster, in which rock is an important ingredient.

Reading Check Name some types of rock that have been used to construct buildings. *(See the Appendix for answers to Reading Checks.)*

Figure 1 *The ancient Egyptians used a sedimentary rock called* limestone *to construct the pyramids at Giza (left). Granite, an igneous rock, was used to construct the Texas state capitol building in Austin (right).*

248 Chapter 10 Rocks: Mineral Mixtures

Be Resourceful—Use the Web

SciLinks boxes in your textbook take you to resources that you can use for science projects, reports, and research papers. Go to **scilinks.org** and type in the **SciLinks code** to find information on a topic.

Visit go.hrw.com
Check out the **Current Science**® magazine articles and other materials that go with your textbook at **go.hrw.com.** Click on the textbook icon and the table of contents to see all of the resources for each chapter.

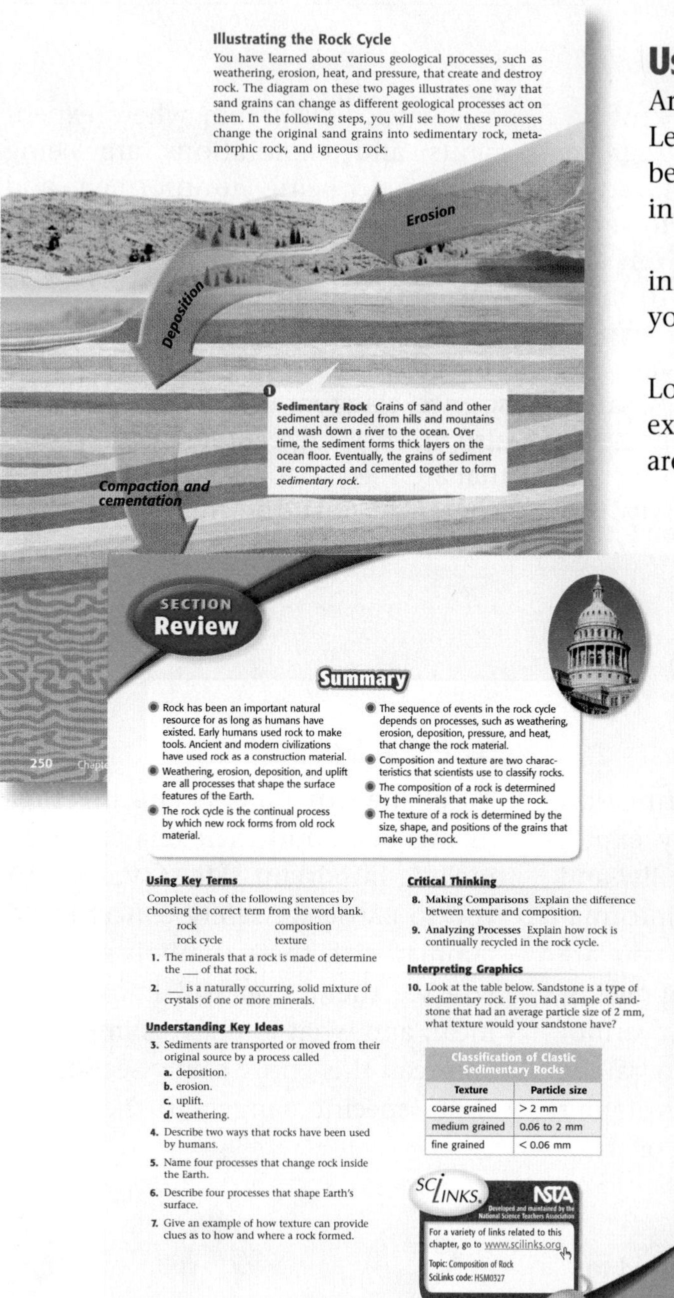

Illustrating the Rock Cycle

You have learned about various geological processes, such as weathering, erosion, heat, and pressure, that create and destroy rock. The diagram on these two pages illustrates one way that sand grains can change as different geological processes act on them. In the following steps, you will see how these processes change the original sand grains into sedimentary rock, metamorphic rock, and igneous rock.

1 **Sedimentary Rock** Grains of sand and other sediment are eroded from hills and mountains and wash down a river to the ocean. Over time, the sediment forms thick layers on the ocean floor. Eventually, the grains of sediment are compacted and cemented together to form *sedimentary rock*.

250 Chapter

SECTION Review

Summary

- Rock has been an important natural resource for as long as humans have existed. Early humans used rock to make tools. Ancient and modern civilizations have used rock as a construction material.
- Weathering, erosion, deposition, and uplift are all processes that shape the surface features of the Earth.
- The rock cycle is the continual process by which new rock forms from old rock material.
- The sequence of events in the rock cycle depends on processes, such as weathering, erosion, deposition, pressure, and heat, that change the rock material.
- Composition and texture are two characteristics that scientists use to classify rocks.
- The composition of a rock is determined by the minerals that make up the rock.
- The texture of a rock is determined by the size, shape, and positions of the grains that make up the rock.

Using Key Terms

Complete each of the following sentences by choosing the correct term from the word bank.

rock composition
rock cycle texture

1. The minerals that a rock is made of determine the ___ of that rock.
2. ___ is a naturally occurring, solid mixture of crystals of one or more minerals.

Understanding Key Ideas

3. Sediments are transported or moved from their original source by a process called
   a. deposition.
   b. erosion.
   c. uplift.
   d. weathering.
4. Describe two ways that rocks have been used by humans.
5. Name four processes that change rock inside the Earth.
6. Describe four processes that shape Earth's surface.
7. Give an example of how texture can provide clues as to how and where a rock formed.

Critical Thinking

8. **Making Comparisons** Explain the difference between texture and composition.
9. **Analyzing Processes** Explain how rock is continually recycled in the rock cycle.

Interpreting Graphics

10. Look at the table below. Sandstone is a type of sedimentary rock. If you had a sample of sandstone that had an average particle size of 2 mm, what texture would your sandstone have?

Classification of Clastic Sedimentary Rocks

Texture	Particle size
coarse grained	> 2 mm
medium grained	0.06 to 2 mm
fine grained	< 0.06 mm

SciLinks. NSTA Developed and maintained by the National Science Teachers Association

For a variety of links related to this chapter, go to www.scilinks.org

Topic: Composition of Rock
SciLinks code: HSM0327

255

Use the Illustrations and Photos

Art shows complex ideas and processes. Learn to analyze the art so that you better understand the material you read in the text.

Tables and graphs display important information in an organized way to help you see relationships.

A picture is worth a thousand words. Look at the photographs to see relevant examples of science concepts that you are reading about.

Answer the Section Reviews

Section Reviews test your knowledge of the main points of the section. Critical Thinking items challenge you to think about the material in greater depth and to find connections that you infer from the text.

STUDY TIP When you can't answer a question, reread the section. The answer is usually there.

Do Your Homework

Your teacher may assign worksheets to help you understand and remember the material in the chapter.

STUDY TIP Don't try to answer the questions without reading the text and reviewing your class notes. A little preparation up front will make your homework assignments a lot easier. Answering the items in the Chapter Review will help prepare you for the chapter test.

Visit Holt Online Learning

If your teacher gives you a special password to log onto the **Holt Online Learning** site, you'll find your complete textbook on the Web. In addition, you'll find some great learning tools and practice quizzes. You'll be able to see how well you know the material from your textbook.

Exploring, inventing, and investigating are essential to the study of science. However, these activities can also be dangerous. To make sure that your experiments and explorations are safe, you must be aware of a variety of safety guidelines. You have probably heard of the saying, "It is better to be safe than sorry." This is particularly true in a science classroom where experiments and explorations are being performed. Being uninformed and careless can result in serious injuries. Don't take chances with your own safety or with anyone else's.

The following pages describe important guidelines for staying safe in the science classroom. Your teacher may also have safety guidelines and tips that are specific to your classroom and laboratory. Take the time to be safe.

Safety Rules!

Start Out Right

Always get your teacher's permission before attempting any laboratory exploration. Read the procedures carefully, and pay particular attention to safety information and caution statements. If you are unsure about what a safety symbol means, look it up or ask your teacher. You cannot be too careful when it comes to safety. If an accident does occur, inform your teacher immediately regardless of how minor you think the accident is.

If you are instructed to note the odor of a substance, wave the fumes toward your nose with your hand. Never put your nose close to the source.

Safety Symbols

All of the experiments and investigations in this book and their related worksheets include important safety symbols to alert you to particular safety concerns. Become familiar with these symbols so that when you see them, you will know what they mean and what to do. It is important that you read this entire safety section to learn about specific dangers in the laboratory.

Eye protection

Clothing protection

Hand safety

Heating safety

Electric safety

Chemical safety

Animal safety

Sharp object

Plant safety

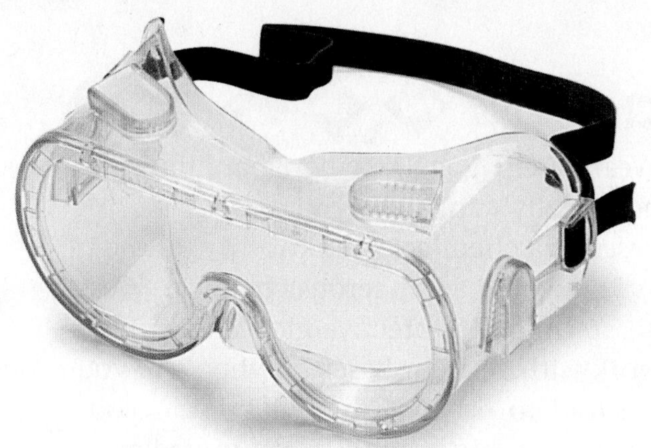

Eye Safety

Wear safety goggles when working around chemicals, acids, bases, or any type of flame or heating device. Wear safety goggles any time there is even the slightest chance that harm could come to your eyes. If any substance gets into your eyes, notify your teacher immediately and flush your eyes with running water for at least 15 minutes. Treat any unknown chemical as if it were a dangerous chemical. Never look directly into the sun. Doing so could cause permanent blindness.

Avoid wearing contact lenses in a laboratory situation. Even if you are wearing safety goggles, chemicals can get between the contact lenses and your eyes. If your doctor requires that you wear contact lenses instead of glasses, wear eye-cup safety goggles in the lab.

Safety Equipment

Know the locations of the nearest fire alarms and any other safety equipment, such as fire blankets and eyewash fountains, as identified by your teacher, and know the procedures for using the equipment.

Neatness

Keep your work area free of all unnecessary books and papers. Tie back long hair, and secure loose sleeves or other loose articles of clothing, such as ties and bows. Remove dangling jewelry. Don't wear open-toed shoes or sandals in the laboratory. Never eat, drink, or apply cosmetics in a laboratory setting. Food, drink, and cosmetics can easily become contaminated with dangerous materials.

Certain hair products (such as aerosol hair spray) are flammable and should not be worn while working near an open flame. Avoid wearing hair spray or hair gel on lab days.

Sharp/Pointed Objects 

Use knives and other sharp instruments with extreme care. Never cut objects while holding them in your hands. Place objects on a suitable work surface for cutting.

Be extra careful when using any glassware. When adding a heavy object to a graduated cylinder, tilt the cylinder so that the object slides slowly to the bottom.

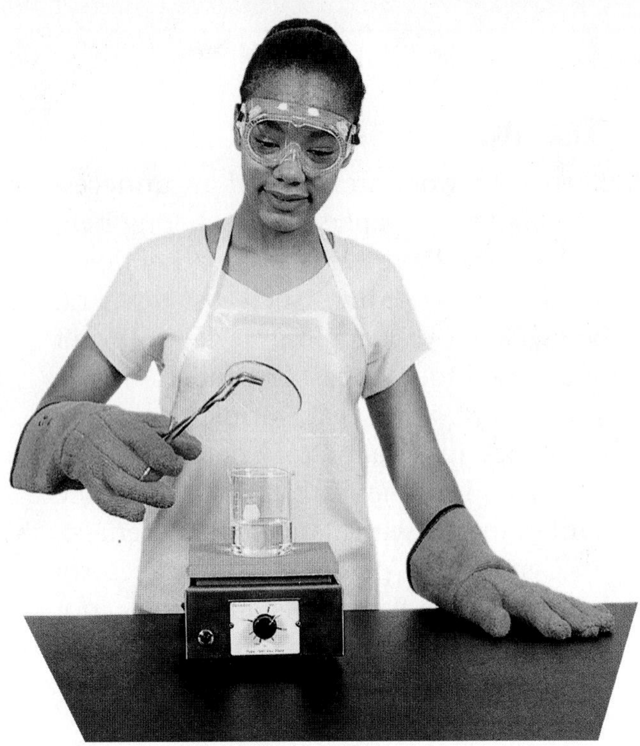

Heat

Wear safety goggles when using a heating device or a flame. Whenever possible, use an electric hot plate as a heat source instead of using an open flame. When heating materials in a test tube, always angle the test tube away from yourself and others. To avoid burns, wear heat-resistant gloves whenever instructed to do so.

Electricity

Be careful with electrical cords. When using a microscope with a lamp, do not place the cord where it could trip someone. Do not let cords hang over a table edge in a way that could cause equipment to fall if the cord is accidentally pulled. Do not use equipment with damaged cords. Be sure that your hands are dry and that the electrical equipment is in the "off" position before plugging it in. Turn off and unplug electrical equipment when you are finished.

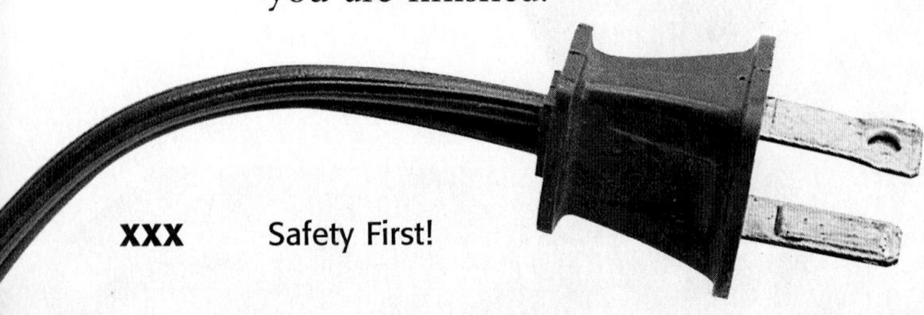

Chemicals

Wear safety goggles when handling any potentially dangerous chemicals, acids, or bases. If a chemical is unknown, handle it as you would a dangerous chemical. Wear an apron and protective gloves when you work with acids or bases or whenever you are told to do so. If a spill gets on your skin or clothing, rinse it off immediately with water for at least 5 minutes while calling to your teacher.

Never mix chemicals unless your teacher tells you to do so. Never taste, touch, or smell chemicals unless you are specifically directed to do so. Before working with a flammable liquid or gas, check for the presence of any source of flame, spark, or heat.

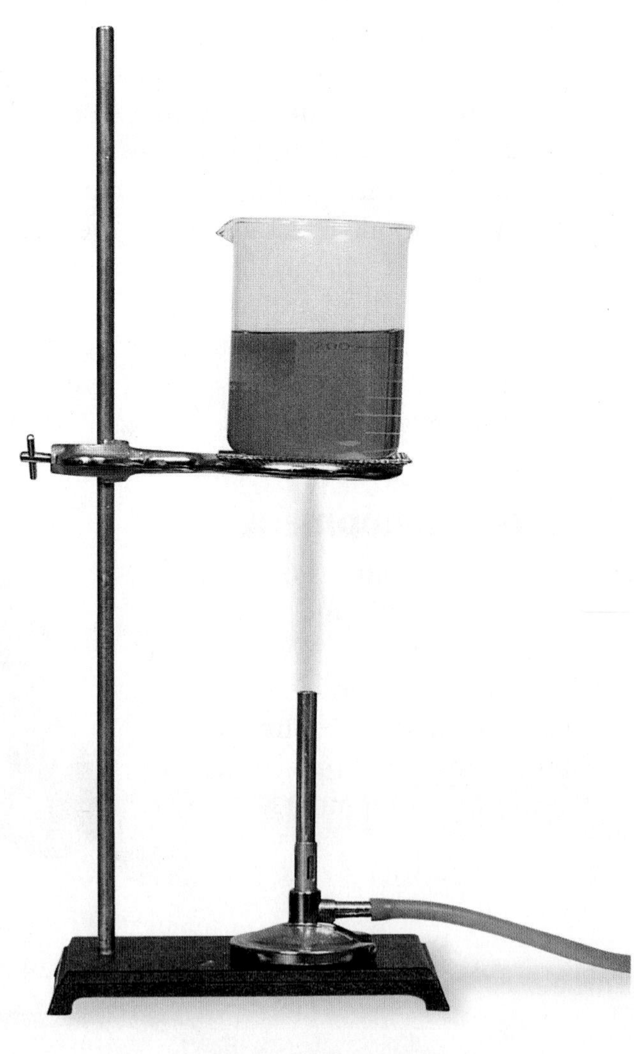

Animal Safety

Always obtain your teacher's permission before bringing any animal into the school building. Handle animals only as your teacher directs. Always treat animals carefully and respectfully. Wash your hands thoroughly after handling any animal.

Plant Safety 

Do not eat any part of a plant or plant seed used in the laboratory. Wash your hands thoroughly after handling any part of a plant. When in nature, do not pick any wild plants unless your teacher instructs you to do so.

Glassware

Examine all glassware before use. Be sure that glassware is clean and free of chips and cracks. Report damaged glassware to your teacher. Glass containers used for heating should be made of heat-resistant glass.

1

Science in Our World

The Big Idea Scientists use scientific processes to study the patterns of natural events and to solve problems.

SECTION

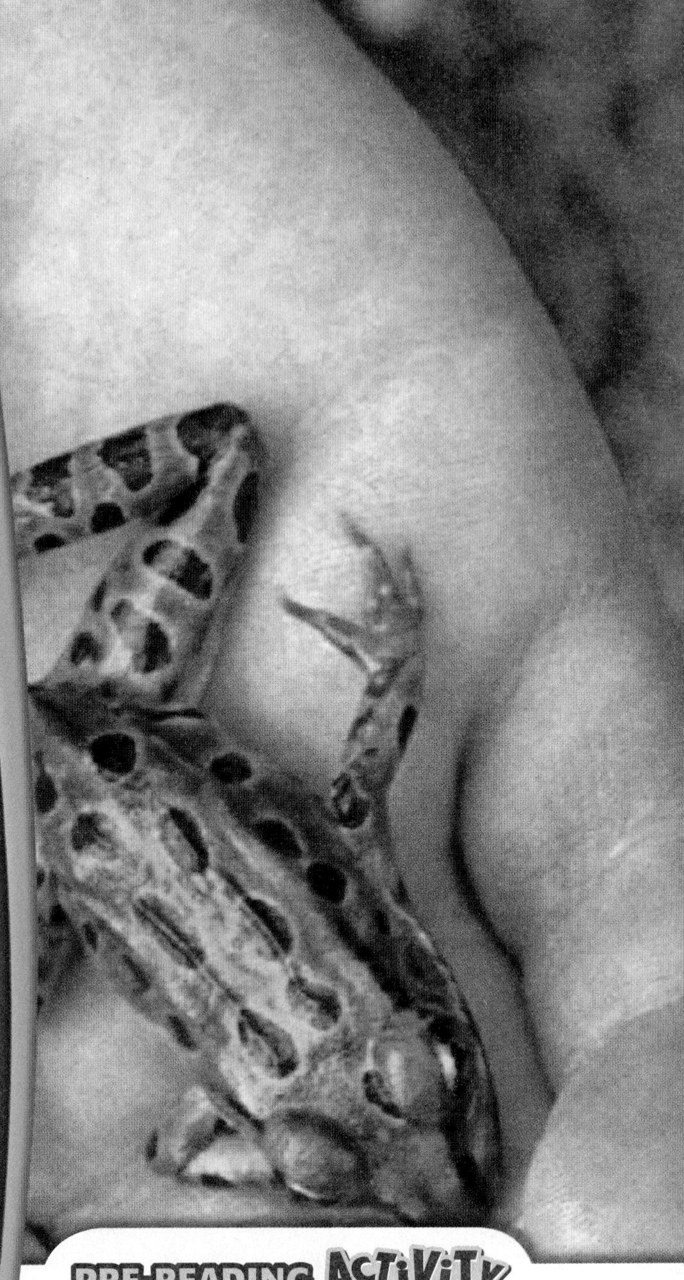

About the Photo

What happened to the legs of these frogs? Science can help answer this question. Deformed frogs, such as the ones in this photo, have been found in the northern United States and southern Canada. Scientists and students like you have been using science to find out how frogs may develop deformities.

PRE-READING ACTIVITY

FOLDNOTES **Layered Book** Before you read the chapter, create the FoldNote entitled "Layered Book" described in the **Study Skills** section of the Appendix. Label the tabs of the layered book with "Examples of life scientists," "Scientific methods," "Scientific models," and "Tools, measurement, and safety." As you read the chapter, write information you learn about each category under the appropriate tab.

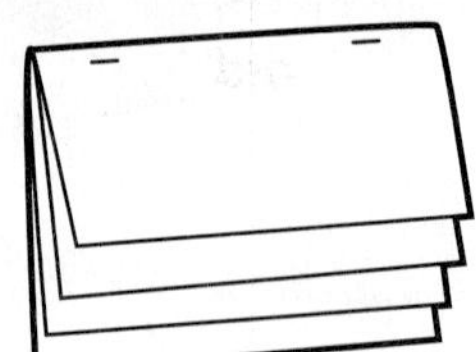

START-UP ACTIVITY

A Little Bit of Science

In this activity, you'll find out that you can learn about the unknown without having to see it.

Procedure

1. Your teacher will give you a **coffee can** to which a **sock** has been attached. Do not look into the can.
2. Reach through the opening in the sock. You will feel **several objects** inside the can.
3. Record observations you make about the objects by feeling them, shaking the can, and so on.
4. What do you think is in the can? List your guesses. State some reasons for your guesses.
5. Pour the contents of the can onto your desk. Compare your list with what was in the can.

Analysis

1. Did you guess the contents of the can correctly? What might have caused you to guess wrongly?
2. What observations did you make about each of the objects while they were in the can? Which of your senses did you use?

SECTION 1

Science and Scientists

What You Will Learn

- Describe three methods of investigation.
- Identify benefits of science in the world around you.
- Describe five jobs that use science.

Vocabulary

science

READING STRATEGY

Prediction Guide Before reading this section, write the title of each heading in this section. Next, under each heading, write what you think you will learn.

You are enjoying a picnic on a summer day. Crumbs from your sandwich fall to the ground, and ants carry the crumbs away. You wonder, Why do ants show up at picnics?

Congratulations! You just took one of the first steps of being a scientist. How did you do it? You observed the world around you. Then, you asked a question about your observations. And asking a question is part of what science is all about.

Start with a Question

The world around you is full of amazing things. Single-celled algae float unseen in ponds. Volcanoes erupt with explosive force. Mars may have had water in the past. And 40-ton whales glide through the oceans. These things or others, such as those shown in **Figure 1,** may lead you to ask a question. A question is the beginning of science. **Science** is the knowledge obtained by observing the natural world in order to discover facts and to formulate laws and principles that can be verified or tested.

Reading Check **What is science?** (*See the Appendix for answers to Reading Checks.*)

science the knowledge obtained by observing natural events and conditions in order to discover facts and formulate laws or principles that can be verified or tested

In Your Own Neighborhood

Take a look around your home, school, and neighborhood. Often, you take things that you use or see every day for granted. But one day you might look at something in a new way. That's when a question hits you! The student in **Figure 1** didn't have to look very far to realize that he had some questions to ask.

The World and Beyond

You don't have to stop at questions about things in your neighborhood. Ask questions about atoms or galaxies, pandas and bamboo, or earthquakes. A variety of plants and animals live in a variety of places. And each place has a unique combination of rocks, soil, and water.

You can even ask questions about places other than those on Earth. Look outward to the moon, the sun, and the planets in our solar system. Beyond that, you have the rest of the universe! There are enough questions to keep scientists busy for a long time.

Figure 1 *Part of science is asking questions about the world around you.*

Investigation: The Search for Answers

After you ask a question, it's time to look for an answer. But how do you start your investigation? Several methods may be used.

Research

You can find answers to some of your questions by doing research, as **Figure 2** shows. You can ask someone who knows a lot about the subject of your question. You can find information in textbooks, encyclopedias, and magazines. You can search on the Internet. You might read a report of an experiment that someone did. But be sure to think about the sources of your information. Use information only from reliable sources.

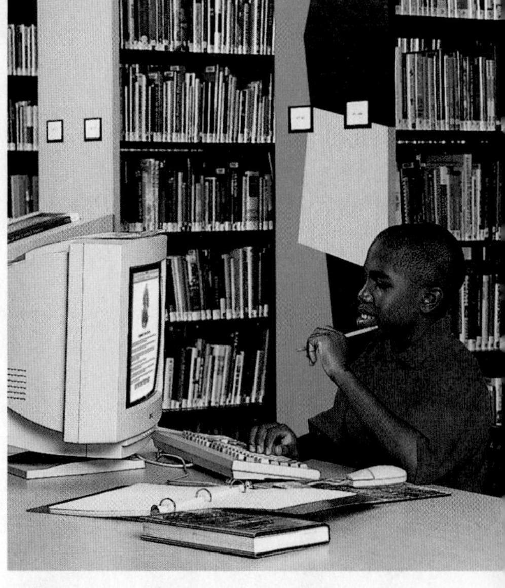

Figure 2 *A library is a good place to begin your search for answers.*

Observation

You can also find answers to questions by making careful observations. For example, if you want to know how spiders spin their webs, look for a web. When you find one, return to observe the spider as it spins. But be careful in making observations. Sometimes, what people expect to observe affects what they do observe. For example, most plants need light to grow. Does that mean that all plants need bright sunlight? Do some plants prefer shade? Some people might "observe" that bright light is the only answer. To test an observation, you may have to do an experiment.

Ask a Question

The next time you're outside, look carefully around you. Think of a science-related question that you would like to answer. Write the question in your **science journal.** Discuss with a parent which methods of investigation would be most likely to help you answer your question.

Experimentation

You might answer the question about light and shade by doing a simple experiment, such as the one shown in **Figure 3.** Your research and your observations can help you plan your experiment. What should you do if your experiment needs something that is hard to get? For example, what do you do if you want to know whether a certain plant grows in space? Don't give up! Try to find results from someone else's experiment!

Figure 3 *This student is doing an experiment to find out whether this type of plant grows better in shade or in direct sunlight.*

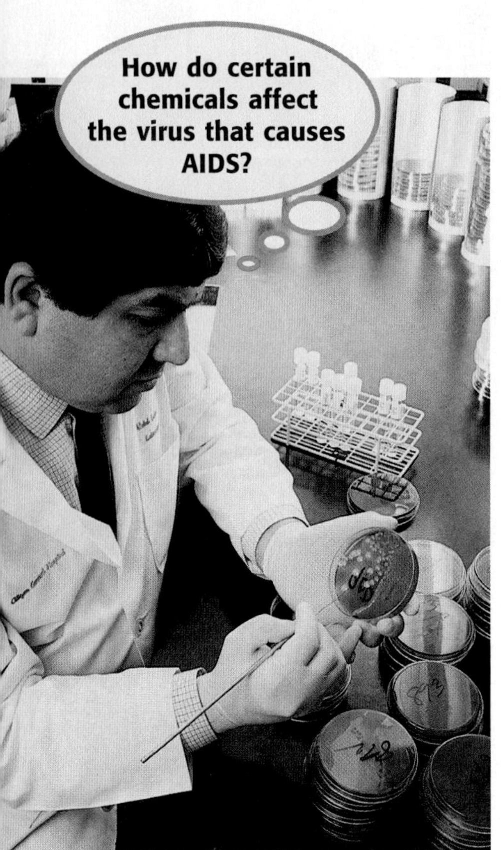

How do certain chemicals affect the virus that causes AIDS?

Figure 4 *Abdul Lakhani studies AIDS to find a cure for the disease.*

Why Ask Questions?

Although scientists cannot answer every question immediately, they do find some interesting answers. Do any of the answers really matter? Absolutely! As you study science, you will see how science affects you and society around you.

Fighting Diseases

Polio is a disease that can cause paralysis by affecting the brain and nerves. Do you know anyone who has had polio? You probably don't. But in 1952, polio infected 58,000 Americans. Fortunately, vaccines developed in 1955 and 1956 have eliminated polio in the United States. In fact, the virus that causes polio has been wiped out in most of the world.

Today, scientists are searching for cures for diseases such as mad cow disease, tuberculosis, and acquired immune deficiency syndrome (AIDS). The scientist in **Figure 4** is learning more about AIDS, which kills millions of people every year.

Saving Resources

Science also helps answer the question, How can we make resources last longer? Recycling is one answer. Think about the last time that you recycled an aluminum can. By recycling that can, you saved more than just the aluminum, as **Figure 5** shows. Using science, people have developed more-efficient methods and better equipment for recycling aluminum, paper, steel, glass, and even some plastics. In this way, science helps make resources last longer.

Figure 5 **Resources Saved Through Recycling**

Compared with producing aluminum from its ore, recycling 1 metric ton (1.1 tons) of aluminum:

produces 95% less air pollution

saves 4 metric tons (4.4 tons) of ore

produces 4 metric tons (4.4 tons) fewer chemical products

uses 14,000 kWh less energy

produces 97% less water pollution

Answering Society's Questions

Sometimes, society faces a question that does not seem to have an immediate answer. For example, at one time, the question of how to reduce air pollution did not have any obvious, reasonable answers. The millions of people who depended on their cars could not just stop driving. As the problem of air pollution became more important to people, scientists developed different technologies to address it. For example, one source of air pollution is exhaust from cars. Through science, people have developed cleaner-burning gasoline. People have even developed new ways to clean up exhaust before it leaves the tailpipe of a car!

Reading Check **How can society influence the types of technologies that are developed?**

CONNECTION TO Biology

Technology and Aging People are living longer than ever before. Research some of the health problems that elderly people may face, such as heart or vision problems. Then, research how these health problems are influencing the development of new technologies. Make a poster illustrating one of these problems and one or more technologies being developed to address it.

ACTIVITY

Scientists All Around You

Believe it or not, scientists work in many different places. If you think about it, any person who asks questions and looks for answers could be called a scientist! Keep reading to learn about just a few people who use science in their jobs.

Zoologist

A *zoologist* (zoh AHL uh jist) is a person who studies the lives of animals. Dale Miquelle, shown in **Figure 6,** is part of a team of Russian and American zoologists studying the Siberian tiger. The tigers have almost become extinct after being hunted and losing their homes. By learning about the tigers' living space and food needs, zoologists hope to make a plan that will help the tigers survive better in the wild.

Figure 6 *To learn how much land a Siberian tiger covers, Dale Miquelle tracks a tiger that is wearing a radio-transmitting collar.*

Figure 7 *This geochemist may work outdoors when collecting rock samples from the field. Then, he may work indoors as he analyzes the samples in his laboratory.*

Geochemist

Some scientists work outdoors most of the time. Other scientists spend much of their time in the laboratory. A geochemist (JEE oh KEM ist), such as the one shown in **Figure 7,** may work in both places. A *geochemist* is a person who specializes in the chemistry of rocks, minerals, and soil.

Geochemists determine the economic value of these materials. They also try to find out what the environment was like when these materials formed and what has happened to the materials since they first formed.

Mechanic

Do you have a machine that needs repairs? Call a mechanic, such as Gene Webb in **Figure 8.** Mechanics work on everything from cars to the space shuttle. Mechanics use science to solve problems. Mechanics must find answers to questions about why a machine is not working. Then, they must find a way to make it work. Mechanics also think of ways to improve the machine, to make it work faster or more efficiently.

Figure 8 *A mechanic can help keep a car's engine running smoothly.*

Oceanographer

An *oceanographer* studies the ocean. Some oceanographers study waves and ocean currents. Others study plants and animals that live in the ocean. Still others study the ocean floor, including how it forms.

While studying the ocean floor, oceanographers discovered black smokers. Black smokers are cracks where hot water (around 300°C!) from beneath Earth's surface comes up. These vents in the ocean floor are home to some strange animals, including red-tipped tube worms and blind white crabs.

Volcanologist

If black smokers aren't hot enough for you, perhaps you would like to become a volcanologist (VAHL kuh NAHL uh jist). A *volcanologist* studies one of Earth's most interesting processes—volcanoes. The volcanologist shown in **Figure 9** is photographing lava flowing from Mt. Etna, a volcano in Italy. Mt. Etna's lava may reach temperatures of 1,050°C. By learning more about volcanoes, volcanologists hope to get better at predicting when a volcano will erupt. Being able to predict eruptions would help save lives.

Reading Check What does a volcanologist do?

Figure 9 *Volcanologists gain a better understanding of the inside of the Earth by studying the makeup of lava.*

SECTION Review

Summary

- Science is a process of gathering knowledge about the natural world by making observations and asking questions.
- Science begins by asking a question.
- Even if science cannot answer the question right away, the answers that scientists find may be very important.
- A question may lead to a scientific investigation, including research, observations, and experimentation.
- Science can help save lives, fight diseases, save resources, and protect the environment.
- A variety of people may become scientists for a variety of reasons.

Using Key Terms

1. In your own words, write a definition for the term *science*.

Understanding Key Ideas

2. A zoologist might study any of the following EXCEPT
   a. shellfish living in ponds.
   b. the reason that mole rats live in large groups underground.
   c. environmental threats to sea turtles.
   d. rocks and minerals in the Painted Desert.
3. Describe five careers that use science.
4. How are observation and experimentation different?
5. How may what people expect to observe affect what they do observe? How can people avoid this problem?

Math Skills

6. Students in a science class collected 50 frogs from a pond. They found that 15 of the frogs had serious deformities. What percentage of the frogs had deformities?

Critical Thinking

7. **Making Inferences** An ad for deluxe garbage bags says that the bags are 30% stronger than regular garbage bags. Describe how science can help you find out if this claim is true.
8. **Identifying Relationships** Make a list of three things that you consider to be a problem in society. Give an example of how new technology might solve these problems.
9. **Applying Concepts** Look at **Figure 9.** Write five questions about what you see. Describe how science might help you answer your questions. Share your questions with your classmates.

SCI LINKS.
NSTA
Developed and maintained by the National Science Teachers Association
For a variety of links related to this chapter, go to www.scilinks.org
Topic: Careers in Science
SciLinks code: HSM0244

SECTION 2

Scientific Methods

What You Will Learn

- Explain why scientists use scientific methods.
- Determine the appropriate design of a controlled experiment.
- Use information in tables and graphs to analyze experimental results.
- Explain how scientific knowledge can change.

Vocabulary

scientific methods
hypothesis
controlled experiment
variable

READING STRATEGY

Reading Organizer As you read this section, make a flowchart of the possible steps in scientific methods.

Imagine that your class is on a field trip to a wildlife refuge. You discover several deformed frogs. You wonder what could be causing the frogs' deformities.

A group of students from Le Sueur, Minnesota, actually made this discovery! By making observations and asking questions about the observations, the students used scientific methods.

What Are Scientific Methods?

When scientists observe the natural world, they often think of a question or problem. But scientists don't just guess at answers. They use scientific methods. **Scientific methods** are the ways in which scientists follow steps to answer questions and solve problems. The steps used for all investigations are the same. But the order in which the steps are followed may vary, as shown in **Figure 1.** Scientists may use all of the steps or just some of the steps during an investigation. They may even repeat some of the steps. The order depends on what works best to answer the question. No matter where scientists work or what questions they try to answer, all scientists have two things in common. They are curious about the natural world, and they use similar methods to investigate it.

Reading Check What are scientific methods? (*See the Appendix for answers to Reading Checks.*)

scientific methods a series of steps followed to solve problems

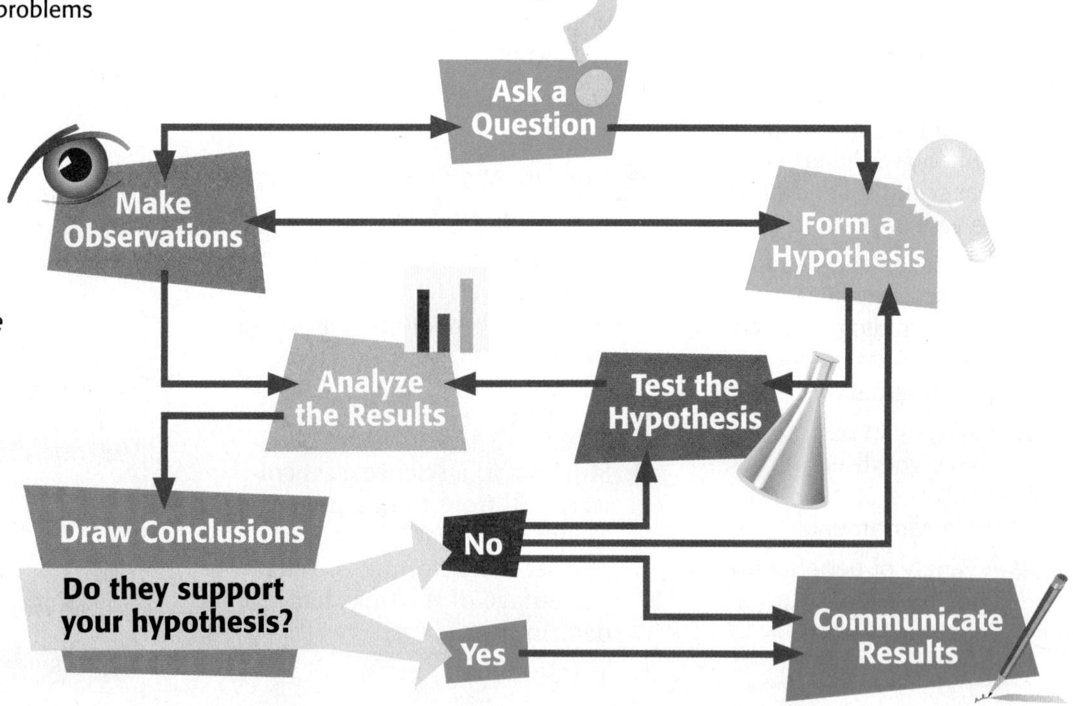

Figure 1 *Scientific methods often include the same steps, but the steps may not be used in the same order every time.*

Ask a Question

Have you ever observed something out of the ordinary or difficult to explain? Such an observation usually raises questions. For example, about the deformed frogs you might ask, "Could something in the water be causing the frog deformities?" Looking for answers may include making more observations.

Make Observations

After the students in Minnesota realized something was wrong with the frogs, they decided to make additional, careful observations, as shown in **Figure 2.** They counted the number of deformed frogs and the number of normal frogs they caught. They also photographed the frogs, took measurements, and wrote a thorough description of each frog.

In addition, the students collected data on other organisms living in the pond. They also conducted many tests on the pond water and measured things such as the level of acidity. The students carefully recorded their data and observations.

Figure 2 *Making careful observations is often the first step in an investigation.*

Accurate Observations

Any information that you gather through your senses is an observation. Observations can take many forms. They may be measurements of length, volume, time, speed, or loudness. They may describe the color or shape of an organism. Or they may record the behavior of organisms in an area. The range of observations that a scientist can make is endless. But no matter what observations reveal, they are useful only if they are accurately made and recorded. Scientists use many standard tools and methods to make and record observations. Examples of these tools are shown in **Figure 3.**

Figure 3 *Microscopes, rulers, and thermometers are some of the many tools scientists use to collect information.*

Form a Hypothesis

After asking questions and making observations, scientists may form a hypothesis. A **hypothesis** (hie PAHTH uh sis) is a possible explanation or answer to a question. A good hypothesis is based on observation and can be tested. When scientists form hypotheses, they think logically and creatively and consider what they already know.

To be useful, a hypothesis must be testable. A hypothesis is testable if an experiment can be designed to test the hypothesis. Yet if a hypothesis is not testable, it is not always wrong. An untestable hypothesis is simply one that cannot be supported or disproved. Sometimes, it may be impossible to gather enough observations to test a hypothesis.

Scientists may form different hypotheses for the same problem. In the case of the Minnesota frogs, scientists formed the hypotheses shown in **Figure 4.** Were any of these explanations correct? To find out, scientists had to test each hypothesis.

Reading Check **What makes a hypothesis testable?**

CONNECTION TO Environmental Science

WRITING SKILL **Minnesota's Deformed Frogs**

Deformed frogs were first noticed in Minnesota in 1995. In 1996, the Minnesota Pollution Control Agency (MPCA) began studying the problem. It funded and coordinated studies searching for the causes of the deformities. Find out what the MPCA is doing about the deformed frogs today, and write a short summary of what the MPCA has discovered.

hypothesis an explanation that is based on prior scientific research or observations and that can be tested

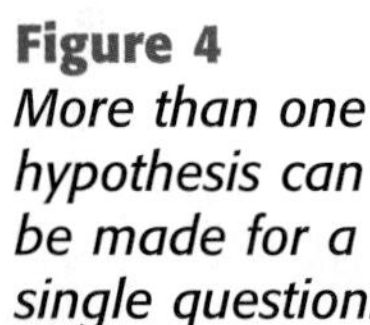

Hypothesis 1:
The deformities were caused by one or more chemical pollutants in the water.
Hypothesis 2:
The deformities were caused by attacks from parasites or other frogs.
Hypothesis 3:
The deformities were caused by an increase in exposure to ultraviolet light from the sun.

Figure 4 *More than one hypothesis can be made for a single question.*

Predictions

Before scientists can test a hypothesis, they must first make predictions. A prediction is a statement of cause and effect that can be used to set up a test for a hypothesis. Predictions are usually stated in an if-then format, as shown in **Figure 5.**

Figure 5 lists the predictions made for the hypotheses shown in **Figure 4.** More than one prediction may be made for each hypothesis. After predictions are made, scientists can conduct experiments to see which predictions, if any, prove to be true and support the hypotheses.

Figure 5 *More than one prediction may be made for a single hypothesis.*

Hypothesis 1:
Prediction: If a substance in the pond water is causing the deformities, then the water from ponds that have deformed frogs will be different from the water from ponds in which no abnormal frogs have been found.
Prediction: If a substance in the pond water is causing the deformities, then some tadpoles will develop deformities when they are raised in pond water collected from ponds that have deformed frogs.

Hypothesis 2:
Prediction: If a parasite is causing the deformities, then this parasite will be found more often in frogs that have deformities.

Hypothesis 3:
Prediction: If an increase in exposure to ultraviolet light is causing the deformities, then some frog eggs exposed to ultraviolet light in a laboratory will develop into deformed frogs.

CONNECTION TO Language Arts

WRITING SKILL **"Leading doctors say . . ."** Suppose that you and a friend see an ad for a cold remedy on TV. According to the ad, "Leading doctors recommend this product for their patients." Then, a famous actor comes on and says that he or she uses the product, too. Write a dialogue of the debate you might have with your friend about whether these claims are believable.

Test the Hypothesis

Figure 6 *Many factors affect this tadpole in the wild. These factors include chemicals, light, temperature, and parasites.*

After scientists make a prediction, they test the hypothesis. Scientists try to design experiments that will clearly show whether a particular factor caused an observed outcome. In an experiment, a *factor* is anything that can influence the experiment's outcome. Factors can be anything from temperature to the type of organism being studied.

Under Control

Scientists studying the frogs in Minnesota observed many factors that affect the development of frogs in the wild, as shown in **Figure 6.** But it was hard to tell which factor could be causing the deformities. To sort factors out, scientists perform controlled experiments. A **controlled experiment** tests only one factor at a time and consists of a control group and one or more experimental groups. All of the factors for the control group and the experimental groups are the same except for one. The one factor that differs is called the **variable.** Because only the variable differs between the control group and the experimental groups, any differences observed in the outcome of the experiment are probably caused by the variable.

Reading Check How many factors should an experiment test?

controlled experiment an experiment that tests only one factor at a time by using a comparison of a control group with an experimental group

variable a factor that changes in an experiment in order to test a hypothesis

Designing an Experiment

Designing a good experiment requires planning. Every factor should be considered. Examine the prediction for Hypothesis 3: *If an increase in exposure to ultraviolet light is causing the deformities, then some frog eggs exposed to ultraviolet light in a laboratory will develop into deformed frogs.* An experiment to test this hypothesis is summarized in **Table 1.** In this case, the variable is the length of time the eggs are exposed to ultraviolet (UV) light. All other factors, such as the temperature of the water, are the same in the control group and in the experimental groups.

Table 1 Experiment to Test Effect of UV Light on Frogs

	Control factors			Variable
Group	Kind of frog	Number of Eggs	Temperature of water	UV light exposure
#1 (control)	leopard frog	100	25°C	0 days
#2 (experimental)	leopard frog	100	25°C	15 days
#3 (experimental)	leopard frog	100	25°C	24 days

Figure 7 UV Light Experiment

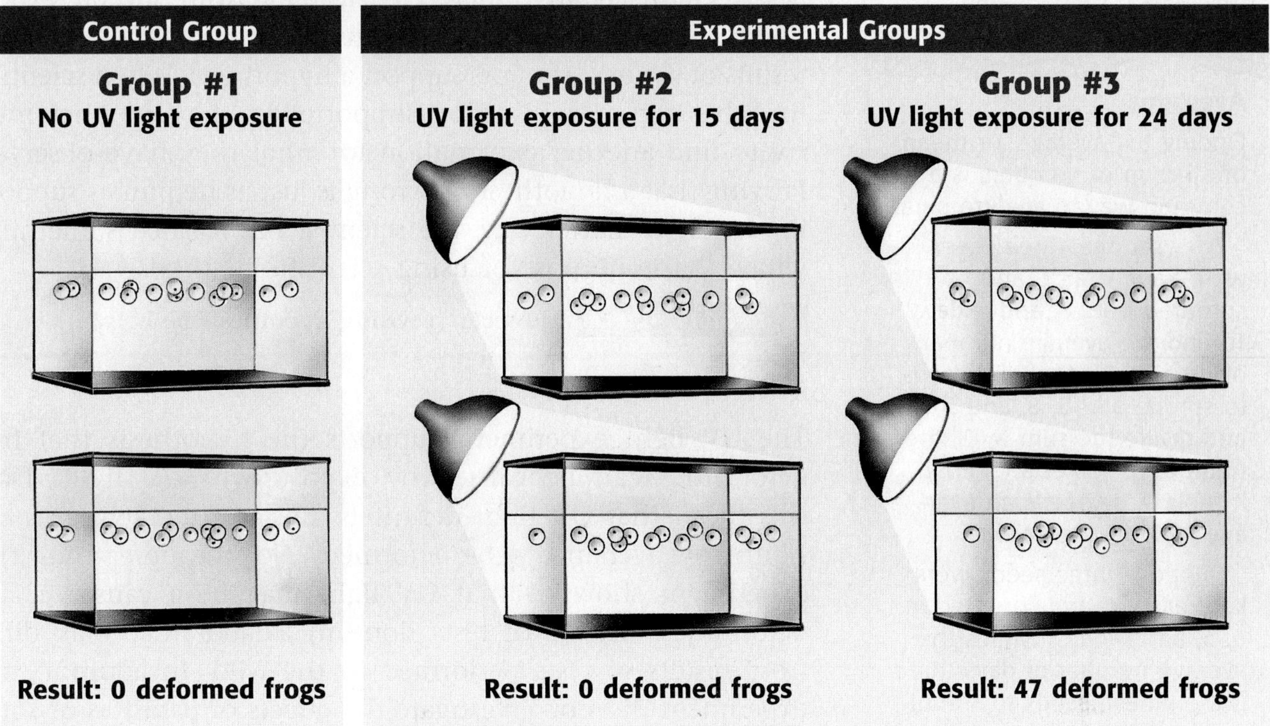

Collecting Data

Figure 7 shows the experimental setup to test Hypothesis 3. As **Table 1** shows, there are 100 eggs in each group. Scientists always try to test many individuals. They want to be sure that differences between control and experimental groups are caused by the variable and not by differences between individuals. The larger the groups are, the smaller the effect of a difference between individual frogs will be. The larger the groups are, the more likely it is that the variable is responsible for any changes and the more accurate the data collected are likely to be.

Scientists test a result by repeating the experiment. If an experiment gives the same results each time, scientists are more certain about the variable's effect on the outcome. Scientists keep clear, accurate, honest records of their data so that other scientists can repeat the experiment and verify the results.

Analyze the Results

After scientists finish their tests, they must organize their data and analyze the results. Scientists may organize data in a table or a graph. The data collected from the UV light experiment are shown in the bar graph in **Figure 8.** Analyzing the results helps scientists explain and focus on the effect of the variable. For example, the graph shows that the length of UV exposure has an effect on the development of frog deformities.

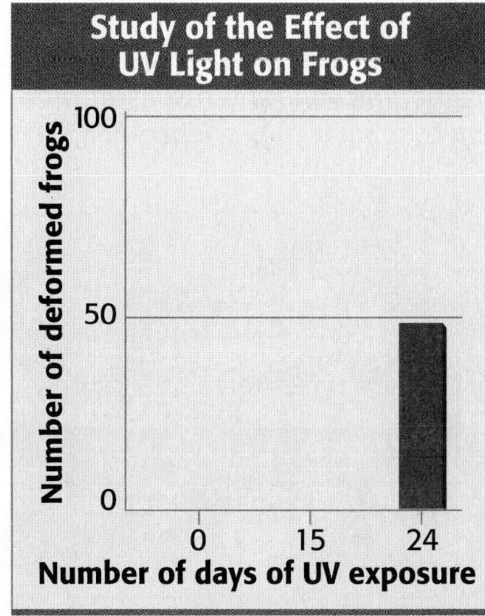

Figure 8 *This graph shows that 24 days of UV exposure had an effect on frog deformities, while less exposure had no effect.*

Averages

Finding the average, or mean, of a group of numbers is a common way to analyze data.

For example, three seeds were kept at 25°C and sprouted in 8, 8, and 5 days. To find the average number of days that it took the seeds to sprout, add 8, 8, and 5 and divide the sum by 3, the number of subjects (seeds). It took these seeds an average of 7 days to sprout.

Suppose three seeds were kept at 30°C and sprouted in 6, 5, and 4 days. What's the average number of days that it took these seeds to sprout?

Draw Conclusions

After scientists have analyzed the data from several experiments, they can draw conclusions. They decide whether the results of the experiments support a hypothesis. When scientists find that a hypothesis is not supported by the tests, they must try to find another explanation for what they have observed. Proving that a hypothesis is wrong is just as helpful as supporting it. Why? Either way, the scientist has learned something, which is the purpose of using scientific methods.

Reading Check **How can a wrong hypothesis be helpful?**

Is It the Answer?

The UV light experiment supports the hypothesis that frog deformities can be caused by exposure to UV light. Does this mean that UV light definitely caused frogs living in the Minnesota wetland to be deformed? No, the only thing this experiment shows is that UV light may be a cause of frog deformities. Results of tests done in a laboratory may differ from results of tests performed in the wild. In addition, the experiment did not investigate the effects of parasites or some other substance on the frogs. In fact, many scientists now think that more than one factor could be causing the deformities.

Sometimes, similar investigations or experiments give different results. For example, another research team may have had results that did not support the UV light hypothesis. In such a case, scientists must work together to decide if the differences in the results are scientifically significant. Often, making that decision takes more experiments and more evidence.

Figure 9 *This student scientist is communicating the results of his investigation at a science fair.*

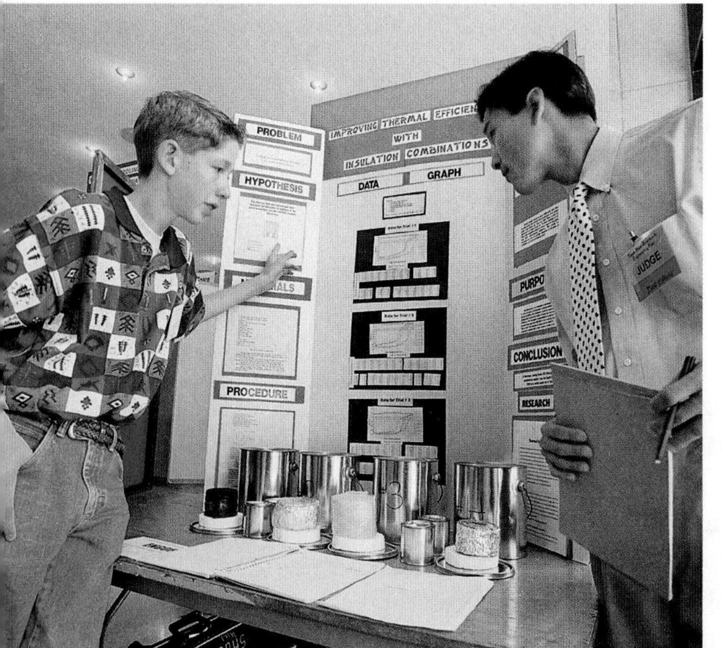

Communicate Results

Scientists form a global community. After scientists complete their investigations, they communicate their results to other scientists. The student in **Figure 9** is explaining the results of a science project.

Scientists regularly share their results for several reasons. First, other scientists may then repeat the experiments to see if they get the same results. Second, the information can be considered by other scientists with similar interests. The scientists can then compare hypotheses and form consistent explanations. New data may strengthen existing hypotheses or show that the hypotheses need to be altered. There are many paths from observations and questions to communicating results.

SECTION Review

Summary

- Scientific methods are the ways in which scientists follow steps to answer questions and solve problems.
- Any information you gather through your senses is an observation. Observations often lead to the formation of questions and hypotheses.
- A hypothesis is a possible explanation or answer to a question. A well-formed hypothesis is testable by experiment.
- A controlled experiment tests only one factor at a time and consists of a control group and one or more experimental groups.
- After testing a hypothesis, scientists analyze the results and draw conclusions about whether the hypothesis is supported.
- Communicating results allows others to check the results, add to their knowledge, and design new experiments.

Using Key Terms

1. Use the following terms in the same sentence: *hypothesis, controlled experiment,* and *variable.*

Understanding Key Ideas

2. The steps of scientific methods
   a. are exactly the same in every investigation.
   b. must be used in the same order every time.
   c. are not used in the same order every time.
   d. always end with a conclusion.
3. What is the appropriate design of a controlled experiment?
4. What causes scientific knowledge to change?

Math Skills

5. Calculate the average of the following values: 4, 5, 6, 6, and 9.

Critical Thinking

6. **Analyzing Methods** Why was UV light chosen to be the variable in the frog experiment?
7. **Analyzing Processes** Why are there many ways to follow the steps of scientific methods?
8. **Making Inferences** Why might two scientists working on the same problem draw different conclusions?
9. **Making Inferences** Why do scientists use scientific methods?

Interpreting Graphics

10. The table below shows how long it takes for bacteria to double. Plot the information on a graph. Put temperature on the *x*-axis and the time to double on the *y*-axis. Do not graph values for which there is no growth. At what temperature do the bacteria multiply the fastest?

Temperature (°C)	Time to double (min)
10	130
20	60
25	40
30	29
37	17
40	19
45	32
50	no growth

11. What would happen if you changed the scale of the graph by using values of 0 to 300 minutes on the *y*-axis? How might that change affect your interpretation of the data?

SCILINKS
NSTA
Developed and maintained by the National Science Teachers Association
For a variety of links related to this chapter, go to www.scilinks.org
Topic: Scientific Methods; Deformed Frogs
SciLinks code: HSM1359; HSM0383

SECTION 3

Scientific Models

What You Will Learn

- Give examples of three types of models.
- Identify the benefits and limitations of models.
- Compare the ways that scientists use hypotheses, theories, and laws.

Vocabulary

model
theory
law

READING STRATEGY

Reading Organizer As you read this section, create an outline of the section. Use the headings from the section in your outline.

How can you see the parts of a cell? Unless you had superhuman eyesight, you couldn't see inside most cells without using a microscope.

What would you do if you didn't have a microscope? Looking at a model of a cell would help! A model of a cell can help you understand what the parts of a cell look like.

Types of Scientific Models

A **model** is a representation of an object or system. Scientific models are used to help explain how something works or to describe the structure of something. A model may be used to predict future events. However, models have limitations. A model is never exactly like the real thing. If it were, it would not be a model. Three major kinds of scientific models are physical, mathematical, and conceptual models.

model a pattern, plan, representation, or description designed to show the structure or workings of an object, system, or concept

Physical Models

A model volcano and a miniature steam engine are examples of physical models. Some physical models, such as a model of a cell, look like the thing that they model. But a limitation of the model of a cell is that the model is not alive and doesn't act exactly like a cell. Other physical models, such as the model of a skyscraper in **Figure 1,** look and act at least somewhat like the thing that they model. Scientists often use the model that is simplest to use but that still serves their purpose.

Figure 1 *The model of the skyscraper doesn't act like the real building in every way, which is both a benefit and a limitation of the model.*

Figure 2 Mathematical Model: A Punnett Square

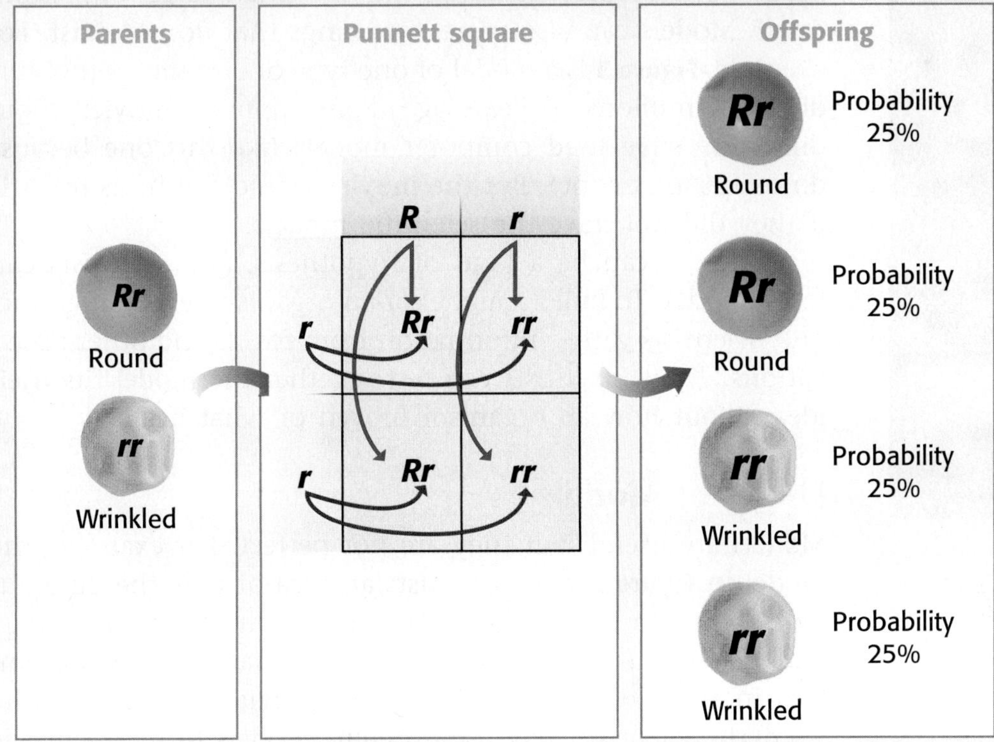

Mathematical Models

A mathematical model may be made up of numbers, equations, and other forms of data. Some mathematical models are simple and can be used easily. The Punnett square shown in **Figure 2** helps scientists study the passing of traits from parents to offspring. Using this model, scientists can predict how often certain traits will appear in the offspring of certain parents.

Computers are useful for creating and manipulating mathematical models. They make fewer mistakes and can keep track of more variables than a person can. But a computer model can also be incorrect in many ways. The more complex a model is, the more carefully scientists must build and test the model.

Reading Check **What type of model is a Punnett square?** (*See the Appendix for answers to Reading Checks.*)

Conceptual Models

The third type of model is the conceptual model. Some conceptual models are systems of ideas. Others compare unfamiliar things with familiar things to help explain unfamiliar ideas. The idea that the solar system formed from a spinning disk of gas is a conceptual model. Scientists also use conceptual models to classify behaviors of animals. Scientists can then predict how an animal might respond to a certain action based on behaviors that have already been observed.

CONNECTION TO Environmental Science

Samples Scientists studying deformed frogs in Minnesota wanted to know at what stage in the frogs' development the deformities happened. So, the scientists collected a large sample of frogs in all stages of development.

The larger a sample is, the more accurately it represents the whole population. If, for example, a sample of frogs is too small, one unusual frog may make the results of the study inaccurate. If the sample has too many old frogs or too many tadpoles, the sample is unrepresentative of the whole population. Give an example of an unrepresentative sample. Make a poster describing how that sample might make the experimental results inaccurate.

ACTIVITY

Figure 3 *This computer-generated model doesn't just look like a dinosaur. It may also open and close its jaws in much the same way that a dinosaur does.*

Benefits of Models

Models often represent things that are small, large, or complicated. Models can also represent things that do not exist. For example, **Figure 3** is a model of one type of dinosaur. Dinosaurs died out millions of years ago. Some popular movies about dinosaurs have used computer models like this one because dinosaurs are extinct. But the movies would not be as realistic if they did not have the scientific models.

A model can be a kind of hypothesis, and scientists can test a model. To build a model of an organism, even an extinct one, scientists gather information from fossils and other observations. Then, scientists can test whether the model fits their ideas about how an organism moved or what it ate.

Limits of Models

Models are useful, but they are not perfect. For example, the model in **Figure 3** gives scientists an idea of how the dinosaur looked. But to find out how strong the dinosaur's jaws were, scientists might build a physical model that has pressure sensors in the jaw. That model would provide data about bite strength. Scientists may use different models to represent the same thing, such as the dinosaur's jaw. But the kind of model and the model's complexity depend on the model's purpose.

Even a model jaw that has pressure sensors is not perfect. Scientists can compare the dinosaur bite with the bite of a crocodile. Next, scientists use their model to conduct tests. Scientists might then estimate how hard the dinosaur could bite. But without a live dinosaur, the result is still a hypothesis.

Building Scientific Knowledge

Sometimes, scientists draw different conclusions from the same data. Other times, new results show that old conclusions are wrong. Scientists are always asking new questions or looking at old questions from a different angle. As scientists find new answers, scientific knowledge continues to grow and change.

Scientific Theories

For every hypothesis, more than one prediction can be made. Each time another prediction is proven true, the hypothesis gains more support. Over time, scientists tie together everything that they have learned. An explanation that ties together many related observations, facts, and tested hypotheses is called a **theory.** Theories are conceptual models that help organize scientific thinking. Theories are used to explain observations and to predict what might happen in the future.

theory an explanation that ties together many hypotheses and observations

law a summary of many experimental results and observations; a law tells how things work

Reading Check **How do scientists use theories?**

Scientific Laws

What happens when a theory and its models correctly predict the results of many experiments? A scientific law may be formed. In science, a **law** is a summary of many experimental results and observations. A scientific law is a statement of what *will* happen in a specific situation. A law tells you how things work.

Scientific laws are at work around you every day. For example, the law of gravity states that objects will always fall toward the center of Earth. And inside your cells, many laws of chemistry are at work to keep you alive.

Scientific Change

New scientific ideas may take time to be accepted as facts, scientific theories, or scientific laws. Scientists should be open to new ideas but should always test new ideas by using scientific methods. If new evidence challenges an accepted idea, scientists must reexamine the old evidence and reevaluate the old idea. In this way, the process of building scientific knowledge never ends.

CONNECTION TO Chemistry

Model Cocaine in the Brain Analyze and evaluate information from a scientifically literate viewpoint by reading scientific texts, magazine articles, and newspaper articles about how drugs, such as cocaine, affect brain chemistry. Create a model to show what you have learned. Use your model to describe possible treatments for drug addiction.

ACTIVITY

SECTION Review

Summary

- Models represent objects or systems. Often, they use familiar things to represent unfamiliar things. Three main types of models are physical, mathematical, and conceptual models. Models have limitations but are useful and can be changed based on new evidence.
- Scientific knowledge is built as scientists form and revise scientific hypotheses, models, theories, and laws.

Using Key Terms

In each of the following sentences, replace the incorrect term with the correct term from the word bank.

theory law hypothesis

1. A conclusion is an explanation that matches many hypotheses but may still change.
2. A model tells you exactly what to expect in certain situations.

Understanding Key Ideas

3. A limitation of models is that
   a. they are large enough to see.
   b. they do not act exactly like the things that they model.
   c. they are smaller than the things that they model.
   d. they model unfamiliar things.
4. What type of model would you use to test the hypothesis that global warming is causing polar icecaps to melt? Explain.

Math Skills

5. If Jerry is 2.1 m tall, how tall is a scale model of Jerry that is 10% of his size?

Critical Thinking

6. **Applying Concepts** You want to make a model of an extinct plant. What are two kinds of models that you might use? Describe the advantages and disadvantages of each type of model.

SCILINKS
NSTA
Developed and maintained by the National Science Teachers Association
For a variety of links related to this chapter, go to www.scilinks.org
Topic: Using Models
SciLinks code: HSM1588

Tools, Measurement, and Safety

What You Will Learn

- Collect, record, and analyze information by using various tools.
- Explain the importance of the International System of Units.
- Calculate area and density.
- Identify lab safety symbols, and demonstrate safe practices during lab investigations.

Vocabulary

meter
area
mass
volume
temperature
density

READING STRATEGY

Reading Organizer As you read this section, make a concept map by using the terms above.

Would you use a hammer to tighten a bolt on a bicycle? No, you wouldn't. You need the right tools to fix a bike.

Scientists use a variety of tools in their experiments. A tool is anything that helps you do a task.

Tools for Measuring

You might remember that one way to collect data is to take measurements. To get the best measurements, you need the proper tools. Stopwatches, metersticks, and balances are tools that you can use to make measurements. Thermometers, spring scales, and graduated cylinders are also helpful tools. Some of the uses of these tools are shown in **Figure 1.**

Reading Check **Name six tools used for taking measurements.** *(See the Appendix for answers to Reading Checks.)*

Tools for Analyzing

After you collect data, you need to analyze them. Perhaps you need to find the average of your data. Calculators are handy tools to help you do calculations quickly. Or you might show your data in a graph or a figure. A computer that has the correct software can help you make neat, colorful figures. Of course, even a pencil and graph paper are tools that you can use to graph your data.

Figure 1 **Measurement Tools**

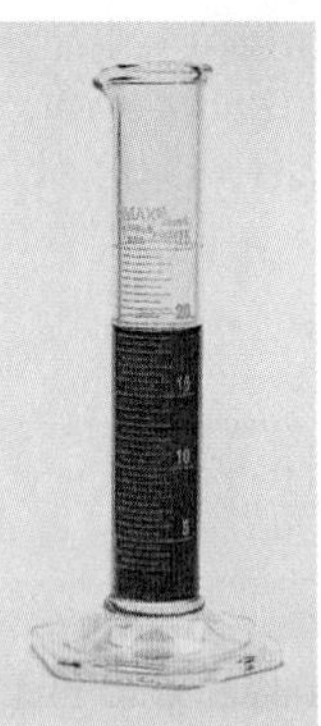

You can use a **graduated cylinder** to measure volume.

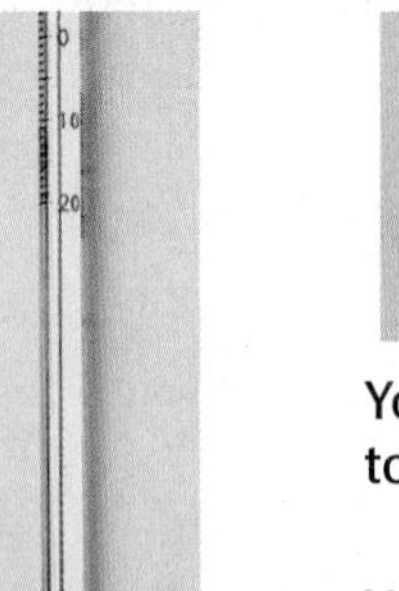

You can use a **thermometer** to measure temperature.

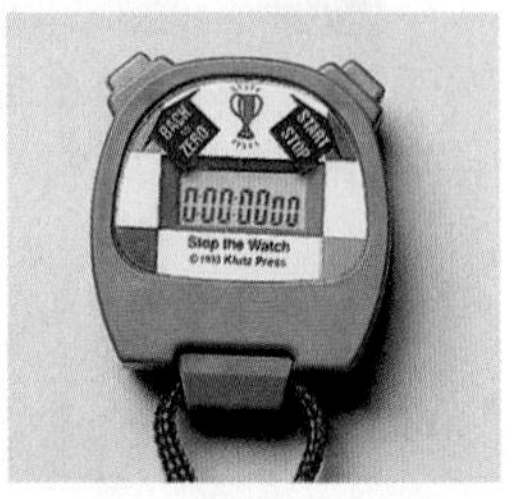

You can use a **stopwatch** to measure time.

You can use a **meterstick** to measure length.

You can use a **balance** to measure mass.

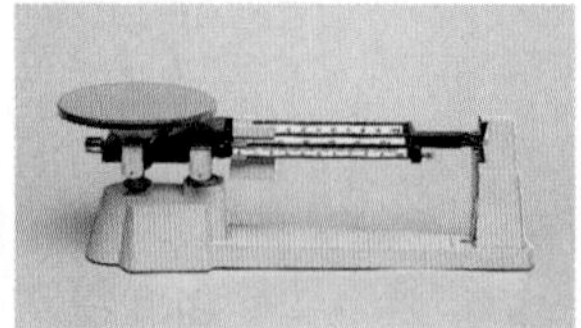

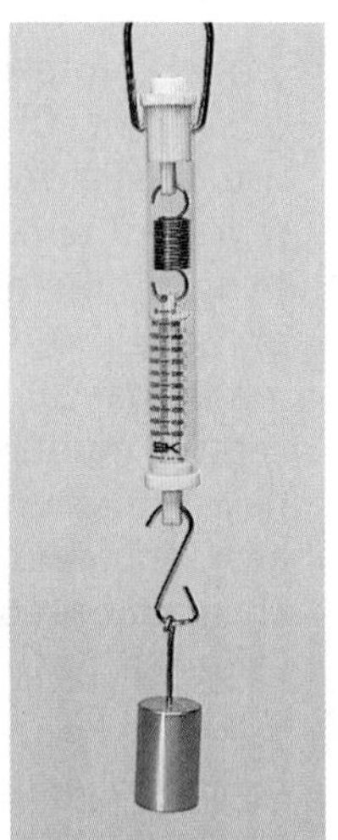

You can use a **spring scale** to measure force.

Units of Measurement

The ability to make accurate and reliable measurements is an important skill in science. Many systems of measurement are used throughout the world. At one time in England, the standard for an inch was three grains of barley placed end to end. Other modern standardized units were originally based on parts of the body, such as the foot. Such systems were not very reliable. Their units were based on objects that had different sizes.

No Rulers Allowed

1. Measure the width of your desk, but don't use a ruler.
2. Select another object to use as your unit of measurement.
3. Compare your measurement with those of your classmates.
4. Explain why it is important to use standard units of measurement.

The International System of Units

In the late 1700s, the French Academy of Sciences began to form a global measurement system now known as the *International System of Units,* or SI. Today, most scientists and almost all countries use this system. One advantage of using SI measurements is that doing so helps scientists share and compare their observations and results.

Another advantage of SI units is that all units are based on the number 10, which makes conversions from one unit to another easy. The table in **Table 1** contains commonly used SI units for length, volume, mass, and temperature.

Table 1 **Common SI Units and Conversions**

Length	**meter (m)** kilometer (km) decimeter (dm) centimeter (cm) millimeter (mm) micrometer (μm) nanometer (nm)	 1 km = 1,000 m 1 dm = 0.1 m 1 cm = 0.01 m 1 mm = 0.001 m 1 μm = 0.000001 m 1 nm = 0.000000001 m
Volume	**cubic meter (m^3)** cubic centimeter (cm^3) liter (L) milliliter (mL)	 1 cm^3 = 0.000001 m^3 1 L = 1 dm^3 = 0.001 m^3 1 mL = 0.001 L = 1 cm^3
Mass	**kilogram (kg)** gram (g) milligram (mg)	 1 g = 0.001 kg 1 mg = 0.000001 kg
Temperature	**Kelvin (K)** **Celsius (°C)**	0°C = 273 K 100°C = 373 K

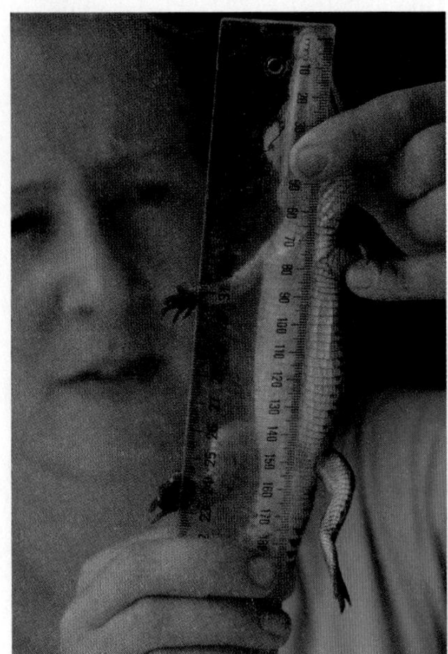

Figure 2 *This scientist is using a metric ruler to measure a lizard's length. The unit chosen to describe an object, such as this lizard, depends on the size of the object being measured.*

meter the basic unit of length in the SI (symbol, m)

area a measure of the size of a surface or a region

Measurement

Scientists report measured quantities in a way that shows the precision of the measurement. To do so, they use significant figures. *Significant figures* are the digits in a measurement that are known with certainty. The Math Focus below will help you understand significant figures and will teach you how to use the correct number of digits. Now that you have a standardized system of units for measuring things, you can use the system to measure length, area, mass, volume, and temperature.

Length

How long is a lizard? Well, a **meter** (m) is the basic SI unit of length. However, a scientist, such as the one in **Figure 2,** would use centimeters (cm) to describe a small lizard's length. If you divide 1 m into 100 parts, each part equals 1 cm. So, 1 cm is one-hundredth of a meter. Even though 1 cm seems small, some things are even smaller. Scientists describe the length of very small objects in micrometers (μm) or nanometers (nm). To see these small objects, scientists use powerful microscopes.

Area

How much paper would you need to cover the top of your desk? To answer this question, you must find the area of the desk. **Area** is a measure of the size of the surface of an object. To calculate the area of a square or a rectangle, measure the length and width. Then, use the following equation:

$$area = length \times width$$

Units for area are square units, such as square meters (m^2), square centimeters (cm^2), and square kilometers (km^2).

Significant Figures Calculate the area of a carpet that is 3.145 m long (four significant figures) and 5.75 m (three significant figures) wide. (Hint: In multiplication and division problems, the answer cannot have more significant figures than the measurement that has the smallest number of significant figures does.)

Step 1: Write the equation for area.

$$area = length \times width$$

Step 2: Replace *length* and *width* with the measurements given, and solve.

$$area = 3.125 \text{ m} \times 5.75 \text{ m} = 18.08375 \text{ m}^2$$

Step 3: Round the answer to get the correct number of significant figures. Here, the correct number of significant figures is three, because the value with the smallest number of significant figures has three significant figures.

$$area = 18.1 \text{ m}^2$$

Now Its Your Turn

1. Use a calculator to perform the following calculation: 125.5 km × 8.225 km. Write the answer with the correct number of significant figures.

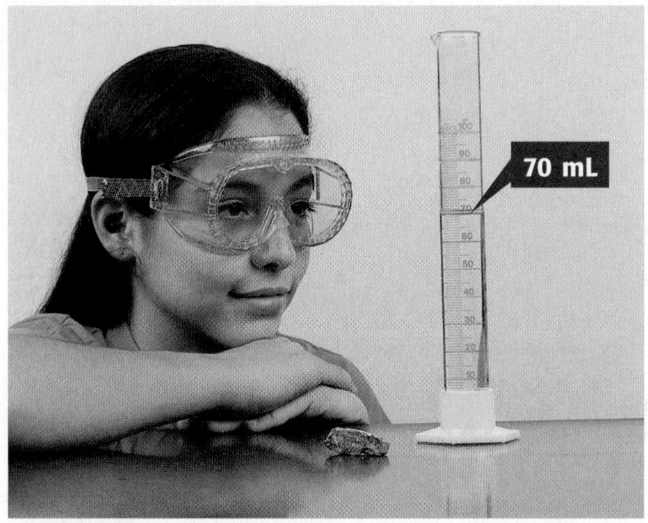

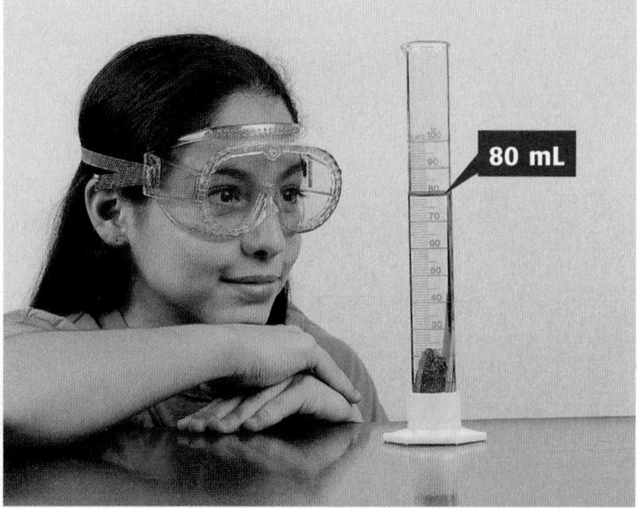

Figure 3 *Adding the rock changes the water level from 70 mL to 80 mL. So, the rock displaces 10 mL of water. Because 1 mL = 1 cm^3, the volume of the rock is 10 cm^3.*

Mass

How large a rock can a rushing stream move? The answer depends on the energy of the stream and the mass of the rock. **Mass** is a measure of the amount of matter in an object. The kilogram (kg) is the basic unit for mass in the SI. Kilograms are used to describe the mass of a large rock. Grams are used to measure the mass of smaller objects. One thousand grams equals 1 kg. For example, a medium-sized apple has a mass of about 100 g. Masses of very large objects are given in metric tons. A metric ton equals 1,000 kg.

Reading Check **What is the basic SI unit for mass?**

Volume

Think about moving some magnets to a laboratory. How many magnets will fit into a box? The answer depends on the volume of the box and the volume of each magnet. **Volume** is a measure of the size of a body in three-dimensional space. In this case, you need the volumes of the box and of the magnets.

mass a measure of the amount of matter in an object

volume a measure of the size of a body or region in three-dimensional space

The volume of a liquid is often given in liters (L). Liters are based on the meter. A cubic meter (1 m^3) is equal to 1,000 L. So, 1,000 L will fit into a box measuring 1 m on each side. A milliliter (mL) will fit into a box measuring 1 cm on each side. So, 1 mL = 1 cm^3. Graduated cylinders are used to measure the volume of liquids.

The volume of a large, solid object is given in cubic meters (m^3). The volumes of smaller objects can be given in cubic centimeters (cm^3) or cubic millimeters (mm^3). The volume of a box can be calculated by multiplying the object's length, width, and height. The volume of an irregularly shaped object can be found by measuring the volume of liquid that the object displaces. You can see how this works in **Figure 3.**

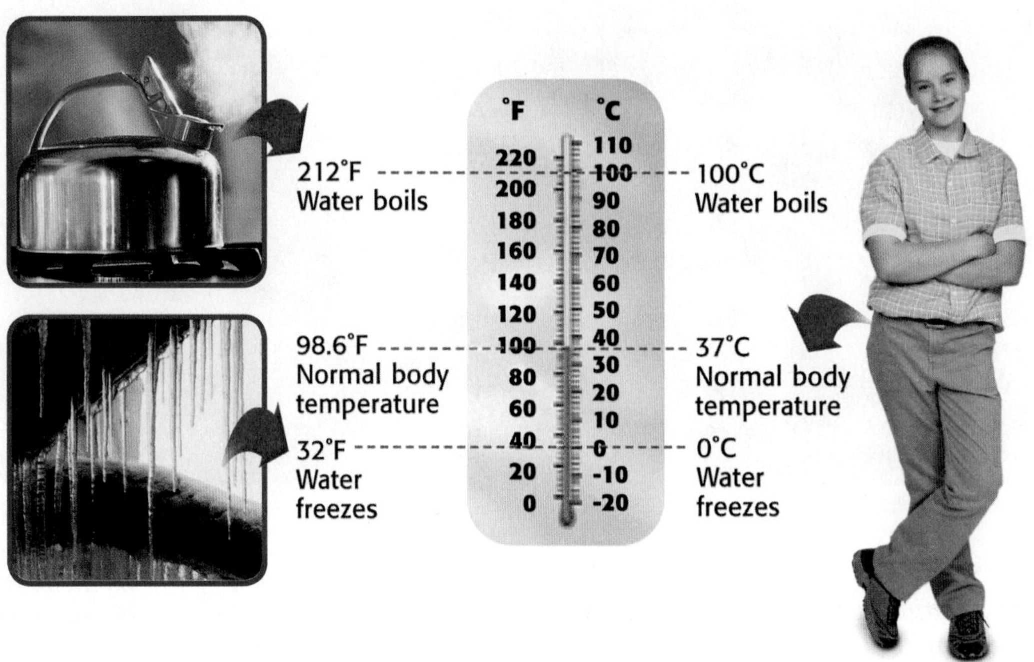

Figure 4 *This thermometer shows the relationship between degrees Fahrenheit and degrees Celsius.*

temperature the measure of how hot (or cold) something is

density the ratio of the mass of a substance to the volume of the substance

Temperature

How hot is melted iron? To answer this question, a scientist would measure the temperature of the liquid metal. **Temperature** is a measure of how hot or cold something is. You probably use degrees Fahrenheit (°F) to describe temperature. Scientists commonly use degrees Celsius (°C), although the kelvin (K) is the official SI base unit for temperature. You will use degrees Celsius in this book. The thermometer in **Figure 4** compares the Fahrenheit and Celsius scales.

Density

If you measure the mass and volume of an object, you have the measurements that you need to find the density of the object. **Density** is the amount of matter in a given volume. You cannot measure density directly. But after you have measured the mass and the volume, you can use the following equation to calculate density:

$$density = \frac{mass}{volume}$$

Density is the ratio of mass to volume, so units often used for density are grams per milliliter (g/mL) and grams per cubic centimeter (g/cm^3). Density may be difficult to understand. Think of a table-tennis ball and a golf ball. They have similar volumes. But a golf ball has more mass than a table-tennis ball does. So the golf ball has a greater density.

CONNECTION TO Social Studies

Archimedes (287 BCE–212 BCE) Archimedes was a Greek mathematician. He was probably the greatest mathematician and scientist that classical Greek civilization produced and is considered to be one of the greatest mathematicians of all time. Archimedes was very interested in putting his theoretical discoveries to practical use. Use the library or Internet to research Archimedes. Make a poster that illustrates one of his scientific or mathematical discoveries.

Safety Rules!

Science is exciting and fun, but it can also be dangerous. Don't take any chances! Always follow your teacher's instructions. Don't take shortcuts—even when you think there is no danger. Before starting an experiment, get your teacher's permission. Read the lab procedures carefully. Pay special attention to safety information and caution statements. **Figure 5** shows the safety symbols used in this book. Get to know these symbols and their meanings. Do so by reading the safety information in the front of this book. **This is important!** If you are still unsure about what a safety symbol means, ask your teacher.

✓ *Reading Check* **Why are safety symbols important?**

Figure 5 Safety Symbols

Eye Protection

Clothing Protection

Hand Safety

Heating Safety

Electric Safety

Sharp Object

Chemical Safety

Animal Safety

Plant Safety

SECTION Review

Summary

- Scientists use a variety of tools to measure and analyze the world around them.
- The International System of Units (SI) is a simple, reliable, and uniform system of measurement that is used by most scientists.
- The basic units of measurement in the SI are the meter (for length), the kilogram (for mass), and the kelvin (for temperature).
- Before starting any science activity or science lab, review the safety symbols and the safety rules for that activity or lab. Don't take chances with your health and safety.

Using Key Terms

Complete each of the following sentences by choosing the correct term from the word bank.

mass	area
volume	temperature

1. A measure of the size of a surface or a region is called ___.
2. Scientists use kilograms when measuring an object's ___.
3. The ___ of a liquid is usually described in liters.

Understanding Key Ideas

4. SI units are
   a. based on standardized measurements of body parts.
   b. almost always based on the number 10.
   c. used to measure only length.
   d. used only in France.
5. What is temperature?
6. If you wanted to measure the mass of a fly, which SI unit would be most appropriate?

Math Skills

7. What is the area of a soccer field that is 110 m long and 85 m wide?
8. What is the density of silver if a 6 cm^3 piece of silver has a mass of 63 g?

Critical Thinking

9. **Applying Concepts** Some people are thinking about sending humans to the moon and then to the planet Mars. Why is it important for scientists around the world to use the International System of Units as they make these plans?
10. **Making Inferences** Give an example of something that can happen if you do not follow safety rules.
11. **Applying Concepts** What tool would you use to measure the mass of the air in a basketball?

SCILINKS
NSTA
Developed and maintained by the National Science Teachers Association
For a variety of links related to this chapter, go to www.scilinks.org
Topic: Tools of Science; SI Units
SciLinks code: HSM1535; HSM1390

Using Scientific Methods

Skills Practice Lab

Does It All Add Up?

OBJECTIVES

Apply scientific methods to predict, measure, and observe the mixing of two unknown liquids.

MATERIALS

- beakers, 100 mL (2)
- Celsius thermometer
- glass-labeling marker
- graduated cylinders, 50 mL (3)
- liquid A, 75 mL
- liquid B, 75 mL
- protective gloves

SAFETY

Your math teacher won't tell you this, but did you know that sometimes 2 + 2 does not appear to equal 4?! In this experiment, you will use scientific methods to predict, measure, and observe the mixing of two unknown liquids. You will learn that a scientist does not set out to prove a hypothesis but to test it and that sometimes the results just don't seem to add up!

Make Observations

1. Put on your safety goggles, gloves, and lab apron. Examine the beakers of liquids A and B provided by your teacher. Write down as many observations as you can about each liquid. **Caution:** Do not taste, touch, or smell the liquids.

2. Pour exactly 25 mL of liquid A from the beaker into each of two 50 mL graduated cylinders. Combine these samples in one of the graduated cylinders. Record the final volume. Pour the liquid back into the beaker of liquid A. Rinse the graduated cylinders. Repeat this step for liquid B.

Form a Hypothesis

3. Based on your observations and on prior experience, formulate a testable hypothesis that states what you expect the volume to be when you combine 25 mL of liquid A with 25 mL of liquid B.

4. Make a prediction based on your hypothesis. Use an if-then format. Explain the basis for your prediction.

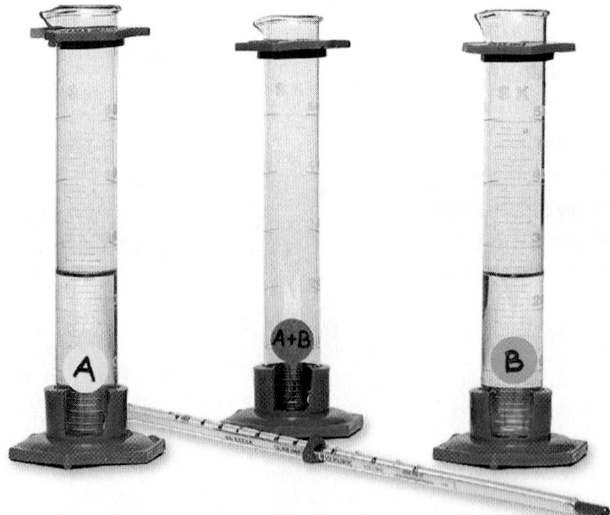

Data Table				
	Contents of cylinder A	Contents of cylinder B	Mixing results: predictions	Mixing results: observations
Volume				
Appearance				
Temperature				

Test the Hypothesis

5. Make a data table like the one above.
6. Mark one graduated cylinder "A." Carefully pour exactly 25 mL of liquid A into this cylinder. In your data table, record its volume, appearance, and temperature.
7. Mark another graduated cylinder "B." Carefully pour exactly 25 mL of liquid B into this cylinder. Record its volume, appearance, and temperature in your data table.
8. Mark the empty third cylinder "A + B."
9. In the "Mixing results: predictions" column in your table, record the prediction you made earlier. Each classmate may have made a different prediction.
10. Carefully pour the contents of both cylinders into the third graduated cylinder.
11. Observe and record the total volume, appearance, and temperature in the "Mixing results: observations" column of your table.

Analyze the Results

1. **Analyzing Data** Discuss your predictions as a class. How many different predictions were there? Which predictions were supported by testing? Did any measurements surprise you?

Draw Conclusions

2. **Drawing Conclusions** Was your hypothesis supported or disproven? Either way, explain your thinking. Describe everything that you think you learned from this experiment.
3. **Analyzing Methods** Explain the value of incorrect predictions.

Chapter Review

USING KEY TERMS

1. Use the following terms in the same sentence: *science* and *scientific methods*.

2. Use the following terms in the same sentence: *controlled experiment* and *variable*.

For each pair of terms, explain how the meanings of the terms differ.

3. *theory* and *hypothesis*

4. *controlled experiment* and *variable*

5. *area* and *volume*

6. *physical model* and *conceptual model*

UNDERSTANDING KEY IDEAS

Multiple Choice

7. The steps of scientific methods
   - **a.** must all be used in every scientific investigation.
   - **b.** must always be used in the same order.
   - **c.** often start with a question.
   - **d.** always result in the development of a theory.

8. In a controlled experiment,
   - **a.** a control group is compared with one or more experimental groups.
   - **b.** there are at least two variables.
   - **c.** all factors should be different.
   - **d.** a variable is not needed.

9. Which of the following tools is best for measuring 100 mL of water?
   - **a.** 10 mL graduated cylinder
   - **b.** 150 mL graduated cylinder
   - **c.** 250 mL beaker
   - **d.** 500 mL beaker

10. Which of the following is NOT an SI unit?
    - **a.** meter
    - **b.** foot
    - **c.** liter
    - **d.** kilogram

11. A pencil is 14 cm long. How many millimeters long is it?
    - **a.** 1.4 mm
    - **b.** 140 mm
    - **c.** 1,400 mm
    - **d.** 1,400,000 mm

12. The directions for a lab include the safety icons shown below. These icons mean that

    - **a.** you should be careful.
    - **b.** you are going into the laboratory.
    - **c.** you should wash your hands first.
    - **d.** you should wear safety goggles, a lab apron, and gloves during the lab.

Short Answer

13. List three ways that science is beneficial to living things.

14. Why do hypotheses need to be testable?

15. Give an example of how a scientist might use computers and technology.

16. List three types of models, and give an example of each.

17. What are some advantages and limitations of models?

18. Which SI units can be used to describe the volume of an object? Which SI units can be used to describe the mass of an object?

19. In a controlled experiment, why should there be several individuals in the control group and in each of the experimental groups?

CRITICAL THINKING

20. **Concept Mapping** Use the following terms to create a concept map: *observations, predictions, questions, controlled experiments, variable,* and *hypothesis*.

21. **Making Inferences** Investigations often begin with observation. What limits the observations that scientists can make?

22. **Forming Hypotheses** A scientist who studies mice makes the following observation: On the day the mice are fed vitamins with their meals, they perform better in mazes. What hypothesis would you form to explain this phenomenon? Write a testable prediction based on your hypothesis.

INTERPRETING GRAPHICS

The pictures below show how an egg can be measured by using a beaker and water. Use the pictures below to answer the questions that follow.

23. What kind of measurement is being taken?

a. area
b. length
c. mass
d. volume

24. Which of the following is an accurate measurement of the egg in the picture?

a. 75 cm^3
b. 125 cm^3
c. 125 mL
d. 200 mL

25. Make a double line graph using the data in the table below.

Number of Frogs		
Date	**Normal**	**Deformed**
1995	25	0
1996	21	0
1997	19	1
1998	20	2
1999	17	3
2000	20	5

Standardized Test Preparation

Multiple Choice

Use the diagram below to answer question 1.

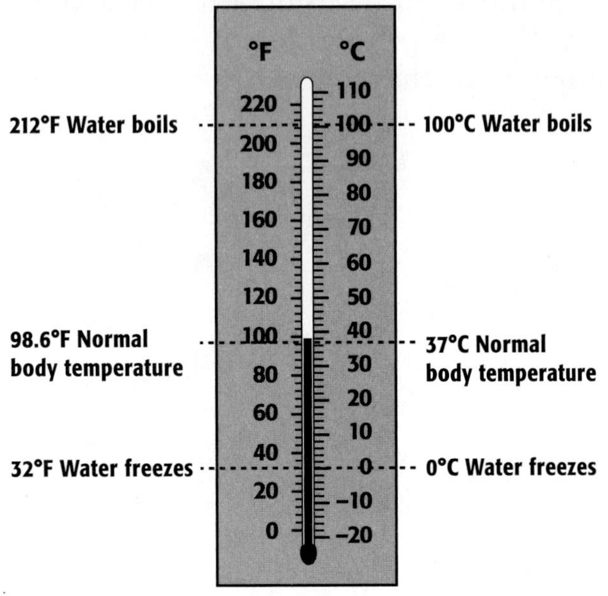

1. The thermometer above correlates Fahrenheit and Celsius temperature scales. According to the thermometer, which of the following sentences is true?

A. You can swim in water that is 100°C.

B. You can boil eggs in water that is 150°F.

C. You can skate on water that is 10°C.

D. Your body temperature is about 37°C.

2. What is the purpose of scientific investigation?

A. to demonstrate how science works

B. to ask questions and make observations

C. to perform experiments

D. to answer certain kinds of questions about the world

3. Which of the following is a tool for measuring the volume of a liquid?

A. graduated cylinder

B. cubic centimeter

C. liter

D. meterstick

4. Which of the following is a feature of a scale model?

A. An unfamiliar thing is explained by comparing the unfamiliar thing to something that is familiar.

B. The measurements of the model are proportional to the measurements of the real object.

C. The mass of an object is measured using a scale or balance and represented on the model through labels.

D. Numbers, equations, and data are used to find patterns within combinations of variables.

5. A scientist hypothesizes new factories are raising pollution levels in several nearby lakes. What is the best way to test the hypothesis?

A. to do library research on the harmful effects of acid precipitation in lakes

B. to experiment with how pollution affects water plants that are native to Georgia

C. to count the number of water plant species found in a Georgia lake

D. to collect lake water samples and test each sample for pollution levels

Use the table below to answer question 6.

Testing Matrix: Effect of UV Light on Leopard Frogs			
Group	Number of eggs	Temperature of water (°C)	UV light exposure (days)
#1 (control)	100	25	0
#2 (experimental)	100	25	15
#3 (experimental)	100	25	24

6. The data in the table above were collected during an experiment to test the effects of ultraviolet (UV) light on frogs. What is the independent variable in the experiment?

A. water temperature

B. length of exposure to UV light

C. number of eggs

D. kind of frog

7. Which of these common steps in a scientific inquiry involves coming up with a possible answer to a question about the world?

A. communication of results

B. formation of a hypothesis

C. making observations

D. testing a hypothesis

8. How many grams are in 1.2 kg?

A. 12 g

B. 120 g

C. 1,200 g

D. 12,000 g

9. Which of the following is a symbol for an SI unit of length?

A. m

B. cm^3

C. L

D. kg

Open Response

10. A biologist designs an experiment to determine the eating habits of cardinals. She performs her tests on 20 captured birds that live in identical cages. She feeds half of the cardinals a set amount of food each day. She lets the other half of the birds eat as much as they would like. All other aspects of their care are the same. Is this a controlled experiment? What is the variable in the experiment? Explain your answer.

11. From a scientific point of view, what is the problem with the following claim about an animal that is native to Kentucky? "Slender Glass Lizards are happy for eight hours each day."

Science in Action

Scientific Debate

Should We Stop All Forest Fires?

Since 1972, the policy of the National Park Service has been to manage the national parks as naturally as possible. Because fire is a natural event in forests, this policy includes allowing most fires caused by lightning to burn. The only lightning-caused fires that are put out are those that threaten lives, property, uniquely scenic areas, or endangered species. All human-caused fires are put out. However, this policy has caused some controversy. Some people want this policy followed in all public forests and even grasslands. Others think that all fires should be put out.

Social Studies ACTIVITY

WRITING SKILL Research a location where there is a debate about controlling forest fires. You might look into national forests or parks. Write a newspaper article about the issue. Be sure to present all sides of the debate.

Science Fiction

"The Homesick Chicken" by Edward D. Hoch

Why did the chicken cross the road? You think you know the answer to this old riddle, don't you? But "The Homesick Chicken," by Edward D. Hoch, may surprise you. That old chicken may not be exactly what it seems.

You see, one of the chickens at the high-tech Tangaway Research Farms has escaped. Then, it was found in a vacant lot across the highway from Tangaway, pecking away contentedly. Why did it bother to escape? Barnabus Rex, a specialist in solving scientific riddles, is called in to work on this mystery. As he investigates, he finds clues and forms a hypothesis. Read the story, and see if you can explain the mystery before Mr. Rex does.

Language Arts ACTIVITY

WRITING SKILL Write your own short story about a chicken crossing a road for a mysterious reason. Give clues (evidence) to the reader about the mysterious reason but do not reveal the truth until the end of the story. Be sure the story makes sense scientifically.

People in Science

George Archibald

Dancing with Cranes Imagine a man flapping his arms in a dance with a whooping crane. Does this sound funny? When Dr. George Archibald danced with a crane named Tex, he wasn't joking around. To help this endangered species survive, Archibald wanted cranes to mate in captivity so that he could release cranes into the wild. But the captive cranes wouldn't do their courtship dance. Archibald's cranes had imprinted on the humans that raised them. *Imprinting* is a process in which birds learn to recognize their species by looking at their parents. The birds saw humans as their own species, and could only reproduce if a human did the courtship dance. So, Archibald decided to dance. His plan worked! After some time, Tex hatched a baby crane.

After that, Archibald found a way to help the captive cranes imprint on other cranes. He and his staff now feed baby cranes with hand puppets that look like crane heads. They play recordings of real crane sounds for the young cranes. They even wear crane suits when they are near older birds. These cranes are happy to do their courtship dance with each other instead of with Archibald.

Math Activity

Suppose you want to drive a group of cranes from Madison, Wisconsin, to Orlando, Florida. Find and measure this distance on a map. If your truck goes 500 km per gas tank and a tank costs $30, how much would gas cost on your trip?

To learn more about these Science in Action topics, visit go.hrw.com and type in the keyword **HZ5SW7F.**

Current Science

Check out Current Science® articles related to this chapter by visiting go.hrw.com. Just type in the keyword HZ5CS01.

TIMELINE

Life Processes

Life science is the study of living things—from the tiniest bacterium to the largest tree! In this unit, you will discover the similarities of all living things. You will learn about important processes such as cellular respiration and photosynthesis. These life processes make life possible on Earth.

This timeline includes a few of the many people who have studied living things and a few events that have shaped the history of life science. And there's always more to be learned, so keep your eyes open.

Around 2700 BCE

Si Ling-Chi, empress of China, observes silkworms in her garden and develops a process to cultivate them and make silk.

1931

The first electron microscope is developed.

1934

Dorothy Crowfoot Hodgkin uses X-ray techniques to determine the protein structure of insulin.

1970

Floppy disks for computer data storage are introduced.

1983

Dian Fossey writes *Gorillas in the Mist*, a book about her research on mountain gorillas in Africa and her efforts to save them from poachers.

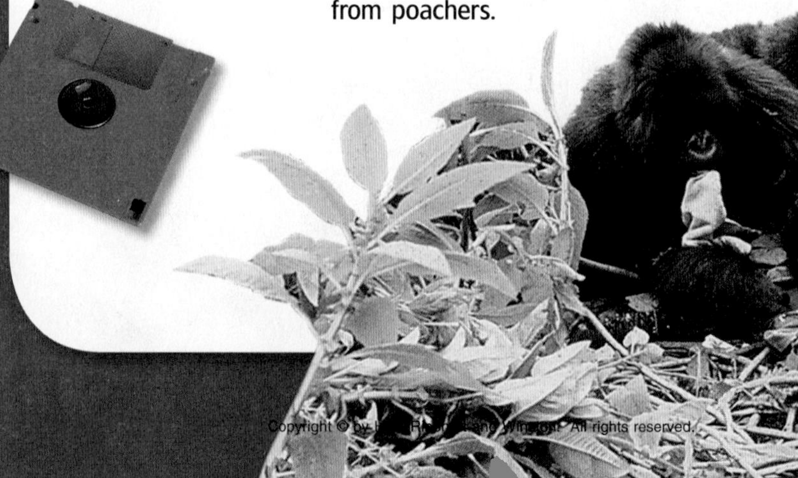

Around 1000
Arab mathematician and physicist Ibn al Haytham discovers that vision is caused by the reflection of light from objects into the eye.

1684
Improvements to microscopes allow the first observation of red blood cells.

1914
His studies on agriculture and soil conservation lead George Washington Carver to perform research on peanuts.

1944
Oswald T. Avery demonstrates that DNA is the material that carries genetic properties in living organisms.

1946
ENIAC, the first entirely electronic computer, is built. It weighs 30 tons.

1967
Dr. Christiaan Barnard performs the first successful human heart transplant.

1984
A process known as DNA fingerprinting is developed by Alec Jeffreys.

1998
In China, scientists discover a fossil of a dinosaur that had feathers.

2001
A team of scientists led by Philippa Uwins announces that tiny nanobes that are 20 to 150 nanometers wide have been found in Australia. Scientists debate whether these particles are living.

2

The Cell in Action

The Big Idea

Cells carry out important life functions including taking in nutrients and releasing materials, obtaining energy, and growing.

SECTION

About the Photo

This adult katydid is emerging from its last immature, or nymph, stage. As the katydid changed from a nymph to an adult, every structure of its body changed. To grow and change, an organism must produce new cells. When a cell divides, it makes a copy of its genetic material.

PRE-READING ACTIVITY

FOLDNOTES

Tri-Fold Before you read the chapter, create the FoldNote entitled "Tri-Fold" described in the **Study Skills** section of the Appendix. Write what you know about the actions of cells in the column labeled "Know." Then, write what you want to know in the column labeled "Want." As you read the chapter, write what you learn about the actions of cells in the column labeled "Learn."

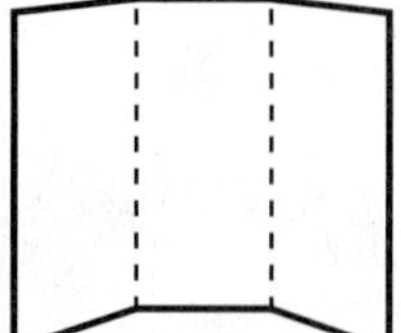

START-UP ACTIVITY

Cells in Action

Yeast are single-celled fungi that are an important ingredient in bread. Yeast cells break down sugar molecules to release energy. In the process, carbon dioxide gas is produced, which causes bread dough to rise.

Procedure

1. Add **4 mL of a sugar solution** to **10 mL of a yeast-and-water mixture**. Use a **stirring rod** to thoroughly mix the two liquids.
2. Pour the stirred mixture into a small test tube.
3. Place a slightly **larger test tube** over the **small test tube.** The top of the small test tube should touch the bottom of the larger test tube.
4. Hold the test tubes together, and quickly turn both test tubes over. Place the test tubes in a test-tube rack.
5. Use a **ruler** to measure the height of the fluid in the large test tube. Wait 20 min, and then measure the height of the liquid again.

Analysis

1. What is the difference between the first height measurement and the second height measurement?
2. What do you think caused the change in the fluid's height?

SECTION 1

Exchange with the Environment

What You Will Learn

- Explain the process of diffusion.
- Describe how osmosis occurs.
- Compare passive transport with active transport.
- Explain how large particles get into and out of cells.

Vocabulary

diffusion
osmosis
passive transport
active transport
endocytosis
exocytosis

READING STRATEGY

Reading Organizer As you read this section, make a table comparing active transport and passive transport.

What would happen to a factory if its power were shut off or its supply of raw materials never arrived? What would happen if the factory couldn't get rid of its garbage?

Like a factory, an organism must be able to obtain energy and raw materials and get rid of wastes. An organism's cells perform all of these functions. These functions keep cells healthy so that they can divide. Cell division allows organisms to grow and repair injuries.

The exchange of materials between a cell and its environment takes place at the cell's membrane. To understand how materials move into and out of the cell, you need to know about diffusion.

What Is Diffusion?

What happens if you pour dye on top of a layer of gelatin? At first, it is easy to see where the dye ends and the gelatin begins. But over time, the line between the two layers will blur, as shown in **Figure 1.** Why? Everything, including the gelatin and the dye, is made up of tiny moving particles. Particles travel from where they are crowded to where they are less crowded. This movement from areas of high concentration (crowded) to areas of low concentration (less crowded) is called **diffusion** (di FYOO zhuhn). Dye particles diffuse from where they are crowded (near the top of the glass) to where they are less crowded (in the gelatin). Diffusion also happens within and between living cells. Cells do not need to use energy for diffusion.

diffusion the movement of particles from regions of higher density to regions of lower density

Figure 1 *The particles of the dye and the gelatin slowly mix by diffusion.*

Figure 2 Osmosis

❶ The side that holds only pure water has the higher concentration of water particles.

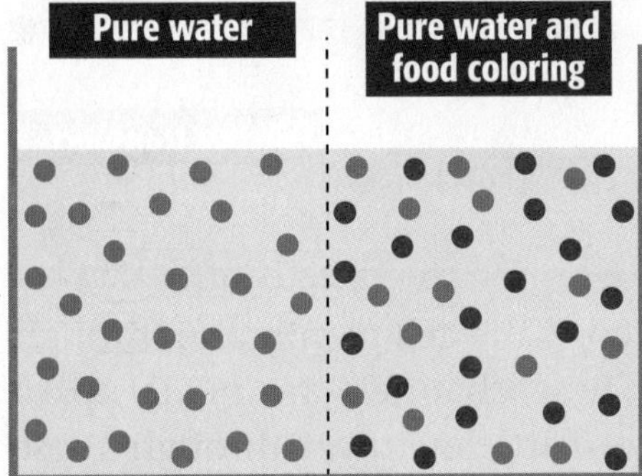

❷ During osmosis, water particles move to where they are less concentrated.

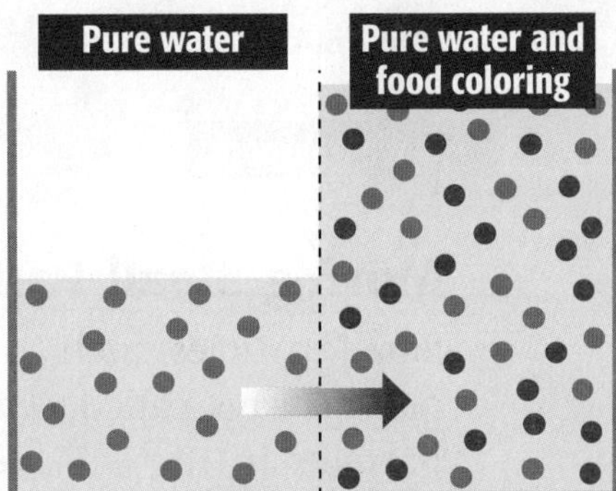

Diffusion of Water

The cells of organisms are surrounded by and filled with fluids that are made mostly of water. The diffusion of water through cell membranes is so important to life processes that it has been given a special name—**osmosis** (ahs MOH sis).

osmosis the diffusion of water through a semipermeable membrane

Water is made up of particles, called *molecules*. Pure water has the highest concentration of water molecules. When you mix something, such as food coloring, sugar, or salt, with water, you lower the concentration of water molecules. **Figure 2** shows how water molecules move through a membrane that is semipermeable (SEM i PUHR mee uh buhl). *Semipermeable* means that only certain substances can pass through. The picture on the left in **Figure 2** shows liquids that have different concentrations of water. Over time, the water molecules move from the liquid with the high concentration of water molecules to the liquid with the lower concentration of water molecules.

The Cell and Osmosis

Osmosis is important to cell functions. For example, red blood cells are surrounded by plasma. Plasma is made up of water, salts, sugars, and other particles. The concentration of these particles is kept in balance by osmosis. If red blood cells were in pure water, water molecules would flood into the cells and cause them to burst. When red blood cells are put into a salty solution, the concentration of water molecules inside the cell is higher than the concentration of water outside. This difference makes water move out of the cells, and the cells shrivel up. Osmosis also occurs in plant cells. When a wilted plant is watered, osmosis makes the plant firm again.

✓ Reading Check **Why would red blood cells burst if you placed them in pure water?** (*See the Appendix for answers to Reading Checks.*)

Bead Diffusion

1. Put three groups of **colored beads** on the bottom of a **plastic bowl.** Each group should be made up of five beads of the same color.
2. Stretch some **clear plastic wrap** tightly over the top of the bowl. Gently shake the bowl for 10 seconds while watching the beads.
3. How is the scattering of the beads like the diffusion of particles? How is it different from the diffusion of particles?

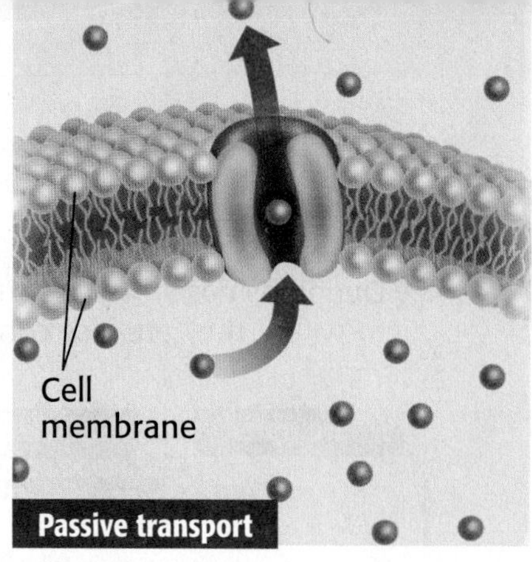

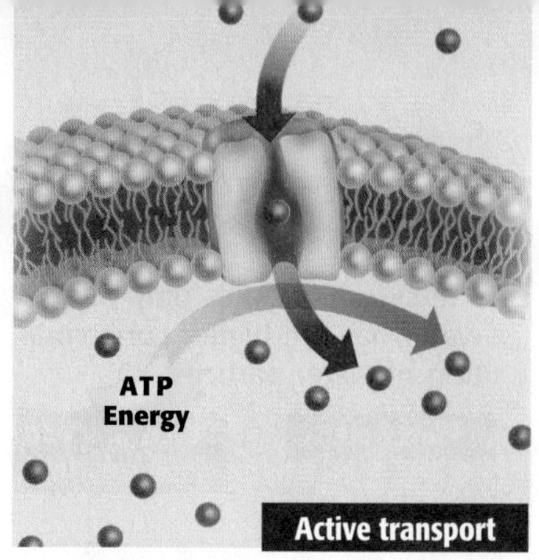

Figure 3 *In passive transport, particles travel through proteins to areas of lower concentration. In active transport, cells use energy to move particles, usually to areas of higher concentration.*

Moving Small Particles

Small particles, such as sugars, cross the cell membrane through passageways called *channels*. These channels are made up of proteins in the cell membrane. Particles travel through these channels by either passive or active transport. The movement of particles across a cell membrane without the use of energy by the cell is called **passive transport**, and is shown in **Figure 3.** During passive transport, particles move from an area of high concentration to an area of low concentration. Diffusion and osmosis are examples of passive transport.

A process of transporting particles that requires the cell to use energy is called **active transport.** Active transport usually involves the movement of particles from an area of low concentration to an area of high concentration.

passive transport the movement of substances across a cell membrane without the use of energy by the cell

active transport the movement of substances across the cell membrane that requires the cell to use energy

endocytosis the process by which a cell membrane surrounds a particle and encloses the particle in a vesicle to bring the particle into the cell

Moving Large Particles

Small particles cross the cell membrane by diffusion, passive transport, and active transport. Large particles move into and out of the cell by processes called *endocytosis* and *exocytosis.*

Endocytosis

The active-transport process by which a cell surrounds a large particle, such as a large protein, and encloses the particle in a vesicle to bring the particle into the cell is called **endocytosis** (EN doh sie TOH sis). *Vesicles* are sacs formed from pieces of cell membrane. **Figure 4** shows endocytosis.

Figure 4 **Endocytosis**

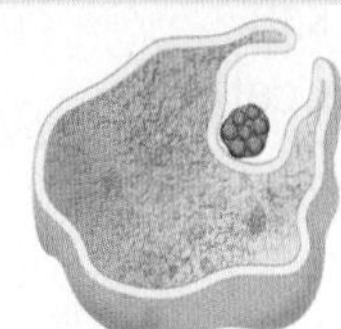

1. The cell comes into contact with a particle.

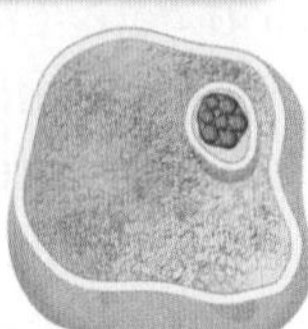

2. The cell membrane begins to wrap around the particle.

3. Once the particle is completely surrounded, a vesicle pinches off.

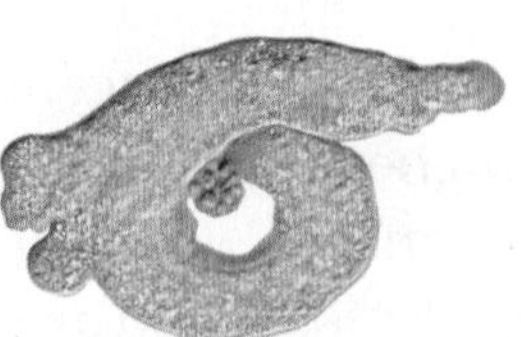

This photo shows the end of *endocytosis,* which means "within the cell."

Figure 5 **Exocytosis**

❶ Large particles that must leave the cell are packaged in vesicles.

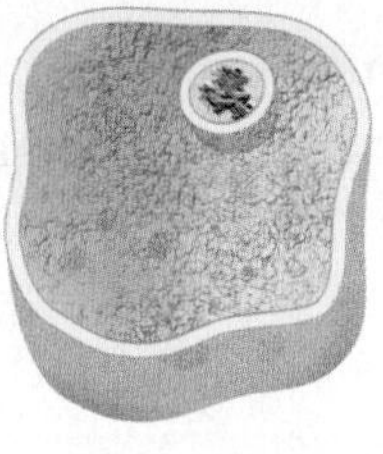

❷ The vesicle travels to the cell membrane and fuses with it.

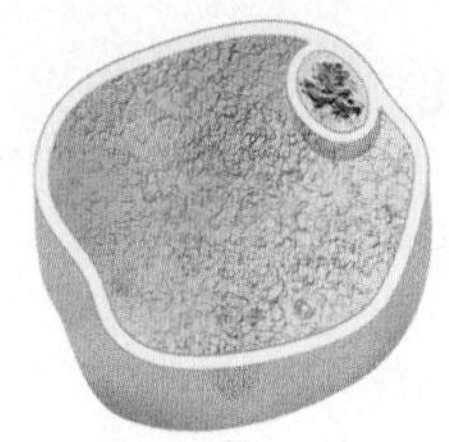

❸ The cell releases the particle to the outside of the cell.

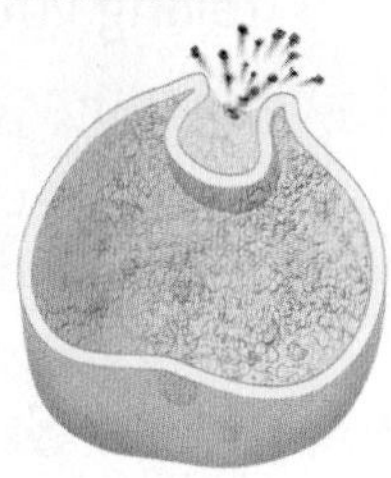

Exocytosis means "outside the cell."

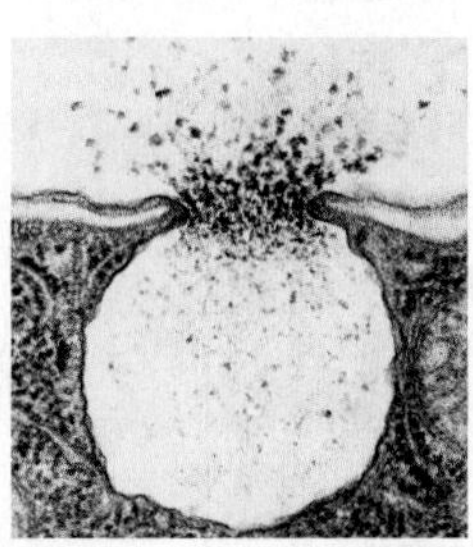

Exocytosis

When large particles, such as wastes, leave the cell, the cell uses an active-transport process called **exocytosis** (EK soh sie TOH sis). During exocytosis, a vesicle forms around a large particle within the cell. The vesicle carries the particle to the cell membrane. The vesicle fuses with the cell membrane and releases the particle to the outside of the cell. **Figure 5** shows exocytosis.

exocytosis the process in which a cell releases a particle by enclosing the particle in a vesicle that then moves to the cell surface and fuses with the cell membrane

Reading Check What is exocytosis?

SECTION Review

Summary

- Diffusion is the movement of particles from an area of high concentration to an area of low concentration.
- Osmosis is the diffusion of water through a semipermeable membrane.
- Cells move small particles by diffusion, which is an example of passive transport, and by active transport.
- Large particles enter the cell by endocytosis, and exit the cell by exocytosis.

Using Key Terms

For each pair of terms, explain how the meanings of the terms differ.

1. *diffusion* and *osmosis*
2. *active transport* and *passive transport*
3. *endocytosis* and *exocytosis*

Understanding Key Ideas

4. The movement of particles from a less crowded area to a more crowded area requires
   a. sunlight. **c.** a membrane.
   b. energy. **d.** osmosis.
5. What structures allow small particles to cross cell membranes?

Math Skills

6. The area of particle 1 is 2.5 mm^2. The area of particle 2 is 0.5 mm^2. The area of particle 1 is how many times as big as the area of particle 2?

Critical Thinking

7. **Predicting Consequences** What would happen to a cell if its channel proteins were damaged and unable to transport particles? What would happen to the organism if many of its cells were damaged in this way? Explain your answer.
8. **Analyzing Ideas** Why does active transport require energy?

SCILINKS.
NSTA
Developed and maintained by the National Science Teachers Association
For a variety of links related to this chapter, go to www.scilinks.org
Topics: Diffusion; Osmosis
SciLinks code: HSM0406; HSM1090

SECTION 2

Cell Energy

Why do you get hungry? Feeling hungry is your body's way of telling you that your cells need energy.

All cells need energy to live, grow, and reproduce. Plant cells get their energy from the sun. Many animal cells get the energy they need from food.

What You Will Learn

- Describe photosynthesis and cellular respiration.
- Compare cellular respiration with fermentation.

Vocabulary

photosynthesis
cellular respiration
fermentation

READING STRATEGY

Discussion Read this section silently. Write down questions that you have about this section. Discuss your questions in a small group.

From Sun to Cell

Nearly all of the energy that fuels life comes from the sun. Plants capture energy from the sun and change it into food through a process called **photosynthesis.** The food that plants make supplies them with energy. This food also becomes a source of energy for the organisms that eat the plants.

photosynthesis the process by which plants, algae, and some bacteria use sunlight, carbon dioxide, and water to make food

Photosynthesis

Plant cells have molecules that absorb light energy. These molecules are called *pigments*. Chlorophyll (KLAWR uh FIL), the main pigment used in photosynthesis, gives plants their green color. Chlorophyll is found in chloroplasts.

Plants use the energy captured by chlorophyll to change carbon dioxide and water into food. The food is in the form of the simple sugar glucose. Glucose is a carbohydrate. When plants make glucose, they convert the sun's energy into a form of energy that can be stored. The energy in glucose is used by the plant's cells. Photosynthesis also produces oxygen. Photosynthesis is summarized in **Figure 1.**

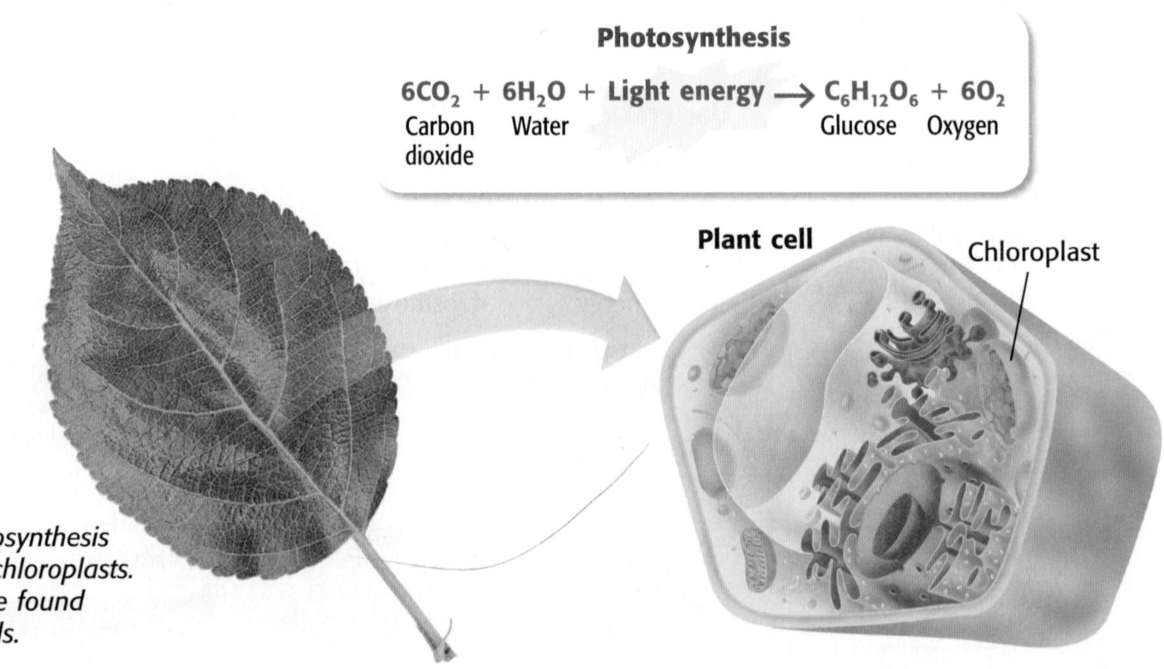

Figure 1 *Photosynthesis takes place in chloroplasts. Chloroplasts are found inside plant cells.*

Getting Energy from Food

Animal cells have different ways of getting energy from food. One way, called **cellular respiration,** uses oxygen to break down food. Many cells can get energy without using oxygen through a process called **fermentation.** Cellular respiration will release more energy from a given food than fermentation will.

Cellular Respiration

The word *respiration* means "breathing," but cellular respiration is different from breathing. Breathing supplies the oxygen needed for cellular respiration. Breathing also removes carbon dioxide, which is a waste product of cellular respiration. But cellular respiration is a chemical process that occurs in cells.

Most complex organisms, such as plants and animals, obtain energy through cellular respiration. During cellular respiration, food (such as glucose) is broken down into CO_2 and H_2O, and energy is released. In animals, most of the energy released maintains body temperature. Some of the energy is used to form adenosine triphosphate (ATP). ATP supplies energy that fuels cell activities.

Most of the process of cellular respiration takes place in the cell membrane of prokaryotic cells. But in the cells of eukaryotes, cellular respiration takes place mostly in the mitochondria. The process of cellular respiration is summarized in **Figure 2.** Does the equation in the figure remind you of the equation for photosynthesis? **Figure 3** on the next page shows how photosynthesis and respiration are related.

Reading Check **What is the difference between cellular respiration and breathing?** (*See the Appendix for answers to Reading Checks.*)

CONNECTION TO Chemistry

Earth's Early Atmosphere

Scientists think that Earth's early atmosphere lacked oxygen. Because of this lack of oxygen, early organisms used fermentation to get energy from food. When organisms began to photosynthesize, the oxygen they produced entered the atmosphere. How do you think this oxygen changed how other organisms got energy?

cellular respiration the process by which cells use oxygen to produce energy from food

fermentation the breakdown of food without the use of oxygen

Cellular Respiration

$$C_6H_{12}O_6 + 6O_2 \rightarrow 6CO_2 + 6H_2O + \text{energy (ATP)}$$

Glucose, Oxygen, Carbon dioxide, Water

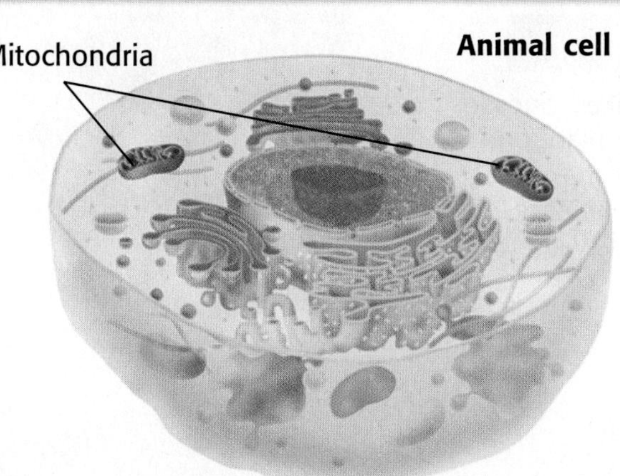

Figure 2 *The mitochondria in the cells of this cow will use cellular respiration to release the energy stored in the grass.*

Figure 3 The Connection Between Photosynthesis and Respiration

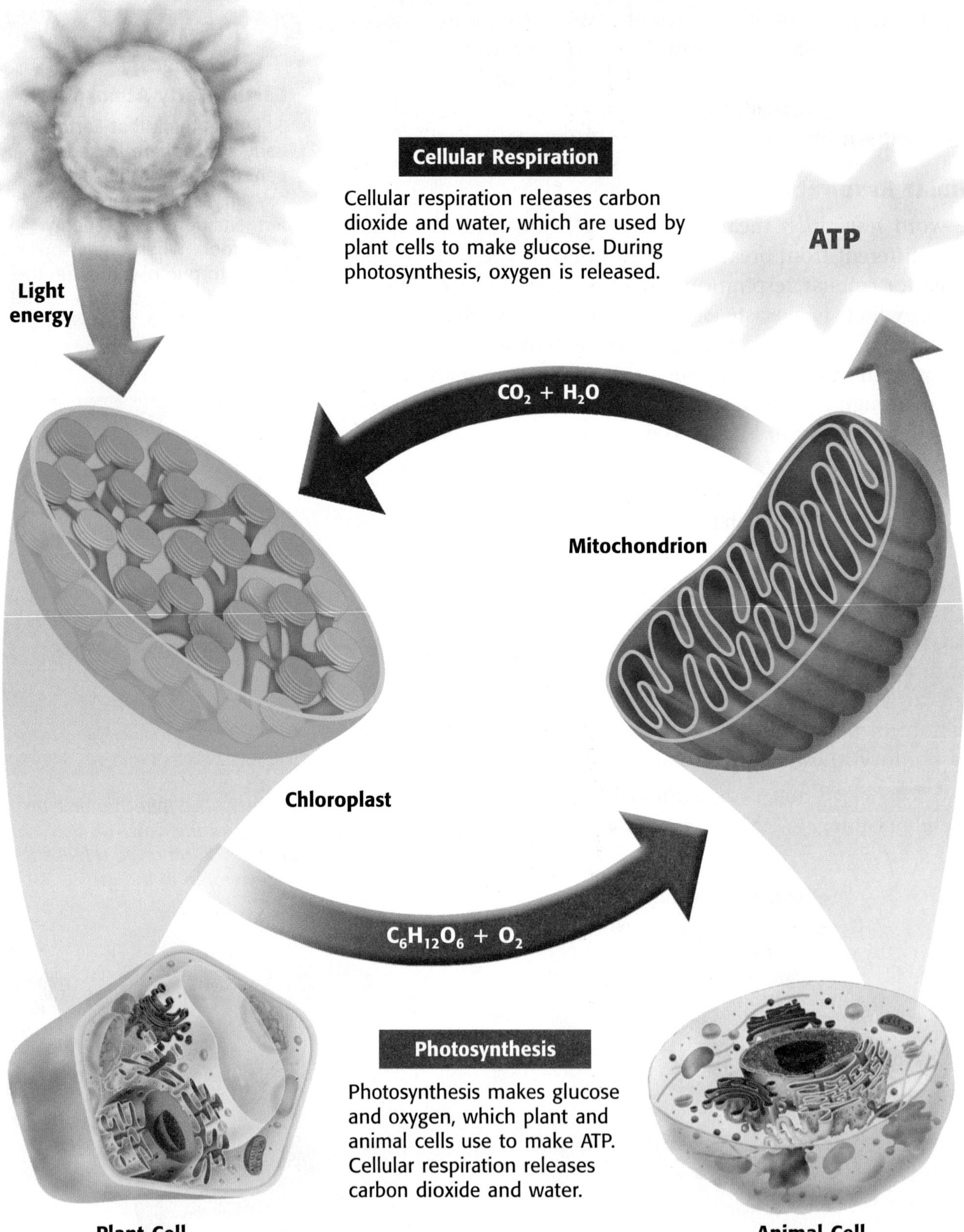
Cellular Respiration
Cellular respiration releases carbon dioxide and water, which are used by plant cells to make glucose. During photosynthesis, oxygen is released.
ATP
Light energy
$CO_2 + H_2O$
Mitochondrion
Chloroplast
$C_6H_{12}O_6 + O_2$
Photosynthesis
Photosynthesis makes glucose and oxygen, which plant and animal cells use to make ATP. Cellular respiration releases carbon dioxide and water.
Plant Cell
Animal Cell

Connection Between Photosynthesis and Respiration

As shown in **Figure 3,** photosynthesis transforms energy from the sun into glucose. During photosynthesis, cells use CO_2 to make glucose, and the cells release O_2. During cellular respiration, cells use O_2 to break down glucose and release energy and CO_2. Each process makes the materials that are needed for the other process to occur elsewhere.

Fermentation

Have you ever felt a burning sensation in your leg muscles while you were running? When muscle cells can't get the oxygen needed for cellular respiration, they use the process of fermentation to get energy. One kind of fermentation happens in your muscles and produces lactic acid. The buildup of lactic acid contributes to muscle fatigue and causes a burning sensation. This kind of fermentation also happens in the muscle cells of other animals and in some fungi and bacteria. Another type of fermentation occurs in some types of bacteria and in yeast as described in **Figure 4.**

Figure 4 *Yeast forms carbon dioxide during fermentation. The bubbles of CO_2 gas cause the dough to rise and leave small holes in bread after it is baked.*

Reading Check **What are two kinds of fermentation?**

SECTION Review

Summary

- Most of the energy that fuels life processes comes from the sun.
- The sun's energy is converted into food by the process of photosynthesis.
- Cellular respiration breaks down glucose into water, carbon dioxide, and energy.
- Fermentation is a way that cells get energy from their food without using oxygen.

Using Key Terms

1. In your own words, write a definition for the term *fermentation*.

Understanding Key Ideas

2. O_2 is released during
   a. cellular respiration.
   b. photosynthesis.
   c. breathing.
   d. fermentation.
3. How are photosynthesis and cellular respiration related?
4. How are respiration and fermentation similar? How are they different?

Math Skills

5. Cells of plant A make 120 molecules of glucose an hour. Cells of plant B make half as much glucose as plant A does. How much glucose does plant B make every minute?

Critical Thinking

6. **Analyzing Relationships** Why are plants important to the survival of all other organisms?
7. **Applying Concepts** You have been given the job of restoring life to a barren island. What types of organisms would you put on the island? If you want to have animals on the island, what other organisms must you bring? Explain your answer.

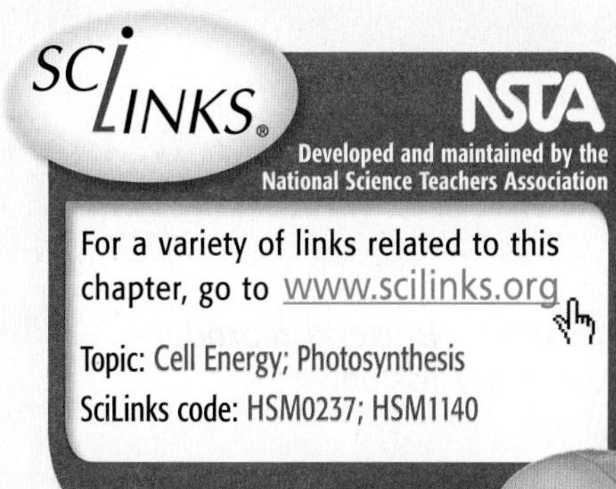

SCILINKS
NSTA
Developed and maintained by the National Science Teachers Association
For a variety of links related to this chapter, go to www.scilinks.org
Topic: Cell Energy; Photosynthesis
SciLinks code: HSM0237; HSM1140

SECTION 3

The Cell Cycle

What You Will Learn

- Explain how cells produce more cells.
- Describe the process of mitosis.
- Explain how cell division differs in animals and plants.

Vocabulary

cell cycle
chromosome
homologous chromosomes
mitosis
cytokinesis

READING STRATEGY

Paired Summarizing Read this section silently. In pairs, take turns summarizing the material. Stop to discuss ideas that seem confusing.

In the time that it takes you to read this sentence, your body will have made millions of new cells! Making new cells allows you to grow and replace cells that have died.

The environment in your stomach is so acidic that the cells lining your stomach must be replaced every few days. Other cells are replaced less often, but your body is constantly making new cells.

The Life of a Cell

As you grow, you pass through different stages in life. Your cells also pass through different stages in their life cycle. The life cycle of a cell is called the **cell cycle.**

The cell cycle begins when the cell is formed and ends when the cell divides and forms new cells. Before a cell divides, it must make a copy of its deoxyribonucleic acid (DNA). DNA is the hereditary material that controls all cell activities, including the making of new cells. The DNA of a cell is organized into structures called **chromosomes.** Copying chromosomes ensures that each new cell will be an exact copy of its parent cell. How does a cell make more cells? It depends on whether the cell is prokaryotic (with no nucleus) or eukaryotic (with a nucleus).

cell cycle the life cycle of a cell

chromosome in a eukaryotic cell, one of the structures in the nucleus that are made up of DNA and protein; in a prokaryotic cell, the main ring of DNA

Making More Prokaryotic Cells

Prokaryotic cells are less complex than eukaryotic cells are. Bacteria, which are prokaryotes, have ribosomes and a single, circular DNA molecule but don't have membrane-enclosed organelles. Cell division in bacteria is called *binary fission,* which means "splitting into two parts." Binary fission results in two cells that each contain one copy of the circle of DNA. A few of the bacteria in **Figure 1** are undergoing binary fission.

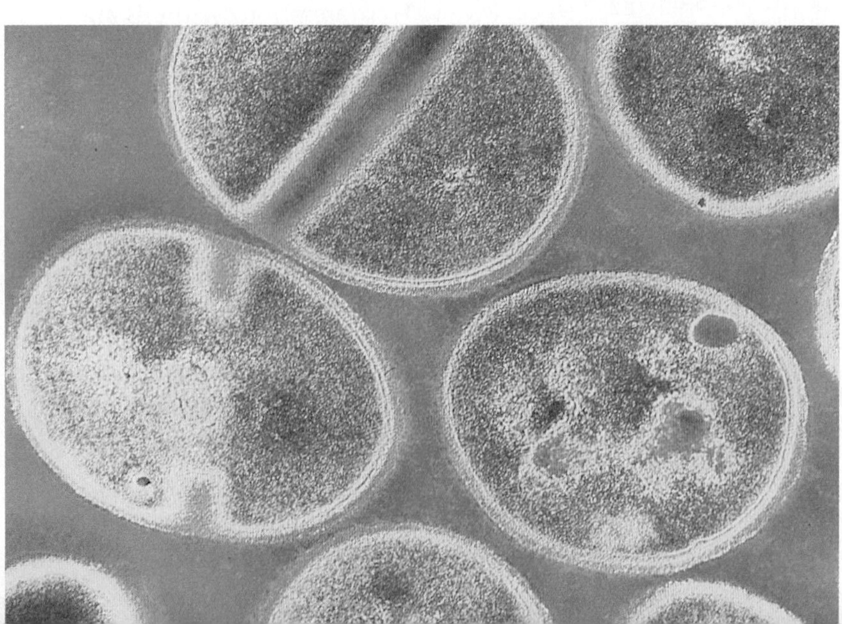

Figure 1 *Bacteria reproduce by binary fission.*

Eukaryotic Cells and Their DNA

Eukaryotic cells are more complex than prokaryotic cells are. The chromosomes of eukaryotic cells contain more DNA than those of prokaryotic cells do. Different kinds of eukaryotes have different numbers of chromosomes. More-complex eukaryotes do not necessarily have more chromosomes than simpler eukaryotes do. For example, fruit flies have 8 chromosomes, potatoes have 48, and humans have 46. **Figure 2** shows the 46 chromosomes of a human body cell lined up in pairs. These pairs are made up of similar chromosomes known as **homologous chromosomes** (hoh MAHL uh guhs KROH muh SOHMZ).

Reading Check **Do more-complex organisms always have more chromosomes than simpler organisms do?** *(See the Appendix for answers to Reading Checks.)*

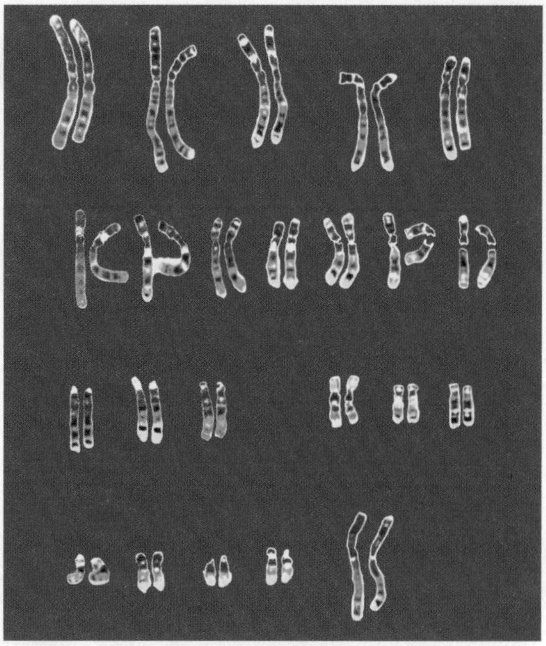

Figure 2 *Human body cells have 46 chromosomes, or 23 pairs of chromosomes.*

Making More Eukaryotic Cells

The eukaryotic cell cycle includes three stages. In the first stage, called *interphase,* the cell grows and copies its organelles and chromosomes. After each chromosome is duplicated, the cell enters the second stage of the cell cycle.

In the second stage, each chromosome twists, coils, and condenses into an X shape, as shown in **Figure 3.** The X shape is made up of two *chromatids,* which are held together at a region called the *centromere.* After this step, the chromatids separate. The complicated process by which chromosomes condense and separate is called **mitosis.** Mitosis ensures that each new cell receives a copy of each chromosome. Mitosis is divided into four phases, as shown on the following pages.

In the third stage, the cell splits into two cells. These cells are identical to each other and to the original cell.

homologous chromosomes chromosomes that have the same sequence of genes and the same structure

mitosis in eukaryotic cells, a process of cell division that forms two new nuclei, each of which has the same number of chromosomes

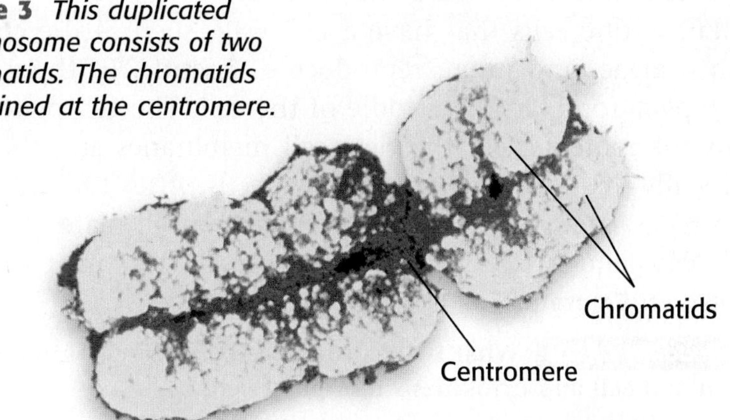

Figure 3 *This duplicated chromosome consists of two chromatids. The chromatids are joined at the centromere.*

CONNECTION TO Language Arts

Picking Apart Vocabulary

Brainstorm what words are similar to the parts of the term *homologous chromosome.* What can you guess about the meaning of the term's root words? Look up the roots of the words, and explain how they help describe the concept.

ACTIVITY

Figure 4 **The Cell Cycle**

Copying DNA (Interphase)

Before mitosis begins, chromosomes are copied.

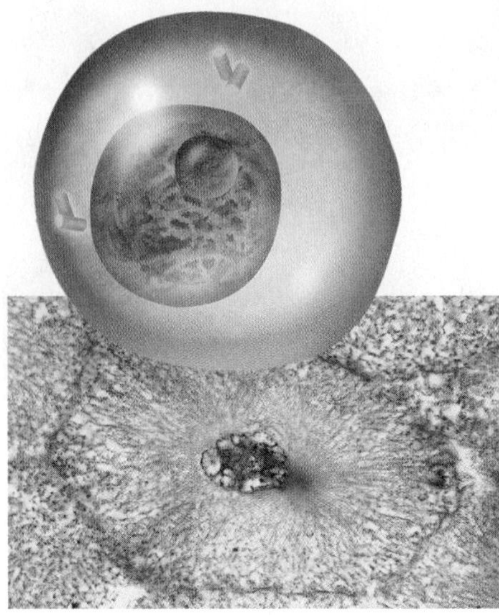

Mitosis Phase 1 (Prophase)

Mitosis begins. Chromosomes condense from long strands into rodlike structures.

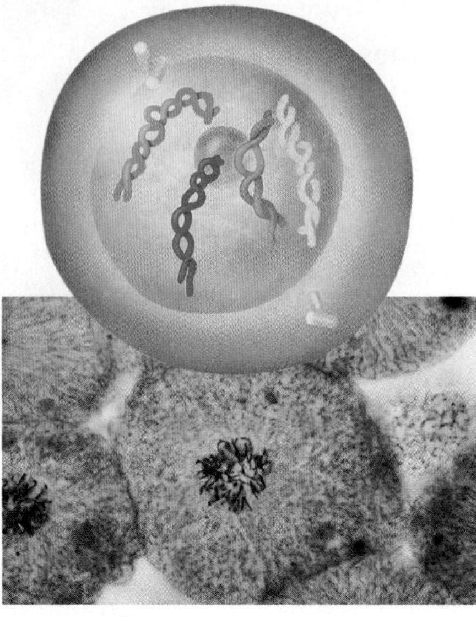

Mitosis Phase 2 (Metaphase)

The nuclear membrane is dissolved. Paired chromatids align at the cell's equator.

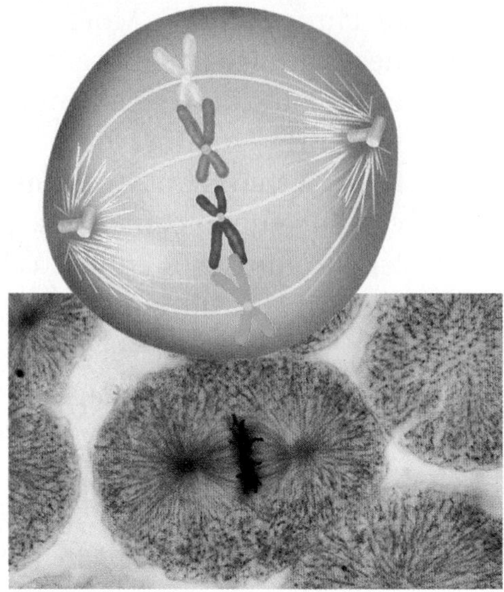

Mitosis and the Cell Cycle

cytokinesis the division of the cytoplasm of a cell

Figure 4 shows the cell cycle and the phases of mitosis in an animal cell. Mitosis has four phases that are shown and described above. This diagram shows only four chromosomes to make it easy to see what's happening inside the cell.

Cytokinesis

In animal cells and other eukaryotes that do not have cell walls, division of the cytoplasm begins at the cell membrane. The cell membrane begins to pinch inward to form a groove, which eventually pinches all the way through the cell, and two daughter cells form. The division of cytoplasm is called **cytokinesis** and is shown at the last step of **Figure 4.**

Eukaryotic cells that have a cell wall, such as the cells of plants, algae, and fungi, reproduce differently. In these cells, a *cell plate* forms in the middle of the cell. The cell plate contains the materials for the new cell membranes and the new cell walls that will separate the new cells. After the cell splits into two, a new cell wall forms where the cell plate was. The cell plate and a late stage of cytokinesis in a plant cell are shown in **Figure 5.**

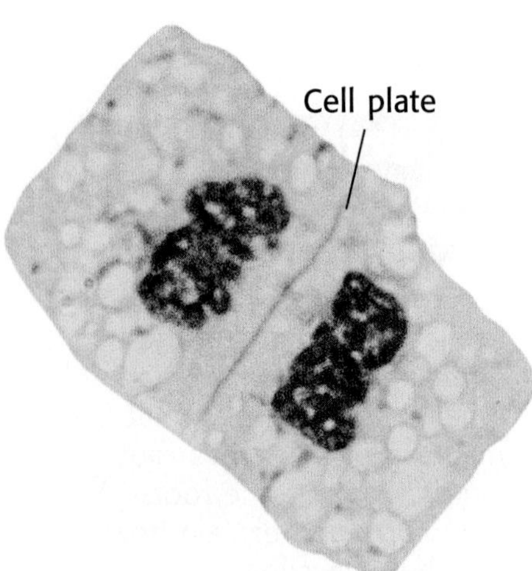

Figure 5 *When a plant cell divides, a cell plate forms and the cell splits into two cells.*

Reading Check **What is the difference between cytokinesis in an animal cell and cytokinesis in a plant cell?**

Mitosis Phase 3 (Anaphase)

The chromatids separate and move to opposite sides of the cell.

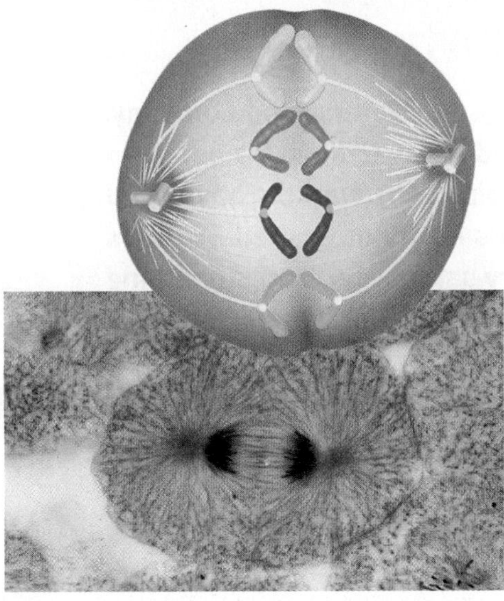

Mitosis Phase 4 (Telophase)

A nuclear membrane forms around each set of chromosomes, and the chromosomes unwind. Mitosis is complete.

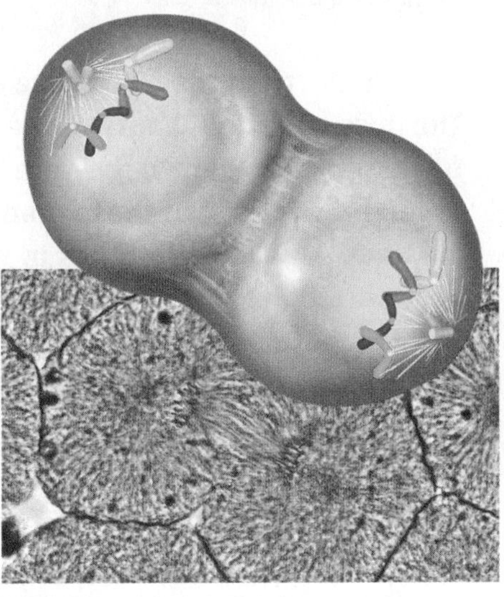

Cytokinesis

In cells that lack a cell wall, the cell pinches in two. In cells that have a cell wall, a cell plate forms between the two new cells.

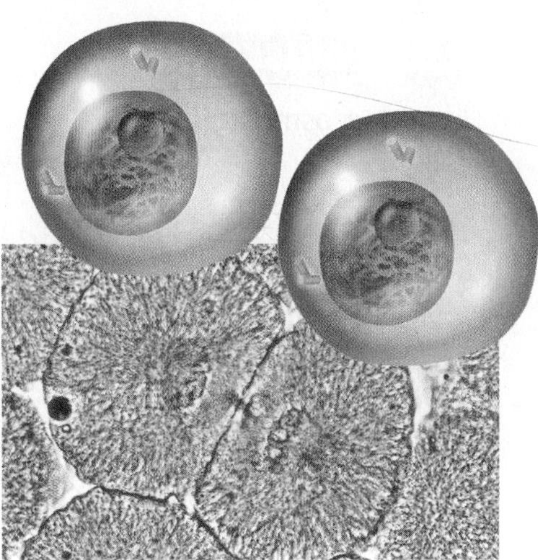

SECTION Review

Summary

- A cell produces more cells by first copying its DNA.
- Eukaryotic cells produce more cells through the four phases of mitosis.
- Mitosis produces two cells that have the same number of chromosomes as the parent cell.
- At the end of mitosis, a cell divides the cytoplasm by cytokinesis.
- In plant cells, a cell plate forms between the two new cells during cytokinesis.

Using Key Terms

1. In your own words, write a definition for each of the following terms: *cell cycle* and *cytokinesis*.

Understanding Key Ideas

2. Eukaryotic cells
   - **a.** do not divide.
   - **b.** undergo binary fission.
   - **c.** undergo mitosis.
   - **d.** have cell walls.

3. Why is it important for chromosomes to be copied before cell division?

4. Describe mitosis.

Math Skills

5. Cell A takes 6 h to complete division. Cell B takes 8 h to complete division. After 24 h, how many more copies of cell A would there be than cell B?

Critical Thinking

6. Predicting Consequences What would happen if cytokinesis occurred without mitosis?

7. Applying Concepts How does mitosis ensure that a new cell is just like its parent cell?

8. Making Comparisons Compare the processes that animal cells and plant cells use to make new cells. How are the processes different?

SCILINKS.
NSTA
Developed and maintained by the National Science Teachers Association
For a variety of links related to this chapter, go to www.scilinks.org
Topic: Cell Cycle
SciLinks code: HSM0235

Using Scientific Methods

Inquiry Lab

The Perfect Taters Mystery

OBJECTIVES

Examine osmosis in potato cells.

Design a procedure that will give the best results.

MATERIALS

- cups, clear plastic, small
- potato pieces, freshly cut
- potato samples (A, B, and C)
- salt
- water, distilled

SAFETY

You are the chief food detective at Perfect Taters Food Company. The boss, Mr. Fries, wants you to find a way to keep his potatoes fresh and crisp before they are cooked. His workers have tried several methods, but these methods have not worked. Workers in Group A put the potatoes in very salty water, and something unexpected happened to the potatoes. Workers in Group B put the potatoes in water that did not contain any salt, and something else happened! Workers in Group C didn't put the potatoes in any water, and that didn't work either. Now, you must design an experiment to find out what can be done to make the potatoes stay crisp and fresh.

- Before you plan your experiment, review what you know. You know that potatoes are made of cells. Plant cells contain a large amount of water. Cells have membranes that hold water and other materials inside and keep some things out. Water and other materials must travel across cell membranes to get into and out of the cell.
- Mr. Fries has told you that you can obtain as many samples as you need from the workers in Groups A, B, and C. Your teacher will have these samples ready for you to observe.
- Make a data table like the one below. List your observations in the data table. Make as many observations as you can about the potatoes tested by workers in Groups A, B, and C.

Observations	
Group A	
Group B	
Group C	

Ask a Question

1. Now that you have made your observations, state Mr. Fries's problem in the form of a question that can be answered by your experiment.

Form a Hypothesis

2. Form a hypothesis based on your observations and your questions. The hypothesis should be a statement about what causes the potatoes not to be crisp and fresh. Based on your hypothesis, make a prediction about the outcome of your experiment. State your prediction in an if-then format.

Test the Hypothesis

3. Once you have made a prediction, design your investigation. Check your experimental design with your teacher before you begin. Mr. Fries will give you potato pieces, water, salt, and no more than six containers.

4. Keep very accurate records. Write your plan and procedure. Make data tables. To be sure your data is accurate, measure all materials carefully and make drawings of the potato pieces before and after the experiment.

Analyze the Results

1. **Explaining Events** Explain what happened to the potato cells in Groups A, B, and C in your experiment. Include a discussion of the cell membrane and the process of osmosis.

Draw Conclusions

2. **Analyzing Results** Write a letter to Mr. Fries that explains your experimental method, results, and conclusion. Then, make a recommendation about how he should handle the potatoes so that they will stay fresh and crisp.

Chapter Review

USING KEY TERMS

1. Use the following terms in the same sentence: *diffusion* and *osmosis*.

2. In your own words, write a definition for each of the following terms: *exocytosis* and *endocytosis*.

Complete each of the following sentences by choosing the correct term from the word bank.

cellular respiration
photosynthesis
fermentation

3. Plants use ___ to make glucose.

4. During ___, oxygen is used to break down food molecules releasing large amounts of energy.

For each pair of terms, explain how the meanings of the terms differ.

5. *cytokinesis* and *mitosis*

6. *active transport* and *passive transport*

7. *cellular respiration* and *fermentation*

UNDERSTANDING KEY IDEAS

Multiple Choice

8. The process in which particles move through a membrane from a region of low concentration to a region of high concentration is
   a. diffusion.
   b. passive transport.
   c. active transport.
   d. fermentation.

9. What is the result of mitosis and cytokinesis?
   a. two identical cells
   b. two nuclei
   c. chloroplasts
   d. two different cells

10. Before the energy in food can be used by a cell, the energy must first be transferred to molecules of
   a. proteins.
   b. carbohydrates.
   c. DNA.
   d. ATP.

11. Which of the following cells would form a cell plate during the cell cycle?
   a. a human cell
   b. a prokaryotic cell
   c. a plant cell
   d. All of the above

Short Answer

12. Are exocytosis and endocytosis examples of active or passive transport? Explain your answer.

13. Name the cell structures that are needed for photosynthesis and the cell structures that are needed for cellular respiration.

14. Describe the three stages of the cell cycle of a eukaryotic cell.

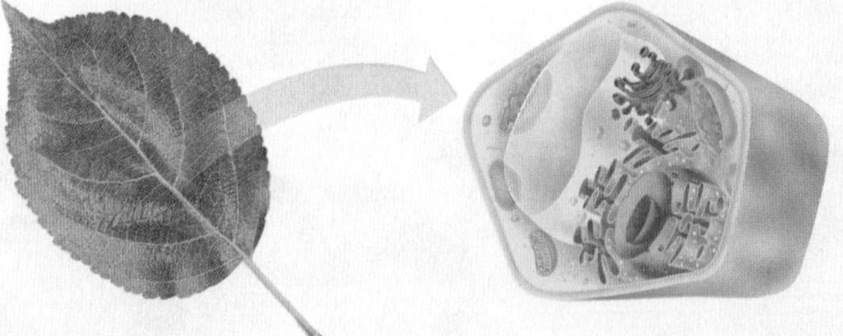

CRITICAL THINKING

15 **Concept Mapping** Use the following terms to create a concept map: *chromosome duplication, cytokinesis, prokaryote, mitosis, cell cycle, binary fission,* and *eukaryote.*

16 **Making Inferences** Which one of the plants pictured below was given water mixed with salt, and which one was given pure water? Explain how you know, and be sure to use the word *osmosis* in your answer.

17 **Identifying Relationships** Why would your muscle cells need to be supplied with more food when there is a lack of oxygen than when there is plenty of oxygen present?

18 **Applying Concepts** A parent cell has 10 chromosomes.

a. Will the cell go through binary fission or mitosis and cytokinesis to produce new cells?

b. How many chromosomes will each new cell have after the parent cell divides?

INTERPRETING GRAPHICS

The picture below shows a cell. Use the picture below to answer the questions that follow.

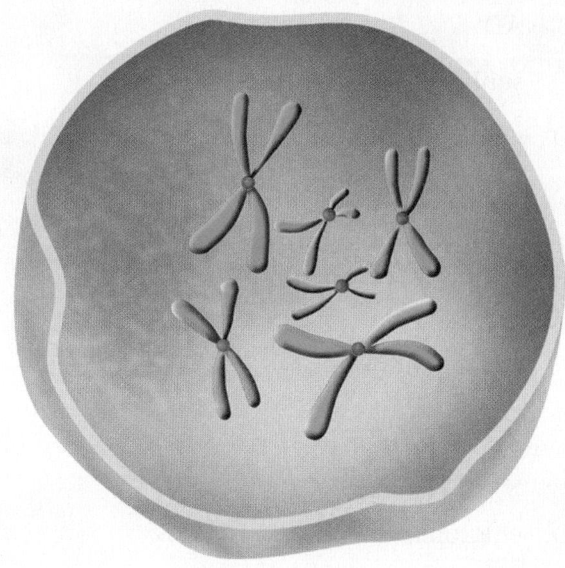

19 Is the cell prokaryotic or eukaryotic?

20 Which stage of the cell cycle is this cell in?

21 How many chromatids are present? How many pairs of homologous chromosomes are present?

22 How many chromosomes will be present in each of the new cells after the cell divides?

Standardized Test Preparation

Multiple Choice

1. What is the primary source of energy for all organisms?

A. carbohydrates

B. ATP

C. sunlight

D. glucose

2. In eukaryotic organisms, which cell part converts the energy stored in food to ATP?

A. mitochondrion

B. chromosome

C. cell membrane

D. chloroplast

3. Plants are producers. Which of the following statements best describes producers?

A. They obtain their food by eating other organisms.

B. They use a process known as cellular respiration to make their own food.

C. They capture light energy from the sun and use it to make food.

D. They take in oxygen and produce carbon dioxide.

Use the diagram below to answer question 4.

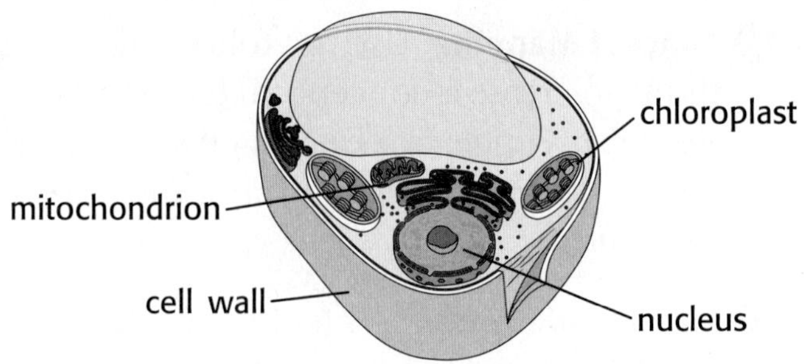

4. What structure in the cell above can convert energy from the sun into chemical energy that can be used by plants and animals?

A. mitochondrion

B. cell wall

C. nucleus

D. chloroplast

5. Which of the following correctly displays the cell cycle and division?

A. interphase, prophase, metaphase, anaphase, telophase, cytokinesis

B. interphase, cytokinesis, anaphase, mitosis, telophase

C. prophase, metaphase, interphase, anaphase, telophase

D. prophase, mitosis, interphase, metaphase, cytokinesis

6. When plants make glucose, they are converting the sun's radiant energy

A. into ATP.

B. into chemical energy that can be stored.

C. in a process known as cellular respiration.

D. into chlorophyll.

Use the illustration below to answer question 7.

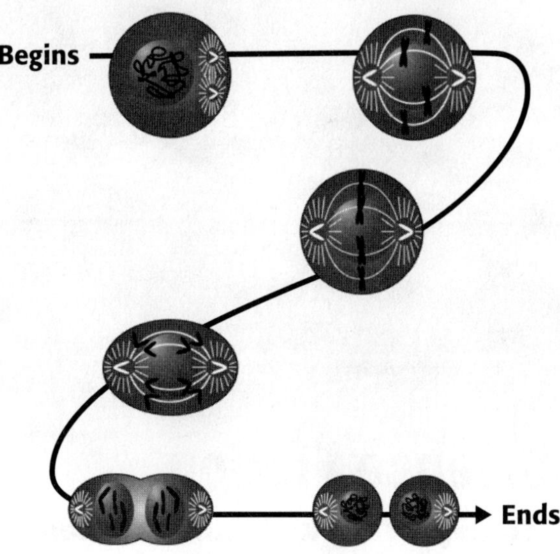

7. **Based on the process shown in Katie's sketches of cell division, which of the following is a valid conclusion?**

   A. Cytokinesis occurs right after the chromosomes are copied.

   B. Two daughter cells form during mitosis.

   C. Chromosomes are condensed only during metaphase.

   D. The cells shown in the diagram are prokaryotic cells.

8. **How is the process of cellular respiration in eukaryotic cells different than cellular respiration in prokaryotic cells? Cellular respiration**

   A. requires oxygen in eukaryotic cells but not in prokaryotic cells.

   B. occurs in mitochondria in eukaryotic cells, but in the cell membrane in prokaryotic cells.

   C. produces lactic acid in eukaryotic cells, but carbon dioxide gas in prokaryotic cells.

   D. is not possible in prokaryotic cells.

9. **During mitosis, chromosomes condense from long strands into rodlike structures. What must happen before this stage of the cell cycle?**

   A. The paired chromatids separate and move to opposite sides of the cell.

   B. The paired chromatids align at the cell's equator.

   C. The cell grows and copies its organelles.

   D. The nuclear membrane dissolves.

Open Response

10. **Kudzu is a vine that was planted during the Great Depression in order to control soil erosion. This fast-growing plant is now considered a weed. In the southeastern United States, kudzu can grow up to 20 m in one year. Kudzu cells undergo rapid cell division. Draw a diagram and describe the cell cycle for kudzu cells.**

11. **The Longleaf Pine Forest is a fire-adapted ecosystem that once covered 70–90 million acres along the coast of the southeastern U.S. Less than 5% of this forest now remains. Plants in this ecosystem include longleaf pine, wiregrass, and native legumes. Animals include scarab beetles and other invertebrates, striped newts, dusky gopher frogs, indigo snakes, and bobwhite quail. Describe how energy would move through organisms in this ecosystem.**

Science in Action

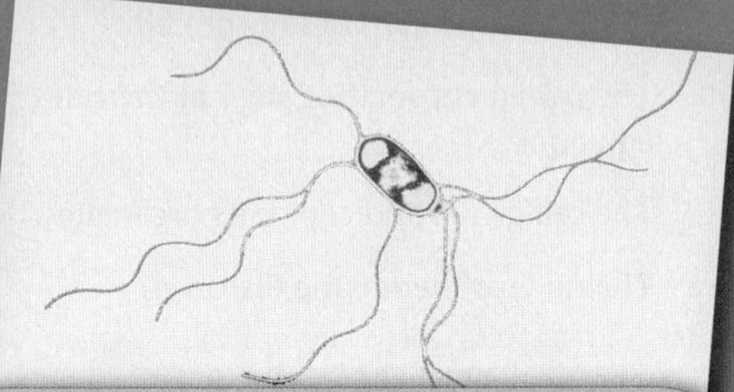

Scientific Discoveries

Electrifying News About Microbes

Your car is out of fuel, and there isn't a service station in sight. This is not a problem! Your car's motor runs on electricity supplied by trillions of microorganisms. Some chemists think that "living" batteries will someday operate everything from watches to entire cities. A group of scientists at King's College in London have demonstrated that microorganisms can convert food into usable electrical energy. The microorganisms convert foods such as table sugar and molasses most efficiently. An efficient microorganism can convert more than 90% of its food into compounds that will fuel an electric reaction. A less efficient microbe will only convert 50% of its food into these types of compounds.

Math Activity

An efficient microorganism converts 90% of its food into fuel compounds, and an inefficient microorganism converts only 50%. If the inefficient microorganism makes 60 g of fuel out of a possible 120 g of food, how much fuel would an efficient microorganism make out of the same amount of food?

Science Fiction

"Contagion" by Katherine MacLean

A quarter mile from their spaceship, the *Explorer,* a team of doctors walk carefully along a narrow forest trail. Around them, the forest looks like a forest on Earth in the fall—the leaves are green, copper, purple, and fiery red. But it isn't fall. And the team is not on Earth.

Minos is enough like Earth to be the home of another colony of humans. But Minos might also be home to unknown organisms that could cause severe illness or death among the crew of *Explorer*. These diseases might be enough like diseases on Earth to be contagious, but they might be different enough to be very difficult to treat.

Something large moves among the shadows—it looks like a man. What happens next? Read Katherine's MacLean's "Contagion" in the *Holt Anthology of Science Fiction* to find out.

Language Arts Activity

WRITING SKILL Write two to three paragraphs that describe what you think might happen next in the story.

Careers

Jerry Yakel

Neuroscientist Jerry Yakel credits a sea slug for making him a neuroscientist. In a college class studying neurons, or nerve cells, Yakel got to see firsthand how ions move across the cell membrane of *Aplysia californica,* also known as a sea hare. He says, "I was totally hooked. I knew that I wanted to be a neurophysiologist then and there. I haven't wavered since."

Today, Yakel is a senior investigator for the National Institutes of Environmental Health Sciences, which is part of the U.S. government's National Institutes of Health. "We try to understand how the normal brain works," says Yakel of his team. "Then, when we look at a diseased brain, we train to understand where the deficits are. Eventually, someone will have an idea about a drug that will tweak the system in this or that way."

Yakel studies the ways in which nicotine affects the human brain. "It is one of the most prevalent and potent neurotoxins in the environment," says Yakel. "I'm amazed that it isn't higher on the list of worries for the general public."

Social Studies ACTIVITY

WRITING SKILL Research a famous or historical figure in science. Write a short report that outlines how he or she became interested in science.

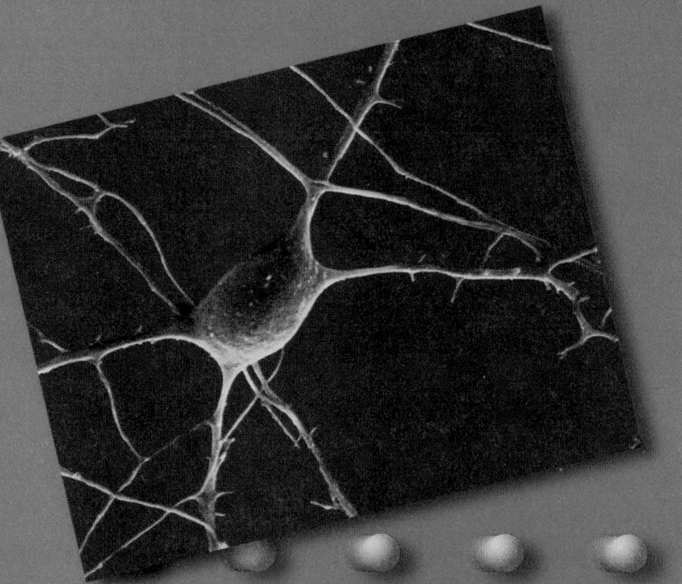

To learn more about these Science in Action topics, visit go.hrw.com and type in the keyword HL5ACTF.

Current Science

Check out Current Science® articles related to this chapter by visiting go.hrw.com. Just type in the keyword HL5CS04.

3

Plant Processes

The Big Idea

Like all living things, plants need nourishment, reproduce, and respond to stimuli.

SECTION

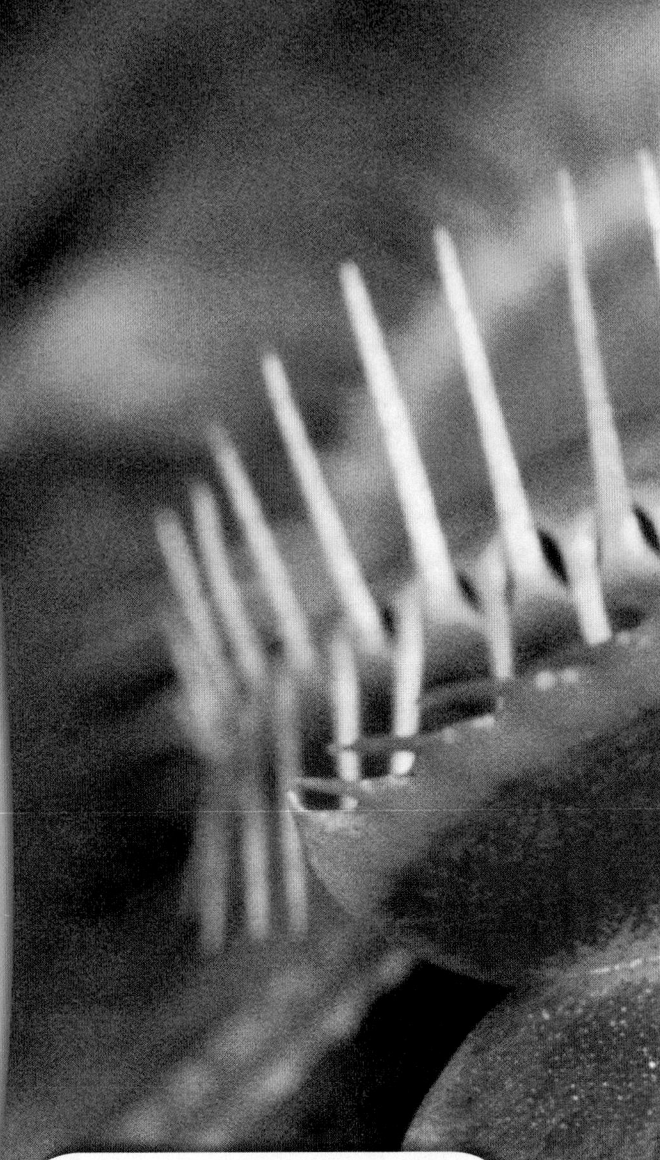

About the Photo

The plant in this photo is a Venus' flytrap. Those red and green spiny pads are its leaves. Like other plants, Venus' flytraps rely on photosynthesis to get energy. What is so unusual about the Venus' flytrap? Unlike most plants, the Venus' flytrap gets important nutrients, such as nitrogen, by capturing and digesting insects or other small animals.

PRE-READING ACTIVITY

FOLDNOTES **Booklet** Before you read the chapter, create the FoldNote entitled "Booklet" described in the **Study Skills** section of the Appendix. Label each page of the booklet with a main idea from the chapter. As you read the chapter, write what you learn about each main idea on the appropriate page of the booklet.

START-UP ACTIVITY

Which End Is Up?

If you plant seeds with their "tops" facing in different directions, will their stems all grow upward? Do this activity to find out.

Procedure

1. Pack a **clear, medium-sized plastic cup** with slightly moistened **paper towels.**
2. Place **five or six corn seeds,** equally spaced, around the cup between the side of the cup and the paper towels. Point the tip of each seed in a different direction.
3. Using a **marker,** draw arrows on the outside of the cup to show the direction each seed tip points.
4. Place the cup in a well-lit location for 1 week. Keep the seeds moist by adding **water** to the paper towels as needed.
5. After 1 week, observe the seeds. Record the direction in which each shoot grew.

Analysis

1. In which direction did each of your shoots grow?
2. What might explain why your shoots grew the way they did?

SECTION 1

Photosynthesis

Plants don't have lungs. But like you, plants need air. Air contains oxygen, carbon dioxide, and other gases. Your body needs oxygen, and plants need oxygen. But what other gas is important to plants?

What You Will Learn

- Describe photosynthesis.
- Compare photosynthesis and cellular respiration.
- Describe how gas is exchanged in the leaves of plants.
- Describe two ways in which photosynthesis is important.

Vocabulary

photosynthesis
chlorophyll
cellular respiration
stoma
transpiration

READING STRATEGY

Discussion Read this section silently. Write down questions that you have about this section. Discuss your questions in a small group.

If you guessed *carbon dioxide,* you are correct. Plants use carbon dioxide for photosynthesis (FOHT oh SIN thuh sis). **Photosynthesis** is the process by which plants make their own food. Plants capture energy from sunlight during photosynthesis. This energy is used to make the sugar glucose ($C_6H_{12}O_6$) from carbon dioxide (CO_2) and water (H_2O).

Capturing Light Energy

Plant cells have organelles called *chloroplasts* (KLAWR uh PLASTS), shown in **Figure 1.** Chloroplasts are surrounded by two membranes. Inside the chloroplast, another membrane forms stacks called *grana* (GRAY nuh). Grana contain a green pigment, called **chlorophyll** (KLAWR uh FIL), that absorbs light energy.

Sunlight is made up of many different wavelengths of light. Chlorophyll absorbs many of these wavelengths. But it reflects more wavelengths of green light than wavelengths of other colors of light. So, most plants look green.

Reading Check **Why are most plants green?** (*See the Appendix for answers to Reading Checks.*)

Figure 1 Chloroplast Structure

The grana found in chloroplasts contain chlorophyll, which captures energy from sunlight.

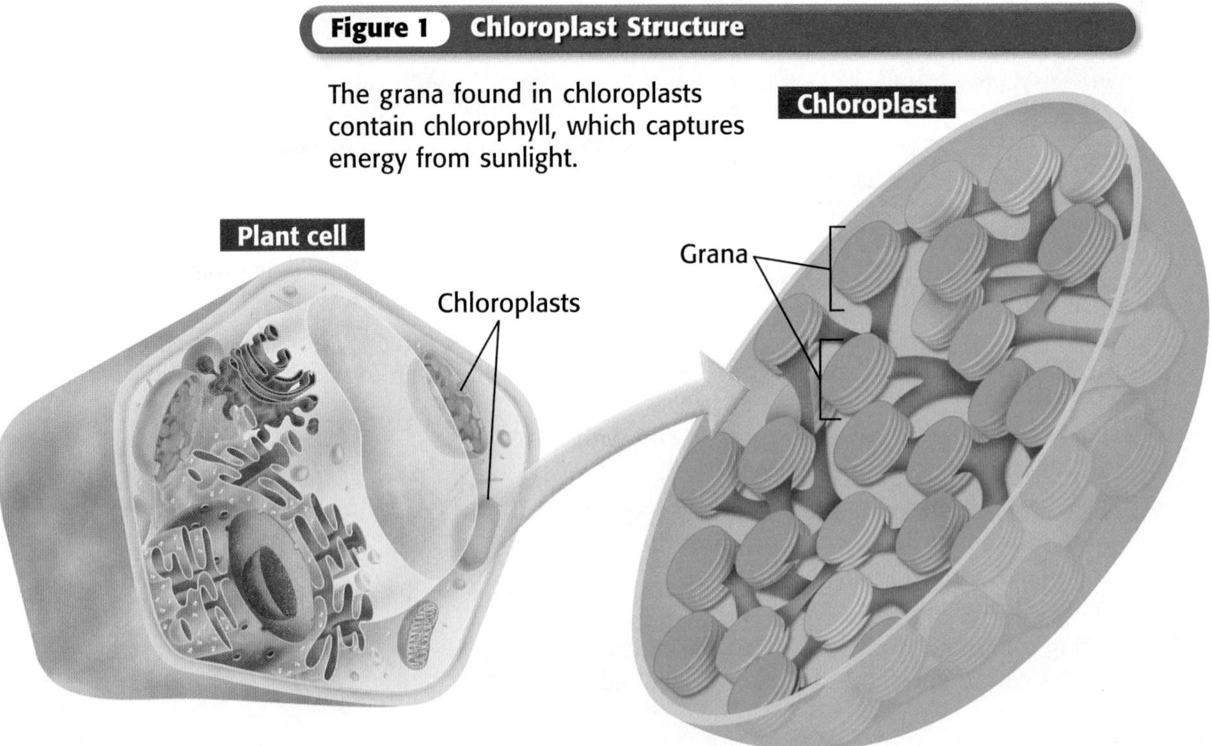

Making Sugar

The light energy captured by chlorophyll is used to help form glucose molecules. In turn, oxygen gas (O_2) is given off by plant cells. Photosynthesis is a complicated process made up of many steps. But photosynthesis can be summarized by the following chemical equation:

$$6CO_2 + 6H_2O \xrightarrow{\text{light energy}} C_6H_{12}O_6 + 6O_2$$

Six molecules of carbon dioxide and six molecules of water are needed to form one molecule of glucose and six molecules of oxygen. **Figure 2** shows where plants get the materials for photosynthesis.

Getting Energy from Sugar

Glucose molecules store energy. Plant cells use this energy for their life processes. To get energy, plant cells break down glucose and other food molecules in a process called **cellular respiration.** During this process, plant cells use oxygen. The cells give off carbon dioxide and water. Excess glucose is converted to another sugar called *sucrose* or stored as starch.

CONNECTION TO Social Studies

WRITING SKILL **Sugar** Some plants make and store large amounts of sucrose, or table sugar, during photosynthesis. People harvest these plants for sucrose. Identify a plant that produces large amounts of sucrose. Then, identify how people use the plant and which countries are major growers of the plant. Write an article about your findings in your **science journal.**

photosynthesis the process by which plants, algae, and some bacteria use sunlight, carbon dioxide, and water to make food

chlorophyll a green pigment that captures light energy for photosynthesis

cellular respiration the process by which cells use oxygen to produce energy from food

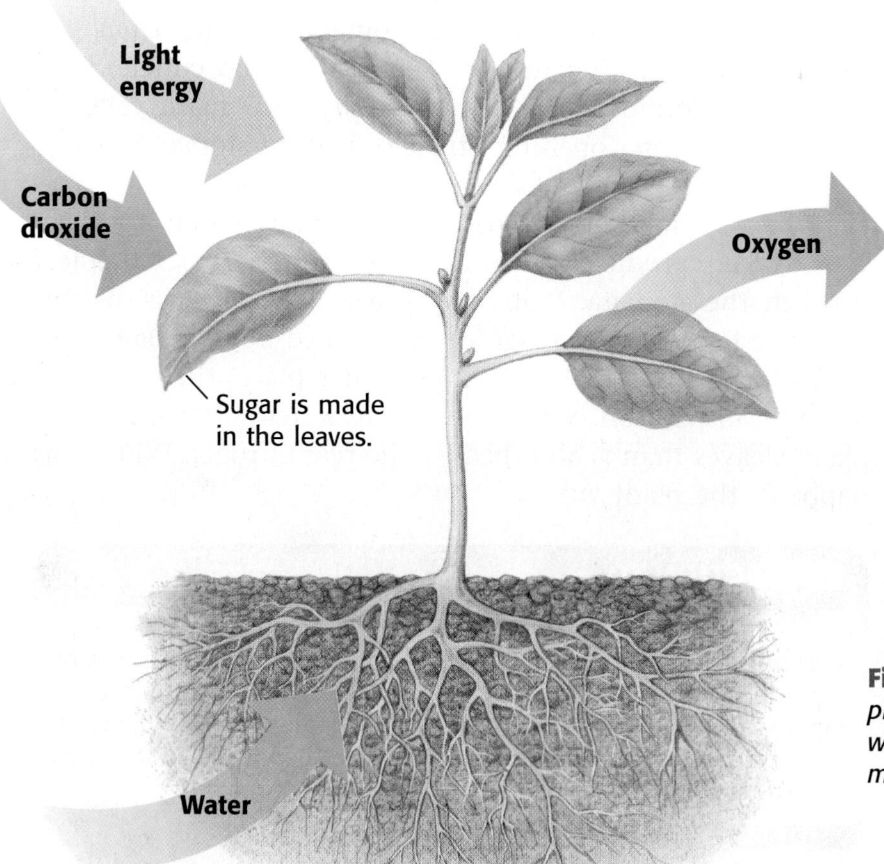

Figure 2 *During photosynthesis, plants take in carbon dioxide and water and absorb light energy. They make sugar and release oxygen.*

Figure 3 Gas Exchange in Leaves

When light is available for photosynthesis, the stomata are usually open. At nighttime, the stomata close to conserve water.

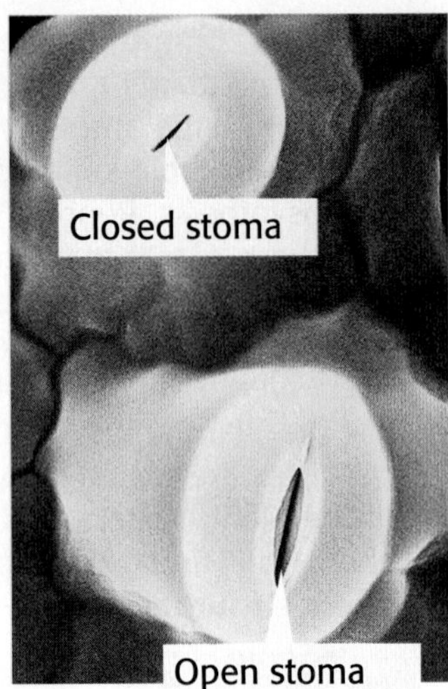

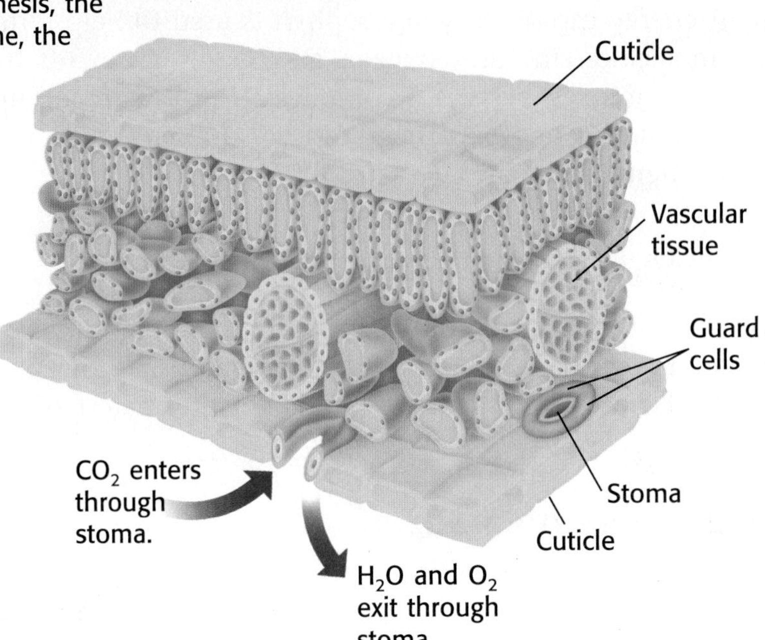

Gas Exchange

Many above-ground plant surfaces are covered by a waxy cuticle. The cuticle protects the plant from water loss. How does a plant get carbon dioxide through this barrier? Carbon dioxide enters the plant's leaves through stomata (singular, *stoma*). A **stoma** is an opening in the leaf's epidermis and cuticle. Each stoma is surrounded by two *guard cells*. The guard cells act like double doors, opening and closing the stoma. You can see stomata in **Figure 3.**

stoma one of many openings in a leaf or a stem of a plant that enable gas exchange to occur (plural, *stomata*)

transpiration the process by which plants release water vapor into the air through stomata

When stomata are open, carbon dioxide enters the leaf. The oxygen produced during photosynthesis exits the leaf through the stomata. Water vapor also exits the leaf in this way. The loss of water from leaves is called **transpiration.** Most of the water absorbed by a plant's roots replaces the water lost during transpiration. Sometimes, more water is lost through a plant's leaves than is absorbed by the plant's roots. When this happens, the plant wilts.

CONNECTION TO Chemistry

Transpiration Wrap a plastic bag around the branch of a tree or a portion of a potted plant. Secure the bag closed with a piece of tape or a rubber band, but be sure not to injure the plant. Record what happens over the next few days. What happened to the bag? How does this illustrate transpiration?

ACTIVITY

The Importance of Photosynthesis

Plants and other photosynthetic organisms, such as some bacteria and many protists, form the base of nearly all food chains on Earth. An example of one food chain is shown in **Figure 4.** During photosynthesis, plants store light energy as chemical energy. Some animals use this chemical energy when they eat plants. Other animals get energy from plants indirectly. These animals eat animals that eat plants. Most organisms could not survive without photosynthetic organisms.

Plants, animals, and most other organisms rely on cellular respiration to get energy. Cellular respiration requires oxygen. Oxygen is a byproduct of photosynthesis. So, photosynthesis provides the oxygen that animals and plants need for cellular respiration.

Reading Check **What are two ways in which photosynthesis is important?**

Figure 4 *Mice rely on plants for food. In turn, cats get energy from mice.*

SECTION Review

Summary

- During photosynthesis, plants use energy from sunlight, carbon dioxide, and water to make food.
- Plants get energy from food by cellular respiration, which uses oxygen and releases carbon dioxide and water.
- Transpiration, or the loss of water through the leaves, happens when stomata are open.
- Photosynthesis provides oxygen. Most animals rely on photosynthetic organisms for food.

Using Key Terms

1. In your own words, write a definition for each of the following terms: *photosynthesis*, *chlorophyll*, and *cellular respiration*.

Understanding Key Ideas

2. During photosynthesis, plants
   a. absorb energy from sunlight.
   b. use carbon dioxide and water.
   c. make food and oxygen.
   d. All of the above
3. How is cellular respiration related to photosynthesis?
4. Describe gas exchange in plants.

Math Skills

5. Plants use 6 carbon dioxide molecules and 6 water molecules to make 1 glucose molecule. How many carbon dioxide and water molecules would be needed to make 12 glucose molecules?

Critical Thinking

6. **Predicting Consequences** Predict what might happen if plants and other photosynthetic organisms disappeared.
7. **Applying Concepts** Light filters let through certain colors of light. Predict what would happen if you grew a plant under a green light filter.

SCILINKS.
NSTA
Developed and maintained by the National Science Teachers Association
For a variety of links related to this chapter, go to www.scilinks.org
Topic: Photosynthesis
SciLinks code: HSM1140

SECTION 2

Reproduction of Flowering Plants

What You Will Learn

- Describe pollination and fertilization in flowering plants.
- Explain how fruits and seeds are formed from flowers.
- List three reasons why a seed might be dormant.
- List three examples of asexual reproduction in plants.

Vocabulary

dormant

READING STRATEGY

Reading Organizer As you read this section, make a table comparing sexual reproduction and asexual reproduction in plants.

Imagine you are standing in a field of wildflowers. You're surrounded by bright colors and sweet fragrances. You can hear bees buzzing from flower to flower.

Flowering plants are the largest and most diverse group of plants. Their success is partly due to their flowers. Flowers are adaptations for sexual reproduction. During sexual reproduction, an egg is fertilized by a sperm.

Fertilization

In flowering plants, fertilization takes place within flowers. *Pollination* happens when pollen is moved from anthers to stigmas. Usually, wind or animals move pollen from one flower to another flower. Pollen contains sperm. After pollen lands on the stigma, a tube grows from each pollen grain. The tube grows through the style to an ovule. Ovules are found inside the ovary. Each ovule contains an egg. Sperm from the pollen grain move down the pollen tube and into an ovule. Fertilization happens when a sperm fuses with the egg inside an ovule. **Figure 1** shows pollination and fertilization.

Figure 1 Pollination and Fertilization

1 Pollen grains land on the stigma and begin to grow pollen tubes.
Stigma
Anther
Pollen
Style
Ovary
Ovule
2 Sperm travel down pollen tubes and fertilize the eggs.
Pollen tube
Sperm
Ovary
Ovule containing egg

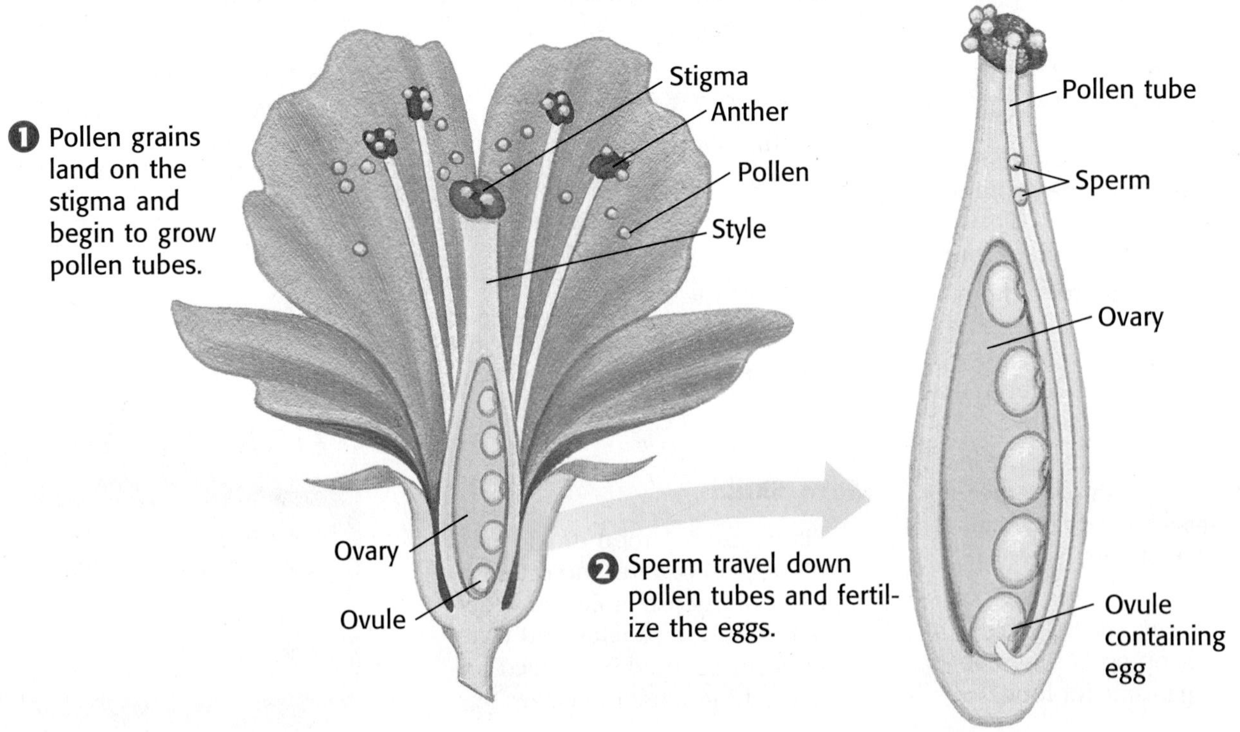

Figure 2 Seed Production

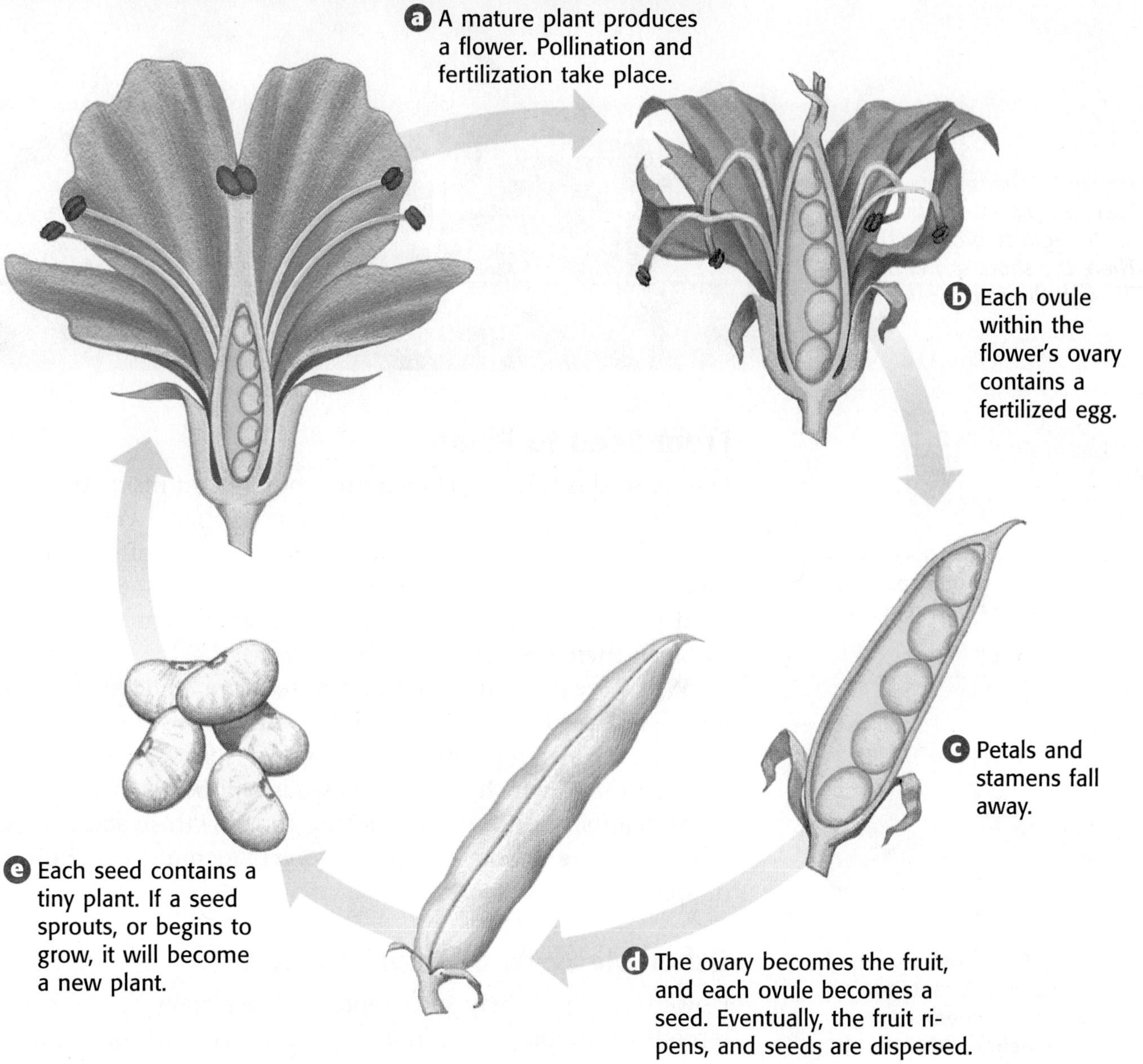

a A mature plant produces a flower. Pollination and fertilization take place.

b Each ovule within the flower's ovary contains a fertilized egg.

c Petals and stamens fall away.

d The ovary becomes the fruit, and each ovule becomes a seed. Eventually, the fruit ripens, and seeds are dispersed.

e Each seed contains a tiny plant. If a seed sprouts, or begins to grow, it will become a new plant.

From Flower to Fruit

After fertilization takes place, the ovule develops into a seed. The seed contains a tiny, undeveloped plant. The ovary surrounding the ovule becomes a fruit, as shown in **Figure 2.**

As a fruit swells and ripens, it protects the developing seeds. **Figure 3** shows a common fruit. Fruits often help a plant spread its seeds. Many fruits are edible. Animals may eat these fruits. Then, the animals discard the seeds away from the parent plant. Other fruits, such as burrs, get caught in an animal's fur. Some fruits are carried by the wind.

Reading Check **How do fruits help a plant spread its seeds?** (*See the Appendix for answers to Reading Checks.*)

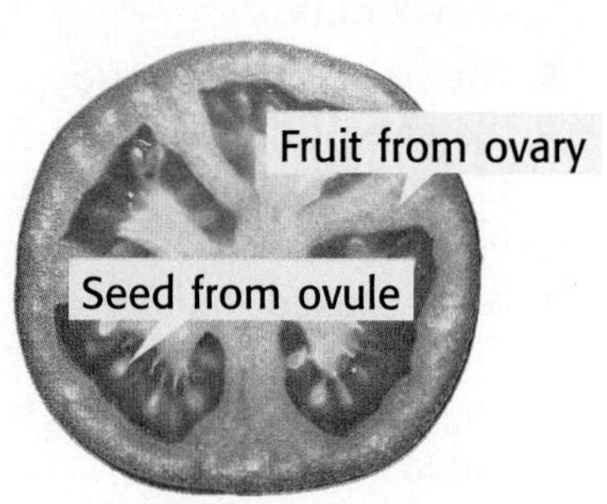

Figure 3 *Tomatoes develop from a flower's ovary and ovules.*

Figure 4 *Seeds grow into new plants. The roots begin to grow first. Then, the shoot grows up through the soil.*

From Seed to Plant

Once a seed is fully developed, the young plant inside the seed stops growing. The seed may become dormant. When seeds are **dormant,** they are inactive. Dormant seeds often survive long periods of drought or freezing temperatures. Some seeds need extreme conditions, such as cold winters or forest fires, to break their dormancy.

dormant describes the inactive state of a seed or other plant part when conditions are unfavorable to growth

When seeds are dropped or planted in a suitable environment, the seeds sprout. To sprout, most seeds need water, air, and warm temperatures. Each plant species has an ideal temperature at which most of its seeds will begin to grow. For many plants, the ideal temperature for growth is about 27°C (80.6°F). **Figure 4** shows the *germination* (JUHR muh NAY shuhn), or sprouting, of a bean seed.

Thirsty Seeds

1. Fill a **Petri dish** two-thirds full of **water,** and add **six dry bean seeds.** Using a **wax pencil,** label the dish "Water."
2. Add **six dry bean seeds** to a dry **Petri dish.** Label this dish "Control."
3. The next day, compare the size of the two sets of seeds. Record your observations.
4. What caused the size of the seeds to change? Why might this be important to the seed's survival?

Other Methods of Reproduction

Flowering plants may also reproduce asexually. For asexual reproduction, plants do not need flowers. Part of a plant, such as a stem or root, produces a new plant. The following are three structures plants use to reproduce asexually:

- **Plantlets** Tiny plants grow along the edges of a plant's leaves. These plantlets fall off and grow on their own.
- **Tubers** Underground stems, or tubers, can produce new plants after a dormant season.
- **Runners** Above-ground stems from which new plants can grow are called *runners*.

You can see an example of each kind of asexual reproduction in **Figure 5.**

Reading Check **What are three structures plants use to reproduce asexually?**

Figure 5 Three Structures for Asexual Reproduction

Kalanchoe plants produce **plantlets** along the edges of their leaves. The plantlets eventually fall off and root in the soil to grow on their own.

A potato is a **tuber,** or underground stem. The "eyes" of potatoes are buds that can grow into new plants.

The strawberry plant produces **runners,** or stems that grow horizontally along the ground. Buds along the runners take root and grow into new plants.

SECTION Review

Summary

- After pollination, a pollen tube forms from the stigma to an ovule. This tube allows a sperm to fertilize an egg.
- After fertilization, seeds and fruit form. The seeds are protected by fruit.
- A dormant seed can survive drought and freezing temperatures. Some seeds need extreme conditions to break their dormancy.
- Some plants use plantlets, tubers, or runners to reproduce asexually.

Using Key Terms

1. In your own words, write a definition for the term *dormant*.

Understanding Key Ideas

2. Pollination happens when
   a. a pollen tube forms.
   b. a sperm cell fuses with an egg.
   c. pollen is transferred from the anther to the stigma.
   d. None of the above
3. Which part of a flower develops into a fruit? into a seed?
4. Why do seeds become dormant?
5. Describe how plants reproduce asexually.

Math Skills

6. A seed sprouts when the temperature is 27°C. If the temperature is now 20°C and it rises 1.5°C per week, in how many weeks will the seed sprout?

Critical Thinking

7. **Making Inferences** What do flowers and runners have in common? How do they differ?
8. **Identifying Relationships** When might asexual reproduction be important for the survival of some flowering plants?
9. **Analyzing Ideas** Sexual reproduction produces more genetic variety than asexual reproduction. Why is variety important?

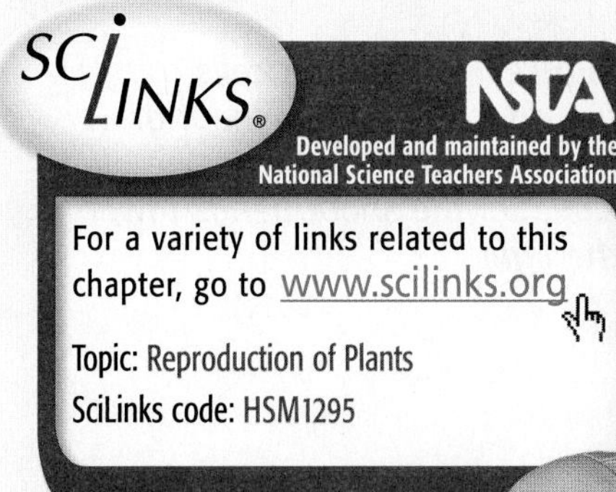

For a variety of links related to this chapter, go to www.scilinks.org

Topic: Reproduction of Plants
SciLinks code: HSM1295

SECTION 3

Plant Responses to the Environment

What You Will Learn

- Describe how plants may respond to light and gravity.
- Explain how some plants respond to night length.
- Describe how some plants respond to the changes of season.

Vocabulary

tropism

READING STRATEGY

Discussion Read this section silently. Write down questions that you have about this section. Discuss your questions in a small group.

What happens when you get really cold? Do your teeth chatter? Or do you shiver? Anything that causes a reaction in your body is a **stimulus** (plural, **stimuli**). But would a plant respond to a stimulus?

Plants do respond to stimuli! For example, they respond to light, gravity, and changing seasons.

Plant Tropisms

Some plants respond to an environmental stimulus by growing in a particular direction. Growth in response to a stimulus is called a **tropism** (TROH PIZ uhm). Tropisms are either positive or negative. Plant growth toward a stimulus is a positive tropism. Plant growth away from a stimulus is a negative tropism.

tropism the growth of all or part of an organism in response to an external stimulus, such as light

Light

What happens if you place a houseplant so that it gets light from only one direction, such as from a window? The shoot tips probably bend toward the light. Bending toward the light is a positive tropism. A change in the direction a plant grows that is caused by light is called *phototropism* (FOH toh TROH PIZ uhm). The result of phototropism is shown in **Figure 1.** Shoots bend because cells on one side of the shoot grow longer than cells on the other side of the shoot.

Reading Check **What happens when a plant gets light from only one direction?** (*See the Appendix for answers to Reading Checks.*)

Figure 1 *The plant cells on the dark side of the shoot grow longer than the cells on the other side. So, the shoot bends toward the light.*

Figure 2 Gravitropism

▼ To grow away from the pull of gravity, this plant has grown upward.

▼ This plant has recently been upside down.

Gravity

Plant growth also changes in response to the direction of gravity. This change is called *gravitropism* (GRAV i TROH PIZ uhm). The effect of gravitropism is demonstrated by the plants in **Figure 2.** A few days after a plant is placed on its side or turned upside down, the roots and shoots change direction of growth. Most shoot tips have negative gravitropism. They grow upward, away from the center of the Earth. In contrast, most root tips have positive gravitropism. Roots grow downward, toward the center of the Earth.

Seasonal Responses

What would happen if a plant living in an area that has very cold winters flowered in December? Would the plant be able to successfully produce seeds and fruits? Probably not. The plant's flowers would likely freeze and die. So, the flowers would never produce mature seeds.

Plants living in regions with cold winters can detect the change in seasons. How do plants do this? As fall and winter approach, the days get shorter, and the nights get longer. The opposite happens when spring and summer approach. Plants respond to the change in the length of day.

Reading Check **How do plants detect seasonal changes?**

MATH PRACTICE

Bending by Degrees

Suppose a plant has a positive phototropism and bends toward light at a rate of 0.3° per minute. In how many hours will the plant bend 90°?

For another activity related to this chapter, go to **go.hrw.com** and type in the keyword **HL5PL2W.**

Figure 3 **Night Length and Flower Color**

Early summer

Night length

Day length

In the early summer, night length is short. At this time, poinsettia leaves are all green, and there are no flowers.

Late fall

Poinsettias flower in the fall, when nights are longer. The leaves surrounding the flower clusters turn red. Professional growers use artificial lighting to control the timing of this color change.

Length of Day

The difference between day length and night length is an important environmental stimulus for many plants. This stimulus can cause plants to begin reproducing. For example, some plants flower in fall or winter. At this time, night length is long. These plants are called *short-day plants*. Poinsettias, such as those shown in **Figure 3,** are short-day plants. Chrysanthemums are also short-day plants. Other plants flower in spring or early summer, when night length is short. These plants are called *long-day plants*. Clover, spinach, and lettuce are examples of long-day plants.

Seasons and Leaf Loss

All trees lose their leaves. Some trees, such as pine and holly, shed some of their leaves year-round so that some leaves are always on the tree. These trees are called *evergreen trees*. Evergreen trees have leaves adapted to survive throughout the year. The leaves are often covered with a thick cuticle. This cuticle protects the leaves from cold and dry weather.

Other trees, such as maple, oak, and elm trees, are called *deciduous* (dee SIJ oo uhs) *trees*. These trees lose all of their leaves around the same time each year. In colder areas, deciduous trees usually lose their leaves before winter begins. In warmer climates that have wet and dry seasons, deciduous trees lose their leaves before the dry season. The loss of leaves helps plants survive low temperatures or long periods without rain.

Reading Check **Compare evergreen trees and deciduous trees.**

Earth's Orbit and the Seasons

The seasons are caused by Earth's tilt and its orbit around the sun. Research how Earth's orbit determines the seasons. With a parent, make a model of the Earth's orbit around the sun to illustrate your findings.

Figure 4 Amount of Pigment Based on Season

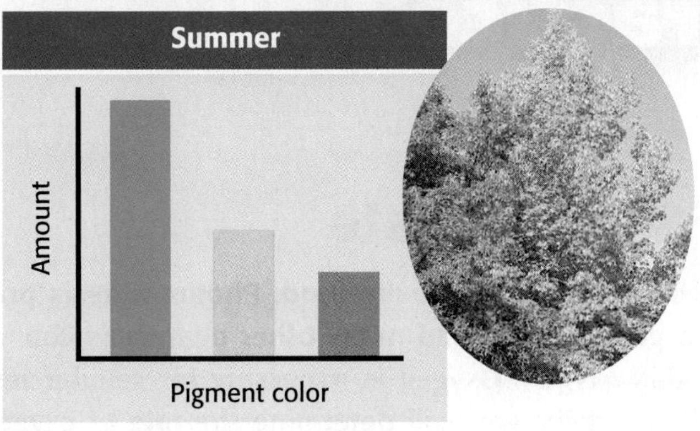

Seasons and Leaf Color

As shown in **Figure 4,** the leaves of deciduous trees may change color before they are lost. As fall approaches, green chlorophyll breaks down. Orange or yellow pigments in the leaves are then revealed. These pigments were always present in the leaves. But they were hidden by green chlorophyll.

SECTION Review

Summary

- Plant growth in response to a stimulus is called a tropism. Tropisms are positive or negative.
- Plants react to light, gravity, and changing seasons.
- Short-day plants flower when night length is long. Long-day plants flower when night length is short.
- Evergreen trees do not lose all their leaves at one time. Deciduous trees lose their leaves at the same time each year.

Using Key Terms

1. In your own words, write a definition for the term *tropism.*

Understanding Key Ideas

2. Deciduous trees lose their leaves
   a. to conserve water during the dry season.
   b. around the same time each year.
   c. to survive low winter temperatures.
   d. All of the above
3. How do light and gravity affect plants?
4. Describe how day length can affect the flowering of plants.

Math Skills

5. A certain plant won't bloom until it is dark for 70% of a 24 h period. How long is the day when the plant will bloom?

Critical Thinking

6. **Making Inferences** Many evergreen trees live in areas with long, cold winters. Why might these evergreen trees keep their leaves all year?
7. **Analyzing Ideas** Some short-day plants bloom during the winter. If cold weather reduces the chances that a plant will produce seeds, what might you conclude about where these short-day plants are found?

Skills Practice Lab

Food Factory Waste

OBJECTIVES

Measure the amount of gas produced over time by photosynthesis.

Draw a graph of the amount of gas produced versus time.

MATERIALS

- baking-soda-and-water solution, 5% (500 mL)
- beaker (600 mL)
- *Elodea* sprigs, 20 cm long (2–3)
- funnel
- gloves, protective
- ruler, metric
- test tube

SAFETY

Plants use photosynthesis to make food. Photosynthesis produces oxygen gas. Humans and many other organisms cannot live without this oxygen. Oxygen is necessary for cellular respiration. In this activity, you will determine the rate of oxygen production for an *Elodea* plant.

Procedure

1. Add 450 mL of baking-soda-and-water solution to a beaker.
2. Put two or three sprigs of *Elodea* in the beaker. The baking soda will provide the *Elodea* with the carbon dioxide it needs for photosynthesis.
3. Place the wide end of the funnel over the *Elodea*. The small end of the funnel should be pointing up. The *Elodea* and the funnel should be completely under the solution.
4. Fill a test tube with the remaining baking-soda-and-water solution. Place your thumb over the end of the test tube, and turn the test tube upside down. Make sure no air enters the test tube. Hold the opening of the test tube under the solution. Place the test tube over the small end of the funnel. Try not to let any solution out of the test tube.

5. Place the beaker setup in a well-lit area.
6. Prepare a data table similar to the one below.

Amount of Gas Present in the Test Tube		
Days of exposure to light	**Total amount of gas present (mm)**	**Amount of gas produced per day (mm)**
0		
1		
2		
3		
4		
5		

DO NOT WRITE IN BOOK

7. If no air entered the test tube, record that there was 0 mm of gas in the test tube on day 0. If air got into the tube while you were placing it, measure the height of the column of air in the test tube in millimeters. Measure the gas in the test tube from the middle of the curve on the bottom of the upside-down test tube to the level of the solution. Record this number for day 0.
8. As described in the previous step, measure the amount of gas in the test tube each day for the next 5 days. Record your measurements in the second column of your data table.
9. Calculate the amount of gas produced each day. Subtract the amount of gas present on the previous day from the amount of gas present on the current day. Record these amounts in the third column of your data table.

Analyze the Results

1. **Constructing Graphs** Make a graph similar to the one below. Based on your measurements, your graph should show the amount of gas produced versus time.

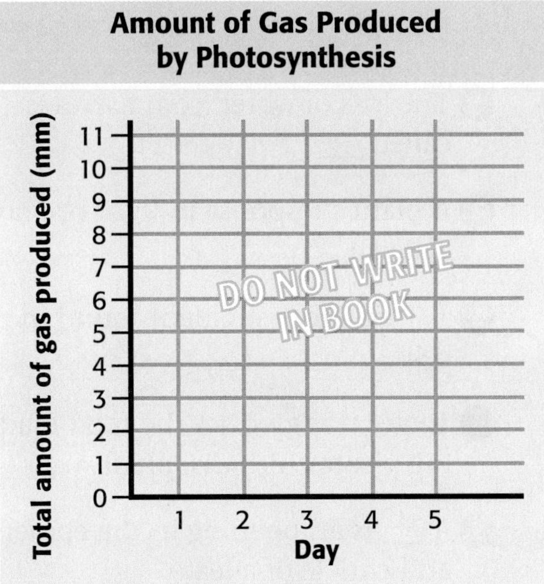

2. **Describing Events** Based on your graph, what happened to the amount of gas in the test tube?

Draw Conclusions

3. **Interpreting Information** Write the equation for photosynthesis. Then, relate each part of your experiment to the part of the equation it represents.

Applying Your Data

As you can see from your results, *Elodea* produces oxygen gas as a byproduct of photosynthesis. Research photosynthesis. Find out if there are factors that affect the rate of photosynthesis. Then, predict what would happen to the production of oxygen gas.

Chapter Review

USING KEY TERMS

Complete each of the following sentences by choosing the correct term from the word bank.

stoma	photosynthesis
dormant	cellular respiration
tropism	chlorophyll
transpiration	

1. The loss of water from leaves is called ___.
2. A plant's response to light or gravity is called a ___.
3. ___ is a green pigment found in plant cells.
4. To get energy from the food made during photosynthesis, plants use ___.
5. A ___ is an opening in the epidermis and cuticle of a leaf.
6. An inactive seed is ___.
7. ___ is the process by which plants make their own food.

UNDERSTANDING KEY IDEAS

Multiple Choice

8. During gas exchange in plants,
   - **a.** carbon dioxide exits while oxygen and water enter the leaf.
   - **b.** oxygen and water exit while carbon dioxide enters the leaf.
   - **c.** carbon dioxide and water enter while oxygen exits the leaf.
   - **d.** carbon dioxide and oxygen enter while water exits the leaf.
9. Plants often respond to light from one direction by
   - **a.** bending away from the light.
   - **b.** bending toward the light.
   - **c.** wilting.
   - **d.** None of the above
10. Which of the following is NOT a way that plants reproduce asexually?
    - **a.** runners
    - **b.** tubers
    - **c.** flowers
    - **d.** plantlets

Short Answer

11. Compare short-day plants and long-day plants.
12. How do potted plants respond to gravity if placed on their sides?
13. Describe the pollination and fertilization of flowering plants.
14. What three things do seeds need before they will sprout?
15. Explain how fruits and seeds form from flowers.
16. Compare photosynthesis and cellular respiration.
17. What are two ways in which photosynthesis is important?

CRITICAL THINKING

18 **Concept Mapping** Use the following terms to create a concept map: *plants, cellular respiration, light energy, photosynthesis, chemical energy, carbon dioxide,* and *oxygen.*

19 **Making Inferences** Many plants live in areas that have severe winters. Some of these plants have seeds that will not germinate unless the seeds have first been exposed to a long period of cold. How might this characteristic help new plants survive?

20 **Analyzing Ideas** Most plant shoots have positive phototropism. Plant roots have positive gravitropism. What might be the benefits of each of these characteristics?

21 **Applying Concepts** If you wanted to make poinsettias bloom and the leaves turn red in the summer, what would you have to do?

22 **Making Inferences** Imagine that someone discovered a new flowering plant. The plant has yellow flowers and underground stems. How might this plant reproduce asexually?

INTERPRETING GRAPHICS

The graph below shows seed germination rates for different seed companies. Use the graph below to answer the questions that follow.

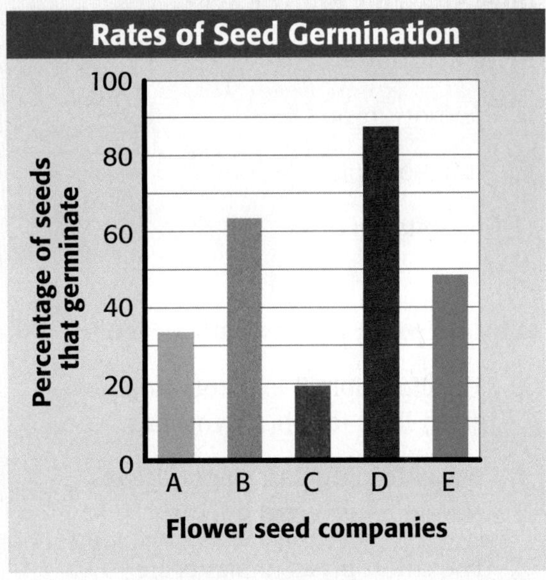

23 Which seed company had the highest rate of seed germination? the lowest rate of seed germination?

24 Which seed companies had seed germination rates higher than 50%?

25 If Elaine wanted to buy seeds that had a germination rate higher than 60%, which seed companies would she buy seeds from? Why might Elaine want to buy seeds with a higher germination rate?

Multiple Choice

1. Shawn recently placed his houseplant next to a window. After a week, Shawn noticed that the shoot tips of the plant started to bend toward the light coming from the window. What kind of tropism does Shawn's plant have?

A. gravitropism

B. phototropism

C. thigmotropism

D. seasonal tropism

2. Why do most plants look green?

A. The chlorophyll in plants captures green light for photosynthesis.

B. The chlorophyll in plants reflects wavelengths of green light.

C. The chloroplasts in plants are surrounded by two green membranes.

D. The chloroplasts in plants make green sugar during photosynthesis.

3. What must happen for sexual reproduction to occur in flowering plants?

A. Plantlets must fall from the parent.

B. The fruit of the plant must be edible.

C. An egg must be fertilized by a sperm.

D. Pollen must be produced.

Use the diagram below to answer question 4.

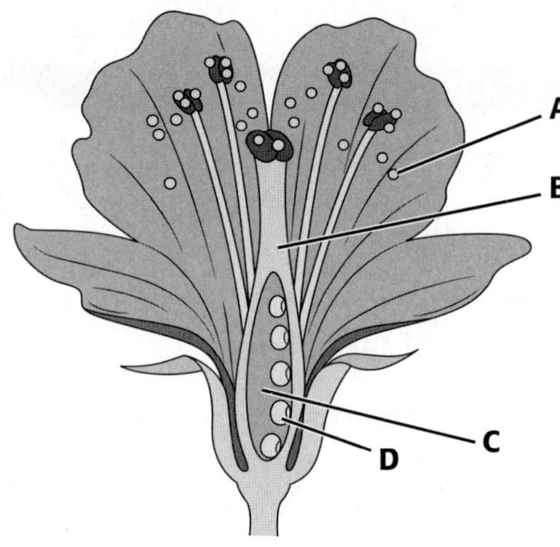

4. In which structure could a fertilized egg be found?

A. structure A

B. structure B

C. structure C

D. structure D

5. The chemical equation for cellular respiration is shown below. What happens on the right side of the arrow?

$$C_6H_{12}O_6 + 6O_2 \longrightarrow 6CO_2 + 6H_2O$$

A. Sugar is produced.

B. Carbon dioxide and water are produced.

C. Sugar and oxygen react.

D. Carbon dioxide and oxygen are produced.

6. What kind of energy is transferred into chemical energy by photosynthesis?

A. radiant energy from the sun

B. potential energy of the ground

C. kinetic energy of a plant's leaves

D. kinetic energy from wind

7. **Why do the leaves of some deciduous trees change color in the fall?**

   A. More of the colored pigments enter the leaves in the fall.

   B. Cold weather causes chlorophyll to change color.

   C. Chlorophyll changes into different colors in cold weather.

   D. Chlorophyll breaks down, revealing pigments that were always there.

8. **What is an advantage of seed dormancy for a plant?**

   A. The seeds can be eaten by animals.

   B. The seed gets the rest it needs to grow.

   C. The seed only begins to grow when the right conditions exist.

   D. The seed doesn't die until the parent plant has died.

9. **In photosynthesis, what energy source is converted into chemical energy and stored as glucose ($C_6H_{12}O_6$)?**

   A. chemical energy

   B. H_2O

   C. light energy

   D. CO_2

10. **Pollination occurs in angiosperms when**

   A. pollen moves from anthers to stigmas.

   B. the ovule develops into a seed.

   C. the ovary becomes the fruit.

   D. sperm moves down the pollen tube.

Use the table below to answer question 11.

$6CO_2 + 6H_2O$	Light Energy $\longrightarrow$	$C_6H_{12}O_6 + 6O_2$

11. **Analyze the equation for photosynthesis above and identify which of the following is a valid conclusion.**

   A. The process of photosynthesis produces carbon dioxide.

   B. Carbon dioxide combines with the hydrogen in the water.

   C. Six hydrogen atoms disappear during photosynthesis.

   D. Six oxygen atoms are destroyed during photosynthesis.

Open Response

12. **Wetlands, such as Kentucky's bald cypress swamps, are often thick with vegetation. Such locations are usually much more humid than cities. One cause is greater evaporation from the open water found in wetlands. What is another cause?**

13. **In Kentucky, strawberries are planted in the early spring. In the first year, blooms are removed to encourage the growth of runners. Would these runners work in another garden?**

Science in Action

Weird Science

What's That Smell?

Imagine that you are walking through a tropical rain forest. You're surrounded by green—green leaves, green vines, and green trees. You can hear monkeys and birds calling to each other. When you touch the plants nearby, they are wet from a recent rain shower. But what's that horrible smell? You don't see any rotting garbage around, but you do see a huge flower spike. As you get closer, the smell gets stronger. Then, you realize the flower is what smells so bad! The flower is called a *corpse flower*. The corpse flower is just one plant that uses bad odors to attract pollinators.

Math Activity

A corpse flower sprouts and grows to a maximum height of 2.35 m in 28 days. In centimeters, what is the average growth of the corpse flower per day?

Scientific Debate

Are Exotic Species Helpful or Harmful?

Have you visited the coast of California? If so, you may have seen large eucalyptus trees. You may be surprised to know that those trees are an exotic species. An *exotic species* is an organism that makes a new home for itself in a new place. People brought eucalyptus trees to California to use them in their yards and gardens. Since then, eucalyptus trees have spread to other areas. Exotic species often take over areas. Exotic species may compete with native species. Sometimes, exotic species keep native species from surviving. But in urban areas, exotic species are sometimes the only plants that will grow. So, are exotic species helpful or harmful?

Social Studies Activity

Identify an exotic species that people imported to grow in their gardens. Find out where the exotic species came from and the effect it is having on the environment.

Careers

Nalini Nadkarni

Canopy Scientist As a child, Nalini Nadkarni loved to climb trees. She still does. Nadkarni is a biologist who studies the forest canopy. The canopy is the uppermost layer of the trees. It includes leaves, twigs, and branches and the air among them. Far above the ground, the canopy is home to many different plants, birds, insects, and other animals.

Canopy science was a new field of study when Nadkarni started her research 20 years ago. Because most canopies are tall, few scientists visited them. Most field biologists did their research with both feet planted firmly on the ground. Today, scientists know that the canopy is an important habitat for wildlife.

Nadkarni tells others about the importance of forests. As she puts it, "I can have a real impact in raising public awareness of the need to save forests." Nadkarni has invited artists and musicians to visit the canopy. "In my job, I try to understand the science of the canopy, but artists and musicians help capture the aesthetic value of the canopy."

Language Arts ACTIVITY

WRITING SKILL Imagine that you are a canopy scientist. Then, write a creative story about something that you would like to study in the canopy.

To learn more about these Science in Action topics, visit go.hrw.com and type in the keyword HL5PL2F.

Current Science

Check out Current Science® articles related to this chapter by visiting go.hrw.com. Just type in the keyword HL5CS13.

TIMELINE

Heredity and Evolution

The differences and similarities between living things are the subject of this unit. You will learn how characteristics are passed from one generation to another, how living things are classified based on their characteristics, and how these characteristics help living things survive.

Scientists have not always understood these topics, and there is still much to be learned. This timeline will give you an idea of some things that have been learned so far.

1753
Carolus Linnaeus publishes the first of two volumes containing the classification of all known species.

1905
Nettie Stevens describes how human gender is determined by the X and Y chromosomes.

1930
The planet Pluto is discovered.

1969
Apollo 11 lands on the moon. Neil Armstrong becomes the first person to walk on the lunar surface.

1859

Charles Darwin suggests that natural selection is a mechanism of evolution.

1860

Abraham Lincoln is elected the 16th president of the United States.

1865

Gregor Mendel publishes the results of his studies of genetic inheritance in pea plants.

1951

Rosalind Franklin photographs DNA.

1953

James Watson and Francis Crick figure out the structure of DNA.

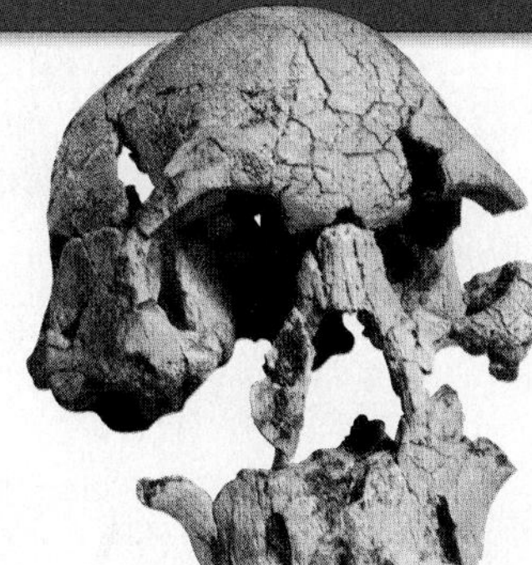

1960

Mary and Jonathan Leakey discover fossil bones of the human ancestor *Homo habilis* in Olduvai Gorge, Tanzania.

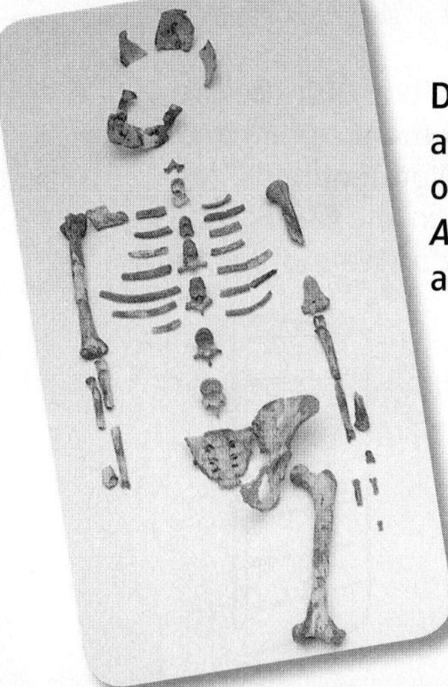

1974

Donald Johanson discovers a fossilized skeleton of one of the first hominids, *Australopithecus afarensis,* also called "Lucy."

1990

Ashanti DeSilva's white blood cells are genetically engineered to treat her immune deficiency disease.

2003

The Human Genome Project is completed. Scientists spent 13 years mapping out the 3 billion DNA subunits of chromosomes.

Heredity

The Big Idea

Heredity is the passage of traits from one generation to the next.

SECTION

About the Photo

The guinea pig in the middle has dark fur, and the other two have light orange fur. The guinea pig on the right has longer hair than the other two. Why do these guinea pigs look different from one another? The length and color of their fur was determined before they were born. These are just two of the many traits determined by genetic information. Genetic information is passed on from parents to their offspring.

PRE-READING ACTIVITY

FOLDNOTES **Key-Term Fold** Before you read the chapter, create the FoldNote entitled "Key-Term Fold" described in the **Study Skills** section of the Appendix. Write a key term from the chapter on each tab of the key-term fold. Under each tab, write the definition of the key term.

START-UP ACTIVITY

Clothing Combos

How do the same parents have children with many different traits?

Procedure

1. Gather **three boxes**. Put **five hats** in the first box, **five gloves** in the second, and **five scarves** in the third.
2. Without looking in the boxes, select one item from each box. Repeat this process, five students at a time, until the entire class has picked "an outfit." Record what outfit each student chooses.

Analysis

1. Were any two outfits exactly alike? Did you see all possible combinations? Explain your answer.
2. Choose a partner. Using your outfits, how many different combinations could you make by giving a third person one hat, one glove, and one scarf? How is this process like parents passing traits to their children?
3. After completing this activity, why do you think parents often have children who look very different from each other?

SECTION 1

Mendel and His Peas

What You Will Learn

- Explain the relationship between traits and heredity.
- Describe the experiments of Gregor Mendel.
- Explain the difference between dominant and recessive traits.

Vocabulary

heredity
dominant trait
recessive trait

READING STRATEGY

Brainstorming The key idea of this section is heredity. Brainstorm words and phrases related to heredity.

Why don't you look like a rhinoceros? The answer to this question seems simple: Neither of your parents is a rhinoceros. But there is more to this answer than meets the eye.

As it turns out, **heredity,** or the passing of traits from parents to offspring, is more complicated than you might think. For example, you might have curly hair, while both of your parents have straight hair. You might have blue eyes even though both of your parents have brown eyes. How does this happen? People have investigated this question for a long time. About 150 years ago, Gregor Mendel performed important experiments. His discoveries helped scientists begin to find some answers to these questions.

Reading Check What is heredity? (*See the Appendix for answers to Reading Checks.*)

Who Was Gregor Mendel?

Gregor Mendel, shown in **Figure 1,** was born in 1822 in Heinzendorf, Austria. Mendel grew up on a farm and learned a lot about flowers and fruit trees.

When he was 21 years old, Mendel entered a monastery. The monks taught science and performed many scientific experiments. From there, Mendel was sent to Vienna where he could receive training in teaching. However, Mendel had trouble taking tests. Although he did well in school, he was unable to pass the final exam. He returned to the monastery and put most of his energy into research. Mendel discovered the principles of heredity in the monastery garden.

Figure 1 *Gregor Mendel discovered the principles of heredity while studying pea plants.*

Unraveling the Mystery

From working with plants, Mendel knew that the patterns of inheritance were not always clear. For example, sometimes a trait that appeared in one generation (parents) was not present in the next generation (offspring). In the generation after that, though, the trait showed up again. Mendel noticed these kinds of patterns in several other living things, too. Mendel wanted to learn more about what caused these patterns.

To keep his investigation simple, Mendel decided to study only one kind of organism. Because he had studied garden pea plants before, they seemed like a good choice.

Self-Pollinating Peas

In fact, garden peas were a good choice for several reasons. Pea plants grow quickly, and there are many different kinds available. They are also able to self-pollinate. A *self-pollinating plant* has both male and female reproductive structures. So, pollen from one flower can fertilize the ovule of the same flower or the ovule of another flower on the same plant. The flower on the right side of **Figure 2** is self-pollinating.

Why is it important that pea plants can self-pollinate? Because eggs (in an ovule) and sperm (in pollen) from the same plant combine to make a new plant, Mendel was able to grow true-breeding plants. When a *true-breeding plant* self-pollinates, all of its offspring will have the same trait as the parent. For example, a true-breeding plant with purple flowers will always have offspring with purple flowers.

Pea plants can also cross-pollinate. In *cross-pollination,* pollen from one plant fertilizes the ovule of a flower on a different plant. There are several ways that this can happen. Pollen may be carried by insects to a flower on a different plant. Pollen can also be carried by the wind from one flower to another. The left side of **Figure 2** shows these kinds of cross-pollination.

Describing Traits

How would you describe yourself? Would you say that you are tall or short, have curly hair or straight hair? Make a list of some of your physical traits. Make a second list of traits that you were not born with, such as "caring" or "good at soccer." Talk to your family about your lists. Do they agree with your descriptions?

heredity the passing of genetic traits from parent to offspring

Figure 2 *During pollination, pollen from the anthers (male) is transferred to the stigma (female). Fertilization occurs when a sperm from the pollen travels through the stigma and enters the egg in an ovule.*

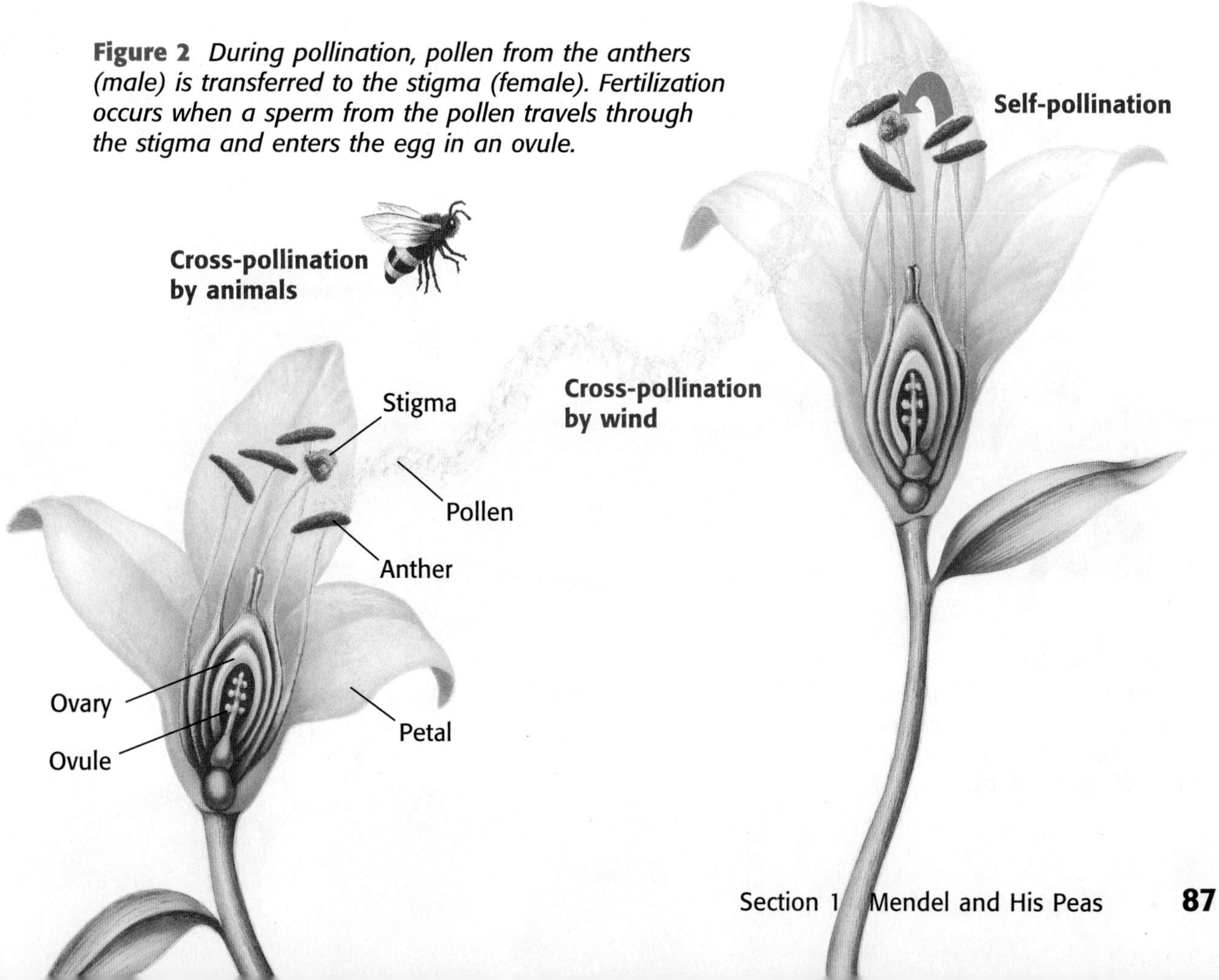

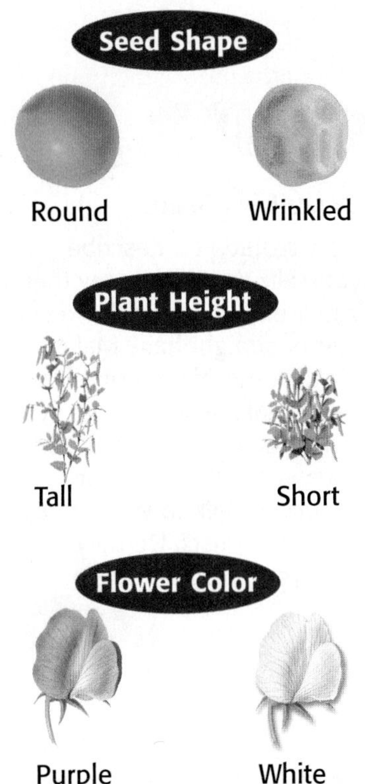

Figure 3 *These are some of the plant characteristics that Mendel studied.*

Characteristics

Mendel studied only one characteristic at a time. A *characteristic* is a feature that has different forms in a population. For example, hair color is a characteristic in humans. The different forms, such as brown or red hair, are called *traits.* Mendel used plants that had different traits for each of the characteristics he studied. For instance, for the characteristic of flower color, he chose plants that had purple flowers and plants that had white flowers. Three of the characteristics Mendel studied are shown in **Figure 3.**

Mix and Match

Mendel was careful to use plants that were true breeding for each of the traits he was studying. By doing so, he would know what to expect if his plants were to self-pollinate. He decided to find out what would happen if he bred, or crossed, two plants that had different traits of a single characteristic. To be sure the plants cross-pollinated, he removed the anthers of one plant so that the plant could not self-pollinate. Then, he used pollen from another plant to fertilize the plant, as shown in **Figure 4.** This step allowed Mendel to select which plants would be crossed to produce offspring.

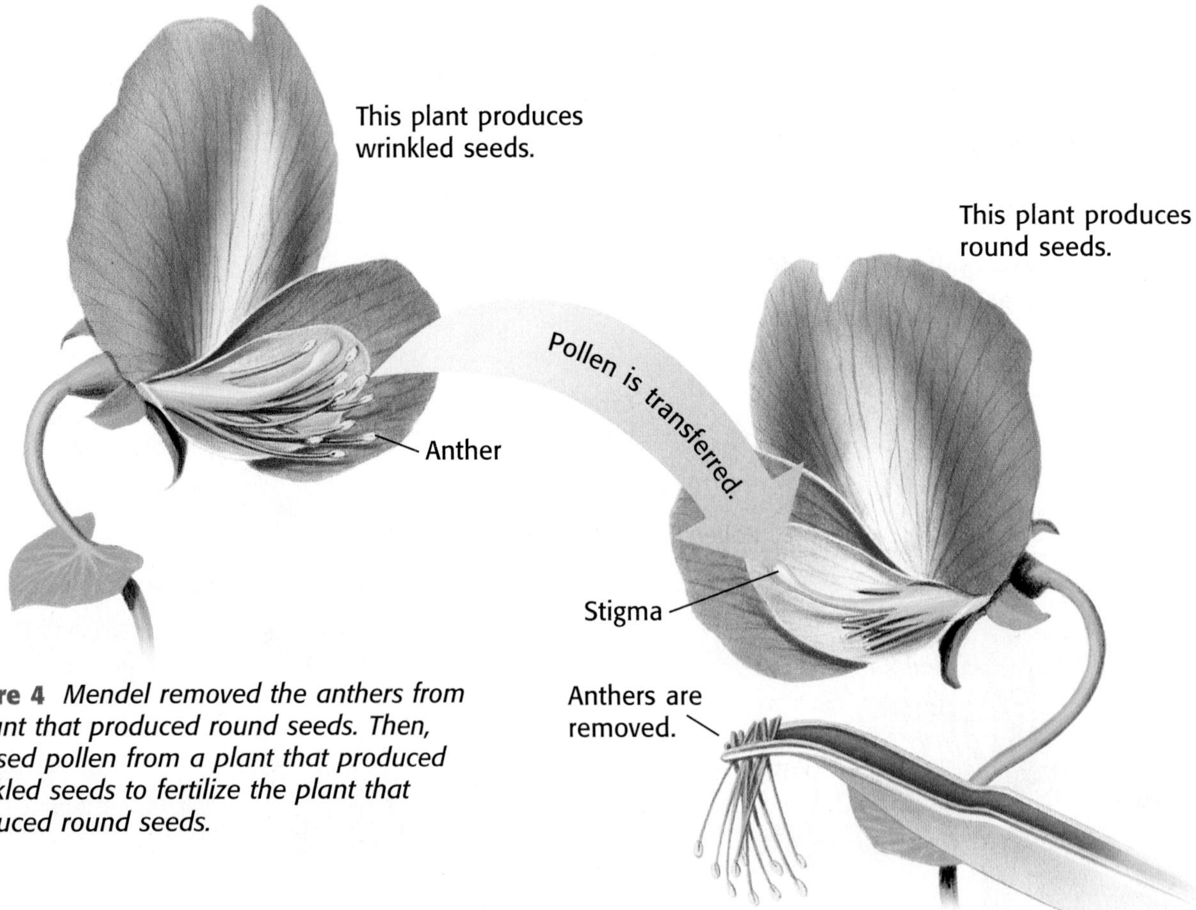

This plant produces wrinkled seeds.

This plant produces round seeds.

Pollen is transferred.

Anther

Stigma

Anthers are removed.

Figure 4 *Mendel removed the anthers from a plant that produced round seeds. Then, he used pollen from a plant that produced wrinkled seeds to fertilize the plant that produced round seeds.*

Mendel's First Experiments

In his first experiments, Mendel crossed pea plants to study seven different characteristics. In each cross, Mendel used plants that were true breeding for different traits for each characteristic. For example, he crossed plants that had purple flowers with plants that had white flowers. This cross is shown in the first part of **Figure 5.** The offspring from such a cross are called *first-generation plants*. All of the first-generation plants in this cross had purple flowers. Are you surprised by the results? What happened to the trait for white flowers?

Mendel got similar results for each cross. One trait was always present in the first generation, and the other trait seemed to disappear. Mendel chose to call the trait that appeared the **dominant trait.** Because the other trait seemed to fade into the background, Mendel called it the **recessive trait.** (To *recede* means "to go away or back off.") To find out what might have happened to the recessive trait, Mendel decided to do another set of experiments.

dominant trait the trait observed in the first generation when parents that have different traits are bred

recessive trait a trait that reappears in the second generation after disappearing in the first generation when parents with different traits are bred

Mendel's Second Experiments

Mendel allowed the first-generation plants to self-pollinate. **Figure 5** also shows what happened when a first-generation plant with purple flowers was allowed to self-pollinate. As you can see, the recessive trait for white flowers reappeared in the second generation.

Mendel did this same experiment on each of the seven characteristics. In each case, some of the second-generation plants had the recessive trait.

Reading Check **Describe Mendel's second set of experiments.**

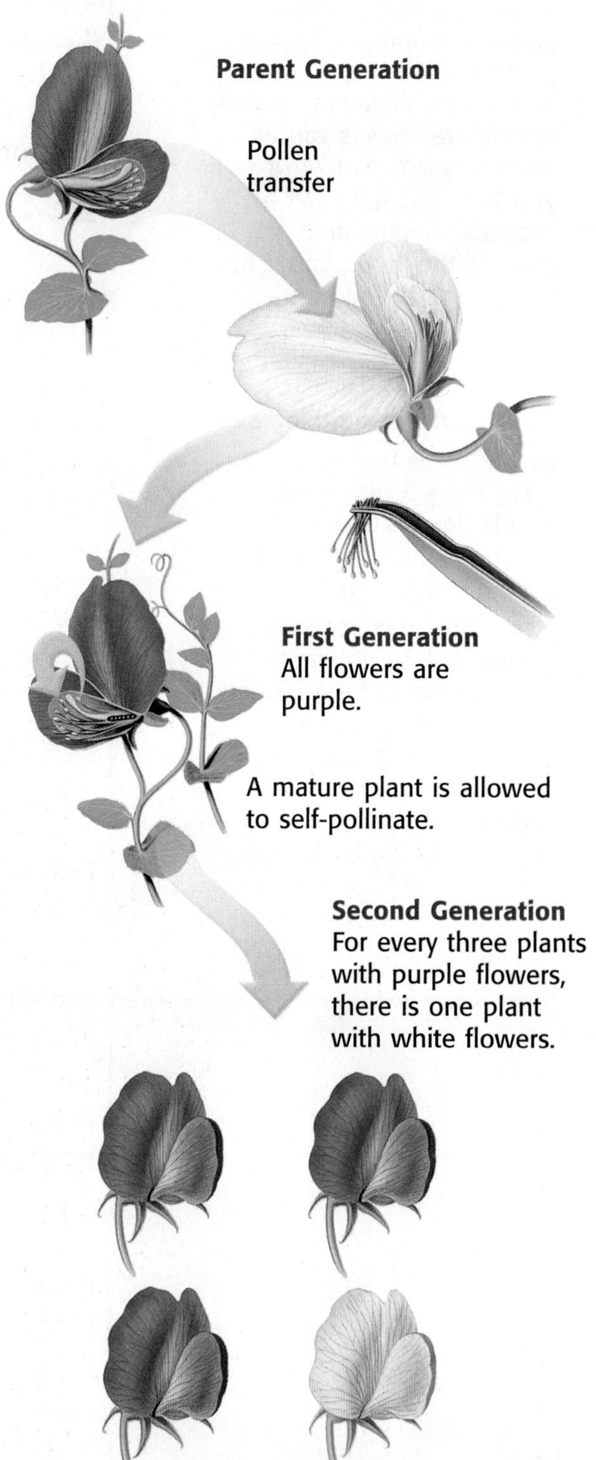
Parent Generation
Pollen transfer
First Generation
All flowers are purple.
A mature plant is allowed to self-pollinate.
Second Generation
For every three plants with purple flowers, there is one plant with white flowers.

Figure 5 *Mendel used the pollen from a plant with purple flowers to fertilize a plant with white flowers. Then, he allowed the offspring to self-pollinate.*

Ratios in Mendel's Experiments

Mendel then decided to count the number of plants with each trait that turned up in the second generation. He hoped that this might help him explain his results. Take a look at Mendel's results, shown in **Table 1.**

As you can see, the recessive trait did not show up as often as the dominant trait. Mendel decided to figure out the ratio of dominant traits to recessive traits. A *ratio* is a relationship between two different numbers that is often expressed as a fraction. Calculate the dominant-to-recessive ratio for each characteristic. (If you need help, look at the Math Practice at left.) Do you notice anything interesting about the ratios? Round to the nearest whole number. Are the ratios all the same, or are they different?

Reading Check What is a ratio?

Understanding Ratios

A ratio is a way to compare two numbers. Look at **Table 1.** The ratio of plants with purple flowers to plants with white flowers can be written as 705 to 224 or 705:224. This ratio can be reduced, or simplified, by dividing the first number by the second as follows:

$$\frac{705}{224} = \frac{3.15}{1}$$

which is the same thing as a ratio of 3.15:1.

For every 3 plants with purple flowers, there will be roughly 1 plant with white flowers. Try this problem:

In a box of chocolates, there are 18 nougat-filled chocolates and 6 caramel-filled chocolates. What is the ratio of nougat-filled chocolates to caramel-filled chocolates?

Table 1 Mendel's Results

Characteristic	Dominant traits	Recessive traits	Ratio
Flower color	705 purple	224 white	3.15:1
Seed color	6,002 yellow	2,001 green	?
Seed shape	5,474 round	1,850 wrinkled	?
Pod color	428 green	152 yellow	?
Pod shape	882 smooth	299 bumpy	?
Flower position	651 along stem	207 at tip	?
Plant height	787 tall	277 short	?

Gregor Mendel—Gone but Not Forgotten

Mendel realized that his results could be explained only if each plant had two sets of instructions for each characteristic. Each parent would then donate one set of instructions. In 1865, Mendel published his findings. But good ideas are sometimes overlooked or misunderstood at first. It wasn't until after his death, more than 30 years later, that Mendel's work was widely recognized. Once Mendel's ideas were rediscovered and understood, the door was opened to modern genetics. Genetic research, as shown in **Figure 6,** is one of the fastest changing fields in science today.

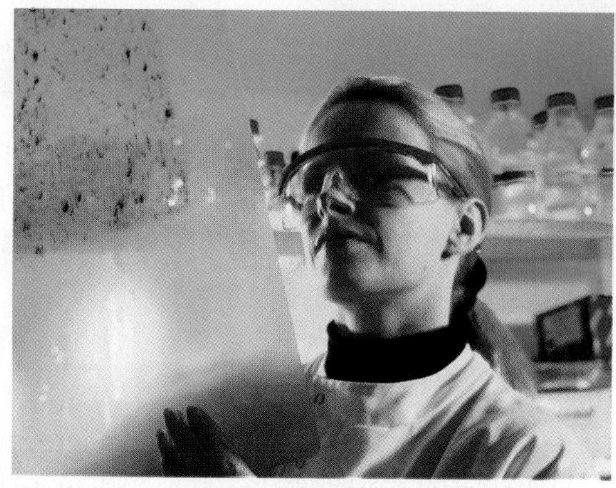

Figure 6 *This researcher is continuing the work started by Gregor Mendel more than 100 years ago.*

SECTION Review

Summary

- Heredity is the passing of traits from parents to offspring.
- Gregor Mendel made carefully planned experiments using pea plants that could self-pollinate.
- When parents with different traits are bred, dominant traits are always present in the first generation. Recessive traits are not visible in the first generation but reappear in the second generation.
- Mendel found a 3:1 ratio of dominant-to-recessive traits in the second generation.

Using Key Terms

1. Use each of the following terms in a separate sentence: *heredity, dominant trait,* and *recessive trait.*

Understanding Key Ideas

2. A plant that has both male and female reproductive structures is able to
   a. self-replicate.
   b. self-pollinate.
   c. change colors.
   d. None of the above
3. Explain the difference between self-pollination and cross-pollination.
4. What is the difference between a trait and a characteristic? Give one example of each.
5. Describe Mendel's first set of experiments.
6. Describe Mendel's second set of experiments.

Math Skills

7. In a bag of chocolate candies, there are 21 brown candies and 6 green candies. What is the ratio of brown to green? What is the ratio of green to brown?

Critical Thinking

8. **Predicting Consequences** Gregor Mendel used only true-breeding plants. If he had used plants that were not true breeding, do you think he would have discovered dominant and recessive traits? Explain.
9. **Applying Concepts** In cats, there are two types of ears: normal and curly. A curly-eared cat mated with a normal-eared cat, and all of the kittens had curly ears. Are curly ears a dominant or recessive trait? Explain.
10. **Identifying Relationships** List three other fields of study that use ratios.

SCILINKS.
NSTA
Developed and maintained by the National Science Teachers Association
For a variety of links related to this chapter, go to www.scilinks.org
Topic: Heredity; Dominant and Recessive Traits
SciLinks code: HSM0738; HSM0423

SECTION 2

Traits and Inheritance

Mendel calculated the ratio of dominant traits to recessive traits. He found a ratio of 3:1. What did this tell him about how traits are passed from parents to offspring?

What You Will Learn

- Explain how genes and alleles are related to genotype and phenotype.
- Use the information in a Punnett square.
- Explain how probability can be used to predict possible genotypes in offspring.
- Describe three exceptions to Mendel's observations.

Vocabulary

gene
allele
phenotype
genotype
probability

READING STRATEGY

Paired Summarizing Read this section silently. In pairs, take turns summarizing the material. Stop to discuss ideas that seem confusing.

A Great Idea

Mendel knew from his experiments with pea plants that there must be two sets of instructions for each characteristic. The first-generation plants carried the instructions for both the dominant trait and the recessive trait. Scientists now call these instructions for an inherited trait **genes.** Each parent gives one set of genes to the offspring. The offspring then has two forms of the same gene for every characteristic—one from each parent. The different forms (often dominant and recessive) of a gene are known as **alleles** (uh LEELZ). Dominant alleles are shown with a capital letter. Recessive alleles are shown with a lowercase letter.

Reading Check **What is the difference between a gene and an allele?** *(See the Appendix for answers to Reading Checks.)*

Phenotype

Genes affect the traits of offspring. An organism's appearance is known as its **phenotype** (FEE noh TIEP). In pea plants, possible phenotypes for the characteristic of flower color would be purple flowers or white flowers. For seed color, yellow and green seeds are the different phenotypes.

Phenotypes of humans are much more complicated than those of peas. Look at **Figure 1** below. The man has an inherited condition called *albinism* (AL buh NIZ uhm). Albinism prevents hair, skin, and eyes from having normal coloring.

gene one set of instructions for an inherited trait

allele one of the alternative forms of a gene that governs a characteristic, such as hair color

phenotype an organism's appearance or other detectable characteristic

Figure 1 *Albinism is an inherited disorder that affects a person's phenotype in many ways.*

Genotype

Both inherited alleles together form an organism's **genotype.** Because the allele for purple flowers (*P*) is dominant, only one *P* allele is needed for the plant to have purple flowers. A plant with two dominant or two recessive alleles is said to be *homozygous* (HOH moh ZIE guhs). A plant that has the genotype *Pp* is said to be *heterozygous* (HET uhr OH ZIE guhs).

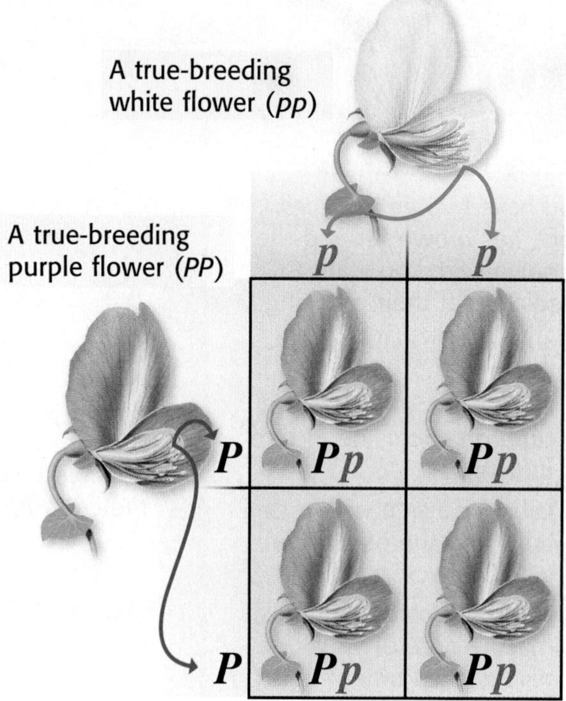

Figure 2 *All of the offspring for this cross have the same genotype—*Pp.

Punnett Squares

A Punnett square is used to organize all the possible combinations of offspring from particular parents. The alleles for a true-breeding, purple-flowered plant are written as *PP*. The alleles for a true-breeding, white-flowered plant are written as *pp*. The Punnett square for this cross is shown in **Figure 2.** All of the offspring have the same genotype: *Pp*. The dominant allele, *P*, in each genotype ensures that all of the offspring will be purple-flowered plants. The recessive allele, *p*, may be passed on to the next generation. This Punnett square shows the results of Mendel's first experiments.

genotype the entire genetic makeup of an organism; also the combination of genes for one or more specific traits

Making a Punnett Square

1. Draw a square, and divide it into four sections.
2. Write the letters that represent alleles from one parent along the top of the box.
3. Write the letters that represent alleles from the other parent along the side of the box.
4. The cross shown at right is between two plants that produce round seeds. The genotype for each is *Rr*. Round seeds are dominant, and wrinkled seeds are recessive. Follow the arrows to see how the inside of the box was filled. The resulting alleles inside the box show all the possible genotypes for the offspring from this cross. What would the phenotypes for these offspring be?

Taking Your Chances

You have two guinea pigs. Each has brown fur and the genotype *Bb*. You want to predict what their offspring might look like. Try this to find out.

1. Stick a **piece of masking tape** on each side of **two quarters.**
2. Label one side with a capital *B* and the other side with a lowercase *b*.
3. Toss both coins 10 times, making note of your results each time.
4. How many times did you get the *bb* combination?
5. What is the probability that the next toss will result in *bb*?
6. What are the chances that the guinea pigs' offspring will have white fur (with the genotype *bb*)?

Figure 3 *This Punnett square shows the possible results from the cross* Pp × Pp.

More Evidence for Inheritance

In Mendel's second experiments, he allowed the first generation plants to self-pollinate. **Figure 3** shows a self-pollination cross of a plant with the genotype *Pp*. What are the possible genotypes of the offspring?

Notice that one square shows the genotype *Pp,* while another shows *pP*. These are exactly the same genotype. The other possible genotypes of the offspring are *PP* and *pp*. The combinations *PP, Pp,* and *pP* have the same phenotype—purple flowers. This is because each contains at least one dominant allele (*P*).

Only one combination, *pp,* produces plants that have white flowers. The ratio of dominant to recessive is 3:1, just as Mendel calculated from his data.

What Are the Chances?

Each parent has two alleles for each gene. When these alleles are different, as in *Pp,* offspring are equally likely to receive either allele. Think of a coin toss. There is a 50% chance you'll get heads and a 50% chance you'll get tails. The chance of receiving one allele or another is as random as a coin toss.

Probability

The mathematical chance that something will happen is known as **probability.** Probability is most often written as a fraction or percentage. If you toss a coin, the probability of tossing tails is 1/2—you will get tails half the time.

probability the likelihood that a possible future event will occur in any given instance of the event

Reading Check **What is probability?**

Probability If you roll a pair of dice, what is the probability that you will roll 2 threes?

Step 1: Count the number of faces on a single die. Put this number in the denominator: 6.

Step 2: Count how many ways you can roll a three with one die. Put this number in the numerator: 1/6.

Step 3: To find the probability that you will throw 2 threes, multiply the probability of throwing the first three by the probability of throwing the second three: $1/6 \times 1/6 = 1/36$.

Now It's Your Turn

If you roll a single die, what is the probability that you will roll an even number?

Calculating Probabilities

To find the probability that you will toss two heads in a row, multiply the probability of tossing the first head (1/2) by the probability of tossing the second head (1/2). The probability of tossing two heads in a row is 1/4.

Genotype Probability

To have white flowers, a pea plant must receive a *p* allele from each parent. Each offspring of a $Pp \times Pp$ cross has a 50% chance of receiving either allele from either parent. So, the probability of inheriting two *p* alleles is $1/2 \times 1/2$, which equals 1/4, or 25%. Traits in pea plants are easy to predict because there are only two choices for each trait, such as purple or white flowers and round or wrinkled seeds. Look at **Figure 4.** Do you see only two distinct choices for fur color?

Figure 4 *These kittens inherited one allele from their mother for each trait.*

CONNECTION TO Chemistry

Round and Wrinkled Round seeds may look better, but wrinkled seeds taste sweeter. The dominant allele for seed shape, *R*, causes sugar to be changed into starch (which is a storage molecule for sugar). This change makes the seed round. Seeds with the genotype *rr* do not make or store this starch. Because the sugar has not been changed into starch, the seed tastes sweeter. If you had a pea plant with round seeds (*Rr*), what would you cross it with to get some offspring with wrinkled seeds? Draw a Punnett square showing your cross.

ACTIVITY

More About Traits

As you may have already discovered, things are often more complicated than they first appear to be. Gregor Mendel uncovered the basic principles of how genes are passed from one generation to the next. But as scientists learned more about heredity, they began to find exceptions to Mendel's principles. A few of these exceptions are explained below.

Incomplete Dominance

Since Mendel's discoveries, researchers have found that sometimes one trait is not completely dominant over another. These traits do not blend together, but each allele has its own degree of influence. This is known as *incomplete dominance.*

One example of incomplete dominance is found in the snapdragon flower. **Figure 5** shows a cross between a true-breeding red snapdragon (R^1R^1) and a true-breeding white snapdragon (R^2R^2). As you can see, all of the possible phenotypes for their offspring are pink because both alleles of the gene have some degree of influence.

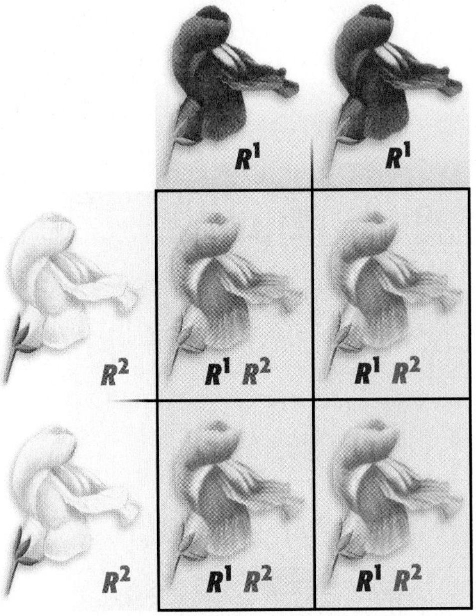

Figure 5 *Cross-breeding two true-breeding snapdragons provides a good example of incomplete dominance.*

Reading Check What is incomplete dominance?

One Gene, Many Traits

Sometimes one gene influences more than one trait. An example of this phenomenon is shown by the white tiger in **Figure 6.** The white fur is caused by a single gene, but this gene influences more than just fur color. Do you see anything else unusual about the tiger? If you look closely, you'll see that the tiger has blue eyes. Here, the gene that controls fur color also influences eye color.

Figure 6 *The gene that gave this tiger white fur also influenced its eye color.*

Many Genes, One Trait

Some traits, such as the color of your skin, hair, and eyes, are the result of several genes acting together. Therefore, it's difficult to tell if some traits are the result of a dominant or a recessive gene. Different combinations of alleles result in different eye-color shades, as shown in **Figure 7.**

The Importance of Environment

Genes aren't the only influences on traits. A guinea pig could have the genes for long fur, but its fur could be cut. In the same way, your environment influences how you grow. Your genes may make it possible that you will grow to be tall, but you need a healthy diet to reach your full potential height.

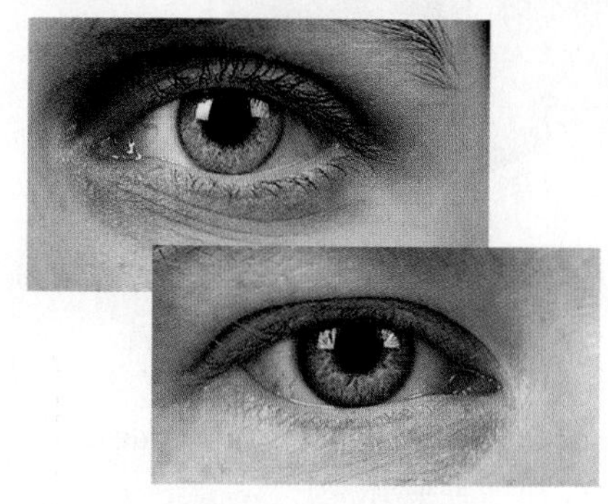

Figure 7 *At least two genes determine human eye color. That's why many shades of a single color are possible.*

SECTION Review

Summary

- Instructions for an inherited trait are called *genes*. For each gene, there are two alleles, one inherited from each parent. Both alleles make up an organism's genotype. Phenotype is an organism's appearance.
- Punnett squares show all possible offspring genotypes.
- Probability can be used to describe possible outcomes in offspring and the likelihood of each outcome.
- Incomplete dominance occurs when one allele is not completely dominant over the other allele.
- Some genes influence more than one trait.

Using Key Terms

1. Use the following terms in the same sentence: *gene* and *allele*.
2. In your own words, write a definition for each of the following terms: *genotype* and *phenotype*.

Understanding Key Ideas

3. Use a Punnett square to determine the possible genotypes of the offspring of a *BB* × *Bb* cross.
   a. all *BB*
   b. *BB*, *Bb*
   c. *BB*, *Bb*, *bb*
   d. all *bb*
4. How are genes and alleles related to genotype and phenotype?
5. Describe three exceptions to Mendel's observations.

Math Skills

6. What is the probability of rolling a five on one die three times in a row?

Critical Thinking

7. **Applying Concepts** The allele for a cleft chin, *C*, is dominant among humans. What are the results of a cross between parents with genotypes *Cc* and *cc*?

Interpreting Graphics

The Punnett square below shows the alleles for fur color in rabbits. Black fur, *B*, is dominant over white fur, *b*.

	?	?
?	*Bb*	*Bb*
?	*Bb*	*Bb*

8. Given the combinations shown, what are the genotypes of the parents?
9. If black fur had incomplete dominance over white fur, what color would the offspring be?

SCILINKS
NSTA
Developed and maintained by the National Science Teachers Association
For a variety of links related to this chapter, go to www.scilinks.org
Topic: Genotypes; Phenotypes
SciLinks code: HSM0664; HSM1135

SECTION 3

Meiosis

What You Will Learn

- Explain the difference between mitosis and meiosis.
- Describe how chromosomes determine sex.
- Explain why sex-linked disorders occur in one sex more often than in the other.
- Interpret a pedigree.

Vocabulary

homologous chromosomes
meiosis
sex chromosome
pedigree

READING STRATEGY

Reading Organizer As you read this section, make a flowchart of the steps of meiosis.

Where are genes located, and how do they pass information? Understanding reproduction is the first step to finding the answers.

There are two kinds of reproduction: asexual and sexual. Asexual reproduction results in offspring with genotypes that are exact copies of their parent's genotype. Sexual reproduction produces offspring that share traits with their parents but are not exactly like either parent.

Asexual Reproduction

In *asexual reproduction,* only one parent cell is needed. The structures inside the cell are copied, and then the parent cell divides, making two exact copies. This type of cell reproduction is known as *mitosis*. Most of the cells in your body and most single-celled organisms reproduce in this way.

Sexual Reproduction

In sexual reproduction, two parent cells join together to form offspring that are different from both parents. The parent cells are called *sex cells*. Sex cells are different from ordinary body cells. Human body cells have 46, or 23 pairs of, chromosomes. One set of human chromosomes is shown in **Figure 1.** Chromosomes that carry the same sets of genes are called **homologous** (hoh MAHL uh guhs) **chromosomes.** Imagine a pair of shoes. Each shoe is like a homologous chromosome. The pair represents a homologous pair of chromosomes. But human sex cells are different. They have 23 chromosomes—half the usual number. Each sex cell has only one of the chromosomes from each homologous pair. Sex cells have only one "shoe."

homologous chromosomes chromosomes that have the same sequence of genes and the same structure

meiosis a process in cell division during which the number of chromosomes decreases to half the original number by two divisions of the nucleus, which results in the production of sex cells

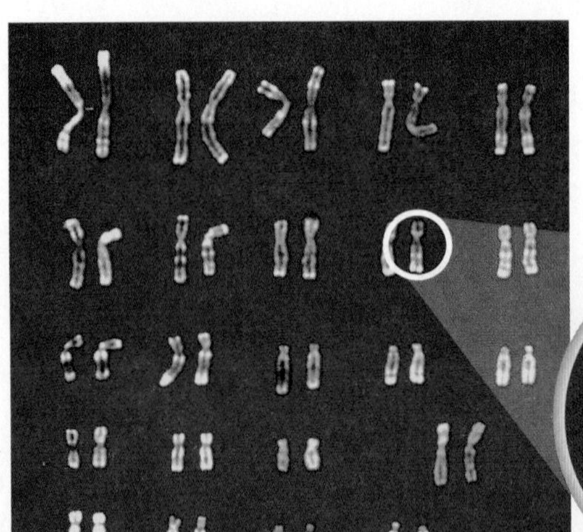

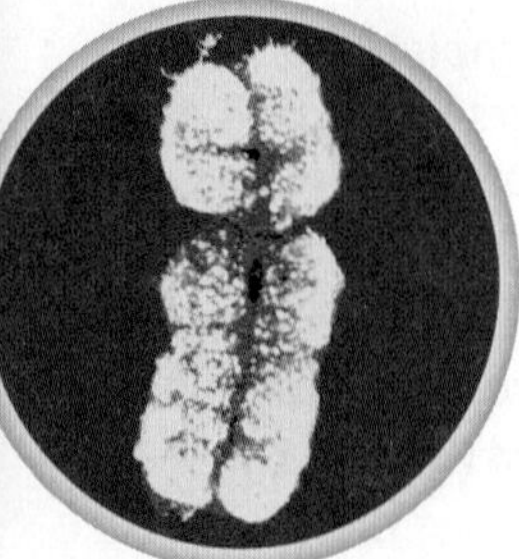

Figure 1 *Human body cells have 23 pairs of chromosomes. One member of a pair of homologous chromosomes is shown below.*

Meiosis

Sex cells are made during meiosis (mie OH sis). **Meiosis** is a copying process that produces cells with half the usual number of chromosomes. Each sex cell receives one-half of each homologous pair. For example, a human egg cell has 23 chromosomes, and a sperm cell has 23 chromosomes. The new cell that forms when an egg cell and a sperm cell join has 46 chromosomes.

✓ *Reading Check* **How many chromosomes does a human egg cell have?** *(See the Appendix for answers to Reading Checks.)*

Genes and Chromosomes

What does all of this have to do with the location of genes? Not long after Mendel's work was rediscovered, a graduate student named Walter Sutton made an important observation. Sutton was studying sperm cells in grasshoppers. Sutton knew of Mendel's studies, which showed that the egg and sperm must each contribute the same amount of information to the offspring. That was the only way the 3:1 ratio found in the second generation could be explained. Sutton also knew from his own studies that although eggs and sperm were different, they did have something in common: Their chromosomes were located inside a nucleus. Using his observations of meiosis, his understanding of Mendel's work, and some creative thinking, Sutton proposed something very important:

Genes are located on chromosomes!

Understanding meiosis was critical to finding the location of genes. Before you learn about meiosis, review mitosis, shown in **Figure 2.** Meiosis is outlined in **Figure 3** on the next two pages.

CONNECTION TO Language Arts

Greek Roots The word *mitosis* is related to a Greek word that means "threads." Threadlike spindles are visible during mitosis. The word *meiosis* comes from a Greek word that means "to make smaller." How do you think meiosis got its name?

Figure 2 **Mitosis Revisited**

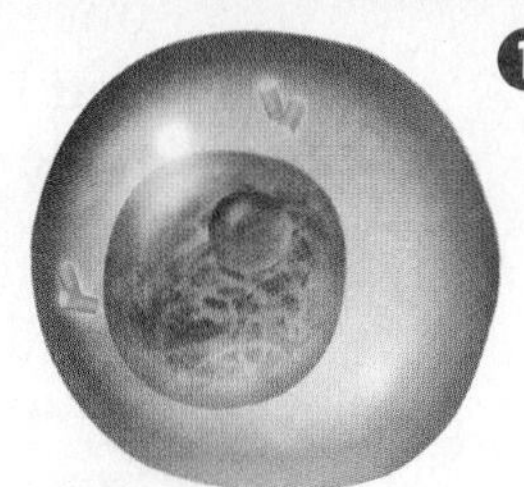

1. Each chromosome is copied.

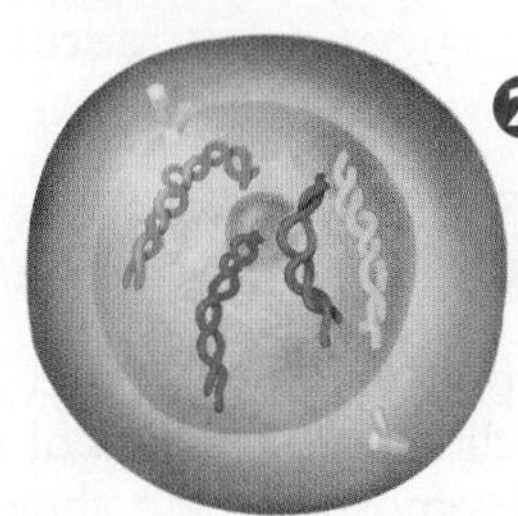

2. The chromosomes thicken and shorten. Each chromosome consists of two identical copies, called *chromatids.*

3. The nuclear membrane is dissolved. The chromatids line up along the equator (center) of the cell.

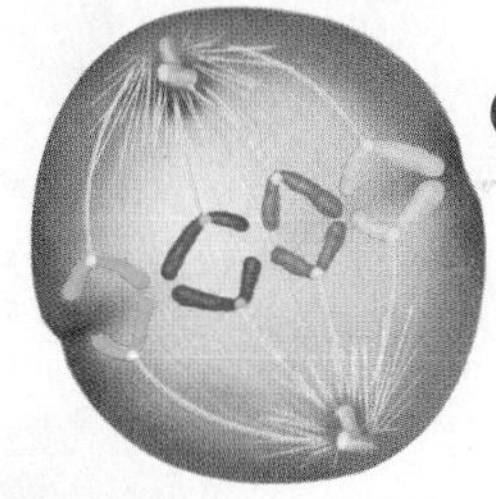

4. The chromatids pull apart.

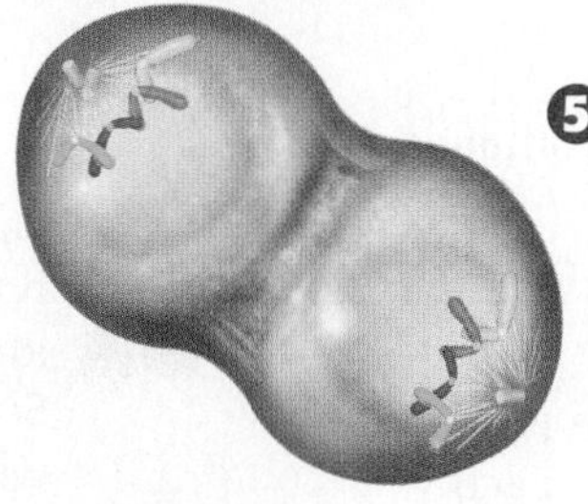

5. The nuclear membrane forms around the separated chromatids. The chromosomes unwind, and the cell divides.

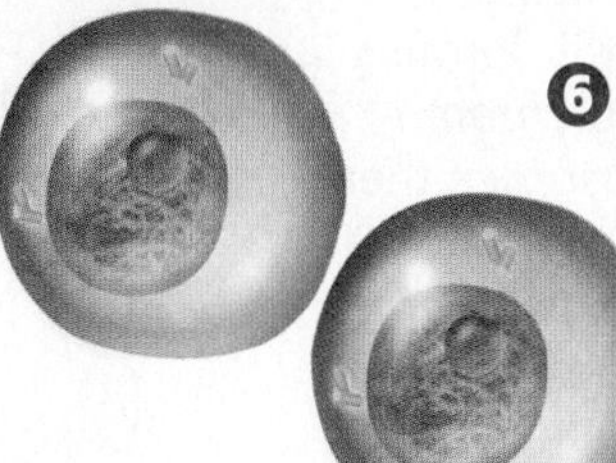

6. The result is two identical copies of the original cell.

The Steps of Meiosis

During mitosis, chromosomes are copied once, and then the nucleus divides once. During meiosis, chromosomes are copied once, and then the nucleus divides twice. The resulting sperm and eggs have half the number of chromosomes of a normal body cell. **Figure 3** shows all eight steps of meiosis. Read about each step as you look at the figure. Different types of living things have different numbers of chromosomes. In this illustration, only four chromosomes are shown.

Reading Check **How many cells are made from one parent cell during meiosis?**

Figure 3 **Steps of Meiosis**

Read about each step as you look at the diagram. Different types of living things have different numbers of chromosomes. In this diagram, only four chromosomes are shown.

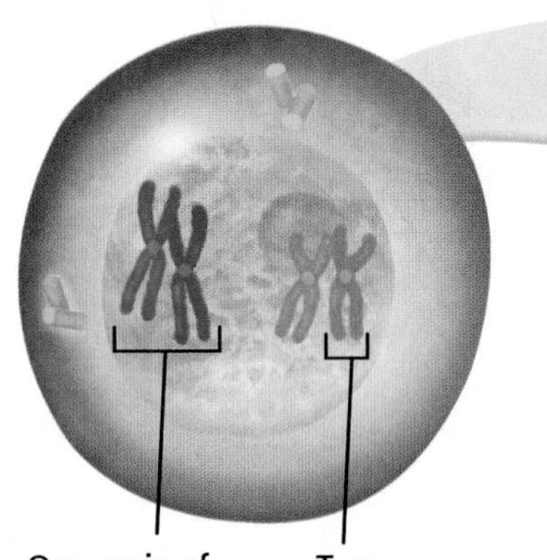

1 Before meiosis begins, the chromosomes are in a threadlike form. Each chromosome makes an exact copy of itself, forming two halves called *chromatids*. The chromosomes then thicken and shorten into a form that is visible under a microscope. The nuclear membrane disappears.

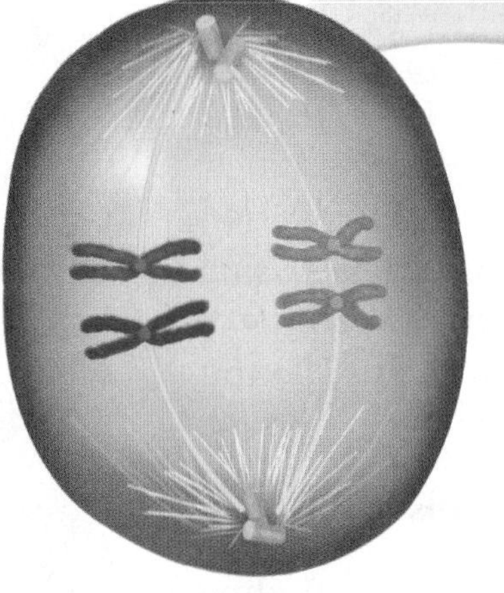

2 Each chromosome is now made up of two identical chromatids. Similar chromosomes pair with one another, and the paired homologous chromosomes line up at the equator of the cell.

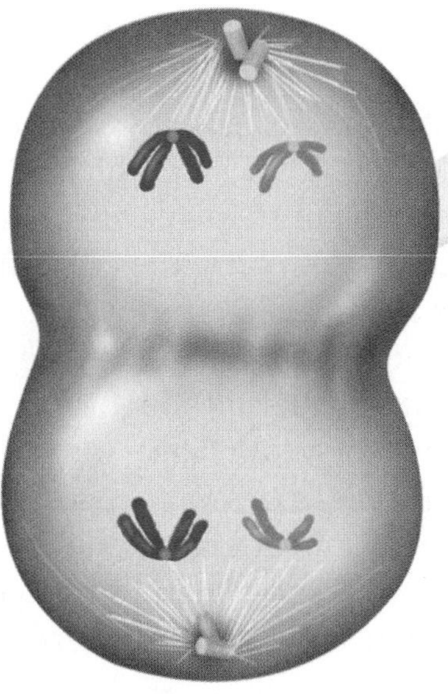

3 The chromosomes separate from their homologous partners and then move to opposite ends of the cell.

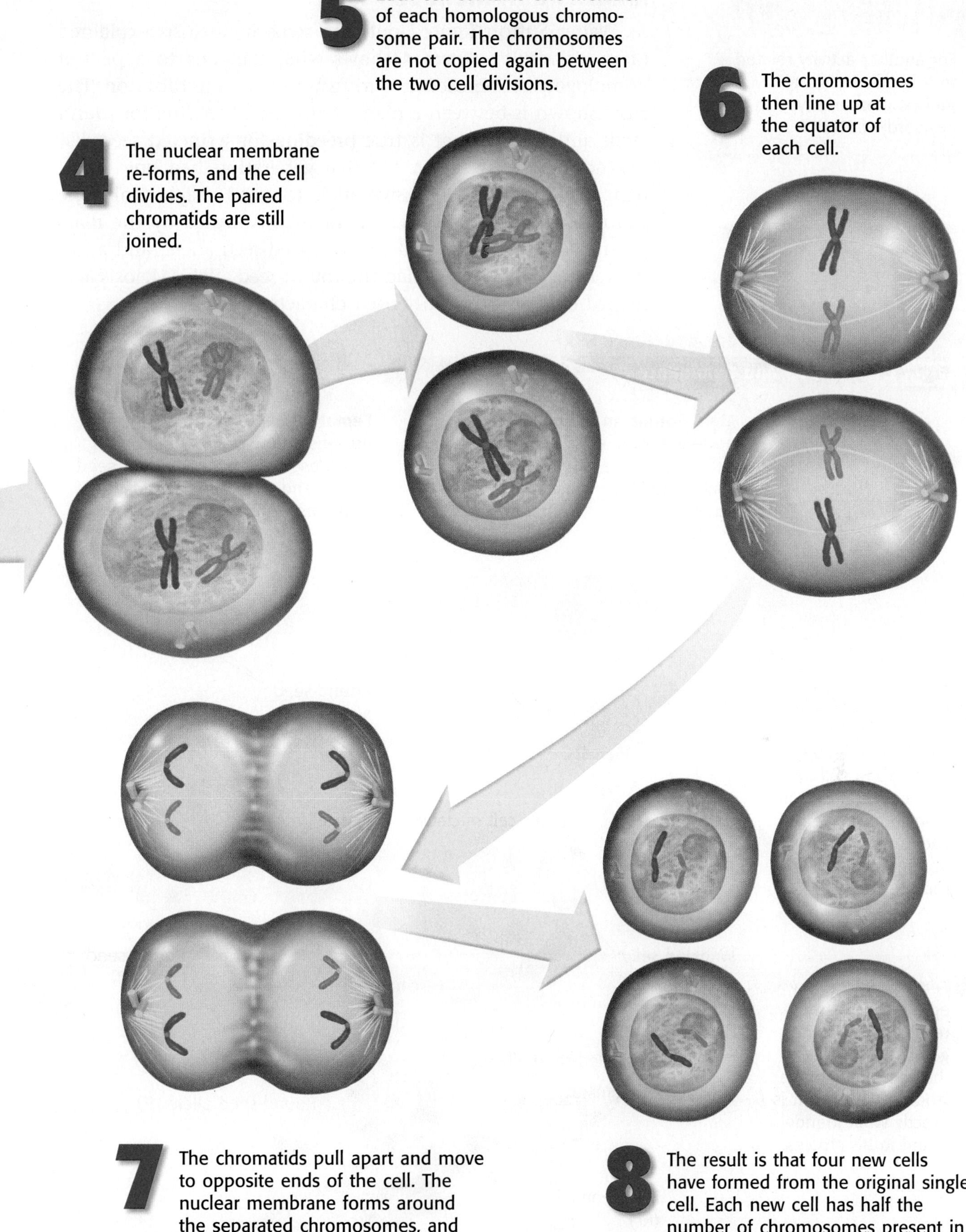
4
The nuclear membrane re-forms, and the cell divides. The paired chromatids are still joined.
5
Each cell contains one member of each homologous chromosome pair. The chromosomes are not copied again between the two cell divisions.
6
The chromosomes then line up at the equator of each cell.
7
The chromatids pull apart and move to opposite ends of the cell. The nuclear membrane forms around the separated chromosomes, and the cells divide.
8
The result is that four new cells have formed from the original single cell. Each new cell has half the number of chromosomes present in the original cell.

For another activity related to this chapter, go to **go.hrw.com** and type in the keyword **HL5HERW.**

Meiosis and Mendel

As Walter Sutton figured out, the steps in meiosis explained Mendel's results. **Figure 4** shows what happens to a pair of homologous chromosomes during meiosis and fertilization. The cross shown is between a plant that is true breeding for round seeds and a plant that is true breeding for wrinkled seeds.

Each fertilized egg in the first generation had one dominant allele and one recessive allele for seed shape. Only one genotype was possible because all sperm formed by the male parent during meiosis had the wrinkled-seed allele, and all of the female parent's eggs had the round-seed allele. Meiosis also helped explain other inherited characteristics.

Figure 4 **Meiosis and Dominance**

Male Parent In the plant-cell nucleus below, each homologous chromosome has an allele for seed shape, and each allele carries the same instructions: to make wrinkled seeds.

Female Parent In the plant-cell nucleus below, each homologous chromosome has an allele for seed shape, and each allele carries the same instructions: to make round seeds.

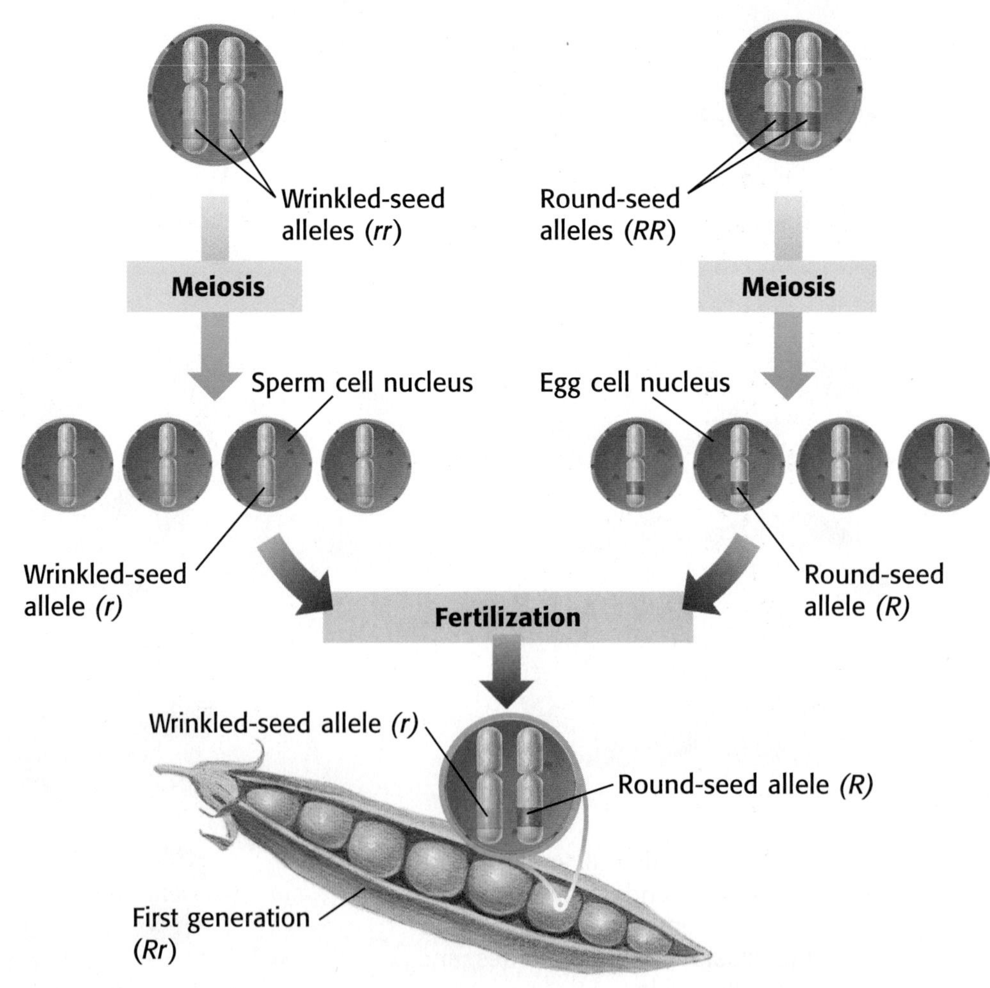

a Following **meiosis,** each sperm cell has a recessive allele for wrinkled seeds, and each egg cell has a dominant allele for round seeds.

b **Fertilization** of any egg by any sperm results in the same genotype (*Rr*) and the same phenotype (round). This result is exactly what Mendel found in his studies.

Sex Chromosomes

Information contained on chromosomes determines many of our traits. **Sex chromosomes** carry genes that determine sex. In humans, females have two X chromosomes. But human males have one X chromosome and one Y chromosome.

During meiosis, one of each of the chromosome pairs ends up in a sex cell. Females have two X chromosomes in each body cell. When meiosis produces the egg cells, each egg gets one X chromosome. Males have both an X chromosome and a Y chromosome in each body cell. Meiosis produces sperm with either an X or a Y chromosome. An egg fertilized by a sperm with an X chromosome will produce a female. If the sperm contains a Y chromosome, the offspring will be male, as shown in **Figure 5.**

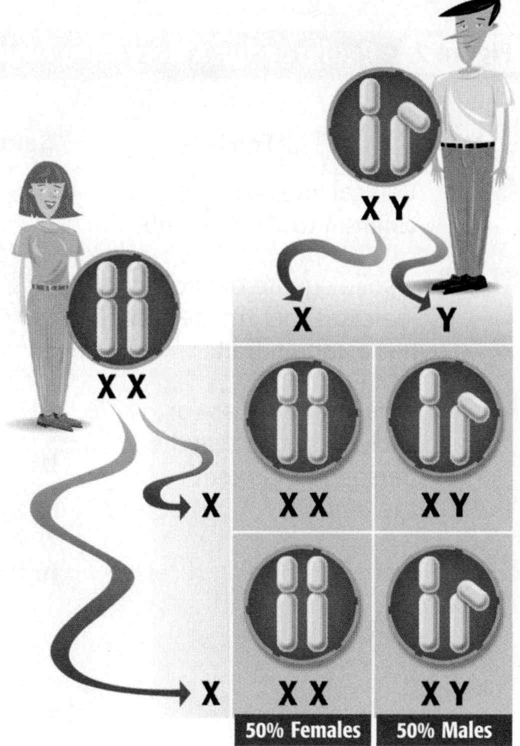

Figure 5 *Egg and sperm combine to form either the XX or XY combination.*

Sex-Linked Disorders

The Y chromosome does not carry all of the genes of an X chromosome. Females have two X chromosomes, so they carry two copies of each gene found on the X chromosome. This makes a backup gene available if one becomes damaged. Males have only one copy of each gene on their one X chromosome. The genes for certain disorders, such as colorblindness, are carried on the X chromosome. These disorders are called *sex-linked disorders*. Because the gene for such disorders is recessive, men are more likely to have sex-linked disorders.

sex chromosome one of the pair of chromosomes that determine the sex of an individual

People who are colorblind can have trouble distinguishing between shades of red and green. To help the colorblind, some cities have added shapes to their street lights, as shown in **Figure 6.** Hemophilia (HEE moh FIL ee uh) is another sex-linked disorder. Hemophilia prevents blood from clotting, and people with hemophilia bleed for a long time after small cuts. Hemophilia can be fatal.

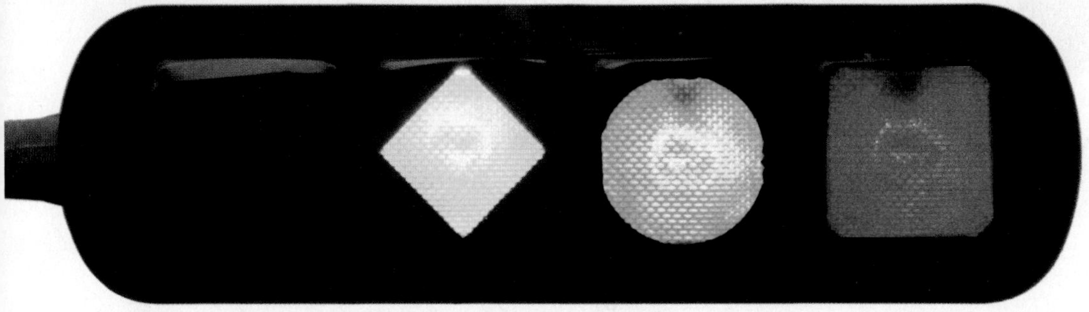

Figure 6 *This stoplight in Canada is designed to help the colorblind see signals easily. This photograph was taken over a few minutes to show all three shapes.*

Figure 7 **Pedigree for a Recessive Disease**

Males   Females

Vertical lines connect children to their parents.

A solid square or circle indicates that the person has a certain trait.

A half-filled square or circle indicates that the person is a carrier of the trait.

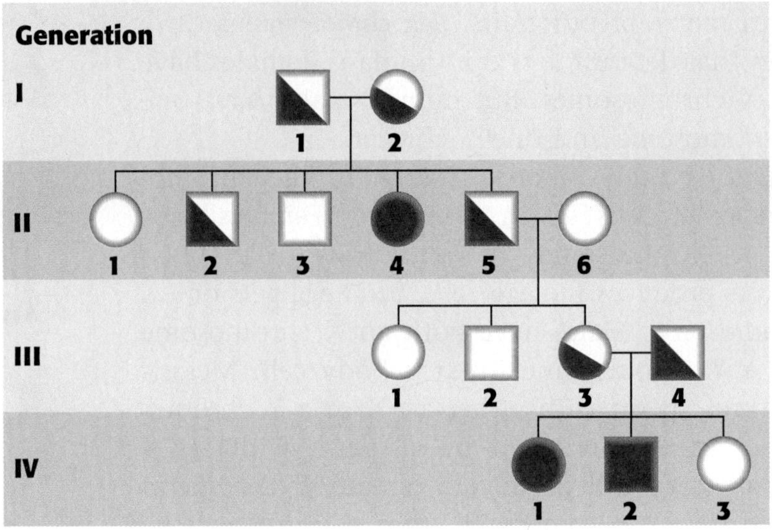

Generation

I: 1 2

II: 1 2 3 4 5 6

III: 1 2 3 4

IV: 1 2 3

Genetic Counseling

Hemophilia and other genetic disorders can be traced through a family tree. If people are worried that they might pass a disease to their children, they may consult a genetic counselor. These counselors often make use of a diagram known as a **pedigree,** which is a tool for tracing a trait through generations of a family. By making a pedigree, a counselor can often predict whether a person is a carrier of a hereditary disease. The pedigree shown in **Figure 7** traces a disease called *cystic fibrosis* (SIS tik FIE broh sis). Cystic fibrosis causes serious lung problems. People with this disease have inherited two recessive alleles. Both parents need to be carriers of the gene for the disease to show up in their children.

pedigree a diagram that shows the occurrence of a genetic trait in several generations of a family

Pedigrees can be drawn up to trace any trait through a family tree. You could even draw a pedigree that would show how you inherited your hair color. Many different pedigrees could be drawn for a typical family.

Figure 8 *Roses have been selectively bred to create large, bright flowers.*

Selective Breeding

For thousands of years, humans have seen the benefits of the careful breeding of plants and animals. In *selective breeding,* organisms with desirable characteristics are mated. You have probably enjoyed the benefits of selective breeding, although you may not have realized it. For example, you have probably eaten an egg from a chicken that was bred to produce more eggs. Your pet dog may be a result of selective breeding. Roses, like the one shown in **Figure 8,** have been selectively bred to produce large flowers. Wild roses are much smaller and have fewer petals than roses that you could buy at a nursery.

SECTION Review

Summary

- In mitosis, chromosomes are copied once, and then the nucleus divides once. In meiosis, chromosomes are copied once, and then the nucleus divides twice.
- The process of meiosis produces sex cells, which have half the number of chromosomes. These two halves combine during reproduction.
- In humans, females have two X chromosomes. So, each egg contains one X chromosome. Males have both an X and a Y chromosome. So, each sperm cell contains either an X or a Y chromosome.
- Sex-linked disorders occur in males more often than in females. Colorblindness and hemophilia are examples of sex-linked disorders.
- A pedigree is a diagram used to trace a trait through many generations of a family.

Using Key Terms

1. Use each of the following terms in the same sentence: *meiosis* and *sex chromosomes*.

In each of the following sentences, replace the incorrect term with the correct term from the word bank.

pedigree	homologous chromosomes
meiosis	mitosis

2. During fertilization, chromosomes are copied, and then the nucleus divides twice.
3. A Punnett square is used to show how inherited traits move through a family.
4. During meiosis, sex cells line up in the middle of the cell.

Understanding Key Ideas

5. Genes are found on
   a. chromosomes.
   b. proteins.
   c. alleles.
   d. sex cells.
6. If there are 14 chromosomes in pea plant cells, how many chromosomes are present in a sex cell of a pea plant?
7. Draw the eight steps of meiosis. Label one chromosome, and show its position in each step.

Interpreting Graphics

Use this pedigree to answer the question below.

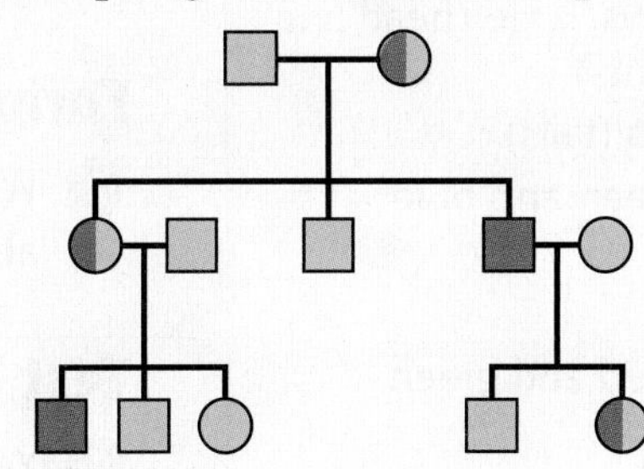

8. Is this disorder sex linked? Explain your reasoning.

Critical Thinking

9. **Identifying Relationships** Put the following in order of smallest to largest: chromosome, gene, and cell.
10. **Applying Concepts** A pea plant has purple flowers. What alleles for flower color could the sex cells carry?

SCILINKS
NSTA
Developed and maintained by the National Science Teachers Association
For a variety of links related to this chapter, go to www.scilinks.org
Topic: Meiosis; Genetic Diseases, Screening, Counseling
SciLinks code: HSM0935; HSM0651

Using Scientific Methods

Model-Making Lab

Bug Builders, Inc.

OBJECTIVES

Build models to further your understanding of inheritance.

Examine the traits of a population of offspring.

MATERIALS

- allele sacks (14) (supplied by your teacher)
- gumdrops, green and black (feet)
- map pins (eyes)
- marshmallows, large (head and body segments)
- pipe cleaners (tails)
- pushpins, green and blue (noses)
- scissors
- toothpicks, red and green (antennae)

SAFETY

Imagine that you are a designer for a toy company that makes toy alien bugs. The president of Bug Builders, Inc., wants new versions of the wildly popular Space Bugs, but he wants to use the bug parts that are already in the warehouse. It's your job to come up with a new bug design. You have studied how traits are passed from one generation to another. You will use this knowledge to come up with new combinations of traits and assemble the bug parts in new ways. Model A and Model B, shown below, will act as the "parent" bugs.

Ask a Question

1. If there are two forms of each of the seven traits, then how many possible combinations are there?

Form a Hypothesis

2. Write a hypothesis that is a possible answer to the question above. Explain your reasoning.

Test the Hypothesis

3. Your teacher will display 14 allele sacks. The sacks will contain slips of paper with capital or lowercase letters on them. Take one piece of paper from each sack. (Remember: Capital letters represent dominant alleles, and lowercase letters represent recessive alleles.) One allele is from "Mom," and one allele is from "Dad." After you have recorded the alleles you have drawn, place the slips of paper back into the sack.

Model A ("Mom")

- red antennae
- 3 body segments
- curly tail
- 2 pairs of legs
- green nose
- black feet
- 3 eyes

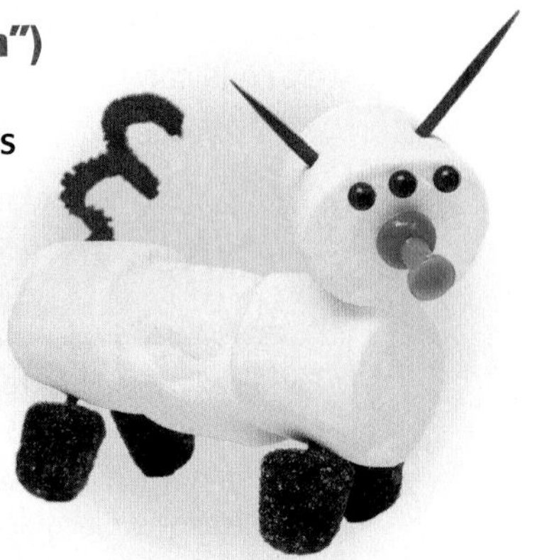

Model B ("Dad")

- green antennae
- 2 body segments
- straight tail
- 3 pairs of legs
- blue nose
- green feet
- 2 eyes

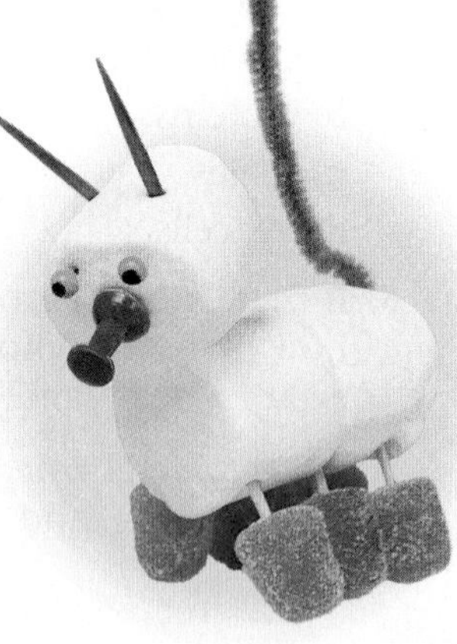

Bug Family Traits				
Trait	Model A "Mom" allele	Model B "Dad" allele	New model "Baby" genotype	New model "Baby" phenotype
Antennae color				
Number of body segments				
Tail shape				
Number of leg pairs		DO NOT WRITE IN BOOK		
Nose color				
Foot color				
Number of eyes				

4. Create a table like the one above. Fill in the first two columns with the alleles that you selected from the sacks. Next, fill in the third column with the genotype of the new model ("Baby").

5. Use the information below to fill in the last column of the table.

Genotypes and Phenotypes	
RR or *Rr*—red antennae	*rr*—green antennae
SS or *Ss*—3 body segments	*ss*—2 body segments
CC or *Cc*—curly tail	*cc*—straight tail
LL or *Ll*—3 pairs of legs	*ll*—2 pairs of legs
BB or *Bb*—blue nose	*bb*—green nose
GG or *Gg*—green feet	*gg*—black feet
EE or *Ee*—2 eyes	*ee*—3 eyes

6. Now that you have filled out your table, you are ready to pick the parts you need to assemble your bug. (Toothpicks can be used to hold the head and body segments together and as legs to attach the feet to the body.)

Analyze the Results

1. **Organizing Data** Take a poll of the traits of the offspring. What are the ratios for each trait?

2. **Examining Data** Do any of the new models look exactly like the parents? Explain.

Draw Conclusions

3. **Interpreting Information** What are the possible genotypes of the parent bugs?

4. **Making Predictions** How many different genotypes are possible in the offspring?

Applying Your Data

Find a mate for your "Baby" bug. What are the possible genotypes and phenotypes of the offspring from this match?

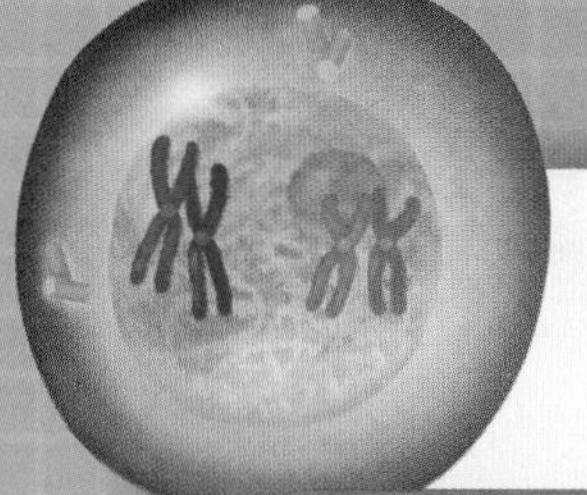

Chapter Review

USING KEY TERMS

Complete each of the following sentences by choosing the correct term from the word bank.

sex cells	genotype
sex chromosomes	alleles
phenotype	meiosis

1. Sperm and eggs are known as _____.

2. The _____ is the expression of a trait and is determined by the combination of alleles called the _____.

3. _____ produces cells with half the normal number of chromosomes.

4. Different versions of the same genes are called _____.

UNDERSTANDING KEY IDEAS

Multiple Choice

5. Genes carry information that determines
   a. alleles.
   b. ribosomes.
   c. chromosomes.
   d. traits.

6. The process that produces sex cells is
   a. mitosis.
   b. photosynthesis.
   c. meiosis.
   d. probability.

7. The passing of traits from parents to offspring is called
   a. probability.
   b. heredity.
   c. recessive.
   d. meiosis.

8. If you cross a white flower with the genotype *pp* with a purple flower with the genotype *PP,* the possible genotypes in the offspring are
   a. *PP* and *pp*.
   b. all *Pp*.
   c. all *PP*.
   d. all *pp*.

9. For the cross in item 8, what would the phenotypes be?
   a. all white
   b. 3 purple and 1 white
   c. all purple
   d. half white, half purple

10. In meiosis,
   a. chromosomes are copied twice.
   b. the nucleus divides once.
   c. four cells are produced from a single cell.
   d. two cells are produced from a single cell.

11. When one trait is not completely dominant over another, it is called
   a. recessive.
   b. incomplete dominance.
   c. environmental factors.
   d. uncertain dominance.

Short Answer

12. Which sex chromosomes do females have? Which do males have?

13. In one or two sentences, define the term *recessive trait* in your own words.

14. How are sex cells different from other body cells?

15. What is a sex-linked disorder? Give one example of a sex-linked disorder that is found in humans.

CRITICAL THINKING

16. **Concept Mapping** Use the following terms to create a concept map: *meiosis, eggs, cell division, X chromosome, mitosis, Y chromosome, sperm,* and *sex cells.*

17. **Identifying Relationships** If you were a carrier of one allele for a certain recessive disorder, how could genetic counseling help you prepare for the future?

18. **Applying Concepts** If a child has blond hair and both of her parents have brown hair, what does that tell you about the allele for blond hair? Explain.

19. **Applying Concepts** What is the genotype of a pea plant that is true-breeding for purple flowers?

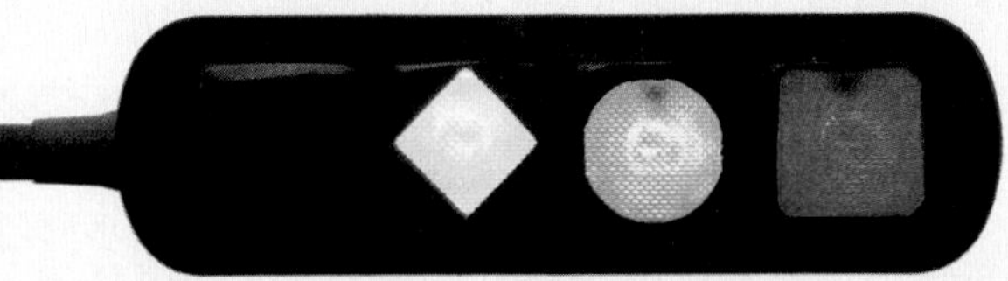

INTERPRETING GRAPHICS

Use the Punnett square below to answer the questions that follow.

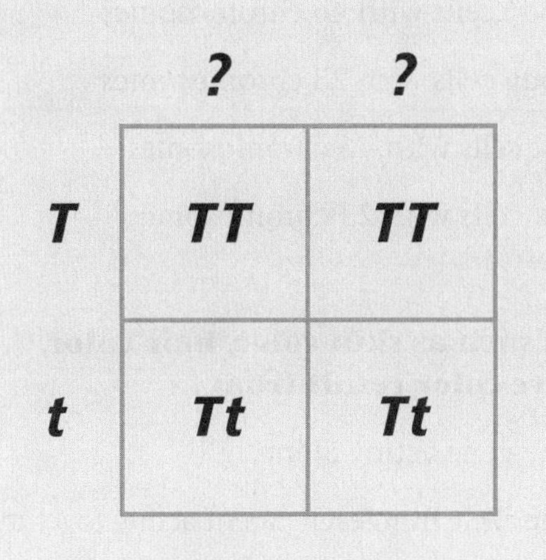

20. What is the unknown genotype?

21. If *T* represents the allele for tall pea plants and *t* represents the allele for short pea plants, what is the phenotype of each parent and of the offspring?

22. If each of the offspring were allowed to self-fertilize, what are the possible genotypes in the next generation?

23. What is the probability of each genotype in item 22?

Multiple Choice

1. **What kind of cells are created during meiosis in humans?**

   A. body cells with 46 chromosomes

   B. body cells with 23 chromosomes

   C. sex cells with 46 chromosomes

   D. sex cells with 23 chromosomes

2. **Traits such as skin color, hair color, and eye color result from**

   A. one gene acting alone.

   B. one allele from each parent acting together.

   C. several genes acting together.

   D. one dominant allele.

3. **The allele for freckles, *F*, is dominant. If a woman with freckles *(FF)* and a man without freckles *(ff)* have children, what are the possible genotypes of the children?**

   A. *Ff, ff*

   B. *FF, Ff, ff*

   C. *Ff*

   D. *ff*

4. **People who wish to achieve desirable traits in organisms, such as dogs or roses, use which of the following processes?**

   A. selective breeding

   B. sexual reproduction

   C. genetic typing

   D. genetic counseling

5. **Homologous chromosomes contain**

   A. the same alleles, but no genes.

   B. the same genes, but possibly different alleles for the genes.

   C. the same genes and the same alleles for the genes.

   D. different genes and different alleles.

Use the graph below to answer question 6.

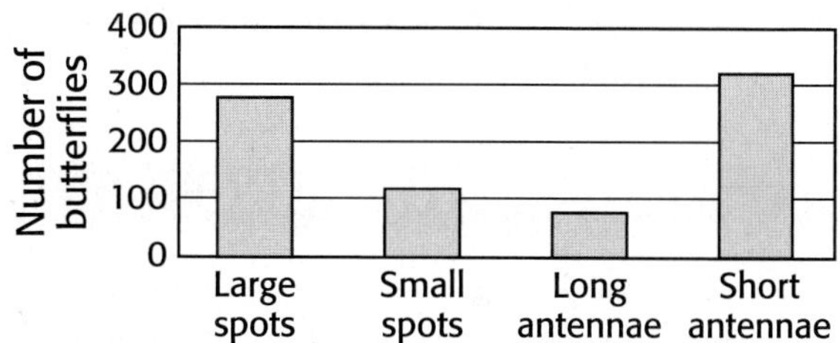

6. **Mai-lin created the graph above as part of a field experiment studying traits of Viceroy butterflies. Based on the data in the graph, which traits seem to be the dominant traits?**

   A. large spots and long antennae

   B. small spots and long antennae

   C. large spots and short antennae

   D. small spots and short antennae

7. **Which of the following statements is true?**

   A. A phenotype is the entire genetic makeup of an organism, whereas a genotype is the combination of genes for one specific trait.

   B. A phenotype is the result of the environment on appearance, whereas a genotype is the result of genes on appearance.

   C. A phenotype is the appearance of an organism, whereas a genotype is the genetic makeup of the organism.

   D. A phenotype is the result of heterozygous alleles, whereas a genotype is the result of homozygous alleles.

Use the diagram below to answer question 8.

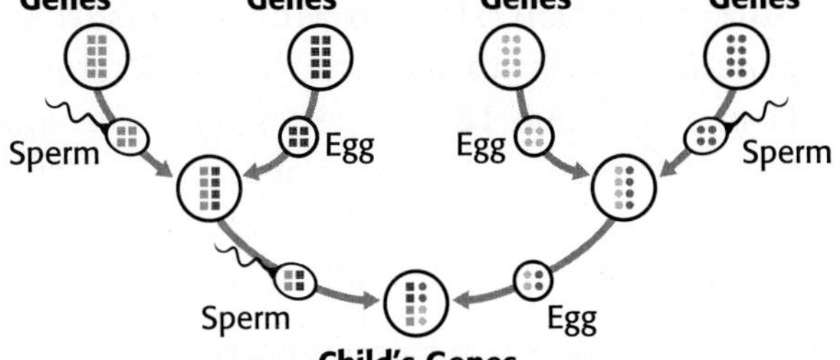

INHERITING GENES

8. **Colorblindness is a sex-linked trait found on the X chromosome. If the grandfather on the mother's side is colorblind, how likely is it that the child will be colorblind?**

   A. highly likely regardless of the child's gender

   B. more likely if the child is a boy

   C. more likely if the child is a girl

   D. highly unlikely regardless of the child's gender

9. **Why do identical twins have the same genotype?**

   A. They have the same sets of alleles.

   B. They come from two similar eggs.

   C. They look exactly alike.

   D. They have heterozygous genotypes.

10. **When Mendel crossed true-breeding tall pea plants with true-breeding short pea plants, all of the offspring were tall. When he allowed the first-generation pea plants to self-pollinate, some of the offspring were tall and some were short. What should Mendel have concluded from these results?**

    A. Only dominant traits appear in every generation.

    B. Both dominant and recessive traits appear in each generation.

    C. Dominant and recessive traits appear at random from one generation to the next.

    D. Dominant and recessive traits appear in predictable patterns from one generation to the next.

Open Response

11. **Suppose a grower bred a blackberry bush that produces more fruit than a normal blackberry bush, but it also becomes susceptible to disease. If this bush self-pollinates, what are the chances (25%, 50%, 75%, or 100%) that its seedlings will also be susceptible to the disease? Explain your answer.**

12. **What are the differences between the sexual and asexual reproduction of cells?**

Science in Action

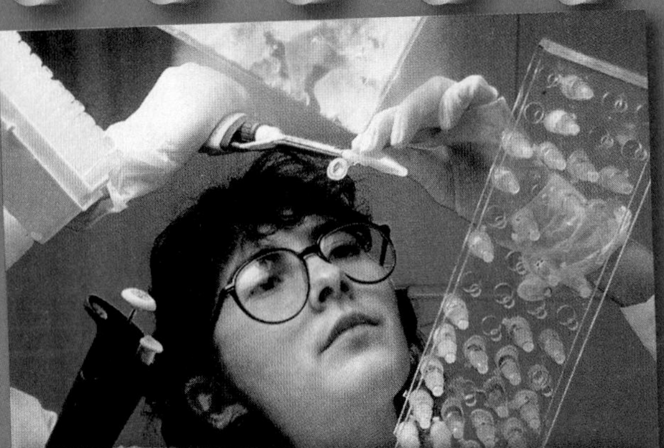

Science, Technology, and Society

Mapping the Human Genome

In 2003, scientists finished one of the most ambitious research projects ever. Researchers with the Human Genome Project (HGP) mapped the human body's complete set of genetic instructions, which is called the *genome*. You might be wondering whose genome the scientists are decoding. Actually, it doesn't matter—only 0.1% of each person's genetic material is unique. The researchers' goals are to identify how tiny differences in that 0.1% make each of us who we are and to begin to understand how some differences can cause disease. Scientists are already using the map to think of new ways to treat genetic diseases, such as asthma, diabetes, and kidney disease.

Social Studies ACTIVITY

WRITING SKILL Research DNA fingerprinting. Write a short report describing how DNA fingerprinting has affected the way criminals are caught.

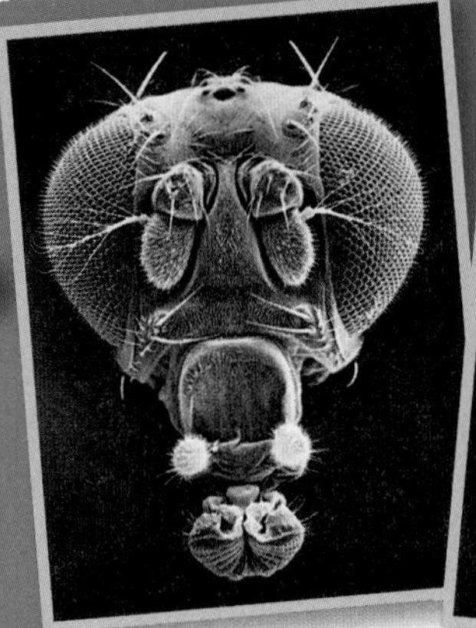

This is a normal fruit fly under a scanning electron microscope.

This fruit fly has legs growing where its antennae should be.

Weird Science

Lab Rats with Wings

Drosophila melanogaster (droh SAHF i luh muh LAN uh GAS tuhr) is the scientific name for the fruit fly. This tiny insect has played a big role in helping scientists understand many illnesses. Because fruit flies reproduce every 2 weeks, scientists can alter a fruit fly gene and see the results of the experiment very quickly. Another important reason for using these "lab rats with wings" is that their genetic code is simple and well understood. Fruit flies have 12,000 genes, but humans have more than 25,000. Scientists use fruit flies to find out about diseases like cancer, Alzheimer's, and muscular dystrophy.

Language Arts ACTIVITY

WRITING SKILL The mythical creature called the *Chimera* (kie MIR uh) was said to be part lion, part goat, and part serpent. According to legend, the Chimera terrorized people for years until it was killed by a brave hero. The word *chimera* now refers to any organism that has parts from many organisms. Write a short story about the Chimera that describes what it looks like and how it came to be.

Careers

Stacey Wong

Genetic Counselor If your family had a history of a particular disease, what would you do? Would you eat healthier foods, get more exercise, or visit your doctor regularly? All of those are good ideas, but Stacey Wong went a step farther. Her family's history of cancer helped her decide to become a genetic counselor. "Genetic counselors are usually part of a team of health professionals," she says, which can include physicians, nurses, dieticians, social workers, laboratory personnel, and others. "If a diagnosis is made by the geneticist," says Wong, "then I provide genetic counseling." When a patient visits a genetic counselor, the counselor asks many questions and builds a family medical history. Although counseling involves discussing what it means to have a genetic condition, Wong says "the most important part is to get to know the patient or family we are working with, listen to their concerns, gain an understanding of their values, help them to make decisions, and be their advocate."

Math Activity

The probability of inheriting genetic disease *A* is 1/10,000. The probability of inheriting genetic disease *B* is also 1/10,000. What is the probability that one person would inherit both genetic diseases *A* and *B*?

To learn more about these Science in Action topics, visit go.hrw.com and type in the keyword **HL5HERF.**

Current Science

Check out Current Science® articles related to this chapter by visiting go.hrw.com. Just type in the keyword HL5CS05.

5

Genes and DNA

The Big Idea

DNA is the genetic material of living organisms and is located in the chromosomes of each cell.

SECTION

About the Photo

These adult mice have no hair—not because their hair was shaved off but because these mice do not grow hair. In cells of these mice, the genes that normally cause hair to grow are not working. The genes were "turned off" by scientists who have learned to control the function of some genes. Scientists changed the genes of these mice to research medical problems such as cancer.

PRE-READING ACTIVITY

Graphic Organizer

Concept Map Before you read the chapter, create the graphic organizer entitled "Concept Map" described in the **Study Skills** section of the Appendix. As you read the chapter, fill in the concept map with details about DNA.

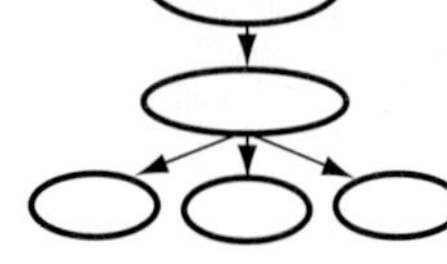

START-UP ACTIVITY

Fingerprint Your Friends

One way to identify people is by taking their fingerprints. Does it really work? Are everyone's fingerprints unique? Try this activity to find out.

Procedure

1. Rub the tip of a **pencil** back and forth across a **piece of tracing paper.** Make a large, dark mark.
2. Rub the tip of one of your fingers on the pencil mark. Then place a small **piece of transparent tape** over the darkened area on your finger.
3. Remove the tape, and stick it on **a piece of white paper.** Repeat steps 1–3 for the rest of your fingers.
4. Look at the fingerprints with a **magnifying lens.** What patterns do you see? Is the pattern the same on every finger?

Analysis

1. Compare your fingerprints with those of your classmates. Do any two people in your class have the same prints? Try to explain your findings.

SECTION 1

What Does DNA Look Like?

For many years, the structure of a DNA molecule was a puzzle to scientists. In the 1950s, two scientists deduced the structure while experimenting with chemical models. They later won a Nobel Prize for helping solve this puzzle!

What You Will Learn

- List three important events that led to understanding the structure of DNA.
- Describe the basic structure of a DNA molecule.
- Explain how DNA molecules can be copied.

Vocabulary

DNA
nucleotide

READING STRATEGY

Prediction Guide Before reading this section, write the title of each heading in this section. Next, under each heading, write what you think you will learn.

Inherited characteristics are determined by genes, and genes are passed from one generation to the next. Genes are parts of chromosomes, which are structures in the nucleus of most cells. Chromosomes are made of protein and DNA. **DNA** stands for *deoxyribonucleic acid* (dee AHKS ee RIE boh noo KLEE ik AS id). DNA is the genetic material—the material that determines inherited characteristics. But what does DNA look like?

The Pieces of the Puzzle

Scientists knew that the material that makes up genes must be able to do two things. First, it must be able to give instructions for building and maintaining cells. Second, it must be able to be copied each time a cell divides, so that each cell contains identical genes. Scientists thought that these things could be done only by complex molecules, such as proteins. They were surprised to learn how much the DNA molecule could do.

Nucleotides: The Subunits of DNA

DNA is made of subunits called nucleotides. A **nucleotide** consists of a sugar, a phosphate, and a base. The nucleotides are identical except for the base. The four bases are *adenine, thymine, guanine,* and *cytosine.* Each base has a different shape. Scientists often refer to a base by the first letter of the base, *A, T, G,* and *C.* **Figure 1** shows models of the four nucleotides.

DNA **d**eoxyribo**n**ucleic **a**cid, a molecule that is present in all living cells and that contains the information that determines the traits that a living thing inherits and needs to live

nucleotide in a nucleic-acid chain, a subunit that consists of a sugar, a phosphate, and a nitrogenous base

Figure 1 The Four Nucleotides of DNA

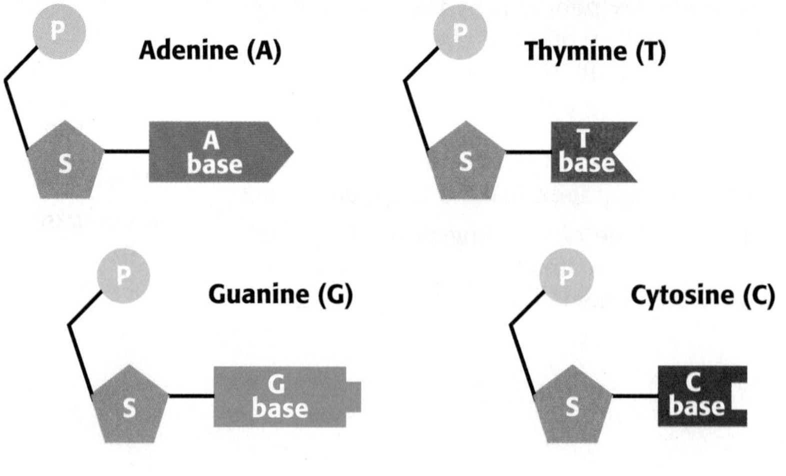

Adenine (A) — P, S, A base

Thymine (T) — P, S, T base

Guanine (G) — P, S, G base

Cytosine (C) — P, S, C base

Chargaff's Rules

In the 1950s, a biochemist named Erwin Chargaff found that the amount of adenine in DNA always equals the amount of thymine. And he found that the amount of guanine always equals the amount of cytosine. His findings are known as *Chargaff's rules*. At the time of his discovery, no one knew the importance of these findings. But Chargaff's rules later helped scientists understand the structure of DNA.

Reading Check **Summarize Chargaff's rules.** (*See the Appendix for answers to Reading Checks.*)

Franklin's Discovery

More clues about the structure of DNA came from scientists in Britain. There, chemist Rosalind Franklin, shown in **Figure 2,** was able to make images of DNA molecules. She used a process known as *X-ray diffraction* to make these images. In this process, X rays are aimed at the DNA molecule. When an X ray hits a part of the molecule, the ray bounces off. The pattern made by the bouncing rays is captured on film. Franklin's images suggested that DNA has a spiral shape.

Watson and Crick's Model

At about the same time, two other scientists were also trying to solve the mystery of DNA's structure. They were James Watson and Francis Crick, shown in **Figure 3.** After seeing Franklin's X-ray images, Watson and Crick concluded that DNA must look like a long, twisted ladder. They were then able to build a model of DNA by using simple materials from their laboratory. Their model perfectly fit with both Chargaff's and Franklin's findings. The model eventually helped explain how DNA is copied and how it functions in the cell.

CONNECTION TO Chemistry

WRITING SKILL **Linus Pauling** Many scientists contributed to the discovery of DNA's structure. In fact, some scientists competed to be the first to make the discovery. One of these competitors was a chemist named Linus Pauling. Research and write a paragraph about how Pauling's work helped Watson and Crick.

Figure 2 *Rosalind Franklin used X-ray diffraction to make images of DNA that helped reveal the structure of DNA.*

Figure 3 *This photo shows James Watson (left) and Francis Crick (right) with their model of DNA.*

Making a Model of DNA

1. Gather assorted simple materials that you could use to build a basic model of DNA. You might use **clay, string, toothpicks, paper, tape, plastic foam,** or **pieces of food.**
2. Work with a partner or a small team to build your model. Use your book and other resources to check the details of your model.
3. Show your model to your classmates. Give your classmates feedback about the scientific aspects of their models.

DNA's Double Structure

The shape of DNA is shown in **Figure 4.** As you can see, a strand of DNA looks like a twisted ladder. This shape is known as a *double helix* (DUB uhl HEE LIKS). The two sides of the ladder are made of alternating sugar parts and phosphate parts. The rungs of the ladder are made of a pair of bases. Adenine on one side of a rung always pairs with thymine on the other side. Guanine always pairs with cytosine.

Notice how the double helix structure matches Chargaff's observations. When Chargaff separated the parts of a sample of DNA, he found that the matching bases were always present in equal amounts. To model how the bases pair, Watson and Crick tried to match Chargaff's observations. They also used information from chemists about the size and shape of each of the nucleotides. As it turned out, the width of the DNA ladder matches the combined width of the matching bases. Only the correct pairs of bases fit within the ladder's width.

Making Copies of DNA

The pairing of bases allows the cell to *replicate*, or make copies of, DNA. Each base always bonds with only one other base. Thus, pairs of bases are *complementary* to each other, and both sides of a DNA molecule are complementary. For example, the sequence CGAC will bond to the sequence GCTG.

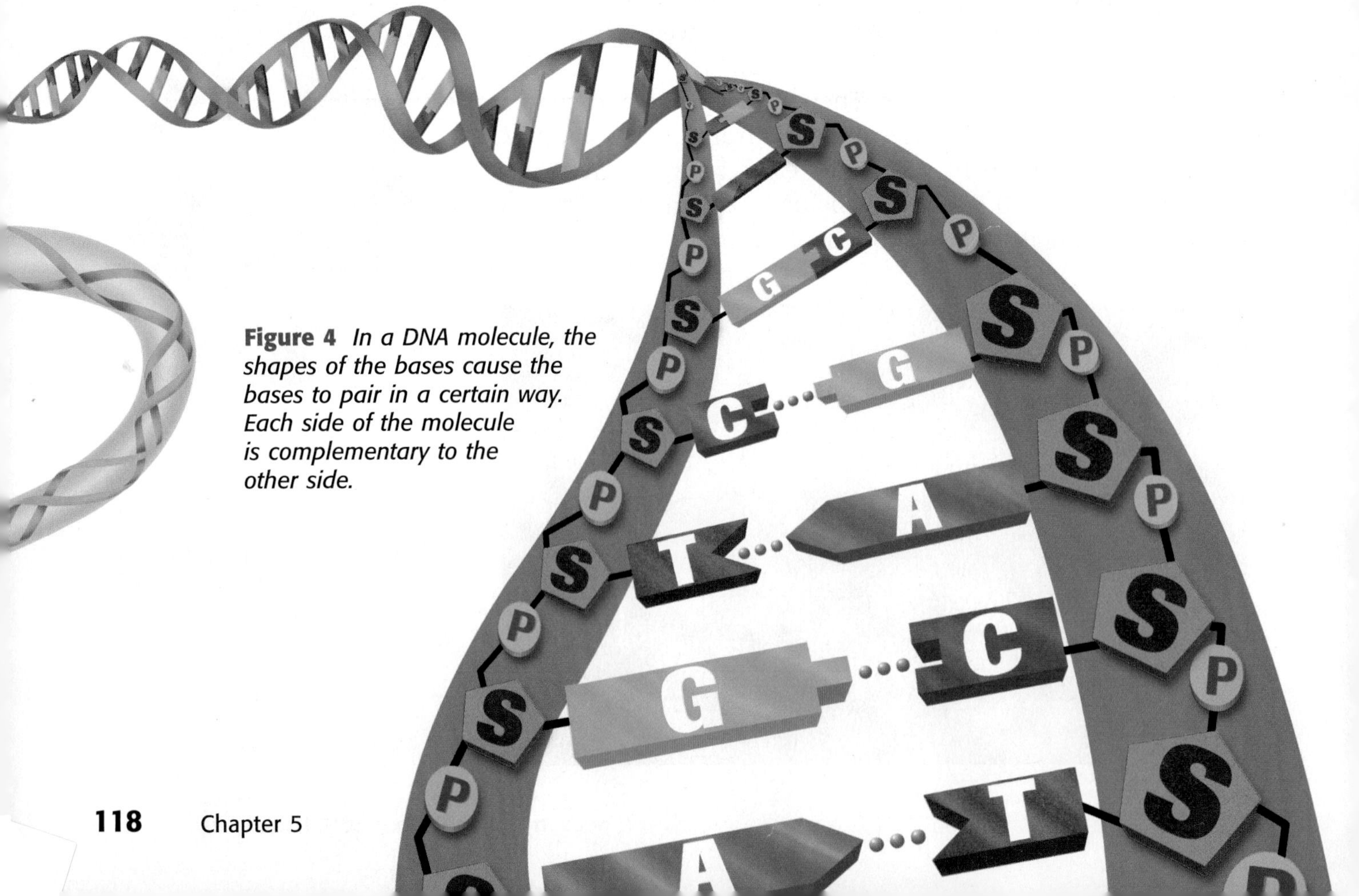

Figure 4 *In a DNA molecule, the shapes of the bases cause the bases to pair in a certain way. Each side of the molecule is complementary to the other side.*

How Copies Are Made

During replication, as shown in **Figure 5,** a DNA molecule is split down the middle, where the bases meet. The bases on each side of the molecule are used as a pattern for a new strand. As the bases on the original molecule are exposed, complementary nucleotides are added to each side of the ladder. Two DNA molecules are formed. Half of each of the molecules is old DNA, and half is new DNA.

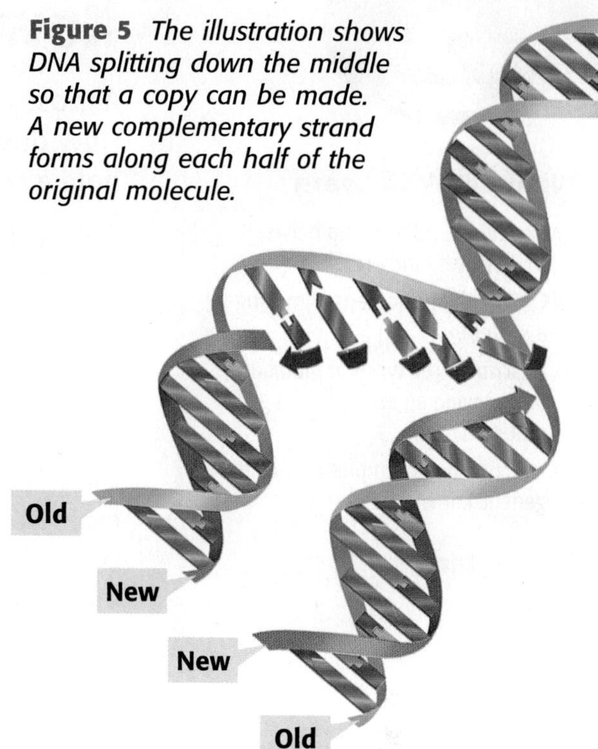

Figure 5 *The illustration shows DNA splitting down the middle so that a copy can be made. A new complementary strand forms along each half of the original molecule.*

When Copies Are Made

DNA is copied every time a cell divides. Each new cell gets a complete copy of all the DNA. The job of unwinding, copying, and re-winding the DNA is done by proteins within the cell. So, DNA is usually found with several kinds of proteins. Other proteins help with the process of carrying out the instructions written in the code of the DNA.

Reading Check How often is DNA copied?

SECTION Review

Summary

- DNA is the material that makes up genes. It carries coded information that is copied in each new cell.
- The DNA molecule looks like a twisted ladder. The two halves are long strings of nucleotides. The rungs are complementary pairs of bases.
- Because each base has a complementary base, DNA can be replicated accurately.

Using Key Terms

1. Use the term *DNA* in a sentence.
2. In your own words, write a definition for the term *nucleotide*.

Understanding Key Ideas

3. List three important events that led to understanding the structure of DNA.
4. Which of the following is NOT part of a nucleotide?
   - **a.** base
   - **b.** sugar
   - **c.** fat
   - **d.** phosphate

Math Skills

5. If a sample of DNA contained 20% cytosine, what percentage of guanine would be in this sample? What percentage of adenine would be in the sample? Explain.

Critical Thinking

6. **Making Inferences** Explain what is meant by the statement "DNA unites all organisms."
7. **Applying Concepts** What would the complementary strand of DNA be for the sequence of bases below?

   C T T A G G C T T A C C A

8. **Analyzing Processes** How are copies of DNA made? Draw a picture as part of your answer.

For a variety of links related to this chapter, go to www.scilinks.org

Topic: DNA; Genes and Traits
SciLinks code: HSM0418; HSM0647

SECTION 2

How DNA Works

What You Will Learn

- Explain the relationship between DNA, genes, and proteins.
- Outline the basic steps in making a protein.
- Describe three types of mutations, and provide an example of a gene mutation.
- Describe two examples of uses of genetic knowledge.

Vocabulary

RNA
ribosome
mutation

READING STRATEGY

Reading Organizer As you read this section, make a flowchart of the steps of how DNA codes for proteins.

Almost every cell in your body contains about 2 m of DNA. How does all of the DNA fit in a cell? And how does the DNA hold a code that affects your traits?

DNA is found in the cells of all organisms, including bacteria, mosquitoes, and humans. Each organism has a unique set of DNA. But DNA functions the same way in all organisms.

Unraveling DNA

DNA is often wound around proteins, coiled into strands, and then bundled up even more. In a cell that lacks a nucleus, each strand of DNA forms a loose loop within the cell. In a cell that has a nucleus, the strands of DNA and proteins are bundled into chromosomes, as shown in **Figure 1.**

The structure of DNA allows DNA to hold information. The order of the bases on one side of the molecule is a code that carries information. A *gene* consists of a string of nucleotides that give the cell information about how to make a specific trait. There is an enormous amount of DNA, so there can be a large variety of genes.

Reading Check **What makes up a gene?** (*See the Appendix for answers to Reading Checks.*)

Figure 1 **Unraveling DNA**

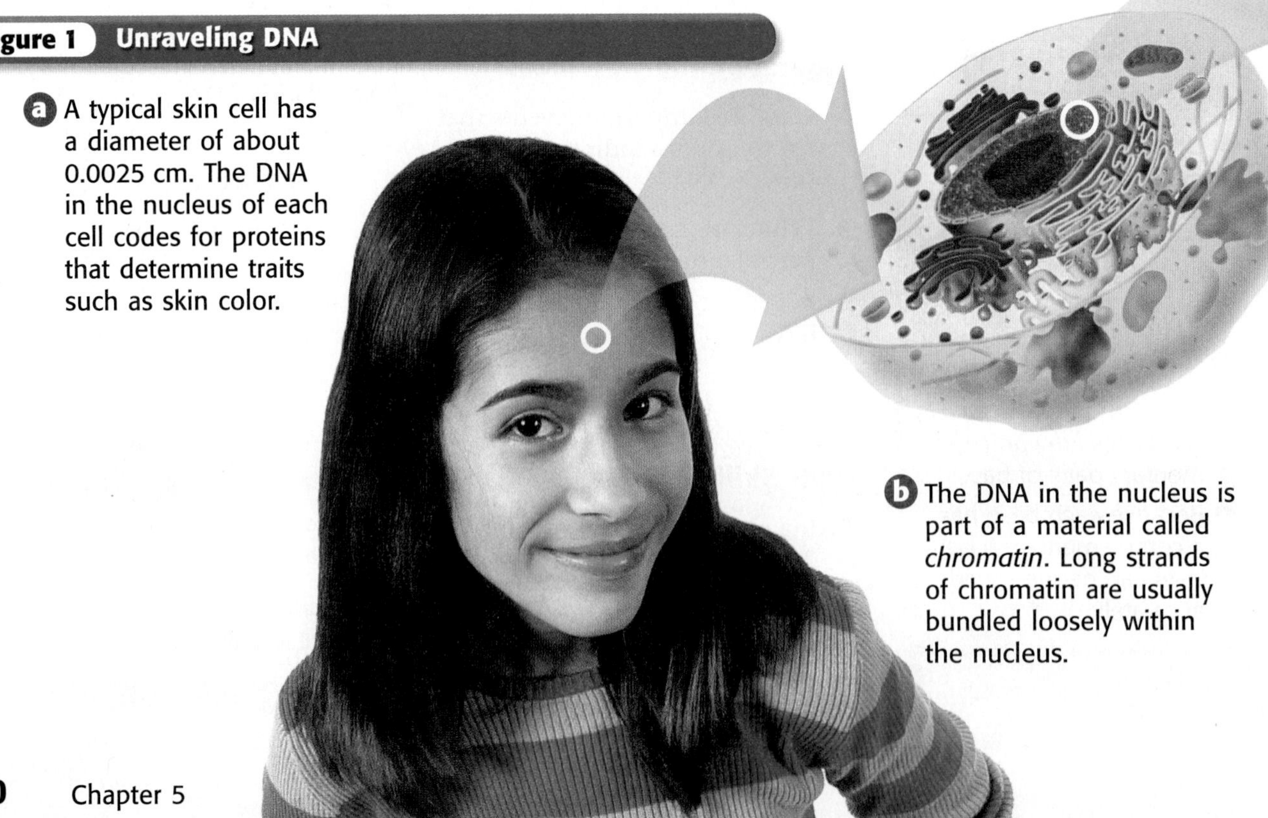

a A typical skin cell has a diameter of about 0.0025 cm. The DNA in the nucleus of each cell codes for proteins that determine traits such as skin color.

b The DNA in the nucleus is part of a material called *chromatin*. Long strands of chromatin are usually bundled loosely within the nucleus.

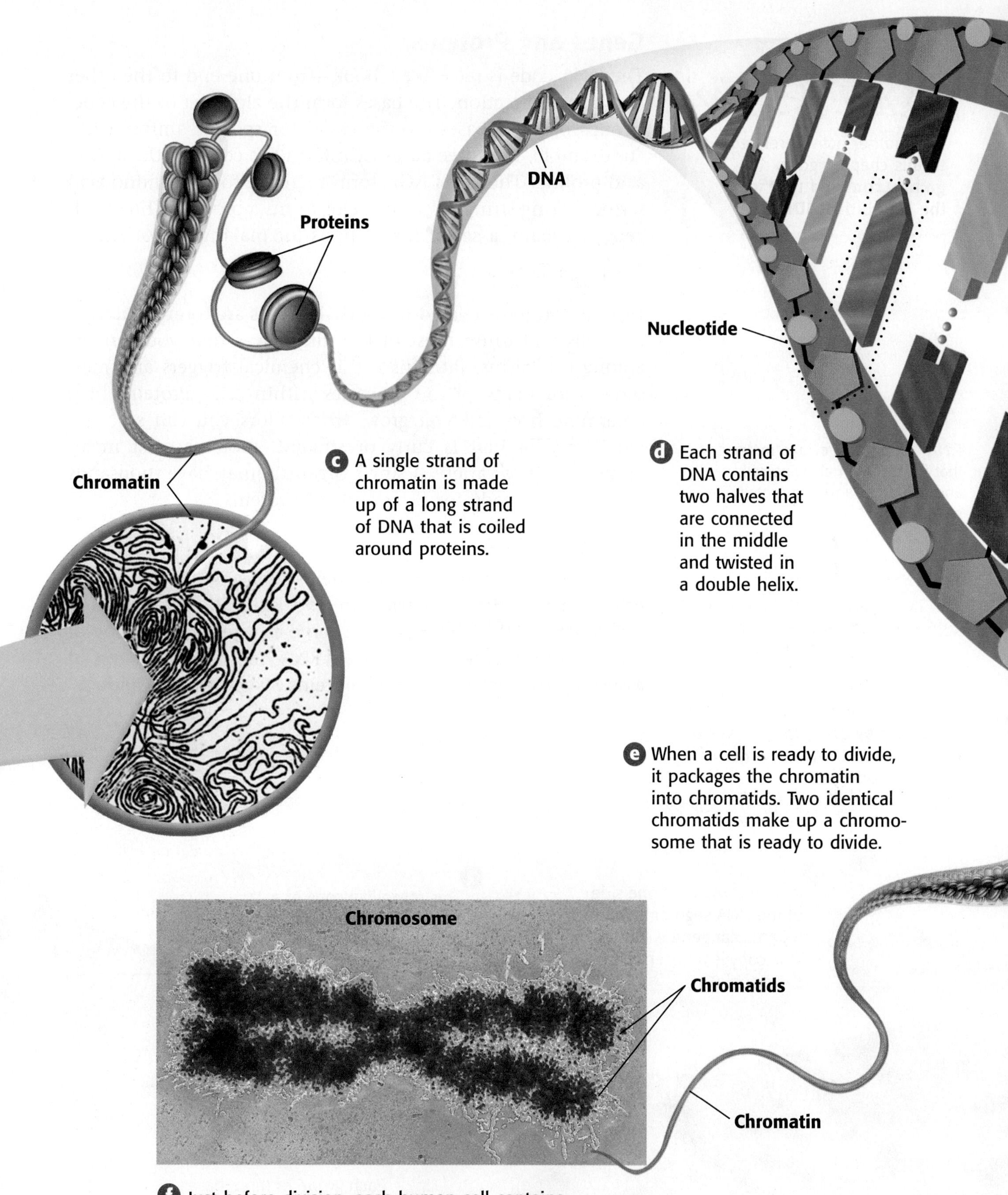

c A single strand of chromatin is made up of a long strand of DNA that is coiled around proteins.

d Each strand of DNA contains two halves that are connected in the middle and twisted in a double helix.

e When a cell is ready to divide, it packages the chromatin into chromatids. Two identical chromatids make up a chromosome that is ready to divide.

f Just before division, each human cell contains 46 chromosomes. These chromosomes contain two identical copies of all of the cell's genetic material.

Genes and Proteins

INTERNET ACTIVITY

For another activity related to this chapter, go to **go.hrw.com** and type in the keyword **HL5DNAW.**

The DNA code is read like a book—from one end to the other and in one direction. The bases form the alphabet of the code. Groups of three bases are the codes for specific amino acids. For example, the three bases CCA form the code for the amino acid proline. The bases AGC form the code for the amino acid serine. A long string of amino acids forms a protein. Thus, each gene is usually a set of instructions for making a protein.

Proteins and Traits

How are proteins related to traits? Proteins are found throughout cells and cause most of the differences that you can see among organisms. Proteins act as chemical triggers and messengers for many of the processes within cells. Proteins help determine how tall you grow, what colors you can see, and whether your hair is curly or straight. Proteins exist in an almost limitless variety. A single organism may have thousands of genes that code for thousands of proteins.

Help from RNA

RNA ribonucleic acid, a molecule that is present in all living cells and that plays a role in protein production

Another type of molecule that helps make proteins is called **RNA,** or *ribonucleic acid* (RIE boh noo KLEE ik AS id). RNA is so similar to DNA that RNA can serve as a temporary copy of a DNA sequence. Several forms of RNA help in the process of changing the DNA code into proteins, as shown in **Figure 2.**

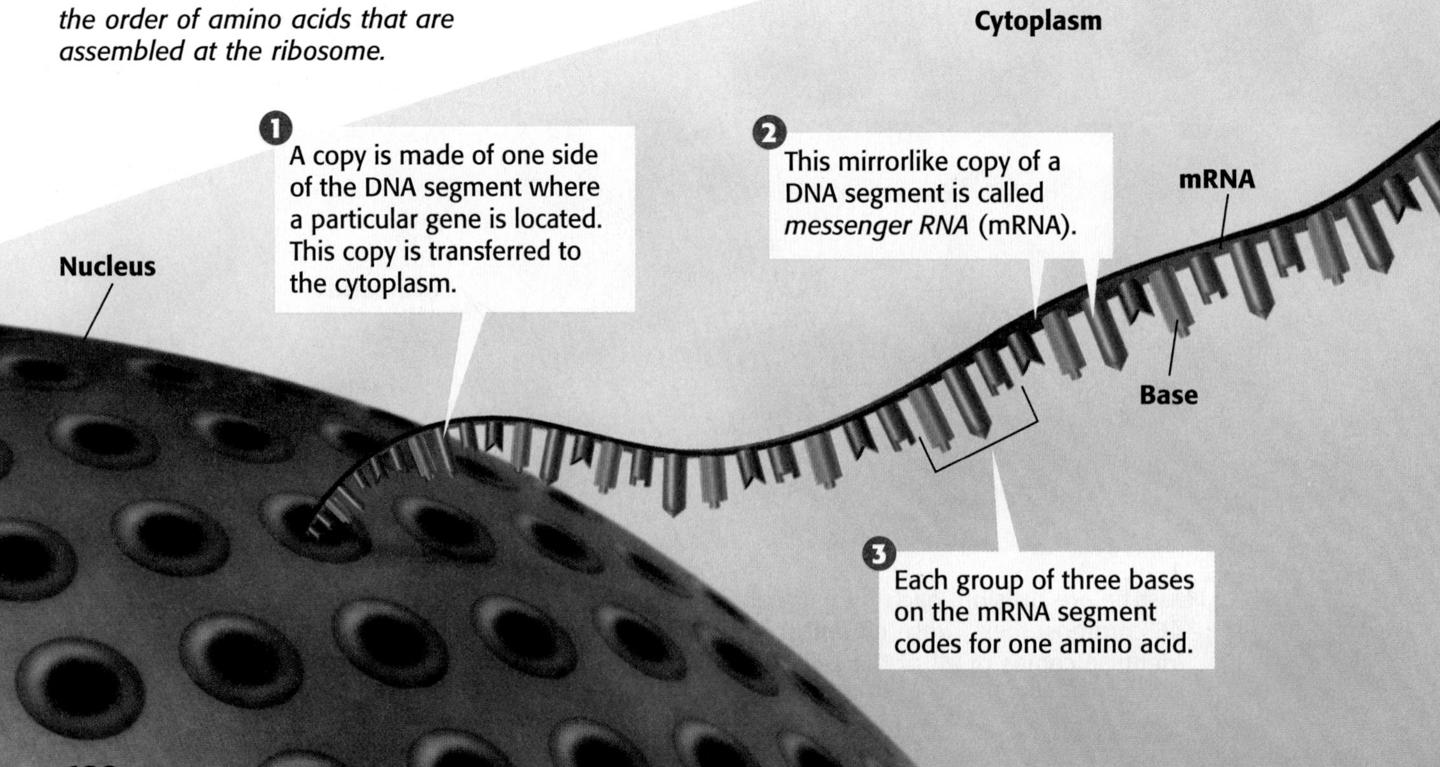
Cytoplasm
1 A copy is made of one side of the DNA segment where a particular gene is located. This copy is transferred to the cytoplasm.
2 This mirrorlike copy of a DNA segment is called *messenger RNA* (mRNA).
mRNA
Nucleus
Base
3 Each group of three bases on the mRNA segment codes for one amino acid.

Figure 2 *Proteins are built in the cytoplasm by using RNA copies of a segment of DNA. The order of the bases on the RNA determines the order of amino acids that are assembled at the ribosome.*

The Making of a Protein

The first step in making a protein is to copy one side of the segment of DNA containing a gene. A mirrorlike copy of the DNA segment is made out of RNA. This copy of the DNA segment is called *messenger RNA* (mRNA). It moves out of the nucleus and into the cytoplasm of the cell.

In the cytoplasm, the messenger RNA is fed through a protein assembly line. The "factory" that runs this assembly line is known as a ribosome. A **ribosome** is a cell organelle composed of RNA and protein. The messenger RNA is fed through the ribosome three bases at a time. Then, molecules of *transfer RNA* (tRNA) translate the RNA message. Each transfer RNA molecule picks up a specific amino acid from the cytoplasm. Inside the ribosome, bases on the transfer RNA match up with bases on the messenger RNA like pieces of a puzzle. The transfer RNA molecules then release their amino acids. The amino acids become linked in a growing chain. As the entire segment of messenger RNA passes through the ribosome, the growing chain of amino acids folds up into a new protein molecule.

Reading Check **What do the transfer RNA molecules transfer?**

Code Combinations

A given sequence of three bases codes for one amino acid. For example, AGT is one possible sequence. How many different sequences of the four DNA base types are possible? (Hint: Make a list.)

ribosome a cell organelle composed of RNA and protein; the site of protein synthesis

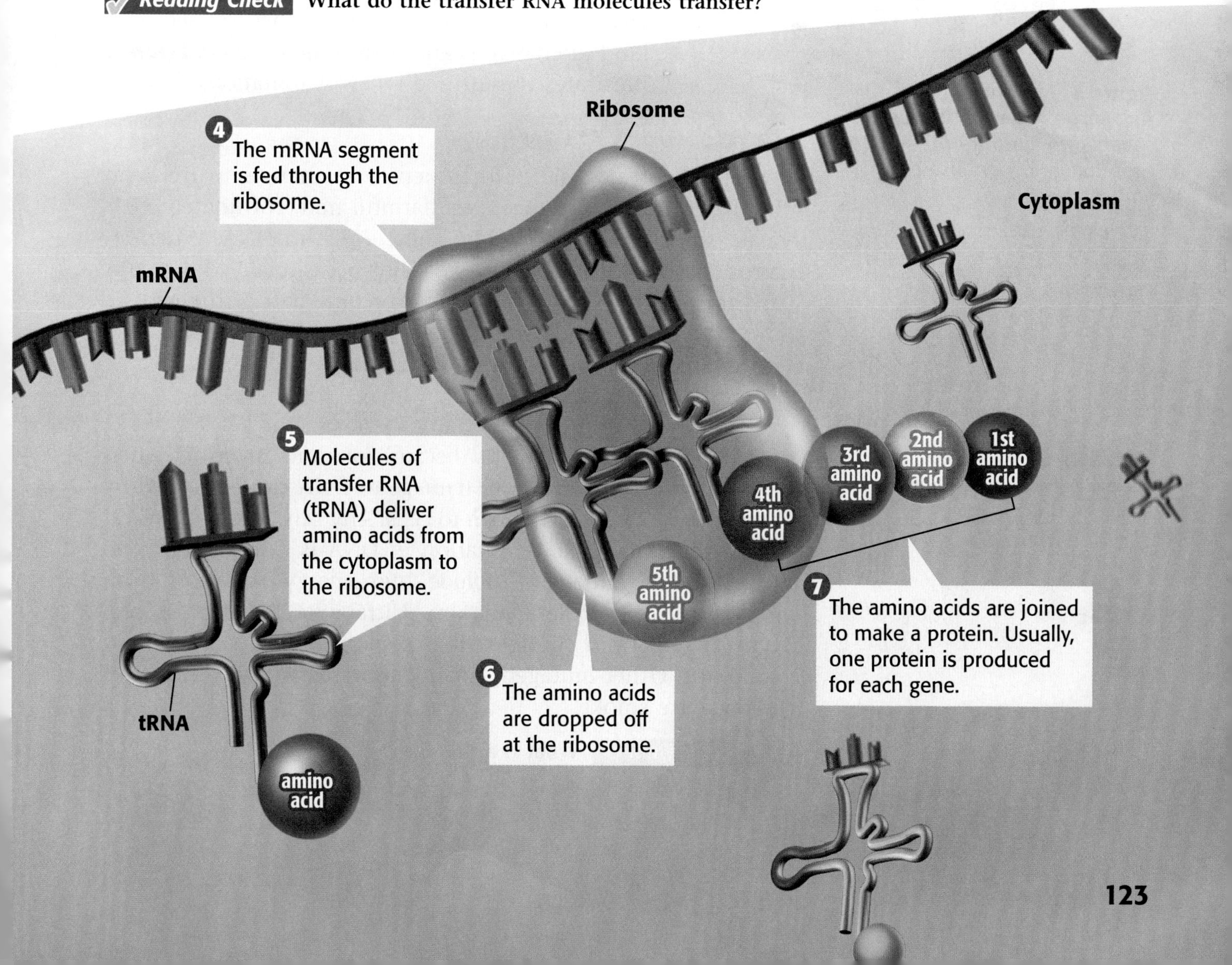

Ribosome

Cytoplasm

mRNA

tRNA

4 The mRNA segment is fed through the ribosome.

5 Molecules of transfer RNA (tRNA) deliver amino acids from the cytoplasm to the ribosome.

6 The amino acids are dropped off at the ribosome.

7 The amino acids are joined to make a protein. Usually, one protein is produced for each gene.

1st amino acid

2nd amino acid

3rd amino acid

4th amino acid

5th amino acid

amino acid

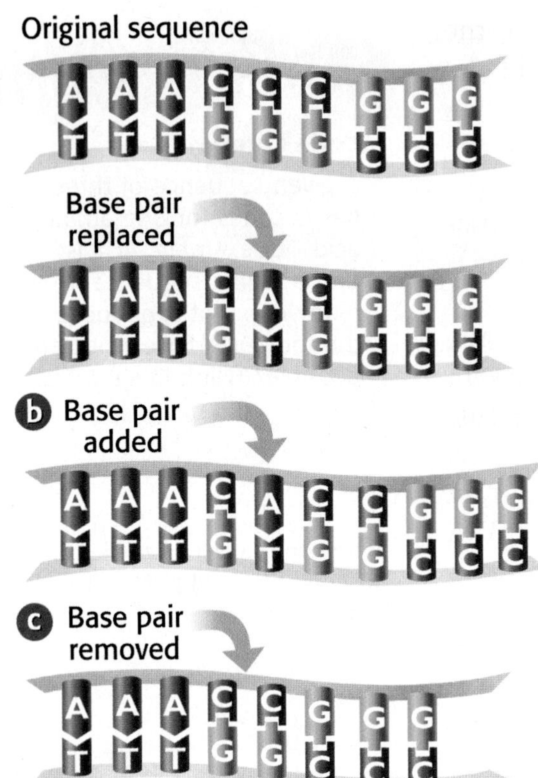

Figure 3 *The original base sequence on the top has been changed to illustrate (a) a substitution, (b) an insertion, and (c) a deletion.*

Changes in Genes

Imagine that you have been invited to ride on a new roller coaster at the state fair. Before you climb into the front car, you are told that some of the metal parts on the coaster have been replaced by parts made of a different substance. Would you still want to ride this roller coaster? Perhaps a strong metal was used as a substitute. Or perhaps a material that is not strong enough was used. Imagine what would happen if cardboard were used instead of metal!

Mutations

Substitutions like the ones in the roller coaster can accidentally happen in DNA. Changes in the number, type, or order of bases on a piece of DNA are known as **mutations.** Sometimes, a base is left out. This kind of change is known as a *deletion.* Or an extra base might be added. This kind of change is known as an *insertion.* The most common change happens when the wrong base is used. This kind of change is known as a *substitution.* **Figure 3** illustrates these three types of mutations.

mutation a change in the nucleotide-base sequence of a gene or DNA molecule

Do Mutations Matter?

There are three possible consequences to changes in DNA: an improved trait, no change, or a harmful trait. Fortunately, cells make some proteins that can detect errors in DNA. When an error is found, it is usually fixed. But occasionally the repairs are not accurate, and the mistakes become part of the genetic message. If the mutation occurs in the sex cells, the changed gene can be passed from one generation to the next.

How Do Mutations Happen?

Mutations happen regularly because of random errors when DNA is copied. In addition, damage to DNA can be caused by abnormal things that happen to cells. Any physical or chemical agent that can cause a mutation in DNA is called a *mutagen.* Examples of mutagens include high-energy radiation from X rays and ultraviolet radiation. Ultraviolet radiation is one type of energy in sunlight. It is responsible for suntans and sunburns. Other mutagens include asbestos and the chemicals in cigarette smoke.

Reading Check **What is a mutagen?**

An Example of a Substitution

A mutation, such as a substitution, can be harmful because it may cause a gene to produce the wrong protein. Consider the DNA sequence GAA. When copied as mRNA, this sequence gives the instructions to place the amino acid glutamic acid into the growing protein. If a mistake happens and the original DNA sequence is changed to GTA, the sequence will code for the amino acid valine instead.

This simple change in an amino acid can cause the disease *sickle cell disease.* Sickle cell disease affects red blood cells. When valine is substituted for glutamic acid in a blood protein, as shown in **Figure 4,** the red blood cells are changed into a sickle shape.

The sickle cells are not as good at carrying oxygen as normal red blood cells are. Sickle cells are also likely to get stuck in blood vessels and cause painful and dangerous clots.

Reading Check What causes sickle cell disease?

An Error in the Message

The sentence below is the result of an error similar to a DNA mutation. The original sentence was made up of three-letter words, but an error was made in this copy. Explain the idea of mutations to your parent or guardian. Then, work together to find the mutation, and write the sentence correctly.

THE IGB ADC ATA TET HEB IGR EDR AT.

ACTIVITY

Figure 4 How Sickle Cell Disease Results from a Mutation

Original DNA: A C T C C T G A A G A A A A A / T G A G G A C T T C T T T T T

mRNA

Resulting amino acid chain: Threonine – Proline – Glutamic acid – Glutamic acid – Lysine

Normal red blood cell

Substitution

Mutated DNA: A C T C C T G T A G A A A A A / T G A G G A C A T C T T T T T

mRNA

Resulting amino acid chain: Threonine – Proline – Valine – Glutamic acid – Lysine

Sickle-shaped red blood cell

Uses of Genetic Knowledge

In the years since Watson and Crick made their model, scientists have learned a lot about genetics. This knowledge is often used in ways that benefit humans. But some uses of genetic knowledge also cause ethical and scientific debates.

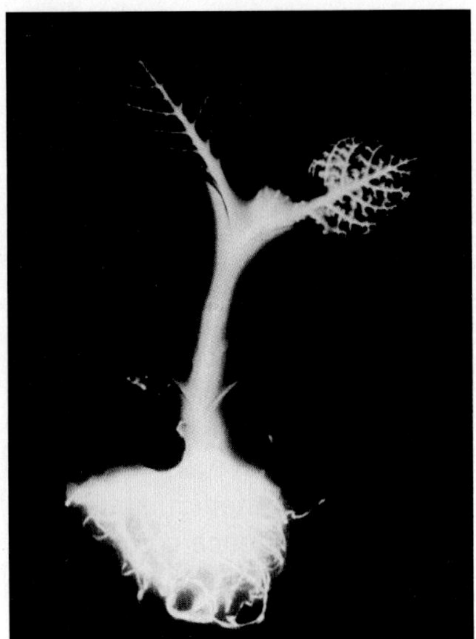

Figure 5 *This genetically engineered tobacco plant contains firefly genes.*

Genetic Engineering

Scientists can manipulate individual genes within organisms. This kind of manipulation is called *genetic engineering*. In some cases, genes may be transferred from one type of organism to another. An example of a genetically engineered plant is shown in **Figure 5.** Scientists added a gene from fireflies to this plant. The gene produces a protein that causes the plant to glow.

Scientists may use genetic engineering to create new products, such as drugs, foods, or fabrics. For example, bacteria may be used to make the proteins found in spider's silk. Or cows may be used to produce human proteins. In some cases, this practice could produce a protein that is needed by a person who has a genetic disease. However, some scientists worry about the dangers of creating genetically engineered organisms.

Genetic Identification

Your DNA is unique, so it can be used like a fingerprint to identify you. *DNA fingerprinting* identifies the unique patterns in an individual's DNA. DNA samples are now used as evidence in crimes, as shown in **Figure 6.** Similarities between people's DNA can reveal other information, too. For example, DNA can be used to identify family relations or hereditary diseases.

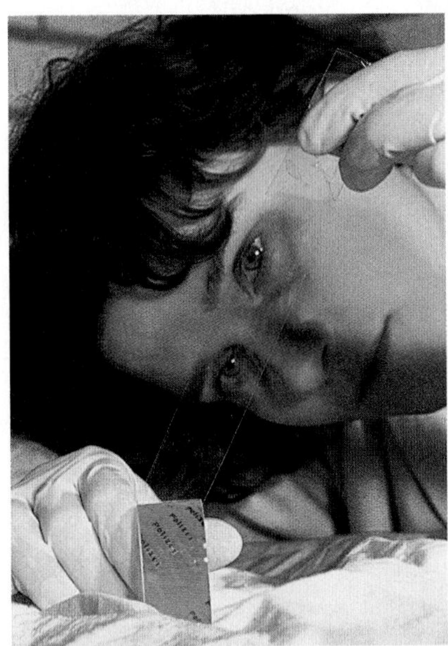

Figure 6 *This scientist is gathering dead skin cells from a crime scene. DNA from the cells could be used as evidence of a criminal's identity.*

Identical twins have truly identical DNA. Scientists are now able to create something like a twin, called a clone. A *clone* is a new organism that has an exact copy of another organism's genes. Clones of several types of organisms, including some mammals, have been developed by scientists. However, the possibility of cloning humans is still being debated among both scientists and politicians.

Reading Check **What is a clone?**

CONNECTION TO Social Studies

Genetic Property Could you sell your DNA code? Using current laws and technology, someone could sell genetic information like authors sell books. It is also possible to file a patent to establish ownership of the information used to make a product. Thus, a patent can be filed for a unique sequence of DNA or for new genetic engineering technology. Conduct research to find an existing patent on a genetic sequence or genetic engineering technology.

SECTION Review

Summary

- A gene is a set of instructions for assembling a protein. DNA is the molecular carrier of these genetic instructions.
- Every organism has DNA in its cells. Humans have about 2 m of DNA in each cell.
- Within a gene, each group of three bases codes for one amino acid. A sequence of amino acids is linked to make a protein.
- Proteins are fundamental to the function of cells and the expression of traits.
- Proteins are assembled within the cytoplasm through a multi-step process that is assisted by several forms of RNA.
- Genes can become mutated when the order of the bases is changed. Three main types of mutations are possible: insertion, deletion, and substitution.
- Genetic knowledge has many practical uses. Some applications of genetic knowledge are controversial.

Using Key Terms

1. Use each of the following terms in the same sentence: *ribosome* and *RNA*.
2. In your own words, write a definition for the term *mutation*.

Understanding Key Ideas

3. Explain the relationship between genes and proteins.
4. List three possible types of mutations.
5. Which type of mutation causes sickle cell anemia?
   a. substitution
   b. insertion
   c. deletion
   d. mutagen

Math Skills

6. A set of 23 chromosomes in a human cell contains 3.2 billion pairs of DNA bases in sequence. On average, about how many pairs of bases are in each chromosome?

Critical Thinking

7. **Applying Concepts** In which cell type might a mutation be passed from generation to generation? Explain.
8. **Making Comparisons** How is genetic engineering different from natural reproduction?

Interpreting Graphics

The illustration below shows a sequence of bases on one strand of a DNA molecule. Use the illustration below to answer the questions that follow.

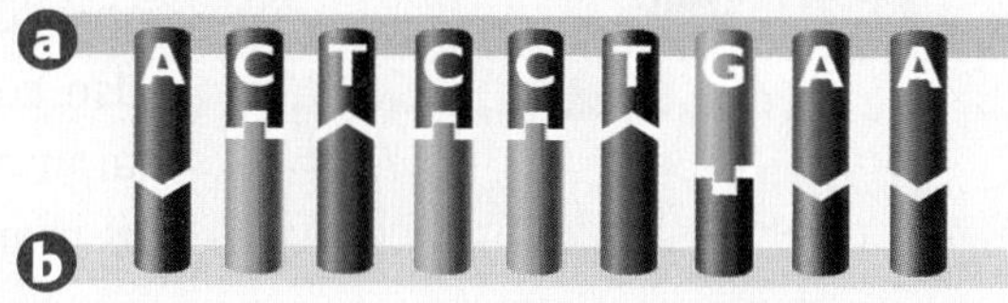

9. How many amino acids are coded for by the sequence on one side (A) of this DNA strand?
10. What is the order of bases on the complementary side of the strand (B), from left to right?
11. If a G were inserted as the first base on the top side (A), what would the order of bases be on the complementary side (B)?

SCILINKS.
NSTA
Developed and maintained by the National Science Teachers Association
For a variety of links related to this chapter, go to www.scilinks.org
Topic: Genetic Engineering
SciLinks code: HSM0654

Model-Making Lab

Base-Pair Basics

OBJECTIVES

Construct a model of a DNA strand.

Model the process of DNA replication.

MATERIALS

- bag, large paper
- paper, colored (4 colors)
- paper, white
- scissors

SAFETY

You have learned that DNA is shaped something like a twisted ladder. The side rails of the ladder are made of sugar parts and phosphate parts. The two side rails are connected to each other by parts called *bases*. The bases join in pairs to form the rungs of the ladder. Within DNA, each base can pair with only one other base. Each of these pairs is called a *base pair*. When DNA replicates, enzymes separate the base pairs, which breaks the rungs of the ladder in half. Then, each half of the DNA ladder can be used as a template for building a new half. In this activity, you will construct a paper model of DNA and use it to model the replication process.

Procedure

1. Trace the models of nucleotides below onto white paper. Label the pieces "A" (**a**denine), "T" (**t**hymine), "C" (**c**ytosine), and "G" (**g**uanine). Draw the pieces again on colored paper. Use a different color for each type of base. Draw the pieces as large as you want, and draw as many of the white pieces and as many of the colored pieces as time will allow.
2. Carefully cut out all of the pieces.
3. Put all of the colored pieces in the classroom into a large paper bag. Spread all of the white pieces in the classroom onto a large table.
4. Remove nine colored pieces from the bag. Arrange the colored pieces in any order in a straight column so that the letters *A, T, C,* and *G* are right side up. Be sure to fit the sugar notches to the phosphate tabs. Draw this arrangement.
5. Find the white bases that correctly pair with the nine colored bases. Remember the base-pairing rules, and pair the bases according to those rules.
6. Pair the pieces by fitting tabs to notches. The letters on the white pieces should be upside down. You now have a model of a double-stranded piece of DNA. The strand contains nine pairs of complementary nucleotides. Draw your model.

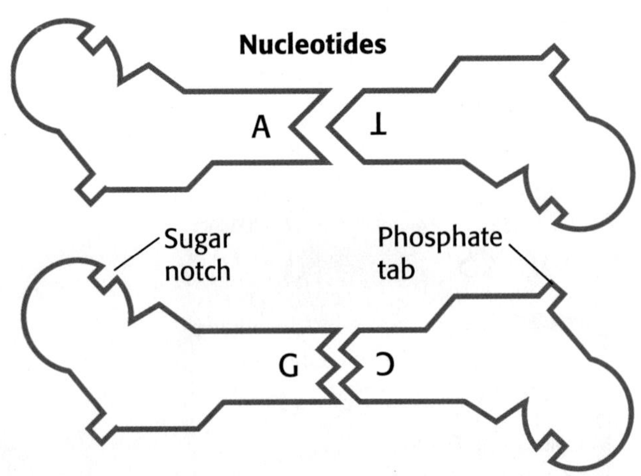

Analyze the Results

1. **Identifying Patterns** Now, separate the two halves of your DNA strand along the middle of the base pair rungs of the ladder. Keep the side rails together by keeping the sugar notches fitted to the phosphate tabs. Draw this arrangement.

2. **Recognizing Patterns** Look at the drawing made in the previous step. Along each strand in the drawing, write the letters of the bases that complement the bases in that strand.

3. **Examining Data** Find all of the bases that you need to complete replication. Find white pieces to pair with the bases on the left, and find colored pieces to pair with the bases on the right. Be sure that the tabs and notches fit and the sides are straight. You have now replicated your model of DNA. Are the two models identical? Draw your results.

Draw Conclusions

4. **Interpreting Information** State the correct base-pairing rules. How do these rules make DNA replication possible?

5. **Evaluating Models** What happens when you attempt to pair thymine with guanine? Do they fit together? Are the sides straight? Do all of the tabs and notches fit? Explain.

Applying Your Data

Construct a 3-D model of a DNA molecule that shows DNA's twisted-ladder structure. Use your imagination and creativity to select materials. You may want to use licorice, gum balls, and toothpicks or pipe cleaners and paper clips.

1. Display your model in your classroom.
2. Take a vote to decide which models are the most accurate and the most creative.

Chapter Review

USING KEY TERMS

1. Use the following terms in the same sentence: *mutation* and *mutagen*.

The statements below are false. For each statement, replace the underlined term to make a true statement.

2. The information in DNA is coded in the order of <u>amino acids</u> along one side of the DNA molecule.

3. The "factory" that assembles proteins based on the DNA code is called a <u>gene</u>.

UNDERSTANDING KEY IDEAS

Multiple Choice

4. James Watson and Francis Crick
   - **a.** took X-ray pictures of DNA.
   - **b.** discovered that genes are in chromosomes.
   - **c.** bred pea plants to study heredity.
   - **d.** made models to figure out DNA's shape.

5. In a DNA molecule, which of the following bases pair together?
   - **a.** adenine and cytosine
   - **b.** thymine and adenine
   - **c.** thymine and guanine
   - **d.** cytosine and thymine

6. A gene can be all of the following EXCEPT
   - **a.** a set of instructions for a trait.
   - **b.** a complete chromosome.
   - **c.** instructions for making a protein.
   - **d.** a portion of a strand of DNA.

7. Which of the following statements about DNA is NOT true?
   - **a.** DNA is found in all organisms.
   - **b.** DNA is made up of five subunits.
   - **c.** DNA has a structure like a twisted ladder.
   - **d.** Mistakes can be made when DNA is copied.

8. Within the cell, where are proteins assembled?
   - **a.** the cytoplasm
   - **b.** the nucleus
   - **c.** the amino acids
   - **d.** the chromosomes

9. Changes in the type or order of the bases in DNA are called
   - **a.** nucleotides.
   - **b.** mutations.
   - **c.** RNA.
   - **d.** genes.

Short Answer

10. What would be the complementary strand of DNA for the following sequence of bases?

    C T T A G G C T T A C C A

11. If the DNA sequence TGAGCCATGA is changed to TGAGCACATGA, what kind of mutation has occurred?

12. Explain how the DNA in genes relates to the traits of an organism.

13. Why is DNA frequently found associated with proteins inside of cells?

14. What is the difference between DNA and RNA?

CRITICAL THINKING

15. **Concept Mapping** Use the following terms to create a concept map: *bases, adenine, thymine, nucleotides, guanine, DNA,* and *cytosine*.

16. **Analyzing Processes** Draw and label a picture that explains how DNA is copied.

17. **Analyzing Processes** Draw and label a picture that explains how proteins are made.

18. **Applying Concepts** The following DNA sequence codes for how many amino acids?

    T C A G C C A C C T A T G G A

19. **Making Inferences** Why does the government make laws about the use of chemicals that are known to be mutagens?

INTERPRETING GRAPHICS

The illustration below shows the process of replication of a DNA strand. Use this illustration to answer the questions that follow.

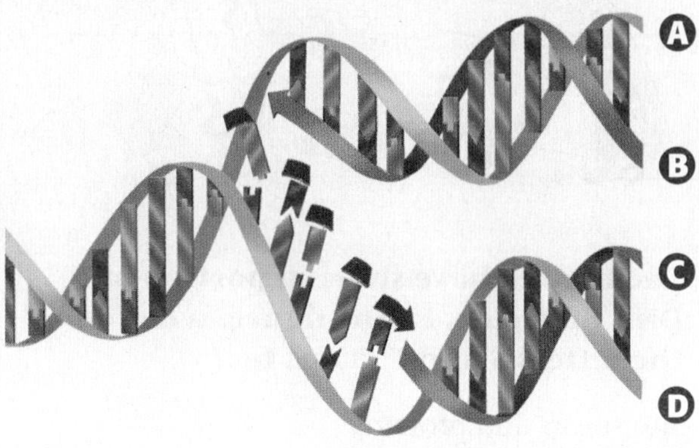

20. Which strands are part of the original molecule?
    - **a.** A and B
    - **b.** A and C
    - **c.** A and D
    - **d.** None of the above

21. Which strands are new?
    - **a.** A and B
    - **b.** B and C
    - **c.** C and D
    - **d.** None of the above

22. Which strands are complementary?
    - **a.** A and C
    - **b.** B and C
    - **c.** All of the strands
    - **d.** None of the strands

Multiple Choice

Use the figure below to answer question 1.

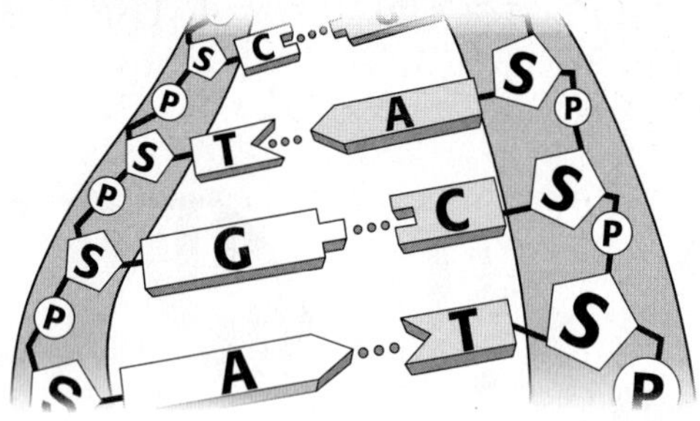

1. **The figure above shows a portion of a DNA molecule. In the figure, what do the letters S and P stand for?**

   A. sugars and proteins

   B. sodium and proteins

   C. sugars and phosphates

   D. sodium and phosphates

2. **Which of the following is the best description of the structure of DNA?**

   A. DNA has two strands that form a branched chain called a *branched helix.*

   B. DNA is in the shape of a twisted ladder called a *double helix.*

   C. DNA is in the shape of a straight ladder called a *straight helix.*

   D. DNA has three strands that form a *triple helix.*

3. **What three components make up a nucleotide?**

   A. a sugar, a protein, and a nitrogenous base

   B. a sucrose, a protein, and a nitrogenous base

   C. a sugar, a proton, and a nitrogenous base

   D. a sugar, a phosphate, and a nitrogenous base

4. **Which pattern shows how bases pair in complementary strands of DNA?**

   A. A–A and C–C

   B. A–G and T–C

   C. A–T and C–G

   D. A–C and T–G

5. **How are copies of DNA made?**

   A. DNA strands unwind and complementary nucleotides are added.

   B. DNA strands unwind and amino acids are joined together to form the copies.

   C. DNA strands are assembled by ribosomes.

   D. DNA strands are made using mRNA templates.

Use the figure below to answer question 6.

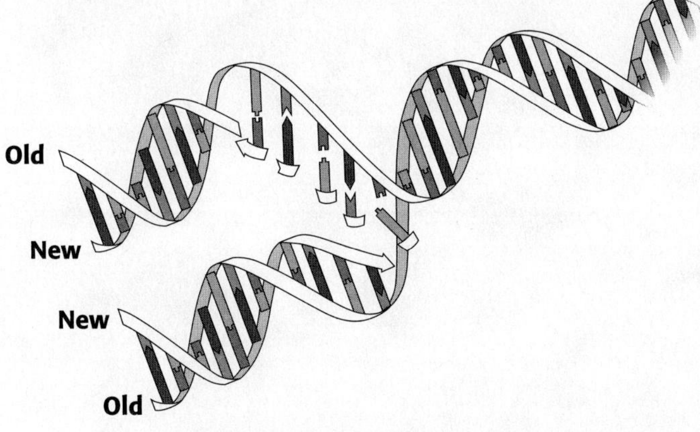

6. **DNA replication results in the formation of two molecules of DNA, as shown in the figure above. Based on the figure, which of the following statements is true?**

   A. Both molecules of DNA have one new strand and one strand from the original DNA molecule.

   B. One molecule is made up of two new strands and the other molecule is made up of old strands.

   C. Each strand in each new DNA molecule is a mixture of portions of old strands and portions of the new strands.

   D. Both molecules of DNA can have one new and one old strand, or they can have two new or two old strands.

7. **What are the structures that are in the nuclei of most cells and that are made of protein and DNA?**

   A. cytosine

   B. molecules

   C. chromosomes

   D. nucleotides

8. **A scientist conducts research on a sample of DNA that contains 200 nucleotides. Her results show that adenine makes up 30% of the sample and cytosine makes up 20% of the sample. The remaining 50% of the sample is made up of thymine and guanine. How many of the nucleotides are thymine?**

   A. 30

   B. 40

   C. 50

   D. 60

9. **How are proteins formed?**

   A. Amino acids assemble along strands of genes in the nucleus to form proteins.

   B. Genes are fed through ribosomes where amino acids assemble to form proteins.

   C. Mirrorlike copies of genes are fed through ribosomes where amino acids assemble to form proteins.

   D. Mirrorlike copies of a gene, called tRNA, are made. tRNA is fed through ribosomes where amino acids assemble to form proteins.

Open Response

10. **Why is it important for a cell to replicate its DNA before cellular division?**

11. **How do the genes in DNA determine the characteristics of living things?**

Science in Action

Scientific Debate

Supersquash or Frankenfruit?

Some food that you buy may have been developed in a new way. Food producers may use genetic engineering to make food crops easier to grow or sell, more nutritious, or resistant to pests and disease. More than half of the packaged foods sold in the United States are likely to contain ingredients from genetically modified organisms.

The U.S. government has stated that research shows that these foods are safe. But some scientists are concerned that genes introduced into crop plants could cause new environmental or health problems. For example, people who are allergic to peanuts might also be allergic to tomato plants that contain peanut genes.

Math Activity

Write a survey about genetically altered foods. Ask your teacher to approve your questions. Ask at least 15 people to answer your survey. Create graphs to summarize your results.

Science Fiction

"Moby James" by Patricia A. McKillip

Rob Trask and his family live on a space station. Rob thinks that his real brother was sent back to Earth. The person who claims to be his brother, James, is really either some sort of mutated plant or a mutant pair of dirty sweat socks.

Now, Rob has another problem—his class is reading Herman Melville's novel *Moby Dick*. As he reads the novel, Rob becomes convinced that his brother is a great white mutant whale—Moby James. To see how Rob solves his problems, read "Moby James" in the *Holt Anthology of Science Fiction*.

Language Arts Activity

WRITING SKILL Read "Moby James" by Patricia A. McKillip. Then, write your own short science-fiction story about a mutant organism. Be sure to incorporate some science into your science fiction.

People in Science

Lydia Villa-Komaroff

Genetic Researcher When Lydia Villa-Komaroff was young, science represented "a kind of refuge" for her. She grew up in a very large family that lived in a very small house. "I always wanted to find things out. I was one of those kids who took things apart."

In college, Villa-Komaroff became very interested in the process of embryonic development—how a simple egg grows into a complex animal. This interest led her to study genes and the way that genes code for proteins. For example, insulin is a protein that is normally produced by the human body. Often, people who suffer from diabetes lack the insulin gene, so their bodies can't make insulin. These people may need to inject insulin into their blood as a drug treatment.

Before the research by Villa-Komaroff's team was done, insulin was difficult to produce. Villa-Komaroff's team isolated the human gene that codes for insulin. Then, the scientists inserted the normal human insulin gene into the DNA of bacteria. This inserted gene caused the bacteria to produce insulin. This technique was a new and more efficient way to produce insulin. Now, most of the insulin used for diabetes treatment is made in this way. Many genetic researchers dream of making breakthroughs like the one that Villa-Komaroff made in her work with insulin.

Social Studies ACTIVITY

WRITING SKILL Do some research about several women, such as Marie Curie, Barbara McClintock, or Maxine Frank Singer, who have done important scientific research. Write a short biography about one of these women.

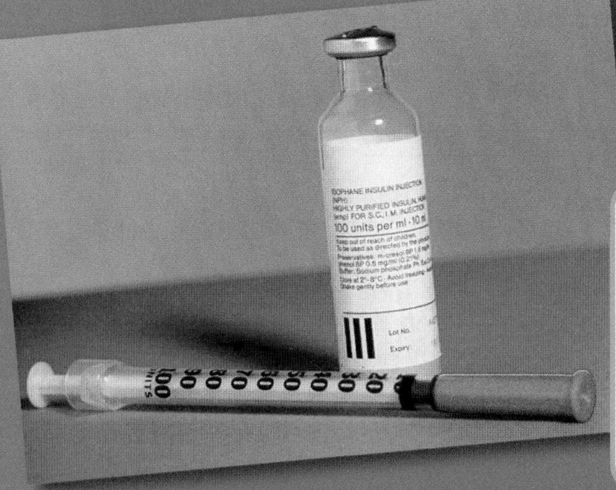

To learn more about these Science in Action topics, visit go.hrw.com and type in the keyword **HL5DNAF.**

Current Science

Check out Current Science® articles related to this chapter by visiting go.hrw.com. Just type in the keyword HL5CS06.

The Evolution of Living Things

The Big Idea

Biological evolution explains how populations change over time.

SECTION

About the Photo

Can you find two eyes and a mouth in this photo? The eyes and mouth belong to an adult flounder. Adult flounders swim on their sides and have both eyes on one side of their body. These characteristics allow flounders to lie flat and still see all of their surroundings. Flounders also look like the sandy bottoms of coastal areas. These adaptations help flounders survive in their environment.

PRE-READING ACTIVITY

Graphic Organizer

Concept Map Before you read the chapter, create the graphic organizer entitled "Concept Map" described in the **Study Skills** section of the Appendix. As you read the chapter, fill in the concept map with details about evolution and natural selection.

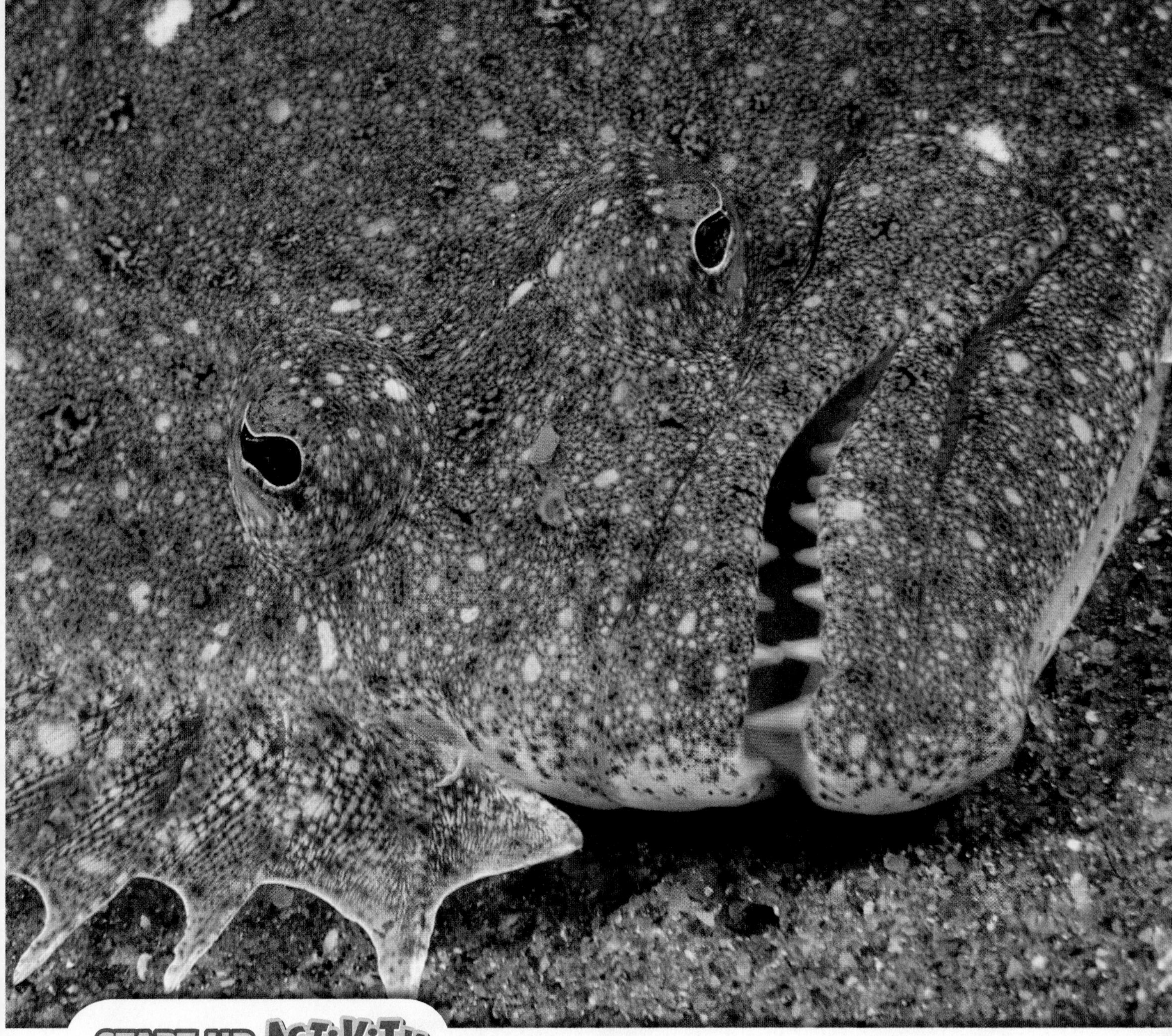

START-UP ACTIVITY

Out of Sight, Out of Mind

In this activity, you will see how traits can affect the success of an organism in a particular environment.

Procedure

1. Count out **25 colored marshmallows** and **25 white marshmallows.**
2. Ask your partner to look away while you spread the marshmallows out on a **white cloth.** Do not make a pattern with the marshmallows. Now, ask your partner to turn around and pick the first marshmallow that he or she sees.
3. Repeat step 2 ten times.

Analysis

1. How many white marshmallows did your partner pick? How many colored marshmallows did he or she pick?
2. What did the marshmallows and the cloth represent in your investigation? What effect did the color of the cloth have?
3. When an organism blends into its environment, the organism is *camouflaged*. How does this activity model camouflaged organisms in the wild? What are some weaknesses of this model?

SECTION 1

Change over Time

If someone asked you to describe a frog, you might say that a frog has long hind legs, has bulging eyes, and croaks. But what color skin would you say that a frog has?

What You Will Learn

- Identify two kinds of evidence that show that organisms have evolved.
- Describe one pathway through which a modern whale could have evolved from an ancient mammal.
- Explain how comparing organisms can provide evidence that they have ancestors in common.

Vocabulary

adaptation
species
evolution
fossil
fossil record

READING STRATEGY

Paired Summarizing Read this section silently. In pairs, take turns summarizing the material. Stop to discuss ideas that seem confusing.

Once you start to think about frogs, you realize that frogs differ in many ways. These differences set one kind of frog apart from another. The frogs in **Figures 1, 2,** and **3** look different from each other, yet they may live in the same areas.

Differences Among Organisms

As you can see, each frog has a different characteristic that might help the frog survive. A characteristic that helps an organism survive and reproduce in its environment is called an **adaptation.** Adaptations may be physical, such as a long neck or striped fur. Or adaptations may be behaviors that help an organism find food, protect itself, or reproduce.

Living things that have the same characteristics may be members of the same species. A **species** is a group of organisms that can mate with one another to produce fertile offspring. For example, all strawberry poison arrow frogs are members of the same species and can mate with each other to produce more strawberry poison arrow frogs. Groups of individuals of the same species living in the same place make up a *population.*

Reading Check How can you tell that organisms are members of the same species? (*See the Appendix for answers to Reading Checks.*)

Figure 1 The red-eyed tree frog hides among a tree's leaves during the day and comes out at night.

Figure 2 The bright coloring of the strawberry poison arrow frog warns predators that the frog is poisonous.

Figure 3 The smokey jungle frog blends into the forest floor.

Do Species Change over Time?

In a single square mile of rain forest, there may be dozens of species of frogs. Across the Earth, there are millions of different species of organisms. The species that live on Earth today range from single-celled bacteria, which lack cell nuclei, to multicellular fungi, plants, and animals. Have these species always existed on Earth?

Scientists think that Earth has changed a great deal during its history, and that living things have changed, too. Scientists estimate that the planet is 4.6 billion years old. Since life first appeared on Earth, many species have died out, and many new species have appeared. **Figure 4** shows some of the species that have existed during Earth's history.

Scientists observe that species have changed over time. They also observe that the inherited characteristics in populations change over time. Scientists think that as populations change over time, new species form. Thus, newer species descend from older species. The process in which populations gradually change over time is called **evolution.** Scientists continue to develop theories to explain exactly how evolution happens.

adaptation a characteristic that improves an individual's ability to survive and reproduce in a particular environment

species a group of organisms that are closely related and can mate to produce fertile offspring

evolution the process in which inherited characteristics within a population change over generations such that new species sometimes arise

Figure 4 *This diagram shows some of the many kinds of organisms that have lived on Earth since the planet formed 4.6 billion years ago.*

Figure 5 *The fossil on the left is of a trilobite, an ancient aquatic animal. The fossils on the right are of seed ferns.*

Evidence of Changes over Time

Evidence that organisms have changed over time is buried within Earth's crust. The layers are made up of different kinds of rock and soil stacked on top of each other. These layers form when *sediments*, particles of sand, dust, or soil, are carried by wind and water and are deposited in an orderly fashion. Older layers are deposited before newer layers and are buried deeper within Earth.

Fossils

The remains or imprints of once-living organisms found in layers of rock called **fossils.** Examples of fossils are shown in **Figure 5.** Fossils can be complete organisms, parts of organisms, or just a set of footprints. Fossils usually form when a dead organism is covered by a layer of sediment. Over time, more sediment settles on top of the organism. Minerals in the sediment may seep into the organism and gradually replace the organism with stone. If the organism rots away completely after being covered, it may leave an imprint of itself in the rock.

fossil the trace or remains of an organism that lived long ago, most commonly preserved in sedimentary rock

fossil record a historical sequence of life indicated by fossils found in layers of the Earth's crust

The Fossil Record

By studying fossils, scientists have made a timeline of life known as the **fossil record.** The fossil record organizes fossils by their estimated ages and physical similarities. Fossils found in newer layers of Earth's crust tend to be similar to present-day organisms. This similarity indicates that the fossilized organisms were close relatives of present-day organisms. Fossils from older layers are less similar to present-day organisms than fossils from newer layers are. The older fossils are of earlier life-forms, which may not exist anymore.

Reading Check **How does the fossil record organize fossils?**

Evidence of Ancestry

The fossil record provides evidence about the order in which species have existed. Scientists observe that all living organisms have characteristics in common and inherit characteristics in similar ways. So, scientists think that all living species descended from common ancestors. Evidence of common ancestors can be found in fossils and in living organisms.

Drawing Connections

Scientists examine the fossil record to figure out the relationships between extinct and living organisms. Scientists draw models, such as the one shown in **Figure 6,** that illustrate their hypotheses. The short horizontal line at the top left in the diagram represents a species that lived in the past. Each branch in the diagram represents a group of organisms that descended from that species.

Scientists think that whales and some types of hoofed mammals have a common ancestor, as **Figure 6** shows. This ancestor was probably a mammal that lived on land between 50 million and 70 million years ago. During this time period, the dinosaurs died out and a variety of mammals appeared in the fossil record. The first ocean-dwelling mammals appeared about 50 million years ago. Scientists think that all mammal species alive today evolved from common ancestors.

Scientists have named and described hundreds of thousands of living and ancient species. Scientists use information about these species to sketch out a "tree of life" that includes all known organisms. But scientists know that their information is incomplete. For example, parts of Earth's history lack a fossil record. In fact, fossils are rare because specific conditions are necessary for fossils to form.

Sedimentary Rock Fossils are most often found in sedimentary rock. *Sedimentary rock* usually forms when rock is broken into sediment by wind, water, and other means. The wind and water move the sediment around and deposit it. Over time, layers of sediment pile up. Lower layers are compressed and changed into rock. Find out if your area has any sedimentary rocks that contain fossils. Mark the location of such rocks on a copy of a local map.

ACTIVITY

Figure 6 *This diagram is a model of the proposed relationships between ancient and modern mammals that have characteristics similar to whales.*

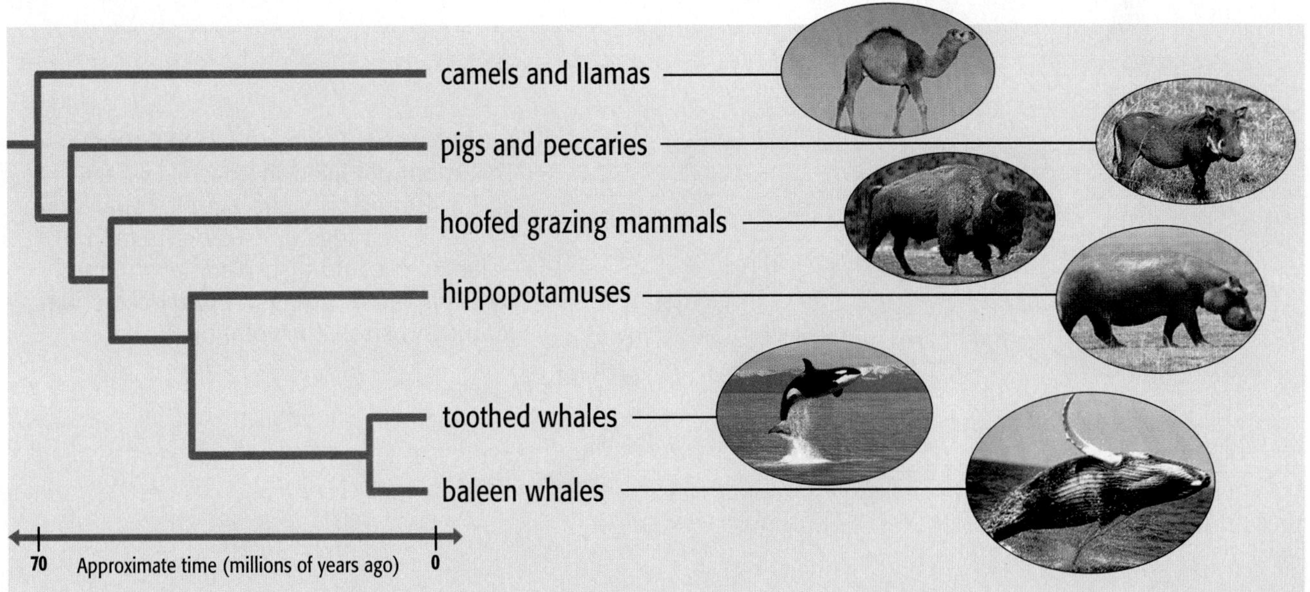

Examining Organisms

Examining an organism carefully can give scientists clues about its ancestors. For example, whales seem similar to fish. But unlike fish, whales breathe air, give birth to live young, and produce milk. These traits show that whales are *mammals*. Thus, scientists think that whales evolved from ancient mammals.

Case Study: Evolution of the Whale

Scientists think that the ancient ancestor of whales was probably a mammal that lived on land and that could run on four legs. A more recent ancestor was probably a mammal that spent time both on land and in water. Comparisons of modern whales and a large number of fossils have supported this hypothesis. **Figure 7** illustrates some of this evidence.

Reading Check **What kind of organism do scientists think was an ancient ancestor of whales?**

Figure 7 **Evidence of Whale Evolution**

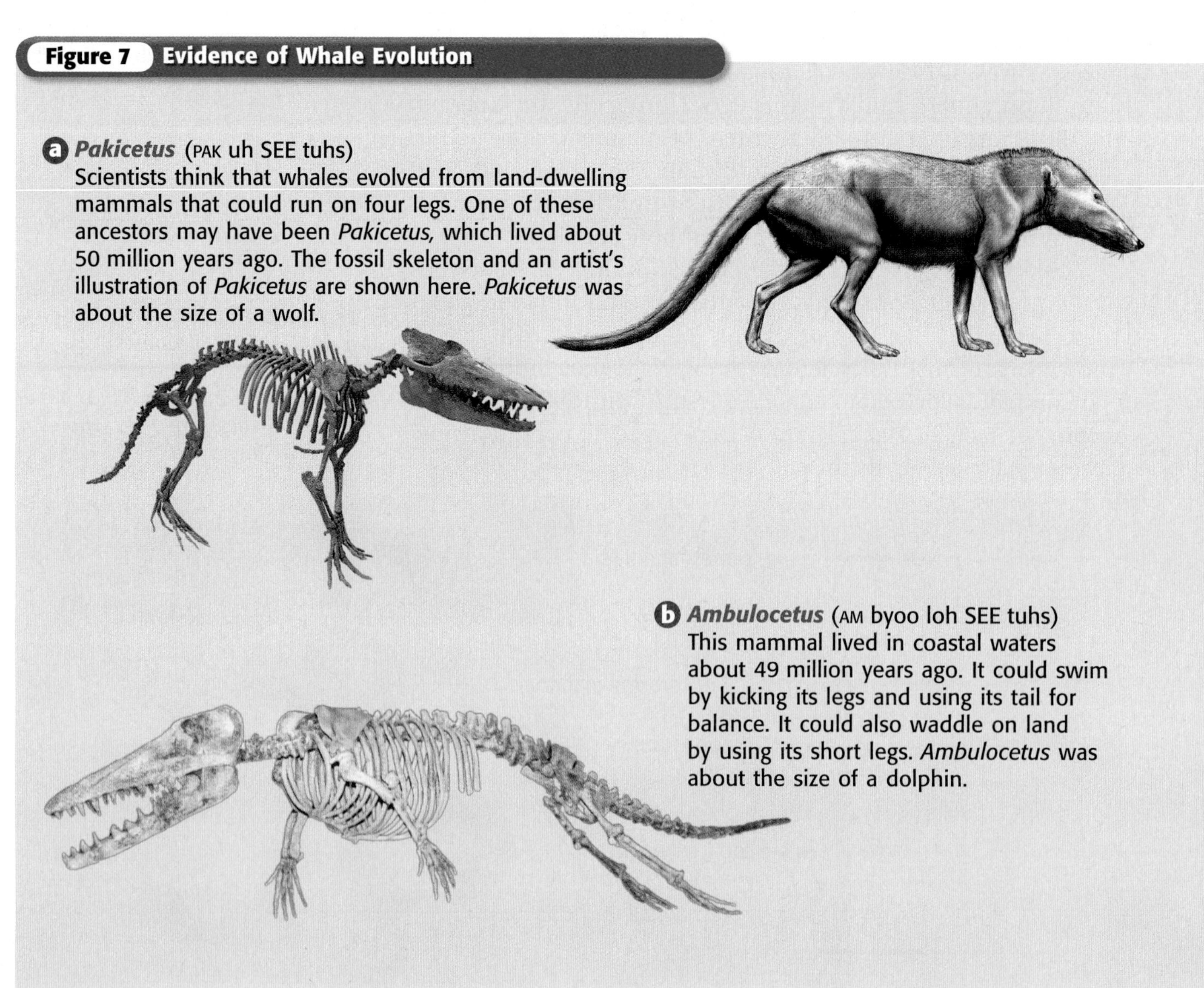

a ***Pakicetus*** (PAK uh SEE tuhs) Scientists think that whales evolved from land-dwelling mammals that could run on four legs. One of these ancestors may have been *Pakicetus,* which lived about 50 million years ago. The fossil skeleton and an artist's illustration of *Pakicetus* are shown here. *Pakicetus* was about the size of a wolf.

b ***Ambulocetus*** (AM byoo loh SEE tuhs) This mammal lived in coastal waters about 49 million years ago. It could swim by kicking its legs and using its tail for balance. It could also waddle on land by using its short legs. *Ambulocetus* was about the size of a dolphin.

Walking Whales

The organisms in **Figure 7** form a sequence between ancient four-legged mammals and modern whales. Several pieces of evidence indicate that these species are related by ancestry. Each species shared some traits with an earlier species. However, some species had new traits that were shared with later species. Yet, each species had traits that allowed it to survive in a particular time and place in Earth's history.

Further evidence can be found inside the bodies of living whales. For example, although modern whales do not have hind limbs, inside their bodies are tiny hip bones, as shown in **Figure 7.** Scientists think that these hip bones were inherited from the whales' four-legged ancestors. Scientists often look at this kind of evidence when they want to determine the relationships between organisms.

The Weight of Whales

Whales are the largest animals ever known on Earth. One reason whales can grow so large is that they live in water, which supports their weight in a way that their bones could not. The blue whale—the largest type of whale in existence—is about 24 m long and has a mass of about 99,800 kg. Convert these measurements into feet and pounds, and round to whole numbers.

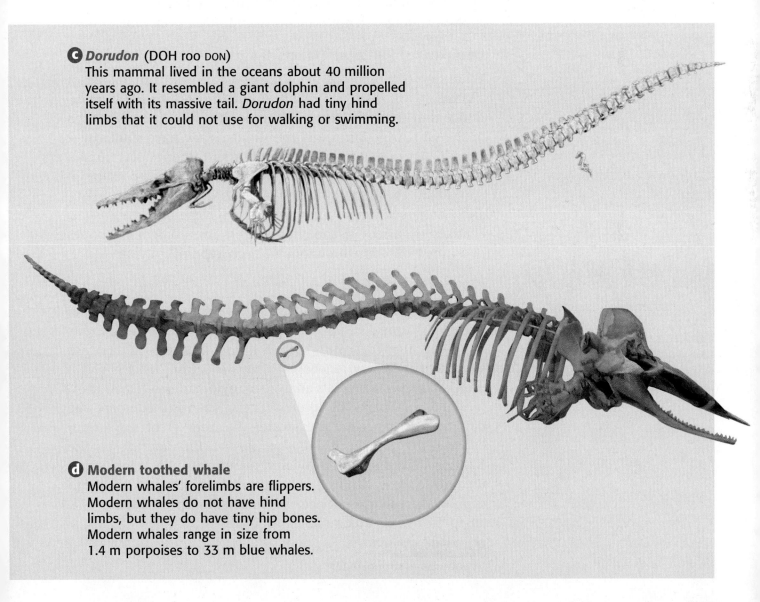

c ***Dorudon*** (DOH roo DON)
This mammal lived in the oceans about 40 million years ago. It resembled a giant dolphin and propelled itself with its massive tail. *Dorudon* had tiny hind limbs that it could not use for walking or swimming.

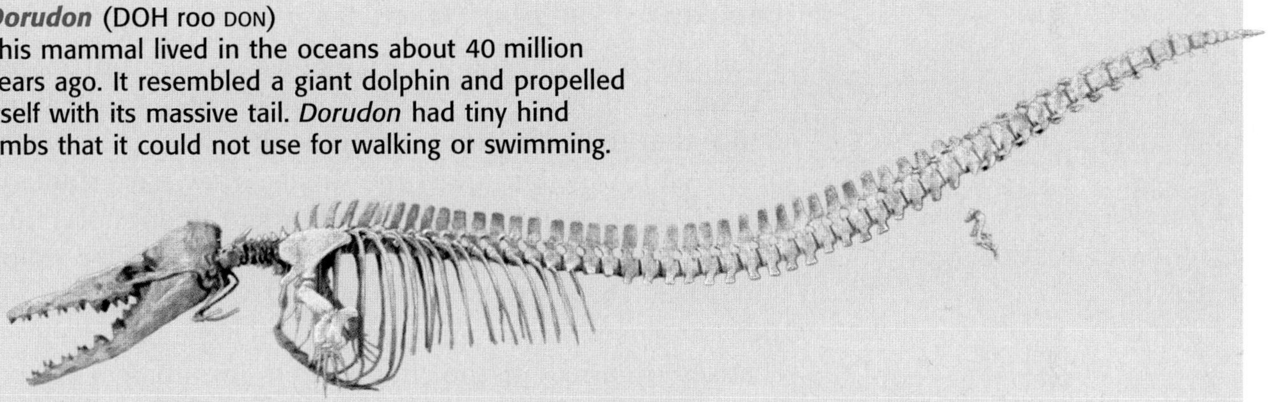

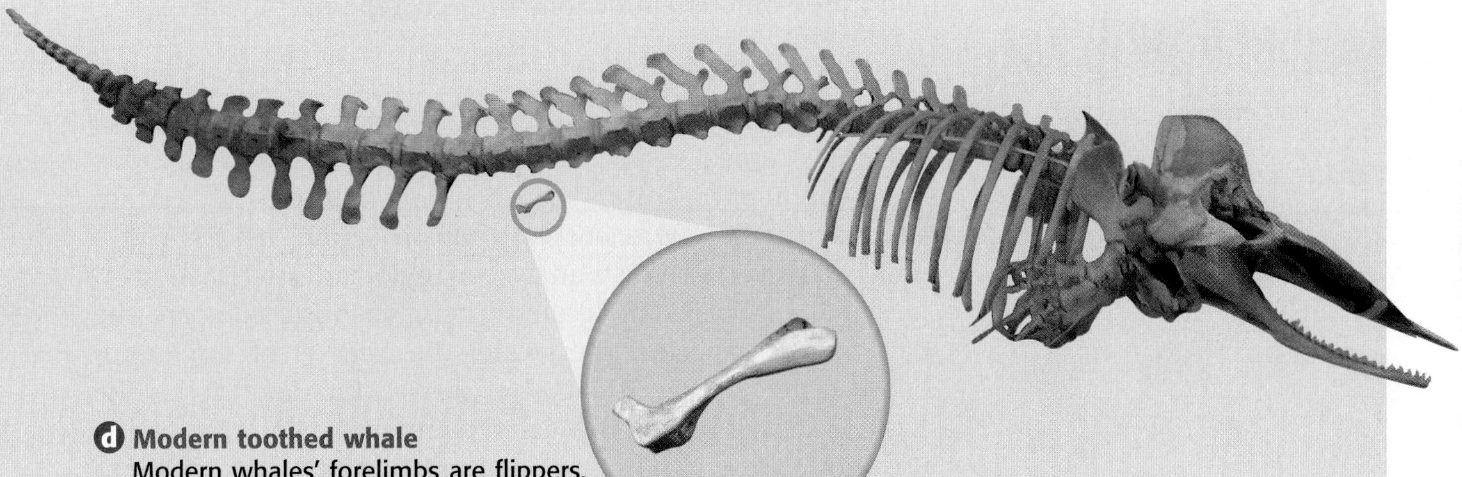

d **Modern toothed whale**
Modern whales' forelimbs are flippers. Modern whales do not have hind limbs, but they do have tiny hip bones. Modern whales range in size from 1.4 m porpoises to 33 m blue whales.

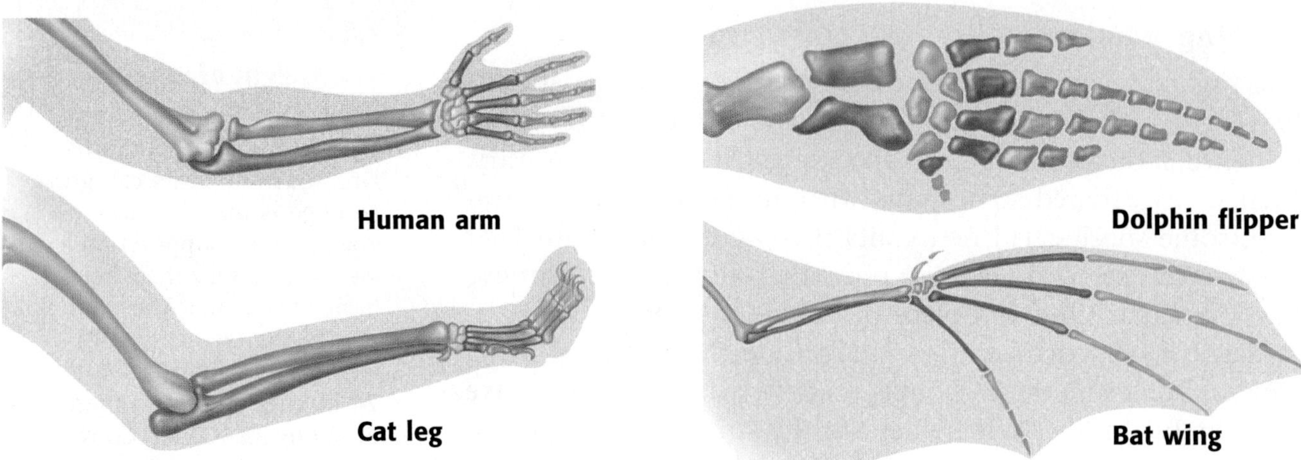

Figure 8 *The bones in the front limbs of these animals are similar. Similar bones are shown in the same color. These limbs are different sizes in life.*

Comparing Organisms

Evidence that groups of organisms have common ancestry can be found by comparing the groups' DNA. Because every organism inherits DNA, every organism inherits the traits determined by DNA. Organisms contain evidence that populations and species undergo changes in traits and DNA over time.

Comparing Skeletal Structures

What do your arm, the front leg of a cat, the front flipper of a dolphin, and the wing of a bat have in common? You might notice that these structures do not look alike and are not used in the same way. But under the surface, they have similarities. Look at **Figure 8.** The structure and order of bones of a human arm are similar to those of the front limbs of a cat, a dolphin, and a bat. These similarities suggest that cats, dolphins, bats, and humans had a common ancestor. Over millions of years, changes occurred in the limb bones. Eventually, the bones performed different functions in each type of animal.

For another activity related to this chapter, go to **go.hrw.com** and type in the keyword **HL5EVOW.**

Comparing DNA

When scientists compare organism's traits, such as skeletal structures, much of the information that they get supports the theory that organisms share a common ancestor. To further support this theory, scientists compare organisms' DNA at a molecular level. Scientists analyze many organisms' DNA, RNA, proteins, and other molecules. Then, scientists compare the data for each species. The greater the number of similarities between the data sets for any two species, the more closely the two species are related through a common ancestor. Scientists use molecular data, the comparison of traits, and fossils to support the theory that because all existing species have DNA, all species share a common ancestor.

Reading Check **If two species have similar DNA, what hypothesis is supported?**

SECTION Review

- Evolution is the process in which inherited characteristics within a population change over generations, sometimes giving rise to new species. Scientists continue to develop theories to explain how evolution happens.
- Evidence that organisms evolve can be found by comparing living organisms to each other and to the fossil record. Such comparisons provide evidence of common ancestry.
- Scientists think that modern whales evolved from an ancient, land-dwelling mammal ancestor. Fossil organisms that support this hypothesis have been found.
- Evidence of common ancestry among living organisms is provided by comparing DNA and inherited traits. Species that have a common ancestor will have traits and DNA that are more similar to each other than to those of distantly related species.

Using Key Terms

Complete each of the following sentences by choosing the correct term from the word bank.

adaptation	species
fossil	evolution

1. Members of the same ___ can mate with one another to produce offspring.
2. A(n) ___ helps an organism survive.
3. When populations change over time, ___ has occurred.

Understanding Key Ideas

4. A human's arm, a cat's front leg, a dolphin's front flipper, and a bat's wing
   a. have similar kinds of bones.
   b. are used in similar ways.
   c. are very similar to insect wings and jellyfish tentacles.
   d. have nothing in common.
5. How does the fossil record show that species have changed over time?
6. What evidence do fossils provide about the ancestors of whales?

Critical Thinking

7. **Making Comparisons** Other than the examples provided in the text, how are whales different from fishes?
8. **Forming Hypotheses** Is a person's DNA likely to be more similar to the DNA of his or her biological parents or to the DNA of one of his or her cousins? Explain your answer.

Interpreting Graphics

9. The photograph below shows the layers of sedimentary rock exposed during the construction of a road. Imagine that a species that lived 200 million years ago is found in layer **b.** Would the species' ancestor, which lived 250 million years ago, most likely be found in layer **a** or in layer **c**? Explain your answer.

SCILINKS.
NSTA
Developed and maintained by the National Science Teachers Association
For a variety of links related to this chapter, go to www.scilinks.org
Topic: Species and Adaptation; Fossil Record
SciLinks code: HSM1433; HSM0615

SECTION 2

How Does Evolution Happen?

What You Will Learn

- List four sources of Charles Darwin's ideas about evolution.
- Describe the four parts of Darwin's theory of evolution by natural selection.
- Relate genetics to evolution.

Vocabulary

trait
selective breeding
natural selection

READING STRATEGY

Brainstorming The key idea of this section is natural selection. Brainstorm words and phrases related to natural selection.

Imagine that you are a scientist in the 1800s. Fossils of some very strange animals have been found. And some familiar fossils have been found where you would least expect them. How did seashells end up on the tops of mountains?

In the 1800s, geologists began to realize that the Earth is much older than anyone had previously thought. Evidence showed that gradual processes had changed the Earth's surface over millions of years. Some scientists saw evidence of evolution in the fossil record. However, no one had been able to explain *how* evolution happens—until Charles Darwin.

Charles Darwin

In 1831, 21-year-old Charles Darwin, shown in **Figure 1,** graduated from college. Like many young people just out of college, Darwin didn't know what he wanted to do with his life. His father wanted him to become a doctor, but seeing blood made Darwin sick. Although he eventually earned a degree in theology, Darwin was most interested in the study of plants and animals.

So, Darwin signed on for a five-year voyage around the world. He served as the *naturalist*—a scientist who studies nature—on the British ship the HMS *Beagle,* similar to the ship in **Figure 2.** During the trip, Darwin made observations that helped him form a theory about how evolution happens.

Figure 1 *Charles Darwin wanted to understand the natural world.*

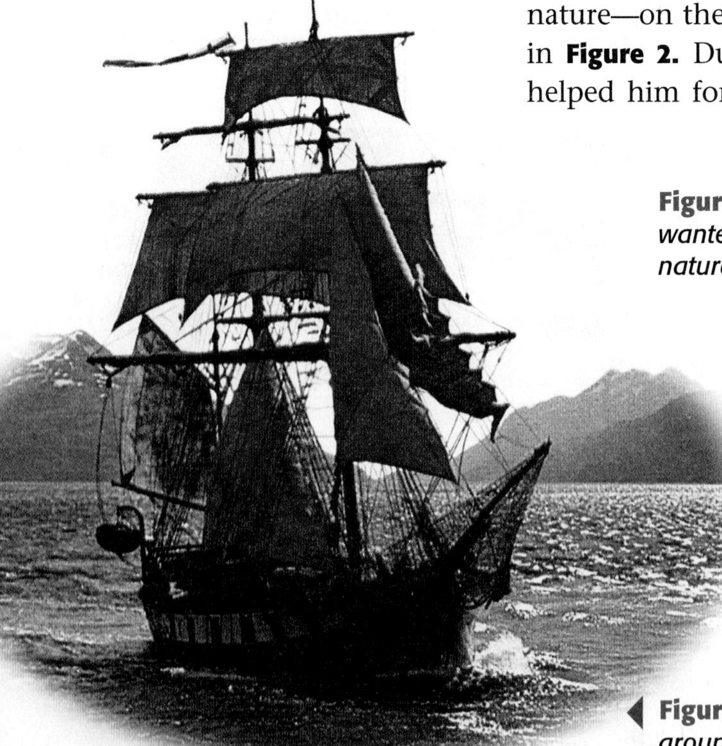

Figure 2 *Darwin sailed around the world on a ship similar to this one.*

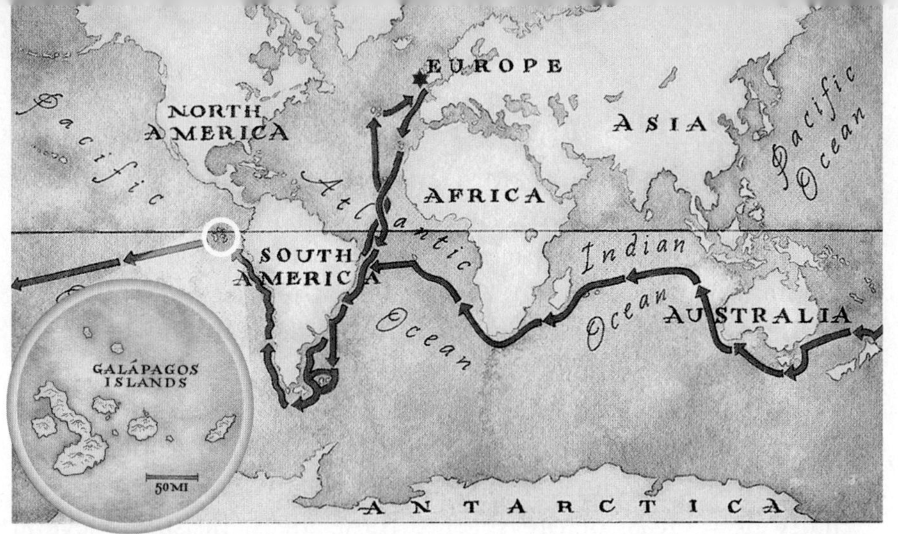

Figure 3 *The course of the HMS* Beagle *is shown by the red line. The journey began and ended in England.*

Darwin's Excellent Adventure

The *Beagle*'s journey is charted in **Figure 3.** Along the way, Darwin collected thousands of plant and animal samples. He kept careful notes of his observations. One interesting place that the ship visited was the Galápagos Islands. These islands are found 965 km (600 mi) west of Ecuador, a country in South America.

✓ Reading Check **Where are the Galápagos Islands?** (*See the Appendix for answers to Reading Checks.*)

Darwin's Finches

Darwin noticed that the animals and plants on the Galápagos Islands were a lot like those in Ecuador. However, they were not exactly the same. The finches of the Galápagos Islands, for example, were a little different from the finches in Ecuador. And the finches on each island differed from the finches on the other islands. As **Figure 4** shows, the beak of each finch is adapted to the way the bird usually gets food.

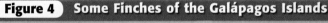

Figure 4 **Some Finches of the Galápagos Islands**

The **large ground finch** has a wide, strong beak that it uses to crack open big, hard seeds. This beak works like a nutcracker.

The **cactus finch** has a tough beak that it uses for eating cactus parts and insects. This beak works like a pair of needle-nose pliers.

The **warbler finch** has a small, narrow beak that it uses to catch small insects. This beak works like a pair of tweezers.

Darwin's Thinking

After returning to England, Darwin puzzled over the animals of the Galápagos Islands. He tried to explain why the animals seemed so similar to each other yet had so many different adaptations. For example, Darwin hypothesized that the island finches were descended from South American finches. The first finches on the islands may have been blown from South America by a storm. Over many generations, the finches may have evolved adaptations for the various island environments.

During the course of his travels, Darwin came up with many new ideas. Before sharing these ideas, he spent several years analyzing his evidence and gathering ideas from other people.

Ideas About Breeding

trait a genetically determined characteristic

selective breeding the human practice of breeding animals or plants that have certain desired traits

In Darwin's time, farmers and breeders had produced many kinds of farm animals and plants. These plants and animals had traits that were desired by the farmers and breeders. A **trait** is a characteristic that can be passed from parent to offspring through genes. The process in which humans select which plants or animals to reproduce based on certain desired traits is called **selective breeding.** Most pets, such as the dogs in **Figure 5,** have been bred for various desired traits.

You can see the results of selective breeding in many kinds of organisms. For example, people have bred horses that are particularly fast or strong. And farmers have bred crops that produce large fruit or that grow in specific climates.

Figure 5 *Over the past 12,000 years, dogs have been selectively bred to produce more than 150 breeds.*

Population Growth Versus Food Supply

1. Get an **egg carton** and a **bag of rice.** Use a **marker** to label one row of the carton "Food supply." Then, label the second row "Human population."
2. In the row labeled "Food supply," place one grain of rice in the first cup. Place two grains of rice in the second cup, and place three grains of rice in the third cup. In each subsequent cup, place one more grain than you placed in the previous cup. Imagine that each grain represents enough food for one person's lifetime.
3. In the row labeled "Human population," place one grain of rice in the first cup. Place two grains in the second cup, and place four grains in the third cup. In each subsequent cup, place twice as many grains as you placed in the previous cup. This rice represents people.
4. How many units of food are in the sixth cup? How many "people" are in the sixth cup? If this pattern continued, what would happen?
5. Describe how the patterns in the food supply and in the human population differ. Explain how the patterns relate to Malthus's hypothesis.

Ideas About Population

During Darwin's time, Thomas Malthus wrote a famous book entitled *An Essay on the Principle of Population.* Malthus noted that humans have the potential to reproduce rapidly. He warned that food supplies could not support unlimited population growth. **Figure 6** illustrates this relationship. However, Malthus pointed out that human populations are limited by choices that humans make or by problems such as starvation and disease.

After reading Malthus's work, Darwin realized that any species can produce many offspring. He also knew that the populations of all species are limited by starvation, disease, competition, and predation. Only a limited number of individuals survive to reproduce. Thus, there is something special about the survivors. Darwin reasoned that the offspring of the survivors inherit traits that help the offspring survive in their environment.

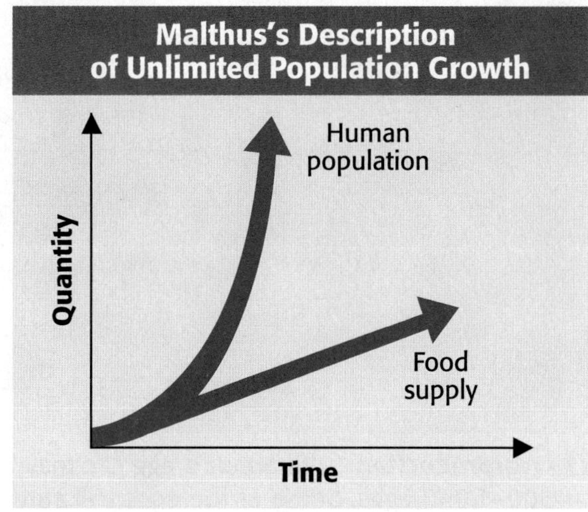

Figure 6 *Malthus thought that the human population could increase more quickly than the food supply, with the result that there would not be enough food for everyone.*

Ideas About Earth's History

Darwin had begun to think that species could evolve over time. But most geologists at the time did not think that Earth was old enough to allow for slow changes. Darwin learned new ideas from *Principles of Geology,* a book by Charles Lyell. This book presented evidence that Earth had formed by natural processes over a long period of time. It became clear to Darwin that Earth was much older than anyone had imagined.

Reading Check **What did Darwin learn from Charles Lyell?**

Darwin's Theory of Natural Selection

natural selection the process by which individuals that are better adapted to their environment survive and reproduce more successfully than less well adapted individuals do; a theory to explain the mechanism of evolution

After his voyage on the HMS *Beagle*, Darwin privately struggled with his ideas for about 20 years. Then, in 1858, Darwin received a letter from a fellow naturalist named Alfred Russel Wallace. Wallace had arrived at the same ideas about evolution that Darwin had. In 1859, Darwin published a famous book called *On the Origin of Species by Means of Natural Selection.* In his book, Darwin proposed the theory that evolution happens through *natural selection.* **Natural selection** is the process by which organisms that are better adapted to their environment survive and reproduce more successfully than less well adapted organisms do. The process has four parts and is explained in **Figure 7.**

Reading Check What is natural selection?

Figure 7 **Four Parts of Natural Selection**

1 Overproduction A tarantula's egg sac may hold 500–1,000 eggs. Some of the eggs will survive and develop into adult spiders. Some will not.

2 Inherited Variation Every individual has its own combination of traits. Each tarantula is similar to, but not identical to, its parents.

3 Struggle to Survive Some tarantulas may be caught by predators, such as this wasp. Other tarantulas may starve or get a disease. Only some of the tarantulas will survive to adulthood.

4 Successful Reproduction The tarantulas that are best adapted to their environment are likely to have many offspring that survive.

Genetics and Evolution

Darwin lacked evidence for parts of his theory. For example, he knew that organisms inherit traits, but not *how* they inherit traits. He knew that there is great variation among organisms, but not *how* that variation occurs. Today, scientists have found most of the evidence that Darwin lacked. They know that variation happens as a result of differences in genes. Changes in genes may happen whenever organisms produce offspring. Some genes make an organism more likely to survive to reproduce. The process called *selection* happens when only organisms that carry these genes can survive to reproduce. New fossil discoveries and new information about genes add to scientists' understanding of natural selection and evolution.

SECTION Review

Summary

- Darwin explained that evolution occurs through natural selection. His theory has four parts:
  1. Each species produces more offspring than will survive to reproduce.
  2. Individuals within a population have slightly different traits.
  3. Individuals within a population compete with each other for limited resources.
  4. Individuals that are better equipped to live in an environment are more likely to survive to reproduce.
- Modern genetics helps explain the theory of natural selection.

Using Key Terms

1. In your own words, write a definition for the term *trait.*
2. Use the following terms in the same sentence: *selective breeding* and *natural selection.*

Understanding Key Ideas

3. Modern scientific explanations of evolution
   a. have replaced Darwin's theory.
   b. rely on genetics instead of natural selection.
   c. fail to explain how traits are inherited.
   d. combine the principles of natural selection and genetic inheritance.
4. Describe the observations that Darwin made about the species on the Galápagos Islands.
5. Summarize the ideas that Darwin developed from books by Malthus and Lyell.
6. Describe the four parts of Darwin's theory of evolution by natural selection.
7. What knowledge did Darwin lack that modern scientists now use to explain evolution?

Math Skills

8. In a sample of 80 beetles, 50 beetles had 4 spots each, and the rest had 6 spots each. What was the average number of spots per beetle?

Critical Thinking

9. **Making Comparisons** In selective breeding, humans influence the course of evolution. What determines the course of evolution in natural selection?
10. **Predicting Consequences** Suppose that an island in the Pacific Ocean was just formed by a volcano. Over the next million years, how might species evolve on this island?

SCILINKS.
NSTA
Developed and maintained by the National Science Teachers Association
For a variety of links related to this chapter, go to www.scilinks.org
Topic: Galápagos Islands; Darwin and Natural Selection
SciLinks code: HSM0631; HSM0378

SECTION 3

Natural Selection in Action

Have you ever had to take an antibiotic? Antibiotics are supposed to kill bacteria. But sometimes, bacteria are not killed by the medicine. Do you know why?

What You Will Learn

- Give three examples of natural selection in action.
- Outline the process of speciation.

Vocabulary

generation time
speciation

READING STRATEGY

Prediction Guide Before reading this section, write the title of each heading in this section. Next, under each heading, write what you think you will learn.

A population of bacteria might develop an adaptation through natural selection. Most bacteria are killed by the chemicals in antibiotics. But a few of the bacteria have an adaptation that makes them naturally *resistant to,* or not killed by, the antibiotic. These few bacteria survive antibiotic treatment, continue to reproduce, and pass the adaptation to their offspring. After several generations, almost all the bacteria in the population carry the adaptation of antibiotic resistance.

Changes in Populations

The theory of natural selection explains how a population changes in response to its environment. Through ongoing natural selection, a population adapts to its environment. Well-adapted individuals will likely survive and reproduce.

Adaptation to Hunting

Changes in populations are sometimes observed when a new force affects the survival of individuals. Scientists think that hunting in Uganda is affecting Uganda's elephant population. In 1930, about 99% of the male elephants in one area had tusks. Only 1% of the elephants were born without tusks. Today, as many as 15% of the male elephants in that area lack tusks. What happened?

A male African elephant that has tusks is shown in **Figure 1.** The ivory of an elephant's tusks is very valuable. People hunt the elephants for their tusks. As a result, fewer of the elephants that have tusks survive to reproduce, and more of the tuskless elephants survive. When the tuskless elephants reproduce, they pass the tuskless trait to their offspring.

Figure 1 *The ivory tusks of African elephants are very valuable. Some elephants are born without tusks.*

Figure 2 Natural Selection of Insecticide Resistance

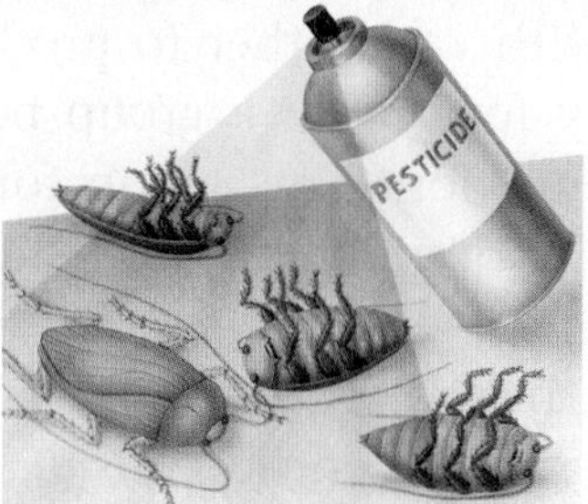

1 An insecticide will kill most insects, but a few may survive. These survivors have genes that make them resistant to the insecticide.

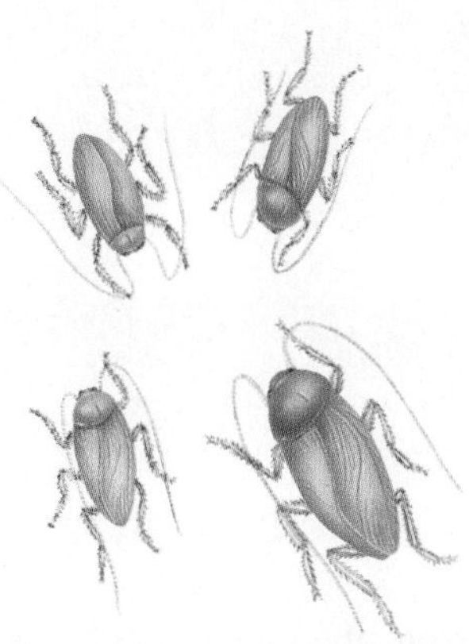

2 The survivors then reproduce, passing the insecticide-resistance genes to their offspring.

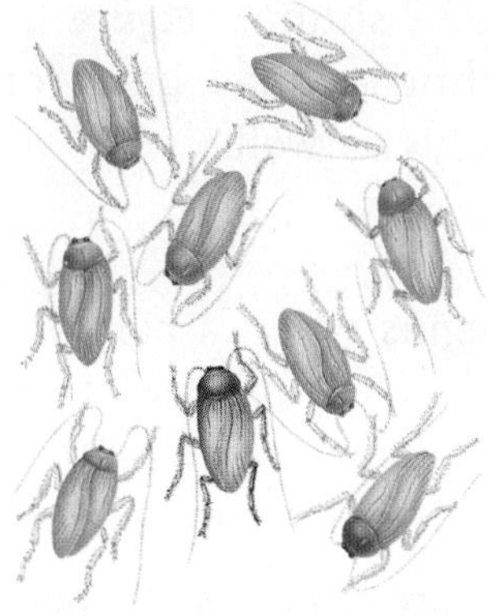

3 In time, the replacement population of insects is made up mostly of individuals that have the insecticide-resistance genes.

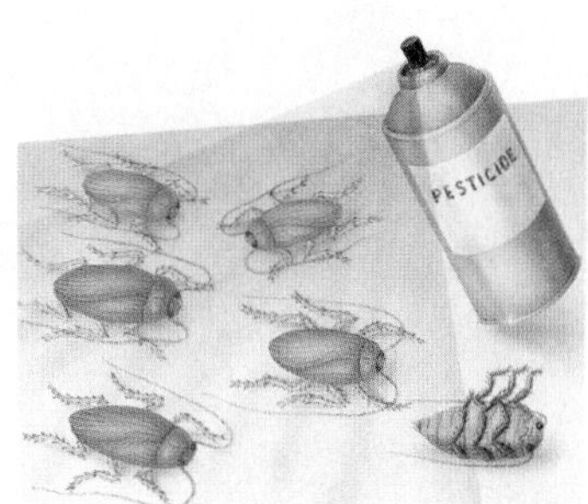

4 When the same kind of insecticide is used on the insects, only a few are killed because most of them are resistant to that insecticide.

Insecticide Resistance

To control insect pests, many people use insecticides, chemicals that kill insects. Sometimes, an insecticide that used to work well no longer affects an insect population. The reason is that a few insects in the population are resistant to the chemical. These insects survive insecticide treatment and pass the resistance trait to their offspring. **Figure 2** shows how an insect population becomes resistant to some insecticides.

Insect populations can evolve quickly because insects produce many offspring and have a short generation time. **Generation time** is the average time between one generation and the next.

generation time the period between the birth of one generation and the birth of the next generation

Reading Check **Why do insects quickly develop resistance to insecticides?** (*See the Appendix for answers to Reading Checks.*)

Competition for Mates

For organisms that reproduce sexually, competition for mates can select for adaptations. For example, in many bird species, females prefer to mate with colorful males. So, colorful males have more offspring than noncolorful males do. Because colorful males are more likely to pass on their genes to the next generation, the proportion of colorful males is likely to increase from generation to generation.

Forming a New Species

Sometimes, drastic changes that can form a new species take place. In the animal kingdom, a *species* is a group of organisms that can mate with each other to produce fertile offspring. A new species may form after a group becomes separated from the original population. This group forms a new population. Over time, the new population adapts to its new environment. Eventually, the new population and the original population differ so greatly that they can no longer mate successfully. The new population may then be considered a new species. The formation of a new species as a result of evolution is called **speciation** (SPEE shee AY shuhn). **Figure 3** shows how new species of Galápagos finches may have formed. Speciation may happen in other ways as well.

speciation the formation of new species as a result of evolution

Separation

Speciation often begins when a part of a population becomes separated from the rest. The process of separation can happen in several ways. For example, a newly formed canyon, mountain range, or lake can divide the members of a population.

Reading Check How can parts of a population become separated?

Figure 3 The Evolution of Galápagos Finch Species

1 Some finches left the mainland and reached one of the islands (separation).

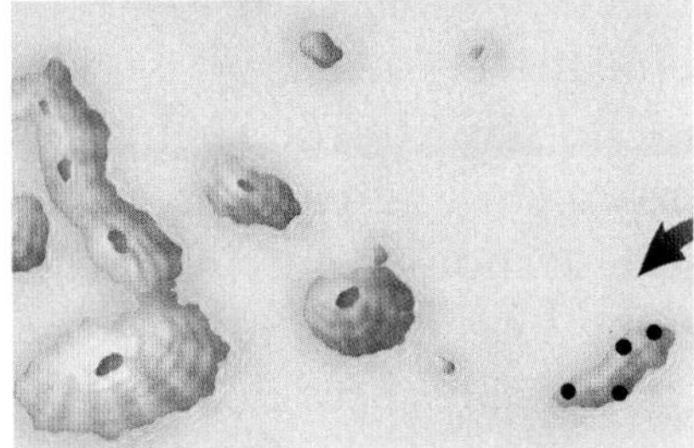

2 The finches reproduced and adapted to the environment (adaptation).

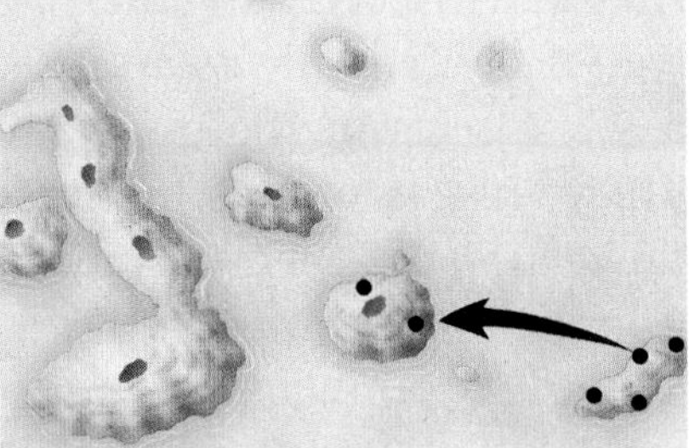

3 Some finches flew to a second island (separation).

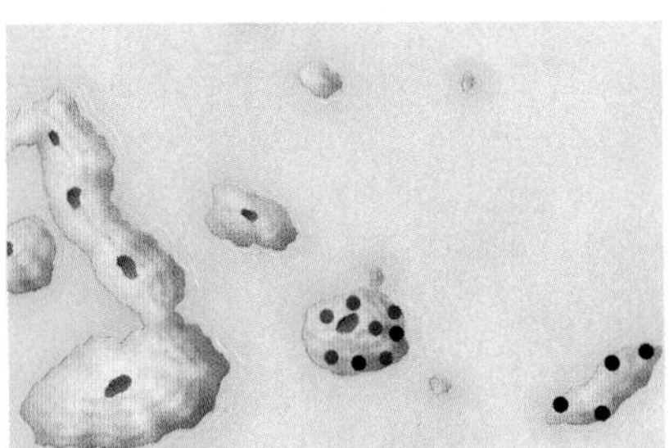

4 The finches reproduced and adapted to the different environment (adaptation).

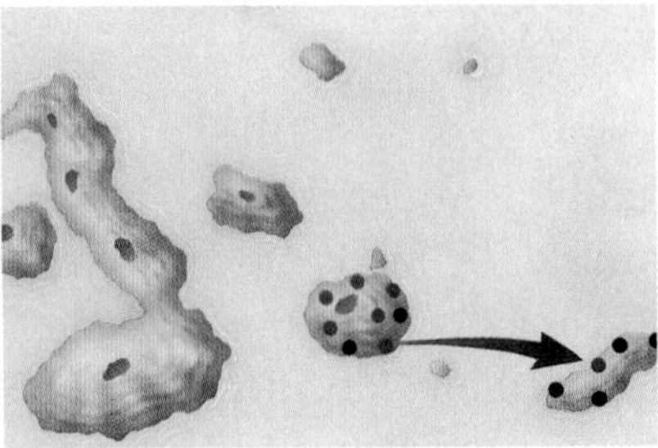

5 Some finches flew back to the first island but could no longer interbreed with the finches there (division).

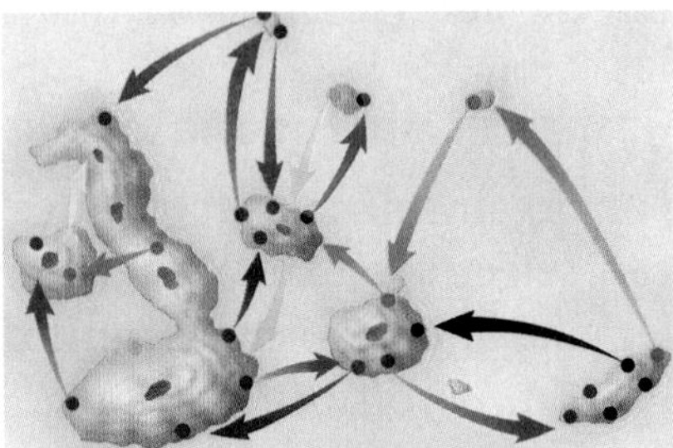

6 This process may have occurred over and over again as the finches flew to the other islands.

Adaptation

Populations constantly undergo natural selection. After two groups have separated, natural selection may act on each group in different ways. Over many generations, the separated groups may evolve different sets of traits. If the environmental conditions for each group differ, the adaptations in the groups will also differ.

Division

Over many generations, two separated groups of a population may become very different. Even if a geographical barrier is removed, the groups may not be able to interbreed anymore. At this point, the two groups are no longer the same species.

Figure 4 shows another way that populations may stop interbreeding. Leopard frogs and pickerel frogs probably had the same ancestor species. Then, at some point, some of these frogs began to mate at different times during the year.

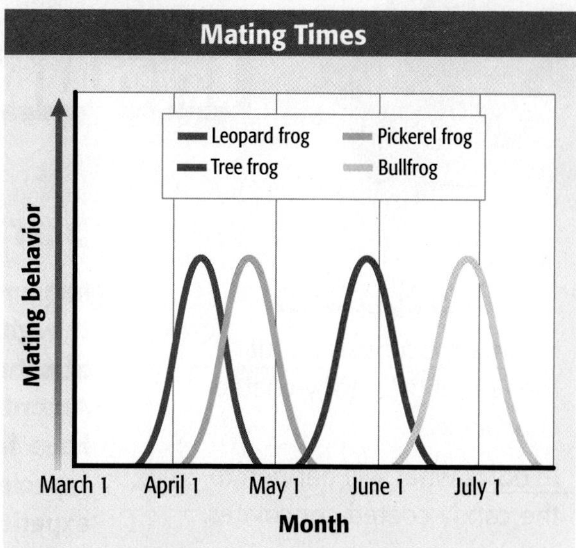

Figure 4 *The leopard frog and the pickerel frog are similar species. However, leopard frogs do not search for mates at the same time of year that pickerel frogs do.*

SECTION Review

Summary

- Natural selection explains how populations adapt to changes in their environment. A variety of examples of such adaptations can be found.
- Natural selection also explains how one species may evolve into another. Speciation occurs as populations undergo separation, adaptation, and division.

Using Key Terms

1. In your own words, write a definition for the term *speciation*.

Understanding Key Ideas

2. Two populations have evolved into two species when
   a. the populations are separated.
   b. the populations look different.
   c. the populations can no longer interbreed.
   d. the populations adapt.
3. Explain why the number of tuskless elephants in Uganda may be increasing.

Math Skills

4. A female cockroach can produce 80 offspring at a time. If half of the offspring produced by a certain female are female and each female produces 80 offspring, how many cockroaches are there in the third generation?

Critical Thinking

5. **Forming Hypotheses** Most kinds of cactus have leaves that grow in the form of spines. The stems or trunks become thick, juicy pads or barrels. Explain how these cactus parts might have evolved.
6. **Making Comparisons** Suggest an organism other than an insect that might evolve an adaptation to human activities.

Using Scientific Methods

Inquiry Lab

Survival of the Chocolates

OBJECTIVES

Form a hypothesis about the fate of the candy-coated chocolates.

Predict what will happen to the candy-coated chocolates.

Design and conduct an experiment to test your hypothesis.

MATERIALS

- chocolates, candy-coated, small, in a variety of colors (about 100)
- items to be determined by the students and approved by the teacher

SAFETY

Imagine a world populated with candy, and hold that delicious thought in your head for just a moment. Try to apply the idea of natural selection to a population of candy-coated chocolates. According to the theory of natural selection, individuals who have favorable adaptations are more likely to survive. In the "species" of candy-coated chocolates you will study in this experiment, the characteristics of individual chocolates may help them "survive." For example, shell strength (the strength of the candy coating) could be an adaptive advantage. Plan an experiment to find out which characteristics of the chocolates are favorable "adaptations."

Ask a Question

1. What might "survival" mean for a candy-coated chocolate? What are some ways you can test which chocolates are the "strongest" or "most fit" for their environment? Also, write down any other questions that you could ask about the "survival" of the chocolates.

Form a Hypothesis

2. Form a hypothesis, and make a prediction. For example, if you chose to study candy color, your prediction might be similar to this: If the ___ colored shell is the strongest, then fewer of the chocolates with this color of shell will ___ when ___.

Test the Hypothesis

3. Design a procedure to determine which type of candy-coated chocolate is most likely to survive. In your plan, be sure to include materials and tools you may need to complete this procedure.

4. Check your experimental design with your teacher before you begin. Your teacher will supply the candy and assist you in gathering materials and tools.

5. Record your results in a data table. Be sure to organize your data in a clear and understandable way.

Analyze the Results

1. **Describing Events** Write a report that describes your experiment. Be sure to include tables and graphs of the data you collected.

Draw Conclusions

2. **Evaluating Data** In your report, explain how your data either support or do not support your hypothesis. Include possible errors and ways to improve your procedure.

Applying Your Data

Can you think of another characteristic of the chocolates that can be tested to determine which type is best adapted to survive? Explain your idea, and describe how you might test it.

Chapter Review

USING KEY TERMS

Complete each of the following sentences by choosing the correct term from the word bank.

adaptation
evolution
generation time
species
speciation
fossil record
selective breeding
natural selection

1. When a single population evolves into two populations that cannot interbreed anymore, ___ has occurred.
2. Darwin's theory of ___ explained the process by which organisms become well-adapted to their environment.
3. A group of organisms that can mate with each other to produce offspring is known as a(n) ___.
4. The ___ provides information about organisms that have lived in the past.
5. In ___, humans select organisms with desirable traits that will be passed from one generation to another.
6. A(n) ___ helps an organism survive better in its environment.
7. Populations of insects and bacteria can evolve quickly because they usually have a short ___.

UNDERSTANDING KEY IDEAS

Multiple Choice

8. Fossils are commonly found in
   - **a.** sedimentary rock.
   - **b.** all kinds of rock.
   - **c.** granite.
   - **d.** loose sand.
9. The fact that all organisms have DNA as their genetic material is evidence that
   - **a.** all organisms undergo natural selection.
   - **b.** all organisms may have descended from a common ancestor.
   - **c.** selective breeding takes place every day.
   - **d.** genetic resistance rarely occurs.
10. Charles Darwin puzzled over differences in the ___ of the different species of Galápagos finches.
    - **a.** webbed feet
    - **b.** beaks
    - **c.** bone structure of the wings
    - **d.** eye color
11. Darwin observed variations among individuals within a population, but he did not realize that these variations were caused by
    - **a.** interbreeding.
    - **b.** differences in food.
    - **c.** differences in genes.
    - **d.** selective breeding.

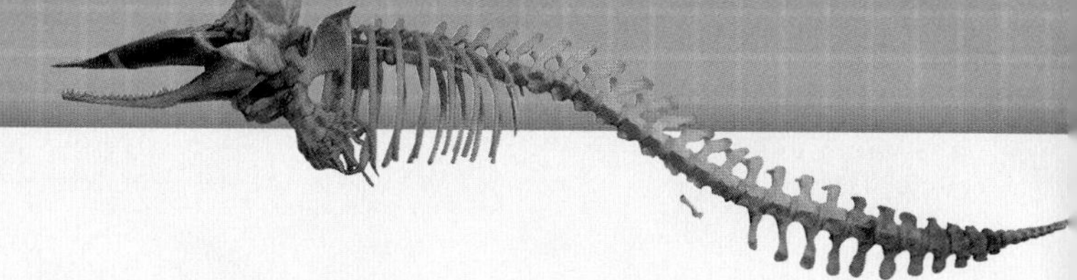

Short Answer

12 Identify two ways that organisms can be compared to provide evidence of evolution from a common ancestor.

13 Describe evidence that supports the hypothesis that whales evolved from land-dwelling mammals.

14 Why are some animals more likely to survive to adulthood than other animals are?

15 Explain how genetics is related to evolution.

16 Outline an example of the process of speciation.

CRITICAL THINKING

17 **Concept Mapping** Use the following terms to create a concept map: *struggle to survive, theory, genetic variation, Darwin, overpopulation, natural selection,* and *successful reproduction.*

18 **Making Inferences** How could natural selection affect the songs that birds sing?

19 **Forming Hypotheses** In Australia, many animals look like mammals from other parts of the world. But most of the mammals in Australia are marsupials, which carry their young in pouches after birth. Few kinds of marsupials are found anywhere else in the world. What is a possible explanation for the presence of so many of these unique mammals in Australia?

20 **Analyzing Relationships** Geologists have evidence that the continents were once a single giant continent. This giant landform eventually split apart, and the individual continents moved to their current positions. What role might this drifting of continents have played in evolution?

INTERPRETING GRAPHICS

The graphs below show information about the infants that are born and the infants that have died in a population. The weight of each infant was measured at birth. Use the graphs to answer the questions that follow.

Infant Births by Birth Weight

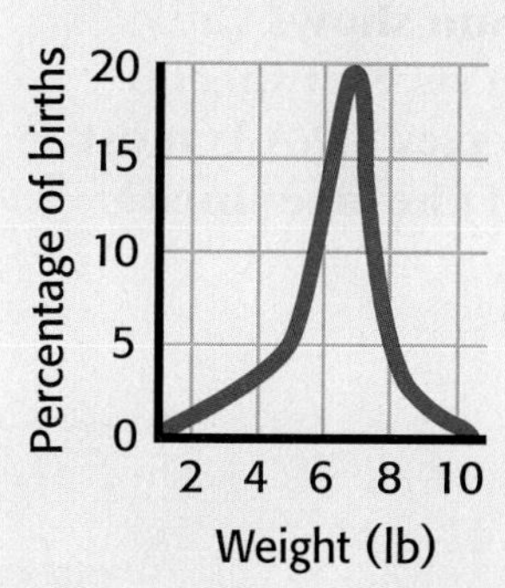

Infant Deaths by Birth Weight

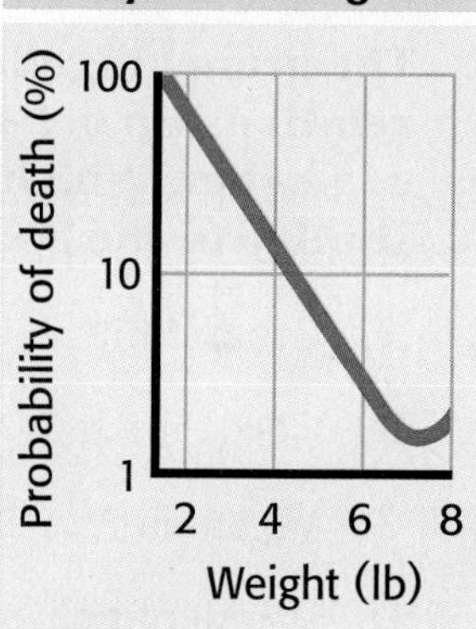

21 What is the most common birth weight?

22 At which birth weight is an infant most likely to survive?

23 How do the principles of natural selection help explain why there are more deaths among babies whose birth weights are low than among babies whose birth weights are average?

Multiple Choice

1. **Which of the following factors is necessary for natural selection to occur in a species?**

   A. genetic variation within a population

   B. an abundance of food resources

   C. a hospitable environment

   D. a strong family structure

Use the diagram below to answer question 2.

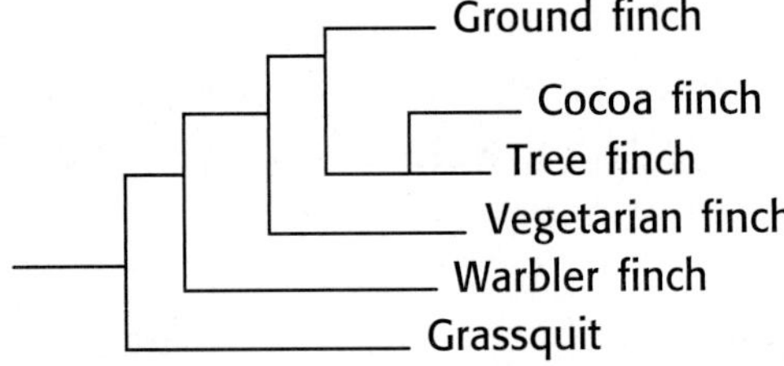

2. **The branching diagram shows the relationship between several species of finches. Which species' DNA is most similar to the DNA of the tree finch?**

   A. Ground finch

   B. Cocoa finch

   C. Vegetarian finch

   D. Warbler finch

3. **Which of the following is an example of natural selection?**

   A. Bears moving into a new part of a forest over many generations.

   B. A tree growing toward sunlight.

   C. Shrubs growing longer thorns over many generations.

   D. A plant growing between rocks.

4. **Charles Darwin noticed that finches on different islands of the Galápagos Islands were similar but that their beaks differed. What explanation for these differences did he propose?**

   A. The beaks of the finches are adapted to the way the bird usually gets food.

   B. The beaks of the finches are a randomly selected trait caused by genetic mutation.

   C. The different beaks of the finches would one day evolve into identical beaks.

   D. Beak size is related to the size of the finch.

5. **A scientist is studying fossils from different layers of sedimentary rock. From which rock layer would the fossils tend to resemble present-day organisms most closely?**

   A. older rock layers

   B. newer rock layers

   C. All rock layers would contain the same fossils.

   D. None of the fossils would resemble present-day organisms.

6. **A population of organisms is separated into two groups for many years. When would the two populations be considered two different species?**

   A. when the populations live in different habitats and look different

   B. when the populations eat different food

   C. when the populations behave differently

   D. when the populations can no longer interbreed and produce fertile offspring

7. Which of the following is an example of selective breeding?

A. Populations of lizards with a certain trait become more numerous after a change in climate.

B. Farmers allow only sheep that produce the best wool to breed.

C. A population of bacteria develops resistance to an antibiotic.

D. A population of insects develops resistance to a pesticide after farmers repeatedly use the same pesticide to kill the insects.

8. Alia purchased fruit flies from a biological supply company. One population of fruit flies had straight wings. The other population had wrinkled wings. The fruit flies with straight wings were able to fly, but the flies with wrinkled wings could not fly. Which is the best prediction about what would happen if all of the fruit flies were released into the natural environment?

A. The two types of flies would interbreed and produce flies with only slightly wrinkled wings.

B. The flies with straight wings would lack the correct traits to survive.

C. The flies with the wrinkled wings would lack the correct traits to survive.

D. None of the flies would survive.

Use the diagram below to answer question 9.

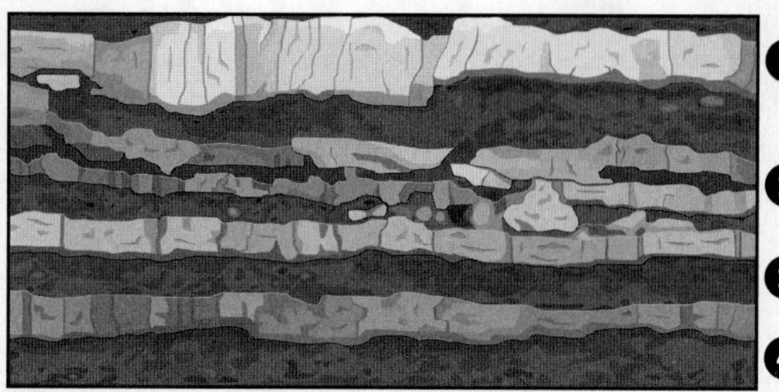

9. The diagram above shows the layers of sedimentary rock exposed during an archaeological dig. In layer 2, archaeologists discovered the fossil of a *Pakicetus*, a mammal that lived around 50 million years ago. In what layer would you expect to find the remains of an *Ambulocetus*, which existed after *Pakicetus* did?

A. layer 1

B. layer 2

C. layer 3

D. layer 4

Open Response

10. What is the relationship between genetics and evolution?

11. A scientist is studying several layers of rock at Big Black Mountain, the highest point in Kentucky. He finds several fossils in each layer. How can these fossils provide evidence of evolution?

Science in Action

Science, Technology, and Society

Seed Banks

All over the world, scientists are making deposits in a special kind of bank. These banks are not for money, but for seeds. Why should seeds be saved? Saving seeds saves plants that may someday save human lives. These plants could provide food or medicine in the future. Throughout human history, many medicines have been developed from plants. And scientists keep searching for new chemicals among the incredible variety of plants in the world. But time is running out. Many plant species are becoming extinct before they have even been studied.

Math ACTIVITY

Many drugs were originally developed from plants. Suppose that 100 plants are used for medicines this year, but 5% of plant species become extinct each year. How many of the medicinal plants would be left after 1 year? after 10 years? Round your answers to whole numbers.

Science Fiction

"The Anatomy Lesson" by Scott Sanders

Do you know the feeling you get when you have an important test? A medical student faces a similar situation in this story. The student needs to learn the bones of the human body for an anatomy exam the next day. The student goes to the anatomy library to study. The librarian lets him check out a box of bones that are supposed to be from a human skeleton. But something is wrong. There are too many bones. They are the wrong shape. They don't fit together correctly. Somebody must be playing a joke! Find out what's going on and why the student and the librarian will never be the same after "The Anatomy Lesson." You can read it in the *Holt Anthology of Science Fiction*.

Language Arts ACTIVITY

WRITING SKILL Before you read this story, predict what you think will happen. Write a paragraph that "gives away" the ending that you predict. After you have read the story, listen to some of the predictions made by your classmates. Discuss your opinions about the possible endings.

People in Science

Raymond Pierotti

Canine Evolution Raymond Pierotti thinks that it's natural that he became an evolutionary biologist. He grew up exploring the desert around his home in New Mexico. He was fascinated by the abundant wildlife surviving in the bleak landscape. "One of my earliest memories is getting coyotes to sing with me from my backyard," he says.

Pierotti now studies the evolutionary relationships between wolves, coyotes, and domestic dogs. Some of his ideas come from the traditions of the Comanches. According to the Comanche creation story, humans came from wolves. Although Pierotti doesn't believe that humans evolved from wolves, he sees the creation story as a suggestion that humans and wolves have evolved together. "Wolves are very similar to humans in many ways," says Pierotti. "They live in family groups and hunt together. It is possible that wolves actually taught humans how to hunt in packs, and there are ancient stories of wolves and humans hunting together and sharing the food. I think it was this relationship that inspired the Comanche creation stories."

Social Studies ACTIVITY

WRITING SKILL Research a story of creation that comes from a Greek, Roman, or Native American civilization. Write a paragraph summarizing the myth, and share it with a classmate.

To learn more about these Science in Action topics, visit **go.hrw.com** and type in the keyword **HL5EVOF.**

Current Science

Check out Current Science® articles related to this chapter by visiting go.hrw.com. Just type in the keyword HL5CS07.

The History of Life on Earth

The Big Idea

Geologic evidence allows us to understand the evolution of life on Earth.

SECTION

About the Photo

What is 23,000 years old and 9 ft tall? The partial remains of the woolly mammoth in this picture! The mammoth was found in the frozen ground in Siberia in 1999. Scientists think that several types of woolly mammoths roamed the northern hemisphere until about 4,000 years ago.

PRE-READING ACTIVITY

FOLDNOTES **Layered Book** Before you read the chapter, create the Foldnote entitled "Layered Book" described in the **Study Skills** section of the Appendix. Label the tabs of the layered book with "Precambrian time," "Paleozoic era," "Mesozoic era," and "Cenozoic era." As you read the chapter, write information you learn about each category under the appropriate tab.

START-UP ACTIVITY

Making a Fossil

In this activity, you will make a model of a fossil.

Procedure

1. Get a **paper plate,** some **modeling clay,** and a **leaf** or a **shell** from your teacher.
2. Flatten some of the modeling clay on the paper plate. Push the leaf or shell into the clay. Be sure that your leaf or shell has made a mark in the clay. Remove the leaf or shell carefully.
3. Ask your teacher to cover the clay with **plaster of Paris.** Allow the plaster to dry overnight.
4. Carefully remove the paper plate and the clay from the plaster the next day.

Analysis

1. Consider the following objects—a clam, a seed, a jellyfish, a crab, a leaf, and a mushroom. Which of the objects do you think would make good fossils? Explain your answers.
2. In nature, fossils form only under certain conditions. For example, fossils may form when a dead organism is covered by tiny bits of sand or dirt for a long period of time. The presence of oxygen can prevent fossils from forming. Considering these facts, what are some limitations of your model of how a fossil is formed?

SECTION 1

Evidence of the Past

What You Will Learn

- Explain how fossils can be formed and how their age can be estimated.
- Describe the geologic time scale and the way that scientists use it.
- Compare two ways that conditions for life on Earth have changed over time.

Vocabulary

fossil
relative dating
absolute dating
geologic time scale
extinct
plate tectonics

READING STRATEGY

Reading Organizer As you read this section, make a concept map by using the terms above.

In 1995, scientist Paul Sereno found a dinosaur skull that was 1.5 m long in the Sahara, a desert in Africa. The dinosaur may have been the largest land predator that has ever existed!

Scientists such as Paul Sereno look for clues to help them reconstruct what happened in the past. These scientists, called *paleontologists* (PAY lee uhn TAHL uh jists), use fossils to reconstruct the history of life before humans existed. Fossils show us that life on Earth has changed a great deal. They also provide us clues about how those changes happened.

Fossils

Fossils are traces or imprints of living things—such as animals, plants, bacteria, and fungi—that are preserved by geological processes. Fossils sometimes form when a dead organism is covered by a layer of sediment. The sediment may later be pressed together to form sedimentary rock. **Figure 1** shows one way that fossils can form in sedimentary rock.

fossil the trace or remains of an organism that lived long ago, most commonly preserved in sedimentary rock

Figure 1 One Way Fossils Can Form

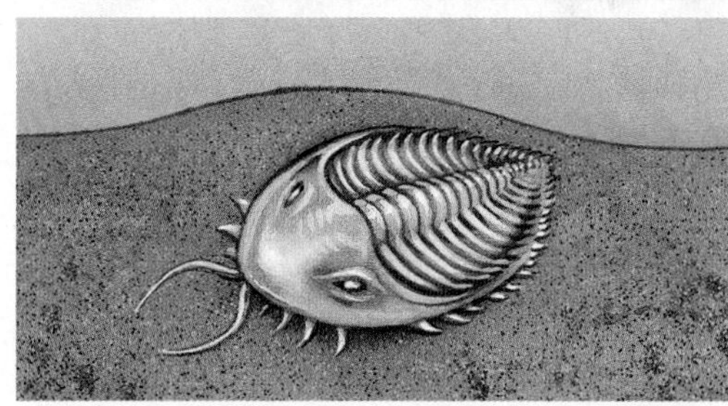

1 Fossils can form in several ways. The most common way is when an organism dies and becomes buried in sediment.

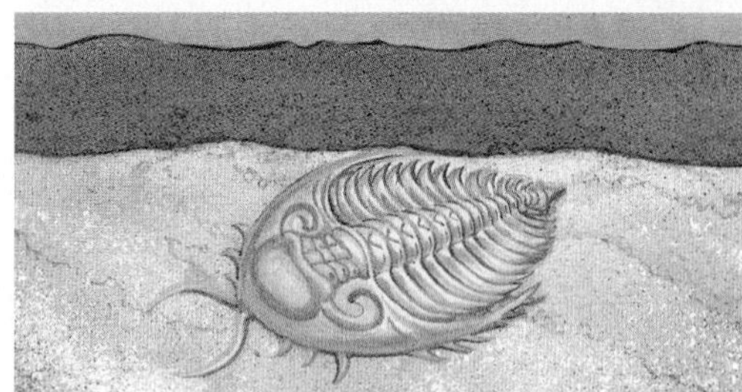

2 The organism gradually decomposes and leaves a hollow impression, or *mold*, in the sediment.

3 Over time, the mold fills with sediment, which forms a *cast* of the organism.

Figure 2 Using Half-Lives to Date Fossils

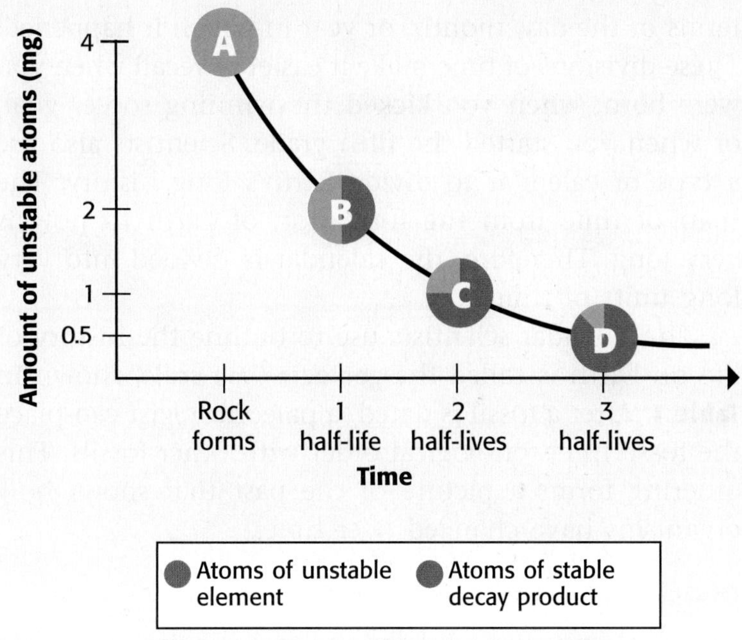

A The unstable atoms in this sample of rock have a half-life of 1.3 billion years. The sample contained 4 mg of unstable atoms when it formed.

B After 1.3 billion years, (one half-life for this type of unstable atom), 2 mg of the unstable atoms have decayed to become stable atoms, and 2 mg of unstable atoms remain.

C After 2.6 billion years (two half-lives for this sample), the rock sample contains 3 mg of stable decay atoms and 1 mg of unstable atoms.

D After three half-lives, only 0.5 mg of unstable atoms remain in the rock sample. This is equal to one-eighth of the original amount.

The Age of Fossils

Sedimentary rock has many layers. The oldest layers are usually on the bottom. The newest layers are usually on the top. The layers can tell a scientist the relative age of fossils. Fossils found in the bottom layers are usually older than the fossils in the top layers. So, scientists can determine whether a fossil is older or younger than other fossils based on its position in sedimentary rock. Estimating the age of rocks and fossils in this way is called **relative dating.**

In addition, scientists can determine the age of a fossil more precisely. **Absolute dating** is a method that measures the age of fossils or rocks in years. In one type of absolute dating, scientists examine atoms. *Atoms* are the particles that make up all matter. Atoms, in turn, are made of smaller particles. Some atoms are unstable and will decay by releasing energy, particles, or both. When an atom decays it becomes a different, and more stable, kind of atom. Each kind of unstable atom decays at its own rate. As shown in **Figure 2,** the time it takes for half of the unstable atoms in a sample to decay is the *half-life* of that type of unstable atom. By measuring the ratio of unstable atoms to stable atoms, scientists can determine the approximate age of a sample of rock.

Reading Check **Which type of fossil dating is more precise?** (*See the Appendix for answers to Reading Checks.*)

relative dating any method of determining whether an event or object is older or younger than other events or objects

absolute dating any method of measuring the age of an object or event in years

Fractions of Fractions

Find the answer to each of the following problems. Be sure to show your work. You may want to draw pictures.

1. 1/2 × 1/2 × 1/2 × 1/2

2. 1/2 × 1/8

3. 1/4 × 1/4

Table 1 Geologic Time Scale		
Era	**Period**	**Time***
Cenozoic era	Quaternary	1.8
	Tertiary	65.5
Mesozoic era	Cretaceous	146
	Jurassic	200
	Triassic	251
Paleozoic era	Permian	299
	Carboniferous	359
	Devonian	416
	Silurian	444
	Ordovician	488
	Cambrian	542
Precambrian time		4,600

**indicates how many millions of years ago the period began*

The Geologic Time Scale

Think about important events that have happened during your lifetime. You usually recall each event in terms of the day, month, or year in which it happened. These divisions of time make it easier to recall when you were born, when you kicked the winning soccer goal, or when you started the fifth grade. Scientists also use a type of calendar to divide Earth's long history. The span of time from the formation of Earth to now is very long. Therefore, the calendar is divided into very long units of time.

The calendar scientists use to outline the history of life on Earth is called the **geologic time scale,** shown in **Table 1.** After a fossil is dated, a paleontologist can place the fossil in chronological order with other fossils. This ordering forms a picture of the past that shows how organisms have changed over time.

Divisions in the Geologic Time Scale

Paleontologists have divided the geologic time scale into large blocks of time. Each block may be divided into smaller blocks of time as scientists continue to find more fossil information.

The divisions known as *eras* are characterized by the type of organism that dominated Earth at the time. For instance, the Mesozoic era—dominated by dinosaurs and other reptiles—is referred to as the *Age of Reptiles.* Eras began with a change in the type of organism that was most dominant.

Paleontologists sometimes adjust and add details to the geologic time scale. The early history of Earth has been poorly understood because fossils from this period are rare. So, the earliest part of the geologic time scale is not named as an era. But more evidence of life before the Paleozoic era is being gathered. Scientists have proposed using this evidence to name new eras before the Paleozoic era.

CONNECTION TO Social Studies

A Place in Time Most of the periods of the Paleozoic era were named by geologists for places where rocks from that period are found. Research the name of each period of the Paleozoic era listed in **Table 1.** On a copy of a world map, label the locations related to each name.

ACTIVITY

Figure 3 *Scientists think that a meteorite hit Earth about 65 million years ago and caused major climate changes.*

Mass Extinctions

Some of the important divisions in the geologic time scale mark times when rapid changes happened on Earth. During these times, many species died out completely, or became **extinct**. When a species is extinct, it does not reappear. At certain points in the Earth's history, a large number of species disappeared from the fossil record. These periods when many species suddenly become extinct are called *mass extinctions*.

Scientists are not sure what caused each of the mass extinctions. Most scientists think that the extinction of the dinosaurs happened because of extreme changes in the climate on Earth. These changes could have resulted from a giant meteorite hitting the Earth, as shown in **Figure 3.** Or, forces within the Earth could have caused many volcanoes and earthquakes.

geologic time scale the standard method used to divide the Earth's long natural history into manageable parts

extinct describes a species that has died out completely

Reading Check What are mass extinctions?

Making a Geologic Timeline

1. Use a **metric ruler** to mark 10 cm sections on a **strip of paper** that is 46 cm long.
2. Label each 10 cm section in order from top to bottom as follows: 1 bya (billion years ago), 2 bya, etc. The timeline begins at 4.6 bya.
3. Divide each 10 cm section into 10 equal subsections. Divide the top 1 cm into 10 subsections. Calculate the number of years that are represented by 1 mm on this scale.
4. On your timeline, label the following events:
   a. Earth forms. (4.6 billion years ago)
   b. First animals appear. (600 million years ago)
   c. Dinosaurs appear. (251 million years ago)
   d. Dinosaurs are extinct. (65 million years ago)
   e. Humans appear. (160,000 years ago)
5. Label other events from the chapter.
6. Describe what most of the timeline looks like.
7. Compare the length of time dinosaurs existed with the length of time humans have existed.

Figure 4 *The continents have been slowly moving throughout the history of Earth. The colored areas show the location of the continents 245 million years ago, and blue outlines show where the continents are today.*

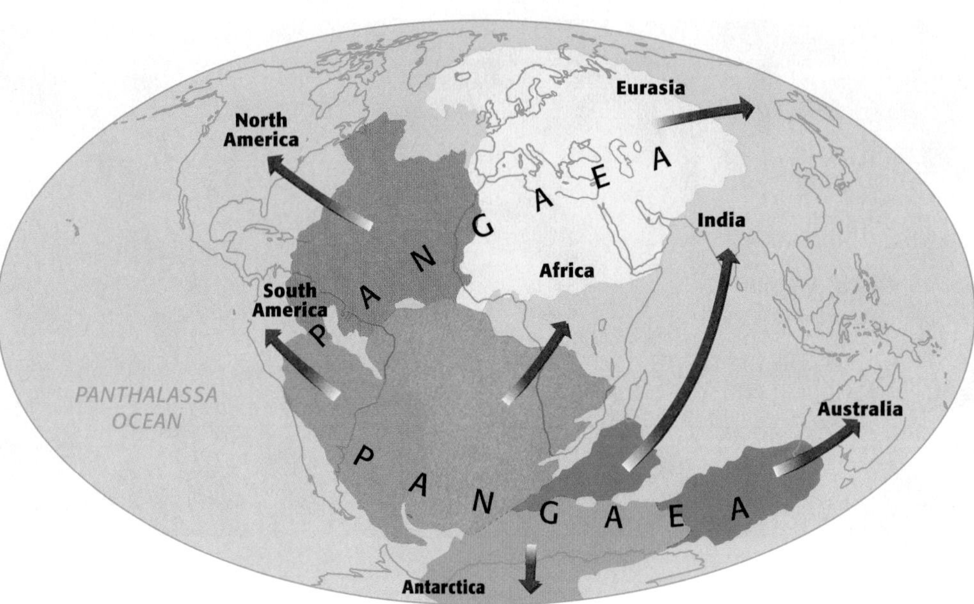

The Changing Earth

Did you know that fossils of tropical plants have been found in Antarctica? Antarctica, now frozen, must have once had a warm climate to support these plants. The fossils provide evidence that Antarctica was once located near the equator!

plate tectonics the theory that explains how large pieces of the Earth's outermost layer, called *tectonic plates,* move and change shape

Pangaea

Have you ever noticed that the continents look like pieces of a puzzle? German scientist Alfred Wegener had a similar thought in the early 1900s. He proposed that long ago the continents formed one landmass surrounded by a gigantic ocean. Wegener called that single landmass *Pangaea* (pan JEE uh), which means "all Earth." **Figure 4** shows how the continents may have formed from Pangaea.

Reading Check **What idea did Alfred Wegener propose?**

Do the Continents Move?

In the mid-1960s, J. Tuzo Wilson of Canada came up with the idea that the continents were not moving by themselves. Wilson thought that huge pieces of the Earth's crust were pushed around by forces within the planet. Each huge piece of crust is called a *tectonic plate.* Wilson's theory of how these huge pieces of crust move around the Earth is called **plate tectonics.**

According to Wilson, the outer crust of the Earth is broken into seven large, rigid plates and several smaller ones. The continents and oceans ride on top of these plates. The motion of the plates causes the continents to move. For example, the plates that carry South America and Africa are slowly moving apart, as shown in **Figure 5.**

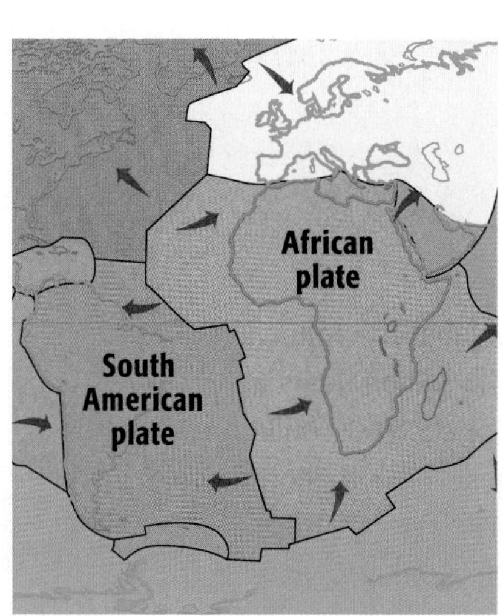

Figure 5 *The continents ride on tectonic plates, outlined here in black. The plates are still moving about 1 to 10 cm per year.*

Adaptation to Slow Changes

When conditions on the Earth change, organisms may become extinct. A rapid change, such as a meteorite impact, may cause a mass extinction. But slow changes, such as moving continents, allow time for adaptation.

Anywhere on Earth, you are able to see living things that are well adapted to the location where they live. Yet in the same location, you may find evidence of organisms that lived there in the past that were very different. For example, the animals currently living in Antarctica are able to survive very cold temperatures. But under the frozen surface of Antarctica are the remains of tropical forests. Conditions on Earth have changed many times in history, and life has changed, too.

Mid-Atlantic Ridge In 1947, scientists examined rock from a ridge that runs down the middle of the Atlantic Ocean, between Africa and the Americas. They found that this rock was much younger than the rock on the continents. Explain what this finding indicates about the tectonic plates.

SECTION Review

Summary

- Fossils are formed most often in sedimentary rock. The age of a fossil can be determined using relative dating and absolute dating.
- The geologic time scale is a timeline that is used by scientists to outline the history of Earth and life on Earth.
- Conditions for life on Earth have changed many times. Rapid changes, such as a meteorite impact, might have caused mass extinctions. But many groups of organisms have adapted to changes such as the movement of tectonic plates.

Using Key Terms

1. Use the following terms in the same sentence: *fossil* and *extinct*.
2. In your own words, write a definition for the term *plate tectonics*.

Understanding Key Ideas

3. Explain how a fossil forms in sedimentary rock.
4. What kind of information does the geologic time scale show?
5. About how many years of Earth's history was Precambrian time?
6. What are two possible causes of mass extinctions?

Math Skills

7. The Earth formed 4.6 billion years ago. Modern humans have existed for about 160,000 years. Simple worms have existed for at least 500 million years. For what fraction of the history of Earth have humans existed? have worms existed?

Critical Thinking

8. **Identifying Relationships** Why are both absolute dating and relative dating used to determine the age of fossils?
9. **Making Inferences** Fossils of *Mesosaurus,* the small aquatic reptile shown below, have been found only in Africa and South America. Using what you know about plate tectonics, how would you explain this finding?

SECTION 2

Eras of the Geologic Time Scale

What You Will Learn

- Outline the major developments that allowed life to exist on Earth.
- Describe the types of organisms that arose during the four major divisions of the geologic time scale.

Vocabulary

Precambrian time
Paleozoic era
Mesozoic era
Cenozoic era

READING STRATEGY

Mnemonics As you read this section, create a mnemonic device to help you remember the eras of geologic time.

The walls of the Grand Canyon are layered with different kinds and colors of rocks. The deeper down into the canyon you go, the older the layers of rocks. Try to imagine a time when the bottom layer was the only layer that existed.

Each layer of rock tells a story about what was happening on Earth when that layer was on top. The rocks and fossils in each layer tell the story. Scientists have compared the stories told by fossils and rocks all over the Earth. From these stories, scientists have divided geologic history into four major parts. These divisions are Precambrian time, the Paleozoic era, the Mesozoic era, and the Cenozoic era.

Precambrian Time

The layers at the bottom of the Grand Canyon are from the oldest part of the geologic time scale. **Precambrian time** (pree KAM bree UHN TIEM) is the time from the formation of Earth 4.6 billion years ago to about 542 million years ago. Life on Earth began during this time.

Scientists think that the early Earth was very different than it is today. The atmosphere was made of gases such as water vapor, carbon dioxide, and nitrogen. Also, the early Earth was a place of great turmoil, as illustrated in **Figure 1.** Volcanic eruptions, meteorite impacts, and violent storms were common. Intense radiation from the sun bombarded Earth's surface.

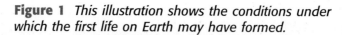

Precambrian time the period in the geologic time scale from the formation of the Earth to the beginning of the Paleozoic era, from about 4.6 billion to 542 million years ago

Reading Check **Describe the early Earth.** (*See the Appendix for answers to Reading Checks.*)

Figure 1 *This illustration shows the conditions under which the first life on Earth may have formed.*

How Did Life Begin?

Scientists think that life developed from simple chemicals in the oceans and in the atmosphere. Energy from radiation and storms could have caused these chemicals to react. Some of these reactions formed the complex molecules that made life possible. Eventually, these molecules may have joined to form structures such as cells.

The early atmosphere of the Earth did not contain oxygen gas. The first organisms did not need oxygen to survive. These organisms were *prokaryotes* (proh KAR ee OHTS), or single-celled organisms that lack a nucleus.

For another activity related to this chapter, go to **go.hrw.com** and type in the keyword **HL5HISW.**

Photosynthesis and Oxygen

There is evidence that *cyanobacteria,* a new kind of prokaryotic organism, appeared more than 3 billion years ago. Some cyanobacteria are shown in **Figure 2.** Cyanobacteria use sunlight to produce their own food. Along with doing other things, this process releases oxygen. The first cyanobacteria began to release oxygen gas into the oceans and air.

Eventually, some of the oxygen formed a new layer of gas in the upper atmosphere. This gas, called *ozone,* absorbs harmful radiation from the sun, as shown in **Figure 3.** Before ozone formed, life existed only in the oceans and underground. The new ozone layer reduced the radiation on Earth's surface.

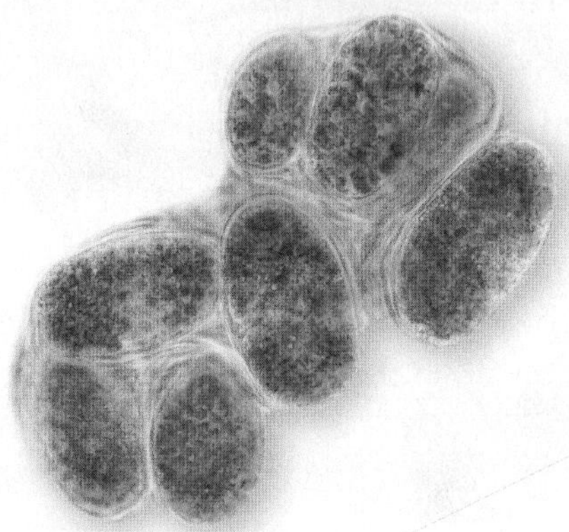

Figure 2 *Cyanobacteria are the simplest living organisms that use the sun's energy to produce their own food.*

Multicellular Organisms

After about 1 billion years, organisms that were larger and more complex than prokaryotes appeared in the fossil record. These organisms, known as *eukaryotes* (yoo KAR ee OHTS), contain a nucleus and other complex structures in their cells. Eventually, eukaryotic cells may have evolved into organisms that are composed of many cells.

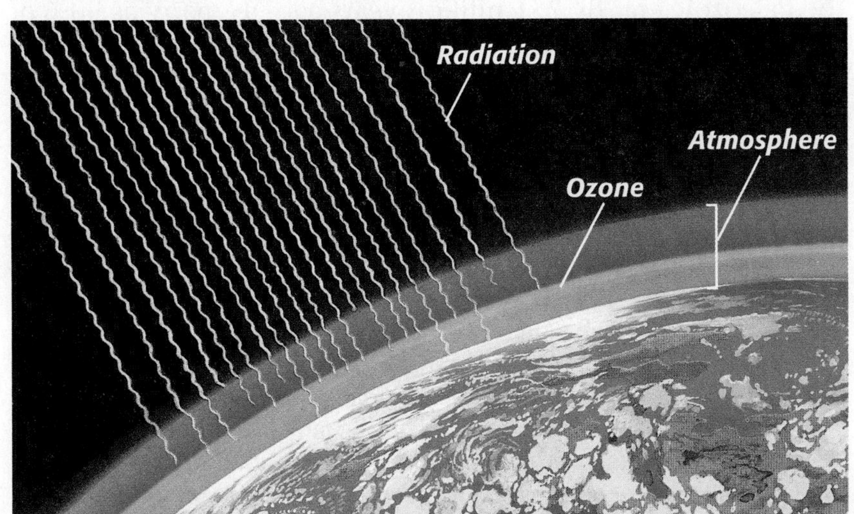

Figure 3 *Oxygen in the atmosphere formed a layer of ozone, which helps to absorb harmful radiation from the sun.*

The Paleozoic Era

The **Paleozoic era** (PAY lee OH ZOH ik ER uh) began about 542 million years ago and ended about 251 million years ago. Considering the length of Precambrian time, you can see that the Paleozoic era was relatively recent. Rocks from the Paleozoic era are rich in fossils of animals such as sponges, corals, snails, clams, squids, and trilobites. Fishes, the earliest animals with backbones, appeared during this era, and sharks became abundant. **Figure 4** shows an artist's depiction of life in the Paleozoic era.

The word *Paleozoic* comes from Greek words that mean "ancient life." When scientists first named this era, they thought it held the earliest forms of life. Scientists now think that earlier forms of life existed, but less is known about those life-forms. Before the Paleozoic era, most organisms lived in the oceans and left few fossils.

Figure 4 *Organisms that first appeared in the Paleozoic era include reptiles, amphibians, fishes, worms, and ferns.*

Life on Land

During the 300 million years of the Paleozoic era, plants, fungi, and air-breathing animals slowly colonized land. By the end of the era, forests of giant ferns, club mosses, horsetails, and conifers covered much of the Earth. All major plant groups except for flowering plants appeared during this era. These plants provided food and shelter for animals.

Fossils indicate that crawling insects were some of the first animals to live on land. They were followed by large salamander-like animals. Near the end of the Paleozoic era, reptiles and winged insects appeared.

The largest mass extinction known took place at the end of the Paleozoic era. By 251 million years ago, as many as 90% of marine species had become extinct. The mass extinction wiped out entire groups of marine organisms, such as trilobites. The oceans were completely changed.

Paleozoic era the geologic era that followed Precambrian time and that lasted from 542 million to 251 million years ago

CONNECTION TO Oceanography

Prehistoric Marine Organisms Find a variety of pictures and descriptions of marine organisms from the Cambrian period of the Paleozoic era. Choose three organisms that you find interesting. Draw or write a description of each organism. Find out whether scientists think the organism is related to any living group of organisms, and add this information to your description.

The Mesozoic Era

The **Mesozoic era** (MES oh ZOH ik ER uh) began about 251 million years ago and lasted about 185.5 million years. *Mesozoic* comes from Greek words that mean "middle life." Scientists think that the surviving reptiles evolved into many different species after the Paleozoic era. Therefore, the Mesozoic era is commonly called the *Age of Reptiles*.

Life in the Mesozoic Era

Dinosaurs are the most well known reptiles that evolved during the Mesozoic era. Dinosaurs dominated the Earth for about 150 million years. A great variety of dinosaurs lived on Earth. Some had unique adaptations, such as ducklike bills for feeding or large spines on their bodies for defense. In addition to dinosaurs roaming the land, giant marine lizards swam in the ocean. The first birds also appeared during the Mesozoic era. In fact, scientists think that some of the dinosaurs became the ancestors of birds.

The most important plants during the early part of the Mesozoic era were conifers, which formed large forests. Flowering plants appeared later in the Mesozoic era. Some of the organisms of the Mesozoic era are illustrated in **Figure 5.**

Figure 5 *The Mesozoic era was dominated by dinosaurs. The era ended with the mass extinction of many species.*

The Extinction of Dinosaurs

At the end of the Mesozoic era, 65.5 million years ago, dinosaurs and many other animal and plant species became extinct. What happened to the dinosaurs? According to one hypothesis, a large meteorite hit the Earth and generated giant dust clouds and enough heat to cause worldwide fires. The dust and smoke from these fires blocked out much of the sunlight and caused many plants to die out. Without enough plants to eat, the plant-eating dinosaurs died out. And the meat-eating dinosaurs that fed on the plant-eating dinosaurs died. Global temperatures may have dropped for many years. However, some mammals and birds survived.

Reading Check **What kind of event happened at the end of both the Paleozoic and Mesozoic eras?**

Mesozoic era the geologic era that lasted from 251 million to 65.5 million years ago; also called the *Age of Reptiles*

Figure 6 *Many types of mammals evolved during the Cenozoic era.*

The Cenozoic Era

The **Cenozoic era** (SEN uh ZOH ik ER uh) began about 65 million years ago and continues today. *Cenozoic* comes from Greek words that mean "recent life." Scientists have more information about the Cenozoic era than about any of the previous eras. Fossils from the Cenozoic era formed recently in geologic time, so they are found in rock layers closer to the Earth's surface. The closer the fossils are to the surface, the easier they are to find.

During the Cenozoic era, many kinds of mammals, birds, insects, and flowering plants appeared. Some organisms that appeared in the Cenozoic era are shown in **Figure 6.**

Reading Check What does *Cenozoic* mean?

The Age of Mammals

The Cenozoic era is sometimes called the *Age of Mammals*. Mammals have dominated the Cenozoic era the way reptiles dominated the Mesozoic era. Early Cenozoic mammals were small, forest dwellers. Larger mammals appeared later in the era. Some of these larger mammals had long legs for running, teeth that were specialized for eating different kinds of food, and large brains. Cenozoic mammals have included mastodons, saber-toothed cats, camels, giant ground sloths, and small horses.

MATH FOCUS

Relative Scale It's hard to imagine 4.6 billion years. One way is to use a *relative scale*. For example, we can represent all of Earth's history by using the 12 h shown on a clock. The scale would begin at noon, representing 4.6 billion years ago, and end at midnight, representing the present. Because 12 h represent 4.6 billion years, 1 h represents about 383 million years. (Hint: 4.6 billion ÷ 12 = 383 million) So, what time on the clock represents the beginning of the Paleozoic era, 543 million years ago?

Step 1: Write the ratio.

$$\frac{x}{543{,}000{,}000 \text{ years}} = \frac{1 \text{ h}}{383{,}000{,}000 \text{ years}}$$

Step 2: Solve for x.

$$x = \frac{543{,}000{,}000 \text{ years} \times 1 \text{ h}}{383{,}000{,}000 \text{ years}} = 1.42 \text{ h}$$

Step 3: Convert the answer to the clock scale.

$$1.42 \text{ h} = 1 \text{ h} + (0.42 \times 60 \text{ min/h})$$

$$1.42 \text{ h} = 1 \text{ h } 25 \text{ min}$$

So, the Paleozoic era began 1 h 25 min before midnight, at about 10:35.

Now It's Your Turn

1. Use this method to calculate the relative times at which the Mesozoic and Cenozoic eras began.

The Cenozoic Era Today

We are currently living in the Cenozoic era. Modern humans appeared during this era. The environment and landscapes that we see around us today are part of this era.

However, the climate has changed many times during the Cenozoic era. Earth's history includes some periods called *ice ages,* during which the climate was very cold. During the ice ages, ice sheets and glaciers extended from the Earth's poles. To survive, many organisms migrated toward the equator. Other organisms adapted to the cold or became extinct.

When will the Cenozoic era end? No one knows. In the future, geologists might draw the line at a time when life on Earth again undergoes major changes.

Cenozoic era the most recent geologic era, beginning 65 million years ago; also called the *Age of Mammals*

SECTION Review

Summary

- The Earth is about 4.6 billion years old. Life formed from nonliving matter long ago.
- Precambrian time includes the formation of the Earth and the appearance of simple organisms.
- The first cells did not need oxygen. Later, photosynthetic cells evolved and released oxygen into the atmosphere.
- During the Paleozoic era, animals appeared in the oceans and on land, and plants grew on land.
- Dinosaurs dominated the Earth during the Mesozoic era.
- Mammals have dominated the Cenozoic era. This era continues today.

Using Key Terms

1. Use each of the following terms in a separate sentence: *Precambrian time, Paleozoic era, Mesozoic era,* and *Cenozoic era.*

Understanding Key Ideas

2. Unlike the atmosphere today, the atmosphere 3.5 billion years ago did not contain
   - **a.** carbon dioxide.
   - **b.** nitrogen.
   - **c.** gases.
   - **d.** ozone.
3. How do prokaryotic cells and eukaryotic cells differ?
4. Explain why cyanobacteria were important to the development of life on Earth.
5. Place in chronological order the following events on Earth:
   - **a.** The first cells appeared that could make their own food from sunlight.
   - **b.** The ozone layer formed.
   - **c.** Simple chemicals reacted to form the molecules of life.
   - **d.** Animals appeared.
   - **e.** The first organisms appeared.
   - **f.** Humans appeared.
   - **g.** The Earth formed.

Math Skills

6. Calculate the total number of years that each of the geologic eras lasted, rounding to the nearest 100 million. Then, calculate each of these values as a percentage of the total 4.6 billion years of Earth's history. Round your answer to the units place.

Critical Thinking

7. **Making Inferences** Which chemicals probably made up the first cells on Earth?
8. **Forming Hypotheses** Think of your own hypothesis to explain the disappearance of the dinosaurs. Explain your hypothesis.

SCILINKS.
NSTA
Developed and maintained by the National Science Teachers Association
For a variety of links related to this chapter, go to www.scilinks.org
Topic: Geologic Time Scale
SciLinks code: HSM0669

SECTION 3

Humans and Other Primates

What You Will Learn

- Describe two characteristics that all primates share.
- Describe three major groups of hominids.

Vocabulary

primate
hominid
Homo sapiens

READING STRATEGY

Discussion Read this section silently. Write down questions that you have about this section. Discuss your questions in a small group.

Have you ever heard someone say that humans descended from monkeys or apes? Well, scientists would not exactly say that. The scientific theory is that humans, apes, and monkeys share a common ancestor. This common ancestor probably lived more than 45 million years ago.

Most scientists agree that there is enough evidence to support this theory. Many fossils of organisms have been found that show traits of both humans and apes. Also, comparisons of modern humans and apes support this theory.

Primates

What characteristics make us human? Humans are classified as primates. **Primates** are a group of mammals that includes humans, apes, monkeys, and lemurs. Primates have the characteristics illustrated in **Figure 1.**

The First Primates

The ancestors of primates may have co-existed with the dinosaurs. These ancestors were probably mouselike mammals that were active at night, lived in trees, and ate insects. The first primates did not exist until after the dinosaurs died out. About 45 million years ago, primates that had larger brains appeared. These were the first primates that had traits similar to monkeys, apes, and humans.

Figure 1 Characteristics of Primates

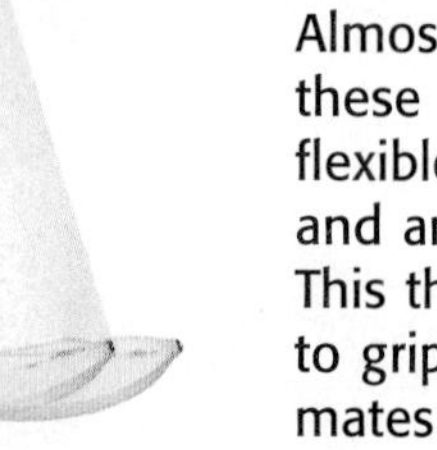

Both eyes are located at the front of the head, and they provide binocular, or three-dimensional, vision.

Almost all primates, such as these orangutans, have five flexible fingers—four fingers and an opposable thumb. This thumb enables primates to grip objects. Most primates besides humans also have opposable big toes.

Apes and Chimpanzees

Scientists think that the chimpanzee, a type of ape, is the closest living relative of humans. This theory does not mean humans descended from chimpanzees. It means that humans and chimpanzees share a common ancestor. Sometime between 6 million and 30 million years ago, the ancestors of humans, chimpanzees, and other apes began to evolve along different lines.

primate a type of mammal characterized by opposable thumbs and binocular vision

Hominids

Humans are in a family separate from other primates. This family, called **hominids,** includes only humans and their human-like ancestors. The main characteristic that separates hominids from other primates is bipedalism. *Bipedalism* means "walking primarily upright on two feet." Evidence of bipedalism can be seen in a primate's skeletal structure. **Figure 2** shows a comparison of the skeletal features of apes and hominids.

hominid a type of primate characterized by bipedalism, relatively long lower limbs, and lack of a tail

Reading Check **In which family are humans classified?** (*See the Appendix for answers to Reading Checks.*)

Figure 2 **Comparison of Primate Skeletons**

The bones of gorillas (a type of ape) and humans (a type of hominid) have a very similar form, but the human skeleton is adapted for walking upright.

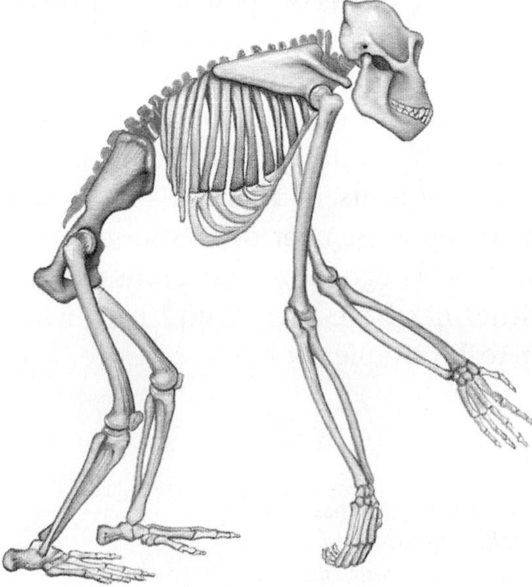

▲ The gorilla pelvis tilts the ape's large rib cage and heavy neck and head forward. The gorilla spine is curved in a C shape. The arms are long to provide balance on the ground.

The human pelvis is vertical and helps hold the entire skeleton upright. The human spine is curved in an S shape. The arms are shorter than the legs. ▶

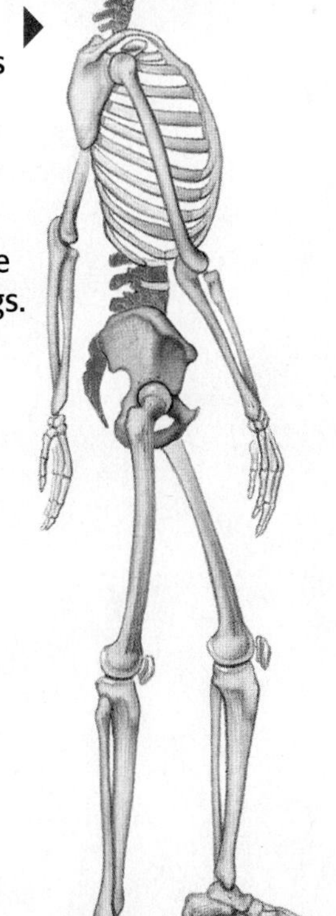

Hominids Through Time

Scientists are constantly filling in pieces of the hominid family picture. They have found many different fossils of ancient hominids and have named at least 18 types of hominids. However, scientists do not agree on the classification of every fossil. Fossils are classified as hominids when they share some of the characteristics of modern humans. But each type of hominid was unique in terms of size, the way it walked, the shape of its skull, and other characteristics.

Figure 3 *This skull was found in the Sahel desert in Chad, Africa. The skull is estimated to be 6 million to 7 million years old.*

The Earliest Hominids

The earliest hominids had traits that were more humanlike than apelike. These traits include the ability to walk upright as well as smaller teeth, flatter faces, and larger brains than earlier primates. The oldest hominid fossils have been found in Africa. So, scientists think hominid evolution began in Africa. **Figure 3** shows a fossil that may be from one of the earliest hominids. It is 6 million to 7 million years old.

Reading Check **Where are the earliest hominid fossils found?**

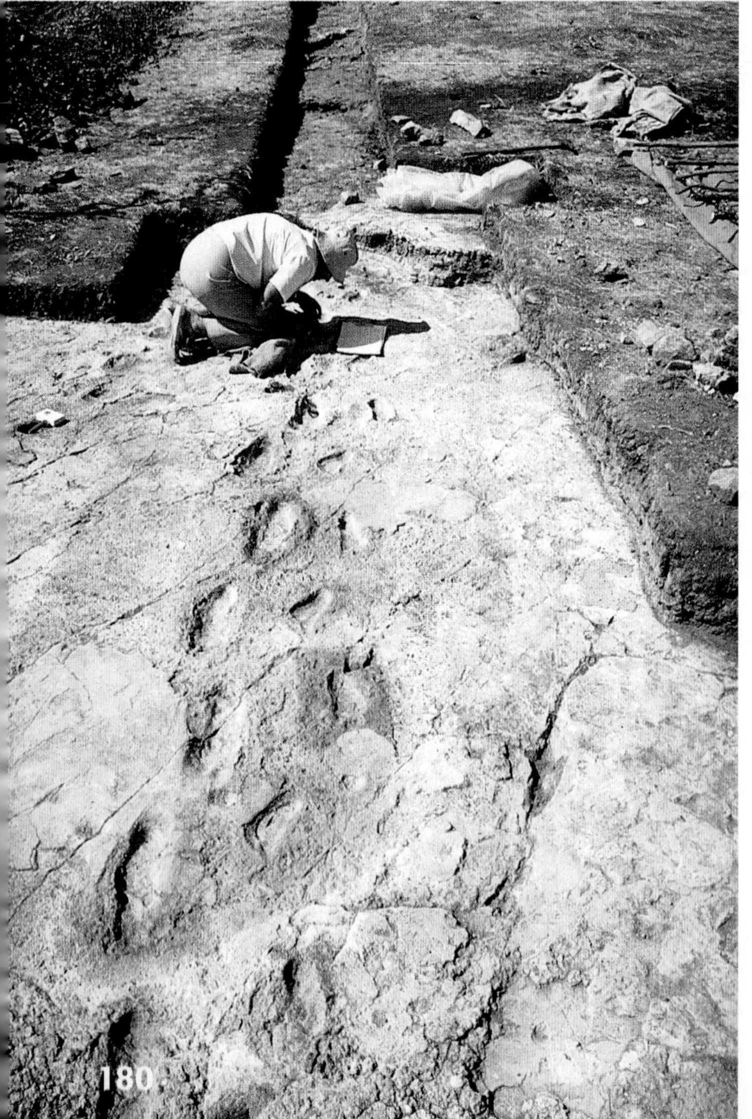

Australopithecines

Many early hominids are classified as *australopithecines* (AW struh LOH PITH uh SEENS). Members of this group were similar to apes but were different from apes in several ways. For example, their brains were slightly larger than the brains of apes. Some of them may have used stone tools. They climbed trees but also walked on two legs.

Fossil evidence of australopithecines has been found in several places in Africa. The fossilized footprints in **Figure 4** were probably made by a member of this group over 3 million years ago. Some skeletons of australopithecines have been found near what appear to be simple tools.

Figure 4 *Anthropologist Mary Leakey discovered these 3.6 million year old footprints in Tanzania, Africa.*

A Variety of Early Hominids

Many australopithecines and other types of hominids lived at the same time. Some australopithecines had slender bodies. They had humanlike jaws and teeth but had small, apelike skulls. They probably lived in forests and grasslands and ate a vegetarian diet. Scientists think that some of these types of hominids may have been the ancestors of modern humans.

Some early hominids had large bodies and massive teeth and jaws. They had a unique skull structure and relatively small brains. Most of these types of hominids lived in tropical forests and probably ate tough plant material, such as roots. Scientists do not think that these large-bodied hominids are the ancestors of modern humans.

Global Hominids

About 2.4 million years ago, a new group of hominids appeared. These hominids were similar to the slender australopithecines but were more humanlike. These new hominids had larger and more complex brains, rounder skulls, and flatter faces than early hominids. They showed advanced tool-making abilities and walked upright.

These new hominids were members of the group *Homo,* which includes modern humans. Fossil evidence indicates that several members of the *Homo* group existed at the same time and on several continents. Members of this group were probably scavengers that ate a variety of foods. Some of these hominids may have adapted to climate change by migrating and changing the way they lived.

An early member of this new group was *Homo habilis* (HOH moh HAB uh luhs), which lived about 2.4 million years ago. About 1.8 million years ago, a hominid called *Homo erectus* (HOH moh i REK tuhs) appeared. This type of hominid could grow as tall as modern humans do. A museum creation of a member of *Homo erectus* is shown in **Figure 5.** No one knows what early hominids looked like. Scientists construct models based on skulls and other evidence.

Thumb Through This

1. Keep your thumbs from moving by attaching them to the sides of your hands with **tape.**
2. Attempt each of the following tasks: using a **pencil sharpener,** using **scissors,** tying your **shoelaces,** buttoning **buttons.**
3. After each attempt, answer the following questions:
   a. Is the task more difficult with an opposable thumb or without one?
   b. Do you think you would carry out this task on a regular basis if you did not have an opposable thumb?

ACTIVITY

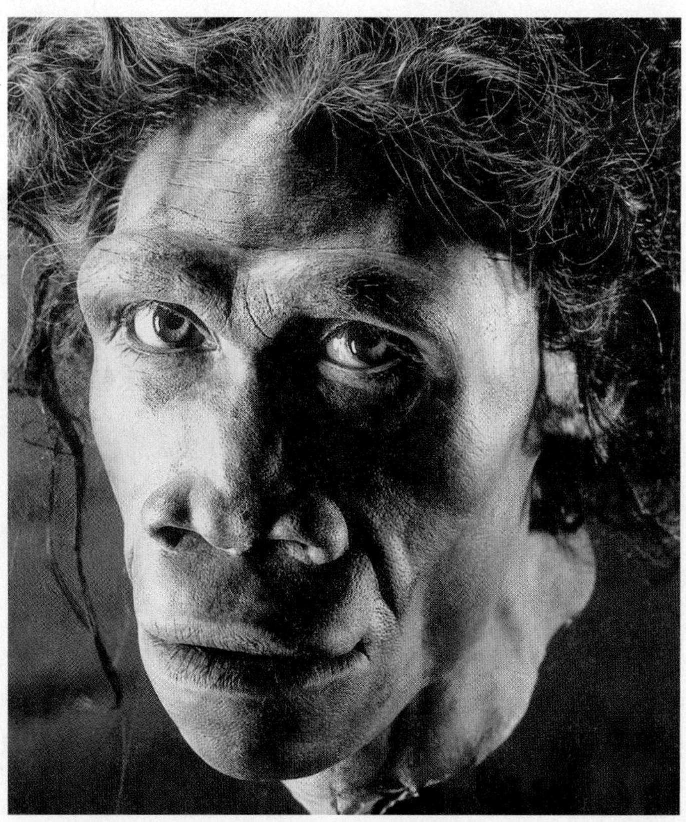

Figure 5 *Fossils of a hominid known as* Homo erectus *have been found in Africa, Europe, and Asia.*

Recent Hominids

As recently as 30,000 years ago, two types of hominids may have lived in the same areas at the same time. Both had the largest brains of any hominids and made advanced tools, clothing, and art. Scientists think that modern humans may have descended from one of these two types of hominids.

Neanderthals

One recent hominid is known as *Neanderthal* (nee AN duhr TAWL). Neanderthals lived in Europe and western Asia. They may have lived as early as 230,000 years ago. They hunted large animals, made fires, and wore clothing. They also may have cared for the sick and elderly and buried their dead with cultural rituals. About 30,000 years ago, Neanderthals disappeared. No one knows what caused their extinction.

Homo sapiens the species of hominids that includes modern humans and their closest ancestors and that first appeared about 100,000 to 160,000 years ago

Early and Modern Humans

Modern humans are classified as the species ***Homo sapiens*** (HOH moh SAY pee UHNZ). The earliest *Homo sapiens* existed in Africa 100,000 to 160,000 years ago. The group migrated out of Africa sometime between 40,000 and 100,000 years ago. Compared with Neanderthals, *Homo sapiens* has a smaller and flatter face, and has a skull that is more rounded. Of all known hominids, only *Homo sapiens* still exists.

Early *Homo sapiens* created large amounts of art. Early humans produced sculptures, carvings, paintings, and clothing such as that shown in **Figure 6.** The preserved villages and burial grounds of early humans show that they had an organized and complex society.

Figure 6 *These photos show museum recreations of early* Homo sapiens.

Drawing the Hominid Family Tree

Scientists review their hypotheses when they learn something new about a group of organisms and their related fossils. As more hominid fossils are discovered, there are more features to compare. Sometimes, scientists add details to the relationships they see between each group. Sometimes, new groups of hominids are recognized. Human evolution was once thought to be a line of descent from ancient primates to modern humans. But scientists now speak of a "tree" or even a "bush" to describe the evolution of various hominids in the fossil record.

Reading Check **What is likely to happen when a new hominid fossil is discovered?**

SECTION Review

Summary

- Humans, apes, and monkeys are primates. Almost all primates have opposable thumbs and binocular vision.
- Hominids, a subgroup of primates, include humans and their humanlike ancestors. The oldest known hominid fossils may be 7 million years old.
- Early hominids included australopithecines and the *Homo* group.
- Early *Homo sapiens* did not differ very much from present-day humans. *Homo sapiens* is the only type of hominid living today.

Using Key Terms

1. Use each of the following words in the same sentence: *primate, hominid,* and *Homo sapiens.*

Understanding Key Ideas

2. The unique characteristics of primates are
   a. bipedalism and thumbs.
   b. opposable thumbs.
   c. opposable thumbs and binocular vision.
   d. opposable toes and thumbs.
3. Describe the major evolutionary developments from early hominids to modern humans.
4. Compare members of the *Homo* group with australopithecines.

Critical Thinking

5. **Forming Hypotheses** Suggest some reasons why Neanderthals might have become extinct.
6. **Making Inferences** Imagine you are a scientist excavating an ancient campsite. What might you infer about the people who used the site if you found the charred bones of large animals and various stone blades among human fossils?

Interpreting Graphics

The figure below shows a possible ancestral relationships between humans and some modern apes. Use this figure to answer the questions that follow.

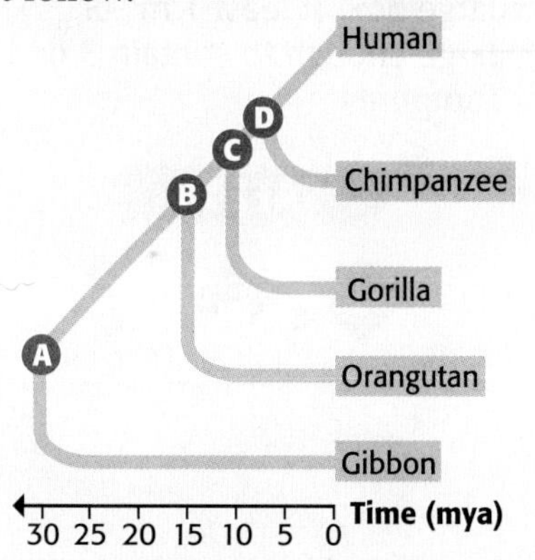

7. Which letter represents the ancestor of all the apes?
8. To which living ape are gorillas most closely related?

Using Scientific Methods

Inquiry Lab

Mystery Footprints

Sometimes, scientists find clues preserved in rocks that are evidence of the activities of organisms that lived thousands of years ago. Evidence such as preserved footprints can provide important information about an organism. Imagine that your class has been asked by a group of scientists to help study some human footprints. These footprints were found embedded in rocks in an area just outside of town.

OBJECTIVES

Form a hypothesis to explain observations of traces left by other organisms.

Design and **conduct** an experiment to test one of these hypotheses.

Analyze and **communicate** the results in a scientific way.

MATERIALS

- ruler, metric or meterstick
- sand, slightly damp
- large box, at least 1 m^2 or large enough to contain 3 or 4 footprints

SAFETY

Ask a Question

1. Your teacher will give you some mystery footprints in sand. Examine the mystery footprints. Brainstorm what you might learn about the people who walked on this patch of sand.

Form a Hypothesis

2. As a class, formulate several testable hypotheses about the people who left the footprints. Form groups of three people, and choose one hypothesis for your group to investigate.

Test the Hypothesis

3. Draw a table for recording your data. For example, if you have two sets of mystery footprints, your table might look similar to the one below.

Mystery Footprints		
	Footprint set 1	**Footprint set 2**
Length		
Width		
Depth of toe	DO NOT WRITE IN BOOK	
Depth of heel		
Length of stride		

4. With the help of your group, you may first want to analyze your own footprints to help you draw conclusions about the mystery footprints. For example, use a meterstick to measure your stride when you are running. Is your stride different when you are walking? What part of your foot touches the ground first when you are running? When you are running, which part of your footprint is deeper?

5. Make a list of the kind of footprint each different activity produces. For example, you might write, "When I am running, my footprints are deep near the toe area and 110 cm apart."

Analyze the Results

1. **Classifying** Compare the data from your footprints with the data from the mystery footprints. How are the footprints alike? How are they different?

2. **Identifying Patterns** How many people do you think made the mystery footprints? Explain your interpretation.

3. **Analyzing Data** Can you tell if the mystery footprints were made by men, women, children, or a combination? Can you tell if they were standing still, walking, or running? Explain your interpretation.

Draw Conclusions

4. **Drawing Conclusions** Do your data support your hypothesis? Explain.

5. **Evaluating Methods** How could you improve your experiment?

Communicating Your Data

WRITING SKILL Summarize your group's conclusions in a report for the scientists who asked for your help. Begin by stating your hypothesis. Then, summarize the methods you used to study the footprints. Include the comparisons you made between your footprints and the mystery footprints. Add pictures if you wish. State your conclusions. Finally, offer some suggestions about how you could improve your investigation.

Chapter Review

USING KEY TERMS

Complete each of the following sentences by choosing the correct term from the word bank.

Precambrian time	Paleozoic era
Mesozoic era	Cenozoic era

1. During ___, life is thought to have originated from nonliving matter.
2. The Age of Mammals refers to the ___.
3. The Age of Reptiles refers to the ___.
4. Plants colonized land during the ___.

For each pair of terms, explain how the meanings of the terms differ.

5. *relative dating* and *absolute dating*
6. *primates* and *hominids*

UNDERSTANDING KEY IDEAS

Multiple Choice

7. If the half-life of an unstable element is 5,000 years, what percentage of the parent material will be left after 10,000 years?
   - **a.** 100%
   - **b.** 75%
   - **c.** 50%
   - **d.** 25%
8. The first cells on Earth appeared in
   - **a.** Precambrian time.
   - **b.** the Paleozoic era.
   - **c.** the Mesozoic era.
   - **d.** the Cenozoic era.
9. In which era are we currently living?
   - **a.** Precambrian time
   - **b.** Paleozoic era
   - **c.** Mesozoic era
   - **d.** Cenozoic era
10. Scientists think that the closest living relatives of humans are
    - **a.** lemurs.
    - **b.** monkeys.
    - **c.** gorillas.
    - **d.** chimpanzees.

Short Answer

11. Describe how plant and animal remains can become fossils.
12. What information do fossils provide about the history of life?
13. List three important steps in the early development of life on Earth.
14. List two important groups of organisms that appeared during each of the three most recent geologic eras.
15. Describe the event that scientists think caused the mass extinction at the end of the Mesozoic era.

16 From which geologic era are fossils most commonly found?

17 Describe two characteristics that are shared by all primates.

18 Which hominid species is alive today?

CRITICAL THINKING

19 **Concept Mapping** Use the following terms to create a concept map: *Earth's history, humans, Paleozoic era, dinosaurs, Precambrian time, land plants, Mesozoic era, cyanobacteria,* and *Cenozoic era.*

20 **Applying Concepts** Can footprints be fossils? Explain your answer.

21 **Making Inferences** If you find rock layers containing fish fossils in a desert, what can you infer about the history of the desert?

22 **Applying Concepts** Explain how an environmental change can threaten the survival of a species. Give two examples.

23 **Analyzing Ideas** Why do scientists think the first cells did not need oxygen to survive?

24 **Identifying Relationships** How does the extinction that occurred at the end of the Mesozoic era relate to the Age of Mammals?

25 **Making Comparisons** Make a table listing the similarities and differences between australopithecines, early members of the group *Homo*, and modern members of the species *Homo sapiens*.

INTERPRETING GRAPHICS

The graph below shows data about fossilized teeth that were found within a series of rock layers. Use this graph to answer the questions that follow.

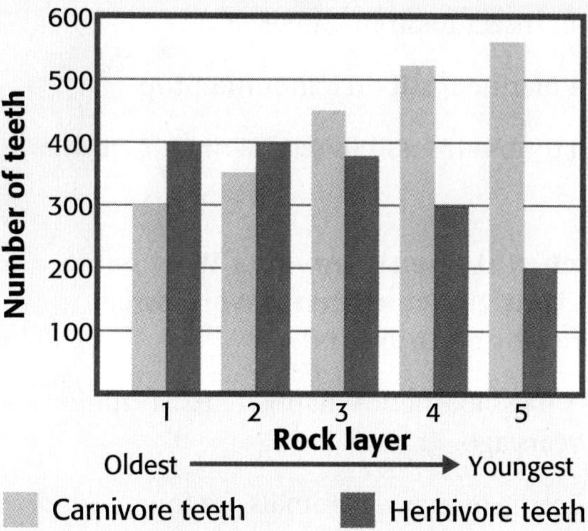

26 Which of the following statements best describes the information presented in the graph?

a. Over time, the number of carnivores decreased and the number of herbivores increased.

b. Over time, the number of carnivores increased and the number of herbivores increased.

c. Over time, the number of carnivores and herbivores remained the same.

d. Over time, the number of carnivores increased and the number of herbivores decreased.

27 At what point did carnivore teeth begin to outnumber herbivore teeth?

a. between layer 1 and layer 2

b. between layer 2 and layer 3

c. between layer 3 and layer 4

d. between layer 4 and layer 5

Standardized Test Preparation

Multiple Choice

1. Which of the following events provides evidence that environmental conditions on Earth have changed?

A. a fossilized footprint in lava rock

B. an insect fossil in amber

C. a marine fossil on a mountaintop

D. a dinosaur fossil in sedimentary rock

2. Which statement supports Wegener's idea that the continents were once part of one landmass?

A. A mass extinction happened 251 million years ago.

B. Fossils of marine animals are found on mountaintops.

C. Fossils of tropical plants have been found in Antarctica.

D. The half-lives of unstable elements throughout Earth are the same.

3. A scientist is trying to determine the age of a fossil. If the scientist wants to find the fossil's age in years, which method should she use?

A. The scientist should examine the rock layers.

B. The scientist should examine atoms in the rock.

C. The scientist should examine the fossil's position in the rock.

D. The scientist should examine how deep in the rock the fossil was located.

4. Based on the fossil record, which of the following statements describes a way in which primates changed over time?

A. Primate brains became larger.

B. Humans evolved from Neanderthals.

C. Fewer primates exist today than before.

D. Primates arose with the dinosaurs.

Use the figure below to answer question 5.

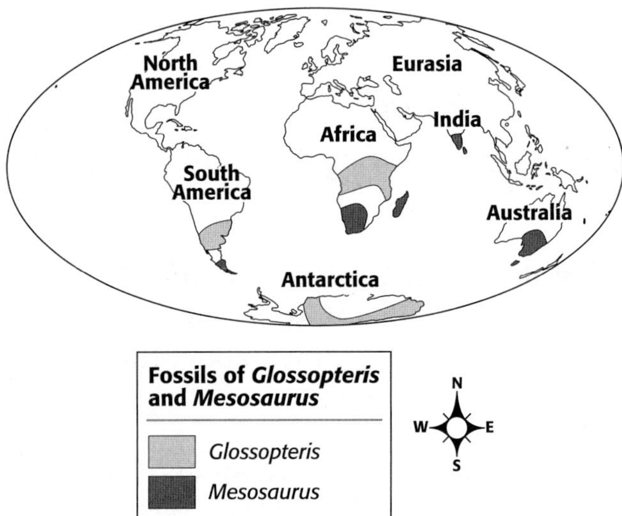

5. *Mesosaurus* was a small, aquatic reptile and *Glossopteris* was an ancient plant species. Based on the map above, which of the following statements is true?

A. Australia was once much colder.

B. Antarctica was once much warmer.

C. Central Africa was once covered by water.

D. North America was once covered by water.

6. **Which of the following organisms will most likely become a fossil?**

   A. a plant covered by a lava flow

   B. a small lizard covered by tree sap

   C. a deer killed and eaten by predators

   D. a bacterium dead on the bottom of the ocean

7. **Why are fossils from the Cenozoic Era, which began 65 million years ago, the easiest fossils to find?**

   A. Fossils of the largest creatures are from this era.

   B. The number of species greatly increased during this era.

   C. Life on Earth, in the form of cyanobacteria, began during this era.

   D. Fossils from this era are found in layers closest to Earth's surface.

8. **A mass extinction occurs when a large number of species become extinct. Which of the following events might lead to a mass extinction?**

   A. A volcano erupts.

   B. A comet or asteroid strikes Earth.

   C. An island forms in the ocean.

   D. Two continents move away from each other.

Use the figure below to answer question 9.

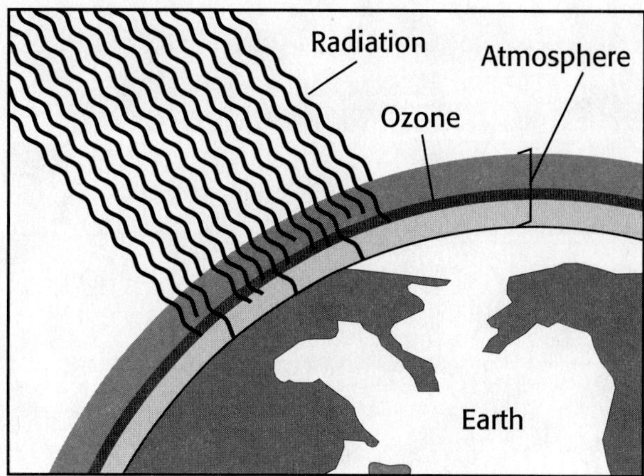

9. **The figure above shows the ozone layer, which became part of the upper atmosphere as Earth developed. Based on the figure, which of the following statements about ozone is true?**

   A. The ozone layer absorbs radiation, which can harm organisms, making life possible.

   B. The ozone layer reflects radiation, which can harm organisms, making life possible.

   C. The ozone layer allows large amounts of radiation to warm Earth, making life possible.

   D. The ozone layer made the atmosphere thicker, blocking radiation and making life possible.

Open Response

10. **What changes in Earth's atmosphere made life on Earth possible?**

11. **What fossil evidence indicates a mass extinction?**

Standardized Test Preparation

Science in Action

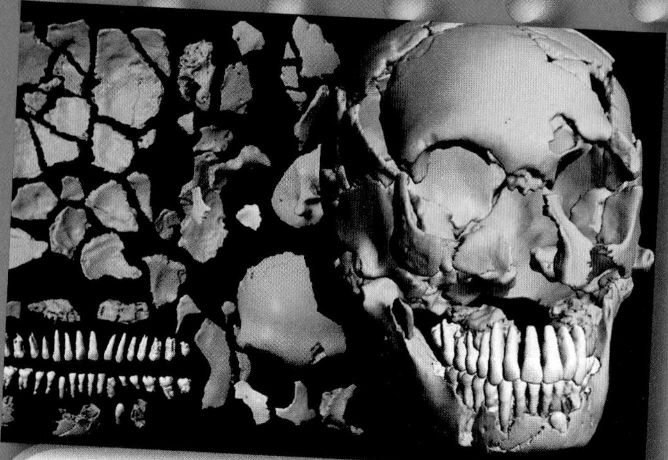

Residents of this neighborhood in Jerusalem, Israel, objected when anthropologists started to dig in the area.

Science, Technology, and Society

Using Computers to Examine Fossils

Paleontologists want to examine fossils without taking apart or damaging the fossils. Fortunately, they can now use a technology called *computerized axial tomography*, or *CAT scanning,* which provides views inside objects without touching the objects. A CAT scan is a series of cross-section pictures of an object. A computer can assemble these "slices" to create a three-dimensional picture of the entire object. Computer graphic programs can also be used to move pictures of fossil pieces around to see how the pieces fit together. The fossil skull above was reconstructed using CAT scans and computers.

Math ACTIVITY

The average volume of a Neanderthal adult's brain was about 1,400 cm^3, while that of an adult gorilla is about 400 cm^3. Calculate how much larger a Neanderthal brain was than a gorilla brain. Express your answer as a percentage.

Scientific Debate

Who Owns the Past?

Does a piece of land include all the layers below it? If you start digging, you may find evidence of past life. In areas that have been inhabited by human ancestors, you may find artifacts that they left behind. But who has the right to dig up these "leftovers" from the past? And who owns them?

In areas that contain many remains of the past, digging up land often leads to conflicts. Landowners may want to build on their own land. But when remains of ancient human cultures are found, living relatives of those cultures may lay claim to the remains. Scientists are often caught in the middle, because they want to study and preserve evidence of past life.

Social Studies ACTIVITY

WRITING SKILL Research an area where there is a debate over what to do with fossils or remains of human ancestors. Write a newspaper article about the issue. Be sure to present all sides of the debate.

People in Science

The Leakey Family

A Family of Fossil Hunters In some families, a business is passed down from one generation to the next. For the Leakey's, the family business is paleoanthropology (PAY lee OH AN thruh PAWL uh jee)—the study of the origin of humans. The first famous Leakey was Dr. Louis Leakey, who was known for his hominid fossil discoveries in Africa in the 1950s. Louis formed many important hypotheses about human evolution. Louis' wife, Mary, made some of the most-important hominid fossil finds of her day.

Louis and Mary's son, Richard, carried on the family tradition of fossil hunting. He found his first fossil, which was of an extinct pig, when he was six years old. As a young man, he went on safari expeditions in which he collected photographs and specimens of African wildlife. Later, he met and married a zoologist named Meave. The photo at right shows Richard (right), Meave (left), and their daughter Louise (middle) Each of the Leakeys has contributed important finds to the study of ancient hominids.

Language Arts ACTIVITY

WRITING SKILL Visit the library and look for a book by or about the Leakey family and other scientists who have worked with them. Write a short book review to encourage your classmates to read the book.

go.hrw.com

To learn more about these Science in Action topics, visit **go.hrw.com** and type in the keyword **HL5HISF.**

Current Science

Check out Current Science® articles related to this chapter by visiting go.hrw.com. Just type in the keyword HL5CS08.

TIMELINE

Earth's Resources

In this unit, you will learn about the basic components of the solid Earth—rocks and the minerals from which they are made. You will also learn about other resources the Earth contains. The ground beneath your feet is a treasure-trove of interesting materials, some of which are very valuable. Secrets of Earth's history are also hidden within the ground's depths. This timeline shows some of the events that have occurred through human history as scientists have come to understand more about our planet.

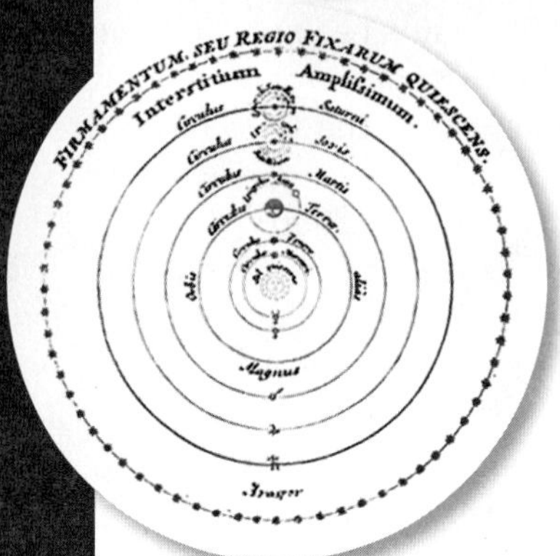

1543

Nicolaus Copernicus argues that the sun rather than the Earth is the center of the universe.

1860

Fossil remains of *Archaeopteryx*, a species that may link reptiles and birds, are discovered in Germany.

1936

Hoover Dam is completed. This massive hydroelectric dam, standing more than 221 m, required 3.25 million cubic yards of concrete to build.

1975

Tabei Junko of Japan becomes the first woman to successfully climb Mount Everest, 22 years after Edmund Hillary and Tenzing Norgay first conquered the mountain in 1953.

1681

The dodo, a flightless bird, is driven to extinction by the actions of humans.

1739

Georg Brandt identifies a new element and names it cobalt.

1848

James Marshall discovers gold at Sutter's Mill, in California, beginning the California gold rush. Prospectors during the gold rush of the following year are referred to as "forty-niners."

1947

Willard F. Libby develops a method of dating prehistoric objects by using radioactive carbon.

1955

Using 1 million pounds of pressure per square inch and temperatures of more than 1,700°C, General Electric creates the first artificial diamonds from graphite.

1969

Apollo 11 astronauts Neil Armstrong and Edwin "Buzz" Aldrin bring 22 kg of moon rocks and soil back to the Earth.

1989

Russian engineers drill a borehole 12 km into the Earth's crust. The borehole is more than 3 times deeper than the deepest mine shaft.

1997

Sojourner, a roving probe on Mars, investigates a Martian boulder nicknamed Yogi.

1999

A Japanese automaker introduces the first hybrid car into the U.S. market.

Maps as Models of the Earth

The Big Idea

Maps are models of Earth that are important tools in both science and society.

SECTION

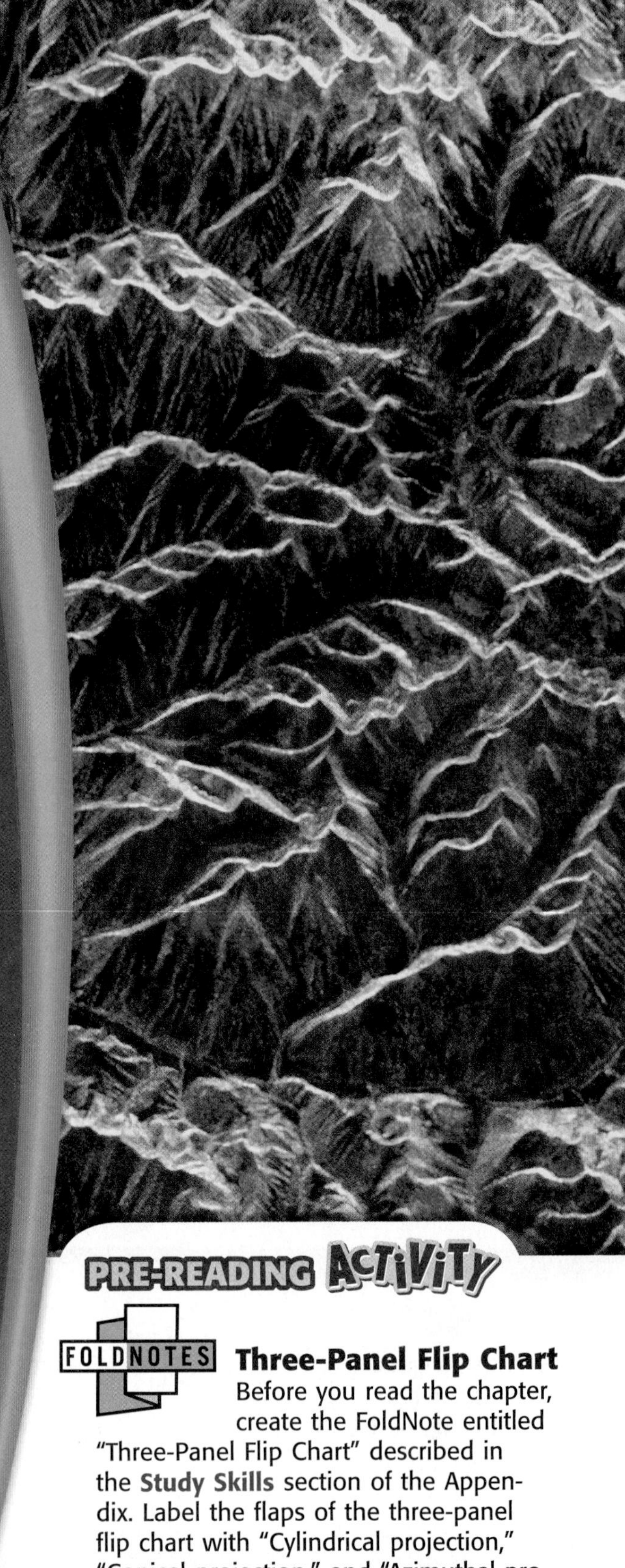

About the Photo

No ordinary camera took this picture! In fact, a camera wasn't used at all. This image is a radar image of a mountainous area of Tibet. It was taken from the space shuttle. Radar imaging is a method that scientists use to map areas of the Earth from far above the Earth's surface.

PRE-READING ACTIVITY

FOLDNOTES

Three-Panel Flip Chart

Before you read the chapter, create the FoldNote entitled "Three-Panel Flip Chart" described in the **Study Skills** section of the Appendix. Label the flaps of the three-panel flip chart with "Cylindrical projection," "Conical projection," and "Azimuthal projection." As you read the chapter, write information you learn about each category under the appropriate flap.

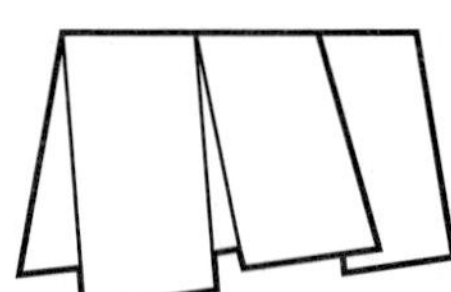

START-UP ACTIVITY

Follow the Yellow Brick Road

In this activity, you will not only learn how to read a map but you will also make a map that someone else can read.

Procedure

1. Use a **computer drawing program or colored pencils and paper** to draw a map that shows how to get from your classroom to another place in your school, such as the gym. Make sure you include enough information for someone unfamiliar with your school to find his or her way.
2. After you finish drawing your map, switch maps with a partner. Examine your classmate's map, and try to figure out where the map is leading you.

Analysis

1. Is your map an accurate picture of your school? Explain your answer.
2. What could you do to make your map better? What are some limitations of your map?
3. Compare your map with your partner's map. How are your maps alike? How are they different?

SECTION 1

You Are Here

Have you ever noticed the curve of the Earth's surface? You probably haven't. When you walk across the Earth, it does not appear to be curved. It looks flat.

What You Will Learn

- Explain how a magnetic compass can be used to find directions on Earth.
- Explain the difference between true north and magnetic north.
- Compare latitude and longitude.
- Explain how latitude and longitude are used to locate places on Earth.

Vocabulary

map	latitude
true north	equator
magnetic declination	longitude
	prime meridian

READING STRATEGY

Reading Organizer As you read this section, create an outline of the section. Use the headings from the section in your outline.

Over time, ideas about Earth's shape have changed. Maps reflected how people saw the world and what technology was available. A **map** is a representation of the features of a physical body such as Earth. If you look at Ptolemy's (TAHL uh meez) world map from the second century, as shown in **Figure 1**, you might not know what you are looking at. Today satellites give us more accurate images of the Earth. In this section, you will learn how early scientists knew Earth was round long before pictures from space were taken. You will also learn how to find location and direction on Earth's surface.

What Does Earth Really Look Like?

The Greeks thought of Earth as a sphere almost 2,000 years before Christopher Columbus made his voyage in 1492. The observation that a ship sinks below the horizon as it sails into the distance supported the idea of a spherical Earth. If Earth were flat, the ship would not sink below the horizon.

Eratosthenes (ER uh TAHS thuh NEEZ), a Greek mathematician, wanted to know the size of Earth. In about 240 BCE, he calculated Earth's circumference using math and observations of the sun. There were no satellites or computers back then. We now know his calculation was wrong by only 6,250 km!

map a representation of the features of a physical body such as Earth

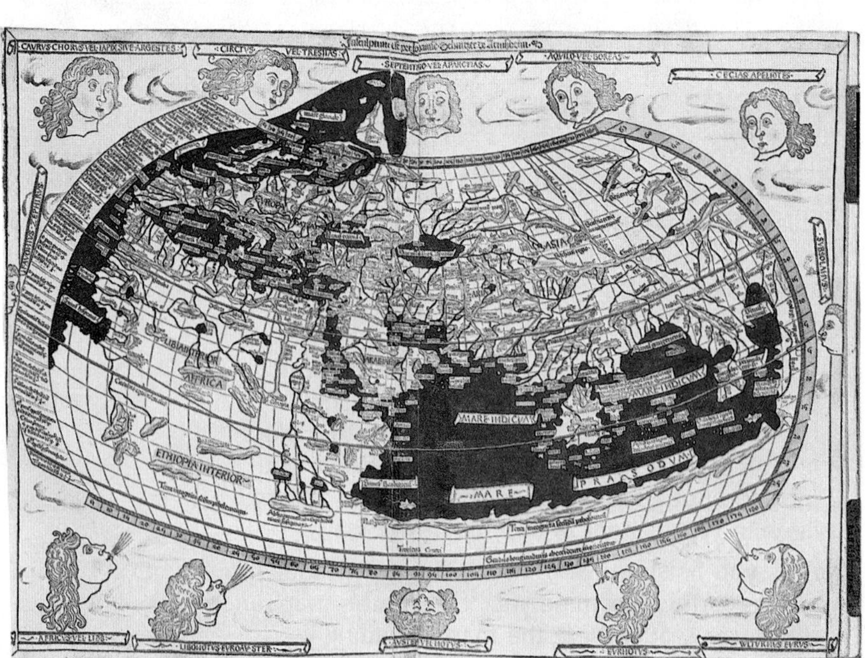

Figure 1 *This map shows what explorers thought the world looked like 1,800 years ago.*

Figure 2 *The North Pole is a good reference point for describing locations in North America.*

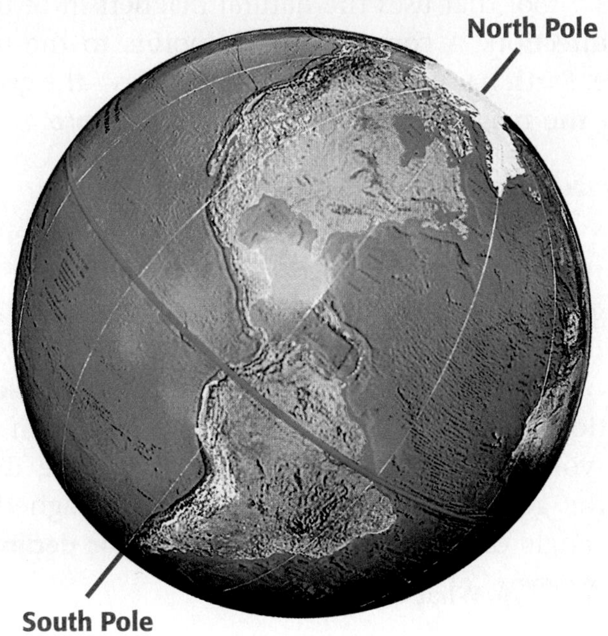

WRITING SKILL **Columbus's Voyage**

Did Christopher Columbus discover that Earth was a sphere only after he completed his voyage in 1492? Or did he know before he left? With a parent or guardian, use the Internet or the library to find out more information about Columbus's voyage. Then, write a paragraph describing what you learned.

Finding Direction on Earth

When giving directions to your home, you might name a landmark, such as a grocery store, as a reference point. A *reference point* is a fixed place on the Earth's surface from which direction and location can be described.

The Earth is spherical, so it has no top, bottom, or sides for people to use as reference points for determining locations on its surface. However, the Earth does rotate, or spin, on its axis. The Earth's axis is an imaginary line that runs through the Earth. At either end of the axis is a geographic pole. The North and South Poles are used as reference points when describing direction and location on the Earth, as shown in **Figure 2.**

Reading Check **What is a reference point?** (*See the Appendix for answers to Reading Checks.*)

Cardinal Directions

A reference point alone will not help you give good directions. You will need to be able to describe how to get to your home from the reference point. You will need to use the directions north, south, east, and west. These directions are called *cardinal directions*. Using cardinal directions is much more precise than saying "Turn left," "Go straight," or "Turn right." So, you may tell a friend to walk a block north of the gas station to get to your home. To use cardinal directions properly, you will need a compass, shown in **Figure 3.**

Figure 3 *A compass shows the cardinal directions north, south, east and west, as well as combinations of these directions.*

Using a Compass

A magnetic compass will show you which direction is north. A *compass* is a tool that uses the natural magnetism of the Earth to show direction. A compass needle points to the magnetic north pole. Earth has two different sets of poles—the geographic poles and the magnetic poles, as shown in **Figure 4.**

True North and Magnetic Declination

Remember that the Earth's geographic poles are on either end of the Earth's axis. Earth has its own magnetic field, which produces magnetic poles. Earth's magnetic poles are not lined up exactly with Earth's axis. So, there is a difference between the locations of Earth's magnetic and geographic poles. **True north** is the direction to the geographic North Pole. When using a compass, you need to make a correction for the difference between the geographic North Pole and the magnetic north pole. The angle of correction is called **magnetic declination.**

true north the direction to the geographic North Pole

magnetic declination the difference between the magnetic north and the true north

Reading Check What is true north?

Figure 4 *Unlike the geographic poles, which are always in the same place, the magnetic poles have changed location throughout the history of the Earth.*

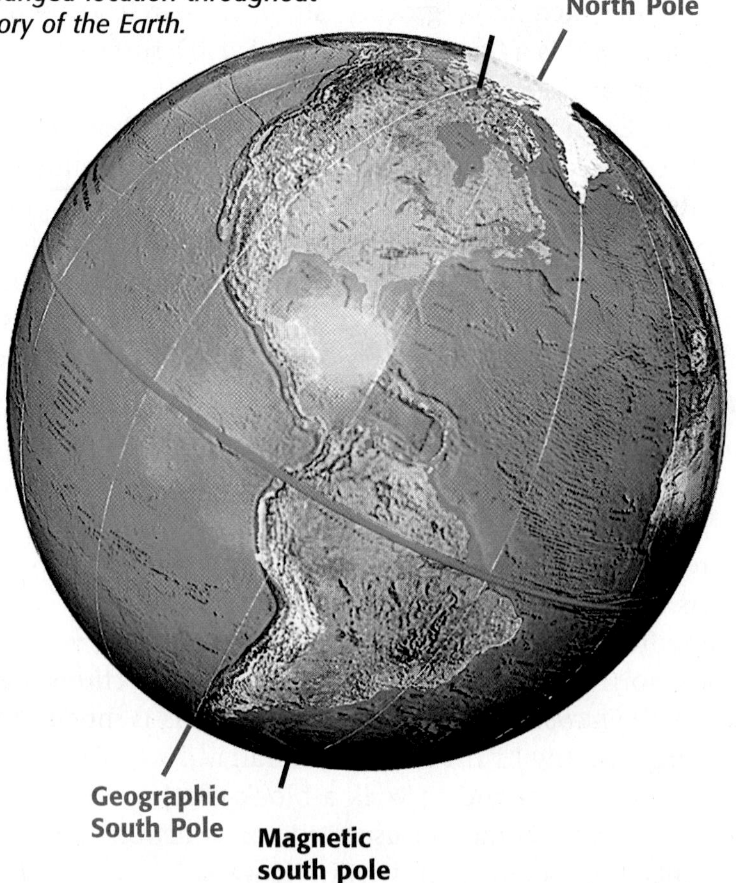

Making a Compass

1. Do this lab outside. Carefully rub a **steel sewing needle** against a **magnet** in the same direction 40 times.
2. Float a **1 cm × 3 cm piece of tissue paper** in a **bowl of water.**
3. Place the needle in the center of the tissue paper.
4. Compare your compass with a **regular compass.** Are both compasses pointing in the same direction?
5. How would you improve your compass?

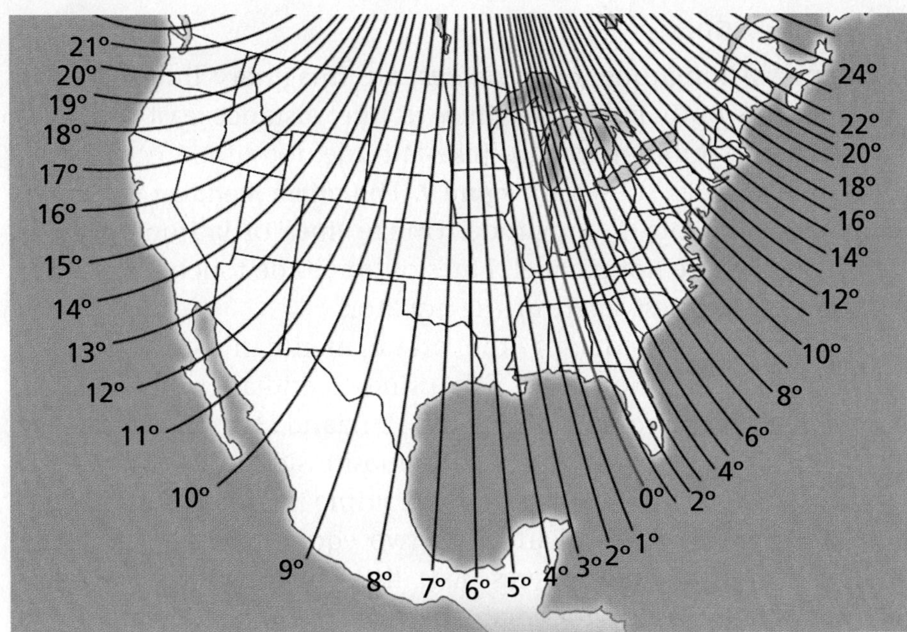

Figure 5 *The lines on the map connect points that have the same magnetic declination.*

Using Magnetic Declination

Magnetic declination is measured in degrees east or west of true north. Magnetic declination has been determined for different points on the Earth's surface. Once you know the declination for your area, you can use a compass to determine true north. This correction is like the correction you would make to the handlebars of a bike with a bent front wheel. You have to turn the handlebars a certain amount to make the bicycle go straight. **Figure 5** shows a map of the magnetic declination of the United States. What is the approximate magnetic declination of your city or town?

latitude the distance north or south from the equator; expressed in degrees

equator the imaginary circle halfway between the poles that divides the Earth into the Northern and Southern Hemispheres

Finding Locations on the Earth

All of the houses and buildings in your neighborhood have addresses that give their location. But how would you find the location of something such as a city or an island? These places can be given an "address" using *latitude* and *longitude.* Latitude and longitude are shown by intersecting lines on a globe or map that allow you to find exact locations.

Latitude

Imaginary lines drawn around the Earth parallel to the equator are called lines of latitude, or *parallels.* **Latitude** is the distance north or south from the equator. Latitude is expressed in degrees, as shown in **Figure 6.** The **equator** is a circle halfway between the North and South Poles that divides the Earth into the Northern and Southern Hemispheres. The equator represents 0° latitude. The North Pole is 90° north latitude, and the South Pole is 90° south latitude.

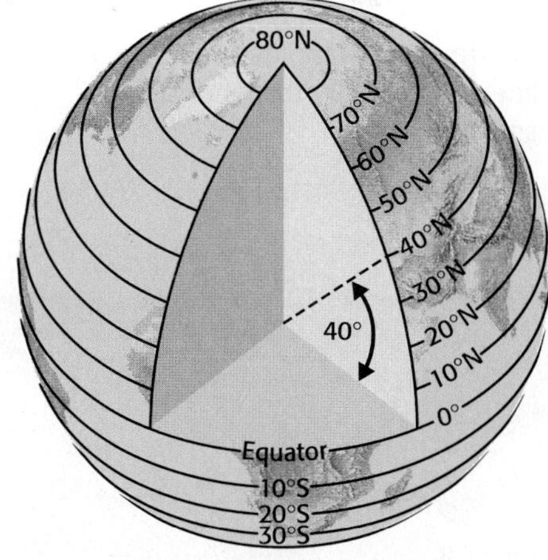

Figure 6 *Degrees latitude are a measure of the angle made by the equator and the location on the Earth's surface, as measured from the center of the Earth.*

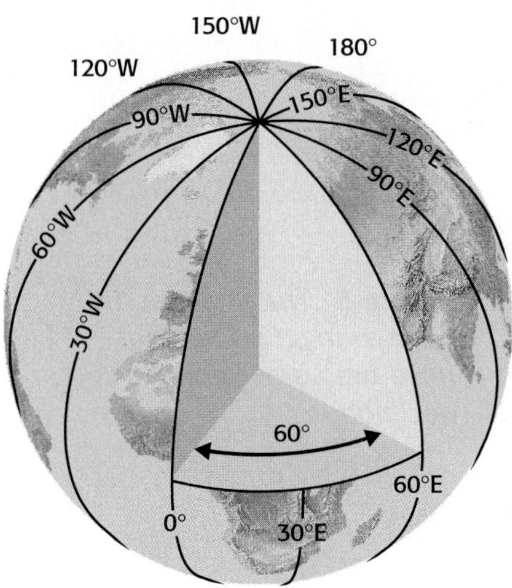

Figure 7 *Degrees longitude are a measure of the angle made by the prime meridian and the location on the Earth's surface, as measured from the center of the Earth.*

Longitude

Lines of longitude, or *meridians*, are imaginary lines that pass through both poles. **Longitude** is the distance east and west from the prime meridian. Like latitude, longitude is expressed in degrees, as shown in **Figure 7.** The **prime meridian** is the line that represents 0° longitude. Unlike lines of latitude, lines of longitude are not parallel. Lines of longitude touch at the poles and are farthest apart at the equator.

Unlike the equator, the prime meridian does not completely circle the globe. The prime meridian runs from the North Pole through Greenwich, England, to the South Pole. The 180° meridian lies on the opposite side of the Earth from the prime meridian. Together, the prime meridian and the 180° meridian divide the Earth into two equal halves—the Eastern and Western Hemispheres. East lines of longitude are found east of the prime meridian, between 0° and 180° longitude. West lines of longitude are found west of the prime meridian, between 0° and 180° longitude.

longitude the distance east and west from the prime meridian; expressed in degrees

prime meridian the meridian, or line of longitude, that is designated as 0° longitude

Using Latitude and Longitude

Points on the Earth's surface can be located by using latitude and longitude. Lines of latitude and lines of longitude cross and form a grid system on globes and maps. This grid system can be used to find locations north or south of the equator and east or west of the prime meridian.

Figure 8 shows you how latitude and longitude can be used to find the location of your state capital. First, locate the star representing your state capital on the appropriate map. Then, use the lines of latitude and longitude closest to your state capital to estimate its approximate latitude and longitude.

Reading Check **Which set of imaginary lines are referred to as meridians: lines of latitude or lines of longitude?**

CONNECTION TO Social Studies

Global Addresses You can find the location of any place on Earth by finding the coordinates of the place, or latitude and longitude, on a globe or a map. Using a globe or an atlas, find the coordinates of the following cities:

New York, New York	Madrid, Spain
Sao Paulo, Brazil	Paris, France
Sydney, Australia	Cairo, Egypt

Then, find the latitude and longitude coordinates of your own city. Can you find another city that shares the same latitude as your city? Can you find another city that shares the same longitude?

ACTIVITY

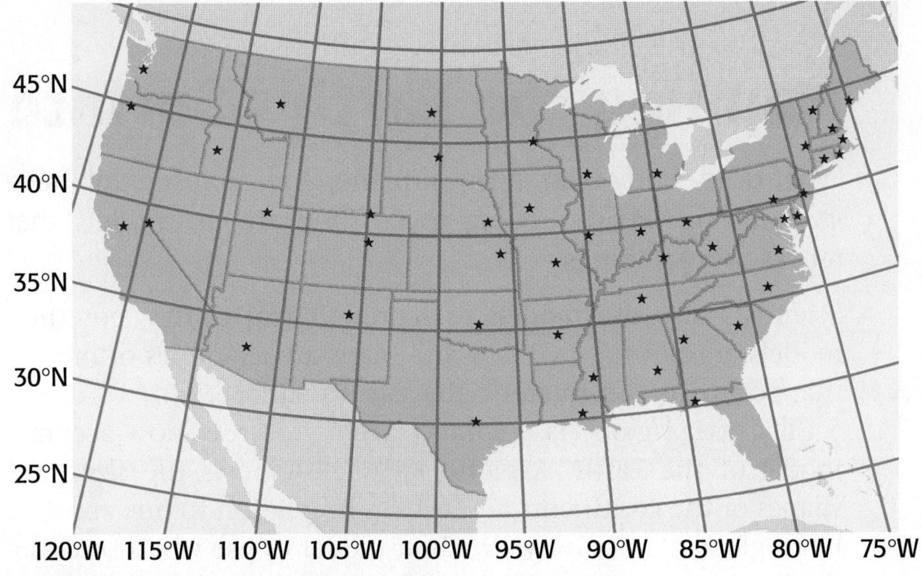

Figure 8 *The grid pattern formed by lines of latitude and longitude allows you to pinpoint any location on the Earth's surface.*

SECTION Review

Summary

- Magnetic compasses are used to find direction on Earth's surface. A compass needle points to the magnetic north pole.
- True north is the direction to the geographic North Pole, which never changes. The magnetic north pole may change over time. Magnetic declination is the difference between true north and magnetic north.
- Latitude and longitude help you find locations on a map or a globe. Lines of latitude run east and west. Lines of longitude run north and south through the poles. These lines cross and form a grid system on globes and maps.

Using Key Terms

1. Use each of the following terms in a separate sentence: *latitude, longitude, equator,* and *prime meridian.*
2. In your own words, write a definition for the term *true north.*

Understanding Key Ideas

3. The geographic poles are
   a. used as reference points when describing direction and location on Earth.
   b. formed because of the Earth's magnetic field.
   c. at either end of the Earth's axis.
   d. Both (a) and (c)
4. How are lines of latitude and lines of longitude alike? How are they different?
5. How can you use a magnetic compass to find directions on Earth?
6. What is the difference between true north and magnetic north?
7. How do lines of latitude and longitude help you find locations on the Earth's surface?

Math Skills

8. The distance between 40°N latitude and 41°N latitude is 69 mi. What is this distance in km? (Hint: 1 km = 0.621 mi)

Critical Thinking

9. **Applying Concepts** While exploring the attic, you find a treasure map. The map shows that the treasure is buried at 97°N and 188°E. Explain why this location is incorrect.
10. **Making Inferences** When using a compass to explore an area, why do you need to know an area's magnetic declination?

SCILINKS
NSTA
Developed and maintained by the National Science Teachers Association
For a variety of links related to this chapter, go to www.scilinks.org
Topic: Latitude and Longitude
SciLinks code: HSM0854

SECTION 2

Mapping the Earth's Surface

What You Will Learn

- Explain why maps of the Earth show distortion.
- Describe four types of map projections.
- Identify five pieces of information that should be shown on a map.
- Describe four methods modern mapmakers use to make accurate maps.

Vocabulary

cylindrical projection
conic projection
azimuthal projection
remote sensing

READING STRATEGY

Discussion Read this section silently. Write down questions that you have about this section. Discuss your questions in a small group.

What do a teddy bear, a toy airplane, and a plastic doll have in common besides being toys? They are all models that represent real things.

Scientists also use models to represent real things, but their models are not toys. Globes and maps are examples of models that scientists use to study the Earth's surface.

Because a globe is a sphere, a globe is the most accurate model of the Earth. A globe accurately shows the sizes and shapes of the continents and oceans in relation to one another. But a globe is not always the best model to use when studying the Earth's surface. A globe is too small to show many details, such as roads and rivers. It is much easier to show details on maps. But how do you show the Earth's curved surface on a flat surface? Keep reading to find out.

A Flat Sphere?

A map is a flat representation of the Earth's curved surface. However, when you move information from a curved surface to a flat surface, you lose some accuracy. Changes called *distortions* happen in the shapes and sizes of landmasses and oceans on maps. Direction and distance can also be distorted. Consider the example of the orange peel shown in **Figure 1.**

Reading Check What are distortions on maps? *(See the Appendix for answers to Reading Checks.)*

Figure 1 *If you remove and flatten the peel from an orange, the peel will stretch and tear. Notice how shapes as well as distances between points on the peel are distorted.*

Map Projections

Mapmakers use map projections to move the image of Earth's curved surface onto a flat surface. No map projection of Earth can show the surface of a sphere in the correct proportions. All flat maps have distortion. However, a map showing a smaller area, such as a city, has less distortion than a map showing a larger area, such as the world.

To understand how map projections are made, think of Earth as a translucent globe that has a light inside. If you hold a piece of paper against the globe, shadows appear on the paper. These shadows show marks on the globe, such as continents, oceans, and lines of latitude and longitude. The way the paper is held against the globe determines the kind of map projection that is made. The most common map projections are based on three shapes—cylinders, cones, and planes.

INTERNET ACTIVITY

For another activity related to this chapter, go to **go.hrw.com** and type in the keyword **HZ5MAPW.**

Cylindrical Projection

A map projection that is made when the contents of the globe are moved onto a cylinder of paper is called a **cylindrical projection** (suh LIN dri kuhl proh JEK shuhn). The most common cylindrical projection is called a *Mercator projection* (muhr KAYT uhr proh JEK shuhn). The Mercator projection shows the globe's latitude and longitude lines as straight lines. Equal amounts of space are used between longitude lines. Latitude lines are spaced farther apart north and south of the equator. Because of the spacing, areas near the poles look wider and longer on the map than they look on the globe. In **Figure 2,** Greenland appears almost as large as Africa!

cylindrical projection a map projection that is made by moving the surface features of the globe onto a cylinder

Figure 2 **Cylindrical Projection**

This cylindrical projection is a Mercator projection. It is accurate near the equator but distorts areas near the North and South Poles.

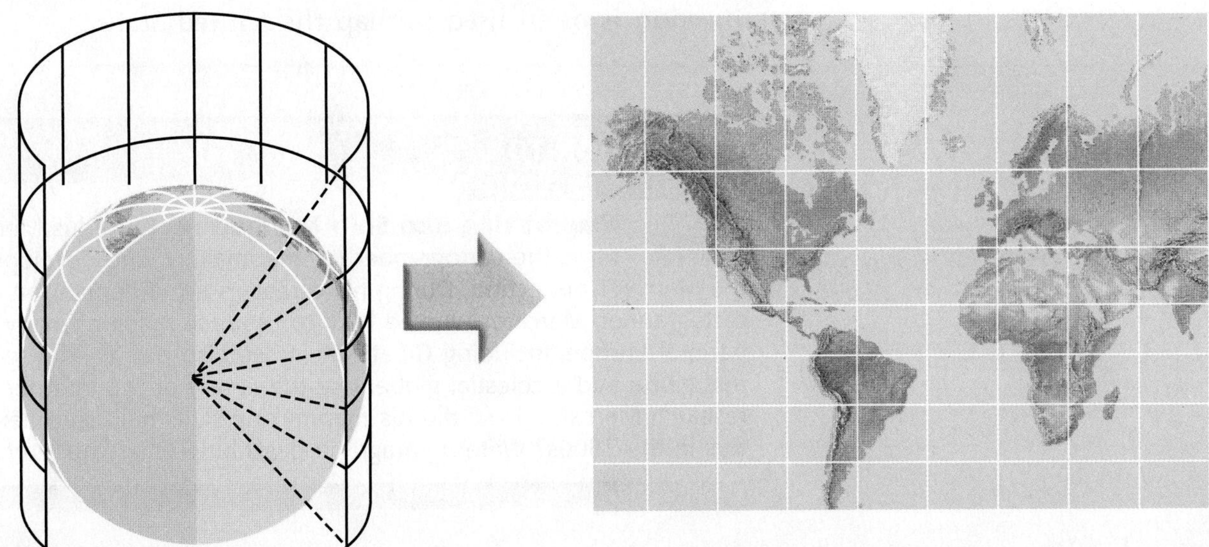

Figure 3 **Conic Projection**

A series of conic projections can be used to map a large area. Because each cone touches the globe at a different latitude, conic projections reduce distortion.

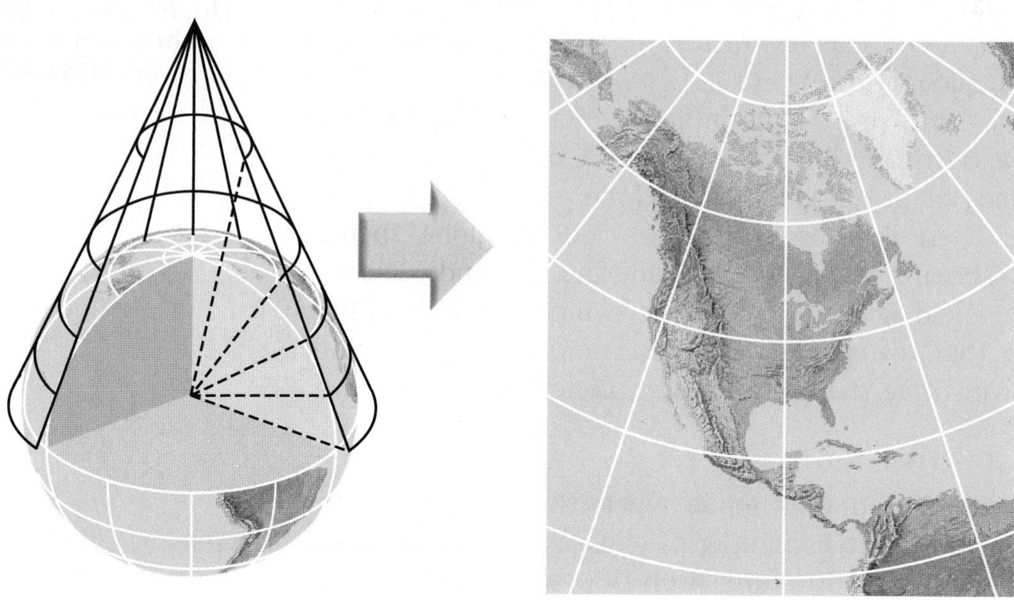

conic projection a map projection that is made by moving the surface features of the globe onto a cone

Conic Projection

A map projection that is made by moving the contents of the globe onto a cone is a **conic projection,** shown in **Figure 3.** This cone is then unrolled to form a flat plane.

The cone touches the globe at each line of longitude but at only one line of latitude. There is no distortion along the line of latitude where the globe touches the cone. Areas near this line of latitude are distorted less than other areas are. Because the cone touches many lines of longitude and only one line of latitude, conic projections are best for mapping large masses of land that have more area east to west. For example, a conic projection is often used to map the United States.

CONNECTION TO Social Studies

WRITING SKILL **Mapmaking and Ship Navigation** Gerardus Mercator is the cartographer (or mapmaker) who developed the Mercator projection. During his career as a mathematician and cartographer, Mercator worked hard to produce maps of many parts of Europe, including Great Britain. He also produced a terrestrial globe and a celestial globe. Use the library or the Internet to research Mercator. How did his mapmaking skills help ship navigators in the 1500s? Write a paragraph describing what you learn.

Figure 4 **Azimuthal Projection**

On this azimuthal projection, distortion increases as you move farther from the North Pole.

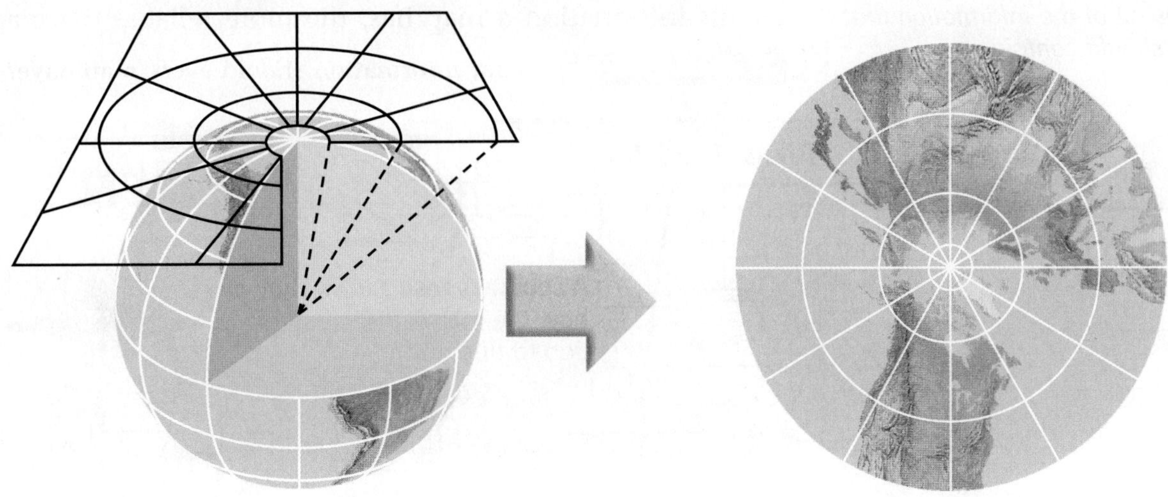

Azimuthal Projection

An **azimuthal projection** (AZ uh MYOOTH uhl proh JEK shuhn) is a map projection that is made by moving the contents of the globe onto a flat plane. Look at **Figure 4.** On an azimuthal projection, the plane touches the globe at only one point. There is little distortion at this point of contact. The point of contact for an azimuthal projection is usually one of the poles. However, distortion of direction, distance, and shape increases as you move away from the point of contact. Azimuthal projections are most often used to map areas of the globe that are near the North and South Poles.

azimuthal projection a map projection that is made by moving the surface features of the globe onto a plane

Reading Check **How are azimuthal and conic projections alike? How are they different?**

Equal-Area Projection

A map projection that shows the area between the latitude and longitude lines the same size as that area on a globe is called an *equal-area projection*. Equal-area projections can be made by using cylindrical, conic, or azimuthal projections. Equal-area projections are often used to map large land areas, such as continents. The shapes of the continents and oceans are distorted on equal-area projections. But because the scale used on equal-area projections is constant throughout the map, this type of projection is good for determining distance on a map. **Figure 5** is an example of an equal-area projection.

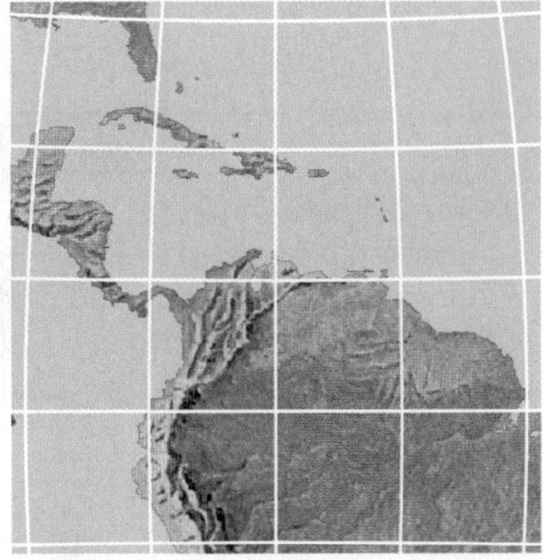

Figure 5 *Equal-area projections are useful for determining distance on a map.*

Information Shown on Maps

Regardless of the kind of map you are reading, the map should contain the information shown in **Figure 6.** This information includes a title, a compass rose, a scale, a legend, and a date. Unfortunately, not all maps have all this information. The more of this information a map has, the more reliable the map is.

Reading Check **What information should every map have?**

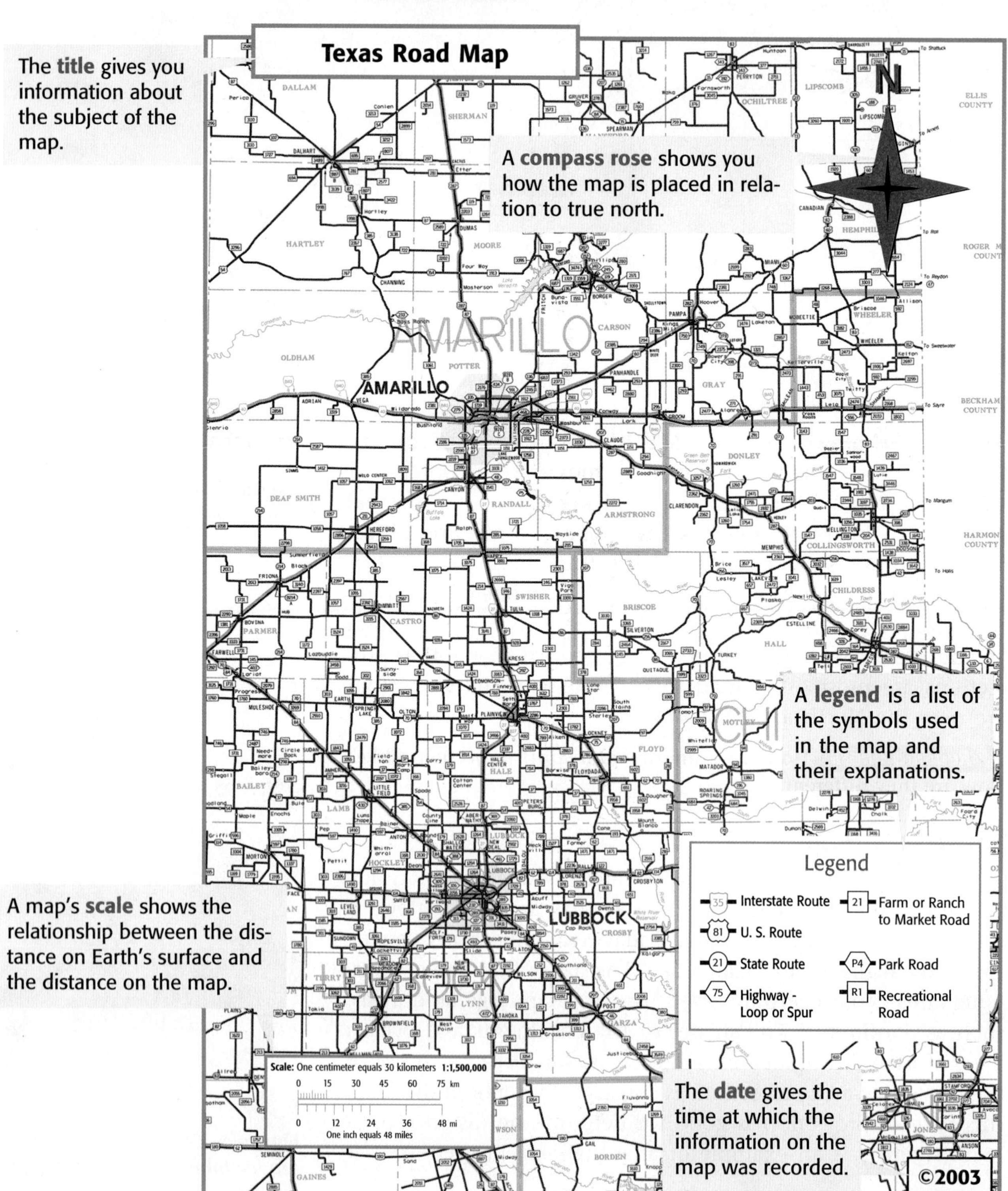

Texas Road Map
The **title** gives you information about the subject of the map.
A **compass rose** shows you how the map is placed in relation to true north.
N
AMARILLO
LUBBOCK
A **legend** is a list of the symbols used in the map and their explanations.
Legend
35 Interstate Route
81 U. S. Route
21 State Route
75 Highway - Loop or Spur
21 Farm or Ranch to Market Road
P4 Park Road
R1 Recreational Road
A map's **scale** shows the relationship between the distance on Earth's surface and the distance on the map.
Scale: One centimeter equals 30 kilometers 1:1,500,000
0 15 30 45 60 75 km
0 12 24 36 48 mi
One inch equals 48 miles
The **date** gives the time at which the information on the map was recorded.
©2003

Figure 6 *This Texas road map includes all of the information that a map should contain.*

Modern Mapmaking

For many centuries mapmakers relied on the observations of explorers to make maps. Today, however, mapmakers have far more technologically advanced tools for mapmaking.

Many of today's maps are made by remote sensing. **Remote sensing** is a way to collect information about something without physically being there. Remote sensing can be as basic as putting cameras on airplanes. However, many mapmakers rely on more sophisticated technology, such as satellites.

remote sensing the process of gathering and analyzing information about an object without physically being in touch with the object

Remote Sensing and Satellites

The image shown in **Figure 7** is a photograph taken by a satellite. Satellites can also detect energy that your eyes cannot. Remote sensors gather data about energy coming from Earth's surface and send the data back to receiving stations on Earth. A computer is then used to process the information to make a picture you can see.

Remote Sensing Using Radar

Radar is a tool that uses waves of energy to map Earth's surface. Waves of energy are sent from a satellite to the area being observed. The waves are then reflected from the area to a receiver on the satellite. The distance and the speed in which the waves travel to the area and back are measured and analyzed to create a map of the area. The waves used in radar can move through clouds and water. Because of this ability, radar has been used to map the surface of Venus, whose atmosphere is thick and cloudy.

Figure 7 *Satellites can produce very detailed images of the Earth's surface. The satellite that took this picture was 423 mi above the Earth's surface!*

Figure 8 *This tiny GPS unit may come in handy if you are ever lost.*

Global Positioning System

Did you know that satellite technology can actually help you from getting lost? The *global positioning system* (GPS) can help you find where you are on Earth. GPS is a system of orbiting satellites that send radio signals to receivers on Earth. The receivers calculate a given place's latitude, longitude, and elevation.

GPS was invented in the 1970s by the U.S. Department of Defense for military use. However, during the last 30 years, GPS has made its way into people's daily lives. Mapmakers use GPS to verify the location of boundary lines between countries and states. Airplane and boat pilots use GPS for navigation. Businesses and state agencies use GPS for mapping and environmental planning. Many new cars have GPS units that show information on a screen on the dashboard. Some GPS units are small enough to wear on your wrist, as shown in **Figure 8,** so you can know your location anywhere you go!

Geographic Information Systems

Mapmakers now use geographic information systems to store, use, and view geographic information. A *geographic information system*, or GIS, is a computerized system that allows a user to enter different types of information about an area. This information is entered and stored as layers. The user can then use the stored information to make complex analyses or display maps. **Figure 9** shows three GIS images of Seattle, Washington.

Reading Check **Explain how information is stored using GIS.**

Figure 9 *The images at right show the location of sewer lines, roads, and parks in Seattle, Washington.*

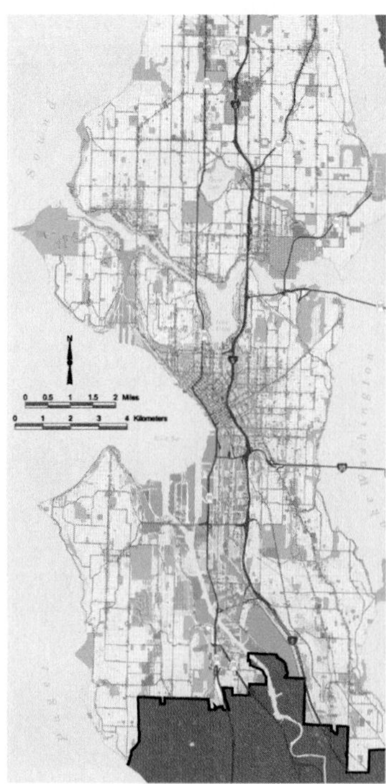

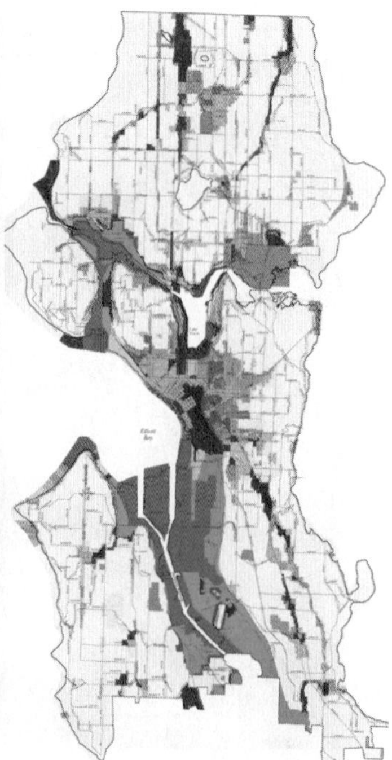

SECTION Review

Summary

- When information is moved from a curved surface to a flat surface, distortion occurs.
- Three main types of projections are used to show Earth's surface on a flat map: cylindrical, conic, and azimuthal projections.
- Equal-area maps are used to show the area of a piece of land in relation to the area of other landmasses and oceans.
- Maps should contain a title, a scale, a legend, a compass rose, and a date.
- Modern mapmakers use remote sensing technology, such as satellites and radar.
- The Global positioning system, or GPS, is a system of satellites that can help you determine your location no matter where you are.
- Geographical information systems, or GIS, are computerized systems that allow mapmakers to store and use many types of data about an area.

Using Key Terms

1. In your own words, write a definition for each of the following terms: *cylindrical projection, azimuthal projection,* and *conic projection.*

Understanding Key Ideas

2. Which of the following map projections is most often used to map the United States?
   a. cylindrical projection
   b. conic projection
   c. azimuthal projection
   d. equal-area projection
3. List five things found on maps. Explain how each thing is important to reading a map.
4. Describe how GPS can help you find your location on Earth.
5. Why is radar useful when mapping areas that tend to be covered in clouds?

Critical Thinking

6. **Analyzing Ideas** Imagine you are a mapmaker. You have been asked to map a landmass that has more area from east to west than from north to south. What type of map projection would you use? Explain.
7. **Making Inferences** Imagine looking at a map of North America. Would this map have a large scale or a small scale? Would a map of your city have a large scale or a small scale? Explain.

Interpreting Graphics

Use the map below to answer the questions that follow.

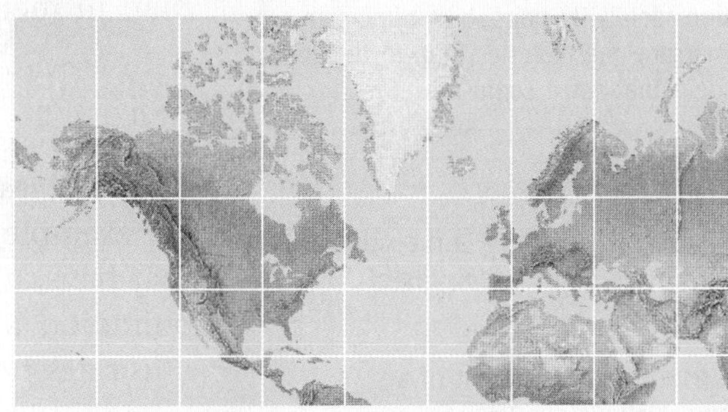

8. What type of projection was used to make this map?
9. Which areas of this map are the most distorted? Explain.
10. Which areas of this map are the least distorted? Explain.

SCI LINKS
NSTA
Developed and maintained by the National Science Teachers Association
For a variety of links related to this chapter, go to www.scilinks.org
Topic: Mapmaking
SciLinks code: HSM0909

SECTION 3

Topographic Maps

What You Will Learn

- Explain how contour lines show elevation and landforms on a map.
- Explain how the relief of an area determines the contour interval used on a map.
- List the rules of contour lines.

Vocabulary

topographic map
elevation
contour line
contour interval
relief
index contour

READING STRATEGY

Paired Summarizing Read this section silently. In pairs, take turns summarizing the material. Stop to discuss ideas that seem confusing.

Imagine you are going on a camping trip in the wilderness. To be prepared, you want to take a compass and a map. But what kind of map should you take? Because there won't be any roads in the wilderness, you can forget about a road map. Instead, you will need a topographic map.

A **topographic map** (TAHP uh GRAF ik MAP) is a map that shows surface features, or topography (tuh PAHG ruh fee), of the Earth. Topographic maps show both natural features, such as rivers, lakes, and mountains, and features made by humans, such as cities, roads, and bridges. Topographic maps also show elevation. **Elevation** is the height of an object above sea level. The elevation at sea level is 0. In this section, you will learn how to read a topographic map.

Elements of Elevation

The United States Geological Survey (USGS), a federal government agency, has made topographic maps for most of the United States. These maps show elevation in feet (ft) rather than in meters, the SI unit usually used by scientists.

Contour Lines

On a topographic map, *contour lines* are used to show elevation. **Contour lines** are lines that connect points of equal elevation. For example, one contour line would connect points on a map that have an elevation of 100 ft. Another line would connect points on a map that have an elevation of 200 ft. **Figure 1** illustrates how contour lines appear on a map.

topographic map a map that shows the surface features of Earth

elevation the height of an object above sea level

contour line a line that connects points of equal elevation

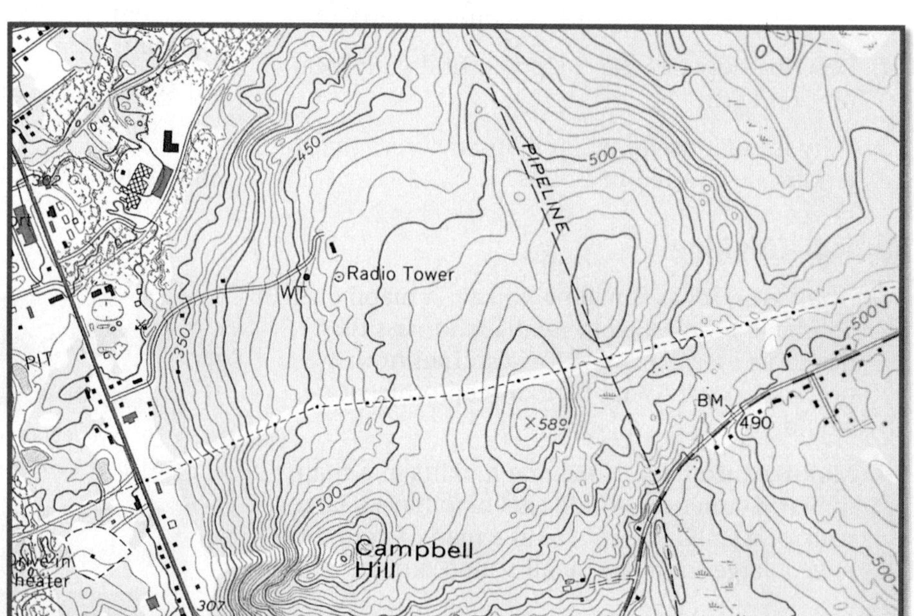

Figure 1 *Because contour lines connect points of equal elevation, the shape of the contour lines reflects the shape of the land.*

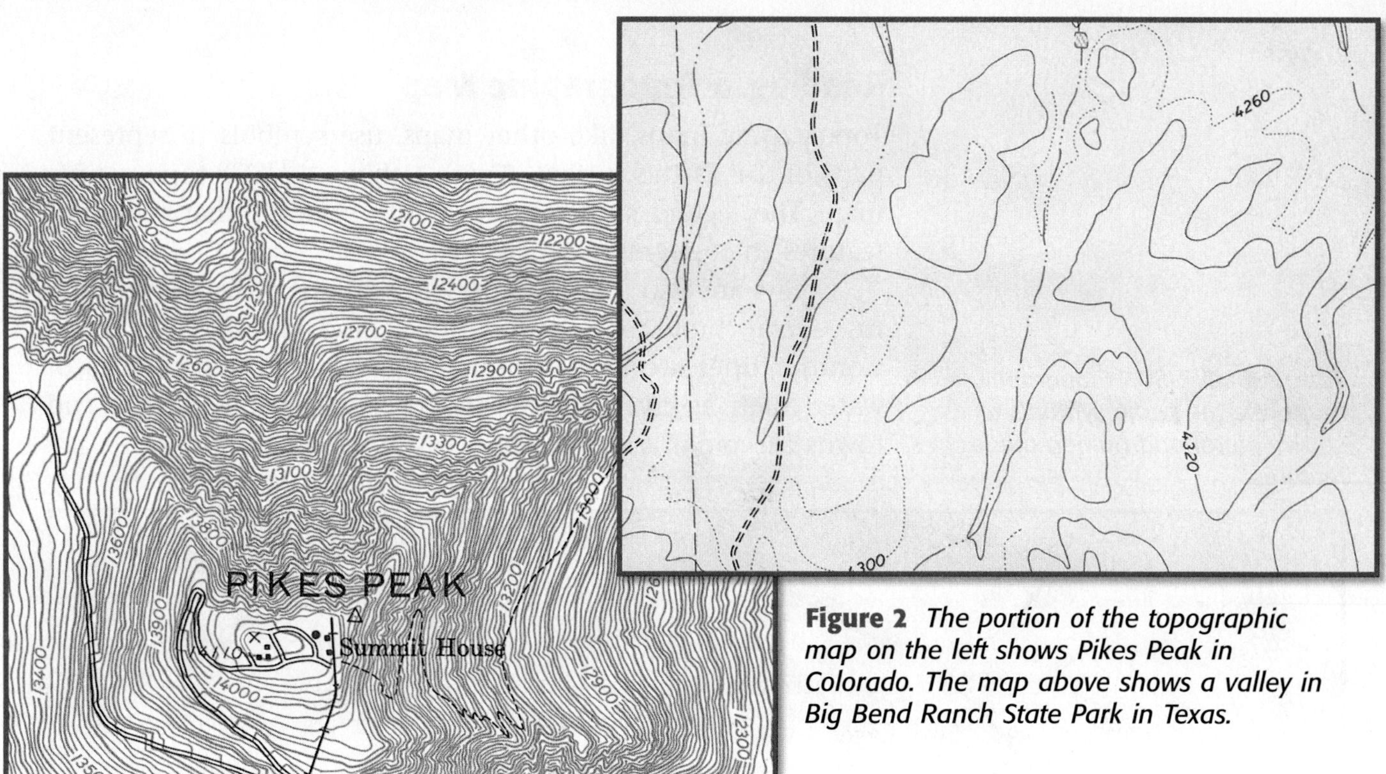

Figure 2 *The portion of the topographic map on the left shows Pikes Peak in Colorado. The map above shows a valley in Big Bend Ranch State Park in Texas.*

Contour Interval

The difference in elevation between one contour line and the next is called the **contour interval.** For example, a map with a contour interval of 20 ft would have contour lines every 20 ft of elevation change, such as 0 ft, 20 ft, 40 ft, and 60 ft. A mapmaker chooses a contour interval based on the area's relief. **Relief** is the difference in elevation between the highest and lowest points of the area being mapped. Because the relief of an area with mountains is large, the relief might be shown on a map using a large contour interval, such as 100 ft. However, a flat area has small relief and might be shown on a map by using a small contour interval, such as 10 ft.

The spacing of contour lines also indicates slope, as shown in **Figure 2.** Contour lines that are close together show a steep slope. Contour lines that are spaced far apart show a gentle slope.

contour interval the difference in elevation between one contour line and the next

relief the variations in elevation of a land surface

index contour on a map, a darker, heavier contour line that is usually every fifth line and that indicates a change in elevation

Index Contour

On USGS topographic maps, an index contour is used to make reading the map easier. An **index contour** is a darker, heavier contour line that is usually every fifth line and that is labeled by elevation. Find an index contour on both of the topographic maps shown in **Figure 2.**

Reading Check **What is an index contour?** (*See the Appendix for answers to Reading Checks.*)

CONNECTION TO Oceanography

Mapping the Ocean Floor
Oceanographers use topographic maps to map the topography of the ocean floor. Use the Internet or the library to find a topographic map of the ocean floor. How are maps of the ocean floor similar to maps of the continents? How are they different?

Reading a Topographic Map

Topographic maps, like other maps, use symbols to represent parts of the Earth's surface. **Figure 3** shows a USGS topographic map. The legend shows some of the symbols that represent features in topographic maps.

Colors are also used to represent features of Earth's surface. In general, buildings, roads, bridges, and railroads are black. Contour lines are brown. Major highways are red. Bodies of water, such as rivers, lakes, and oceans are blue. Cities and towns are pink, and wooded areas are green.

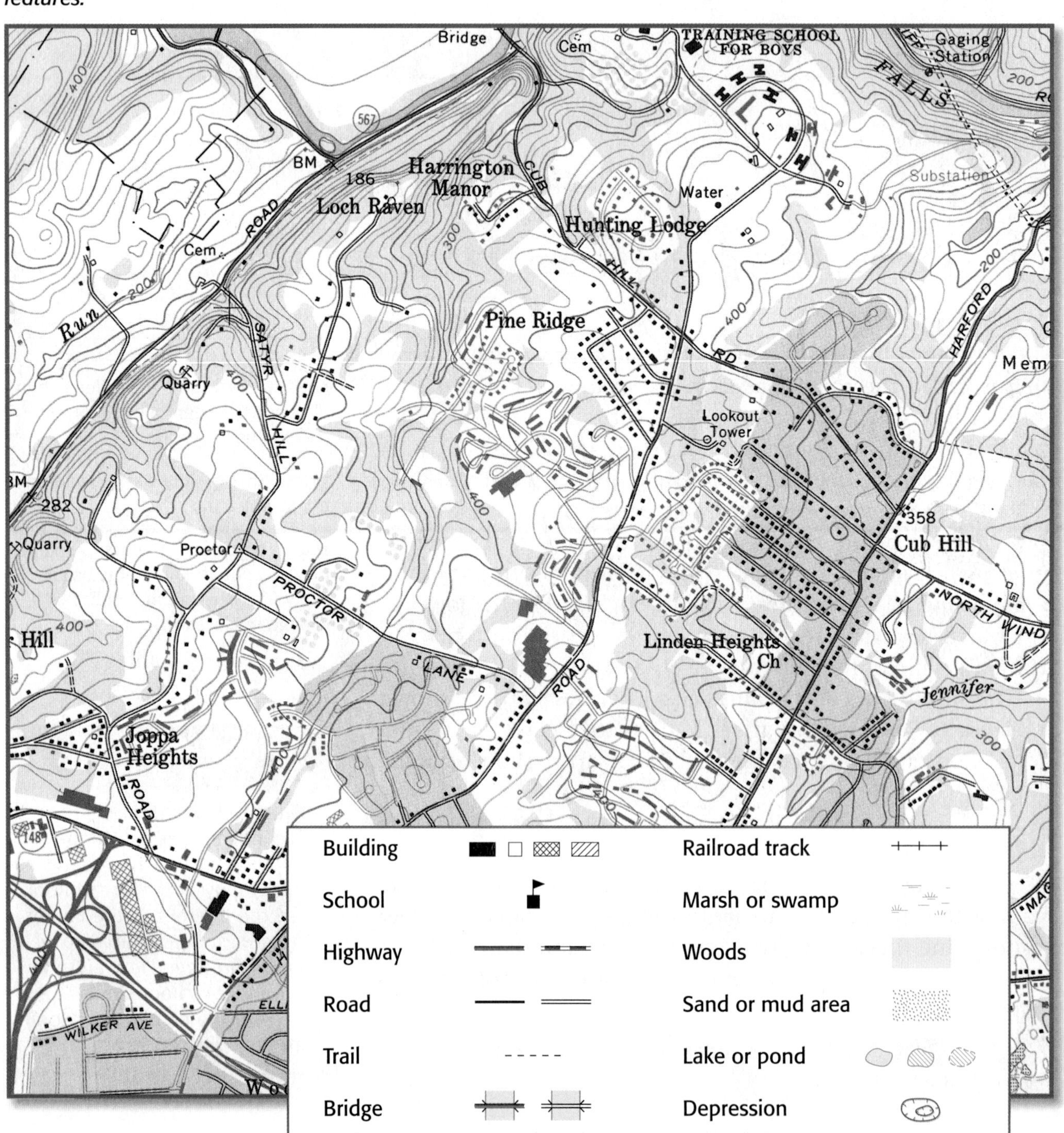

Figure 3 *All USGS topographic maps use the same symbols to show natural and human-made features.*

The Golden Rules of Contour Lines

Contour lines are the key to explaining the size and shape of landforms on a topographic map. Reading a topographic map takes training and practice. The following rules will help you understand how to read topographic maps:

- Contour lines never cross. All points along a contour line represent one elevation.
- The spacing of contour lines depends on slope characteristics. Contour lines that are close together show a steep slope. Contour lines that are far apart show a gentle slope.
- Contour lines that cross a valley or stream are V shaped. The V points toward the area of highest elevation. If a stream or river flows through the valley, the V points upstream.
- The tops of hills, mountains, and depressions are shown by closed circles. Depressions are marked with short, straight lines inside the circle that point downslope to the depression.

CONNECTION TO Environmental Science

Endangered Species State agencies, such as the Texas Parks and Wildlife Department, use topographic maps to mark where endangered plant and animal species are. By marking the location of the endangered plants and animals, these agencies can record and protect these places. Use the Internet or another source to find out if there is an agency in your state that tracks endangered species by using topographic maps.

SECTION Review

Summary

- Contour lines are used to show elevation and landforms by connecting points of equal elevation.
- The contour interval is determined by the relief of an area.
- Contour lines never cross. Contour lines that cross a valley or a stream are V shaped and point upstream. The tops of hills, mountains, and depressions are shown by closed circles.

Using Key Terms

1. In your own words, write a definition for each of the following terms: *topographic map, contour interval,* and *relief.*

Understanding Key Ideas

2. An index contour
   a. is a heavier contour line that shows a change in elevation.
   b. points in the direction of higher elevation.
   c. indicates a depression.
   d. indicates a hill.
3. How do topographic maps represent the Earth's surface?
4. How does the relief of an area determine the contour interval used on a map?
5. What are the rules of contour lines?

Math Skills

6. The contour line at the base of a hill reads 90 ft. There are five contour lines between the base of the hill and the top of the hill. If the contour interval is 30 ft, what is the elevation of the highest contour line?

Critical Thinking

7. **Making Inferences** Why isn't the highest point on a hill represented by a contour line?

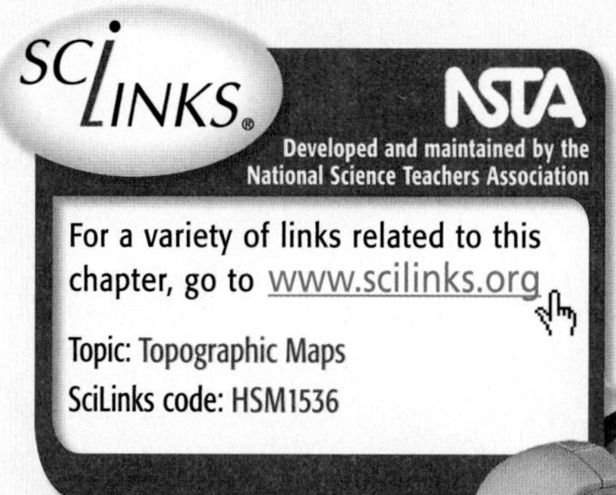

SCILINKS.
NSTA
Developed and maintained by the National Science Teachers Association
For a variety of links related to this chapter, go to www.scilinks.org
Topic: Topographic Maps
SciLinks code: HSM1536

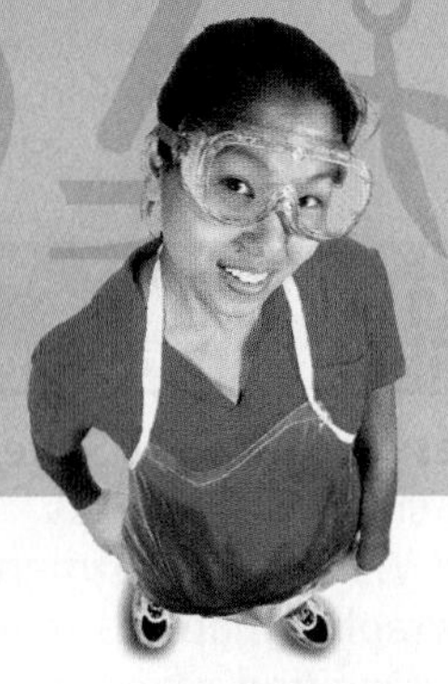

Using Scientific Methods

Skills Practice Lab

Round or Flat?

OBJECTIVES

Construct a tool to measure the circumference of the Earth.

Calculate the circumference of the Earth.

MATERIALS

- basketball
- books or notebooks (2)
- calculator (optional)
- clay, modeling
- flashlight or small lamp
- meterstick
- pencils, unsharpened (2)
- protractor
- ruler, metric
- string, 10 cm long
- tape, masking
- tape measure

SAFETY

Eratosthenes thought of a way to measure the circumference of Earth. He came up with the idea when he read that a well in southern Egypt was entirely lit by the sun at noon once each year. He realized that to shine on the entire surface of the well water, the sun must be directly over the well. At the same time, in a city just north of the well, a tall monument cast a shadow. Thus, Eratosthenes reasoned that the sun could not be directly over both the monument and the well at noon on the same day. In this experiment, you will see how Eratosthenes' way of measuring works.

Ask a Question

1. How could I use Eratosthenes' method of investigation to measure the size of the Earth?

Form a Hypothesis

2. Formulate a hypothesis that answers the question above. Record your hypothesis.

Test the Hypothesis

3. Set the basketball on a table. Place a book or notebook on either side of the basketball to hold the ball in place. The ball represents Earth.

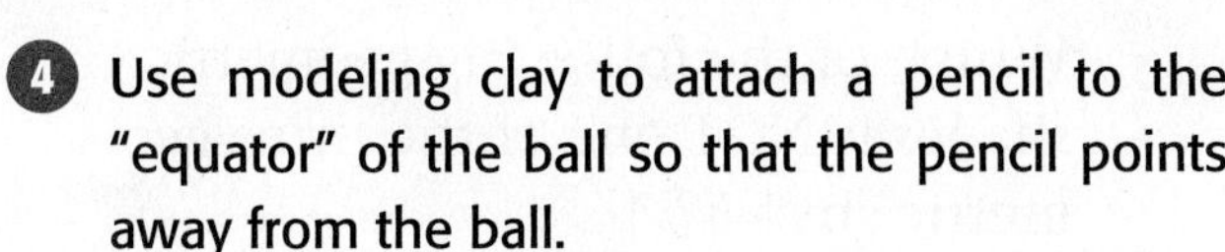

4. Use modeling clay to attach a pencil to the "equator" of the ball so that the pencil points away from the ball.

5. Attach the second pencil to the ball at a point that is 5 cm above the first pencil. This second pencil should also point away from the ball.

6. Use a meterstick to measure 1 m away from the ball. Mark the 1 m position with masking tape. Label the position "Sun." Hold the flashlight so that its front edge is above the masking tape.

7. When your teacher turns out the lights, turn on your flashlight and point it so that the pencil on the equator does not cast a shadow. Ask a partner to hold the flashlight in this position. The second pencil should cast a shadow on the ball.

8. Tape one end of the string to the top of the second pencil. Hold the other end of the string against the ball at the far edge of the shadow. Make sure that the string is tight. But be careful not to pull the pencil over.

9. Use a protractor to measure the angle between the string and the pencil. Record this angle.

10. Use the following formula to calculate the experimental circumference of the ball.

$$\textit{Circumference} = \frac{360° \times 5 \text{ cm}}{\text{angle between pencil and string}}$$

11. Record the experimental circumference you calculated in step 10. Wrap the tape measure around the ball's equator to measure the actual circumference of the ball. Record this circumference.

Analyze the Results

1. **Examining Data** Compare the experimental circumference with the actual circumference.

2. **Analyzing Data** What could have caused your experimental circumference to differ from the actual circumference?

3. **Analyzing Data** What are some of the advantages and disadvantages of taking measurements this way?

Draw Conclusions

4. **Evaluating Methods** Was Eratosthenes' method an effective way to measure Earth's circumference? Explain your answer.

Chapter Review

USING KEY TERMS

For each pair of terms, explain how the meanings of the terms differ.

1. *true north* and *magnetic north*
2. *latitude* and *longitude*
3. *equator* and *prime meridian*
4. *cylindrical projection* and *azimuthal projection*
5. *contour interval* and *index contour*
6. *global positioning system* and *geographic information system*

UNDERSTANDING KEY IDEAS

Multiple Choice

7. A point whose latitude is 0° is located on the
   - **a.** North Pole.
   - **b.** equator.
   - **c.** South Pole.
   - **d.** prime meridian.
8. The distance in degrees east or west of the prime meridian is
   - **a.** latitude.
   - **b.** declination.
   - **c.** longitude.
   - **d.** projection.
9. Widely spaced contour lines indicate a
   - **a.** steep slope.
   - **b.** gentle slope.
   - **c.** hill.
   - **d.** river.
10. The most common map projections are based on three geometric shapes. Which of the following geometric shapes is NOT one of the three geometric shapes?
    - **a.** cylinder
    - **b.** square
    - **c.** cone
    - **d.** plane
11. A cylindrical projection is distorted near the
    - **a.** equator.
    - **b.** poles.
    - **c.** prime meridian.
    - **d.** date line.
12. What is the relationship between the distance on a map and the actual distance on Earth called?
    - **a.** legend
    - **b.** elevation
    - **c.** relief
    - **d.** scale
13. ___ is the height of an object above sea level.
    - **a.** Contour interval
    - **b.** Elevation
    - **c.** Declination
    - **d.** Index contour

Short Answer

14. List four methods that modern mapmakers use to make accurate maps.
15. Why is a map legend important?

16 Why does Greenland appear so large in relation to other landmasses on a map made using a cylindrical projection?

17 What is the function of contour lines on a topographic map?

18 How can GPS help you find your location on Earth?

19 What is GIS?

CRITICAL THINKING

20 **Concept Mapping** Use the following terms to create a concept map: *maps, legend, map projection, map parts, scale, cylinder, title, cone, plane, date,* and *compass rose.*

21 **Making Inferences** One of the important parts of a map is its date. Why is the date important?

22 **Analyzing Ideas** Why is it important for maps to have scales?

23 **Applying Concepts** Imagine that you are looking at a topographic map of the Grand Canyon. Would the contour lines be spaced close together or far apart? Explain your answer.

24 **Analyzing Processes** How would a GIS system help a team of engineers plan a new highway system for a city?

25 **Making Inferences** If you were stranded in a national park, what kind of map of the park would you want to have with you? Explain your answer.

INTERPRETING GRAPHICS

Use the topographic map below to answer the questions that follow.

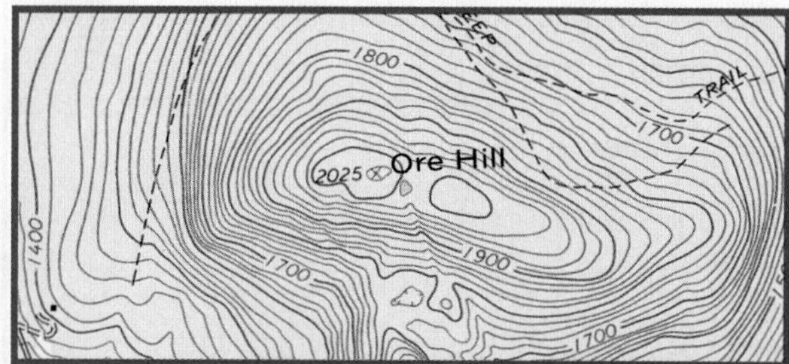

26 What is the elevation change between two adjacent lines on this map?

27 What type of relief does this area have?

28 What surface features are shown on this map?

29 What is the elevation at the top of Ore Hill?

Standardized Test Preparation

Multiple Choice

1. Which of the following shapes most accurately represents Earth?

A. a cone

B. a plane

C. a sphere

D. a pyramid

2. Which of the following types of projections is best for determining distance on a map?

A. azimuthal projection

B. conic projection

C. cylindrical projection

D. equal-area projection

3. Which of the following types of projections shows increasing distortion as you move away from the poles?

A. azimuthal projection

B. conic projection

C. cylindrical projection

D. equal-area projection

4. Which of the following types of projections shows increasing distortion as you move away from the equator?

A. azimuthal projection

B. conic projection

C. cylindrical projection

D. equal-area projection

Use the table below to answer question 5.

	Scale
Map A	1 cm = 0.5 mile
Map B	1 cm = 25 miles
Map C	1 cm = 250 miles

5. Ayanna is using Map B to plan a trip from her house in Cleveland, Ohio, to another location. Based on the map's scale, for which of the following trips would Map B be most useful?

A. to go to a restaurant 4 miles away

B. to go to a mall 10 miles away

C. to go to a stadium 75 miles away

D. to go to a university 2530 miles away

6. Which of the following observations led the ancient Greeks to think that Earth was a sphere?

A. Winds and ocean currents travel in curved paths over Earth's surface.

B. A ship sinks below the horizon as it sails into the distance.

C. Gravity keeps the moon in orbit around Earth.

D. High tides occur on the side of Earth facing the moon.

7. Topographic maps are primarily used to show which of the following features?

A. the shapes of continents and oceans

B. lines of latitude and longitude

C. highways and other roads

D. the elevation of surface features

8. Lines that connect points of equal elevation on topographic maps are called

A. index contours.

B. contour intervals.

C. contour lines.

D. relief.

9. Which of the following statements regarding contour lines on topographic maps is true?

A. Contour lines that are far apart show a steep slope.

B. If a stream flows through a valley, the V of a contour line points downstream.

C. The highest point of a hill or mountain is shown by a contour line.

D. All points along a contour line represent equal elevation.

Use the map below to answer question 10.

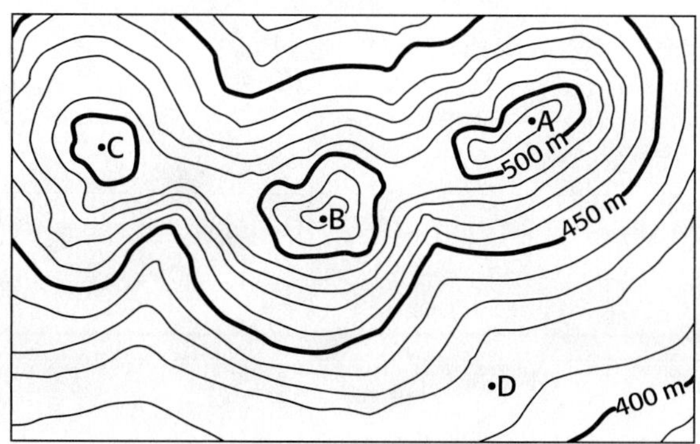

10. Which of the points on the topographic map has the lowest elevation?

A. point A

B. point B

C. point C

D. point D

11. On a map, what is scale used for?

A. to show the location of boundary lines on the map

B. to show the relationship between distance on a map and actual distance

C. to aid in navigation at sea or in the air by approximating elevation of objects

D. to aid in navigation across a state by providing directions

Open Response

12. An area that has one of the highest earthquake risks in the country might surprise you: It's the New Madrid seismic zone that is almost in the center of the country. An earthquake there will immediately affect southeast Missouri, the southern tip of Illinois, northeast Arkansas, and parts of Tennessee and Kentucky. In which layer of the Earth do earthquakes occur? What structures in the layer cause many earthquakes?

13. The coordinates of Frankfort, Kentucky, are 38°, 12 minutes North latitude and 84°, 52 minutes West longitude. Each degree of latitude is about 69 miles. At the equator, each degree of longitude is also about 69 miles. At the coordinates of Frankfort, which distance is greater, 55° of longitude or 55° of latitude? Why?

Science in Action

Scientific Discoveries

The Lost City of Ubar

According to legend, the city of Ubar was a prosperous ancient city. Ubar was most famous for its frankincense, a tree sap that had many uses. As Ubar was in its decline, however, something strange happened. The city disappeared! It was a great myth that Ubar was swallowed up by the desert. It wasn't until present-day scientists used information from a Shuttle Imaging Radar system aboard the space shuttle that this lost city was found! Using radar, scientists were able to "see" beneath the huge dunes of the desert, where they finally found the lost city of Ubar.

Roads appear as purple lines on this computer-generated remote-sensing image.

Social Studies ACTIVITY

WRITING SKILL Ubar was once a very wealthy, magnificent city. Its riches were built on the frankincense trade. Research the history of frankincense, and write a paragraph describing how frankincense was used in ancient times and how it is used today.

Science, Technology, and Society

Geocaching

Wouldn't it be exciting to go on a hunt for buried treasure? Thousands of people around the world participate in geocaching, which is an adventure game for GPS users. In this adventure game, individuals and groups of people put caches, or hidden treasures, in places all over the world. Once the cache is hidden, the coordinates of the cache's location are posted on the Internet. Then, geocaching teams compete to find the cache. Geocaching should only be attempted with parental supervision.

Language Arts ACTIVITY

Why was the word *geocaching* chosen for this adventure game? Use the Internet or another source to find the origin and meaning of the word *geocaching*.

People in Science

Matthew Henson

Arctic Explorer Matthew Henson was born in Maryland in 1866. His parents were freeborn sharecroppers. When Henson was a young boy, his parents died. He then went to look for work as a cabin boy on a ship. Several years later, Henson had traveled around the world and had become educated in the areas of geography, history, and mathematics. In 1898, Henson met U.S. Naval Lieutenant Robert E. Peary. Peary was the leader of Arctic expeditions between 1886 and 1909.

Peary asked Henson to accompany him as a navigator on several trips, including trips to Central America and Greenland. One of Peary's passions was to be the first person to reach the North Pole. It was Henson's vast knowledge of mathematics and carpentry that made Peary's trek to the North Pole possible. In 1909, Henson was the first person to reach the North Pole. Part of Henson's job as navigator was to drive ahead of the party and blaze the first trail. As a result, he often arrived ahead of everyone else. On April 6, 1909, Henson reached the approximate North Pole 45 minutes ahead of Peary. Upon his arrival, he exclaimed, "I think I'm the first man to sit on top of the world!"

Math ACTIVITY

On the last leg of their journey, Henson and Peary traveled 664.5 km in 16 days! On average, how far did Henson and Peary travel each day?

To learn more about these Science in Action topics, visit go.hrw.com and type in the keyword **HZ5MAPF.**

Current Science

Check out Current Science® articles related to this chapter by visiting go.hrw.com. Just type in the keyword HZ5CS02.

Minerals of the Earth's Crust

The Big Idea

Minerals have characteristic physical and chemical properties that determine how each mineral is used by humans.

SECTION

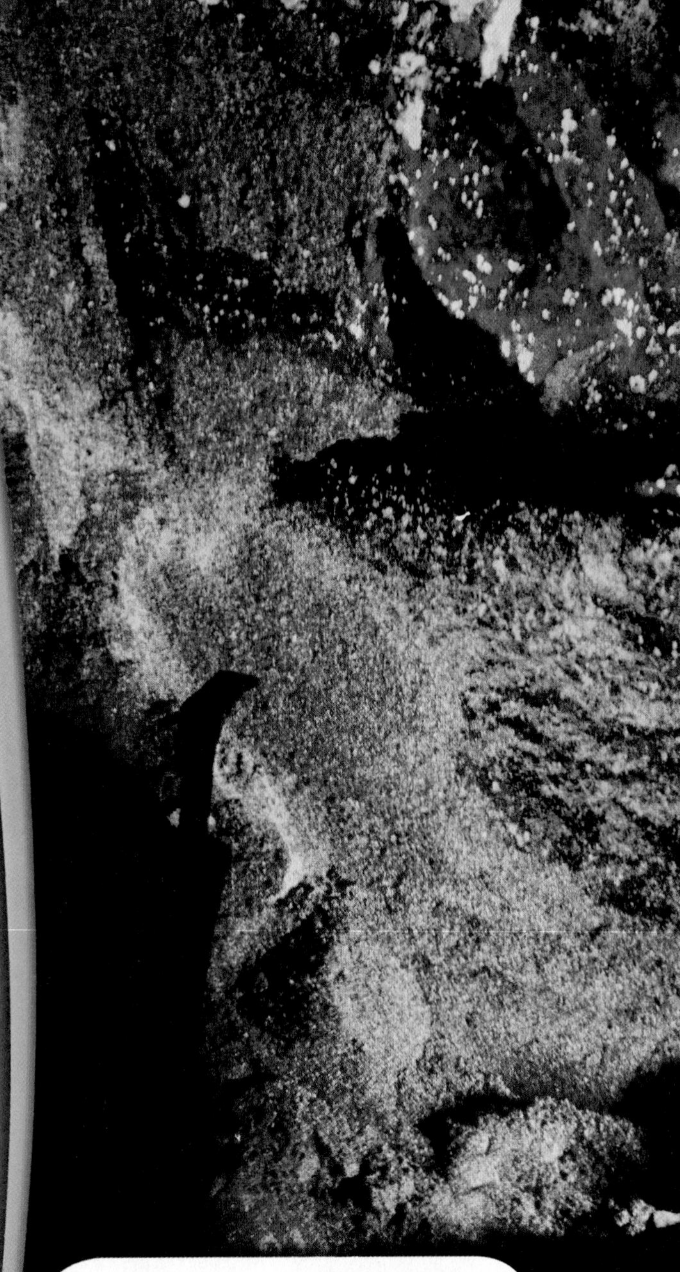

About the Photo

Fluorescence is the ability that some minerals have to glow under ultraviolet light. The beauty of mineral fluorescence is well represented at the Sterling Hill Mine in Franklin, New Jersey. In this picture taken at the mine, minerals in the rock glow as brightly as if they had been freshly painted by an artist.

PRE-READING ACTIVITY

Graphic Organizer

Concept Map Before you read the chapter, create the graphic organizer entitled "Concept Map" described in the **Study Skills** section of the Appendix. As you read the chapter, fill in the concept map with details about minerals.

START-UP ACTIVITY

What Is Your Classroom Made Of?

One of the properties of minerals is that minerals are made from nonliving material. Complete the following activity to see if you can determine whether items in your classroom are made from living or nonliving materials.

Procedure

1. On a **sheet of paper,** make two columns. Label one column "Materials made from living things." Label the second column "Materials made from nonliving things."
2. Look around your classroom. Choose a variety of items to put on your list. Some items that you might select are your clothing, your desk, books, notebook paper, pencils, the classroom windows, doors, walls, the ceiling, and the floor.
3. With a partner, discuss each item that you have chosen. Decide into which column each item should be placed. Write down the reason for your decision.

Analysis

1. Are most of the items that you chose made of living or nonliving materials?

SECTION 1

What Is a Mineral?

You may think that all minerals look like gems. But, in fact, most minerals look more like rocks. Does this mean that minerals are the same as rocks? Well, not really. So, what's the difference?

For one thing, rocks are made of minerals, but minerals are not made of rocks. A **mineral** is a naturally formed, inorganic solid that has a definite crystalline structure.

What You Will Learn

- Describe the structure of minerals.
- Describe the two major groups of minerals.

Vocabulary

mineral
element
compound
crystal
silicate mineral
nonsilicate mineral

READING STRATEGY

Paired Summarizing Read this section silently. In pairs, take turns summarizing the material. Stop to discuss ideas that seem confusing.

Mineral Structure

By answering the four questions in **Figure 1,** you can tell whether an object is a mineral. If you cannot answer "yes" to all four questions, you don't have a mineral. Three of the four questions may be easy to answer. The question about crystalline structure may be more difficult. To understand what crystalline structure is, you need to know a little about the elements that make up a mineral. **Elements** are pure substances that cannot be broken down into simpler substances by ordinary chemical means. All minerals contain one or more of the 92 naturally occurring elements.

Is it nonliving material?
A mineral is inorganic, meaning it isn't made of living things.
Is it a solid?
Minerals can't be gases or liquids.
Does it have a crystalline structure?
Minerals are crystals, which have a repeating inner structure that is often reflected in the shape of the crystal. Minerals generally have the same chemical composition throughout.
Is it formed in nature?
Crystalline materials made by people aren't classified as minerals.

Figure 1 *The answers to these four questions will determine whether an object is a mineral.*

Atoms and Compounds

Each element is made of only one kind of atom. An *atom* is the smallest part of an element that has all the properties of that element. Like other substances, minerals are made up of atoms of one or more elements.

Most minerals are made of compounds of several different elements. A **compound** is a substance made of two or more elements that have been chemically joined, or bonded. Halite, NaCl, for example, is a compound of sodium, Na, and chlorine, Cl, as shown in **Figure 2.** A few minerals, such as gold and silver, are composed of only one element. A mineral that is composed of only one element is called a *native element.*

Reading Check **How does a compound differ from an element?** (*See the Appendix for answers to Reading Checks.*)

Figure 2 *When atoms of sodium (purple) and chlorine (green) join, they form a compound commonly known as rock salt, or the mineral halite.*

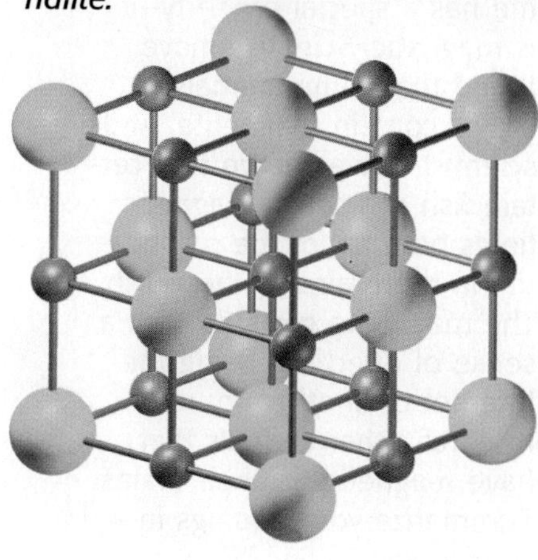

Crystals

Solid, geometric forms of minerals produced by a repeating pattern of atoms or molecules that is present throughout the mineral are called **crystals.** A crystal's shape is determined by the arrangement of the atoms or molecules within the crystal. The arrangement of atoms or molecules in turn is determined by the kinds of atoms or molecules that make up the mineral. Each mineral has a definite crystalline structure. All minerals can be grouped into crystal classes according to the kinds of crystals they form. **Figure 3** shows how the arrangement of atoms in gold may form cubic crystals.

mineral a naturally formed, inorganic solid that has a definite crystalline structure

element a substance that cannot be separated or broken down into simpler substances by chemical means

compound a substance made up of atoms of two or more different elements joined by chemical bonds

crystal a solid whose atoms, ions, or molecules are arranged in a definite pattern

Figure 3 Composition of the Mineral Gold

The mineral gold is composed of gold atoms arranged in a crystalline structure.

The arrangement of gold atoms

The shape of a gold crystal

Crystals of the mineral gold

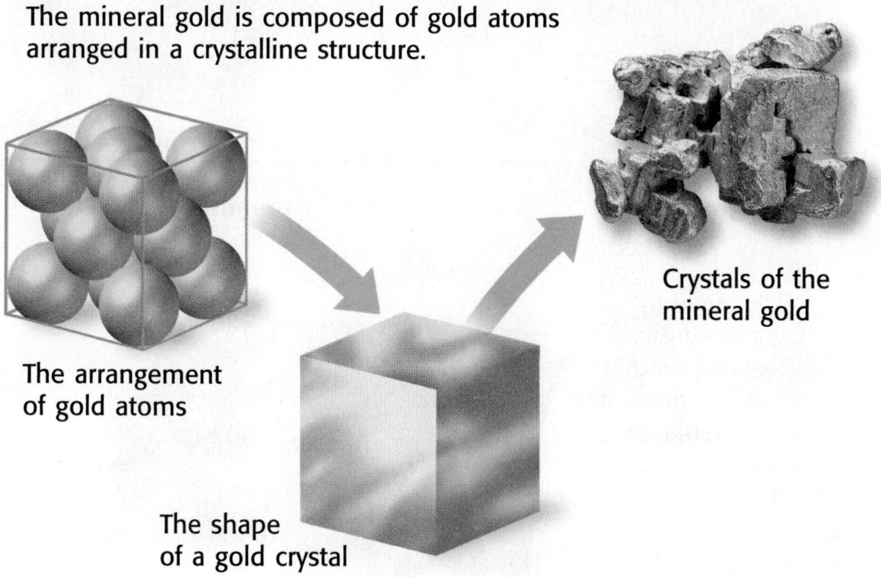

CONNECTION TO Biology

WRITING SKILL **Magnetite** The mineral magnetite has a special property—it is magnetic. Scientists have found that some animals' brains contain magnetite. And scientists have shown that certain fish can sense magnetic fields because of the magnetite in the brains of these fish. The magnetite gives the fish a sense of direction. Using the Internet or another source, research other animals that have magnetite in their brains. Summarize your findings in a short essay.

Two Groups of Minerals

The most common classification of minerals is based on chemical composition. Minerals are divided into two groups based on their chemical composition. These groups are the silicate minerals and the nonsilicate minerals.

Silicate Minerals

Silicon and oxygen are the two most common elements in the Earth's crust. Minerals that contain a combination of these two elements are called **silicate minerals.** Silicate minerals make up more than 90% of the Earth's crust. The rest of the Earth's crust is made up of nonsilicate minerals. Silicon and oxygen usually combine with other elements, such as aluminum, iron, magnesium, and potassium, to make up silicate minerals. Some of the more common silicate minerals are shown in **Figure 4.**

Nonsilicate Minerals

Minerals that do not contain a combination of the elements silicon and oxygen form a group called the **nonsilicate minerals.** Some of these minerals are made up of elements such as carbon, oxygen, fluorine, and sulfur. **Figure 5** on the following page shows the most important classes of nonsilicate minerals.

Reading Check How do silicate minerals differ from nonsilicate minerals?

silicate mineral a mineral that contains a combination of silicon, oxygen, and one or more metals

nonsilicate mineral a mineral that does not contain compounds of silicon and oxygen

Figure 4 **Common Silicate Minerals**

Quartz is the basic building block of many rocks.

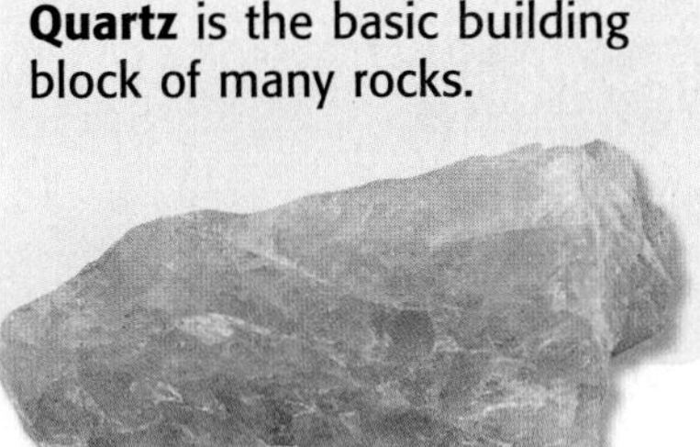

Feldspar minerals are the main component of most rocks on the Earth's surface.

Mica minerals separate easily into sheets when they break. Biotite is one of several kinds of mica.

Figure 5 Classes of Nonsilicate Minerals

Native elements are minerals that are composed of only one element. Some examples are copper, Cu, gold, Au, and silver, Ag. Native elements are used in communications and electronics equipment.

Copper

Oxides are compounds that form when an element, such as aluminum or iron, combines chemically with oxygen. Oxide minerals are used to make abrasives, aircraft parts, and paint.

Corundum

Carbonates are minerals that contain combinations of carbon and oxygen in their chemical structure. We use carbonate minerals in cement, building stones, and fireworks.

Calcite

Sulfates are minerals that contain sulfur and oxygen, SO_4. Sulfates are used in cosmetics, toothpaste, cement, and paint.

Gypsum

Halides are compounds that form when fluorine, chlorine, iodine, or bromine combine with sodium, potassium, or calcium. Halide minerals are used in the chemical industry and in detergents.

Fluorite

Sulfides are minerals that contain one or more elements, such as lead, iron, or nickel, combined with sulfur. Sulfide minerals are used to make batteries, medicines, and electronic parts.

Galena

SECTION Review

Summary

- A mineral is a naturally formed, inorganic solid that has a definite crystalline structure.
- Minerals may be either elements or compounds.
- Mineral crystals are solid, geometric forms that are produced by a repeating pattern of atoms.
- Minerals are classified as either silicate minerals or nonsilicate minerals based on the elements of which they are composed.

Using Key Terms

1. In your own words, write a definition for each of the following terms: *element, compound,* and *mineral.*

Understanding Key Ideas

2. Which of the following minerals is a nonsilicate mineral?
   a. mica
   b. quartz
   c. gypsum
   d. feldspar
3. What is a crystal, and what determines a crystal's shape?
4. Describe the two major groups of minerals.

Math Skills

5. If there are approximately 3,600 known minerals and about 20 of the minerals are native elements, what percentage of all minerals are native elements?

Critical Thinking

6. **Applying Concepts** Explain why each of the following is not considered a mineral: water, oxygen, honey, and teeth.
7. **Applying Concepts** Explain why scientists consider ice to be a mineral.
8. **Making Comparisons** In what ways are sulfate and sulfide minerals the same. In what ways are they different?

SCILINKS®
NSTA
Developed and maintained by the National Science Teachers Association
For a variety of links related to this chapter, go to www.scilinks.org
Topic: Gems
SciLinks code: HSM0640

SECTION 2

Identifying Minerals

What You Will Learn

- Identify seven ways to determine the identity of minerals.
- Explain special properties of minerals.

Vocabulary

luster, fracture, streak, hardness, cleavage, density

READING STRATEGY

Reading Organizer As you read this section, create an outline of the section. Use the headings from the section in your outline.

If you closed your eyes and tasted different foods, you could probably determine what the foods are by noting properties such as saltiness or sweetness. You can also determine the identity of a mineral by noting different properties.

In this section, you will learn about the properties that will help you identify minerals.

Color

The same mineral can come in a variety of colors. For example, in its purest state quartz is clear. Samples of quartz that contain various types of and various amounts of impurities, however, can be a variety of colors.

Besides impurities, other factors can change the appearance of minerals. The mineral pyrite, often called fool's gold, normally has a golden color. But if pyrite is exposed to air and water for a long period, it can turn brown or black. Because of factors such as impurities, color usually is not the best way to identify a mineral.

Luster

luster the way in which a mineral reflects light

The way a surface reflects light is called **luster.** When you say an object is shiny or dull, you are describing its luster. Minerals have metallic, submetallic, or nonmetallic luster. If a mineral is shiny, it has a metallic luster. If the mineral is dull, its luster is either submetallic or nonmetallic. The different types of lusters are shown in **Figure 1.**

Figure 1 Types of Mineral Luster

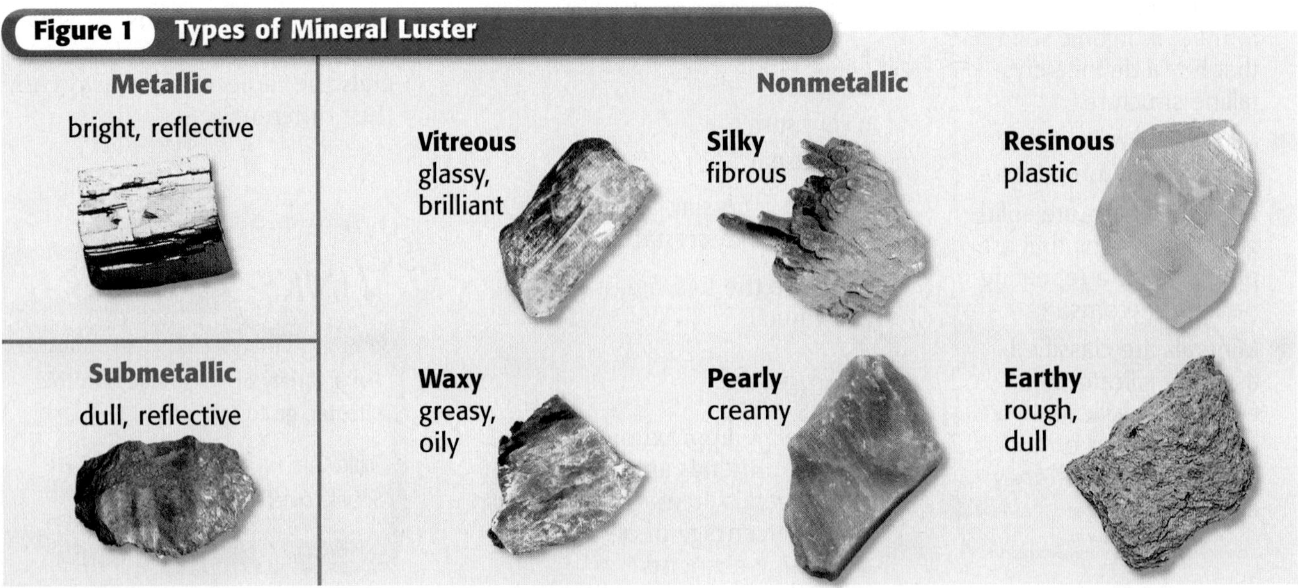

Streak

The color of a mineral in powdered form is called the mineral's **streak.** A mineral's streak can be found by rubbing the mineral against a piece of unglazed porcelain called a *streak plate.* The mark left on the streak plate is the streak. The streak is a thin layer of powdered mineral. The color of a mineral's streak is not always the same as the color of the mineral sample. The difference between color and streak is shown in **Figure 2.** Unlike the surface of a mineral sample, the streak is not affected by air or water. For this reason, using streak is more reliable than using color in identifying a mineral.

Figure 2 *The color of the mineral hematite may vary, but hematite's streak is always red-brown.*

Reading Check **Why is using streak more reliable in identifying a mineral than using color is?** (*See the Appendix for answers to Reading Checks.*)

Cleavage and Fracture

Different types of minerals break in different ways. The way a mineral breaks is determined by the arrangement of its atoms. **Cleavage** is the tendency of some minerals to break along smooth, flat surfaces. **Figure 3** shows the cleavage patterns of the minerals mica and halite.

Fracture is the tendency of some minerals to break unevenly along curved or irregular surfaces. One type of fracture is shown in **Figure 4.**

streak the color of the powder of a mineral

cleavage the splitting of a mineral along smooth, flat surfaces

fracture the manner in which a mineral breaks along either curved or irregular surfaces

Figure 3 *Cleavage varies with mineral type.*

Mica breaks easily into distinct sheets.

Halite breaks at 90° angles in three directions.

Figure 4 *This sample of quartz shows a curved fracture pattern called* conchoidal fracture *(kahn KOYD uhl FRAK chuhr).*

Figure 5 Mohs Hardness Scale

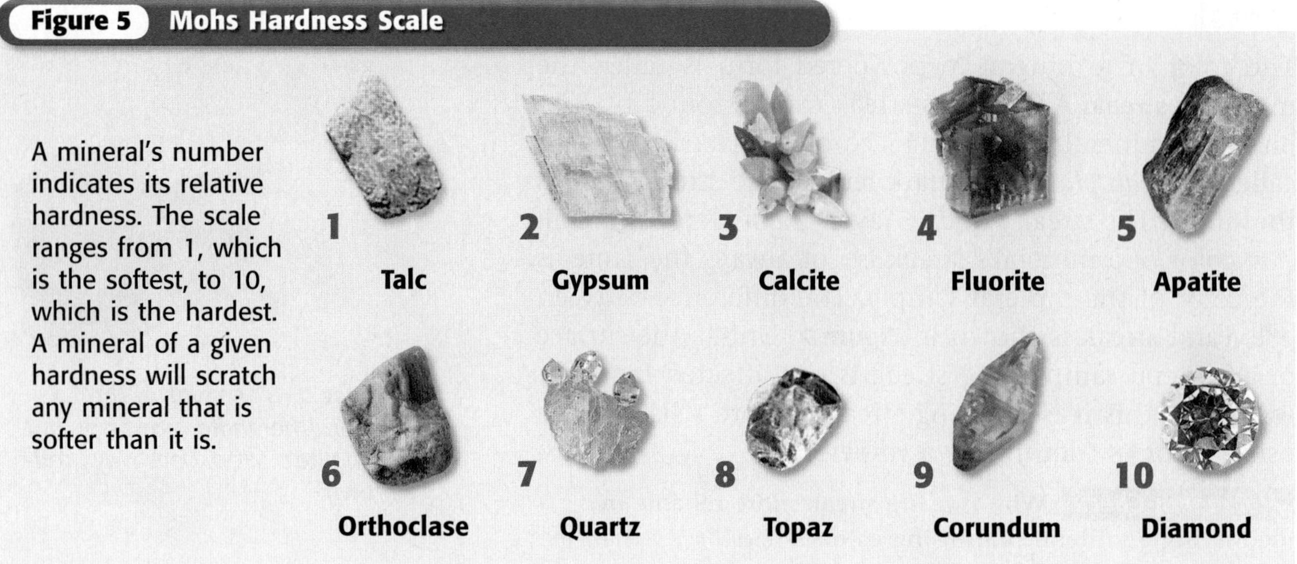

A mineral's number indicates its relative hardness. The scale ranges from 1, which is the softest, to 10, which is the hardest. A mineral of a given hardness will scratch any mineral that is softer than it is.

hardness a measure of the ability of a mineral to resist scratching

density the ratio of the mass of a substance to the volume of the substance

Hardness

A mineral's resistance to being scratched is called **hardness**. To determine the hardness of minerals, scientists use *Mohs hardness scale,* shown in **Figure 5.** Notice that talc has a rating of 1 and diamond has a rating of 10. The greater a mineral's resistance to being scratched is, the higher the mineral's rating is. To identify a mineral by using Mohs scale, try to scratch the surface of a mineral with the edge of one of the 10 reference minerals. If the reference mineral scratches your mineral, the reference mineral is harder than your mineral.

Reading Check **How would you determine the hardness of an unidentified mineral sample?**

Scratch Test

1. You will need a **penny,** a **pencil,** and your **fingernail.** Which one of these three materials is the hardest?
2. Use your fingernail to try to scratch the graphite at the tip of a pencil.
3. Now try to scratch the penny with your fingernail.
4. Rank the three materials in order from softest to hardest.

Density

If you pick up a golf ball and a table-tennis ball, which will feel heavier? Although the balls are of similar size, the golf ball will feel heavier because it is denser. **Density** is the measure of how much matter is in a given amount of space. In other words, density is a ratio of an object's mass to its volume. Density is usually measured in grams per cubic centimeter. Because water has a density of 1 g/cm^3, it is used as a reference point for other substances. The ratio of an object's density to the density of water is called the object's *specific gravity.* The specific gravity of gold, for example, is 19. So, gold has a density of 19 g/cm^3. In other words, 1 cm^3 of gold contains 19 times as much matter than 1 cm^3 of water contains.

Special Properties

Some properties are particular to only a few types of minerals. The properties shown in **Figure 6** can help you quickly identify the minerals shown. To identify some properties, however, you will need specialized equipment.

Figure 6 **Special Properties of Some Minerals**

Fluorescence
Calcite and fluorite glow under ultraviolet light. The same fluorite sample is shown in ultraviolet light (top) and in white light (bottom).

Chemical Reaction
Calcite will become bubbly, or "fizz," when a drop of weak acid is placed on it.

Optical Properties
A thin, clear piece of calcite placed over an image will cause a double image.

Magnetism
Both magnetite and pyrrhotite are natural magnets that attract iron.

Taste
Halite has a salty taste.

Radioactivity
Minerals that contain radium or uranium can be detected by a Geiger counter.

SECTION Review

Summary

- Properties that can be used to identify minerals are color, luster, streak, cleavage, fracture, hardness, and density.
- Some minerals can be identified by special properties they have, such as taste, magnetism, fluorescence, radioactivity, chemical reaction, and optical properties.

Using Key Terms

1. Use each of the following terms in a separate sentence: *luster, streak,* and *cleavage.*

Understanding Key Ideas

2. Which of the following properties of minerals is expressed in numbers?
   a. fracture
   b. cleavage
   c. hardness
   d. streak
3. How do you determine a mineral's streak?
4. Briefly describe the special properties of minerals.

Math Skills

5. If a mineral has a specific gravity of 5.5, how much more matter is there in 1 cm^3 of this mineral than in 1 cm^3 of water?

Critical Thinking

6. **Applying Concepts** What properties would you use to determine whether two mineral samples are different minerals?
7. **Applying Concepts** If a mineral scratches calcite but is scratched by apatite, what is the mineral's hardness?
8. **Analyzing Methods** What would be the easiest way to identify calcite?

For a variety of links related to this chapter, go to www.scilinks.org

Topic: Identifying Minerals
SciLinks code: HSM0782

SECTION 3

The Formation, Mining, and Use of Minerals

What You Will Learn

- Describe the environments in which minerals form.
- Compare the two types of mining.
- Describe two ways to reduce the effects of mining.
- Describe different uses for metallic and nonmetallic minerals.

Vocabulary

ore
reclamation

READING STRATEGY

Discussion Read this section silently. Write down questions that you have about this section. Discuss your questions in a small group.

If you wanted to find a mineral, where do you think you would look?

Minerals form in a variety of environments in the Earth's crust. Each of these environments has a different set of physical and chemical conditions. Therefore, the environment in which a mineral forms determines the mineral's properties. Environments in which minerals form may be on or near the Earth's surface or deep beneath the Earth's surface.

Limestones Surface water and groundwater carry dissolved materials into lakes and seas, where they crystallize on the bottom. Minerals that form in this environment include calcite and dolomite.

Evaporating Salt Water When a body of salt water dries up, minerals such as gypsum and halite are left behind. As the salt water evaporates, these minerals crystallize.

Metamorphic Rocks When changes in pressure, temperature, or chemical makeup alter a rock, *metamorphism* takes place. Minerals that form in metamorphic rock include calcite, garnet, graphite, hematite, magnetite, mica, and talc.

INTERNET ACTIVITY

For another activity related to this chapter, go to go.hrw.com and type in the keyword **HZ5MINW.**

Hot-Water Solutions Groundwater works its way downward and is heated by magma. It then reacts with minerals to form a hot liquid solution. Dissolved metals and other elements crystallize out of the hot fluid to form new minerals. Gold, copper, sulfur, pyrite, and galena form in such hot-water environments.

Pegmatites As magma moves upward, it can form teardrop-shaped bodies called *pegmatites.* The mineral crystals in pegmatites become extremely large, sometimes growing to several meters across! Many gemstones, such as topaz and tourmaline, form in pegmatites.

Plutons As magma rises upward through the crust, it sometimes stops moving before it reaches the surface and cools slowly, forming millions of mineral crystals. Eventually, the entire magma body solidifies to form a *pluton.* Mica, feldspar, magnetite, and quartz are some of the minerals that form from magma.

Surface Coal Mining

Producing 1 metric ton of coal requires that up to 30 metric tons of earth be removed first. Some surface coal mines produce up to 50,000 metric tons of coal per day. How many metric tons of earth might have to be removed in order to mine 50,000 metric tons of coal?

Mining

Many kinds of rocks and minerals must be mined to extract the valuable elements they contain. Geologists use the term **ore** to describe a mineral deposit large enough and pure enough to be mined for profit. Rocks and minerals are removed from the ground by one of two methods—surface mining or subsurface mining. The method miners choose depends on how close to the surface or how far down in the Earth the mineral is located.

ore a natural material whose concentration of economically valuable minerals is high enough for the material to be mined profitably

Surface Mining

When mineral deposits are located at or near the surface of the Earth, surface-mining methods are used to remove the minerals. Types of surface mines include open pits, surface coal mines, and quarries.

Open-pit mining is used to remove large, near-surface deposits of economically important minerals such as gold and copper. As shown in **Figure 1,** ore is mined downward, layer by layer, in an open-pit mine. Explosives are often used to break up the ore. The ore is then loaded into haul trucks and transported from the mine for processing. Quarries are open pits that are used to mine building stone, crushed rock, sand, and gravel. Coal that is near the surface is removed by surface coal mining. Surface coal mining is sometimes known as strip mining because the coal is removed in strips that may be as wide as 50 m and as long as 1 km.

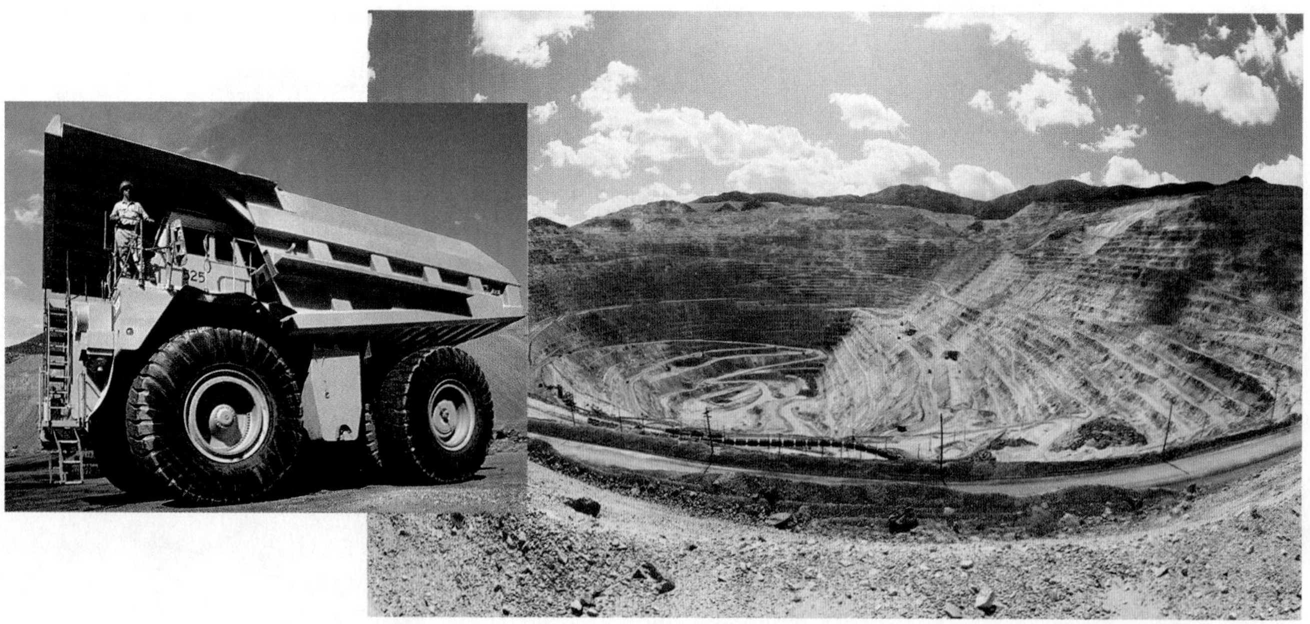

Figure 1 *In open-pit mines, the ore is mined downward in layers. The stair-step excavation of the walls keeps the sides of the mine from collapsing. Giant haul trucks (inset) are used to transport ore from the mine.*

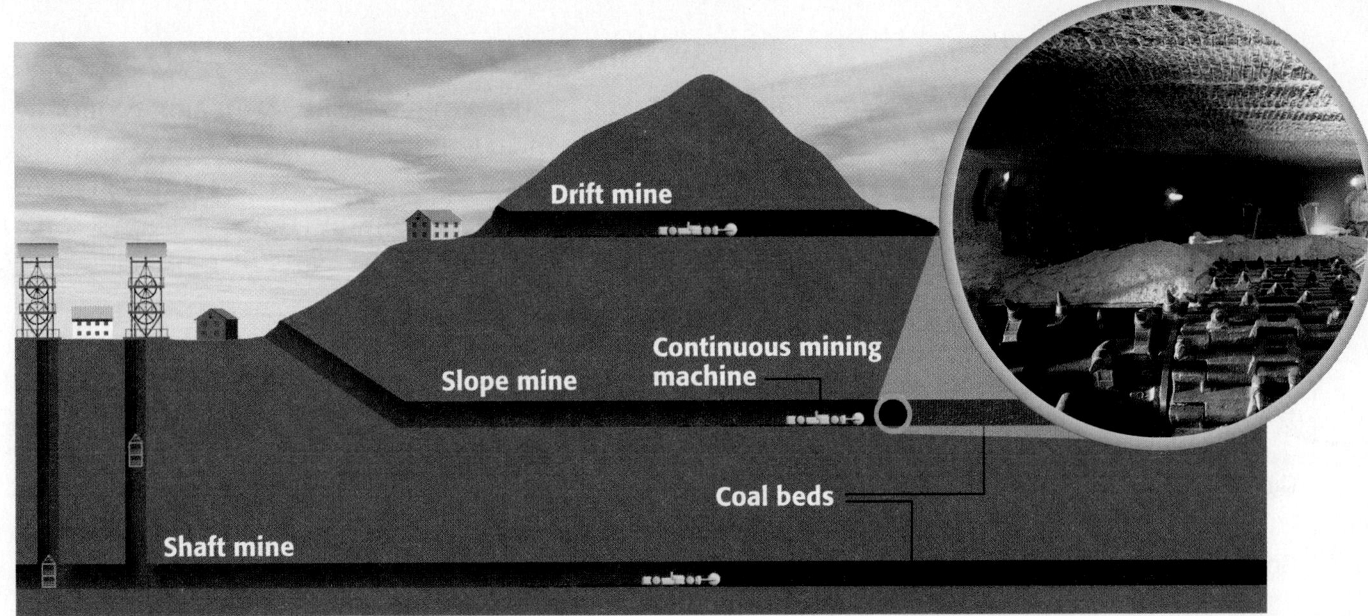

Figure 2 *Subsurface mining is the removal of minerals or other materials from deep within the Earth. Passageways must be dug underground to reach the ore. Machines such as continuous mining machines (inset) are used to mine ore in subsurface mines.*

Subsurface Mining

Subsurface mining methods are used when mineral deposits are located too deep within the Earth to be surface mined. Subsurface mining often requires that passageways be dug into the Earth to reach the ore. As shown in **Figure 2,** these passageways may be dug horizontally or at an angle. If a mineral deposit extends deep within the Earth, however, a vertical shaft is sunk. This shaft may connect a number of passageways that intersect the ore at different levels.

Reading Check **Compare surface and subsurface mining.** (*See the Appendix for answers to Reading Checks.*)

reclamation the process of returning land to its original condition after mining is completed

Responsible Mining

Mining gives us the minerals we need, but it may also create problems. Mining can destroy or disturb the habitats of plants and animals. Also, the waste products from a mine may get into water sources, which pollutes surface water and groundwater.

Mine Reclamation

One way to reduce the potential harmful effects of mining is to return the land to its original state after the mining is completed. The process by which land used for mining is returned to its original state or better is called **reclamation.** Reclamation of mined public and private land has been required by law since the mid-1970s. Another way to reduce the effects of mining is to reduce our need for minerals. We reduce our need for minerals by recycling many of the mineral products that we currently use, such as aluminum.

Recycling Minerals at Home

With a parent or guardian, locate products in your home that are made of minerals. Decide which of these products could be recycled. In your **science journal,** make a list of the products that could be recycled to save minerals.

Table 1 Common Uses of Minerals	
Mineral	**Uses**
Copper	electrical wire, plumbing, coins
Diamond	jewelry, cutting tools, drill bits
Galena	batteries, ammunition
Gibbsite	cans, foil, appliances, utensils
Gold	jewelry, computers, spacecraft, dentistry
Gypsum	wallboards, plaster, cement
Halite	nutrition, highway de-icer, water softener
Quartz	glass, computer chips
Silver	photography, electronics products, jewelry
Sphalerite	jet aircraft, spacecraft, paints

The Use of Minerals

As shown in **Table 1,** some minerals are of major economic and industrial importance. Some minerals can be used just as they are. Other minerals must be processed to get the element or elements that the minerals contain. **Figure 3** shows some processed minerals used to make the parts of a bicycle.

Metallic Minerals

Some minerals are metallic. Metallic minerals have shiny surfaces, do not let light pass through them, and are good conductors of heat and electricity. Metallic minerals can be processed into metals that are strong and do not rust. Other metals can be pounded or pressed into various shapes or stretched thinly without breaking. These properties make metals desirable for use in aircraft, automobiles, computers, communications and electronic equipment, and spacecraft. Examples of metallic minerals that have many industrial uses are gold, silver, and copper.

Nonmetallic Minerals

Other minerals are nonmetals. Nonmetallic minerals have shiny or dull surfaces, may let light pass through them, and are good insulators of electricity. Nonmetallic minerals are some of the most widely used minerals in industry. For example, calcite is a major component of concrete, which is used in building roads, buildings, bridges, and other structures. Industrial sand and gravel, or silica, have uses that range from glassmaking to producing computer chips.

Figure 3 Some Materials Used in the Parts of a Bicycle

Gemstones

Some nonmetallic minerals, called *gemstones*, are highly valued for their beauty and rarity rather than for their usefulness. Important gemstones include diamond, ruby, sapphire, emerald, aquamarine, topaz, and tourmaline. An example of a diamond is shown in **Figure 4.** Color is the most important characteristic of a gemstone. The more attractive the color is, the more valuable the gem is. Gemstones must also be durable. That is, they must be hard enough to be cut and polished. The mass of a gemstone is expressed in a unit known as a *carat*. One carat is equal to 200 mg.

Reading Check **In your own words, define the term *gemstone*.**

Figure 4 *The Cullinan diamond, at the center of this scepter, is part of the largest diamond ever found.*

SECTION Review

Summary

- Environments in which minerals form may be located at or near the Earth's surface or deep below the surface.
- The two types of mining are surface mining and subsurface mining.
- Two ways to reduce the effects of mining are the reclamation of mined land and the recycling of mineral products.
- Some metallic and nonmetallic minerals have many important economic and industrial uses.

Using Key Terms

Complete each of the following sentences by choosing the correct term from the word bank.

ore reclamation

1. _____ is the process of returning land to its original condition after mining is completed.
2. _____ is the term used to describe a mineral deposit that is large enough and pure enough to be mined for profit.

Understanding Key Ideas

3. Which of the following conditions is NOT important in the formation of minerals?
   a. presence of groundwater
   b. evaporation
   c. volcanic activity
   d. wind
4. What are the two main types of mining, and how do they differ?
5. List some uses of metallic minerals.
6. List some uses of nonmetallic minerals.

Math Skills

7. A diamond cutter has a raw diamond that weighs 19.5 carats and from which two 5-carat diamonds will be cut. How much did the raw diamond weigh in milligrams? How much will each of the two cut diamonds weigh in milligrams?

Critical Thinking

8. **Analyzing Ideas** How does reclamation protect the environment around a mine?
9. **Applying Concepts** Suppose you find a mineral crystal that is as tall as you are. What kinds of environmental factors would cause such a crystal to form?

SCILINKS.
NSTA
Developed and maintained by the National Science Teachers Association
For a variety of links related to this chapter, go to www.scilinks.org
Topic: Mining Minerals
SciLinks code: HSM0968

Using Scientific Methods

Skills Practice Lab

Is It Fool's Gold? A Dense Situation

OBJECTIVES

Calculate the density and specific gravity of a mineral.

Explain how density and specific gravity can be used to identify a mineral specimen.

MATERIALS

- balance
- beaker, 400 mL
- galena sample
- pyrite sample
- ring stand
- spring scale
- string
- water, 400 mL

SAFETY

Have you heard of fool's gold? Maybe you've seen a piece of it. This mineral is actually pyrite, and it was often passed off as real gold. However, there are simple tests that you can do to keep from being tricked. Minerals can be identified by their properties. Some properties, such as color, vary from sample to sample. Other properties, such as density and specific gravity, remain consistent across samples. In this activity, you will try to verify the identity of some mineral samples.

Ask a Question

1. How can I determine if an unknown mineral is not gold or silver?

Form a Hypothesis

2. Write a hypothesis that is a possible answer to the question above. Explain your reasoning.

Test the Hypothesis

3. Copy the data table. Use it to record your observations.

Observation Chart

Measurement	Galena	Pyrite
Mass in air (g)		
Weight in air (N)		
Volume of mineral (mL)	DO NOT WRITE IN BOOK	
Weight in water (N)		

4. Find the mass of each sample by laying the mineral on the balance. Record the mass of each sample in your data table.
5. Attach the spring scale to the ring stand.
6. Tie a string around the sample of galena, and leave a loop at the loose end. Suspend the galena from the spring scale, and find its mass and weight in air. Do not remove the sample from the spring scale yet. Enter these data in your data table.

Galena

Pyrite

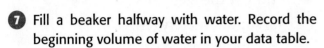

7. Fill a beaker halfway with water. Record the beginning volume of water in your data table.
8. Carefully lift the beaker around the galena until the mineral is completely submerged. Be careful not to splash any water out of the beaker! Do not allow the mineral to touch the beaker.
9. Record the new volume and weight in your data table.
10. Subtract the original volume of water from the new volume to find the amount of water displaced by the mineral. This is the volume of the mineral sample itself. Record this value in your data table.
11. Repeat steps 6–10 for the sample of pyrite.

Analyze the Results

1. **Constructing Tables** Copy the data table below. (Note: 1 mL = 1 cm^3)

Density Data Table

Mineral	Density (g/cm^3)	Specific gravity
Silver	10.5	10.5
Galena	DO NOT WRITE IN BOOK	
Pyrite		
Gold	19.0	19.0

2. **Organizing Data** Use the following equations to calculate the density and specific gravity of each mineral, and record your answers in your data table.

$$density = \frac{mass\ in\ air}{volume}$$

$$specific\ gravity = \frac{weight\ in\ air}{weight\ in\ air - weight\ in\ water}$$

Draw Conclusions

3. **Drawing Conclusions** The density of pure gold is 19 g/cm^3. How can you use this information to prove that your sample of pyrite is not gold?
4. **Drawing Conclusions** The density of pure silver is 10.5 g/cm^3. How can you use this information to prove that your sample of galena is not silver?
5. **Applying Conclusions** If you found a gold-colored nugget, how could you find out if the nugget was real gold or fool's gold?

Chapter Review

USING KEY TERMS

1. Use each of the following terms in a separate sentence: *element, compound,* and *mineral.*

For each pair of terms, explain how the meanings of the terms differ.

2. *color* and *streak*

3. *mineral* and *ore*

4. *silicate mineral* and *nonsilicate mineral*

UNDERSTANDING KEY IDEAS

Multiple Choice

5. Which of the following properties of minerals does Mohs scale measure?
   - **a.** luster
   - **b.** hardness
   - **c.** density
   - **d.** streak

6. Pure substances that cannot be broken down into simpler substances by ordinary chemical means are called
   - **a.** molecules.
   - **b.** elements.
   - **c.** compounds.
   - **d.** crystals.

7. Which of the following properties is considered a special property that applies to only a few minerals?
   - **a.** luster
   - **b.** hardness
   - **c.** taste
   - **d.** density

8. Silicate minerals contain a combination of the elements
   - **a.** sulfur and oxygen.
   - **b.** carbon and oxygen.
   - **c.** iron and oxygen.
   - **d.** silicon and oxygen.

9. The process by which land used for mining is returned to its original state is called
   - **a.** recycling.
   - **b.** regeneration.
   - **c.** reclamation.
   - **d.** renovation.

10. Which of the following minerals is an example of a gemstone?
    - **a.** mica
    - **b.** diamond
    - **c.** gypsum
    - **d.** copper

Short Answer

11. Compare surface and subsurface mining.

12. Explain the four characteristics of a mineral.

13. Describe two environments in which minerals form.

14. List two uses for metallic minerals and two uses for nonmetallic minerals.

15. Describe two ways to reduce the effects of mining.

16. Describe three special properties of minerals.

CRITICAL THINKING

17 **Concept Mapping** Use the following terms to create a concept map: *minerals, calcite, silicate minerals, gypsum, carbonates, nonsilicate minerals, quartz,* and *sulfates.*

18 **Making Inferences** Imagine that you are trying to determine the identity of a mineral. You decide to do a streak test. You rub the mineral across the streak plate, but the mineral does not leave a streak. Has your test failed? Explain your answer.

19 **Applying Concepts** Why would cleavage be important to gem cutters, who cut and shape gemstones?

20 **Applying Concepts** Imagine that you work at a jeweler's shop and someone brings in some gold nuggets for sale. You are not sure if the nuggets are real gold. Which identification tests would help you decide whether the nuggets are gold?

21 **Identifying Relationships** Suppose you are in a desert. You are walking across the floor of a dry lake, and you see crusts of cubic halite crystals. How do you suppose the halite crystals formed? Explain your answer.

INTERPRETING GRAPHICS

The table below shows the temperatures at which various minerals melt. Use the table below to answer the questions that follow.

Melting Points of Various Minerals

Mineral	Melting Point (°C)
Mercury	−39
Sulfur	+113
Halite	801
Silver	961
Gold	1,062
Copper	1,083
Pyrite	1,171
Fluorite	1,360
Quartz	1,710
Zircon	2,500

22 According to the table, what is the approximate difference in temperature between the melting points of the mineral that has the lowest melting point and the mineral that has the highest melting point?

23 Which of the minerals listed in the table do you think is a liquid at room temperature?

24 Pyrite is often called *fool's gold.* Using the information in the table, how could you determine if a mineral sample is pyrite or gold?

25 Convert the melting points of the minerals shown in the table from degrees Celsius to degrees Fahrenheit. Use the formula $°F = (9/5 \times °C) + 32$.

Standardized Test Preparation

Multiple Choice

1. **Which of the following statements best defines a mineral?**

   A. a substance that cannot by chemical means be separated or broken down into simpler substances

   B. a substance made up of the atoms of two or more elements that are joined by chemical bonds

   C. a naturally formed solid with a regular crystalline structure and a defined chemical composition

   D. a solid whose atoms, ions, or molecules are arranged in a regular pattern

2. **Which of the following substances is a mineral?**

   A. coal, which is formed with the remains of living things

   B. fluorite, which is a crystalline solid with the chemical formula CaF_2

   C. obsidian, which is a volcanic glass and is not crystalline

   D. brass, which is a metal that is made by humans

3. **Minerals that contain one or more elements combined with silicon and oxygen are called**

   A. sulfides.

   B. silicates.

   C. oxides.

   D. halides.

Use the table below to answer question 4.

Chemical symbol	Mineral	Mineral Class
Au	gold	native element
$CaCO_3$	calcite	________
FeS_2	pyrite	sulfide
SiO_2	quartz	silicate

4. **Which of the following terms correctly completes the table above?**

   A. sulfate

   B. oxide

   C. carbonate

   D. halide

5. **Which of the following is a nonsilicate mineral?**

   A. orthoclase, $KAlSi_3O_8$

   B. talc, $Mg_3Si_4O_{10}(OH)_2$

   C. almandine, $Fe_3Al_2(SiO_4)_3$

   D. magnetite, Fe_3O_4

6. **Which of the following minerals can be identified by taste?**

   A. magnetite

   B. fluorite

   C. calcite

   D. halite

7. **Minerals such as gypsum and halite form**

A. from hot-water solutions.

B. when a rock is altered by metamorphism.

C. when bodies of salt water evaporate.

D. from the cooling of magma that rises upward through the crust.

8. **Which of the following statements about metallic minerals is true?**

A. Metallic minerals can be pounded or pressed into various shapes.

B. Metallic minerals have dull lusters.

C. Metallic minerals let light pass through them.

D. Metallic minerals are poor conductors of electricity.

9. **Why are gemstones valuable?**

A. They can be used to strengthen concrete and to build buildings.

B. They are good conductors of heat and electricity.

C. They are beautiful and rare.

D. They taste good.

10. **Which of the following would be considered an ore?**

A. a small deposit of a mineral that is rare and has no known use

B. a large deposit of a mineral that has many uses and costs little to mine

C. a small deposit of a mineral that is rare, valuable, and very expensive to mine

D. a large deposit of a mineral that is abundant but that has no known use

Use the graph below to answer question 11.

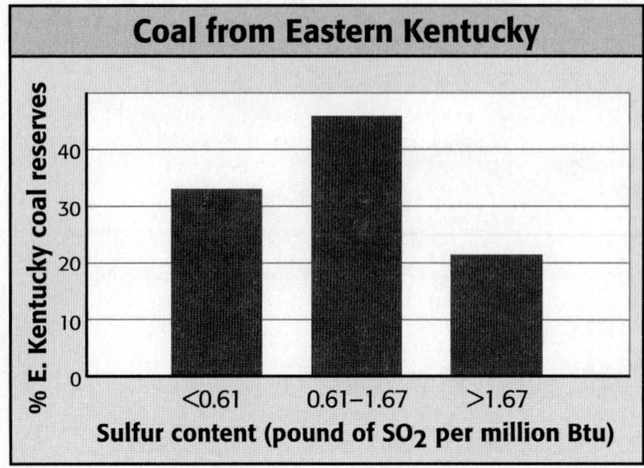

11. **Eastern Kentucky's coal fields contain large amounts of coal, but not all of it has a low enough sulfur content to meet government pollution-reduction goals. If the emissions limit was set at a maximum of 1.67 pounds of SO_2 per million Btu, how much of Eastern Kentucky's coal could be used?**

A. 13.6%

B. 32.3%

C. 45.9%

D. 78.2%

Open Response

12. **What is the difference between an element and a mineral?**

13. **The state rock of Kentucky happens to be a mineral, Kentucky agate. Its chemical composition is SiO_2. In what group of minerals does agate belong? How do you know?**

Science in Action

Science Fiction

"The Metal Man" by Jack Williamson

In a dark, dusty corner of Tyburn College Museum stands a life-sized statue of a man. Except for its strange greenish color, the statue looks quite ordinary. But if you look closely, you will see the perfect detail of the hair and skin. On the statue's chest, you will also see a strange mark—a dark crimson shape with six sides. No one knows how the statue ended up in the dark corner. But most people in Tyburn believe that the metal man is, or once was, Professor Thomas Kelvin of Tyburn College's geology department. Read for yourself the strange story of Professor Kelvin and the Metal Man, which is in the *Holt Anthology of Science Fiction*.

Language Arts Activity

WRITING SKILL Read "The Metal Man" by Jack Williamson. Write a short essay explaining how the ideas in the story are related to what you are learning.

Weird Science

Wieliczka Salt Mine

Imagine an underground city that is made entirely of salt. Within the city are churches, chapels, rooms of many kinds, and salt lakes. Sculptures of biblical scenes, saints, and famous historical figures carved from salt are found throughout the city. Even chandeliers of salt hang from the ceilings. Such a city is located 16 km southeast of Krakow, Poland, inside the Wieliczka (VEE uh LEETS kuh) Salt Mine. As the mine grew over the past 700 years, it turned into an elaborate underground city. Miners constructed chapels to patron saints so they could pray for a safe day in the mine. Miners also developed superstitions about the mine. So, images that were meant to bring good luck were carved in salt. In 1978, the mine was added to UNESCO's list of endangered world heritage sites. Many of the sculptures in the mine have begun to dissolve because of the humidity in the air. Efforts to save the treasures in the mine from further damage were begun in 1996.

Social Studies Activity

WRITING SKILL Research some aspect of the role of salt in human history. For example, subjects might include the Saharan and Tibetan salt trade or the use of salt as a form of money in ancient Poland. Report your findings in a one-page essay.

Jamie Hill

The Emerald Man Jamie Hill was raised in the Brushy Mountains of North Carolina. While growing up, Hill gained firsthand knowledge of the fabulous green crystals that could be found in the mountains. These green crystals were emeralds. Emerald is the green variety of the silicate mineral beryl and is a valuable gemstone. Emerald crystals form in pockets, or openings, in rock known as *pegmatite*.

Since 1985, Hill has been searching for pockets containing emeralds in rock near the small town of Hiddenite, North Carolina. He has been amazingly successful. Hill has discovered some spectacular emerald crystals. The largest of these crystals weighs 858 carats and is on display at the North Carolina Museum of Natural Science. Estimates of the total value of the emeralds that Hill has discovered so far are well in the millions of dollars. Hill's discoveries have made him a celebrity, and he has appeared both on national TV and in magazines.

Math ACTIVITY

An emerald discovered by Jamie Hill in 1999 was cut into a 7.85-carat stone that sold for $64,000 per carat. What was the total value of the cut stone?

To learn more about these Science in Action topics, visit go.hrw.com and type in the keyword HZ5MINF.

Current Science

Check out Current Science® articles related to this chapter by visiting go.hrw.com. Just type in the keyword HZ5CS03.

10

Rocks: Mineral Mixtures

The Big Idea

Rock changes through the rock cycle and is classified by how it formed, by its composition, and by its texture.

SECTION

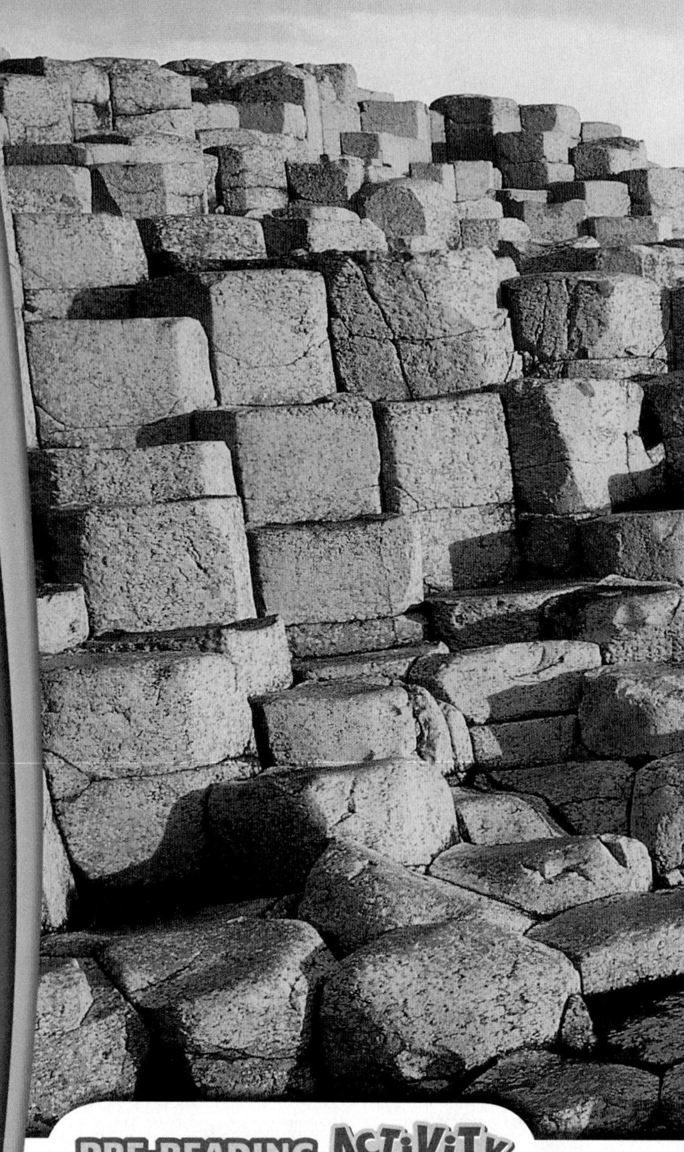

About the Photo

Irish legend claims that the mythical hero Finn MacCool built the Giant's Causeway, shown here. But this rock formation is the result of the cooling of huge amounts of molten rock. As the molten rock cooled, it formed tall pillars separated by cracks called *columnar joints*.

PRE-READING ACTIVITY

Graphic Organizer

Spider Map Before you read the chapter, create the graphic organizer entitled "Spider Map" described in the **Study Skills** section of the Appendix. Label the circle "Rock." Create a leg for each of the sections in this chapter. As you read the chapter, fill in the map with details about the material presented in each section of the chapter.

START-UP ACTIVITY

Classifying Objects

Scientists use the physical and chemical properties of rocks to classify rocks. Classifying objects such as rocks requires looking at many properties. Do this exercise for some classification practice.

Procedure

1. Your teacher will give you a **bag** containing **several objects.** Examine the objects, and note features such as size, color, shape, texture, smell, and any unique properties.
2. Develop three different ways to sort these objects.
3. Create a chart that organizes objects by properties.

Analysis

1. What properties did you use to sort the items?
2. Were there any objects that could fit into more than one group? How did you solve this problem?
3. Which properties might you use to classify rocks? Explain your answer.

SECTION 1

The Rock Cycle

What You Will Learn

- Describe two ways rocks have been used by humans.
- Describe four processes that shape Earth's features.
- Describe how each type of rock changes into another type as it moves through the rock cycle.
- List two characteristics of rock that are used to help classify it.

Vocabulary

rock cycle	deposition
rock	composition
erosion	texture

READING STRATEGY

Reading Organizer As you read this section, make a flowchart of the steps of the rock cycle.

You know that paper, plastic, and aluminum can be recycled. But did you know that the Earth also recycles? And one of the things that Earth recycles is rock.

Scientists define **rock** as a naturally occurring solid mixture of one or more minerals and organic matter. It may be hard to believe, but rocks are always changing. The continual process by which new rock forms from old rock material is called the **rock cycle.**

The Value of Rock

Rock has been an important natural resource as long as humans have existed. Early humans used rocks as hammers to make other tools. They discovered that they could make arrowheads, spear points, knives, and scrapers by carefully shaping rocks such as chert and obsidian.

Rock has also been used for centuries to make buildings, monuments, and roads. **Figure 1** shows how rock has been used as a construction material by both ancient and modern civilizations. Buildings have been made out of granite, limestone, marble, sandstone, slate, and other rocks. Modern buildings also contain concrete and plaster, in which rock is an important ingredient.

Reading Check **Name some types of rock that have been used to construct buildings.** *(See the Appendix for answers to Reading Checks.)*

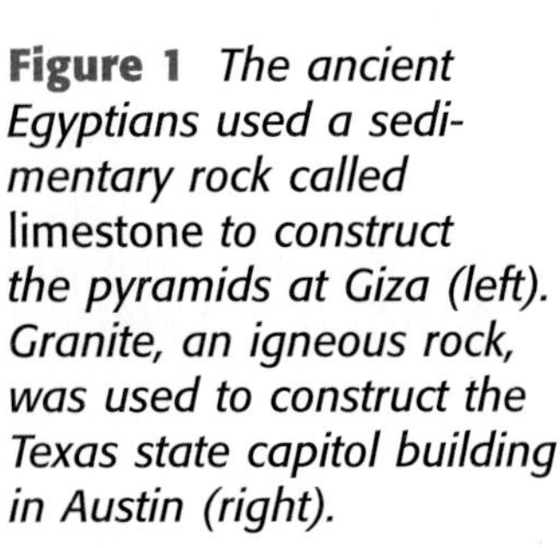

Figure 1 *The ancient Egyptians used a sedimentary rock called* limestone *to construct the pyramids at Giza (left).* Granite, *an igneous rock, was used to construct the Texas state capitol building in Austin (right).*

Processes That Shape the Earth

Certain geological processes make and destroy rock. These processes shape the features of our planet. These processes also influence the type of rock that is found in a certain area of Earth's surface.

rock a naturally occurring solid mixture of one or more minerals or organic matter

rock cycle the series of processes in which a rock forms, changes from one type to another, is destroyed, and forms again by geological processes

erosion the process by which wind, water, ice, or gravity transports soil and sediment from one location to another

deposition the process in which material is laid down

Weathering, Erosion, and Deposition

The process in which water, wind, ice, and heat break down rock is called *weathering*. Weathering is important because it breaks down rock into fragments. These rock and mineral fragments are the sediment of which much sedimentary rock is made.

The process by which sediment is removed from its source is called **erosion.** Water, wind, ice, and gravity can erode and move sediments and cause them to collect. **Figure 2** shows an example of the way land looks after weathering and erosion.

The process in which sediment moved by erosion is dropped and comes to rest is called **deposition.** Sediment is deposited in bodies of water and other low-lying areas. In those places, sediment may be pressed and cemented together by minerals dissolved in water to form sedimentary rock.

Heat and Pressure

Sedimentary rock made of sediment can also form when buried sediment is squeezed by the weight of overlying layers of sediment. If the temperature and pressure are high enough at the bottom of the sediment, the rock can change into metamorphic rock. In some cases, the rock gets hot enough to melt. This melting creates the magma that eventually cools to form igneous rock.

How the Cycle Continues

Buried rock is exposed at the Earth's surface by a combination of uplift and erosion. *Uplift* is movement within the Earth that causes rocks inside the Earth to be moved to the Earth's surface. When uplifted rock reaches the Earth's surface, weathering, erosion, and deposition begin.

Figure 2 *Bryce Canyon, in Utah, is an excellent example of how the processes of weathering and erosion shape the face of our planet.*

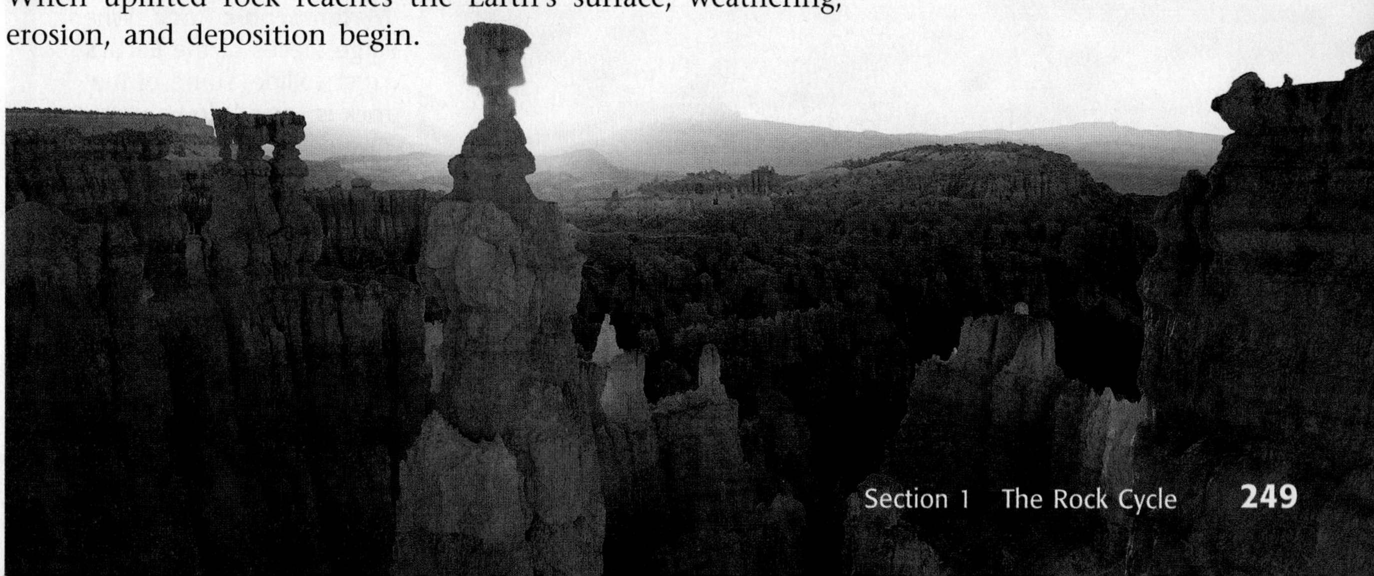

Illustrating the Rock Cycle

You have learned about various geological processes, such as weathering, erosion, heat, and pressure, that create and destroy rock. The diagram on these two pages illustrates one way that sand grains can change as different geological processes act on them. In the following steps, you will see how these processes change the original sand grains into sedimentary rock, metamorphic rock, and igneous rock.

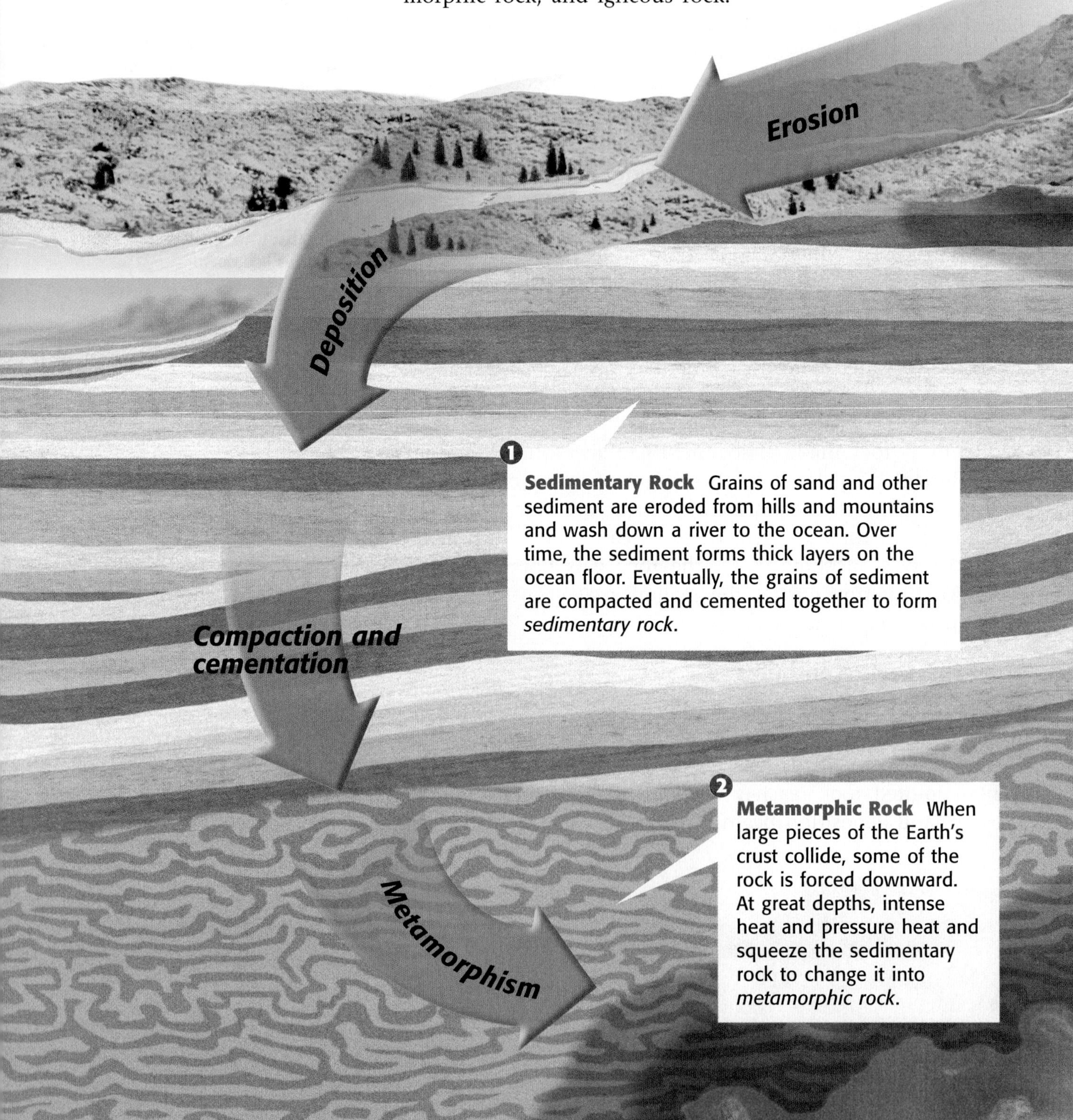

1 **Sedimentary Rock** Grains of sand and other sediment are eroded from hills and mountains and wash down a river to the ocean. Over time, the sediment forms thick layers on the ocean floor. Eventually, the grains of sediment are compacted and cemented together to form *sedimentary rock*.

2 **Metamorphic Rock** When large pieces of the Earth's crust collide, some of the rock is forced downward. At great depths, intense heat and pressure heat and squeeze the sedimentary rock to change it into *metamorphic rock*.

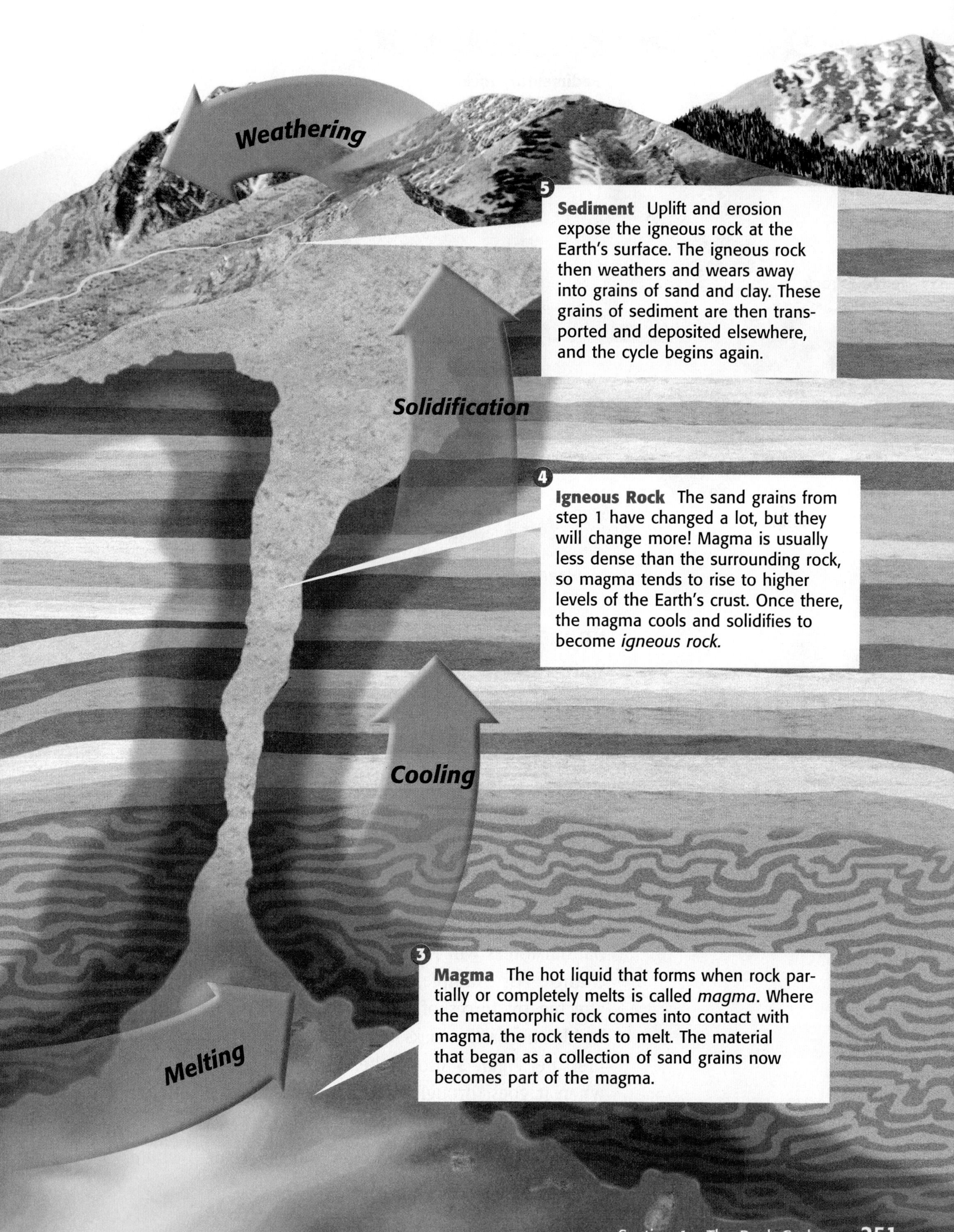
Weathering
Solidification
Cooling
Melting
5
Sediment Uplift and erosion expose the igneous rock at the Earth's surface. The igneous rock then weathers and wears away into grains of sand and clay. These grains of sediment are then transported and deposited elsewhere, and the cycle begins again.
4
Igneous Rock The sand grains from step 1 have changed a lot, but they will change more! Magma is usually less dense than the surrounding rock, so magma tends to rise to higher levels of the Earth's crust. Once there, the magma cools and solidifies to become *igneous rock.*
3
Magma The hot liquid that forms when rock partially or completely melts is called *magma*. Where the metamorphic rock comes into contact with magma, the rock tends to melt. The material that began as a collection of sand grains now becomes part of the magma.

Figure 3 The Rock Cycle

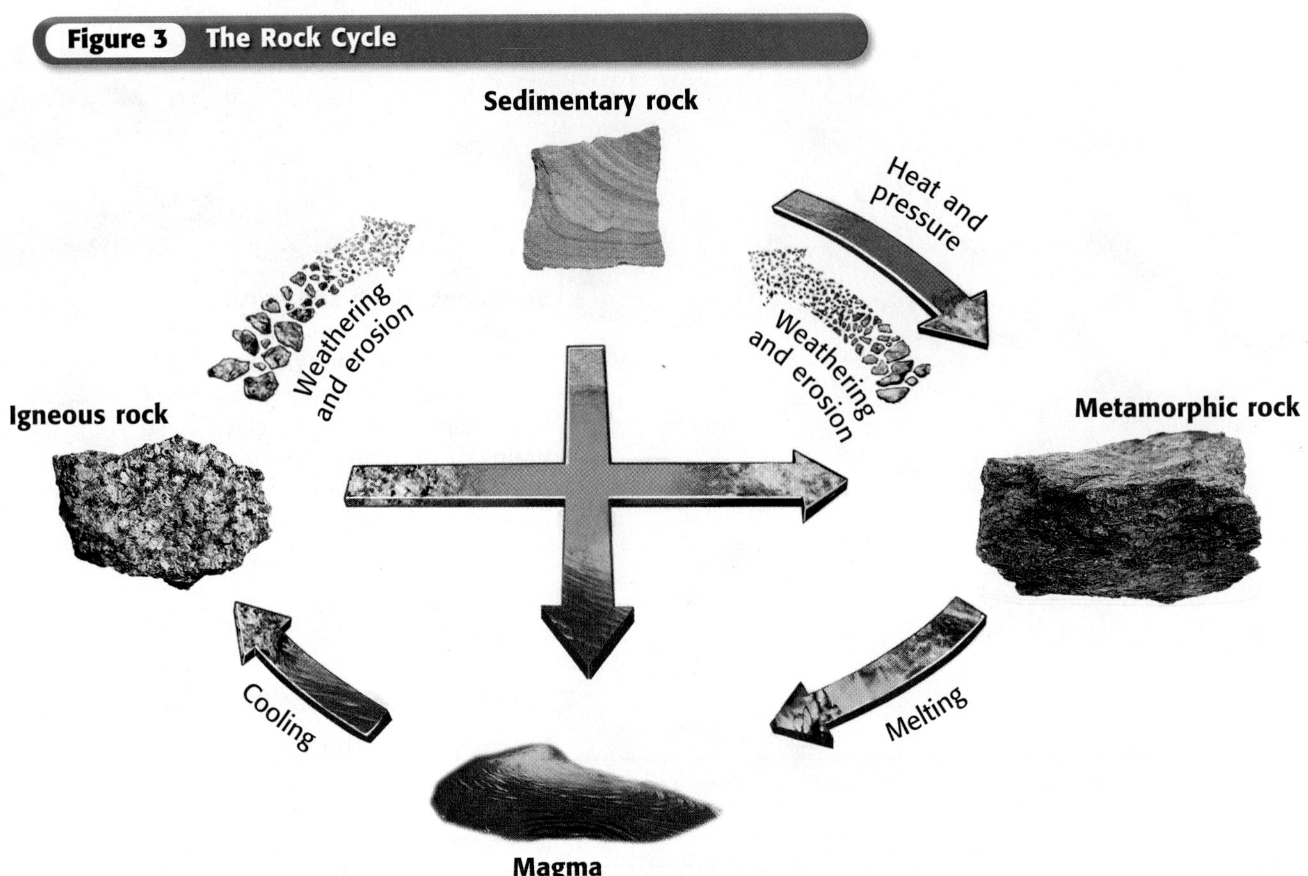

Round and Round It Goes

You have seen how different geological processes can change rock. Each rock type can change into one of the three types of rock. For example, igneous rock can change into sedimentary rock, metamorphic rock, or even back into igneous rock. This cycle, in which rock is changed by geological processes into different types of rock, is known as the rock cycle.

Rocks may follow various pathways in the rock cycle. As one rock type is changed to another type, several variables, including time, heat, pressure, weathering, and erosion may alter a rock's identity. The location of a rock determines which natural forces will have the biggest impact on the process of change. For example, rock at the Earth's surface is primarily affected by forces of weathering and erosion, whereas deep inside the Earth, rocks change because of extreme heat and pressure. **Figure 3** shows the different ways rock may change when it goes through the rock cycle and the different forces that affect rock during the cycle.

✓ *Reading Check* **What processes change rock deep within the Earth?**

Rock Classification

You have already learned that scientists divide all rock into three main classes based on how the rock formed: igneous, sedimentary, and metamorphic. But did you know that each class of rock can be divided further? These divisions are also based on differences in the way rocks form. For example, all igneous rock forms when magma cools and solidifies. But some igneous rocks form when magma cools *on* the Earth's surface, and others form when magma cools deep *beneath* the surface. Therefore, igneous rock can be divided again based on how and where it forms. Sedimentary and metamorphic rocks are also divided into groups. How do scientists know how to classify rocks? They study rocks in detail using two important criteria—composition and texture.

What's in It?

Assume that a granite sample you are studying is made of 30% quartz and 55% feldspar by volume. The rest is made of biotite mica. What percentage of the sample is biotite mica?

Composition

The minerals a rock contains determine the **composition** of that rock, as shown in **Figure 4.** For example, a rock made of mostly the mineral quartz will have a composition very similar to that of quartz. But a rock made of 50% quartz and 50% feldspar will have a very different composition than quartz does.

composition the chemical makeup of a rock; describes either the minerals or other materials in the rock

Reading Check **What determines a rock's composition?**

Figure 4 **Two Examples of Rock Composition**

The composition of a rock depends on the minerals the rock contains.

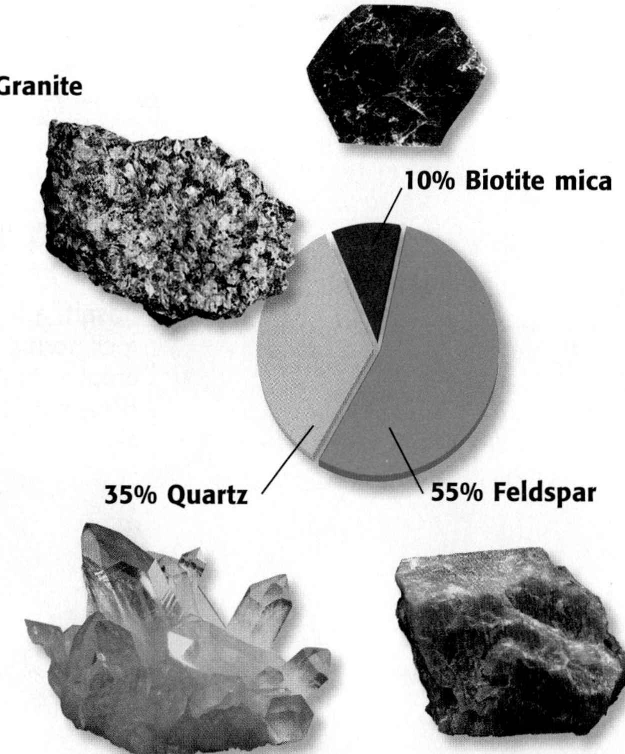

Figure 5 Three Examples of Sedimentary Rock Texture

Fine-grained

Siltstone

Medium-grained

Sandstone

Coarse-grained

Conglomerate

Texture

texture the quality of a rock that is based on the sizes, shapes, and positions of the rock's grains

The size, shape, and positions of the grains that make up a rock determine a rock's **texture.** Sedimentary rock can have a fine-grained, medium-grained, or coarse-grained texture, depending on the size of the grains that make up the rock. Three samples of textures are shown in **Figure 5.** The texture of igneous rock can be fine-grained or coarse-grained, depending on how much time magma has to cool. Based on the degree of temperature and pressure a rock is exposed to, metamorphic rock can also have a fine-grained or coarse-grained texture.

The texture of a rock can provide clues as to how and where the rock formed. Look at the rocks shown in **Figure 6.** The rocks look different because they formed in very different ways. The texture of a rock can reveal the process that formed it.

Reading Check **Give three examples of sedimentary rock textures.**

Figure 6 Texture and Rock Formation

Basalt, a fine-grained igneous rock, forms when lava that erupts onto Earth's surface cools rapidly.

Sandstone, a medium-grained sedimentary rock, forms when sand grains deposited in dunes, on beaches, or on the ocean floor are buried and cemented.

SECTION Review

Summary

- Rock has been an important natural resource for as long as humans have existed. Early humans used rock to make tools. Ancient and modern civilizations have used rock as a construction material.
- Weathering, erosion, deposition, and uplift are all processes that shape the surface features of the Earth.
- The rock cycle is the continual process by which new rock forms from old rock material.
- The sequence of events in the rock cycle depends on processes, such as weathering, erosion, deposition, pressure, and heat, that change the rock material.
- Composition and texture are two characteristics that scientists use to classify rocks.
- The composition of a rock is determined by the minerals that make up the rock.
- The texture of a rock is determined by the size, shape, and positions of the grains that make up the rock.

Using Key Terms

Complete each of the following sentences by choosing the correct term from the word bank.

rock	composition
rock cycle	texture

1. The minerals that a rock is made of determine the ___ of that rock.
2. ___ is a naturally occurring, solid mixture of crystals of one or more minerals.

Understanding Key Ideas

3. Sediments are transported or moved from their original source by a process called
   a. deposition.
   b. erosion.
   c. uplift.
   d. weathering.
4. Describe two ways that rocks have been used by humans.
5. Name four processes that change rock inside the Earth.
6. Describe four processes that shape Earth's surface.
7. Give an example of how texture can provide clues as to how and where a rock formed.

Critical Thinking

8. **Making Comparisons** Explain the difference between texture and composition.
9. **Analyzing Processes** Explain how rock is continually recycled in the rock cycle.

Interpreting Graphics

10. Look at the table below. Sandstone is a type of sedimentary rock. If you had a sample of sandstone that had an average particle size of 2 mm, what texture would your sandstone have?

Classification of Clastic Sedimentary Rocks

Texture	Particle size
coarse grained	> 2 mm
medium grained	0.06 to 2 mm
fine grained	< 0.06 mm

SCILINKS.
NSTA
Developed and maintained by the National Science Teachers Association
For a variety of links related to this chapter, go to www.scilinks.org
Topic: Composition of Rock
SciLinks code: HSM0327

SECTION 2

Igneous Rock

What You Will Learn

- Describe three ways that igneous rock forms.
- Explain how the cooling rate of magma affects the texture of igneous rock.
- Distinguish between igneous rock that cools within Earth's crust and igneous rock that cools at Earth's surface.

Vocabulary

intrusive igneous rock
extrusive igneous rock

READING STRATEGY

Reading Organizer As you read this section, make a table comparing intrusive rock and extrusive rock.

Where do igneous rocks come from? Here's a hint: The word **igneous** comes from a Latin word that means "fire."

Igneous rock forms when hot, liquid rock, or *magma,* cools and solidifies. The type of igneous rock that forms depends on the composition of the magma and the amount of time it takes the magma to cool.

Origins of Igneous Rock

Igneous rock begins as magma. As shown in **Figure 1,** there are three ways magma can form: when rock is heated, when pressure is released, or when rock changes composition.

When magma cools enough, it solidifies to form igneous rock. Magma solidifies in much the same way that water freezes. But there are also differences between the way magma freezes and the way water freezes. One main difference is that water freezes at 0°C. Magma freezes between 700°C and 1,250°C. Also, liquid magma is a complex mixture containing many melted minerals. Because these minerals have different melting points, some minerals in the magma will freeze or become solid before other minerals do.

Figure 1 **The Formation of Magma**

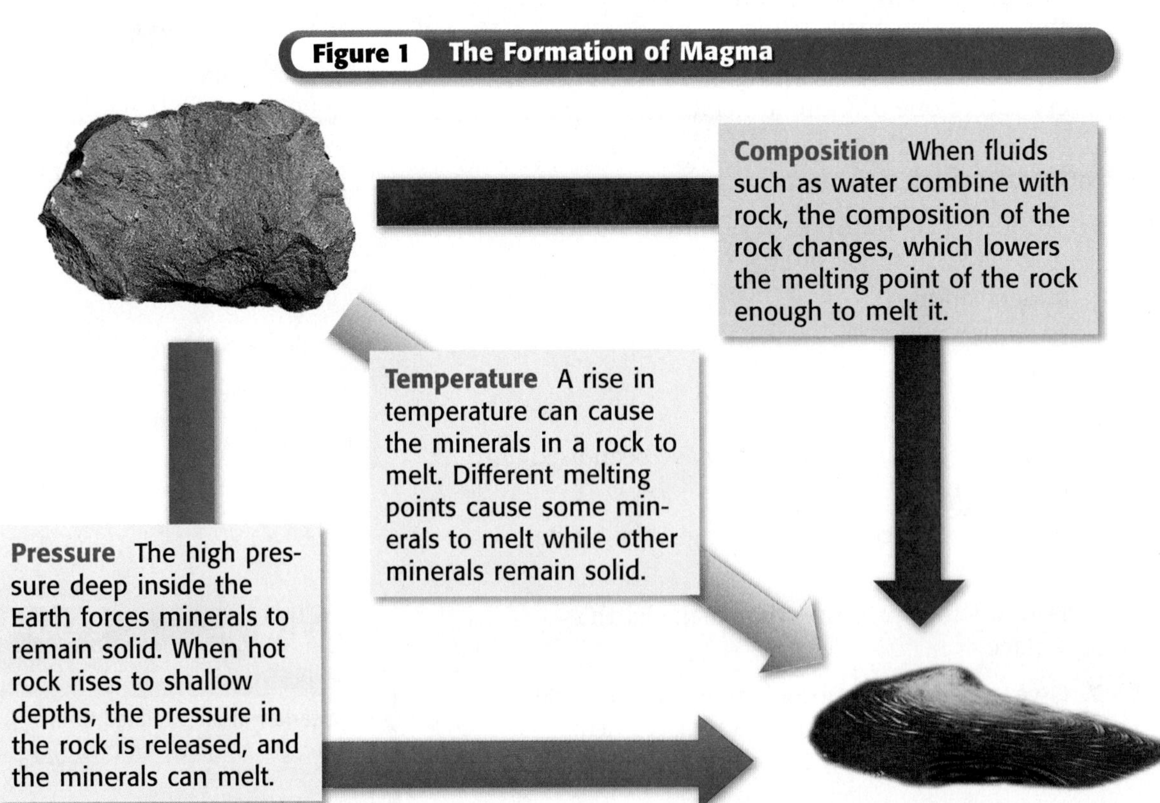

Composition When fluids such as water combine with rock, the composition of the rock changes, which lowers the melting point of the rock enough to melt it.
Temperature A rise in temperature can cause the minerals in a rock to melt. Different melting points cause some minerals to melt while other minerals remain solid.
Pressure The high pressure deep inside the Earth forces minerals to remain solid. When hot rock rises to shallow depths, the pressure in the rock is released, and the minerals can melt.

Figure 2 Igneous Rock Texture

	Coarse-grained	Fine-grained
Felsic	Granite	Rhyolite
Mafic	Gabbro	Basalt

Composition and Texture of Igneous Rock

Look at the rocks in **Figure 2.** All of the rocks are igneous rocks even though they look different from one another. These rocks differ from one another in what they are made of and how fast they cooled.

The light-colored rocks are less dense than the dark-colored rocks are. The light-colored rocks are rich in elements such as aluminum, potassium, silicon, and sodium. These rocks are called *felsic rocks*. The dark-colored rocks, called *mafic rocks,* are rich in calcium, iron, and magnesium, and poor in silicon.

Figure 3 shows what happens to magma when it cools at different rates. The longer it takes for the magma or lava to cool, the more time mineral crystals have to grow. The more time the crystals have to grow, the larger the crystals are and the coarser the texture of the resulting igneous rock is.

In contrast, the less time magma takes to cool, the less time crystals have to grow. Therefore, the rock that is formed will be fine grained. Fine-grained igneous rock contains very small crystals, or if the cooling is very rapid, it contains no crystals.

Reading Check **Explain the difference between felsic rock and mafic rock.** (*See the Appendix for answers to Reading Checks.*)

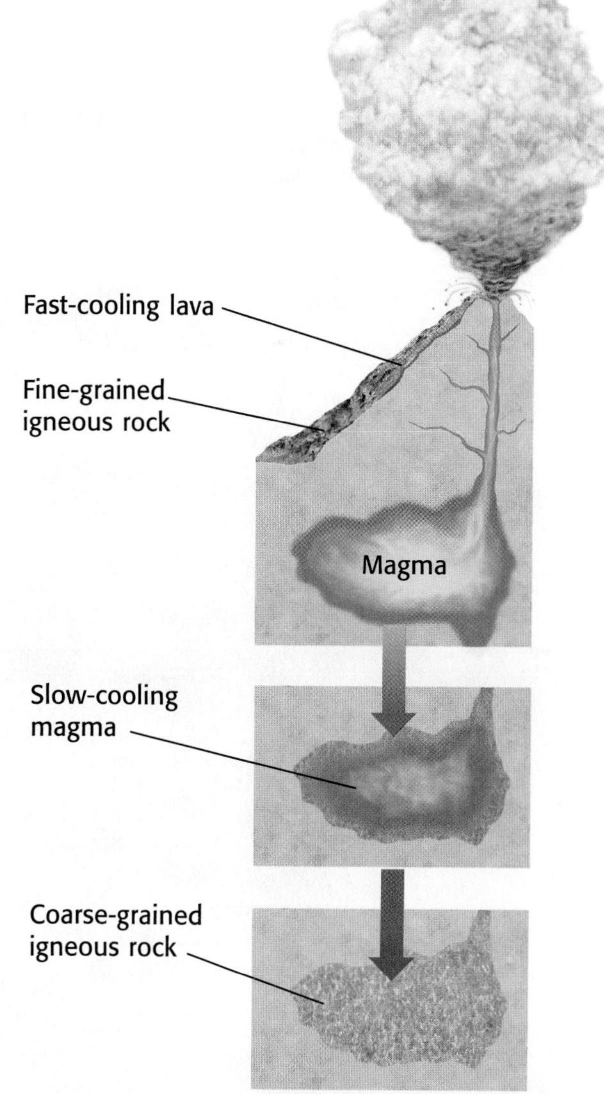

Figure 3 *The amount of time it takes for magma or lava to cool determines the texture of igneous rock.*

INTERNET ACTIVITY

For another activity related to this chapter, go to **go.hrw.com** and type in the keyword **HZ5RCKW.**

Igneous Rock Formations

Igneous rock formations are located above and below the surface of the Earth. You may be familiar with igneous rock formations that were caused by lava cooling on the Earth's surface, such as volcanoes. But not all magma reaches the surface. Some magma cools and solidifies deep within the Earth's crust.

Intrusive Igneous Rock

intrusive igneous rock rock formed from the cooling and solidification of magma beneath the Earth's surface

When magma *intrudes,* or pushes, into surrounding rock below the Earth's surface and cools, the rock that forms is called **intrusive igneous rock.** Intrusive igneous rock usually has a coarse-grained texture because it is well insulated by surrounding rock and cools very slowly. The minerals that form are large, visible crystals.

Masses of intrusive igneous rock are named for their size and shape. Common intrusive shapes are shown in **Figure 4.** *Plutons* are large, irregular-shaped intrusive bodies. The largest of all igneous intrusions are *batholiths. Stocks* are intrusive bodies that are exposed over smaller areas than batholiths. Sheetlike intrusions that cut across previous rock units are called *dikes,* whereas *sills* are sheetlike intrusions that are oriented parallel to previous rock units.

Figure 4 *Igneous intrusive bodies have different shapes and sizes.*

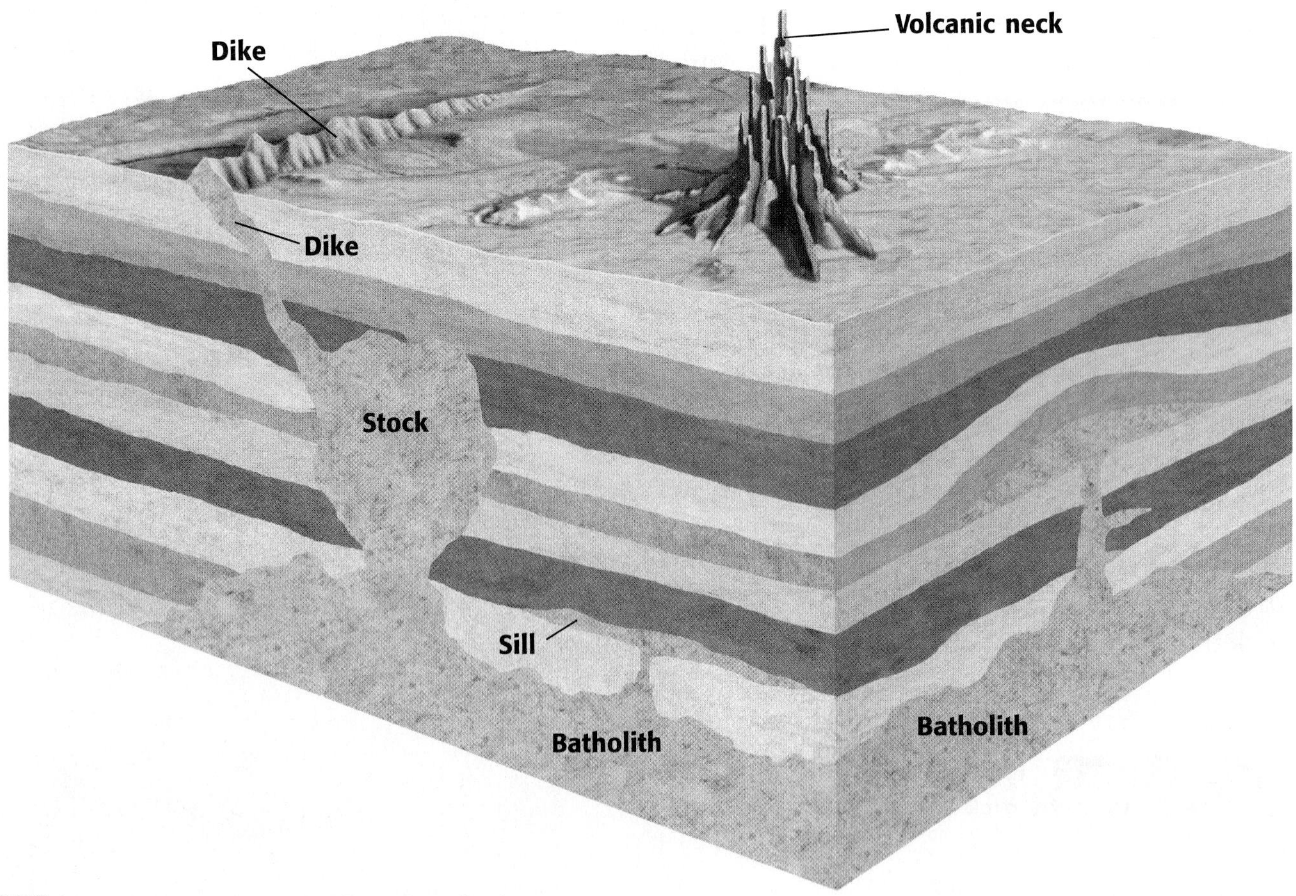

Extrusive Igneous Rock

Igneous rock that forms from magma that erupts, or extrudes, onto the Earth's surface is called **extrusive igneous rock.** Extrusive rock is common around volcanoes. It cools quickly on the surface and contains very small crystals or no crystals.

When lava erupts from a volcano, a *lava flow* forms. **Figure 5** shows an active lava flow. Lava does not always flow from volcanoes. Sometimes lava erupts and flows from long cracks in the Earth's crust called *fissures*. Lava flows from fissures on the ocean floor at places where tension is causing the ocean floor to be pulled apart. This lava cools to form new ocean floor. When a large amount of lava flows out of fissures onto land, the lava can cover a large area and form a plain called a *lava plateau*. Pre-existing landforms are often buried by these lava flows.

Reading Check How does new ocean floor form?

Figure 5 *An active lava flow is shown in this photo. When exposed to Earth's surface conditions, lava quickly cools and solidifies to form a fine-grained igneous rock.*

extrusive igneous rock rock that forms as a result of volcanic activity at or near the Earth's surface

SECTION Review

Summary

- Igneous rock forms when magma cools and hardens.
- The texture of igneous rock is determined by the rate at which the rock cools.
- Igneous rock that solidifies at Earth's surface is extrusive. Igneous rock that solidifies within Earth's surface is intrusive.
- Shapes of common igneous intrusive bodies include batholiths, stocks, sills, and dikes.

Using Key Terms

1. In your own words, write a definition for each of the following terms: *intrusive igneous rock* and *extrusive igneous rock.*

Understanding Key Ideas

2. ___ is an example of a coarse-grained, felsic, igneous rock.
   a. Basalt
   b. Gabbro
   c. Granite
   d. Rhyolite
3. Explain three ways in which magma can form.
4. What determines the texture of igneous rocks?

Math Skills

5. The summit of a granite batholith has an elevation of 1,825 ft. What is the height of the batholith in meters?

Critical Thinking

6. **Making Comparisons** Dikes and sills are both types of igneous intrusive bodies. What is the difference between a dike and a sill?
7. **Predicting Consequences** An igneous rock forms from slow-cooling magma deep beneath the surface of the Earth. What type of texture is this rock most likely to have? Explain.

SCILINKS.
NSTA
Developed and maintained by the National Science Teachers Association
For a variety of links related to this chapter, go to www.scilinks.org
Topic: Igneous Rock
SciLinks code: HSM0783

SECTION 3

Sedimentary Rock

Have you ever tried to build a sand castle at the beach? Did you ever wonder where the sand came from?

What You Will Learn

- Describe the origin of sedimentary rock.
- Describe the three main categories of sedimentary rock.
- Describe three types of sedimentary structures.

Vocabulary

strata
stratification

READING STRATEGY

Reading Organizer As you read this section, create an outline of this section. Use the headings from the section in your outline.

Sand is a product of weathering, which breaks rock into pieces. Over time, sand grains may be compacted, or compressed, and then cemented together to form a rock called *sandstone*. Sandstone is just one of many types of sedimentary rock.

Origins of Sedimentary Rock

Wind, water, ice, sunlight, and gravity all cause rock to physically weather into fragments. Through the process of erosion, these rock and mineral fragments, called *sediment*, are moved from one place to another. Eventually, the sediment is deposited in layers. As new layers of sediment are deposited, they cover older layers. Older layers become compacted. Dissolved minerals, such as calcite and quartz, separate from water that passes through the sediment to form a natural cement that binds the rock and mineral fragments together into sedimentary rock.

Sedimentary rock forms at or near the Earth's surface. It forms without the heat and pressure that are involved in the formation of igneous and metamorphic rocks.

The most noticeable feature of sedimentary rock is its layers, or **strata.** A single, horizontal layer of rock is sometimes visible for many miles. Road cuts are good places to observe strata. **Figure 1** shows the spectacular views that sedimentary rock formations carved by erosion can provide.

Figure 1 *The red sandstone "monuments" for which Monument Valley in Arizona has been named are the products of millions of years of erosion.*

Figure 2 Classification of Clastic Sedimentary Rock

Composition of Sedimentary Rock

Sedimentary rock is classified by the way it forms. *Clastic sedimentary rock* forms when rock or mineral fragments, called *clasts,* are cemented together. *Chemical sedimentary rock* forms when minerals crystallize out of a solution, such as sea water, to become rock. *Organic sedimentary rock* forms from the remains of once-living plants and animals.

strata layers of rock (singular, *stratum*)

Clastic Sedimentary Rock

Clastic sedimentary rock is made of fragments of rocks cemented together by a mineral such as calcite or quartz. **Figure 2** shows how clastic sedimentary rock is classified according to the size of the fragments from which the rock is made. Clastic sedimentary rocks can have coarse-grained, medium-grained, or fine-grained textures.

Chemical Sedimentary Rock

Chemical sedimentary rock forms from solutions of dissolved minerals and water. As rainwater slowly makes its way to the ocean, it dissolves some of the rock material it passes through. Some of this dissolved material eventually crystallizes and forms the minerals that make up chemical sedimentary rock. Halite, one type of chemical sedimentary rock, is made of sodium chloride, NaCl, or table salt. Halite forms when sodium ions and chlorine ions in shallow bodies of water become so concentrated that halite crystallizes from solution.

Reading Check **How does a chemical sedimentary rock such as halite form?** (*See the Appendix for answers to Reading Checks.*)

CONNECTION TO Language Arts

WRITING SKILL **Salty Expressions** The word salt is used in many expressions in the English language. Some common examples include "the salt of the earth," "taken with a grain of salt," not worth his salt," "the salt of truth," "rubbing salt into a wound," and "old salt." Use the Internet or another source to research one these expressions. In your research, attempt to find the origin of the expression. Write a short paragraph that summarizes what you found.

Organic Sedimentary Rock

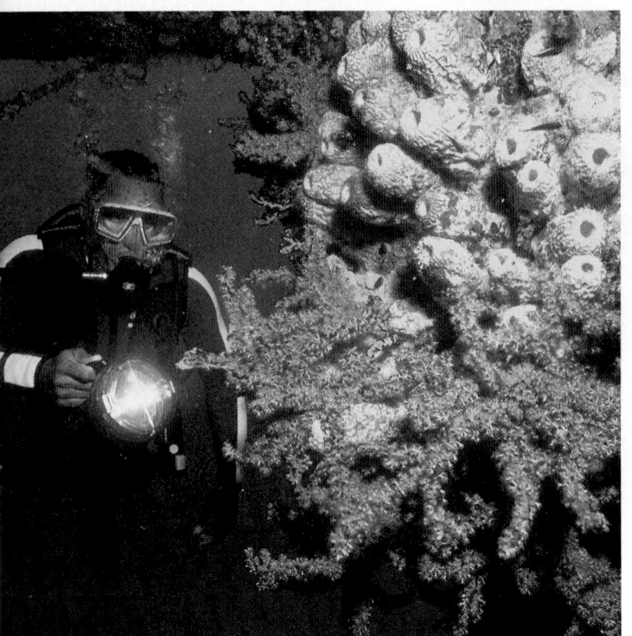

Figure 3 *Ocean animals called* coral *create huge deposits of limestone. As they die, their skeletons collect on the ocean floor.*

Most limestone forms from the remains, or *fossils*, of animals that once lived in the ocean. For example, some limestone is made of the skeletons of tiny organisms called *coral*. Coral are very small, but they live in huge colonies called *reefs*, shown in **Figure 3.** Over time, the skeletons of these sea animals, which are made of calcium carbonate, collect on the ocean floor. These animal remains eventually become cemented together to form *fossiliferous limestone* (FAH suhl IF uhr uhs LIEM STOHN).

Corals are not the only animals whose remains are found in fossiliferous limestone. The shells of mollusks, such as clams and oysters, commonly form fossiliferous limestone. An example of fossiliferous limestone that contains mollusks is shown in **Figure 4.**

Another type of organic sedimentary rock is *coal*. Coal forms underground when partially decomposed plant material is buried beneath sediment and is changed into coal by increasing heat and pressure. This process occurs over millions of years.

Figure 4 **The Formation of Organic Sedimentary Rock**

Marine organisms, such as brachiopods, get the calcium carbonate for their shells from ocean water. When these organisms die, their shells collect on the ocean floor and eventually form fossiliferous limestone (inset). Over time, huge rock formations that contain the remains of large numbers of organisms, such as brachiopods, form.

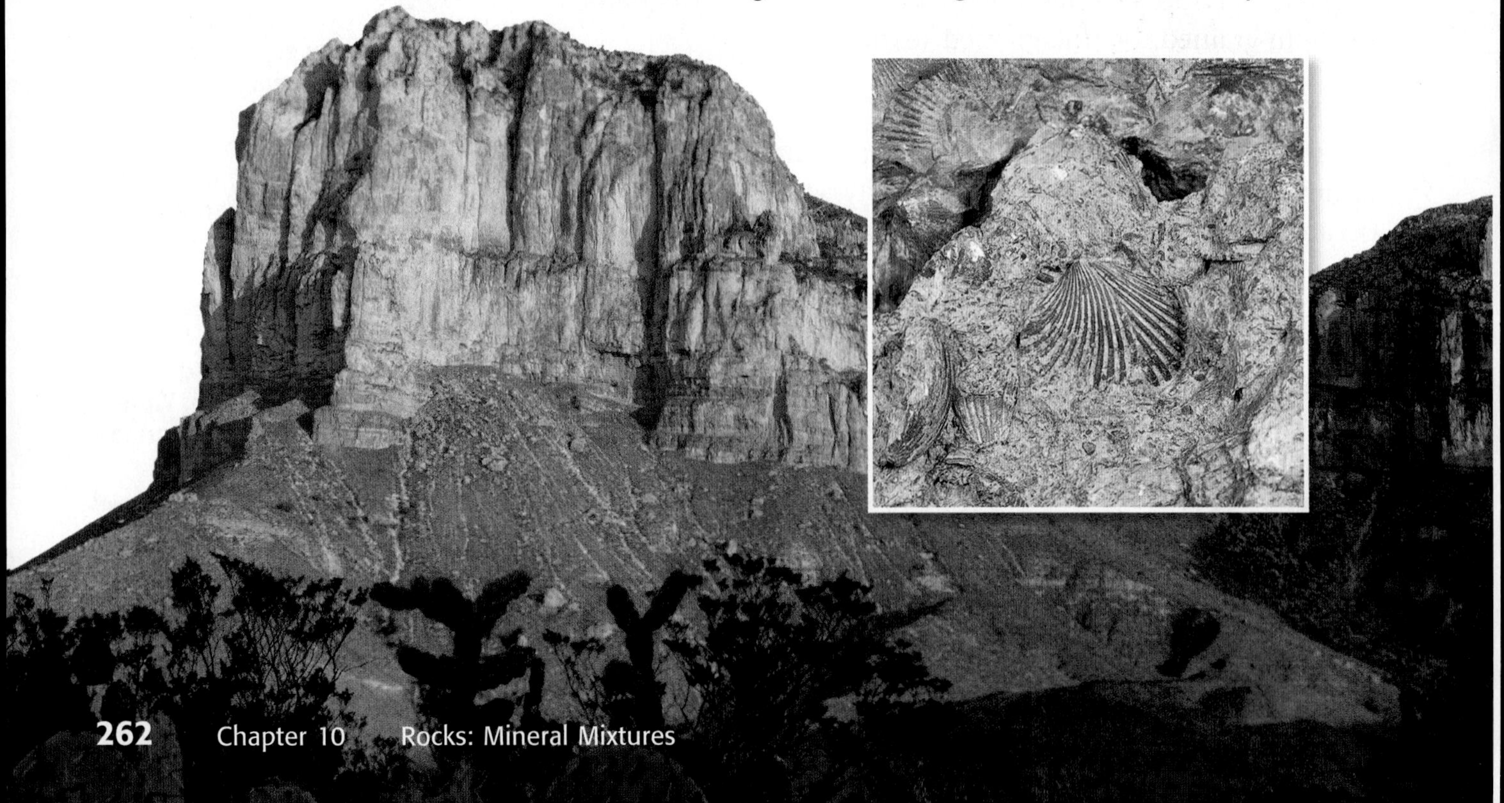

Sedimentary Rock Structures

Many features can tell you about the way sedimentary rock formed. The most important feature of sedimentary rock is stratification. **Stratification** is the process in which sedimentary rocks are arranged in layers. Strata differ from one another depending on the kind, size, and color of their sediment.

Sedimentary rocks sometimes record the motion of wind and water waves on lakes, oceans, rivers, and sand dunes in features called *ripple marks*, as shown in **Figure 5.** Structures called *mud cracks* form when fine-grained sediments at the bottom of a shallow body of water are exposed to the air and dry out. Mud cracks indicate the location of an ancient lake, stream, or ocean shoreline. Even raindrop impressions can be preserved in fine-grained sediments, as small pits with raised rims.

Reading Check What are ripple marks?

Figure 5 *These ripple marks were made by flowing water and were preserved when the sediments became sedimentary rock. Ripple marks can also form from the action of wind.*

stratification the process in which sedimentary rocks are arranged in layers

SECTION Review

Summary

- Sedimentary rock forms at or near the Earth's surface.
- Clastic sedimentary rock forms when rock or mineral fragments are cemented together.
- Chemical sedimentary rock forms from solutions of dissolved minerals and water.
- Organic limestone forms from the remains of plants and animals.
- Sedimentary structures include ripple marks, mud cracks, and raindrop impressions.

Using Key Terms

1. In your own words, write a definition for each of the following terms: *strata* and *stratification.*

Understanding Key Ideas

2. Which of the following is an organic sedimentary rock?
   a. chemical limestone
   b. shale
   c. fossiliferous limestone
   d. conglomerate
3. Explain the process by which clastic sedimentary rock forms.
4. Describe the three main categories of sedimentary rock.

Math Skills

5. A layer of a sedimentary rock is 2 m thick. How many years did it take for this layer to form if an average of 4 mm of sediment accumulated per year?

Critical Thinking

6. **Identifying Relationships** Rocks are classified based on texture and composition. Which of these two properties would be more important for classifying clastic sedimentary rock?
7. **Analyzing Processes** Why do you think raindrop impressions are more likely to be preserved in fine-grained sedimentary rock rather than in coarse-grained sedimentary rock?

For a variety of links related to this chapter, go to www.scilinks.org

Topic: Sedimentary Rock
SciLinks code: HSM1365

SECTION 4

Metamorphic Rock

Have you ever watched a caterpillar change into a butterfly? Some caterpillars go through a biological process called metamorphosis in which they completely change their shape.

What You Will Learn

- Describe two ways a rock can undergo metamorphism.
- Explain how the mineral composition of rocks changes as the rocks undergo metamorphism.
- Describe the difference between foliated and nonfoliated metamorphic rock.
- Explain how metamorphic rock structures are related to deformation.

Vocabulary

foliated
nonfoliated

READING STRATEGY

Discussion Read this section silently. Write down questions that you have about this section. Discuss your questions in a small group.

Rocks can also go through a process called *metamorphism*. The word *metamorphism* comes from the Greek words *meta,* which means "changed," and *morphos,* which means "shape." Metamorphic rocks are rocks in which the structure, texture, or composition of the rock have changed. All three types of rock can be changed by heat, pressure, or a combination of both.

Origins of Metamorphic Rock

The texture or mineral composition of a rock can change when its surroundings change. If the temperature or pressure of the new environment is different from the one in which the rock formed, the rock will undergo metamorphism.

The temperature at which most metamorphism occurs ranges from 50°C to 1,000°C. However, the metamorphism of some rocks takes place at temperatures above 1,000°C. It seems that at these temperatures the rock would melt, but this is not true of metamorphic rock. It is the depth and pressure at which metamorphic rocks form that allows the rock to heat to this temperature and maintain its solid nature. Most metamorphic change takes place at depths greater than 2 km. But at depths greater than 16 km, the pressure can be 4,000 times greater than the pressure of the atmosphere at Earth's surface.

Large movements within the crust of the Earth cause additional pressure to be exerted on a rock during metamorphism. This pressure can cause the mineral grains in rock to align themselves in certain directions. The alignment of mineral grains into parallel bands is shown in the metamorphic rock in **Figure 1.**

Figure 1 *This metamorphic rock is an example of how mineral grains were aligned into distinct bands when the rock underwent metamorphism.*

Figure 2 *Metamorphism occurs over small areas, such as next to bodies of magma, and over large areas, such as mountain ranges.*

Contact metamorphism

Sedimentary rock

Magma

Regional metamorphism

Contact Metamorphism

One way rock can undergo metamorphism is by being heated by nearby magma. When magma moves through the crust, the magma heats the surrounding rock and changes it. Some minerals in the surrounding rock are changed into other minerals by this increase in temperature. The greatest change takes place where magma comes into direct contact with the surrounding rock. The effect of heat on rock gradually decreases as the rock's distance from the magma increases and as temperature decreases. *Contact metamorphism* occurs near igneous intrusions, as shown in **Figure 2.**

Regional Metamorphism

When pressure builds up in rock that is buried deep below other rock formations or when large pieces of the Earth's crust collide with each other, *regional metamorphism* occurs. The increased pressure and temperature causes rock to become deformed and chemically changed. Unlike contact metamorphism, which happens near bodies of magma, regional metamorphism occurs over thousands of cubic kilometers deep within Earth's crust. Rocks that have undergone regional metamorphism are found beneath most continental rock formations.

Reading Check **Explain how and where regional metamorphism takes place.** (*See the Appendix for answers to Reading Checks.*)

Stretching Out

1. Sketch the crystals in granite rock on a **piece of paper** with a **black-ink pen.** Be sure to include the outline of the rock, and fill it in with different crystal shapes.
2. Flatten some **plastic play putty** over your drawing, and slowly peel it off.
3. After making sure that the outline of your granite has been transferred to the putty, squeeze and stretch the putty. What happened to the crystals in the granite? What happened to the granite?

Figure 3 *The minerals calcite, quartz, and hematite combine and recrystallize to form the metamorphic mineral garnet.*

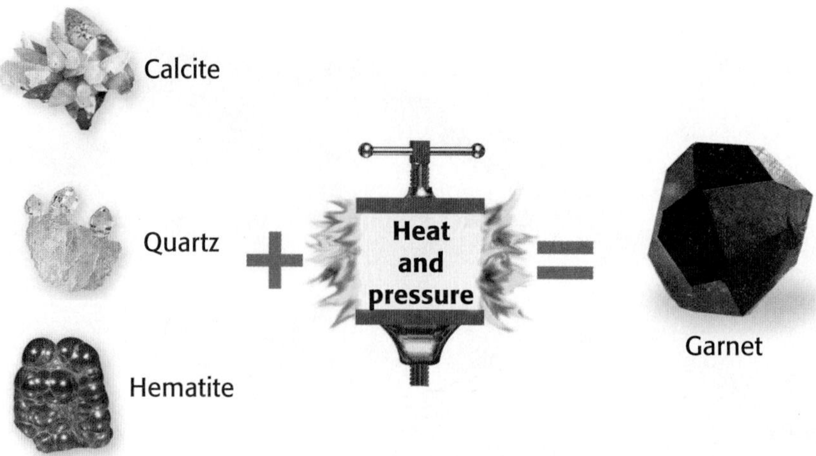

Making a Rock Collection

With a parent or guardian, try to collect a sample of each class of rock described in this chapter. You may wish to collect rocks from road cuts or simply collect pebbles from your garden or driveway. Try to collect samples that show the composition and texture of each rock. Classify the rocks in your collection, and bring it to class. With other members of the class, discuss your rock samples and see if they are accurately identified.

Composition of Metamorphic Rock

Metamorphism occurs when temperature and pressure inside the Earth's crust change. Minerals that were present in the rock when it formed may not be stable in the new temperature and pressure conditions. The original minerals change into minerals that are more stable in these new conditions. Look at **Figure 3** to see an example of how this change happens.

Many of these new minerals form only in metamorphic rock. As shown in **Figure 4,** some metamorphic minerals form only at certain temperatures and pressures. These minerals, known as *index minerals,* are used to estimate the temperature, depth, and pressure at which a rock undergoes metamorphism. Index minerals include biotite mica, chlorite, garnet, kyanite, muscovite mica, sillimanite, and staurolite.

Reading Check What is an index mineral?

Figure 4 *Scientists can understand a metamorphic rock's history by observing the minerals the rock contains. For example, a metamorphic rock that contains garnet formed at a greater depth and under greater heat and pressure than a rock that contains only chlorite.*

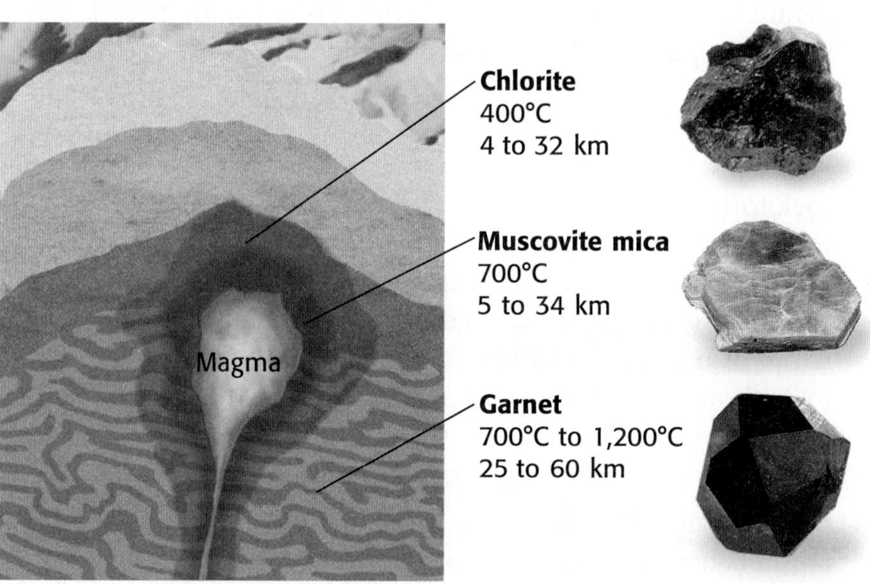

Textures of Metamorphic Rock

You have learned that texture helps scientists classify igneous and sedimentary rock. The same is true of metamorphic rock. All metamorphic rock has one of two textures—foliated or nonfoliated. Take a closer look at each of these types of metamorphic rock to find out how each type forms.

foliated the texture of metamorphic rock in which the mineral grains are arranged in planes or bands

Foliated Metamorphic Rock

The texture of metamorphic rock in which the mineral grains are arranged in planes or bands is called **foliated.** Foliated metamorphic rock usually contains aligned grains of flat minerals, such as biotite mica or chlorite. Look at **Figure 5.** Shale is a sedimentary rock made of layers of clay minerals. When shale is exposed to slight heat and pressure, the clay minerals change into mica minerals. The shale becomes a foliated metamorphic rock called *slate*.

Metamorphic rocks can become other metamorphic rocks if the environment changes again. If slate is exposed to more heat and pressure, the slate can change into rock called *phyllite*. When phyllite is exposed to heat and pressure, it can change into *schist*.

If metamorphism continues, the arrangement of minerals in the rock changes. More heat and pressure cause minerals to separate into distinct bands in a metamorphic rock called *gneiss* (NIES).

Sedimentary shale

Slate

Phyllite

Schist

Gneiss

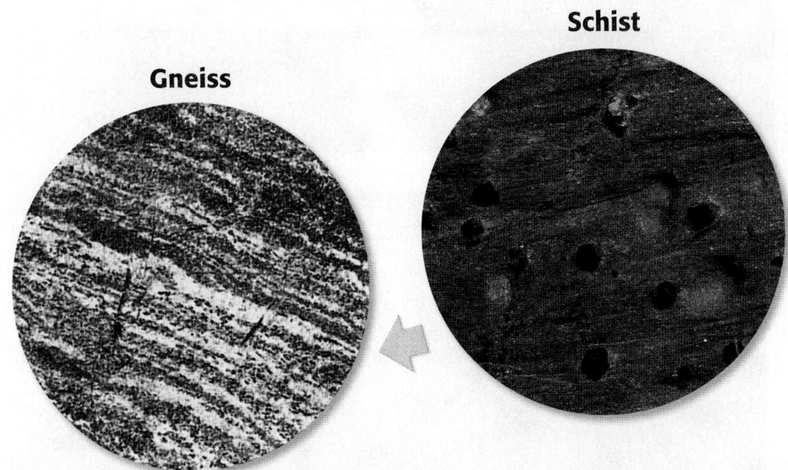

Figure 5 *The effects of metamorphism depend on the heat and pressure applied to the rock. Here you can see what happens to shale, a sedimentary rock, when it is exposed to more and more heat and pressure.*

Nonfoliated Metamorphic Rock

The texture of metamorphic rock in which the mineral grains are not arranged in planes or bands is called **nonfoliated.** Notice that the rocks shown in **Figure 6** do not have mineral grains that are aligned. This lack of aligned mineral grains is the reason these rocks are called *nonfoliated rocks.*

Nonfoliated rocks are commonly made of one or only a few minerals. During metamorphism, the crystals of these minerals may change in size or the mineral may change in composition in a process called *recrystallization.* The quartzite and marble shown in **Figure 6** are examples of sedimentary rocks that have recrystallized during metamorphism.

Quartz sandstone is a sedimentary rock made of quartz sand grains that have been cemented together. When quartz sandstone is exposed to the heat and pressure, the spaces between the sand grains disappear as the grains recrystallize to form quartzite. Quartzite has a shiny, glittery appearance. Like quartz sandstone, it is made of quartz. But during recrystallization, the mineral grains have grown larger than the original grains in the sandstone.

When limestone undergoes metamorphism, the same process that happened to the quartz happens to the calcite, and the limestone becomes marble. The calcite crystals in the marble are larger than the calcite grains in the original limestone.

CONNECTION TO Biology

WRITING SKILL **Metamorphosis** The term *metamorphosis* means "change in form." When some animals undergo a dramatic change in the shape of their body, they are said to have undergone a metamorphosis. As part of their natural life cycle, moths and butterflies go through four stages. After they hatch from an egg, they are in the larval stage in the form of a caterpillar. In the next stage, they build a cocoon or become a chrysalis. This stage is called the *pupal stage*. They finally emerge into the adult stage of their life, in which they have wings, antennae, and legs! Research other animals that undergo a metamorphosis, and summarize your findings in a short essay.

nonfoliated the texture of metamorphic rock in which the mineral grains are not arranged in planes or bands

Figure 6 Two Examples of Nonfoliated Metamorphic Rock

Marble and quartzite are nonfoliated metamorphic rocks. As you can see in the views through a microscope, the mineral crystals are not well aligned.

Metamorphic Rock Structures

Like igneous and sedimentary rock, metamorphic rock also has features that tell you about its history. In metamorphic rocks, these features are caused by deformation. *Deformation* is a change in the shape of a rock caused by a force placed on it. These forces may cause a rock to be squeezed or stretched.

Folds, or bends, in metamorphic rock are structures that indicate that a rock has been deformed. Some folds are not visible to the naked eye. But, as shown in **Figure 7,** some folds may be kilometers or even hundreds of kilometers in size.

Reading Check **How are metamorphic rock structures related to deformation?**

Figure 7 *These large folds occur in metamorphosed sedimentary rock along Saglet Fiord in Labrador, Canada.*

SECTION Review

Summary

- Metamorphic rocks are rocks in which the structure, texture, or composition has changed.
- Two ways rocks can undergo metamorphism are by contact metamorphism and regional metamorphism.
- As rocks undergo metamorphism, the original minerals in a rock change into new minerals that are more stable in new pressure and temperature conditions.
- Foliated metamorphic rock has mineral crystals aligned in planes or bands, whereas nonfoliated rocks have unaligned mineral crystals.
- Metamorphic rock structures are caused by deformation.

Using Key Terms

1. In your own words, define the following terms: *foliated* and *nonfoliated.*

Understanding Key Ideas

2. Which of the following is not a type of foliated metamorphic rock?
   - **a.** gneiss
   - **b.** slate
   - **c.** marble
   - **d.** schist
3. Explain the difference between contact metamorphism and regional metamorphism.
4. Explain how index minerals allow a scientist to understand the history of a metamorphic rock.

Math Skills

5. For every 3.3 km a rock is buried, the pressure placed upon it increases 0.1 gigapascal (100 million pascals). If rock undergoing metamorphosis is buried at 16 km, what is the pressure placed on that rock? (Hint: The pressure at Earth's surface is .101 gigapascal.)

Critical Thinking

6. **Making Inferences** If you had two metamorphic rocks, one that has garnet crystals and the other that has chlorite crystals, which one could have formed at a deeper level in the Earth's crust? Explain your answer.
7. **Applying Concepts** Which do you think would be easier to break, a foliated rock, such as slate, or a nonfoliated rock, such as quartzite? Explain.
8. **Analyzing Processes** A mountain range is located at a boundary where two tectonic plates are colliding. Would most of the metamorphic rock in the mountain range be a product of contact metamorphism or regional metamorphism? Explain.

SCILINKS.
NSTA
Developed and maintained by the National Science Teachers Association
For a variety of links related to this chapter, go to www.scilinks.org
Topic: Metamorphic Rock
SciLinks code: HSM0949

Skills Practice Lab

Let's Get Sedimental

How do we determine if sedimentary rock layers are undisturbed? The best way to do this is to be sure that fine-grained sediments near the top of a layer lie above coarse-grained sediments near the bottom of the layer. This lab activity will show you how to read rock features that will help you distinguish individual sedimentary rock layers. Then, you can look for the features in real rock layers.

OBJECTIVES

Model the process of sedimentation.

Determine whether sedimentary rock layers are undisturbed.

MATERIALS

- clay
- dropper pipet
- gravel
- magnifying lens
- mixing bowl, 2 qt
- sand
- scissors
- soda bottle with a cap, plastic, 2 L
- soil, clay rich, if available
- water

SAFETY

Procedure

1. In a mixing bowl, thoroughly mix the sand, gravel, and soil. Fill the soda bottle about one-third full of the mixture.
2. Add water to the soda bottle until the bottle is two-thirds full. Twist the cap back onto the bottle, and shake the bottle vigorously until all of the sediment is mixed in the rapidly moving water.
3. Place the bottle on a tabletop. Using the scissors, carefully cut the top off the bottle a few centimeters above the water, as shown. The open bottle will allow water to evaporate.
4. Immediately after you set the bottle on the tabletop, describe what you see from above and through the sides of the bottle.
5. Do not disturb the container. Allow the water to evaporate. (You may speed up the process by carefully using the dropper pipet to siphon off some of the clear water after you allow the container to sit for at least 24 hours.) You may also set the bottle in the sun or under a desk lamp to speed up evaporation.
6. After the sediment has dried and hardened, describe its surface.
7. Carefully lay the container on its side, and cut a wide, vertical strip of plastic down the length of the bottle to expose the sediments in the container. You may find it easier if you place pieces of clay on either side of the container to stabilize it. (If the bottle is clear along its length, this step may not be required.)
8. Brush away the loose material from the sediment, and gently blow on the surface until it is clean. Examine the surface, and record your observations.

Analyze the Results

1. **Identifying Patterns** Do you see anything through the side of the bottle that could help you determine if a sedimentary rock is undisturbed? Explain your answer.

2. **Identifying Patterns** Can you observe a pattern of deposition? If so, describe the pattern of deposition of sediment that you observe from top to bottom.

3. **Explaining Events** Explain how these features might be used to identify the top of a sedimentary layer in real rock and to decide if the layer has been disturbed.

4. **Identifying Patterns** Do you see any structures through the side of the bottle that might indicate which direction is up, such as a change in particle density or size?

5. **Identifying Patterns** Use the magnifying lens to examine the boundaries between the gravel, sand, and silt. Do the size of the particles and the type of sediment change dramatically in each layer?

Draw Conclusions

6. **Making Predictions** Imagine that a layer was deposited directly above the sediment in your bottle. Describe the composition of this new layer. Will it have the same composition as the mixture in steps 1–5 in the Procedure?

Applying Your Data

With your class or with a parent, visit an outcrop of sedimentary rock. Apply the information that you have learned in this lab to see if you can determine whether the sedimentary rock layers are disturbed or undisturbed.

Chapter Review

USING KEY TERMS

1. In your own words, write a definition for the term *rock cycle.*

Complete each of the following sentences by choosing the correct term from the word bank.

stratification	foliated
extrusive igneous rock	texture

2. The ___ of a rock is determined by the sizes, shapes, and positions of the minerals the rock contains.

3. ___ metamorphic rock contains minerals that are arranged in plates or bands.

4. The most characteristic property of sedimentary rock is ___.

5. ___ forms plains called *lava plateaus.*

UNDERSTANDING KEY IDEAS

Multiple Choice

6. Sedimentary rock is classified into all of the following main categories except
   - **a.** clastic sedimentary rock.
   - **b.** chemical sedimentary rock.
   - **c.** nonfoliated sedimentary rock.
   - **d.** organic sedimentary rock.

7. An igneous rock that cools very slowly has a ___ texture.
   - **a.** foliated
   - **b.** fine-grained
   - **c.** nonfoliated
   - **d.** coarse-grained

8. Igneous rock forms when
   - **a.** minerals crystallize from a solution.
   - **b.** sand grains are cemented together.
   - **c.** magma cools and solidifies.
   - **d.** mineral grains in a rock recrystallize.

9. A ___ is a common structure found in metamorphic rock.
   - **a.** ripple mark
   - **b.** fold
   - **c.** sill
   - **d.** layer

10. The process in which sediment is removed from its source and transported is called
    - **a.** deposition.
    - **b.** erosion.
    - **c.** weathering.
    - **d.** uplift.

11. Mafic rocks are
    - **a.** light-colored rocks rich in calcium, iron, and magnesium.
    - **b.** dark-colored rocks rich in aluminum, potassium, silica, and sodium.
    - **c.** light-colored rocks rich in aluminum, potassium, silica, and sodium.
    - **d.** dark-colored rocks rich in calcium, iron, and magnesium.

Short Answer

12. Explain how composition and texture are used by scientists to classify rocks.

13. Describe two ways a rock can undergo metamorphism.

14. Explain why some minerals only occur in metamorphic rocks.

15. Describe how each type of rock changes as it moves through the rock cycle.

16 Describe two ways rocks were used by early humans and ancient civilizations.

CRITICAL THINKING

17 **Concept Mapping** Use the following terms to construct a concept map: *rocks, metamorphic, sedimentary, igneous, foliated, nonfoliated, organic, clastic, chemical, intrusive,* and *extrusive.*

18 **Making Inferences** If you were looking for fossils in the rocks around your home and the rock type that was closest to your home was metamorphic, do you think that you would find many fossils? Explain your answer.

19 **Applying Concepts** Imagine that you want to quarry, or mine, granite. You have all of the equipment, but you have two pieces of land to choose from. One area has a granite batholith underneath it. The other has a granite sill. If both intrusive bodies are at the same depth, which one would be the better choice for you to quarry? Explain your answer.

20 **Applying Concepts** The sedimentary rock coquina is made up of pieces of seashells. Which of the three kinds of sedimentary rock could coquina be? Explain your answer.

21 **Analyzing Processes** If a rock is buried deep inside the Earth, which geological processes cannot change the rock? Explain your answer.

INTERPRETING GRAPHICS

The bar graph below shows the percentage of minerals by mass that compose a sample of granite. Use the graph below to answer the questions that follow.

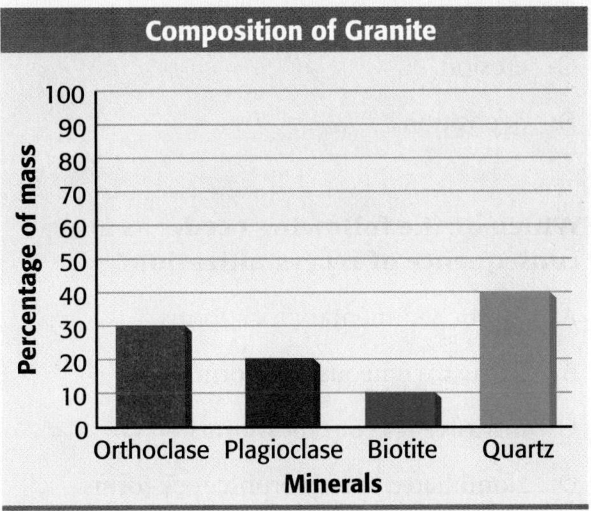

22 Your rock sample is made of four minerals. What percentage of each mineral makes up your sample?

23 Both plagioclase and orthoclase are feldspar minerals. What percentage of the minerals in your sample of granite are not feldspar minerals?

24 If your rock sample has a mass of 10 g, how many grams of quartz does it contain?

25 Use paper, a compass, and a protractor or a computer to make a pie chart. Show the percentage of each of the four minerals your sample of granite contains. (Look in the Appendix of this book for help on making a pie chart.)

Standardized Test Preparation

Multiple Choice

1. The process by which water, wind, ice, or gravity transports soil and sediment from one location to another is called

A. uplift.

B. weathering.

C. erosion.

D. deposition.

2. Which of the following occurs as a consequence of recrystallization?

A. Clastic sedimentary rock forms.

B. Extrusive igneous rock forms.

C. Intrusive igneous rock forms.

D. Nonfoliated metamorphic rock forms.

3. Igneous rock forms when

A. magma cools and hardens.

B. minerals crystallize out of seawater.

C. heat and pressure change the composition and texture of a rock.

D. natural cement binds rock fragments together.

4. Volcanic activity on Earth's surface would most likely result in the formation of which of the following types of rock?

A. intrusive igneous rock

B. extrusive igneous rock

C. clastic sedimentary rock

D. chemical sedimentary rock

Use the diagram below to answer question 5.

The Rock Cycle

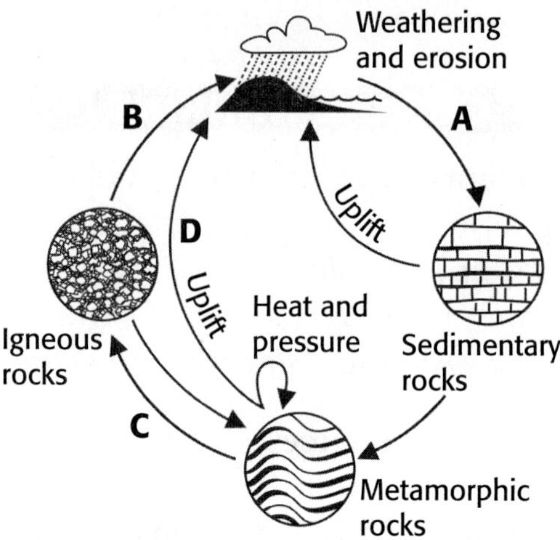

5. Which of the following processes occurs at point C on the diagram of the rock cycle shown above?

A. deposition

B. uplift

C. heat and pressure

D. melting and cooling

6. During metamorphism, limestone changes to become a metamorphic rock called marble. What happens to the calcite in the limestone during this process?

A. The calcite crystals change in chemical composition.

B. The calcite crystals separate to form bonds.

C. The calcite crystals become quartz crystals.

D. The calcite crystals recrystallize and grow larger.

7. A rock that forms from the melting and cooling of rock has which of the following characteristics?

A. It is made of crystals.

B. It is made of fragments of other rocks.

C. It has bands of minerals.

D. It is dark in color.

8. Buried rock is exposed at Earth's surface by the combination of which two processes?

A. weathering and deposition

B. uplift and erosion

C. erosion and deposition

D. deposition and uplift

9. How does clastic sedimentary rock form?

A. Rock fragments are cemented together by a mineral such as calcite or quartz.

B. Dissolved minerals crystallize out of solution in water to form solid minerals.

C. Partially decomposed plant material is turned into rock by heat and pressure.

D. Skeletons of sea animals that collected on the ocean floor are cemented together.

10. Stratification would occur as the result of which of the following processes?

A. the cooling and solidification of magma

B. the partial or complete melting of rock

C. the deformation of rock by heat and pressure

D. the deposition of sediments in a body of water

Use the table below to answer question 11.

Rock Type		
Rock Sample	**Texture**	**Composition**
Sample A	coarse-grained	mica, quartz, and feldspar
Sample B	medium-grained	quartz sand in quartz cement
Sample C	foliated	biotite mica
Sample D	fine-grained	olivine, pyroxene, feldspar

11. Which of the four rock samples in the table above most likely formed through the process of heating and cooling beneath Earth's surface?

A. Sample A

B. Sample B

C. Sample C

D. Sample D

Open Response

12. Kaolin is a white claystone that is composed of kaolinite and other minerals. Kaolin is used as a coating on glossy paper. It is also used in the production of ceramics, paints, plastics, and rubber. What type of rock is kaolin? How is kaolin rock formed?

13. Elberton granite can be seen all over the United States in buildings, monuments, and gravestones. The stone consists of coarse light-gray and dark-gray grains, which give it a speckled appearance. What was the process that formed Elberton granite? What can you infer about the properties of this stone from its uses?

Science in Action

Science, Technology, and Society

The Moai of Easter Island

Easter island is located in the Pacific Ocean more than 3,200 km from the coast of Chile. The island is home to mysterious statues that were carved from volcanic ash. The statues, called *moai,* have human heads and large torsos. The average moai weighs 14 tons and is more than 4.5 m tall, though some are as tall as 10 m! Altogether, 887 moai have been discovered. How old are the moai? Scientists believe that the moai were built between 500 and 1,000 years ago. What purpose did moai serve for their creators? The moai may have been religious symbols or gods.

Social Studies ACTIVITY

WRITING SKILL Research another ancient society or civilization, such as the ancient Egyptians, who are believed to have used stone to construct monuments to their gods or to important people. Report your findings in a short essay.

Scientific Discoveries

Shock Metamorphism

When a large asteroid, meteoroid, or comet collides with the Earth, extremely high temperatures and pressures are created in Earth's surface rock. These high pressures and temperatures cause minerals in the surface rock to shatter and recrystallize. The new minerals that result from this recrystallization cannot be created under any other conditions. This process is called *shock metamorphism.*

When large objects from space collide with the Earth, craters are formed by the impact. However, impact craters are not always easy to find on Earth. Scientists use shock metamorphism as a clue to locate ancient impact craters.

Language Arts ACTIVITY

WRITING SKILL The impact site caused by the asteroid strike in the Yucatán 65 million years ago has been named the Chicxulub (cheeks OO loob) structure. Research the origin of the name Chicxulub, and report your findings in a short paper.

Careers

Robert L. Folk

Petrologist For Dr. Robert Folk, the study of rock takes place on the microscopic level. Dr. Folk is searching for tiny life-forms he has named nannobacteria, or dwarf bacteria, in rock. *Nannobacteria* may also be spelled *nanobacteria.* Because nannobacteria are so incredibly small, only 0.05 to 0.2 µm in diameter, Folk must use an extremely powerful 100,000× microscope, called a *scanning electron microscope,* to see the shape of the bacteria in rock. Folk's research had already led him to discover that a certain type of Italian limestone is produced by bacteria. The bacteria were consuming the minerals, and the waste of the bacteria was forming the limestone. Further research led Folk to the discovery of the tiny nannobacteria. The spherical or oval-shaped nannobacteria appeared as chains and grapelike clusters. From his research, Folk hypothesized that nannobacteria are responsible for many inorganic reactions that occur in rock. Many scientists are skeptical of Folk's nannobacteria. Some skeptics believe that the tiny size of nannobacteria makes the bacteria simply too small to contain the chemistry of life. Others believe that nannobacteria actually represent structures that do not come from living things.

If a nannobacterium is 1/10 the length, 1/10 the width, and 1/10 the height of an ordinary bacterium, how many nannobacteria can fit within an ordinary bacterium? (Hint: Draw block diagrams of both a nannobacterium and an ordinary bacterium.)

To learn more about these Science in Action topics, visit **go.hrw.com** and type in the keyword **HZ5RCKF.**

Current Science

Check out Current Science® articles related to this chapter by visiting go.hrw.com. Just type in the keyword HZ5CS04.

The Rock and Fossil Record

The Big Idea Studying the rock and fossil record helps us understand Earth's history and the history of life on Earth.

SECTION

About the Photo

This extremely well preserved crocodile fossil has been out of water for 49 million years. Its skeleton was collected in an abandoned mine pit in Messel, Germany.

PRE-READING ACTIVITY

FOLDNOTES **Layered Book** Before you read the chapter, create the FoldNote entitled "Layered Book" described in the **Study Skills** section of the Appendix. Label the tabs of the layered book with "Earth's history," "Relative dating," "Absolute dating," "Fossils," and "Geologic time." As you read the chapter, write information you learn about each category under the appropriate tab.

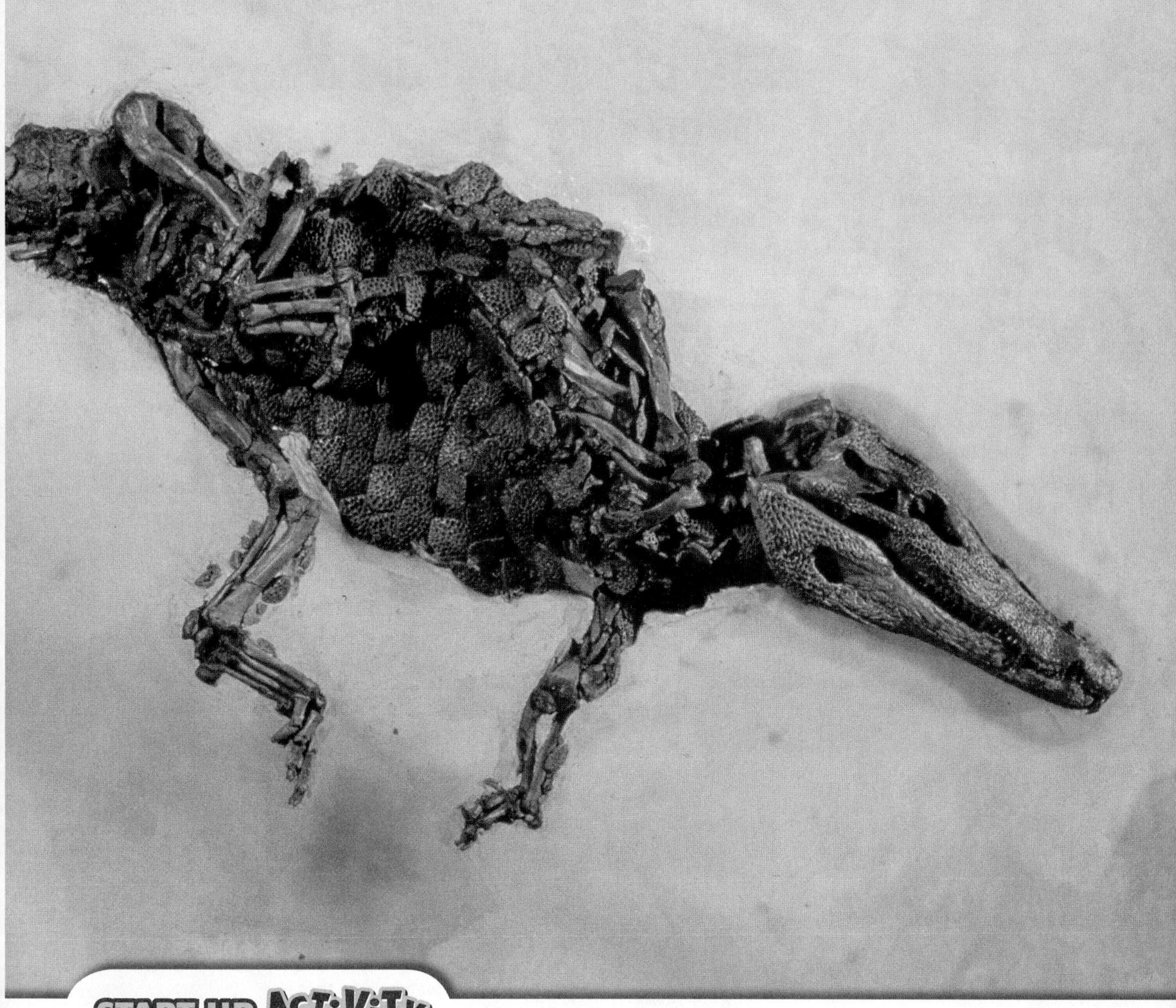

START-UP ACTIVITY

Making Fossils

How do scientists learn from fossils? In this activity, you will study "fossils" and identify the object that made each.

Procedure

1. You and three or four of your classmates will be given **several pieces** of **modeling clay** and a **paper sack** containing a few **small objects.**
2. Press each object firmly into a piece of clay. Try to leave a "fossil" imprint showing as much detail as possible.
3. After you have made an imprint of each object, exchange your model fossils with another group.
4. On a **sheet of paper,** describe the fossils you have received. List as many details as possible. What patterns and textures do you observe?
5. Work as a group to identify each fossil, and check your results. Were you right?

Analysis

1. What kinds of details were important in identifying your fossils? What kinds of details were not preserved in the imprints? For example, can you tell the materials from which the objects are made or their color?
2. Explain how scientists follow similar methods when studying fossils.

SECTION 1

Earth's Story and Those Who First Listened

What You Will Learn

- Compare uniformitarianism and catastrophism.
- Describe how the science of geology has changed over the past 200 years.
- Explain the role of paleontology in the study of Earth's history.

Vocabulary

uniformitarianism
catastrophism
paleontology

READING STRATEGY

Reading Organizer As you read this section, make a table comparing uniformitarianism and catastrophism.

How do mountains form? How is new rock created? How old is the Earth? Have you ever asked these questions? Nearly 250 years ago, a Scottish farmer and scientist named James Hutton did.

Searching for answers to his questions, Hutton spent more than 30 years studying rock formations in Scotland and England. His observations led to the foundation of modern geology.

The Principle of Uniformitarianism

In 1788, James Hutton collected his notes and wrote *Theory of the Earth*. In *Theory of the Earth,* he stated that the key to understanding Earth's history was all around us. In other words, processes that we observe today—such as erosion and deposition—remain uniform, or do not change, over time. This assumption is now called uniformitarianism. **Uniformitarianism** is the idea that the same geologic processes shaping the Earth today have been at work throughout Earth's history. **Figure 1** shows how Hutton developed the idea of uniformitarianism.

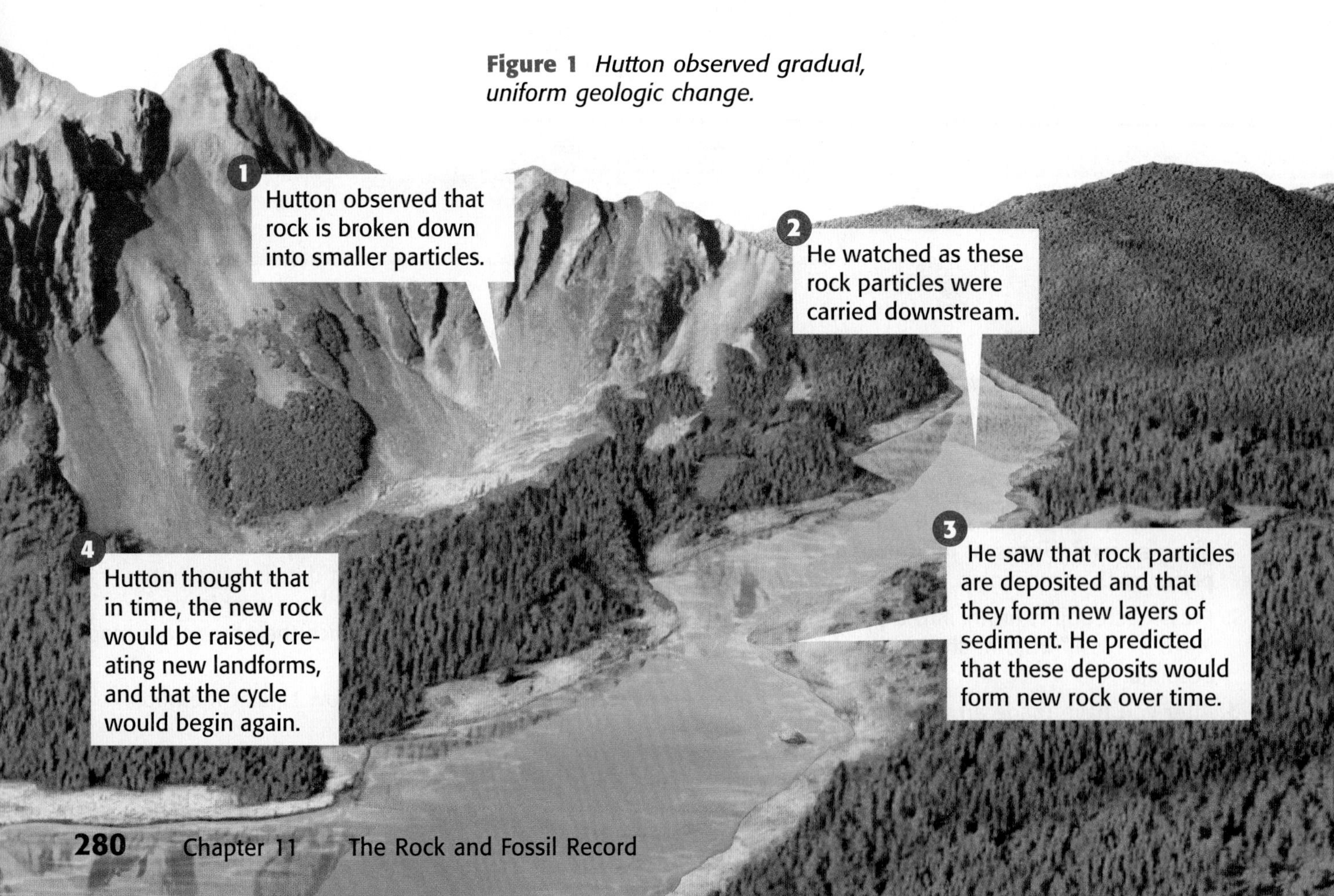

1
Hutton observed that rock is broken down into smaller particles.
2
He watched as these rock particles were carried downstream.
3
He saw that rock particles are deposited and that they form new layers of sediment. He predicted that these deposits would form new rock over time.
4
Hutton thought that in time, the new rock would be raised, creating new landforms, and that the cycle would begin again.

Figure 1 *Hutton observed gradual, uniform geologic change.*

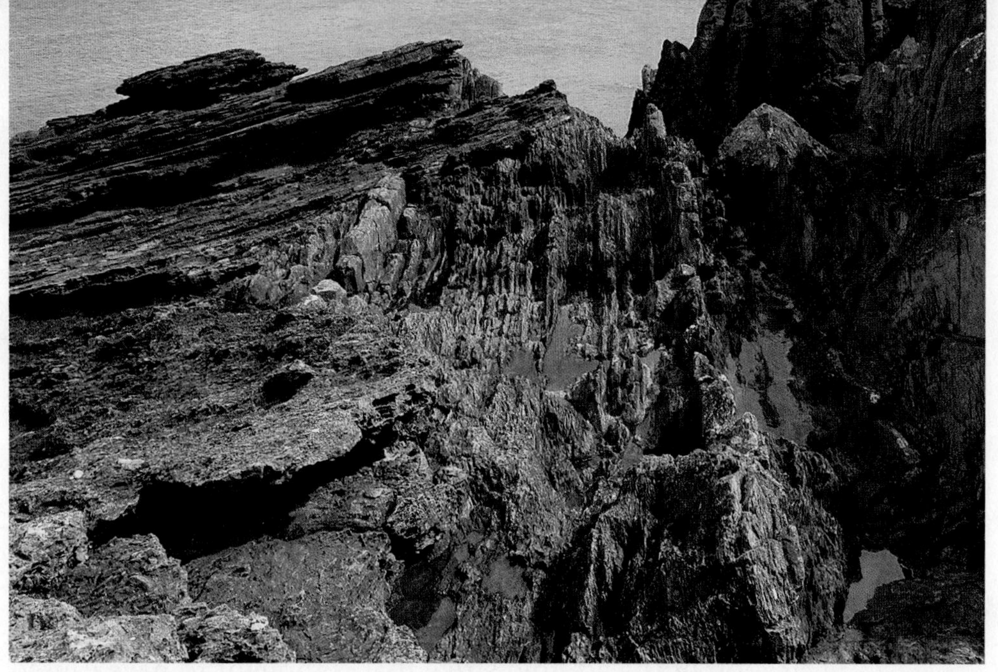

Figure 2 *This photograph shows Siccar Point on the coast of Scotland. Siccar Point is one of the places where Hutton observed results of geologic processes that would lead him to form his principle of uniformitarianism.*

Uniformitarianism Versus Catastrophism

Hutton's theories sparked a scientific debate by suggesting that Earth was much older than previously thought. In Hutton's time, most people thought that Earth was only a few thousand years old. A few thousand years was not nearly enough time for the gradual geologic processes that Hutton described to have shaped our planet. The rocks that he observed at Siccar Point, shown in **Figure 2,** were deposited and folded, indicating a long geological history. To explain Earth's history, most scientists supported catastrophism. **Catastrophism** is the principle that states that all geologic change occurs suddenly. Supporters of catastrophism thought that Earth's features, such as its mountains, canyons, and seas, formed during rare, sudden events called *catastrophes.* These unpredictable events caused rapid geologic change over large areas—sometimes even globally.

uniformitarianism a principle that states that geologic processes that occurred in the past can be explained by current geologic processes

catastrophism a principle that states that geologic change occurs suddenly

Reading Check **According to catastrophists, what was the rate of geologic change?** (*See the Appendix for answers to Reading Checks.*)

A Victory for Uniformitarianism

Despite Hutton's work, catastrophism remained geology's guiding principle for decades. Only after the work of British geologist Charles Lyell did people seriously consider uniformitarianism as geology's guiding principle.

From 1830 to 1833, Lyell published three volumes, collectively titled *Principles of Geology,* in which he reintroduced uniformitarianism. Armed with Hutton's notes and new evidence of his own, Lyell successfully challenged the principle of catastrophism. Lyell saw no reason to doubt that major geologic change happened at the same rate in the past as it happens in the present—gradually.

CONNECTION TO Biology

WRITING SKILL **Darwin and Lyell** The theory of evolution was developed soon after Lyell introduced his ideas, which was no coincidence. Lyell and Charles Darwin were good friends, and their talks greatly influenced Darwin's theories. Similar to uniformitarianism, Darwin's theory of evolution proposes that changes in species occur gradually over long periods of time. Write a short essay comparing uniformitarianism and evolution.

Modern Geology—A Happy Medium

During the late 20th century, scientists such as Stephen J. Gould challenged Lyell's uniformitarianism. They believed that catastrophes do, at times, play an important role in shaping Earth's history.

Today, scientists realize that neither uniformitarianism nor catastrophism accounts for all geologic change throughout Earth's history. Although most geologic change is gradual and uniform, catastrophes that cause geologic change have occurred during Earth's long history. For example, huge craters have been found where asteroids and comets are thought to have struck Earth in the past. Some scientists think one such asteroid strike, approximately 65 million years ago, may have caused the dinosaurs to become extinct. **Figure 3** is an imaginary re-creation of the asteroid strike that is thought to have caused the extinction of the dinosaurs. The impact of this asteroid is thought to have thrown debris into the atmosphere. The debris spread around the entire planet and rained down on Earth for decades. This global debris cloud may have blocked the sun's rays, causing major changes in the global climate that doomed the dinosaurs.

Reading Check **How can a catastrophe affect life on Earth?**

Figure 3 *Today, scientists think that sudden events are responsible for some changes during Earth's past. An asteroid hitting Earth, for example, may have led to the extinction of the dinosaurs about 65 million years ago.*

Paleontology—The Study of Past Life

The history of the Earth would be incomplete without a knowledge of the organisms that have inhabited our planet and the conditions under which they lived. The science involved with the study of past life is called **paleontology.** Scientists who study this life are called *paleontologists*. The data paleontologists use are fossils. Fossils are the remains of organisms preserved by geologic processes. Some paleontologists specialize in the study of particular organisms. Invertebrate paleontologists study animals without backbones, whereas vertebrate paleontologists, such as the scientist in **Figure 4,** study animals with backbones. Paleobotanists study fossils of plants. Other paleontologists reconstruct past ecosystems, study the traces left behind by animals, and piece together the conditions under which fossils were formed. As you see, the study of past life is as varied and complex as Earth's history itself.

Figure 4 *Edwin Colbert was a 20th-century vertebrate paleontologist who made important contributions to the study of dinosaurs.*

paleontology the scientific study of fossils

SECTION Review

Summary

- Uniformitarianism assumes that geologic change is gradual. Catastrophism is based on the idea that geologic change is sudden.
- Modern geology is based on the idea that gradual geologic change is interrupted by catastrophes.
- Using fossils to study past life is called *paleontology*.

Using Key Terms

1. Use each of the following terms in a separate sentence: *uniformitarianism, catastrophism,* and *paleontology.*

Understanding Key Ideas

2. Which of the following words describes change according to the principle of uniformitarianism?
   a. sudden
   b. rare
   c. global
   d. gradual
3. What is the difference between uniformitarianism and catastrophism?
4. Describe how the science of geology has changed.
5. Give one example of catastrophic global change.
6. Describe the work of three types of paleontologists.

Math Skills

7. An impact crater left by an asteroid strike has a radius of 85 km. What is the area of the crater? (Hint: The area of a circle is πr^2.)

Critical Thinking

8. **Analyzing Ideas** Why is uniformitarianism considered to be the foundation of modern geology?
9. **Applying Concepts** Give an example of a type of recent catastrophe.

For a variety of links related to this chapter, go to www.scilinks.org

Topic: Earth's Story
SciLinks code: HSM0450

SECTION 2

Relative Dating: Which Came First?

What You Will Learn

- Explain how relative dating is used in geology.
- Explain the principle of superposition.
- Describe how the geologic column is used in relative dating.
- Identify two events and two features that disrupt rock layers.
- Explain how physical features are used to determine relative ages.

Vocabulary

relative dating
superposition
geologic column
unconformity

READING STRATEGY

Reading Organizer As you read this section, create an outline of the section. Use the headings from the section in your outline.

Imagine that you are a detective investigating a crime scene. What is the first thing you would do?

You might begin by dusting the scene for fingerprints or by searching for witnesses. As a detective, you must figure out the sequence of events that took place before you reached the crime scene.

Geologists have a similar goal when investigating the Earth. They try to determine the order in which events have happened during Earth's history. But instead of relying on fingerprints and witnesses, geologists rely on rocks and fossils to help them in their investigation. Determining whether an object or event is older or younger than other objects or events is called **relative dating.**

The Principle of Superposition

Suppose that you have an older brother who takes a lot of photographs of your family and piles them in a box. Over the years, he keeps adding new photographs to the top of the stack. Think about the family history recorded in those photos. Where are the oldest photographs—the ones taken when you were a baby? Where are the most recent photographs—those taken last week?

Layers of sedimentary rock, such as the ones shown in **Figure 1,** are like stacked photographs. As you move from top to bottom, the layers are older. The principle that states that younger rocks lie above older rocks in undisturbed sequences is called **superposition.**

Figure 1 *Rock layers are like photos stacked over time–the younger ones lie above the older ones.*

Disturbing Forces

Not all rock sequences are arranged with the oldest layers on the bottom and the youngest layers on top. Some rock sequences are disturbed by forces within the Earth. These forces can push other rocks into a sequence, tilt or fold rock layers, and break sequences into movable parts. Sometimes, geologists even find rock sequences that are upside down! The disruptions of rock sequences pose a challenge to geologists trying to determine the relative ages of rocks. Fortunately, geologists can get help from a very valuable tool—the geologic column.

relative dating any method of determining whether an event or object is older or younger than other events or objects

superposition a principle that states that younger rocks lie above older rocks if the layers have not been disturbed

geologic column an arrangement of rock layers in which the oldest rocks are at the bottom

The Geologic Column

To make their job easier, geologists combine data from all the known undisturbed rock sequences around the world. From this information, geologists create the geologic column, as illustrated in **Figure 2.** The **geologic column** is an ideal sequence of rock layers that contains all the known fossils and rock formations on Earth, arranged from oldest to youngest.

Geologists rely on the geologic column to interpret rock sequences. Geologists also use the geologic column to identify the layers in puzzling rock sequences.

Reading Check **List two ways in which geologists use the geologic column.** (*See the Appendix for answers to Reading Checks.*)

Figure 2 **Constructing the Geologic Column**

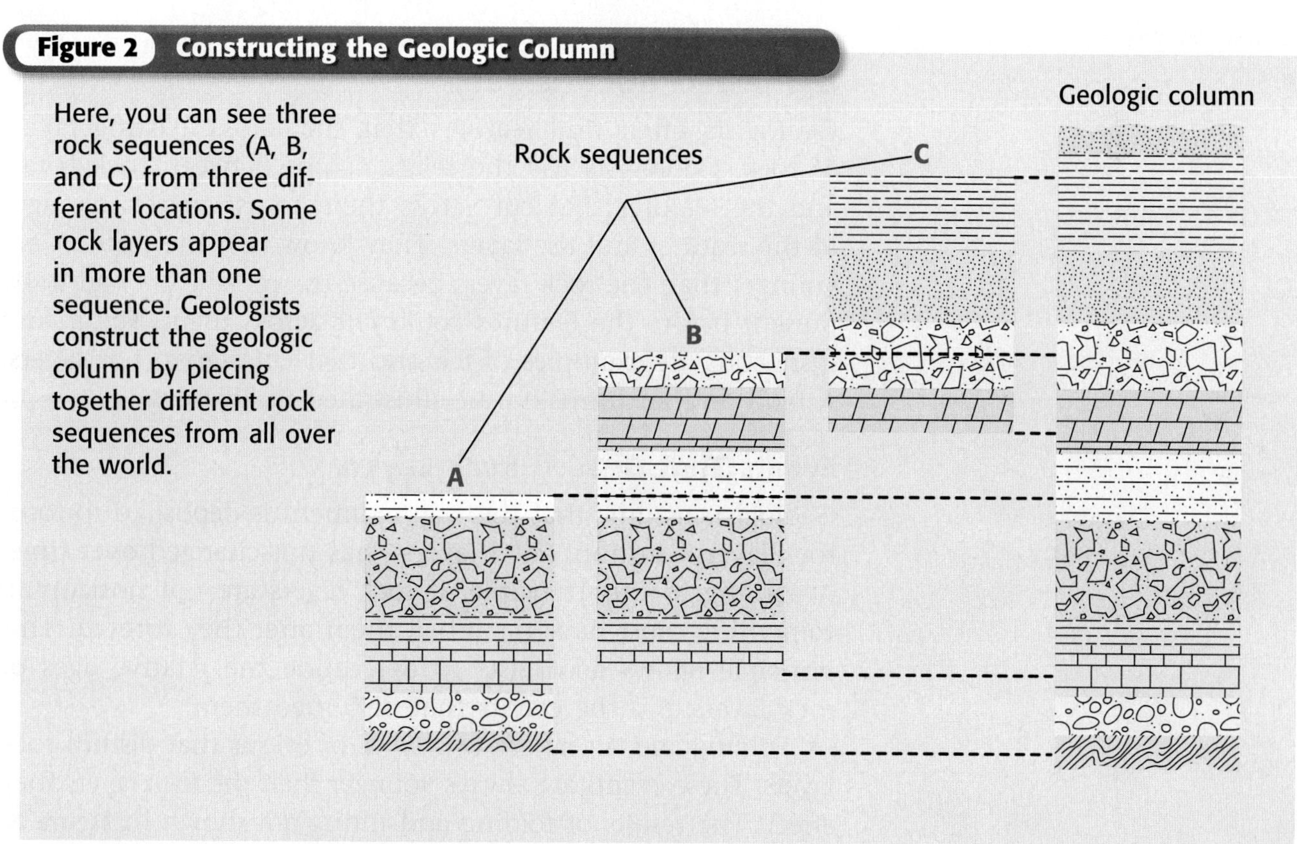

Here, you can see three rock sequences (A, B, and C) from three different locations. Some rock layers appear in more than one sequence. Geologists construct the geologic column by piecing together different rock sequences from all over the world.

Figure 3 How Rock Layers Become Disturbed

Fault A *fault* is a break in the Earth's crust along which blocks of the crust slide relative to one another.

Intrusion An *intrusion* is molten rock from the Earth's interior that squeezes into existing rock and cools.

Folding *Folding* occurs when rock layers bend and buckle from Earth's internal forces.

Tilting *Tilting* occurs when internal forces in the Earth slant rock layers.

Disturbed Rock Layers

Geologists often find features that cut across existing layers of rock. Geologists use the relationships between rock layers and the features that cut across them to assign relative ages to the features and the layers. They know that the features are younger than the rock layers because the rock layers had to be present before the features could cut across them. Faults and intrusions are examples of features that cut across rock layers. A fault and an intrusion are illustrated in **Figure 3.**

Events That Disturb Rock Layers

Geologists assume that the way sediment is deposited to form rock layers—in horizontal layers—has not changed over time. According to this principle, if rock layers are not horizontal, something must have disturbed them after they formed. This principle allows geologists to determine the relative ages of rock layers and the events that disturbed them.

Folding and tilting are two types of events that disturb rock layers. These events are always younger than the rock layers they affect. The results of folding and tilting are shown in **Figure 3.**

Gaps in the Record—Unconformities

Faults, intrusions, and the effects of folding and tilting can make dating rock layers a challenge. Sometimes, layers of rock are missing altogether, creating a gap in the geologic record. To think of this another way, let's say that you stack your newspapers every day after reading them. Now, let's suppose you want to look at a paper you read 10 days ago. You know that the paper should be 10 papers deep in the stack. But when you look, the paper is not there. What happened? Perhaps you forgot to put the paper in the stack. Now, imagine a missing rock layer instead of a missing newspaper.

Missing Evidence

Missing rock layers create breaks in rock-layer sequences called unconformities. An **unconformity** is a surface that represents a missing part of the geologic column. Unconformities also represent missing time—time that was not recorded in layers of rock. When geologists find an unconformity, they must question whether the "missing layer" was never present or whether it was somehow removed. **Figure 4** shows how *nondeposition,* or the stoppage of deposition when a supply of sediment is cut off, and *erosion* create unconformities.

unconformity a break in the geologic record created when rock layers are eroded or when sediment is not deposited for a long period of time

Reading Check Define the term unconformity.

Figure 4 How Unconformities Are Created

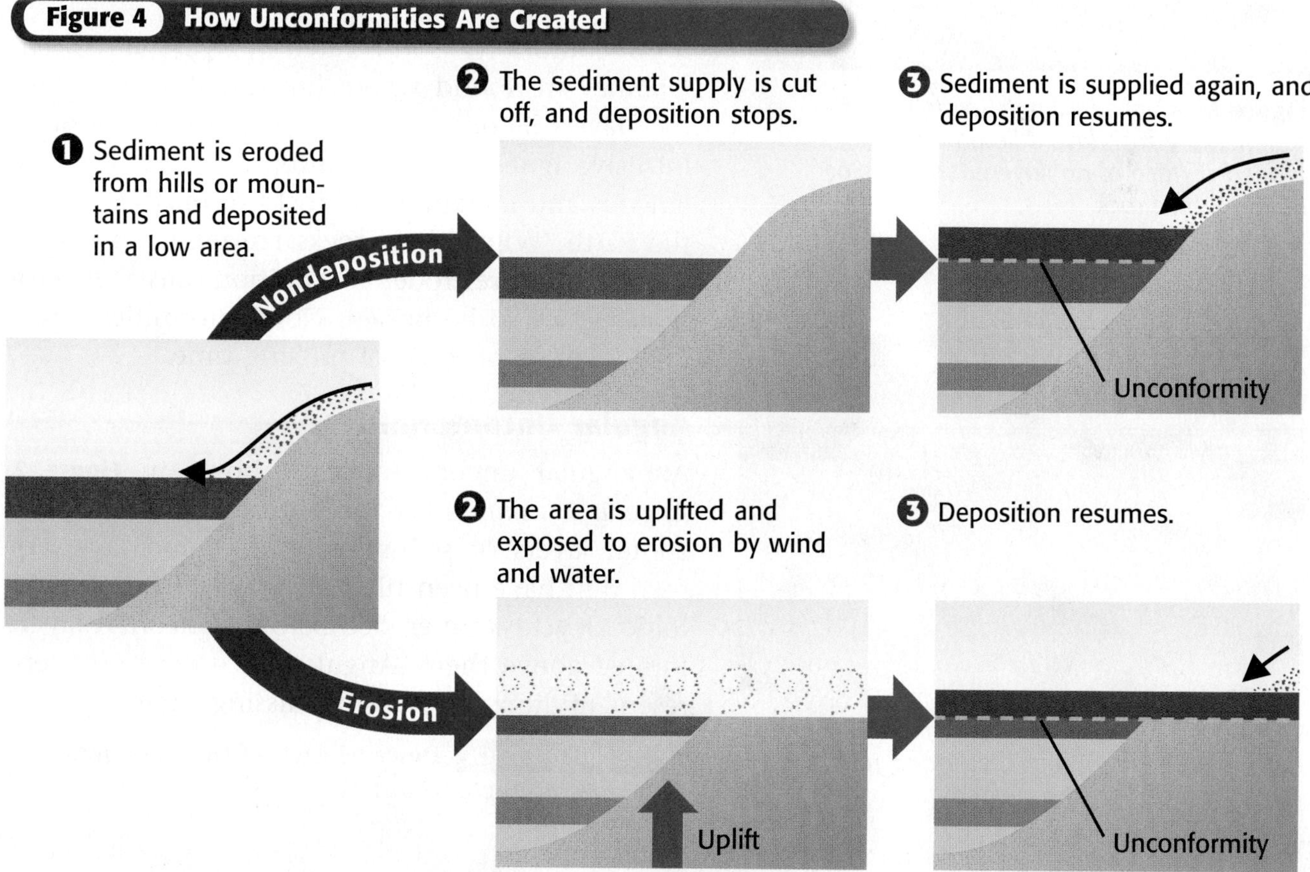
❶ Sediment is eroded from hills or mountains and deposited in a low area.
Nondeposition
❷ The sediment supply is cut off, and deposition stops.
❸ Sediment is supplied again, and deposition resumes.
Unconformity
Erosion
❷ The area is uplifted and exposed to erosion by wind and water.
Uplift
❸ Deposition resumes.
Unconformity

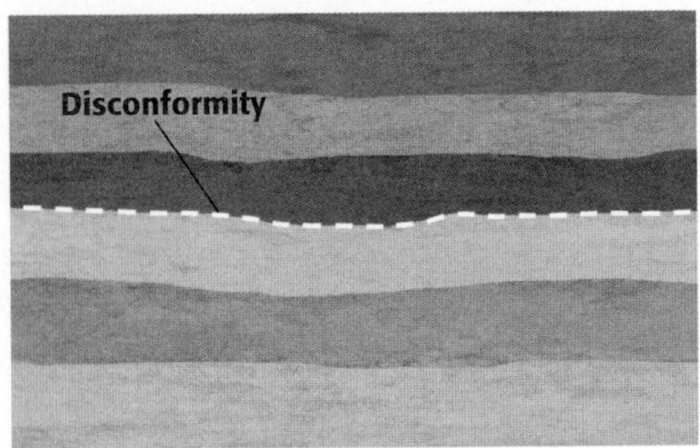

Figure 5 *A disconformity exists where part of a sequence of parallel rock layers is missing.*

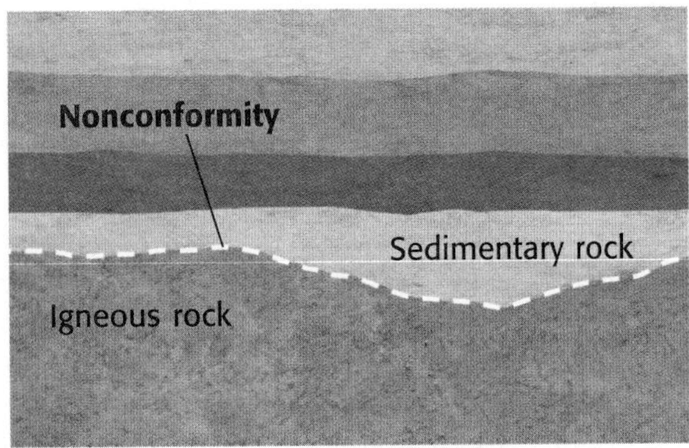

Figure 6 *A nonconformity exists where sedimentary rock layers lie on top of an eroded surface of nonlayered igneous or metamorphic rock.*

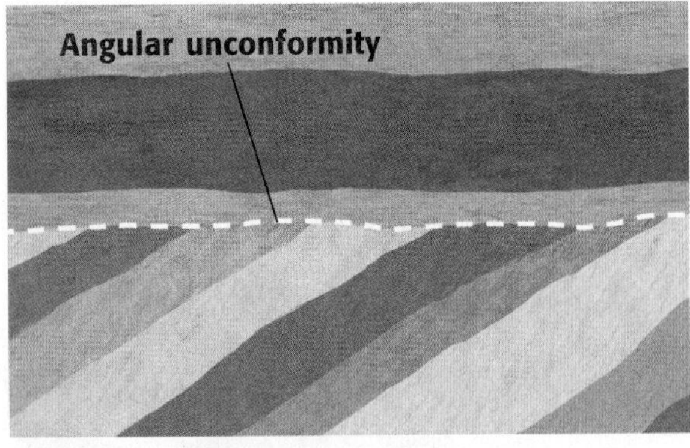

Figure 7 *An angular unconformity exists between horizontal rock layers and rock layers that are tilted or folded.*

Types of Unconformities

Most unconformities form by both erosion and nondeposition. But other factors can complicate matters. To simplify the study of unconformities, geologists place them into three major categories: disconformities, nonconformities, and angular unconformities. The three diagrams at left illustrate these three categories.

Disconformities

The most common type of unconformity is a disconformity, which is illustrated in **Figure 5.** *Disconformities* are found where part of a sequence of parallel rock layers is missing. A disconformity can form in the following way. A sequence of rock layers is uplifted. Younger layers at the top of the sequence are removed by erosion, and the eroded material is deposited elsewhere. At some future time, deposition resumes, and sediment buries the old erosion surface. The disconformity that results shows where erosion has taken place and rock layers are missing. A disconformity represents thousands to many millions of years of missing time.

Nonconformities

A nonconformity is illustrated in **Figure 6.** *Nonconformities* are found where horizontal sedimentary rock layers lie on top of an eroded surface of older intrusive igneous or metamorphic rock. Intrusive igneous and metamorphic rocks form deep within the Earth. When these rocks are raised to Earth's surface, they are eroded. Deposition causes the erosion surface to be buried. Nonconformities represent millions of years of missing time.

Angular Unconformities

An angular unconformity is shown in **Figure 7.** *Angular unconformities* are found between horizontal layers of sedimentary rock and layers of rock that have been tilted or folded. The tilted or folded layers were eroded before horizontal layers formed above them. Angular unconformities represent millions of years of missing time.

Reading Check **Describe each of the three major categories of unconformities.**

Rock-Layer Puzzles

Geologists often find rock-layer sequences that have been affected by more than one of the events and features mentioned in this section. For example, as shown in **Figure 8,** intrusions may squeeze into rock layers that contain an unconformity. Determining the order of events that led to such a sequence is like piecing together a jigsaw puzzle. Geologists must use their knowledge of the events that disturb or remove rock-layer sequences to help piece together the history of Earth as told by the rock record.

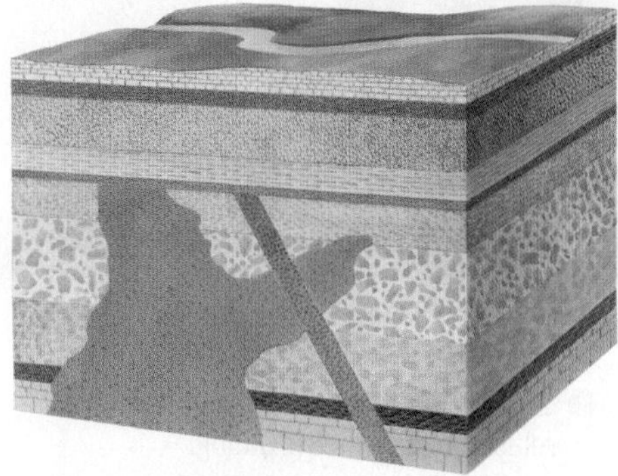

Figure 8 *Rock-layer sequences are often disturbed by more than one rock-disturbing feature.*

SECTION Review

Summary

- Geologists use relative dating to determine the order in which events happen.
- The principle of superposition states that in undisturbed rock sequences, younger layers lie above older layers.
- Folding and tilting are two events that disturb rock layers. Faults and intrusions are two features that disturb rock layers.
- The known rock and fossil record is indicated by the geologic column.
- Geologists examine the relationships between rock layers and the structures that cut across them in order to determine relative ages.

Using Key Terms

1. In your own words, write a definition for each of the following terms: *relative dating, superposition,* and *geologic column.*

Understanding Key Ideas

2. Molten rock that squeezes into existing rock and cools is called a(n)
   a. fold.
   b. fault.
   c. intrusion.
   d. unconformity.
3. List two events and two features that can disturb rock-layer sequences.
4. Explain how physical features are used to determine relative ages.

Critical Thinking

5. **Analyzing Concepts** Is there a place on Earth that has all the layers of the geologic column? Explain.
6. **Analyzing Ideas** Disconformities are hard to recognize because all of the layers are horizontal. How does a geologist know when he or she is looking at a disconformity?

Interpreting Graphics

Use the illustration below to answer the question that follows.

7. If the top rock layer were eroded and deposition later resumed, what type of unconformity would mark the boundary between older rock layers and the newly deposited rock layers?

SCILINKS.
NSTA
Developed and maintained by the National Science Teachers Association
For a variety of links related to this chapter, go to www.scilinks.org
Topic: Relative Dating
SciLinks code: HSM1288

SECTION 3

Absolute Dating: A Measure of Time

What You Will Learn

- Describe how radioactive decay occurs.
- Explain how radioactive decay relates to radiometric dating.
- Identify four types of radiometric dating.
- Determine the best type of radiometric dating to use to date an object.

Vocabulary

absolute dating
isotope
radioactive decay
radiometric dating
half-life

READING STRATEGY

Reading Organizer As you read this section, make a concept map by using the terms above.

Have you ever heard the expression "turning back the clock"? With the discovery of the natural decay of uranium in 1896, French physicist Henri Becquerel provided a means of doing just that. Scientists could use radioactive elements as clocks to measure geologic time.

The process of establishing the age of an object by determining the number of years it has existed is called **absolute dating.** In this section, you will learn about radiometric dating, which is the most common method of absolute dating.

Radioactive Decay

To determine the absolute ages of fossils and rocks, scientists analyze isotopes of radioactive elements. Atoms of the same element that have the same number of protons but have different numbers of neutrons are called **isotopes.** Most isotopes are stable, meaning that they stay in their original form. But some isotopes are unstable. Scientists call unstable isotopes *radioactive*. Radioactive isotopes tend to break down into stable isotopes of the same or other elements in a process called **radioactive decay. Figure 1** shows an example of how radioactive decay occurs. Because radioactive decay occurs at a steady rate, scientists can use the relative amounts of stable and unstable isotopes present in an object to determine the object's age.

Figure 1 Radioactive Decay

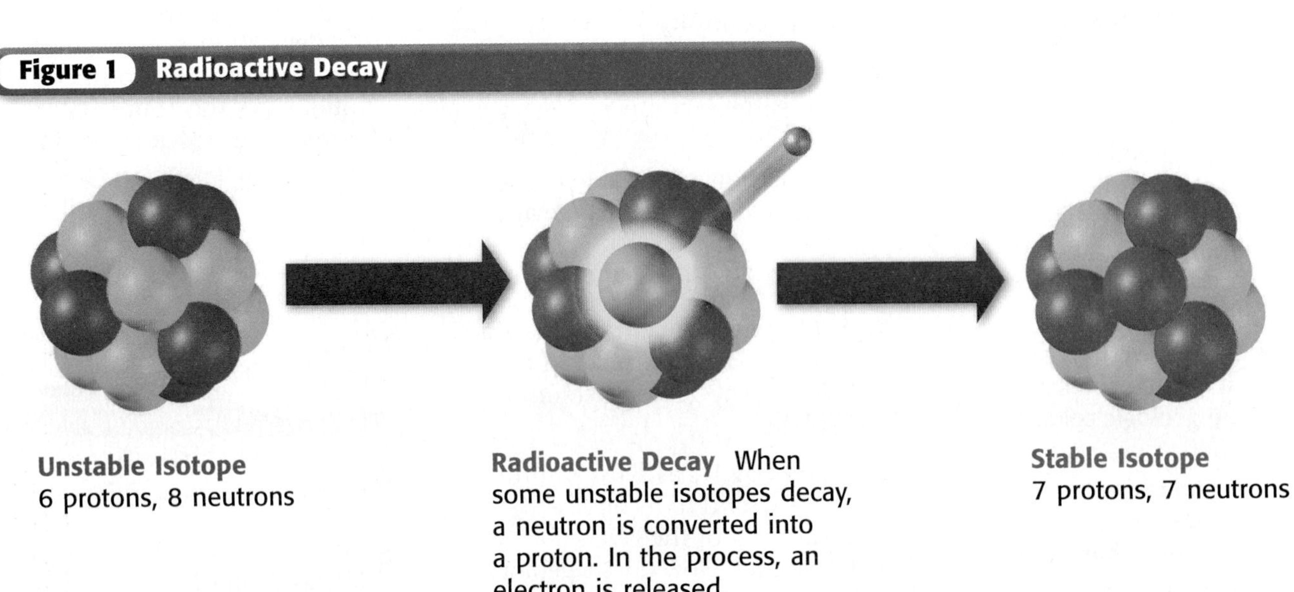

Unstable Isotope
6 protons, 8 neutrons

Radioactive Decay When some unstable isotopes decay, a neutron is converted into a proton. In the process, an electron is released.

Stable Isotope
7 protons, 7 neutrons

Dating Rocks—How Does It Work?

In the process of radioactive decay, an unstable radioactive isotope of one element breaks down into a stable isotope. The stable isotope may be of the same element or, more commonly, a different element. The unstable radioactive isotope is called the *parent isotope*. The stable isotope produced by the radioactive decay of the parent isotope is called the *daughter isotope*. The radioactive decay of a parent isotope into a stable daughter isotope can occur in a single step or a series of steps. In either case, the rate of decay is constant. Therefore, to date rock, scientists compare the amount of parent material with the amount of daughter material. The more daughter material there is, the older the rock is.

Radiometric Dating

If you know the rate of decay for a radioactive element in a rock, you can figure out the absolute age of the rock. Determining the absolute age of a sample, based on the ratio of parent material to daughter material, is called **radiometric dating.** For example, let's say that a rock sample contains an isotope with a half-life of 10,000 years. A **half-life** is the time that it takes one-half of a radioactive sample to decay. So, for this rock sample, in 10,000 years, half the parent material will have decayed and become daughter material. You analyze the sample and find equal amounts of parent material and daughter material. This means that half the original radioactive isotope has decayed and that the sample must be about 10,000 years old.

What if one-fourth of your sample is parent material and three-fourths is daughter material? You would know that it took 10,000 years for half the original sample to decay and another 10,000 years for half of what remained to decay. The age of your sample would be 2 × 10,000, or 20,000, years. **Figure 2** shows how this steady decay happens.

Reading Check What is a half-life? (*See the Appendix for answers to Reading Checks.*)

absolute dating any method of measuring the age of an event or object in years

isotope an atom that has the same number of protons (or the same atomic number) as other atoms of the same element do but that has a different number of neutrons (and thus a different atomic mass)

radioactive decay the process in which a radioactive isotope tends to break down into a stable isotope of the same element or another element

radiometric dating a method of determining the age of an object by estimating the relative percentages of a radioactive (parent) isotope and a stable (daughter) isotope

half-life the time needed for half of a sample of a radioactive substance to undergo radioactive decay

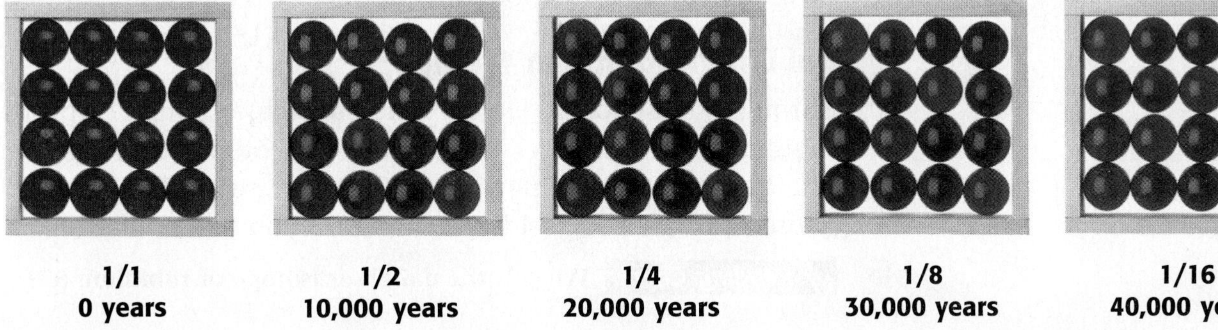

Figure 2 *After every half-life, the amount of parent material decreases by one-half.*

Figure 3 *This burial mound at Effigy Mounds resembles a snake.*

Types of Radiometric Dating

Imagine traveling back through the centuries to a time before Columbus arrived in America. You are standing along the bluffs of what will one day be called the Mississippi River. You see dozens of people building large mounds. Who are these people, and what are they building?

The people you saw in your time travel were Native Americans, and the structures they were building were burial mounds. The area you imagined is now an archaeological site called Effigy Mounds National Monument. **Figure 3** shows one of these mounds.

According to archaeologists, people lived at Effigy Mounds from 2,500 years ago to 600 years ago. How do archaeologists know these dates? They have dated bones and other objects in the mounds by using radiometric dating. Scientists use different radiometric-dating techniques based on the estimated age of an object. As you read on, think about how the half-life of an isotope relates to the age of the object being dated. Which technique would you use to date the burial mounds?

Potassium-Argon Method

One isotope that is used for radiometric dating is potassium-40. Potassium-40 has a half-life of 1.3 billion years, and it decays to argon and calcium. Geologists measure argon as the daughter material. This method is used mainly to date rocks older than 100,000 years.

Uranium-Lead Method

Uranium-238 is a radioactive isotope that decays in a series of steps to lead-206. The half-life of uranium-238 is 4.5 billion years. The older the rock is, the more daughter material (lead-206) there will be in the rock. Uranium-lead dating can be used for rocks more than 10 million years old. Younger rocks do not contain enough daughter material to be accurately measured by this method.

Rubidium-Strontium Method

Through radioactive decay, the unstable parent isotope rubidium-87 forms the stable daughter isotope strontium-87. The half-life of rubidium-87 is 49 billion years. This method is used to date rocks older than 10 million years.

Reading Check **What is the daughter isotope of rubidium-87?**

Carbon-14 Method

The element carbon is normally found in three forms, the stable isotopes carbon-12 and carbon-13 and the radioactive isotope carbon-14. These carbon isotopes combine with oxygen to form the gas carbon dioxide, which is taken in by plants during photosynthesis. As long as a plant is alive, new carbon dioxide with a constant carbon-14 to carbon-12 ratio is continually taken in. Animals that eat plants contain the same ratio of carbon isotopes.

Once a plant or an animal dies, however, no new carbon is taken in. The amount of carbon-14 begins to decrease as the plant or animal decays, and the ratio of carbon-14 to carbon-12 decreases. This decrease can be measured in a laboratory, such as the one shown in **Figure 4.** Because the half-life of carbon-14 is only 5,730 years, this dating method is used mainly for dating things that lived within the last 50,000 years.

Figure 4 *Some samples containing carbon must be cleaned and burned before their age can be determined.*

SECTION Review

Summary

- During radioactive decay, an unstable isotope decays at a constant rate and becomes a stable isotope of the same or a different element.
- Radiometric dating, based on the ratio of parent to daughter material, is used to determine the absolute age of a sample.
- Methods of radiometric dating include potassium-argon, uranium-lead, rubidium-strontium, and carbon-14 dating.

Using Key Terms

1. Use each of the following terms in a separate sentence: *absolute dating, isotope,* and *half-life.*

Understanding Key Ideas

2. Rubidium-87 has a half-life of
   - **a.** 5,730 years.
   - **b.** 4.5 billion years.
   - **c.** 49 billion years.
   - **d.** 1.3 billion years.
3. Explain how radioactive decay occurs.
4. How does radioactive decay relate to radiometric dating?
5. List four types of radiometric dating.

Math Skills

6. A radioactive isotope has a half-life of 1.3 billion years. After 3.9 billion years, how much of the parent material will be left?

Critical Thinking

7. **Analyzing Methods** Explain why radioactive decay must be constant in order for radiometric dating to be accurate.
8. **Applying Concepts** Which radiometric-dating method would be most appropriate for dating artifacts found at Effigy Mounds? Explain.

SCILINKS
NSTA
Developed and maintained by the National Science Teachers Association
For a variety of links related to this chapter, go to www.scilinks.org
Topic: Absolute Dating
SciLinks code: HSM0003

SECTION 4

Looking at Fossils

What You Will Learn

- Describe five ways that different types of fossils form.
- List three types of fossils that are not part of organisms.
- Explain how fossils can be used to determine the history of changes in environments and organisms.
- Explain how index fossils can be used to date rock layers.

Vocabulary

fossil
trace fossil
mold
cast
index fossil

READING STRATEGY

Reading Organizer As you read this section, create an outline of the section. Use the headings from this section in your outline.

Descending from the top of a ridge in the badlands of Argentina, your expedition team suddenly stops. You look down and realize that you are walking on eggshells—dinosaur eggshells!

A paleontologist named Luis Chiappe had this experience. He had found an enormous dinosaur nesting ground.

Fossilized Organisms

The remains or physical evidence of an organism preserved by geologic processes is called a **fossil.** Fossils are most often preserved in sedimentary rock. But as you will see, other materials can also preserve evidence of past life.

Fossils in Rocks

When an organism dies, it either immediately begins to decay or is consumed by other organisms. Sometimes, however, organisms are quickly buried by sediment when they die. The sediment slows down decay. Hard parts of organisms, such as shells and bones, are more resistant to decay than soft tissues are. So, when sediments become rock, the hard parts of animals are much more commonly preserved than are soft tissues.

Fossils in Amber

Imagine that an insect is caught in soft, sticky tree sap. Suppose that the insect gets covered by more sap, which quickly hardens and preserves the insect inside. Hardened tree sap is called *amber.* Some of our best insect fossils are found in amber, as shown in **Figure 1.** Frogs and lizards have also been found in amber.

Reading Check **Describe how organisms are preserved in amber.** (*See the Appendix for answers to Reading Checks.*)

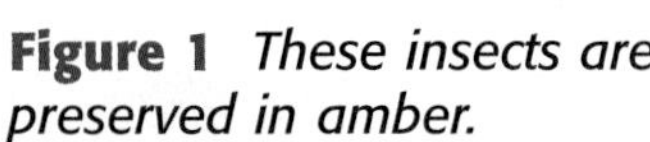

Figure 1 *These insects are preserved in amber.*

Figure 2 *Scientist Vladimir Eisner studies the upper molars of a 20,000-year-old woolly mammoth found in Siberia, Russia. The almost perfectly preserved male mammoth was excavated from a block of ice in October 1999.*

Petrifaction

Another way that organisms are preserved is by petrifaction. *Petrifaction* is a process in which minerals replace an organism's tissues. One form of petrifaction is called permineralization. *Permineralization* is a process in which the pore space in an organism's hard tissue—for example, bone or wood—is filled up with mineral. Another form of petrifaction is called *replacement,* a process in which the organism's tissues are completely replaced by minerals. For example, in some specimens of petrified wood, all of the wood has been replaced by minerals.

fossil the remains or physical evidence of an organism preserved by geological processes

Fossils in Asphalt

There are places where asphalt wells up at the Earth's surface in thick, sticky pools. The La Brea asphalt deposits in Los Angeles, California, for example, are at least 38,000 years old. These pools of thick, sticky asphalt have trapped and preserved many kinds of organisms for the past 38,000 years. From these fossils, scientists have learned about the past environment in southern California.

Frozen Fossils

In October 1999, scientists removed a 20,000-year-old woolly mammoth frozen in the Siberian tundra. The remains of this mammoth are shown in **Figure 2.** Woolly mammoths, relatives of modern elephants, became extinct approximately 10,000 years ago. Because cold temperatures slow down decay, many types of frozen fossils are preserved from the last ice age. Scientists hope to find out more about the mammoth and the environment in which it lived.

CONNECTION TO Environmental Science

WRITING SKILL **Preservation in Ice** Subfreezing climates contain almost no decomposing bacteria. The well-preserved body of John Torrington, a member of an expedition that explored the Northwest Passage in Canada in the 1840s, was uncovered in 1984. His body appeared much as it did at the time he died, more than 160 years earlier. Research another well-preserved discovery, and write a report for your class.

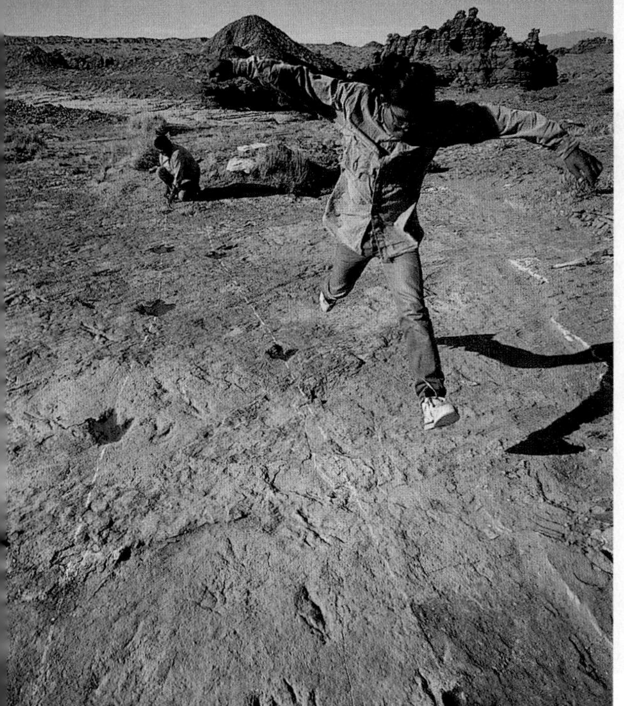

Figure 3 *These dinosaur tracks are located in Arizona. They leave a trace of a dinosaur that had longer legs than humans do.*

Other Types of Fossils

Besides their hard parts—and in rare cases their soft parts—do organisms leave behind any other clues about their existence? What other evidence of past life do paleontologists look for?

Trace Fossils

Any naturally preserved evidence of animal activity is called a **trace fossil.** Tracks like the ones shown in **Figure 3** are a fascinating example of a trace fossil. These fossils form when animal footprints fill with sediment and are preserved in rock. Tracks reveal a lot about the animal that made them, including how big it was and how fast it was moving. Parallel trackways showing dinosaurs moving in the same direction have led paleontologists to hypothesize that dinosaurs moved in herds.

Burrows are another trace fossil. Burrows are shelters made by animals, such as clams, that bury in sediment. Like tracks, burrows are preserved when they are filled in with sediment and buried quickly. A *coprolite* (KAHP roh LIET), a third type of trace fossil, is preserved animal dung.

trace fossil a fossilized mark that is formed in soft sediment by the movement of an animal

mold a mark or cavity made in a sedimentary surface by a shell or other body

cast a type of fossil that forms when sediments fill in the cavity left by a decomposed organism

Molds and Casts

Molds and casts are two more examples of fossils. A cavity in rock where a plant or animal was buried is called a **mold.** A **cast** is an object created when sediment fills a mold and becomes rock. A cast shows what the outside of the organism looked like. **Figure 4** shows two types of molds from the same organism—and internal mold and an external mold.

Reading Check How are a cast and a mold different?

Figure 4 *This photograph shows two molds from an ammonite. The image on the left is the internal mold of the ammonite, which formed when sediment filled the ammonite's shell, which later dissolved away. The image on the right is the external mold of the ammonite, which preserves the external features of the shell.*

Figure 5 *This scientist has found marine fossils on mountaintops in the Yoho National Park in Canada. The fossil of* Marrella, *shown above, tells the scientist that these rocks were pushed up from below sea level millions of years ago.*

Using Fossils to Interpret the Past

Think about your favorite outdoor place. Now, imagine that you are a paleontologist at the same site 65 million years from now. What types of fossils would you dig up? Based on the fossils you found, how would you reconstruct this place?

The Information in the Fossil Record

The fossil record offers only a rough sketch of the history of life on Earth. Some parts of this history are more complete than others. For example, scientists know more about organisms that had hard body parts than about organisms that had soft body parts. Scientists also know more about organisms that lived in environments that favored fossilization. The fossil record is incomplete because most organisms never became fossils. And of course, many fossils have yet to be discovered.

History of Environmental Changes

Would you expect to find marine fossils on the mountaintop shown in **Figure 5**? The presence of marine fossils means that the rocks of these mountaintops in Canada formed in a totally different environment—at the bottom of an ocean.

The fossil record reveals a history of environmental change. For example, marine fossils help scientists reconstruct ancient coastlines and the deepening and shallowing of ancient seas. Using the fossils of plants and land animals, scientists can reconstruct past climates. They can tell whether the climate in an area was cooler or wetter than it is at present.

Make a Fossil

1. Find a **common object,** such as a shell, a button, or a pencil, to use to make a mold. Keep the object hidden from your classmates.
2. To create a mold, press the items down into **modeling clay** in a **shallow pan or tray.**
3. Trade your tray with a classmate's tray, and try to identify the item that made the mold.
4. Describe how a cast could be formed from your mold.

Fossil Hunt

Go on a fossil hunt with a parent or guardian. Find out what kinds of rocks in your local area might contain fossils. Take pictures or draw sketches of your trip and any fossils that you find.

History of Changing Organisms

By studying the relationships between fossils, scientists can interpret how life has changed over time. For example, older rock layers contain organisms that often differ from the organisms found in younger rock layers.

Only a small fraction of the organisms that have existed in Earth's history have been fossilized. Because the fossil record is incomplete, it does not provide paleontologists with a continuous record of change. Instead, they look for similarities between fossils, or between fossilized organisms and their closest living relatives, and try to fill in the blanks in the fossil record.

Reading Check **How do paleontologists fill in missing information about changes in organisms in the fossil record?**

Using Fossils to Date Rocks

index fossil a fossil that is found in the rock layers of only one geologic age and that is used to establish the age of the rock layers

Scientists have found that particular types of fossils appear only in certain layers of rock. By dating the rock layers above and below these fossils, scientists can determine the time span in which the organisms that formed the fossils lived. If a type of organism existed for only a short period of time, its fossils would show up in a limited range of rock layers. These types of fossils are called index fossils. **Index fossils** are fossils of organisms that lived during a relatively short, well-defined geologic time span.

Ammonites

To be considered an index fossil, a fossil must be found in rock layers throughout the world. One example of an index fossil is the fossil of a genus of ammonites (AM uh NIETS) called *Tropites*, shown in **Figure 6.** *Tropites* was a marine mollusk similar to a modern squid. It lived in a coiled shell. *Tropites* lived between 230 million and 208 million years ago and is an index fossil for that period of time.

Figure 6 Tropites *is a genus of coiled ammonites.* Tropites *existed for only about 20 million years, which makes this genus a good index fossil.*

Trilobites

Fossils of a genus of trilobites (TRIE loh BIETS) called *Phacops* are another example of an index fossil. Trilobites are extinct. Their closest living relative is the horseshoe crab. Through the dating of rock, paleontologists have determined that *Phacops* lived approximately 400 million years ago. So, when scientists find *Phacops* in rock layers anywhere on Earth, they assume that these rock layers are also approximately 400 million years old. An example of a *Phacops* fossil is shown in **Figure 7.**

Reading Check **Explain how fossils of *Phacops* can be used to establish the age of rock layers.**

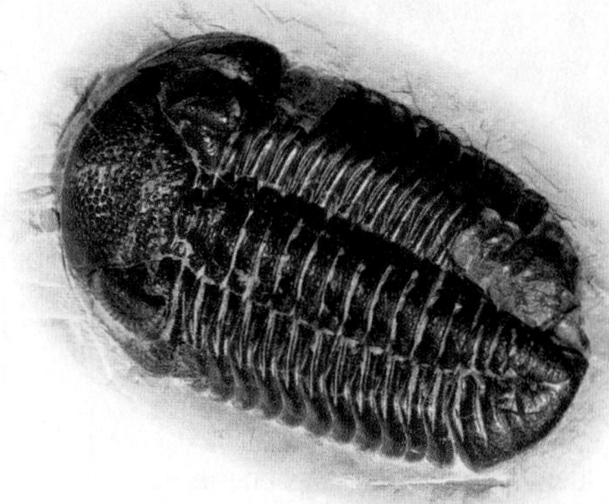

Figure 7 *Paleontologists assume that any rock layer containing a fossil of the trilobite* Phacops *is about 400 million years old.*

SECTION Review

Summary

- Fossils are the remains or physical evidence of an organism preserved by geologic processes.
- Fossils can be preserved in rock, amber, asphalt, and ice and by petrifaction.
- Trace fossils are any naturally preserved evidence of animal activity. Tracks, burrows, and coprolites are examples of trace fossils.
- Scientists study fossils to determine how environments and organisms have changed over time.
- An index fossil is a fossil of an organism that lived during a relatively short, well-defined time span. Index fossils can be used to establish the age of rock layers.

Using Key Terms

Complete each of the following sentences by choosing the correct term from the word bank.

cast	index fossils
mold	trace fossils

1. A ___ is a cavity in rock where a plant or animal was buried.
2. ___ can be used to establish the age of rock layers.

Understanding Key Ideas

3. Fossils are most often preserved in
   - **a.** ice.
   - **b.** amber.
   - **c.** asphalt.
   - **d.** rock.
4. Describe three types of trace fossils.
5. Explain how an index fossil can be used to date rock.
6. Explain why the fossil record contains an incomplete record of the history of life on Earth.
7. Explain how fossils can be used to determine the history of changes in environments and organisms.

Math Skills

8. If a scientist finds the remains of a plant between a rock layer that contains 400 million–year-old *Phacops* fossils and a rock layer that contains 230 million–year-old *Tropites* fossils, how old could the plant fossil be?

Critical Thinking

9. **Making Inferences** If you find rock layers containing fish fossils in a desert, what can you infer about the history of the desert?
10. **Identifying Bias** Because information in the fossil record is incomplete, scientists are left with certain biases concerning fossil preservation. Explain two of these biases.

SCILINKS.
NSTA
Developed and maintained by the National Science Teachers Association
For a variety of links related to this chapter, go to www.scilinks.org
Topic: Looking at Fossils
SciLinks code: HSM0886

SECTION 5

Time Marches On

What You Will Learn

- Explain how geologic time is recorded in rock layers.
- Identify important dates on the geologic time scale.
- Explain how environmental changes resulted in the extinction of some species.

Vocabulary

geologic time scale	period
eon	epoch
era	extinction

READING STRATEGY

Brainstorming The key idea of this section is the geologic time scale. Brainstorm words and phrases related to the geologic time scale.

How old is the Earth? Well, if the Earth celebrated its birthday every million years, there would be 4,600 candles on its birthday cake! Humans have been around only long enough to light the last candle on the cake.

Try to think of the Earth's history in "fast-forward." If you could watch the Earth change from this perspective, you would see mountains rise up like wrinkles in fabric and quickly wear away. You would see life-forms appear and then go extinct. In this section, you will learn that geologists must "fast-forward" the Earth's history when they write or talk about it. You will also learn about some incredible events in the history of life on Earth.

Geologic Time

Shown in **Figure 1** is the rock wall at the Dinosaur Quarry Visitor Center in Dinosaur National Monument, Utah. Contained within this wall are approximately 1,500 fossil bones that have been excavated by paleontologists. These are the remains of dinosaurs that inhabited the area about 150 million years ago. Granted, 150 million years seems to be an incredibly long period of time. However, in terms of the Earth's history, 150 million years is little more than 3% of the time our planet has existed. It is a little less than 4% of the time represented by the Earth's oldest known rocks.

Figure 1 *Bones of dinosaurs that lived about 150 million years ago are exposed in the quarry wall at Dinosaur National Monument in Utah.*

Figure 2 *Well-preserved plant and animal fossils are common in the Green River formation. Clockwise from the upper right are a fossil leaf, a dragonfly, a fish, and a turtle.*

The Rock Record and Geologic Time

One of the best places in North America to see the Earth's history recorded in rock layers is in Grand Canyon National Park. The Colorado River has cut the canyon nearly 2 km deep in some places. Over the course of 6 million years, the river has eroded countless layers of rock. These layers represent almost half, or nearly 2 billion years, of Earth's history.

Reading Check **How much geologic time is represented by the rock layers in the Grand Canyon?** (*See the Appendix for answers to Reading Checks.*)

The Fossil Record and Geologic Time

Figure 2 shows sedimentary rocks that belong to the Green River formation. These rocks, which are found in parts of Wyoming, Utah, and Colorado, are thousands of meters thick. These rocks were once part of a system of ancient lakes that existed for a period of millions of years. Fossils of plants and animals are common in these rocks and are very well preserved. Burial in the fine-grained lake-bed sediments preserved even the most delicate structures.

For another activity related to this chapter, go to **go.hrw.com** and type in the keyword **HZ5FOSW.**

Geologic Time Scale

Eon	Era	Period	Epoch	Millions of years ago
PHANEROZOIC EON	Cenozoic	Quaternary	Holocene	0.01
			Pleistocene	1.8
		Tertiary	Pliocene	5.3
			Miocene	23
			Oligocene	33.9
			Eocene	55.8
			Paleocene	65.5
	Mesozoic	Cretaceous		146
		Jurassic		200
		Triassic		251
	Paleozoic	Permian		299
		Pennsylvanian		318
		Mississippian		359
		Devonian		416
		Silurian		444
		Ordovician		488
		Cambrian		542
PROTEROZOIC EON				2,500
ARCHEAN EON				3,800
HADEAN EON				4,600

Phanerozoic Eon

(542 million years ago to the present)
The rock and fossil record represents mainly the Phanerozoic eon, which is the eon in which we live.

Proterozoic Eon

(2.5 billion years ago to 542 million years ago)
The first organisms with well-developed cells appeared during this eon.

Archean Eon

(3.8 billion years ago to 2.5 billion years ago)
The earliest known rocks on Earth formed during this eon.

Hadean Eon

(4.6 billion years ago to 3.8 billion years ago)
The only rocks that scientists have found from this eon are meteorites and rocks from the moon.

Figure 3 *The geologic time scale accounts for Earth's entire history. It is divided into four major parts called* eons. *Dates given for intervals on the geologic time scale are estimates.*

The Geologic Time Scale

The geologic column represents the billions of years that have passed since the first rocks formed on Earth. Altogether, geologists study 4.6 billion years of Earth's history! To make their job easier, geologists have created the geologic time scale. The **geologic time scale,** which is shown in **Figure 3,** is a scale that divides Earth's 4.6 billion–year history into distinct intervals of time.

Reading Check **Define the term *geologic time scale.***

Divisions of Time

Geologists have divided Earth's history into sections of time, as shown on the geologic time scale in **Figure 3.** The largest divisions of geologic time are **eons** (EE AHNZ). There are four eons—the Hadean eon, the Archean eon, the Proterozoic eon, and the Phanerozoic eon. The Phanerozoic eon is divided into three **eras,** which are the second-largest divisions of geologic time. The three eras are further divided into **periods,** which are the third-largest divisions of geologic time. Periods are divided into **epochs** (EP uhks), which are the fourth-largest divisions of geologic time.

The boundaries between geologic time intervals represent shorter intervals in which visible changes took place on Earth. Some changes are marked by the disappearance of index fossil species, while others are recognized only by detailed paleontological studies.

geologic time scale the standard method used to divide the Earth's long natural history into manageable parts

eon the largest division of geologic time

era a unit of geologic time that includes two or more periods

period a unit of geologic time into which eras are divided

epoch a subdivision of a geologic period

extinction the death of every member of a species

The Appearance and Disappearance of Species

At certain times during Earth's history, the number of species has increased or decreased dramatically. An increase in the number of species often comes as a result of either a relatively sudden increase or decrease in competition among species. *Hallucigenia,* shown in **Figure 4,** appeared during the Cambrian period, when the number of marine species greatly increased. On the other hand, the number of species decreases dramatically over a relatively short period of time during a mass extinction event. **Extinction** is the death of every member of a species. Gradual events, such as global climate change and changes in ocean currents, can cause mass extinctions. A combination of these events can also cause mass extinctions.

Figure 4 Hallucigenia, *named for its "bizarre and dreamlike quality," was one of numerous marine organisms to make its appearance during the early Cambrian period.*

Figure 5 *Jungles were present during the Paleozoic era, but there were no birds singing in the trees and no monkeys swinging from the branches. Birds and mammals didn't evolve until much later.*

The Paleozoic Era—Old Life

The Paleozoic era lasted from about 542 million to 251 million years ago. It is the first era well represented by fossils.

Marine life flourished at the beginning of the Paleozoic era. The oceans became home to a diversity of life. However, there were few land organisms. By the middle of the Paleozoic, all modern groups of land plants had appeared. By the end of the era, amphibians and reptiles lived on the land, and insects were abundant. **Figure 5** shows what the Earth might have looked like late in the Paleozoic era. The Paleozoic era came to an end with the largest mass extinction in Earth's history. Some scientists believe that ocean changes were a likely cause of this extinction, which killed nearly 90% of all marine species.

The Mesozoic Era—The Age of Reptiles

The Mesozoic era began about 251 million years ago. The Mesozoic is known as the *Age of Reptiles* because reptiles, such as the dinosaurs shown in **Figure 6,** inhabited the land.

During this time, reptiles dominated. Small mammals appeared about the same time as dinosaurs, and birds appeared late in the Mesozoic era. Many scientists think that birds evolved directly from a type of dinosaur. At the end of the Mesozoic era, about 15% to 20% of all species on Earth, including the dinosaurs, became extinct. Global climate change may have been the cause.

Reading Check **Why is the Mesozoic known as the *Age of Reptiles*?**

Figure 6 *Imagine walking in the desert and bumping into these fierce creatures! It's a good thing humans didn't evolve in the Mesozoic era, which was dominated by dinosaurs.*

The Cenozoic Era—The Age of Mammals

The Cenozoic era, as shown in **Figure 7,** began about 65.5 million years ago and continues to the present. This era is known as the *Age of Mammals.* During the Mesozoic era, mammals had to compete with dinosaurs and other animals for food and habitat. After the mass extinction at the end of the Mesozoic era, mammals flourished. Unique traits, such as regulating body temperature internally and bearing young that develop inside the mother, may have helped mammals survive the environmental changes that probably caused the extinction of the dinosaurs.

Figure 7 *Thousands of species of mammals evolved during the Cenozoic era. This scene shows species from the early Cenozoic era that are now extinct.*

SECTION Review

Summary

- The geologic time scale divides Earth's 4.6 billion–year history into distinct intervals of time. Divisions of geologic time include eons, eras, periods, and epochs.
- The boundaries between geologic time intervals represent visible changes that have taken place on Earth.
- The rock and fossil record represents mainly the Phanerozoic eon, which is the eon in which we live.
- At certain times in Earth's history, the number of life-forms has increased or decreased dramatically.

Using Key Terms

1. Use each of the following terms in the same sentence: *era, period,* and *epoch.*

Understanding Key Ideas

2. The unit of geologic time that began 65.5 million years ago and continues to the present is the
   a. Holocene epoch.
   b. Cenozoic era.
   c. Phanerozoic eon.
   d. Quaternary period.
3. What are the major time intervals represented by the geologic time scale?
4. Explain how geologic time is recorded in rock layers.
5. What kinds of environmental changes cause mass extinctions?

Critical Thinking

6. **Making Inferences** What future event might mark the end of the Cenozoic era?
7. **Identifying Relationships** How might a decrease in competition between species lead to the sudden appearance of many new species?

Interpreting Graphics

8. Look at the illustration below. On the Earth-history clock shown, 1 h equals 383 million years, and 1 min equals 6.4 million years. In millions of years, how much more time is represented by the Proterozoic eon than by the Phanerozoic eon?

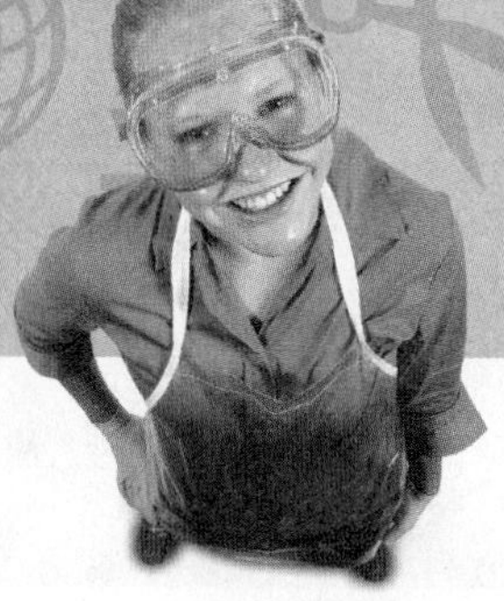

Model-Making Lab

How Do You Stack Up?

OBJECTIVES

Make a model of a geologic column.

Interpret the geologic history represented by the geologic column you have made.

MATERIALS

- paper, white
- pencil
- pencils or crayons, assorted colors
- ruler, metric
- scissors
- tape, transparent

SAFETY

According to the principle of superposition, in undisturbed sequences of sedimentary rock, the oldest layers are on the bottom. Geologists use this principle to determine the relative age of the rocks in a small area. In this activity, you will model what geologists do by drawing sections of different rock outcrops. Then, you will create a part of the geologic column, showing the geologic history of the area that contains all of the outcrops.

Procedure

1. Use a metric ruler and a pencil to draw four boxes on a blank piece of paper. Each box should be 3 cm wide and at least 6 cm tall. (You can trace the boxes shown on the next page.)
2. With colored pencils, copy the illustrations of the four outcrops on the next page. Copy one illustration in each of the four boxes. Use colors and patterns similar to those shown.
3. Pay close attention to the contact between layers—straight or wavy. Straight lines represent bedding planes, where deposition was continuous. Wavy lines represent unconformities, where rock layers may be missing. The top of each outcrop is incomplete, so it should be a jagged line. (Assume that the bottom of the lowest layer is a bedding plane.)
4. Use a black crayon or pencil to add the symbols representing fossils to the layers in your drawings. Pay attention to the shapes of the fossils and the layers that they are in.
5. Write the outcrop number on the back of each section.
6. Carefully cut the outcrops out of the paper, and lay the individual outcrops next to each other on your desk or table.
7. Find layers that have the same rocks and contain the same fossils. Move each outcrop up or down to line up similar layers next to each other.
8. If unconformities appear in any of the outcrops, there may be rock layers missing. You may need to examine other sections to find out what fits between the layers above and below the unconformities. Leave room for these layers by cutting the outcrops along the unconformities (wavy lines).

9. Eventually, you should be able to make a geologic column that represents all four of the outcrops. It will show rock types and fossils for all the known layers in the area.

10. Tape the pieces of paper together in a pattern that represents the complete geologic column.

Analyze the Results

1. **Examining Data** How many layers are in the part of the geologic column that you modeled?

2. **Examining Data** Which is the oldest layer in your column? Which rock layer is the youngest? How do you know? Describe these layers in terms of rock type or the fossils they contain.

3. **Classifying** List the fossils in your column from oldest to youngest. Label the youngest and oldest fossils.

4. **Analyzing Data** Look at the unconformity in outcrop 2. Which rock layers are partially or completely missing? How do you know?

Draw Conclusions

5. **Drawing Conclusions** Which (if any) fossils can be used as index fossils for a single layer? Why are these fossils considered index fossils? What method(s) would be required to determine the absolute age of these fossils?

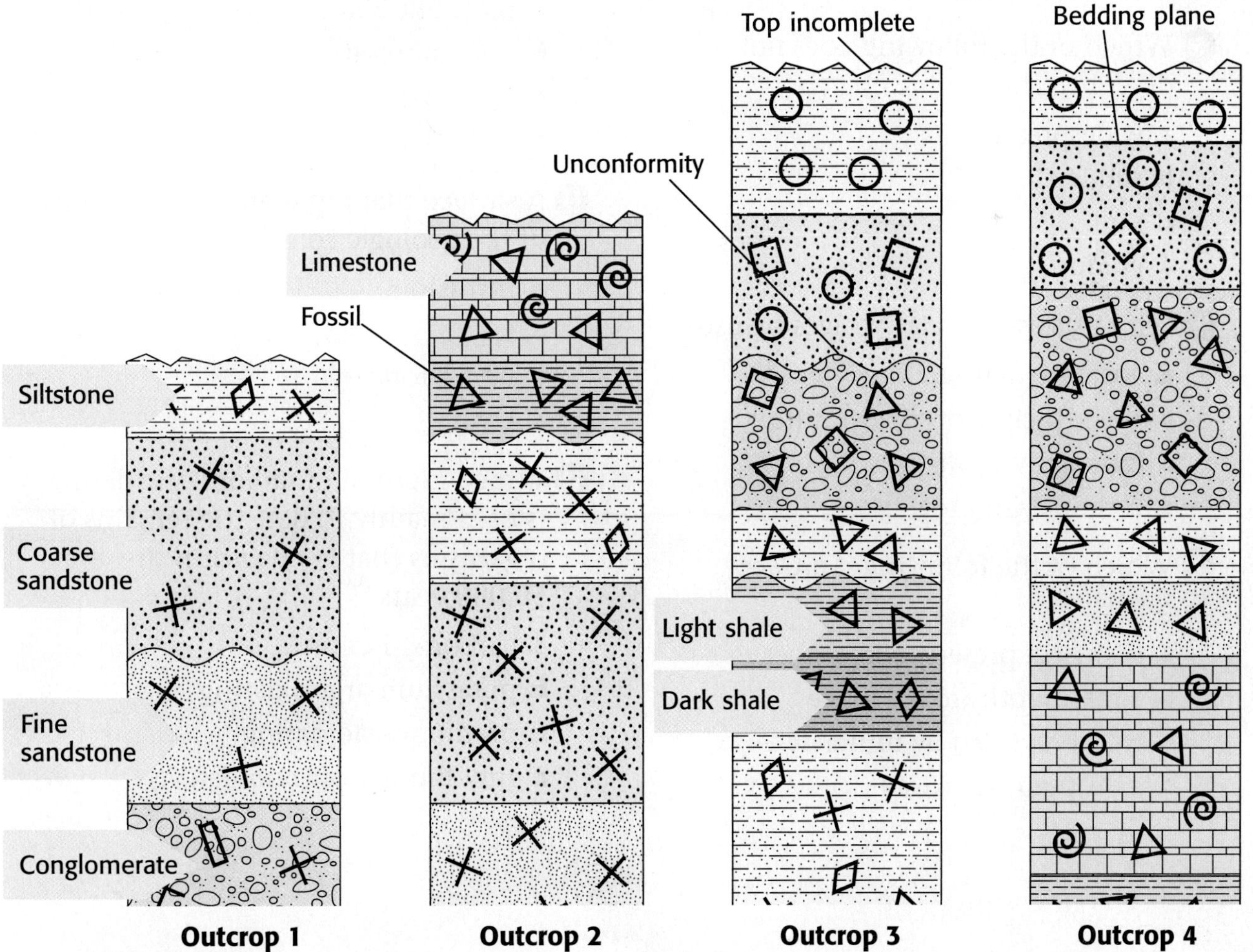

Chapter Review

USING KEY TERMS

1. In your own words, write a definition for each of the following terms: *superposition, geologic column,* and *geologic time scale.*

For each pair of terms, explain how the meanings of the terms differ.

2. *uniformitarianism* and *catastrophism*
3. *relative dating* and *absolute dating*
4. *trace fossil* and *index fossil*

UNDERSTANDING KEY IDEAS

Multiple Choice

5. Which of the following does not describe catastrophic change?
   - **a.** widespread
   - **b.** sudden
   - **c.** rare
   - **d.** gradual
6. Scientists assign relative ages by using
   - **a.** absolute dating.
   - **b.** the principle of superposition.
   - **c.** radioactive half-lives.
   - **d.** carbon-14 dating.
7. Which of the following is a trace fossil?
   - **a.** an insect preserved in amber
   - **b.** a mammoth frozen in ice
   - **c.** wood replaced by minerals
   - **d.** a dinosaur trackway
8. The largest divisions of geologic time are called
   - **a.** periods.
   - **b.** eras.
   - **c.** eons.
   - **d.** epochs.
9. Rock layers cut by a fault formed
   - **a.** after the fault.
   - **b.** before the fault.
   - **c.** at the same time as the fault.
   - **d.** There is not enough information to determine the answer.
10. Of the following isotopes, which is stable?
    - **a.** uranium-238
    - **b.** potassium-40
    - **c.** carbon-12
    - **d.** carbon-14
11. A surface that represents a missing part of the geologic column is called a(n)
    - **a.** intrusion.
    - **b.** fault.
    - **c.** unconformity.
    - **d.** fold.
12. Which method of radiometric dating is used mainly to date the remains of organisms that lived within the last 50,000 years?
    - **a.** carbon-14 dating
    - **b.** potassium-argon dating
    - **c.** uranium-lead dating
    - **d.** rubidium-strontium dating

Short Answer

13. Describe three processes by which fossils form.

14. Identify the role of uniformitarianism in Earth science.

15. Explain how radioactive decay occurs.

16. Describe two ways in which scientists use fossils to determine environmental change.

17. Explain the role of paleontology in the study of Earth's history.

CRITICAL THINKING

18. **Concept Mapping** Use the following terms to create a concept map: *age, half-life, absolute dating, radioactive decay, radiometric dating, relative dating, superposition, geologic column,* and *isotopes.*

19. **Applying Concepts** Identify how changes in environmental conditions can affect the survival of a species. Give two examples.

20. **Identifying Relationships** Why do paleontologists know more about hard-bodied organisms than about soft-bodied organisms?

21. **Analyzing Processes** Why isn't a 100 million–year-old fossilized tree made of wood?

INTERPRETING GRAPHICS

Use the diagram below to answer the questions that follow.

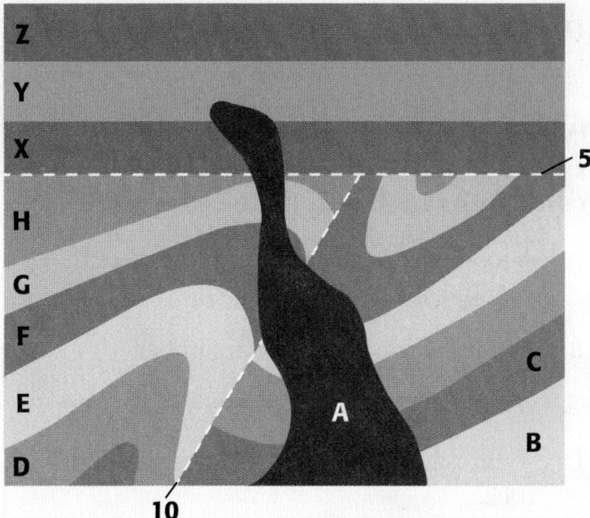

22. Is intrusion **A** younger or older than layer **X**? Explain.

23. What feature is marked by **5**?

24. Is intrusion **A** younger or older than fault **10**? Explain.

25. Other than the intrusion and faulting, what event happened in layers **B, C, D, E, F, G,** and **H**? Number this event, the intrusion, and the faulting in the order that they happened.

Standardized Test Preparation

Multiple Choice

1. **Which of the following does NOT refer to a geological process?**
   A. catastrophism.
   B. uniformitarianism.
   C. superposition.
   D. extinction.

2. **Which of the following provides evidence that environmental conditions on Earth have changed?**
   A. A fossilized footprint is found in volcanic ash.
   B. An insect fossil is found in amber.
   C. A marine fossil is found on a mountaintop.
   D. A dinosaur fossil is found in sedimentary rock.

3. **Which of the following animals dominated Earth during the Mesozoic Era?**
   A. reptiles
   B. amphibians
   C. mammals
   D. birds

4. **The carbon-14 method of radiometric dating would most likely be used to date**
   A. archaeological artifacts.
   B. meteorites that have struck Earth.
   C. Earth's oldest rocks.
   D. dinosaur bones and teeth.

5. **Which of the following statements best describes present ideas about geologic change?**
   A. All geologic change occurs gradually and uniformly.
   B. Most geologic change occurs gradually and uniformly.
   C. All geologic change occurs rapidly and catastrophically.
   D. Most geologic change occurs rapidly and catastrophically.

Use the graph below to answer question 6.

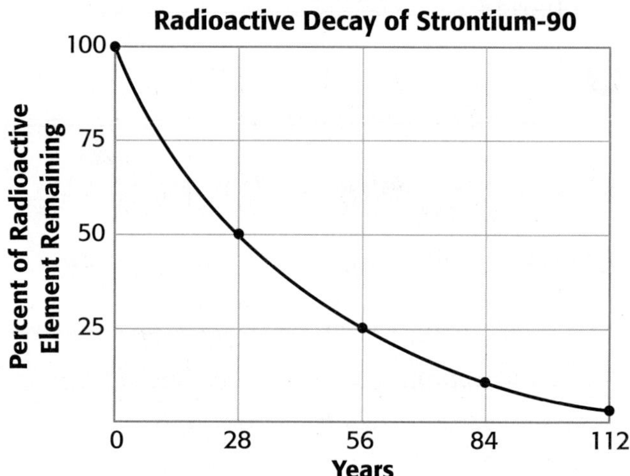

6. **Ramona was studying the radioactive decay of isotopes from the uranium-enrichment facility in Paducah, Kentucky. One isotope she studied was strontium-90. According to the graph, what is the half-life of strontium-90?**
   A. 28 years
   B. 56 years
   C. 84 years
   D. 112 years

Use the diagram below to answer question 7.

7. **Fossils have been found in layers A, B, C, D, and E. Which fossils are the oldest?**

   A. The fossils found in Level A are the oldest.

   B. The fossils are all the same age.

   C. It is impossible to tell because of the intrusion.

   D. The fossils found in Level E are the oldest.

8. **A small reptile called *Mesosaurus* lived 260 million years ago and is now extinct. Fossils of this reptile have been found in both South America and southern Africa. Which of the following statements best explains why the fossils were found on both continents?**

   A. At one time, the continents were joined.

   B. The reptile swam across the Atlantic Ocean.

   C. The reptile traveled across a land bridge.

   D. People brought the reptile to South America.

9. **Which of the following would be an example of gradual geologic change?**

   A. a volcanic eruption

   B. an earthquake-generated tsunami

   C. accumulation of sediment in a river delta

   D. an asteroid striking Earth

10. **A fossilized mark that is formed in soft sediment by the movement of an animal is called a(n)**

    A. trace fossil.

    B. index fossil.

    C. mold.

    D. cast.

Open Response

11. **Across the Ohio River from Louisville, Kentucky, is the state park called Falls of the Ohio. Visitors can walk across acre after acre of fossils of sea creatures from 386 million years ago. What do the fossil beds suggest about the geologic history of the area around Louisville?**

12. **The oldest rocks in Kentucky are found above the surface in the center of the state, but they are far beneath the surface in the western and eastern parts of the state. Yet the elevation at the center of the state is higher than in the western part of the state. How can this be explained?**

Science in Action

Scientific Debate

Feathered Dinosaurs

One day in 1996, a Chinese farmer broke open a rock he found in the bed of an ancient dry lake. What he found inside the rock became one of the most exciting paleontological discoveries of the 20th century. Preserved inside were the remains of a dinosaur. The dinosaur had a large head; powerful jaws; sharp, jagged teeth; and, most important of all, a row of featherlike structures along the backbone. Scientists named the dinosaur *Sinosauropteryx*, or "Chinese dragon wing." *Sinosauropteryx* and the remains of other "feathered" dinosaurs recently discovered in China have led some scientists to hypothesize that feathers evolved through theropod (three-toed) dinosaurs. Other paleontologists disagree. They believe the structures along the backbone of these dinosaurs are not feathers but the remains of elongated spines, like those that run down the head and back of an iguana.

Language Arts ACTIVITY

Paleontologists often give dinosaurs names that describe something unusual about the animal's head, body, feet, or size. These names have Greek or Latin roots. Research the names of some dinosaurs, and find out what the names mean. Create a list of dinosaur names and their meanings.

Science, Technology, and Society

DNA and a Mammoth Discovery

In recent years, scientists have unearthed several mammoths that had been frozen in ice in Siberia and other remote northern locations. Bones, fur, food in the stomach, and even dung have all been found in good condition. Some scientists hoped that DNA extracted from the mammoths might lead to the cloning of this animal, which became extinct about 10,000 years ago. But the DNA might not be able to be duplicated by scientists. However, DNA samples may nevertheless help scientists understand why mammoths became extinct. One theory about why mammoths became extinct is that they were killed off by disease. Using DNA taken from fossilized mammoth bone, hair, or dung, scientists can check to see if it contains the DNA of a disease-causing pathogen that led to the extinction of the mammoths.

Math ACTIVITY

The male Siberian mammoth reached a height of about 3 m at the shoulder. Females reached a height of about 2.5 m at the shoulder. What is the ratio of the maximum height of a female Siberian mammoth to the height of a male Siberian mammoth?

People in Science

Lizzie May

Amateur Paleontologist For Lizzie May, summer vacations have meant trips into the Alaskan wilderness with her stepfather, geologist/paleontologist Kevin May. The purpose of these trips has not been for fun. Instead, Kevin and Lizzie have been exploring the Alaskan wilderness for the remains of ancient life—dinosaurs, in particular.

At age 18, Lizzie May has gained the reputation of being Alaska's most famous teenage paleontologist. It is a reputation that is well deserved. To date, Lizzie has collected hundreds of dinosaur bones and located important sites of dinosaur, bird, and mammal tracks. In her honor and as a result of her hard work in the field, scientists named the skeleton of a dinosaur discovered by the Mays "Lizzie." "Lizzie" is a duckbill dinosaur, or hadrosaur, that lived approximately 90 million years ago. "Lizzie" is the oldest dinosaur ever found in Alaska and one of the earliest known duckbill dinosaurs in North America.

The Mays have made other, equally exciting discoveries. On one summer trip, Kevin and Lizzie located six dinosaur and bird track sites that dated back 97 million to 144 million years. On another trip, the Mays found a fossil marine reptile more than 200 million years old—an ichthyosaur—that had to be removed with the help of a military helicopter. You have to wonder what other exciting adventures are in store for Lizzie and Kevin!

Social Studies ACTIVITY

WRITING SKILL Lizzie May is not the only young person to have made a mark in dinosaur paleontology. Using the Internet or another source, research people such as Bucky Derflinger, Johnny Maurice, Brad Riney, and Wendy Sloboda, who as young people made contributions to the field of dinosaur study. Write a short essay summarizing your findings.

To learn more about these Science in Action topics, visit **go.hrw.com** and type in the keyword **HZ5FOSF.**

Current Science

Check out Current Science® articles related to this chapter by visiting go.hrw.com. Just type in the keyword HZ5CS06.

TIMELINE

The Restless Earth

In this unit, you will learn what a dynamic planet the Earth is. Earth's landmasses are changing position continuously as they travel across Earth's surface on tremendous blocks of rock. As these blocks collide with each other, mountain ranges are formed. As these blocks pull apart, magma is released from below, sometimes explosively in volcanic eruptions. When these blocks grind slowly past one another, long breaks in the Earth are created, where devastating earthquakes can take place. This timeline shows some of the events that have occurred as scientists have tried to understand our dynamic Earth.

1864

Jules Verne's *A Journey to the Center of the Earth* is published. In this fictional story, the heroes enter and exit the Earth through volcanoes.

1912

Alfred Wegener proposes his theory of continental drift.

1979

Volcanoes are discovered on Io, one of Jupiter's moons.

1980

Mount St. Helens erupts after an earthquake triggers a landslide on the volcano's north face.

Io, one of Jupiter's moons

1883

When Krakatau erupts, more than 36,000 people are killed.

1896

Henry Ford builds his first car.

The Quadricycle, Henry Ford's first car

1906

San Francisco burns in the aftermath of an earthquake.

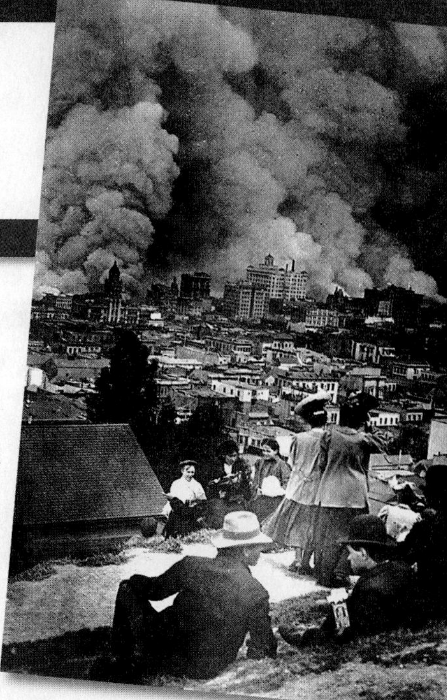

1935

Charles Richter devises a system of measuring the magnitude of earthquakes.

1951

Color television programming is introduced in the United States.

1962

A worldwide network of seismographs is established.

1982

Compact discs (CDs) and compact-disc players are made available to the public.

1994

An eight-legged robot named Dante II descends into the crater of an active volcano in Alaska.

Dante II

1997

The population of the Caribbean island of Montserrat dwindles to less than half its original size as frequent eruptions of the Soufriere Hills volcano force evacuations.

2003

An earthquake of magnitude 4.6 strikes Alabama. It is one of the largest earthquakes ever recorded for this area.

12

The Earth's Ecosystems

The Big Idea

Earth's ecosystems are characterized by their living and nonliving parts.

SECTION

About the Photo

Is this animal a movie monster? No! The thorny devil is a lizard that lives in the desert of Australia. The thorny devil's rough skin is an adaptation that helps it survive in the hot, dry desert. Grooves in the thorny devil's skin collect water that the lizard later drinks. Water lands on its back and runs along the tiny grooves to the thorny devil's mouth.

PRE-READING ACTIVITY

Three-Panel Flip Chart Before you read the chapter, create the FoldNote entitled "Three-Panel Flip Chart" described in the **Study Skills** section of the Appendix. Label the flaps of the three-panel flip chart with "Land biomes," "Marine ecosystems," and "Freshwater ecosystems." As you read the chapter, write information you learn about each category under the appropriate flap.

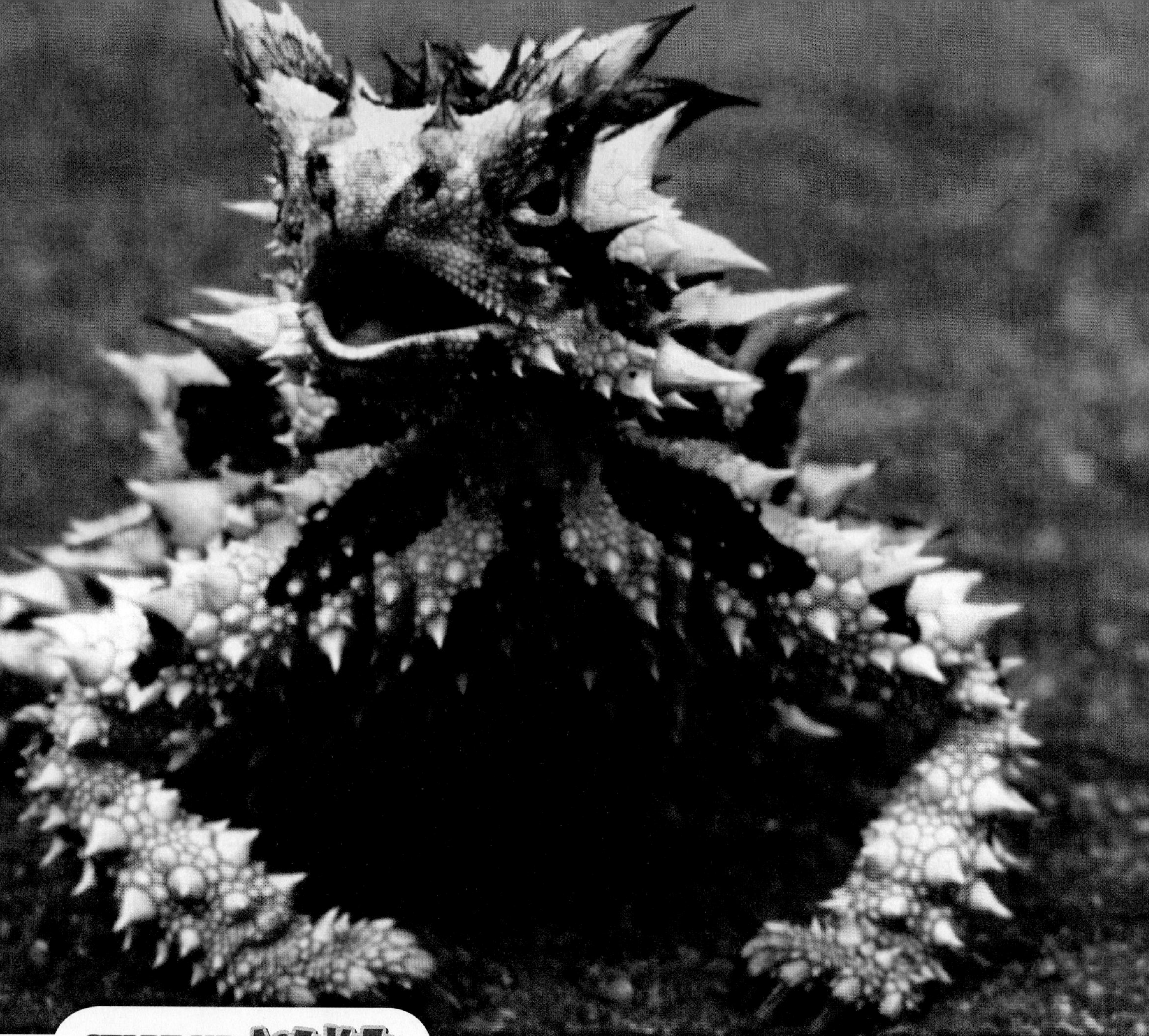

START-UP ACTIVITY

A Mini-Ecosystem

In this activity, you will build and observe a miniature ecosystem.

Procedure

1. Place a layer of **gravel** at the bottom of a **container,** such as a **large, wide-mouthed jar** or a **2 L soda bottle** with the top cut off. Then, add a layer of **soil.**
2. Add a variety of **plants** that need similar growing conditions. Choose small plants that will not grow too quickly.
3. Spray **water** inside the container to moisten the soil.
4. Loosely cover the container with a **lid** or **plastic wrap.** Place the container in indirect light.
5. Describe the appearance of your ecosystem.
6. Let your mini-ecosystem grow for 6 weeks. Add more water when the soil is dry.
7. Observe your mini-ecosystem every week. Record your observations.

Analysis

1. List the nonliving factors that make up the ecosystem that you built.
2. List the living factors that make up your ecosystem.
3. How is your mini-ecosystem similar to a real ecosystem? How is it different?

SECTION 1

Land Biomes

What You Will Learn

- Distinguish between abiotic factors and biotic factors in biomes.
- Identify seven land biomes on Earth.

Vocabulary

biome
savanna
desert
tundra

READING STRATEGY

Reading Organizer As you read this section, create an outline of the section. Use the headings from the section in your outline.

What do you think of when you think of polar bears? You probably imagine them in a snow-covered setting. Why don't polar bears live in the desert?

Different ecosystems are home to different kinds of organisms. Polar bears don't live in the desert because they are adapted to very cold environments. Polar bears have thick fur. This fur keeps polar bears warm. It also hides them in the snow.

The Earth's Land Biomes

Imagine yourself in a hot, dry, dusty place. You see a cactus on your right. A lizard sits on a rock to your left. Where are you? You may not know exactly, but you probably think you are in a desert.

A desert is different from other places because of its abiotic (AY bie AHT ik) factors and biotic (bie AHT ik) factors. *Abiotic factors* are the nonliving parts of an environment. Soil, water, and climate are abiotic factors. Climate is the average weather conditions for an area over a long period of time. *Biotic factors* are the living parts of an environment. Plants and animals are biotic factors. Areas that have similar abiotic factors usually have similar biotic factors. A **biome** (BIE OHM) is a large area characterized by its climate and the plants and animals that live in the area. A biome contains related ecosystems. For example, a tropical rain forest biome contains treetop ecosystems and forest-floor ecosystems. The major land biomes on Earth are shown in **Figure 1.**

biome a large region characterized by a specific type of climate and certain types of plant and animal communities

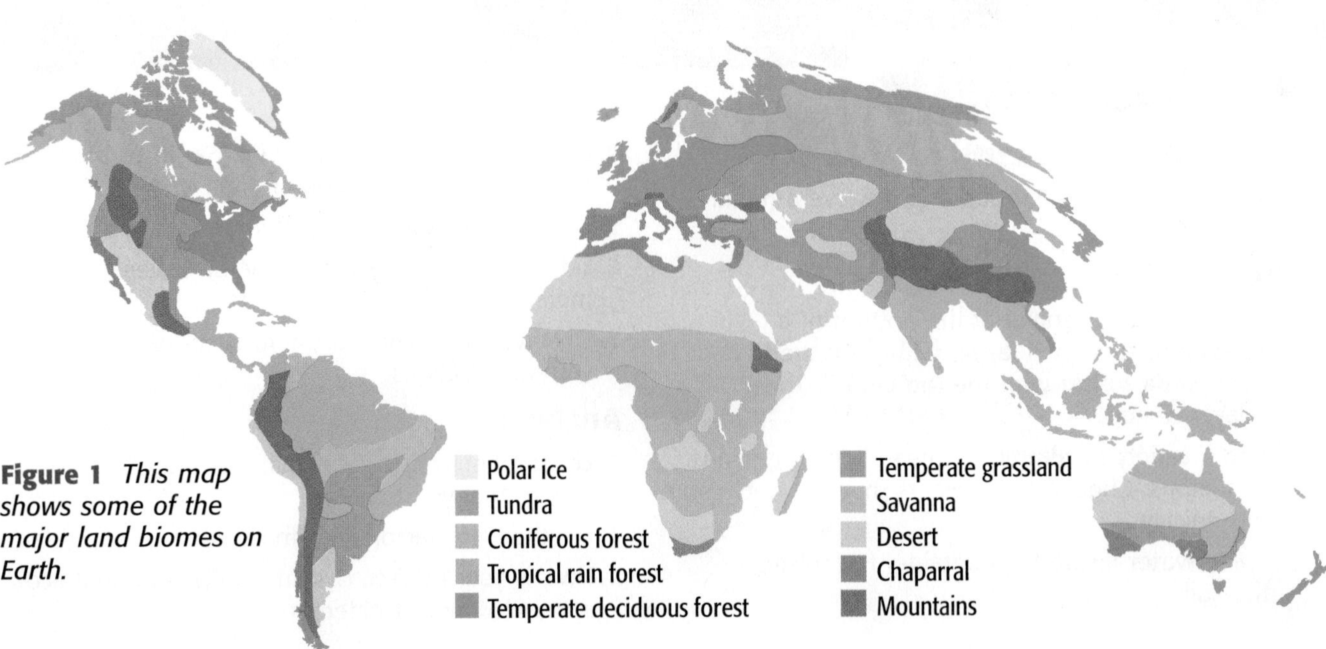

Figure 1 *This map shows some of the major land biomes on Earth.*

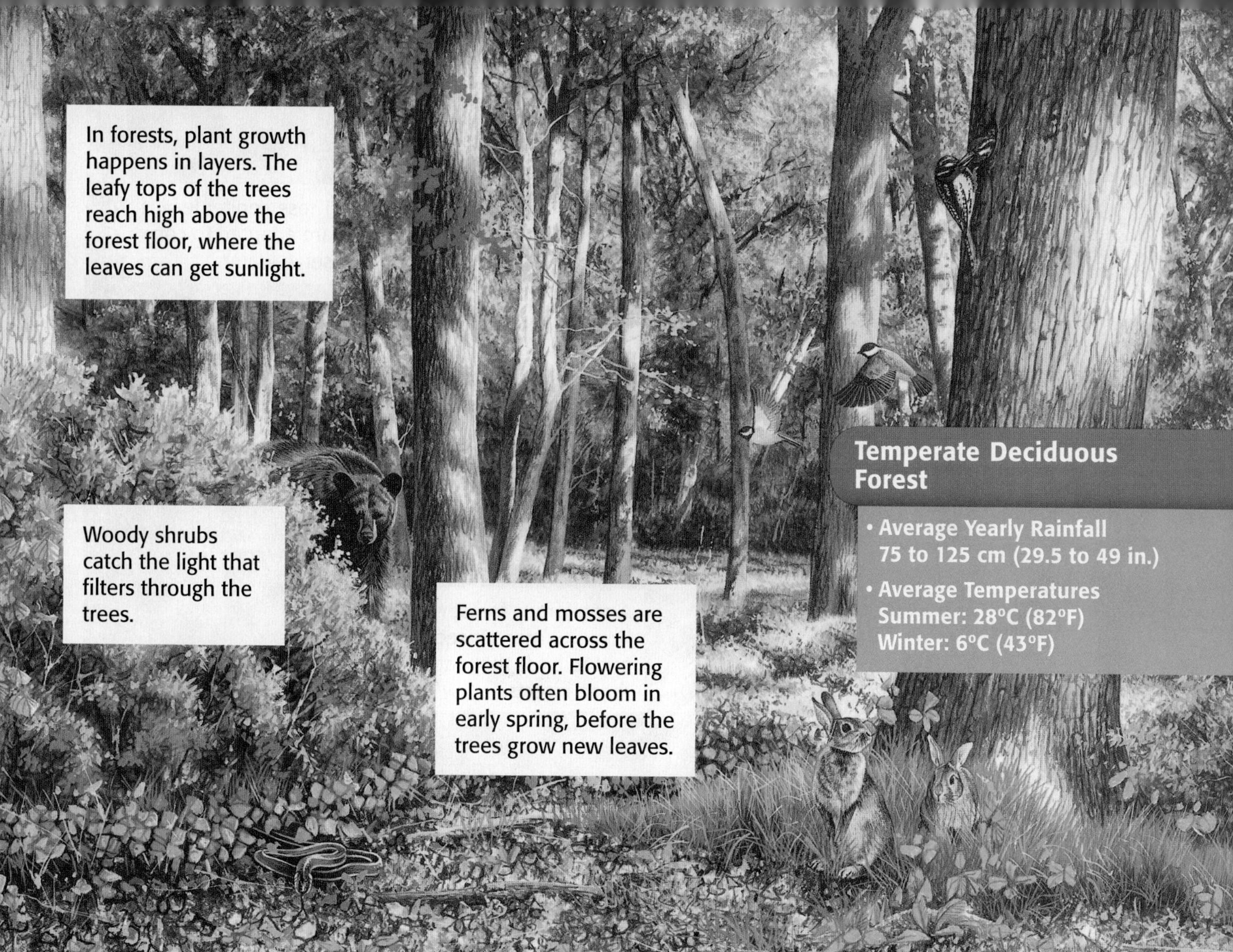

In forests, plant growth happens in layers. The leafy tops of the trees reach high above the forest floor, where the leaves can get sunlight.
Woody shrubs catch the light that filters through the trees.
Ferns and mosses are scattered across the forest floor. Flowering plants often bloom in early spring, before the trees grow new leaves.
Temperate Deciduous Forest
• Average Yearly Rainfall 75 to 125 cm (29.5 to 49 in.)
• Average Temperatures Summer: 28°C (82°F) Winter: 6°C (43°F)

Figure 2 *In a temperate deciduous forest, mammals, birds, and reptiles thrive on the many leaves, seeds, nuts, and insects.*

Forests

Forest biomes are often found in areas that have mild temperatures and plenty of rain. The kind of forest biome that develops depends on an area's temperatures and rainfall. Three forest biomes are temperate deciduous (dee SIJ oo uhs) forests, coniferous (koh NIF uhr uhs) forests, and tropical rain forests.

Temperate Deciduous Forests

Have you seen leaves change colors in the fall? Have you seen trees lose all of their leaves? If so, you have seen trees that are deciduous. The word *deciduous* comes from a Latin word that means "to fall off." Deciduous trees shed their leaves to save water during the winter or during the dry season. As shown in **Figure 2,** a variety of animals, such as bears, snakes, and woodpeckers, live in temperate deciduous forests.

Reading Check **How does the word *deciduous* describe temperate deciduous forests?** (*See the Appendix for answers to Reading Checks.*)

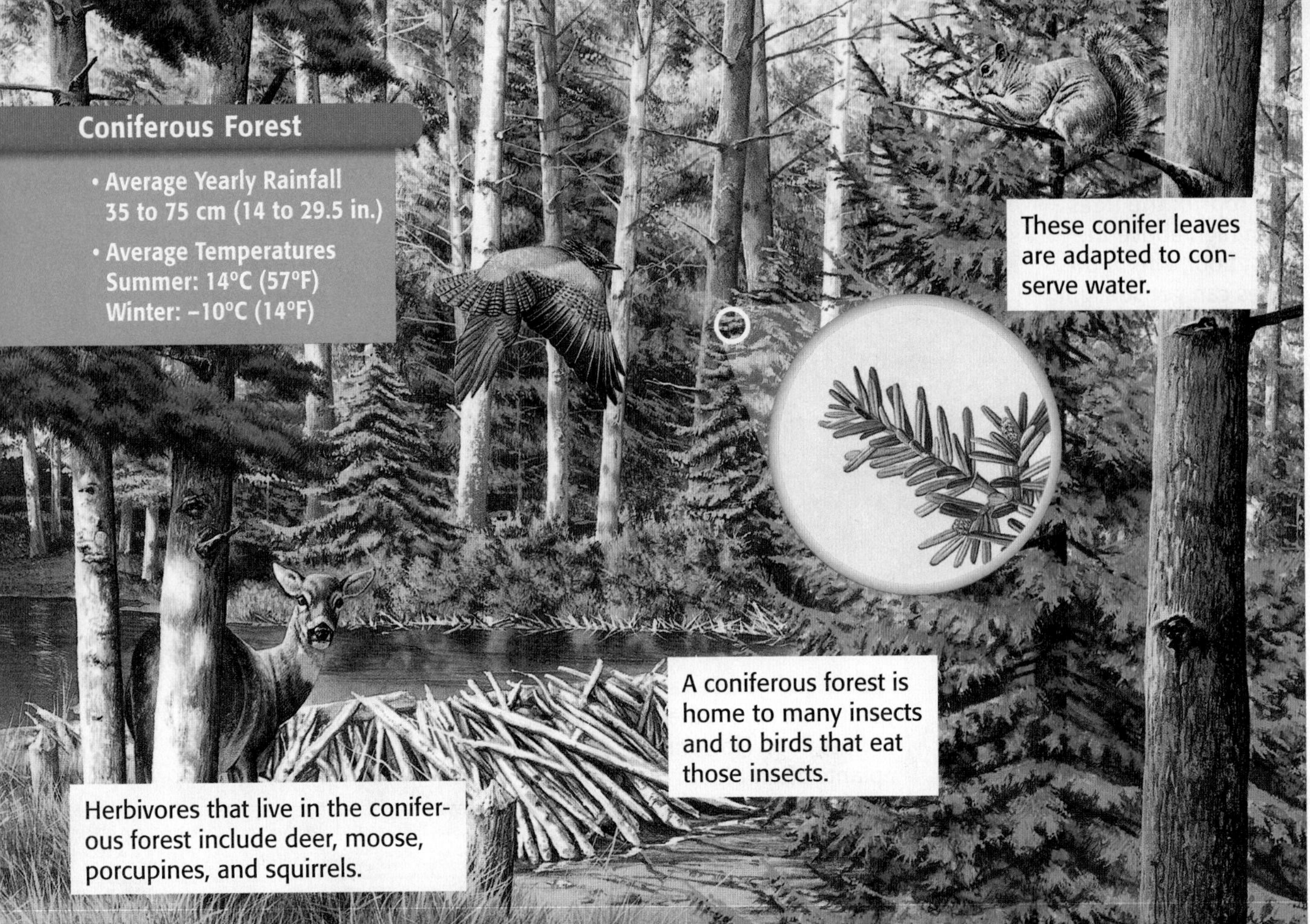

Coniferous Forest
• Average Yearly Rainfall 35 to 75 cm (14 to 29.5 in.)
• Average Temperatures Summer: 14°C (57°F) Winter: −10°C (14°F)
These conifer leaves are adapted to conserve water.
A coniferous forest is home to many insects and to birds that eat those insects.
Herbivores that live in the coniferous forest include deer, moose, porcupines, and squirrels.

Figure 3 *Many animals that live in a coniferous forest survive the harsh winters by hibernating or migrating to a warmer climate for the winter.*

Coniferous Forests

Most of the trees in a coniferous forest are called *conifers*. Conifers produce seeds in cones. Conifers also have special leaves that are shaped like needles. The leaves have a thick, waxy coating. This waxy coating has three functions. First, it helps keep conifer leaves from drying out. Second, the waxy coating protects needles from being damaged by cold winter temperatures. Finally, the waxy coating allows most conifers to keep many of their leaves year-round. So, most conifers do not change very much from summer to winter. Trees that stay green all year and do not lose all of their leaves at one time are known as *evergreen trees*.

Figure 3 shows a coniferous forest and some of the animals that live there. Squirrels and insects live in coniferous forests. Birds, such as finches, chickadees, and jays, are common in these forests. Herbivores, such as porcupines, elk, and moose, also live in coniferous forests. The ground beneath large conifers is often covered by a thick layer of needles. Also, very little light reaches the ground. So, few large plants can grow beneath these trees.

✓ Reading Check **What is another name for most conifers? What are some animals that live in coniferous forests?**

Tropical Rain Forests

Tropical rain forests have more biological diversity than other places on Earth have. This means that rain forests have more kinds of plants and animals than any other land biome. For example, more than 100 different kinds of trees may grow in an area about one-fourth the size of a football field. Many animals live on the ground. But most animals live in the *canopy,* or the treetops. Many different animals live in the canopy. For example, nearly 1,400 species of birds live in the rain-forest canopy. **Figure 4** shows some of the diversity of the tropical rain forest.

Because of its diversity, the rain forest may seem as if it has nutrient-rich soil. But most of the nutrients in the tropical rain forest are found in the plants. The soil is actually very thin and poor in nutrients. Because the soil is so thin, many trees grow above-ground roots for extra support.

Figure 4 *Tropical rain forests have a greater variety of organisms than any other biome.*

Trees form a continuous green roof, or canopy, that may extend 60 m above the forest floor.
Woody vines climb the tree trunks to reach sunlight.
Little light reaches the ground. Low-growing plants in the rain forest don't need a lot of light.
Tropical Rain Forest
• Average Yearly Rainfall up to 400 cm (157.5 in.)
• Average Temperatures Daytime: 34°C (93°F) Nighttime: 20°C (68°F)

Grasslands

Grasslands have many names, such as *steppes, prairies,* and *pampas*. Grasslands are found on every continent but Antarctica. They are often flat or have gently rolling hills.

Temperate Grassland

- Average Yearly Rainfall 25 to 75 cm (10 to 29.5 in.)
- Average Temperatures Summer: 30°C (86°F) Winter: 0°C (32°F)

Figure 5 *Bison once roamed North American temperate grasslands in great herds.*

Temperate Grasslands

Temperate grassland plants include grasses and other flowering plants. Temperate grasslands have few trees. Fires, drought, and grazing prevent the growth of trees and shrubs. Temperate grasslands support small seed-eating animals, such as prairie dogs and mice. Large grass eaters, such as the North American bison shown in **Figure 5,** also live in temperate grasslands.

Savannas

A grassland that has scattered clumps of trees and seasonal rains is called a **savanna.** Savannas are found in parts of Africa, India, and South America. During the dry season, savanna grasses dry out and turn yellow. But the grasses' deep roots survive for many months without water. The African savanna is home to many large herbivores, such as elephants, giraffes, zebras, and wildebeests. Some of these animals are shown in **Figure 6.**

Reading Check What happens to grasses on a savanna during the dry season?

savanna a grassland that often has scattered trees and that is found in tropical and subtropical areas where seasonal rains, fires, and drought happen

Figure 6 *In the African savanna, lions and leopards hunt zebras and wildebeests.*

CONNECTION TO Environmental Science

WRITING SKILL **Mountains and Climate**
Mountains can affect the climate of the land around them. Research the ecosystems around a mountain range. In your **science journal,** write a report describing how the mountains affect the climate of the surrounding land.

Desert
• Average Yearly Rainfall less than 25 cm (10 in.)
• Average Temperatures Summer: 38°C (100°F) Winter: 7°C (45°F)
Cactuses store water in their stems and roots.
Some flowering plants bloom, bear seeds, and die within a few weeks after a heavy rain.
Deep-rooted plants can reach groundwater as deep as 30 m.
Huge ears help jack rabbits get rid of body heat.
Kangaroo rats never need to drink. They recycle water from the foods that they eat.

Figure 7 *The residents of the desert biome have special adaptations to survive in a dry climate.*

Deserts

Biomes that are very dry and often very hot are called **deserts.** Many kinds of plants and animals are found only in deserts. These organisms have special adaptations to live in a hot, dry climate. For example, plants grow far apart so that the plants won't have to compete with each other for water. Some plants have shallow, widespread roots that grow just under the surface. These roots let plants take up water during a storm. Other desert plants, such as cactuses, have fleshy stems and leaves. These fleshy structures store water. The leaves of desert plants also have a waxy coating that helps prevent water loss.

desert a region that has little or no plant life, long periods without rain, and extreme temperatures; usually found in hot climates

Animals also have adaptations for living in the desert. Most desert animals are active only at night, when temperatures are cooler. Some animals, such as the spadefoot toad, bury themselves in the ground and are dormant during the dry season. Doing so helps these animals escape the heat of summer. Animals such as desert tortoises eat flowers or leaves and store the water under their shells. **Figure 7** shows how some desert plants and animals live in the heat with little water.

Reading Check What are some adaptations of desert plants?

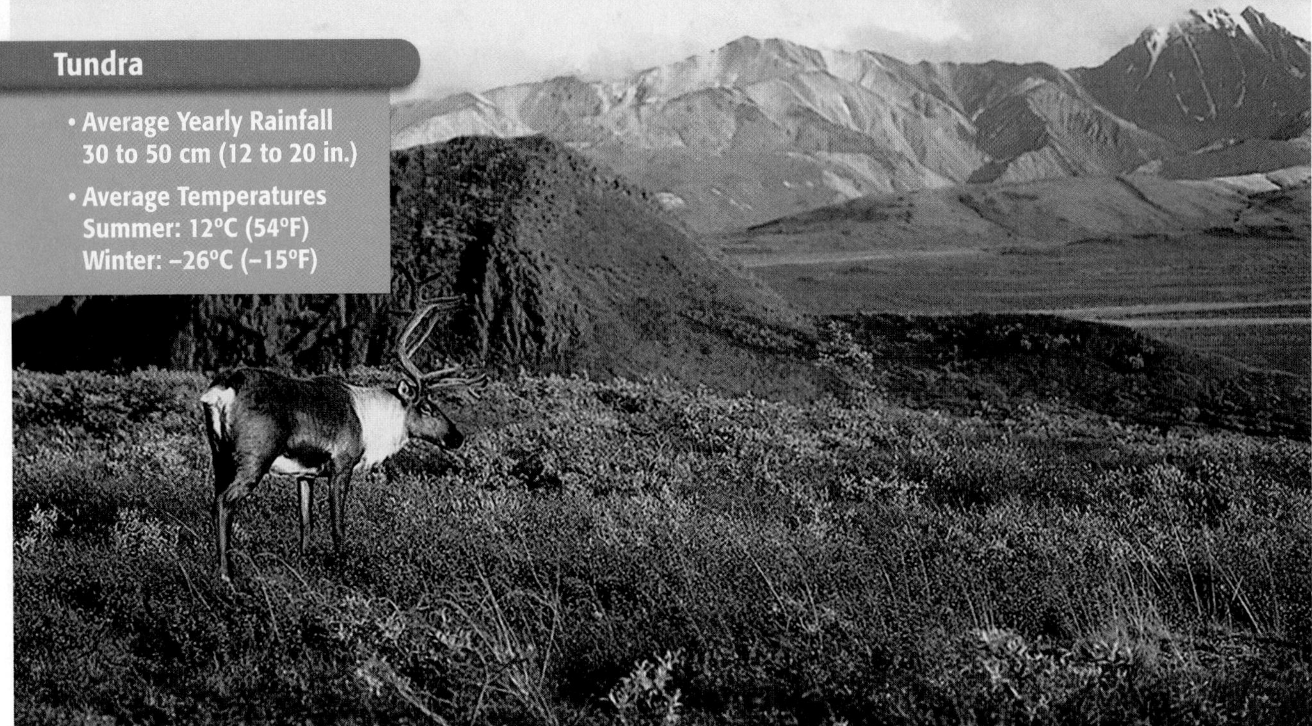

Figure 8 *During winters in the tundra, caribou migrate to grazing grounds that have a more-plentiful supply of food.*

Tundra

Imagine a place on Earth where it is so cold that trees do not grow. A biome that has very cold temperatures and little rainfall is called a **tundra.** Two types of tundra are polar tundra and alpine tundra.

tundra a treeless plain found in the Arctic, in the Antarctic, or on the tops of mountains that is characterized by very low winter temperatures and short, cool summers

Polar Tundra

Polar tundra is found near the North and South Poles. In polar tundra, the layer of soil beneath the surface soil stays frozen all the time. This layer is called *permafrost*. During the short, cool summers, only the surface soil thaws. The layer of thawed soil is too shallow for deep-rooted plants to live. So, shallow-rooted plants, such as grasses and small shrubs, are common. Mosses and lichens (LIE kuhnz) grow beneath these plants. The thawed soil above the permafrost becomes muddy. Insects, such as mosquitoes, lay eggs in the mud. Birds feed on these insects. Other tundra animals include musk oxen, wolves, and caribou, such as the one shown in **Figure 8.**

Local Ecosystems

WRITING SKILL With a family member, explore the ecosystems around your home. What kinds of plants and animals live in your area? In your **science journal,** write a short essay describing the plants and animals in the ecosystems near your home.

Alpine Tundra

Alpine tundra is similar to arctic tundra. Alpine tundra also has permafrost. But alpine tundra is found at the top of tall mountains. Above an elevation called the *tree line*, trees cannot grow on a mountain. Alpine tundra is found above the tree line. Alpine tundra gets plenty of sunlight and precipitation.

✓ *Reading Check* **What is alpine tundra?**

SECTION Review

- A biome is characterized by abiotic factors, such as climate, and biotic factors, such as plant and animal communities.
- Three forest biomes are temperate deciduous forests, coniferous forests, and tropical rain forests.
- Grasslands are areas where grasses are the main plants. Temperate grasslands have hot summers and cold winters. Savannas have wet and dry seasons.
- Deserts are very dry and often very hot. Desert plants and animals competing for the limited water supply have special adaptations for survival.
- Tundras are cold areas that have very little rainfall. Permafrost, the layer of frozen soil below the surface of arctic tundra, determines the kinds of plants and animals that live on the tundra.

Using Key Terms

1. Use each of the following terms in a separate sentence: *biome* and *tundra*.
2. In your own words, write a definition for each of the following terms: *savanna* and *desert*.

Understanding Key Ideas

3. If you visited a savanna, you would most likely see
   - **a.** large herds of grazing animals, such as zebras, gazelles, and wildebeests.
   - **b.** dense forests stretching from horizon to horizon.
   - **c.** snow and ice throughout most of the year.
   - **d.** trees that form a continuous green roof, called the *canopy*.
4. Components of a desert ecosystem include
   - **a.** a hot, dry climate.
   - **b.** plants that grow far apart.
   - **c.** animals that are active mostly at night.
   - **d.** All of the above
5. List seven land biomes that are found on Earth.
6. What are two things that characterize a biome?

Critical Thinking

7. **Making Inferences** While excavating an area in the desert, a scientist discovers the fossils of very large trees and ferns. What might the scientist conclude about biomes in this area?
8. **Analyzing Ideas** Tundra receives very little rainfall. Could tundra accurately be called a *frozen desert*? Explain your answer.

Interpreting Graphics

Use the bar graph below to answer the questions that follow.

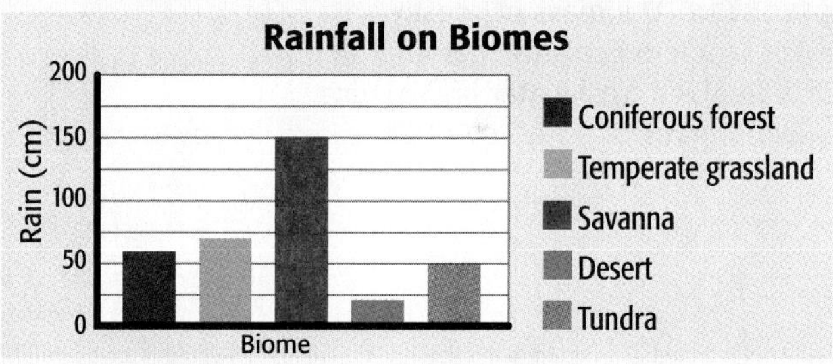

9. Which biomes receive 50 cm or more of rain each year?
10. Which biome receives the smallest amount of rain? the largest amount of rain?

SCILINKS.
NSTA
Developed and maintained by the National Science Teachers Association
For a variety of links related to this chapter, go to www.scilinks.org
Topic: Forests
SciLinks code: HSM0609

SECTION 2

Marine Ecosystems

What You Will Learn

- List three abiotic factors that shape marine ecosystems.
- Describe four major ocean zones.
- Describe five marine ecosystems.

Vocabulary

plankton
estuary

READING STRATEGY

Prediction Guide Before reading this section, write the title of each heading in this section. Next, under each heading, write what you think you will learn.

What covers almost three-fourths of Earth's surface? What holds both the largest animals and some of the smallest organisms on Earth?

If your answer to both questions is *oceans,* you are correct! Earth's oceans contain many different ecosystems. Scientists call ecosystems in the ocean *marine ecosystems.*

Life in the Ocean

Marine ecosystems are shaped by abiotic factors. These factors include water temperature, water depth, and the amount of sunlight that passes into the water. The animals and plants that live in the ocean come in all shapes and sizes. The largest animals on Earth, blue whales, live in the ocean. So do trillions of tiny plankton. **Plankton** are tiny organisms that float near the surface of the water. Many plankton are producers. They use photosynthesis to make their own food. Plankton form the base of the ocean's food chains. **Figure 1** shows plankton and an animal that relies on plankton for food.

Reading Check What are plankton? How are they important to marine ecosystems? (*See the Appendix for answers to Reading Checks.*)

plankton the mass of mostly microscopic organisms that float or drift freely in freshwater and marine environments

Figure 1 *Marine ecosystems support a broad diversity of life. Humpback whales rely on plankton for food.*

Temperature

The temperature of ocean water decreases as the depth of the water increases. However, the temperature change is not gradual. **Figure 2** shows the three temperature zones of ocean water. Notice that the temperature of the water in the surface zone is much warmer than in the rest of the ocean. Temperatures in the surface zone vary with latitude. Areas of the ocean along the equator are warmer than areas closer to the poles. Surface zone temperatures also vary with the time of year. During the summer, the Northern Hemisphere is tilted toward the sun. So, the surface zone is warmer than it is during the winter.

Temperature affects the animals that live in marine ecosystems. For example, fishes that live near the poles have adaptations to live in near-freezing water. In contrast, animals that live in coral reefs need warm water to live. Some animals, such as whales, migrate from cold areas to warm areas of the ocean to reproduce. Water temperature also affects whether some animals, such as barnacles, can eat. If the water is too hot or too cold, these animals may not be able to eat. A sudden change in temperature may cause these animals to die.

Reading Check **How does temperature affect marine animals?**

Figure 2 **Ocean Temperature Zones**

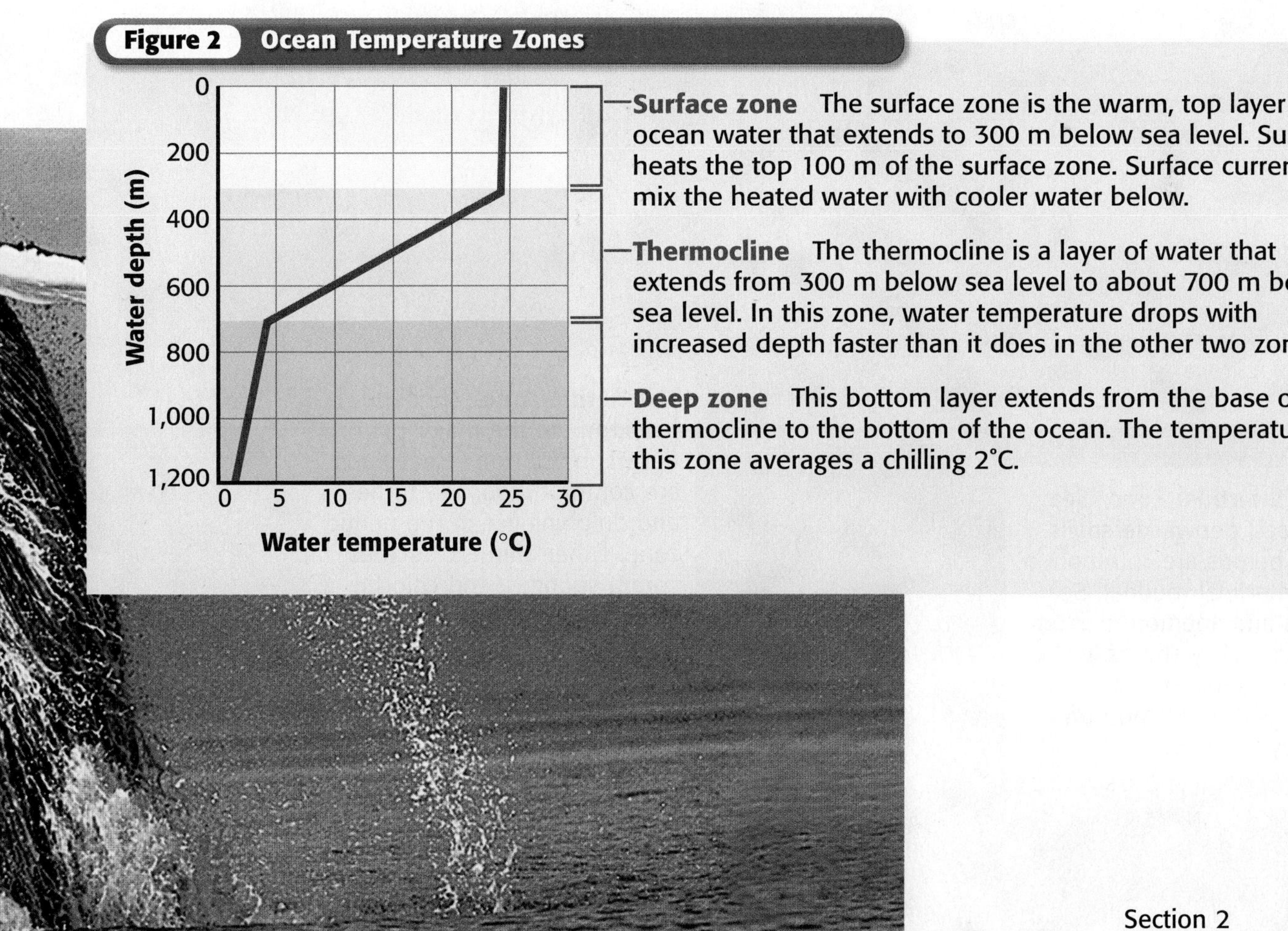

Surface zone The surface zone is the warm, top layer of ocean water that extends to 300 m below sea level. Sunlight heats the top 100 m of the surface zone. Surface currents mix the heated water with cooler water below.

Thermocline The thermocline is a layer of water that extends from 300 m below sea level to about 700 m below sea level. In this zone, water temperature drops with increased depth faster than it does in the other two zones.

Deep zone This bottom layer extends from the base of the thermocline to the bottom of the ocean. The temperature in this zone averages a chilling 2°C.

Depth and Sunlight

In addition to water temperature, life in the ocean is affected by water depth and the amount of sunlight that passes into the water. The major ocean zones are shown in **Figure 3.**

The Intertidal Zone

The intertidal zone is the place where the ocean meets the land. This area is exposed to the air for part of the day. Waves are always crashing on the rock and sand. The animals that live in the intertidal zone have adaptations to survive exposure to air and to keep from being washed away by the waves.

The Neritic Zone

As you move farther away from shore, into the neritic zone (nee RIT ik ZOHN), the water becomes deeper. The ocean floor starts to slope downward. The water is warm and receives a lot of sunlight. Many interesting plants and animals, such as corals, sea turtles, fishes, and dolphins, live in this zone.

Figure 3 *The life in a marine ecosystem depends on water temperature, water depth, and the amount of sunlight the area receives.*

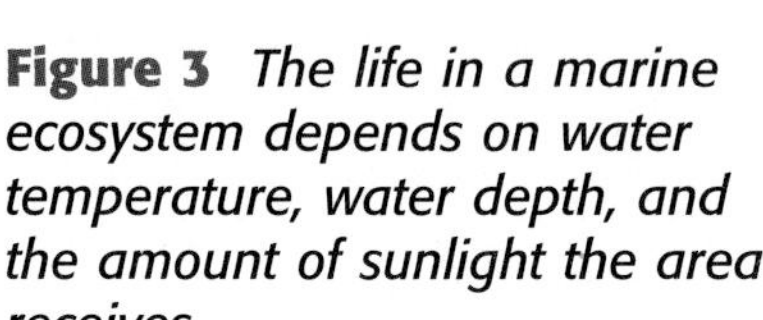

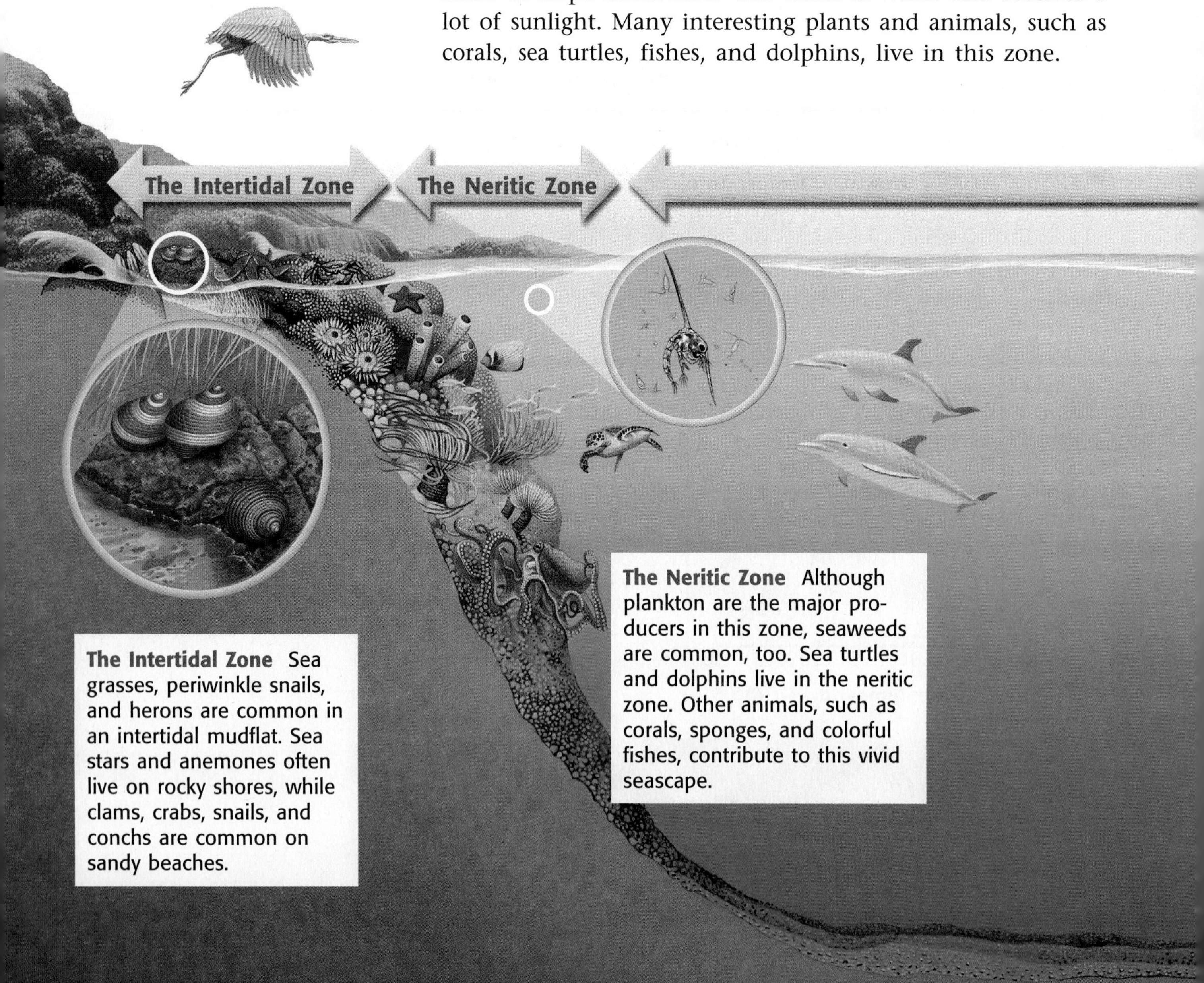

The Intertidal Zone

The Neritic Zone

The Intertidal Zone Sea grasses, periwinkle snails, and herons are common in an intertidal mudflat. Sea stars and anemones often live on rocky shores, while clams, crabs, snails, and conchs are common on sandy beaches.

The Neritic Zone Although plankton are the major producers in this zone, seaweeds are common, too. Sea turtles and dolphins live in the neritic zone. Other animals, such as corals, sponges, and colorful fishes, contribute to this vivid seascape.

The Oceanic Zone

In the oceanic zone, the sea floor drops sharply. This zone contains the deep water of the open ocean. Plankton can be found near the water surface. Animals, such as fishes, whales, and sharks, are found in the oceanic zone. Some animals in this zone live in very deep water. These animals often get food from material that sinks down from the ocean surface.

The Benthic Zone

The benthic zone is the ocean floor. The deepest parts of the benthic zone do not get any sunlight. They are also very cold. Animals, such as fishes, worms, and crabs, have special adaptations to the deep, dark water. Many of these organisms get food by eating material that sinks from above. Some organisms, such as bacteria, get energy from chemicals that escape from thermal vents on the ocean floor. Thermal vents form at cracks in the Earth's crust.

Reading Check **How do animals in the benthic zone get food?**

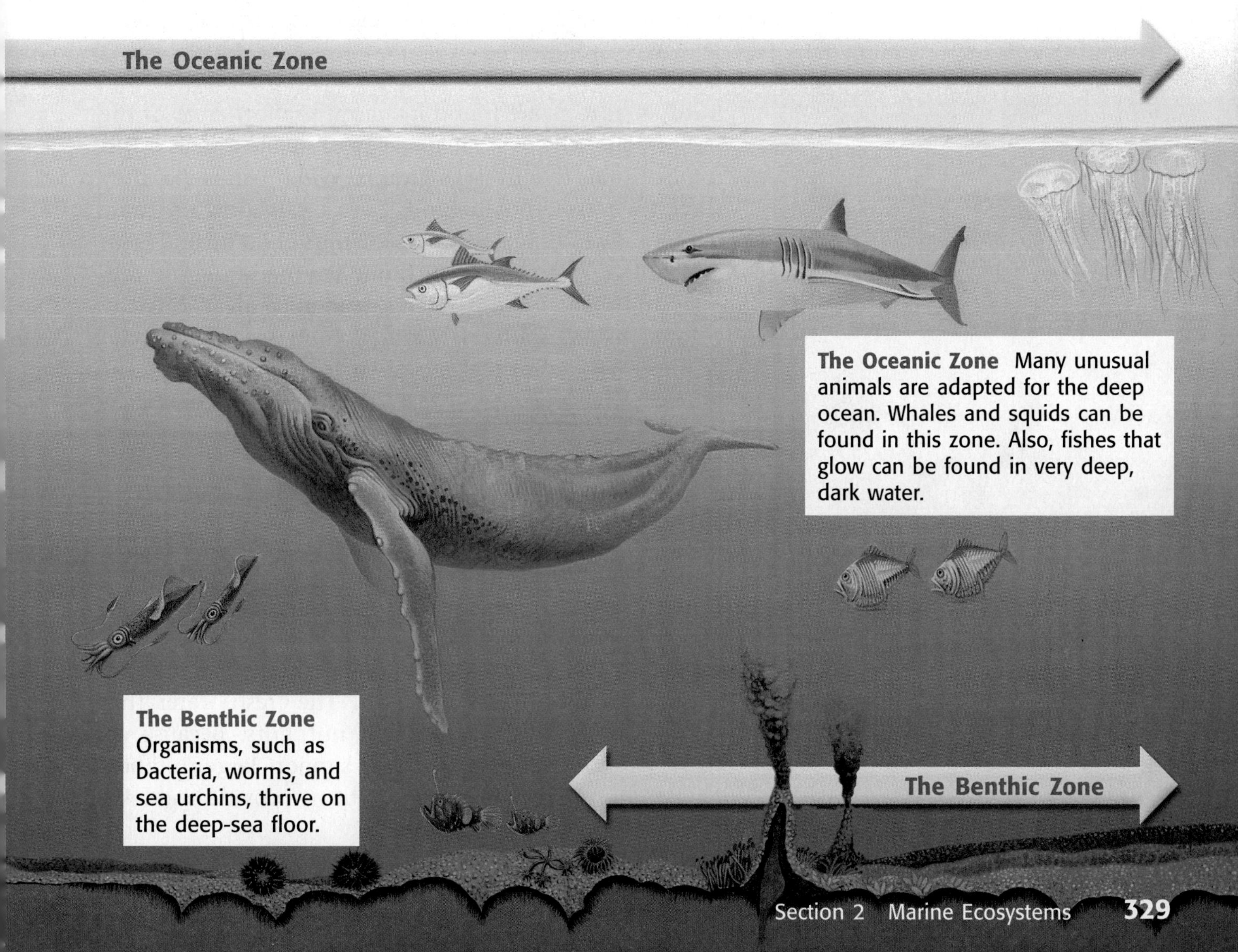

The Oceanic Zone Many unusual animals are adapted for the deep ocean. Whales and squids can be found in this zone. Also, fishes that glow can be found in very deep, dark water.

The Benthic Zone Organisms, such as bacteria, worms, and sea urchins, thrive on the deep-sea floor.

A Closer Look

Life on Earth depends on the ocean. Through evaporation, the ocean provides most of the water that makes up Earth's precipitation. Ocean temperatures and currents can affect world climates and wind patterns. Humans and many animals depend on the ocean for food.

Many ecosystems exist in the ocean. Some of these ecosystems are found on or near the shore. Other ecosystems are found in the middle of the ocean or near the poles.

Intertidal Areas

estuary an area where fresh water from rivers mixes with salt water from the ocean

Intertidal areas are found near the shore. These areas include mudflats, sandy beaches, and rocky shores. Intertidal organisms must be able to live both underwater and out of water. The organisms that live in mudflats include worms and crabs. Shorebirds feed on these animals. Organisms that live on sandy beaches include worms, clams, crabs, and plankton. On rocky shores, organisms have adaptations to keep from being swept away by crashing waves. Some organisms use rootlike structures called *holdfasts* to attach themselves to the rocks. Other organisms attach themselves to rocks by releasing a special glue.

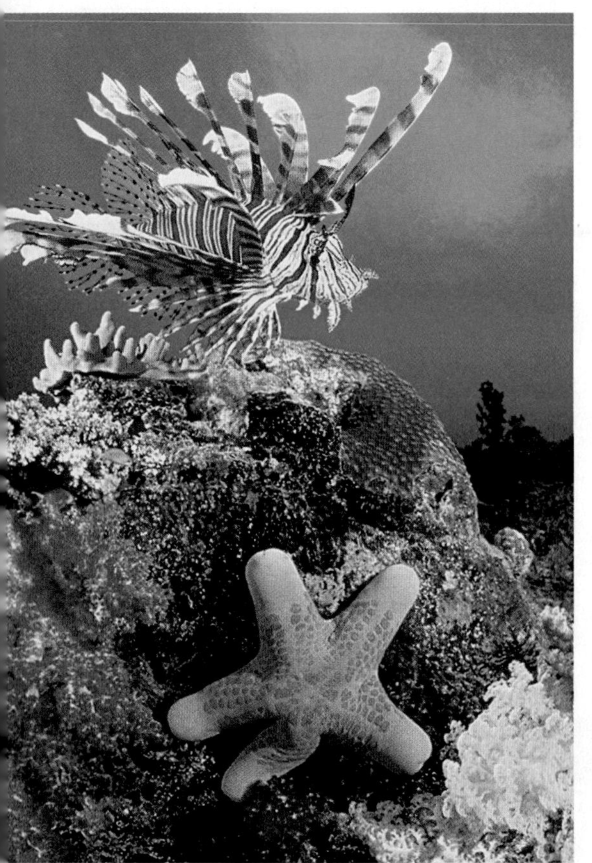

Figure 4 *A coral reef is one of the most biologically diverse ecosystems on Earth.*

Coral Reefs

Most coral reefs are found in warm, shallow areas of the neritic zone. The reefs are made up of small animals called *corals*. Corals live in large groups. When corals die, they leave their skeletons behind. New corals grow on these remains. Over time, layers of skeletons build up and form a reef. This reef provides a home for many marine animals and plants. These organisms include algae, brightly colored fishes, sponges, sea stars, and sea urchins. An example of a coral reef is shown in **Figure 4.**

Reading Check How do coral reefs develop?

Estuaries

An area where fresh water from streams and rivers spills into the ocean is called an **estuary** (ES tyoo er ee). In estuaries, the fresh water from rivers and the salt water from the ocean are always mixing. Therefore, the amount of salt in the water is always changing. Plants and animals that live in estuaries must be able to survive the changing concentrations of salt. The fresh water that spills into an estuary is rich in nutrients. Because estuaries are so nutrient rich, they support large numbers of plankton. The plankton, in turn, provide food for many animals.

The Sargasso Sea

An ecosystem called the *Sargasso Sea* (sahr GAS oh SEE) is found in the middle of the Atlantic Ocean. This ecosystem contains floating rafts of algae called *sargassums* (sahr GAS uhmz). Many of the animals that live in the Sargasso Sea are the same color as sargassums, which helps the animals hide from predators.

Polar Ice

The Arctic Ocean and the ocean around Antarctica make up another marine ecosystem. These icy waters are rich in nutrients, which support large numbers of plankton. Many fishes, birds, and mammals rely on the plankton for food. Animals, such as polar bears and penguins, live on the polar ice.

SECTION Review

Summary

- Abiotic factors that affect marine ecosystems are water temperature, water depth, and the amount of light that passes into the water.
- Plankton form the base of the ocean's food chains.
- Four ocean zones are the intertidal zone, the neritic zone, the oceanic zone, and the benthic zone.
- The ocean contains unique ecosystems, including intertidal areas, coral reefs, estuaries, the Sargasso Sea, and polar ice.

Using Key Terms

1. Use each of the following terms in a separate sentence: *plankton* and *estuary*.

Understanding Key Ideas

2. Water temperature
   a. has no effect on the animals in a marine ecosystem.
   b. affects the types of organisms that can live in a marine ecosystem.
   c. decreases gradually as water gets deeper.
   d. increases as water gets deeper.
3. What are three abiotic factors that affect marine ecosystems?
4. Describe four major ocean zones.
5. Describe five marine ecosystems. For each ecosystem, list an organism that lives there.

Math Skills

6. The ocean covers about 71% of the Earth's surface. If the total surface area of the Earth is about 510 million square kilometers, how many square kilometers are covered by the ocean?

Critical Thinking

7. **Making Inferences** Animals in the Sargasso Sea hide from predators by blending in with the sargassum. Color is only one way to blend in. What is another way that animals can blend in with sargassum?
8. **Identifying Relationships** Many fishes and other organisms that live in the deep ocean produce light. What are two ways in which this light might be useful?
9. **Applying Concepts** Imagine that you are studying animals that live in intertidal zones. You just discovered a new animal. Describe the animal and adaptations the animal has to survive in the intertidal zone.

SCILINKS
NSTA
Developed and maintained by the National Science Teachers Association
For a variety of links related to this chapter, go to www.scilinks.org
Topic: Marine Ecosystems
SciLinks code: HSM0911

SECTION 3

Freshwater Ecosystems

A brook bubbles over rocks. A mighty river thunders through a canyon. A calm swamp echoes with the sounds of frogs and birds. What do these places have in common?

What You Will Learn

- Describe one abiotic factor that affects freshwater ecosystems.
- Describe the three zones of a lake.
- Describe two wetland ecosystems.
- Explain how a lake becomes a forest.

Vocabulary

littoral zone
open-water zone
deep-water zone
wetland
marsh
swamp

READING STRATEGY

Paired Summarizing Read this section silently. In pairs, take turns summarizing the material. Stop to discuss ideas that seem confusing.

Brooks, rivers, and swamps are examples of freshwater ecosystems. The water in brooks and rivers is often fast moving. In swamps, water moves very slowly. Also, water in swamps is often found in standing pools.

Stream and River Ecosystems

The water in brooks, streams, and rivers may flow from melting ice or snow. Or the water may come from a spring. A spring is a place where water flows from underground to the Earth's surface. Each stream of water that joins a larger stream is called a *tributary* (TRIB yoo TER ee). As more tributaries join a stream, the stream contains more water. The stream becomes stronger and wider. A very strong, wide stream is called a *river*. **Figure 1** shows how a river develops.

Like other ecosystems, freshwater ecosystems are characterized by their abiotic factors. An important abiotic factor in freshwater ecosystems is how quickly water moves.

Streams and rivers are full of life. Plants line the edges of streams and rivers. Fish live in the open waters. And clams and snails live in the mud at the bottom of a stream or river. Organisms that live in fast-moving water have adaptations to keep from being washed away. Some producers, such as algae and moss, are attached to rocks. Consumers, such as tadpoles, use suction disks to hold themselves to rocks. Other consumers, such as insects, live under rocks.

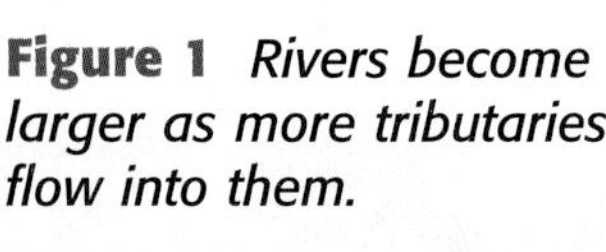

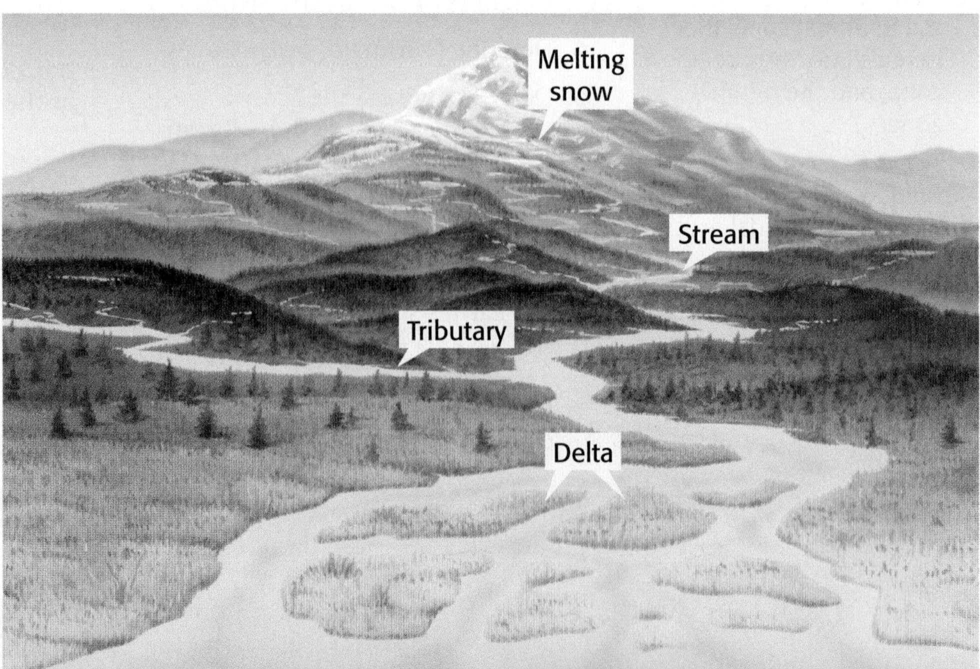

Figure 1 *Rivers become larger as more tributaries flow into them.*

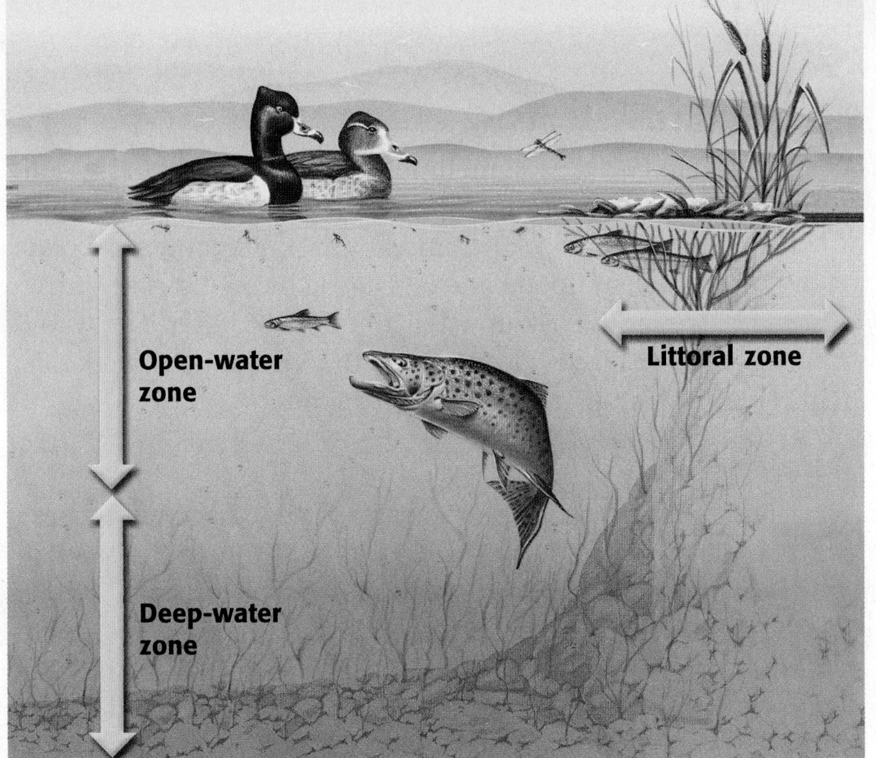

Figure 2 *Ponds and lakes can be divided into three zones. Each zone has different organisms and abiotic factors.*

Pond and Lake Ecosystems

Ponds and lakes have different ecosystems than streams and rivers do. **Figure 2** shows the zones of a typical lake.

Life near Shore

The area of water closest to the edge of a lake or pond is called the **littoral zone** (LIT uh ruhl ZOHN). Sunlight reaches the bottom of the littoral zone. This sunlight makes it possible for algae and plants to grow in the littoral zone. Algae grow beneath the surface of the water in the littoral zone. Plants that grow near the shore include cattails and rushes. Floating leaf plants, such as water lilies, grow farther from the shore. The plants of the littoral zone are home to small animals, such as snails and insects. Clams and worms bury themselves in the mud. Frogs, salamanders, turtles, fish, and snakes also live in this zone.

Life Away from Shore

The area of a lake or pond that extends from the littoral zone across the top of the water is called the **open-water zone.** The open-water zone goes as deep as sunlight can reach. This zone is home to bass, lake trout, and other fishes. Many photosynthetic plankton also live in this area. Beneath the open-water zone is the **deep-water zone,** where no sunlight reaches. Catfish, carp, worms, crustaceans, fungi, and bacteria live here. These organisms often feed on dead organisms that sink from above.

Reading Check **Describe the three zones of a lake.** (*See the Appendix for answers to Reading Checks.*)

Pond-Food Relationships

1. On **index cards,** write the names of some of the plants and animals that live in a typical freshwater pond or small lake. Write one type of organism on each card.
2. Use **yarn** or **string** to connect each organism to its food sources.
3. Describe the food relationships in a pond.

littoral zone the shallow zone of a lake or pond where light reaches the bottom and nurtures plants

open-water zone the zone of a pond or lake that extends from the littoral zone and that is only as deep as light can reach

deep-water zone the zone of a lake or pond below the open-water zone, where no light reaches

Figure 3 *This painted turtle suns itself on a log in a freshwater marsh.*

Wetland Ecosystems

An area of land that is sometimes underwater or whose soil contains a great deal of moisture is called a **wetland.** Wetlands support many different plants and animals. Wetlands also play an important role in flood control. During heavy rains or spring snow melt, wetlands soak up large amounts of water. The water in wetlands also moves deeper into the ground. So, wetlands help replenish underground water supplies.

Marshes

A treeless wetland ecosystem where plants, such as grasses, grow is called a **marsh.** A freshwater marsh is shown in **Figure 3.** Freshwater marshes are often found in shallow areas along the shores of lakes, ponds, rivers, and streams. The plants in a marsh vary depending on the depth of the water and the location of the marsh. Grasses, reeds, bulrushes, and wild rice are common marsh plants. Muskrats, turtles, frogs, and birds also live in marshes.

wetland an area of land that is periodically underwater or whose soil contains a great deal of moisture

marsh a treeless wetland ecosystem where plants such as grasses grow

swamp a wetland ecosystem in which shrubs and trees grow

Swamps

A wetland ecosystem in which trees and vines grow is called a **swamp.** Swamps, as shown in **Figure 4,** are found in low-lying areas and beside slow-moving rivers. Most swamps are flooded part of the year, depending on rainfall. Willows, bald cypresses, and oaks are common swamp trees. Vines, such as poison ivy, grow up tree trunks. Plants, such as orchids, may hang from tree branches. Water lilies and other plants grow in standing water. Many fishes, snakes, and birds also live in swamps.

Reading Check What is a swamp?

CONNECTION TO Language Arts

Compound Words A compound word is a word made up of two or more single words. In your **science journal,** define the two words that make up the word *wetland.* Then, define three more compound words.

Figure 4 *The trunks of these trees are adapted to give the trees more support in the wet, soft soil of a swamp.*

From a Lake to a Forest

Did you know that a lake or pond can disappear? How can this happen? Water entering a standing body of water usually carries nutrients and sediment. These materials settle to the bottom of the pond or lake. Dead leaves from overhanging trees and decaying plant and animal life also settle to the bottom. Then, bacteria decompose this material. This process uses oxygen in the water. The loss of oxygen affects the kinds of animals that can survive in the pond or lake. For example, many fishes would not be able to survive with less oxygen in the water.

Over time, the pond or lake is filled with sediment. Plants grow in the new soil. Shallow areas fill in first. So, plants slowly grow closer and closer to the center of the pond or lake. What is left of the lake or pond becomes a wetland, such as a marsh or swamp. Eventually, the wetland can become a forest.

✓ *Reading Check* **What happens to some of the animals in a pond as the pond becomes a forest?**

For another activity related to this chapter, go to **go.hrw.com** and type in the keyword **HL5ECOW.**

SECTION Review

Summary

- An important abiotic factor in freshwater ecosystems is how quickly water moves.
- The three zones of a pond or lake are the littoral zone, the open-water zone, and the deep-water zone.
- Wetlands include marshes and swamps.
- Sediments and decaying plant and animal matter build up in a pond. Over time, the pond may fill completely and become a forest.

Using Key Terms

1. Use the following terms in the same sentence: *wetland, marsh,* and *swamp.*

Understanding Key Ideas

2. A major abiotic factor in freshwater ecosystems is the
   a. source of the water.
   b. speed of the water.
   c. width of the stream or river.
   d. None of the above
3. Describe the three zones of a lake.
4. Explain how a lake can become a forest over time.

Math Skills

5. Sunlight can penetrate a certain lake to a depth of 15 m. The lake is five and a half times deeper than the depth to which light can penetrate. In meters, how deep is the lake?

Critical Thinking

6. **Making Inferences** When bacteria decompose material in a pond, the oxygen in the water may be used up. So, fishes in the pond die. How might the absence of fish lead to a pond filling faster?
7. **Applying Concepts** Imagine a steep, rocky stream. What kinds of adaptations might animals living in this stream have? Explain your answer.

For a variety of links related to this chapter, go to www.scilinks.org

Topic: Freshwater Ecosystems
SciLinks code: HSM0621

Skills Practice Lab

OBJECTIVES

Draw common pond-water organisms.

Observe the effect of fertilizer on pond-water organisms.

Describe how fertilizer affects the number and type of pond-water organisms over time.

MATERIALS

- beaker, 500 mL
- distilled water, 2.25 L
- eyedropper
- fertilizer
- gloves, protective
- graduated cylinder, 100 mL
- jars, 1 qt or 1 L (3)
- microscope
- microscope slides with coverslips
- pencil, wax
- plastic wrap
- pond water containing living organisms, 300 mL
- stirring rod

SAFETY

    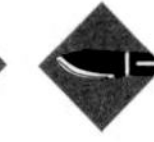

Too Much of a Good Thing?

Plants need nutrients, such as phosphates and nitrates, to grow. Phosphates are often found in detergents. Nitrates are often found in animal wastes and fertilizers. When large amounts of these nutrients enter rivers and lakes, algae and plants grow rapidly and then die off. Microorganisms that decompose the dead matter use up oxygen in the water. Without oxygen, fish and other animals die. In this activity, you will observe the effect of fertilizers on organisms that live in pond water.

Procedure

1. Label one jar "Control," the second jar "Fertilizer," and the third jar "Excess fertilizer."
2. Pour 750 mL of distilled water into each jar. To the "Fertilizer" jar, add the amount of fertilizer recommended for 750 mL of water. To the "Excess fertilizer" jar, add 10 times the amount recommended for 750 mL of water. Stir the contents of each jar to dissolve the fertilizer.
3. Obtain a sample of pond water. Stir it gently to make sure that the organisms in it are evenly distributed. Pour 100 mL of pond water into each of the three jars.
4. Observe a drop of water from each jar under the microscope. Draw at least four of the organisms. Determine whether the organisms you see are producers, which are usually green, or consumers, which are usually able to move. Describe the number and type of organisms in the pond water.

Common Pond-Water Organisms

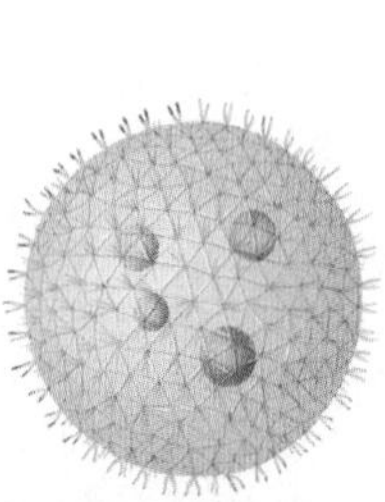

Volvox (producer)

Spirogyra (producer)

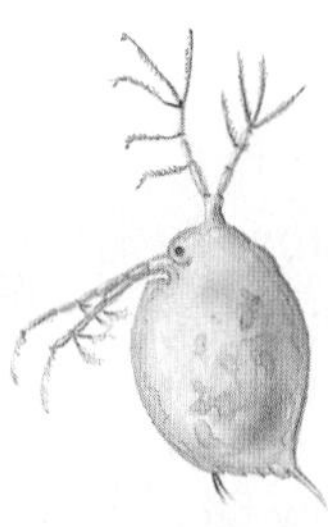

Daphnia (consumer)

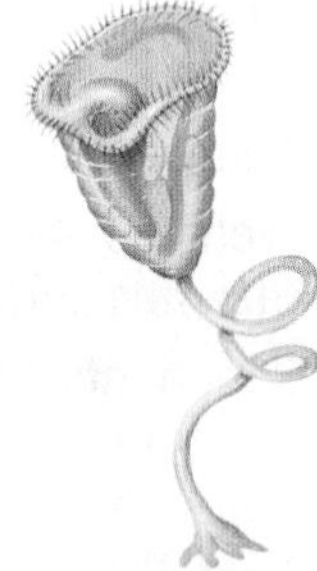

Vorticella (consumer)

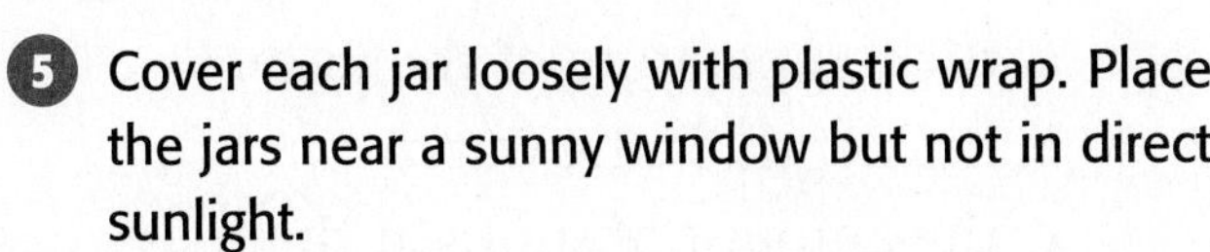

5. Cover each jar loosely with plastic wrap. Place the jars near a sunny window but not in direct sunlight.

6. Make a prediction about how the pond organisms will grow in each of the three jars.

7. Make three data tables. Title one table "Control," as shown below. Title another table "Fertilizer," and title the third table "Excess fertilizer."

Control			
Date	Color	Odor	Other observations

DO NOT WRITE IN BOOK

8. Observe the jars when you first set them up and once every 3 days for the next 3 weeks. Note the color, the odor, and the presence of organisms. Record your observations.

9. When organisms become visible in the jars, use an eyedropper to remove a sample from each jar. Observe the sample under the microscope. How have the number and type of organisms changed since you first looked at the pond water?

10. At the end of the 3-week period, observe a sample from each jar under the microscope. Draw at least four of the most abundant organisms, and describe how the number and type of organisms have changed since your last microscope observation.

Analyze the Results

1. **Describing Events** After 3 weeks, which jar has the most abundant growth of algae?

2. **Analyzing Data** Did you observe any effects on organisms (other than algae) in the jar with the most abundant algal growth? Explain your answer.

Draw Conclusions

3. **Drawing Conclusions** What may have caused increased growth in the jars?

4. **Evaluating Results** Did your observations match your predictions? Explain your answer.

5. **Interpreting Information** Decaying plant and animal life contribute to the filling of lakes and ponds. How might the rapid filling of lakes and ponds be prevented or slowed?

Chapter Review

USING KEY TERMS

1. In your own words, write a definition for the following terms: *biome* and *tundra*.

2. Use each of the following terms in a separate sentence: *intertidal zone, neritic zone,* and *oceanic zone.*

For each pair of terms, explain how the meanings of the terms differ.

3. *savanna* and *desert*

4. *open-water zone* and *deep-water zone*

5. *marsh* and *swamp*

UNDERSTANDING KEY IDEAS

Multiple Choice

6. Trees that lose their leaves in the winter are called
   - **a.** evergreen trees.
   - **b.** coniferous trees.
   - **c.** deciduous trees.
   - **d.** None of the above

7. In which major ocean zone are plants and animals exposed to air for part of the day?
   - **a.** intertidal zone
   - **b.** neritic zone
   - **c.** oceanic zone
   - **d.** benthic zone

8. An abiotic factor that affects marine ecosystems is
   - **a.** the temperature of the water.
   - **b.** the depth of the water.
   - **c.** the amount of sunlight that passes through the water.
   - **d.** All of the above

9. _____ is a marine ecosystem that includes mudflats, sandy beaches, and rocky shores.
   - **a.** An intertidal area
   - **b.** Polar ice
   - **c.** A coral reef
   - **d.** The Sargasso Sea

Short Answer

10. What are seven land biomes?

11. Explain how a small lake can become a forest.

12. What are two factors that characterize biomes?

13. Describe the three zones of a lake.

14. How do rivers form?

15. What are three abiotic factors in land biomes? three abiotic factors in marine ecosystems? an abiotic factor in fresh-water ecosystems?

CRITICAL THINKING

16 **Concept Mapping** Use the following terms to create a concept map: *plants and animals, tropical rain forest, tundra, biomes, permafrost, canopy, desert,* and *abiotic factors.*

17 **Making Inferences** Plankton use photosynthesis to make their own food. They need sunlight for photosynthesis. Which of the four major ocean zones can support plankton growth? Explain your answer.

18 **Predicting Consequences** Wetlands, such as marshes and swamps, play an important role in flood control. Wetlands also help replenish underground water supplies. Predict what might happen if a wetland dries out.

19 **Analyzing Ideas** A scientist has a new hypothesis. He or she thinks that savannas and deserts are part of one biome rather than two separate biomes. Based on what you've learned, decide if the scientist's hypothesis is correct. Explain your answer.

20 **Applying Concepts** Imagine that you are a scientist. You are studying an area that gets about 100 cm of rain each year. The average summer temperatures are near 30°C. What biome are you in? What are some plants and animals you will likely encounter? If you stayed in this area for the winter, what kind of preparations might you need to make?

INTERPRETING GRAPHICS

Use the graphs below to answer the questions that follow.

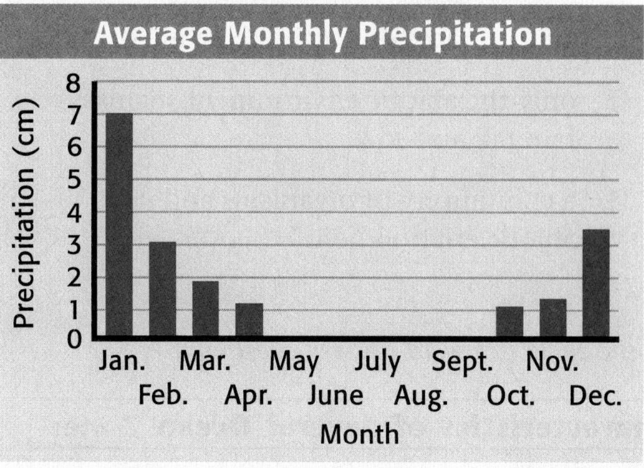

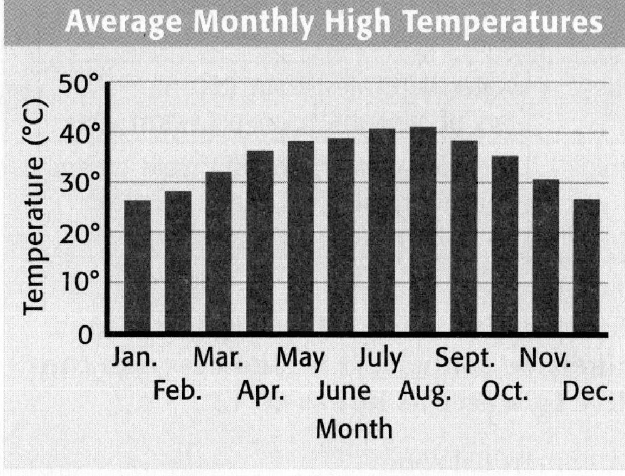

21 Which biome is most likely found in the region described by the graphs above? Explain your answer.

22 How many centimeters of rain fell in the region during the course of the year?

23 Which month is the hottest in the region? the coolest in the region?

24 What is the average monthly precipitation for the month that has the highest average high temperature?

Multiple Choice

1. **An ecosystem consists of**

   A. many populations of a number of species.

   B. all the places on Earth where life exists.

   C. only the abiotic environment such as rain fall and soil.

   D. a community of organisms and its abiotic environment.

Use the table below to answer question 2.

Characteristics of Several Ocean Zones	
Zone	Description
Intertidal	air, sun, and water exposure; crashing waves
Neritic	water depth less than 200 m; lots of sunlight; relatively warm water
Benthic	very deep water; no light; cold except near thermal vents that emit heat and chemicals

2. **In which zone would an organism most likely be found if it has no eyes and can live in water as hot as 80°C?**

   A. intertidal zone

   B. neritic zone

   C. benthic zone

   D. It would not live in the ocean.

3. **Plants that cannot tolerate water with a constantly changing salt content are NOT likely to be found in**

   A. a freshwater stream.

   B. a pond.

   C. the neritic zone.

   D. an estuary.

4. **Trout thrive in the oxygen-rich waters of cool, fast-moving streams. Which of the following events might reduce the population of trout in a mountain stream?**

   A. There is unusually heavy snowfall in the winter.

   B. The flow of a tributary stream slows slightly.

   C. The movement of a boulder forms a new waterfall.

   D. Ash and silt from a forest fire cover the surface of the stream.

5. **Why are savannas well-suited to supporting large herbivores?**

   A. They have very little biodiversity, only large herbivores live there.

   B. They are areas where grasses are the main plants.

   C. They are dry and hot.

   D. They are cold and dry.

6. **Tim saw a flock of pelicans flying inland above the Savannah River. What part of an ecosystem did Tim see?**

   A. organism

   B. population

   C. community

   D. abiotic environment

Use the graphs below to answer question 7.

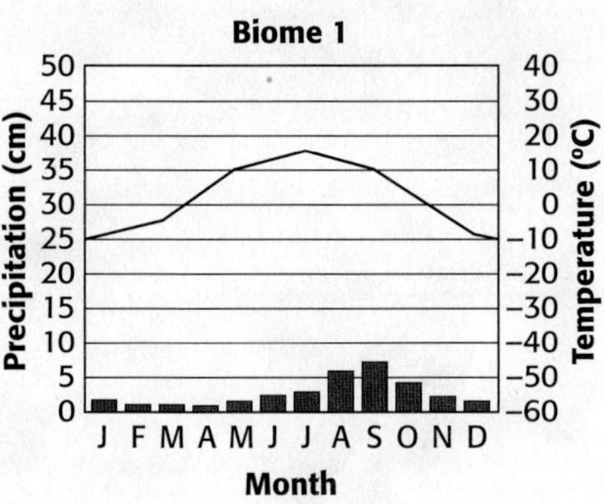

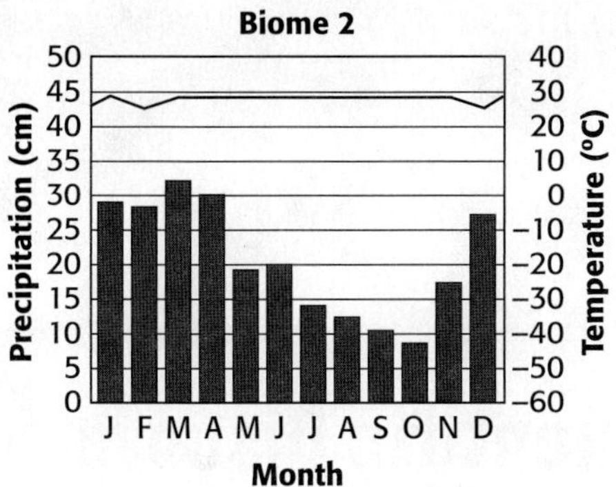

7. Scientists involved in a field study produced the two precipitation and temperature graphs shown above. On each graph, the line represents temperature and the bars represent precipitation. Based on the graph of biome 2, which of the following is a reasonable conclusion?

A. Biome 2 is most likely tundra.

B. Biome 2 is most likely located near the equator.

C. Biome 2 receives most of its annual rainfall within a three-month period.

D. Biome 2 has wild temperature swings.

8. Chantrell is making a terrarium for a praying mantis she wants to study. Praying mantises are carnivores. Chantrell has placed the following in her terrarium: soil, twigs, a rock, a small dish of water, and the praying mantis. What is missing from Chantrell's terrarium?

A. plants for the praying mantis to eat

B. other insects for the praying mantis to eat

C. a mouse for the praying mantis to eat, and grains for the mouse to eat

D. other insects for the praying mantis to eat, and plants for the other insects to eat

Open Response

9. Biomes can be used to classify living systems because similar organisms live in a particular biome regardless of where that biome is located. Like all of the eastern United States, Kentucky's biome is temperate deciduous forest. What are the characteristics of temperate deciduous forest?

10. Versailles, Kentucky, is in the heart of the state's "bluegrass" region. The average yearly rainfall is 114 cm. The average yearly rainfall in a desert is 25 cm. What kind of change would have to occur for this region of Kentucky to become a desert?

Science in Action

Scientific Debate

Developing Wetlands

Wetlands are home to many flowering plants, birds, and turtles. Wetlands also play important roles in flood control and maintaining water quality. However, as more people need homes, grocery stores, and other facilities, some wetlands are being developed for construction. State governments often regulate the development of wetlands. Development is not allowed on many environmentally sensitive wetlands. But it is sometimes allowed on wetlands that are less sensitive. However, some people think that all wetlands should be protected, regardless of how sensitive an area is.

Language Arts ACTIVITY

WRITING SKILL Research wetland development on your own. Then, write a letter in which you describe your opinion about the development of wetlands.

Scientific Discoveries

Ocean Vents

Imagine the deepest parts of the ocean. There is no light at all, and it is very cold. Some of the animals that live here have found a unique place to live—vents on the ocean floor. Water seeps into the Earth between plates on the ocean floor. The water is heated and absorbs sulfuric gases. When the water blasts up through ocean vents, it raises the temperature of the ocean hundreds of degrees! Bacteria use the gases from the ocean vents to survive. In turn, mussels and clams feed on the bacteria. Without ocean vents, it would be much more difficult for these organisms to survive.

Math ACTIVITY

A thermal vent increases the temperature of the water around it to 360°C. If the temperature of the water was 2°C, what is the difference in temperature? By what percentage did the water temperature increase?

Careers

Alfonso Alonso-Mejía

Ecologist During the winter, ecologist Alfonso Alonso-Mejía visits sites in central Mexico where millions of monarch butterflies spend the winter. Unfortunately, the monarchs' winter habitat is threatened by human activity. Only nine of the monarchs' wintering sites remain. Five of the sites are set aside as sanctuaries for monarchs, but these sites are threatened by people who cut down fir trees for firewood or for commercial purposes.

Alonso-Mejía discovered that monarchs depend on understory vegetation, bushlike plants that grow beneath fir trees, to survive. When the temperature is low, monarchs can climb understory vegetation until they are at least 10 cm above the ground. This tiny difference in elevation can ensure that monarchs are warm enough to survive. Because of Alonso-Mejía's discovery, Mexican conservationists are working to protect understory vegetation and monarchs.

Social Studies ACTIVITY

Use your school library or the Internet to research the routes that monarchs use to migrate to Mexico. Draw a map illustrating your findings.

To learn more about these Science in Action topics, visit go.hrw.com and type in the keyword HL5ECOF.

Current Science

Check out Current Science® articles related to this chapter by visiting go.hrw.com. Just type in the keyword HL5CS20.

13

Earth's Systems and Cycles

The Big Idea Processes in the lithosphere, atmosphere, hydrosphere, and biosphere interact to shape Earth.

SECTION

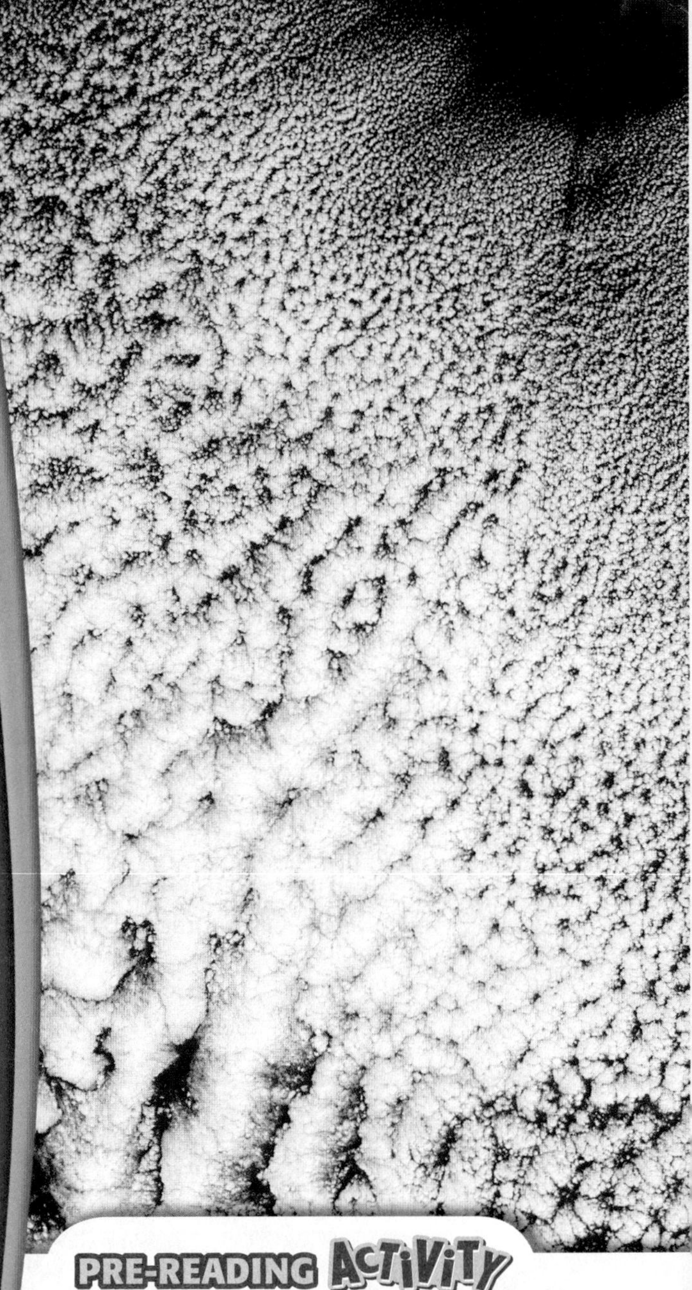

About the Photo

From space, the land, ocean, and atmosphere appear to be distinct. However, each of these three spheres interact to form a system that sustains life on Earth. Shown here is the Florida Peninsula in the southeastern United States.

PRE-READING ACTIVITY

Layered Book Before you read the chapter, create the FoldNote entitled "Layered Book" described in the **Study Skills** section of the Appendix. Label the tabs of the layered book with "Geosphere," "Atmosphere," "Hydrosphere," and "Biosphere." As you read the chapter, write information you learn about each category under the appropriate tab.

START-UP ACTIVITY

Make a Hydrothermal Vent

In this activity, you will model a hydrothermal vent. Hydrothermal vents are openings in the ocean floor where superhot, mineral-rich waters stream through structures known as *chimneys*. Hydrothermal vents generally occur where large pieces of Earth's lithosphere, called *tectonic plates,* are separating.

Procedure

1. Fill a **large glass container** or **aquarium** with very **cold water.**
2. Tie one end of a **piece of string** around the neck of a **small bottle.**
3. Fill the small bottle with very **hot water,** and add a few drops of **food coloring.**
4. Keep the small bottle upright while you lower it into the glass container until it rests on the bottom.

Analysis

1. Did the food coloring indicate that the hot water and cold water mixed?
2. Based on your results, what do you predict happens to the superhot water from a hydrothermal vent when it encounters the cold water of the ocean floor?

SECTION 1

The Geosphere

Stop and look at the sky above you and the earth beneath your feet. What do they have in common? They are constantly changing.

Some changes on Earth happen slowly, and others happen quickly. Some changes are driven by energy from within Earth. Others are driven by energy from the sun. But these changes are related, because Earth is an interconnected, global system.

What You Will Learn

- Identify the four major divisions of Earth.
- Identify the layers of Earth based on composition and physical properties.
- Describe the rate at which tectonic plates move.
- Explain the causes of earthquakes and volcanoes.
- Explain how water and wind reshape Earth's surface.

Vocabulary

geosphere
atmosphere
hydrosphere
biosphere
crust
mantle
core
erosion

READING STRATEGY

Paired Summarizing Read this section silently. In pairs, take turns summarizing the material. Stop to discuss ideas that seem confusing.

Earth as a System

In this chapter, you will learn about the four major divisions, or spheres, of Earth and how they work together as a system. The four divisions of Earth are the geosphere, atmosphere, hydrosphere, and biosphere. The **geosphere** is the solid rocks of Earth. The geosphere is surrounded by the **atmosphere,** which is made up of invisible gases and water vapor. The **hydrosphere** consists of the global ocean, polar ice caps, glaciers, lakes, rivers, water vapor, clouds, and rain. The **biosphere** is the area where all life on Earth exists.

As seen in **Figure 1,** Earth's spheres are overlapping and share some of the same physical space. But each of these spheres has a different composition and different energy relations.

Reading Check **Briefly define each of the four major divisions of Earth.** (*See the Appendix for answers to Reading Checks.*)

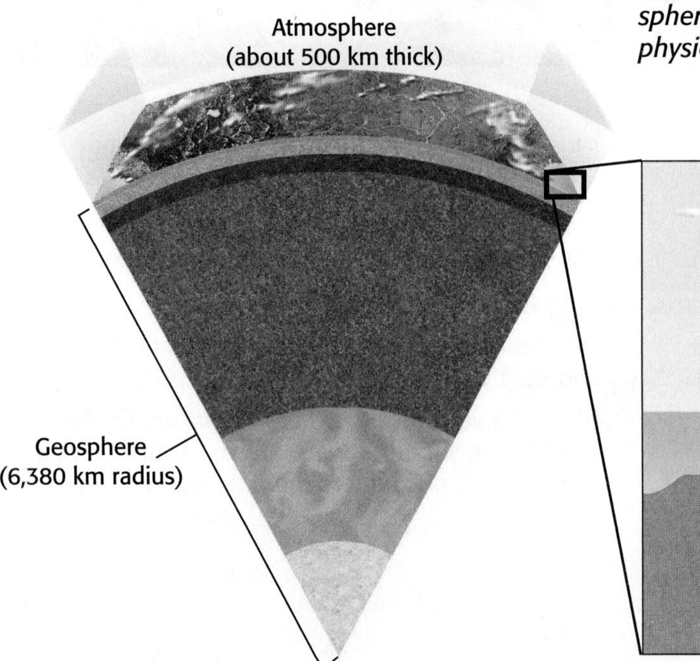

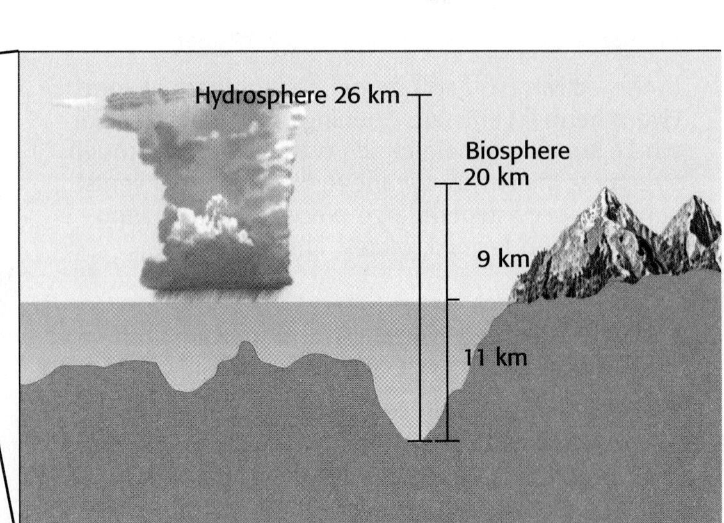

Figure 1 *Earth is divided into four spheres, some of which overlap in physical space.*

Earth's Compositional Layers

Crust The crust is the solid, brittle, outermost layer of Earth and is 5 to 100 km thick. Continental crust is thick and made of less dense silicate minerals; oceanic crust is thin and made of denser minerals.

Mantle The mantle is 2,900 km thick. It is made of silicate minerals and contains much less aluminum and much more magnesium than the crust does. The mantle is slightly denser than the crust is.

Core The core has a radius of 3,400 km. This sphere, which contains an iron-nickel alloy, is about twice as dense as the mantle is.

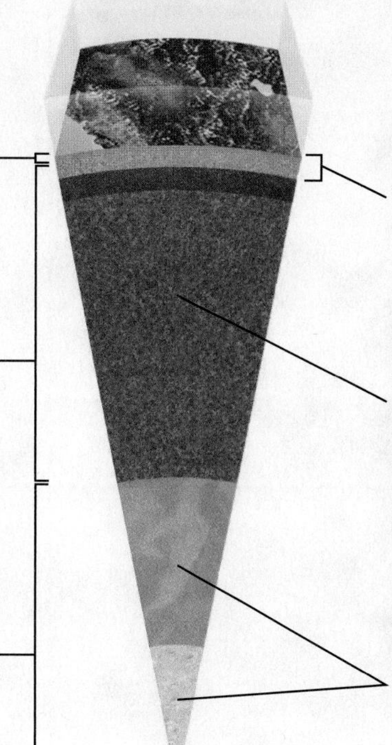

Earth's Physical Layers

Lithosphere The lithosphere is 15 to 300 km thick. This cool, rigid, outermost layer of Earth is divided into huge slabs called *tectonic plates*.

Mantle The mantle is 2,900 km thick. It is made up of the lower part of the lithosphere, the asthenosphere—a semi-solid layer that is 250 km thick upon which the lithospheric plates move—and the mesosphere—a lower, more rigid layer that is 2,550 km thick.

Core The core has a radius of 3,400 km. It is composed of the outer core and inner core. The outer core is molten iron and nickel alloy; the inner core is also iron and nickel but is under so much pressure that it is solid.

Figure 2 *The geosphere is divided into compositional and physical layers.*

The Layers of Earth

The geosphere is the solid Earth, as shown in **Figure 2.** Scientists have learned a lot about Earth's layers by measuring seismic waves generated by earthquakes. They know that Earth's layers differ by chemical composition and physical properties.

geosphere the mostly solid, rocky part of the Earth; extends from the center of the core to the surface of the crust

atmosphere a mixture of gases that surrounds a planet or moon

hydrosphere the portion of Earth that is water

biosphere the part of Earth where life exists

crust the thin and solid outermost layer of the Earth above the mantle

mantle the layer of rock between the Earth's crust and core

core the central part of the Earth below the mantle

The Composition of Earth

Earth is divided into three layers based on chemical composition. The surface layer, or **crust,** is composed largely of silicon, oxygen, and aluminum and represents less than 1% of Earth's mass. The **mantle,** the layer below the crust, is made up largely of silicon, oxygen, and magnesium. Because the mantle contains more magnesium, it is denser than the crust. It accounts for 64% of Earth's mass. In the center of Earth is the **core.** The core is made up mainly of the metal iron, which accounts for the core's high density. Even though the core is the thickest and densest layer, it accounts for only about 35% of Earth's mass.

The Physical Structure of Earth

Earth is also divided into five layers based on physical properties. Earth's rigid, outermost layer, the *lithosphere,* is divided into pieces called *tectonic plates*. These plates move slowly around Earth's surface on the underlying semisolid mantle layer called the *asthenosphere*. The *mesosphere,* the lower layer of the mantle, lies below the asthenosphere. At Earth's center are the *outer core,* which is made of liquid iron and nickel, and the *inner core,* which is made of solid iron and nickel.

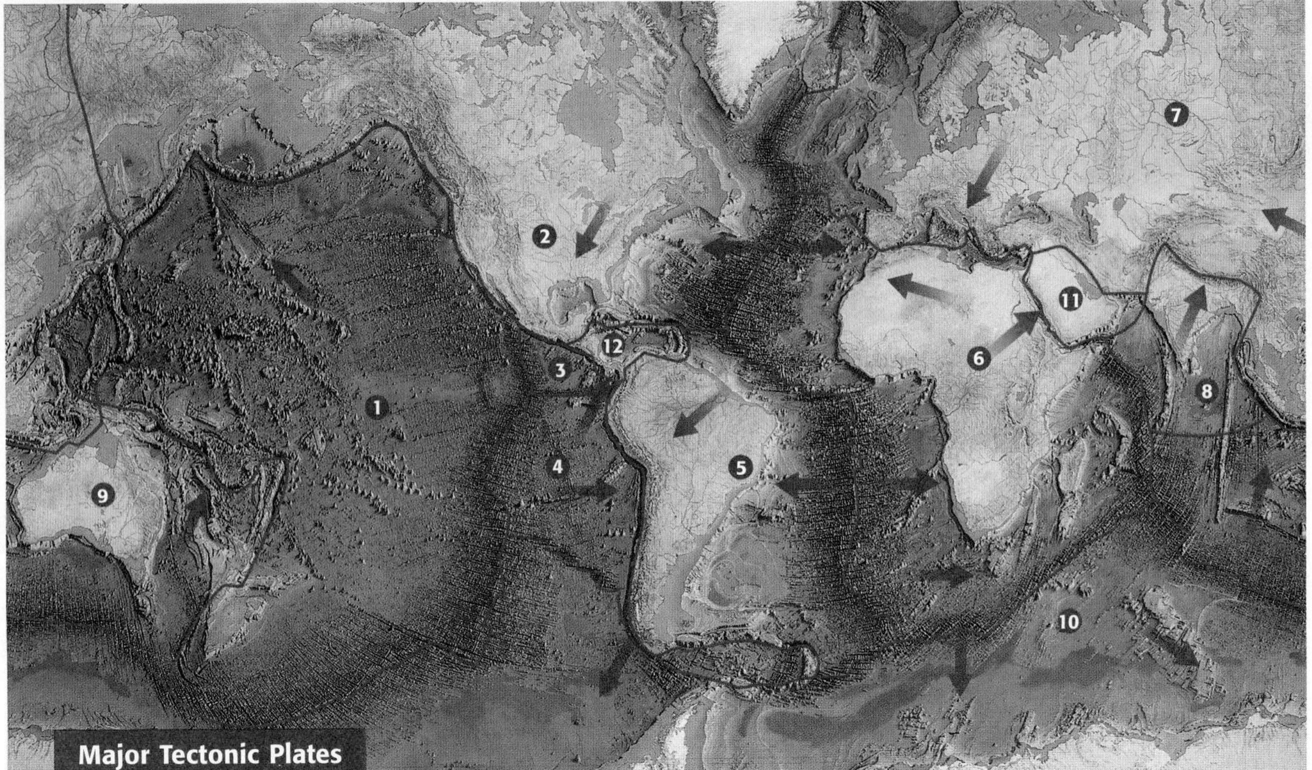

Major Tectonic Plates

1. Pacific plate
2. North American plate
3. Cocos plate
4. Nazca plate
5. South American plate
6. African plate
7. Eurasian plate
8. Indian plate
9. Australian plate
10. Antarctic plate
11. Arabian plate
12. Caribbean plate

Figure 3 *Earth's tectonic plates fit together like a giant jigsaw puzzle.*

Plate Tectonics

As you have learned, Earth's lithosphere is divided into tectonic plates. These tectonic plates, which are shown in **Figure 3,** have different sizes, shapes, and thicknesses. A single plate usually includes both continent and ocean. For example, the North American plate includes North America, part of the North Atlantic Ocean, and the island of Greenland. Tectonic plates move around Earth's surface at rates of millimeters to centimeters per year.

Tectonic Plate Boundaries

Plate boundaries are zones of geologic activity at the surface of Earth. Three plate motions are possible at plate boundaries. Plates can separate from each other, such as in the mid-Atlantic Ocean. Plates can also collide with each other and move past each other. The forces generated by these plate motions are responsible for mountain building, earthquakes, and volcanoes.

Mountain Building at Plate Boundaries

Although tectonic plates move slowly, the forces generated in movement are strong enough to cause rock to deform, buckle, and break. These forces are responsible for building major mountain ranges. The Himalaya Mountains were formed during the last 50 million years when the Indian plate moved north and collided with the Eurasian plate.

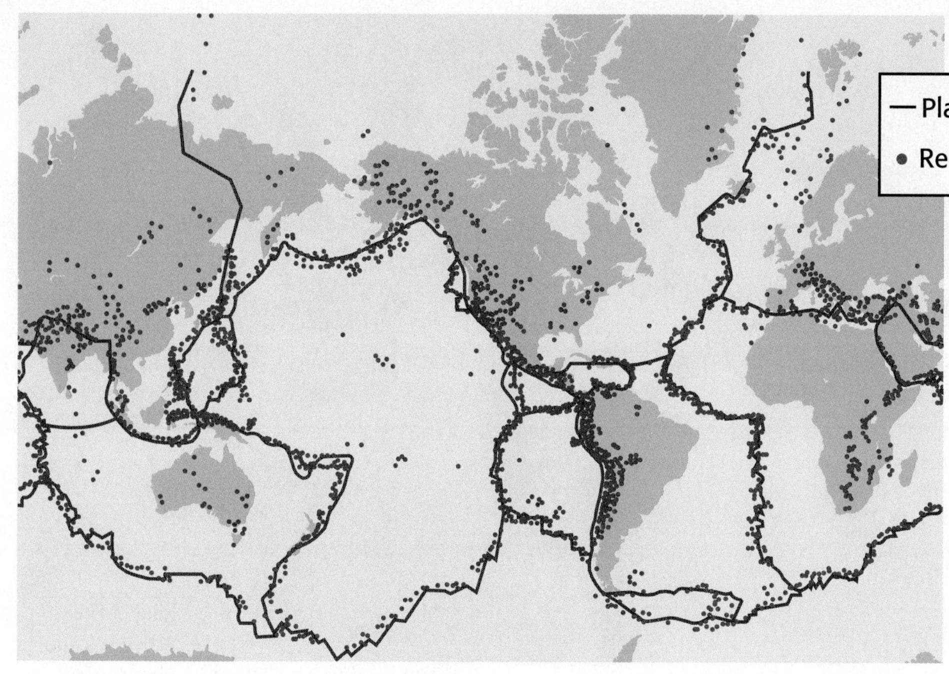

Figure 4 *The red dots in this figure indicate major earthquakes, which mainly occur very close to the tectonic plate boundaries. These boundaries are shown as thick, black lines.*

Earthquakes

Plate boundaries are also where most earthquakes occur. **Figure 4** shows where earthquakes have happened along plate boundaries. When plates move, solid rock is deformed and broken. When this happens, some of the huge amount of energy that is generated is released as vibrations that travel through the ground and shake it. This shaking is an earthquake. Some earthquakes are too small to be felt by humans. Others can be thousands or millions of times stronger. The largest earthquakes can do tremendous damage, as shown in **Figure 5.** These types of earthquakes can be responsible for loss of life and the destruction of buildings and highway overpasses.

Alien Planet Adventure
Create a planet that might be described in a science fiction book. Describe the interactions of the planet's core, mantle, and crust! Go to **go.hrw.com,** and type in the keyword **HZ5TECW.**

Reading Check **Explain how earthquakes are caused by the energy released in tectonic plate movement.**

Earthquake Zones and Hazards

Earthquake zones are places where large numbers of earthquakes occur. Most earthquake zones are located along plate boundaries. For example, the boundary between the Pacific plate and North American plate along the west coast of North America is an earthquake zone. However, large earthquakes can and do occur in the interior regions of continents. Two large earthquakes occurred within the continental United States in Charleston, South Carolina, in 1886 and in New Madrid, Missouri, in 1812.

Figure 5 *In 1995, a large earthquake shook the area in and around Kobe, Japan. Large sections of the Hanshin Expressway collapsed when the columns supporting the expressway failed.*

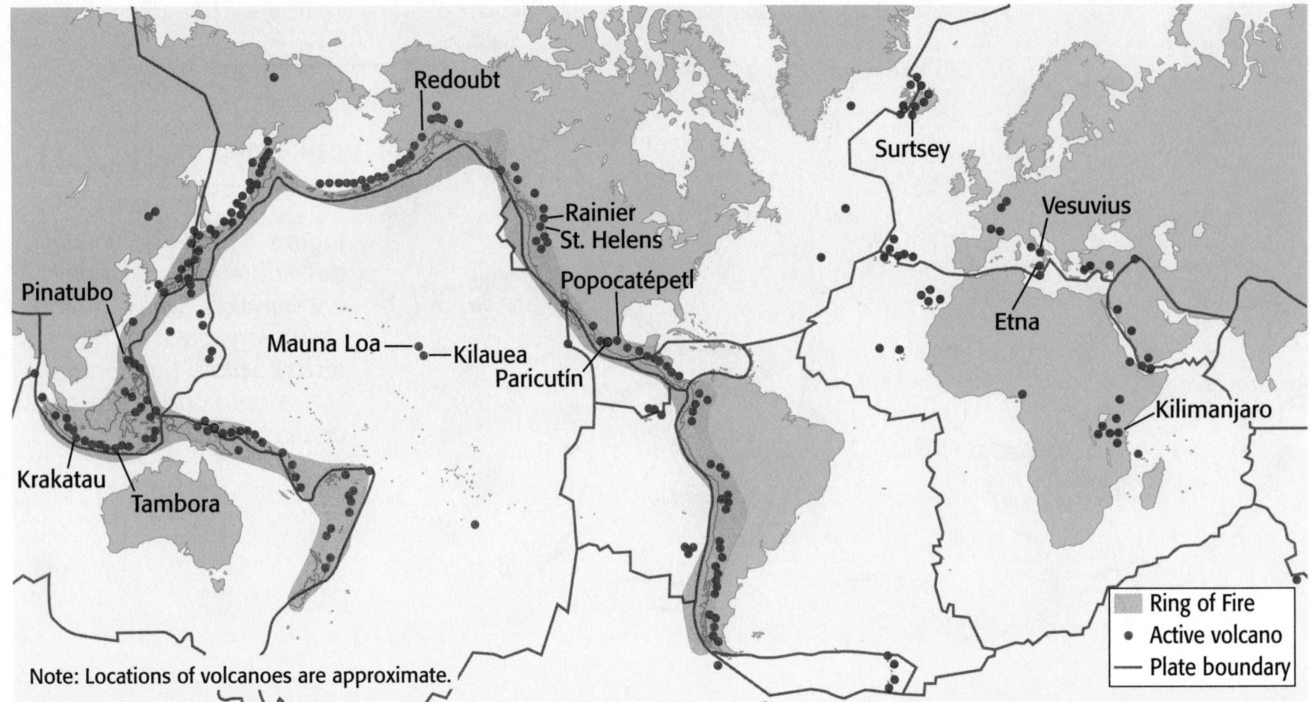

Figure 6 *Tectonic plate boundaries are also areas of volcanic activity. Nearly 75% of the active volcanoes on Earth are located around the Pacific Ocean, which has caused this area to be named the* Ring of Fire.

Volcanoes

Volcanoes are mountains that form when magma rises from Earth's interior to Earth's surface, where the magma cools and solidifies. As shown in **Figure 6,** volcanoes often occur near tectonic plate boundaries. On the ocean floor, volcanoes are located directly on the boundaries where plates pull apart. On continents, volcanoes are often located inland from the plate boundary, where the ocean plate is forced below the continent. Examples of places where volcanoes occur on continents are the west coasts of North America and South America.

Effects of Volcanic Eruptions

erosion the process by which wind, water, ice, or gravity transports soil and sediment from one location to another

Local effects of volcanic eruptions include the loss of lives and property and the destruction of the surrounding environment. Damage can be caused by flowing lava and by volcanic ash that is ejected during an eruption. This wind-carried volcanic ash and dust can also cause problems regionally or even globally.

Large volcanic eruptions can affect Earth's climate when ash blocks sunlight from reaching Earth's surface and sulfur gases reflect sunlight. Both of these effects can lower Earth's temperature. After the eruption of Mount Pinatubo in the Philippines in 1991, the amount of sunlight reaching the surface of the entire Earth was decreased by about 3%. This decrease in sunlight lowered the average global temperature by several tenths of a degree for a few years.

Reading Check **Explain how a large volcanic eruption can affect the average global temperature.**

Erosion

The process by which soil and sediment are transported from one location to another is called **erosion.** In the process of erosion, moving water, ice, and wind constantly move soil and sediment and reshape Earth's surface. Water is a very powerful force for reshaping Earth's surface. Although erosion happens over millions of years, moving water can create surface features such as the Grand Canyon, shown in **Figure 7.** Wind can move soil, especially in places where vegetation and roots do not hold the soil in place. Loose, sandy soil is most affected by wind erosion.

Figure 7 *These cliffs in the Grand Canyon were formed by the action of moving water and by wind over millions of years.*

SECTION Review

Summary

- Earth can be divided into four spheres that work together as a global system.
- The solid Earth can be divided into layers based on chemical composition and physical properties.
- Earth's lithosphere is divided into tectonic plates, which move slowly around Earth's surface.
- Tectonic plate movement can release energy in the form of earthquakes.
- Volcanic eruptions can reduce the amount of sunlight that reaches Earth's surface.
- Wind and water are erosional forces that reshape Earth's surface.

Using Key Terms

1. Use *geosphere, atmosphere, hydrosphere,* and *biosphere* in the same sentence.

Understanding Key Ideas

2. Identify the layers of Earth by their composition and physical properties.
3. Describe the rate at which tectonic plates move.
4. Explain what causes earthquakes.
5. Describe local and global effects of volcanic eruptions.
6. Explain how water and wind reshape Earth's surface.
7. Describe a tectonic plate.
8. Identify what kind of measurements helped scientists determine the structure of Earth's interior.

Critical Thinking

9. **Predicting Consequences** How might the lowering of average global temperature over a period of several years affect life on Earth?
10. **Identifying Relationships** Identify two or more of Earth's spheres that overlap in the same physical space.
11. **Making Comparisons** Compare Earth's crust with Earth's mantle.
12. **Analyzing Ideas** A volcanic eruption ejects large quantities of ash and gas into Earth's upper atmosphere. What will be the most likely consequence of this cloud of gas and ash?

For a variety of links related to this chapter, go to www.scilinks.org

Topic: Earth's Geologic Layers
SciLinks code: HSM0447

SECTION 2

The Atmosphere

What You Will Learn

- Compare and contrast the different layers of Earth's atmosphere.
- Explain how energy in Earth's atmosphere is transferred by radiation, conduction, and convection.
- Explain how the greenhouse effect warms Earth's surface.
- Explain how the ozone layer protects Earth from damaging UV radiation.

Vocabulary

radiation
conduction
convection

READING STRATEGY

Reading Organizer As you read this section, create an outline of the section. Use the headings from the section in your outline.

When you think of Earth's atmosphere, you probably think of sunlight, clouds, wind, rain, and many other phenomena that you can see. However, Earth's atmosphere affects our planet in very important ways that are not immediately visible.

For example, changes in atmospheric temperature and pressure influence Earth's weather. Atmospheric gases, such as carbon dioxide, water vapor, and methane, absorb energy and keep Earth warm. And ozone—a molecule of oxygen that contains three oxygen atoms, O_3—forms a layer in the atmosphere that absorbs harmful ultraviolet radiation.

Composition of the Atmosphere

Earth is surrounded by a mixture of gases called the *atmosphere.* Earth's atmosphere extends outward some 500 km from the surface of Earth. However, the majority of atmospheric gases are concentrated within 12 km of Earth's surface.

Figure 1 shows the gases that compose the atmosphere. Nitrogen, N_2, makes up 78% of the atmosphere by volume. Nitrogen is put into the atmosphere mostly by microorganisms and volcanic eruptions. Oxygen, O_2, makes up 21% of the atmosphere by volume. Oxygen is released by plants through photosynthesis. Oxygen is used by both plants and animals during respiration. Other important gases in the atmosphere include water vapor, carbon dioxide, and argon. These three gases make up nearly 1% of atmospheric gases. The atmosphere also contains small particles, which include dust, volcanic ash, sea salt, and smoke.

Figure 1 Composition of the Atmosphere

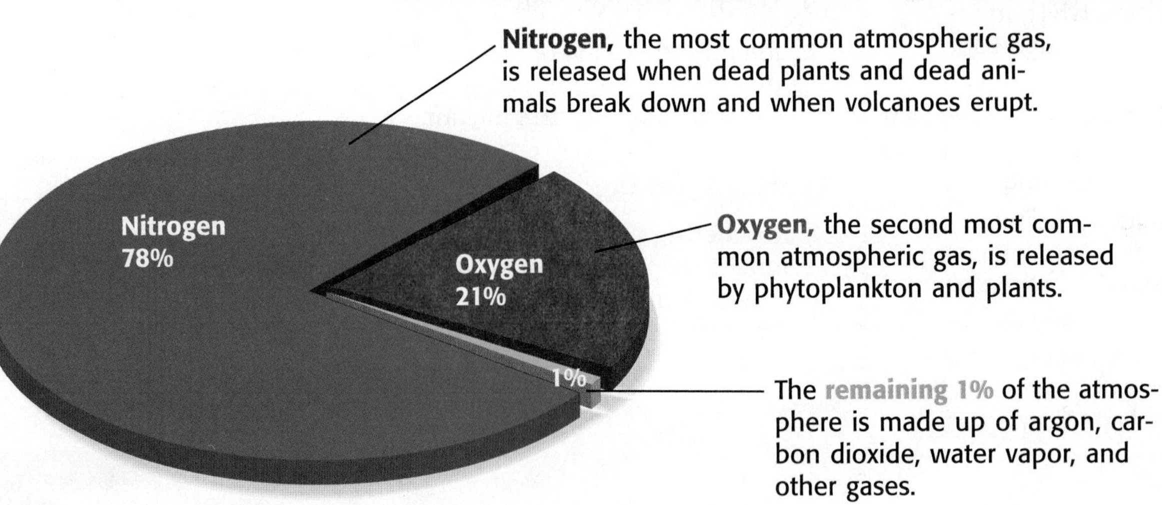

Nitrogen, the most common atmospheric gas, is released when dead plants and dead animals break down and when volcanoes erupt.

Oxygen, the second most common atmospheric gas, is released by phytoplankton and plants.

The remaining 1% of the atmosphere is made up of argon, carbon dioxide, water vapor, and other gases.

Layers in the Atmosphere

Earth's atmosphere is made up of four layers, which are classified by their altitude and temperature, as shown in **Figure 2.** The major gases, nitrogen and oxygen, occur in the same proportions throughout the atmosphere. Carbon dioxide is also well mixed. Some other gases, such as water vapor and ozone, have varying concentrations.

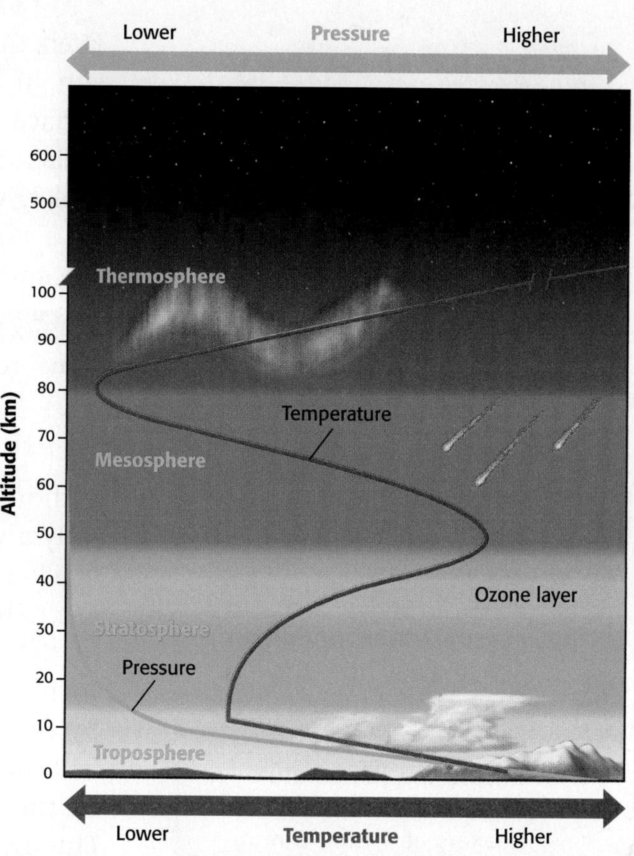

Figure 2 *Scientists divide Earth's atmosphere into four distinct layers. The way temperature varies with altitude is easy to see in this diagram.*

The Troposphere

The *troposphere* is the atmospheric layer in which we live. It extends from the surface of Earth to an altitude of about 12 km. **Figure 2** shows that as altitude increases in the troposphere, temperature and atmospheric pressure decrease. Water vapor is restricted mainly to the troposphere. Thus, weather, such as rain, snow, and clouds, is also restricted to the troposphere. Depending on location and temperature, water vapor varies from 0.1% to 3% of atmospheric gases in the troposphere.

The Stratosphere

The atmospheric layer immediately above the troposphere is the *stratosphere,* which extends up to about 50 km. Here, temperature rises with altitude. The reason is that incoming solar ultraviolet (UV) radiation interacts with oxygen to form ozone. This stratospheric ozone forms a layer from about 15 km to 40 km in altitude in the middle of the stratosphere. The ozone layer is very important because it absorbs ultraviolet radiation from the sun that can damage or kill organisms.

The Mesosphere

Above the stratosphere is the *mesosphere.* The mesosphere extends up to 80 km. It is the coldest layer of the atmosphere. Temperatures can reach –93°C at the top of the mesosphere.

The Thermosphere

The layer farthest from Earth's surface is the *thermosphere.* This layer extends from 80 km to 500 km. Oxygen molecules in the thermosphere absorb incoming solar UV radiation, causing temperatures to reach 2,000°C. Oxygen and nitrogen also absorb harmful X-ray and gamma-ray radiation from space.

Reading Check **Show that you can differentiate the layers of Earth's atmosphere by stating one fact about each layer.** *(See the Appendix for answers to Reading Checks.)*

The Heat Is On!

1. Fill **two 250 mL beakers** with **water.** Use a **thermometer** to record the initial temperature of the water in both beakers. The temperature of the water should be the same for both beakers.
2. Wrap one beaker with **white paper,** and wrap one with **black paper.** Secure the paper with a piece of **tape.**
3. Place a **150 W floodlight** 50 cm away from the beakers, and turn the light on.
4. Record the temperature of the water in both beakers at 1 min, 5 min, and 10 min.
5. Is energy being transferred to the beakers by radiation, conduction, or convection? Explain your answer.

Energy from the Sun to Earth

Even though we live almost 150 million kilometers from the sun, it is the source of 99% of the thermal energy on the surface of Earth. The energy from the sun is transmitted by **radiation** as electromagnetic waves. These waves include ultraviolet, visible light, and infrared (IR). When you are outside on a sunny day, you can feel the radiation from the sun warm the surface of your body.

Reading Check **Identify the various forms in which energy comes to Earth from the sun.**

Heating the Atmosphere and Earth's Surface

Although the sun releases an enormous amount of energy, only a very small percentage of the sun's total energy actually reaches Earth's surface. As shown in **Figure 3,** about 25% of the radiant energy that Earth receives from the sun is *reflected* by the atmosphere. Sources of reflection in Earth's atmosphere include clouds and air. Another 5% of solar energy is *reflected* by the surface of Earth, particularly by ice and snow. Another 25% of the energy that Earth receives from the sun is *absorbed* by the atmosphere—by atmospheric gases, clouds, and ozone. Finally, 45% of the solar energy that Earth receives is *absorbed* by Earth's surface—the land and the oceans.

Figure 3 *Energy from the sun is absorbed by the atmosphere, land, and water and is changed into thermal energy.*

About **25%** is scattered and reflected by clouds and air.

About **25%** is absorbed by ozone, clouds, and atmospheric gases.

About **5%** is reflected by Earth's surface.

About **45%** is absorbed by Earth's surface.

Energy Transfer

As you have already learned, the energy from the sun is transmitted to Earth in the form of radiation. When this energy reaches Earth, the energy is transferred in two other ways. One way energy is transferred is by conduction. **Conduction** is the transfer of thermal energy through a material. Thermal energy is always transferred from a hotter area to a colder area, such as your warm feet to a cold floor. When air molecules come into direct contact with the warm surface of Earth, thermal energy is transferred to the atmosphere.

The second and more common way energy is transferred in Earth's atmosphere is by convection. **Convection** is the transfer of thermal energy by the circulation of a liquid or a gas.

In Earth's atmosphere, as a general rule, currents of warm, less dense air rise into the atmosphere, and currents of cold, dense air sink toward Earth's surface. As a current of warm air rises into the atmosphere from Earth's surface, the current begins to cool. As the air current cools, it becomes denser than the air that surrounds it. When the current can no longer rise, it begins sinking back toward Earth's surface. As this cool air sinks, it pushes currents of warm air away from Earth's surface. This continuous cycle of warm air rising and cool air sinking is called a *convection current* and is shown in **Figure 4.**

radiation the transfer of energy as electromagnetic waves

conduction the transfer of energy as heat through a material

convection the transfer of thermal energy by the circulation or movement of a liquid or gas

Figure 4 *The processes of radiation, conduction, and convection heat Earth and its atmosphere.*

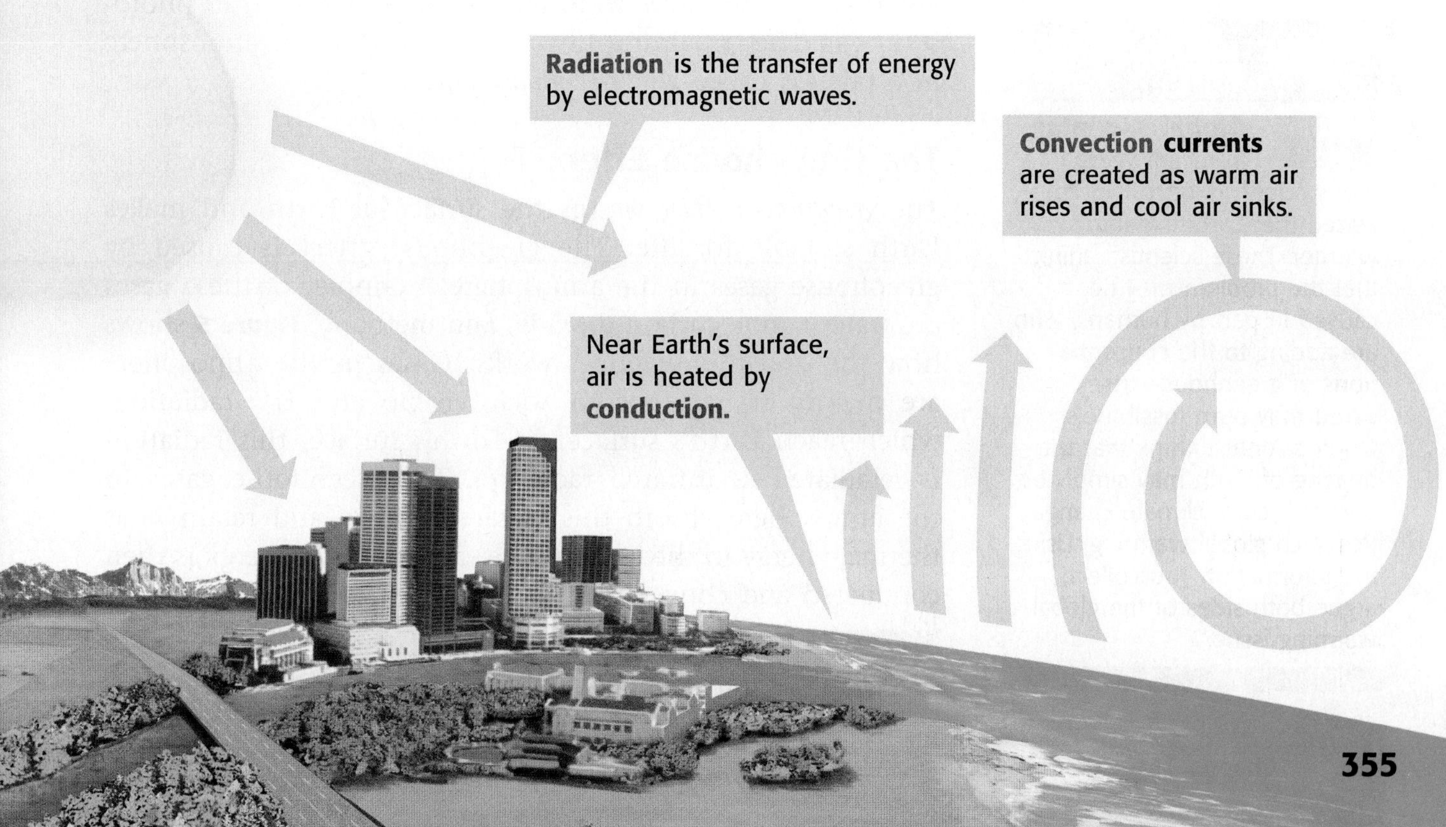
Radiation is the transfer of energy by electromagnetic waves.
Convection currents are created as warm air rises and cool air sinks.
Near Earth's surface, air is heated by **conduction.**

Figure 5 The Greenhouse Effect

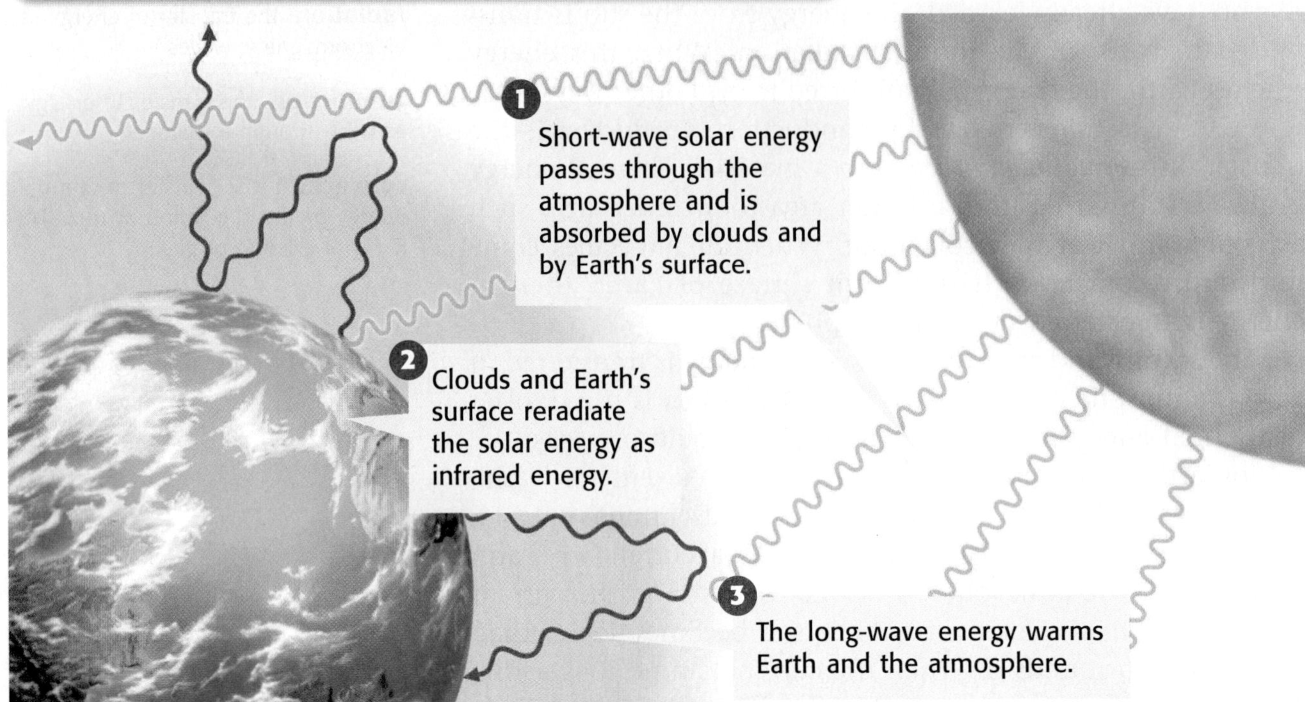

1
Short-wave solar energy passes through the atmosphere and is absorbed by clouds and by Earth's surface.
2
Clouds and Earth's surface reradiate the solar energy as infrared energy.
3
The long-wave energy warms Earth and the atmosphere.

Earth's Energy Budget

The 45% of solar energy that is absorbed by Earth's surface is important for Earth's processes. Approximately 20% of this energy causes water to evaporate from the ocean. Evaporation transfers water vapor to the atmosphere. About 6% of the energy is transferred from the land to the atmosphere as rising air masses. Another 5% is reradiated into the atmosphere, and less than 1% produces wind and waves and is used in photosynthesis. The remaining 13% is reabsorbed by the atmosphere in a process called the *greenhouse effect.*

CONNECTION TO Environmental Science

WRITING SKILL **Global Warming** In recent years, many scientists have hypothesized that Earth is getting warmer. These scientists think that the problem may be caused in part by humans, who are adding to the concentrations of greenhouse gases when they burn fossil fuels. Other scientists think that the heating of Earth may simply be part of cyclical climate change. Research global warming. Using the information you collect, argue both sides of the global-warming issue.

The Greenhouse Effect

The *greenhouse effect* warms the surface of Earth and makes Earth suitable for life. The greenhouse effect is caused by greenhouse gases in the atmosphere. Examples of these gases are water vapor, carbon dioxide, and methane. **Figure 5** shows how the greenhouse effect works. Gases in the atmosphere are mainly transparent to solar visible and UV radiation, which reach Earth's surface. At Earth's surface, this radiation is reradiated as infrared radiation. The greenhouse gases in the atmosphere absorb this infrared energy and retain it as thermal energy in the atmosphere. This thermal energy is then conducted and convected to the surface, warming it.

Reading Check **Explain how the reradiation of infrared radiation from Earth's surface affects Earth's temperature.**

The Ozone Shield

As you have already learned, concentrated ozone forms a layer in the stratosphere. This layer of ozone is found from approximately 15 km to 40 km above Earth's surface. This layer of ozone is very important because it protects life from damage caused by UV radiation from the sun. Ozone forms a shield that absorbs 95% to 99% of this harmful UV radiation.

UV radiation can damage the DNA of an organism. DNA contains the information that determines the traits that an organism inherits and needs to live. The damaging effects of UV light on humans can include skin cancer, wrinkling of the skin, and a weakening of the immune response.

Making Ozone

How many molecules of ozone, O_3, can be made from 12 molecules of oxygen gas, O_2?

SECTION Review

Summary

- The atmosphere is made up of mostly nitrogen gas and oxygen gas.
- Earth's atmosphere is divided into layers based on altitude and temperature.
- The processes of radiation, conduction, and convection heat Earth and its atmosphere.
- The greenhouse effect warms Earth's surface and makes Earth suitable for life.
- The ozone layer protects life on Earth from damage caused by UV radiation from the sun.

Using Key Terms

1. Use *radiation, conduction,* and *convection* in the same sentence.

Understanding Key Ideas

2. What is the best example of thermal conduction?
   - **a.** a light bulb warming a lampshade
   - **b.** an egg cooking on a frying pan
   - **c.** water boiling in a pot
   - **d.** gasses circulating in the atmosphere
3. Identify the gases that compose Earth's atmosphere.
4. Compare and contrast the layers of Earth's atmosphere.
5. Explain how the greenhouse effect warms Earth.
6. Explain the importance of the ozone layer to life on Earth.

Math Skills

7. If an average cloud has a density of 0.5 g/m^3 and has a volume of 1,000,000,000 m^3. What is the mass of an average cloud?

Critical Thinking

8. **Making Comparisons** Compare the ways in which conduction and convection transfer heat in the atmosphere.
9. **Making Predictions** Predict how the temperatures on Earth might be affected if the percentage of greenhouse gases in the atmosphere were to increase.

SCILINKS
NSTA
Developed and maintained by the National Science Teachers Association
For a variety of links related to this chapter, go to www.scilinks.org
Topic: The Atmosphere
SciLinks code: HSM0112

SECTION 3

The Hydrosphere and Biosphere

What You Will Learn

- Describe the global pattern of ocean currents.
- Describe how thermal energy is transferred globally and locally by ocean water.
- Explain how groundwater is stored in aquifers underground.
- Explain why life on Earth is dependent on energy from the sun.
- Describe how energy in the biosphere is cycled by decomposition.

Vocabulary

surface current
deep current
aquifer

READING STRATEGY

Discussion Read this section silently. Write down questions that you have about this section. Discuss your questions in a small group.

"Water, water, everywhere." You have probably heard this expression before, but do you realize how great the amount of water on Earth really is?

Earth's hydrosphere covers 71% of Earth's surface. It includes the water that is visible in the oceans, lakes, rivers, glaciers, and polar ice caps. However, the hydrosphere also includes clouds, rain, and snow in the atmosphere and water in the pores of underground rocks.

The Global Ocean

The global ocean, a portion of which is shown in **Figure 1,** is the largest reservoir of water on Earth. The global ocean contains more than 97% of all water on Earth and covers a surface area of approximately 335 million square kilometers.

As you know, the water in the global ocean is salty. If you evaporate a 1,000 g sample of ocean water, you are left with 35 g of salts. For this reason, ocean water is denser than fresh water. The majority of these salts are table salt, which is made up of the elements sodium and chlorine.

The temperature of surface ocean water varies from warm at the equator to near freezing at the poles. Ocean water temperature also decreases with depth. The surface water located in the top 100 to 200 m of the ocean is much warmer than deeper water.

Figure 1 *In this satellite view of Earth, the Florida Peninsula separates the Gulf of Mexico (above) from the Atlantic Ocean (below).*

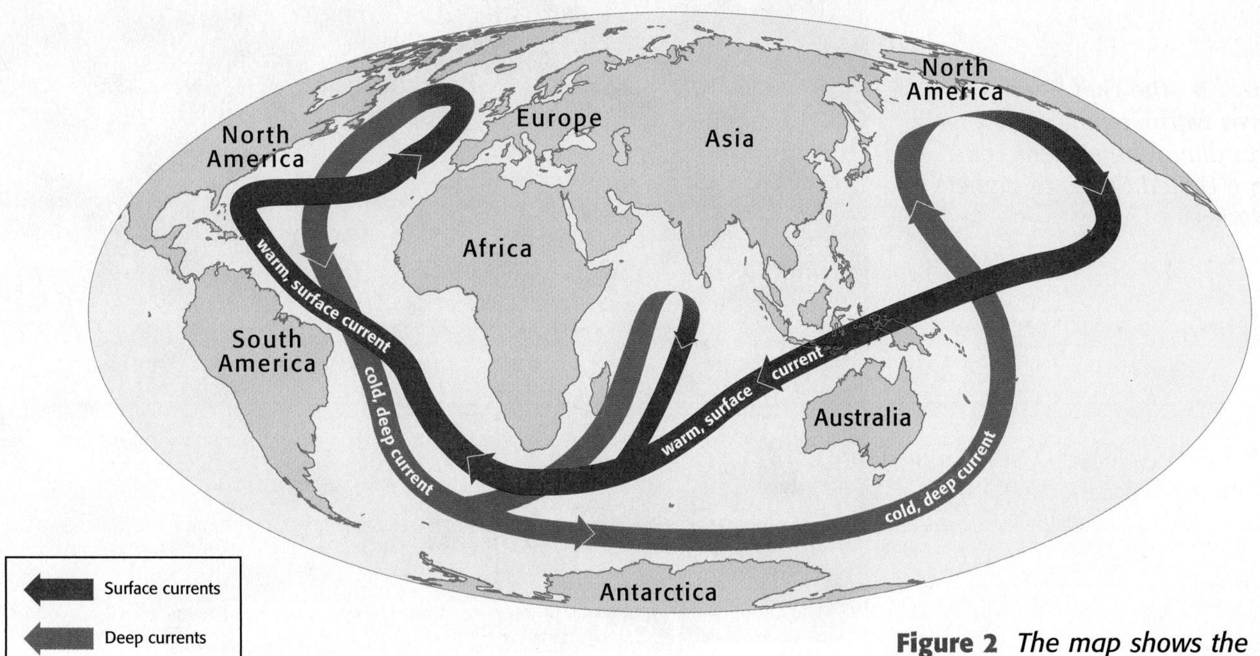

Figure 2 *The map shows the flow directions of ocean currents–the ocean conveyor belt. Warm-water currents are shown as red arrows; cold-water currents are shown as blue arrows.*

Ocean Currents

Ocean water contains streamlike movements of water called *ocean currents*. Ocean currents are either surface currents or deep currents. Both types of currents are part of the global pattern of ocean currents known as the *ocean conveyor belt*.

Surface Currents

The surface currents of the global ocean are shown above in **Figure 2. Surface currents** are horizontal, streamlike movements of water that occur at or near the surface of the ocean. Surface currents are driven mainly by winds. They can reach depths of several hundred meters and lengths of several thousand kilometers, and they can travel across oceans.

surface current a horizontal movement of ocean water that is caused by wind and that occurs at or near the ocean's surface

deep current a streamlike movement of ocean water far below the surface

Deep Currents

Deep currents, also shown in **Figure 2,** are streamlike movements of water that are located far below the ocean surface. Because deep currents are located near the ocean bottom, they are not controlled by the wind. Instead, these currents result when cold and, therefore, dense surface water sinks and flows along the bottom of the ocean. As shown in **Figure 2,** deep currents flow from the North Atlantic Ocean to Antarctica and then into the Pacific Ocean. Bottom water then flows northward toward Alaska, where the water rises to the surface again. This journey takes more than a thousand years.

Reading Check **Explain how ocean currents form the global pattern known as the *ocean conveyor belt*.** (*See the Appendix for answers to Reading Checks.*)

Figure 3 *The Gulf Stream moves warm, equatorial water north along the eastern coast of the United States to higher latitudes.*

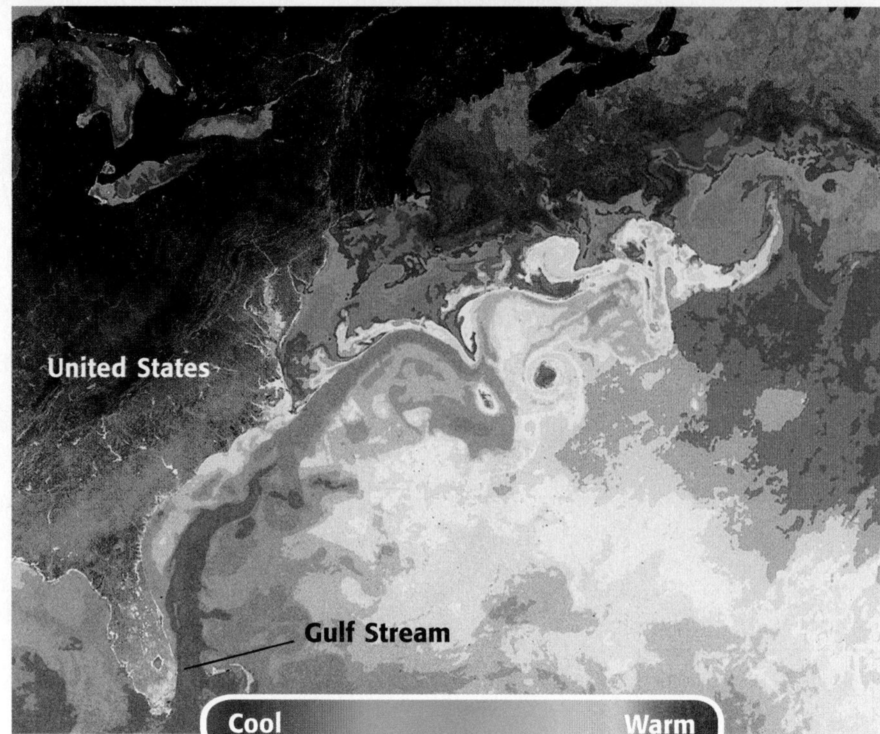

A Global Temperature Regulator

The global ocean is a reservoir for thermal energy from the sun. Because the global ocean covers such a large area of the surface of Earth, the global ocean absorbs much of the 45% of solar energy that reaches Earth.

Ocean water warms as it absorbs thermal energy near the equator. As the surface currents flow, this energy is transferred to midlatitudes. **Figure 3** shows how a surface current called the *Gulf Stream* transports warm, equatorial water northward. As a result of this thermal energy transfer by the Gulf Stream, Florida and even the British Isles are several degrees warmer than are other coastal areas at similar latitudes.

The transfer of thermal energy by flowing water is much more efficient than the transfer of thermal energy stored on land. The reason for this difference lies in the fact that thermal energy from the land is moved by wind. Unlike ocean water, wind does not distribute thermal energy evenly over Earth's surface.

Comparing Temperature
With a parent or guardian, check your local newspaper for the high and low temperatures in your town on a specific date. Check the same temperatures for another town that is located at the same or a similar latitude. Try to choose a town that is located closer to or farther from the ocean than the town in which you live. Are the temperatures in your town higher or lower than those of the other town? Do the temperatures of the town located nearer to the ocean appear to be influenced by the moderating effect of the ocean?

Local Climate

Ocean water warms and cools more slowly than the land nearby. Therefore, the ocean can keep the summer temperatures of land near the water cooler. It can also make winter temperatures warmer. Coastal areas can be many degrees warmer or cooler than areas that are located 30 or more kilometers inland.

Reading Check **Explain how heat from the ocean can affect temperatures on land.**

Fresh Water

Only 2.8% of all the water on Earth is fresh water. Fresh water occurs as polar ice caps, glaciers, lakes, rivers, and streams. Polar ice caps and glaciers contain about 77% of Earth's fresh water. Lakes, such as the five Great Lakes of North America, are another reservoir of fresh water. Surprisingly, all lakes account for only about 0.003% of fresh water. Rivers and streams compose another 0.00004% of fresh water.

In Florida, much of the surface fresh water is found in the Everglades. The Everglades is a giant, slow-moving wetland that flows south from Lake Okeechobee to Florida Bay. A small portion of the Everglades is shown in **Figure 4.**

Figure 4 *The wetlands known as* the Everglades *cover more than 19,000 km^2 of South Florida.*

Groundwater

Groundwater is surface water that has seeped into the ground over time. Below ground, groundwater is stored in microscopic cracks in rocks and in the pores between rock grains. Although we cannot see this groundwater, it represents 22% of the fresh water on Earth.

Bodies of rock below the ground that contain groundwater are called **aquifers.** Groundwater aquifers that occur in the continental United States are shown on the map in **Figure 5.** The groundwater from aquifers is made available for human use by pumping from wells. Groundwater that is pumped from aquifers must be replaced. The process by which groundwater seeps back into aquifers from Earth's surface is called *recharge.* Recharge is part of Earth's groundwater cycling process.

aquifer a body of rock or sediment that stores groundwater and allows the flow of groundwater

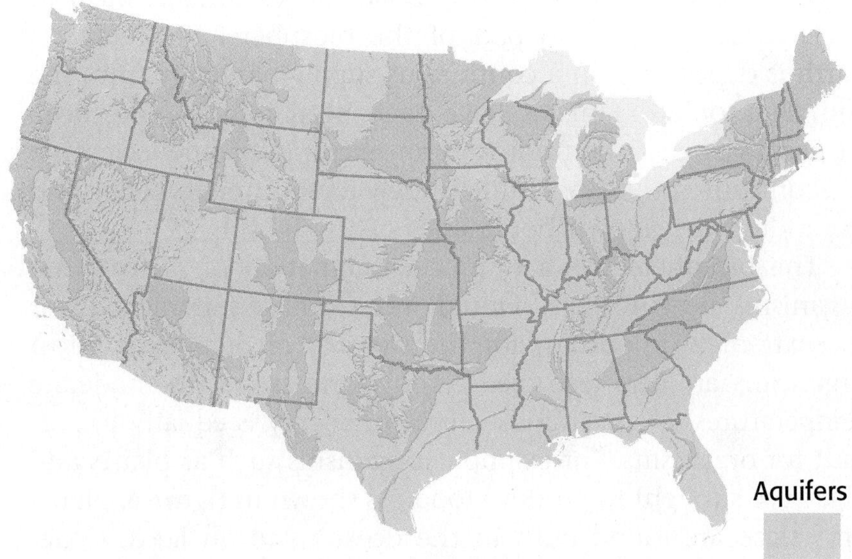

Figure 5 *The continental United States has extensive groundwater aquifers. The water from these aquifers has many agricultural, industrial, and municipal uses.*

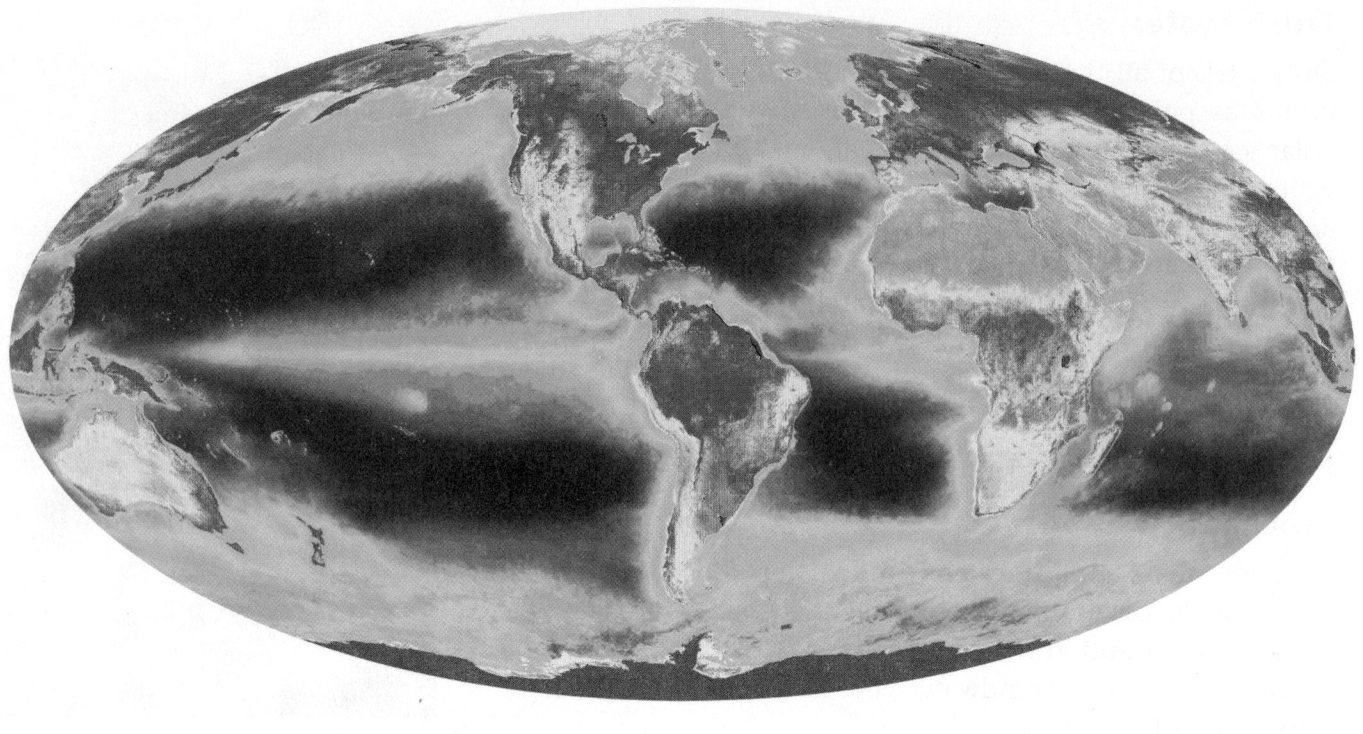

Figure 6 *The colors in this image of Earth indicate the concentrations of plant life in the oceans and on land.*

The Biosphere

Life on Earth is found in a variety of habitats. These habitats are collectively called *the biosphere.* The biosphere includes the part of the atmosphere that extends from the surface of Earth to approximately 11 km above Earth's surface. Most of the hydrosphere is also part of the biosphere. Most life on Earth is dependent on a continuous supply of energy from the sun. But some organisms have even been found living deep in Earth's crust. This finding is an example of how scientists are continuing to discover life in new environments today and expanding the known boundaries of the biosphere.

The biosphere has a unique combination of factors that organisms need for life. Liquid water and a suitable habitat are extremely important for the survival of organisms. Most organisms are also restricted to environments with moderate temperatures. A continuous source of energy is equally important for organisms. For example, organisms such as plants and algae use sunlight to produce food. As shown in **Figure 6,** plants and algae are found both in the oceans and on land. Other organisms get their food from consuming plants and algae.

✓ *Reading Check* **Explain why organisms are dependent on a continuous supply of energy from the sun.**

Energy Flow in the Biosphere

What happens to plants and animals when they die? Dead organisms are consumed by decomposers, such as bacteria and insects. By breaking down dead plant and animal matter, decomposers obtain the energy that they need to live. The process of decomposition releases carbon dioxide and water. Some of this carbon dioxide will be used by plants during photosynthesis to make sugars. During decomposition, some bacteria release nitrogen into the soil in a form that plants can use. Plants use this form of nitrogen in many activities, such as making new proteins.

Reading Check **Explain how energy in the biosphere is cycled by the process of decomposition.**

SECTION Review

Summary

- The largest reservoir of water on Earth is the global ocean.
- Ocean currents form a global pattern known as the ocean conveyor belt.
- Thermal energy is transferred both globally and locally by ocean water.
- Fresh water represents 2.8% of all water on Earth. Groundwater for human use is located underground in aquifers.
- The biosphere is the part of Earth where all life is found. Energy in the biosphere is cycled by the process of decomposition.

Using Key Terms

1. Write an original definition for *surface current* and *deep current*.

Understanding Key Ideas

2. Describe the global pattern of ocean currents.
3. Describe how thermal energy is transferred globally and locally by ocean currents.
4. Explain how groundwater is stored underground in aquifers.
5. Explain the importance of energy from the sun to life on Earth.
6. Explain how decomposers recycle energy in the biosphere.

Math Skills

7. Groundwater flows at a speed of 4km/h. At this rate, how long will it take water to flow 10km?

Critical Thinking

8. **Analyzing Processes** Why can the process of aquifer recharge be considered a natural event that occurs in a pattern?
9. **Analyzing Ideas** Identify a new environment on Earth whose discovery would cause scientists to expand the known boundaries of the biosphere. Explain.
10. **Identifing Relationships** Explain how urban growth might affect the recharge of an area's groundwater.

SECTION 4

The Cycling of Matter

What You Will Learn

- Explain how rock is continuously recycled in the rock cycle.
- Identify the steps in the water cycle.
- Describe how carbon cycles through the carbon cycle.
- Describe how nitrogen cycles through the nitrogen cycle.

Vocabulary

rock cycle
water cycle
carbon cycle
nitrogen cycle

READING STRATEGY

Prediction Guide Before reading this section, write the title of each heading in this section. Next, under each heading, write what you think you will learn.

Have you ever asked yourself, Why is it that I always have water to drink and air to breathe? Why don't we run out of resources?

The answer is that matter on Earth is recycled. Earth is a closed system into which very little new matter enters. So, existing matter must cycle continuously for this planet to support life. Water, carbon, nitrogen, and even rocks move through cycles. If these materials did not cycle, Earth could not support life.

The Rock Cycle

Rocks in Earth's crust are classified into three types: sedimentary, metamorphic, and igneous. Different geologic processes can change each of these rock types into one of the three types of rocks. This cycle, in which rock is changed by geologic processes into different types of rock, is called the **rock cycle.** As shown in **Figure 1,** rock may cycle through the rock cycle in various ways. As a rock moves through the rock cycle, heat, pressure, weathering, erosion, melting, cooling, or a combination of these variables can change a rock's identity. The process of change a rock goes through next depends on where the rock is in the rock cycle.

Figure 1 The Rock Cycle

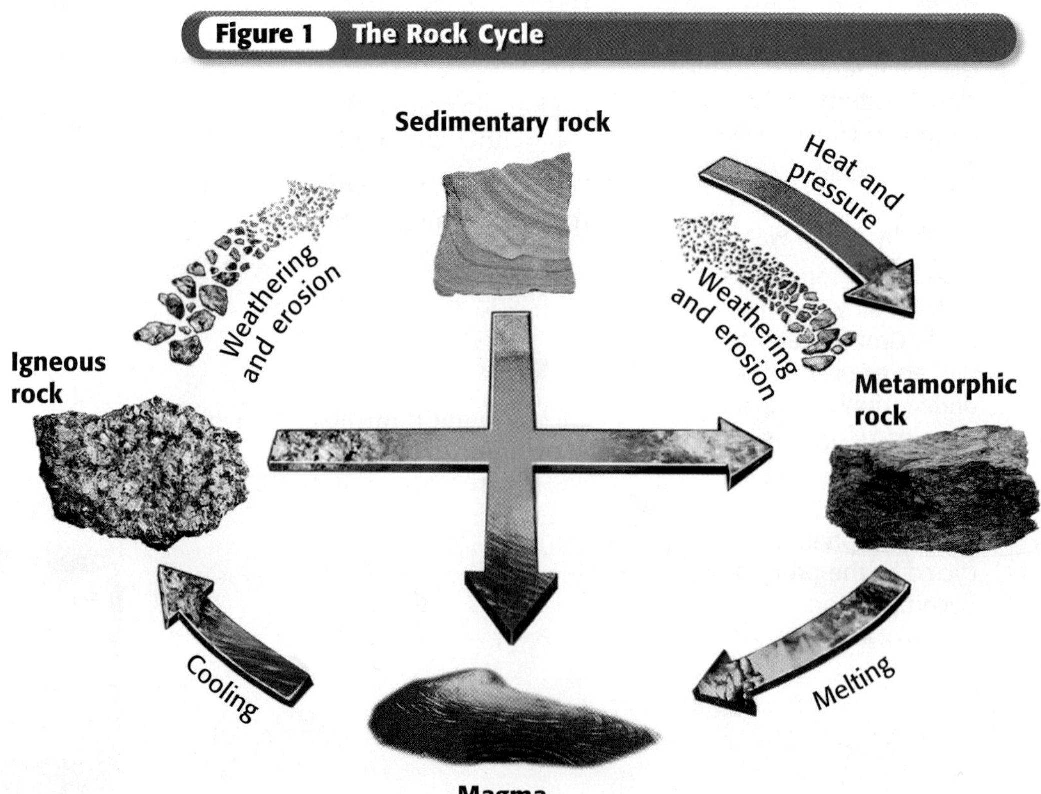

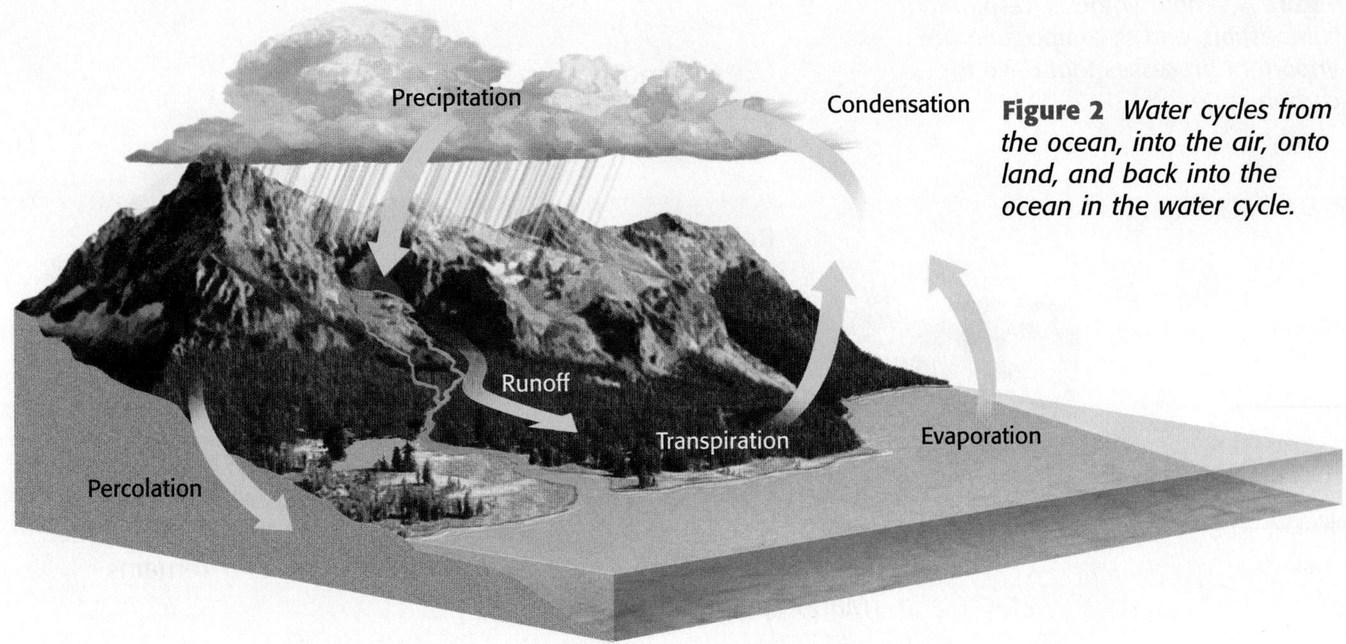

Figure 2 *Water cycles from the ocean, into the air, onto land, and back into the ocean in the water cycle.*

The Water Cycle

Water moves continuously from the ocean, to the atmosphere, to the land, and back to the ocean. This process is called the **water cycle,** and is shown in **Figure 2.**

Steps in the water cycle include evaporation, transpiration, condensation, precipitation, runoff, and percolation. *Evaporation* occurs when liquid water in the ocean and on Earth's surface changes into water vapor, a gas. Water vapor is also released into the air through pores, called *stomata,* on the leaves of plants. This process is known as *transpiration.* After water vapor is released, it rises into the atmosphere. There, it cools and turns into liquid water droplets. This change in water from a gas to a liquid is called *condensation.* When water droplets become heavy enough, gravity causes them to fall back to Earth as *precipitation.* Rain, snow, and hail are all forms of precipitation. The majority of precipitation never reaches the land surface. It falls directly into the ocean.

Precipitation that does reach the land surface may fill lakes, streams, and rivers and eventually return to the ocean. This movement of water over the land surface is called *runoff.* Water moves across Earth's land surface from higher to lower elevations under the influence of gravity.

Some water does not run off the land surface. Gravity may move the water downward through spaces in rock or soil to become groundwater. This downward movement of groundwater is called *percolation.*

Reading Check **Describe the process by which water moves through the water cycle.** (*See the Appendix for answers to Reading Checks.*)

rock cycle the series of processes in which a rock forms, changes from one type to another, is destroyed, and forms again by geologic processes

water cycle the continuous movement of water between the atmosphere, the land, and the oceans

Figure 3 *Photosynthesis, respiration, combustion, and decomposition are important processes that drive the carbon cycle.*

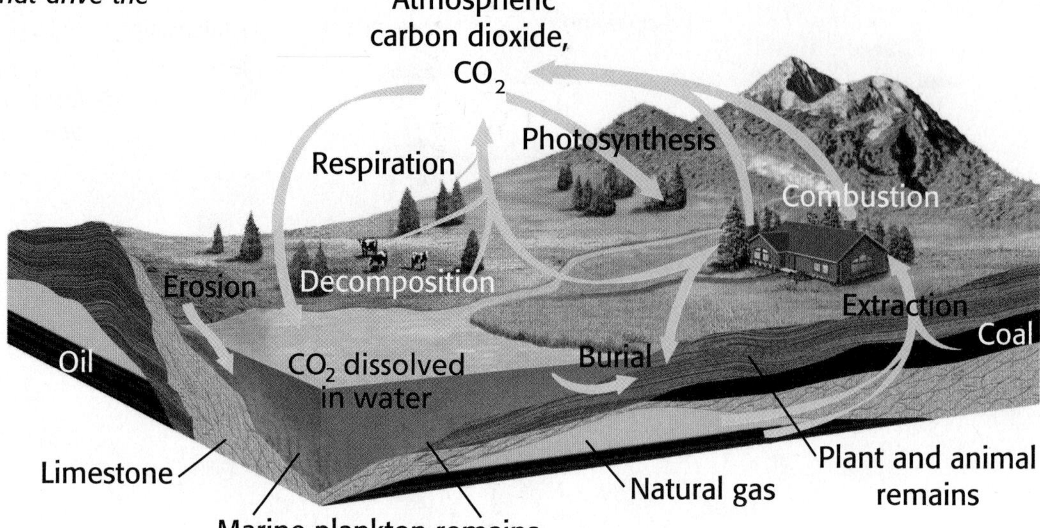

CONNECTION TO Biology

Deep-Sea Dining Some deep-sea tube worms have bacteria living inside them. These bacteria use gases to produce nutrition in the form of organic carbon. Any extra nutrition is transferred to the tube worms. This relationship that is beneficial to the tube worm and the bacteria is called *mutualism*. Research other organisms that benefit from mutualism, and write a report on what you have learned.

The Carbon Cycle

With the exception of water molecules, the most common molecules in organisms are molecules that contain carbon. The cycling of carbon between the atmosphere, land, water, and organisms is called the **carbon cycle.**

Photosynthesis plays a key role in the carbon cycle. During the process of photosynthesis, plants use sunlight, atmospheric carbon dioxide, and water to make sugars for nutrition. Most organisms obtain the carbon and the energy they need by consuming plants or by consuming other organisms. When organisms break down sugar molecules to release energy, carbon is returned to the environment as carbon dioxide. This process, called *respiration,* occurs in the cells of organisms. The byproducts of respiration are carbon dioxide and water. These byproducts can be reused in photosynthesis.

Carbon dioxide is also released into the environment during the process of decomposition. *Decomposition* occurs when organisms such as bacteria, fungi, or insects break down organic matter into simple molecules. When partially decomposed organic matter is deeply buried and heated, it is chemically transformed over millions of years into fuels, such as coal, gas, and oil. When humans burn these fuels, carbon returns to the atmosphere as carbon dioxide. This is an example of *combustion,* the process by which substances are burned to release energy.

Reading Check **Explain why the carbon cycle is important to Earth's organisms.**

The Nitrogen Cycle

The movement of nitrogen between the environment and organisms is called the **nitrogen cycle,** which is shown in **Figure 4.** Certain bacteria in soil change atmospheric nitrogen into forms of nitrogen that plants can use. Other organisms obtain the nitrogen they need from plants. When organisms die, decomposers release this nitrogen back into the soil. Plants then take up some of this nitrogen. Some bacteria in soil change this nitrogen into atmospheric nitrogen, which returns to the atmosphere.

carbon cycle the movement of carbon from the nonliving environment into living things and back

nitrogen cycle the process in which nitrogen circulates among the air, soil, water, plants, and animals in an ecosystem

Nitrogen in plants is consumed by animals.

Bacteria in soil change nitrogen into N_2.

Bacteria in soil change N_2 into nitrogen plants can use.

Decomposition releases nitrogen into the soil.

Figure 4 *The nitrogen cycle includes bacteria, plants, and animals.*

SECTION Review

Summary

- The process in which a rock forms, changes from one type to another, is destroyed, and forms again by geologic processes is called the *rock cycle*.
- In the water cycle, water moves continuously from the ocean, to the atmosphere, to land, and back to the ocean.
- Substances that are necessary for life are continuously cycled in the carbon cycle and nitrogen cycle.

Using Key Terms

1. Use *rock cycle, water cycle, carbon cycle,* and *nitrogen cycle* in the same sentence.

Understanding Key Ideas

2. Explain how rock is continuously recycled in the rock cycle.
3. Identify the steps in the water cycle.
4. Describe how carbon cycles through the carbon cycle.
5. Describe how nitrogen cycles through the nitrogen cycle.

Critical Thinking

6. **Analyzing Ideas** What is the importance of gravity in the movement of water in the water cycle?
7. **Identifing Relationships** The processes of photosynthesis, respiration, combustion, and decomposition are all part of the carbon cycle. In which process do organisms take up carbon? Explain.

SCILINKS
NSTA
Developed and maintained by the National Science Teachers Association
For a variety of links related to this chapter, go to www.scilinks.org
Topic: Water Cycle, Cycles of Matter
SciLinks code: HSM1626; HSM0303

Model-Making Lab

Metamorphic Mash

OBJECTIVES

Model the process of metamorphism.

Describe how the process of metamorphism can reorganize the mineral grains within a rock.

MATERIALS

- cardboard (or plywood), very stiff, small pieces
- clay, modeling
- knife, plastic
- sequins (or other small flat objects)

SAFETY

Metamorphism is a complex process that takes place deep within the Earth, where the temperature and pressure would turn a human into a crispy pancake. The effects of this extreme temperature and pressure are obvious in some metamorphic rocks. One of these effects is the reorganization of mineral grains within the rock. This reorganization of mineral grains can result in a metamorphic rock that has a foliated texture. A foliated metamorphic rock has its mineral grains arranged in planes or bands. Examples of foliated metamorphic rocks are slate, phyllite, schist, and gneiss. In this activity, you will investigate the process of metamorphism without being charred, flattened, or buried.

Procedure

1. Flatten the clay into a layer about 1 cm thick.
2. Sprinkle the surface of the clay with sequins.
3. Roll the corners of the clay toward the middle to form a neat ball.
4. Carefully use the plastic knife to cut the ball in half.
5. On a separate sheet of paper, describe the position and location of the sequins inside the ball that you cut in half.
6. Put the ball back together, and use the sheets of cardboard or plywood to flatten the ball until it is a slab that is about 2 cm thick.
7. Using the plastic knife, slice open the slab of clay in several places.
8. Describe the position and location of the sequins in the slab.

Analyze the Results

1. What physical process does flattening the ball represent?
2. Describe any changes in the position and location of the sequins that occurred as the clay ball was flattened into a slab.

Draw Conclusions

3. How are the sequins oriented in relation to the force you put on the ball to flatten it?

4. How does the orientation of the sequins in your clay ball model the reorganization of mineral grains in a metamorphic rock with a foliated texture? Explain your answer.

5. Do you think the orientation of the mineral grains in a foliated metamorphic rock tells you anything about the rock? (Think in terms of temperature and pressure.) Defend your answer.

Foliation

Applying Your Data

Suppose that you find a foliated metamorphic rock that has grains running in two distinct directions. Use what you have learned in this activity to offer a possible explanation for this observation.

Chapter Review

USING KEY TERMS

For each pair of terms, explain how the meanings of the terms differ.

1. *atmosphere* and *hydrosphere*
2. *deep current* and *surface current*
3. *crust* and *mantle*
4. *convection* and *conduction*
5. *rock cycle* and *water cycle*
6. *carbon cycle* and *nitrogen cycle*

UNDERSTANDING KEY IDEAS

Multiple Choice

7. The sphere of Earth in which all life is contained is called the
   a. geosphere. **c.** hydrosphere.
   b. atmosphere. **d.** biosphere.

8. At which rate do tectonic plates move around Earth's surface?
   a. meters per year
   b. kilometers per year
   c. centimeters per year
   d. micrometers per year

9. Which of the following types of radiant energy that comes from the sun can damage an organism's DNA?
   a. UV radiation **c.** infrared radiaton
   b. visible light **d.** microwaves

10. How is most thermal energy in the atmosphere transferred?
    a. by radiation **c.** by conduction
    b. by convection **d.** by diffusion

11. Which of the following is a property of deep currents?
    a. Deep currents contain warm water.
    b. Deep currents flow along the ocean bottom.
    c. Deep currents are controlled by the wind.
    d. Deep currents form when cold water rises to the ocean surfaces.

12. Which of the following processes in the water cycle takes place in the geosphere?
    a. condensation **c.** percolation
    b. evaporation **d.** precipitation

13. In which cycle does decomposition release carbon dioxide into the atmosphere?
    a. the water cycle
    b. the nitrogen cycle
    c. the rock cycle
    d. the carbon cycle

14. Only a small fraction of the energy radiated by the sun reaches Earth. What happens to the majority of the sun's energy that reaches Earth?
    a. It is absorbed by the land and ocean.
    b. It is reflected by clouds and air.
    c. It is reflected by Earth's surface.
    d. It is absorbed by ozone, clouds, and atmospheric gases.

Short Answer

15. Describe the way in which wind and moving water reshape Earth's surface.

16. Explain how the greenhouse effect makes life on Earth possible.

17 Describe the way in which thermal energy is transferred globally and locally by ocean water.

18 Explain why animals are dependent on a continuous supply of energy from the sun.

Math Skills

19 If the radius of Earth is 6,500 km and the radius of the core is 3,400 km, what percentage of Earth's radius does the core represent?

CRITICAL THINKING

20 **Concept Mapping** Use the following terms to create a concept map: *geosphere, crust, mantle, inner core, outer core, core, lithosphere, asthenosphere, mesosphere, compositional layer,* and *physical layer.*

21 **Analyzing Ideas** How do differences in density cause currents to flow both in the surface waters of the ocean and in the bottom waters of the ocean?

22 **Predicting Consequences** What might the consequences be for humans if groundwater is pumped from an aquifer at a much faster rate than the aquifer is recharging?

INTERPRETING GRAPHICS

The illustration below shows how temperature and pressure change with altitude in Earth's atmosphere. Use the illustration below to answer the questions that follow.

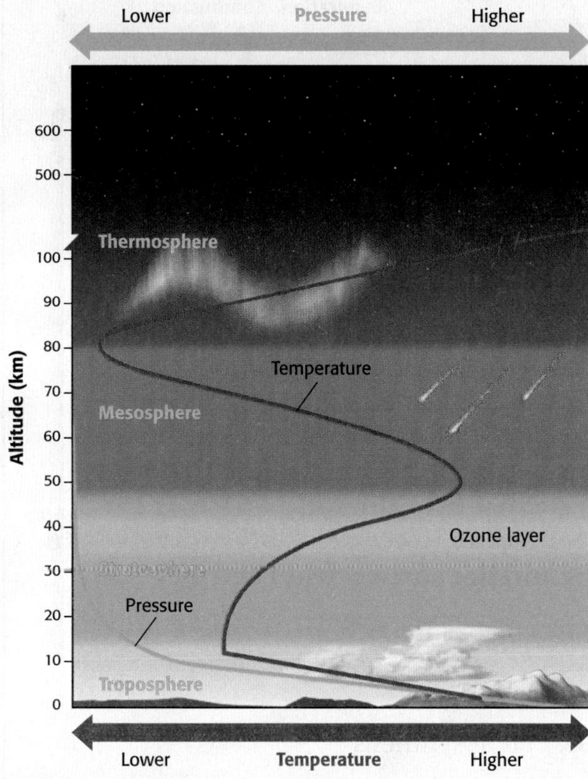

23 In which atmospheric layer is the temperature the coldest?

a. the troposphere
b. the stratosphere
c. the mesophere
d. the thermosphere

24 In which atmospheric layer is the pressure the highest?

a. the troposphere
b. the stratosphere
c. the mesophere
d. the thermosphere

Standardized Test Preparation

Multiple Choice

Use the illustration below to answer question 1.

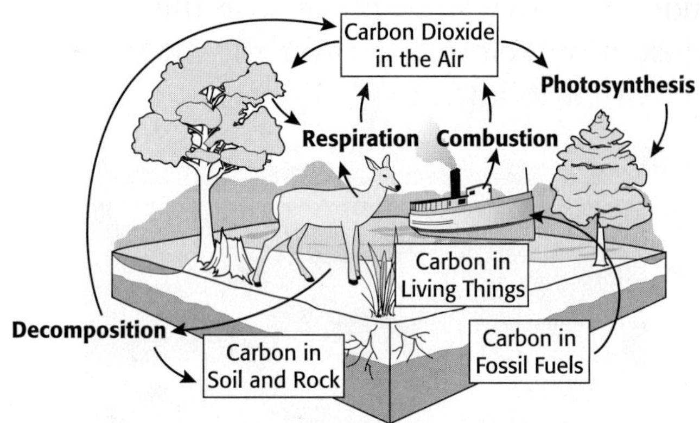

1. The illustration above shows the carbon cycle. During the carbon cycle, some carbon is released into the atmosphere and some carbon is released into the soil. Which of the following processes is most involved in removing carbon from the air?

A. combustion

B. decomposition

C. photosynthesis

D. respiration

2. In which layer of the atmosphere do people live?

A. stratosphere

B. mesosphere

C. troposphere

D. thermosphere

3. Which of the following occurs as a result of the forces generated by plate motion at tectonic plate boundaries?

A. erosion

B. earthquakes

C. sediment deposition

D. warm surface currents

4. Thermal energy flows from hot areas to cold areas. By what process is air near the Earth's surface heated by the surface?

A. conduction

B. convection

C. diffusion

D. radiation

5. Ocean currents are streamlike movements of ocean water. Ocean currents can either be deep currents or surface currents. Which of the following is true of surface currents?

A. They contain dense water.

B. They are cold-water currents.

C. They reach depths of several hundred meters.

D. They flow from the North Atlantic Ocean to the Pacific Ocean.

Use the illustration below to answer question 6.

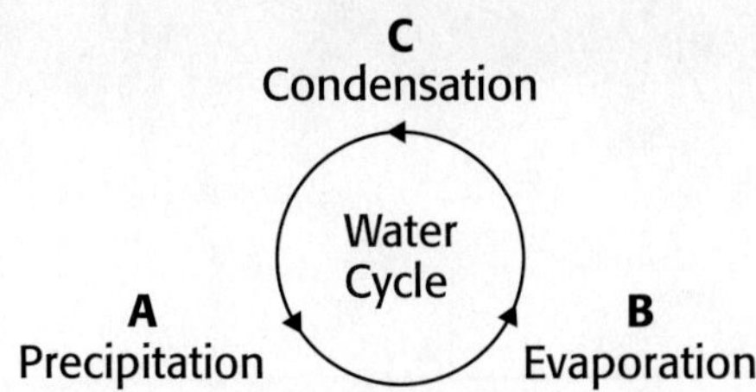

6. The water cycle depicted above involves energy changes and the continuous movement of water between the ground and the atmosphere. At which stage can water be in a solid state?

A. precipitation

B. evaporation

C. condensation

D. Both stages B and C.

7. In the rock cycle, which type of rock is formed by heating and pressure?

A. igneous rock

B. sedimentary rock

C. magma

D. metamorphic rock

8. The four divisions of the Earth are the geosphere, the atmosphere, the hydrosphere, and the biosphere. Conditions in one of the Earth's spheres can influence the conditions in one or more of the other three spheres. Which of the following statements is an example of how conditions that exist in the atmosphere directly influence the conditions that exist in the biosphere?

A. Evaporation transfers ocean water to the atmosphere.

B. A volcanic eruption ejects ash and gas into the atmosphere.

C. Partially decomposed organic matter is chemically transformed into fossil fuel over millions of years.

D. The ozone layer blocks much of the harmful ultraviolet radiation that would reach the Earth's surface.

Open Response

9. During the nitrogen cycle, nitrogen-fixing bacteria change nitrogen gas into a form of nitrogen that can be used by plants. Some pesticides that are used on soil can kill these helpful bacteria. How would the nitrogen cycle be affected if nitrogen-fixing bacteria were destroyed?

10. The ozone shield is a layer in the stratosphere. Why is it important to life on Earth?

Science in Action

Science, Technology, and Society

A "Ship" That Flips?

Does your school's laboratory have doors on the floor or tables bolted sideways to the walls? A lab like this exists, and you can find it floating in the ocean. *FLIP,* or *Floating Instrument Platform,* is a 108 m long ocean research vessel that can tilt 90°. *FLIP* is towed to an area that scientists want to study. To flip the vessel, empty chambers within the vessel are filled with water. The *FLIP* begins tilting until almost all of the vessel is underwater. Having most of the vessel below the ocean's surface stabilizes the vessel against wind and waves. Scientists can collect accurate data from the ocean, even during a hurricane!

Social Studies ACTIVITY

Design your own *FLIP*. Make a map on poster board. Draw the layout of a living room, bathroom, and bedroom before your *FLIP* is tilted 90°. Include entrances and walkways to use when *FLIP* is not flipped.

Weird Science

It's Raining Fish and Frogs

What forms of precipitation have you seen fall from the sky? Rain, snow, hail, sleet, or fish? Wait a minute! Fish? Fish and frogs might not be a form of precipitation, but as early as the second century, they have been reported to fall from the sky during rainstorms. Scientists theorize that tornadoes or waterspouts that suck water into clouds can also suck up unsuspecting fish, frogs, or tadpoles that are near the surface of the water. After being sucked up into the clouds and carried a few miles, these reluctant travelers then rain down from the sky.

Language Arts ACTIVITY

WRITING SKILL You are a reporter for your local newspaper. On a rainy day in spring, while driving to work, you witness a downpour of frogs and fish. You pull off to the side of the road and interview other witnesses. Write an article describing this event for your local newspaper.

People in Science

Ashanti Johnson Pyrtle

Chemical Oceanographer Growing up in Dallas, Texas, Ashanti Johnson Pyrtle loved everything associated with science—especially marine science. This interest led her to become the first African American female chemical oceanographer and the first African American to obtain a Ph.D. in oceanography from Texas A&M University.

Pyrtle is now an assistant professor in the College of Marine Science at the University of South Florida. She studies the distribution, transport, and behavior of radionuclides—radioactive particles—found in lakes, rivers, and oceans. Pyrtle's work has focused on a variety of places around the world, including the Lena River estuary in northern Russia. There, she studied sediments taken from the estuary and found evidence of radioactive contamination. Pyrtle's research has shown that currents carry radionuclides from the estuary eastward toward Alaska. The radionuclides could potentially harm fish that are economically important to Alaskan fisherman. Pyrtle has also studied radionuclide distribution in Georgia's Savannah River estuary. The results of these studies will help scientists understand the way in which radionuclides would spread through the aquatic environment if radiation leaked from a nuclear facility.

In addition to working as an oceanographer, Pyrtle participates in programs that help students excel in science. To Pyrtle, research is important, but so is helping others achieve their goals and dreams.

Math Activity

Dr. Pyrtle has discovered the radionuclide cesium-137 in the Savannah River estuary. If half of the cesium-137 decays in 30 years, what percentage of cesium-137 will remain after 150 years?

To learn more about these Science in Action topics, visit go.hrw.com and type in the keyword **HT6FSYFF.**

Current Science

Check out Current Science® articles related to this chapter by visiting go.hrw.com. Just type in the keyword HZ5CS14.

Plate Tectonics

The Big Idea

Plate tectonics accounts for important features of Earth's surface and major geologic events.

SECTION

About the Photo

The San Andreas fault stretches across the California landscape like a giant wound. The fault, which is 1,000 km long, breaks the Earth's crust from Northern California to Mexico. Because the North American plate and Pacific plate are slipping past one another along the fault, many earthquakes happen.

PRE-READING ACTIVITY

Key-Term Fold Before you read the chapter, create the FoldNote entitled "Key-Term Fold" described in the **Study Skills** section of the Appendix. Write a key term from the chapter on each tab of the key-term fold. Under each tab, write the definition of the key term.

START-UP ACTIVITY

Continental Collisions

As you can see, continents not only move but can also crash into each other. In this activity, you will model the collision of two continents.

Procedure

1. Obtain **two stacks of paper** that are each about 1 cm thick.
2. Place the two stacks of paper on a **flat surface,** such as a desk.
3. Very slowly, push the stacks of paper together so that they collide. Continue to push the stacks until the paper in one of the stacks folds over.

Analysis

1. What happens to the stacks of paper when they collide with each other?
2. Are all of the pieces of paper pushed upward? If not, what happens to the pieces that are not pushed upward?
3. What type of landform will most likely result from this continental collision?

SECTION 1

Inside the Earth

If you tried to dig to the center of the Earth, what do you think you would find? Would the Earth be solid or hollow? Would it be made of the same material throughout?

Actually, the Earth is made of several layers. Each layer is made of different materials that have different properties. Scientists think about physical layers in two ways—by their chemical composition and by their physical properties.

What You Will Learn

- Identify the layers of the Earth by their chemical composition.
- Identify the layers of the Earth by their physical properties.
- Describe a tectonic plate.
- Explain how scientists know about the structure of Earth's interior.

Vocabulary

crust
mantle
core
lithosphere
asthenosphere
mesosphere
tectonic plate

READING STRATEGY

Reading Organizer As you read this section, create an outline of the section. Use the headings from the section in your outline.

The Composition of the Earth

The Earth is divided into three layers—the crust, the mantle, and the core—based on the compounds that make up each layer. A *compound* is a substance composed of two or more elements. The less dense compounds make up the crust and mantle, and the densest compounds make up the core. The layers form because heavier elements are pulled toward the center of the Earth by gravity, and elements of lesser mass are found farther from the center.

The Crust

The outermost layer of the Earth is the **crust.** The crust is 5 to 100 km thick. It is the thinnest layer of the Earth.

As **Figure 1** shows, there are two types of crust—continental and oceanic. Both continental crust and oceanic crust are made mainly of the elements oxygen, silicon, and aluminum. However, the denser oceanic crust has almost twice as much iron, calcium, and magnesium, which form minerals that are denser than those in the continental crust.

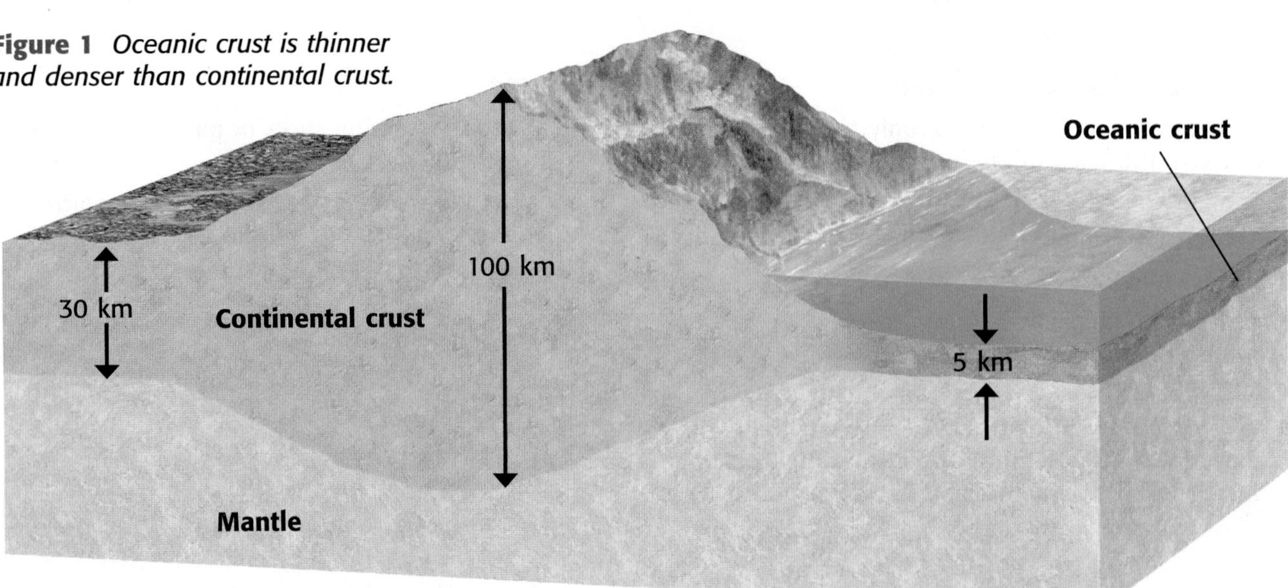

Figure 1 *Oceanic crust is thinner and denser than continental crust.*

The Mantle

The layer of the Earth between the crust and the core is the **mantle.** The mantle is much thicker than the crust and contains most of the Earth's mass.

No one has ever visited the mantle. The crust is too thick to drill through to reach the mantle. Scientists must draw conclusions about the composition and other physical properties of the mantle from observations made on the Earth's surface. In some places, mantle rock pushes to the surface, which allows scientists to study the rock directly.

As you can see in **Figure 2,** another place scientists look for clues about the mantle is the ocean floor. Magma from the mantle flows out of active volcanoes on the ocean floor. These underwater volcanoes have given scientists many clues about the composition of the mantle. Because the mantle has more magnesium and less aluminum and silicon than the crust does, the mantle is denser than the crust.

Figure 2 *Volcanic vents on the ocean floor, such as this vent off the coast of Hawaii, allow magma to rise up through the crust from the mantle.*

The Core

The layer of the Earth that extends from below the mantle to the center of the Earth is the **core.** Scientists think that the Earth's core is made mostly of iron and contains smaller amounts of nickel but almost no oxygen, silicon, aluminum, or magnesium. As shown in **Figure 3,** the core makes up roughly one-third of the Earth's mass.

crust the thin and solid outermost layer of the Earth above the mantle

mantle the layer of rock between the Earth's crust and core

core the central part of the Earth below the mantle

Reading Check **Briefly describe the layers that make up the Earth.** (*See the Appendix for answers to Reading Checks.*)

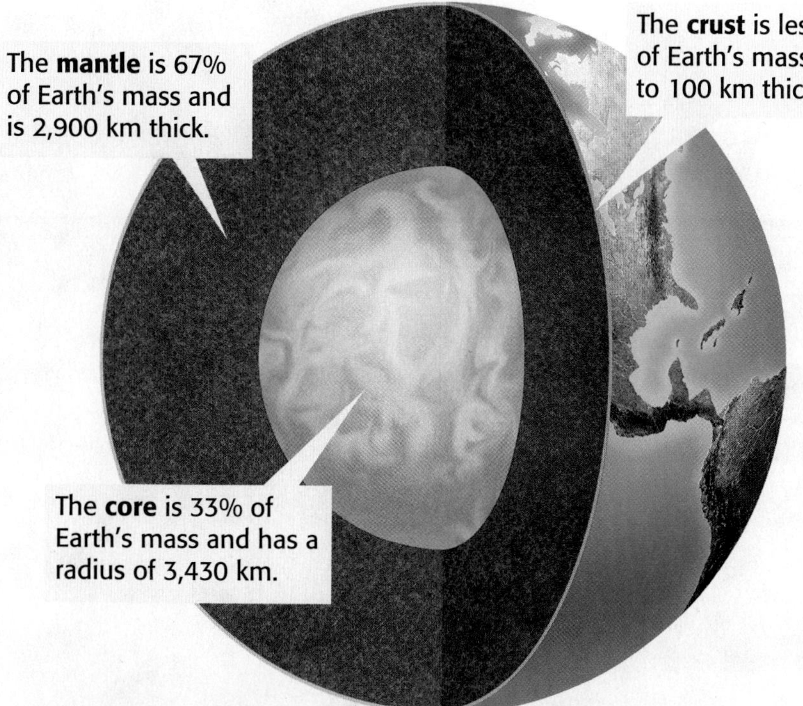
The **mantle** is 67% of Earth's mass and is 2,900 km thick.
The **crust** is less than 1% of Earth's mass and is 5 to 100 km thick.
The **core** is 33% of Earth's mass and has a radius of 3,430 km.

Figure 3 *The Earth is made up of three layers based on the composition of each layer.*

Using Models

Imagine that you are building a model of the Earth that will have a radius of 1 m. You find out that the average radius of the Earth is 6,380 km and that the thickness of the lithosphere is about 150 km. What percentage of the Earth's radius is the lithosphere? How thick (in centimeters) would you make the lithosphere in your model?

The Physical Structure of the Earth

Another way to look at the Earth is to examine the physical properties of its layers. The Earth is divided into five physical layers—the lithosphere, asthenosphere, mesosphere, outer core, and inner core. As shown in the figure below, each layer has its own set of physical properties.

Reading Check **What are the five physical layers of the Earth?**

Lithosphere The outermost, rigid layer of the Earth is the **lithosphere.** The lithosphere is made of two parts—the crust and the rigid upper part of the mantle. The lithosphere is divided into pieces called *tectonic plates.*

Asthenosphere The **asthenosphere** is a plastic layer of the mantle on which pieces of the lithosphere move. The asthenosphere is made of solid rock that flows very slowly.

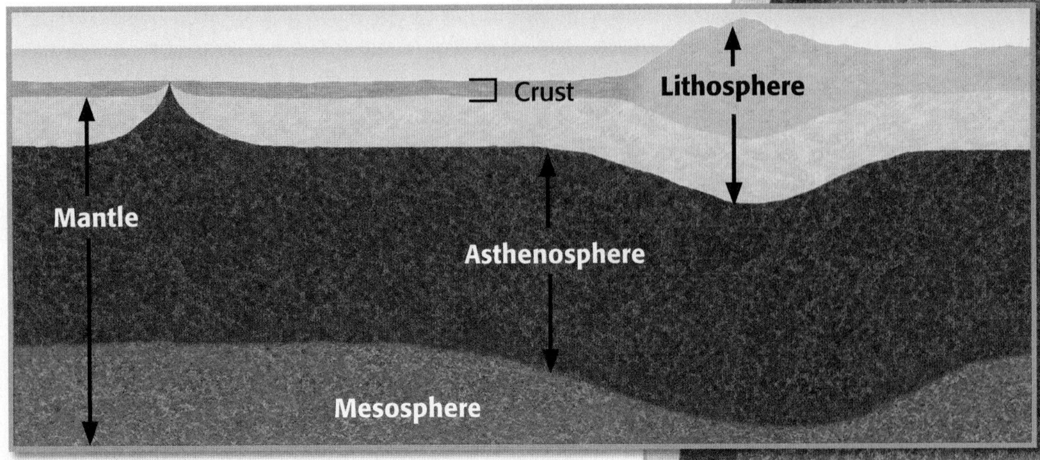

lithosphere the solid, outer layer of the Earth that consists of the crust and the rigid upper part of the mantle

asthenosphere the soft layer of the mantle on which the tectonic plates move

mesosphere the strong, lower part of the mantle between the asthenosphere and the outer core

Mesosphere Beneath the asthenosphere is the strong, lower part of the mantle called the **mesosphere.** The mesosphere extends from the bottom of the asthenosphere to the Earth's core.

Lithosphere
15–300 km

Asthenosphere
250 km

Mesosphere
2,550 km

Outer Core The Earth's core is divided into two parts—the outer core and the inner core. The outer core is the liquid layer of the Earth's core that lies beneath the mantle and surrounds the inner core.

Inner Core The inner core is the solid, dense center of our planet that extends from the bottom of the outer core to the center of the Earth, which is about 6,380 km beneath the surface.

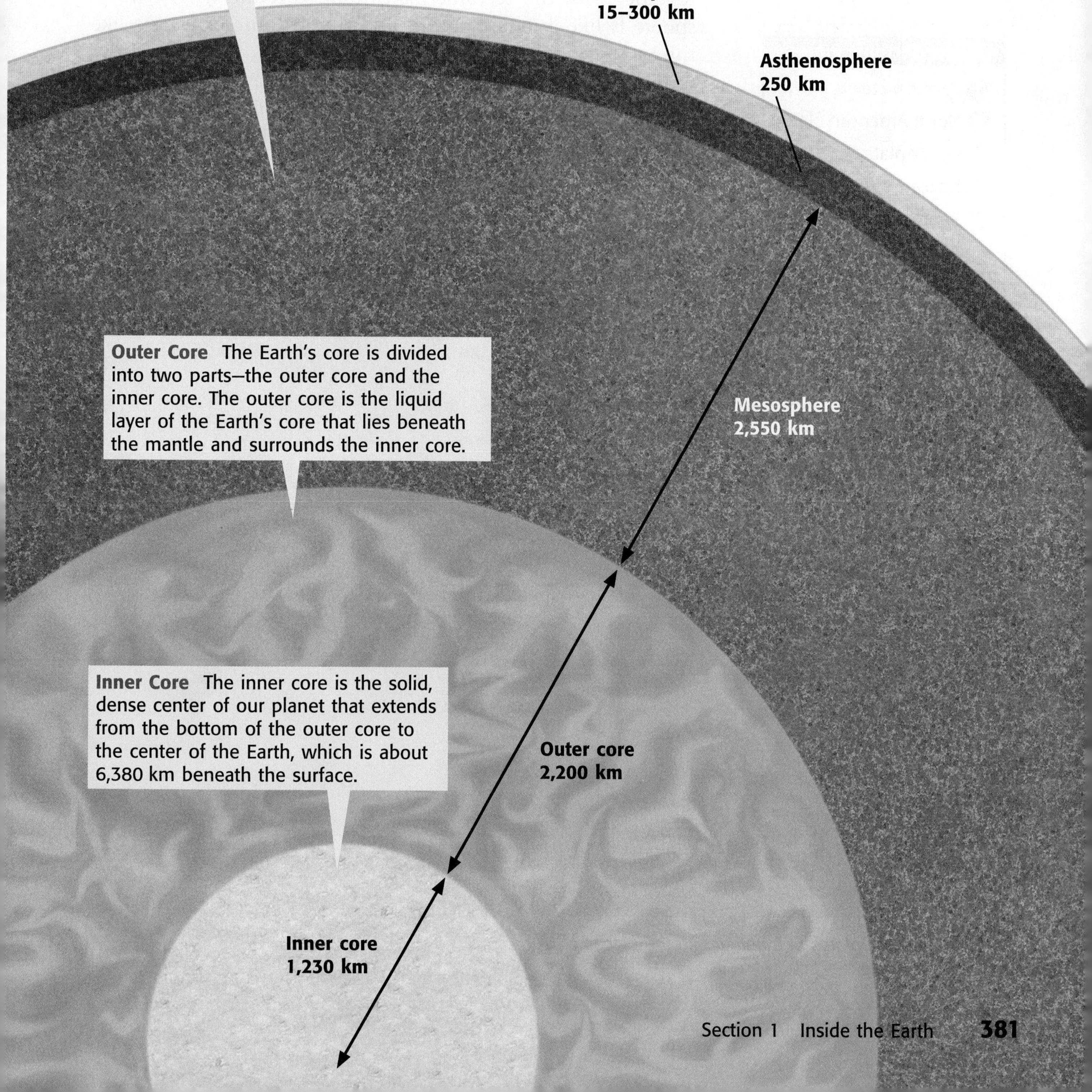

Outer core
2,200 km

Inner core
1,230 km

Tectonic Plates

tectonic plate a block of lithosphere that consists of the crust and the rigid, outermost part of the mantle

Pieces of the lithosphere that move around on top of the asthenosphere are called **tectonic plates**. But what exactly does a tectonic plate look like? How big are tectonic plates? How and why do they move around? To answer these questions, begin by thinking of the lithosphere as a giant jigsaw puzzle.

A Giant Jigsaw Puzzle

All of the tectonic plates have names, some of which you may already know. Some of the major tectonic plates are named on the map in **Figure 4.** Notice that each tectonic plate fits together with the tectonic plates that surround it. The lithosphere is like a jigsaw puzzle, and the tectonic plates are like the pieces of a jigsaw puzzle.

Notice that not all tectonic plates are the same. For example, compare the size of the South American plate with that of the Cocos plate. Tectonic plates differ in other ways, too. For example, the South American plate has an entire continent on it and has oceanic crust, but the Cocos plate has only oceanic crust. Some tectonic plates, such as the South American plate, include both continental and oceanic crust.

Major Tectonic Plates

1. Pacific plate
2. North American plate
3. Cocos plate
4. Nazca plate
5. South American plate
6. African plate
7. Eurasian plate
8. Indian plate
9. Australian plate
10. Antarctic plate

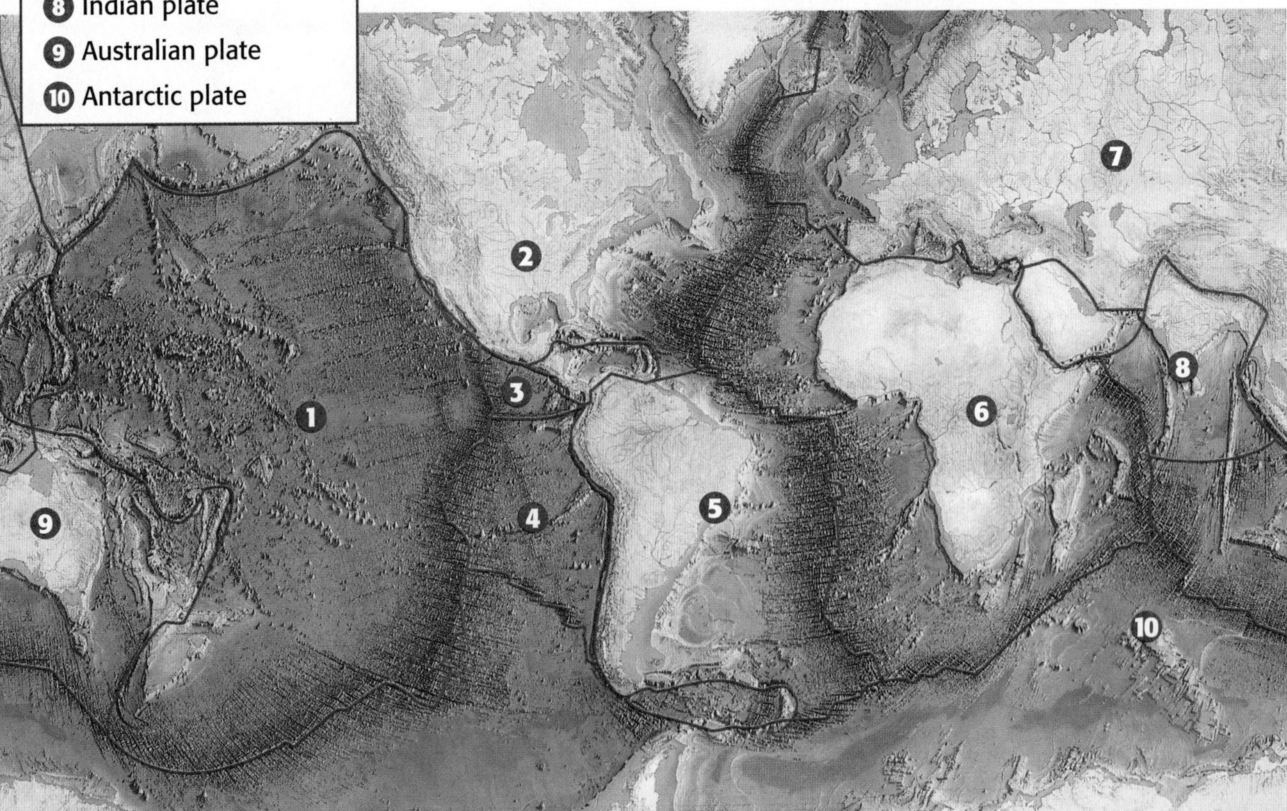

Figure 4 *Tectonic plates fit together like the pieces of a giant jigsaw puzzle.*

Figure 5 **The South American Plate**

This image shows what you might see if you could lift the South American plate out of its position between other tectonic plates.

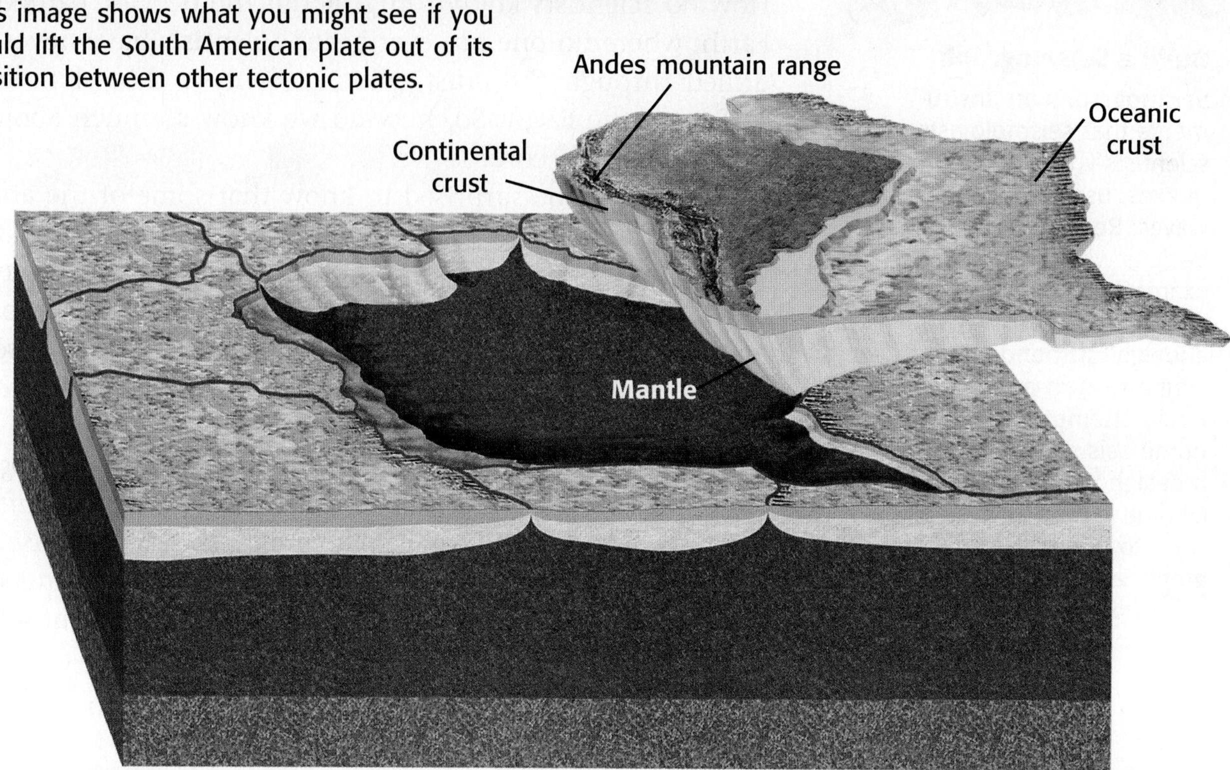

A Tectonic Plate Close-Up

What would a tectonic plate look like if you could lift it out of its place? **Figure 5** shows what the South American plate might look like if you could. Notice that this tectonic plate not only consists of the upper part of the mantle but also consists of both oceanic crust and continental crust. The thickest part of the South American plate is the continental crust. The thinnest part of this plate is in the mid-Atlantic Ocean.

Like Ice Cubes in a Bowl of Punch

Think about ice cubes floating in a bowl of punch. If there are enough cubes, they will cover the surface of the punch and bump into one another. Parts of the ice cubes are below the surface of the punch and displace the punch. Large pieces of ice displace more punch than small pieces of ice. Tectonic plates "float" on the asthenosphere in a similar way. The plates cover the surface of the asthenosphere, and they touch one another and move around. The lithosphere displaces the asthenosphere. Thick tectonic plates, such as those made of continental crust, displace more asthenosphere than do thin plates, such as those made of oceanic lithosphere.

Reading Check **Why do tectonic plates made of continental lithosphere displace more asthenosphere than tectonic plates made of oceanic lithosphere do?**

Tectonic Ice Cubes

1. Take the bottom half of a clear, **2 L soda bottle** that has been cut in half. Make sure that the label has been removed.
2. Fill the bottle with **water** to about 1 cm below the top edge of the bottle.
3. Get **three pieces of irregularly shaped ice** that are small, medium, and large.
4. Float the ice in the water, and note how much of each piece is below the surface of the water.
5. Do all pieces of ice float mostly below the surface? Which piece is mostly below the surface? Why?

Build a Seismograph

Seismographs are instruments that seismologists, scientists who study earthquakes, use to detect seismic waves. Research seismograph designs with an adult. For example, a simple seismograph can be built by using a weight suspended by a spring next to a ruler. With an adult, attempt to construct a home seismograph based on a design you have selected. Outline each of the steps used to build your seismograph, and present the written outline to your teacher.

Mapping the Earth's Interior

How do scientists know things about the deepest parts of the Earth, where no one has ever been? Scientists have never even drilled through the crust, which is only a thin skin on the surface of the Earth. So, how do we know so much about the mantle and the core?

Would you be surprised to know that some of the answers come from earthquakes? When an earthquake happens, vibrations called *seismic waves* are produced. Seismic waves travel at different speeds through the Earth. Their speed depends on the density and composition of material that they pass through. For example, a seismic wave traveling through a solid will go faster than a seismic wave traveling through a liquid.

When an earthquake happens, machines called *seismographs* measure the times at which seismic waves arrive at different distances from an earthquake. Seismologists can then use these distances and travel times to calculate the density and thickness of each physical layer of the Earth. **Figure 6** shows how seismic waves travel through the Earth.

Reading Check What are some properties of seismic waves?

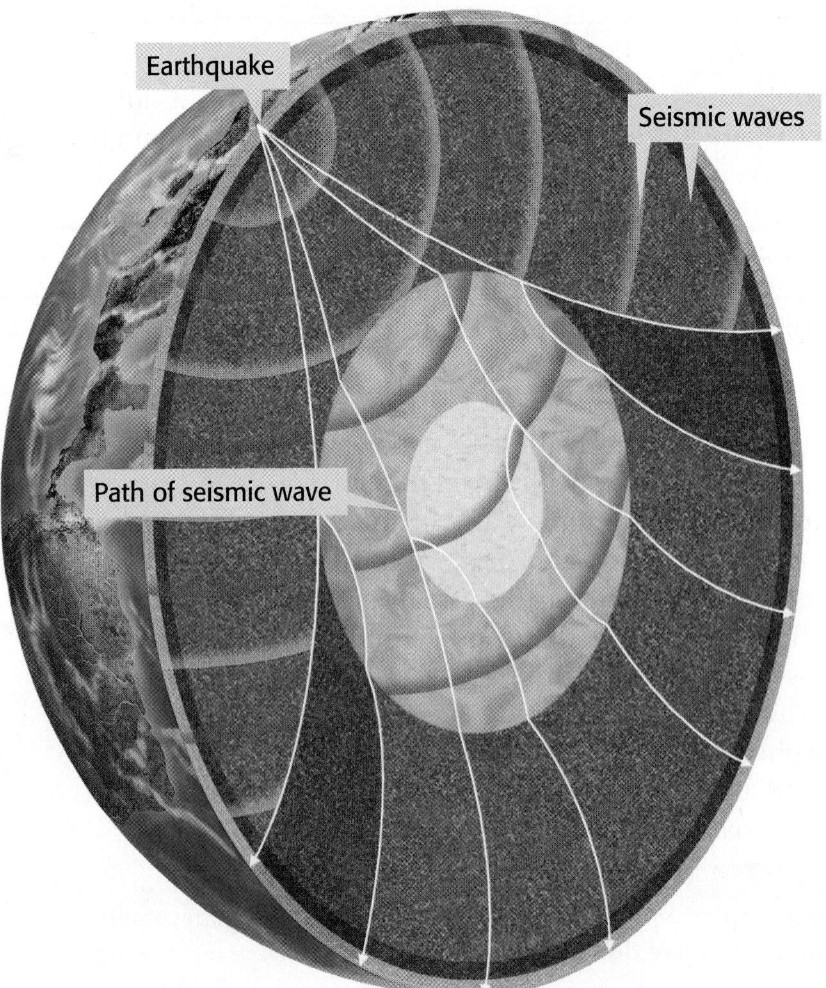

Figure 6 *By measuring changes in the speed of seismic waves that travel through Earth's interior, seismologists have learned that the Earth is made of different layers.*

SECTION Review

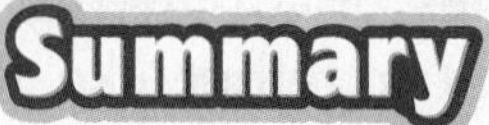

- The Earth is made up of three layers—the crust, the mantle, and the core—based on chemical composition. Less dense compounds make up the crust and mantle. Denser compounds make up the core.
- The Earth is made up of five main physical layers: the lithosphere, the asthenosphere, the mesosphere, the outer core, and the inner core.
- Tectonic plates are large pieces of the lithosphere that move around on the Earth's surface.
- The crust in some tectonic plates is mainly continental. Other plates have only oceanic crust. Still other plates include both continental and oceanic crust.
- Thick tectonic plates, such as those in which the crust is mainly continental, displace more asthenosphere than do thin plates, such as those in which the crust is mainly oceanic.
- Knowledge about the layers of the Earth comes from the study of seismic waves caused by earthquakes.

Using Key Terms

For each pair of terms, explain how the meanings of the terms differ.

1. *crust* and *mantle*
2. *lithosphere* and *asthenosphere*

Understanding Key Ideas

3. The part of the Earth that is molten is the
   - **a.** crust.
   - **b.** mantle.
   - **c.** outer core.
   - **d.** inner core.
4. The part of the Earth on which the tectonic plates move is the
   - **a.** lithosphere.
   - **b.** asthenosphere.
   - **c.** mesosphere.
   - **d.** crust.
5. Identify the layers of the Earth by their chemical composition.
6. Identify the layers of the Earth by their physical properties.
7. Describe a tectonic plate.
8. Explain how scientists know about the structure of the Earth's interior.

Interpreting Graphics

9. According to the wave speeds shown in the table below, which two physical layers of the Earth are densest?

Speed of Seismic Waves in Earth's Interior

Physical layer	Wave speed
Lithosphere	7 to 8 km/s
Asthenosphere	7 to 11 km/s
Mesosphere	11 to 13 km/s
Outer core	8 to 10 km/s
Inner core	11 to 12 km/s

Critical Thinking

10. **Making Comparisons** Explain the difference between the crust and the lithosphere.
11. **Analyzing Ideas** Why does a seismic wave travel faster through solid rock than through water?

For a variety of links related to this chapter, go to www.scilinks.org
Topic: Composition of the Earth; Structure of the Earth
SciLinks code: HSM0329; HSM1468

SECTION 2

Restless Continents

Have you ever looked at a map of the world and noticed how the coastlines of continents on opposite sides of the oceans appear to fit together like the pieces of a puzzle? Is it just coincidence that the coastlines fit together well? Is it possible that the continents were actually together sometime in the past?

What You Will Learn

- Describe Wegener's hypothesis of continental drift.
- Explain how sea-floor spreading provides a way for continents to move.
- Describe how new oceanic lithosphere forms at mid-ocean ridges.
- Explain how magnetic reversals provide evidence for sea-floor spreading.

Vocabulary

continental drift
sea-floor spreading

READING STRATEGY

Paired Summarizing Read this section silently. In pairs, take turns summarizing the material. Stop to discuss ideas that seem confusing.

Wegener's Continental Drift Hypothesis

One scientist who looked at the pieces of this puzzle was Alfred Wegener (VAY guh nuhr). In the early 1900s, he wrote about his hypothesis of *continental drift.* **Continental drift** is the hypothesis that states that the continents once formed a single landmass, broke up, and drifted to their present locations. This hypothesis seemed to explain a lot of puzzling observations, including the observation of how well continents fit together.

Continental drift also explained why fossils of the same plant and animal species are found on continents that are on different sides of the Atlantic Ocean. Many of these ancient species could not have crossed the Atlantic Ocean. As you can see in **Figure 1,** without continental drift, this pattern of fossils would be hard to explain. In addition to fossils, similar types of rock and evidence of the same ancient climatic conditions were found on several continents.

Reading Check **How did fossils provide evidence for Wegener's hypothesis of continental drift?** (*See the Appendix for answers to Reading Checks.*)

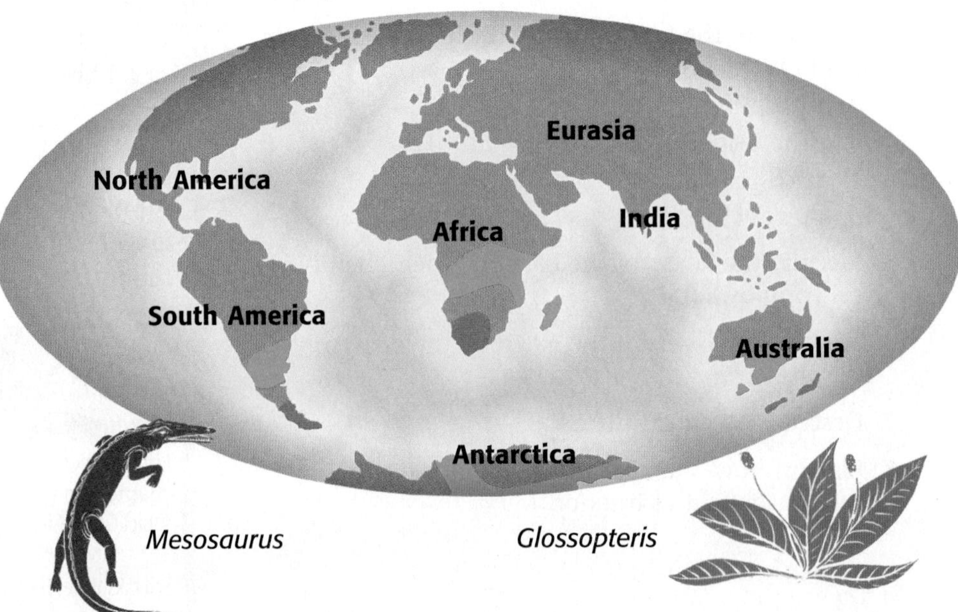

Figure 1 *Fossils of* Mesosaurus, *a small, aquatic reptile, and* Glossopteris, *an ancient plant species, have been found on several continents.*

Figure 2 The Drifting Continents

245 Million Years Ago
Pangaea existed when some of the earliest dinosaurs were roaming the Earth. The continent was surrounded by a sea called *Panthalassa*, which means "all sea."

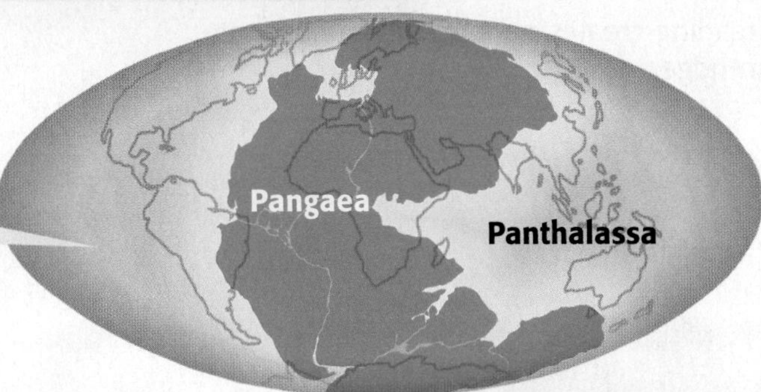

180 Million Years Ago
Gradually, Pangaea broke into two big pieces. The northern piece is called *Laurasia*. The southern piece is called *Gondwana*.

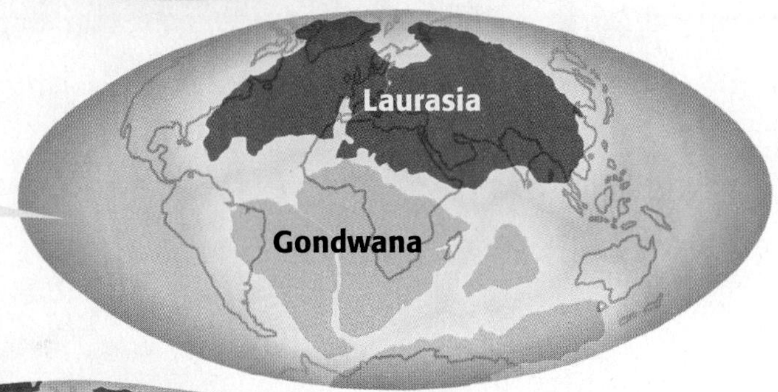

65 Million Years Ago
By the time the dinosaurs became extinct, Laurasia and Gondwana had split into smaller pieces.

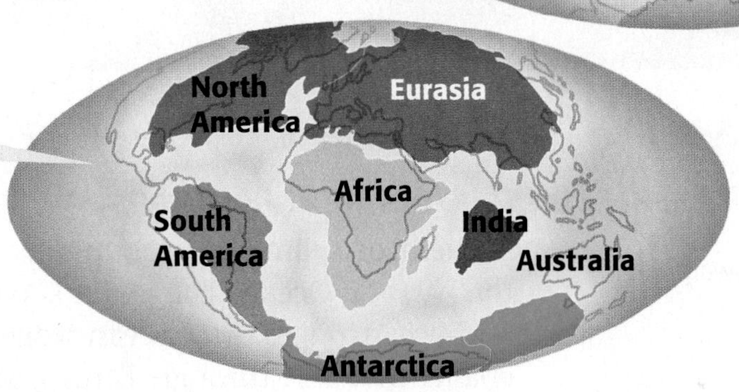

The Breakup of Pangaea

Wegener made many observations before proposing his hypothesis of continental drift. He thought that all of the present continents were once joined in a single, huge continent. Wegener called this continent *Pangaea* (pan JEE uh), which is Greek for "all earth." We now know from the hypothesis of plate tectonics that Pangaea existed about 245 million years ago. We also know that Pangaea further split into two huge continents—Laurasia and Gondwana—about 180 million years ago. As shown in **Figure 2,** these two continents split again and formed the continents we know today.

continental drift the hypothesis that states that the continents once formed a single landmass, broke up, and drifted to their present locations

Sea-Floor Spreading

When Wegener put forth his hypothesis of continental drift, many scientists would not accept his hypothesis. From the calculated strength of the rocks, it did not seem possible for the crust to move in this way. During Wegener's life, no one knew the answer. It wasn't until many years later that evidence provided some clues to the forces that moved the continents.

Figure 3 Sea-Floor Spreading

Sea-floor spreading creates new oceanic lithosphere at mid-ocean ridges.

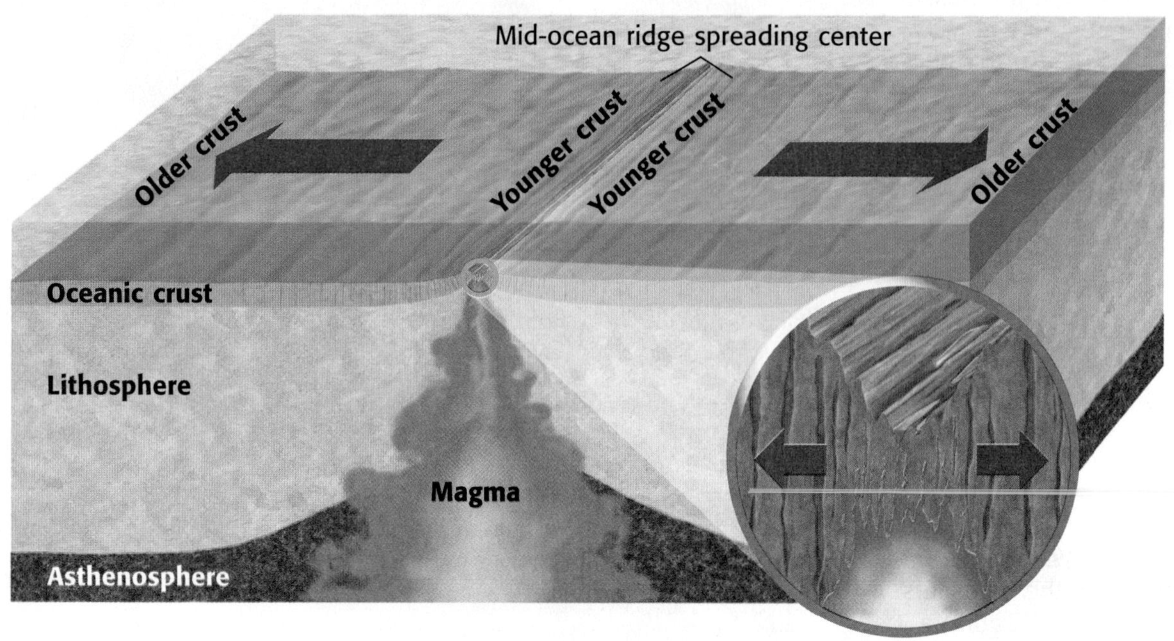

sea-floor spreading the process by which new oceanic lithosphere forms as magma rises toward the surface and solidifies

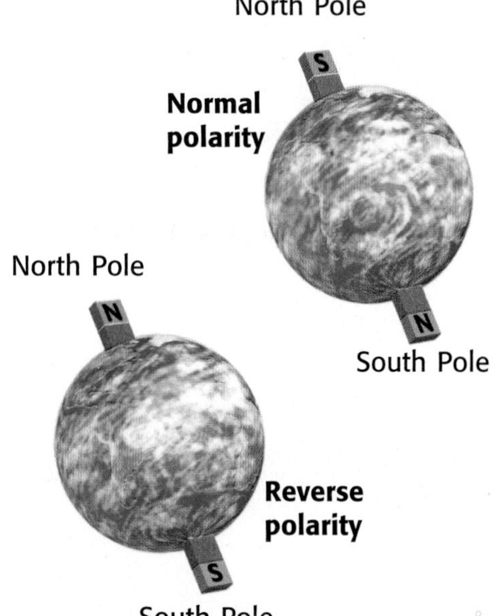

Figure 4 *The polarity of Earth's magnetic field changes over time.*

Mid-Ocean Ridges and Sea-Floor Spreading

A chain of submerged mountains runs through the center of the Atlantic Ocean. The chain is part of a worldwide system of mid-ocean ridges. Mid-ocean ridges are underwater mountain chains that run through Earth's ocean basins.

Mid-ocean ridges are places where sea-floor spreading takes place. **Sea-floor spreading** is the process by which new oceanic lithosphere forms as magma rises toward the surface and solidifies. As the tectonic plates move away from each other, the sea floor spreads apart and magma fills in the gap. As this new crust forms, the older crust gets pushed away from the mid-ocean ridge. As **Figure 3** shows, the older crust is farther away from the mid-ocean ridge than the younger crust is.

Evidence for Sea-Floor Spreading: Magnetic Reversals

Some of the most important evidence of sea-floor spreading comes from magnetic reversals recorded in the ocean floor. Throughout Earth's history, the north and south magnetic poles have changed places many times. When the poles change places, the polarity of Earth's magnetic poles changes, as shown in **Figure 4.** When Earth's magnetic poles change places, this change is called a *magnetic reversal.*

Magnetic Reversals and Sea-Floor Spreading

The molten rock at the mid-ocean ridges contains tiny grains of magnetic minerals. These mineral grains contain iron and are like compasses. They align with the magnetic field of the Earth. When the molten rock cools, the record of these tiny compasses remains in the rock. This record is then carried slowly away from the spreading center of the ridge as sea-floor spreading occurs.

As you can see in **Figure 5,** when the Earth's magnetic field reverses, the magnetic mineral grains align in the opposite direction. The new rock records the direction of the Earth's magnetic field. As the sea floor spreads away from a mid-ocean ridge, it carries with it a record of magnetic reversals. This record of magnetic reversals was the final proof that sea-floor spreading does occur.

Reading Check **How is a record of magnetic reversals recorded in molten rock at mid-ocean ridges?**

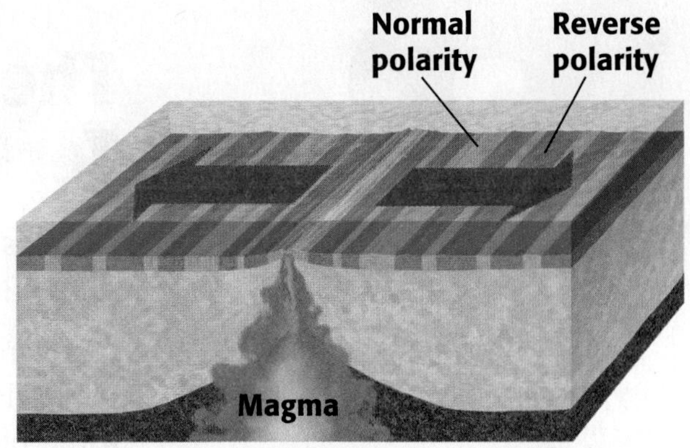

Figure 5 *Magnetic reversals in oceanic crust are shown as bands of light blue and dark blue oceanic crust. Light blue bands indicate normal polarity, and dark blue bands indicate reverse polarity.*

SECTION Review

Summary

- Wegener hypothesized that continents drift apart from one another and have done so in the past.
- The process by which new oceanic lithosphere forms at mid-ocean ridges is called sea-floor spreading.
- As tectonic plates separate, the sea floor spreads apart and magma fills in the gap.
- Magnetic reversals are recorded over time in oceanic crust.

Using Key Terms

1. In your own words, write a definition for each of the following terms: *continental drift* and *sea-floor spreading.*

Understanding Key Ideas

2. At mid-ocean ridges,
   a. the crust is older.
   b. sea-floor spreading occurs.
   c. oceanic lithosphere is destroyed.
   d. tectonic plates are colliding.
3. Explain how oceanic lithosphere forms at mid-ocean ridges.
4. What is magnetic reversal?

Math Skills

5. If a piece of sea floor has moved 50 km in 5 million years, what is the yearly rate of sea-floor motion?

Critical Thinking

6. **Identifying Relationships** Explain how magnetic reversals provide evidence for sea-floor spreading.
7. **Applying Concepts** Why do bands indicating magnetic reversals appear to be of similar width on both sides of a mid-ocean ridge?
8. **Applying Concepts** Why do you think that old rocks are rare on the ocean floor?

SCILINKS
NSTA
Developed and maintained by the National Science Teachers Association
For a variety of links related to this chapter, go to www.scilinks.org
Topic: Tectonic Plates
SciLinks code: HSM1497

SECTION 3

The Theory of Plate Tectonics

What You Will Learn

- Describe the three types of tectonic plate boundaries.
- Describe the three forces thought to move tectonic plates.
- Explain how scientists measure the rate at which tectonic plates move.

Vocabulary

plate tectonics
convergent boundary
divergent boundary
transform boundary

READING STRATEGY

Brainstorming The key idea of this section is plate tectonics. Brainstorm words and phrases related to plate tectonics.

It takes an incredible amount of force to move a tectonic plate! But where does this force come from?

As scientists' understanding of mid-ocean ridges and magnetic reversals grew, scientists formed a theory to explain how tectonic plates move. **Plate tectonics** is the theory that the Earth's lithosphere is divided into tectonic plates that move around on top of the asthenosphere. In this section, you will learn what causes tectonic plates to move. But first you will learn about the different types of tectonic plate boundaries.

Tectonic Plate Boundaries

A boundary is a place where tectonic plates touch. All tectonic plates share boundaries with other tectonic plates. These boundaries are divided into three types: convergent, divergent, and transform. The type of boundary depends on how the tectonic plates move relative to one another. Tectonic plates can collide, separate, or slide past each other. Earthquakes can occur at all three types of plate boundaries. The figure below shows examples of tectonic plate boundaries.

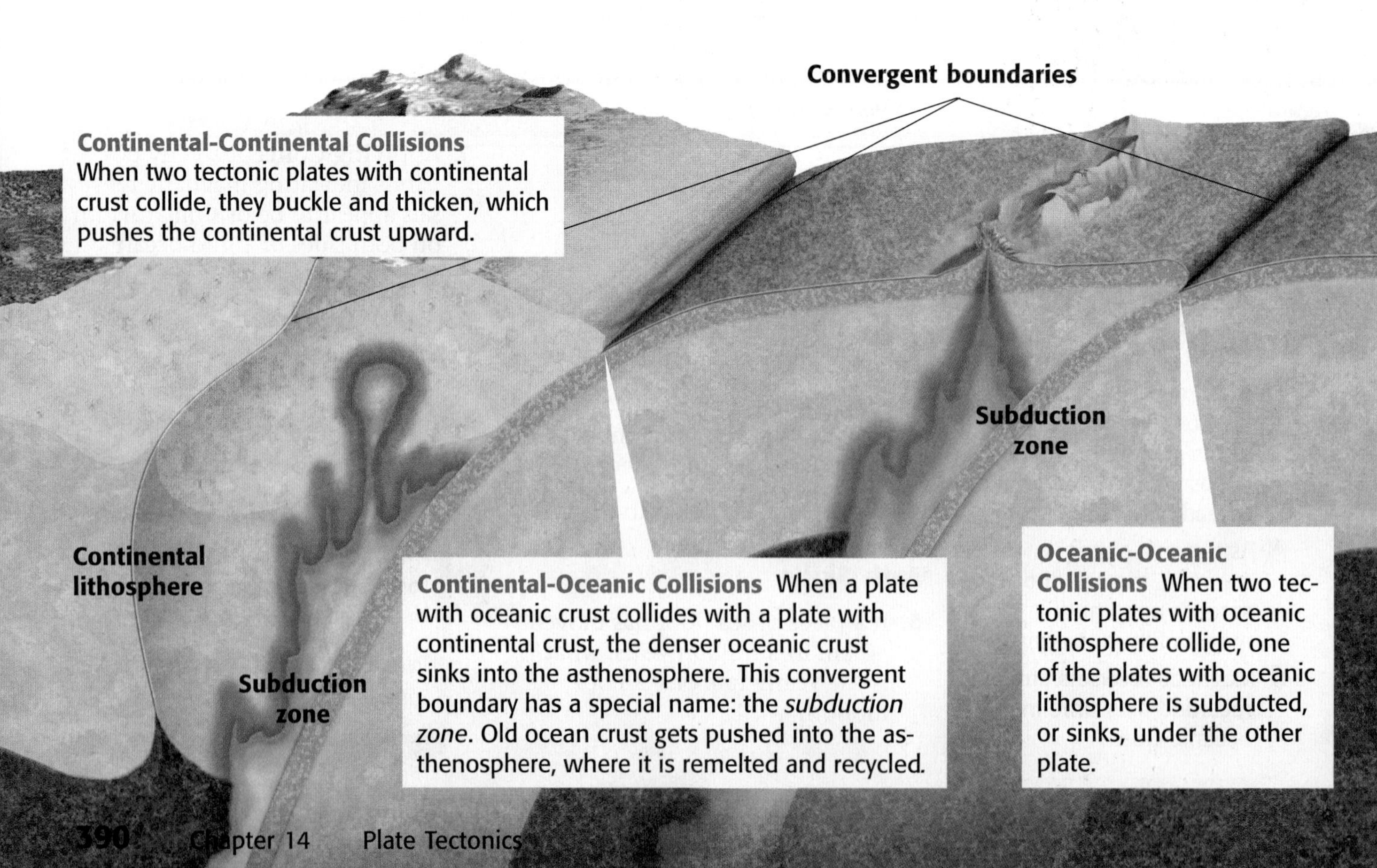

Continental-Continental Collisions When two tectonic plates with continental crust collide, they buckle and thicken, which pushes the continental crust upward.

Continental-Oceanic Collisions When a plate with oceanic crust collides with a plate with continental crust, the denser oceanic crust sinks into the asthenosphere. This convergent boundary has a special name: the *subduction zone*. Old ocean crust gets pushed into the asthenosphere, where it is remelted and recycled.

Oceanic-Oceanic Collisions When two tectonic plates with oceanic lithosphere collide, one of the plates with oceanic lithosphere is subducted, or sinks, under the other plate.

Convergent Boundaries

When two tectonic plates collide, the boundary between them is a **convergent boundary.** What happens at a convergent boundary depends on the kind of crust at the leading edge of each tectonic plate. The three types of convergent boundaries are continental-continental boundaries, continental-oceanic boundaries, and oceanic-oceanic boundaries.

Divergent Boundaries

When two tectonic plates separate, the boundary between them is called a **divergent boundary.** New sea floor forms at divergent boundaries. Mid-ocean ridges are the most common type of divergent boundary.

Transform Boundaries

When two tectonic plates slide past each other horizontally, the boundary between them is a **transform boundary.** The San Andreas Fault in California is a good example of a transform boundary. This fault marks the place where the Pacific and North American plates are sliding past each other.

Reading Check **Define the term *transform boundary*.** *(See the Appendix for answers to Reading Checks.)*

plate tectonics the theory that explains how large pieces of the Earth's outermost layer, called *tectonic plates,* move and change shape

convergent boundary the boundary formed by the collision of two lithospheric plates

divergent boundary the boundary between two tectonic plates that are moving away from each other

transform boundary the boundary between tectonic plates that are sliding past each other horizontally

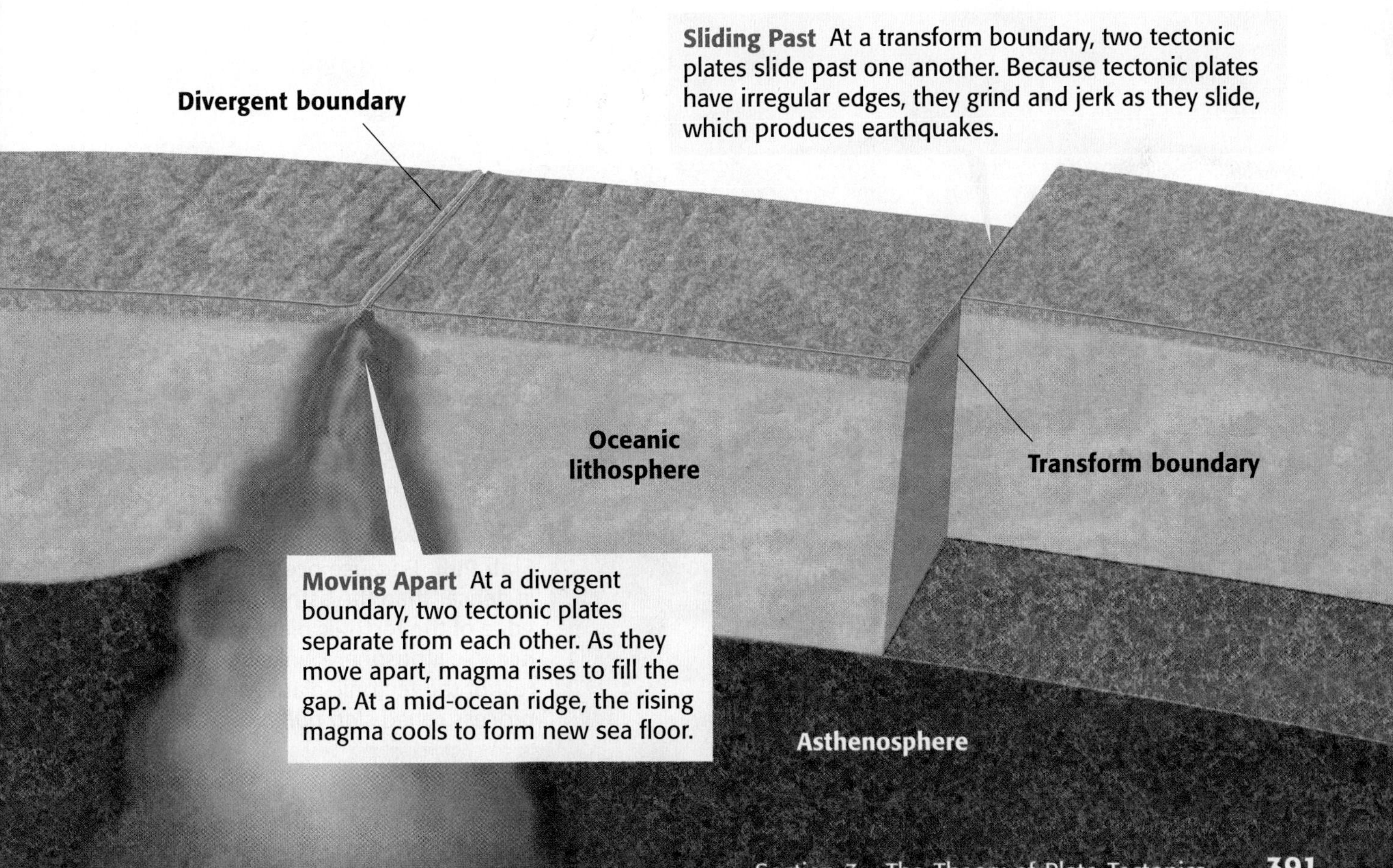

Sliding Past At a transform boundary, two tectonic plates slide past one another. Because tectonic plates have irregular edges, they grind and jerk as they slide, which produces earthquakes.

Moving Apart At a divergent boundary, two tectonic plates separate from each other. As they move apart, magma rises to fill the gap. At a mid-ocean ridge, the rising magma cools to form new sea floor.

Possible Causes of Tectonic Plate Motion

You have learned that plate tectonics is the theory that the lithosphere is divided into tectonic plates that move around on top of the asthenosphere. What causes the motion of tectonic plates? Remember that the solid rock of the asthenosphere flows very slowly. This movement occurs because of changes in density within the asthenosphere. These density changes are caused by the outward flow of thermal energy from deep within the Earth. When rock is heated, it expands, becomes less dense, and tends to rise to the surface of the Earth. As the rock gets near the surface, the rock cools, becomes more dense, and tends to sink. **Figure 1** shows three possible causes of tectonic plate motion.

Reading Check **What causes changes in density in the asthenosphere?**

Figure 1 **Three Possible Driving Forces of Plate Tectonics**

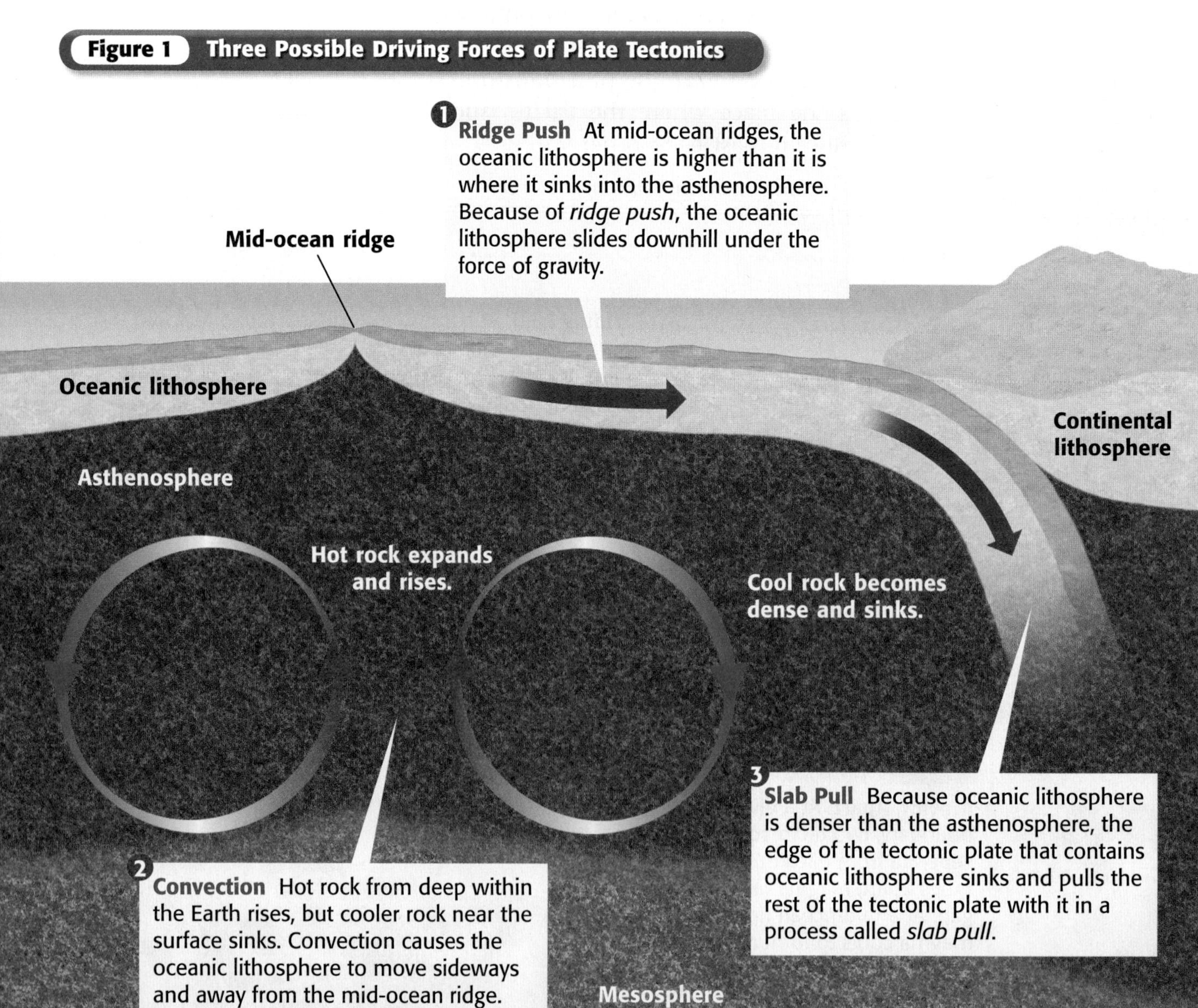

1 **Ridge Push** At mid-ocean ridges, the oceanic lithosphere is higher than it is where it sinks into the asthenosphere. Because of *ridge push*, the oceanic lithosphere slides downhill under the force of gravity.
Mid-ocean ridge
Oceanic lithosphere
Continental lithosphere
Asthenosphere
Hot rock expands and rises.
Cool rock becomes dense and sinks.
3 **Slab Pull** Because oceanic lithosphere is denser than the asthenosphere, the edge of the tectonic plate that contains oceanic lithosphere sinks and pulls the rest of the tectonic plate with it in a process called *slab pull*.
2 **Convection** Hot rock from deep within the Earth rises, but cooler rock near the surface sinks. Convection causes the oceanic lithosphere to move sideways and away from the mid-ocean ridge.
Mesosphere

Tracking Tectonic Plate Motion

How fast do tectonic plates move? The answer to this question depends on many factors, such as the type and shape of the tectonic plate and the way that the tectonic plate interacts with the tectonic plates that surround it. Tectonic plate movements are so slow and gradual that you can't see or feel them—the movement is measured in centimeters per year.

The Global Positioning System

Scientists use a system of satellites called the *global positioning system* (GPS), shown in **Figure 2,** to measure the rate of tectonic plate movement. Radio signals are continuously beamed from satellites to GPS ground stations, which record the exact distance between the satellites and the ground station. Over time, these distances change slightly. By recording the time it takes for the GPS ground stations to move a given distance, scientists can measure the speed at which each tectonic plate moves.

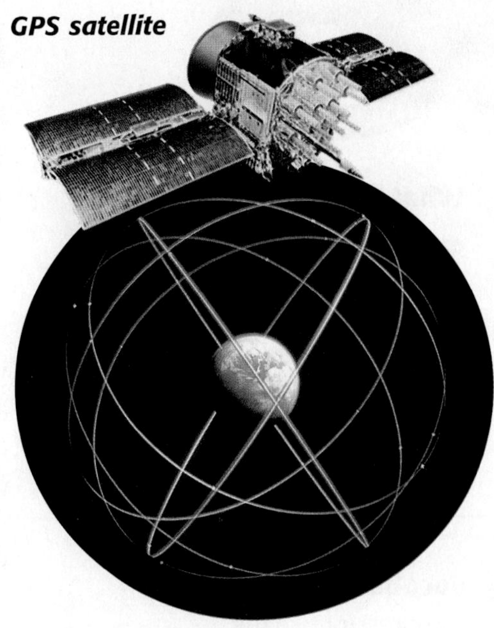
GPS satellite

Figure 2 *The image above shows the orbits of the GPS satellites.*

SECTION Review

Summary

- Boundaries between tectonic plates are classified as convergent, divergent, or transform.
- Ridge push, convection, and slab pull are three possible driving forces of plate tectonics.
- Scientists use data from a system of satellites called the global positioning system to measure the rate of motion of tectonic plates.

Using Key Terms

1. In your own words, write a definition for the term *plate tectonics*.

Understanding Key Ideas

2. The speed a tectonic plate moves per year is best measured in
   a. kilometers per year.
   b. centimeters per year.
   c. meters per year.
   d. millimeters per year.
3. Briefly describe three possible driving forces of tectonic plate movement.
4. Explain how scientists use GPS to measure the rate of tectonic plate movement.

Math Skills

5. If an orbiting satellite has a diameter of 60 cm, what is the total surface area of the satellite? (Hint: *surface area* = $4\pi r^2$)

Critical Thinking

6. **Identifying Relationships** When convection takes place in the mantle, why does cool rock material sink and warm rock material rise?
7. **Analyzing Processes** Why does oceanic crust sink beneath continental crust at convergent boundaries?

SCILINKS
NSTA
Developed and maintained by the National Science Teachers Association
For a variety of links related to this chapter, go to www.scilinks.org
Topic: Plate Tectonics
SciLinks code: HSM1171

SECTION 4

Deforming the Earth's Crust

What You Will Learn

- Describe two types of stress that deform rocks.
- Describe three major types of folds.
- Explain the differences between the three major types of faults.
- Identify the most common types of mountains.
- Explain the difference between uplift and subsidence.

Vocabulary

compression
tension
folding
fault
uplift
subsidence

READING STRATEGY

Discussion Read this section silently. Write down questions that you have about this section. Discuss your questions in a small group.

Have you ever tried to bend something, only to have it break? Take long, uncooked pieces of spaghetti, and bend them very slowly but only a little. Now, bend them again, but this time, bend them much farther and faster. What happened?

How can a material bend at one time and break at another time? The answer is that the stress you put on the material was different each time. *Stress* is the amount of force per unit area on a given material. The same principle applies to the rocks in the Earth's crust. Different things happen to rock when different types of stress are applied.

Deformation

The process by which the shape of a rock changes because of stress is called *deformation*. In the example above, the spaghetti deformed in two different ways—by bending and by breaking. **Figure 1** illustrates this concept. The same thing happens in rock layers. Rock layers bend when stress is placed on them. But when enough stress is placed on rocks, they can reach their elastic limit and break.

Compression and Tension

The type of stress that occurs when an object is squeezed, such as when two tectonic plates collide, is called **compression.** When compression occurs at a convergent boundary, large mountain ranges can form.

Another form of stress is *tension*. **Tension** is stress that occurs when forces act to stretch an object. As you might guess, tension occurs at divergent plate boundaries, such as mid-ocean ridges, when two tectonic plates pull away from each other.

Reading Check **How do the forces of plate tectonics cause rock to deform?** (*See the Appendix for answers to Reading Checks.*)

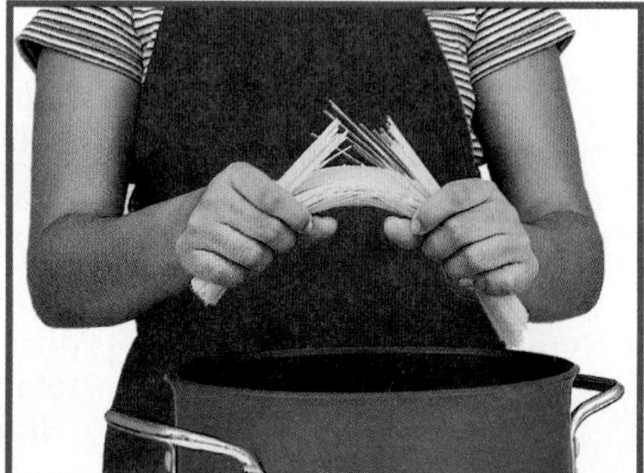

Figure 1 *When a small amount of stress is placed on uncooked spaghetti, the spaghetti bends. Additional stress causes the spaghetti to break.*

Figure 2 Folding: When Rock Layers Bend Because of Stress

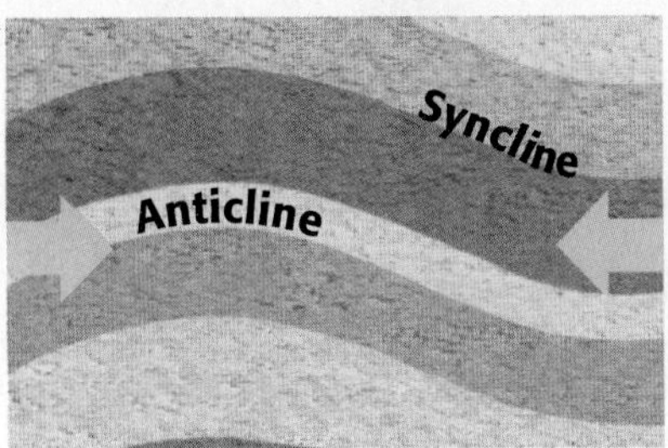

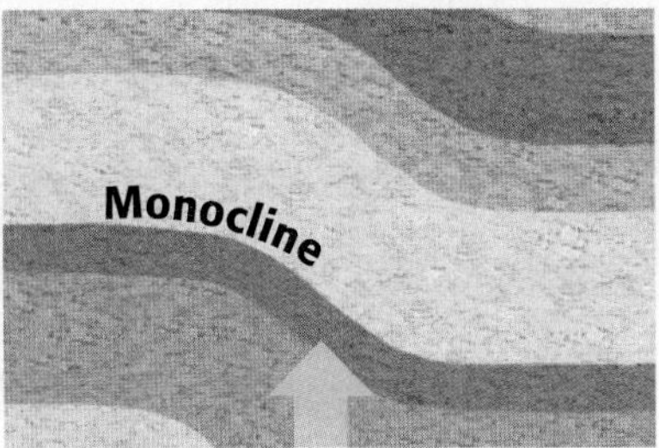

Folding

The bending of rock layers because of stress in the Earth's crust is called **folding.** Scientists assume that all rock layers started as horizontal layers. So, when scientists see a fold, they know that deformation has taken place.

compression stress that occurs when forces act to squeeze an object

tension stress that occurs when forces act to stretch an object

folding the bending of rock layers due to stress

Types of Folds

Depending on how the rock layers deform, different types of folds are made. **Figure 2** shows the two most common types of folds—*anticlines*, or upward-arching folds, and *synclines,* downward, troughlike folds. Another type of fold is a *monocline*. In a monocline, rock layers are folded so that both ends of the fold are horizontal. Imagine taking a stack of paper and laying it on a table. Think of the sheets of paper as different rock layers. Now put a book under one end of the stack. You can see that both ends of the sheets are horizontal, but all of the sheets are bent in the middle.

Folds can be large or small. The largest folds are measured in kilometers. Other folds are also obvious but are much smaller. These small folds can be measured in centimeters. **Figure 3** shows examples of large and small folds.

Figure 3 *The large photo shows mountain-sized folds in the Rocky Mountains. The small photo shows a rock that has folds smaller than a penknife.*

Figure 4 *The position of a fault block determines whether it is a hanging wall or a footwall.*

Faulting

Some rock layers break when stress is applied to them. The surface along which rocks break and slide past each other is called a **fault.** The blocks of crust on each side of the fault are called *fault blocks*.

When a fault is not vertical, understanding the difference between its two sides—the *hanging wall* and the *footwall*—is useful. **Figure 4** shows the difference between a hanging wall and a footwall. Two main types of faults can form. The type of fault that forms depends on how the hanging wall and footwall move in relationship to each other.

fault a break in a body of rock along which one block slides relative to another

Normal Faults

A *normal fault* is shown in **Figure 5.** When a normal fault moves, it causes the hanging wall to move down relative to the footwall. Normal faults usually occur when tectonic forces cause tension that pulls rocks apart.

Reverse Faults

A *reverse fault* is shown in **Figure 5.** When a reverse fault moves, it causes the hanging wall to move up relative to the footwall. This movement is the reverse of a normal fault. Reverse faults usually happen when tectonic forces cause compression that pushes rocks together.

Reading Check **How does the hanging wall in a normal fault move in relation to a reverse fault?**

Figure 5 **Normal and Reverse Faults**

Normal Fault When rocks are pulled apart because of tension, normal faults often form.

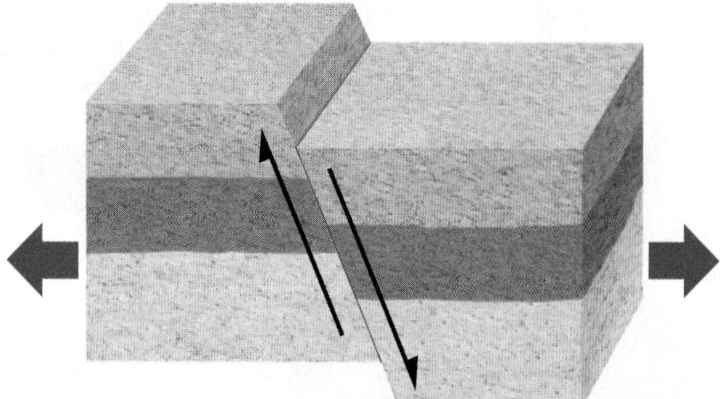

Reverse Fault When rocks are pushed together by compression, reverse faults often form.

Figure 6 *The photo at left is a normal fault. The photo at right is a reverse fault.*

Telling the Difference Between Faults

It's easy to tell the difference between a normal fault and a reverse fault in drawings with arrows. But what types of faults are shown in **Figure 6**? You can certainly see the faults, but which one is a normal fault, and which one is a reverse fault? In the top left photo in **Figure 6,** one side has obviously moved relative to the other side. You can tell this fault is a normal fault by looking at the order of sedimentary rock layers. If you compare the two dark layers near the surface, you can see that the hanging wall has moved down relative to the footwall.

Strike-Slip Faults

A third major type of fault is called a *strike-slip fault*. An illustration of a strike-slip fault is shown in **Figure 7.** *Strike-slip faults* form when opposing forces cause rock to break and move horizontally. If you were standing on one side of a strike-slip fault looking across the fault when it moved, the ground on the other side would appear to move to your left or right. The San Andreas Fault in California is a spectacular example of a strike-slip fault.

Modeling Strike-Slip Faults

1. Use **modeling clay** to construct a box that is 6 in. × 6 in. × 4 in. Use different colors of clay to represent different horizontal layers.
2. Using **scissors,** cut the box down the middle. Place **two 4 in. × 6 in. index cards** inside the cut so that the two sides of the box slide freely.
3. Using gentle pressure, slide the two sides horizontally past one another.
4. How does this model illustrate the motion that occurs along a strike-slip fault?

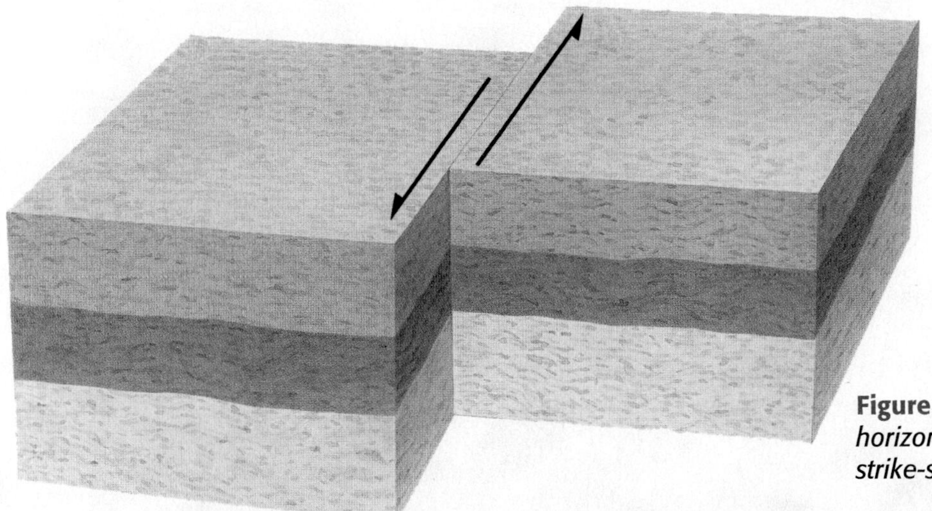

Figure 7 *When rocks are moved horizontally by opposing forces, strike-slip faults often form.*

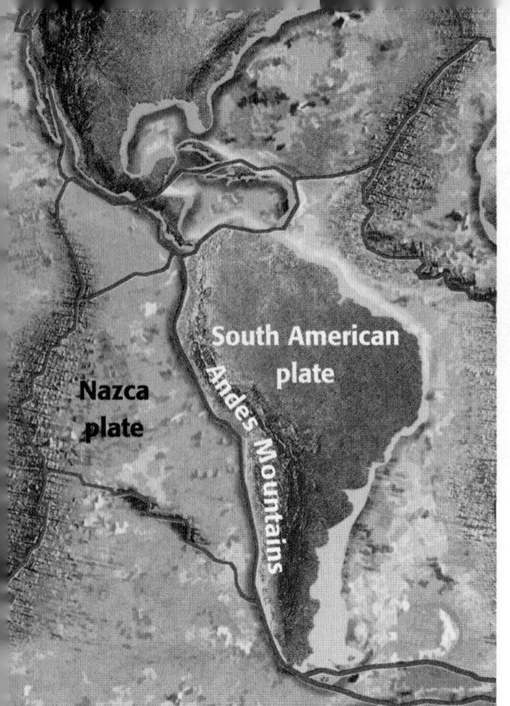

Figure 8 *The Andes Mountains formed on the edge of the South American plate where it converges with the Nazca plate.*

Plate Tectonics and Mountain Building

You have just learned about several ways the Earth's crust changes because of the forces of plate tectonics. When tectonic plates collide, land features that start as folds and faults can eventually become large mountain ranges. Mountains exist because tectonic plates are continually moving around and colliding with one another. As shown in **Figure 8,** the Andes Mountains formed above the subduction zone where two tectonic plates converge.

When tectonic plates undergo compression or tension, they can form mountains in several ways. Take a look at three of the most common types of mountains—folded mountains, fault-block mountains, and volcanic mountains.

Folded Mountains

The highest mountain ranges in the world are made up of folded mountains. These ranges form at convergent boundaries where continents have collided. *Folded mountains* form when rock layers are squeezed together and pushed upward. If you place a pile of paper on a table and push on opposite edges of the pile, you will see how folded mountains form.

An example of a folded mountain range that formed at a convergent boundary is shown in **Figure 9.** About 390 million years ago, the Appalachian Mountains formed when the landmasses that are now North America and Africa collided. Other examples of mountain ranges that consist of very large and complex folds are the Alps in central Europe, the Ural Mountains in Russia, and the Himalayas in Asia.

Reading Check **Explain how folded mountains form.**

Figure 9 *The Appalachian Mountains were once as tall as the Himalaya Mountains but have been worn down by hundreds of millions of years of weathering and erosion.*

Figure 10 *When the crust is subjected to tension, the rock can break along a series of normal faults, which creates fault-block mountains.*

Fault-Block Mountains

When tectonic forces put enough tension on the Earth's crust, a large number of normal faults can result. *Fault-block mountains* form when this tension causes large blocks of the Earth's crust to drop down relative to other blocks. **Figure 10** shows one way that fault-block mountains form.

When sedimentary rock layers are tilted up by faulting, they can produce mountains that have sharp, jagged peaks. As shown in **Figure 11,** the Tetons in western Wyoming are a spectacular example of fault-block mountains.

Volcanic Mountains

Most of the world's major volcanic mountains are located at convergent boundaries where oceanic crust sinks into the asthenosphere at subduction zones. The rock that is melted in subduction zones forms magma, which rises to the Earth's surface and erupts to form *volcanic mountains*. Volcanic mountains can also form under the sea. Sometimes these mountains can rise above the ocean surface to become islands. The majority of tectonically active volcanic mountains on the Earth have formed around the tectonically active rim of the Pacific Ocean. The rim has become known as the *Ring of Fire*.

CONNECTION TO Social Studies

WRITING SKILL **The Naming of the Appalachian Mountains** How did the Appalachian Mountains get their name? It is believed that the Appalachian Mountains were named by Spanish explorers in North America during the 16th century. It is thought that the name was taken from a Native American tribe called *Appalachee,* who lived in northern Florida. Research other geological features in the United States, including mountains and rivers, whose names are of Native American origin. Write the results of your research in a short essay.

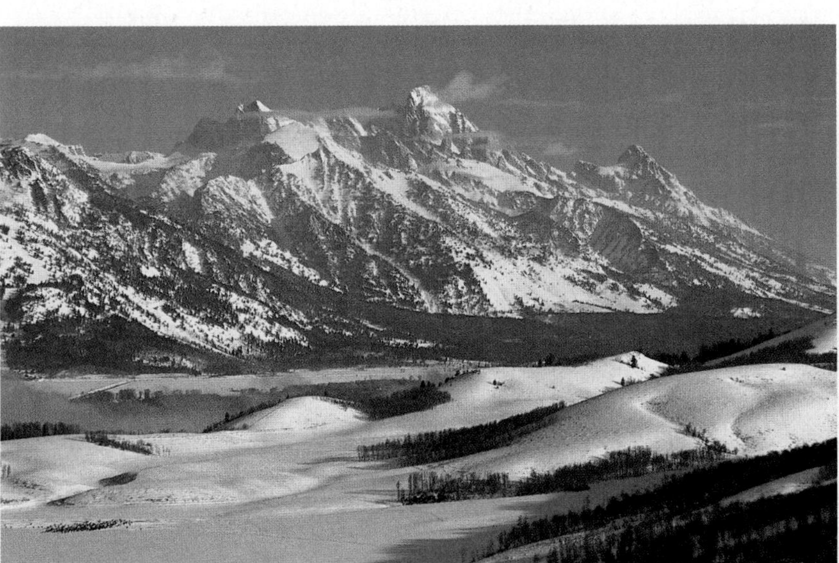

Figure 11 *The Tetons formed as a result of tectonic forces that stretched the Earth's crust and caused it to break in a series of normal faults.*

For another activity related to this chapter, go to **go.hrw.com** and type in the keyword **HZ5TECW.**

Uplift and Subsidence

Vertical movements in the crust are divided into two types—uplift and subsidence. The rising of regions of Earth's crust to higher elevations is called **uplift.** Rocks that are uplifted may or may not be highly deformed. The sinking of regions of Earth's crust to lower elevations is known as **subsidence** (suhb SIED'ns). Unlike some uplifted rocks, rocks that subside do not undergo much deformation.

uplift the rising of regions of the Earth's crust to higher elevations

subsidence the sinking of regions of the Earth's crust to lower elevations

Uplifting of Depressed Rocks

The formation of mountains is one type of uplift. Uplift can also occur when large areas of land rise without deforming. One way areas rise without deforming is a process known as *rebound.* When the crust rebounds, it slowly springs back to its previous elevation. Uplift often happens when a weight is removed from the crust.

Subsidence of Cooler Rocks

Rocks that are hot take up more space than cooler rocks. For example, the lithosphere is relatively hot at mid-ocean ridges. The farther the lithosphere is from the ridge, the cooler and denser the lithosphere becomes. Because the oceanic lithosphere now takes up less volume, the ocean floor subsides.

Tectonic Letdown

Subsidence can also occur when the lithosphere becomes stretched in rift zones. A *rift zone* is a set of deep cracks that forms between two tectonic plates that are pulling away from each other. As tectonic plates pull apart, stress between the plates causes a series of faults to form along the rift zone. As shown in **Figure 12,** the blocks of crust in the center of the rift zone subside.

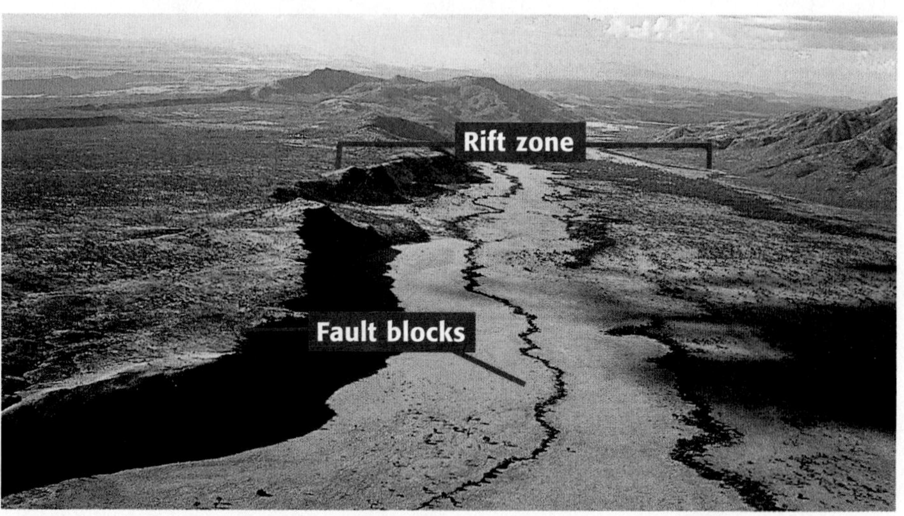

Figure 12 *The East African Rift, from Ethiopia to Kenya, is part of a divergent boundary, but you can see how the crust has subsided relative to the blocks at the edge of the rift zone.*

SECTION Review

Summary

- Compression and tension are two forces of plate tectonics that can cause rock to deform.
- Folding occurs when rock layers bend because of stress.
- Faulting occurs when rock layers break because of stress and then move on either side of the break.
- Mountains are classified as either folded, fault-block, or volcanic depending on how they form.
- Mountain building is caused by the movement of tectonic plates. Folded mountains and volcanic mountains form at convergent boundaries. Fault-block mountains form at divergent boundaries.
- Uplift and subsidence are the two types of vertical movement in the Earth's crust. Uplift occurs when regions of the crust rise to higher elevations. Subsidence occurs when regions of the crust sink to lower elevations.

Using Key Terms

For each pair of key terms, explain how the meanings of the terms differ.

1. *compression* and *tension*
2. *uplift* and *subsidence*

Understanding Key Ideas

3. The type of fault in which the hanging wall moves up relative to the footwall is called a
   - **a.** strike-slip fault.
   - **b.** fault-block fault.
   - **c.** normal fault.
   - **d.** reverse fault.
4. Describe three types of folds.
5. Describe three types of faults.
6. Identify the most common types of mountains.
7. What is rebound?
8. What are rift zones, and how do they form?

Critical Thinking

9. **Predicting Consequences** If a fault occurs in an area where rock layers have been folded, which type of fault is it likely to be? Why?
10. **Identifying Relationships** Would you expect to see a folded mountain range at a mid-ocean ridge? Explain your answer.

Interpreting Graphics

Use the diagram below to answer the questions that follow.

11. What type of fault is shown in the diagram?
12. At what kind of tectonic boundary would you most likely find this fault?

SCILINKS.
NSTA
Developed and maintained by the National Science Teachers Association
For a variety of links related to this chapter, go to www.scilinks.org
Topic: Faults; Mountain Building
SciLinks code: HSM0566; HSM0999

Using Scientific Methods

Model-Making Lab

Convection Connection

Some scientists think that convection currents within the Earth's mantle cause tectonic plates to move. Because these convection currents cannot be observed directly, scientists use models to simulate the process. In this activity, you will make your own model to simulate tectonic plate movement.

OBJECTIVES

Model convection currents to simulate plate tectonic movement.

Draw conclusions about the role of convection in plate tectonics.

MATERIALS

- craft sticks (2)
- food coloring
- gloves, heat-resistant
- hot plates, small (2)
- pan, aluminum, rectangular
- pencil
- ruler, metric
- thermometers (3)
- water, cold
- wooden blocks

SAFETY

Ask a Question

1. How can I make a model of convection currents in the Earth's mantle?

Form a Hypothesis

2. Turn the question above into a statement in which you give your best guess about what factors will have the greatest effect on your convection model.

Test the Hypothesis

3. Place two hot plates side by side in the center of your lab table. Be sure that they are away from the edge of the table.
4. Place the pan on top of the hot plates. Slide the wooden blocks under the pan to support the ends. Make sure that the pan is level and secure.
5. Fill the pan with cold water. The water should be at least 4 cm deep. Turn on the hot plates, and put on your gloves.
6. After a minute or two, tiny bubbles will begin to rise in the water above the hot plates. Gently place two craft sticks on the water's surface.
7. Use the pencil to align the sticks parallel to the short ends of the pan. The sticks should be about 3 cm apart and near the center of the pan.
8. As soon as the sticks begin to move, place a drop of food coloring in the center of the pan. Observe what happens to the food coloring.

9. With the help of a partner, hold one thermometer bulb just under the water at the center of the pan. Hold the other two thermometers just under the water near the ends of the pan. Record the temperatures.

10. When you are finished, turn off the hot plates. After the water has cooled, carefully empty the water into a sink.

Analyze the Results

1. **Explaining Events** Based on your observations of the motion of the food coloring, how does the temperature of the water affect the direction in which the craft sticks move?

Draw Conclusions

2. **Drawing Conclusions** How does the motion of the craft sticks relate to the motion of the water?

3. **Applying Conclusions** How does this model relate to plate tectonics and the movement of the continents?

4. **Applying Conclusions** Based on your observations, what can you conclude about the role of convection in plate tectonics?

Applying Your Data

Suggest a substance other than water that might be used to model convection in the mantle. Consider using a substance that flows more slowly than water.

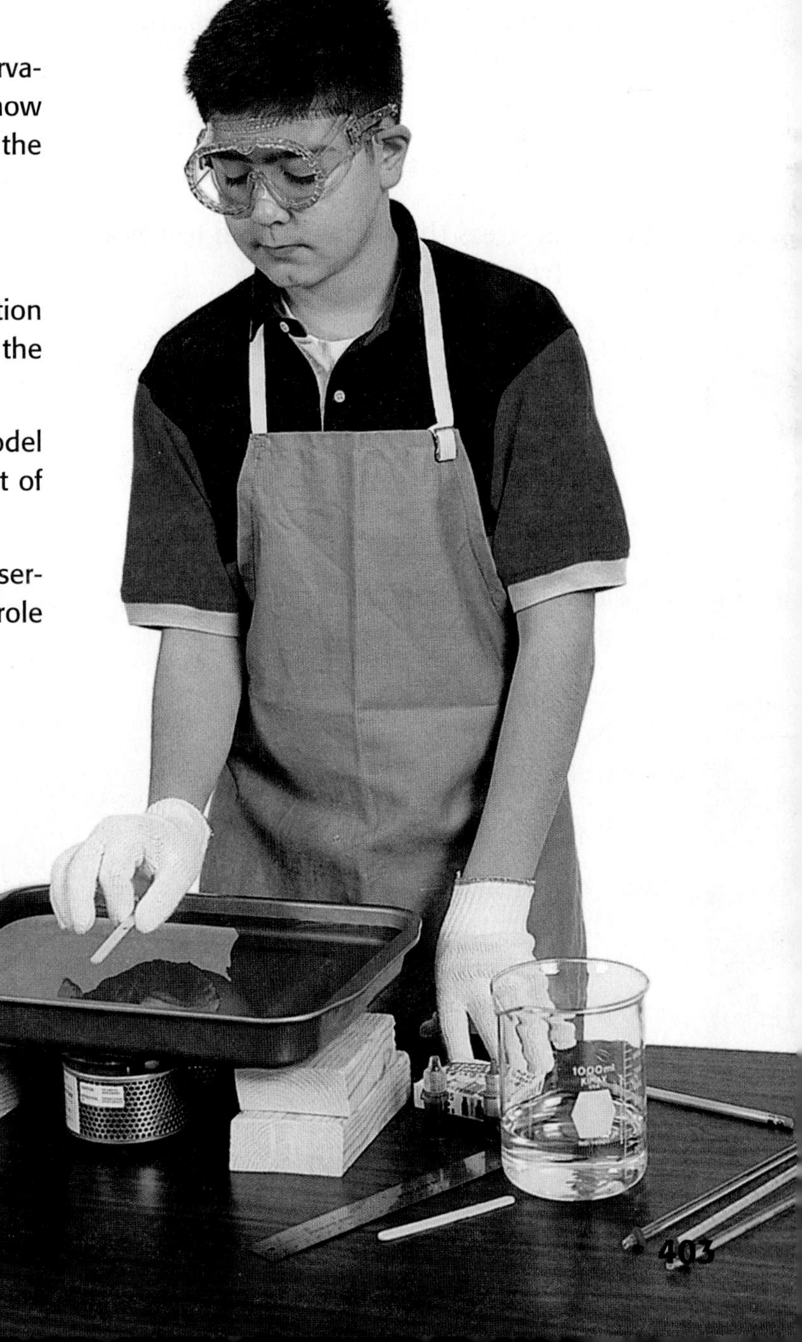

Chapter Review

USING KEY TERMS

1. Use the following terms in the same sentence: *crust, mantle,* and *core.*

Complete each of the following sentences by choosing the correct term from the word bank.

asthenosphere	uplift
tension	continental drift

2. The hypothesis that continents can drift apart and have done so in the past is known as ___.

3. The ___ is the soft layer of the mantle on which the tectonic plates move.

4. ___ is stress that occurs when forces act to stretch an object.

5. The rising of regions of the Earth's crust to higher elevations is called ___.

UNDERSTANDING KEY IDEAS

Multiple Choice

6. The strong, lower part of the mantle is a physical layer called the
   a. lithosphere.
   b. mesosphere.
   c. asthenosphere.
   d. outer core.

7. The type of tectonic plate boundary that forms from a collision between two tectonic plates is a
   a. divergent plate boundary.
   b. transform plate boundary.
   c. convergent plate boundary.
   d. normal plate boundary.

8. The bending of rock layers due to stress in the Earth's crust is known as
   a. uplift.
   b. folding.
   c. faulting.
   d. subsidence.

9. The type of fault in which the hanging wall moves up relative to the footwall is called a
   a. strike-slip fault.
   b. fault-block fault.
   c. normal fault.
   d. reverse fault.

10. The type of mountain that forms when rock layers are squeezed together and pushed upward is the
    a. folded mountain.
    b. fault-block mountain.
    c. volcanic mountain.
    d. strike-slip mountain.

11. Scientists' knowledge of the Earth's interior has come primarily from
    a. studying magnetic reversals in oceanic crust.
    b. using a system of satellites called the *global positioning system.*
    c. studying seismic waves generated by earthquakes.
    d. studying the pattern of fossils on different continents.

Short Answer

12. Explain how scientists use seismic waves to map the Earth's interior.

13. How do magnetic reversals provide evidence of sea-floor spreading?

14. Explain how sea-floor spreading provides a way for continents to move.

15. Describe two types of stress that deform rock.

16. What is the global positioning system (GPS), and how does GPS allow scientists to measure the rate of motion of tectonic plates?

CRITICAL THINKING

17. **Concept Mapping** Use the following terms to create a concept map: *sea-floor spreading, convergent boundary, divergent boundary, subduction zone, transform boundary,* and *tectonic plates.*

18. **Applying Concepts** Why does oceanic lithosphere sink at subduction zones but not at mid-ocean ridges?

19. **Identifying Relationships** New tectonic material continually forms at divergent boundaries. Tectonic plate material is also continually destroyed in subduction zones at convergent boundaries. Do you think that the total amount of lithosphere formed on the Earth is about equal to the amount destroyed? Why?

20. **Applying Concepts** Folded mountains usually form at the edge of a tectonic plate. How can you explain folded mountain ranges located in the middle of a tectonic plate?

INTERPRETING GRAPHICS

Imagine that you could travel to the center of the Earth. Use the diagram below to answer the questions that follow.

Composition	Structure
Crust (50 km)	Lithosphere (150 km)
Mantle (2,900 km)	Asthenosphere (250 km)
	Mesosphere (2,550 km)
Core (3,430 km)	Outer core (2,200 km)
	Inner core (1,228 km)

21. How far beneath the Earth's surface would you have to go before you were no longer passing through rock that had the composition of granite?

22. How far beneath the Earth's surface would you have to go to find liquid material in the Earth's core?

23. At what depth would you find mantle material but still be within the lithosphere?

24. How far beneath the Earth's surface would you have to go to find solid iron and nickel in the Earth's core?

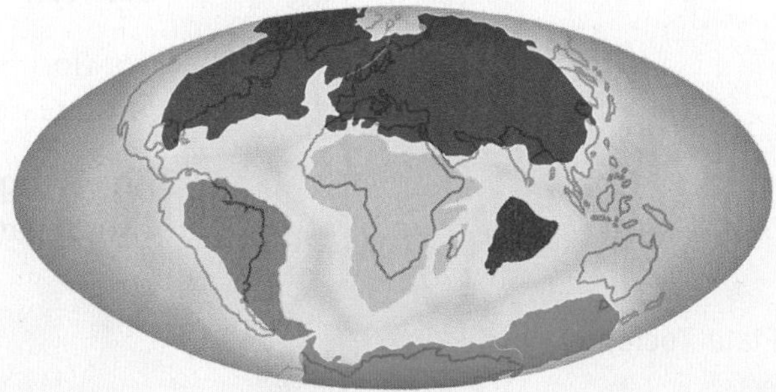

Multiple Choice

1. How do mid-ocean ridges support both the idea of continental drift and the theory of plate tectonics?

A. Oceanic lithosphere is destroyed at mid-ocean ridges.

B. New crust forms at mid-ocean ridges.

C. Tectonic plates collide at mid-ocean ridges.

D. The crust at mid-ocean ridges is old oceanic lithosphere.

2. Which of the following compositional layers makes up the greatest percentage of Earth's mass?

A. continental crust

B. oceanic crust

C. the mantle

D. the core

3. How does fossil evidence support Wegener's hypothesis of continental drift?

A. Similar fossils found on widely separated landmasses suggest that the continents were once a single landmass.

B. Fossil evidence suggests that the continents were always in their current positions.

C. No similarities exist between fossils on different continents.

D. Plant and animal fossils show evidence of changes in Earth's polarity.

4. Some of the world's folded mountains formed as a result of

A. oceanic-oceanic separation at mid-ocean ridges.

B. continental-continental separation at rift zones.

C. continental-oceanic collision at subduction zones.

D. continental-continental collision at convergent boundaries.

5. Which of the following geologic features is formed as a result of tension?

A. an anticline

B. a syncline

C. a normal fault

D. a reverse fault

Use the diagram below to answer question 6.

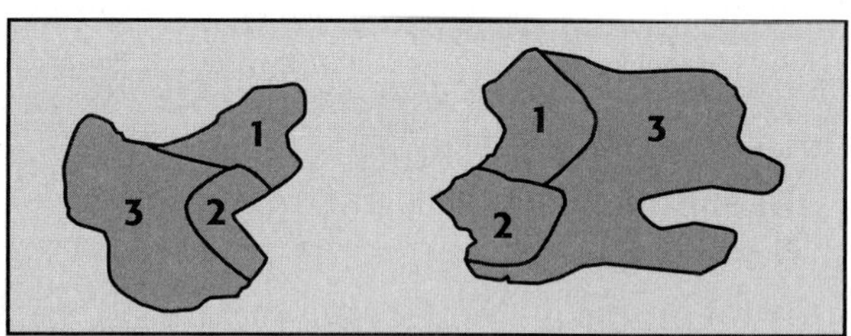

6. Which of the following statements best explains the relative positions of the two landmasses above?

A. The landmasses slid away from each other at a transform boundary.

B. Subduction occurred, causing the land between the two landmasses to sink.

C. Sea-floor spreading pushed the two landmasses apart.

D. An earthquake split the tectonic plate in two, separating the landmasses.

Use the illustration below to answer question 7.

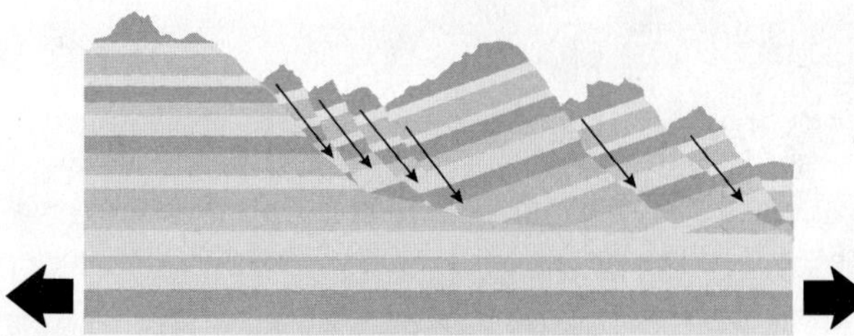

Mountain Formation

7. How were these mountains formed?

A. Rock layers were squeezed and folded by tectonic forces.

B. Volcanoes formed rock layers that then cooled and subsided.

C. Rocks pushed past each other at a transform boundary.

D. Tension caused some rock blocks to drop and tilt upward.

8. Sea-floor spreading occurs at which of the following types of tectonic plate boundaries?

A. transform

B. convergent

C. divergent

D. strike-slip

9. The process by which hot rock from deep within Earth rises and cooler rock near the surface sinks is called

A. ridge push.

B. slab pull.

C. subduction.

D. convection.

10. The sinking of Earth's crust to lower elevations is called

A. rebound.

B. subsidence.

C. uplift.

D. deformation.

11. Strike-slip faults generally form as a result of tectonic forces that cause

A. rock to break and move horizontally.

B. compression that pushes rock together.

C. tension that pulls rock apart.

D. rock layers to bend.

Open Response

12. Both the Appalachian Mountains and the Himalayas in Asia were formed by folding. However, the Himalayas are still growing, while the Appalachian Mountains are losing height and becoming more rounded. Why are these mountains changing in different ways?

13. The Cartersville fault is one section of a huge fault zone that extends from Pennsylvania to Alabama. The Cartersville fault formed when metamorphic rocks from Georgia's Piedmont region were pushed over sedimentary rock layers. This collision most likely occurred during the formation of Pangaea. What kind of fault is the Cartersville fault? Explain your answer.

Science in Action

Science, Technology, and Society

Using Satellites to Track Plate Motion

When you think of laser beams firing, you may think of science fiction movies. However, scientists use laser beams to determine the rate and direction of motion of tectonic plates. From ground stations on Earth, laser beams are fired at several small satellites orbiting 5,900 km above Earth. From the satellites, the laser beams are reflected back to ground stations. Differences in the time it takes signals to be reflected from targets are measured over a period of time. From these differences, scientists can determine the rate and direction of plate motion.

Social Studies ACTIVITY

WRITING SKILL Research a society that lives at an active plate boundary. Find out how the people live with dangers such as volcanoes and earthquakes. Include your findings in a short report.

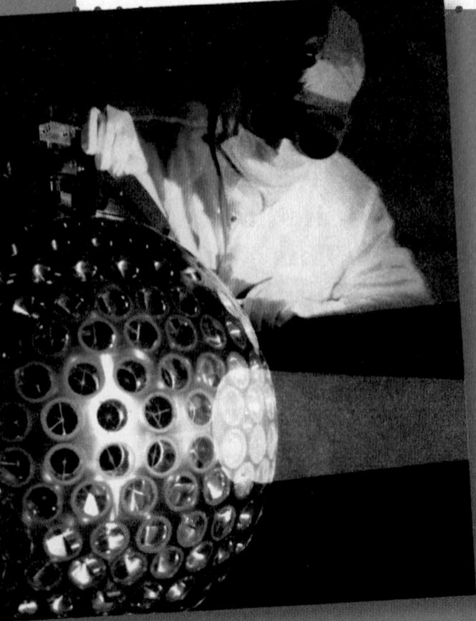

This scientist is using a laser to test one of the satellites that will be used to track plate motion.

Scientific Discoveries

Megaplumes

Eruptions of boiling water from the sea floor form giant, spiral disks that twist through the oceans. Do you think it's impossible? Oceanographers have discovered these disks at eight locations at mid-ocean ridges over the past 20 years. These disks, which may be tens of kilometers across, are called *megaplumes*. Megaplumes are like blenders. They mix hot water with cold water in the oceans. Megaplumes can rise hundreds of meters from the ocean floor to the upper layers of the ocean. They carry gases and minerals and provide extra energy and food to animals in the upper layers of the ocean.

Language Arts ACTIVITY

WRITING SKILL Did you ever wonder about the origin of the name *Himalaya*? Research the origin of the name *Himalaya*, and write a short report about what you find.

People in Science

Alfred Wegener

Continental Drift Alfred Wegener's greatest contribution to science was the hypothesis of continental drift. This hypothesis states that continents drift apart from one another and have done so in the past. To support his hypothesis, Wegener used geologic, fossil, and glacial evidence gathered on both sides of the Atlantic Ocean. For example, Wegener recognized similarities between rock layers in North America and Europe and between rock layers in South America and Africa. He believed that these similarities could be explained only if these geologic features were once part of the same continent.

Although continental drift explained many of his observations, Wegener could not find scientific evidence to develop a complete explanation of how continents move. Most scientists were skeptical of Wegener's hypothesis and dismissed it as foolishness. It was not until the 1950s and 1960s that the discoveries of magnetic reversals and sea-floor spreading provided evidence of continental drift.

Math ACTIVITY

The distance between South America and Africa is 7,200 km. As new crust is created at the mid-ocean ridge, South America and Africa are moving away from each other at a rate of about 3.5 cm per year. How many millions of years ago were South America and Africa joined?

To learn more about these Science in Action topics, visit go.hrw.com and type in the keyword HZ5TECF.

Current Science

Check out Current Science® articles related to this chapter by visiting go.hrw.com. Just type in the keyword HZ5CS07.

15

Earthquakes

The Big Idea Earthquakes result from sudden motions along breaks in Earth's crust and can affect landforms and societies.

SECTION

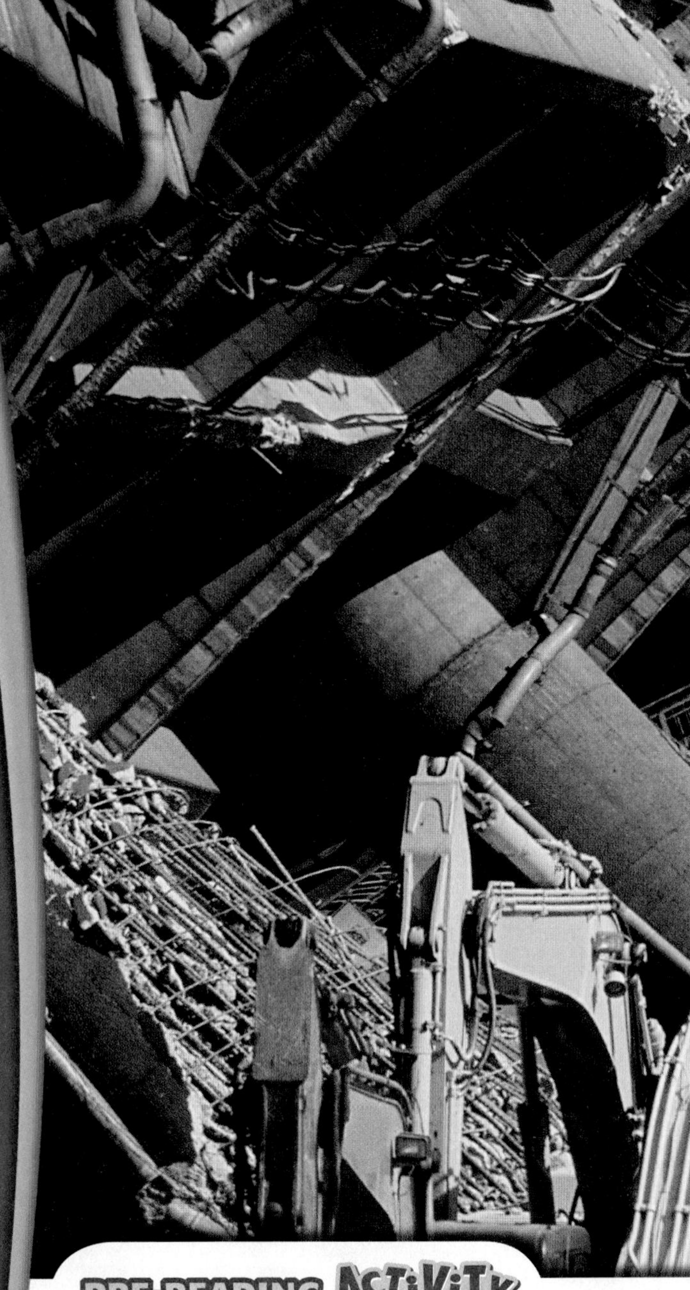

About the Photo

On January 17, 1995, an earthquake of magnitude 7.0 shook the area in and around Kobe, Japan. Though the earthquake lasted for less than a minute, more than 5,000 people lost their lives and another 300,000 people were left homeless. More than 200,000 buildings were damaged or destroyed. Large sections of the elevated Hanshin Expressway, shown in the photo, toppled when the columns supporting the expressway failed. The expressway passed over ground that was soft and wet, where the shaking was stronger and longer lasting.

PRE-READING ACTIVITY

Graphic Organizer

Spider Map Before you read the chapter, create the graphic organizer entitled "Spider Map" described in the **Study Skills** section of the Appendix. Label the circle "Earthquakes." Create a leg for each of the sections in this chapter. As you read the chapter, fill in the map with details about the material presented in each section of the chapter.

START-UP ACTIVITY

Bend, Break, or Shake

In this activity, you will test different materials in a model earthquake setting.

Procedure

1. Gather a **small wooden stick,** a **wire clothes hanger,** and a **plastic clothes hanger.**
2. Draw a straight line on a **sheet of paper.** Use a **protractor** to measure and draw the following angles from the line: 20°, 45°, and 90°.
3. Put on your **safety goggles.** Using the angles that you drew as a guide, try bending each item 20° and then releasing it. What happens? Does it break? If it bends, does it return to its original shape?
4. Repeat step 3, but bend each item 45°. Repeat the test again, but bend each item 90°.

Analysis

1. How do the different materials' responses to bending compare?
2. Where earthquakes happen, engineers use building materials that are flexible but that do not break or stay bent. Which materials from this experiment would you want building materials to behave like? Explain your answer.

SECTION 1

What Are Earthquakes?

What You Will Learn

- Explain where earthquakes take place.
- Explain what causes earthquakes.
- Identify three different types of faults that occur at plate boundaries.
- Describe how energy from earthquakes travels through the Earth.

Vocabulary

seismology
deformation
elastic rebound
seismic waves
P waves
S waves

READING STRATEGY

Paired Summarizing Read this section silently. In pairs, take turns summarizing the material. Stop to discuss ideas that seem confusing.

Have you ever felt the earth move under your feet? Many people have. Every day, somewhere within this planet, an earthquake is happening.

The word *earthquake* defines itself fairly well. But there is more to earthquakes than just the shaking of the ground. An entire branch of Earth science, called **seismology** (siez MAHL uh jee), is devoted to studying earthquakes. Earthquakes are complex, and they present many questions for *seismologists,* the scientists who study earthquakes.

Where Do Earthquakes Occur?

Most earthquakes take place near the edges of tectonic plates. *Tectonic plates* are giant pieces of Earth's thin, outermost layer. Tectonic plates move around on top of a layer of plastic rock. **Figure 1** shows the Earth's tectonic plates and the locations of recent major earthquakes.

Tectonic plates move in different directions and at different speeds. Two plates can push toward or pull away from each other. They can also slip slowly past each other. As a result of these movements, numerous features called faults exist in the Earth's crust. A *fault* is a break in the Earth's crust along which blocks of the crust slide relative to one another. Earthquakes occur along faults because of this sliding.

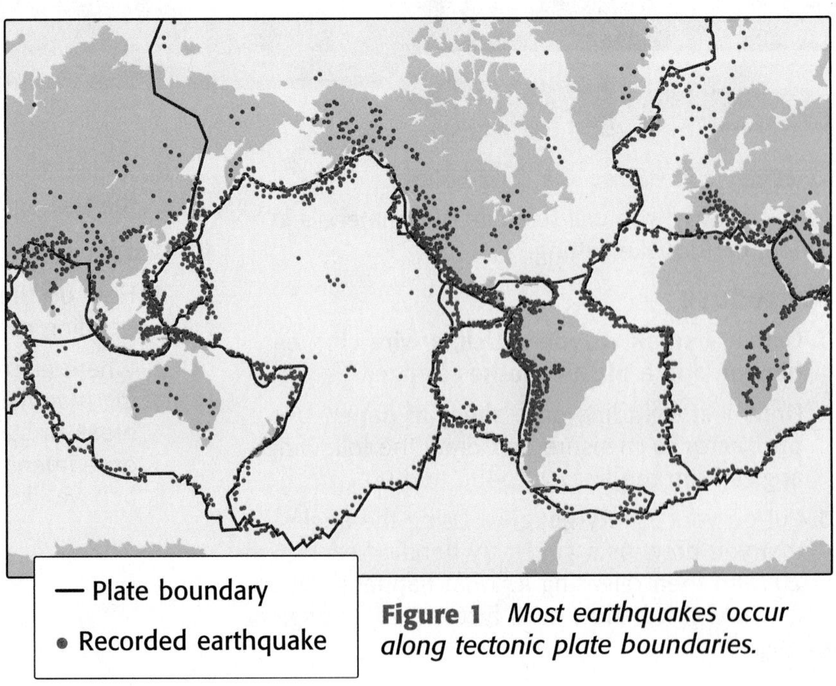

Figure 1 *Most earthquakes occur along tectonic plate boundaries.*

What Causes Earthquakes?

As tectonic plates push, pull, or slip past each other, stress increases along faults near the plates' edges. In response to this stress, rock in the plates deforms. **Deformation** is the change in the shape of rock in response to stress. Rock along a fault deforms in mainly two ways. It deforms in a plastic manner, like a piece of molded clay, or in an elastic manner, like a rubber band. *Plastic deformation,* which is shown in **Figure 2,** does not lead to earthquakes.

Elastic deformation, however, does lead to earthquakes. Rock can stretch farther without breaking than steel can, but rock will break at some point. Think of elastically deformed rock as a stretched rubber band. You can stretch a rubber band only so far before it breaks. When the rubber band breaks, it releases energy. Then, the broken pieces return to their unstretched shape.

Figure 2 *This road cut is adjacent to the San Andreas Fault in southern California. The rocks in the cut have undergone deformation because of the continuous motion of the fault.*

Elastic Rebound

The sudden return of elastically deformed rock to its original shape is called **elastic rebound.** Elastic rebound is like the return of the broken rubber-band pieces to their unstretched shape. Elastic rebound occurs when more stress is applied to rock than the rock can withstand. During elastic rebound, energy is released. Some of this energy travels as seismic waves. These seismic waves cause an earthquake, as shown in **Figure 3.**

Reading Check **How does elastic rebound relate to earthquakes?** (*See the Appendix for answers to Reading Checks.*)

seismology the study of earthquakes

deformation the bending, tilting, and breaking of the Earth's crust; the change in the shape of rock in response to stress

elastic rebound the sudden return of elastically deformed rock to its undeformed shape

Figure 3 **Elastic Rebound and Earthquakes**

Before earthquake

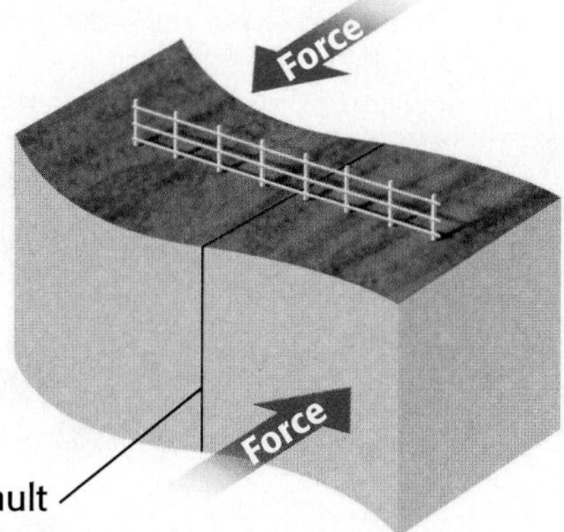

1. Tectonic forces push rock on either side of the fault in opposite directions, but the rock is locked together and does not move. The rock deforms in an elastic manner.

After earthquake

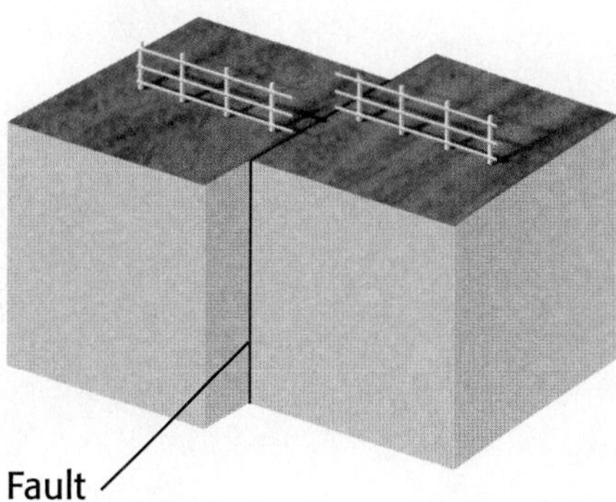

2. When enough stress is applied, the rock slips along the fault and releases energy.

Faults at Tectonic Plate Boundaries

A specific type of plate motion takes place at different tectonic plate boundaries. Each type of motion creates a particular kind of fault that can produce earthquakes. Examine **Table 1** and the diagram below to learn more about plate motion.

Table 1 Plate Motion and Fault Types	
Plate motion	**Major fault type**
Transform	strike-slip fault
Convergent	reverse fault
Divergent	normal fault

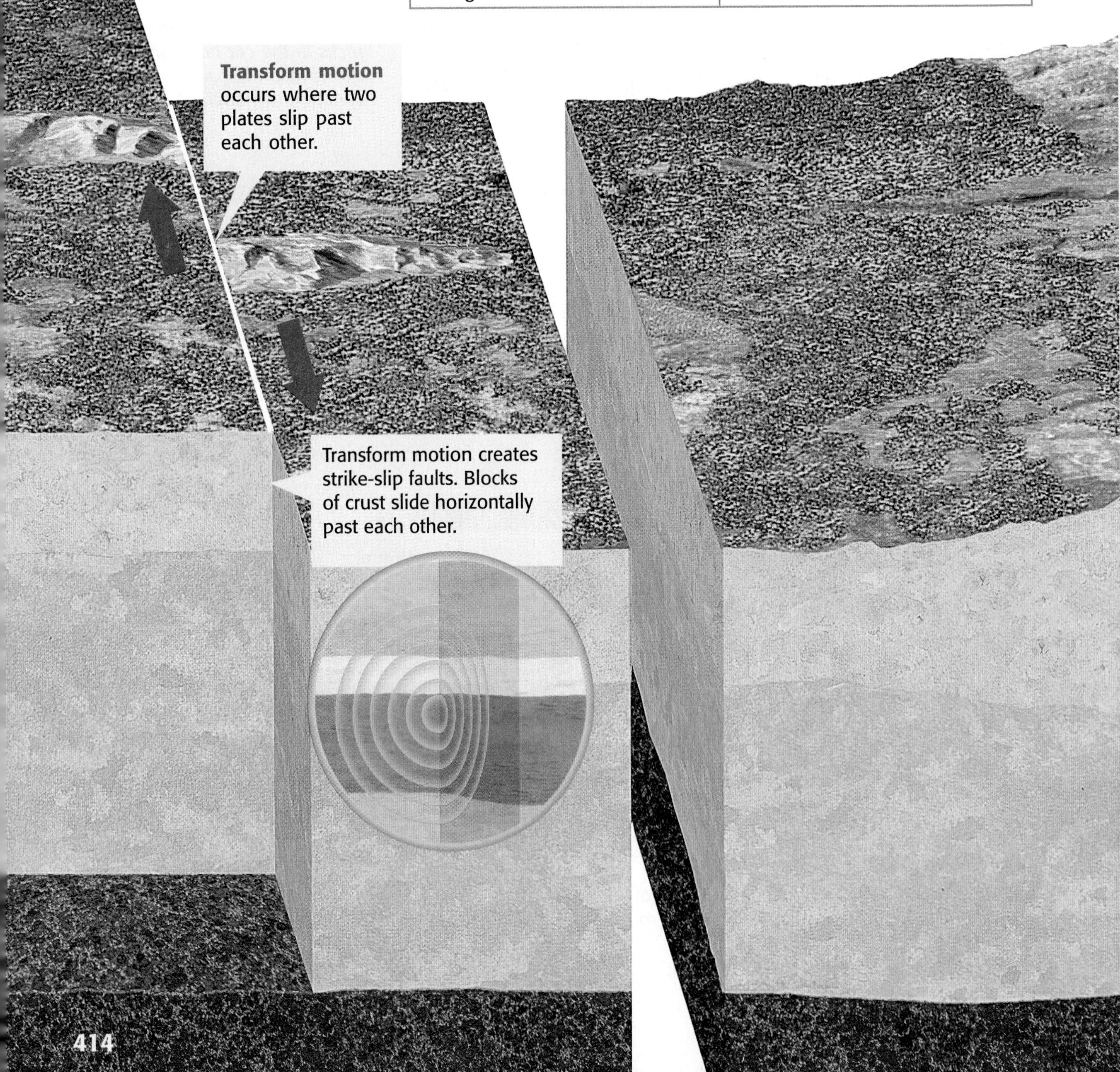

Transform motion occurs where two plates slip past each other.
Transform motion creates strike-slip faults. Blocks of crust slide horizontally past each other.

Earthquake Zones

Earthquakes can happen both near Earth's surface or far below it. Most earthquakes happen in the earthquake zones along tectonic plate boundaries. Earthquake zones are places where a large number of faults are located. The San Andreas Fault Zone in California is an example of an earthquake zone. But not all faults are located at tectonic plate boundaries. Sometimes, earthquakes happen along faults in the middle of tectonic plates.

Reading Check **Where are earthquake zones located?**

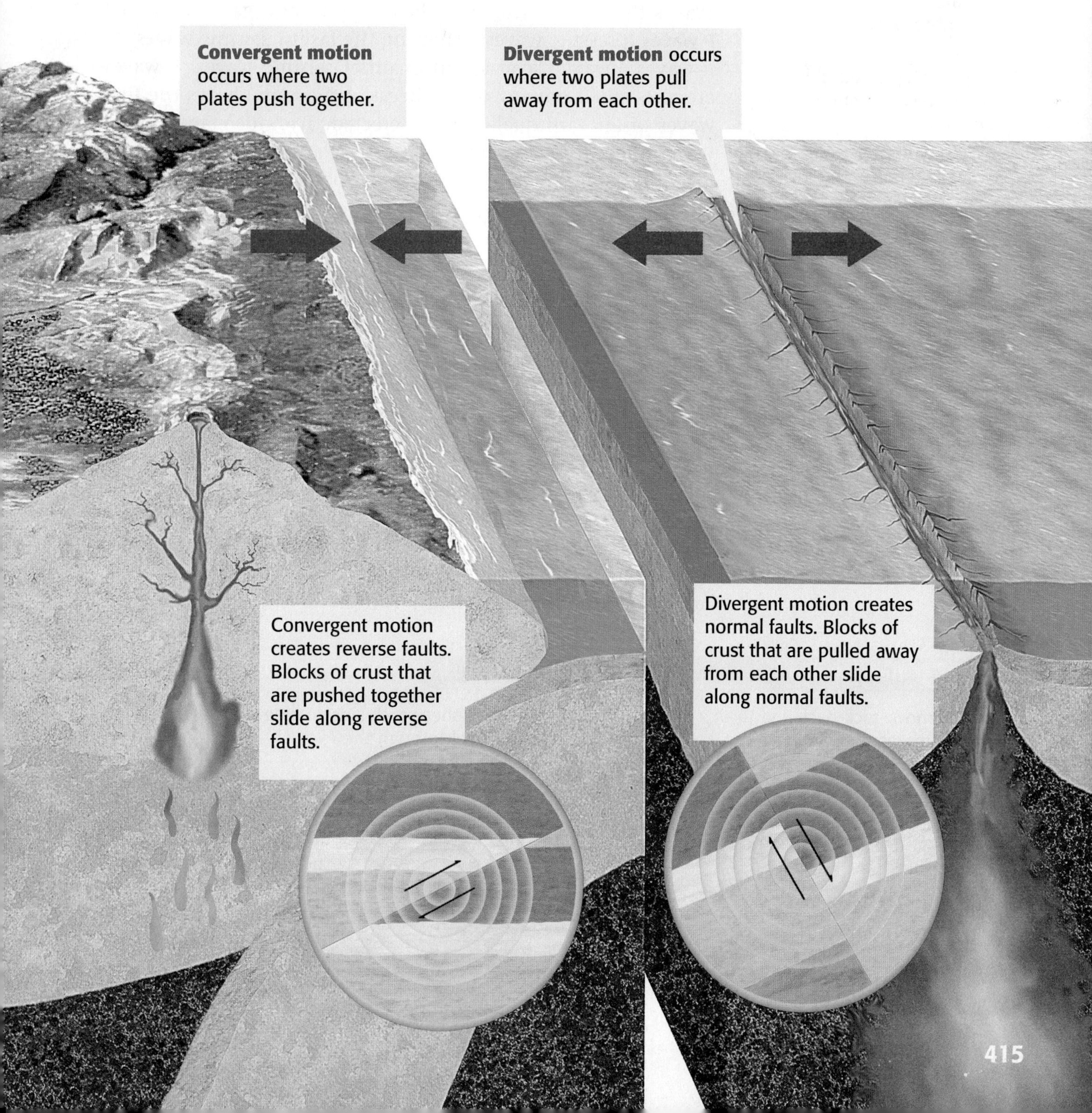

Convergent motion occurs where two plates push together.
Divergent motion occurs where two plates pull away from each other.
Convergent motion creates reverse faults. Blocks of crust that are pushed together slide along reverse faults.
Divergent motion creates normal faults. Blocks of crust that are pulled away from each other slide along normal faults.

How Do Earthquake Waves Travel?

Waves of energy that travel through the Earth are called **seismic waves.** Seismic waves that travel through the Earth's interior are called *body waves*. There are two types of body waves: P waves and S waves. Seismic waves that travel along the Earth's surface are called *surface waves*. Each type of seismic wave travels through Earth's layers in a different way and at a different speed. Also, the speed of a seismic wave depends on the kind of material the wave travels through.

Modeling Seismic Waves

1. Stretch a **spring toy** lengthwise on a **table.**
2. Hold one end of the spring while a partner holds the other end. Push your end toward your partner's end, and observe what happens.
3. Repeat step 2, but this time shake the spring from side to side.
4. Which type of seismic wave is represented in step 2? in step 3?

P Waves

Waves that travel through solids, liquids, and gases are called **P waves** (pressure waves). They are the fastest seismic waves, so P waves always travel ahead of other seismic waves. P waves are also called *primary waves,* because they are always the first waves of an earthquake to be detected. To understand how P waves affect rock, imagine a cube of gelatin sitting on a plate. Like most solids, gelatin is an elastic material. It wiggles if you tap it. Tapping the cube of gelatin changes the pressure inside the cube, which momentarily deforms the cube. The gelatin then reacts by springing back to its original shape. This process is how P waves affect rock, as shown in **Figure 4.**

seismic wave a wave of energy that travels through the Earth, away from an earthquake in all directions

P wave a seismic wave that causes particles of rock to move in a back-and-forth direction

S wave a seismic wave that causes particles of rock to move in a side-to-side direction

S Waves

Rock can also be deformed from side to side. After being deformed from side to side, the rock springs back to its original position and S waves are created. **S waves,** or shear waves, are the second-fastest seismic waves. S waves shear rock side to side, as shown in **Figure 4,** which means they stretch the rock sideways. Unlike P waves, S waves cannot travel through parts of the Earth that are completely liquid. Also, S waves are slower than P waves and always arrive later. Thus, another name for S waves is *secondary waves*.

Figure 4 **Body Waves**

P waves move rock back and forth, which squeezes and stretches the rock, as they travel through the rock.

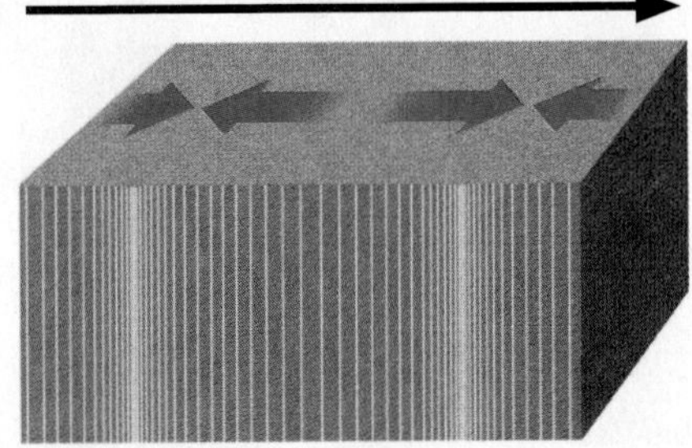

S waves shear rock side to side as they travel through the rock.

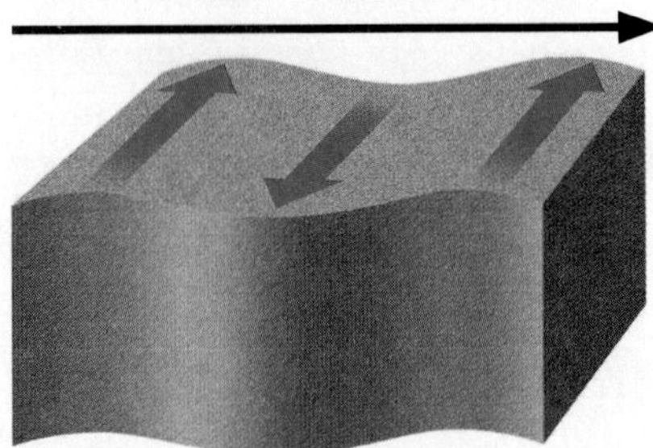

Surface Waves

Surface waves move along the Earth's surface and produce motion mostly in the upper few kilometers of Earth's crust. There are two types of surface waves. One type of surface wave produces motion up, down, and around, as shown in **Figure 5.** The other type produces back-and-forth motion like the motion produced by S waves. Surface waves are different from body waves in that surface waves travel more slowly and are more destructive.

Reading Check **Explain the differences between surface waves and body waves.**

Figure 5 **Surface Waves**

Surface waves move the ground much like ocean waves move water particles.

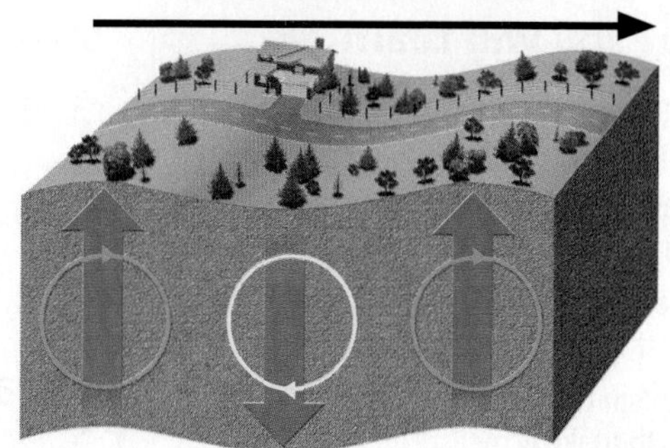

SECTION Review

Summary

- Earthquakes occur mainly near the edges of tectonic plates.
- Elastic rebound is the direct cause of earthquakes.
- Three major types of faults occur at tectonic plate boundaries: normal faults, reverse faults, and strike-slip faults.
- Earthquake energy travels as body waves through the Earth's interior or as surface waves along the surface of the Earth.

Using Key Terms

Complete each of the following sentences by choosing the correct term from the word bank.

Deformation	P waves
Elastic rebound	S waves

1. _____ is the change in shape of rock due to stress.
2. _____ always travel ahead of other waves.

Understanding Key Ideas

3. Seismic waves that shear rock side to side are called
   a. surface waves.
   b. S waves.
   c. P waves.
   d. Both (b) and (c)
4. Where do earthquakes occur?
5. What is the direct cause of earthquakes?
6. Describe the three types of plate motion and the faults that are characteristic of each type of motion.
7. What is an earthquake zone?

Math Skills

8. A seismic wave is traveling through the Earth at an average rate of speed of 8 km/s. How long will it take the wave to travel 480 km?

Critical Thinking

9. **Applying Concepts** Given what you know about elastic rebound, why do you think some earthquakes are stronger than others?
10. **Identifying Relationships** Why are surface waves more destructive to buildings than P waves or S waves are?
11. **Identifying Relationships** Why do you think the majority of earthquake zones are located at tectonic plate boundaries?

For a variety of links related to this chapter, go to www.scilinks.org

Topic: What Is an Earthquake?
SciLinks code: HSM1658

SECTION 2

Earthquake Measurement

What You Will Learn

- Explain how earthquakes are detected.
- Describe how to locate an earthquake's epicenter.
- Explain how the strength of an earthquake is measured.
- Explain how the intensity of an earthquake is measured.

Vocabulary

seismograph
seismogram
epicenter
focus

READING STRATEGY

Reading Organizer As you read this section, create an outline of the section. Use the headings from the section in your outline.

Imagine walls shaking, windows rattling, and glassware and dishes clinking and clanking. After only seconds, the vibrating stops and the sounds die away.

Within minutes, news reports give information about the strength, the time, and the location of the earthquake. You are amazed at how scientists could have learned this information so quickly.

Locating Earthquakes

How do seismologists know when and where earthquakes begin? They depend on earthquake-sensing instruments called seismographs. **Seismographs** are instruments located at or near the surface of the Earth that record seismic waves. When the waves reach a seismograph, the seismograph creates a seismogram. A **seismogram** is a tracing of earthquake motion and is created by a seismograph.

Determining Time and Location of Earthquakes

Seismologists use seismograms to calculate when an earthquake began. Seismologists find an earthquake's start time by comparing seismograms and noting the differences in arrival times of P waves and S waves. Seismologists also use seismograms to find an earthquake's epicenter. An **epicenter** is the point on the Earth's surface directly above an earthquake's starting point. A **focus** is the point inside the Earth where an earthquake begins. **Figure 1** shows the location of an earthquake's epicenter and its focus.

Reading Check How do seismologists determine an earthquake's start time? (*See the Appendix for answers to Reading Checks.*)

seismograph an instrument that records vibrations in the ground and determines the location and strength of an earthquake

seismogram a tracing of earthquake motion that is created by a seismograph

epicenter the point on Earth's surface directly above an earthquake's starting point, or focus

focus the point along a fault at which the first motion of an earthquake occurs

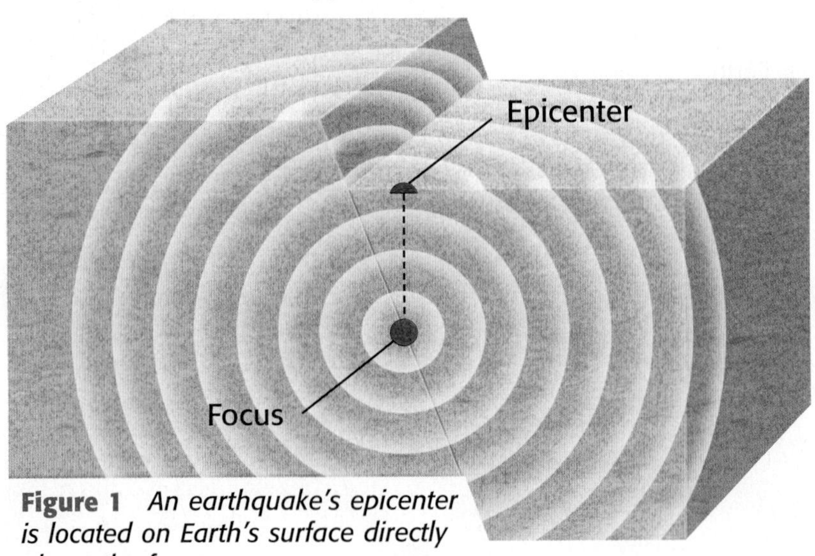

Figure 1 *An earthquake's epicenter is located on Earth's surface directly above the focus.*

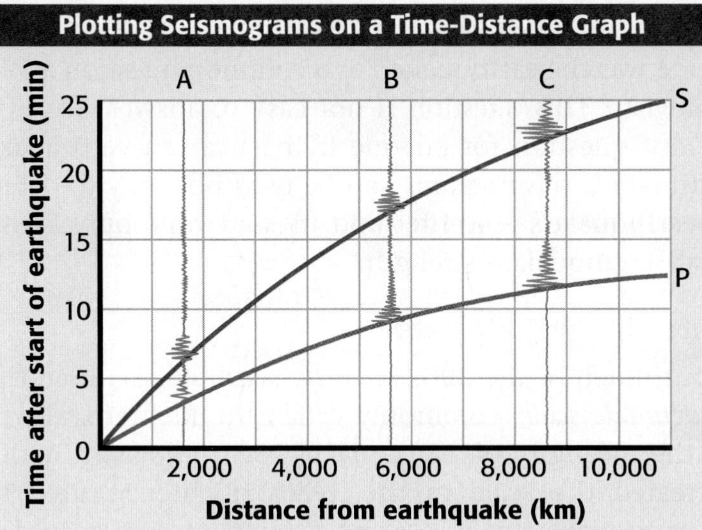

Figure 2 *After identifying P and S waves, seismologists can use the time difference to determine an earthquake's start time and the distance from the epicenter to each station. The vertical axis tells how much time passed between the start of the earthquake and the arrival of seismic waves at a station. The horizontal axis tells the distance between a station and the earthquake's epicenter.*

The S-P Time Method

Perhaps the simplest method by which seismologists find an earthquake's epicenter is the *S-P time method.* The first step in this method is to collect several seismograms of the same earthquake from different locations. Then, the seismograms are placed on a time-distance graph. The seismogram tracing of the first P wave is lined up with the P-wave time-distance curve, and the tracing of the first S wave is lined up with the S-wave curve, as shown in **Figure 2.** The distance of each station from the earthquake can be found by reading the horizontal axis. After finding out the distances, a seismologist can locate an earthquake's epicenter, as shown in **Figure 3.**

Figure 3 **Finding an Earthquake's Epicenter**

1. A circle is drawn around a seismograph station. The radius of the circle equals the distance from the seismograph to the epicenter. (This distance is taken from the time-distance graph.)

2. When a second circle is drawn around another seismograph station, the circle overlaps the first circle in two spots. One of these spots is the earthquake's epicenter.

3. When a circle is drawn around a third seismograph station, all three circles intersect in one spot—the earthquake's epicenter. In this case, the epicenter was in San Francisco.

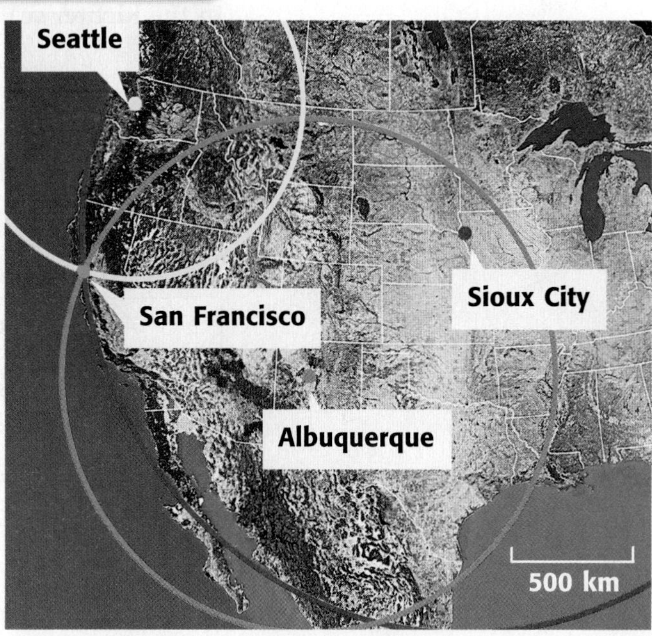

Measuring Earthquake Strength and Intensity

"How strong was the earthquake?" is a common question asked of seismologists. This question is not easy to answer. But it is an important question for anyone living near an earthquake zone. Fortunately, seismograms can be used not only to determine an earthquake's epicenter and its start time but also to find out an earthquake's strength.

CONNECTION TO Social Studies

WRITING SKILL **New Madrid Earthquakes**

During the winter of 1811–1812, three of the most powerful earthquakes in U.S. history were centered near New Madrid, Missouri, thousands of miles from the nearest tectonic plate boundary. Research the New Madrid earthquakes, and summarize your findings in a one-page essay.

The Richter Magnitude Scale

Throughout much of the 20th century, seismologists used the *Richter magnitude scale*, commonly called the Richter scale, to measure the strength of earthquakes. Seismologist Charles Richter created the scale in the 1930s. Richter wanted to compare earthquakes by measuring ground motion recorded by seismograms at seismograph stations.

Earthquake Ground Motion

A measure of the strength of an earthquake is called *magnitude*. The Richter scale measures the ground motion from an earthquake and adjusts for distance to find its strength. Each time the magnitude increases by one unit, the measured ground motion becomes 10 times larger. For example, an earthquake with a magnitude of 5.0 on the Richter scale will produce 10 times as much ground motion as an earthquake with a magnitude of 4.0. Furthermore, an earthquake with a magnitude of 6.0 will produce 100 times as much ground motion (10 × 10) as an earthquake with a magnitude of 4.0. **Table 1** shows the differences in the estimated effects of earthquakes with each increase of one unit of magnitude.

Reading Check **How are magnitude and ground motion related in the Richter scale?**

Table 1 **Effects of Different-Sized Earthquakes**

Magnitude	Estimated effects
2.0	can be detected only by seismograph
3.0	can be felt at epicenter
4.0	can be felt by most people in the area
5.0	causes damage at epicenter
6.0	can cause widespread damage
7.0	can cause great, widespread damage

Modified Mercalli Intensity Scale

A measure of the degree to which an earthquake is felt by people and the amount of damage caused by the earthquake, if any, is called *intensity*. Currently, seismologists in the United States use the Modified Mercalli Intensity Scale to measure earthquake intensity. This scale is a numerical scale that uses Roman numerals from I to XII to describe increasing earthquake intensity levels. An intensity level of I describes an earthquake that is not felt by most people. An intensity level of XII indicates total damage of an area. **Figure 4** shows the type of damage caused by an earthquake that has a Modified Mercalli intensity level of XI.

Because the effects of an earthquake vary from place to place, any earthquake will have more than one intensity value. Intensity values are usually higher near an earthquake's epicenter.

Figure 4 *Intensity values for the 1906 San Francisco earthquake varied from place to place. The maximum intensity level was XI.*

SECTION Review

Summary

- Seismologists detect seismic waves and record them as seismograms.
- The S-P time method is the simplest method to use to find an earthquake's epicenter.
- Seismologists use the Richter scale to measure an earthquake's strength.
- Seismologists use the Modified Mercalli Intensity Scale to measure an earthquake's intensity.

Using Key Terms

1. In your own words, write a definition for each of the following terms: *epicenter* and *focus*.

Understanding Key Ideas

2. What is the difference between a seismograph and a seismogram?
3. Explain how earthquakes are detected.
4. Briefly explain the steps of the S-P time method for locating an earthquake's epicenter.
5. Why might an earthquake have more than one intensity value?

Math Skills

6. How much more ground motion is produced by an earthquake of magnitude 7.0 than by an earthquake of magnitude 4.0?

Critical Thinking

7. **Making Inferences** Why is a 6.0 magnitude earthquake so much more destructive than a 5.0 magnitude earthquake?
8. **Identifying Bias** Which do you think is the more important measure of earthquakes, strength or intensity? Explain.
9. **Making Inferences** Do you think an earthquake of moderate magnitude can produce high Modified Mercalli intensity values?

SCILINKS.
NSTA
Developed and maintained by the National Science Teachers Association
For a variety of links related to this chapter, go to www.scilinks.org
Topic: Earthquake Measurement
SciLinks code: HSM0452

SECTION 3

Earthquakes and Society

What You Will Learn

- Explain how earthquake-hazard level is determined.
- Compare methods of earthquake forecasting.
- Describe five ways to safeguard buildings against earthquakes.
- Outline earthquake safety procedures.

Vocabulary

gap hypothesis
seismic gap

READING STRATEGY

Discussion Read this section silently. Write down questions that you have about this section. Discuss your questions in a small group.

Imagine that you are in class and the ground begins to shake beneath your feet. What do you do?

Seismologists are not able to predict the exact time when and place where an earthquake will occur. They can, at best, make forecasts based on the frequency with which earthquakes take place. Therefore, seismologists are always looking for better ways to forecast when and where earthquakes will happen. In the meantime, it is important for people in earthquake zones to be prepared before an earthquake strikes.

Earthquake Hazard

Earthquake hazard is a measurement of how likely an area is to have damaging earthquakes in the future. An area's earthquake-hazard level is determined by past and present seismic activity. The map in **Figure 1** shows that some areas of the United States have a higher earthquake-hazard level than others do. This variation is caused by differences in seismic activity. The greater the seismic activity, the higher the earthquake-hazard level. The West Coast, for example, has a very high earthquake-hazard level because it has a lot of seismic activity.

Look at the map. What earthquake-hazard level or levels are shown in the area in which you live? How do the hazard levels of nearby areas compare with your area's hazard level?

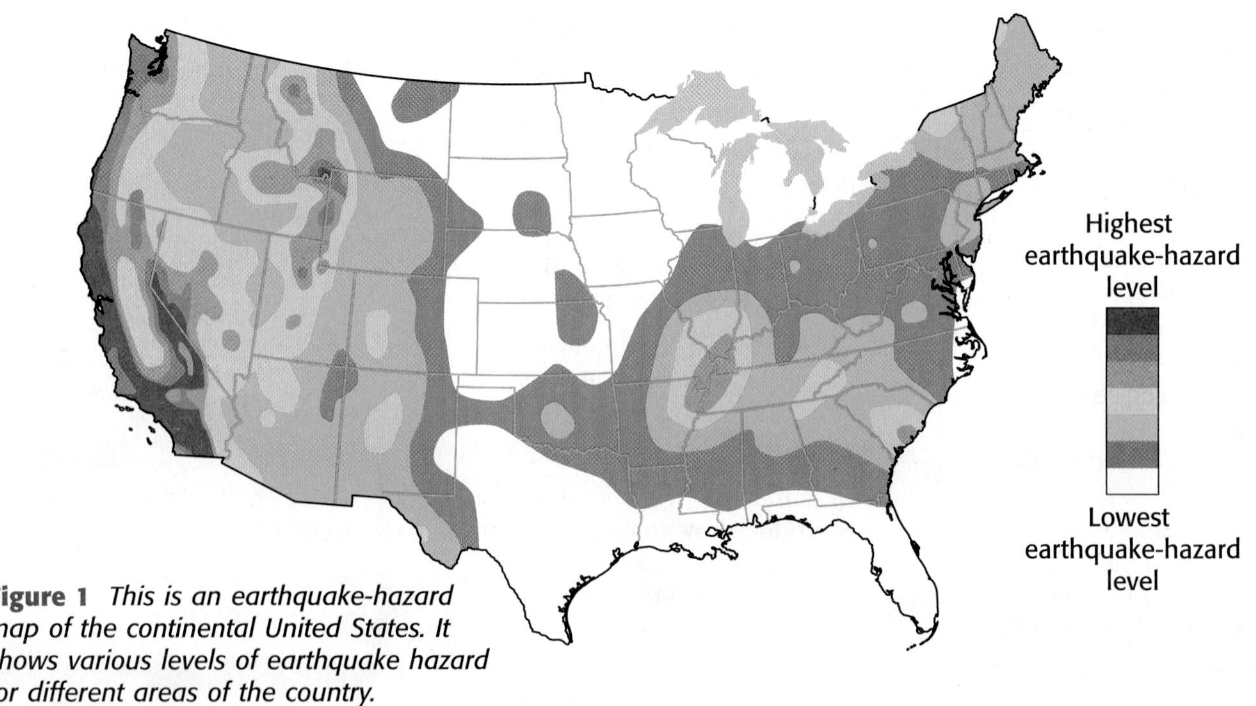

Figure 1 *This is an earthquake-hazard map of the continental United States. It shows various levels of earthquake hazard for different areas of the country.*

Table 1 Worldwide Earthquake Frequency (Based on Observations Since 1900)		
Descriptor	**Magnitude**	**Average number annually**
Great	8.0 and higher	1
Major	7.0–7.9	18
Strong	6.0–6.9	120
Moderate	5.0–5.9	800
Light	4.0–4.9	about 6,200
Minor	3.0–3.9	about 49,000
Very minor	2.0–2.9	about 365,000

Earthquake Forecasting

Forecasting when and where earthquakes will occur and their strength is difficult. By looking carefully at areas of seismic activity, seismologists have discovered some patterns in earthquakes that allow them to make some general predictions.

For another activity related to this chapter, go to **go.hrw.com** and type in the keyword **HZ5EQKW.**

Strength and Frequency

Earthquakes vary in strength. And you can probably guess that earthquakes don't occur on a set schedule. But what you may not know is that the strength of earthquakes is related to how often they occur. **Table 1** provides more detail about this relationship worldwide.

The relationship between earthquake strength and frequency is also at work on a local scale. For example, each year approximately 1.6 earthquakes with a magnitude of 4.0 on the Richter scale occur in the Puget Sound area of Washington State. Over this same time period, approximately 10 times as many earthquakes with a magnitude of 3.0 occur in this area. Scientists use these statistics to make forecasts about the strength, location, and frequency of future earthquakes.

Reading Check **What is the relationship between the strength of earthquakes and earthquake frequency?** (*See the Appendix for answers to Reading Checks.*)

gap hypothesis a hypothesis that is based on the idea that a major earthquake is more likely to occur along the part of an active fault where no earthquakes have occurred for a certain period of time

seismic gap an area along a fault where relatively few earthquakes have occurred recently but where strong earthquakes have occurred in the past

The Gap Hypothesis

Another method of forecasting an earthquake's strength, location, and frequency is based on the gap hypothesis. The **gap hypothesis** is a hypothesis that states that sections of active faults that have had relatively few earthquakes are likely to be the sites of strong earthquakes in the future. The areas along a fault where relatively few earthquakes have occurred are called **seismic gaps.**

Figure 2 **A Seismic Gap on the San Andreas Fault**

This diagram shows a cross section of the San Andreas Fault. Note how the seismic gap was filled by the 1989 Loma Prieta earthquake and its aftershocks. *Aftershocks* are weaker earthquakes that follow a stronger earthquake.

- Earthquakes prior to 1989 earthquake
- 1989 earthquake and aftershocks

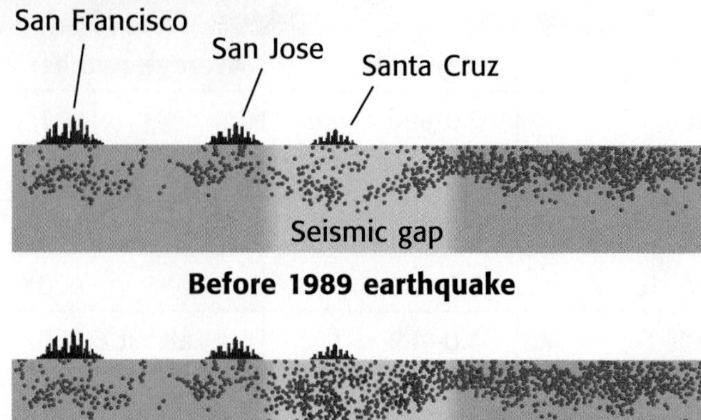

Using the Gap Hypothesis

Not all seismologists believe the gap hypothesis is an accurate method of forecasting earthquakes. But some seismologists think the gap hypothesis helped forecast the approximate location and strength of the 1989 Loma Prieta earthquake in the San Francisco Bay area. The seismic gap that they identified is illustrated in **Figure 2.** In 1988, these seismologists predicted that over the next 30 years there was a 30% chance that an earthquake with a magnitude of at least 6.5 would fill this seismic gap. Were they correct? The Loma Prieta earthquake, which filled in the seismic gap in 1989, measured 6.9 on the Richter scale. Their prediction was very close, considering how complicated the forecasting of earthquakes is.

Figure 3 *During the January 17, 1995, earthquake, the fronts of entire buildings collapsed into the streets of Kobe, Japan.*

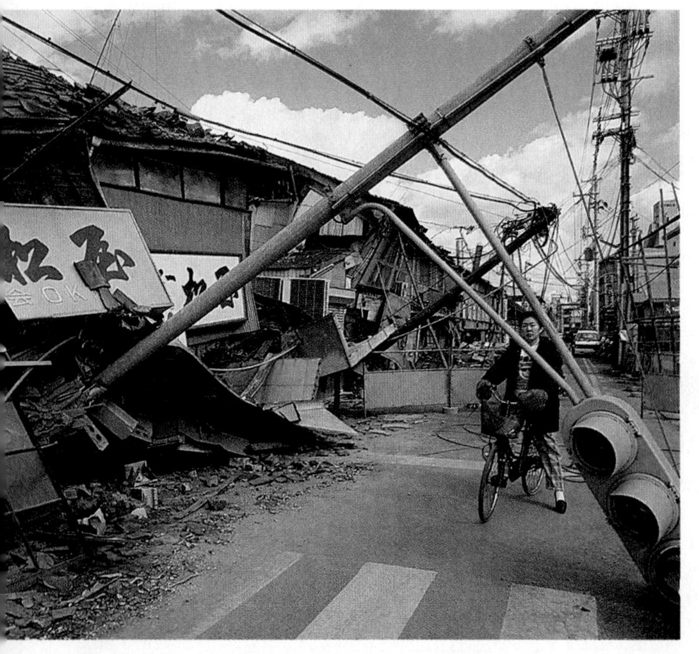

Earthquakes and Buildings

Figure 3 shows what can happen to buildings during an earthquake. These buildings were not designed or constructed to withstand the forces of an earthquake.

Today, older structures in seismically active places, such as California, are being made more earthquake resistant. The process of making older structures more earthquake resistant is called *retrofitting*. A common way to retrofit an older home is to securely fasten it to its foundation. Steel can be used to strengthen structures made of brick.

Reading Check **Explain the meaning of the term *retrofitting*.**

Earthquake-Resistant Buildings

A lot has been learned from building failure during earthquakes. Armed with this knowledge, architects and engineers use the newest technology to design and construct buildings and bridges to better withstand earthquakes. Carefully study **Figure 4** to learn more about this modern technology.

Figure 4 Earthquake-Resistant Building Technology

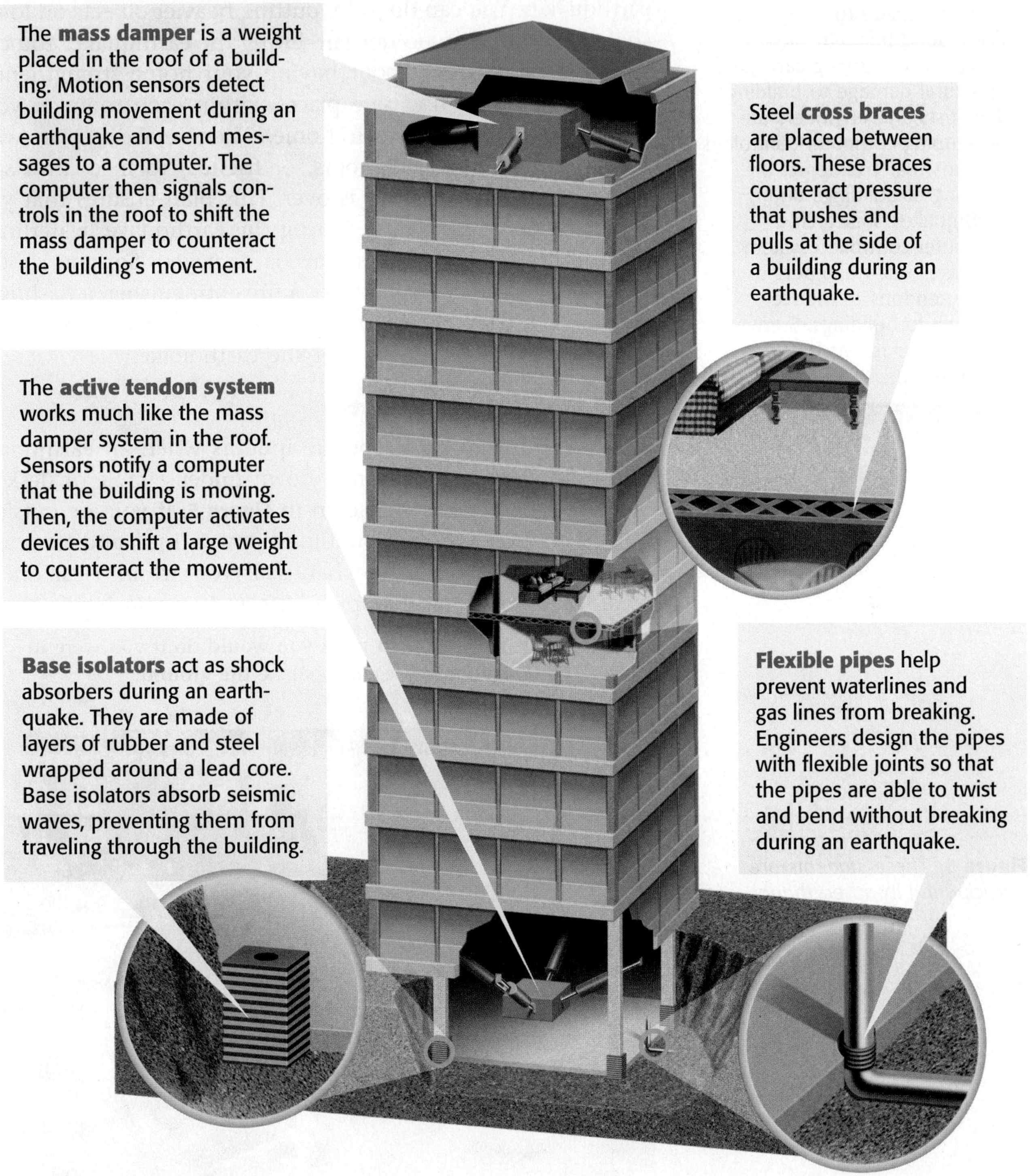

The **mass damper** is a weight placed in the roof of a building. Motion sensors detect building movement during an earthquake and send messages to a computer. The computer then signals controls in the roof to shift the mass damper to counteract the building's movement.

Steel **cross braces** are placed between floors. These braces counteract pressure that pushes and pulls at the side of a building during an earthquake.

The **active tendon system** works much like the mass damper system in the roof. Sensors notify a computer that the building is moving. Then, the computer activates devices to shift a large weight to counteract the movement.

Base isolators act as shock absorbers during an earthquake. They are made of layers of rubber and steel wrapped around a lead core. Base isolators absorb seismic waves, preventing them from traveling through the building.

Flexible pipes help prevent waterlines and gas lines from breaking. Engineers design the pipes with flexible joints so that the pipes are able to twist and bend without breaking during an earthquake.

Are You Prepared for an Earthquake?

If you live in an area where earthquakes are common, there are many things you can do to protect yourself and your property from earthquakes. Plan ahead so that you will know what to do before, during, and after an earthquake. Stick to your plan as closely as possible.

CONNECTION TO Physics

WRITING SKILL **Earthquake Proof Buildings** During earthquakes, buildings often sway from side to side when the ground beneath them moves. This swaying can cause structural damage to buildings. Scientists and engineers are developing computer-controlled systems that counteract the swaying of buildings during earthquakes. Research a computer-controlled system that uses mass dampers or active tendons to reduce damage to buildings. Summarize your research in a short essay.

Before the Shaking Starts

The first thing you should do is safeguard your home against earthquakes. You can do so by putting heavier objects on lower shelves so that they do not fall during the earthquake. You can also talk to a parent about having your home strengthened. Next, you should find safe places within each room of your home and outside of your home. Then, make a plan with others (your family, neighbors, or friends) to meet in a safe place after the earthquake is over. This plan ensures that you will all know who is safe. During the earthquake, waterlines, power lines, and roadways may be damaged. So, you should store water, nonperishable food, a fire extinguisher, a flashlight with batteries, a portable radio, medicines, and a first-aid kit in a place you can access after the earthquake.

When the Shaking Starts

The best thing to do if you are indoors when an earthquake begins is to crouch or lie face down under a table or desk in the center of a room, as shown in **Figure 5.** If you are outside, lie face down away from buildings, power lines, and trees and cover your head with your hands. If you are in a car on an open road, you should stop the car and remain inside.

Reading Check **Explain what you would do if you were in class and an earthquake began to shake the ground.**

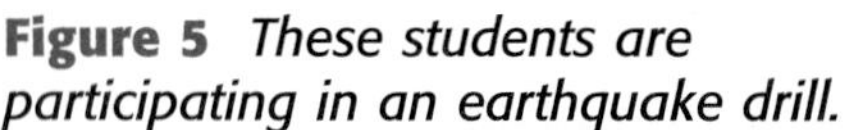

Figure 5 *These students are participating in an earthquake drill.*

After the Shaking Stops

Being in an earthquake is a startling and often frightening experience for most people. After being in an earthquake, you should not be surprised to find yourself and others puzzled about what took place. You should try to calm down and get your bearings as quickly as possible. Then, remove yourself from immediate danger, such as downed power lines, broken glass, and fire hazards. Always stay out of damaged buildings, and return home only when you are told that it is safe to do so by someone in authority. Be aware that there may be aftershocks, which may cause more damage to structures. Recall your earthquake plan, and follow it.

Disaster Planning

With an adult, create a plan that will protect your family in the event of a natural disaster, such as an earthquake. The plan should include steps to take before, during, and after a disaster. Present your disaster plan in the form of an oral report to your class.

ACTIVITY

SECTION Review

Summary

- Earthquake hazard is a measure of how likely an area is to have earthquakes in the future.
- Seismologists use their knowledge of the relationship between earthquake strength and frequency and of the gap hypothesis to forecast earthquakes.
- Homes and buildings and bridges can be strengthened to decrease earthquake damage.
- People who live in earthquake zones should safeguard their home against earthquakes.

Using Key Terms

1. In your own words, write a definition for each of the following terms: *gap hypothesis* and *seismic gap*.

Understanding Key Ideas

2. A weight that is placed on a building to make the building earthquake resistant is called a(n)
   a. active tendon system.
   b. cross brace.
   c. mass damper.
   d. base isolator.
3. How is an area's earthquake-hazard level determined?
4. Compare the strength and frequency method with the gap hypothesis method for predicting earthquakes.
5. What is a common way of making homes more earthquake resistant?
6. Describe four pieces of technology that are designed to make buildings earthquake resistant.
7. Name five items that you should store in case of an earthquake.

Math Skills

8. Of the approximately 420,000 earthquakes recorded each year, about 140 have a magnitude greater than 6.0. What percentage of total earthquakes have a magnitude greater than 6.0?

Critical Thinking

9. **Evaluating Hypotheses** Seismologists predict that there is a 20% chance that an earthquake of magnitude 7.0 or greater will fill a seismic gap during the next 50 years. Is the hypothesis incorrect if the earthquake does not happen? Explain your answer.
10. **Applying Concepts** Why is a large earthquake often followed by numerous aftershocks?

For a variety of links related to this chapter, go to www.scilinks.org

Topic: Earthquakes and Society
SciLinks code: HSM0455

Using Scientific Methods

Inquiry Lab

Quake Challenge

In many parts of the world, people must have earthquakes in mind when they construct buildings. Each building must be designed so that the structure is protected during an earthquake. Architects have greatly improved the design of buildings since 1906, when an earthquake and the fires it caused destroyed much of San Francisco. In this activity, you will use marshmallows and toothpicks to build a structure that can withstand a simulated earthquake. In the process, you will discover some of the ways a building can be built to withstand an earthquake.

OBJECTIVES

Build a model of a structure that can withstand a simulated earthquake.

Evaluate ways in which you can strengthen your model.

MATERIALS

- gelatin, square, approximately 8 × 8 cm
- marshmallows (10)
- paper plate
- toothpicks (10)

SAFETY

Ask a Question

1. What features help a building withstand an earthquake? How can I use this information to build my structure?

Form a Hypothesis

2. Brainstorm with a classmate to design a structure that will resist the simulated earthquake. Write two or three sentences to describe your design. Explain why you think your design will be able to withstand a simulated earthquake.

Test the Hypothesis

3. Follow your design to build a structure using the toothpicks and marshmallows.
4. Set your structure on a square of gelatin, and place the gelatin on a paper plate.
5. Shake the square of gelatin to test whether your building will remain standing during a quake. Do not pick up the gelatin.
6. If your first design does not work well, change it until you find a design that does. Try to determine why your building is falling so that you can improve your design each time.
7. Sketch your final design.

8. After you have tested your final design, place your structure on the gelatin square on your teacher's desk.

9. When every group has added a structure to the teacher's gelatin, your teacher will simulate an earthquake by shaking the gelatin. Watch to see which buildings withstand the most severe quake.

Analyze the Results

1. **Explaining Events** Which buildings were still standing after the final earthquake? What features made them more stable?

2. **Analyzing Results** How would you change your design in order to make your structure more stable?

Draw Conclusions

3. **Evaluating Models** This was a simple model of a real-life problem for architects. Based on this activity, what advice would you give to architects who design buildings in earthquake zones?

4. **Evaluating Models** What are some limitations of your earthquake model?

5. **Making Predictions** How could your research have an impact on society?

Chapter Review

USING KEY TERMS

1. Use each of the following terms in a separate sentence: *seismic wave, P wave,* and *S wave.*

For each pair of terms, explain how the meanings of the terms differ.

2. *seismograph* and *seismogram*
3. *epicenter* and *focus*
4. *gap hypothesis* and *seismic gap*

UNDERSTANDING KEY IDEAS

Multiple Choice

5. When rock is ___, energy builds up in it. Seismic waves occur as this energy is ___.
   - **a.** plastically deformed, increased
   - **b.** elastically deformed, released
   - **c.** plastically deformed, released
   - **d.** elastically deformed, increased
6. Reverse faults are created
   - **a.** by divergent plate motion.
   - **b.** by convergent plate motion.
   - **c.** by transform plate motion.
   - **d.** All of the above
7. The last seismic waves to arrive are
   - **a.** P waves.
   - **b.** body waves.
   - **c.** S waves.
   - **d.** surface waves.

8. If an earthquake begins while you are in a building, the safest thing for you to do is
   - **a.** to run out into an open space.
   - **b.** to get under the strongest table, chair, or other piece of furniture.
   - **c.** to call home.
   - **d.** to crouch near a wall.
9. How many major earthquakes (magnitude 7.0 to 7.9) happen on average in the world each year?
   - **a.** 1
   - **b.** 18
   - **c.** 120
   - **d.** 800
10. ___ counteract pressure that pushes and pulls at the side of a building during an earthquake.
    - **a.** Base isolators
    - **b.** Mass dampers
    - **c.** Active tendon systems
    - **d.** Cross braces

Short Answer

11. Can the S-P time method be used with one seismograph station to locate the epicenter of an earthquake? Explain your answer.
12. Explain how the Richter scale and the Modified Mercalli Intensity Scale are different.
13. What is the relationship between the strength of earthquakes and earthquake frequency?

14 Explain the way that different seismic waves affect rock as they travel through it.

15 Describe some steps you can take to protect yourself and your property from earthquakes.

CRITICAL THINKING

16 **Concept Mapping** Use the following terms to create a concept map: *focus, epicenter, earthquake start time, seismic waves, P waves,* and *S waves.*

17 **Identifying Relationships** Would a strong or light earthquake be more likely to happen along a major fault where there have not been many recent earthquakes? Explain. (Hint: Think about the average number of earthquakes of different magnitudes that occur annually.)

18 **Applying Concepts** Japan is located near a point where three tectonic plates converge. What would you imagine the earthquake-hazard level in Japan to be? Explain why.

19 **Applying Concepts** You learned that if you are in a car during an earthquake and are out in the open, it is best to stay in the car. Can you think of any situation in which you might want to leave a car during an earthquake?

20 **Identifying Relationships** You use gelatin to simulate rock in an experiment in which you are investigating the way different seismic waves affect rock. In what ways is your gelatin model limited?

INTERPRETING GRAPHICS

The graph below illustrates the relationship between earthquake magnitude and the height of tracings on a seismogram. Charles Richter initially formed his magnitude scale by comparing the heights of seismogram readings for different earthquakes. Use the graph below to answer the questions that follow.

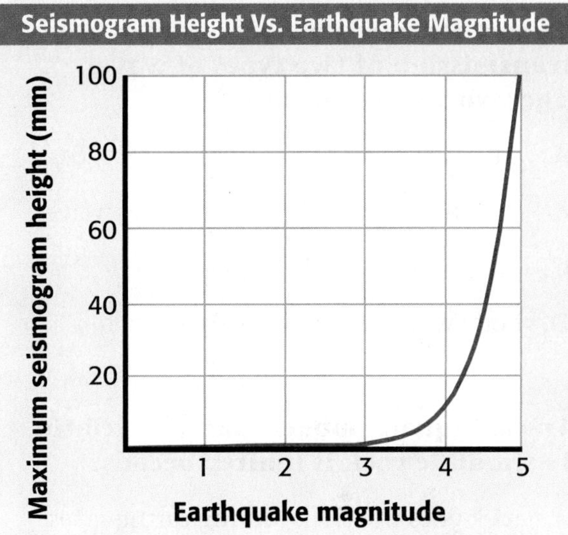

21 According to the graph, what would the magnitude of an earthquake be if its maximum seismogram height is 10 mm?

22 According to the graph, what is the difference in maximum seismogram height (in mm) between an earthquake of magnitude 4.0 and an earthquake of magnitude 5.0?

23 Look at the shape of the curve on the graph. What does this tell you about the relationship between seismogram heights and earthquake magnitudes? Explain.

Standardized Test Preparation

Multiple Choice

1. **The greatest earthquake damage happens at the**

   A. focus.

   B. boundary between tectonic plates.

   C. epicenter.

   D. seismograph station.

2. **An earthquake typically involves the transmission of two types of waves. The two wave types are**

   A. short waves and long waves.

   B. primary waves and complementary waves.

   C. ocean waves and land waves.

   D. body waves and surface waves.

3. **An earthquake model that uses gelatin to simulate rock is limited because**

   A. rock does not shake during earthquakes.

   B. gelatin has different physical properties than rock.

   C. you cannot eat rock.

   D. gelatin has a different color than rock.

4. **Earthquake waves that cause the ground to move up and down, much like ocean waves move water particles, are known as**

   A. S waves.

   B. body waves.

   C. surface waves.

   D. P waves.

5. **What happens when two tectonic plates push against each other but no earthquake takes place?**

   A. Potential energy is released.

   B. Kinetic energy is released.

   C. Potential energy builds up.

   D. Nothing happens.

Use the table below to answer question 6.

Worldwide Earthquake Frequency		
Description	**Magnitude**	**Yearly average**
Great	8.0+	1
Major	7.0–7.9	18
Strong	6.0–6.9	120
Moderate	5.0–5.9	800

6. **The table above summarizes the frequency of several earthquake types throughout the world. Based on the data given in the table, how many earthquakes in the range 4.0–4.9 probably happen each year?**

   A. approximately 900

   B. approximately 1100

   C. several thousand

   D. several million

7. **Density is determined by dividing the mass of the sample by its volume. Which pieces of laboratory equipment would be the best choice for making the necessary measurements to determine the density of sand?**

   A. beaker, graduated cylinder

   B. petri dish, balance

   C. balance, graduated cylinder

   D. graduated cylinder, stopwatch

8. **Which of the following statements reasonably describes the type of information seismologists need to analyze and potentially predict earthquake occurrences in an area?**

   A. Seismologists need to have data on the recent seismic activity of an area.

   B. Seismologists need to have detailed and accurate fault stress data for every meter of the fault line.

   C. Seismologists need to know the exact amount of potential energy a fault can store before causing an earthquake.

   D. Seismologists need to know the locations of all the existing faults in the world.

9. **Herbert is drawing a diagram of an earthquake as part of a field investigation. What label should Herbert apply to the point inside Earth where the earthquake begins?**

   A. epicenter

   B. focus

   C. ground zero

   D. plate boundary

10. **What is one way society benefits from earthquake research?**

    A. We are better able to construct buildings that can withstand shaking from earthquakes.

    B. We can now cause earthquakes to happen.

    C. We can now be certain of exactly when an earthquake will happen.

    D. We can now prevent earthquakes from happening as often.

Use the graph below to answer question 11.

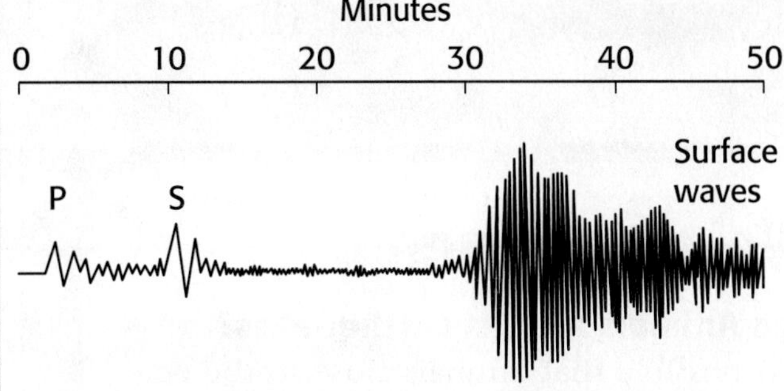

11. **Marcus made the graph above as part of a field investigation at the Kentucky Geological Institute. It shows the ground movement that occurred during a recent earthquake in western Kentucky. Which wave type caused the largest ground movements?**

    A. P waves

    B. S waves

    C. body waves

    D. surface waves

Open Response

12. **The series of major earthquakes that struck New Madrid, Missouri, in the winter of 1811–12 were so violent that Reelfoot Lake, which extends into Kentucky, was formed. Was New Madrid the earthquake's focus or its epicenter? Why?**

13. **On September 5, 2005, a small earthquake struck central Kentucky, just north of Sharpsburg. How is energy converted during an earthquake?**

Science in Action

Weird Science

Can Animals Predict Earthquakes?

Is it possible that animals close to the epicenter of an earthquake are able to sense changes in their environment? And should we be paying attention to such animal behavior? As long ago as the 1700s, unusual animal activity prior to earthquakes has been recorded. Examples include domestic cattle seeking higher ground and zoo animals refusing to enter their shelters at night. Other animals, such as lizards, snakes, and small mammals, evacuate their underground burrows, and wild birds leave their usual habitats. These events occur days, hours, or even minutes before an earthquake.

Language Arts ACTIVITY

WRITING SKILL Create an illustrated field guide of animal activity to show how animal activity can predict earthquakes. Each illustration must have a paragraph that describes the activity of a specific animal.

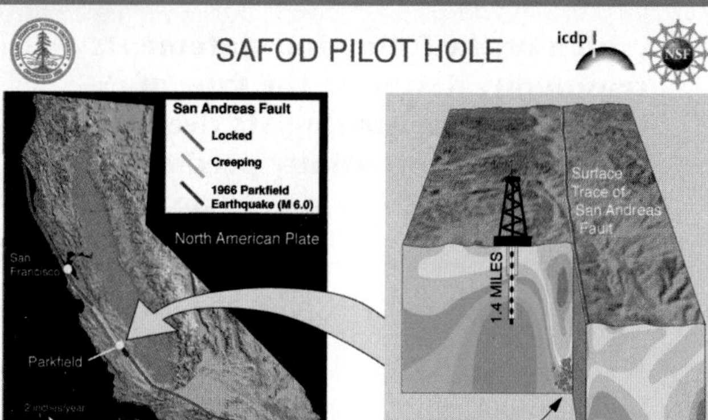

Science, Technology, and Society

San Andreas Fault Observatory at Depth (SAFOD)

Seismologists are creating an underground observatory in Parkfield, California, to study earthquakes along the San Andreas Fault. The observatory will be named the San Andreas Fault Observatory at Depth (SAFOD). A deep hole will be drilled directly into the fault zone near a point where earthquakes of magnitude 6.0 have been recorded. Instruments will be placed at the bottom of the hole, 3 to 4 km beneath Earth's surface. These instruments will make seismological measurements of earthquakes and measure the deformation of rock.

Social Studies ACTIVITY

Research the great San Francisco earthquake of 1906. Find images of the earthquake on the Internet and download them, or cut them out of old magazines. Create a photo collage of the earthquake that shows San Francisco before and after the earthquake.

Hiroo Kanamori

Seismologist Hiroo Kanamori is a seismologist at the California Institute of Technology in Pasadena, California. Dr. Kanamori studies how earthquakes occur and tries to reduce their impact on our society. He also analyzes what the effects of earthquakes on oceans are and how earthquakes create giant ocean waves called *tsunamis* (tsoo NAH meez). Tsunamis are very destructive to life and property when they reach land. Kanamori has discovered that even some weak earthquakes can cause powerful tsunamis. He calls these events *tsunami earthquakes,* and he has learned to predict when tsunamis will form. In short, when tectonic plates grind together slowly, special waves called *long-period seismic waves* are created. When Kanamori sees a long-period wave recorded on a seismogram, he knows a tsunami will form. Because long-period waves travel faster than tsunamis, they arrive at recording stations earlier. When an earthquake station records an earthquake, information about that earthquake is provided to a tsunami warning center. The center determines if the earthquake may cause a tsunami and, if so, issues a tsunami warning to areas that may be affected.

Math ACTIVITY

An undersea earthquake causes a tsunami to form. The tsunami travels across the open ocean at 800 km/h. How long will the tsunami take to travel from the point where it formed to a coastline 3,600 km away?

To learn more about these Science in Action topics, visit go.hrw.com and type in the keyword HZ5EQKF.

Current Science

Check out Current Science® articles related to this chapter by visiting go.hrw.com. Just type in the keyword HZ5CS08.

16

Volcanoes

The Big Idea

Volcanoes are locations where molten rock reaches Earth's surface, and volcanoes can affect landforms and societies.

SECTION

About the Photo

When you think of a volcanic eruption, you probably think of a cone-shaped mountain exploding and sending huge clouds of ash into the air. Some volcanic eruptions do just that! Most volcanic eruptions, such as the one shown here, which is flowing over a road in Hawaii, are slow and quiet. Volcanic eruptions happen throughout the world, and they play a major role in shaping the Earth's surface.

PRE-READING ACTIVITY

FOLDNOTES **Layered Book** Before you read the chapter, create the FoldNote entitled "Layered Book" described in the **Study Skills** section of the Appendix. Label the tabs of the layered book with "Volcanic eruptions," "Effects of eruptions," and "Causes of eruptions." As you read the chapter, write information you learn about each category under the appropriate tab.

START-UP ACTIVITY

Anticipation

In this activity, you will build a simple model of a volcano and you will try to predict an eruption.

Procedure

1. Place **10 mL of baking soda** on a **sheet of tissue.** Fold the corners of the tissue over the baking soda, and place the tissue packet in a **large pan.**
2. Put **modeling clay** around the top edge of a **funnel.** Press that end of the funnel over the tissue packet to make a tight seal.
3. After you put on **safety goggles,** add **50 mL of vinegar** and **several drops of liquid dish soap** to a **200 mL beaker** and stir.
4. Predict how long it will take the volcano to erupt after the liquid is poured into the funnel. Then, carefully pour the liquid into the funnel, and use a **stopwatch** to measure how long the volcano takes to begin erupting.

Analysis

1. Based on your observations, explain what happened to cause the eruption.
2. How accurate was your prediction? By how many seconds did the class predictions vary?
3. How do the size of the funnel opening and the amount of baking soda and vinegar affect the amount of time that the volcano takes to erupt?

SECTION 1

Volcanic Eruptions

What You Will Learn

- Distinguish between nonexplosive and explosive volcanic eruptions.
- Identify the features of a volcano.
- Explain how the composition of magma affects the type of volcanic eruption that will occur.
- Describe four types of lava and four types of pyroclastic material.

Vocabulary

volcano
magma chamber
vent

READING STRATEGY

Reading Organizer As you read this section, make a table comparing types of lava and pyroclastic material.

Think about the force released when the first atomic bomb exploded during World War II. Now imagine an explosion 10,000 times stronger, and you will get an idea of how powerful a volcanic eruption can be.

The explosive pressure of a volcanic eruption can turn an entire mountain into a billowing cloud of ash and rock in a matter of seconds. But eruptions are also creative forces—they help form fertile farmland. They also create some of the largest mountains on Earth. During an eruption, molten rock, or *magma,* is forced to the Earth's surface. Magma that flows onto the Earth's surface is called *lava.* **Volcanoes** are areas of Earth's surface through which magma and volcanic gases pass.

volcano a vent or fissure in the Earth's surface through which magma and gases are expelled

Nonexplosive Eruptions

At this moment, volcanic eruptions are occurring around the world—on the ocean floor and on land. Nonexplosive eruptions are the most common type of eruption. These eruptions produce relatively calm flows of lava, such as those shown in **Figure 1.** Nonexplosive eruptions can release huge amounts of lava. Vast areas of the Earth's surface, including much of the sea floor and the Northwest region of the United States, are covered with lava from nonexplosive eruptions.

Figure 1 Examples of Nonexplosive Eruptions

Sometimes, nonexplosive eruptions can spray lava into the air. Lava fountains, such as this one, pulse with the pressure of escaping gases.

The speed of a lava flow can range from a slow creep to as fast as 60 km/h.

Explosive Eruptions

Explosive eruptions, such as the one shown in **Figure 2,** are much rarer than nonexplosive eruptions. However, the effects of explosive eruptions can be incredibly destructive. During an explosive eruption, clouds of hot debris, ash, and gas rapidly shoot out from a volcano. Instead of producing lava flows, explosive eruptions cause molten rock to be blown into tiny particles that harden in the air. The dust-sized particles, called *ash,* can reach the upper atmosphere and can circle the Earth for years. Larger pieces of debris fall closer to the volcano. An explosive eruption can also blast millions of tons of lava and rock from a volcano. In a matter of seconds, an explosive eruption can demolish an entire mountainside, as shown in **Figure 3.**

✓ Reading Check **List two differences between explosive and nonexplosive eruptions.** (*See the Appendix for answers to Reading Checks.*)

Figure 2 *In what resembles a nuclear explosion, volcanic ash rockets skyward during the 1990 eruption of Mount Redoubt in Alaska.*

Figure 3 *Within seconds, the 1980 eruption of Mount St. Helens in Washington State caused the side of the mountain to collapse. The blast scorched and flattened 600 km^2 of forest.*

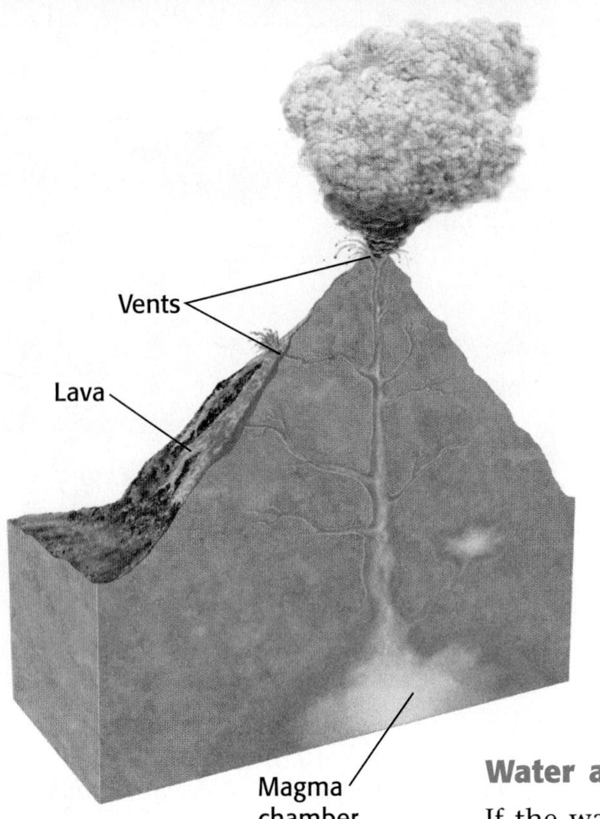

Figure 4 *Volcanoes form when lava is released from vents.*

What Is Inside a Volcano?

If you could look inside an erupting volcano, you would see the features shown in **Figure 4.** A **magma chamber** is a body of molten rock deep underground that feeds a volcano. Magma rises from the magma chamber through cracks in the Earth's crust to openings called **vents.** Magma is released from the vents during an eruption.

magma chamber the body of molten rock that feeds a volcano

vent an opening at the surface of the Earth through which volcanic material passes

What Makes Up Magma?

By comparing the composition of magma from different eruptions, scientists have made an important discovery. The composition of the magma affects how explosive a volcanic eruption is. The key to whether an eruption will be explosive lies in the silica, water, and gas content of the magma.

Water and Magma Are an Explosive Combination

If the water content of magma is high, an explosive eruption is more likely. Because magma is underground, it is under intense pressure and water stays dissolved in the magma. If the magma quickly moves to the surface, the pressure suddenly decreases and the water and other compounds, such as carbon dioxide, become gases. As the gases expand rapidly, an explosion can result. This process is similar to what happens when you shake a can of soda and open it. When a can of soda is shaken, the CO_2 dissolved in the soda is released and pressure builds up. When the can is opened, the soda shoots out, just as lava shoots out of a volcano during an explosive eruption. In fact, some lava is so frothy with gas when it reaches the surface that its solid form, called *pumice,* can float in water!

Silica-Rich Magma Traps Explosive Gases

Magma that has a high silica content also tends to cause explosive eruptions. Silica-rich magma has a stiff consistency. It flows slowly and tends to harden in a volcano's vents. As a result, it plugs the vent. As more magma pushes up from below, pressure increases. If enough pressure builds up, an explosive eruption takes place. Stiff magma also prevents water vapor and other gases from easily escaping. Gas bubbles trapped in magma can expand until they explode. When they explode, the magma shatters and ash and pumice are blasted from the vent. Magma that contains less silica has a more fluid, runnier consistency. Because gases escape this type of magma more easily, explosive eruptions are less likely to occur.

Reading Check How do silica levels affect an eruption?

What Erupts from a Volcano?

Magma erupts as either lava or pyroclastic (PIE roh KLAS tik) material. *Lava* is liquid magma that flows from a volcanic vent. *Pyroclastic material* forms when magma is blasted into the air and hardens. Nonexplosive eruptions produce mostly lava. Explosive eruptions produce mostly pyroclastic material. Over many years—or even during the same eruption—a volcano's eruptions may alternate between lava and pyroclastic eruptions.

Types of Lava

The viscosity of lava, or how lava flows, varies greatly. To understand viscosity, remember that a milkshake has high viscosity and a glass of milk has low viscosity. Lava that has high viscosity is stiff. Lava that has low viscosity is more fluid. The viscosity of lava affects the surface of a lava flow in different ways, as shown in **Figure 5.** *Blocky lava* and *pahoehoe* (puh HOY HOY) have a high viscosity and flow slowly. Other types of lava flows, such as *aa* (AH AH) and *pillow lava,* have lower viscosities and flow more quickly.

CONNECTION TO Social Studies

Fertile Farmlands Volcanic ash helps create some of the most fertile farmland in the world. Use a world map and reference materials to find the location of volcanoes that have helped create farmland in Italy, Africa, South America, and the United States. Make an illustrated map on a piece of poster board to share your findings.

ACTIVITY

Figure 5 Four Types of Lava

Aa lava pours out quickly and forms a brittle crust. The crust is torn into jagged pieces as molten lava continues to flow underneath.

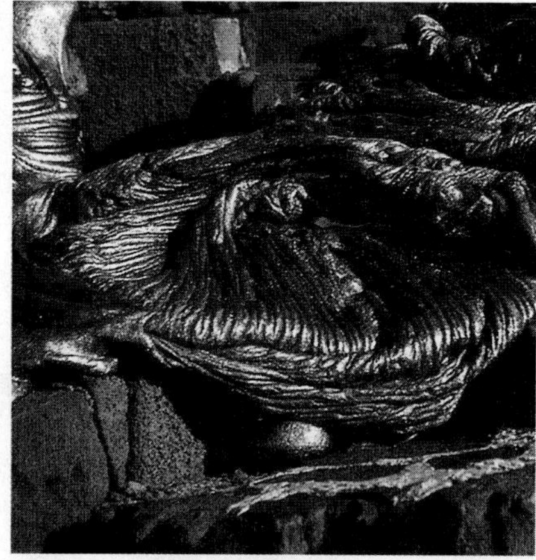

Pahoehoe lava flows slowly, like wax dripping from a candle. Its glassy surface has rounded wrinkles.

Pillow lava forms when lava erupts underwater. As you can see here, this lava forms rounded lumps that are the shape of pillows.

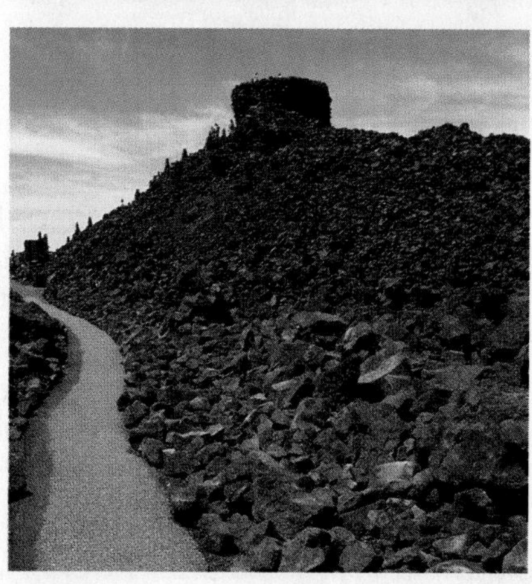

Blocky lava is cool, stiff lava that does not travel far from the erupting vent. Blocky lava usually oozes from a volcano and forms jumbled heaps of sharp-edged chunks.

Figure 6 Four Types of Pyroclastic Material

Volcanic bombs are large blobs of magma that harden in the air. The shape of this bomb was caused by the magma spinning through the air as it cooled.

Lapilli, which means "little stones" in Italian, are pebblelike bits of magma that hardened before they hit the ground.

Volcanic ash forms when the gases in stiff magma expand rapidly and the walls of the gas bubbles explode into tiny, glasslike slivers. Ash makes up most of the pyroclastic material in an eruption.

Volcanic blocks, the largest pieces of pyroclastic material, are pieces of solid rock erupted from a volcano.

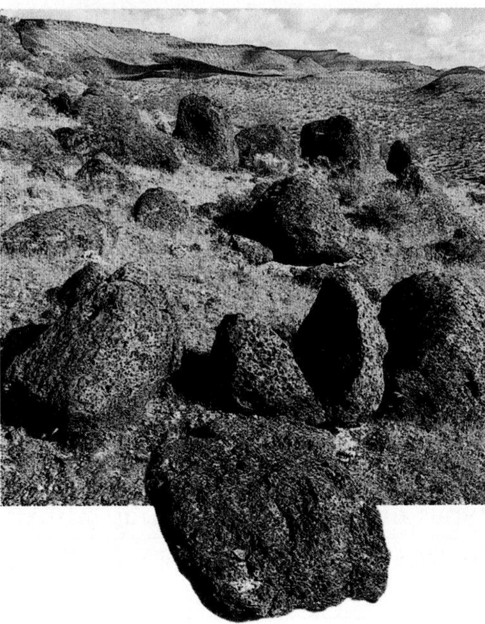

Types of Pyroclastic Material

Pyroclastic material forms when magma explodes from a volcano and solidifies in the air. This material also forms when powerful eruptions shatter existing rock. The size of pyroclastic material ranges from boulders that are the size of houses to tiny particles that can remain suspended in the atmosphere for years. **Figure 6** shows four types of pyroclastic material: volcanic bombs, volcanic blocks, lapilli (lah PIL IE), and volcanic ash.

Reading Check **Describe four types of pyroclastic material.**

Modeling an Explosive Eruption

1. Inflate a **large balloon,** and place it in a **cardboard box.**
2. Spread a **sheet** on the floor. Place the box in the middle of the sheet. Mound a thin layer of **sand** over the balloon to make a volcano that is taller than the edges of the box.
3. Lightly mist the volcano with **water.** Sprinkle **tempera paint** on the volcano until the volcano is completely covered.
4. Place **small objects** such as **raisins** randomly on the volcano. Draw a sketch of the volcano.
5. Put on your **safety goggles.** Pop the balloon with a **pin.**
6. Use a **metric ruler** to calculate the average distance that 10 grains of sand and 10 raisins traveled.
7. How did the relative weight of each type of material affect the average distance that the material traveled?
8. Draw a sketch of the exploded volcano.

Pyroclastic Flows

One particularly dangerous type of volcanic flow is called a *pyroclastic flow*. Pyroclastic flows are produced when enormous amounts of hot ash, dust, and gases are ejected from a volcano. This glowing cloud of pyroclastic material can race downhill at speeds of more than 200 km/h—faster than most hurricane-force winds! The temperature at the center of a pyroclastic flow can exceed 700°C. A pyroclastic flow from the eruption of Mount Pinatubo is shown in **Figure 7.** Fortunately, scientists were able to predict the eruption and a quarter of a million people were evacuated before the eruption.

Figure 7 *The 1991 eruption of Mount Pinatubo in the Philippines released terrifying pyroclastic flows.*

SECTION Review

Summary

- Volcanoes erupt both explosively and nonexplosively.
- Magma that has a high level of water, CO_2, or silica tends to erupt explosively.
- Lava can be classified by its viscosity and by the surface texture of lava flows.
- Pyroclastic material, such as ash and volcanic bombs, forms when magma solidifies as it travels through the air.

Using Key Terms

1. In your own words, write a definition for each of the following terms: *volcano, magma chamber,* and *vent.*

Understanding Key Ideas

2. Which of the following factors influences whether a volcano erupts explosively?
   - **a.** the concentration of volcanic bombs in the magma
   - **b.** the concentration of phosphorus in the magma
   - **c.** the concentration of aa in the magma
   - **d.** the concentration of water in the magma
3. How are lava and pyroclastic material classified? Describe four types of lava.
4. Which produces more pyroclastic material: an explosive eruption or a nonexplosive eruption?
5. Explain how the presence of silica and water in magma increases the chances of an explosive eruption.
6. What is a pyroclastic flow?

Math Skills

7. A sample of magma is 64% silica. Express this percentage as a simplified fraction.

Critical Thinking

8. **Analyzing Ideas** How is an explosive eruption similar to opening a can of soda that has been shaken? Be sure to describe the role of carbon dioxide.
9. **Making Inferences** Predict the silica content of aa, pillow lava, and blocky lava.
10. **Making Inferences** Explain why the names of many types of lava are Hawaiian but the names of many types of pyroclastic material are Italian and Indonesian.

For a variety of links related to this chapter, go to www.scilinks.org

Topic: Volcanic Eruptions
SciLinks code: HSM1616

SECTION 2

Effects of Volcanic Eruptions

What You Will Learn

- Explain how volcanic eruptions can affect climate.
- Compare the three types of volcanoes.
- Compare craters, calderas, and lava plateaus.

Vocabulary

crater
caldera
lava plateau

READING STRATEGY

Paired Summarizing Read this section silently. In pairs, take turns summarizing the material. Stop to discuss ideas that seem confusing.

In 1816, Chauncey Jerome, a resident of Connecticut, wrote that the clothes his wife had laid out to dry the day before had frozen during the night. This event would not have been unusual except that the date was June 10!

At that time, residents of New England did not know that the explosion of a volcanic island on the other side of the world had severely changed the global climate and was causing "The Year Without a Summer."

Volcanic Eruptions and Climate Change

The explosion of Mount Tambora in 1815 blanketed most of Indonesia in darkness for three days. It is estimated that 12,000 people died directly from the explosion and 80,000 people died from the resulting hunger and disease. The global effects of the eruption were not felt until the next year, however.

During large-scale eruptions, enormous amounts of volcanic ash and gases are ejected into the upper atmosphere. As volcanic ash and gases spread throughout the atmosphere, they can block enough sunlight to cause global temperatures to drop. The Tambora eruption affected the global climate enough to cause food shortages in North America and Europe. More recently, the eruption of Mount Pinatubo, shown in **Figure 1**, caused average global temperatures to drop by as much as 0.5°C. Although this may seem insignificant, such a shift can disrupt climates all over the world.

Reading Check How does a volcanic eruption affect climate? *(See the Appendix for answers to Reading Checks.)*

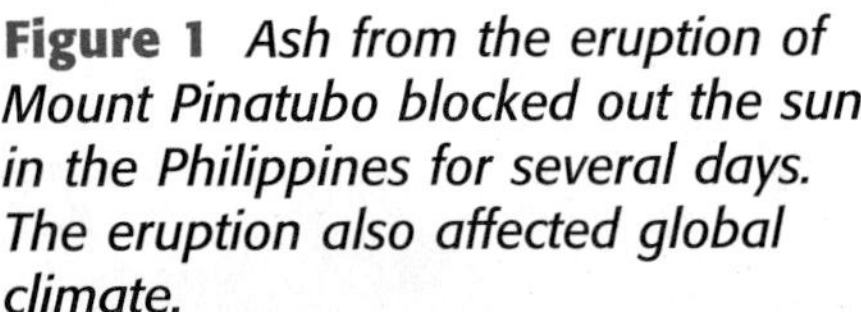

Figure 1 *Ash from the eruption of Mount Pinatubo blocked out the sun in the Philippines for several days. The eruption also affected global climate.*

Different Types of Volcanoes

Volcanic eruptions can cause profound changes in climate. But the changes to Earth's surface caused by eruptions are probably more familiar. Perhaps the best known of all volcanic landforms are the volcanoes themselves. The three basic types of volcanoes are illustrated in **Figure 2.**

Shield Volcanoes

Shield volcanoes are built of layers of lava released from repeated nonexplosive eruptions. Because the lava is very runny, it spreads out over a wide area. Over time, the layers of lava create a volcano that has gently sloping sides. Although their sides are not very steep, shield volcanoes can be enormous. Hawaii's Mauna Kea, the shield volcano shown here, is the tallest mountain on Earth. Measured from its base on the sea floor, Mauna Kea is taller than Mount Everest.

Cinder Cone Volcanoes

Cinder cone volcanoes are made of pyroclastic material usually produced from moderately explosive eruptions. The pyroclastic material forms steep slopes, as shown in this photo of the Mexican volcano Paricutín. Cinder cones are small and usually erupt for only a short time. Paricutín appeared in a cornfield in 1943 and erupted for only nine years before stopping at a height of 400 m. Cinder cones often occur in clusters, commonly on the sides of other volcanoes. They usually erode quickly because the pyroclastic material is not cemented together.

Composite Volcanoes

Composite volcanoes, sometimes called *stratovolcanoes,* are one of the most common types of volcanoes. They form from explosive eruptions of pyroclastic material followed by quieter flows of lava. The combination of both types of eruptions forms alternating layers of pyroclastic material and lava. Composite volcanoes, such as Japan's Mount Fuji (shown here), have broad bases and sides that get steeper toward the top. Composite volcanoes in the western region of the United States include Mount Hood, Mount Rainier, Mount Shasta, and Mount St. Helens.

Figure 2 **Three Types of Volcanoes**

Shield volcano

Cinder cone volcano

Composite volcano

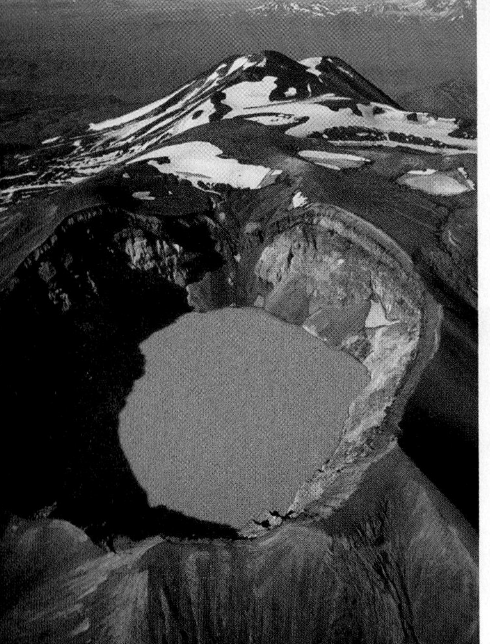

Figure 3 *A crater, such as this one in Kamchatka, Russia, forms around the central vent of a volcano.*

Other Types of Volcanic Landforms

In addition to volcanoes, other landforms are produced by volcanic activity. These landforms include craters, calderas, and lava plateaus. Read on to learn more about these landforms.

Craters

Around the central vent at the top of many volcanoes is a funnel-shaped pit called a **crater.** An example of a crater is shown in **Figure 3.** During less explosive eruptions, lava flows and pyroclastic material can pile up around the vent creating a cone with a central crater. As the eruption stops, the lava that is left in the crater often drains back underground. The vent may then collapse to form a larger crater. If the lava hardens in the crater, the next eruption may blast it away. In this way, a crater becomes larger and deeper.

crater a funnel-shaped pit near the top of the central vent of a volcano

caldera a large, semicircular depression that forms when the magma chamber below a volcano partially empties and causes the ground above to sink

Calderas

Calderas can appear similar to craters, but they are many times larger. A **caldera** is a large, semicircular depression that forms when the chamber that supplies magma to a volcano partially empties and the chamber's roof collapses. As a result, the ground above the magma chamber sinks, as shown in **Figure 4.** Much of Yellowstone Park is made up of three large calderas that formed when volcanoes collapsed between 1.9 million and 0.6 million years ago. Today, hot springs, such as Old Faithful, are heated by the thermal energy left over from those events.

Reading Check How do calderas form?

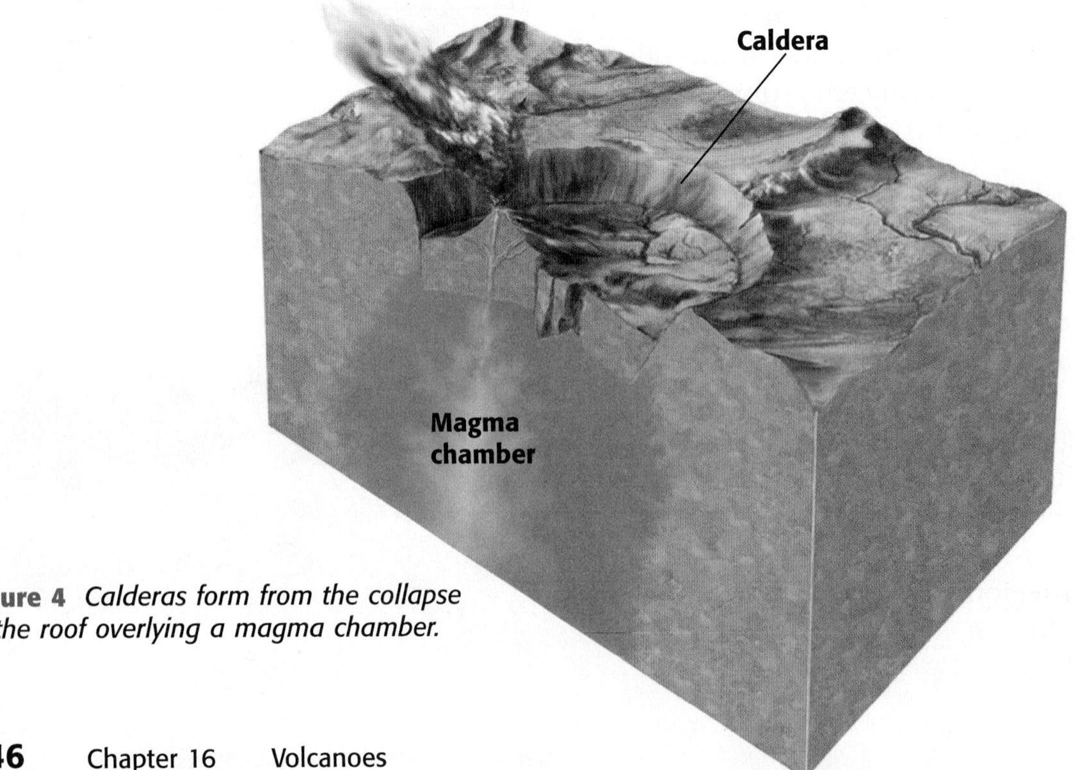

Figure 4 *Calderas form from the collapse of the roof overlying a magma chamber.*

Figure 5 *The Columbia River Plateau formed from a massive outpouring of lava that began 17 million years ago.*

Lava Plateaus

The most massive outpourings of lava do not come from individual volcanoes. Most of the lava on Earth's surface erupted from long cracks, or *rifts,* in the crust. In this type of eruption, runny lava can pour out for millions of years and spread over huge areas. A landform that results from repeated eruptions of lava spread over a large area is called a **lava plateau.** The Columbia River Plateau, part of which is shown in **Figure 5,** is a lava plateau that formed between 17 million and 14 million years ago in the northwestern region of the United States. In some places, the Columbia River Plateau is 3 km thick.

lava plateau a wide, flat landform that results from repeated nonexplosive eruptions of lava that spread over a large area

SECTION Review

Summary

- The large volumes of gas and ash released from volcanic eruptions can affect climate.
- Shield volcanoes result from many eruptions of relatively runny lava.
- Cinder cone volcanoes result from mildly explosive eruptions of pyroclastic material.
- Composite volcanoes result from alternating explosive and nonexplosive eruptions.
- Craters, calderas, and lava plateaus are volcanic landforms.

Using Key Terms

Complete each of the following sentences by choosing the correct term from the word bank.

caldera crater

1. A ___ is a funnel-shaped hole around the central vent.
2. A ___ results when a magma chamber partially empties.

Understanding Key Ideas

3. Which type of volcano results from alternating explosive and nonexplosive eruptions?
   a. composite volcano
   b. cinder cone volcano
   c. rift-zone volcano
   d. shield volcano
4. Why do cinder cone volcanoes have narrower bases and steeper sides than shield volcanoes do?
5. Why does a volcano's crater tend to get larger over time?

Math Skills

6. The fastest lava flow recorded was 60 km/h. A horse can gallop as fast as 48 mi/h. Could a galloping horse outrun the fastest lava flow? (Hint: 1 km = 0.621 mi)

Critical Thinking

7. **Making Inferences** Why did it take a year for the effects of the Tambora eruption to be experienced in New England?

SCILINKS.
NSTA
Developed and maintained by the National Science Teachers Association
For a variety of links related to this chapter, go to www.scilinks.org
Topic: Volcanic Effects
SciLinks code: HSM1615

SECTION 3

Causes of Volcanic Eruptions

What You Will Learn

- Describe the formation and movement of magma.
- Explain the relationship between volcanoes and plate tectonics.
- Summarize the methods scientists use to predict volcanic eruptions.

Vocabulary

rift zone
hot spot

READING STRATEGY

Reading Organizer As you read this section, make a flowchart of the steps of magma formation in different tectonic environments.

More than 2,000 years ago, Pompeii was a busy Roman city near the sleeping volcano Mount Vesuvius. People did not see Vesuvius as much of a threat. Everything changed when Vesuvius suddenly erupted and buried the city in a deadly blanket of ash that was almost 20 ft thick!

Today, even more people are living on and near active volcanoes. Scientists closely monitor volcanoes to avoid this type of disaster. They study the gases coming from active volcanoes and look for slight changes in the volcano's shape that could indicate that an eruption is near. Scientists know much more about the causes of eruptions than the ancient Pompeiians did, but there is much more to be discovered.

The Formation of Magma

Understanding how magma forms helps explain why volcanoes erupt. Magma forms in the deeper regions of the Earth's crust and in the uppermost layers of the mantle where the temperature and pressure are very high. Changes in pressure and temperature cause magma to form.

Pressure and Temperature

Part of the upper mantle is made of very hot, puttylike rock that flows slowly. The rock of the mantle is hot enough to melt at Earth's surface, but it remains a puttylike solid because of pressure. This pressure is caused by the weight of the rock above the mantle. In other words, the rock above the mantle presses the atoms of the mantle so close together that the rock cannot melt. As **Figure 1** shows, rock melts when its temperature increases or when the pressure on the rock decreases.

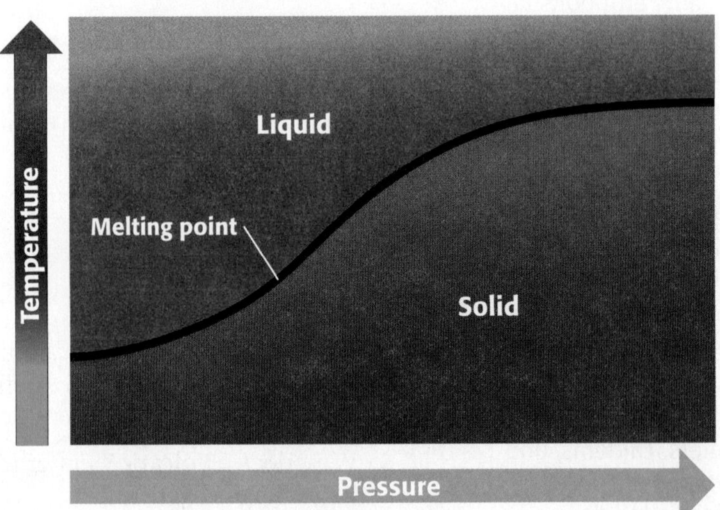

Figure 1 *The curved line indicates the melting point of a rock. As pressure decreases and temperature increases, the rock begins to melt.*

Magma Formation in the Mantle

Because the temperature of the mantle is fairly constant, a decrease in pressure is the most common cause of magma formation. Magma often forms at the boundary between separating tectonic plates, where pressure is decreased. Once formed, the magma is less dense than the surrounding rock, so the magma slowly rises toward the surface like an air bubble in a jar of honey.

Where Volcanoes Form

The locations of volcanoes give clues about how volcanoes form. The map in **Figure 2** shows the location of some of the world's major active volcanoes. The map also shows the boundaries between tectonic plates. A large number of volcanoes lie directly on tectonic plate boundaries. In fact, the plate boundaries surrounding the Pacific Ocean have so many volcanoes that the area is called the *Ring of Fire.*

Tectonic plate boundaries are areas where tectonic plates either collide, separate, or slide past one another. At these boundaries, it is possible for magma to form and travel to the surface. About 80% of active volcanoes on land form where plates collide, and about 15% form where plates separate. The remaining few occur far from tectonic plate boundaries.

Reading Check **Why are most volcanoes on plate boundaries?** (*See the Appendix for answers to Reading Checks.*)

Reaction to Stress

1. Make a pliable "rock" by pouring **60 mL of water** into a **plastic cup** and adding **150 mL of cornstarch,** 15 mL at a time. Stir well each time.
2. Pour half of the cornstarch mixture into a **clear bowl.** Carefully observe how the "rock" flows. Be patient—this process is slow!
3. Scrape the rest of the "rock" out of the cup with a **spoon.** Observe the behavior of the "rock" as you scrape.
4. What happened to the "rock" when you let it flow by itself? What happened when you put stress on the "rock"?
5. How is this pliable "rock" similar to the rock of the upper part of the mantle?

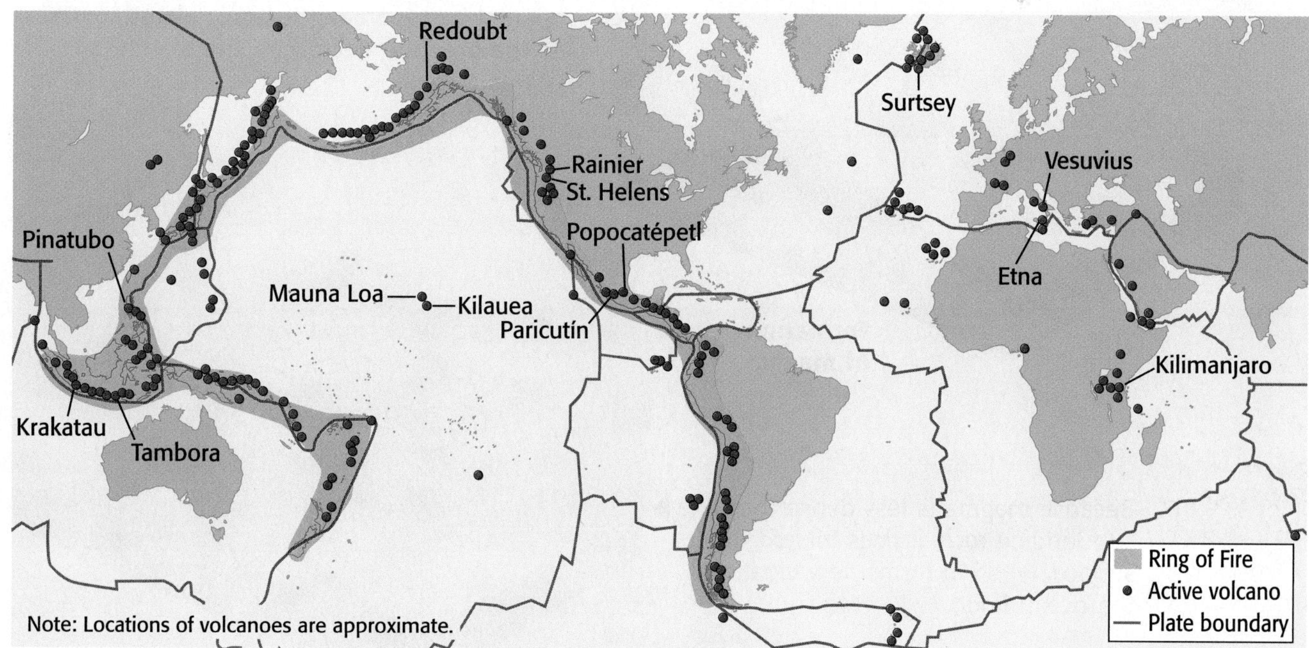

Figure 2 *Tectonic plate boundaries are likely places for volcanoes to form. The Ring of Fire contains nearly 75% of the world's active volcanoes on land.*

How Hot Is Hot?

Inside the Earth, magma can reach a burning-hot 1,400°C! You may be more familiar with Fahrenheit temperatures, so convert 1,400°C to degrees Fahrenheit by using the formula below.

$$°F = (°C \div 5 \times 9) + 32$$

What is the temperature in degrees Fahrenheit?

rift zone an area of deep cracks that forms between two tectonic plates that are pulling away from each other

When Tectonic Plates Separate

At a *divergent boundary,* tectonic plates move away from each other. As tectonic plates separate, a set of deep cracks called a **rift zone** forms between the plates. Mantle rock then rises to fill in the gap. When mantle rock gets closer to the surface, the pressure decreases. The pressure decrease causes the mantle rock to melt and form magma. Because magma is less dense than the surrounding rock, it rises through the rifts. When the magma reaches the surface, it spills out and hardens, creating new crust, as shown in **Figure 3.**

Mid-Ocean Ridges Form at Divergent Boundaries

Lava that flows from undersea rift zones produces volcanoes and mountain chains called *mid-ocean ridges.* Just as a baseball has stitches, the Earth is circled with mid-ocean ridges. At these ridges, lava flows out and creates new crust. Most volcanic activity on Earth occurs at mid-ocean ridges. While most mid-ocean ridges are underwater, Iceland, with its volcanoes and hot springs, was created by lava from the Mid-Atlantic Ridge. In 1963, enough lava poured out of the Mid-Atlantic Ridge near Iceland to form a new island called *Surtsey.* Scientists watched this new island being born!

Figure 3 How Magma Forms at a Divergent Boundary

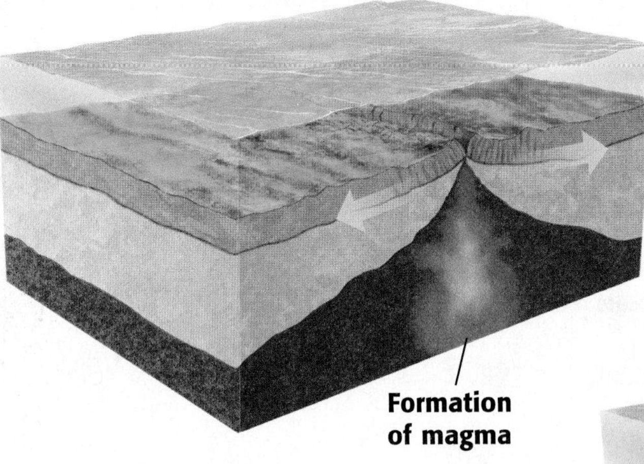

Mantle material rises to fill the space opened by separating tectonic plates. As the pressure decreases, the mantle begins to melt.

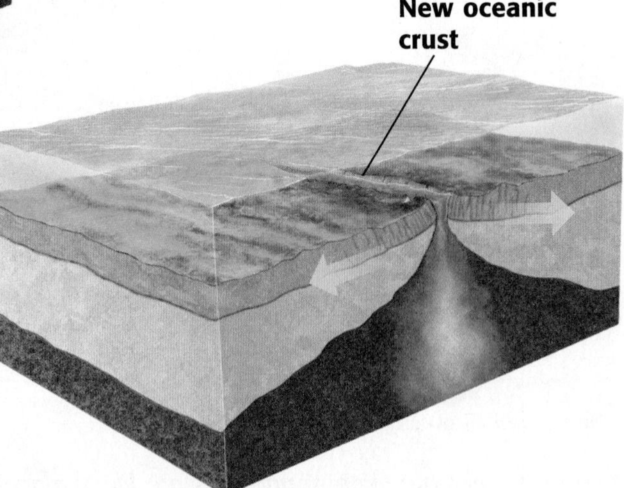

Because magma is less dense than the surrounding rock, it rises toward the surface, where it forms new crust on the ocean floor.

Figure 4 **How Magma Forms at a Convergent Boundary**

Oceanic crust

Continental crust

Magma forms

Release of superheated water

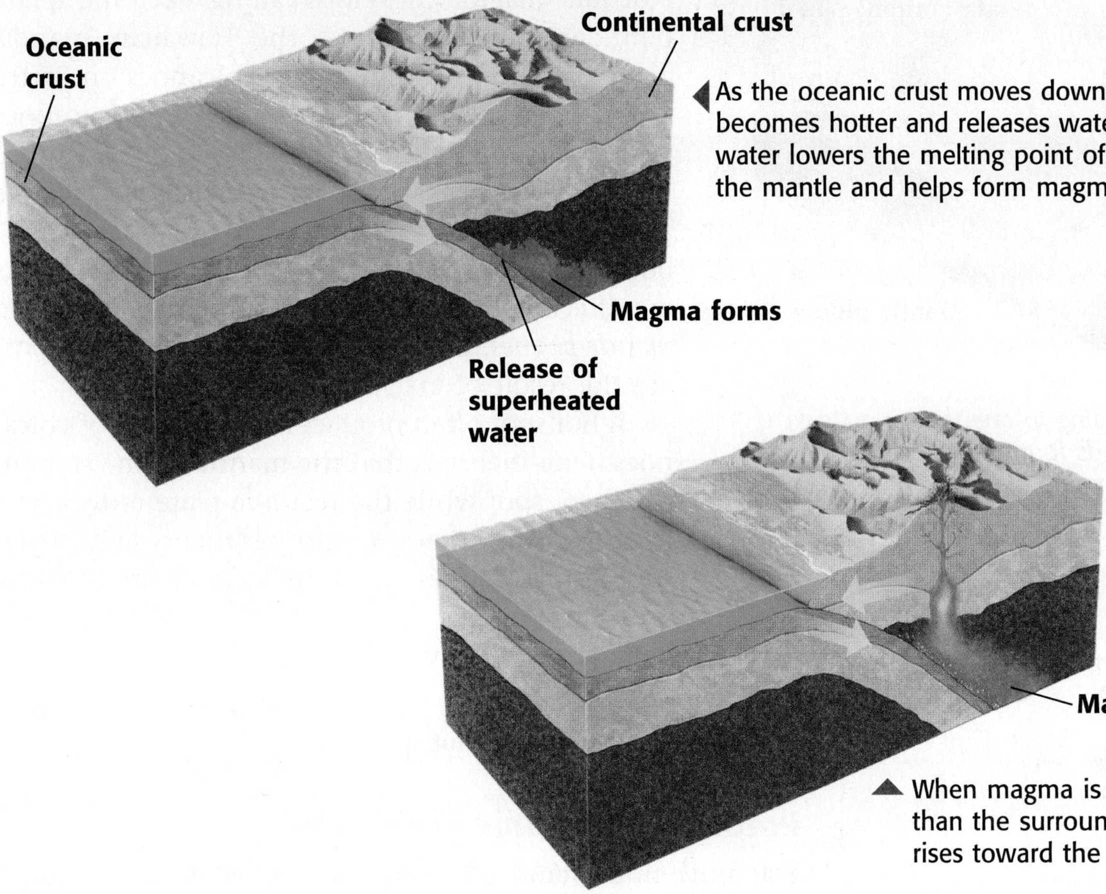

As the oceanic crust moves downward, it becomes hotter and releases water. The water lowers the melting point of rock in the mantle and helps form magma.

Magma rises

When magma is less dense than the surrounding rock, it rises toward the surface.

When Tectonic Plates Collide

If you slide two pieces of notebook paper into one another on a flat desktop, the papers will either buckle upward or one piece of paper will move under the other. This is similar to what happens at a convergent boundary. A *convergent boundary* is a place where tectonic plates collide. When an oceanic plate collides with a continental plate, the oceanic plate usually slides underneath the continental plate. The process of *subduction,* the movement of one tectonic plate underneath another, is shown in **Figure 4.** Oceanic crust is subducted because it is denser and thinner than continental crust.

Subduction Produces Magma

As the descending oceanic crust scrapes past the continental crust, the temperature and pressure increase. The combination of increased heat and pressure causes the water contained in the oceanic crust to be released. The water then mixes with the mantle rock, which lowers the rock's melting point, causing it to melt. This body of magma can rise to form a volcano.

Reading Check How does subduction produce magma?

Tectonic Models

Create models of convergent and divergent boundaries by using materials of your choice. Have your teacher approve your list before you start building your model at home with an adult. In class, use your model to explain how each type of boundary leads to the formation of magma.

ACTIVITY

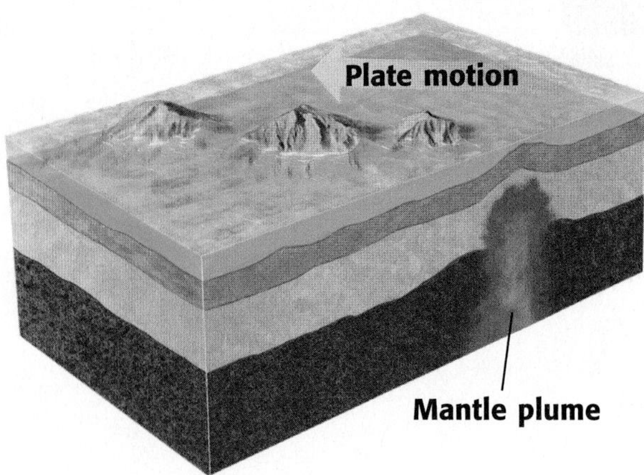

Figure 5 *According to one theory, a string of volcanic islands forms as a tectonic plate passes over a mantle plume.*

Hot Spots

Not all magma develops along tectonic plate boundaries. For example, the Hawaiian Islands, some of the most well-known volcanoes on Earth, are nowhere near a plate boundary. The volcanoes of Hawaii and several other places on Earth are known as *hot spots.* **Hot spots** are volcanically active places on the Earth's surface that are far from plate boundaries. Some scientists think that hot spots are directly above columns of rising magma, called *mantle plumes.* Other scientists think that hot spots are the result of cracks in the Earth's crust.

A hot spot often produces a long chain of volcanoes. One theory is that the mantle plume stays in the same spot while the tectonic plate moves over it, as shown in **Figure 5.** Another theory argues that hot-spot volcanoes occur in long chains because they form along the cracks in the Earth's crust. Both theories may be correct.

hot spot a volcanically active area of Earth's surface far from a tectonic plate boundary

Reading Check **Describe two theories that explain the existence of hot spots.**

Predicting Volcanic Eruptions

You now understand some of the processes that produce volcanoes, but how do scientists predict when a volcano is going to erupt? Volcanoes are classified in three categories. *Extinct volcanoes* have not erupted in recorded history and probably never will erupt again. *Dormant volcanoes* are currently not erupting, but the record of past eruptions suggests that they may erupt again. *Active volcanoes* are currently erupting or show signs of erupting in the near future. Scientists study active and dormant volcanoes for signs of a future eruption.

Figure 6 *As if being this close to an active volcano is not dangerous enough, the gases being collected are extremely poisonous.*

Measuring Small Quakes and Volcanic Gases

Most active volcanoes produce small earthquakes as the magma within them moves upward and causes the surrounding rock to shift. Just before an eruption, the number and intensity of the earthquakes increase and the occurrence of quakes may be continuous. Monitoring these quakes is one of the best ways to predict an eruption.

As **Figure 6** shows, scientists also study the volume and composition of volcanic gases. The ratio of certain gases, especially that of sulfur dioxide, SO_2, to carbon dioxide, CO_2, may be important in predicting eruptions. Changes in this ratio may indicate changes in the magma chamber below.

Measuring Slope and Temperature

As magma moves upward prior to an eruption, it can cause the Earth's surface to swell. The side of a volcano may even bulge as the magma moves upward. An instrument called a *tiltmeter* helps scientists detect small changes in the angle of a volcano's slope. Scientists also use satellite technology such as the Global Positioning System (GPS) to detect the changes in a volcano's slope that may signal an eruption.

One of the newest methods for predicting volcanic eruptions includes using satellite images. Infrared satellite images record changes in the surface temperature and gas emissions of a volcano over time. If the site is getting hotter, the magma below is probably rising!

For another activity related to this chapter, go to **go.hrw.com** and type in the keyword **HZ5VOLW.**

SECTION Review

Summary

- Temperature and pressure influence magma formation.
- Most volcanoes form at tectonic boundaries.
- As tectonic plates separate, magma rises to fill the cracks, or rifts, that develop.
- As oceanic and continental plates collide, the oceanic plate tends to subduct and cause the formation of magma.
- To predict eruptions, scientists study the frequency and type of earthquakes associated with the volcano as well as changes in slope, changes in the gases released, and changes in the volcano's surface temperature.

Using Key Terms

1. Use each of the following terms in a separate sentence: *hot spot* and *rift zone.*

Understanding Key Ideas

2. If the temperature of a rock remains constant but the pressure on the rock decreases, what tends to happen?
   a. The temperature increases.
   b. The rock becomes liquid.
   c. The rock becomes solid.
   d. The rock subducts.
3. Which of the following words is a synonym for *dormant*?
   a. predictable
   b. active
   c. dead
   d. sleeping
4. What is the Ring of Fire?
5. Explain how convergent and divergent plate boundaries cause magma formation.
6. Describe four methods that scientists use to predict volcanic eruptions.
7. Why does a oceanic plate tend to subduct when it collides with a continental plate?

Math Skills

8. If a tectonic plate moves at a rate of 2 km every 1 million years, how long would it take a hot spot to form a chain of volcanoes 100 km long?

Critical Thinking

9. **Making Inferences** New crust is constantly being created at mid-ocean ridges. So, why is the oldest oceanic crust only about 150 million years old?
10. **Identifying Relationships** If you are studying a volcanic deposit, would the youngest layers be more likely to be found on the top or on the bottom? Explain your answer.

For a variety of links related to this chapter, go to www.scilinks.org

Topic: What Causes Volcanoes?
SciLinks code: HSM1654

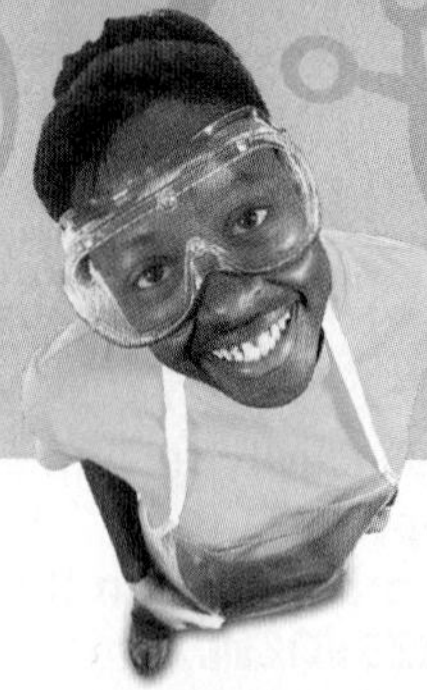

Skills Practice Lab

Volcano Verdict

You will need to pair up with a partner for this exploration. You and your partner will act as geologists who work in a city located near a volcano. City officials are counting on you to predict when the volcano will erupt next. You and your partner have decided to use limewater as a gas-emissions tester. You will use this tester to measure the levels of carbon dioxide emitted from a simulated volcano. The more active the volcano is, the more carbon dioxide it releases.

OBJECTIVES

Build a working apparatus to test carbon dioxide levels.

Test the levels of carbon dioxide emitted from a model volcano.

MATERIALS

- baking soda, 15 mL
- bottle, drinking, 16 oz
- box or stand for plastic cup
- clay, modeling
- coin
- cup, clear plastic, 9 oz
- graduated cylinder
- limewater, 1 L
- straw, drinking, flexible
- tissue, bathroom (2 sheets)
- vinegar, white, 140 mL
- water, 100 mL

SAFETY

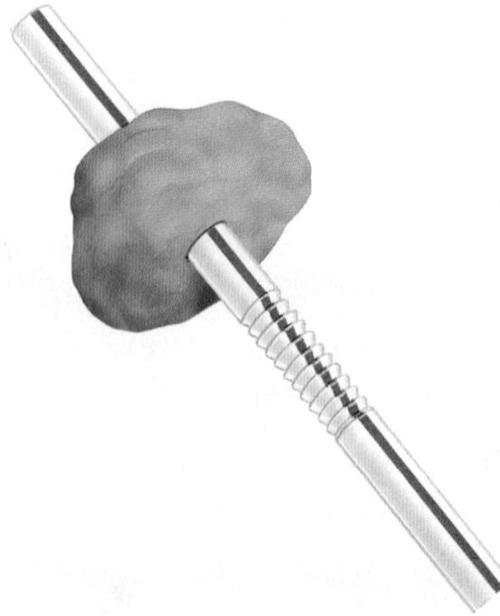

Procedure

1. Put on your safety goggles, and carefully pour limewater into the plastic cup until the cup is three-fourths full. You have just made your gas-emissions tester.
2. Now, build a model volcano. Begin by pouring 50 mL of water and 70 mL of vinegar into the drink bottle.
3. Form a plug of clay around the short end of the straw, as shown at left. The clay plug must be large enough to cover the opening of the bottle. Be careful not to get the clay wet.
4. Sprinkle 5 mL of baking soda along the center of a single section of bathroom tissue. Then, roll the tissue, and twist the ends so that the baking soda can't fall out.

5. Drop the tissue into the drink bottle, and immediately put the short end of the straw inside the bottle to make a seal with the clay.
6. Put the other end of the straw into the limewater, as shown at right.
7. You have just taken your first measurement of gas levels from the volcano. Record your observations.
8. Imagine that it is several days later and you need to test the volcano again to collect more data. Before you continue, toss a coin. If it lands heads up, go to step 9. If it lands tails up, go to step 10. Write down the step that you follow.
9. Repeat steps 1–7. This time, add 2 mL of baking soda to the vinegar and water. (Note: You must use fresh water, vinegar, and limewater.) Write down your observations. Go to step 11.
10. Repeat steps 1–7. This time, add 8 mL of baking soda to the vinegar and water. (Note: You must use fresh water, vinegar, and limewater.) Write down your observations. Go to step 11.
11. Return to step 8 once. Then, answer the questions below.

Analyze the Results

1. **Explaining Events** How do you explain the difference in the appearance of the limewater from one trial to the next?
2. **Recognizing Patterns** What does the data that you collected indicate about the activity in the volcano?

Draw Conclusions

3. **Evaluating Results** Based on your results, do you think it would be necessary to evacuate the city?
4. **Applying Conclusions** How would a geologist use a gas-emissions tester to predict volcanic eruptions?

Chapter Review

USING KEY TERMS

For each pair of terms, explain how the meanings of the terms differ.

1. *caldera* and *crater*
2. *lava* and *magma*
3. *lava* and *pyroclastic material*
4. *vent* and *rift*
5. *cinder cone volcano* and *shield volcano*

UNDERSTANDING KEY IDEAS

Multiple Choice

6. The type of magma that tends to cause explosive eruptions has a
   - **a.** high silica content and high viscosity.
   - **b.** high silica content and low viscosity.
   - **c.** low silica content and low viscosity.
   - **d.** low silica content and high viscosity.
7. Lava that flows slowly to form a glassy surface with rounded wrinkles is called
   - **a.** aa lava.
   - **b.** pahoehoe lava.
   - **c.** pillow lava.
   - **d.** blocky lava.
8. Magma forms within the mantle most often as a result of
   - **a.** high temperature and high pressure.
   - **b.** high temperature and low pressure.
   - **c.** low temperature and high pressure.
   - **d.** low temperature and low pressure.
9. What causes an increase in the number and intensity of small earthquakes before an eruption?
   - **a.** the movement of magma
   - **b.** the formation of pyroclastic material
   - **c.** the hardening of magma
   - **d.** the movement of tectonic plates
10. If volcanic dust and ash remain in the atmosphere for months or years, what do you predict will happen?
    - **a.** Solar reflection will decrease, and temperatures will increase.
    - **b.** Solar reflection will increase, and temperatures will increase.
    - **c.** Solar reflection will decrease, and temperatures will decrease.
    - **d.** Solar reflection will increase, and temperatures will decrease.
11. At divergent plate boundaries,
    - **a.** heat from Earth's core causes mantle plumes.
    - **b.** oceanic plates sink, which causes magma to form.
    - **c.** tectonic plates move apart.
    - **d.** hot spots cause volcanoes.
12. A theory that helps explain the causes of both earthquakes and volcanoes is the theory of
    - **a.** pyroclastics.
    - **b.** plate tectonics.
    - **c.** climatic fluctuation.
    - **d.** mantle plumes.

Short Answer

13. How does the presence of water in magma affect a volcanic eruption?

14. Describe four clues that scientists use to predict eruptions.

15. Identify the characteristics of the three types of volcanoes.

16. Describe the positive effects of volcanic eruptions.

CRITICAL THINKING

17. **Concept Mapping** Use the following terms to create a concept map: *volcanic bombs, aa, pyroclastic material, pahoehoe, lapilli, lava,* and *volcano.*

18. **Identifying Relationships** You are exploring a volcano that has been dormant for some time. You begin to keep notes on the types of volcanic debris that you see as you walk. Your first notes describe volcanic ash. Later, your notes describe lapilli. In what direction are you most likely traveling—toward the crater or away from the crater? Explain your answer.

19. **Making Inferences** Loihi is a submarine Hawaiian volcano that might grow to form a new island. The Hawaiian Islands are located on the Pacific plate, which is moving northwest. Considering how this island chain may have formed, where do you think the new volcanic island will be located? Explain your answer.

20. **Evaluating Hypotheses** What evidence could confirm the existence of mantle plumes?

INTERPRETING GRAPHICS

The graph below illustrates the average change in temperature above or below normal for a community over several years. Use the graph below to answer the questions that follow.

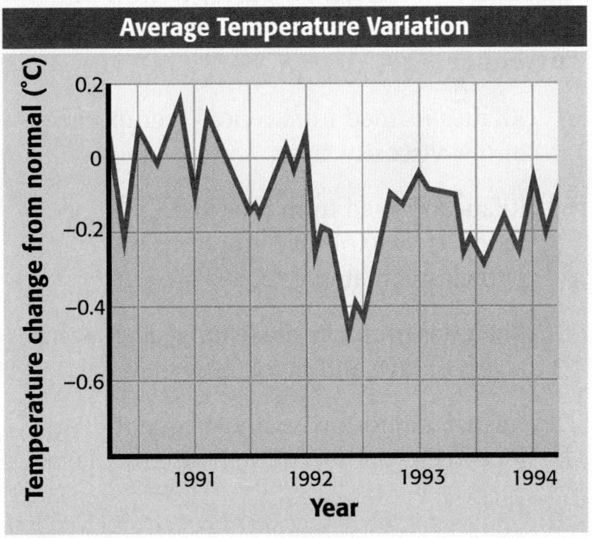

21. If the variation in temperature over the years was influenced by a major volcanic eruption, when did the eruption most likely take place? Explain.

22. If the temperature were measured only once each year (at the beginning of the year), how would your interpretation be different?

Standardized Test Preparation

Multiple Choice

1. **A benefit to society of volcano research is that it allows scientists**

   A. to measure volcanic gases.

   B. to measure temperature changes.

   C. to prevent volcanoes from erupting.

   D. to better predict when eruptions will occur.

2. **One of the active volcanoes on the island of Hawaii is named Kilauea. If Kilauea is a shield volcano, which of the following would be a reasonable inference?**

   A. Kilauea formed from repeated eruptions of low viscosity lava.

   B. Kilauea formed from repeated moderately explosive eruptions of pyroclastic material.

   C. Kilauea is primarily made up of alternating layers of lava and pyroclastic material.

   D. Kilauea has formed a cinder cone through repeated eruptions of high viscosity lava.

3. **Which of the following is a likely result of large amounts of volcanic ash in the atmosphere?**

   A. The average global temperature will decrease.

   B. The average duration of a day will become shorter.

   C. Ocean tide levels will be affected.

   D. Only the area near the volcano will be affected.

4. **When magma builds up beneath a volcano, a large amount of pressure is created. What form does this pressure take?**

   A. kinetic energy

   B. chemical energy

   C. potential energy

   D. explosive energy

Use the table below to answer question 5.

Magma Viscosity	
Magma type	Viscosity
Felsic	High
Intermediate	Intermediate
Mafic	Low

5. **The thicker the magma, the more likely it is to cause an explosive eruption. According to the data collected above, which type of magma is least likely to cause an explosive eruption?**

   A. felsic magma

   B. intermediate magma

   C. mafic

   D. They will all cause explosive eruptions.

6. **If a volcanic eruption covered farmland with several meters of ash, which of the following could be said about the ash?**

   A. It would be an effective fertilizer, causing record crop yields.

   B. It would smother the crops and possibly lead to food shortages.

   C. It would be a nuisance, but it could be easily removed.

   D. Farmers would mix it with water and use it as a substitute for concrete.

7. In which of the following situations would there be the greatest amount of kinetic energy?

A. just prior to eruption, when great pressure has built up inside a volcano

B. during an explosive eruption in which pyroclastic material is blown high into the atmosphere

C. just after an explosive eruption, when most of the debris has settled back to the ground

D. long after an explosive eruption, when the volcanic debris has cooled and erosion of these deposits has started taking place

8. What effect might a volcanic eruption have on climate or weather patterns?

A. The average global temperature would decrease.

B. The average global temperature would increase.

C. The average global rainfall would decrease.

D. The average global rainfall would increase.

9. What happens when tectonic plates pass over mantle plumes?

A. fissures form

B. volcanic hot spots form

C. trenches form

D. mid-ocean ridges form

Use the illustration below to answer question 10.

10. What is the term for the area to which the arrow is pointing?

A. lava

B. crater

C. caldera

D. magma chamber

Open Response

11. Unlike the west coast of North America, Kentucky's position closer to the center of the continental plate makes it free from volcanoes. Yet its climate can still be affected by volcanoes. How?

12. Explain how a volcanist can piece together the history of a volcano by studying the rock that makes up the volcano.

Science in Action

Weird Science

Pele's Hair

It is hard to believe that the fragile specimen shown below is a volcanic rock. This strange type of lava, called *Pele's hair,* forms when volcanic gases spray molten rock high into the air. When conditions are right, the lava can harden into strands of volcanic glass as thin as a human hair. This type of lava is named after Pele, the Hawaiian goddess of volcanoes. Several other types of lava are named in Pele's honor. Pele's tears are tear-shaped globs of volcanic glass often found at the end of strands of Pele's hair. Pele's diamonds are green, gemlike stones found in hardened lava flows.

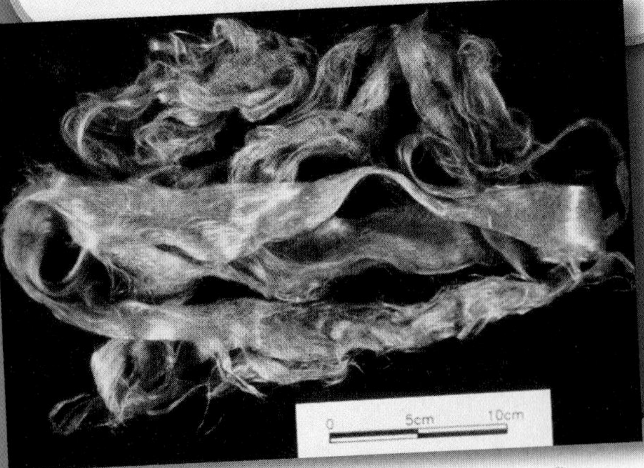

Language Arts ACTIVITY

Volcanic terms come from many languages. Research some volcanic terms on the Internet, and create an illustrated volcanic glossary to share with your class.

Science, Technology, and Society

Fighting Lava with Fire Hoses

What would you do if a 60 ft wall of lava was advancing toward your home? Most people would head for safety. But when an eruption threatened to engulf the Icelandic fishing village of Heimaey in 1973, some villagers held their ground and fought back. Working 14-hour days in conditions so hot that their boots would catch on fire, villagers used fire-hoses to spray sea water on the lava flow. For several weeks, the lava advanced toward the town, and it seemed as if there was no hope. But the water eventually cooled the lava fast enough to divert the flow and save the village. It took 5 months and about 1.5 billion gallons of water to fight the lava flow. When the eruption stopped, villagers found that the island had grown by 20%!

Social Studies ACTIVITY

WRITING SKILL To try to protect the city of Hilo, Hawaii, from an eruption in 1935, planes dropped bombs on the lava. Find out if this mission was successful, and write a report about other attempts to stop lava flows.

Careers

Tina Neal

Volcanologist Would you like to study volcanoes for a living? Tina Neal is a volcanologist at the Alaska Volcano Observatory in Anchorage, Alaska. Her job is to monitor and study some of Alaska's 41 active volcanoes. Much of her work focuses on studying volcanoes in order to protect the public. According to Neal, being near a volcano when it is erupting is a wonderful adventure for the senses. "Sometimes you can get so close to an erupting volcano that you can feel the heat, hear the activity, and smell the lava. It's amazing! In Alaska, erupting volcanoes are too dangerous to get very close to, but they create a stunning visual display even from a distance."

Neal also enjoys the science of volcanoes. "It's fascinating to be near an active volcano and become aware of all the chemical and physical processes taking place. When I'm watching a volcano, I think about everything we understand and don't understand about what is happening. It's mind-boggling!" Neal says that if you are interested in becoming a volcanologist, it is important to be well rounded as a scientist. So, you would have to study math, geology, chemistry, and physics. Having a good understanding of computer tools is also important because volcanologists use computers to manage a lot of data and to create models. Neal also suggests learning a second language, such as Spanish. In her spare time, Neal is learning Russian so that she can better communicate with research partners in Kamchatka, Siberia.

Math Activity

The 1912 eruption of Mt. Katmai in Alaska could be heard 5,620 km away in Atlanta, Georgia. If the average speed of sound in the atmosphere is 342 m/s, how many hours after the eruption did the citizens of Atlanta hear the explosion?

To learn more about these Science in Action topics, visit **go.hrw.com** and type in the keyword **HZ5VOLF**.

Current Science

Check out Current Science® articles related to this chapter by visiting go.hrw.com. Just type in the keyword HZ5CS09.

TIMELINE

Matter and Atoms

In this unit, you will explore a basic question that people have been pondering for centuries: What is the nature of matter? You will learn how to define the word *matter* and the ways to describe matter and the changes it goes through. You will also learn about the different states of matter and how to classify different arrangements of matter as elements, compounds, or mixtures. This timeline shows some of the events and discoveries that have occurred throughout history as scientists have sought to understand the nature of matter.

1661

Robert Boyle, a chemist in England, determines that elements are substances that cannot be broken down into anything simpler by chemical processes.

1712

Thomas Newcomen invents the first practical steam engine.

1937

The *Hindenburg* explodes while docking in Lakehurst, New Jersey. To make it lighter than air, the airship was filled with flammable hydrogen gas.

1971

The first commercially available "pocket" calculator is introduced. It has a mass of nearly 1 kg and a price of about $400, hardly the kind of pocket calculator that exists today.

1766

English chemist Henry Cavendish discovers and describes the properties of a highly flammable substance now known as hydrogen gas.

1800

Current from an electric battery is used to separate water into the elements hydrogen and oxygen for the first time.

1920

American women win the right to vote with the ratification of the 19th Amendment to the Constitution.

1950

Silly Putty® is sold in a toy store for the first time. The soft, gooey substance quickly becomes popular because of its strange properties, including the ability to "pick up" the print from a newspaper page.

1957

The space age begins when the Soviet Union launches *Sputnik I*, the first artificial satellite to circle the Earth.

1989

An oil tanker strikes a reef in Prince William Sound, Alaska, and spills nearly 11 million gallons of oil. The floating oil injures or kills thousands of marine mammals and seabirds and damages the Alaskan coastline.

2000

The World's Fair, an international exhibition featuring exhibits and participants from around the world, is held in Hanover, Germany. The theme is "Humankind, Nature, and Technology."

2003

Sally Ride, the first American woman in space, is inducted into the Astronaut Hall of Fame.

The Properties of Matter

The Big Idea

Matter is described by its properties and may undergo changes.

SECTION

About the Photo

This giant ice dragon began as a 1,700 kg block of ice! Making the blocks of ice takes six weeks. Then, the ice blocks are stored at –30°C until the sculpting begins. The artist has to work at –10°C to keep the ice from melting. An ice sculptor has to be familiar with the many properties of water, including its melting point.

PRE-READING ACTIVITY

FOLDNOTES **Booklet** Before you read the chapter, create the FoldNote entitled "Booklet" described in the **Study Skills** section of the Appendix. Label each page of the booklet with a main idea from the chapter. As you read the chapter, write what you learn about each main idea on the appropriate page of the booklet.

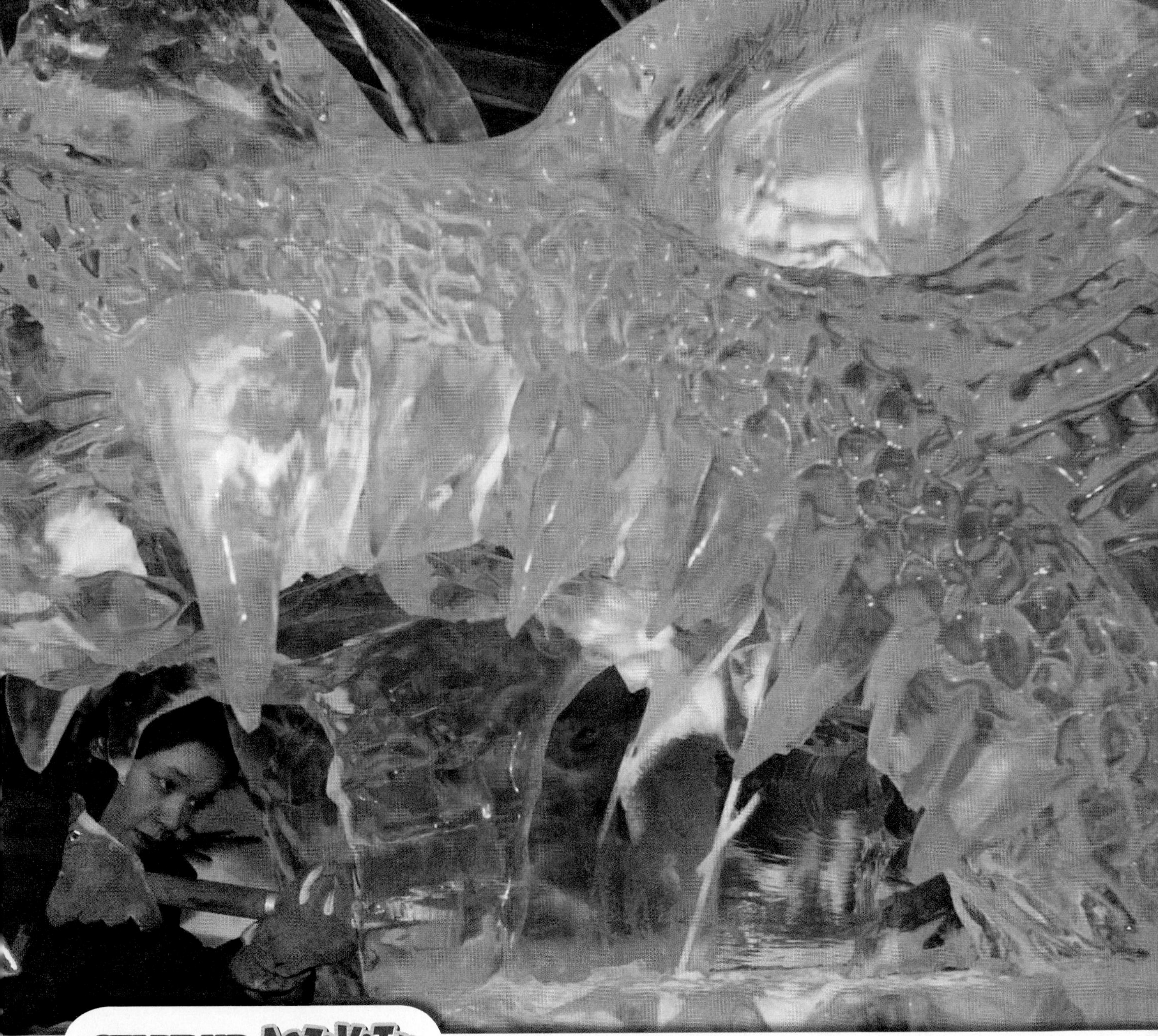

START-UP ACTIVITY

Sack Secrets

In this activity, you will test your skills in determining an object's identity based on the object's properties.

Procedure

1. You and two or three of your classmates will receive a **sealed paper sack** containing a **mystery object.** Do not open the sack!
2. For five minutes, make as many observations about the object as you can without opening the sack. You may touch, smell, shake, or listen to the object through the sack. Record your observations.

Analysis

1. At the end of five minutes, discuss your findings with your partners.
2. List the object's properties that you can identify. Make another list of properties that you cannot identify. Make a conclusion about the object's identity.
3. Share your observations, your list of properties, and your conclusion with the class. Then, open the sack.
4. Did you properly identify the object? If so, how? If not, why not? Record your answers.

SECTION 1

What Is Matter?

What do you have in common with a toaster, a steaming bowl of soup, or a bright neon sign?

What You Will Learn

- Describe the two properties of all matter.
- Identify the units used to measure volume and mass.
- Compare mass and weight.
- Explain the relationship between mass and inertia.

Vocabulary

matter	mass
volume	weight
meniscus	inertia

READING STRATEGY

Prediction Guide Before reading this section, write the title of each heading in this section. Next, under each heading, write what you think you will learn.

You are probably thinking that this is a trick question. It is hard to imagine that a person has anything in common with a kitchen appliance, hot soup, or a glowing neon sign.

Matter

From a scientific point of view, you have at least one characteristic in common with these things. You, the toaster, the bowl, the soup, the steam, the glass tubing of a neon sign, and the glowing gas are made of matter. But exactly what is matter? **Matter** is anything that has mass and takes up space. It's that simple! Everything in the universe that you can see is made up of some type of matter.

Matter and Volume

All matter takes up space. The amount of space taken up, or occupied, by an object is known as the object's **volume.** Your fingernails, the Statue of Liberty, the continent of Africa, and a cloud have volume. And because these things have volume, they cannot share the same space at the same time. Even the tiniest speck of dust takes up space. Another speck of dust cannot fit into that space without somehow bumping the first speck out of the way. **Figure 1** shows an example of how one object cannot share with another object the same space at the same time. Try the Quick Lab on the next page to see for yourself that matter takes up space.

matter anything that has mass and takes up space

volume a measure of the size of a body or region in three-dimensional space

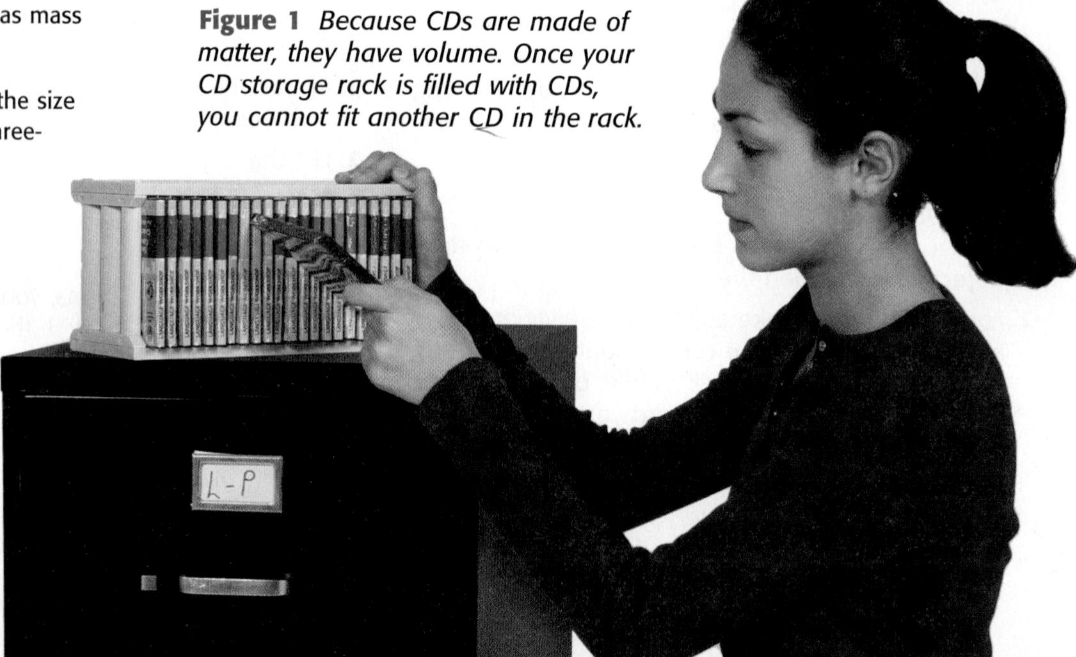

Figure 1 *Because CDs are made of matter, they have volume. Once your CD storage rack is filled with CDs, you cannot fit another CD in the rack.*

Space Case

1. Crumple a **piece of paper.** Fit it tightly in the bottom of a **clear plastic cup** so that it won't fall out.
2. Turn the cup upside down. Lower the cup straight down into a **bucket** half-filled with **water.** Be sure that the cup is completely underwater.
3. Lift the cup straight out of the water. Turn the cup upright, and observe the paper. Record your observations.
4. Use the point of a **pencil** to punch a small hole in the bottom of the cup. Repeat steps 2 and 3.
5. How do the results show that air has volume? Explain your answer.

Liquid Volume

Lake Erie, the smallest of the Great Lakes, has a volume of approximately 483 trillion (that's 483,000,000,000,000) liters of water. Can you imagine that much water? Think of a 2-liter bottle of soda. The water in Lake Erie could fill more than 241 trillion 2-liter soda bottles. That's a lot of water! On a smaller scale, a can of soda has a volume of only 355 milliliters, which is about one-third of a liter. You can check the volume of the soda by using a large measuring cup from your kitchen.

Liters (L) and milliliters (mL) are the units used most often to express the volume of liquids. The volume of any amount of liquid, from one raindrop to a can of soda to an entire ocean, can be expressed in these units.

Reading Check **What are two units used to measure volume?** (*See the Appendix for answers to Reading Checks.*)

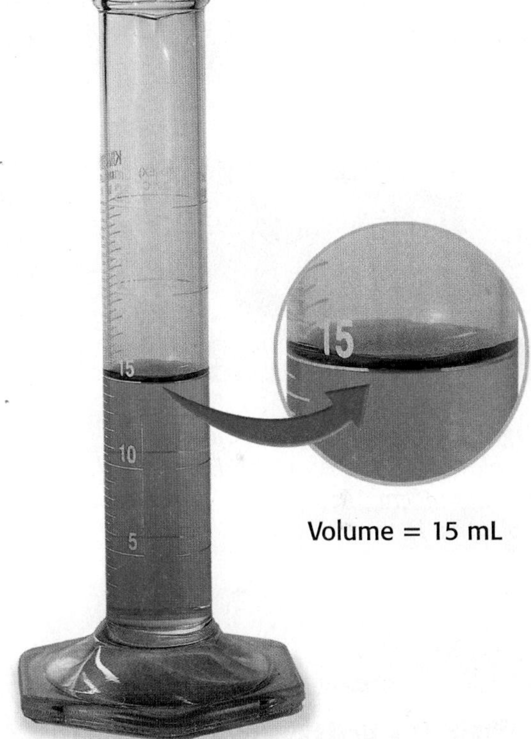

Figure 2 *To measure volume correctly, read the scale of the lowest part of the meniscus (as shown) at eye level.*

Measuring the Volume of Liquids

In your science class, you'll probably use a graduated cylinder instead of a measuring cup to measure the volume of liquids. Graduated cylinders are used to measure the liquid volume when accuracy is important. The surface of a liquid in any container, including a measuring cup or a large beaker, is curved. The curve at the surface of a liquid is called a **meniscus** (muh NIS kuhs). To measure the volume of most liquids, such as water, you must look at the bottom of the meniscus, as shown in **Figure 2.** Note that you may not be able to see a meniscus in a large beaker. The meniscus looks flat because the liquid is in a wide container.

meniscus the curve at a liquid's surface by which one measures the volume of the liquid

Volume of a Regularly Shaped Solid Object

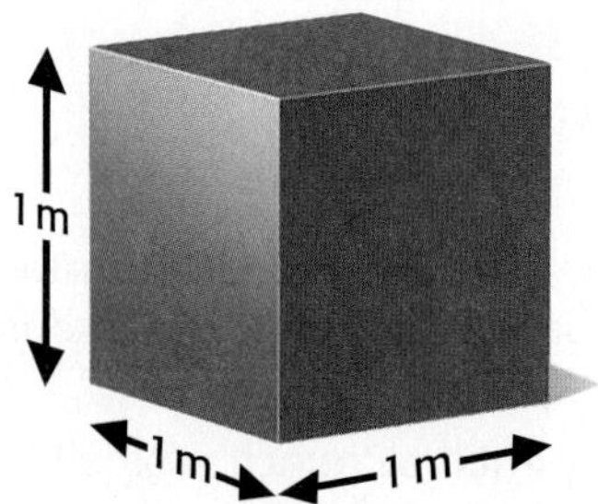

Figure 3 *A cubic meter (1 m^3) is a cube that has a length, width, and height of 1 m.*

The volume of any solid object is expressed in cubic units. The word *cubic* means "having three dimensions." In science, cubic meters (m^3) and cubic centimeters (cm^3) are the units most often used to express the volume of solid things. The 3 in these unit symbols shows that three quantities, or dimensions, were multiplied to get the final result. You can see the three dimensions of a cubic meter in **Figure 3.** There are formulas to find the volume of regularly shaped objects. For example, to find the volume of a cube or a rectangular object, multiply the length, width, and height of the object, as shown in the following equation:

$$volume = length \times width \times height$$

Volume of an Irregularly Shaped Solid Object

Figure 4 *The 12-sided object displaced 15 mL of water. Because 1 mL = 1 cm^3, the volume of the object is 15 cm^3.*

How do you find the volume of a solid that does not have a regular shape? For example, to find the volume of a 12-sided object, you cannot use the equation given above. But you can measure the volume of a solid object by measuring the volume of water that the object displaces. In **Figure 4,** when a 12-sided object is added to the water in a graduated cylinder, the water level rises. The volume of water displaced by the object is equal to its volume. Because 1 mL is equal to 1 cm^3, you can express the volume of the water displaced by the object in cubic centimeters. Although volumes of liquids can be expressed in cubic units, volumes of solids should not be expressed in liters or milliliters.

Reading Check **Explain how you would measure the volume of an apple.**

Volume of a Rectangular Solid What is the volume of a box that has a length of 5 cm, a width of 1 cm, and a height of 2 cm?

Step 1: Write the equation for volume.

$$volume = length \times width \times height$$

Step 2: Replace the variables with the measurements given to you, and solve.

$$volume = 5 \text{ cm} \times 1 \text{ cm} \times 2 \text{ cm} = 10 \text{ cm}^3$$

Now It's Your Turn

1. A book has a length of 25 cm, a width of 18 cm, and a height of 4 cm. What is its volume?
2. What is the volume of a suitcase that has a length of 95 cm, a width of 50 cm, and a height of 20 cm?
3. A CD case is 14.2 cm long, 12.4 cm wide, and 1 cm deep. What is its volume?

Matter and Mass

Another characteristic of all matter is mass. **Mass** is the amount of matter in an object. For example, you and a peanut are made of matter. But you are made of more matter than a peanut is, so you have more mass. The mass of an object is the same no matter where in the universe the object is located. The only way to change the mass of an object is to change the amount of matter that makes up the object.

mass a measure of the amount of matter in an object

weight a measure of the gravitational force exerted on an object; its value can change with the location of the object in the universe

The Difference Between Mass and Weight

The terms *mass* and *weight* are often used as though they mean the same thing, but they don't. **Weight** is a measure of the gravitational (GRAV i TAY shuh nuhl) force exerted on an object. Gravitational force keeps objects on Earth from floating into space. The gravitational force between an object and the Earth depends partly on the object's mass. The more mass an object has, the greater the gravitational force on the object and the greater the object's weight. But an object's weight can change depending on its location in the universe. An object would weigh less on the moon than it does on Earth because the moon has less gravitational force than Earth does. **Figure 5** explains the differences between mass and weight.

Figure 5 Differences Between Mass and Weight

Mass

- Mass is a measure of the amount of matter in an object.
- Mass is always constant for an object no matter where the object is located in the universe.
- Mass is measured by using a balance (shown below).
- Mass is expressed in kilograms (kg), grams (g), and milligrams (mg).

Weight

- Weight is a measure of the gravitational force on an object.
- Weight varies depending on where the object is in relation to the Earth (or any large body in the universe).
- Weight is measured by using a spring scale (shown at right).
- Weight is expressed in newtons (N).

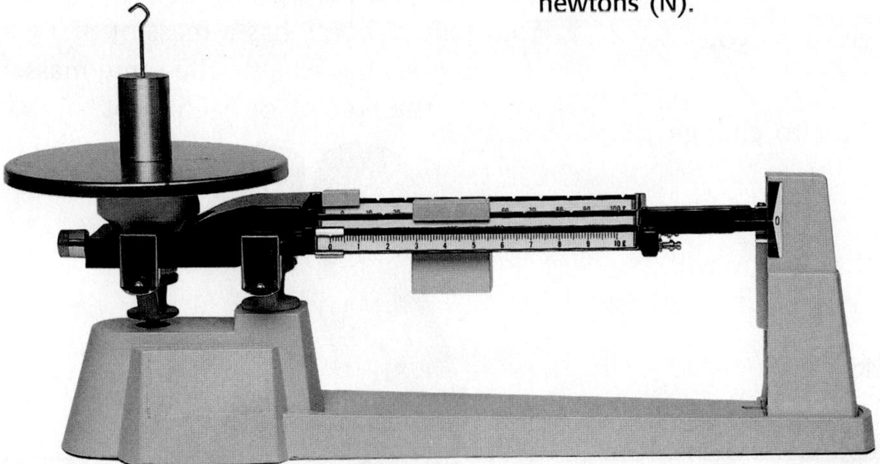

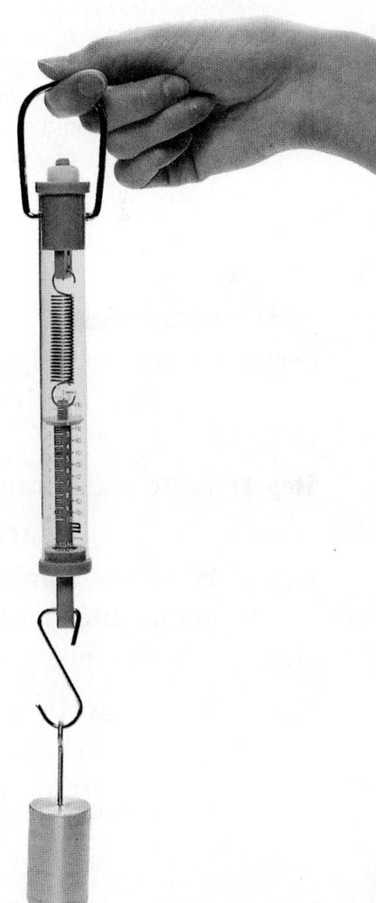

Figure 6 *The brick and the sponge take up the same amount of space. But the brick has more matter in it, so its mass—and thus its weight—is greater.*

Measuring Mass and Weight

The brick and the sponge in **Figure 6** have the same volume. But because the brick has more mass, a greater gravitational force is exerted on the brick than on the sponge. As a result, the brick weighs more than the sponge.

The SI unit of mass is the kilogram (kg), but mass is often expressed in grams (g) and milligrams (mg), too. These units can be used to express the mass of any object in the universe.

Weight is a measure of gravitational force and is expressed in the SI unit of force, the *newton* (N). One newton is about equal to the weight of an object that has a mass of 100 g on Earth. So, if you know the mass of an object, you can calculate the object's weight on Earth. Weight is a good estimate of the mass of an object because, on Earth, gravity doesn't change.

Reading Check **What units are often used to measure mass?**

Inertia

Imagine kicking a soccer ball that has the mass of a bowling ball. It would be not only painful but also very difficult to get the ball moving in the first place! The reason is inertia (in UHR shuh). **Inertia** is the tendency of an object to resist a change in motion. So, an object at rest will remain at rest until something causes the object to move. Also, a moving object will keep moving at the same speed and in the same direction unless something acts on the object to change its speed or direction.

inertia the tendency of an object to resist being moved or, if the object is moving, to resist a change in speed or direction until an outside force acts on the object

MATH FOCUS

Converting Mass to Weight A student has a mass of 45,000 g. How much does this student weigh in newtons?

Step 1: Write the information given to you.

45,000 g

Step 2: Write the conversion factor to change grams into newtons.

1 N = 100 g

Step 3: Write the equation so that grams will cancel.

$$45{,}000 \text{ g} \times \frac{1 \text{ N}}{100 \text{ g}} = 450 \text{ N}$$

Now It's Your Turn

1. What is the weight of a car that has a mass of 1,362,000 g?
2. Your pair of boots has a mass of 850 g. If each boot has exactly the same mass, what is the weight of each boot?

Mass: The Measure of Inertia

Mass is a measure of inertia. An object that has a large mass is harder to get moving and harder to stop than an object that has less mass. The reason is that the object with the large mass has greater inertia. For example, imagine that you are going to push a grocery cart that has only one potato in it. Pushing the cart is easy because the mass and inertia are small. But suppose the grocery cart is stacked with potatoes, as in **Figure 7.** Now the total mass—and the inertia—of the cart full of potatoes is much greater. It will be harder to get the cart moving. And once the cart is moving, stopping the cart will be harder.

Figure 7 *Because of inertia, moving a cart full of potatoes is more difficult than moving a cart that is empty.*

SECTION Review

Summary

- Two properties of matter are volume and mass.
- Volume is the amount of space taken up by an object.
- The SI unit of volume is the liter (L).
- Mass is the amount of matter in an object.
- The SI unit of mass is the kilogram (kg).
- Weight is a measure of the gravitational force on an object, usually in relation to the Earth.
- Inertia is the tendency of an object to resist being moved or, if the object is moving, to resist a change in speed or direction. The more massive an object is, the greater its inertia.

Using Key Terms

1. Use the following terms in the same sentence: *volume* and *meniscus*.
2. In your own words, write a definition for each of the following terms: *mass, weight,* and *inertia*.

Understanding Key Ideas

3. Which of the following is matter?
   a. dust
   b. the moon
   c. strand of hair
   d. All of the above
4. A graduated cylinder is used to measure
   a. volume.
   b. weight.
   c. mass.
   d. inertia.
5. The volume of a solid is measured in
   a. liters.
   b. grams.
   c. cubic centimeters.
   d. All of the above
6. Mass is measured in
   a. liters.
   b. centimeters.
   c. newtons.
   d. kilograms.
7. Explain the relationship between mass and inertia.

Math Skills

8. A nugget of gold is placed in a graduated cylinder that contains 80 mL of water. The water level rises to 225 mL after the nugget is added to the cylinder. What is the volume of the gold nugget?
9. One newton equals about 100 g on Earth. How many newtons would a football weigh if it had a mass of 400 g?

Critical Thinking

10. **Identifying Relationships** Do objects with large masses always have large weights? Explain.
11. **Applying Concepts** Would an elephant weigh more or less on the moon than it would weigh on Earth? Explain your answer.

SCILINKS.
NSTA
Developed and maintained by the National Science Teachers Association
For a variety of links related to this chapter, go to www.scilinks.org
Topic: What Is Matter?
SciLinks code: HSM1662

SECTION 2

Physical Properties

What You Will Learn

- Identify six examples of physical properties of matter.
- Describe how density is used to identify substances.
- List six examples of physical changes.
- Explain what happens to matter during a physical change.

Vocabulary

physical property
density
physical change

READING STRATEGY

Mnemonics As you read this section, create a mnemonic device to help you remember examples of physical properties.

Have you ever played the game 20 Questions? The goal of this game is to figure out what object another person is thinking of by asking 20 yes/no questions or less.

If you can't figure out the object's identity after asking 20 questions, you may not be asking the right kinds of questions. What kinds of questions should you ask? You may want to ask questions about the physical properties of the object. Knowing the properties of an object can help you find out what it is.

Physical Properties

The questions in **Figure 1** help someone gather information about color, odor, mass, and volume. Each piece of information is a physical property of matter. A **physical property** of matter can be observed or measured without changing the matter's identity. For example, you don't have to change an apple's identity to see its color or to measure its volume.

Other physical properties, such as magnetism, the ability to conduct electric current, strength, and flexibility, can help someone identify how to use a substance. For example, think of a scooter with an electric motor. The magnetism produced by the motor is used to convert energy stored in a battery into energy that will turn the wheels.

Reading Check **List four physical properties.** (*See the Appendix for answers to Reading Checks.*)

Could I hold it in my hand? Yes.
Does it have an odor? Yes.
Is it safe to eat? Yes.
Is it orange? No.
Is it yellow? No.
Is it red? Yes.
Is it an apple? Yes!

Figure 1 *Asking questions about the physical properties of an object can help you identify it.*

Figure 2 Examples of Physical Properties

Thermal conductivity (KAHN duhk TIV uh tee) is the rate at which a substance transfers heat. Plastic foam is a poor conductor.

State is the physical form in which a substance exists, such as a solid, liquid, or gas. Ice is water in the solid state.

Density is the mass per unit volume of a substance. Lead is very dense, so it makes a good sinker for a fishing line.

Solubility (SAHL yoo BIL uh tee) is the ability of a substance to dissolve in another substance. Flavored drink mix dissolves in water.

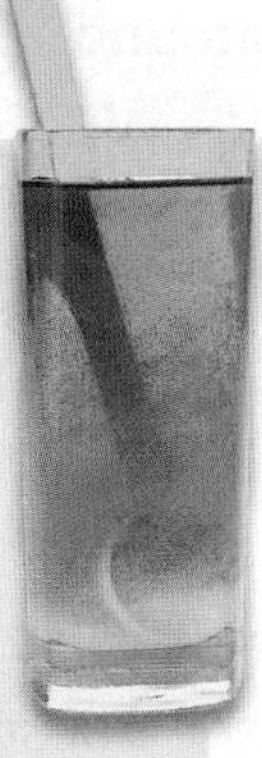

Ductility (duhk TIL uh tee) is the ability of a substance to be pulled into a wire. Copper is often used to make wiring because it is ductile.

Malleability (MAL ee uh BIL uh tee) is the ability of a substance to be rolled or pounded into thin sheets. Aluminum can be rolled into sheets to make foil.

Identifying Matter

You use physical properties every day. For example, physical properties help you determine if your socks are clean (odor), if your books will fit into your backpack (volume), or if your shirt matches your pants (color). **Figure 2** gives more examples of physical properties.

physical property a characteristic of a substance that does not involve a chemical change, such as density, color, or hardness

density the ratio of the mass of a substance to the volume of the substance

Density

Density is a physical property that describes the relationship between mass and volume. **Density** is the amount of matter in a given space, or volume. A golf ball and a table-tennis ball, such as those in **Figure 3**, have similar volumes. But a golf ball has more mass than a table-tennis ball does. So, the golf ball has a greater density.

Figure 3 *A golf ball is denser than a table-tennis ball because the golf ball contains more matter in a similar volume.*

Liquid Layers

Figure 4 *This graduated cylinder contains six liquids. From top to bottom, they are corn oil, water, shampoo, dish detergent, antifreeze, and maple syrup.*

What do you think causes the liquid in **Figure 4** to look the way it does? Is it trick photography? No, it is differences in density! There are six liquids in the graduated cylinder. Each liquid has a different density. If the liquids are carefully poured into the cylinder, they can form six layers because of the differences in density. The densest layer is on the bottom. The least dense layer is on top. The order of the layers shows the order of increasing density. Yellow is the least dense, followed by the colorless layer, red, blue, green, and brown (the densest).

Density of Solids

Which would you rather carry around all day: a kilogram of lead or a kilogram of feathers? At first, you might say feathers. But both the feathers and the lead have the same mass, just as the cotton balls and the tomatoes have the same mass, as shown in **Figure 5.** So, the lead would be less awkward to carry around than the feathers would. The feathers are much less dense than the lead. So, it takes a lot of feathers to equal the same mass of lead.

Knowing the density of a substance can also tell you if the substance will float or sink in water. If the density of an object is less than the density of water, the object will float. Likewise, a solid object whose density is greater than the density of water will sink when the object is placed in water.

Reading Check **What will happen to an object placed in water if the object's density is less than water's density?**

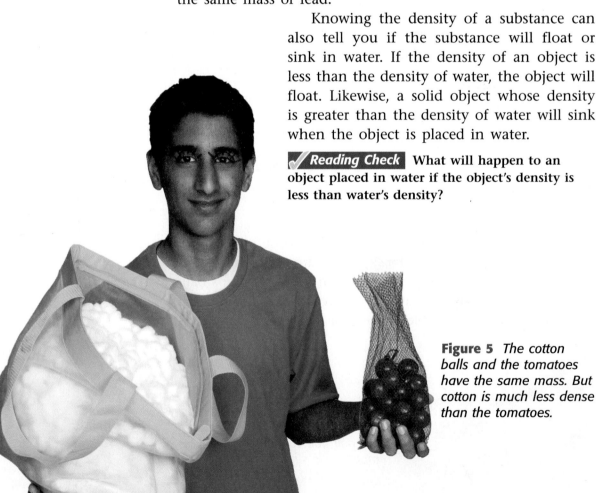

Figure 5 *The cotton balls and the tomatoes have the same mass. But cotton is much less dense than the tomatoes.*

Solving for Density

To find an object's density (D), first measure its mass (m) and volume (V). Then, use the equation below.

$$D = \frac{m}{V}$$

Units for density consist of a mass unit divided by a volume unit. Some units for density are g/cm^3, g/mL, kg/m^3, and kg/L. Remember that the volume of a solid is often given in cubic centimeters or cubic meters. So, the density of a solid should be given in units of g/cm^3 or kg/m^3.

Twenty Questions

Play a game of 20 Questions with an adult. One person will think of an object, and the other person will ask yes/no questions about it. Write the questions in your **science journal** as you play. Put a check mark next to the questions asked about physical properties. When the object is identified or when the 20 questions are up, switch roles.

ACTIVITY

Using Density to Identify Substances

Density is a useful physical property for identifying substances. Each substance has a density that differs from the densities of other substances. And the density of a substance is always the same at a given temperature and pressure. Look at **Table 1** to compare the densities of several common substances.

Table 1* Densities of Common Substances

Substance	Density* (g/cm^3)	Substance	Density* (g/cm^3)
Helium (gas)	0.0001663	Zinc (solid)	7.13
Oxygen (gas)	0.001331	Silver (solid)	10.50
Water (liquid)	1.00	Lead (solid)	11.35
Pyrite (solid)	5.02	Mercury (liquid)	13.55

*at 20°C and 1.0 atm

Calculating Density What is the density of an object whose mass is 25 g and whose volume is 10 cm^3?

Step 1: Write the equation for density.

$$D = \frac{m}{V}$$

Step 2: Replace m and V with the measurements given in the problem, and solve.

$$D = \frac{25\text{ g}}{10\text{ cm}^3} = 2.5\text{ g/cm}^3$$

The equation for density can also be rearranged to find mass and volume, as shown.

$m = D \times V$ (Rearrange by multiplying by V.)

$V = \frac{m}{D}$ (Rearrange by dividing by D.)

Now It's Your Turn

1. Find the density of a substance that has a mass of 45 kg and a volume of 43 m^3. (Hint: Make sure your answer's units are units of density.)
2. Suppose you have a lead ball whose mass is 454 g. What is the ball's volume? (Hint: Use **Table 1** above.)
3. What is the mass of a 15 mL sample of mercury?

Figure 6 Examples of Physical Changes

Changing from a solid to a liquid is a physical change. All changes of state are physical changes.

This aluminum can has gone through the physical change of being crushed. The properties of the can are the same.

Physical Changes Do Not Form New Substances

physical change a change of matter from one form to another without a change in chemical properties

A **physical change** is a change that affects one or more physical properties of a substance. Imagine that a piece of silver is pounded and molded into a heart-shaped pendant. This change is a physical one because only the shape of the silver has changed. The piece of silver is still silver. Its properties are the same. **Figure 6** shows more examples of physical changes.

Reading Check **What is a physical change?**

Examples of Physical Changes

Freezing water to make ice cubes and sanding a piece of wood are examples of physical changes. These changes do not change the identities of the substances. Ice is still water. And sawdust is still wood. Another interesting physical change takes place when certain substances dissolve in other substances. For example, when you dissolve sugar in water, the sugar seems to disappear. But if you heat the mixture, the water evaporates. Then, you will see that the sugar is still there. The sugar went through a physical change when it dissolved.

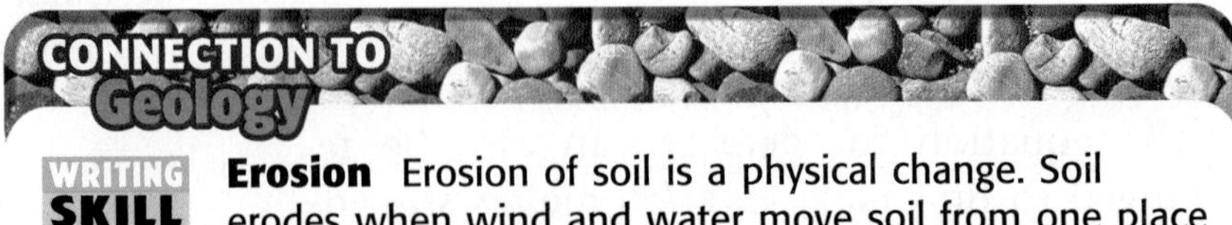

CONNECTION TO Geology

WRITING SKILL **Erosion** Erosion of soil is a physical change. Soil erodes when wind and water move soil from one place to another. Research the history of the Grand Canyon. Write a one-page report about how erosion formed the Grand Canyon.

Matter and Physical Changes

Physical changes do not change the identity of the matter involved. A stick of butter can be melted and poured over a bowl of popcorn, as shown in **Figure 7.** Although the shape of the butter has changed, the butter is still butter, so a physical change has occurred. In the same way, if you make a figure from a lump of clay, you change the clay's shape and cause a physical change. But the identity of the clay does not change. The properties of the figure are the same as those of the lump of clay.

Figure 7 *Melting butter for popcorn involves a physical change.*

SECTION Review

Summary

- Physical properties of matter can be observed without changing the identity of the matter.
- Examples of physical properties are conductivity, state, malleability, ductility, solubility, and density.
- Density is the amount of matter in a given space.
- Density is used to identify substances because the density of a substance is always the same at a given pressure and temperature.
- When a substance undergoes a physical change, its identity stays the same.
- Examples of physical changes are freezing, cutting, bending, dissolving, and melting.

Using Key Terms

1. Use each of the following terms in a separate sentence: *physical property* and *physical change.*

Understanding Key Ideas

2. The units of density for a rectangular piece of wood are
   a. grams per milliliter.
   b. cubic centimeters.
   c. kilograms per liter.
   d. grams per cubic centimeter.
3. Explain why a golf ball is heavier than a table-tennis ball even though the balls are the same size.
4. Describe what happens to a substance when it goes through a physical change.
5. Identify six examples of physical properties.
6. List six physical changes that matter can go through.

Math Skills

7. What is the density of an object that has a mass of 350 g and a volume of 95 cm^3? Would this object float in water? Explain.
8. The density of an object is 5 g/cm^3, and the volume of the object is 10 cm^3. What is the mass of the object?

Critical Thinking

9. **Applying Concepts** How can you determine that a coin is not pure silver if you know the mass and volume of the coin?
10. **Identifying Relationships** What physical property do the following substances have in common: water, oil, mercury, and alcohol?
11. **Analyzing Processes** Explain how you would find the density of an unknown liquid if you have all of the laboratory equipment that you need.

SCILINKS.
NSTA
Developed and maintained by the National Science Teachers Association
For a variety of links related to this chapter, go to www.scilinks.org
Topic: Describing Matter; Physical Changes
SciLinks code: HSM0391; HSM1142

SECTION 3

Chemical Properties

How would you describe a piece of wood before and after it is burned? Has it changed color? Does it have the same texture? The original piece of wood changed, and physical properties alone can't describe what happened to it.

What You Will Learn

- Describe two examples of chemical properties.
- Explain what happens during a chemical change.
- Distinguish between physical and chemical changes.

Vocabulary

chemical property
chemical change

READING STRATEGY

Reading Organizer As you read this section, create an outline of the section. Use the headings from the section in your outline.

Chemical Properties

Physical properties are not the only properties that describe matter. **Chemical properties** describe matter based on its ability to change into new matter that has different properties. For example, when wood is burned, ash and smoke are created. These new substances have very different properties than the original piece of wood had. Wood has the chemical property of flammability. *Flammability* is the ability of a substance to burn. Ash and smoke cannot burn, so they have the chemical property of nonflammability.

Another chemical property is reactivity. *Reactivity* is the ability of two or more substances to combine and form one or more new substances. The photo of the old car in **Figure 1** illustrates reactivity and nonreactivity.

Reading Check **What does the term *reactivity* mean?** (*See the Appendix for answers to Reading Checks.*)

Figure 1 **Reactivity with Oxygen**

The iron used in this old car has the chemical property of **reactivity with oxygen**. When iron is exposed to oxygen, it rusts.

The bumper on this car still looks new because it is coated with chromium. Chromium has the chemical property of **nonreactivity with oxygen.**

Figure 2 Physical Versus Chemical Properties

Physical property

Shape Bending an iron nail will change its shape.

State Rubbing alcohol is a clear liquid at room temperature.

Chemical property

Reactivity with Oxygen An iron nail can react with oxygen in the air to form iron oxide, or rust.

Flammability Rubbing alcohol is able to burn easily.

Comparing Physical and Chemical Properties

How do you tell a physical property from a chemical property? You can observe physical properties without changing the identity of the substance. For example, you can find the density and hardness of wood without changing anything about the wood.

Chemical properties, however, aren't as easy to observe. For example, you can see that wood is flammable only while it is burning. And you can observe that gold is nonflammable only when it won't burn. But a substance always has chemical properties. A piece of wood is flammable even when it's not burning. **Figure 2** shows examples of physical and chemical properties.

Characteristic Properties

The properties that are most useful in identifying a substance are *characteristic properties*. These properties are always the same no matter what size the sample is. Characteristic properties can be physical properties, such as density and solubility, as well as chemical properties, such as flammability and reactivity. Scientists rely on characteristic properties to identify and classify substances.

CONNECTION TO Social Studies

WRITING SKILL **The Right Stuff** When choosing materials to use in manufacturing, you must make sure their properties are suitable for their uses. For example, false teeth can be made from acrylic plastic, porcelain, or gold. According to legend, George Washington wore false teeth made of wood. Do research and find what Washington's false teeth were really made of. In your **science journal,** write a paragraph about what you have learned. Include information about the advantages of the materials used in modern false teeth.

chemical property a property of matter that describes a substance's ability to participate in chemical reactions

Chemical Changes and New Substances

A **chemical change** happens when one or more substances are changed into new substances that have new and different properties. Chemical changes and chemical properties are not the same. Chemical properties of a substance describe which chemical changes will occur and which chemical changes will not occur. But chemical changes are the process by which substances actually change into new substances. You can learn about the chemical properties of a substance by looking at the chemical changes that take place.

You see chemical changes more often than you may think. For example, a chemical reaction happens every time a battery is used. Chemicals failing to react results in a dead battery. Chemical changes also take place within your body when the food you eat is digested. **Figure 3** describes other examples of chemical changes.

Reading Check How does a chemical change differ from a chemical property?

Changing Change

1. Place a folded **paper towel** in a small **pie plate.**
2. Pour **vinegar** into the pie plate until the entire paper towel is damp.
3. Place three shiny **pennies** on top of the paper towel.
4. Put the pie plate in a safe place. Wait 24 hours.
5. Describe and explain the change that took place.

Figure 3 Examples of Chemical Changes

Soured milk smells bad because bacteria have formed new substances in the milk.

Effervescent tablets bubble when the citric acid and baking soda in them react in water.

The **hot gas** formed when hydrogen and oxygen join to make water helps blast the space shuttle into orbit.

The **Statue of Liberty** is made of orange-brown copper but it looks green from the metal's interaction with moist air. New copper compounds formed and these chemical changes made the statue turn green over time.

Figure 4 *Each of the original ingredients has different physical and chemical properties than the final product, the cake, does!*

What Happens During a Chemical Change?

A fun way to see what happens during chemical changes is to bake a cake. You combine eggs, flour, sugar, and other ingredients, as shown in **Figure 4.** When you bake the batter, you end up with something completely different. The heat of the oven and the interaction of the ingredients cause a chemical change. The result is a cake that has properties that differ from the properties of the ingredients.

chemical change a change that occurs when one or more substances change into entirely new substances with different properties

Signs of Chemical Changes

Look back at **Figure 3.** In each picture, at least one sign indicates a chemical change. Other signs that indicate a chemical change include a change in color or odor, production of heat, fizzing and foaming, and sound or light being given off.

In the cake example, you would smell the cake as it baked. You would also see the batter rise and begin to brown. When you cut the finished cake, you would see the air pockets made by gas bubbles that formed in the batter. These signs show that chemical changes have happened.

For another activity related to this chapter, go to **go.hrw.com** and type in keyword **HP5MATW.**

Matter and Chemical Changes

Chemical changes change the identity of the matter involved. So, most of the chemical changes that occur in your daily life, such as a cake baking, would be hard to reverse. Imagine trying to unbake a cake. However, some chemical changes can be reversed by more chemical changes. For example, the water formed in the space shuttle's rockets could be split into hydrogen and oxygen by using an electric current.

Figure 5 Physical and Chemical Changes

Change in Texture Grinding baking soda into a fine, powdery substance is a physical change.

Reactivity with Vinegar Gas bubbles are produced when vinegar is poured into baking soda.

Physical Versus Chemical Changes

The most important question to ask when trying to decide if a physical or chemical change has happened is, Did the composition change? The *composition* of an object is the type of matter that makes up the object and the way that the matter is arranged in the object. **Figure 5** shows both a physical and a chemical change.

A Change in Composition

Physical changes do not change the composition of a substance. For example, water is made of two hydrogen atoms and one oxygen atom. Whether water is a solid, liquid, or gas, its composition is the same. But chemical changes do alter the composition of a substance. For example, through a process called *electrolysis,* water is broken down into hydrogen and oxygen gases. The composition of water has changed, so you know that a chemical change has taken place.

CONNECTION TO Environmental Science

Acid Rain When fossil fuels are burned, a chemical change takes place. Sulfur from fossil fuels and oxygen from the air combine to produce sulfur dioxide, a gas. When sulfur dioxide enters the atmosphere, it undergoes another chemical change by interacting with water and oxygen. Research this chemical reaction. Make a poster describing the reaction and showing how the final product affects the environment.

ACTIVITY

Physical or Chemical Change?

1. Watch as your teacher places a burning **wooden stick** into a **test tube.** Record your observations.
2. Place a mixture of **powdered sulfur** and **iron filings** on a **sheet of paper.** Place a **bar magnet** underneath the paper, and try to separate the iron from the sulfur.
3. Drop an **effervescent tablet** into a **beaker of water.** Record your observations.
4. Identify whether each change is a physical change or a chemical change. Explain your answers.

Reversing Changes

Can physical and chemical changes be reversed? Many physical changes are easily reversed. They do not change the composition of a substance. For example, if an ice cube melts, you could freeze the liquid water to make another ice cube. But composition does change in a chemical change. So, most chemical changes are not easily reversed. Look at **Figure 6.** The chemical changes that happen when a firework explodes would be almost impossible to reverse, even if you collected all of the materials made in the chemical changes.

Figure 6 *This display of fireworks represents many chemical changes happening at the same time.*

SECTION Review

Summary

- Chemical properties describe a substance based on its ability to change into a new substance that has different properties.
- Chemical properties can be observed only when a chemical change might happen.
- Examples of chemical properties are flammability and reactivity.
- New substances form as a result of a chemical change.
- Unlike a chemical change, a physical change does not alter the identity of a substance.

Using Key Terms

1. In your own words, write a definition for each of the following terms: *chemical property* and *chemical change.*

Understanding Key Ideas

2. Rusting is an example of a
   a. physical property.
   b. physical change.
   c. chemical property.
   d. chemical change.
3. Which of the following is a characteristic property?
   a. density
   b. chemical reactivity
   c. solubility in water
   d. All of the above
4. Write two examples of chemical properties and explain what they are.
5. The Statue of Liberty was originally a copper color. After being exposed to the air, she turned a greenish color. What kind of change happened? Explain your answer.
6. Explain how to tell the difference between a physical and a chemical property.

Math Skills

7. The temperature of an acid solution is 25°C. A strip of magnesium is added, and the temperature rises 2°C each minute for the first 3 min. After another 5 min, the temperature has risen two more degrees. What is the final temperature?

Critical Thinking

8. **Making Comparisons** Describe the difference between physical and chemical changes in terms of what happens to the matter involved in each kind of change.
9. **Applying Concepts** Identify two physical properties and two chemical properties of a bag of microwave popcorn before popping and after.

SCILINKS
NSTA
Developed and maintained by the National Science Teachers Association
For a variety of links related to this chapter, go to www.scilinks.org
Topic: Chemical Changes
SciLinks code: HSM0266

Skills Practice Lab

White Before Your Eyes

You have learned how to describe matter based on its physical and chemical properties. You have also learned some signs that can help you determine whether a change in matter is a physical change or a chemical change. In this lab, you'll use what you have learned to describe four substances based on their properties and the changes that they undergo.

OBJECTIVES

Describe the physical properties of four substances.

Identify physical and chemical changes.

Classify four substances by their chemical properties.

MATERIALS

- baking powder
- baking soda
- carton, egg, plastic-foam
- cornstarch
- eyedroppers (3)
- iodine solution
- spatulas (4)
- stirring rod
- sugar
- vinegar
- water

SAFETY

Procedure

1. Copy Table 1 and Table 2 shown on the next page. Be sure to leave plenty of room in each box to write down your observations.
2. Using a spatula, place a small amount of baking powder into three cups of your egg carton. Use just enough baking powder to cover the bottom of each cup. Record your observations about the baking powder's appearance, such as color and texture, in the "Unmixed" column of Table 1.

3. Use an eyedropper to add 60 drops of water to the baking powder in the first cup. Stir with the stirring rod. Record your observations in Table 1 in the column labeled "Mixed with water." Clean your stirring rod.

4. Use a clean dropper to add 20 drops of vinegar to the second cup of baking powder. Stir. Record your observations in Table 1 in the column labeled "Mixed with vinegar." Clean your stirring rod.

5. Use a clean dropper to add five drops of iodine solution to the third cup of baking powder. Stir. Record your observations in Table 1 in the column labeled "Mixed with iodine solution." Clean your stirring rod. **Caution:** Be careful when using iodine. Iodine will stain your skin and clothes.

6. Repeat steps 2–5 for each of the other substances (baking soda, cornstarch, and sugar). Use a clean spatula for each substance.

Analyze the Results

1. **Examining Data** What physical properties do all four substances share?

2. **Analyzing Data** In Table 2, write the type of change—physical or chemical—that you observed for each substance. State the property that the change demonstrates.

Draw Conclusions

3. **Evaluating Results** Classify the four substances by the chemical property of reactivity. For example, which substances are reactive with vinegar (acid)?

***Table 1* Observations**

Substance	Unmixed	Mixed with water	Mixed with vinegar	Mixed with iodine solution
Baking powder				
Baking soda				
Cornstarch				
Sugar				

DO NOT WRITE IN BOOK

***Table 2* Changes and Properties**

	Mixed with water		Mixed with vinegar		Mixed with iodine solution	
Substance	Change	Property	Change	Property	Change	Property
Baking powder						
Baking soda						
Cornstarch						
Sugar						

DO NOT WRITE IN BOOK

Chapter Review

USING KEY TERMS

1. Use each of the following terms in a separate sentence: *physical property, chemical property, physical change,* and *chemical change.*

For each pair of terms, explain how the meanings of the terms differ.

2. *mass* and *weight*
3. *inertia* and *mass*
4. *volume* and *density*

UNDERSTANDING KEY IDEAS

Multiple Choice

5. Which of the following properties is NOT a chemical property?
   a. reactivity with oxygen
   b. malleability
   c. flammability
   d. reactivity with acid
6. The volume of a liquid can be expressed in all of the following units EXCEPT
   a. grams.
   b. liters.
   c. milliliters.
   d. cubic centimeters.
7. The SI unit for the mass of a substance is the
   a. gram.
   b. liter.
   c. milliliter.
   d. kilogram.
8. The best way to measure the volume of an irregularly shaped solid is to
   a. use a ruler to measure the length of each side of the object.
   b. weigh the solid on a balance.
   c. use the water displacement method.
   d. use a spring scale.
9. Which of the following statements about weight is true?
   a. Weight is a measure of the gravitational force on an object.
   b. Weight varies depending on where the object is located in relation to the Earth.
   c. Weight is measured by using a spring scale.
   d. All of the above
10. Which of the following statements does NOT describe a physical property of a piece of chalk?
    a. Chalk is a solid.
    b. Chalk can be broken into pieces.
    c. Chalk is white.
    d. Chalk will bubble in vinegar.
11. Which of the following statements about density is true?
    a. Density is expressed in grams.
    b. Density is mass per unit volume.
    c. Density is expressed in milliliters.
    d. Density is a chemical property.

Short Answer

12. In one or two sentences, explain how the process of measuring the volume of a liquid differs from the process of measuring the volume of a solid.

13 What is the formula for calculating density?

14 List three characteristic properties of matter.

Math Skills

15 What is the volume of a book that has a width of 10 cm, a length that is 2 times the width, and a height that is half the width? Remember to express your answer in cubic units.

16 A jar contains 30 mL of glycerin (whose mass is 37.8 g) and 60 mL of corn syrup (whose mass is 82.8 g). Which liquid is on top? Show your work, and explain your answer.

CRITICAL THINKING

17 **Concept Mapping** Use the following terms to create a concept map: *matter, mass, inertia, volume, milliliters, cubic centimeters, weight,* and *gravity.*

18 **Applying Concepts** Develop a set of questions that would be useful when identifying an unknown substance. The substance may be a liquid, a gas, or a solid.

19 **Analyzing Processes** You are making breakfast for your friend Filbert. When you take the scrambled eggs to the table, he asks, "Would you please poach these eggs instead?" What scientific reason do you give Filbert for not changing his eggs?

20 **Identifying Relationships** You look out your bedroom window and see your new neighbor moving in. Your neighbor bends over to pick up a small cardboard box, but he cannot lift it. What can you conclude about the item(s) in the box? Use the terms *mass* and *inertia* to explain how you came to your conclusion.

21 **Analyzing Ideas** You may sometimes hear on the radio or on TV that astronauts are weightless in space. Explain why this statement is not true.

INTERPRETING GRAPHICS

Use the photograph below to answer the questions that follow.

22 List three physical properties of this aluminum can.

23 When this can was crushed, did it undergo a physical change or a chemical change?

24 How does the density of the metal in the crushed can compare with the density of the metal before the can was crushed?

25 Can you tell what the chemical properties of the can are by looking at the picture? Explain your answer.

Standardized Test Preparation

Multiple Choice

Use the chart below to answer questions 1–2.

Substance	State*	Density* (g/cm^3)	Color
Helium	Gas	0.0001663	Colorless
Iron pyrite	Solid	5.02	Metallic Yellow
Mercury	Liquid	13.55	Metallic Gray
Oxygen	Gas	0.001331	Colorless
Gold	Solid	19.32	Metallic Yellow
Water	Liquid	1.00	Colorless

* at 20° C and 1.0 atm

1. Look at the chart above. Which is true of mercury?

A. It is the densest substance listed.

B. Its density is less than the density of water.

C. It is a solid at 20°C and 1.0 atm.

D. It is the densest liquid listed in the chart.

2. A substance has a mass of 10 g and a volume of 10 cm^3. Based on the chart above, what is the substance?

A. mercury

B. oxygen

C. water

D. helium

3. When oxygen in the air reacts with iron, iron oxide forms. Which statement is correct?

A. This is a physical change.

B. This is a chemical change.

C. Iron and iron oxide have the same properties.

D. Oxygen and iron have similar properties.

4. Which of the following statements regarding chemical properties is true?

A. They can be observed when the identity of a substance changes.

B. They can always be observed without changing the identity of a substance.

C. They are easier to observe than physical properties.

D. They are the properties that are most useful in identifying a substance.

5. A chemical change takes place during a laboratory investigation of the properties of magnesium. Which of the following might have been observed?

A. Magnesium burns in the presence of oxygen.

B. Magnesium melts at 649°C.

C. Magnesium becomes malleable when heated.

D. Magnesium conducts an electric current.

6. Which is a chemical change?

A. Clear water turns red after a dye is added.

B. Ice melts.

C. Salt dissolves in water.

D. Milk sours.

7. Which physical property could be used to classify oxygen, propane, and hydrogen as being similar to one another?

A. flammability

B. state

C. reactivity

D. malleability

Use the diagram below to answer questions 8–9.

Before

After

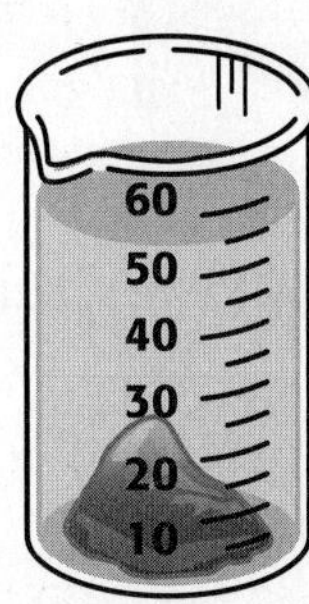

8. An irregular object's volume is determined by displacement of water, as shown above. What is the volume of the object?

A. 15 mL

B. 40 mL

C. 55 mL

D. 95 mL

9. Jonathan finds the mass of the submerged object shown above to be 13.07 g. What can you conclude about the measurement?

A. The measurement cannot be used to determine density without also knowing the force of gravity.

B. The measurement is accurate because the resulting density is 0.87 g/mL, a common density of irregular objects.

C. The measurement can be used to determine density because the object is not completely submerged in the water.

D. The measurement is likely inaccurate because the resulting density, 0.87 g/mL, is less than that of water, 1.0 g/mL, which means it would float.

10. Max drops one effervescent tablet into a beaker of water and places a second tablet on the lab table. He observes bubbles of gas form on the surface of the tablet. The bubbles rise and break on the surface of the water. After several minutes, no more bubbles form and no tablet is visible in the water. The tablet on the lab table is unchanged. What conclusion should Max draw from his observations?

A. The solid tablet changes directly into a gas through a physical change.

B. The tablet breaks down when exposed to light and forms a gas through a chemical change.

C. The tablet causes dissolved gases in the water to be released through a physical change.

D. The tablet interacts with water to form a gas through a chemical change.

Open Response

11. Two ball-shaped objects are made of white plastic. Both balls have the same diameter and are completely solid. One ball has twice the mass of the other. What can you conclude about the material of each ball?

12. What chemical properties would be important to consider when choosing a material to make a safe baking dish?

Science in Action

Scientific Debate

Paper or Plastic?

What do you choose at the grocery store: paper or plastic bags? Plastic bags are waterproof and take up less space. You can use them to line waste cans and to pack lunches. Some places will recycle plastic bags. But making 1 ton of plastic bags uses 11 barrels of oil, which can't be replaced, and produces polluting chemicals. On the other hand, making 1 ton of paper bags destroys 13 to 17 trees, which take years to replace. Paper bags, too, can be reused for lining waste cans and wrapping packages. Recycling paper pollutes less than recycling plastic does. What is the answer? Maybe we should reuse both!

Language Arts ACTIVITY

WRITING SKILL There are advantages and disadvantages of each kind of bag. Write a one-page essay defending your position on this subject. Support your opinion with facts.

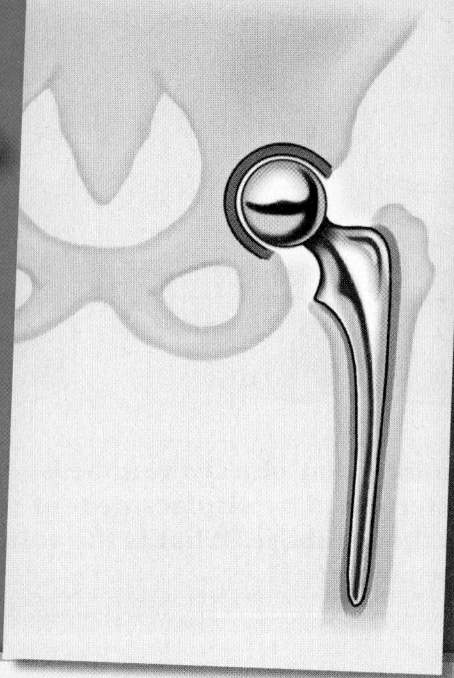

Science, Technology, and Society

Building a Better Body

Have you ever broken a bone? If so, you probably wore a cast while the bone healed. But what happens if the bone is too damaged to heal? Sometimes, a false bone made from titanium can replace the damaged bone. Titanium appears to be a great bone-replacement material. It is a lightweight but strong metal. It can attach to existing bone and resists chemical changes. But, friction can wear away titanium bones. Research has found that implanting a form of nitrogen on the titanium makes the metal last longer.

Social Studies ACTIVITY

Do some research on the history of bone-replacement therapy. Make a poster that shows a timeline of events leading up to current technology.

Careers

Mimi So

Gemologist and Jewelry Designer A typical day for gemologist and jewelry designer Mimi So involves deciding what materials to work with. When she chooses a gemstone for a piece of jewelry, she must consider the size, hardness, color, grade, and cut of the stone. When choosing a metal to use as a setting for a stone, she must look at the hardness, melting point, color, and malleability of the metal. She needs to choose a metal that not only looks good with a particular stone but also has physical properties that will work with that stone. For example, Mimi So says emeralds are soft and fragile. A platinum setting would be too hard and could damage the emerald. So, emeralds are usually set in a softer metal, such as 18-karat gold.

The chemical properties of stones must also be considered. Heating can burn or discolor some gemstones. Mimi So says, "If you are using pearls in a design that requires heating the metal, the pearl is not a stone, so you cannot heat the pearl, because it would destroy the pearl."

Math Activity

Pure gold is 24-karat (24K). Gold that contains 18 parts gold and 6 parts other metals is 18-karat gold. The percentage of gold in 18K gold is found by dividing the amount of gold by the total amount of the material and then multiplying by 100%. For example, (18 parts gold)/(24 parts total) equals $0.75 \times 100\% = 75\%$ gold. Find the percentage of gold in 10K and 14K gold.

To learn more about these Science in Action topics, visit **go.hrw.com** and type in the keyword **HP5MATF.**

Current Science

Check out Current Science® articles related to this chapter by visiting go.hrw.com. Just type in the keyword HP5CS02.

States of Matter

The Big Idea

Matter exists in various physical states, which are determined by the movement of the matter's particles.

About the Photo

This beautiful glass creation by artist Dale Chihuly is entitled "Mille Fiori" (A Thousand Flowers). The pieces that form the sculpture were not always solid and unchanging. Each individual piece started as a blob of melted glass on the end of a hollow pipe. The artist worked with his assistants to quickly form each shape before the molten glass cooled and became a solid again.

PRE-READING ACTIVITY

FOLDNOTES

Three-Panel Flip Chart

Before you read the chapter, create the FoldNote entitled "Three-Panel Flip Chart" described in the **Study Skills** section of the Appendix. Label the flaps of the three-panel flip chart with "Solid," "Liquid," and "Gas." As you read the chapter, write information you learn about each category under the appropriate flap.

START-UP ACTIVITY

Vanishing Act

In this activity, you will use isopropyl alcohol (rubbing alcohol) to investigate a change of state.

Procedure

1. Pour **rubbing alcohol** into a **small plastic cup** until the alcohol just covers the bottom of the cup.
2. Moisten the tip of a **cotton swab** by dipping it into the alcohol in the cup.
3. Rub the cotton swab on the palm of your hand. Make sure there are no cuts or abrasions on your hands.
4. Record your observations.
5. Wash your hands thoroughly.

Analysis

1. Explain what happened to the alcohol after you rubbed the swab on your hand.
2. Did you feel a sensation of hot or cold? If so, how do you explain what you observed?
3. Record your answers.

SECTION 1

Three States of Matter

What You Will Learn

- Describe the properties shared by particles of all matter.
- Describe three states of matter.
- Explain the differences between the states of matter.

Vocabulary

states of matter
solid
liquid
surface tension
viscosity
gas

READING STRATEGY

Paired Summarizing Read this section silently. In pairs, take turns summarizing the material. Stop to discuss ideas that seem confusing.

You've just walked home on one of the coldest days of the year. A fire is blazing in the fireplace. And there is a pot of water on the stove to make hot chocolate.

The water begins to bubble. Steam rises from the pot. You make your hot chocolate, but it is too hot to drink. You don't want to wait for it to cool down. So, you add an ice cube. You watch the ice melt in the hot liquid until the drink is at just the right temperature. Then, you enjoy your hot drink while warming yourself by the fire.

The scene described above has examples of the three most familiar states of matter: solid, liquid, and gas. The **states of matter** are the physical forms in which a substance can exist. For example, water commonly exists in three states of matter: solid (ice), liquid (water), and gas (steam).

Particles of Matter

Matter is made up of tiny particles called *atoms* and *molecules* (MAHL i kyoolz). These particles are too small to see without a very powerful microscope. Atoms and molecules are always in motion and are always bumping into one another. The particles interact with each other, and the way they interact with each other helps determine the state of the matter. **Figure 1** describes three states of matter—solid, liquid, and gas—in terms of the speed and attraction of the particles.

Figure 1 **Models of a Solid, a Liquid, and a Gas**

Particles of a solid do not move fast enough to overcome the strong attraction between them. So, they are close together and vibrate in place.

Particles of a liquid move fast enough to overcome some of the attraction between them. The particles are close together but can slide past one another.

Particles of a gas move fast enough to overcome almost all of the attraction between them. The particles are far apart and move independently of one another.

Solids

Imagine dropping a marble into a bottle. Would anything happen to the shape or size of the marble? Would the shape or size of the marble change if you put it in a larger bottle?

Solids Have Definite Shape and Volume

Even in a bottle, a marble keeps its original shape and volume. The marble's shape and volume stay the same no matter what size bottle you drop it into because the marble is a solid. A **solid** is the state of matter that has a definite shape and volume.

The particles of a substance in a solid state are very close together. The attraction between them is stronger than the attraction between the particles of the same substance in the liquid or gaseous state. The particles in a solid move, but they do not move fast enough to overcome the attraction between them. Each particle vibrates in place. Therefore, each particle is locked in place by the particles around it.

There Are Two Kinds of Solids

There are two kinds of solids—*crystalline* (KRIS tuhl in) and *amorphous* (uh MAWR fuhs). Crystalline solids have a very orderly, three-dimensional arrangement of particles. The particles of crystalline solids are in a repeating pattern of rows. Iron, diamond, and ice are examples of crystalline solids.

Amorphous solids are made of particles that do not have a special arrangement. So, each particle is in one place, but the particles are not arranged in a pattern. Examples of amorphous solids are glass, rubber, and wax. **Figure 2** shows a photo of quartz (a crystalline solid) and glass (an amorphous solid).

Reading Check **How are the particles in a crystalline solid arranged?** (*See the Appendix for answers to Reading Checks.*)

states of matter the physical forms of matter, which include solid, liquid, and gas

solid the state of matter in which the volume and shape of a substance are fixed

CONNECTION TO Physics

Is Glass a Liquid? At one time, there was a theory that glass was a liquid. This theory came about because of the observation that ancient windowpanes were often thicker at the bottom than at the top. People thought that the glass had flowed to the bottom of the pane, so glass must be a liquid. Research this theory. Present your research to your class in an oral presentation.

ACTIVITY

Figure 2 **Crystalline and Amorphous Solids**

The particles of crystalline solids, such as this quartz crystal, have an orderly three-dimensional pattern.

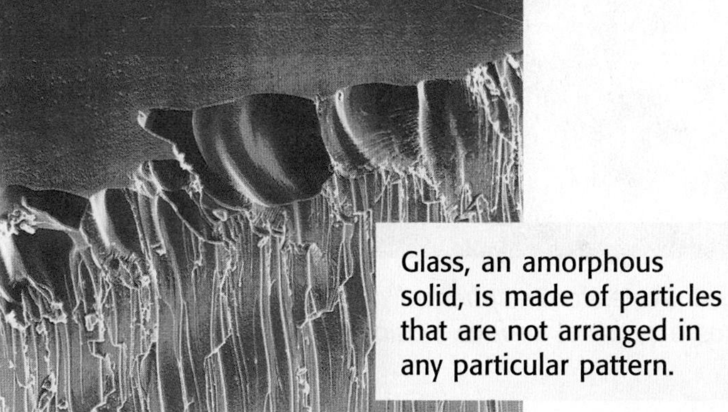

Glass, an amorphous solid, is made of particles that are not arranged in any particular pattern.

Figure 3 *Although their shapes are different, the beaker and the graduated cylinder each contain 350 mL of juice.*

Liquids

What do you think would change about orange juice if you poured the juice from a can into a glass? Would the volume of juice be different? Would the taste of the juice change?

liquid the state of matter that has a definite volume but not a definite shape

surface tension the force that acts on the surface of a liquid and that tends to minimize the area of the surface

viscosity the resistance of a gas or liquid to flow

gas a form of matter that does not have a definite volume or shape

Liquids Change Shape but Not Volume

The only thing that would change when the juice is poured into the glass is the shape of the juice. The shape changes because juice is a liquid. **Liquid** is the state of matter that has a definite volume but takes the shape of its container. The particles in liquids move fast enough to overcome some of the attractions between them. The particles slide past each other until the liquid takes the shape of its container.

Although liquids change shape, they do not easily change volume. A can of juice contains a certain volume of liquid. That volume stays the same if you pour the juice into a large container or a small one. **Figure 3** shows the same volume of liquid in two different containers.

Liquids Have Unique Characteristics

A special property of liquids is surface tension. **Surface tension** is a force that acts on the particles at the surface of a liquid. Surface tension causes some liquids to form spherical drops, like the beads of water shown in **Figure 4.** Different liquids have different surface tensions. For example, gasoline has a very low surface tension and forms flat drops.

Another important property of liquids is viscosity. **Viscosity** is a liquid's resistance to flow. Usually, the stronger the attractions between the molecules of a liquid, the more viscous the liquid is. For example, honey flows more slowly than water. So, honey has a higher viscosity than water.

Figure 4 *Water forms spherical drops as a result of surface tension.*

Reading Check What is viscosity?

Gases

Would you believe that one small tank of helium can fill almost 700 balloons? How is this possible? After all, the volume of a tank is equal to the volume of only about five filled balloons. The answer has to do with helium's state of matter.

Gases Change in Both Shape and Volume

Helium is a gas. **Gas** is the state of matter that has no definite shape or volume. The particles of a gas move quickly. So, they can break away completely from one another. There is less attraction between particles of a gas than between particles of the same substance in the solid or liquid state.

The amount of empty space between gas particles can change. Look at **Figure 5.** The particles of helium in the balloons are farther apart than the particles of helium in the tank. The particles spread out as helium fills the balloon. So, the amount of empty space between the gas particles increases.

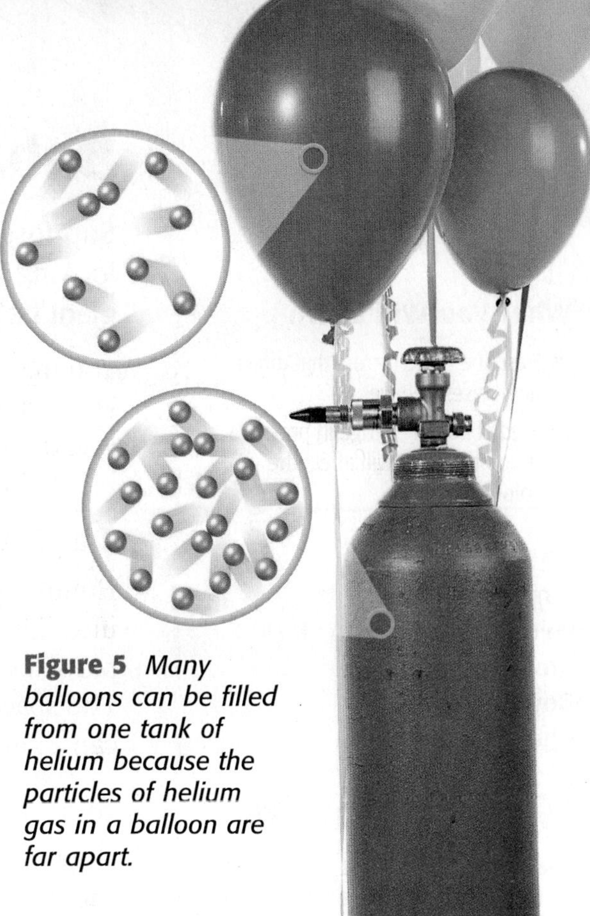

Figure 5 *Many balloons can be filled from one tank of helium because the particles of helium gas in a balloon are far apart.*

SECTION Review

Summary

- The three most familiar states of matter are solid, liquid, and gas.
- All matter is made of tiny particles called atoms and molecules that attract each other and move constantly.
- A solid has a definite shape and volume.
- A liquid has a definite volume but not a definite shape.
- A gas does not have a definite shape or volume.

Using Key Terms

1. Use each of the following terms in a separate sentence: *viscosity* and *surface tension.*

Understanding Key Ideas

2. One property that all particles of matter have in common is they
   a. never move in solids.
   b. only move in gases.
   c. move constantly.
   d. None of the above
3. Describe solids, liquids, and gases in terms of shape and volume.

Critical Thinking

4. **Applying Concepts** Classify each substance according to its state of matter: apple juice, bread, a textbook, and steam.
5. **Identifying Relationships** The volume of a gas can change, but the volume of a solid cannot. Explain why this is true.

Interpreting Graphics

Use the image below to answer the questions that follow.

6. Identify the state of matter shown in the jar.
7. Discuss how the particles in the jar are attracted to each other.

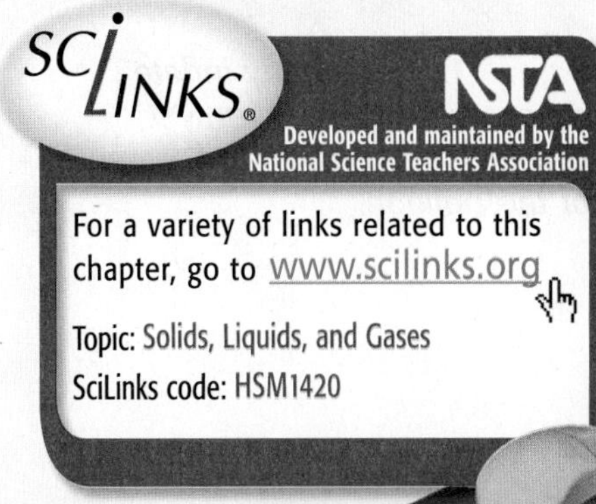

SCILINKS.
NSTA
Developed and maintained by the National Science Teachers Association
For a variety of links related to this chapter, go to www.scilinks.org
Topic: Solids, Liquids, and Gases
SciLinks code: HSM1420

SECTION 2

Behavior of Gases

What You Will Learn

- Describe three factors that affect how gases behave.
- Predict how a change in pressure or temperature will affect the volume of a gas.

Vocabulary

temperature
volume
pressure
Boyle's Law
Charles's Law

READING STRATEGY

Reading Organizer As you read this section, make a table comparing the effects of temperature, volume, and pressure on gases.

Suppose you are watching a parade that you have been looking forward to for weeks. You may be fascinated by the giant balloons floating high overhead.

You may wonder how the balloons were arranged for the parade. How much helium was needed to fill all of the balloons? What role does the weather play in getting the balloons to float?

Describing Gas Behavior

Helium is a gas. Gases behave differently from solids or liquids. Unlike the particles that make up solids and liquids, gas particles have a large amount of empty space between them. The space that gas particles occupy is the gas's volume, which can change because of temperature and pressure.

Temperature

How much helium is needed to fill a parade balloon, like the one in **Figure 1?** The answer depends on the outdoor temperature. **Temperature** is a measure of how fast the particles in an object are moving. The faster the particles are moving, the more energy they have. So, on a hot day, the particles of gas are moving faster and hitting the inside walls of the balloon harder. Thus, the gas is expanding and pushing on the walls of the balloon with greater force. If the gas expands too much, the balloon will explode. But, what will happen if the weather is cool on the day of the parade? The particles of gas in the balloon will have less energy. And, the particles of gas will not push as hard on the walls of the balloon. So, more gas must be used to fill the balloons.

temperature a measure of how hot (or cold) something is; specifically, a measure of the movement of particles.

Figure 1 *To properly inflate a helium balloon, you must consider the temperature outside of the balloon.*

Volume

Volume is the amount of space that an object takes up. But because the particles of a gas spread out, the volume of any gas depends on the container that the gas is in. For example, have you seen inflated balloons that were twisted into different shapes? Shaping the balloons was possible because particles of gas can be compressed, or squeezed together, into a smaller volume. But, if you tried to shape a balloon filled with water, the balloon would probably explode. It would explode because particles of liquids can't be compressed as much as particles of gases.

volume a measure of the size of a body or region in three-dimensional space

pressure the amount of force exerted per unit area of a surface

Pressure

The amount of force exerted on a given area of surface is called **pressure.** You can think of pressure as the number of times the particles of a gas hit the inside of their container.

The balls in **Figure 2** are the same size, which means they can hold the same volume of air, which is a gas. Notice, however, that there are more particles of gas in the basketball than in the beach ball. So, more particles hit the inside surface of the basketball than hit the inside surface of the beach ball. When more particles hit the inside surface of the basketball, the force on the inside surface of the ball increases. This increased force leads to greater pressure, which makes the basketball feel harder than the beach ball.

INTERNET ACTIVITY

For another activity related to this chapter, go to **go.hrw.com** and type in the keyword **HP5STAW**.

Reading Check **Why is the pressure greater in a basketball than in a beach ball?** (*See the Appendix for answers to Reading Checks.*)

Figure 2 **Gas and Pressure**

High pressure

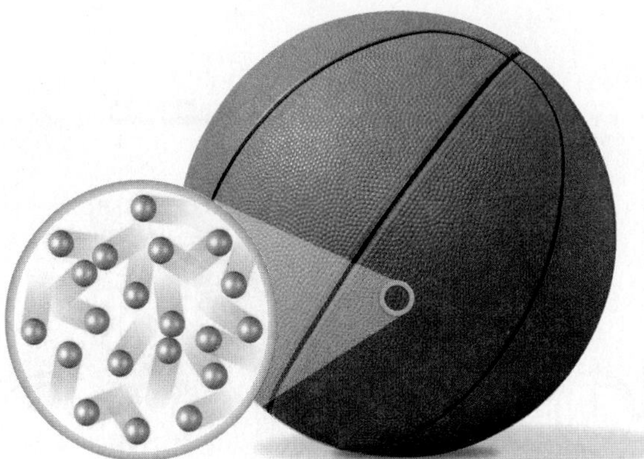

The basketball has a higher pressure because there are more particles of gas in it, and they are closer together. The particles collide with the inside of the ball at a faster rate.

Low pressure

The beach ball has a lower pressure because there are fewer particles of gas, and they are farther apart. The particles in the beach ball collide with the inside of the ball at a slower rate.

Gas Behavior Laws

Scientists found that the temperature, pressure, and volume of a gas are linked. Changing one of the factors changes the other two factors. The relationships between temperature, pressure, and volume are described by gas laws.

Boyle's Law

Imagine that a diver 10 m below the surface of a lake blows a bubble of air. When the bubble reaches the surface, the bubble's volume has doubled. The difference in pressure between the surface and 10 m below the surface caused this change.

The relationship between the volume and pressure of a gas was first described by Robert Boyle, a 17th-century Irish chemist. The relationship is now known as Boyle's law. **Boyle's law** states that for a fixed amount of gas at a constant temperature, the volume of the gas is inversely related to the pressure. So, as the pressure of a gas increases, the volume decreases by the same amount, as shown in **Figure 3.**

Boyle's law the law that states that the volume of a gas is inversely proportional to the pressure of a gas when temperature is constant

Charles's law the law that states that the volume of a gas is directly proportional to the temperature of a gas when pressure is constant

Charles's Law

If you blow air into a balloon and leave it in the hot sun, the balloon might pop. **Charles's law** states that for a fixed amount of gas at a constant pressure, the volume of the gas changes in the same way that the temperature of the gas changes. So, if the temperature increases, the volume of gas also increases by the same amount. Charles's law is shown by the model in **Figure 4.**

Reading Check State Charles's law in your own words.

Figure 3 **Boyle's Law**

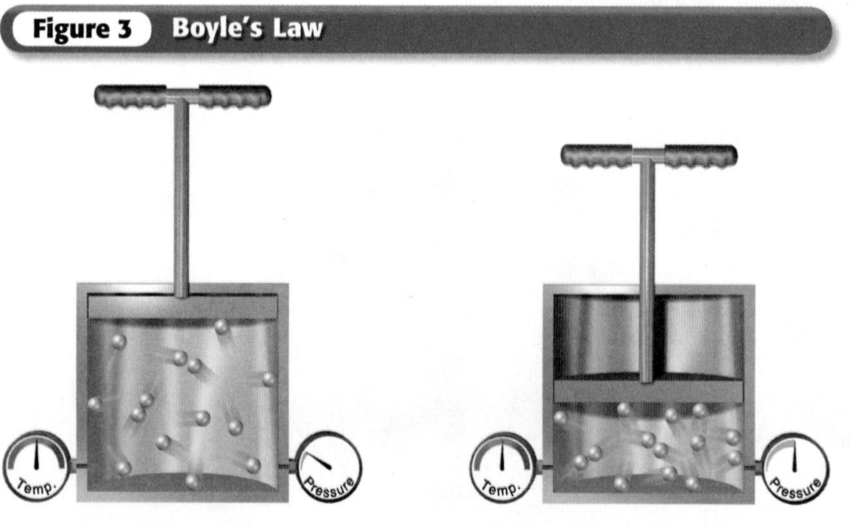

Lifting the piston lets the particles of gas spread far apart. The volume of the gas increases as the pressure decreases.

Releasing the piston allows the particles of gas to return to their original volume and pressure.

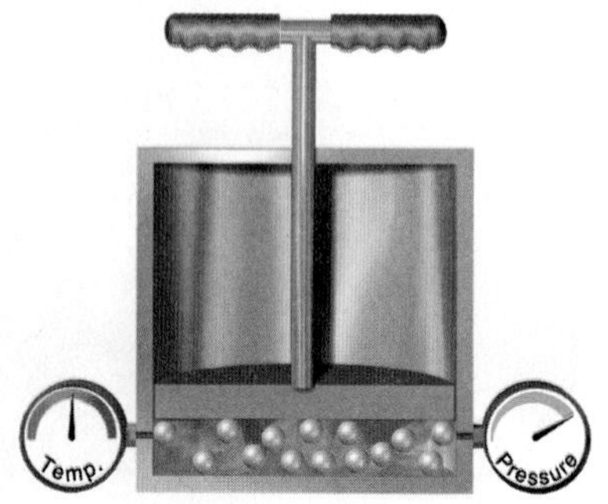

Pushing the piston forces the gas particles close together. The volume of the gas decreases as the pressure increases.

Figure 4 Charles's Law

Decreasing the temperature of the gas causes the particles to move more slowly. The gas particles hit the piston less often and with less force. So, the volume of the gas decreases.

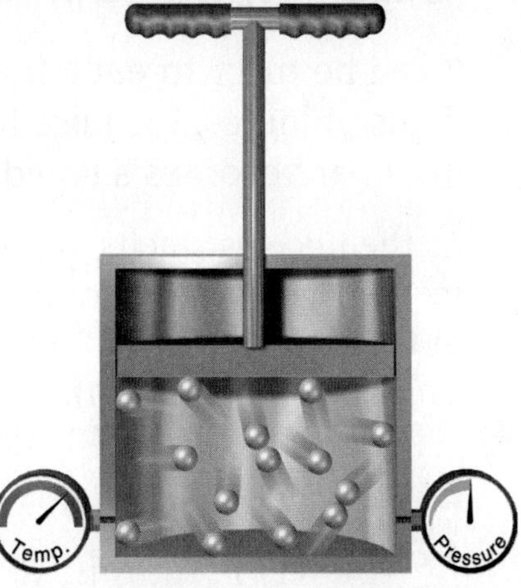

Increasing the temperature of the gas causes the particles to move more quickly. The gas particles hit the piston more often and with greater force. So, the volume of the gas increases.

SECTION Review

Summary

- Temperature measures how fast the particles in an object are moving.
- Gas pressure increases as the number of collisions of gas particles increases.
- Boyle's law states that if the temperature doesn't change, the volume of a gas increases as the pressure decreases.
- Charles's law states that if the pressure doesn't change, the volume of a gas increases as the temperature increases.

Using Key Terms

1. Use each of the following terms in the same sentence: *temperature, pressure, volume,* and *Charles's law.*

Understanding Key Ideas

2. Boyle's law describes the relationship between
   a. volume and pressure.
   b. temperature and pressure.
   c. temperature and volume.
   d. All of the above
3. What are the effects of a warm temperature on gas particles?

Math Skills

4. You have 3 L of gas at a certain temperature and pressure. What would the volume of the gas be if the temperature doubled and the pressure stayed the same?

Critical Thinking

5. **Applying Concepts** What happens to the volume of a balloon that is taken outside on a cold winter day? Explain.
6. **Making Inferences** When scientists record a gas's volume, they also record its temperature and pressure. Why?
7. **Analyzing Ideas** What happens to the pressure of a gas if the volume of gas is tripled at a constant temperature?

For a variety of links related to this chapter, go to www.scilinks.org

Topic: Gas Laws
SciLinks code: HSM0637

SECTION 3

Changes of State

It can be tricky to eat a frozen juice bar outside on a hot day. In just minutes, the juice bar will start to melt. Soon the solid juice bar becomes a liquid mess.

As the juice bar melts, it goes through a change of state. In this section, you will learn about the four changes of state shown in **Figure 1** as well as a fifth change of state called *sublimation* (SUHB luh MAY shuhn).

What You Will Learn

- Describe how energy is involved in changes of state.
- Describe what happens during melting and freezing.
- Compare evaporation and condensation.
- Explain what happens during sublimation.
- Identify the two changes that can happen when a substance loses or gains energy.

Vocabulary

change of state
melting
evaporation
boiling
condensation
sublimation

READING STRATEGY

Mnemonics As you read this section, create a mnemonic device to help you remember the five changes of state.

Energy and Changes of State

A **change of state** is the change of a substance from one physical form to another. All changes of state are physical changes. In a physical change, the identity of a substance does not change. In **Figure 1,** the ice, liquid water, and steam are all the same substance—water.

The particles of a substance move differently depending on the state of the substance. The particles also have different amounts of energy when the substance is in different states. For example, particles in liquid water have more energy than particles in ice. But particles of steam have more energy than particles in liquid water. So, to change a substance from one state to another, you must add or remove energy.

Reading Check What is a change of state? (*See the Appendix for answers to Reading Checks.*)

change of state the change of a substance from one physical state to another

Figure 1 Changes of State

The terms in the arrows are changes of state. Water commonly goes through the changes of state shown here.

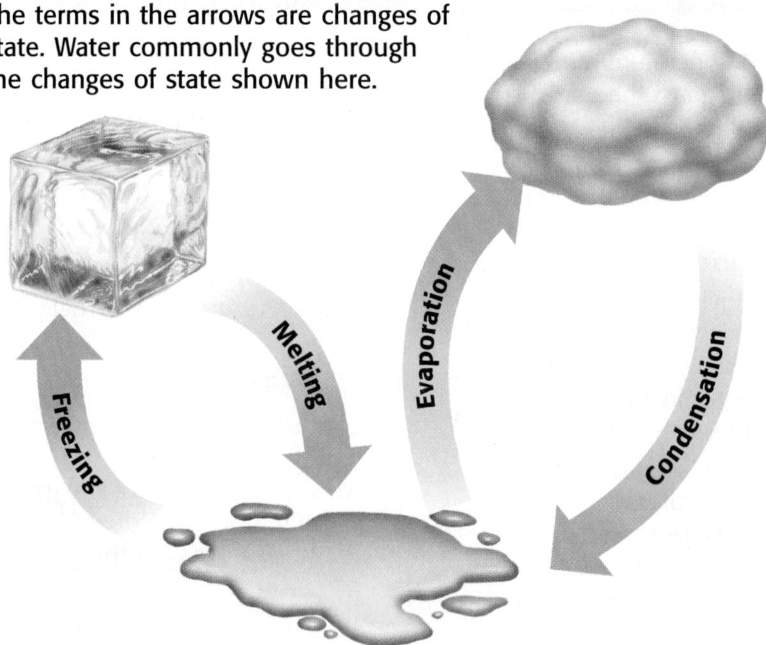

Melting: Solid to Liquid

One change of state that happens when you add energy to a substance is melting. **Melting** is the change of state from a solid to a liquid. This change of state is what happens when ice melts. Adding energy to a solid increases the temperature of the solid. As the temperature increases, the particles of the solid move faster. When a certain temperature is reached, the solid will melt. The temperature at which a substance changes from a solid to a liquid is the *melting point* of the substance. Melting point is a physical property. Different substances have different melting points. For example, gallium melts at about 30°C. Because your normal body temperature is about 37°C, gallium will melt in your hand! This is shown in **Figure 2.** Table salt, however, has a melting point of 801°C, so it will not melt in your hand.

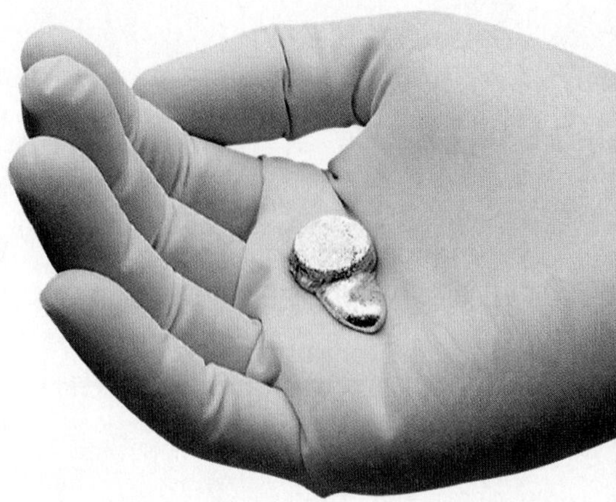

Figure 2 *Even though gallium is a metal, it would not be very useful as jewelry!*

Adding Energy

For a solid to melt, particles must overcome some of their attractions to each other. When a solid is at its melting point, any energy added to it is used to overcome the attractions that hold the particles in place. Melting is an *endothermic* (EN doh THUHR mik) change because energy is gained by the substance as it changes state.

melting the change of state in which a solid becomes a liquid by adding energy

Freezing: Liquid to Solid

The change of state from a liquid to a solid is called *freezing*. The temperature at which a liquid changes into a solid is the liquid's *freezing point*. Freezing is the reverse process of melting. Thus, freezing and melting occur at the same temperature, as shown in **Figure 3.**

Removing Energy

For a liquid to freeze, the attractions between the particles must overcome the motion of the particles. Imagine that a liquid is at its freezing point. Removing energy will cause the particles to begin locking into place. Freezing is an *exothermic* (EK so THUHR mik) change because energy is removed from the substance as it changes state.

Figure 3 *Liquid water freezes at the same temperature at which ice melts—0°C.*

If energy is added at 0°C, the ice will melt.

If energy is removed at 0°C, the liquid water will freeze.

Evaporation: Liquid to Gas

One way to experience evaporation is to iron a shirt using a steam iron. You will notice steam coming up from the iron as the wrinkles disappear. This steam forms when the liquid water in the iron becomes hot and changes to gas.

Boiling and Evaporation

evaporation the change of a substance from a liquid to a gas

boiling the conversion of a liquid to a vapor when the vapor pressure of the liquid equals the atmospheric pressure

Evaporation (ee VAP uh RAY shuhn) is the change of a substance from a liquid to a gas. Evaporation can occur at the surface of a liquid that is below its boiling point. For example, when you sweat, your body is cooled through evaporation. Your sweat is mostly water. Water absorbs energy from your skin as the water evaporates. You feel cooler because your body transfers energy to the water. Evaporation also explains why water in a glass on a table disappears after several days.

Figure 4 explains the difference between boiling and evaporation. **Boiling** is the change of a liquid to a vapor, or gas, throughout the liquid. Boiling occurs when the pressure inside the bubbles, which is called *vapor pressure,* equals the outside pressure on the bubbles, or atmospheric pressure. The temperature at which a liquid boils is called its *boiling point.* No matter how much of a substance is present, neither the boiling point nor the melting point of a substance change. For example, 5 mL and 5 L of water both boil at 100°C.

Reading Check What is evaporation?

Figure 4 **Boiling and Evaporation**

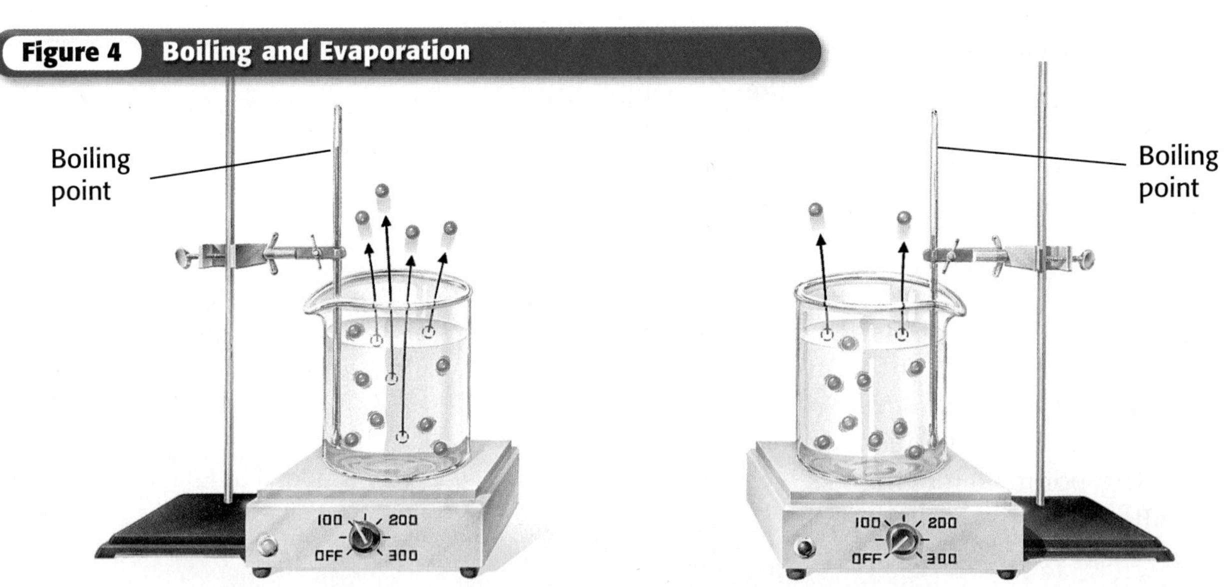

Boiling occurs in a liquid at its boiling point. As energy is added to the liquid, particles throughout the liquid move faster. When they move fast enough to break away from other particles, they evaporate and become a gas.

Evaporation can also occur in a liquid below its boiling point. Some particles at the surface of the liquid move fast enough to break away from the particles around them and become a gas.

Effects of Pressure on Boiling Point

Earlier, you learned that water boils at 100°C. In fact, water boils at 100°C only at sea level, because of atmospheric pressure. Atmospheric pressure is caused by the weight of the gases that make up the atmosphere.

Atmospheric pressure varies depending on where you are in relation to sea level. Atmospheric pressure is lower at higher elevations. The higher you go above sea level, the fewer air particles there are above you. So, the atmospheric pressure is lower. Imagine boiling water at the top of a mountain. The boiling point would be lower than 100°C. For example, Denver, Colorado, is 1.6 km above sea level. In Denver, water boils at about 95°C.

CONNECTION TO Language Arts

WRITING SKILL **Cooking at High Altitudes** Many times, cake mixes and other prepared foods will have special instructions for baking and cooking at high altitudes. Even poaching an egg at a high altitude requires a different amount of cooking time. Imagine that you got a letter from a cousin in Denver. He is upset that a cake he made turned out poorly, even though he followed the recipe. Do research on cooking at high altitudes. Write a letter to your cousin explaining why he may have had problems baking the cake.

Condensation: Gas to Liquid

Look at the dragonfly in **Figure 5.** Notice the beads of water that have formed on the wings. They form because of condensation of gaseous water in the air. **Condensation** is the change of state from a gas to a liquid. Condensation and evaporation are the reverse of each other. The *condensation point* of a substance is the temperature at which the gas becomes a liquid. And the condensation point is the same temperature as the boiling point at a given pressure.

For a gas to become a liquid, large numbers of particles must clump together. Particles clump together when the attraction between them overcomes their motion. For this to happen, energy must be removed from the gas to slow the movement of the particles. Because energy is removed, condensation is an exothermic change.

condensation the change of state from a gas to a liquid

Figure 5 *Beads of water form when water vapor in the air contacts a cool surface, such as the wings of this dragonfly.*

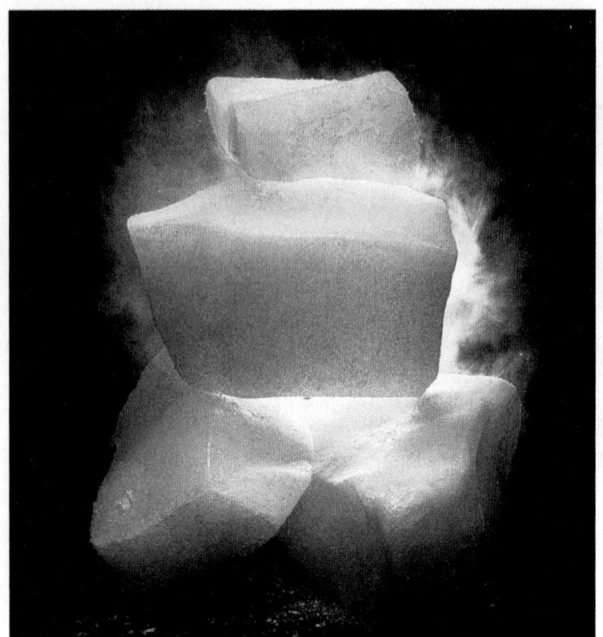

Figure 6 *Dry ice changes directly from a solid to a gas. This change of state is called* sublimation.

Sublimation: Solid to Gas

The solid in **Figure 6** is dry ice. Dry ice is carbon dioxide in a solid state. It is called *dry ice* because instead of melting into a liquid, it goes through sublimation. **Sublimation** is the change of state in which a solid changes directly into a gas. Dry ice is much colder than ice made from water.

For a solid to change directly into a gas, the particles of the substance must move from being very tightly packed to being spread far apart. So, the attractions between the particles must be completely overcome. The substance must gain energy for the particles to overcome their attractions. Thus, sublimation is an endothermic change because energy is gained by the substance as it changes state.

sublimation the process in which a solid changes directly into a gas

Change of Temperature Vs. Change of State

When most substances lose or gain energy, one of two things happens to the substance: its temperature changes or its state changes. The temperature of a substance is related to the speed of the substance's particles. So, when the temperature of a substance changes, the speed of the particles also changes. But the temperature of a substance does not change until the change of state is complete. For example, the temperature of boiling water stays at 100°C until it has all evaporated. In **Figure 7**, you can see what happens to ice as energy is added to the ice.

Reading Check **What happens to the temperature of a substance as it changes state?**

Boiling Water Is Cool

1. Remove the cap from a **syringe.**
2. Place the tip of the syringe in the **warm water** that is provided by your teacher. Pull the plunger out until you have 10 mL of water in the syringe.
3. Tighten the cap on the syringe.
4. Hold the syringe, and slowly pull the plunger out.
5. Observe any changes you see in the water. Record your observations.
6. Why are you not burned by the water in the syringe?

Figure 7 Changing the State of Water

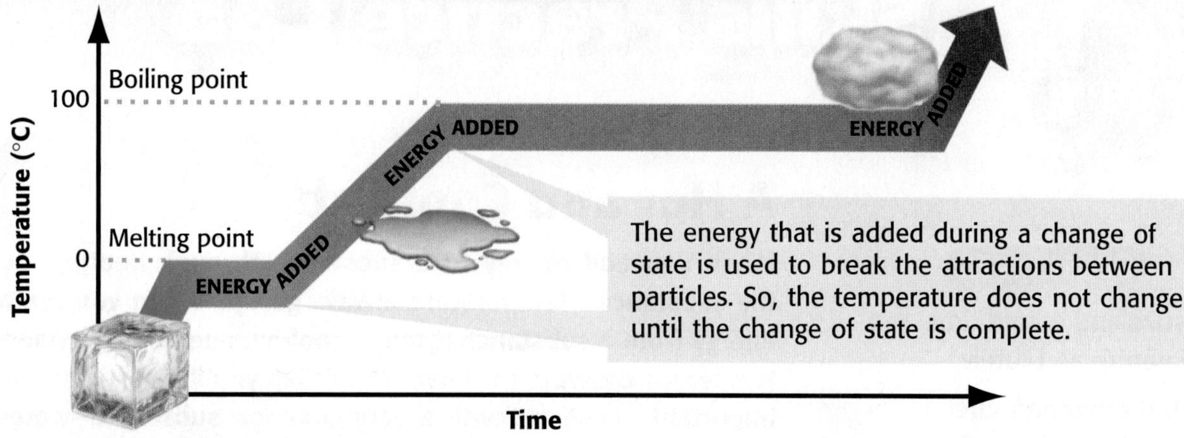

SECTION Review

Summary

- A change of state is the conversion of a substance from one physical form to another.
- Energy is added during endothermic changes. Energy is removed during exothermic changes.
- The freezing point and the melting point of a substance are the same temperature.
- Both boiling and evaporation result in a liquid changing to a gas.
- Condensation is the change of a gas to a liquid. It is the reverse of evaporation.
- Sublimation changes a solid directly to a gas.
- The temperature of a substance does not change during a change of state.

Using Key Terms

For each pair of terms, explain how the meanings of the terms differ.

1. *melting* and *freezing*
2. *condensation* and *evaporation*

Understanding Key Ideas

3. The change from a solid directly to a gas is called
   a. evaporation.
   b. boiling.
   c. melting.
   d. sublimation.
4. Describe how the motion and arrangement of particles in a substance change as the substance freezes.
5. Explain what happens to the temperature of an ice cube as it melts.
6. How are evaporation and boiling different? How are they similar?

Math Skills

7. The volume of a substance in the gaseous state is about 1,000 times the volume of the same substance in the liquid state. How much space would 18 mL of water take up if it evaporated?

Critical Thinking

8. **Evaluating Data** The temperature of water in a beaker is 25°C. After adding a piece of magnesium to the water, the temperature increases to 28°C. Is this an exothermic or endothermic reaction? Explain your answer.
9. **Applying Concepts** Solid crystals of iodine were placed in a flask. The top of the flask was covered with aluminum foil. The flask was gently heated. Soon, the flask was filled with a reddish gas. What change of state took place? Explain your answer.
10. **Predicting Consequences** Would using dry ice in your holiday punch cause it to become watery after several hours? Why or why not?

SCILINKS.
NSTA
Developed and maintained by the National Science Teachers Association
For a variety of links related to this chapter, go to www.scilinks.org
Topic: Changes of State
SciLinks code: HSM0254

Skills Practice Lab

A Hot and Cool Lab

When you add energy to a substance through heating, does the substance's temperature always go up? When you remove energy from a substance through cooling, does the substance's temperature always go down? In this lab you'll investigate these important questions with a very common substance—water.

OBJECTIVES

Measure and record time and temperature accurately.

Graph the temperature change of water as it changes state.

Analyze and interpret graphs of changes of state.

MATERIALS

- beaker, 250 or 400 mL
- coffee can, large
- gloves, heat-resistant
- graduated cylinder, 100 mL
- graph paper
- hot plate
- ice, crushed
- rock salt
- stopwatch
- thermometer
- water
- wire-loop stirring device

SAFETY

Procedure

1. Fill the beaker about one-third to one-half full with water.
2. Put on heat-resistant gloves. Turn on the hot plate, and put the beaker on it. Put the thermometer in the beaker. **Caution:** Be careful not to touch the hot plate.
3. Make a copy of Table l. Record the temperature of the water every 30 seconds. Continue doing this until about one-fourth of the water boils away. Note the first temperature reading at which the water is steadily boiling.

Table 1

Time (s)	30	60	90	120	150	180	210	etc.
Temperature (°C)		DO NOT WRITE IN BOOK						

4. Turn off the hot plate.
5. While the beaker is cooling, make a graph of temperature (*y*-axis) versus time (*x*-axis). Draw an arrow pointing to the first temperature at which the water was steadily boiling.

6. After you finish the graph, use heat-resistant gloves to pick up the beaker. Pour the warm water out, and rinse the warm beaker with cool water.
   Caution: Even after cooling, the beaker is still too warm to handle without gloves.
7. Put approximately 20 mL of water in the graduated cylinder.
8. Put the graduated cylinder in the coffee can, and fill in around the graduated cylinder with crushed ice. Pour rock salt on the ice around the graduated cylinder. Place the thermometer and the wire-loop stirring device in the graduated cylinder.
9. As the ice melts and mixes with the rock salt, the level of ice will decrease. Add ice and rock salt to the can as needed.
10. Make another copy of Table I. Record the temperature of the water in the graduated cylinder every 30 seconds. Stir the water with the stirring device.
   Caution: Do not stir with the thermometer.
11. Once the water begins to freeze, stop stirring. Do not try to pull the thermometer out of the solid ice in the cylinder.
12. Note the temperature when you first notice ice crystals forming in the water. Continue taking readings until the water in the graduated cylinder is completely frozen.
13. Make a graph of temperature (*y*-axis) versus time (*x*-axis). Draw an arrow to the temperature reading at which the first ice crystals form in the water in the graduated cylinder.

Analyze the Results

1. **Describing Events** What happens to the temperature of boiling water when you continue to add energy through heating?
2. **Describing Events** What happens to the temperature of freezing water when you continue to remove energy through cooling?
3. **Analyzing Data** What does the slope of each graph represent?
4. **Analyzing Results** How does the slope of the graph that shows water boiling compare with the slope of the graph before the water starts to boil? Why is the slope different for the two periods?
5. **Analyzing Results** How does the slope of the graph showing water freezing compare with the slope of the graph before the water starts to freeze? Why is the slope different for the two periods?

Draw Conclusions

6. **Evaluating Data** The particles that make up solids, liquids, and gases are in constant motion. Adding or removing energy causes changes in the movement of these particles. Using this idea, explain why the temperature graphs of the two experiments look the way they do.

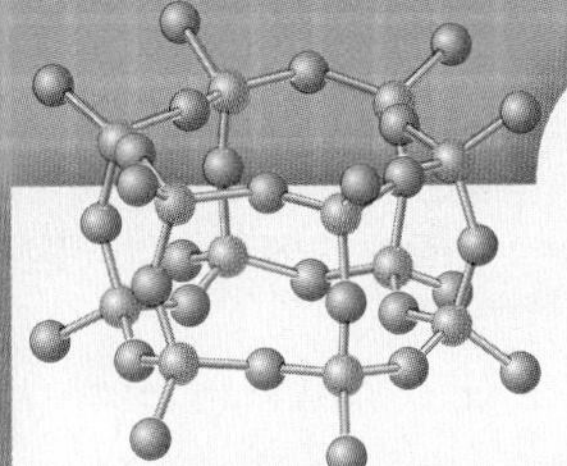

Chapter Review

USING KEY TERMS

For each pair of terms, explain how the meanings of the terms differ.

1 *solid* and *liquid*

2 *Boyle's law* and *Charles's law*

3 *evaporation* and *boiling*

4 *condensation* and *sublimation*

UNDERSTANDING KEY IDEAS

Multiple Choice

5 Which of the following statements best describes the particles of a liquid?

a. The particles are far apart and moving fast.
b. The particles are close together but moving past each other.
c. The particles are far apart and moving slowly.
d. The particles are closely packed and vibrating in place.

6 Which of the following statements describes what happens as the temperature of a gas in a balloon increases?

a. The speed of the particles decreases.
b. The volume of the gas increases, and the speed of the particles increases.
c. The volume of the gas decreases.
d. The pressure of the gas decreases.

7 Boiling points and freezing points are examples of

a. chemical properties. **c.** energy.
b. physical properties. **d.** matter.

8 Dew collecting on a spider web in the early morning is an example of

a. condensation. **c.** sublimation.
b. evaporation. **d.** melting.

9 During which change of state do atoms or molecules become more ordered?

a. boiling **c.** melting
b. condensation **d.** sublimation

10 Which of the following changes of state is exothermic?

a. evaporation **c.** freezing
b. melting **d.** All of the above

11 What happens to the volume of a gas inside a cylinder if the temperature does not change but the pressure is reduced?

a. The volume of the gas increases.
b. The volume of the gas stays the same.
c. The volume of the gas decreases.
d. There is not enough information to determine the answer.

12 The atoms and molecules in matter

a. are attracted to one another.
b. are constantly moving.
c. move faster at higher temperatures.
d. All of the above

Short Answer

13 Explain why liquid water takes the shape of its container but an ice cube does not.

14 Rank solids, liquids, and gases in order of particle speed from the highest speed to the lowest speed.

Math Skills

15. Kate placed 100 mL of water in five different pans, placed the pans on a windowsill for a week, and measured how much water evaporated from each pan. Draw a graph of her data, which is shown below. Place surface area on the *x*-axis and volume evaporated on the *y*-axis. Is the graph linear or non-linear? What does this information tell you?

Pan number	1	2	3	4	5
Surface area (cm^2)	44	82	20	30	65
Volume evaporated (mL)	42	79	19	29	62

CRITICAL THINKING

16. **Concept Mapping** Use the following terms to create a concept map: *states of matter, solid, liquid, gas, changes of state, freezing, evaporation, condensation,* and *melting.*

17. **Analyzing Ideas** In the photo below, water is being split to form two new substances, hydrogen and oxygen. Is this a change of state? Explain your answer.

18. **Applying Concepts** After taking a shower, you notice that small droplets of water cover the mirror. Explain how this happens. Be sure to describe where the water comes from and the changes it goes through.

19. **Analyzing Methods** To protect their crops during freezing temperatures, orange growers spray water onto the trees and allow it to freeze. In terms of energy lost and energy gained, explain why this practice protects the oranges from damage.

20. **Making Inferences** At sea level, water boils at 100°C, while methane boils at –161°C. Which of these substances has a stronger force of attraction between its particles? Explain your reasoning.

INTERPRETING GRAPHICS

Use the graph below to answer the questions that follow.

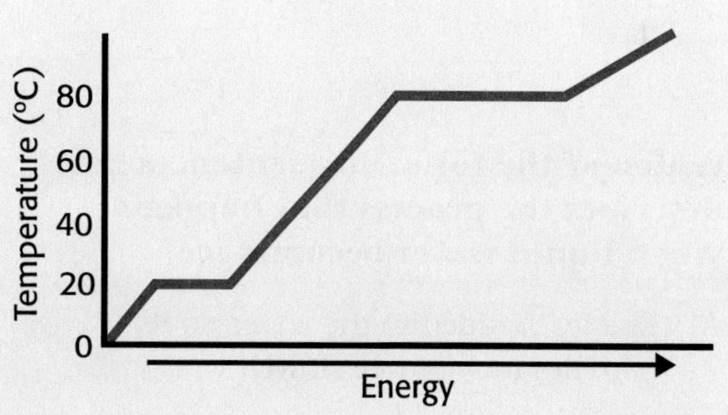

21. What is the boiling point of the substance? What is the melting point?

22. Which state is present at 30°C?

23. How will the substance change if energy is added to the liquid at 20°C?

Multiple Choice

Use the table below to answer question 1.

Substance	Temperature (°C)
Ice	−2
Iced water	0
Water	27
Boiling Water	100

1. The table above shows data from a laboratory experiment in which Andrew measured the temperatures of water in various states. Which of the following would be a correct conclusion from this experiment?

A. The particles in iced water have less energy than the particles in ice have.

B. The particles in ice have more energy than the particles in water have.

C. The particles in iced water have more energy than the particles in boiling water have.

D. The particles in boiling water have more energy than the particles in iced water have.

2. Which of the following sentences best describes the process that happens when liquid water becomes ice?

A. Energy is added to the water, so its particles move more slowly.

B. Energy is added to the water, so its particles move more quickly.

C. Energy is removed from the water, so its particles lock into place.

D. Energy is removed from the water, so its particles move more randomly.

3. Which of the following could describe oxygen at room temperature?

A. It has a constant volume and a definite shape.

B. It has a constant volume but takes the shape of its container.

C. Its particles move fast enough to overcome the attraction between them.

D. Its particles have a very orderly, three-dimensional arrangement.

4. Kevin compared the viscosities of several fluids. Substances A, B, and C flowed at different rates, but substance D did not flow at all. Which of the following is a valid conclusion?

A. Substance D must be at its melting point.

B. Substance D's particles have strong attraction for one another.

C. Substance D is neither a liquid nor a gas.

D. Substance D's particles have little attraction for one another.

5. In a laboratory experiment, Joel observed water as it vaporized, froze, melted, and condensed. Which of the following is a valid conclusion?

A. He observed four different changes of state.

B. Each of these processes happened at different temperatures.

C. All of the changes required energy to be absorbed.

D. All of the changes required energy to be released.

Use the picture below to answer question 6.

6. A cup filled to the rim with water was left at room temperature overnight. The figure above shows how much water was left the next morning. Which of the following is a reasonable hypothesis for what happened to the water?

A. The water at the surface lost enough energy to evaporate.

B. The water at the surface gained enough energy to evaporate.

C. The water at the surface lost enough energy to condense.

D. The water at the surface gained enough energy to sublimate.

7. A sealed, inflated beach ball was placed in a freezer overnight. The next day, the ball was still sealed but had shrunk. Analyze the following hypotheses to determine which is the best.

A. The pressure inside the ball increased, so the gas particles moved faster.

B. The gas inside the ball escaped, which caused the ball to shrink.

C. The temperature of the gas increased, which pushed gas out of the ball.

D. The temperature of the gas decreased, so the particles of gas moved closer together.

8. In a laboratory investigation on changes of state, Rebecca observes that the melting point of water is 0°C and that the freezing point of water is 0°C. What can Rebecca conclude from these observations?

A. Both melting and freezing are exothermic reactions.

B. Water boils at 0°C at normal atmospheric pressure.

C. Melting and freezing can occur at the same temperature.

D. She made an error in her measurements.

9. An ad for a brand of dry ice claims that it keeps food cold without getting it wet. Which of the following is a good explanation for this claim?

A. Dry ice undergoes sublimation.

B. Dry ice is not frozen.

C. Dry ice is colder than regular ice.

D. Dry ice keeps food from freezing.

Open Response

10. Describe how the physical properties of solids, liquids, and gases affect how each state of matter behaves when placed into a new container.

11. Keisha fills a balloon with helium while inside a heated building. She then takes the balloon outside on a cold winter day. The air pressure is the same inside and outside. Predict what will happen to the balloon, and explain your answer.

Science in Action

Science, Technology, and Society

Deep-sea Diving with Helium

Divers who breathe air while deep in the ocean run the risk of suffering from nitrogen narcosis. Nitrogen narcosis produces an alcohol-like effect, which can cause a diver to become disoriented and to use poor judgment. This toxic effect can lead to dangerous behavior. To avoid nitrogen narcosis, divers who work at depths of more than 60 m breathe heliox. *Heliox* is a mixture of helium and oxygen, instead of air. The main disadvantage of heliox is that helium conducts heat about six times faster than nitrogen does, so a diver using heliox will feel cold sooner than a diver who is breathing air.

Math ACTIVITY

There are 2.54 centimeters in one inch. How many feet deep could a diver go before he or she started experiencing nitrogen narcosis?

Scientific Discoveries

The Fourth State of Matter

If you heat water, it will eventually turn into a gas. But what would happen if you kept on heating the gas? Scientists only had to look to the sun for the answer. The sun, like other stars, is made of the fourth state of matter—plasma. Plasma is a superheated gas. Once a gas's temperature rises above 10,000°C to 20,000°C, its particles start to break apart and it becomes plasma. Unlike gas, plasma can create, and be affected by, electrical and magnetic fields. More than 99% of the known universe is made of plasma! Even Earth has some naturally occurring plasma. Plasma can be found in auroras, flames, and lightning.

Social Studies ACTIVITY

Research plasma. Find out how plasma is used in today's technology, such as plasma TVs. How will this new technology affect you and society in general? Describe your findings in a poster.

People in Science

Andy Goldsworthy

Nature Artist Most of the art that Andy Goldsworthy creates will melt, decay, evaporate, or just blow away. He uses leaves, water, sticks, rocks, ice, and snow to create art. Goldsworthy observes how nature works and how it changes over time, and uses what he learns to create his art. For example, on cold, sunny mornings, Goldsworthy makes frost shadows. He stands with his back to the sun, which creates a shadow on the ground. The rising sun warms the ground and melts the frost around his shadow. When he steps away, he can see the shape of his body in the frost that is left on the ground.

In his art, Goldsworthy sometimes shows water in the process of changing states. For example, he made huge snowballs filled with branches, pebbles, and flowers. He then stored these snowballs in a freezer until summer, when they were displayed in a museum. As they melted, the snowballs slowly revealed their contents. Goldsworthy says his art reflects nature, because nature is constantly changing. Fortunately, he takes pictures of his art so we can enjoy it even after it disappears!

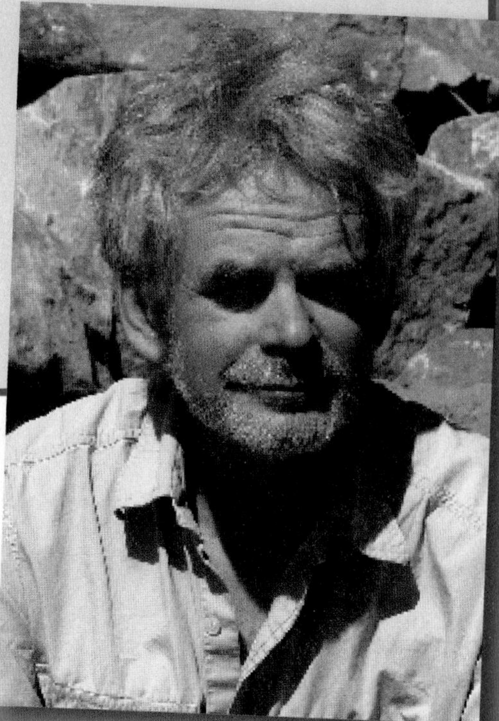

Language Arts ACTIVITY

WRITING SKILL Research Andy Goldsworthy's art. Write a one-page review of one of his creations. Be sure to include what you like or don't like about the art.

To learn more about these Science in Action topics, visit go.hrw.com and type in the keyword HP5STAF.

Current Science

Check out Current Science® articles related to this chapter by visiting go.hrw.com. Just type in the keyword HP5CS03.

Elements, Compounds, and Mixtures

The Big Idea

Matter can be classified into elements, compounds, and mixtures.

SECTION

About the Photo

Within these liquid-filled glass lamps, colored globs slowly rise and fall. But what are these liquids, and what keeps them from mixing together? The liquid inside these lamps is a mixture. This mixture is composed of four compounds, which include mineral oil, wax, water, and alcohol. The water and alcohol mix, but they remain separated from the globs of wax and oil.

PRE-READING ACTIVITY

Key-Term Fold Before you read the chapter, create the FoldNote entitled "Key-Term Fold" described in the **Study Skills** section of the Appendix. Write a key term from the chapter on each tab of the key-term fold. Under each tab, write the definition of the key term.

START-UP ACTIVITY

Mystery Mixture

In this activity, you will separate the different dyes found in an ink mixture.

Procedure

1. Place a **pencil** on top of a **clear plastic cup.** Tear a strip of paper (3 cm × 15 cm) from a **coffee filter.** Wrap one end of the strip around a pencil so that the other end will touch the bottom of the plastic cup. Use **tape** to attach the paper to the pencil.
2. Take the paper out of the cup. Using a **water-soluble black marker,** make a small dot in the center of the strip about 2 cm from the bottom.
3. Pour **water** in the cup to a depth of 1 cm. Lower the paper into the cup. Keep the dot above water.
4. Remove the paper when the water is 1 cm from the top. Record your observations.

Analysis

1. What happened as the paper soaked up the water?
2. Which colors make up the marker's black ink?
3. Compare your results with those of your classmates. Record your observations.
4. Is the process used to make the ink separate a physical or a chemical change? Explain.

SECTION 1

Elements

Imagine that you work for the Break-It-Down Company. Your job is to break down materials into simpler substances.

What You Will Learn

- Describe pure substances.
- Describe the characteristics of elements, and give examples.
- Explain how elements can be identified.
- Classify elements according to their properties.

Vocabulary

element, pure substance, metal, nonmetal, metalloid

READING STRATEGY

Reading Organizer As you read this section, make a concept map by using the terms above.

You haven't had any trouble breaking down materials so far. But one rainy Monday morning, you get a material that seems very hard to break down. First, you try physical changes, such as crushing and melting. But these do not change the material into something simpler. Next, you try some chemical changes, such as passing an electric current through the material. These do not change it either. What's going on?

Elements, the Simplest Substances

You couldn't break down the material described above because it is an element. An **element** is a pure substance that cannot be separated into simpler substances by physical or chemical means. In this section, you'll learn about elements and the properties that help you classify them.

Only One Type of Particle

Elements are pure substances. A **pure substance** is a substance in which there is only one type of particle. So, each element contains only one type of particle. These particles, called *atoms*, are much too small for us to see. For example, every atom in a 5 g nugget of the element gold is like every other atom of gold. The particles of a pure substance are alike no matter where they are found, as shown in **Figure 1.**

Reading Check **Explain why an element is a pure substance.** *(See the Appendix for answers to Reading Checks.)*

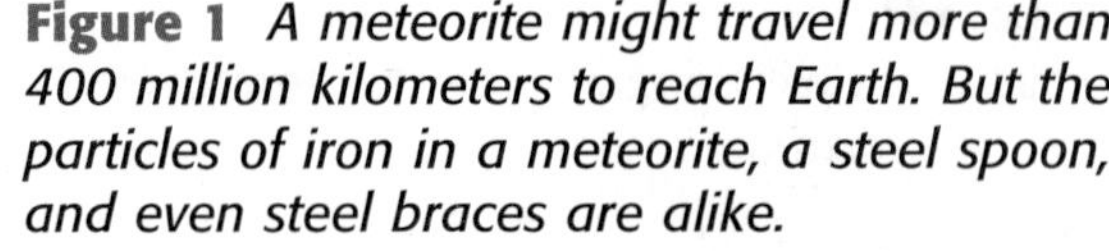

Figure 1 *A meteorite might travel more than 400 million kilometers to reach Earth. But the particles of iron in a meteorite, a steel spoon, and even steel braces are alike.*

Properties of Elements

Each element can be identified by its unique set of properties. For example, each element has its own *characteristic properties.* These properties do not depend on the amount of the element present. Characteristic properties include some physical properties, such as boiling point, melting point, and density. Chemical properties, such as reactivity with acid, are also characteristic properties.

An element may share a property with another element, but other properties can help you tell the elements apart. For example, the elements helium and krypton are both unreactive gases. However, the densities (mass per unit volume) of these elements are different. Helium is less dense than air. A helium-filled balloon will float up if it is released. Krypton is denser than air. A krypton-filled balloon will sink to the ground if it is released.

Identifying Elements by Their Properties

Look at the elements shown in **Figure 2.** These three elements have some similar properties. But each element can be identified by its unique set of properties.

Notice that the physical properties shown in **Figure 2** include melting point and density. Other physical properties, such as color, hardness, and texture, could be added to the list. Chemical properties might also be useful. For example, some elements, such as hydrogen and carbon, are flammable. Other elements, such as sodium, react with oxygen at room temperature. Still other elements, including zinc, are reactive with acid.

Separating Elements

1. Examine a sample of nails provided by your teacher.
2. Your sample has **aluminum nails** and **iron nails.** Try to separate the two kinds of nails. Group similar nails into piles.
3. Pass a **bar magnet** over each pile of nails. Record your results.
4. Were you successful in completely separating the two types of nails? Explain.
5. Based on your observations, explain how the properties of aluminum and iron could be used to separate cans in a recycling plant.

element a substance that cannot be separated or broken down into simpler substances by chemical means

pure substance a sample of matter, either a single element or a single compound, that has definite chemical and physical properties

Figure 2 The Unique Properties of Elements

Cobalt

- Melting point: 1,495°C
- Density: 8.9 g/cm^3
- Conducts electric current and heat energy
- Unreactive with oxygen in the air

Iron

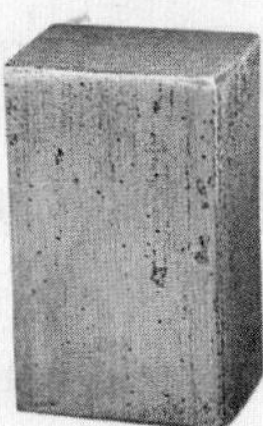

- Melting point: 1,535°C
- Density: 7.9 g/cm^3
- Conducts electric current and heat energy
- Combines slowly with oxygen in the air to form rust

Nickel

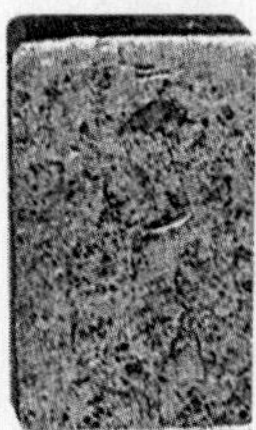

- Melting point: 1,455°C
- Density: 8.9 g/cm^3
- Conducts electric current and heat energy
- Unreactive with oxygen in the air

Figure 3 *Even though these dogs are different breeds, they have enough in common to be classified as terriers.*

Classifying Elements by Their Properties

Think about how many different breeds of dogs there are. Now, think about how you tell one breed from another. Most often, you can tell just by their appearance, or the physical properties, of the dogs. **Figure 3** shows several breeds of terriers. Many terriers are fairly small in size and have short hair. Not all terriers are alike, but they share enough properties to be classified in the same group.

Categories of Elements

Elements are also grouped into categories by the properties they share. There are three major categories of elements: metals, nonmetals, and metalloids. The elements iron, nickel, and cobalt are all metals. Not all metals are exactly alike, but they do have some properties in common. **Metals** are shiny, and they conduct heat energy and electric current. **Nonmetals** make up the second category of elements. They do not conduct heat or electric current, and solid nonmetals are dull in appearance. **Metalloids,** which have properties of both metals and nonmetals, make up the last category.

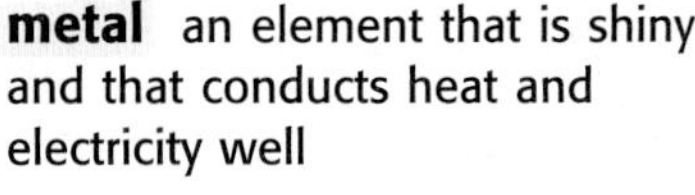

metal an element that is shiny and that conducts heat and electricity well

nonmetal an element that conducts heat and electricity poorly

metalloid an element that has properties of both metals and nonmetals

Reading Check **What are three characteristics of metals?**

Categories Are Similar

Imagine being in a music store. The CDs are categorized by type of music. If you like rock-and-roll, you would go to the rock-and-roll section. You might not know every CD, but you know that a CD has the characteristics of rock-and-roll for it to be in this section.

By knowing the category to which an unfamiliar element belongs, you can predict some of its properties. **Figure 4** shows examples of each category and describes the properties that identify elements in each category.

Figure 4 The Three Major Categories of Elements

Metals

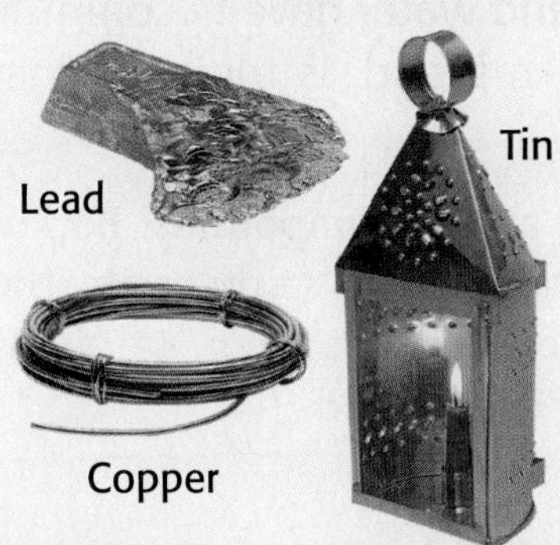

Metals are elements that are shiny and are good conductors of heat and electric current. They are *malleable.* (They can be hammered into thin sheets.) They are also *ductile.* (They can be drawn into thin wires.)

Nonmetals

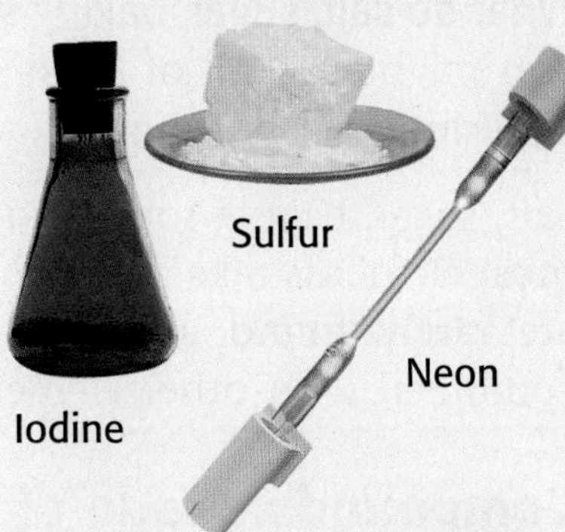

Nonmetals are elements that are dull (not shiny) and that are poor conductors of heat and electric current. Solids tend to be brittle and unmalleable. Few familiar objects are made of only nonmetals.

Metalloids

Metalloids are also called semiconductors. They have properties of both metals and nonmetals. Some metalloids are shiny. Some are dull. Metalloids are somewhat malleable and ductile. Some metalloids conduct heat and electric current as well.

SECTION Review

Summary

- A substance in which all of the particles are alike is a pure substance.
- An element is a pure substance that cannot be broken down into anything simpler by physical or chemical means.
- Each element has a unique set of physical and chemical properties.
- Elements are classified as metals, nonmetals, or metalloids, based on their properties.

Using Key Terms

1. Use the following terms in the same sentence: *element* and *pure substance.*

Understanding Key Ideas

2. A metalloid
   a. may conduct electric current.
   b. can be ductile.
   c. is also called a semiconductor.
   d. All of the above
3. What is a pure substance?

Math Skills

4. There are eight elements that make up 98.5% of the Earth's crust: 46.6% oxygen, 8.1% aluminum, 5.0% iron, 3.6% calcium, 2.8% sodium, 2.6% potassium, and 2.1% magnesium. The rest is silicon. What percentage of the Earth's crust is silicon?

Critical Thinking

5. **Applying Concepts** From which category of elements would you choose to make a container that wouldn't shatter if dropped? Explain your answer.
6. **Making Comparisons** Compare the properties of metals, nonmetals, and metalloids.
7. **Evaluating Assumptions** Your friend tells you that a shiny element has to be a metal. Do you agree? Explain.

SCILINKS.
NSTA
Developed and maintained by the National Science Teachers Association
For a variety of links related to this chapter, go to www.scilinks.org
Topic: Elements
SciLinks code: HSM0496

SECTION 2

Compounds

What do salt, sugar, baking soda, and water have in common? You might use all of these to bake bread. Is there anything else similar about them?

Salt, sugar, baking soda, and water are all compounds. Because most elements take part in chemical changes fairly easily, they are rarely found alone in nature. Instead, they are found combined with other elements as compounds.

Compounds: Made of Elements

A **compound** is a pure substance composed of two or more elements that are chemically combined. Elements combine by reacting, or undergoing a chemical change, with one another. A particle of a compound is a molecule. Molecules of compounds are formed when atoms of two or more elements join together.

In **Figure 1,** you see magnesium reacting with oxygen. A compound called *magnesium oxide* is forming. The compound is a new pure substance. It is different from the elements that make it up. Most of the substances that you see every day are compounds. **Table 1** lists some familiar examples.

The Ratio of Elements in a Compound

Elements do not randomly join to form compounds. Elements join in a specific ratio according to their masses to form a compound. For example, the ratio of the mass of hydrogen to the mass of oxygen in water is 1 to 8. This mass ratio can be written as 1:8. This ratio is always the same. Every sample of water has a 1:8 mass ratio of hydrogen to oxygen. What happens if a sample of a compound has a different mass ratio of hydrogen to oxygen? The compound cannot be water.

What You Will Learn

- Explain how elements make up compounds.
- Describe the properties of compounds.
- Explain how a compound can be broken down into its elements.
- Give examples of common compounds.

Vocabulary

compound

READING STRATEGY

Prediction Guide Before reading this section, write the title of each heading in this section. Next, under each heading, write what you think you will learn.

Figure 1 *As magnesium burns, it reacts with oxygen and forms the compound magnesium oxide.*

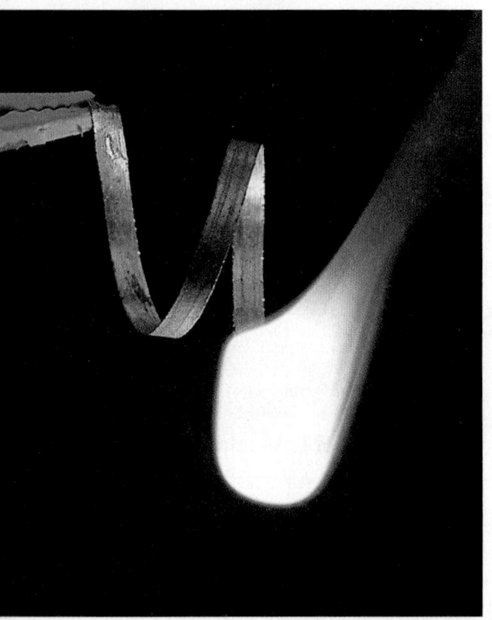

***Table 1* Familiar Compounds**

Compound	Elements combined
Table salt	sodium and chlorine
Water	hydrogen and oxygen
Vinegar	hydrogen, carbon, and oxygen
Carbon dioxide	carbon and oxygen
Baking soda	sodium, hydrogen, carbon, and oxygen

Compound Confusion

1. Measure **4 g of compound A,** and place it in a **clear plastic cup.**
2. Measure **4 g of compound B**, and place it in a **second clear plastic cup.**
3. Observe the color and texture of each compound. Record your observations.
4. Add **5 mL of vinegar** to each cup. Record your observations.
5. Baking soda reacts with vinegar. Powdered sugar does not react with vinegar. Which compound is baking soda, and which compound is powdered sugar? Explain your answer.

Properties of Compounds

As an element does, each compound has its own physical properties. Physical properties include melting point, density, and color. Compounds can also be identified by their different chemical properties. Some compounds react with acid. For example, calcium carbonate, found in chalk, reacts with acid. Other compounds, such as hydrogen peroxide, react when exposed to light.

compound a substance made up of atoms of two or more different elements joined by chemical bonds

Reading Check **What are three physical properties used to identify compounds?** (*See the Appendix for answers to Reading Checks.*)

Properties: Compounds Versus Elements

A compound has properties that differ from those of the elements that form it. Look at **Figure 2.** Sodium chloride, or table salt, is made of two very dangerous elements—sodium and chlorine. Sodium reacts violently with water. Chlorine is a poisonous gas. But when combined, these elements form a harmless compound with unique properties. Sodium chloride is safe to eat. It also dissolves (without exploding!) in water.

Figure 2 **Forming Sodium Chloride**

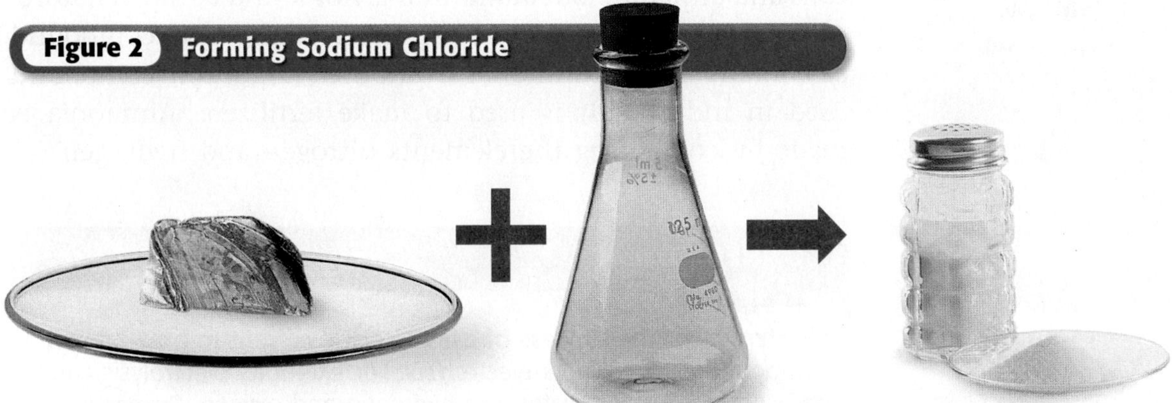

Sodium is a soft, silvery white metal that reacts violently with water.

Chlorine is a poisonous, greenish yellow gas.

Sodium chloride, or table salt, is a white solid. It dissolves easily in water and is safe to eat.

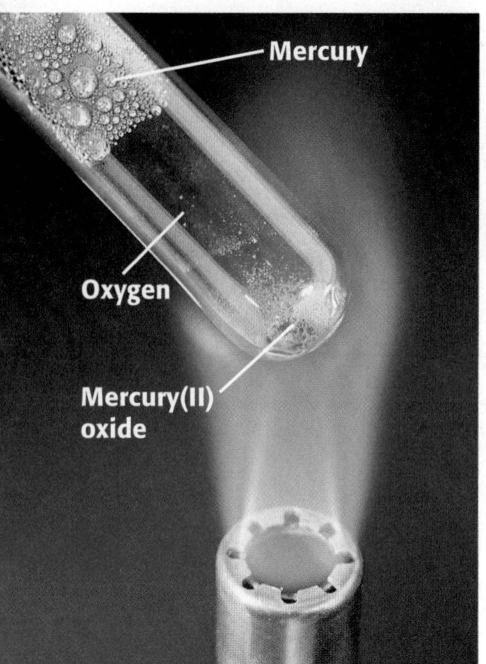

Figure 3 *Heating mercury(II) oxide causes a chemical change that separates it into the elements mercury and oxygen.*

Breaking Down Compounds

Some compounds can be broken down into their elements by chemical changes. Other compounds break down to form simpler compounds instead of elements. These simpler compounds can then be broken down into elements through more chemical changes. For example, carbonic acid is a compound that helps give carbonated beverages their "fizz." When you open a carbonated beverage, carbonic acid breaks down into carbon dioxide and water. Carbon dioxide and water can then be broken down into the elements carbon, oxygen, and hydrogen through chemical changes.

Reading Check **Compounds can be broken down into what two types of substances?**

Methods of Breaking Down Compounds

The only way to break down a compound is through a chemical change. Sometimes, energy is needed for a chemical change to happen. Two ways to add energy to break down a compound are to apply heat and to apply an electric current. For example, heating the compound mercury(II) oxide breaks it down into the elements mercury and oxygen, as shown in **Figure 3.**

Compounds in Your World

You are surrounded by compounds. Compounds make up the food you eat, the school supplies you use, and the clothes you wear—even you!

For another activity related to this chapter, go to **go.hrw.com** and type in the keyword **HP5MIXW.**

Compounds in Industry

The compounds found in nature are not usually the raw materials needed by industry. Often, these compounds must be broken down to provide elements or other compounds that can be used as raw material. For example, aluminum is used in cans and airplanes. But aluminum is not found alone in nature. Aluminum is produced by breaking down the compound aluminum oxide. Ammonia is another important compound used in industry. It is used to make fertilizers. Ammonia is made by combining the elements nitrogen and hydrogen.

CONNECTION TO Physics

Electrolysis The process of using electric current to break down compounds is known as *electrolysis*. For example, electrolysis can be used to separate water into hydrogen and oxygen. Research ways that electrolysis is used in industry. Make a poster of what you learn, and present a report to your class.

ACTIVITY

Compounds in Nature

Proteins are compounds found in all living things. The element nitrogen is one of the elements needed to make proteins. **Figure 4** shows how some plants get the nitrogen they need. Other plants use nitrogen compounds that are in the soil. Animals get the nitrogen they need by eating plants or by eating animals that have eaten plants. The proteins in the food are broken down as an animal digests the food. The simpler compounds that form are used by the animal's cells to make new proteins.

Another compound that plays an important role in life is carbon dioxide. You exhale carbon dioxide that was made in your body. Plants take in carbon dioxide, which is used in photosynthesis. Plants use photosynthesis to make compounds called carbohydrates. These carbohydrates can then be broken down for energy through other chemical changes by plants or animals.

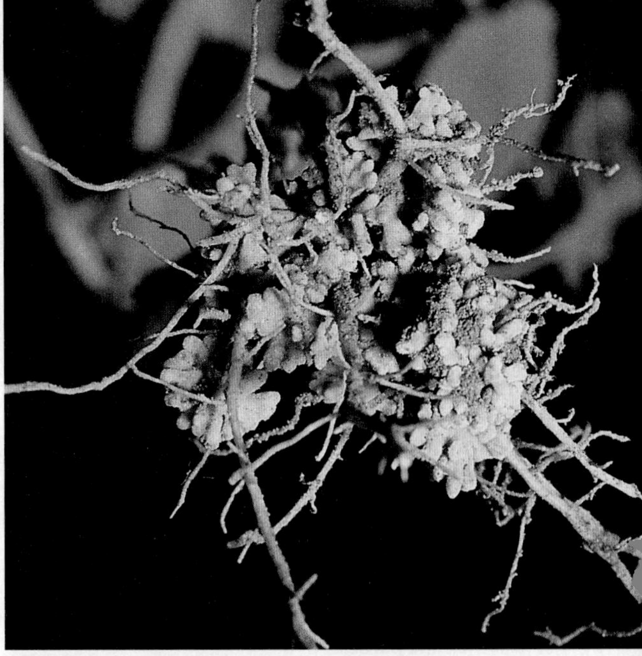

Figure 4 *The bumps on the roots of this pea plant are home to bacteria that form compounds from nitrogen in the air. The pea plant makes proteins from these compounds.*

SECTION Review

Summary

- A compound is a pure substance composed of two or more elements.
- The elements that form a compound always combine in a specific ratio according to their masses.
- Each compound has a unique set of physical and chemical properties that differ from those of the elements that make up the compound.
- Compounds can be broken down into simpler substances only by chemical changes.

Using Key Terms

1. In your own words, write a definition for the term *compound*.

Understanding Key Ideas

2. The elements in a compound
   a. join in a specific ratio according to their masses.
   b. combine by reacting with one another.
   c. can be separated by chemical changes.
   d. All of the above
3. What type of change is needed to break down a compound?

Math Skills

4. Table sugar is a compound made of carbon, hydrogen, and oxygen. If sugar contains 41.86% carbon and 6.98% hydrogen, what percentage of sugar is oxygen?

Critical Thinking

5. **Applying Concepts** Iron is a solid, gray metal. Oxygen is a colorless gas. When they chemically combine, rust is made. Rust has a reddish brown color. Why is rust different from the iron and oxygen that it is made of?
6. **Analyzing Ideas** A jar contains samples of the elements carbon and oxygen. Does the jar contain a compound? Explain your answer.

SCILINKS
NSTA
Developed and maintained by the National Science Teachers Association
For a variety of links related to this chapter, go to www.scilinks.org
Topic: Compounds
SciLinks code: HSM0332

SECTION 3

Mixtures

Imagine that you roll out some dough, add tomato sauce, and sprinkle some cheese on top. Then, you add green peppers, mushrooms, olives, and pepperoni! What have you just made?

A pizza, of course! But that's not all. You have also created a mixture—and a delicious one at that! In this section, you will learn about mixtures and their properties.

What You Will Learn

- Describe three properties of mixtures.
- Describe four methods of separating the parts of a mixture.
- Analyze a solution in terms of its solute and solvent.
- Explain how concentration affects a solution.
- Describe the particles in a suspension.
- Explain how a colloid differs from a solution and a suspension.

Vocabulary

mixture	concentration
solution	solubility
solute	suspension
solvent	colloid

READING STRATEGY

Reading Organizer As you read this section, create an outline of the section. Use the headings from the section in your outline.

Properties of Mixtures

All mixtures—even pizza—share certain properties. A **mixture** is a combination of two or more substances that are not chemically combined. When two or more materials are put together, they form a mixture if they do not react to form a compound. For example, cheese and tomato sauce do not react when they are used to make a pizza. So, a pizza is a mixture.

mixture a combination of two or more substances that are not chemically combined

No Chemical Changes in a Mixture

No chemical change happens when a mixture is made. So, each substance in a mixture has the same chemical makeup it had before the mixture formed. That is, each substance in a mixture keeps its identity. In some mixtures, such as the pizza in **Figure 1,** you can see each of the components. In other mixtures, such as salt water, you cannot see all the components.

✓ Reading Check **Why do substances in a mixture keep their identities?** (*See the Appendix for answers to Reading Checks.*)

Separating Mixtures Through Physical Methods

You don't like mushrooms on your pizza? Just pick them off. This change is a physical change of the mixture. The identities of the substances do not change. But not all mixtures are as easy to separate as a pizza. You cannot just pick salt out of a saltwater mixture. One way to separate the salt from the water is to heat the mixture until the water evaporates. The salt is left behind. Other ways to separate mixtures are shown in **Figure 2.**

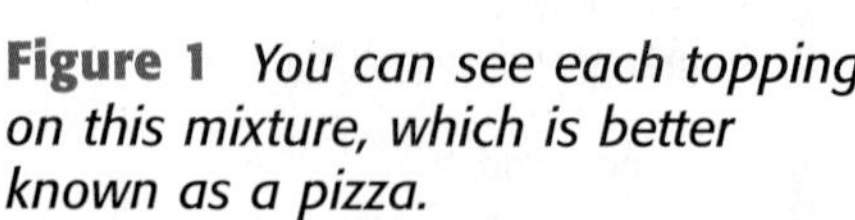

Figure 1 *You can see each topping on this mixture, which is better known as a pizza.*

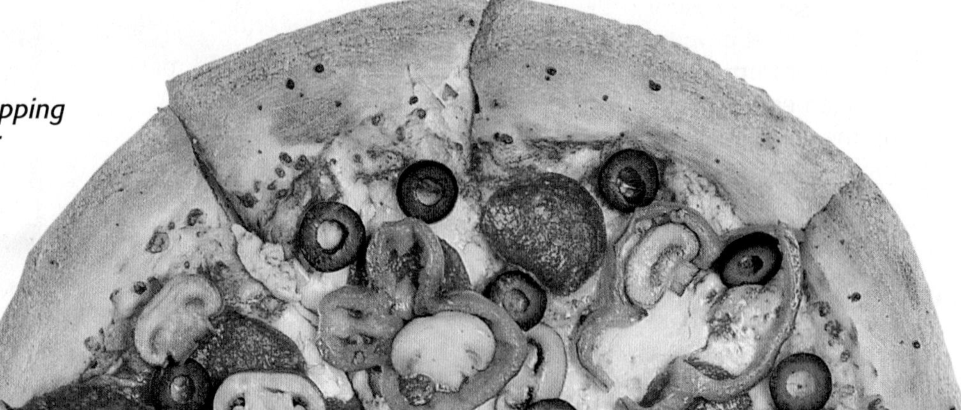

Figure 2 Common Ways to Separate Mixtures

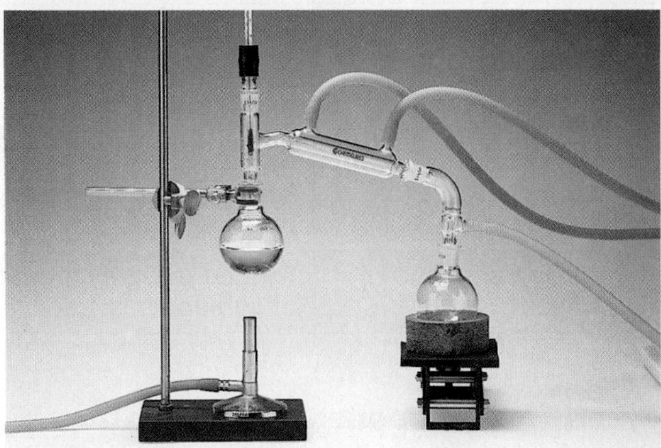

Distillation (DIS tuh LAY shuhn) is a process that separates a mixture based on the boiling points of the components. Here, pure water (at right) is being distilled from a salt-water mixture (at left). Distillation is also used to separate crude oil into components, such as gasoline and kerosene.

A **magnet** can be used to separate a mixture of the elements iron and aluminum. Iron is attracted to the magnet, but aluminum is not.

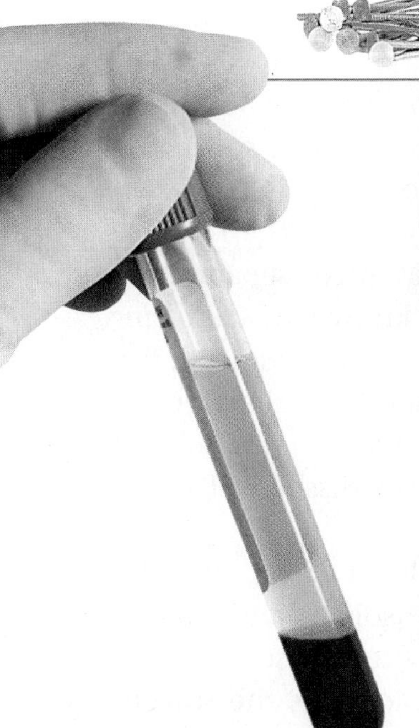

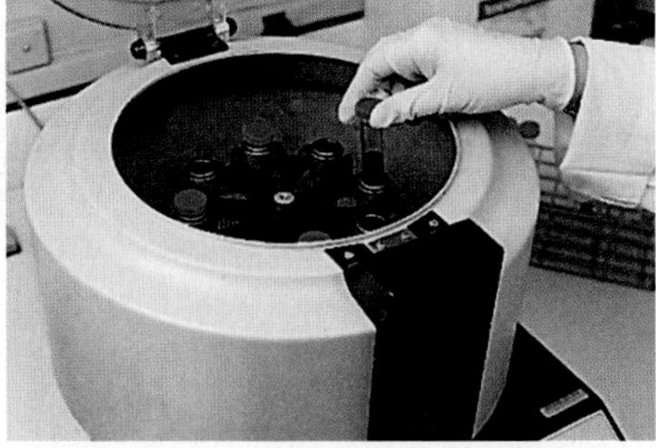

The different parts of blood are separated using a machine called a **centrifuge** (SEN truh FYOOJ). In the test tube at left, a layer of plasma rests above a layer of red blood cells. A centrifuge separates mixtures by the densities of the components.

Separating a mixture of sodium chloride (table salt) and sulfur takes more than one step.

1. In the first step, water is added, and the mixture is stirred. Salt dissolves in water. Sulfur does not.

2. In the second step, the mixture is poured through a filter. The filter traps the solid sulfur.

3. In the third step, the water is evaporated. The sodium chloride is left behind.

Table 1 Mixtures and Compounds

Mixtures	Compounds
Made of elements, compounds, or both	Made of elements
No change in original properties of components	Change in original properties of components
Separated by physical means	Separated by chemical means
Formed using any ratio of components	Formed using a set ratio of components

The Ratio of Components in a Mixture

A compound is made of elements in a specific mass ratio. However, the components of a mixture do not need to be mixed in a definite ratio. For example, granite is a mixture made of three minerals: feldspar, mica, and quartz. Feldspar is pink in color. Mica is black. Quartz is colorless. Look at the egg-shaped paperweights in **Figure 3.** The pink one is made from granite that has more feldspar than mica or quartz. That is why it is pink. The black one is made from granite that has more mica than the other minerals. The gray one is made from granite that has more quartz than the other minerals. Even though the proportions of the minerals change, this combination of minerals is always a mixture called *granite.* **Table 1** above summarizes the differences between mixtures and compounds.

Figure 3 *These paperweights are made of granite. They are different colors because the granite used in each has different ratios of minerals.*

Solutions

solution a homogeneous mixture of two or more substances uniformly dispersed throughout a single phase

solute in a solution, the substance that dissolves in the solvent

solvent in a solution, the substance in which the solute dissolves

A **solution** is a mixture that appears to be a single substance. A solution is composed of particles of two or more substances that are distributed evenly among each other. Solutions have the same appearance and properties throughout the mixture.

The process in which particles of substances separate and spread evenly throughout a mixture is known as *dissolving.* In solutions, the **solute** is the substance that is dissolved. The **solvent** is the substance in which the solute is dissolved. A solute must be *soluble,* or able to dissolve, in the solvent. A substance that is *insoluble,* or unable to dissolve, forms a mixture that is not a solution.

Salt water is a solution. Salt is soluble in water, meaning that salt dissolves in water. So, salt is the solute, and water is the solvent. When two liquids or two gases form a solution, the substance that is present in the largest amount is the solvent.

Table 2 Examples of Different States in Solutions	
States	**Examples**
Gas in gas	dry air (oxygen in nitrogen)
Gas in liquid	soft drinks (carbon dioxide in water)
Liquid in liquid	antifreeze (alcohol in water)
Solid in liquid	salt water (salt in water)
Solid in solid	brass (zinc in copper)

Examples of Solutions

You may think that all solutions are liquids. And in fact, tap water, soft drinks, gasoline, and many cleaning supplies are liquid solutions. However, solutions may also be gases, such as air. Solutions may even be solids, such as steel. *Alloys* are solid solutions of metals or nonmetals dissolved in metals. Brass is an alloy of the metal zinc dissolved in copper. Steel is an alloy made of the nonmetal carbon and other elements dissolved in iron. **Table 2** lists more examples of solutions.

Reading Check What is an alloy?

Particles in Solutions

The particles in solutions are so small that they never settle out. They also cannot be removed by filtering. In fact, the particles are so small that they don't even scatter light. Both of the jars in **Figure 4** contain mixtures. The mixture in the jar on the left is a solution of table salt in water. The jar on the right holds a mixture—but not a solution—of gelatin in water.

CONNECTION TO Language Arts

WRITING SKILL **Alloys** Research an alloy. Find out what the alloy is made of and the amount of each substance in the alloy. Also, identify different ways that the alloy is used. Then, write a song or poem about the alloy to recite in class.

Figure 4 *Both of these jars contain mixtures. The mixture in the jar on the left, however, is a solution. The particles in solutions are so small that they don't scatter light. Therefore, you can't see the path of light through the solution.*

Figure 5 *The dilute solution* (left) *contains less solute than the concentrated solution* (right).

Concentration of Solutions

concentration the amount of a particular substance in a given quantity of a mixture, solution, or ore

solubility the ability of one substance to dissolve in another at a given temperature and pressure

A measure of the amount of solute dissolved in a solvent is **concentration.** Concentration can be expressed in grams of solute per milliliter of solvent (g/mL).

Concentrated or Dilute?

Solutions can be described as being concentrated or dilute. In **Figure 5,** both solutions have the same amount of solvent. However, the solution on the left contains less solute than the solution on the right. The solution on the left is dilute. The solution on the right is concentrated. Keep in mind that the terms *dilute* and *concentrated* do not tell you the amount of solute that is dissolved.

Solubility

If you add too much sugar to a glass of lemonade, not all of the sugar can dissolve. Some of it sinks to the bottom. To find the maximum amount of sugar that can dissolve, you would need to know the solubility of sugar. The **solubility** of a solute is the ability of the solute to dissolve in a solvent at a certain temperature. **Figure 6** shows how the solubility of several different solid substances changes with temperature.

Calculating Concentration What is the concentration of a solution that has 35 g of salt dissolved in 175 mL of water?

Step 1: One equation for finding concentration is the following:

$$concentration = \frac{grams\ of\ solute}{milliliters\ of\ solvent}$$

Step 2: Replace grams of solute and milliliters of solvent with the values given, and solve.

$$\frac{35\ \text{g salt}}{175\ \text{mL water}} = 0.2\ \text{g/mL}$$

Now It's Your Turn

1. What is the concentration of solution A if it has 55 g of sugar dissolved in 500 mL of water?
2. What is the concentration of solution B if it has 36 g of sugar dissolved in 144 mL of water?
3. Which solution is more concentrated?

Figure 6 Solubility of Different Solids In Water

The solubility of most solids increases as the temperature gets higher. So, more solute can dissolve at higher temperatures. However, some solids, such as cerium sulfate, are less soluble at higher temperatures.

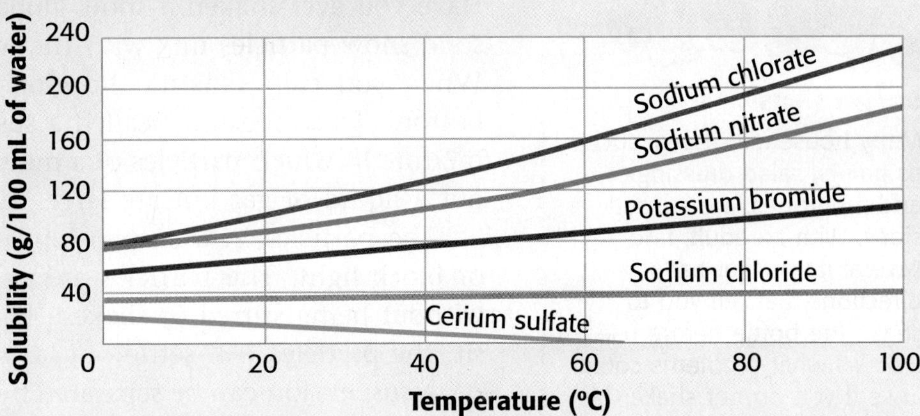

Dissolving Gases in Liquids

Most solids are more soluble in liquids at higher temperatures. But gases become less soluble in liquids as the temperature is raised. A soft drink goes flat faster when warm. The gas that is dissolved in the soft drink cannot stay dissolved when the temperature increases. So, the gas escapes, and the soft drink becomes "flat."

Reading Check **How does the solubility of gases change with temperature?**

Dissolving Solids Faster in Liquids

Several things affect how fast a solid will dissolve. Look at **Figure 7** to see three ways to make a solute dissolve faster. You can see why you will enjoy a glass of lemonade sooner if you stir granulated sugar into the lemonade before adding ice!

Figure 7 How to Dissolve Solids Faster

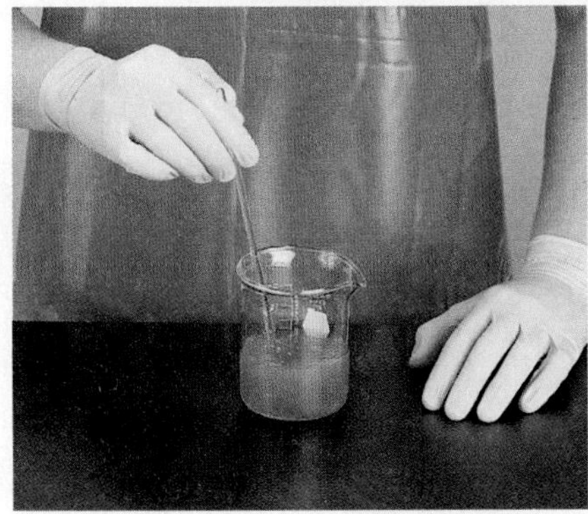

Mixing by stirring or shaking causes the solute particles to separate from one another and spread out more quickly among the solvent particles.

Heating causes particles to move more quickly. The solvent particles can separate the solute particles and spread them out more quickly.

Crushing the solute increases the amount of contact it has with the solvent. The particles of the crushed solute mix with the solvent more quickly.

Suspensions

Many household items, such as paints, salad dressings, and medicines, are suspensions. With an adult, find several items that have directions that tell you to shake the bottle before use. Discuss what problems could arise if you do not shake the container before use.

Suspensions

Have you ever shaken a snow globe? If so, you have seen the solid snow particles mix with the water, as shown in **Figure 8.** When you stop shaking the globe, the snow settles to the bottom. This mixture is called a suspension. A **suspension** is a mixture in which particles of a material are dispersed throughout a liquid or gas but are large enough that they settle out.

The particles in a suspension are large enough to scatter or block light. The particles are also too large to stay mixed without being stirred or shaken. If a suspension is allowed to sit, the particles will settle out, as they do in a snow globe.

A suspension can be separated by passing it through a filter. So, the liquid or gas passes through the filter, but the solid particles are large enough to be trapped by the filter.

Reading Check **How can the particles of a suspension be separated?**

suspension a mixture in which particles of a material are more or less evenly dispersed throughout a liquid or gas

colloid a mixture consisting of tiny particles that are intermediate in size between those in solutions and those in suspensions and that are suspended in a liquid, solid, or gas

Colloids

Some mixtures have properties between those of solutions and suspensions. These mixtures are known as colloids (KAHL OYDZ). A **colloid** is a mixture in which the particles are dispersed throughout but are not heavy enough to settle out. The particles in a colloid are relatively small and are fairly well mixed. You might be surprised at the number of colloids you see each day. Milk, mayonnaise, and stick deodorant—even the gelatin and whipped cream in **Figure 8**—are colloids.

The particles in a colloid are much smaller than the particles in a suspension. However, the particles are large enough to scatter light. A colloid cannot be separated by filtration. The particles are small enough to pass through a filter.

Figure 8 **Properties of Suspensions and Colloids**

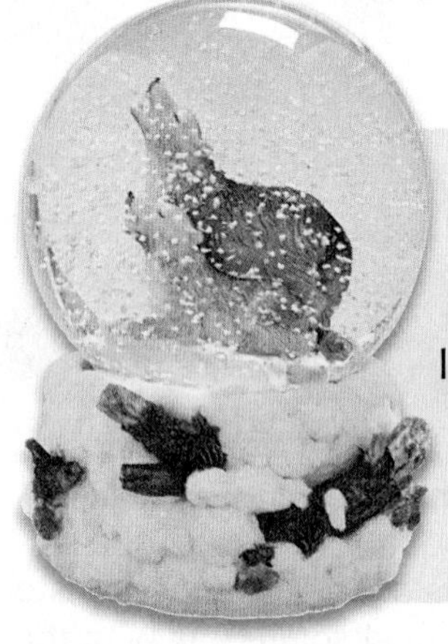

Suspension This snow globe contains solid particles that will mix with the clear liquid when you shake it up. But the particles will soon fall to the bottom when the globe is at rest.

Colloid This dessert includes two tasty examples of colloids—fruity gelatin and whipped cream.

SECTION Review

Summary

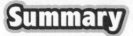

- A mixture is a combination of two or more substances, each of which keeps its own characteristics.
- Mixtures can be separated by physical means, such as filtration and evaporation.
- A solution is a mixture that appears to be a single substance but is composed of a solute dissolved in a solvent.
- Concentration is a measure of the amount of solute dissolved in a solvent.
- The solubility of a solute is the ability of the solute to dissolve in a solvent at a certain temperature.
- Suspensions are mixtures that contain particles large enough to settle out or be filtered and to block or scatter light.
- Colloids are mixtures that contain particles that are too small to settle out or be filtered but are large enough to scatter light.

Using Key Terms

The statements below are false. For each statement, replace the underlined term to make a true statement.

1. The <u>solvent</u> is the substance that is dissolved.
2. A <u>suspension</u> is composed of substances that are spread evenly among each other.
3. A measure of the amount of solute dissolved in a solvent is <u>solubility</u>.
4. A <u>colloid</u> contains particles that will settle out of the mixture if left sitting.

Understanding Key Ideas

5. A mixture
   a. has substances in it that are chemically combined.
   b. can always be separated using filtration.
   c. contains substances that are not mixed in a definite ratio.
   d. All of the above
6. List three ways to dissolve a solid faster.

Critical Thinking

7. **Making Comparisons** How do solutions, suspensions, and colloids differ?
8. **Applying Concepts** Suggest a procedure to separate iron filings from sawdust. Explain why this procedure works.
9. **Analyzing Ideas** Identify the solute and solvent in a solution made of 15 mL of oxygen and 5 mL of helium.

Interpreting Graphics

Use the graph below to answer the questions that follow.

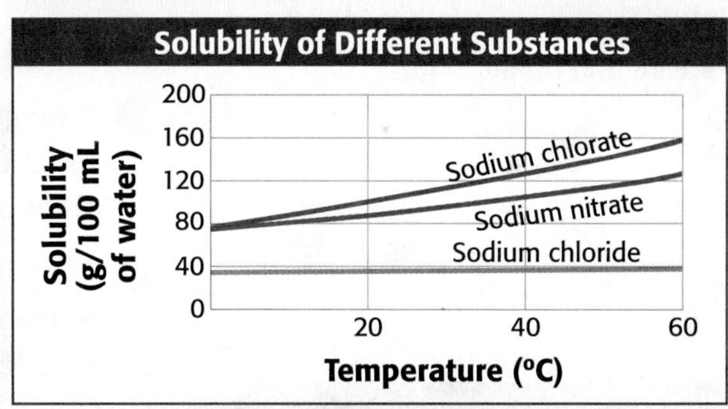

10. At what temperature is 120 g of sodium nitrate soluble in 100 mL of water?
11. At 60°C, how much more sodium chlorate than sodium chloride will dissolve in 100 mL of water?

SCILINKS.
NSTA
Developed and maintained by the National Science Teachers Association
For a variety of links related to this chapter, go to www.scilinks.org
Topic: Mixtures
SciLinks code: HSM0974

Using Scientific Methods

Skills Practice Lab

Flame Tests

OBJECTIVES

Observe flame colors emitted by various compounds.

Determine the composition of an unknown compound.

MATERIALS

- Bunsen burner
- chloride test solutions (4)
- hydrochloric acid, dilute, in a small beaker
- spark igniter
- tape, masking
- test tubes, small (4)
- test-tube rack
- water, distilled, in a small beaker
- wire and holder

SAFETY

Fireworks produce fantastic combinations of color when they are ignited. The different colors are the results of burning different compounds. Imagine that you are the head chemist for a fireworks company. The label has fallen off one box, and you must identify the unknown compound inside so that the fireworks may be used in the correct fireworks display. To identify the compound, you will use your knowledge that every compound has a unique set of properties.

Ask a Question

1. How can you identify an unknown compound by heating it in a flame?

Form a Hypothesis

2. Write a hypothesis that is a possible answer to the question above. Explain your reasoning.

Test the Hypothesis

3. Arrange the test tubes in the test-tube rack. Use masking tape to label each tube with one of the following names: calcium chloride, potassium chloride, sodium chloride, and unknown.
4. Copy the table below. Then, ask your teacher for your portions of the solutions. **Caution:** Be very careful in handling all chemicals. Tell your teacher immediately if you spill a chemical.

Test Results	
Compound	**Color of flame**
Calcium chloride	
Potassium chloride	DO NOT WRITE IN BOOK
Sodium chloride	
Unknown	

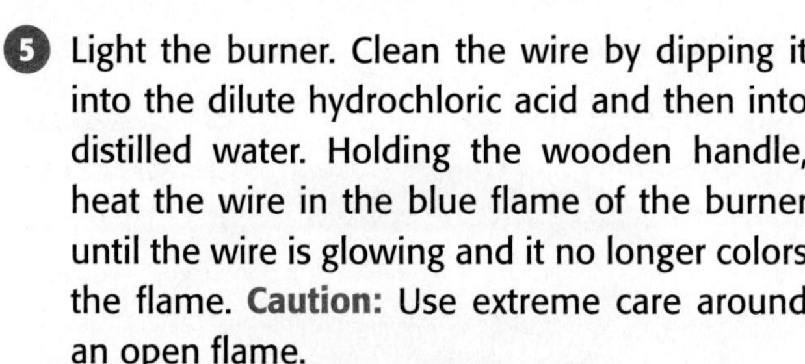

5. Light the burner. Clean the wire by dipping it into the dilute hydrochloric acid and then into distilled water. Holding the wooden handle, heat the wire in the blue flame of the burner until the wire is glowing and it no longer colors the flame. **Caution:** Use extreme care around an open flame.
6. Dip the clean wire into the first test solution. Hold the wire at the tip of the inner cone of the burner flame. Record in the table the color given to the flame.
7. Clean the wire by repeating step 5. Then, repeat steps 5 and 6 for the other solutions.
8. Follow your teacher's instructions for cleanup and disposal.

Analyze the Results

1. **Identifying Patterns** Is the flame color a test for the metal or for the chloride in each compound? Explain your answer.
2. **Analyzing Data** What is the identity of your unknown solution? How do you know?

Draw Conclusions

3. **Evaluating Methods** Why is it necessary to carefully clean the wire before testing each solution?
4. **Making Predictions** Would you expect the compound sodium fluoride to produce the same color as sodium chloride in a flame test? Why or why not?
5. **Interpreting Information** Each of the compounds you tested is made from chlorine, which is a poisonous gas at room temperature. Why is it safe to use these compounds without a gas mask?

Chapter Review

USING KEY TERMS

Complete each of the following sentences by choosing the correct term from the word bank.

compound	element
suspension	solubility
solution	metal
nonmetal	solute

1 A(n) ___ has a definite ratio of components.

2 The ability of one substance to dissolve in another substance is the ___ of the solute.

3 A(n) ___ can be separated by filtration.

4 A(n) ___ is a pure substance that cannot be broken down into simpler substances by chemical means.

5 A(n) ___ is an element that is brittle and dull.

6 The ___ is the substance that dissolves to form a solution.

UNDERSTANDING KEY IDEAS

Multiple Choice

7 Which of the following increases the solubility of a gas in a liquid?

a. increasing the temperature of the liquid
b. increasing the amount of gas in the liquid
c. decreasing the temperature of the liquid
d. decreasing the amount of liquid

8 Which of the following best describes chicken noodle soup?

a. element **c.** compound
b. mixture **d.** solution

9 Which of the following statements describes elements?

a. All of the particles in the same element are different.
b. Elements can be broken down into simpler substances.
c. Elements have unique sets of properties.
d. Elements cannot be joined together in chemical reactions.

10 A solution that contains a large amount of solute is best described as

a. insoluble. **c.** dilute.
b. concentrated. **d.** weak.

11 Which of the following substances can be separated into simpler substances only by chemical means?

a. sodium **c.** water
b. salt water **d.** gold

12 Which of the following would not increase the rate at which a solid dissolves?

a. decreasing the temperature
b. crushing the solid
c. stirring
d. increasing the temperature

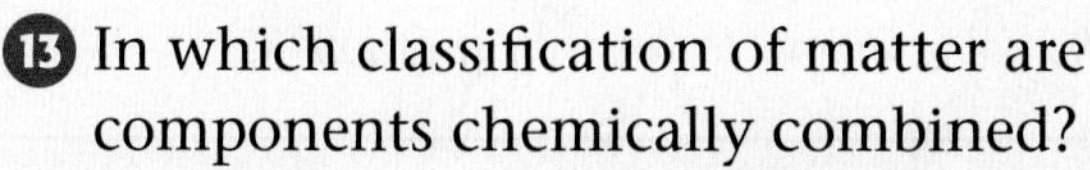

13. In which classification of matter are components chemically combined?
    a. a solution **c.** a compound
    b. a colloid **d.** a suspension

14. An element that conducts thermal energy well and is easily shaped is a
    a. metal.
    b. metalloid.
    c. nonmetal.
    d. None of the above

Short Answer

15. What is the difference between an element and a compound?

16. When nail polish is dissolved in acetone, which substance is the solute, and which is the solvent?

Math Skills

17. What is the concentration of a solution prepared by mixing 50 g of salt with 200 mL of water?

18. How many grams of sugar must be dissolved in 150 mL of water to make a solution that has a concentration of 0.6 g/mL?

CRITICAL THINKING

19. **Concept Mapping** Use the following terms to create a concept map: *matter, element, compound, mixture, solution, suspension,* and *colloid.*

20. **Forming Hypotheses** To keep the "fizz" in carbonated beverages after they have been opened, should you store them in a refrigerator or in a cabinet? Explain.

21. **Making Inferences** A light green powder is heated in a test tube. A gas is given off, and the solid becomes black. In which classification of matter does the green powder belong? Explain your reasoning.

22. **Predicting Consequences** Why is it desirable to know the exact concentration of solutions rather than whether they are concentrated or dilute?

23. **Applying Concepts** Describe a procedure to separate a mixture of salt, finely ground pepper, and pebbles.

INTERPRETING GRAPHICS

Dr. Sol Vent did an experiment to find the solubility of a compound. The data below were collected using 100 mL of water. Use the table below to answer the questions that follow.

Temperature (°C)	10	25	40	60	95
Dissolved solute (g)	150	70	34	25	15

24. Use a computer or graph paper to construct a graph of Dr. Vent's results. Examine the graph. To increase the solubility, would you increase or decrease the temperature? Explain.

25. If 200 mL of water were used instead of 100 mL, how many grams of the compound would dissolve at 40°C?

26. Based on the solubility of this compound, is this compound a solid, liquid, or gas? Explain your answer.

Multiple Choice

Use the pie charts below to answer question 1.

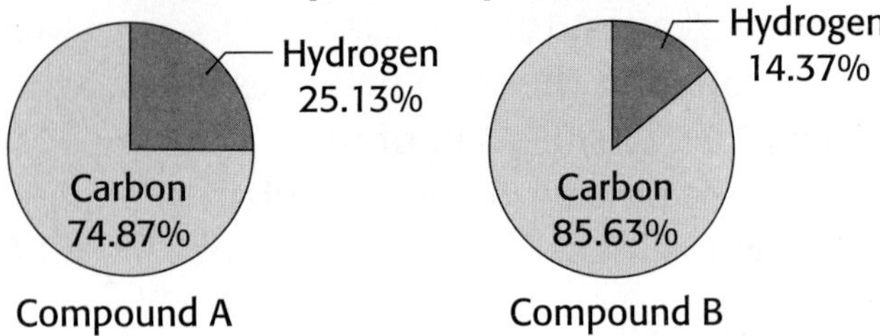

1. **Based on the information given in the pie charts, which of the following statements is true?**

   A. Compound A and compound B are the same compound.

   B. Hydrogen and carbon combine in specific but different ratios in forming compounds A and B.

   C. Although the mass compositions of compounds A and B have different percentages, the two compounds have the same mass ratio of carbon to hydrogen.

   D. The compounds hydrogen and carbon combine to form both compound A and compound B.

2. **Imagine that you were asked to classify four samples of equal and known volume, each of which is made up of a single element. Which factor would be most useful for identifying them?**

   A. mass

   B. shape

   C. hardness

   D. original source

Use the table below to answer question 3.

Property	Substance A	Substance B	Substance C
appearance	shiny yellow solid	powdery yellow solid	shiny gray solid
conductivity	good conductor	poor conductor	conductor
malleability	malleable	not malleable	brittle, not malleable

3. **Which of the following statements is most accurate?**

   A. Substances A and C are metals.

   B. Substance B is a metalloid.

   C. Substances B and C are nonmetals.

   D. Substance C is a metalloid.

4. **If two poisonous elements are combined chemically, which of the following will be true of the resulting compound?**

   A. The compound will be more poisonous than the original elements.

   B. The compound will be as poisonous as the original elements.

   C. The compound may or may not be poisonous.

   D. The compound will not be poisonous.

5. **Which of the following processes could separate the components of a compound?**

   A. dissolving, then filtering

   B. distilling at the boiling points of the compound's components

   C. using a magnet to attract the compound's metallic components

   D. applying an electric current

Use the graph below to answer question 6.

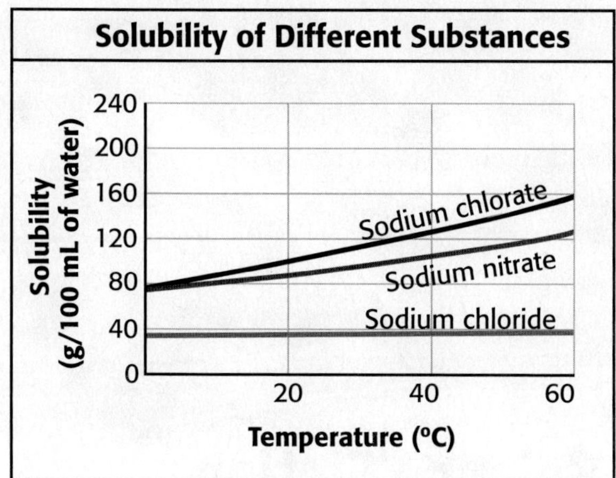

6. Which of the following values is the amount of sodium nitrate that can be dissolved in 100 mL of water at 40°C?

A. 0 g

B. 40 g

C. 100 g

D. 130 g

7. Two different atoms are chemically combined to form a new substance. What kind of substance formed?

A. a compound

B. an element

C. a mixture

D. a solute

8. Which chemical change may be used to break down a compound?

A. boiling

B. freezing

C. distillation

D. combustion

9. You are given two jars, each containing an unknown substance. You are asked to determine whether the substances are different or the same. How should you complete this task?

A. Compare appearances. If the substances look the same, then they are the same.

B. Compare only physical properties. If the substances have the same density or melting point, then they are the same.

C. Compare physical and chemical properties. If the substances perform the same in a variety of tests, then they are the same.

D. Compare physical states. If the substances are in the same state, then they are the same.

Open Response

10. Both vinegar and table sugar are composed of carbon, hydrogen, and oxygen atoms. Compare the properties of these two combinations of elements, and explain why the same elements can produce different substances.

11. Valerie placed 1.0 g of salt into one beaker, 1.0 g of soil into a second beaker, and 1.0 g of sugar into a third beaker. She then added 200 mL of water to each beaker and stirred the contents for 3 minutes. How many solutions did Valerie make? Identify the solvent and solute of each of the solutions.

Science in Action

Science, Technology, and Society

Dry Cleaning: How Stains Are Dissolved

Sometimes, just water and detergent won't remove stains. For example, have you gotten ink on your favorite sweater? Or have you spilled something greasy on your shirt? In that case, your clothes will probably have to be dry-cleaned. In spite of its name, dry cleaning does involve liquids. First, the kind of stain on your clothing must be determined. If the stain will dissolve in water, a stain remover for that particular stain is applied. Then, the stain is removed with a steam gun. But some stains, such as grease or oil, won't dissolve in water. This kind of stain is treated with a liquid solvent. The clothing is then cleaned in a dry-cleaning machine.

Language Arts ACTIVITY

WRITING SKILL Imagine that you are a stained article of clothing. Write a five-paragraph short story describing how you became stained and how the stain was removed by the dry-cleaning process. You may have to research the dry-cleaning process before writing your story.

Science Fiction

"The Strange Case of Dr. Jekyll and Mr. Hyde" by Robert Louis Stevenson

Although Dr. Henry Jekyll was wild as a young man, he has become a respected doctor and scientist. Dr. Jekyll wants to understand the nature of human identity. His theory is that if he can separate his personality into "good" and "evil" parts, he can get rid of his evil side. Then, he can lead a happy, useful life.

Into Dr. Jekyll's life comes the mysterious Mr. Hyde, a man of action and anger. He sparks fear in the hearts of people he meets. Who is he? And what does he have to do with the deaths of two people? To find out more, read Stevenson's "The Strange Case of Dr. Jekyll and Mr. Hyde" in the *Holt Anthology of Science Fiction*.

Social Studies ACTIVITY

"The Strange Case of Dr. Jekyll and Mr. Hyde" was published in 1886. The story takes place in London, England. What was London like in the 1870s and 1880s? Use the library or the Internet to find information about London and its people at that time. Make a chart that compares London in the 1870s with your hometown today.

Careers

Aundra Nix

Metallurgist Aundra Nix is a chief metallurgist for a copper mine in Sahuarita, Arizona, where she supervises laboratories and other engineers. "To be able to look at rock in the ground and follow it through a process of drilling, blasting, hauling, crushing, grinding, and finally mineral separation—where you can hold a mineral that is one-third copper in your hand—is exciting."

Although she is a supervisor, Nix enjoys the flexible nature of her job. "My work environment includes office and computer work, plant work, and outdoor work. In this field you can 'get your hands into it,' which I always prefer," says Nix. "I did not want a career where it may be years before you see the results of your work." Aundra Nix enjoyed math and science, "so engineering seemed to be a natural area to study," she says. Nix's advice to students planning their own career is to learn all they can in science and technology, because that is the future.

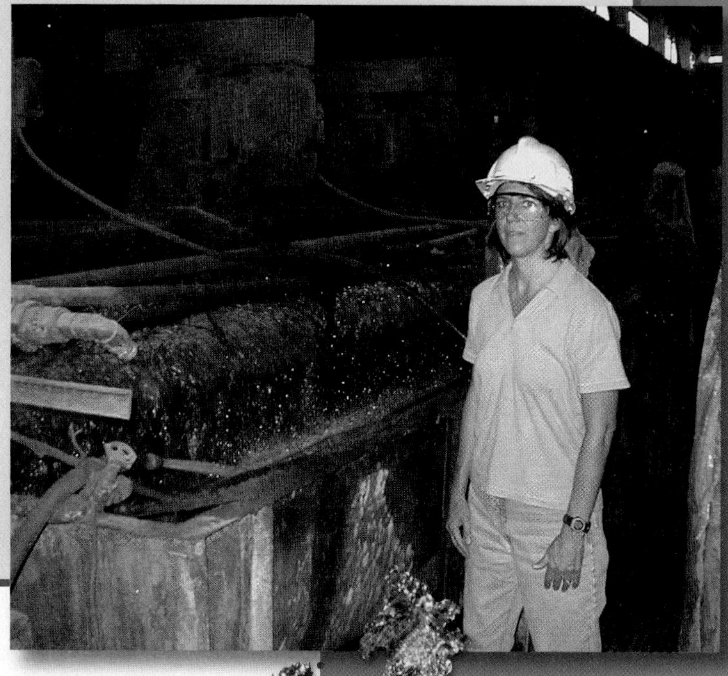

Math ACTIVITY

A large copper-mining company employed about 2,300 people at three locations in New Mexico. Because of an increase in demand for copper, 570 of these workers were hired over a period of a year. Of the 570 new workers, 115 were hired within a three-week period. What percentage of the total work force do the newly hired employees represent? Of the new workers who were hired, what percentage was hired during the three-week hiring period?

To learn more about these Science in Action topics, visit go.hrw.com and type in the keyword HP5MIXF.

Current Science

Check out Current Science® articles related to this chapter by visiting go.hrw.com. Just type in the keyword HP5CS04.

20

Introduction to Atoms

The Big Idea Atoms are composed of small particles that determine the properties of the atom.

SECTION

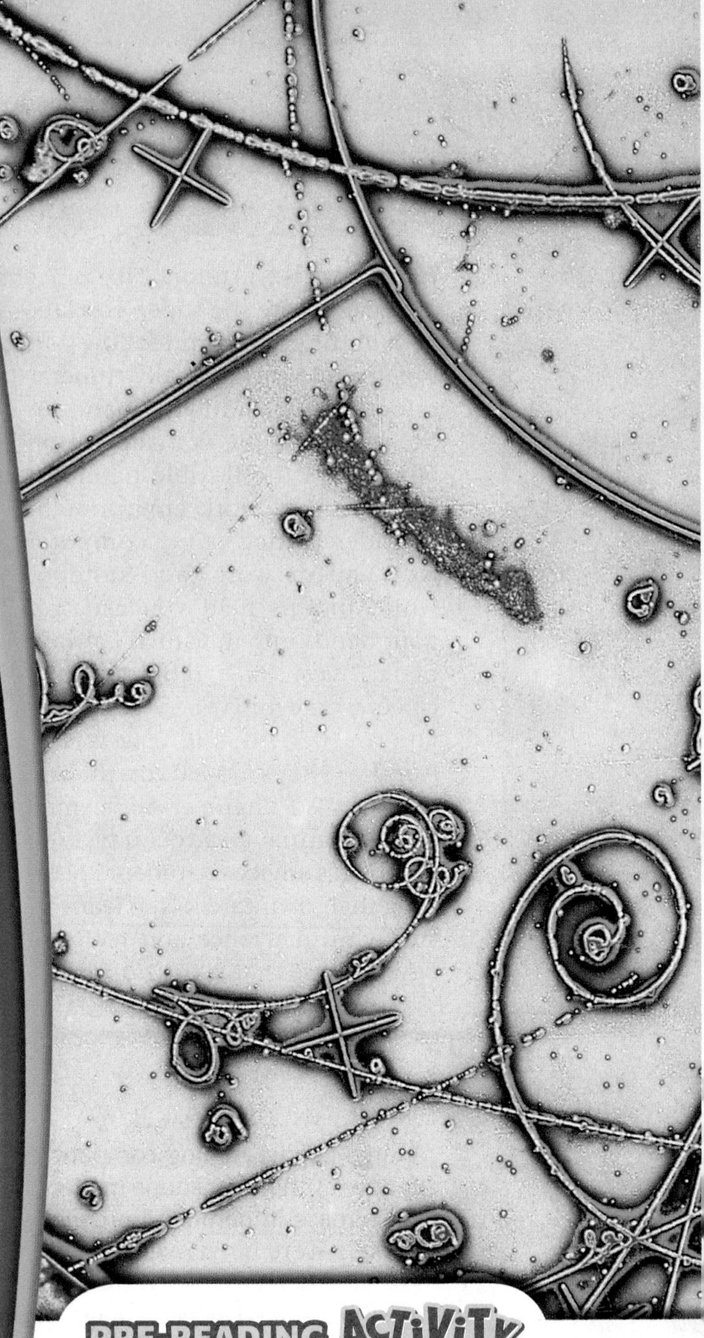

About the Photo

You have probably made bubbles with a plastic wand and a soapy liquid. Some scientists make bubbles by using a bubble chamber. A bubble chamber is filled with a pressurized liquid that forms bubbles when a charged particle moves through it. This photo shows the tracks made by charged particles moving through a bubble chamber. Bubble chambers help scientists learn about particles called ***atoms,*** which make up all objects.

PRE-READING ACTIVITY

Graphic Organizer

Chain-of-Events Chart Before you read the chapter, create the graphic organizer entitled "Chain-of-Events Chart" described in the **Study Skills** section of the Appendix. As you read the chapter, fill in the chart with details about each step in the historical development of ideas about atoms.

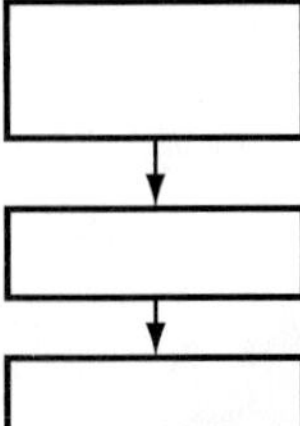

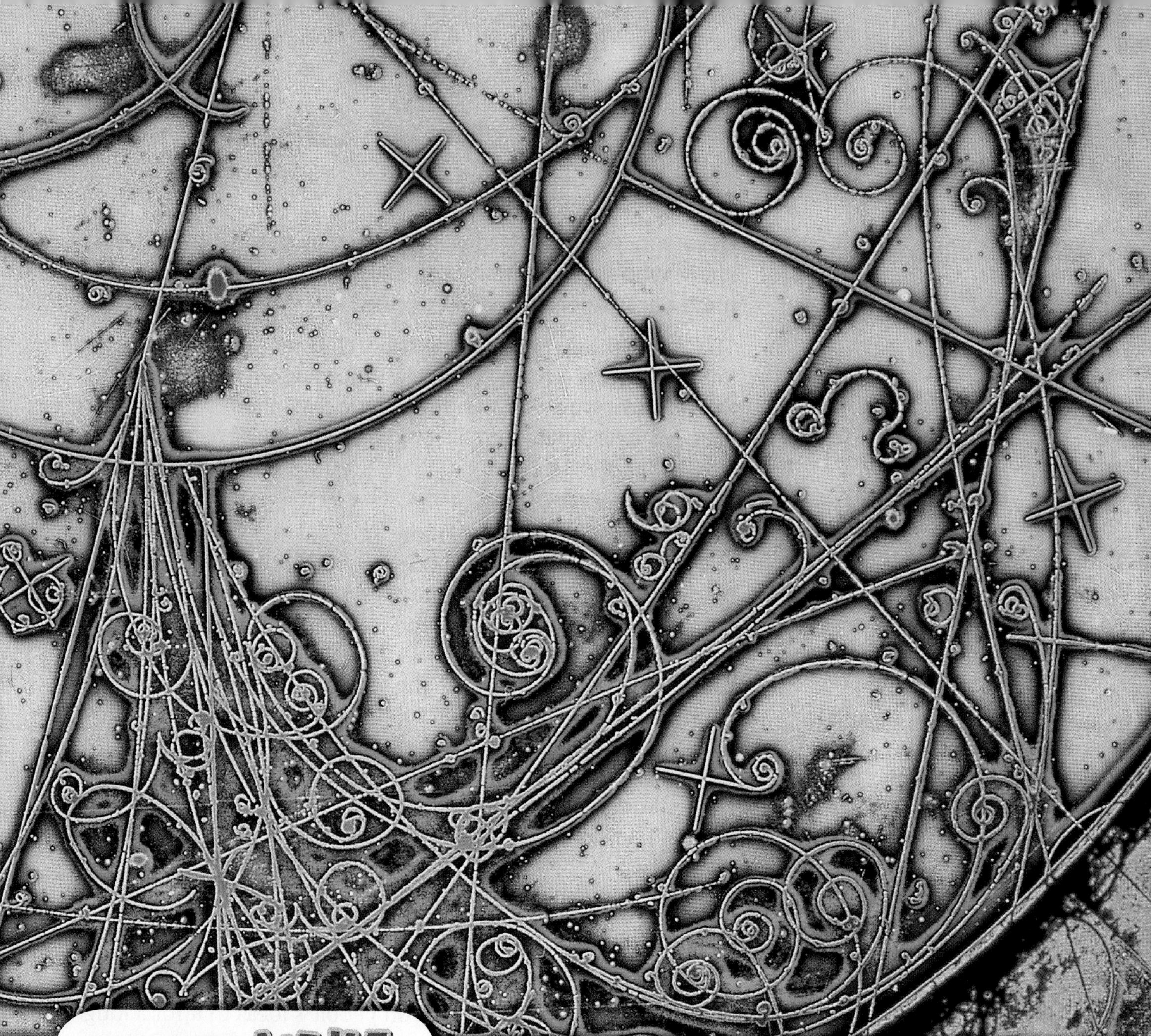

START-UP ACTIVITY

Where Is It?

Scientists have been able to gather information about atoms without actually seeing them. In this activity, you will do something similar: you will form an idea about the location and size of a hidden object by rolling marbles at it.

Procedure

1. Place a **rectangular piece of cardboard** on **four books or blocks** so that each corner of the cardboard rests on a book or block.
2. Your teacher will place an **unknown object** under the cardboard. Be sure that you cannot see the object.
3. Place a **large piece of paper** on top of the cardboard.
4. Carefully roll a **marble** under the cardboard. Record on the paper the position where the marble enters and exits. Also, record the direction it travels.
5. Keep rolling the marble from different directions to collect data about the shape and location of the object. Write down all of your observations.

Analysis

1. Form a conclusion about the object's shape, size, and location. Record your conclusion.
2. Lift the cardboard, and look at the object. Compare your conclusions with the object's actual size, shape, and location.

SECTION 1

Development of the Atomic Theory

What You Will Learn

- Describe some of the experiments that led to the current atomic theory.
- Compare the different models of the atom.
- Explain how the atomic theory has changed as scientists have discovered new information about the atom.

Vocabulary

atom
electron
nucleus
electron cloud

READING STRATEGY

Reading Organizer As you read this section, create an outline of the section. Use the headings from the section in your outline.

Have you ever watched a mystery movie and thought you knew who the criminal was? Have you ever changed your mind because of a new fact or clue?

The same thing happens in science! Sometimes an idea or model must be changed as new information is gathered. In this section, you will see how our ideas about atoms have changed over time. Your first stop is ancient Greece.

The Beginning of Atomic Theory

Imagine that you cut something in half. Then, you cut each half in half again, and so on. Could you keep cutting the pieces in half forever? Around 440 BCE, a Greek philosopher named Democritus (di MAHK ruh tuhs) thought that you would eventually end up with a particle that could not be cut. He called this particle an atom. The word *atom* is from the Greek word *atomos,* meaning "not able to be divided." Democritus said that all atoms are small, hard particles. He thought that atoms were made of a single material formed into different shapes and sizes.

From Aristotle to Modern Science

Aristotle (AR is TAHT'l), another Greek philosopher, disagreed with Democritus's ideas. He believed that you would never end up with a particle that could not be cut. He had such a strong influence on people's ideas that for a long time, most people thought he was right.

Democritus was right, though: Matter is made of particles, which we call atoms. An **atom** is the smallest particle into which an element can be divided and still be the same substance. **Figure 1** shows a picture of aluminum atoms taken with a scanning tunneling electron microscope (STM). Long before actually being able to scan atoms, scientists had ideas about them.

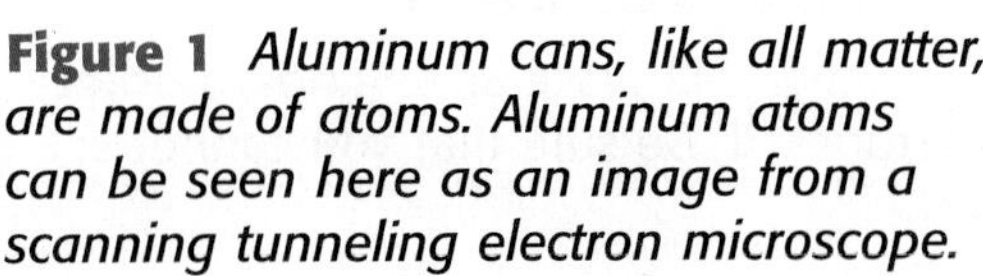

Figure 1 *Aluminum cans, like all matter, are made of atoms. Aluminum atoms can be seen here as an image from a scanning tunneling electron microscope.*

Dalton's Atomic Theory Based on Experiments

By the late 1700s, scientists had learned that elements combine in certain proportions based on mass to form compounds. For example, hydrogen and oxygen always combine in the same proportion to form water. John Dalton, a British chemist and schoolteacher, wanted to know why. He experimented with different substances. His results suggested that elements combine in certain proportions because they are made of single atoms. Dalton, shown in **Figure 2,** published his atomic theory in 1803. His theory stated the following ideas:

atom the smallest unit of an element that maintains the properties of that element

- All substances are made of atoms. Atoms are small particles that cannot be created, divided, or destroyed.
- Atoms of the same element are exactly alike, and atoms of different elements are different.
- Atoms join with other atoms to make new substances.

Reading Check **Why did Dalton think that elements are made of single atoms?** (*See the Appendix for answers to Reading Checks.*)

Not Quite Correct

Toward the end of the 1800s, scientists agreed that Dalton's theory explained much of what they saw. However, new information was found that did not fit some of Dalton's ideas. The atomic theory was then changed to describe the atom more correctly. As you read on, you will learn how Dalton's theory has changed, step by step, into the modern atomic theory.

Figure 2 *John Dalton developed his atomic theory from observations gathered from many experiments.*

Figure 3 Thomson's Cathode-Ray Tube Experiment

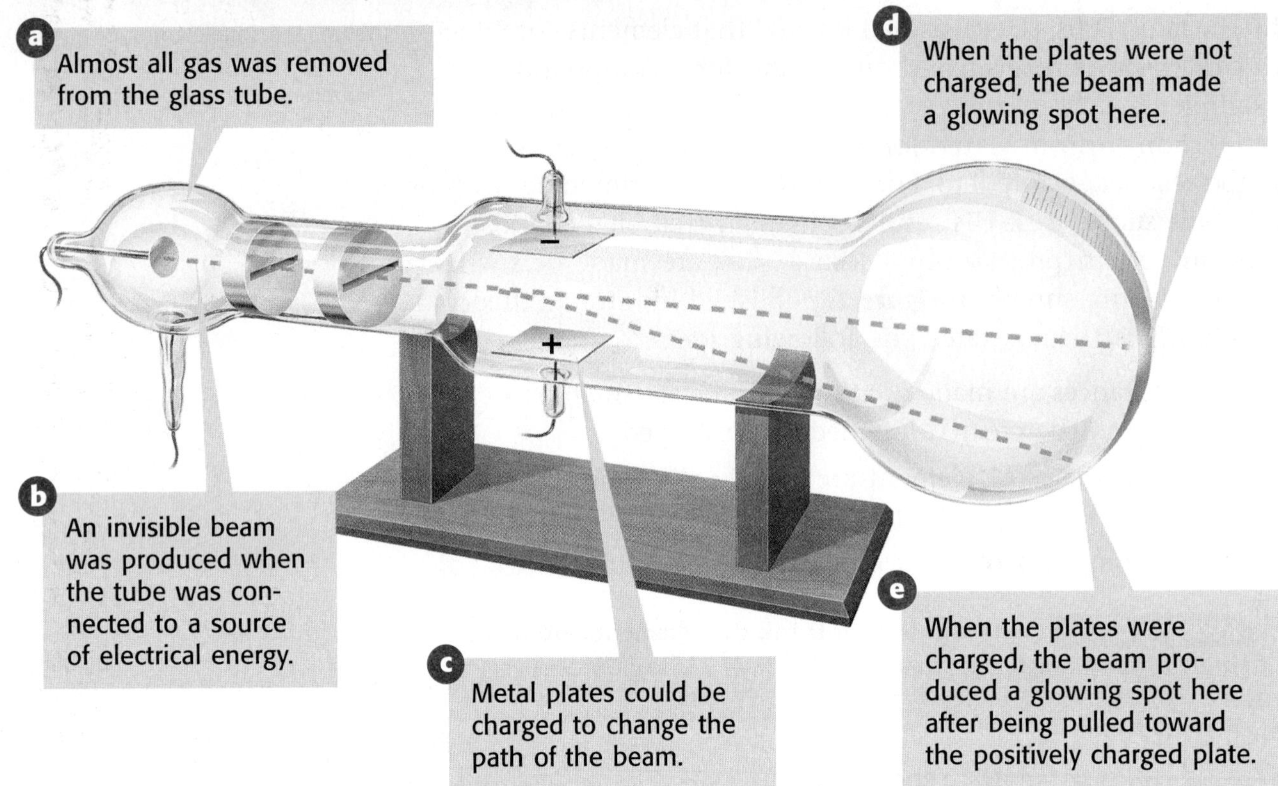
a
Almost all gas was removed from the glass tube.
d
When the plates were not charged, the beam made a glowing spot here.
−
+
b
An invisible beam was produced when the tube was connected to a source of electrical energy.
c
Metal plates could be charged to change the path of the beam.
e
When the plates were charged, the beam produced a glowing spot here after being pulled toward the positively charged plate.

Thomson's Discovery of Electrons

In 1897, a British scientist named J. J. Thomson showed that there was a mistake in Dalton's theory. Thomson discovered that there are small particles *inside* the atom. This means that atoms can be divided into even smaller parts.

electron a subatomic particle that has a negative charge

Thomson experimented with a cathode-ray tube like the one shown in **Figure 3.** He discovered that a positively charged plate (marked with a plus sign in the drawing) attracted the beam. Thomson concluded that the beam was made of particles that have negative electric charges. He also concluded that these negatively charged particles are present in every kind of atom. The negatively charged particles that Thomson discovered are now called **electrons.**

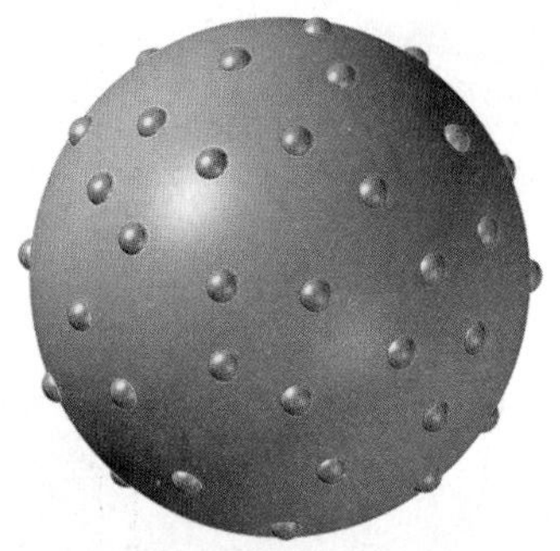

Figure 4 *Thomson proposed that electrons were located throughout an atom like plums in a pudding, as shown in this model.*

Like Plums in a Pudding

After learning that atoms contain electrons, Thomson proposed a new model of the atom. This model is shown in **Figure 4.** It is sometimes called the *plum-pudding model,* after a dessert that was popular in Thomson's day. Thomson thought that electrons were mixed throughout an atom, like plums in a pudding. Today, you might call Thomson's model the *chocolate chip ice-cream model.*

Rutherford's Atomic "Shooting Gallery"

In 1909, a former student of Thomson's named Ernest Rutherford decided to test Thomson's theory. He designed an experiment to study the parts of the atom. He aimed a beam of small, positively charged particles at a thin sheet of gold foil. **Figure 5** shows Rutherford's experiment. Rutherford put a special coating behind the foil. The coating glowed when hit by the positively charged particles. Rutherford could then see where the particles went after hitting the gold.

Reading Check **How could Rutherford tell where the positively charged particles went after hitting the gold foil?**

Surprising Results

Rutherford started with Thomson's idea that atoms are soft "blobs" of matter. He expected the particles to pass right through the gold in a straight line. Most of the particles did just that. But to Rutherford's great surprise, some of the particles were deflected (turned to one side). Some even bounced straight back. Rutherford reportedly said,

"It was quite the most incredible event that has ever happened to me in my life. It was almost as if you fired a fifteen-inch shell into a piece of tissue paper and it came back and hit you."

CONNECTION TO Language Arts

WRITING SKILL **Solving Mysteries** Scientists who made discoveries about the atom had to do so by gathering clues and drawing conclusions from experiments. Read a short mystery story, and write a one-page paper in which you discuss the methods that were used to solve the mystery in the story. Compare these methods with those used by scientists finding out about what atoms are like.

Figure 5 **Rutherford's Gold-Foil Experiment**

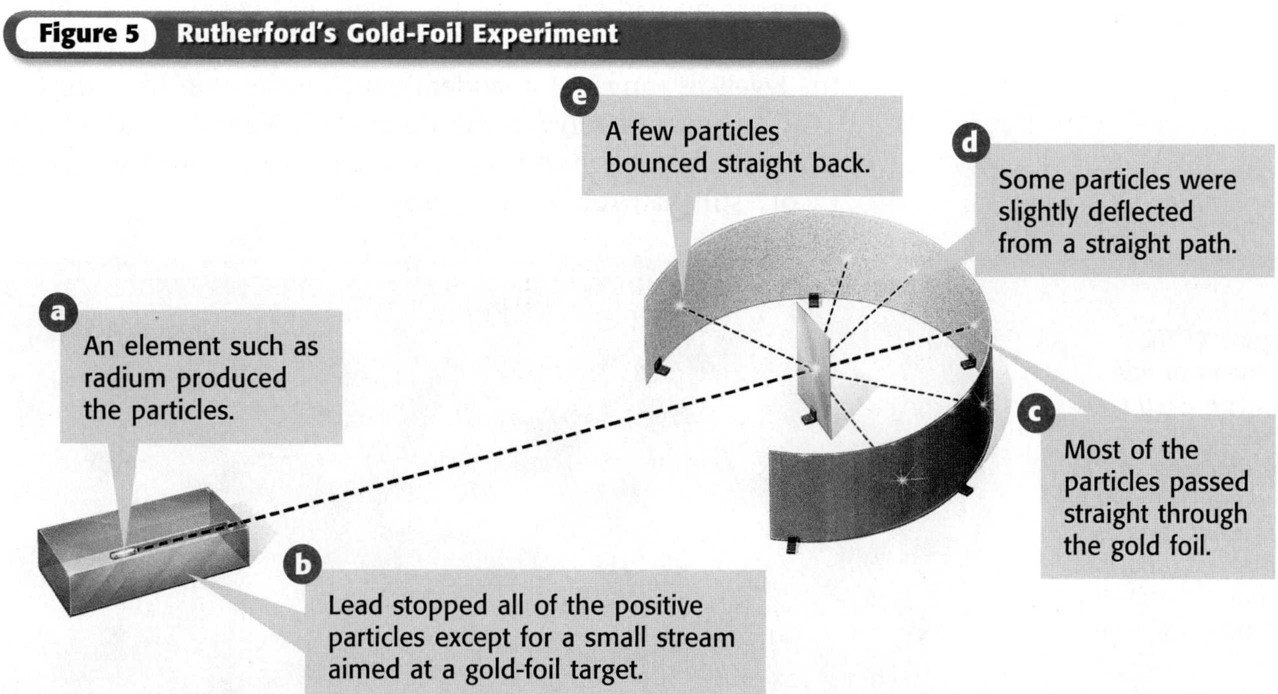
e
A few particles bounced straight back.
d
Some particles were slightly deflected from a straight path.
a
An element such as radium produced the particles.
c
Most of the particles passed straight through the gold foil.
b
Lead stopped all of the positive particles except for a small stream aimed at a gold-foil target.

nucleus in physical science, an atom's central region, which is made up of protons and neutrons

electron cloud a region around the nucleus of an atom where electrons are likely to be found

Where Are the Electrons?

The plum-pudding model of the atom did not explain what Rutherford saw. Most of the tiny particles went straight through the gold foil, with a small number being deflected. He realized that in order to explain this, atoms must be considered mostly empty space, with a tiny part made of highly dense matter.

Far from the Nucleus

In 1911, Rutherford revised the atomic theory. He made a new model of the atom, as shown in **Figure 6.** Rutherford proposed that in the center of the atom is a tiny, extremely dense, positively charged part called the **nucleus** (NOO klee uhs). Because like charges repel, Rutherford reasoned that positively charged particles that passed close by the nucleus were pushed away by the positive charges in the nucleus. A particle that headed straight for a nucleus would be pushed almost straight back in the direction from which it came. From his results, Rutherford calculated that the diameter of the nucleus was 100,000 times smaller than the diameter of the gold atom. To get an idea of this kind of difference in size, look at **Figure 7.**

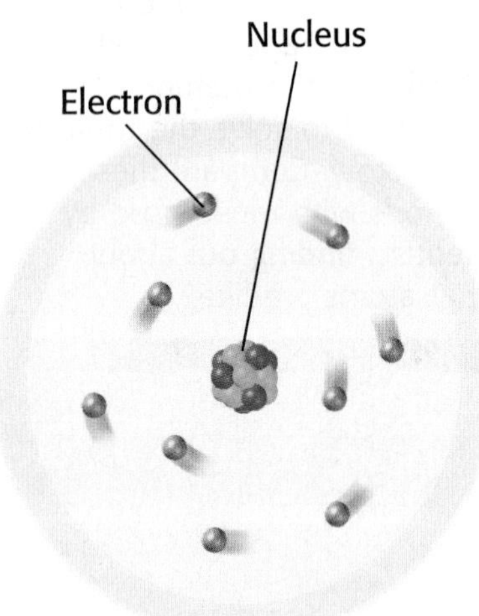

Figure 6 *Rutherford's model of the atom had electrons surrounding the nucleus at a distance. (This model does not show the true scale of sizes and distances.)*

Reading Check **How did Rutherford change Thomson's model of the atom?**

Bohr's Electron Levels

In 1913, Niels Bohr, a Danish scientist who worked with Rutherford, studied the way that atoms react to light. Bohr's results led him to propose that electrons move around the nucleus in certain paths, or energy levels. In Bohr's model, there are no paths between the levels. But electrons can jump from a path in one level to a path in another level. Think of the levels as rungs on a ladder. You can stand on the rungs of a ladder but not *between* the rungs. Bohr's model was a valuable tool in predicting some atomic behavior, but the atomic theory still had room for improvement.

Figure 7 *The diameter of this pinhead is 100,000 times smaller than the diameter of the stadium. The pinhead represents the size of a nucleus, and the stadium represents the size of an atom.*

The Modern Atomic Theory

Many 20th-century scientists added to our current understanding of the atom. An Austrian physicist named Erwin Schrödinger (SHROH ding uhr) and a German physicist named Werner Heisenberg (HIE zuhn berkh) did especially important work. They further explained the nature of electrons in the atom. For example, electrons do not travel in definite paths as Bohr suggested. In fact, the exact path of an electron cannot be predicted. According to the current theory, there are regions inside the atom where electrons are *likely* to be found. These regions are called **electron clouds.** The electron-cloud model of the atom is shown in **Figure 8.**

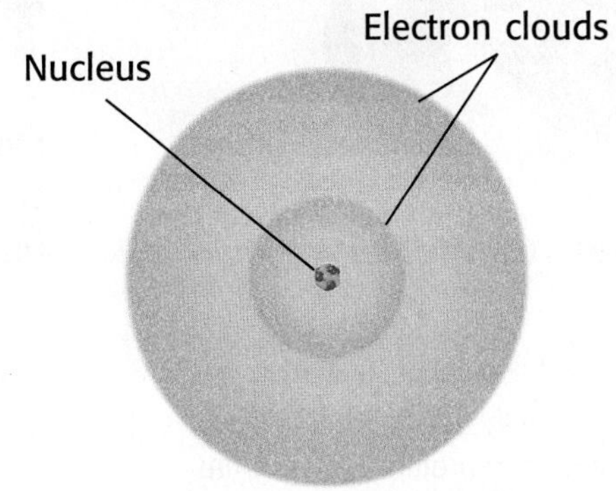

Figure 8 *In the current model of the atom, electrons surround the nucleus in electron clouds.*

SECTION Review

Summary

- Democritus thought that matter is composed of atoms.
- Dalton based his theory on observations of how elements combine.
- Thomson discovered electrons in atoms.
- Rutherford discovered that atoms are mostly empty space with a dense, positive nucleus.
- Bohr proposed that electrons are located in levels at certain distances from the nucleus.
- The electron-cloud model represents the current atomic theory.

Using Key Terms

1. In your own words, write a definition for the term *atom*.

The statements below are false. For each statement, replace the underlined term to make a true statement.

2. A <u>nucleus</u> is a particle with a negative electric charge.
3. The <u>electron</u> is where most of an atom's mass is located.

Understanding Key Ideas

4. Which of the following scientists discovered that atoms contain electrons?
   a. Dalton
   b. Thomson
   c. Rutherford
   d. Bohr
5. What did Dalton do in developing his theory that Democritus did not do?
6. What discovery demonstrated that atoms are mostly empty space?
7. What refinements did Bohr make to Rutherford's proposed atomic theory?

Critical Thinking

8. **Making Comparisons** Compare the location of electrons in Bohr's theory with the location of electrons in the current atomic theory.
9. **Analyzing Methods** How does the design of Rutherford's experiment show what he was trying to find out?

Interpreting Graphics

10. What about the atomic model shown below was shown to be incorrect?

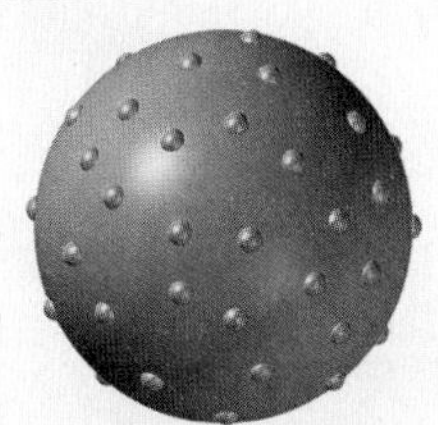

SCILINKS
NSTA
Developed and maintained by the National Science Teachers Association
For a variety of links related to this chapter, go to www.scilinks.org
Topic: Development of the Atomic Theory; Current Atomic Theory
SciLinks code: HSM0399; HSM0371

SECTION 2

The Atom

Even though atoms are very small, they are made up of even smaller things. You can learn a lot about the parts that make up an atom and what holds an atom together.

What You Will Learn

- Describe the size of an atom.
- Name the parts of an atom.
- Describe the relationship between numbers of protons and neutrons and atomic number.
- State how isotopes differ.
- Calculate atomic masses.
- Describe the forces within an atom.

Vocabulary

proton	atomic number
atomic mass unit	isotope
	mass number
neutron	atomic mass

READING STRATEGY

Reading Organizer As you read this section, make a concept map by using the terms above.

In this section, you'll learn about how atoms are alike and how they are different. But first you'll find out just how small an atom really is.

How Small Is an Atom?

Think about a penny. A penny contains about 2×10^{22} atoms (which can be written as 20,000,000,000,000,000,000,000 atoms) of copper and zinc. That's 20 thousand billion billion atoms—over 3,000,000,000,000 times more atoms than there are people on Earth! If there are that many atoms in a penny, each atom must be very small.

Scientists know that aluminum is made of average-sized atoms. An aluminum atom has a diameter of about 0.00000003 cm. That's three one-hundred-millionths of a centimeter. Take a look at **Figure 1.** Even things that are very thin, such as aluminum foil, are made up of very large numbers of atoms.

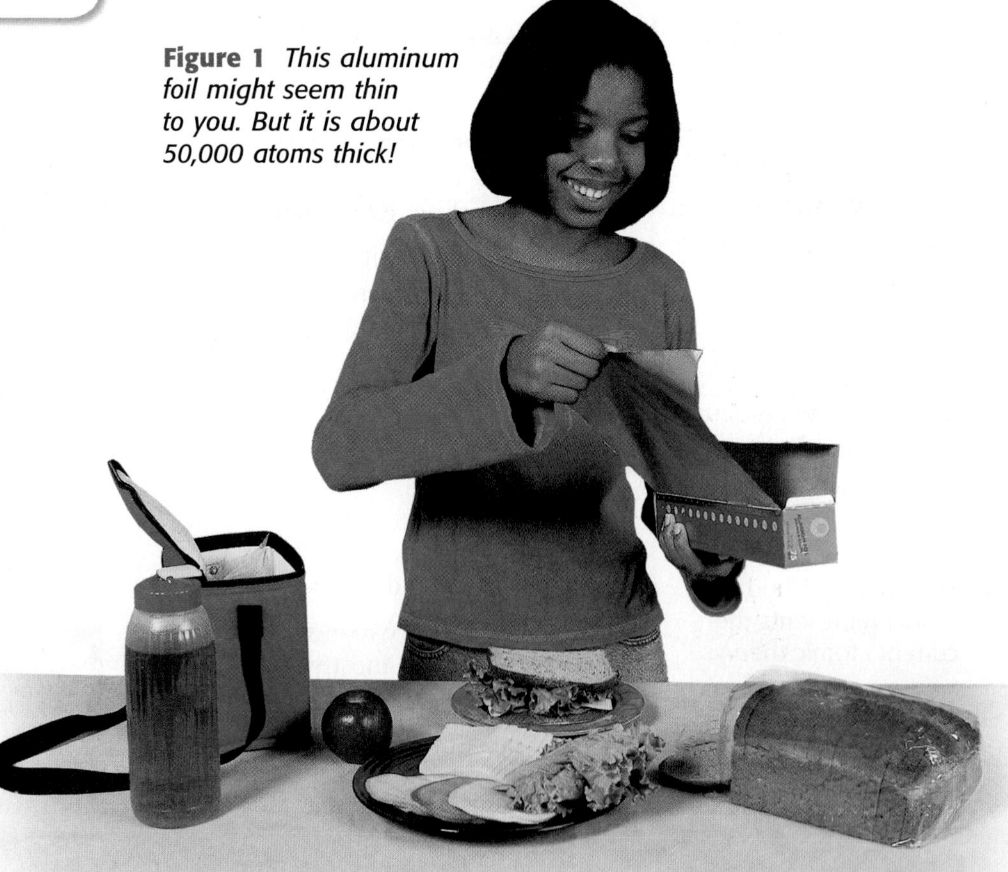

Figure 1 *This aluminum foil might seem thin to you. But it is about 50,000 atoms thick!*

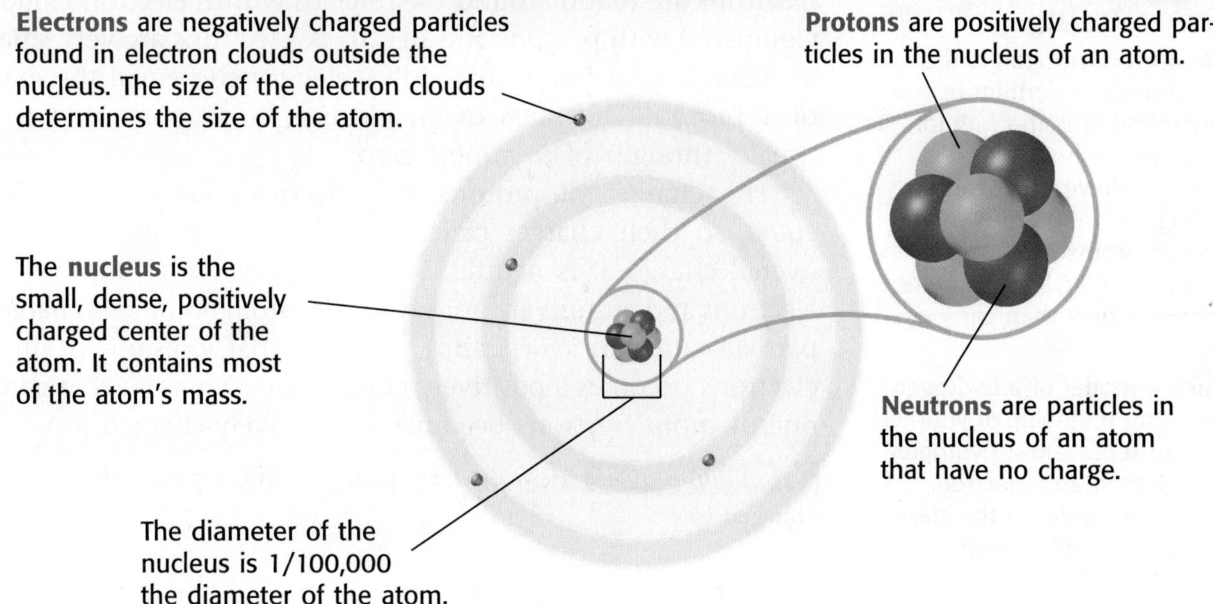

Electrons are negatively charged particles found in electron clouds outside the nucleus. The size of the electron clouds determines the size of the atom.
Protons are positively charged particles in the nucleus of an atom.
The **nucleus** is the small, dense, positively charged center of the atom. It contains most of the atom's mass.
Neutrons are particles in the nucleus of an atom that have no charge.
The diameter of the nucleus is 1/100,000 the diameter of the atom.

What Is an Atom Made Of?

As tiny as an atom is, it is made up of even smaller particles. These particles are protons, neutrons, and electrons, shown in the model in **Figure 2.** (The particles in the pictures are not shown in their correct proportions. If they were, the electrons would be too small to see.)

The Nucleus

Protons are positively charged particles in the nucleus. The mass of a proton is about 1.7×10^{-24} g. This number can also be written as 0.0000000000000000000000017 g. Because the masses of particles in atoms are so small, scientists made a new unit for them. The SI unit used to express the masses of particles in atoms is the **atomic mass unit** (amu). Each proton has a mass of about 1 amu.

Neutrons are the particles of the nucleus that have no electrical charge. Neutrons are a little more massive than protons are. But the difference in mass is so small that the mass of a neutron can be thought of as 1 amu.

Protons and neutrons are the most massive particles in an atom. But the volume of the nucleus is very small. So, the nucleus is very dense. If it were possible to have a nucleus the volume of a grape, that nucleus would have a mass greater than 9 million metric tons!

Reading Check **Name the two kinds of particles that can be found in the nucleus.** (*See the Appendix for answers to Reading Checks.*)

proton a subatomic particle that has a positive charge and that is found in the nucleus of an atom

atomic mass unit a unit of mass that describes the mass of an atom or molecule

neutron a subatomic particle that has no charge and that is found in the nucleus of an atom

CONNECTION TO Astronomy

Hydrogen Hydrogen is the most abundant element in the universe. It is the fuel for the sun and other stars. It is currently believed that there are roughly 2,000 times more hydrogen atoms than oxygen atoms and 10,000 times more hydrogen atoms than carbon atoms.

Make a model of a hydrogen atom using materials of your choice to represent a hydrogen atom's proton and electron. Present the model to the class, and explain in what ways your model resembles a hydrogen atom.

ACTIVITY

Outside the Nucleus

Electrons are the negatively charged particles in atoms. Electrons are found around the nucleus within electron clouds. Compared with protons and neutrons, electrons are very small in mass. It takes more than 1,800 electrons to equal the mass of 1 proton. The mass of an electron is so small that it is usually thought of as almost zero.

The charges of protons and electrons are opposite but equal, so their charges cancel out. Because an atom has no overall charge, it is neutral. What happens if the numbers of electrons and protons are not equal? The atom becomes a charged particle called an *ion* (IE ahn). An atom that loses one or more electrons becomes a positively-charged ion. An atom that gains one or more electrons becomes a negatively-charged ion.

Reading Check **How does an atom become a positively-charged ion?**

How Do Atoms of Different Elements Differ?

There are more than 110 different elements. The atoms of each of these elements are different from the atoms of all other elements. What makes atoms different from each other? To find out, imagine that you could build an atom by putting together protons, neutrons, and electrons.

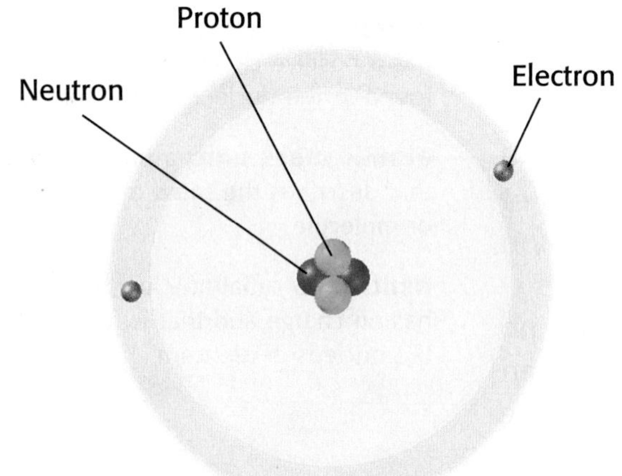

Figure 3 *A helium nucleus must have neutrons in it to keep the protons from moving apart.*

Starting Simply

It's easiest to start with the simplest atom. Protons and electrons are found in all atoms. The simplest atom is made of just one of each. It's so simple it doesn't even have a neutron. To "build" this atom, put just one proton in the center of the atom for the nucleus. Then, put one electron in the electron cloud. Congratulations! You have just made a hydrogen atom.

Now for Some Neutrons

Now, build an atom that has two protons. Both of the protons are positively charged, so they repel one another. You cannot form a nucleus with them unless you add some neutrons. For this atom, two neutrons will do. To have a neutral charge, your new atom will also need two electrons outside the nucleus. What you have is an atom of the element helium. A model of this atom is shown in **Figure 3.**

Building Bigger Atoms

You could build a carbon atom using 6 protons, 6 neutrons, and 6 electrons. You could build an oxygen atom using 8 protons, 9 neutrons, and 8 electrons. You could even build a gold atom with 79 protons, 118 neutrons, and 79 electrons! As you can see, an atom does not have to have equal numbers of protons and neutrons.

For another activity related to this chapter, go to **go.hrw.com** and type in the keyword **HP5ATSW.**

Protons and Atomic Number

How can you tell which elements these atoms represent? The key is the number of protons. The number of protons in the nucleus of an atom is the **atomic number** of that atom. All atoms of an element have the same atomic number. Every hydrogen atom has only one proton in its nucleus, so hydrogen has an atomic number of 1. Every carbon atom has six protons in its nucleus. So, carbon has an atomic number of 6.

Isotopes

An atom that has one proton, one electron, and one neutron is shown in **Figure 4.** The atomic number of this new atom is 1, so the atom is hydrogen. However, this hydrogen atom's nucleus has two particles. Therefore, this atom has a greater mass than the hydrogen atom you made.

The new atom is another isotope (IE suh TOHP) of hydrogen. **Isotopes** are atoms that have the same number of protons but have different numbers of neutrons. Atoms that are isotopes of each other are always the same element, because isotopes always have the same number of protons. They have different numbers of neutrons, however, which gives them different masses.

atomic number the number of protons in the nucleus of an atom; the atomic number is the same for all atoms of an element

isotope an atom that has the same number of protons (or the same atomic number) as other atoms of the same element do but that has a different number of neutrons (and thus a different atomic mass)

Figure 4 Isotopes of Hydrogen

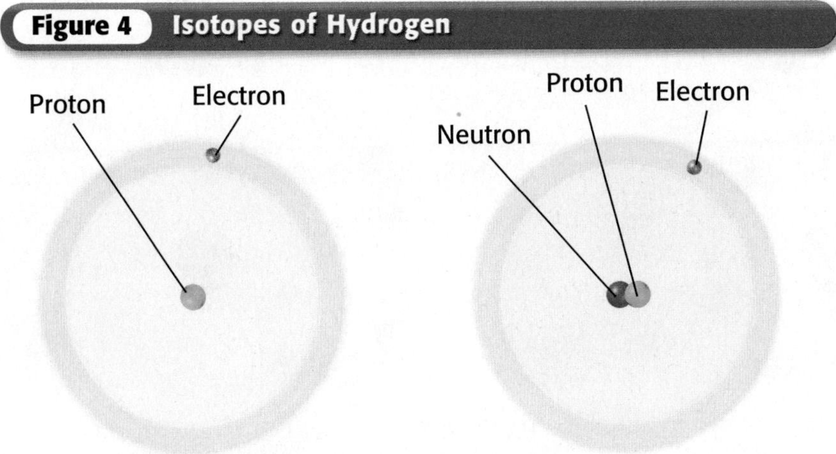

This isotope is a hydrogen atom that has one proton in its nucleus.

This isotope is a hydrogen atom that has one proton and one neutron in its nucleus.

Atomic Diagrams

Explain what you have learned about isotopes to an adult. Together, draw diagrams of hydrogen-2, helium-3, and carbon-14. Show the correct number and location of each type of particle. For the electrons, simply write the total number of electrons in the electron cloud. Use colored pencils or markers to represent the protons, neutrons, and electrons.

Properties of Isotopes

Each element has a limited number of isotopes that are found in nature. Some isotopes of an element have special properties because they are unstable. An unstable atom is an atom with a nucleus that will change over time. This type of isotope is *radioactive*. Radioactive atoms spontaneously fall apart after a certain amount of time. As they do, they give off smaller particles, as well as energy.

However, isotopes of an element share most of the same chemical and physical properties. For example, the most common oxygen isotope has 8 neutrons in the nucleus. Other isotopes of oxygen have 9 or 10 neutrons. All three isotopes are colorless, odorless gases at room temperature. Each isotope has the chemical property of combining with a substance as it burns. Different isotopes of an element even behave the same in chemical changes in your body.

Reading Check **In what cases are differences between isotopes important?**

Telling Isotopes Apart

mass number the sum of the numbers of protons and neutrons in the nucleus of an atom

You can identify each isotope of an element by its mass number. The **mass number** is the sum of the protons and neutrons in an atom. Electrons are not included in an atom's mass number because their mass is so small that they have very little effect on the atom's total mass. Look at the boron isotope models shown in **Figure 5** to see how to calculate an atom's mass number.

Figure 5 **Isotopes of Boron**

Each of these boron isotopes has five protons. But because each has a different number of neutrons, each has a different mass number.

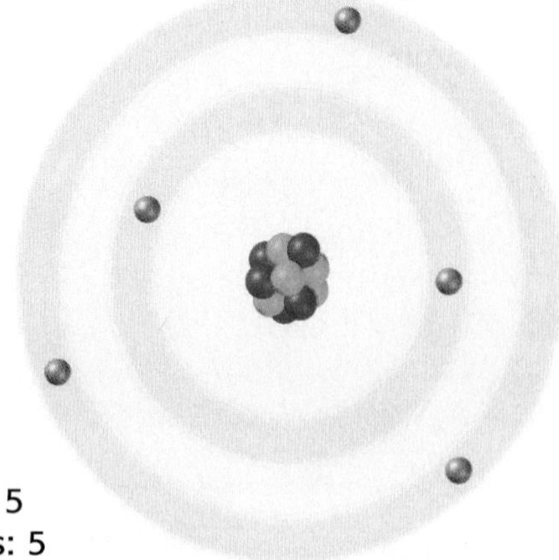

Protons: 5
Neutrons: 5
Electrons: 5
Mass number = protons + neutrons = 10

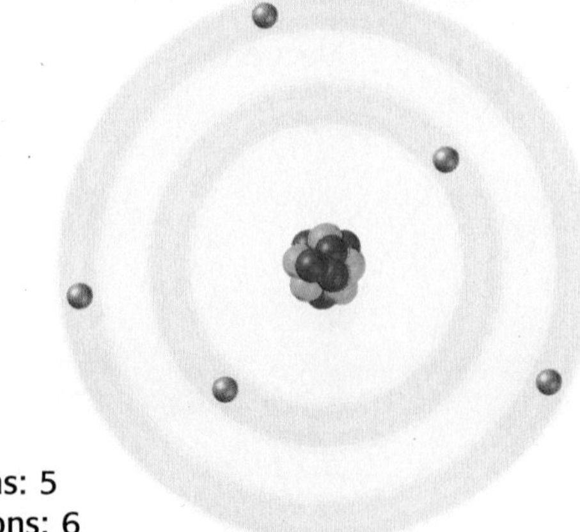

Protons: 5
Neutrons: 6
Electrons: 5
Mass number = protons + neutrons = 11

Naming Isotopes

To identify a specific isotope of an element, write the name of the element followed by a hyphen and the mass number of the isotope. A hydrogen atom with one proton and no neutrons has a mass number of 1. Its name is hydrogen-1. Hydrogen-2 has one proton and one neutron. The carbon isotope with a mass number of 12 is called carbon-12. If you know that the atomic number for carbon is 6, you can calculate the number of neutrons in carbon-12 by subtracting the atomic number from the mass number. For carbon-12, the number of neutrons is 12 − 6, or 6.

  12 Mass number
− 6 Number of protons (atomic number)
  6 Number of neutrons

Figure 6 *The copper used to make the Statue of Liberty includes both copper-63 and copper-65. Copper's atomic mass is 63.6 amu.*

Calculating the Mass of an Element

Most elements contain a mixture of two or more isotopes. For example, all copper is composed of copper-63 atoms and copper-65 atoms. The **atomic mass** of an element is the weighted average of the masses of all the naturally occurring isotopes of that element. A weighted average accounts for the percentages of each isotope that are present. Copper, including the copper in the Statue of Liberty, shown in **Figure 6,** is 69% copper-63 and 31% copper-65. The atomic mass of copper is 63.6 amu.

atomic mass the mass of an atom expressed in atomic mass units

Atomic Mass Chlorine-35 makes up 76% of all the chlorine in nature, and chlorine-37 makes up the other 24%. What is the atomic mass of chlorine?

Step 1: Multiply the mass number of each isotope by its percentage abundance in decimal form.

$$(35 \times 0.76) = 26.60$$
$$(37 \times 0.24) = 8.88$$

Step 2: Add these amounts together to find the atomic mass.

$$(35 \times 0.76) = 26.60$$
$$(37 \times 0.24) = +\ 8.88$$
$$35.48 \text{ amu}$$

Now It's Your Turn

1. Calculate the atomic mass of boron, which occurs naturally as 20% boron-10 and 80% boron-11.
2. Calculate the atomic mass of rubidium, which occurs naturally as 72% rubidium-85 and 28% rubidium-87.
3. Calculate the atomic mass of gallium, which occurs naturally as 60% gallium-69 and 40% gallium-71.
4. Calculate the atomic mass of silver, which occurs naturally as 52% silver-107 and 48% silver-109.
5. Calculate the atomic mass of silicon, which occurs naturally as 92% silicon-28, 5% silicon-29, and 3% silicon-30.

Forces in Atoms

You have seen that atoms are made of smaller particles. But what are the *forces* (the pushes or pulls between objects) acting between these particles? Four basic forces are at work everywhere, even within the atom. These forces are gravitational force, electromagnetic force, strong force, and weak force. These forces work together to give an atom its structure and properties. Look at **Figure 7** to learn about each one.

Reading Check **What are the four basic forces at work everywhere in nature?**

Figure 7 **Forces in the Atom**

Gravitational Force Probably the most familiar of the four forces is *gravitational force*. Gravitational force acts between all objects all the time. The amount of gravitational force between objects depends on their masses and the distance between them. Gravitational force pulls objects, such as the sun, Earth, cars, and books, toward one another. However, because the masses of particles in atoms are so small, the gravitational force within atoms is very small.

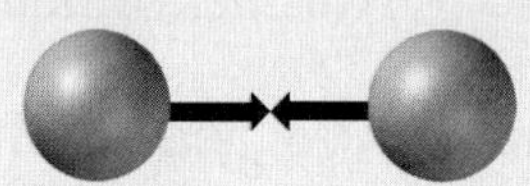

Electromagnetic Force As mentioned earlier, objects that have the same charge repel each other, while objects with opposite charge attract each other. This is due to the *electromagnetic force*. Protons and electrons are attracted to each other because they have opposite charges. The electromagnetic force holds the electrons around the nucleus.

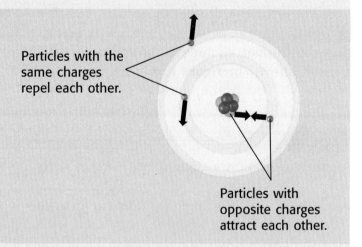

Particles with the same charges repel each other.

Particles with opposite charges attract each other.

Strong Force Protons push away from one another because of the electromagnetic force. A nucleus containing two or more protons would fly apart if it were not for the *strong force*. At the close distances between protons and neutrons in the nucleus, the strong force is greater than the electromagnetic force, so the nucleus stays together.

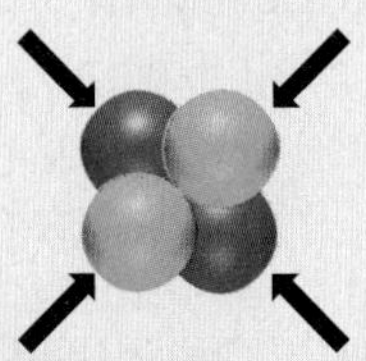

Weak Force The *weak force* is an important force in radioactive atoms. In certain unstable atoms, a neutron can change into a proton and an electron. The weak force plays a key role in this change.

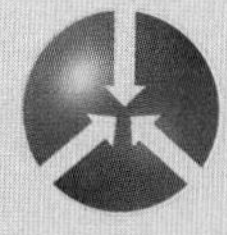

SECTION Review

Summary

- Atoms are extremely small. Ordinary-sized objects are made up of very large numbers of atoms.
- Atoms consist of a nucleus, which has protons and usually neutrons, and electrons, located in electron clouds around the nucleus.
- The number of protons in the nucleus of an atom is that atom's atomic number. All atoms of an element have the same atomic number.
- Different isotopes of an element have different numbers of neutrons in their nuclei. Isotopes of an element share most chemical and physical properties.
- The mass number of an atom is the sum of the atom's neutrons and protons.
- Atomic mass is a weighted average of the masses of natural isotopes of an element.
- The forces at work in an atom are gravitational force, electromagnetic force, strong force, and weak force.

Using Key Terms

1. Use the following terms in the same sentence: *proton, neutron,* and *isotope.*

Complete each of the following sentences by choosing the correct term from the word bank.

atomic mass unit	atomic number
mass number	atomic mass

2. An atom's ___ is equal to the number of protons in its nucleus.
3. An atom's ___ is equal to the weighted average of the masses of all the naturally occurring isotopes of that element.

Understanding Key Ideas

4. Which of the following particles has no electric charge?
   a. proton
   b. neutron
   c. electron
   d. ion
5. Name and describe the four forces that are at work within the nucleus of an atom.

Math Skills

6. The metal thallium occurs naturally as 30% thallium-203 and 70% thallium-205. Calculate the atomic mass of thallium.

Critical Thinking

7. **Analyzing Ideas** Why is gravitational force in the nucleus so small?
8. **Predicting Consequences** Could a nucleus of more than one proton but no neutrons exist? Explain.

Interpreting Graphics

9. Look at the two atomic models below. Do the two atoms represent different elements or different isotopes? Explain.

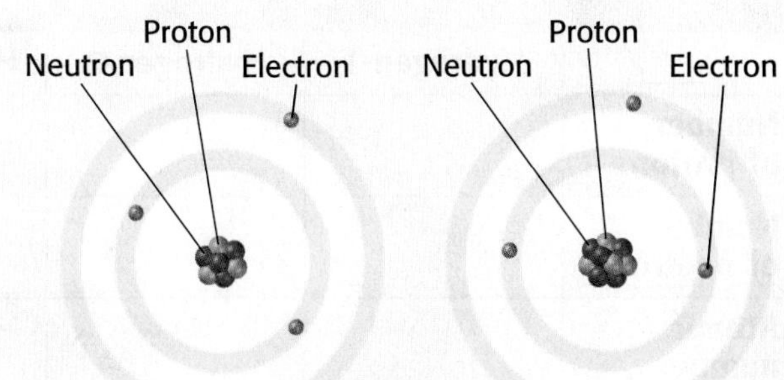
Proton
Neutron
Electron
Proton
Neutron
Electron

SCILINKS
NSTA
Developed and maintained by the National Science Teachers Association
For a variety of links related to this chapter, go to www.scilinks.org
Topic: Inside the Atom; Isotopes
SciLinks code: HSM0799; HSM0820

Model-Making Lab

Made to Order

Imagine that you are an employee at the Elements-4-U Company, which custom builds elements. Your job is to construct the atomic nucleus for each element ordered by your clients. You were hired for the position because of your knowledge about what a nucleus is made of and your understanding of how isotopes of an element differ from each other. Now, it's time to put that knowledge to work!

OBJECTIVES

Build models of nuclei of certain isotopes.

Use the periodic table to determine the composition of atomic nuclei.

MATERIALS

- periodic table
- plastic-foam balls, blue, 2–3 cm in diameter (6)
- plastic-foam balls, white, 2–3 cm in diameter (4)
- toothpicks (20)

SAFETY

Procedure

1. Copy the table below onto another sheet of paper. Be sure to leave room to expand the table to include more elements.
2. Your first assignment is the nucleus of hydrogen-1. Pick up one proton (a white plastic-foam ball). Congratulations! You have built a hydrogen-1 nucleus, the simplest nucleus possible.
3. Count the number of protons and neutrons in the nucleus, and fill in rows 1 and 2 for this element in the table.
4. Use the information in rows 1 and 2 to determine the atomic number and mass number of the element. Record this information in the table.

Data Collection Table

	Hydrogen-1	Hydrogen-2	Helium-3	Helium-4	Beryllium-9	Beryllium-10
Number of protons						
Number of neutrons						
Atomic number						
Mass number						

DO NOT WRITE IN BOOK

5. Draw a picture of your model.

6. Hydrogen-2 is an isotope of hydrogen that has one proton and one neutron. Using a strong-force connector, add a neutron to your hydrogen-1 nucleus. (Remember that in a nucleus, the protons and neutrons are held together by the strong force, which is represented in this activity by the toothpicks.) Repeat steps 3–5.

7. Helium-3 is an isotope of helium that has two protons and one neutron. Add one proton to your hydrogen-2 nucleus to create a helium-3 nucleus. Each particle should be connected to the other two particles so that they make a triangle, not a line. Protons and neutrons always form the smallest arrangement possible because the strong force pulls them together. Then, repeat steps 3–5.

8. For the next part of the lab, you will need to use information from the periodic table of the elements. Look at the illustration below. It shows the periodic table entry for carbon. You can find the atomic number of any element at the top of its entry on the periodic table. For example, the atomic number of carbon is 6.

Atomic number — 6
C
Carbon

9. Use the information in the periodic table to build models of the following isotopes of elements: helium-4, lithium-7, beryllium-9, and beryllium-10. Remember to put the protons and neutrons as close together as possible—each particle should attach to at least two others. Repeat steps 3–5 for each isotope.

Analyze the Results

1. **Examining Data** What is the relationship between the number of protons and the atomic number?

2. **Analyzing Data** If you know the atomic number and the mass number of an isotope, how could you figure out the number of neutrons in its nucleus?

Draw Conclusions

3. **Applying Conclusions** Look up uranium on the periodic table. What is the atomic number of uranium? How many neutrons does the isotope uranium-235 have?

4. **Evaluating Models** Compare your model with the models of your classmates. How are the models similar? How are they different?

Applying Your Data

Combine your model with one that another student has made to create a single nucleus. Identify the element (and isotope) you have created.

Chapter Review

USING KEY TERMS

The statements below are false. For each statement, replace the underlined term to make a true statement.

1. Electrons have a positive charge.
2. All atoms of the same element contain the same number of neutrons.
3. Protons have no electrical charge.
4. The atomic number of an element is the number of protons and neutrons in the nucleus.
5. The mass number is an average of the masses of all naturally occurring isotopes of an element.

UNDERSTANDING KEY IDEAS

Multiple Choice

6. The discovery of which particle proved that the atom is not indivisible?

   a. proton
   b. neutron
   c. electron
   d. nucleus

7. How many protons does an atom with an atomic number of 23 and a mass number of 51 have?

   a. 23
   b. 28
   c. 51
   d. 74

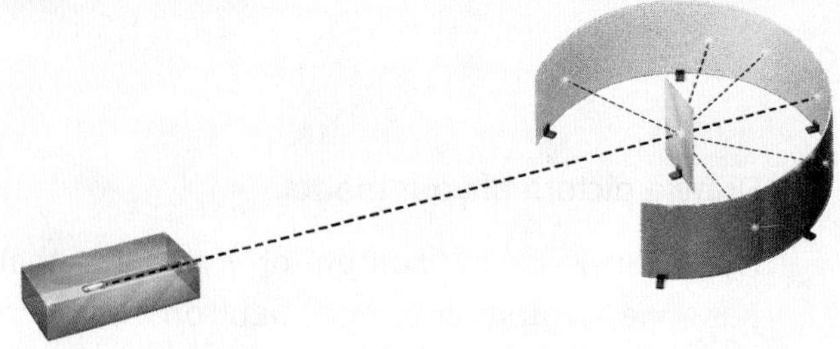

8. In Rutherford's gold-foil experiment, Rutherford concluded that the atom is mostly empty space with a small, massive, positively charged center because

   a. most of the particles passed straight through the foil.
   b. some particles were slightly deflected.
   c. a few particles bounced straight back.
   d. All of the above

9. Which of the following determines the identity of an element?

   a. atomic number
   b. mass number
   c. atomic mass
   d. overall charge

10. Isotopes exist because atoms of the same element can have different numbers of

    a. protons.
    b. neutrons.
    c. electrons.
    d. None of the above

Short Answer

11. What force holds electrons in atoms?
12. In two or three sentences, describe Thomson's plum-pudding model of the atom.

Math Skills

13. Calculate the atomic mass of gallium, which consists of 60% gallium-69 and 40% gallium-71.

14. Calculate the number of protons, neutrons, and electrons in an atom of zirconium-90 that has no overall charge and an atomic number of 40.

CRITICAL THINKING

15. **Concept Mapping** Use the following terms to create a concept map: *atom, nucleus, protons, neutrons, electrons, isotopes, atomic number,* and *mass number.*

16. **Analyzing Processes** Particle accelerators, such as the one below, are devices that speed up charged particles in order to smash them together. Scientists use these devices to make atoms. How can scientists determine whether the atoms formed are a new element or a new isotope of a known element?

17. **Analyzing Ideas** John Dalton made a number of statements about atoms that are now known to be incorrect. Why do you think his atomic theory is still found in science textbooks?

18. **Analyzing Methods** If scientists had tried to repeat Thomson's experiment and found that they could not, would Thomson's conclusion still have been valid? Explain your answer.

INTERPRETING GRAPHICS

Use the diagrams below to answer the questions that follow.

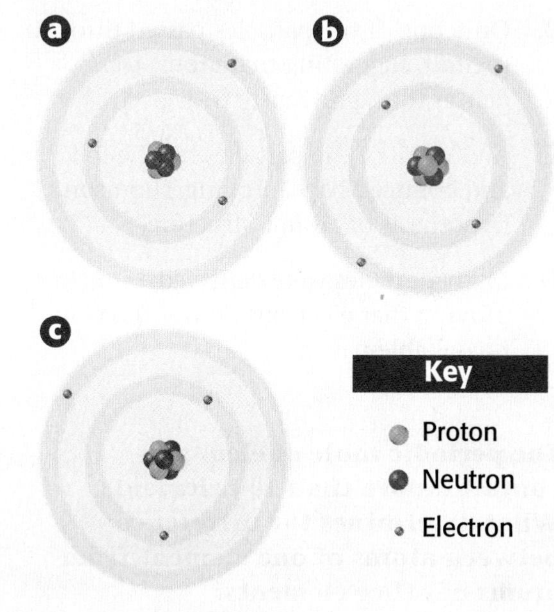

19. Which diagrams represent isotopes of the same element?

20. What is the atomic number for A?

21. What is the mass number for B?

Standardized Test Preparation

Multiple Choice

Use the diagram below to answer question 1.

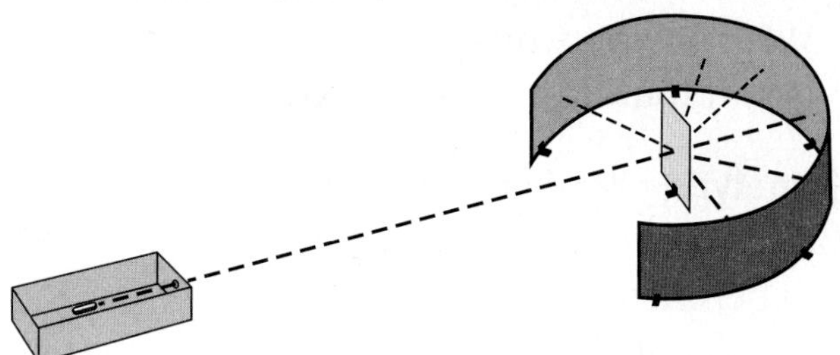

1. In Rutherford's "shooting gallery" experiment, represented in the diagram above, what were the results?

A. Some particles were deflected, some passed through, and some bounced back, suggesting the existence of a nucleus.

B. Only one of the particles passed through the foil, suggesting that atoms were denser than previously thought.

C. Almost all of the particles hit the foil and bounced back, proving Thomson's hypothesis of atomic structure.

D. Many particles were deflected, proving that electrons do not travel in predictable paths.

2. The periodic table of elements contains more than 100 elements. What determines the difference between atoms of one element from atoms of other elements?

A. the number of electrons

B. the number of isotopes

C. the number of neutrons

D. the number of protons

3. The atoms of substance A contain 8 protons and 8 neutrons. The atoms of substance B contain 8 protons and 9 neutrons. The atoms of both substances combine with atoms of hydrogen to form water. What is the best way to classify substances A and B?

A. The atoms of substances A and B are isotopes.

B. The atoms of substances A and B are radioactive.

C. The atoms of substances A and B are atoms of different elements.

D. The atoms of substances A and B have the same mass number.

4. Which of the following pieces of equipment was used by J. J. Thomson to find electrons?

A. an electron microscope

B. a magnifying lens

C. a cathode-ray tube

D. a telescope

5. Which one of the following is true of a neutron?

A. A neutron has half the mass of a proton.

B. A neutron is a little more massive than a proton.

C. A neutron has the same mass as an electron.

D. A neutron is a little more massive than an electron.

6. How many electrons does a neutral atom with an atomic number of 20 and a mass number of 42 have?

A. 20

B. 22

C. 42

D. 62

7. Oxygen has an atomic number of 8. Which of the following could form the nucleus of an isotope of oxygen?

A. 4 protons and 4 neutrons

B. 6 protons and 8 neutrons

C. 8 protons and 10 neutrons

D. 10 protons and 10 neutrons

8. All matter is made up of atoms. Which sentence correctly describes atoms?

A. All substances are made of the same atoms.

B. An atom is the smallest particle of a nucleus.

C. An atom is the smallest particle of an element.

D. An atom is a substance that has been cut in half.

9. What are the negatively charged particles inside an atom called?

A. protons

B. neutrons

C. nuclei

D. electrons

Use the diagram below to answer question 10.

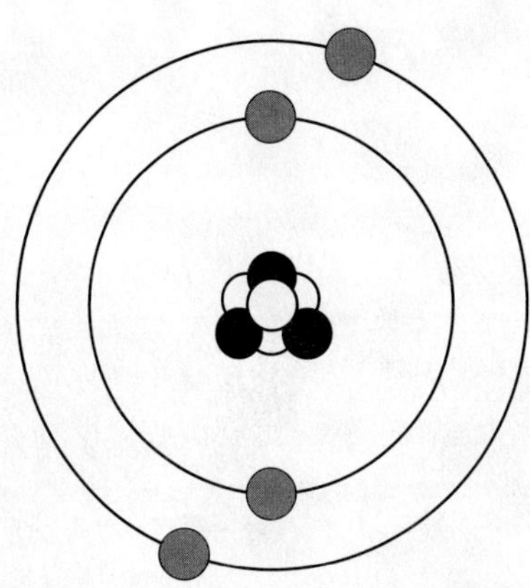

10. The black circles in the Bohr model above represent neutrons. What do the white circles represent?

A. electrons

B. isotopes

C. nuclei

D. protons

Open Response

11. Erwin Schrödinger and Werner Heisenberg expanded atomic theory in the 20th century. They accepted some of the work of earlier scientists, but added to atomic theory with new ideas about electrons. Why was it possible and important for Schrödinger and Heisenberg to accept the work of earlier scientists?

12. The atomic mass of an element and the mass number of an atom of that element often have similar values. However, atomic mass and mass number are not the same thing. Explain the difference.

Science in Action

Weird Science

Mining on the Moon?

Since the end of the Apollo moon missions in 1972, no one has set foot on the surface of the moon. But today, an isotope of helium known as *helium-3* is fueling new interest in returning to the moon. Some scientists speculate that helium-3 can be used as a safe and nonpolluting fuel for a new kind of power plant. Helium-3 is very rare on Earth, but a huge amount of the isotope exists on the surface of the moon. But how can helium-3 be brought to Earth? Some researchers imagine a robotic lunar mining operation that will harvest the helium-3 and transport it to Earth.

Language Arts ACTIVITY

WRITING SKILL Write a paragraph in which you rephrase the information above in your own words. Be sure to include what helium-3 is, where it can be found, and how it could be used.

Scientific Discoveries

Modern Alchemy

Hundreds of years ago, many people thought that if you treated lead with certain chemicals, it would turn into gold. People called *alchemists* often spent their whole lives trying to find a way to make gold from other metals, such as lead. We now know that the methods alchemists tried to change one element to another did not work. But in the 20th century, scientists learned that you really could change one element to another! In a nuclear reaction, small particles can be collided with atomic nuclei. This process makes the nuclei split apart to form two nuclei of different elements.

Math ACTIVITY

If you split apart an atom of lead (atomic number = 82) and one of the atoms left was gold (atomic number = 79), what would be the atomic number of the other atom that resulted from this change?

Careers

Melissa Franklin

Experimental Physicist In the course of a single day, you could find experimental physicist Melissa Franklin running a huge drill or showing her lab to a 10-year-old child. You could see her putting together a huge piece of electronic equipment or even telling a joke. Then you'd see her really get down to business—studying the smallest particles of matter in the universe.

"I am trying to understand the forces that describe how everything in the world moves—especially the smallest things," Franklin explains. Franklin and her team helped discover a particle called the top quark. (Quarks are the tiny particles that make up protons and neutrons.) "You can understand the ideas without having to be a math genius," Franklin says. "Anyone can have ideas," she says, "absolutely anyone." Franklin also has some advice for young people interested in physics. "Go and bug people at the local university. Just call up a physics person and say, 'Can I come visit you for a couple of hours?' Kids do that with me, and it's really fun."

Social Studies ACTIVITY

WRITING SKILL Find out about an experimental physicist who made an important discovery. Write a one-page report about how that discovery affected the

To learn more about these Science in Action topics, visit go.hrw.com and type in the keyword HP5ATSF.

Current Science

Check out Current Science® articles related to this chapter by visiting go.hrw.com. Just type in the keyword HP5CS11.

21

The Periodic Table

The Big Idea

Elements are organized on the periodic table according to their properties.

SECTION

About the Photo

You already know or have heard about elements on the periodic table, such as oxygen, carbon, and neon. Neon gas was discovered in 1898. In 1902, a French engineer, chemist, and inventor named Georges Claude made the first neon lamp. In 1910, Claude made the first neon sign, and in 1923, he introduced neon signs to the United States. Now, artists such as Eric Ehlenberger use glass and neon to create interesting works of art, such as these neon jellyfish.

PRE-READING ACTIVITY

FOLDNOTES **Three-Panel Flip Chart**

Before you read the chapter, create the FoldNote entitled "Three-Panel Flip Chart" described in the **Study Skills** section of the Appendix. Label the flaps of the three-panel flip chart with "Metal," "Nonmetal," and "Metalloid." As you read the chapter, write information you learn about each category under the appropriate flap.

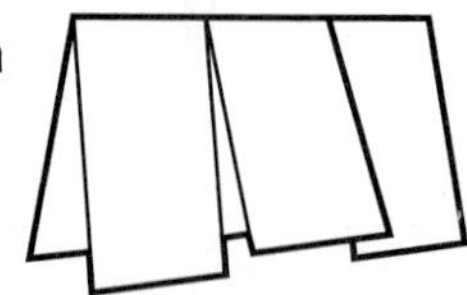

START-UP ACTIVITY

Placement Pattern

In this activity, you will identify the pattern your teacher used to create a new classroom seating arrangement.

Procedure

1. Draw a seating chart for the new classroom arrangement that your teacher gave to you. Write the name of each of your classmates in the place on the chart that corresponds to his or her seat.
2. Write information about yourself, such as your name, date of birth, hair color, and height, in the space that represents you on the chart.
3. Gather the same information about the people near you, and write it in the spaces on the chart.

Analysis

1. From the information you gathered, identify a pattern that might explain the order of people in the chart. Collect more information if needed.
2. Test your pattern by gathering information from a person you did not talk to before.
3. If the new information does not support your pattern, reanalyze your data and collect more information to determine another pattern.

SECTION 1

Arranging the Elements

What You Will Learn

- Describe how Mendeleev arranged elements in the first periodic table.
- Explain how elements are arranged in the modern periodic table.
- Compare metals, nonmetals, and metalloids based on their properties and on their location in the periodic table.
- Describe the difference between a period and a group.

Vocabulary

periodic
periodic law
period
group

READING STRATEGY

Mnemonics As you read this section, create a mnemonic device to help you remember the difference between periods and groups.

Suppose you went to the video store and all the videos were mixed together. How could you tell the comedies from the action movies? If the videos were not arranged in a pattern, you wouldn't know what kind of movie you had chosen!

Scientists in the early 1860s had a similar problem. At that time, scientists knew some of the properties of more than 60 elements. However, no one had organized the elements according to these properties. Organizing the elements according to their properties would help scientists understand how elements interact with each other.

Discovering a Pattern

Dmitri Mendeleev (duh MEE tree MEN duh LAY uhf), a Russian chemist, discovered a pattern to the elements in 1869. First, he wrote the names and properties of the elements on cards. Then, he arranged his cards, as shown in **Figure 1,** by different properties, such as density, appearance, and melting point. After much thought, he arranged the elements in order of increasing atomic mass. When he did so, a pattern appeared.

Reading Check **How had Mendeleev arranged elements when he noticed a pattern?** *(See the Appendix for answers to Reading Checks.)*

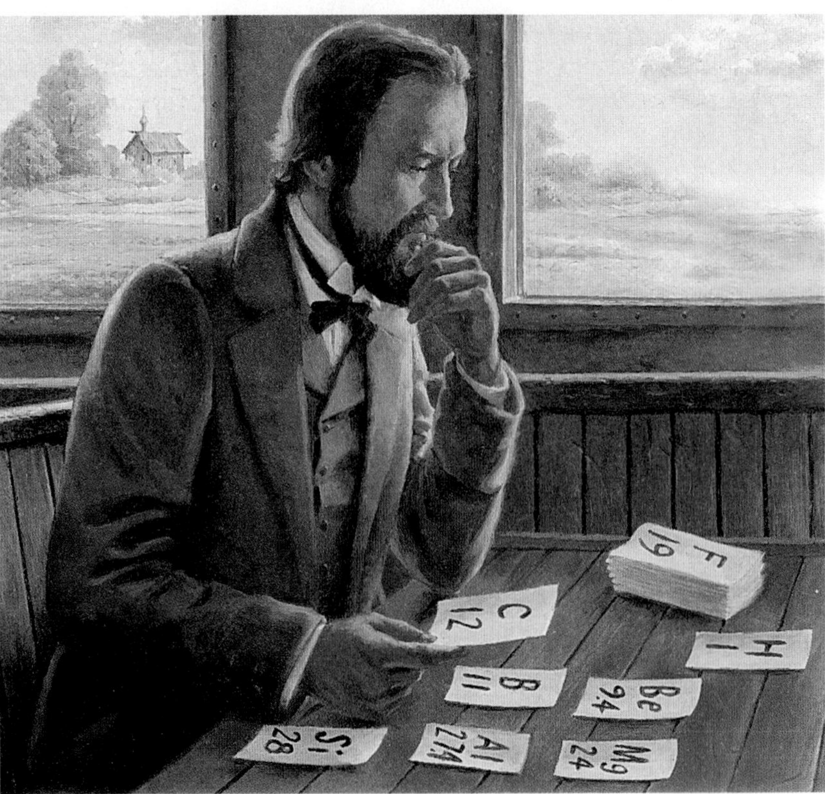

Figure 1 *By playing "chemical solitaire" on long train rides, Mendeleev organized the elements according to their properties.*

Table 1 **Properties of Germanium**		
	Mendeleev's predictions (1869)	**Actual properties**
Atomic mass	70	72.6
Density*	5.5 g/cm^3	5.3 g/cm^3
Appearance	dark gray metal	gray metal
Melting point*	high melting point	937°C

* at room temperature and pressure

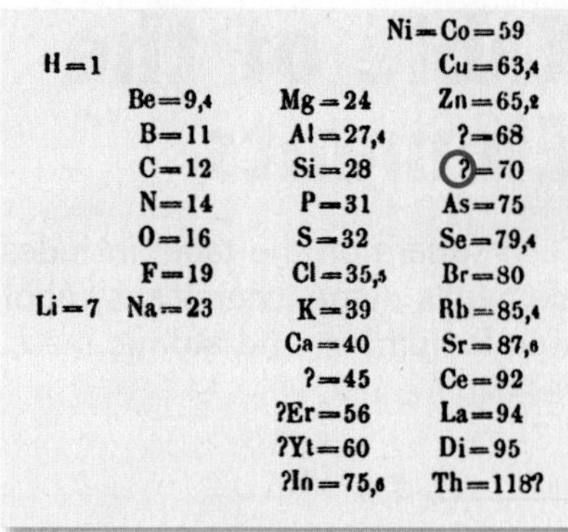

			Ni=Co=59
H=1			Cu=63,4
	Be=9,4	Mg=24	Zn=65,2
	B=11	Al=27,4	?=68
	C=12	Si=28	?=70
	N=14	P=31	As=75
	O=16	S=32	Se=79,4
	F=19	Cl=35,5	Br=80
Li=7	Na=23	K=39	Rb=85,4
		Ca=40	Sr=87,6
		?=45	Ce=92
		?Er=56	La=94
		?Yt=60	Di=95
		?In=75,6	Th=118?

Figure 2 *Mendeleev used question marks to mark some elements that he thought would be found later.*

Periodic Properties of the Elements

Mendeleev saw that when the elements were arranged in order of increasing atomic mass, those that had similar properties occurred in a repeating pattern. That is, the pattern was periodic. **Periodic** means "happening at regular intervals." The days of the week are periodic. They repeat in the same order every 7 days. Similarly, Mendeleev found that the elements' properties followed a pattern that repeated every seven elements. His table became known as the *periodic table of the elements.*

periodic describes something that occurs or repeats at regular intervals

periodic law the law that states that the repeating chemical and physical properties of elements change periodically with the atomic numbers of the elements

Predicting Properties of Missing Elements

Figure 2 shows part of Mendeleev's first try at arranging the elements. The question marks show gaps in the pattern. Mendeleev predicted that elements yet to be found would fill these gaps. He used the pattern he found to predict their properties. **Table 1** compares his predictions for one missing element—germanium—with its actual properties. By 1886, all of the gaps had been filled. His predictions were right.

Changing the Arrangement

A few elements' properties did not fit the pattern in Mendeleev's table. Mendeleev thought that more-accurate atomic masses would fix these flaws in his table. But new atomic mass measurements showed that the masses he had used were correct. In 1914, Henry Moseley (MOHZ lee), a British scientist, determined the number of protons—the atomic number—in an atom. All elements fit the pattern in Mendeleev's periodic table when they were arranged by atomic number.

Look at the periodic table on the next two pages. All of the more than 30 elements discovered since 1914 follow the periodic law. The **periodic law** states that the repeating chemical and physical properties of elements change periodically with the elements' atomic numbers.

Reading Check **What property is used to arrange elements in the periodic table?**

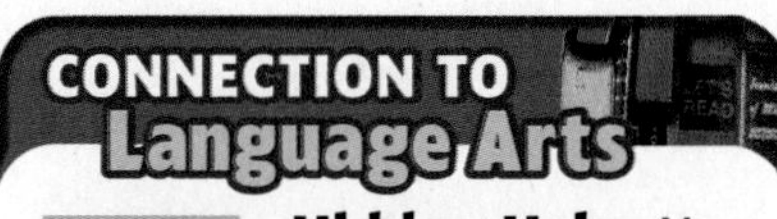

WRITING SKILL **Hidden Help** You may be asked to memorize some of the chemical symbols. A story or poem that uses the symbols might be helpful. In your **science journal,** write a short story, poem, or just a few sentences in which the words correspond to and bring to mind the chemical symbols of the first 20 elements.

Periodic Table of the Elements

Each square on the table includes an element's name, chemical symbol, atomic number, and atomic mass.

6 — Atomic number
C — Chemical symbol
Carbon — Element name
12.0 — Atomic mass

The color of the chemical symbol indicates the physical state at room temperature. Carbon is a solid.

The background color indicates the type of element. Carbon is a nonmetal.

Background
- Metals
- Metalloids
- Nonmetals

Chemical symbol
- Solid
- Liquid
- Gas

	Group 1	Group 2	Group 3	Group 4	Group 5	Group 6	Group 7	Group 8	Group 9
Period 1	1 H Hydrogen 1.0								
Period 2	3 Li Lithium 6.9	4 Be Beryllium 9.0							
Period 3	11 Na Sodium 23.0	12 Mg Magnesium 24.3							
Period 4	19 K Potassium 39.1	20 Ca Calcium 40.1	21 Sc Scandium 45.0	22 Ti Titanium 47.9	23 V Vanadium 50.9	24 Cr Chromium 52.0	25 Mn Manganese 54.9	26 Fe Iron 55.8	27 Co Cobalt 58.9
Period 5	37 Rb Rubidium 85.5	38 Sr Strontium 87.6	39 Y Yttrium 88.9	40 Zr Zirconium 91.2	41 Nb Niobium 92.9	42 Mo Molybdenum 95.9	43 Tc Technetium (98)	44 Ru Ruthenium 101.1	45 Rh Rhodium 102.9
Period 6	55 Cs Cesium 132.9	56 Ba Barium 137.3	57 La Lanthanum 138.9	72 Hf Hafnium 178.5	73 Ta Tantalum 180.9	74 W Tungsten 183.8	75 Re Rhenium 186.2	76 Os Osmium 190.2	77 Ir Iridium 192.2
Period 7	87 Fr Francium (223)	88 Ra Radium (226)	89 Ac Actinium (227)	104 Rf Rutherfordium (261)	105 Db Dubnium (262)	106 Sg Seaborgium (266)	107 Bh Bohrium (264)	108 Hs Hassium (277)	109 Mt Meitnerium (268)

A row of elements is called a *period*.

A column of elements is called a *group* or *family*.

Values in parentheses are the mass numbers of those radioactive elements' most stable or most common isotopes.

Lanthanides	58 Ce Cerium 140.1	59 Pr Praseodymium 140.9	60 Nd Neodymium 144.2	61 Pm Promethium (145)	62 Sm Samarium 150.4
Actinides	90 Th Thorium 232.0	91 Pa Protactinium 231.0	92 U Uranium 238.0	93 Np Neptunium (237)	94 Pu Plutonium (244)

These elements are placed below the table to allow the table to be narrower.

Topic: **Periodic Table**
Go To: **go.hrw.com**
Keyword: **HN0 PERIODIC**
Visit the HRW Web site for updates on the periodic table.

This zigzag line reminds you where the metals, nonmetals, and metalloids are.

Group 10	Group 11	Group 12	Group 13	Group 14	Group 15	Group 16	Group 17	Group 18
								2 **He** Helium 4.0
			5 **B** Boron 10.8	6 **C** Carbon 12.0	7 **N** Nitrogen 14.0	8 **O** Oxygen 16.0	9 **F** Fluorine 19.0	10 **Ne** Neon 20.2
			13 **Al** Aluminum 27.0	14 **Si** Silicon 28.1	15 **P** Phosphorus 31.0	16 **S** Sulfur 32.1	17 **Cl** Chlorine 35.5	18 **Ar** Argon 39.9
28 **Ni** Nickel 58.7	29 **Cu** Copper 63.5	30 **Zn** Zinc 65.4	31 **Ga** Gallium 69.7	32 **Ge** Germanium 72.6	33 **As** Arsenic 74.9	34 **Se** Selenium 79.0	35 **Br** Bromine 79.9	36 **Kr** Krypton 83.8
46 **Pd** Palladium 106.4	47 **Ag** Silver 107.9	48 **Cd** Cadmium 112.4	49 **In** Indium 114.8	50 **Sn** Tin 118.7	51 **Sb** Antimony 121.8	52 **Te** Tellurium 127.6	53 **I** Iodine 126.9	54 **Xe** Xenon 131.3
78 **Pt** Platinum 195.1	79 **Au** Gold 197.0	80 **Hg** Mercury 200.6	81 **Tl** Thallium 204.4	82 **Pb** Lead 207.2	83 **Bi** Bismuth 209.0	84 **Po** Polonium (209)	85 **At** Astatine (210)	86 **Rn** Radon (222)
110 **Ds** Darmstadtium (281)	111 **Uuu** Unununium (272)	112 **Uub** Ununbium (285)	113 **Uut** Ununtrium (284)	114 **Uuq** Ununquadium (289)	115 **Uup** Ununpentium (288)			

The discovery of elements 113, 114, and 115 has been reported but not confirmed.

The names and three-letter symbols of elements are temporary. They are based on the atomic numbers of the elements. Official names and symbols will be approved by an international committee of scientists.

63 **Eu** Europium 152.0	64 **Gd** Gadolinium 157.2	65 **Tb** Terbium 158.9	66 **Dy** Dysprosium 162.5	67 **Ho** Holmium 164.9	68 **Er** Erbium 167.3	69 **Tm** Thulium 168.9	70 **Yb** Ytterbium 173.0	71 **Lu** Lutetium 175.0
95 **Am** Americium (243)	96 **Cm** Curium (247)	97 **Bk** Berkelium (247)	98 **Cf** Californium (251)	99 **Es** Einsteinium (252)	100 **Fm** Fermium (257)	101 **Md** Mendelevium (258)	102 **No** Nobelium (259)	103 **Lr** Lawrencium (262)

Conduction Connection

1. Fill a **plastic-foam cup** with **hot water.**
2. Stand a **piece of copper wire** and a **graphite lead** from a mechanical pencil in the water.
3. After 1 min, touch the top of each object. Record your observations.
4. Which material conducted thermal energy the best? Why?

The Periodic Table and Classes of Elements

At first glance, you might think studying the periodic table is like trying to explore a thick jungle without a guide—you can easily get lost! However, the table itself contains a lot of information that will help you along the way.

Elements are classified as metals, nonmetals, and metalloids, according to their properties. The number of electrons in the outer energy level of an atom is one characteristic that helps determine which category an element belongs in. The zigzag line on the periodic table can help you recognize which elements are metals, which are nonmetals, and which are metalloids.

Metals

Most elements are metals. Metals are found to the left of the zigzag line on the periodic table. Atoms of most metals have few electrons in their outer energy level. Most metals are solid at room temperature. Mercury, however, is a liquid at room temperature. Some additional information on properties shared by most metals is shown in **Figure 3.**

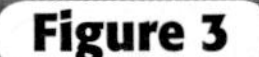

What are four properties shared by most metals?

Figure 3 **Properties of Metals**

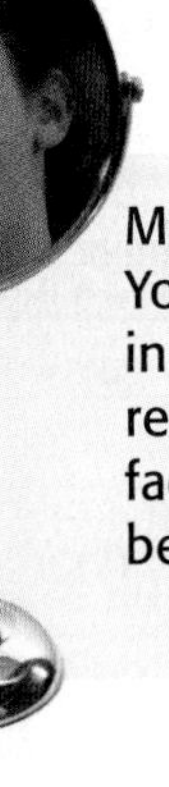

Metals tend to be **shiny.** You can see a reflection in a mirror because light reflects off the shiny surface of a thin layer of silver behind the glass.

Most metals are **ductile,** which means that they can be drawn into thin wires. All metals are **good conductors of electric current.** The wires in the electrical devices in your home are made of copper.

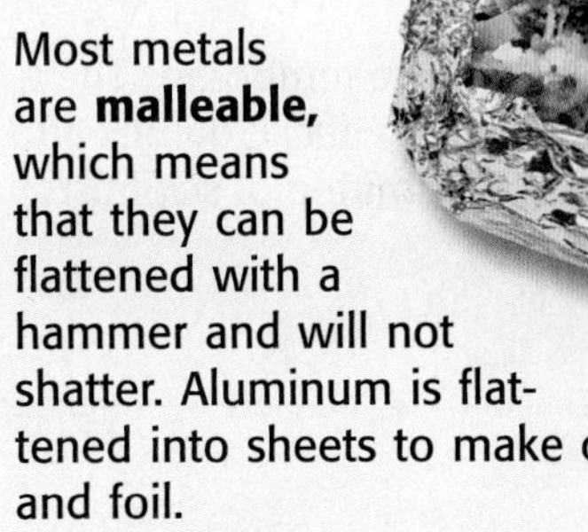

Most metals are **malleable,** which means that they can be flattened with a hammer and will not shatter. Aluminum is flattened into sheets to make cans and foil.

Most metals are **good conductors of thermal energy.** This iron griddle conducts thermal energy from a stove top to cook your favorite foods.

Figure 4 Properties of Nonmetals

Nonmetals are **not malleable or ductile.** In fact, solid nonmetals, such as carbon in the graphite of the pencil lead, are brittle and will break or shatter when hit with a hammer.

Sulfur, like most nonmetals, is **not shiny.**

Nonmetals are **poor conductors of thermal energy and electric current.** If the gap in a spark plug is too wide, the nonmetals nitrogen and oxygen in the air will stop the spark and a car's engine will not run.

Nonmetals

Nonmetals are found to the right of the zigzag line on the periodic table. Atoms of most nonmetals have an almost complete set of electrons in their outer level. Atoms of the elements in Group 18, the noble gases, have a complete set of electrons. More than half of the nonmetals are gases at room temperature. Many properties of nonmetals are the opposite of the properties of metals, as shown in **Figure 4.**

Metalloids

Metalloids, also called *semiconductors,* are the elements that border the zigzag line on the periodic table. Atoms of metalloids have about half of a complete set of electrons in their outer energy level. Metalloids have some properties of metals and some properties of nonmetals, as shown in **Figure 5.**

MATH PRACTICE

Percentages

Elements are classified as metals, nonmetals, and metalloids. Use the periodic table to determine the percentage of elements in each of the three categories.

Figure 5 Properties of Metalloids

Tellurium is **shiny,** but it is **brittle** and can easily be smashed into a powder.

Boron is almost as **hard** as diamond, but it is also **very brittle.** At high temperatures, it is a **good conductor of electric current.**

Patterns of Symbols

Divide a sheet of paper into four columns. Look at the elements whose atomic numbers are 1 to 20 on the periodic table. With a parent, find patterns that describe the relationship between the chemical symbols and names of elements. In each column, write all of the chemical symbols and names that follow a single pattern. At the top of each column, write a sentence describing the pattern.

period in chemistry, a horizontal row of elements in the periodic table

group a vertical column of elements in the periodic table; elements in a group share chemical properties

Decoding the Periodic Table

The periodic table may seem to be in code. In a way, it is. But the colors and symbols will help you decode the table.

Each Element Is Identified by a Chemical Symbol

Each square on the periodic table includes an element's name, chemical symbol, atomic number, and atomic mass. The names of the elements come from many sources. Some elements, such as mendelevium, are named after scientists. Others, such as californium, are named after places. Some element names vary by country. But the chemical symbols are the same worldwide. For most elements, the chemical symbol has one or two letters. The first letter is always capitalized. Any other letter is always lowercase. The newest elements have temporary three-letter symbols.

Rows Are Called *Periods*

Each horizontal row of elements (from left to right) on the periodic table is called a **period.** Look at Period 4 in **Figure 6.** The physical and chemical properties of elements in a row follow a repeating, or periodic, pattern as you move across the period. Properties such as conductivity and reactivity change gradually from left to right in each period.

Columns Are Called *Groups*

Each vertical column of elements (from top to bottom) on the periodic table is called a **group.** Elements in the same group often have similar chemical and physical properties. For this reason, a group is also called a *family.*

Reading Check **Why is a group sometimes called a family?**

Figure 6 *As you move from left to right across a row, the elements become less metallic.*

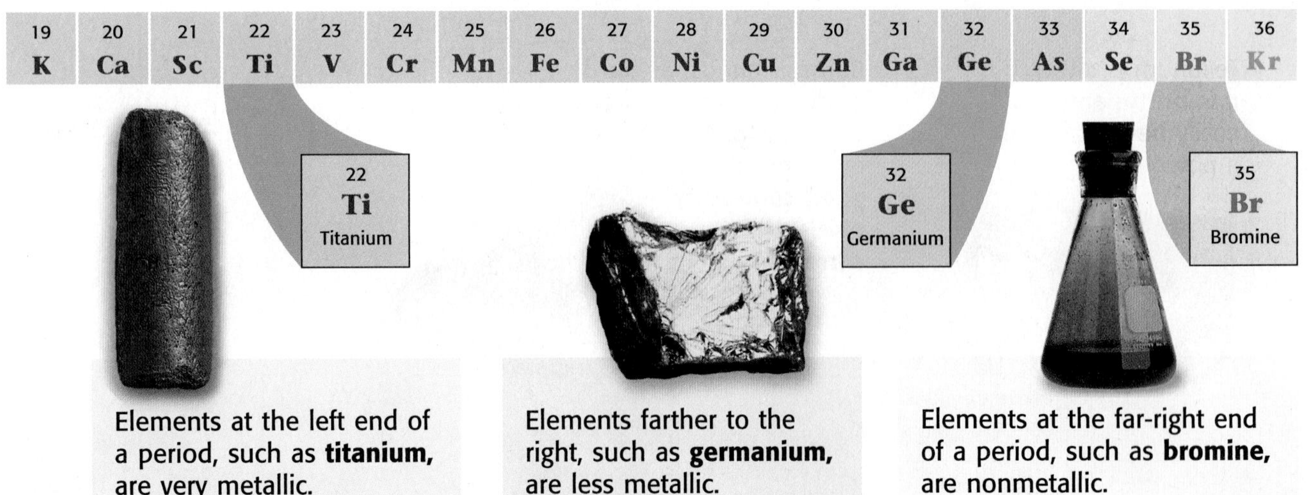

Elements at the left end of a period, such as **titanium,** are very metallic.

Elements farther to the right, such as **germanium,** are less metallic.

Elements at the far-right end of a period, such as **bromine,** are nonmetallic.

SECTION Review

Summary

- Mendeleev developed the first periodic table by listing the elements in order of increasing atomic mass. He used his table to predict that elements with certain properties would be discovered later.
- Properties of elements repeat in a regular, or periodic, pattern.
- Moseley rearranged the elements in order of increasing atomic number.
- The periodic law states that the repeating chemical and physical properties of elements relate to and depend on elements' atomic numbers.
- Elements in the periodic table are classified as metals, nonmetals, and metalloids.
- Each element has a chemical symbol.
- A horizontal row of elements is called a *period.*
- Physical and chemical properties of elements change across each period.
- A vertical column of elements is called a *group* or *family.*
- Elements in a group usually have similar properties.

Using Key Terms

1. In your own words, write a definition for the term *periodic.*

Understanding Key Ideas

2. Which of the following elements should be the best conductor of electric current?
   a. germanium
   b. sulfur
   c. aluminum
   d. helium
3. Compare a period and a group on the periodic table.
4. What property did Mendeleev use to position the elements on the periodic table?
5. State the periodic law.

Critical Thinking

6. **Identifying Relationships** An atom that has 117 protons in its nucleus has not yet been made. Once this atom is made, to which group will element 117 belong? Explain your answer.
7. **Applying Concepts** Are the properties of sodium, Na, more like the properties of lithium, Li, or magnesium, Mg? Explain your answer.

Interpreting Graphics

8. The image below shows part of a periodic table. Compare the image below with the similar part of the periodic table in your book.

1	1 H 1.0079 水素			
2	3 Li 6.941 リチウム	4 Be 9.01218 ベリリウム		
3	11 Na 22.98977 ナトリウム	12 Mg 24.305 マグネシウム		
4	19 K	20 Ca	21 Sc	22 Ti

SCILINKS
NSTA
Developed and maintained by the National Science Teachers Association
For a variety of links related to this chapter, go to www.scilinks.org
Topic: Periodic Table; Metals
SciLinks code: HSM1125; HSM0947

SECTION 2

Grouping the Elements

You probably know a family with several members who look a lot alike. The elements in a family or group in the periodic table often—but not always—have similar properties.

What You Will Learn

- Explain why elements in a group often have similar properties.
- Describe the properties of the elements in the groups of the periodic table.

Vocabulary

alkali metal
alkaline-earth metal
halogen
noble gas

READING STRATEGY

Paired Summarizing Read this section silently. In pairs, take turns summarizing the material. Stop to discuss ideas that seem confusing.

The properties of the elements in a group are similar because the atoms of the elements have the same number of electrons in their outer energy level. Atoms will often take, give, or share electrons with other atoms in order to have a complete set of electrons in their outer energy level. Elements whose atoms undergo such processes are called *reactive* and can combine to form compounds.

Group 1: Alkali Metals

3 **Li** Lithium
11 **Na** Sodium
19 **K** Potassium
37 **Rb** Rubidium
55 **Cs** Cesium
87 **Fr** Francium

Group contains: metals
Electrons in the outer level: 1
Reactivity: very reactive
Other shared properties: softness; color of silver; shininess; low density

Alkali metals (AL kuh LIE MET uhlz) are elements in Group 1 of the periodic table. They share physical and chemical properties, as shown in **Figure 1.** Alkali metals are the most reactive metals because their atoms can easily give away the one outer-level electron. Pure alkali metals are often stored in oil. The oil keeps them from reacting with water and oxygen in the air. Alkali metals are so reactive that in nature they are found only combined with other elements. Compounds formed from alkali metals have many uses. For example, sodium chloride (table salt) is used to flavor your food. Potassium bromide is used in photography.

Hydrogen

Although the element hydrogen appears above the alkali metals on the periodic table, it is not considered a member of Group 1. It will be described separately at the end of this section.

Figure 1 **Properties of Alkali Metals**

▲ Alkali metals are soft enough to be cut with a knife.

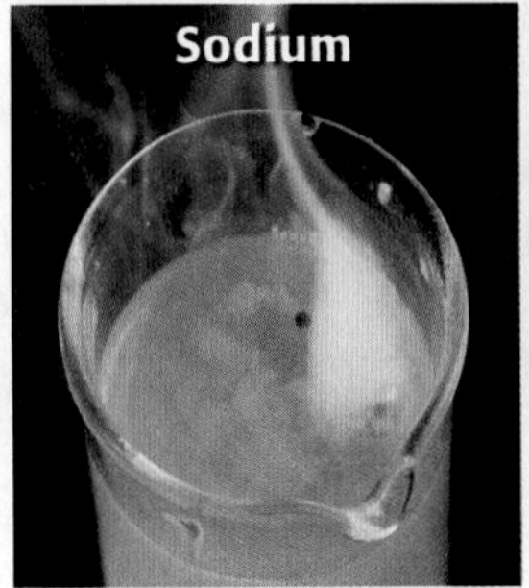

Potassium

▲ Alkali metals react with water to form hydrogen gas.

Group 2: Alkaline-Earth Metals

4 Be Beryllium
12 Mg Magnesium
20 Ca Calcium
38 Sr Strontium
56 Ba Barium
88 Ra Radium

Group contains: metals
Electrons in the outer level: 2
Reactivity: very reactive but less reactive than alkali metals
Other shared properties: color of silver; higher densities than alkali metals

Alkaline-earth metals (AL kuh LIEN UHRTH MET uhlz) are less reactive than alkali metals are. Atoms of alkaline-earth metals have two outer-level electrons. It is more difficult for atoms to give two electrons than to give one when joining with other atoms. Group 2 elements and their compounds have many uses. For example, magnesium can be mixed with other metals to make low-density materials used in airplanes. And compounds of calcium are found in cement, chalk, and even you, as shown in **Figure 2.**

Figure 2 *Calcium, an alkaline-earth metal, is an important part of a compound that keeps your bones and teeth healthy.*

Groups 3–12: Transition Metals

21 Sc	22 Ti	23 V	24 Cr	25 Mn	26 Fe	27 Co	28 Ni	29 Cu	30 Zn
39 Y	40 Zr	41 Nb	42 Mo	43 Tc	44 Ru	45 Rh	46 Pd	47 Ag	48 Cd
57 La	72 Hf	73 Ta	74 W	75 Re	76 Os	77 Ir	78 Pt	79 Au	80 Hg
89 Ac	104 Rf	105 Db	106 Sg	107 Bh	108 Hs	109 Mt	110 Ds	111 Uuu	112 Uub

Group contains: metals
Electrons in the outer level: 1 or 2
Reactivity: less reactive than alkaline-earth metals
Other shared properties: shininess; good conductors of thermal energy and electric current; higher densities and melting points than elements in Groups 1 and 2 (except for mercury)

Groups 3–12 do not have individual names. Instead, all of these groups are called *transition metals*. The atoms of transition metals do not give away their electrons as easily as atoms of the Group 1 and Group 2 metals do. So, transition metals are less reactive than alkali metals and alkaline-earth metals are.

Reading Check **Why are alkali metals more reactive than transition metals are?** (*See the Appendix for answers to Reading Checks.*)

alkali metal one of the elements of Group 1 of the periodic table (lithium, sodium, potassium, rubidium, cesium, and francium)

alkaline-earth metal one of the elements of Group 2 of the periodic table (beryllium, magnesium, calcium, strontium, barium, and radium)

Figure 3 **Properties of Transition Metals**

Mercury is used in thermometers. Unlike the other transition metals, mercury is liquid at room temperature.

Many transition metals—but not all—are silver colored! This **gold** ring proves it!

Some transition metals, such as **titanium** in the artificial hip at right, are not very reactive. But others, such as **iron,** are reactive. The iron in the steel trowel on the left has reacted to form rust.

Properties of Transition Metals

The properties of the transition metals vary widely, as shown in **Figure 3.** But, because these elements are metals, they share the properties of metals. Transition metals tend to be shiny and to conduct thermal energy and electric current well.

Figure 4 *Do you see red? The color red appears on a computer monitor because of a compound formed from europium that coats the back of the screen.*

Lanthanides and Actinides

Some transition metals from Periods 6 and 7 appear in two rows at the bottom of the periodic table to keep the table from being too wide. The elements in each row tend to have similar properties. Elements in the first row follow lanthanum and are called *lanthanides*. The lanthanides are shiny, reactive metals. Some of these elements are used to make steel. An important use of a compound of one lanthanide element is shown in **Figure 4.**

Elements in the second row follow actinium and are called *actinides*. All atoms of actinides are radioactive, or unstable. The atoms of a radioactive element can change into atoms of another element. Elements listed after plutonium, element 94, do not occur in nature. They are made in laboratories. Very small amounts of americium (AM uhr ISH ee uhm), element 95, are used in some smoke detectors.

Reading Check **Are lanthanides and actinides transition metals?**

57 La Lanthanum														
89 Ac Actinium														
Lanthanides	58 Ce	59 Pr	60 Nd	61 Pm	62 Sm	63 Eu	64 Gd	65 Tb	66 Dy	67 Ho	68 Er	69 Tm	70 Yb	71 Lu
Actinides	90 Th	91 Pa	92 U	93 Np	94 Pu	95 Am	96 Cm	97 Bk	98 Cf	99 Es	100 Fm	101 Md	102 No	103 Lr

Group 13: Boron Group

5 **B** Boron	
13 **Al** Aluminum	
31 **Ga** Gallium	
49 **In** Indium	
81 **Tl** Thallium	
113 **Uut** Ununtrium	

Group contains: one metalloid and five metals
Electrons in the outer level: 3
Reactivity: reactive
Other shared properties: solids at room temperature

The most common element from Group 13 is aluminum. In fact, aluminum is the most abundant metal in Earth's crust. Until the 1880s, however, aluminum was considered a precious metal because the process used to make pure aluminum was very expensive. During the 1850s and 1860s, Emperor Napoleon III of France used aluminum dinnerware because aluminum was more valuable than gold.

Today, the process of making pure aluminum is easier and less expensive than it was in the 1800s. Aluminum is now an important metal used in making aircraft parts. Aluminum is also used to make lightweight automobile parts, foil, cans, and siding.

Like the other elements in the boron group, aluminum is reactive. Why can it be used in so many things? A thin layer of aluminum oxide quickly forms on aluminum's surface when aluminum reacts with oxygen in the air. This layer prevents further reaction of the aluminum.

CONNECTION TO Environmental Science

WRITING SKILL **Recycling Aluminum**

Aluminum recycling is a very successful program. In your **science journal,** write a one-page report that describes how aluminum is processed from its ore. In your report, identify the ore and compare the energy needed to extract aluminum from the ore with the energy needed to process recycled aluminum.

Group 14: Carbon Group

6 **C** Carbon	
14 **Si** Silicon	
32 **Ge** Germanium	
50 **Sn** Tin	
82 **Pb** Lead	
114 **Uuq** Ununquadium	

Group contains: one nonmetal, two metalloids, and three metals
Electrons in the outer level: 4
Reactivity: varies among the elements
Other shared properties: solids at room temperature

The nonmetal carbon can be found uncombined in nature, as shown in **Figure 5.** Carbon also forms a wide variety of compounds. Some of these compounds, such as proteins, fats, and carbohydrates, are necessary for living things on Earth.

The metalloids silicon and germanium, also in Group 14, are used to make computer chips. The metal tin is useful because it is not very reactive. For example, a tin can is really made of steel coated with tin. Because the tin is less reactive than the steel is, the tin keeps the iron in the steel from rusting.

Reading Check **What metalloids from Group 14 are used to make computer chips?**

Figure 5 *Diamond and soot have very different properties, yet both are natural forms of carbon.*

Diamond is the hardest material known. It is used as a jewel and on cutting tools, such as saws, drills, and files.

Soot is formed from burning oil, coal, and wood and is used as a pigment in paints and crayons.

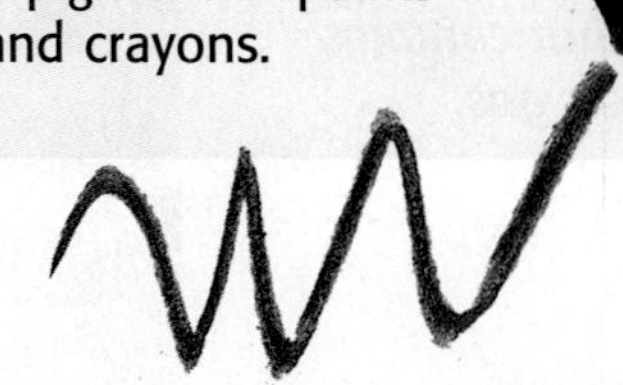

Figure 6 *Simply striking a match on the side of this box causes chemicals on the match to react with phosphorus on the box and begin to burn.*

Group 15: Nitrogen Group

7 N Nitrogen
15 P Phosphorus
33 As Arsenic
51 Sb Antimony
83 Bi Bismuth
115 Uup Ununpentium

Group contains: two nonmetals, two metalloids, and two metals
Electrons in the outer level: 5
Reactivity: varies among the elements
Other shared properties: solids at room temperature (except for nitrogen)

Nitrogen, which is a gas at room temperature, makes up about 80% of the air you breathe. Nitrogen removed from air can be reacted with hydrogen to make ammonia for fertilizers.

Although nitrogen is not very reactive, phosphorus is extremely reactive, as shown in **Figure 6.** In fact, in nature phosphorus is only found combined with other elements.

Group 16: Oxygen Group

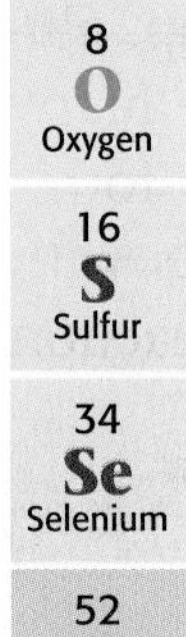

8 O Oxygen
16 S Sulfur
34 Se Selenium
52 Te Tellurium
84 Po Polonium

Group contains: three nonmetals, one metalloid, and one metal
Electrons in the outer level: 6
Reactivity: Reactive
Other shared properties: All but oxygen are solid at room temperature.

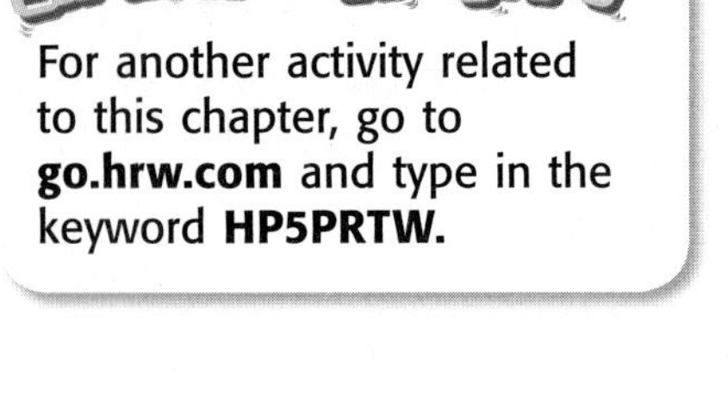

For another activity related to this chapter, go to **go.hrw.com** and type in the keyword **HP5PRTW.**

Oxygen makes up about 20% of air. Oxygen is necessary for substances to burn. Oxygen is also important to most living things, such as the diver in **Figure 7.** Sulfur is another commonly found member of Group 16. Sulfur can be found as a yellow solid in nature. It is used to make sulfuric acid, the most widely used compound in the chemical industry.

Reading Check **Which gases from Groups 15 and 16 make up most of the air you breathe?**

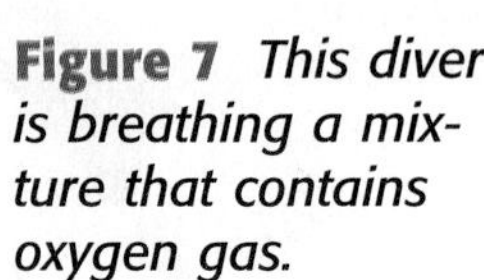

Figure 7 *This diver is breathing a mixture that contains oxygen gas.*

Figure 8 Physical Properties of Some Halogens

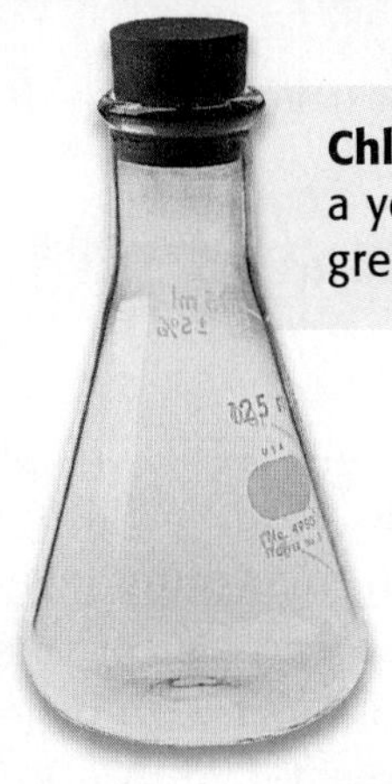

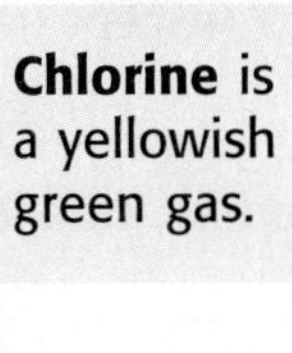

Chlorine is a yellowish green gas.

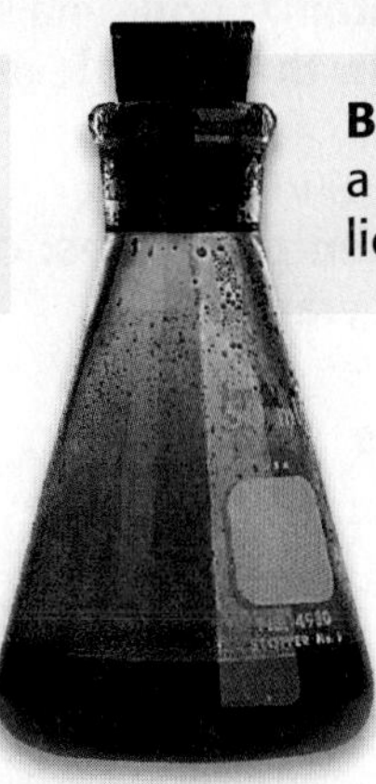

Bromine is a dark red liquid.

Iodine is a dark gray solid.

Group 17: Halogens

9 F Fluorine
17 Cl Chlorine
35 Br Bromine
53 I Iodine
85 At Astatine

Group contains: nonmetals
Electrons in the outer level: 7
Reactivity: very reactive
Other shared properties: poor conductors of electric current; violent reactions with alkali metals to form salts; never in uncombined form in nature

Halogens (HAL oh juhnz) are very reactive nonmetals because their atoms need to gain only one electron to have a complete outer level. The atoms of halogens combine readily with other atoms, especially metals, to gain that missing electron. The reaction of a halogen with a metal makes a salt, such as sodium chloride. Both chlorine and iodine are used as disinfectants. Chlorine is used to treat water. Iodine mixed with alcohol is used in hospitals.

Although the chemical properties of the halogens are similar, the physical properties are quite different, as shown in **Figure 8.**

halogen one of the elements of Group 17 of the periodic table (fluorine, chlorine, bromine, iodine, and astatine); halogens combine with most metals to form salts

CONNECTION TO Biology

Water Treatment Chlorine has been used to treat drinking water since the early 20th century. Chlorinating water helps protect people from many diseases by killing the organisms in water that cause the diseases. But there is much more to water treatment than just adding chlorine. Research how a water treatment plant purifies water for your use. Construct a model of a treatment plant. Use labels to describe the role of each part of the plant in treating the water you use each day.

ACTIVITY

Figure 9 *In addition to neon, other noble gases can be used to make "neon" lights.*

noble gas one of the elements of Group 18 of the periodic table (helium, neon, argon, krypton, xenon, and radon); noble gases are unreactive

Group 18: Noble Gases

2 He Helium
10 Ne Neon
18 Ar Argon
36 Kr Krypton
54 Xe Xenon
86 Rn Radon

Group contains: nonmetals
Electrons in the outer level: 8 (except helium, which has 2)
Reactivity: unreactive
Other shared properties: colorless, odorless gases at room temperature

Noble gases are unreactive nonmetals and are in Group 18 of the periodic table. The atoms of these elements have a full set of electrons in their outer level. So, they do not need to lose or gain any electrons. Under normal conditions, they do not react with other elements. Earth's atmosphere is almost 1% argon. But all the noble gases are found in small amounts.

The unreactivity of the noble gases makes them useful. For example, ordinary light bulbs last longer when they are filled with argon. Because argon is unreactive, it does not react with the metal filament in the light bulb even when the filament gets hot. A more reactive gas might react with the filament, causing the light to burn out. The low density of helium makes blimps and weather balloons float. Another popular use of noble gases is shown in **Figure 9.**

Reading Check **Why are noble gases unreactive?**

Hydrogen

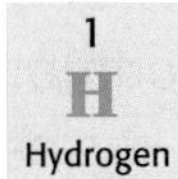
1 H Hydrogen

Electrons in the outer level: 1
Reactivity: reactive
Other properties: colorless, odorless gas at room temperature; low density; explosive reactions with oxygen

The properties of hydrogen do not match the properties of any single group, so hydrogen is set apart from the other elements in the table. Hydrogen is above Group 1 because atoms of the alkali metals also have only one electron in their outer level. Atoms of hydrogen can give away one electron when they join with other atoms. However, the physical properties of hydrogen are more like those of nonmetals than those of metals. So, hydrogen really is in a group of its own. Hydrogen is found in stars. In fact, it is the most abundant element in the universe. Its reactive nature makes it useful as a fuel in rockets, as shown in **Figure 10.**

Figure 10 *Hydrogen reacts violently with oxygen. The hot water vapor that forms as a result of this reaction helps guide the space shuttle into orbit.*

SECTION Review

Summary

- Alkali metals (Group 1) are the most reactive metals. Atoms of the alkali metals have one electron in their outer level.
- Alkaline-earth metals (Group 2) are less reactive than the alkali metals are. Atoms of the alkaline-earth metals have two electrons in their outer level.
- Transition metals (Groups 3–12) include most of the well-known metals and the lanthanides and actinides.
- Groups 13–16 contain the metalloids and some metals and nonmetals.
- Halogens (Group 17) are very reactive non-metals. Atoms of the halogens have seven electrons in their outer level.
- Noble gases (Group 18) are unreactive nonmetals. Atoms of the noble gases have a full set of electrons in their outer level.
- Hydrogen is set off by itself in the periodic table. Its properties do not match the properties of any one group.

Using Key Terms

Complete each of the following sentences by choosing the correct term from the word bank.

noble gas	alkaline-earth metal
halogen	alkali metal

1. An atom of a(n) ___ has a full set of electrons in its outermost energy level.
2. An atom of a(n) ___ has one electron in its outermost energy level.
3. An atom of a(n) ___ tends to gain one electron when it combines with another atom.
4. An atom of a(n) ___ tends to lose two electrons when it combines with another atom.

Understanding Key Ideas

5. Which group contains elements whose atoms have six electrons in their outer level?
   a. Group 2 **c.** Group 16
   b. Group 6 **d.** Group 18
6. What are two properties of the alkali metals?
7. What causes the properties of elements in a group to be similar?
8. What are two properties of the halogens?
9. Why is hydrogen set apart from the other elements in the periodic table?
10. Which group contains elements whose atoms have three electrons in their outer level?

Interpreting Graphics

11. Look at the model of an atom below. Does the model represent a metal atom or a nonmetal atom? Explain your answer.

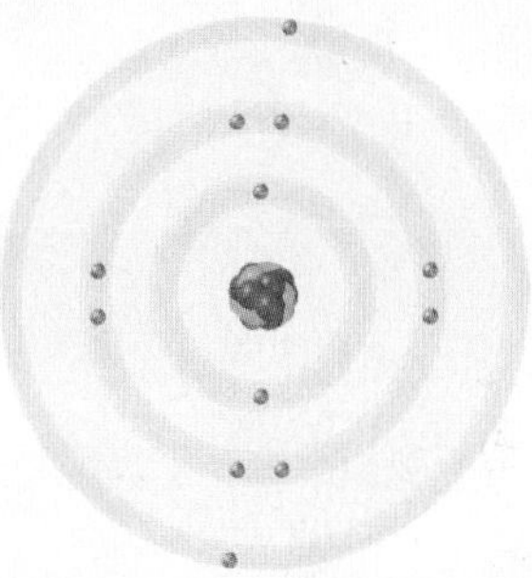

Critical Thinking

12. **Making Inferences** Why are neither the alkali metals nor the alkaline-earth metals found uncombined in nature?
13. **Making Comparisons** Compare the element hydrogen with the alkali metal sodium.

SCILINKS.
NSTA
Developed and maintained by the National Science Teachers Association
For a variety of links related to this chapter, go to www.scilinks.org
Topic: Alkali Metals; Halogens and Noble Gases
SciLinks code: HSM0043; HSM0711

Model-Making Lab

Create a Periodic Table

OBJECTIVES

Classify objects based on their properties.

Identify patterns and trends in data.

MATERIALS

- bag of objects
- balance, metric
- meterstick
- paper, graphing (2 sheets)
- paper, 3 × 3 cm squares (20)

You probably have classification systems for many things in your life, such as your clothes, your books, and your CDs. One of the most important classification systems in science is the periodic table of the elements. In this lab, you will develop your own classification system for a collection of ordinary objects. You will analyze trends in your system and compare your system with the periodic table of the elements.

Procedure

1. Your teacher will give you a bag of objects. Your bag is missing one item. Examine the items carefully. Describe the missing object in as many ways as you can. Be sure to include the reasons why you think the missing object has the characteristics you describe.
2. Lay the paper squares out on your desk or table so that you have a grid of five rows of four squares each.
3. Arrange your objects on the grid in a logical order. (You must decide what order is logical!) You should end up with one blank square for the missing object.
4. Record a description of the basis for your arrangement.

5. Measure the mass (g) and diameter (mm) of each object, and record your results in the appropriate square. Each square (except the empty one) should have one object and two written measurements on it.

6. Examine your pattern again. Does the order in which your objects are arranged still make sense? Explain.

7. Rearrange the squares and their objects if necessary to improve your arrangement. Record a description of the basis for the new arrangement.

8. Working across the rows, number the squares 1 to 20. When you get to the end of a row, continue numbering in the first square of the next row.

9. Copy your grid. In each square, be sure to list the type of object and label all measurements with appropriate units.

Analyze the Results

1. **Constructing Graphs** Make a graph of mass (*y*-axis) versus object number (*x*-axis). Label each axis, and title the graph.

2. **Constructing Graphs** Now make a graph of diameter (*y*-axis) versus object number (*x*-axis).

Draw Conclusions

3. **Analyzing Graphs** Discuss each graph with your classmates. Try to identify any important features of the graph. For example, does the graph form a line or a curve? Is there anything unusual about the graph? What do these features tell you? Record your answers.

4. **Evaluating Models** How is your arrangement of objects similar to the periodic table of the elements found in this textbook? How is your arrangement different from that periodic table?

5. **Making Predictions** Look again at your prediction about the missing object. Do you think your prediction is still accurate? Try to improve your description by estimating the mass and diameter of the missing object. Record your estimates.

6. **Evaluating Methods** Mendeleev created a periodic table of elements and predicted characteristics of missing elements. How is your experiment similar to Mendeleev's work?

Chapter Review

USING KEY TERMS

Complete each of the following sentences by choosing the correct term from the word bank.

group	period
alkali metals	halogens
alkaline-earth metals	noble gases

1. Elements in the same vertical column on the periodic table belong to the same ___.

2. Elements in the same horizontal row on the periodic table belong to the same ___.

3. The most reactive metals are ___.

4. Elements that are unreactive are called ___.

UNDERSTANDING KEY IDEAS

Multiple Choice

5. Mendeleev's periodic table was useful because it
   - **a.** showed the elements arranged by atomic number.
   - **b.** had no empty spaces.
   - **c.** showed the atomic number of the elements.
   - **d.** allowed for the prediction of the properties of missing elements.

6. Most nonmetals are
   - **a.** shiny.
   - **b.** poor conductors of electric current.
   - **c.** flattened when hit with a hammer.
   - **d.** solids at room temperature.

7. Which of the following items is NOT found on the periodic table?
   - **a.** the atomic number of each element
   - **b.** the name of each element
   - **c.** the date that each element was discovered
   - **d.** the atomic mass of each element

8. Which of the following statements about the periodic table is false?
   - **a.** There are more metals than nonmetals on the periodic table.
   - **b.** Atoms of elements in the same group have the same number of electrons in their outer level.
   - **c.** The elements at the far left of the periodic table are nonmetals.
   - **d.** Elements are arranged by increasing atomic number.

9. Which of the following statements about alkali metals is true?
   - **a.** Alkali metals are generally found in their uncombined form.
   - **b.** Alkali metals are Group 1 elements.
   - **c.** Alkali metals should be stored underwater.
   - **d.** Alkali metals are unreactive.

10. Which of the following statements about elements is true?
    - **a.** Every element occurs naturally.
    - **b.** All elements are found in their uncombined form in nature.
    - **c.** Each element has a unique atomic number.
    - **d.** All of the elements exist in approximately equal quantities.

Short Answer

11. How is Moseley's basis for arranging the elements different from Mendeleev's?

12. How is the periodic table like a calendar?

Math Skills

Examine the chart of the percentages of elements in the Earth's crust below. Then, answer the questions that follow.

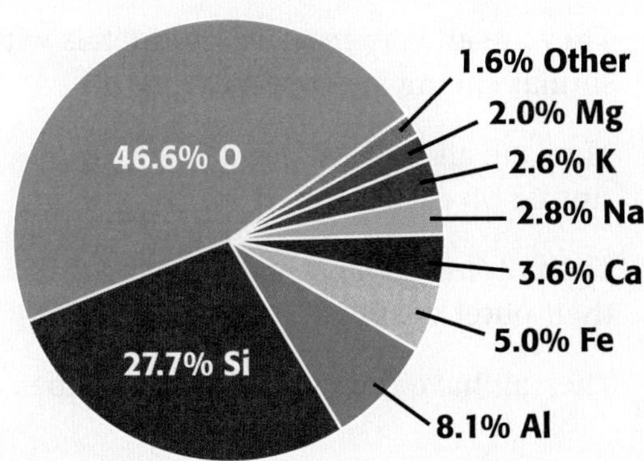

13. Excluding the "Other" category, what percentage of the Earth's crust are alkali metals?

14. Excluding the "Other" category, what percentage of the Earth's crust are alkaline-earth metals?

CRITICAL THINKING

15. **Concept Mapping** Use the following terms to create a concept map: *periodic table, elements, groups, periods, metals, nonmetals,* and *metalloids.*

16. **Forming Hypotheses** Why was Mendeleev unable to make any predictions about the noble gas elements?

17. **Identifying Relationships** When an element that has 115 protons in its nucleus is synthesized, will it be a metal, a nonmetal, or a metalloid? Explain your answer.

18. **Applying Concepts** Your classmate offers to give you a piece of sodium that he found on a hiking trip. What is your response? Explain.

19. **Applying Concepts** Identify each element described below.

    a. This metal is very reactive, has properties similar to those of magnesium, and is in the same period as bromine.

    b. This nonmetal is in the same group as lead.

INTERPRETING GRAPHICS

20. Study the diagram below to determine the pattern of the images. Predict the missing image, and draw it. Identify which properties are periodic and which properties are shared within a group.

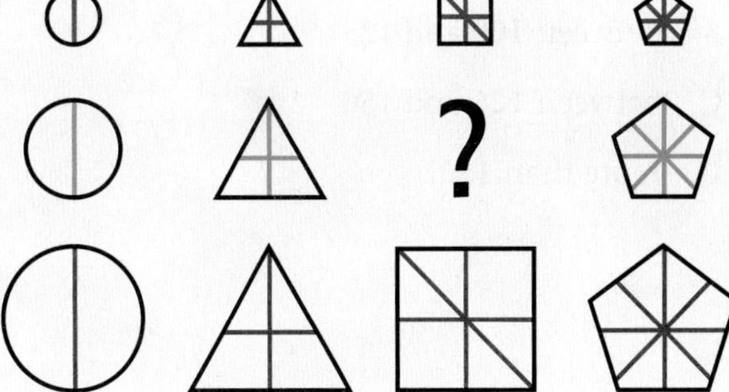

Multiple Choice

Use the diagram below to answer question 1.

Cobalt and Nickel Entries in Periodic Table

27	28
Co	**Ni**
Cobalt	Nickel
58.933	58.693

1. **The diagram above is an enlargement of a section of the periodic table. What is the biggest difference between cobalt (Co) and nickel (Ni) as shown in the periodic table entries?**
   A. Nickel has more protons.
   B. Cobalt has more electrons.
   C. Cobalt has a lower number of neutrons.
   D. Nickel has a higher value for atomic mass.

2. **Approximately how many elements are in the periodic table?**
   A. between 75 and 100
   B. between 100 and 125
   C. between 125 and 150
   D. more than 150

3. **In what order are the regions arranged on the periodic table, reading left to right?**
   A. inert gases, metals, nonmetals, metalloids
   B. metalloids, metals, nonmetals, inert gases
   C. metals, metalloids, nonmetals, inert gases
   D. nonmetals, inert gases, metals, metalloids

4. **Fluorine, chlorine, bromine, iodine, and astatine make up Group 17, the halogens. Why are these elements grouped together?**
   A. They are all very reactive nonmetals with similar chemical properties.
   B. They are all nonreactive gases with similar physical properties.
   C. Their atoms all have eight electrons in their outer energy levels.
   D. They all have the same atomic number.

5. **Which of the following best describes the properties of metals?**
   A. hard, brittle, and unconductive
   B. liquid, dark, and conductive
   C. shiny, malleable, and conductive
   D. soft, oily, and very reactive

6. **Alberto has an element that is a shiny, brittle solid that conducts electricity. The element most likely belongs to which class of elements?**
   A. halogens
   B. metals
   C. nonmetals
   D. metalloids

7. How are the elements in the periodic table arranged?

A. by their atomic mass

B. by their chemical symbol

C. by their chemical name

D. by their atomic number

Use the graph below to answer question 8.

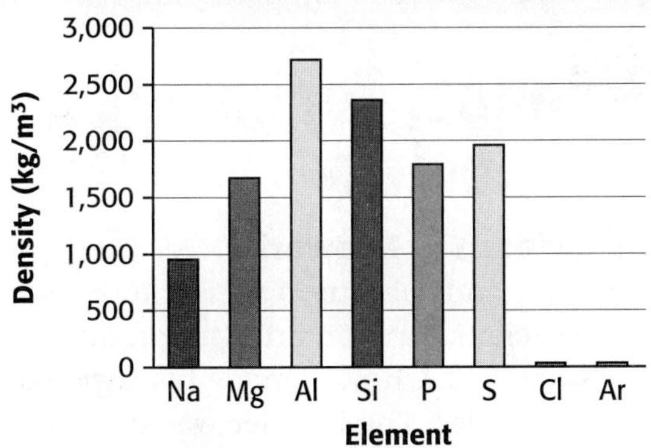

8. The graph above shows the densities in kilograms per cubic meter (kg/m^3) of the elements in Period 2 of the periodic table. Given a 100 m^3 sample of each element in Period 2, which sample would have the greatest mass?

A. the sample of aluminum (Al)

B. the sample of chlorine (Cl)

C. the sample of sulphur (S)

D. the sample of argon (Ar)

9. Which of these statements about a group of elements is true?

A. The elements have a wide range of properties.

B. The elements have the same atomic number.

C. The elements have similar properties.

D. The elements have the same mass number.

10. According to its location on the periodic table, sodium can be described as

A. an alkaline-earth metal.

B. a transition metal.

C. an alkali metal.

D. a metalloid.

Open Response

11. The element hydrogen is usually placed at the top of Group 1 in the periodic table. However, hydrogen is not always considered to be a member of Group 1. Explain why hydrogen is placed in Group 1 and what properties set hydrogen apart from Group 1.

12. The elements in the periodic table can be classified into metals, nonmetals, and metalloids. Describe the properties of these classes, and explain where the elements that fall into these classes can be found on the periodic table.

Science in Action

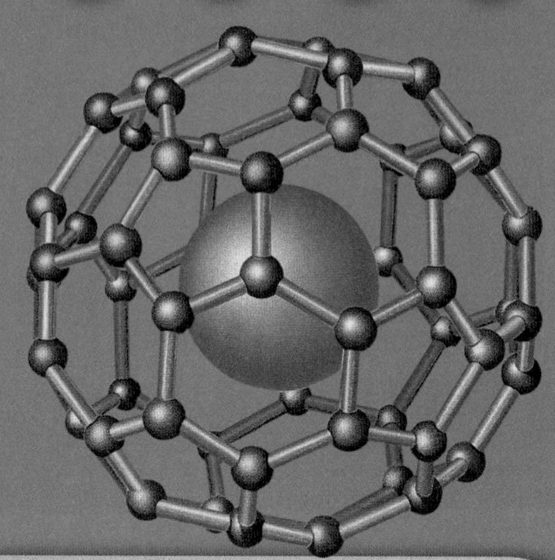

Weird Science

Buckyballs

In 1985, scientists found a completely new kind of molecule! This carbon molecule has 60 carbon atoms linked together in a shape similar to that of a soccer ball. This molecule is called a buckyball. Buckyballs have also been found in the soot from candle flames. And some scientists claim to have detected buckyballs in space. Chemists have been trying to identify the molecules' properties. One property is that a buckyball can act like a cage and hold smaller substances, such as individual atoms. Buckyballs are both slippery and strong. Scientists are exploring their use in tough plastics and cutting tools.

Language Arts ACTiViTy

WRITING SKILL Imagine that you are trapped within a buckyball. Write a one-page short story describing your experience. Describe the windows in your molecular prison.

Science, Technology, and Society

The Science of Fireworks

Explosive and dazzling, a fireworks display is both a science and an art. More than 1,000 years ago, the Chinese made black powder, or gunpowder. The powder was used to set off firecrackers and primitive missiles. The shells of fireworks contain several different chemicals. Black powder at the bottom of the shell launches the shell into the sky. A second layer of black powder ignites the rest of the chemicals and causes an explosion that lights up the sky! Colors can be created by mixing chemicals such as strontium (for red), magnesium (for white), or copper (for blue) with the gunpowder.

Math ACTiViTy

Fireworks can cost between $200 and $2,000 each. If a show uses 20 fireworks that cost $200 each, 12 fireworks that cost $500 each, and 10 fireworks that cost $1,200 each, what is the total cost for the fireworks?

People in Science

Glenn T. Seaborg

Making Elements When you look at the periodic table, you can thank Dr. Glenn Theodore Seaborg and his colleagues for many of the actinide elements. While working at the University of California at Berkeley, Seaborg and his team added a number of elements to the periodic table. His work in identifying properties of plutonium led to his working on the top-secret Manhattan Project at the University of Chicago. He was outspoken about the beneficial uses of atomic energy and, at the same time, opposed the production and use of nuclear weapons.

Seaborg's revision of the layout of the periodic table—the actinide concept—is the most significant since Mendeleev's original design. For his scientific achievements, Dr. Seaborg was awarded the 1951 Nobel Prize in Chemistry jointly with his colleague, Dr. Edwin M. McMillan. Element 106, which Seaborg neither discovered nor created, was named seaborgium in his honor. This was the first time an element had been named after a living person.

Social Studies ACTIVITY

WRITING SKILL Write a newspaper editorial to express an opinion for or against the Manhattan Project. Be sure to include information to support your view.

To learn more about these Science in Action topics, visit go.hrw.com and type in the keyword **HP5PRTF.**

Current Science

Check out Current Science® articles related to this chapter by visiting go.hrw.com. Just type in the keyword HP5CS12.

TIMELINE

Interactions of Matter

In this unit you will study the interactions through which matter can change its identity. You will learn how atoms bond with one another to form compounds and how atoms join in different combinations to form new substances through chemical reactions. You will also learn about the properties of several categories of compounds. Finally, you will learn how nuclear interactions can actually change the identity of an atom. This timeline includes some of the events leading to the current understanding of these interactions of matter.

1828

Urea, a compound found in urine, is produced in a laboratory. Until this time, chemists had believed that compounds created by living organisms could not be produced in the laboratory.

1858

German chemist Friedrich August Kekulé suggests that carbon forms four chemical bonds and can form long chains.

1942

The first nuclear chain reaction is carried out in a squash court under the football stadium at the University of Chicago.

1979

Public fear about nuclear power grows after an accident occurs at the Three Mile Island nuclear power station located in Pennsylvania.

1867

Swedish chemist Alfred Nobel develops dynamite. Dynamite's explosive power is a result of the decomposition reaction of nitroglycerin.

1898

The United States defeats Spain in the Spanish-American War.

1903

Marie Curie, Pierre Curie, and Henri Becquerel are awarded the Nobel Prize in physics for the discovery of radioactivity.

1964

Dr. Martin Luther King, Jr., American civil rights leader, is awarded the Nobel Peace Prize.

1969

The *Nimbus III* weather satellite is launched by the United States, representing the first civilian use of nuclear batteries.

1996

Evidence of organic compounds in a meteorite leads scientists to speculate that life may have existed on Mars more than 3.6 billion years ago.

2001

The first total solar eclipse of the millenium occurs on June 21.

2002

Hy-wire, the world's first drivable vehicle to combine a hydrogen fuel cell with by-wire technology, is introduced.

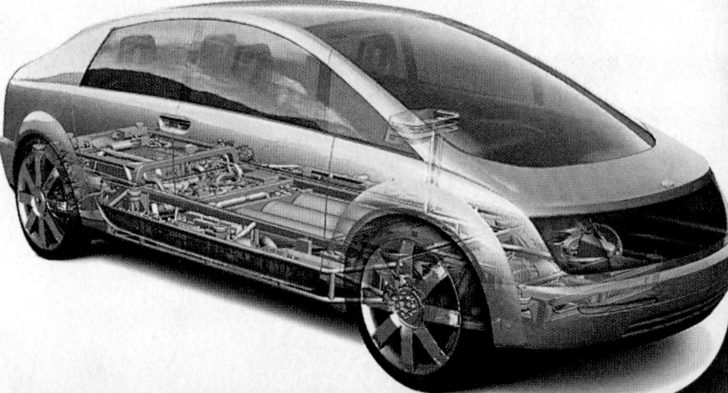

22

Chemical Bonding

The Big Idea

Atoms combine by forming ionic, covalent, and metallic bonds.

SECTION

About the Photo

What looks like a fantastic "sculpture" is really a model of deoxyribonucleic acid (DNA). DNA is one of the most complex molecules in living things. In DNA, atoms are bonded together in two very long spiral strands. These strands join to form a double spiral. The DNA in living cells has all the coding for passing on the traits of that cell and that organism.

PRE-READING ACTIVITY

FOLDNOTES **Three-Panel Flip Chart** Before you read the chapter, create the FoldNote entitled "Three-Panel Flip Chart" described in the **Study Skills** section of the Appendix. Label the flaps of the three-panel flip chart with "Ionic bond," "Covalent bond," and "Metallic bond." As you read the chapter, write information you learn about each category under the appropriate flap.

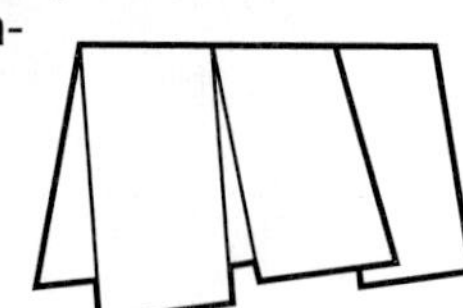

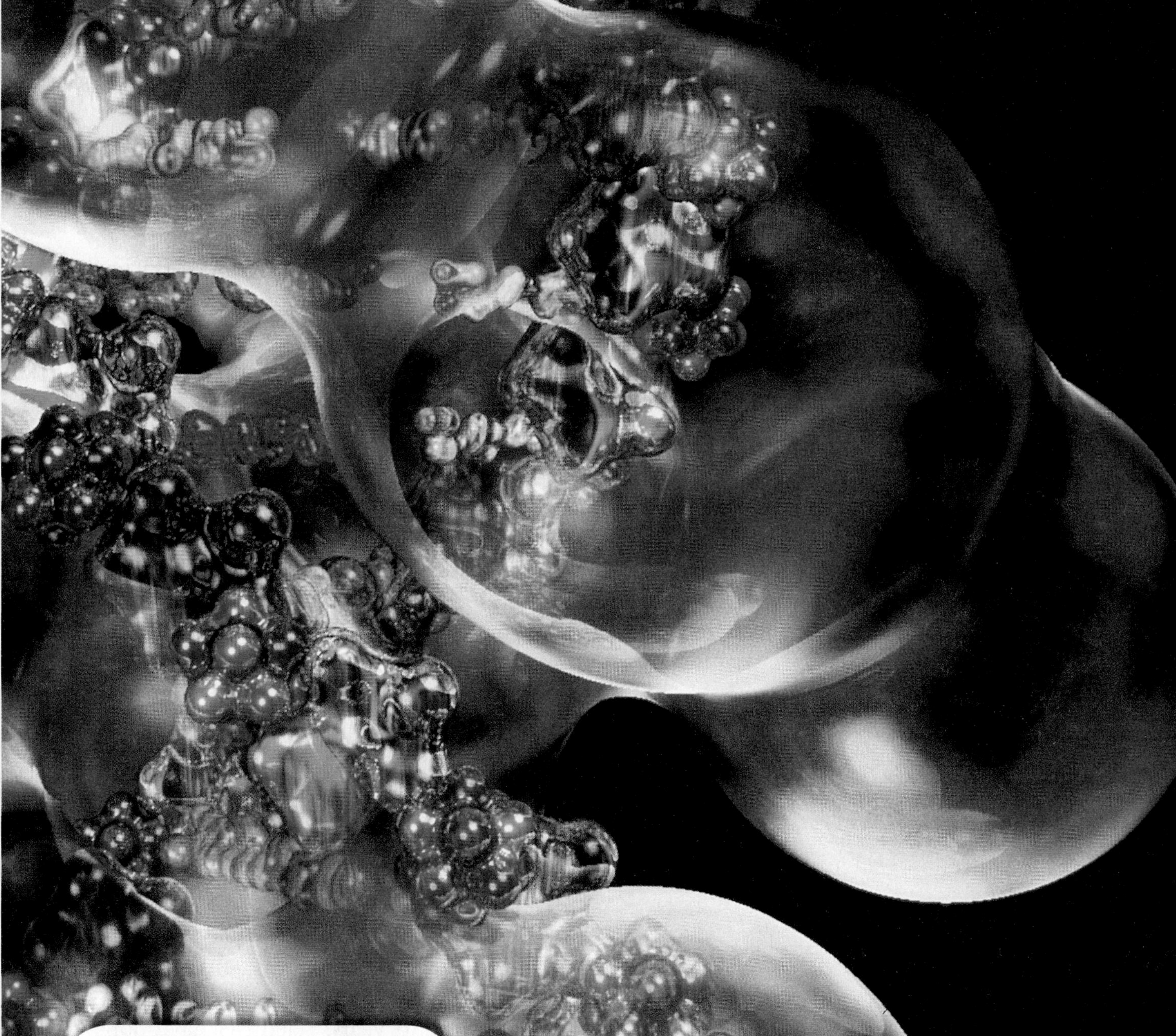

START-UP ACTIVITY

From Glue to Goop

Particles of glue can bond to other particles and hold objects together. Different types of bonds create differences in the properties of substances. In this activity, you will see how the formation of bonds causes a change in the properties of white glue.

Procedure

1. Fill a **small paper cup** 1/4 full of **white glue.** Record the properties of the glue.
2. Fill a **second small paper cup** 1/4 full of **borax solution.**
3. Pour the borax solution into the cup of white glue, and stir well using a **plastic spoon** or a **wooden craft stick.**
4. When the material becomes too thick to stir, remove it from the cup and knead it with your fingers. Record the properties of the material.

Analysis

1. Compare the properties of the glue with those of the new material.
2. The properties of the material resulted from bonds between the borax and the glue. Predict the properties of the material if less borax is used.

SECTION 1

Electrons and Chemical Bonding

What You Will Learn

- Describe chemical bonding.
- Identify the number of valence electrons in an atom.
- Predict whether an atom is likely to form bonds.

Vocabulary

chemical bonding
chemical bond
valence electron

READING STRATEGY

Discussion Read this section silently. Write down questions that you have about this section. Discuss your questions in a small group.

Have you ever stopped to consider that by using only the 26 letters of the alphabet, you make all of the words you use every day?

Although the number of letters is limited, combining the letters in different ways allows you to make a huge number of words. In the same way that words can be formed by combining letters, substances can be formed by combining atoms.

Combining Atoms Through Chemical Bonding

Look at **Figure 1.** Now, look around the room. Everything you see—desks, pencils, paper, and even your friends—is made of atoms of elements. All substances are made of atoms of one or more of the approximately 100 elements. For example, the atoms of carbon, hydrogen, and oxygen combine in different patterns to form sugar, alcohol, and citric acid. **Chemical bonding** is the joining of atoms to form new substances. The properties of these new substances are different from the properties of the original elements. An interaction that holds two atoms together is called a **chemical bond.** When chemical bonds form, electrons are shared, gained, or lost.

Discussing Bonding Using Theories and Models

We cannot see atoms and chemical bonds with the unaided eye. For more than 150 years, scientists have done many experiments that have led to a theory of chemical bonding. Remember that a theory is an explanation for some phenomenon that is based on observation, experimentation, and reasoning. The use of models helps people discuss the theory of how and why atoms form bonds.

Figure 1 *Everything you see in this photo is formed by combining atoms.*

Figure 2 Electron Arrangement in an Atom

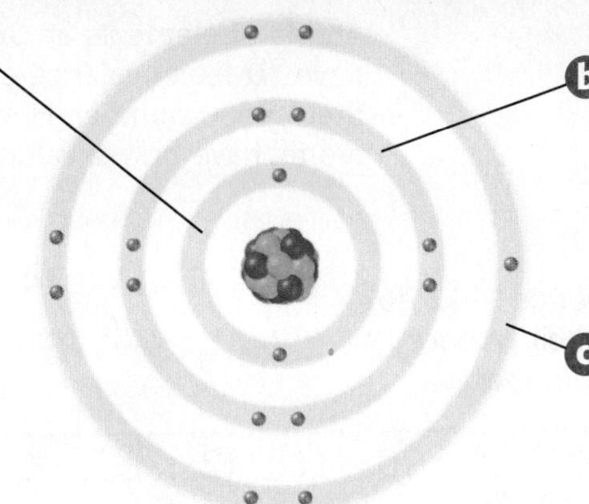

a The **first energy level** is closest to the nucleus and can hold up to 2 electrons.

b Electrons will begin filling the **second energy level** only after the first level is full. The second energy level can hold up to 8 electrons.

c The **third energy level** in this model of a chlorine atom has only 7 electrons, so the atom has a total of 17 electrons. This outer level of the atom is not full.

Electron Number and Organization

To understand how atoms form chemical bonds, you need to know about the electrons in an atom. The number of electrons in an atom can be determined from the atomic number of the element. The *atomic number* is the number of protons in an atom. But atoms have no charge. So, the atomic number also represents the number of electrons in the atom.

Electrons in an atom are organized in energy levels. **Figure 2** shows a model of the arrangement of electrons in a chlorine atom. This model and models like it are useful for counting electrons in energy levels of atoms. But, these models do not show the true structure of atoms.

chemical bonding the combining of atoms to form molecules or ionic compounds

chemical bond an interaction that holds atoms or ions together

valence electron an electron that is found in the outermost shell of an atom and that determines the atom's chemical properties

Outer-Level Electrons and Bonding

Not all of the electrons in an atom make chemical bonds. Most atoms form bonds using only the electrons in the outermost energy level. An electron in the outermost energy level of an atom is a **valence electron** (VAY luhns ee LEK TRAHN). The models in **Figure 3** show the valence electrons for two atoms.

Reading Check **Which electrons are used to form bonds?** (*See the Appendix for answers to Reading Checks.*)

Figure 3 Counting Valence Electrons

Oxygen
Electron total: 8
First level: 2 electrons
Second level: 6 electrons

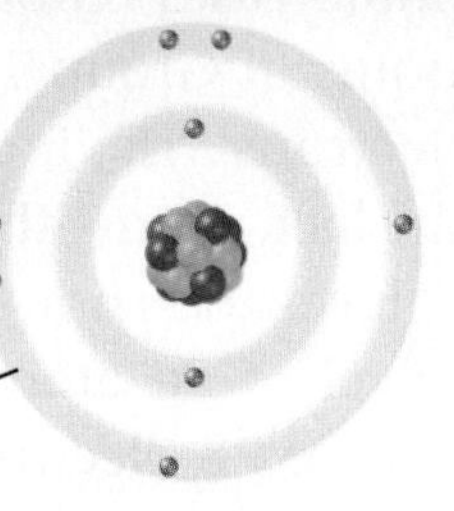

An oxygen atom has 6 valence electrons.

Sodium
Electron total: 11
First level: 2 electrons
Second level: 8 electrons
Third level: 1 electron

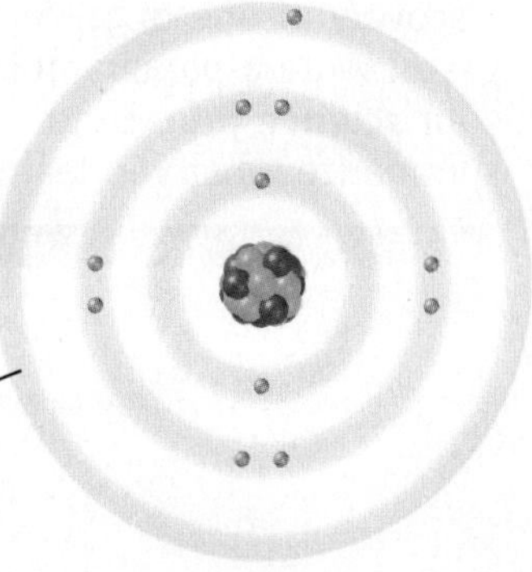

A sodium atom has 1 valence electron.

Figure 4 **Determining the Number of Valence Electrons**

Atoms of elements in **Groups 1 and 2** have the same number of valence electrons as their group number.

Atoms of elements in **Groups 13–18** have 10 fewer valence electrons than their group number. However, helium atoms have only 2 valence electrons.

Atoms of elements in **Groups 3–12** do not have a rule relating their valence electrons to their group number.

1	2	3	4	5	6	7	8	9	10	11	12	13	14	15	16	17	18
H																	He
Li	Be											B	C	N	O	F	Ne
Na	Mg											Al	Si	P	S	Cl	Ar
K	Ca	Sc	Ti	V	Cr	Mn	Fe	Co	Ni	Cu	Zn	Ga	Ge	As	Se	Br	Kr
Rb	Sr	Y	Zr	Nb	Mo	Tc	Ru	Rh	Pd	Ag	Cd	In	Sn	Sb	Te	I	Xe
Cs	Ba	La	Hf	Ta	W	Re	Os	Ir	Pt	Au	Hg	Tl	Pb	Bi	Po	At	Rn
Fr	Ra	Ac	Rf	Db	Sg	Bh	Hs	Mt	Ds	Uuu	Uub	Uut	Uuq	Uup			

CONNECTION TO Social Studies

WRITING SKILL **History of a Noble Gas** When Dmitri Mendeleev organized the first periodic table, he did not include the noble gases. The noble gases had not been discovered at that time. Research the history of the discovery of one of the noble gases. Write a paragraph in your **science journal** to summarize what you learned.

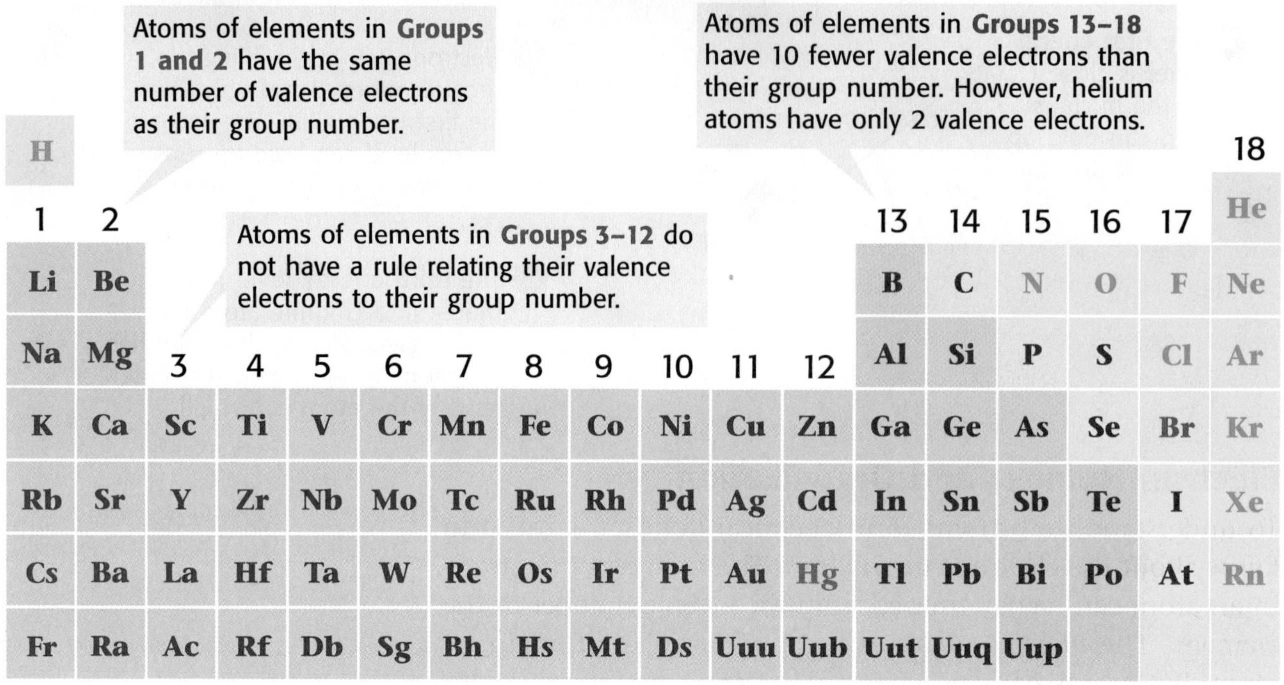

Valence Electrons and the Periodic Table

You can use a model to determine the number of valence electrons of an atom. But what would you do if you didn't have a model? You can use the periodic table to determine the number of valence electrons for atoms of some elements.

Elements are grouped based on similar properties. Within a group, or family, the atoms of each element have the same number of valence electrons. So, the group numbers can help you determine the number of valence electrons for some atoms, as shown in **Figure 4.**

To Bond or Not to Bond

Not all atoms bond in the same manner. In fact, some atoms rarely bond at all! The number of electrons in the outermost energy level of an atom determines whether an atom will form bonds.

Atoms of the noble gases (Group 18) do not usually form chemical bonds. Atoms of Group 18 elements (except helium) have 8 valence electrons. Having 8 valence electrons is a special condition. In fact, atoms that have 8 electrons in their outermost energy level do not usually form bonds. The outermost energy level of an atom is considered to be full if the energy level contains 8 electrons.

Reading Check **The atoms of which group in the periodic table rarely form chemical bonds?**

Filling The Outermost Level

An atom that has fewer than 8 valence electrons is much more likely to form bonds than an atom that has 8 valence electrons is. Atoms bond by gaining, losing, or sharing electrons to have a filled outermost energy level. A filled outermost level contains 8 valence electrons. **Figure 5** describes how atoms can achieve a filled outermost energy level.

Is Two Electrons a Full Set?

Not all atoms need 8 valence electrons to have a filled outermost energy level. Helium atoms need only 2 valence electrons. The outermost energy level in a helium atom is the first energy level. The first energy level of any atom can hold only 2 electrons. So, the outermost energy level of a helium atom is full if the energy level has only 2 electrons. Atoms of hydrogen and lithium also form bonds by gaining, losing, or sharing electrons to achieve 2 electrons in the first energy level.

Figure 5 Filling Outermost Energy Levels

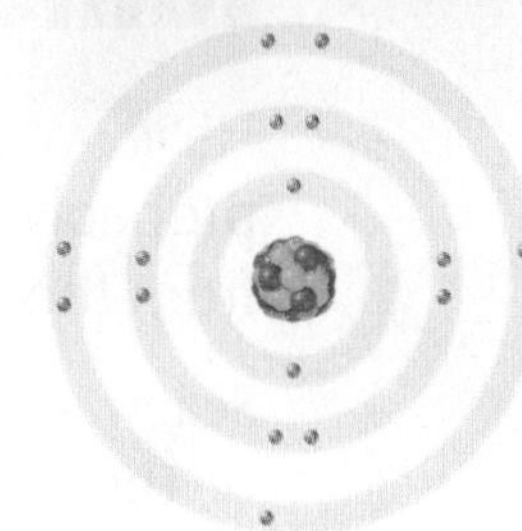

Sulfur An atom of sulfur has 6 valence electrons. It can have 8 valence electrons by sharing 2 electrons with or gaining 2 electrons from other atoms.

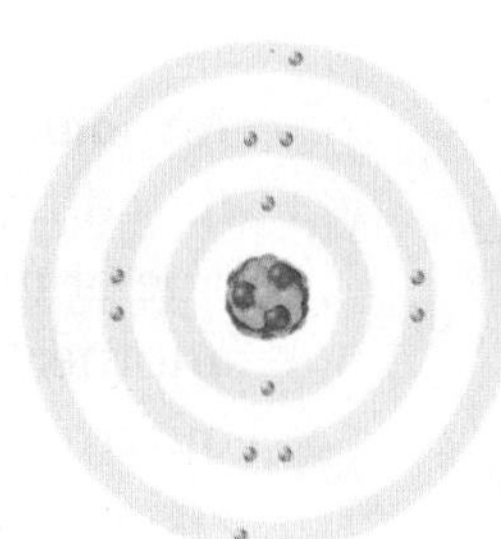

Magnesium An atom of magnesium has 2 valence electrons. It can have a full outer level by losing 2 electrons. The second energy level becomes the outermost energy level and contains 8 electrons.

SECTION Review

Summary

- Chemical bonding is the joining of atoms to form new substances. A chemical bond is an interaction that holds two atoms together.
- A valence electron is an electron in the outermost energy level of an atom.
- Most atoms form bonds by gaining, losing, or sharing electrons until they have 8 valence electrons. Atoms of some elements need only 2 electrons to fill their outermost level.

Using Key Terms

1. Use the following terms in the same sentence: *chemical bond* and *valence electron.*

Understanding Key Ideas

2. Which of the following atoms do not usually form bonds?
   a. calcium **c.** hydrogen
   b. neon **d.** oxygen
3. Describe chemical bonding.
4. Explain how to use the valence electrons in an atom to predict if the atom will form bonds.

Critical Thinking

5. **Making Inferences** How can an atom that has 5 valence electrons achieve a full set of valence electrons?
6. **Applying Concepts** Identify the number of valence electrons in a barium atom.

Interpreting Graphics

7. Look at the model below. How many valence electrons are in a fluorine atom? Will fluorine atoms form bonds? Explain.

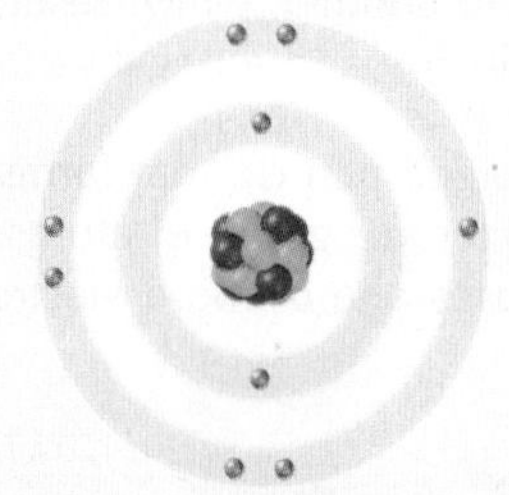

Fluorine

SCILINKS
NSTA
Developed and maintained by the National Science Teachers Association
For a variety of links related to this chapter, go to www.scilinks.org
Topic: The Electron; Periodic Table
SciLinks code: HSM0489; HSM1125

SECTION 2

Ionic Bonds

Have you ever accidentally tasted sea water? If so, you probably didn't enjoy it. What makes sea water taste different from the water in your home?

What You Will Learn

- Explain how ionic bonds form.
- Describe how positive ions form.
- Describe how negative ions form.
- Explain why ionic compounds are neutral.

Vocabulary

ionic bond
ion
crystal lattice

READING STRATEGY

Paired Summarizing Read this section silently. In pairs, take turns summarizing the material. Stop to discuss ideas that seem confusing.

Sea water tastes different because salt is dissolved in it. One of the salts in sea water is the same as the salt that you eat. The chemical bonds in salt are ionic (ie AHN ik) bonds.

Forming Ionic Bonds

An **ionic bond** is a bond that forms when electrons are transferred from one atom to another atom. During ionic bonding, one or more valence electrons are transferred from one atom to another. Like all chemical bonds, ionic bonds form so that the outermost energy levels of the atoms in the bonds are filled. **Figure 1** shows another substance that contains ionic bonds.

Charged Particles

An atom is neutral because the number of electrons in an atom equals the number of protons. So, the charges of the electrons and protons cancel each other. A transfer of electrons between atoms changes the number of electrons in each atom. But the number of protons stays the same in each atom. The negative charges and positive charges no longer cancel out, and the atoms become ions. **Ions** are charged particles that form when atoms gain or lose electrons. An atom normally cannot gain electrons without another atom nearby to lose electrons (or cannot lose electrons without a nearby atom to gain them). But it is easier to study the formation of ions one at a time.

ionic bond a bond that forms when electrons are transferred from one atom to another, which results in a positive ion and a negative ion

ion a charged particle that forms when an atom or group of atoms gains or loses one or more electrons

Reading Check **Why are atoms neutral?** *(See the Appendix for answers to Reading Checks.)*

Figure 1 *Calcium carbonate in this snail's shell contains ionic bonds.*

Figure 2 **Forming Positive Ions**

Here's How It Works: During chemical changes, a sodium atom can lose its 1 electron in the third energy level to another atom. The filled second level becomes the outermost level, so the resulting sodium ion has 8 valence electrons.

Sodium atom (Na)
11+ protons
11− electrons
0 charge

Sodium ion (Na^+)
11+ protons
10− electrons
1+ charge

Here's How It Works: During chemical changes, an aluminum atom can lose its 3 electrons in the third energy level to another atom. The filled second level becomes the outermost level, so the resulting aluminum ion has 8 valence electrons.

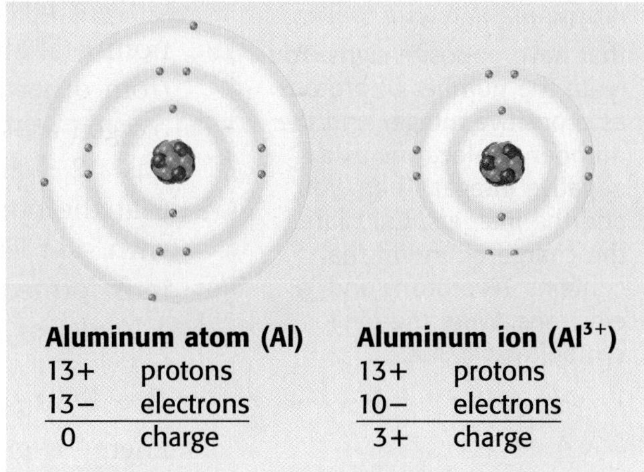

Forming Positive Ions

Ionic bonds form during chemical changes when atoms pull electrons away from other atoms. The atoms that lose electrons form ions that have fewer electrons than protons. Because the positive charges outnumber the negative charges, these ions have a positive charge.

Metal Atoms and the Loss of Electrons

Atoms of most metals have few valence electrons. Metal atoms tend to lose these valence electrons and form positive ions. Look at the models in **Figure 2.** When a sodium atom loses its only valence electron to another atom, the sodium atom becomes a sodium ion. A sodium ion has 1 more proton than it has electrons. So, the sodium ion has a 1+ charge. The chemical symbol for this ion is written as Na^+. Notice that the charge is written to the upper right of the chemical symbol. **Figure 2** also shows a model for the formation of an aluminum ion.

The Energy Needed to Lose Electrons

Energy is needed to pull electrons away from atoms. Only a small amount of energy is needed to take electrons from metal atoms. In fact, the energy needed to remove electrons from atoms of elements in Groups 1 and 2 is so small that these elements react very easily. The energy needed to take electrons from metals comes from the formation of negative ions.

Studying Salt

Spread several grains of salt on a dark sheet of construction paper. Use a magnifying lens to examine the salt. Ask an adult at home to examine the salt. Discuss what you saw. Then, gently tap the salt with a small hammer. Examine the salt again. Describe your observations in your **science journal.**

ACTIVITY

Calculating Charge

Calculating the charge of an ion is the same as adding integers (positive or negative whole numbers and 0) that have opposite signs. You write the number of protons as a positive integer and the number of electrons as a negative integer. Then, you add the integers. Calculate the charge of an ion that contains 16 protons and 18 electrons. Write the ion's symbol and name.

Forming Negative Ions

Some atoms gain electrons from other atoms during chemical changes. The ions that form have more electrons than protons. So, these ions have a negative charge.

Nonmetal Atoms Gain Electrons

The outermost energy level of nonmetal atoms is almost full. Only a few electrons are needed to fill the outer level of a nonmetal atom. So, atoms of nonmetals tend to gain electrons from other atoms. Look at the models in **Figure 3.** When an oxygen atom gains 2 electrons, it becomes an oxide ion that has a 2− charge. The symbol for the oxide ion is O^{2-}. Notice that the name of the negative ion formed from oxygen ends with *-ide*. This ending is used for the names of the negative ions formed when atoms gain electrons. **Figure 3** also shows a model of how a chloride ion is formed.

The Energy of Gaining Electrons

Energy is given off by most nonmetal atoms when they gain electrons. The more easily an atom gains an electron, the more energy the atom releases. Atoms of Group 17 elements give off the most energy when they gain an electron. These elements are very reactive. An ionic bond will form between a metal and a nonmetal if the nonmetal releases more energy than is needed to take electrons from the metal.

Reading Check **Atoms of which group on the periodic table give off the most energy when forming negative ions?**

Figure 3 **Forming Negative Ions**

Here's How It Works: During chemical changes, an oxygen atom gains 2 electrons in the second energy level from another atom. An oxide ion that has 8 valence electrons is formed. Thus, its outermost energy level is filled.

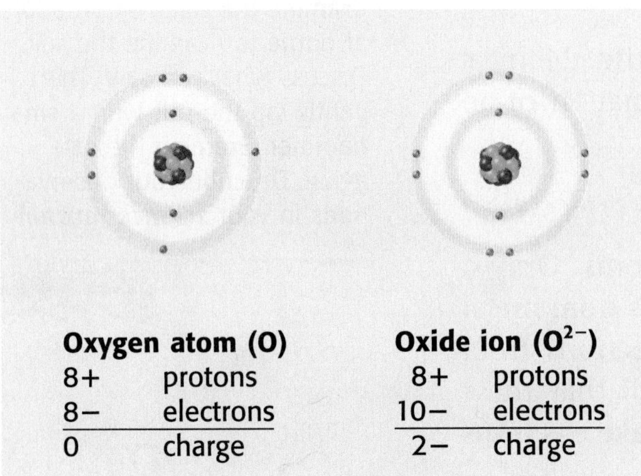

Here's How It Works: During chemical changes, a chlorine atom gains 1 electron in the third energy level from another atom. A chloride ion that has 8 valence electrons is formed. Thus, its outermost energy level is filled.

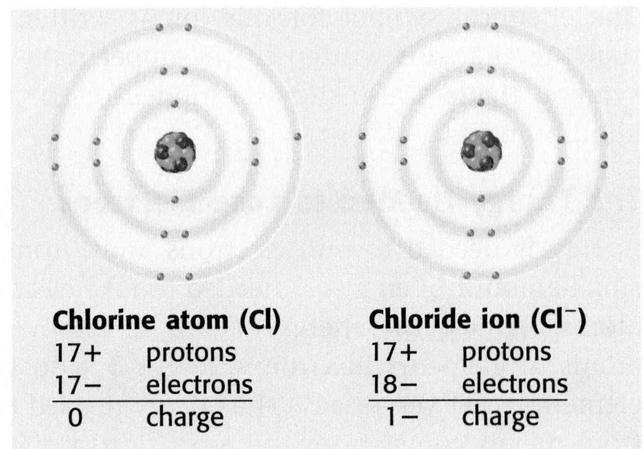

Ionic Compounds

When ionic bonds form, the number of electrons lost by the metal atoms equals the number gained by the nonmetal atoms. The ions that bond are charged, but the compound formed is neutral because the charges of the ions cancel each other. When ions bond, they form a repeating three-dimensional pattern called a **crystal lattice** (KRIS tuhl LAT is), like the one shown in **Figure 4.** The strong attraction between ions in a crystal lattice gives ionic compounds certain properties, which include brittleness, high melting points, and high boiling points.

crystal lattice the regular pattern in which a crystal is arranged

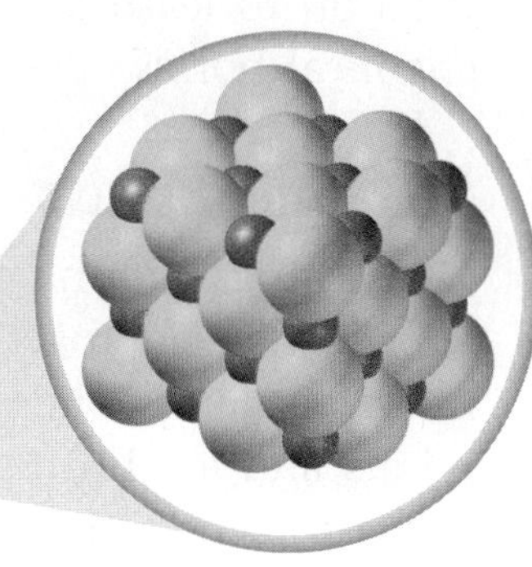

Figure 4 *This model of the crystal lattice of sodium chloride, or table salt, shows a three-dimensional view of the bonded ions. In the model, the sodium ions are pink and the chloride ions are green.*

SECTION Review

Summary

- An ionic bond is a bond that forms when electrons are transferred from one atom to another. During ionic bonding, the atoms become oppositely charged ions.
- Ionic bonding usually occurs between atoms of metals and atoms of nonmetals.
- Energy is needed to remove electrons from metal atoms. Energy is released when most nonmetal atoms gain electrons.

Using Key Terms

1. Use the following terms in the same sentence: *ion* and *ionic bond.*
2. In your own words, write a definition for the term *crystal lattice.*

Understanding Key Ideas

3. Which types of atoms usually become negative ions?
   a. metals
   b. nonmetals
   c. noble gases
   d. All of the above
4. How does an atom become a positive ion? a negative ion?
5. What are two properties of ionic compounds?

Math Skills

6. What is the charge of an ion that has 12 protons and 10 electrons? Write the ion's symbol.

Critical Thinking

7. **Applying Concepts** Which group of elements gains two valence electrons when the atoms form ionic bonds?
8. **Identifying Relationships** Explain why ionic compounds are neutral even though they are made up of charged particles.
9. **Making Comparisons** Compare the formation of positive ions with the formation of negative ions in terms of energy changes.

SCILINKS.
NSTA
Developed and maintained by the National Science Teachers Association
For a variety of links related to this chapter, go to www.scilinks.org
Topic: Types of Chemical Bonds
SciLinks code: HSM1565

SECTION 3

Covalent and Metallic Bonds

What You Will Learn

- Explain how covalent bonds form.
- Describe molecules.
- Explain how metallic bonds form.
- Describe the properties of metals.

Vocabulary

covalent bond
molecule
metallic bond

READING STRATEGY

Reading Organizer As you read this section, create an outline of the section. Use the headings from the section in your outline.

Imagine bending a wooden coat hanger and a wire coat hanger. The wire one would bend easily, but the wooden one would break. Why do these things behave differently?

One reason is that the bonds between the atoms of each object are different. The atoms of the wooden hanger are held together by covalent bonds (KOH VAY luhnt BAHNDZ). But the atoms of the wire hanger are held together by metallic bonds. Read on to learn about the difference between these kinds of chemical bonds.

Covalent Bonds

Most things around you, such as water, sugar, oxygen, and wood, are held together by covalent bonds. Substances that have covalent bonds tend to have low melting and boiling points and are brittle in the solid state. For example, oxygen has a low boiling point, which is why it is a gas at room temperature. And wood is brittle, so it breaks when bent.

A **covalent bond** forms when atoms share one or more pairs of electrons. When two atoms of nonmetals bond, a large amount of energy is needed for either atom to lose an electron. So, two nonmetals don't transfer electrons to fill the outermost energy levels of their atoms. Instead, two nonmetal atoms bond by sharing electrons with each another, as shown in the model in **Figure 1.**

covalent bond a bond formed when atoms share one or more pairs of electrons

Reading Check What is a covalent bond? (*See the Appendix for answers to Reading Checks.*)

Figure 1 *By sharing electrons in a covalent bond, each hydrogen atom (the smallest atom) has a full outermost energy level containing two electrons.*

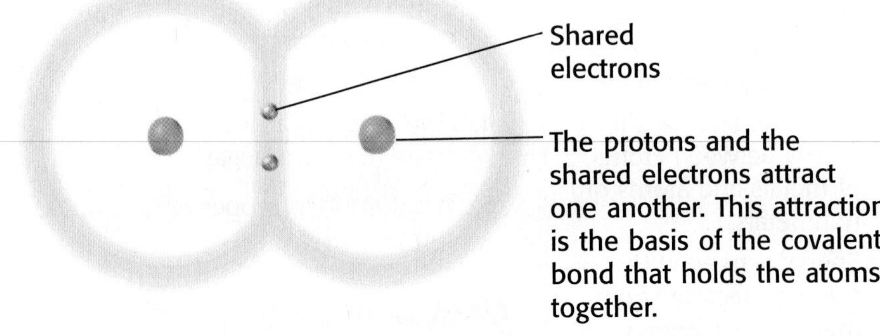
Shared electrons
The protons and the shared electrons attract one another. This attraction is the basis of the covalent bond that holds the atoms together.

Figure 2 Covalent Bonds in a Water Molecule

The oxygen atom shares one of its electrons with each of the two hydrogen atoms. It now has its outermost level filled with 8 electrons.
Each hydrogen atom shares its 1 electron with the oxygen atom. Each hydrogen atom now has an outer level filled with 2 electrons.
:Ö:H
H

This electron-dot diagram for water shows only the outermost level of electrons for each atom. But you still see how the atoms share electrons.

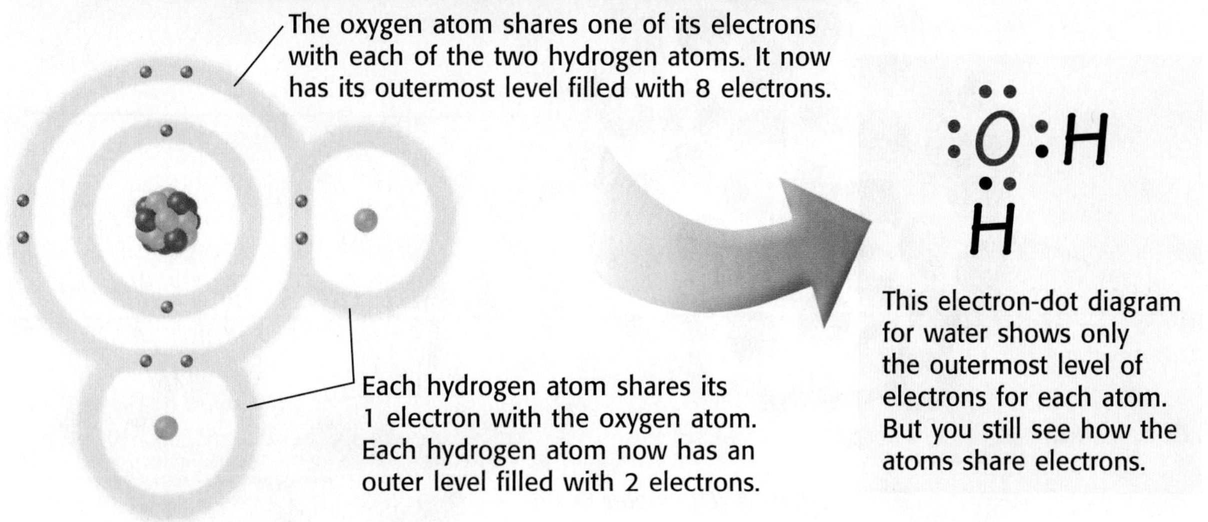

Covalent Bonds and Molecules

Substances containing covalent bonds consist of individual particles called molecules (MAHL i KYOOLZ). A **molecule** usually consists of two or more atoms joined in a definite ratio. A hydrogen molecule is composed of two covalently bonded hydrogen atoms. However, most molecules are composed of atoms of two or more elements. The models in **Figure 2** show two ways to represent the covalent bonds in a water molecule.

molecule the smallest unit of a substance that keeps all of the physical and chemical properties of that substance

One way to represent atoms and molecules is to use electron-dot diagrams. An electron-dot diagram is a model that shows only the valence electrons in an atom. Electron-dot diagrams can help you predict how atoms might bond. To draw an electron-dot diagram, write the symbol of the element and place one dot around the symbol for every valence electron in the atom, as shown in **Figure 3.** Place the first 4 dots alone on each side, and then pair up any remaining dots.

Figure 3 Using Electron-Dot Diagrams

Carbon atoms have 4 valence electrons. A carbon atom needs 4 more electrons to have a filled outermost energy level.

Oxygen atoms have 6 valence electrons. An oxygen atom needs only 2 more electrons to have a filled outer-most energy level.

Krypton atoms have 8 valence electrons. Krypton is nonreactive. Krypton atoms do not need any more electrons.

This diagram rep-resents a hydrogen molecule. The dots between the letters represent a pair of shared electrons.

Figure 4 *The water in this fishbowl is made up of many tiny water molecules. Each molecule is the smallest particle that has the chemical properties of water.*

Covalent Compounds and Molecules

An atom is the smallest particle into which an element can be divided and still be the same element. Likewise, a molecule is the smallest particle into which a covalently bonded compound can be divided and still be the same compound. Look at the three-dimensional models in **Figure 4.** They show how a sample of water is made up of many individual molecules of water. Imagine dividing water over and over. You would eventually end up with a single molecule of water. What would happen if you separated the hydrogen and oxygen atoms that make up a water molecule? Then, you would no longer have water.

For another activity related to this chapter, go to **go.hrw.com** and type in the keyword **HP5BNDW.**

The Simplest Molecules

Molecules are composed of at least two covalently bonded atoms. The simplest molecules are made up of two bonded atoms. Molecules made up of two atoms are called *diatomic molecules*. Elements that are found in nature as diatomic molecules are called *diatomic elements*. Hydrogen is a diatomic element. Oxygen, nitrogen, and the halogens fluorine, chlorine, bromine, and iodine are also diatomic elements. Look at **Figure 5.** The shared electrons are counted as valence electrons for each atom. So, both atoms of the molecule have filled outermost energy levels.

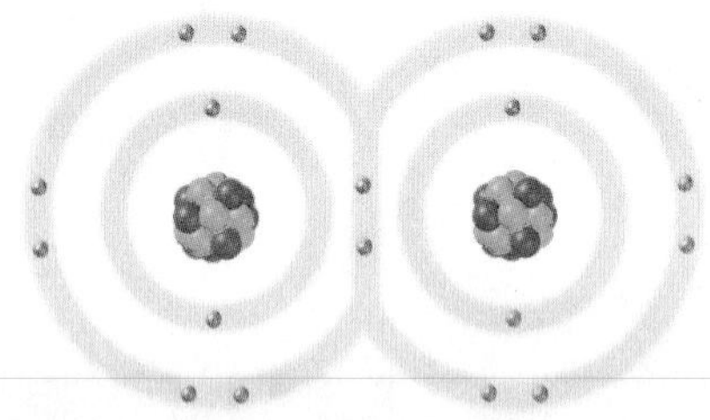

Figure 5 *Two covalently bonded fluorine atoms have filled outermost energy levels. The two electrons shared by the atoms are counted as valence electrons for each atom.*

Reading Check **How many atoms are in a diatomic molecule?**

Figure 6 *A granola bar contains sucrose, or table sugar. A molecule of sucrose is composed of carbon atoms, hydrogen atoms, and oxygen atoms joined by covalent bonds.*

More-Complex Molecules

Diatomic molecules are the simplest molecules. They are also some of the most important molecules. You could not live without diatomic oxygen molecules. But other important molecules are much more complex. Soap, plastic bottles, and even proteins in your body are examples of complex molecules. Carbon atoms are the basis of many of these complex molecules. Each carbon atom needs to make four covalent bonds to have 8 valence electrons. These bonds can be with atoms of other elements or with other carbon atoms, as shown in the model in **Figure 6.**

CONNECTION TO Biology

Proteins Proteins perform many functions throughout your body. A single protein can have thousands of covalently bonded atoms. Proteins are built from smaller molecules called *amino acids.* Make a poster showing how amino acids are joined to make proteins.

ACTIVITY

Metallic Bonds

Look at the unusual metal sculptures shown in **Figure 7.** Some metal pieces have been flattened, while other metal pieces have been shaped into wires. How could the artist change the shape of the metal into all of these different forms without breaking the metal into pieces? Metal can be shaped because of the presence of a metallic bond, a special kind of chemical bond. A **metallic bond** is a bond formed by the attraction between positively charged metal ions and the electrons in the metal. Positively charged metal ions form when metal atoms lose electrons.

metallic bond a bond formed by the attraction between positively charged metal ions and the electrons around them

Figure 7 *The different shapes of metal in these sculptures are possible because of the bonds that hold the metal together.*

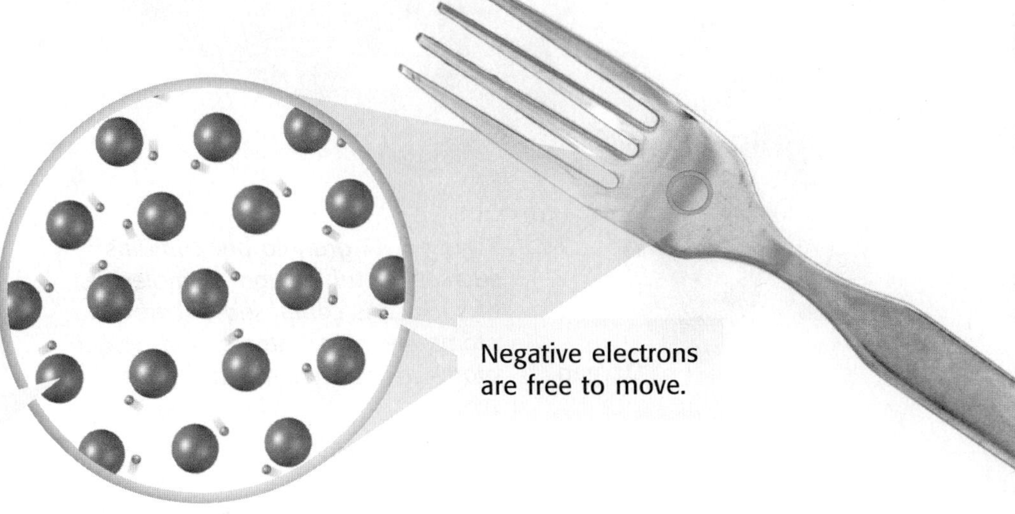
The positive metal ions are in fixed positions in the metal.
Negative electrons are free to move.

Figure 8 *Moving electrons are attracted to the metal ions, and the attraction forms metallic bonds.*

Movement of Electrons Throughout a Metal

Bonding in metals is a result of the metal atoms being so close to one another that their outermost energy levels overlap. This overlapping allows valence electrons to move throughout the metal, as shown in **Figure 8.** You can think of a metal as being made up of positive metal ions that have enough valence electrons "swimming" around to keep the ions together. The electrons also cancel the positive charge of the ions. Metallic bonds extend throughout the metal in all directions.

Quick Lab

Bending with Bonds

1. Straighten out a **wire paper clip.** Record your observations.
2. Bend a **piece of chalk.** Record your observations.
3. Chalk is composed of calcium carbonate, a compound containing ionic bonds. What kind of bond is present in the paper clip?
4. Explain why you could change the shape of the paper clip but could not bend the chalk without breaking it.

Properties of Metals

Metallic bonding is what gives metals their particular properties. These properties include electrical conductivity, malleability, and ductility.

Conducting Electric Current

Metallic bonding allows metals to conduct electric current. For example, when you turn on a lamp, electrons move within the copper wire that connects the lamp to the outlet. The electrons that move are the valence electrons in the copper atoms. These electrons are free to move because the electrons are not connected to any one atom.

Reshaping Metals

Because the electrons swim freely around the metal ions, the atoms in metals can be rearranged. As a result, metals can be reshaped. The properties of *ductility* (the ability to be drawn into wires) and *malleability* (the ability to be hammered into sheets) describe a metal's ability to be reshaped. For example, copper is made into wires for use in electrical cords. Aluminum can be pounded into thin sheets and made into aluminum foil.

Reading Check What is ductility?

Bending Without Breaking

When a piece of metal is bent, some of the metal ions are forced closer together. You might expect the metal to break because all of the metal ions are positively charged. Positively charged ions repel one another. However, positive ions in a metal are always surrounded by and attracted to the electrons in the metal—even if the metal ions move. The electrons constantly move around and between the metal ions. The moving electrons maintain the metallic bonds no matter how the shape of the metal changes. So, metal objects can be bent without being broken, as shown in **Figure 9.**

Figure 9 *Metal can be reshaped without breaking because metallic bonds occur in many directions.*

SECTION Review

Summary

- In covalent bonding, two atoms share electrons. A covalent bond forms when atoms share one or more pairs of electrons.
- Covalently bonded atoms form a particle called a *molecule*. A molecule is the smallest particle of a compound that has the chemical properties of the compound.
- In metallic bonding, the valence electrons move throughout the metal. A bond formed by the attraction between positive metal ions and the electrons in the metal is a metallic bond.
- Properties of metals include conductivity, ductility, and malleability.

Using Key Terms

1. Use each of the following terms in a separate sentence: *covalent bond* and *metallic bond.*
2. In your own words, write a definition for the term *molecule.*

Understanding Key Ideas

3. Between which of the following atoms is a covalent bond most likely to occur?
   a. calcium and lithium
   b. sodium and fluorine
   c. nitrogen and oxygen
   d. helium and argon
4. What happens to the electrons in covalent bonding?
5. How many dots does an electron-dot diagram of a sulfur atom have?
6. List three properties of metals that are a result of metallic bonds.
7. Describe how the valence electrons in a metal move.
8. Explain the difference between ductility and malleability. Give an example of when each property is useful.

Critical Thinking

9. **Identifying Relationships** How do the metallic bonds in a staple allow it to function properly?
10. **Applying Concepts** Draw an electron-dot diagram for ammonia (a nitrogen atom covalently bonded to three hydrogen atoms).

Interpreting Graphics

11. This electron-dot diagram is not complete. Which atom needs to form another bond? Explain.

```
   H
   ••
H: C :H
   •
```

SCILINKS
NSTA
Developed and maintained by the National Science Teachers Association
For a variety of links related to this chapter, go to www.scilinks.org
Topic: Types of Chemical Bonds; Properties of Metals
SciLinks code: HSM1565; HSM1231

Model-Making Lab

Covalent Marshmallows

OBJECTIVES

Build a three-dimensional model of a water molecule.

Draw an electron-dot diagram of a water molecule.

MATERIALS

- marshmallows (two of one color, one of another color)
- toothpicks

SAFETY

A hydrogen atom has 1 electron in its outermost energy level, but 2 electrons are required to fill its outermost level. An oxygen atom has 6 electrons in its outermost level, but 8 electrons are required to fill its outermost level. To fill their outermost energy levels, two atoms of hydrogen and one atom of oxygen can share electrons, as shown below. Such a sharing of electrons to fill the outermost level of atoms is called *covalent bonding*. When hydrogen and oxygen bond in this manner, a molecule of water is formed. In this lab, you will build a three-dimensional model of water to better understand the covalent bonds formed in a water molecule.

A Model of a Water Molecule

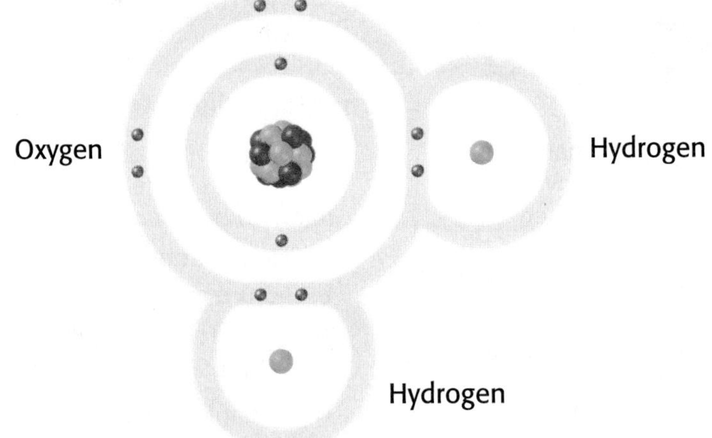

Procedure

1. Using the marshmallows and toothpicks, create a model of a water molecule. Use the diagram above for guidance in building your model.
2. Draw a sketch of your model. Be sure to label the hydrogen and oxygen atoms on your sketch.
3. Draw an electron-dot diagram of the water molecule.

Analyze the Results

1. **Classifying** What do the marshmallows represent? What do the toothpicks represent?

2. **Evaluating Models** Why are the marshmallows different colors?

3. **Analyzing Results** Compare your model with the diagram on the previous page. How might your model be improved to more accurately represent a water molecule?

Draw Conclusions

4. **Making Predictions** Hydrogen in nature can covalently bond to form hydrogen molecules, H_2. How could you use the marshmallows and toothpicks to model this bond?

5. **Applying Conclusions** Draw an electron-dot diagram of a hydrogen molecule.

6. **Drawing Conclusions** Which do you think would be more difficult to create—a model of an ionic bond or a model of a covalent bond? Explain your answer.

Applying Your Data

Create a model of a carbon dioxide molecule, which consists of two oxygen atoms and one carbon atom. The structure is similar to the structure of water, although the three atoms bond in a straight line instead of at angles. The bond between each oxygen atom and the carbon atom in a carbon dioxide molecule is a *double bond,* so use two connections. Do the double bonds in carbon dioxide appear stronger or weaker than the single bonds in water? Explain your answer.

Chapter Review

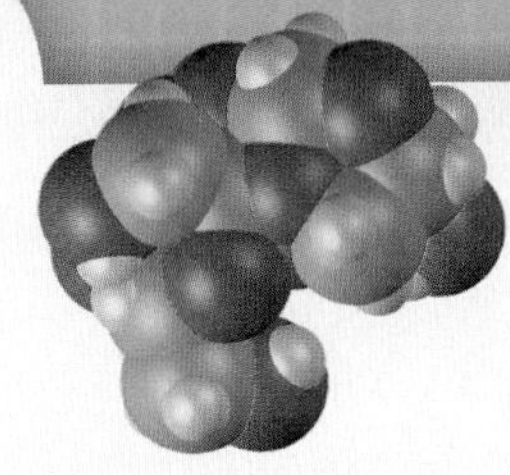

USING KEY TERMS

Complete each of the following sentences by choosing the correct term from the word bank.

crystal lattice	ionic bond
molecule	chemical bond
chemical bonding	metallic bond
valence electron	ion
covalent bond	

1. An interaction that holds two atoms together is a(n) ___.

2. A charged particle that forms when an atom transfers electrons is a(n) ___.

3. A bond formed when atoms share electrons is a(n) ___.

4. Electrons free to move throughout a material are associated with a(n) ___.

5. An electron in the outermost energy level of an atom is a(n) ___.

6. Ionic compounds are bonded in a three-dimensional pattern called a(n) ___.

UNDERSTANDING KEY IDEAS

Multiple Choice

7. Which element has a full outermost energy level containing only two electrons?
   - **a.** fluorine, F
   - **b.** helium, He
   - **c.** hydrogen, H
   - **d.** oxygen, O

8. Which of the following describes what happens when an atom becomes an ion with a 2– charge?
   - **a.** The atom gains 2 protons.
   - **b.** The atom loses 2 protons.
   - **c.** The atom gains 2 electrons.
   - **d.** The atom loses 2 electrons.

9. The properties of ductility and malleability are associated with which type of bonds?
   - **a.** ionic
   - **b.** covalent
   - **c.** metallic
   - **d.** All of the above

10. What type of element tends to lose electrons when it forms bonds?
    - **a.** metal
    - **b.** metalloid
    - **c.** nonmetal
    - **d.** noble gas

11. Which pair of atoms can form an ionic bond?
    - **a.** sodium, Na, and potassium, K
    - **b.** potassium, K, and fluorine, F
    - **c.** fluorine, F, and chlorine, Cl
    - **d.** sodium, Na, and neon, Ne

Short Answer

12. List two properties of covalent compounds.

13. Explain why an iron ion is attracted to a sulfide ion but not to a zinc ion.

14. Compare the three types of bonds based on what happens to the valence electrons of the atoms.

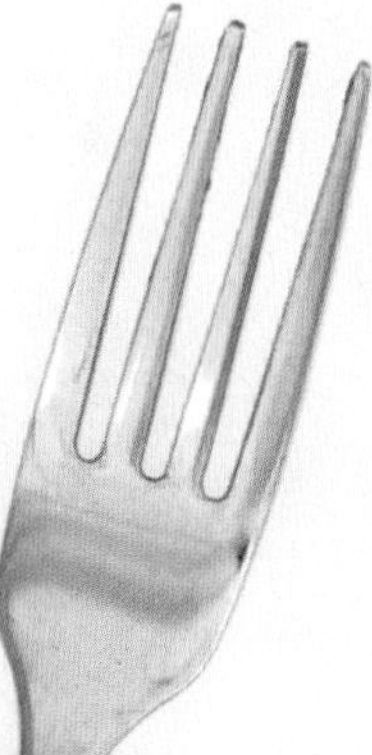

Math Skills

15. For each atom below, write the number of electrons it must gain or lose to have 8 valence electrons. Then, calculate the charge of the ion that would form.
    - **a.** calcium, Ca
    - **b.** phosphorus, P
    - **c.** bromine, Br
    - **d.** sulfur, S

CRITICAL THINKING

16. **Concept Mapping** Use the following terms to create a concept map: *chemical bonds, ionic bonds, covalent bonds, metallic bonds, molecule,* and *ions.*

17. **Identifying Relationships** Predict the type of bond each of the following pairs of atoms would form:
    - **a.** zinc, Zn, and zinc, Zn
    - **b.** oxygen, O, and nitrogen, N
    - **c.** phosphorus, P, and oxygen, O
    - **d.** magnesium, Mg, and chlorine, Cl

18. **Applying Concepts** Draw electron-dot diagrams for each of the following atoms, and state how many bonds it will have to make to fill its outer energy level.
    - **a.** sulfur, S
    - **b.** nitrogen, N
    - **c.** neon, Ne
    - **d.** iodine, I
    - **e.** silicon, Si

19. **Predicting Consequences** Using your knowledge of valence electrons, explain the main reason so many different molecules are made from carbon atoms.

20. **Making Inferences** Does the substance being hit in the photo below contain ionic or metallic bonds? Explain your answer.

INTERPRETING GRAPHICS

Use the picture of a wooden pencil below to answer the questions that follow.

21. In which part of the pencil are metallic bonds found?

22. List three materials in the pencil that are composed of molecules that have covalent bonds.

23. Identify two differences between the properties of the material that has metallic bonds and the materials that have covalent bonds.

Multiple Choice

Use the figure below to answer question 1.

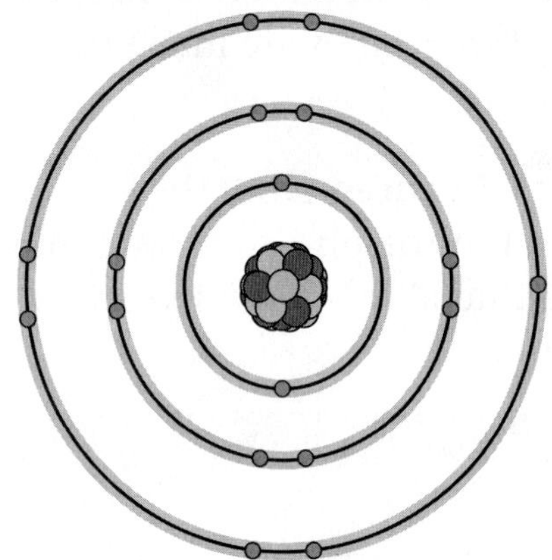

1. **What is the maximum number of electrons that can be held in the second energy level of an atom?**

   A. 2

   B. 7

   C. 8

   D. 9

2. **What happens when a nonmetal atom gains an electron from another atom? Energy is**

   A. given off by the atom losing the electron.

   B. given off by the atom gaining the electron.

   C. absorbed by the atom gaining the electron.

   D. transferred to the atom gaining the electron.

3. **An aluminum ion has 13 protons, 14 neutrons, and 10 electrons. What is the charge of an aluminum ion?**

   A. 10−

   B. 3−

   C. 1+

   D. 3+

4. **The atoms of elements in Group 17 of the periodic table are very reactive. Which of the following best describes the energy transfers that happen with the elements in this group?**

   A. The more easily an atom loses an electron, the less energy the atom releases.

   B. The more easily an atom gains an electron, the less energy the atom releases.

   C. The more easily an atom loses an electron, the more energy the atom releases.

   D. The more easily an atom gains an electron, the more energy the atom releases.

5. **Sodium chloride, or table salt, is formed when a chlorine atom takes an electron from a neighboring sodium atom. Which of the following describes the force that holds the resulting chlorine particle and the resulting sodium particle together?**

   A. an ionic bond

   B. a neutral bond

   C. a metallic bond

   D. a covalent bond

Use the diagram below to answer question 6.

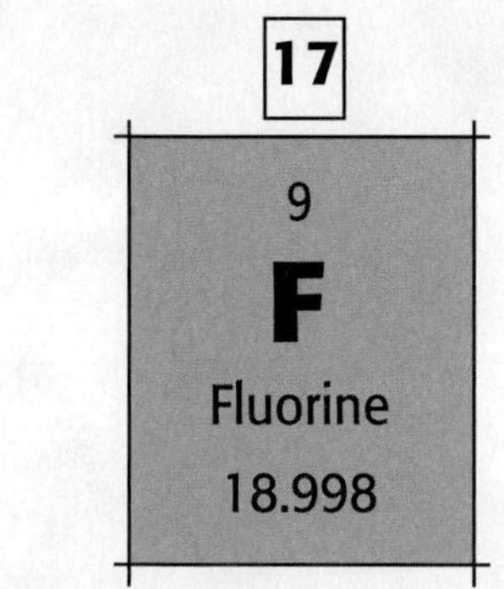

Periodic Table Listing for Fluorine

6. How many neutrons are in a typical fluorine atom?

A. 9

B. 10

C. 17

D. 19

7. What forms when atoms share one or more pairs of electrons?

A. covalent bond

B. ionic bond

C. valence electron

D. nonmetal ion

8. The ions that make up an ionic compound are bonded in a repeating three-dimensional pattern. What is this pattern called?

A. chloride lattice

B. covalent bond

C. crystal lattice

D. crystal pattern

9. What is a molecule?

A. the smallest particle of a substance that cannot be broken down any further by chemical bonding

B. a particle that forms when atoms gain or lose electrons

C. matter of particular or definite chemical composition

D. the smallest unit of a substance that keeps the physical and chemical properties of the substance

10. Juanita observes a model of two bonded atoms. She is told that the atoms are both nonmetals. She is looking at a model of

A. a covalent bond.

B. an acid.

C. an ionic bond.

D. a salt.

Open Response

11. Which of an atom's electrons are most likely to be involved in chemical bonding? Why?

12. Why don't the noble gases in Group 18 on the periodic table form chemical bonds?

Science in Action

Science, Technology, and Society

Superglue Bandages and Stitches

If you aren't careful when using superglue, you may accidentally learn that superglue quickly bonds skin together! This property of superglue led to the development of new kinds of superglue that can be used as alternatives for bandages and stitches. Using superglue to close wounds has several advantages over using bandages and stitches. For example, superglue bandages can cover cuts on parts of the body that are difficult to cover with regular bandages. And superglue stitches are less painful than regular stitches. Finally, wounds closed with superglue are easier to care for than wounds covered by bandages or closed with stitches.

Math ACTIVITY

A wound can be closed 3 times faster with glue than it can be with stitches. If it takes a doctor 27 min to close a wound by using stitches, how long would it take to close the same wound by using glue?

Weird Science

How Geckos Stick to Walls

Geckos are known for their ability to climb up smooth surfaces. Recently, scientists found the secret to the gecko's sticky talent. Geckos have millions of microscopic hairs on the bottom of their feet. Each hair splits into as many as 1,000 tinier hairs called *hairlets*. At the end of each hairlet is a small pad. As the gecko walks, each pad forms a van der Waals force with the surface on which the gecko is walking. A van der Waals force is an attraction similar to an ionic bond, but the van der Waals force is much weaker than an ionic bond and lasts for only an instant. But because there are so many pads on a gecko's foot, the van der Waals forces are strong enough to keep the gecko from falling.

Language Arts ACTIVITY

WRITING SKILL Imagine that you could stick to walls as well as a gecko can. Write a five-paragraph short story describing what you would do with your wall-climbing ability.

Careers

Roberta Jordan

Analytical Chemist Have you ever looked at something and wondered what chemicals it contained? That's what analytical chemists do for a living. They use tests to find the chemical makeup of a sample. Roberta Jordan is an analytical chemist at the Idaho National Engineering and Environmental Laboratory in Idaho Falls, Idaho.

Jordan's work focuses on the study of radioactive waste generated by nuclear power plants and nuclear-powered submarines. Jordan works with engineers to develop safe ways to store the radioactive waste. She tells the engineers which chemicals need to be studied and which techniques to use to study those chemicals.

Jordan enjoys her job because she is always learning new techniques. "One of the things necessary to be a good chemist is you have to be creative. You have to be able to think above and beyond the normal ways of doing things to come up with new ideas, new experiments," she explains. Jordan believes that a person interested in a career in chemistry has many opportunities. "There are a lot of things out there that need to be discovered," says Jordan.

Social Studies ACTIVITY

Many elements in the periodic table were discovered by analytical chemists. Pick an element from the periodic table, and research its history. Make a poster about the discovery of that element.

To learn more about these Science in Action topics, visit go.hrw.com and type in the keyword **HP5BNDF.**

Current Science

Check out Current Science® articles related to this chapter by visiting go.hrw.com. Just type in the keyword HP5CS13.

23

Chemical Reactions

The Big Idea Substances undergo chemical reactions, which form new substances whose properties differ from the properties of the original substances.

SECTION

About the Photo

Dazzling fireworks and the Statue of Liberty are great examples of chemical reactions. Chemical reactions cause fireworks to soar, explode, and light up the sky. And the Statue of Liberty has its distinctive green color because of the reaction between the statue's copper and chemicals in the air.

PRE-READING ACTIVITY

FOLDNOTES

Four-Corner Fold

Before you read the chapter, create the FoldNote entitled "Four-Corner Fold" described in the **Study Skills** section of the Appendix. Label the flaps of the four-corner fold with "Chemical formulas," "Chemical equations," "Types of chemical reactions," and "Rates of chemical reactions." Write what you know about each topic under the appropriate flap. As you read the chapter, add other information that you learn.

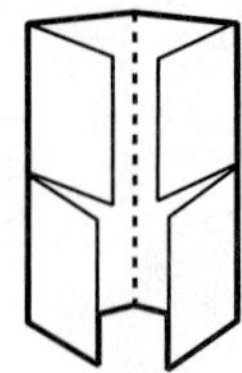

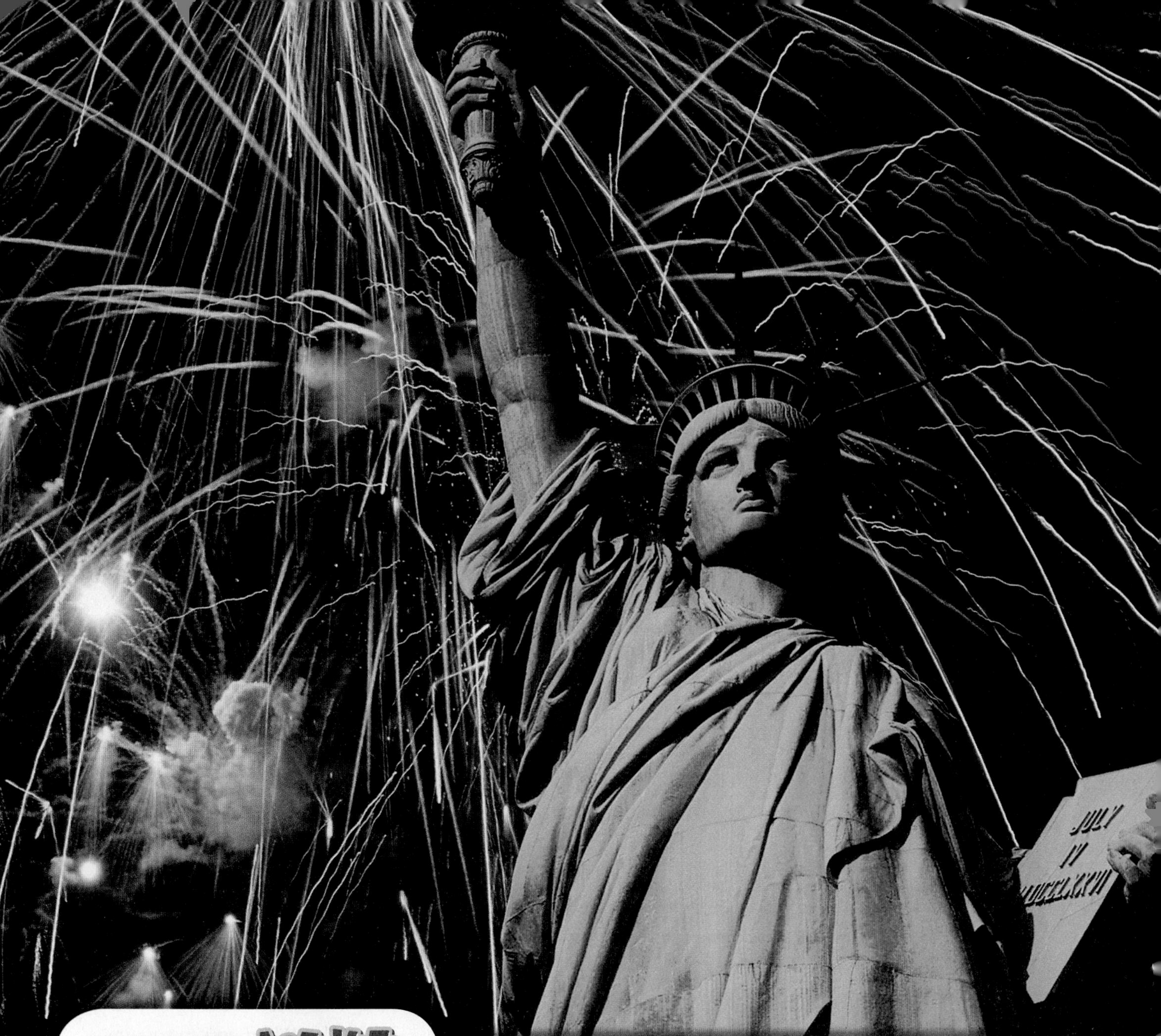

START-UP ACTIVITY

A Model Formula

Chemicals react in very precise ways. In this activity, you will model a chemical reaction and will predict how chemicals react.

Procedure

1. You will receive **several marshmallow models.** The models are marshmallows attached by **toothpicks.** Each of these models is a Model A.
2. Your teacher will show you an example of Model B and Model C. Take apart one or more Model As to make copies of Model B and Model C.
3. If you have marshmallows left over, use them to make more Model Bs and Model Cs. If you need more parts to complete a Model B or Model C, take apart another Model A.
4. Repeat step 3 until you have no parts left over.

Analysis

1. How many Model As did you use to make copies of Model B and Model C?
2. How many Model Bs did you make? How many Model Cs did you make?
3. Suppose you needed to make six Model Bs. How many Model As would you need? How many Model Cs could you make with the leftover marshmallows?

SECTION 1

Forming New Substances

What You Will Learn

- Describe how chemical reactions produce new substances that have different chemical and physical properties.
- Identify four signs that indicate that a chemical reaction might be taking place.
- Explain what happens to chemical bonds during a chemical reaction.

Vocabulary

chemical reaction
precipitate

READING STRATEGY

Reading Organizer As you read this section, create an outline of the section. Use the headings from the section in your outline.

Each fall, a beautiful change takes place when leaves turn colors. You see bright oranges and yellows that had been hidden by green all summer. What causes this change?

To answer this question, you need to know what causes leaves to be green. Leaves are green because they contain a green substance, or *pigment*. This pigment is called *chlorophyll* (KLAWR uh FIL). During the spring and summer, the leaves have a large amount of chlorophyll in them. But in the fall, when temperatures drop and there are fewer hours of sunlight, chlorophyll breaks down to form new substances that have no color. The green chlorophyll is no longer present to hide the other pigments. You can now see the orange and yellow colors that were present all along.

Chemical Reactions

A chemical change takes place when chlorophyll breaks down into new substances. This change is an example of a chemical reaction. A **chemical reaction** is a process in which one or more substances change to make one or more new substances. The chemical and physical properties of the new substances differ from those of the original substances. Some results of chemical reactions are shown in **Figure 1.**

Figure 1 Results of Chemical Reactions

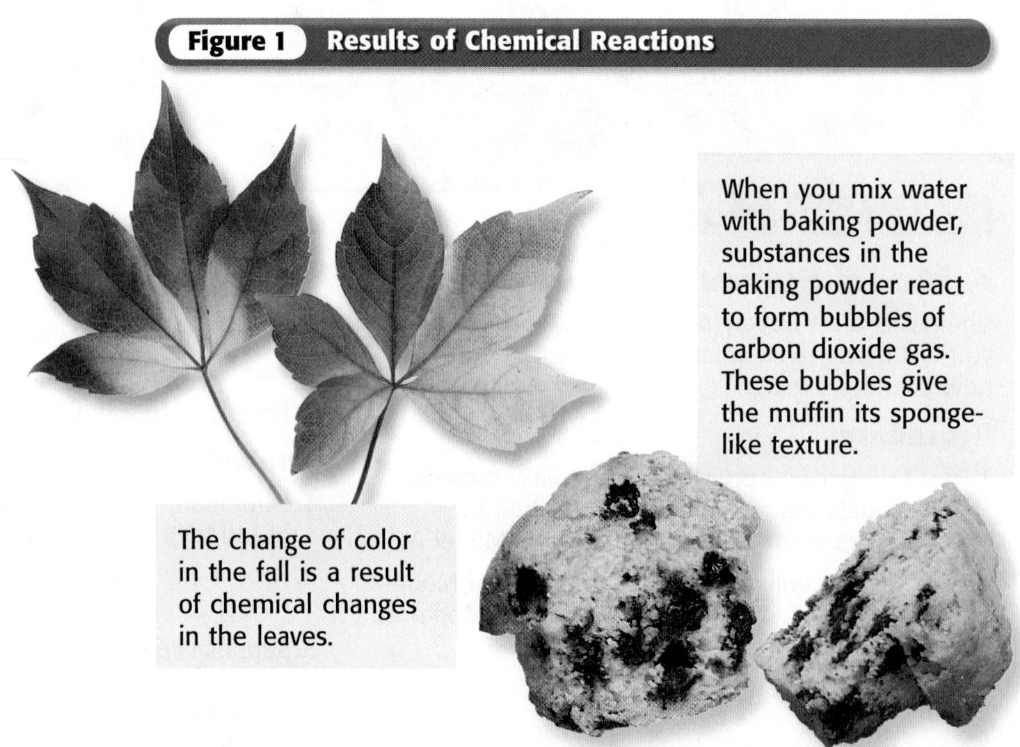

When you mix water with baking powder, substances in the baking powder react to form bubbles of carbon dioxide gas. These bubbles give the muffin its sponge-like texture.

The change of color in the fall is a result of chemical changes in the leaves.

Signs of Chemical Reactions

How can you tell when a chemical reaction is taking place? **Figure 2** shows some signs that tell you that a reaction may be taking place. In some chemical reactions, gas bubbles form. Other reactions form solid precipitates (pree SIP uh TAYTS). A **precipitate** is a solid substance that is formed in a solution. During other chemical reactions, energy is given off. This energy may be in the form of light, thermal energy, or electrical energy. Reactions often have more than one of these signs. And the more of these signs that you see, the more likely that a chemical reaction is taking place.

chemical reaction the process by which one or more substances change to produce one or more different substances

precipitate a solid that is produced as a result of a chemical reaction in solution

Reading Check **What is a precipitate?** (*See the Appendix for answers to Reading Checks.*)

Figure 2 Some Signs of Chemical Reactions

Gas Formation
The chemical reaction in the beaker has formed a brown gas, nitrogen dioxide. This gas is formed when a strip of copper is placed into nitric acid.

Solid Formation
Here you see potassium chromate solution being added to a silver nitrate solution. The dark red solid is a precipitate of silver chromate.

Energy Change
Energy is released during some chemical reactions. The fire in this photo gives off light energy and thermal energy. During some other chemical reactions, energy is taken in.

Color Change
Don't spill chlorine bleach on your jeans! The bleach reacts with the blue dye on the fabric and causes the color of the material to change.

A Change of Properties

Even though the signs we look for to see if a reaction is taking place are good signals of chemical reactions, they do not guarantee that a reaction is happening. For example, gas can be given off when a liquid boils. But this example is a physical change, not a chemical reaction.

So, how can you be sure that a chemical reaction is occurring? The most important sign is the formation of new substances that have different properties. Look at **Figure 3.** The starting materials in this reaction are sugar and sulfuric acid. Several things tell you that a chemical reaction is taking place. Bubbles form, a gas is given off, and the beaker becomes very hot. But most important, new substances form. And the properties of these substances are very different from those of the starting substances.

Figure 3 *The top photo shows the starting substances: table sugar and sulfuric acid, a clear liquid. The substances formed in this chemical reaction are very different from the starting substances.*

Bonds: Holding Molecules Together

A *chemical bond* is a force that holds two atoms together in a molecule. For a chemical reaction to take place, the original bonds must break and new bonds must form.

Breaking and Making Bonds

How do new substances form in a chemical reaction? First, chemical bonds in the starting substances must break. Molecules are always moving. If the molecules bump into each other with enough energy, the chemical bonds in the molecules break. The atoms then rearrange, and new bonds form to make the new substances. **Figure 4** shows how bonds break and form in the reaction between hydrogen and chlorine.

Reading Check **What happens to the bonds of substances during a chemical reaction?**

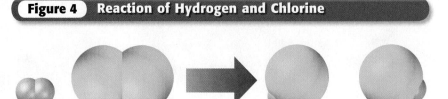

Figure 4 Reaction of Hydrogen and Chlorine

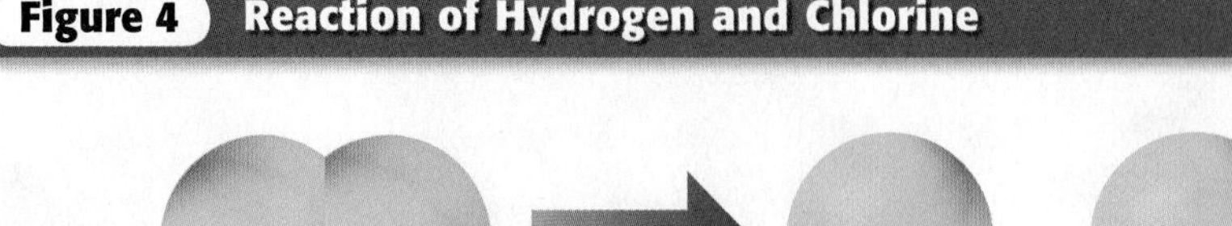

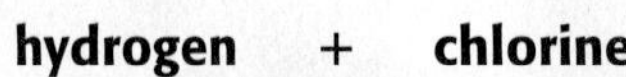

hydrogen chloride

Breaking Bonds Hydrogen and chlorine are diatomic. Diatomic molecules are two atoms bonded together. The bonds joining these atoms must first break before the atoms can react with each other.

Making Bonds A new substance, hydrogen chloride, forms as new bonds are made between hydrogen atoms and chlorine atoms.

New Bonds, New Substances

What happens when hydrogen and chlorine are combined? A chlorine gas molecule is a diatomic (DIE uh TAHM ik) molecule. That is, a chlorine molecule is made of two atoms of chlorine. Chlorine gas has a greenish yellow color. Hydrogen gas is also a diatomic molecule. Hydrogen gas is a flammable, colorless gas. When chlorine gas and hydrogen gas react, the bond between the hydrogen atoms breaks. And the bond between the chlorine atoms also breaks. A new bond forms between each hydrogen and chlorine atom. A new substance, hydrogen chloride, is formed. Hydrogen chloride is a nonflammable, colorless gas. Its properties differ from the properties of both of the starting substances.

Let's look at another example. Sodium is a metal that reacts violently in water. Chlorine gas is poisonous. When chlorine gas and sodium react, the result is a familiar compound—table salt. Sodium chloride, or table salt, is a harmless substance that almost everyone uses. The salt's properties are very different from sodium's or chlorine's. Salt is a new substance.

Reaction Ready

1. Place a **piece of chalk** in a **plastic cup.**
2. Add **5 mL of vinegar** to the cup. Record your observations.
3. What evidence of a chemical reaction do you see?
4. What type of new substance was formed?

SECTION Review

Summary

- A chemical reaction is a process by which substances change to produce new substances with new chemical and physical properties.
- Signs that indicate a chemical reaction has taken place are a color change, formation of a gas or a solid, and release of energy.
- During a reaction, bonds are broken, atoms are rearranged, and new bonds are formed.

Using Key Terms

1. Use the following terms in the same sentence: *chemical reaction* and *precipitate*.

Understanding Key Ideas

2. Most chemical reactions
   a. have starting substances that collide with each other.
   b. do not break bonds.
   c. do not rearrange atoms.
   d. cannot be seen.
3. If the chemical properties of a substance have not changed, has a chemical reaction occurred?

Critical Thinking

4. **Analyzing Processes** Steam is escaping from a teapot. Is this a chemical reaction? Explain.
5. **Applying Concepts** Explain why charcoal burning in a grill is a chemical change.

Interpreting Graphics

Use the photo below to answer the questions that follow.

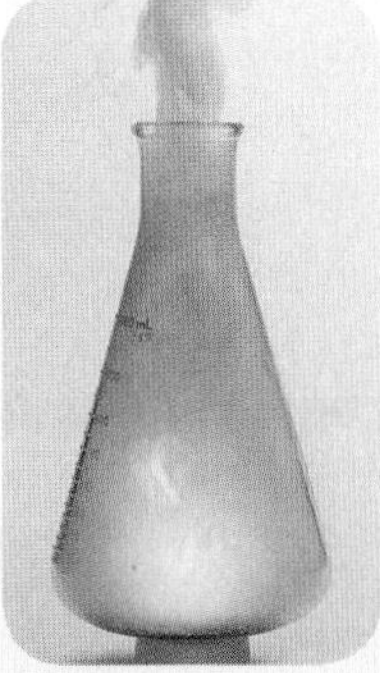

6. What evidence of a chemical reaction is shown in the photo?
7. What is happening to the bonds of the starting substances?

For a variety of links related to this chapter, go to www.scilinks.org

Topic: Chemical Reactions
SciLinks code: HSM0274

SECTION 2

Chemical Formulas and Equations

What You Will Learn

- Interpret and write simple chemical formulas.
- Write and balance simple chemical equations.
- Explain how a balanced equation shows the law of conservation of mass.

Vocabulary

chemical formula
chemical equation
reactant
product
law of conservation of mass

READING STRATEGY

Discussion Read this section silently. Write down questions that you have about this section. Discuss your questions in a small group.

How many words can you make using the 26 letters of the alphabet? Many thousands? Now, think of how many sentences you can make with all of those words.

Letters are used to form words. In the same way, chemical symbols are put together to make chemical formulas that describe substances. Chemical formulas can be placed together to describe a chemical reaction, just like words can be put together to make a sentence.

Chemical Formulas

All substances are formed from about 100 elements. Each element has its own chemical symbol. A **chemical formula** is a shorthand way to use chemical symbols and numbers to represent a substance. A chemical formula shows how many atoms of each kind are present in a molecule.

As shown in **Figure 1,** the chemical formula for water is H_2O. This formula tells you that one water molecule is made of two atoms of hydrogen and one atom of oxygen. The small 2 in the formula is a subscript. A *subscript* is a number written below and to the right of a chemical symbol in a formula. Sometimes, a symbol, such as O for oxygen in water's formula, has no subscript. If there is no subscript, only one atom of that element is present. Look at **Figure 1** for more examples of chemical formulas.

chemical formula a combination of chemical symbols and numbers to represent a substance

Figure 1 Chemical Formulas of Different Substances

Water	Oxygen	Glucose
H_2O	O_2	$C_6H_{12}O_6$
Water molecules are made up of 3 atoms—2 atoms of hydrogen bonded to 1 atom of oxygen.	**Oxygen** is a diatomic molecule. Each molecule has 2 atoms of oxygen bonded together.	**Glucose** molecules have 6 atoms of carbon, 12 atoms of hydrogen, and 6 atoms of oxygen.

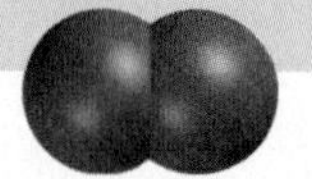

Carbon dioxide

$$CO_2$$

The *absence of a prefix* indicates one carbon atom.

The prefix *di-* indicates two oxygen atoms.

Dinitrogen monoxide

$$N_2O$$

The prefix *di-* indicates two nitrogen atoms.

The prefix *mono-* indicates one oxygen atom.

Figure 2 *The formulas of these covalent compounds can be written by using the prefixes in the names of the compounds.*

Writing Formulas for Covalent Compounds

If you know the name of the covalent compound, you can often write the chemical formula for that compound. Covalent compounds are usually composed of two nonmetals. The names of many covalent compounds use prefixes. Each prefix represents a number, as shown in **Table 1.** The prefixes tell you how many atoms of each element are in a formula. **Figure 2** shows you how to write a chemical formula from the name of a covalent compound.

Table 1 Prefixes Used in Chemical Names

mono-	1	hexa-	6
di-	2	hepta-	7
tri-	3	octa-	8
tetra-	4	nona-	9
penta-	5	deca-	10

Writing Formulas for Ionic Compounds

If the name of a compound contains the name of a metal and the name of a nonmetal, the compound is ionic. To write the formula for an ionic compound, make sure the compound's charge is 0. In other words, the formula must have subscripts that cause the charges of the ions to cancel out. **Figure 3** shows you how to write a chemical formula from the name of an ionic compound.

Reading Check **What kinds of elements make up an ionic compound?** (*See the Appendix for answers to Reading Checks.*)

Sodium chloride

$$NaCl$$

A sodium ion has a **1+ charge.**

A chloride ion has a **1− charge.**

One sodium ion and one chloride ion have an overall **charge of (1+) + (1−) = 0**

Magnesium chloride

$$MgCl_2$$

A magnesium ion has a **2+ charge.**

A chloride ion has a **1− charge.**

One magnesium ion and two chloride ions have an overall **charge of (2+) + 2(1−) = 0.**

Figure 3 *The formula of an ionic compound is written by using enough of each ion so that the overall charge is 0.*

Figure 4 *Like chemical symbols, the symbols on this musical score are understood around the world!*

Chemical Equations

Think about a piece of music, such as the one in **Figure 4.** Someone writing music must tell the musician what notes to play, how long to play each note, and how each note should be played. Words aren't used to describe the musical piece. Instead, musical symbols are used. The symbols can be understood by anyone who can read music.

Describing Reactions by Using Equations

In the same way that composers use musical symbols, chemists around the world use chemical symbols and chemical formulas. Instead of changing words and sentences into other languages to describe reactions, chemists use chemical equations. A **chemical equation** uses chemical symbols and formulas as a shortcut to describe a chemical reaction. A chemical equation is short and is understood by anyone who understands chemical formulas.

chemical equation a representation of a chemical reaction that uses symbols to show the relationship between the reactants and the products

reactant a substance or molecule that participates in a chemical reaction

product the substance that forms in a chemical reaction

From Reactants to Products

When carbon burns, it reacts with oxygen to form carbon dioxide. **Figure 5** shows how a chemist would use an equation to describe this reaction. The starting materials in a chemical reaction are **reactants** (ree AK tuhnts). The substances formed from a reaction are **products.** In this example, carbon and oxygen are reactants. Carbon dioxide is the product.

Reading Check **What is the difference between reactants and products in a chemical reaction?**

Figure 5 **The Parts of a Chemical Equation**

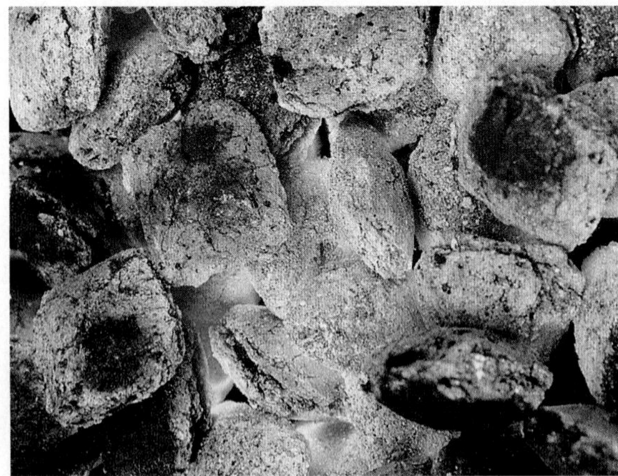

Charcoal is used to cook food on a barbecue grill. When carbon in charcoal reacts with oxygen in the air, the primary product is carbon dioxide, as shown by the chemical equation.

The formulas of the **reactants** are written before the arrow.

The formulas of the **products** are written after the arrow.

$$C + O_2 \longrightarrow CO_2$$

A **plus sign** separates the formulas of two or more reactants or products from one another.

The **arrow,** also called the *yields sign,* separates the formulas of the reactants from the formulas of the products.

Figure 6 Examples of Similar Symbols and Formulas

CO_2

The chemical formula for the compound **carbon dioxide** is CO_2. Carbon dioxide is a colorless, odorless gas that you exhale.

CO

The chemical formula for the compound **carbon monoxide** is CO. Carbon monoxide is a colorless, odorless, and poisonous gas.

Co

The chemical symbol for the element **cobalt** is Co. Cobalt is a hard, bluish gray metal.

The Importance of Accuracy

The symbol or formula for each substance in the equation must be written correctly. For a compound, use the correct chemical formula. For an element, use the proper chemical symbol. An equation that has the wrong chemical symbol or formula will not correctly describe the reaction. In fact, even a simple mistake can make a huge difference. **Figure 6** shows how formulas and symbols can be mistaken.

Counting Atoms

Some chemical formulas contain parentheses. When counting atoms, multiply everything inside the parentheses by the subscript. For example, $Ca(NO_3)_2$ has one calcium atom, two (2 × 1) nitrogen atoms, and six (2 × 3) oxygen atoms. Find the number of atoms of each element in the formulas $Mg(OH)_2$ and $Al_2(SO_4)_3$.

The Reason Equations Must Be Balanced

Atoms are never lost or gained in a chemical reaction. They are just rearranged. Every atom in the reactants becomes part of the products. When writing a chemical equation, make sure the number of atoms of each element in the reactants equals the number of atoms of those elements in the products. This is called balancing the equation.

Balancing equations comes from the work of a French chemist, Antoine Lavoisier (lah vwah ZYAY). In the 1700s, Lavoisier found that the total mass of the reactants was always the same as the total mass of the products. Lavoisier's work led to the **law of conservation of mass.** This law states that mass is neither created nor destroyed in ordinary chemical and physical changes. This law means that a chemical equation must show the same numbers and kinds of atoms on both sides of the arrow.

law of conservation of mass the law that states that mass cannot be created or destroyed in ordinary chemical and physical changes

How to Balance an Equation

To balance an equation, you must use coefficients (KOH uh FISH uhnts). A *coefficient* is a number that is placed in front of a chemical symbol or formula. For example, 2CO represents two carbon monoxide molecules. The number *2* is the coefficient.

For an equation to be balanced, all atoms must be counted. So, you must multiply the subscript of each element in a formula by the formula's coefficient. For example, $2H_2O$ contains a total of four hydrogen atoms and two oxygen atoms. Only coefficients—not subscripts—are changed when balancing equations. Changing the subscripts in the formula of a compound would change the compound. **Figure 7** shows you how to use coefficients to balance an equation.

Reading Check **If you see $4O_2$ in an equation, what is the coefficient?**

CONNECTION TO Language Arts

WRITING SKILL **Diatomic Molecules** Seven of the chemical elements exist as diatomic molecules. Do research to find out which seven elements these are. Write a short report that describes each diatomic molecule. Be sure to include the formula for each molecule.

Figure 7 **Balancing a Chemical Equation**

Follow these steps to write a balanced equation for $H_2 + O_2 \longrightarrow H_2O$.

1. **Count the atoms** of each element in the reactants and in the products. You can see that there are fewer oxygen atoms in the product than in the reactants.

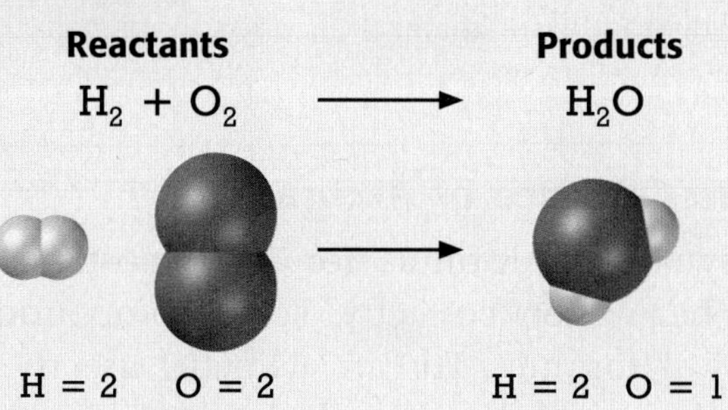

2. **To balance the oxygen atoms,** place the coefficient 2 in front of H_2O. Doing so gives you two oxygen atoms in both the reactants and the products. But now there are too few hydrogen atoms in the reactants.

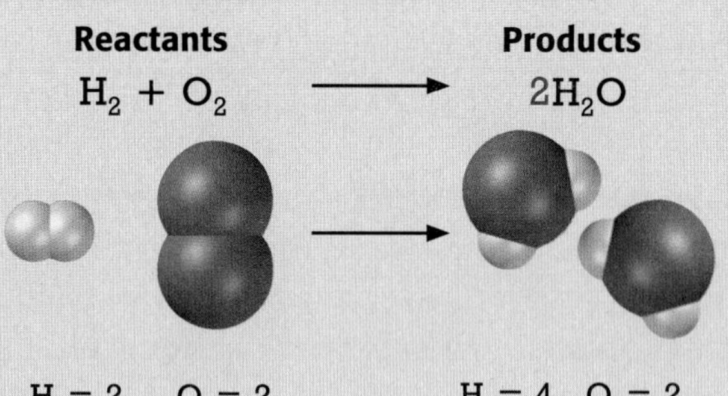

3. **To balance the hydrogen atoms,** place the coefficient 2 in front of H_2. But to be sure that your answer is correct, always double-check your work!

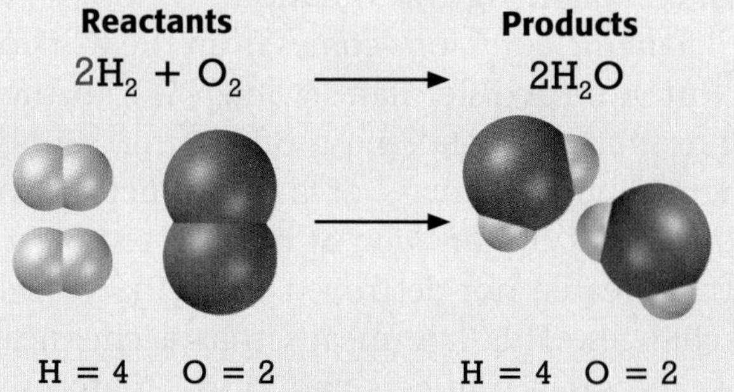

Conservation of Mass

1. Place **5 g of baking soda** into a **sealable plastic bag.**
2. Place **5 mL of vinegar** into a **plastic film canister.** Put the lid on the canister.
3. Place the canister into the bag. Squeeze the air out of the bag. Seal the bag tightly.
4. Use a **balance** to measure the mass of the bag and its contents. Record the mass.
5. Keeping the bag closed, open the canister in the bag. Mix the vinegar with the baking soda. Record your observations.
6. When the reaction has stopped, measure the mass of the bag and its contents. Record the mass.
7. Compare the mass of the materials before the reaction and the mass of the materials after the reaction. Explain your observations.

SECTION Review

Summary

- A chemical formula uses symbols and subscripts to describe the makeup of a compound.
- Chemical formulas can often be written from the names of covalent and ionic compounds.
- A chemical equation uses chemical formulas, chemical symbols, and coefficients to describe a reaction.
- Balancing an equation requires that the same numbers and kinds of atoms be on each side of the equation.
- A balanced equation illustrates the law of conservation of mass: mass is neither created nor destroyed during ordinary physical and chemical changes.

Using Key Terms

The statements below are false. For each statement, replace the underlined word to make a true statement.

1. A chemical <u>formula</u> describes a chemical reaction.
2. The substances formed from a chemical reaction are <u>reactants</u>.

Understanding Key Ideas

3. The correct chemical formula for carbon tetrachloride is
   a. CCl_3.
   b. C_3Cl.
   c. CCl.
   d. CCl_4.
4. Calcium oxide is used to make soil less acidic. Its formula is
   a. Ca_2O_2.
   b. CaO.
   c. CaO_2.
   d. Ca_2O.
5. Balance the following equations by adding the correct coefficients.
   a. $Na + Cl_2 \longrightarrow NaCl$
   b. $Mg + N_2 \longrightarrow Mg_3N_2$
6. How does a balanced chemical equation illustrate that mass is never lost or gained in a chemical reaction?
7. What is the difference between a subscript and a coefficient?

Math Skills

8. Calculate the number of atoms of each element represented in each of the following: $2Na_3PO_4$, $4Al_2(SO_4)_3$, and $6PCl_5$.

Critical Thinking

9. **Analyzing Methods** Describe how to write a formula for a covalent compound. Give an example of a covalent compound.
10. **Applying Concepts** Explain why the subscript in a formula of a chemical compound cannot be changed when balancing an equation.

SCILINKS.
NSTA
Developed and maintained by the National Science Teachers Association
For a variety of links related to this chapter, go to www.scilinks.org
Topic: Chemical Formulas; Chemical Equations
SciLinks code: HSM0271; HSM0269

SECTION 3

Types of Chemical Reactions

What You Will Learn

- Describe four types of chemical reactions.
- Classify a chemical equation as one of four types of chemical reactions.

Vocabulary

synthesis reaction
decomposition reaction
single-displacement reaction
double-displacement reaction

READING STRATEGY

Mnemonics As you read this section, create a mnemonic device to help you remember the four types of chemical reactions.

There are thousands of known chemical reactions. Can you imagine having to memorize even 50 of them?

Remembering all of them would be impossible! But fortunately, there is help. In the same way that the elements are divided into groups based on their properties, reactions can be classified based on what occurs during the reaction.

Most reactions can be placed into one of four categories: synthesis (SIN thuh sis), decomposition, single-displacement, and double-displacement. Each type of reaction has a pattern that shows how reactants become products. One way to remember what happens in each type of reaction is to imagine people at a dance. As you learn about each type of reaction, study the models of students at a dance. The models will help you recognize each type of reaction.

Synthesis Reactions

synthesis reaction a reaction in which two or more substances combine to form a new compound

A **synthesis reaction** is a reaction in which two or more substances combine to form one new compound. For example, a synthesis reaction takes place when sodium reacts with chlorine. This synthesis reaction produces sodium chloride, which you know as table salt. A synthesis reaction would be modeled by two people pairing up to form a dancing couple, as shown in **Figure 1.**

Reading Check What is a synthesis reaction? (*See the Appendix for answers to Reading Checks.*)

Figure 1 *Sodium reacts with chlorine to form sodium chloride in this synthesis reaction.*

Figure 2 *In this decomposition reaction, carbonic acid, H_2CO_3, decomposes to form water and carbon dioxide.*

Decomposition Reactions

A **decomposition reaction** is a reaction in which a single compound breaks down to form two or more simpler substances. Decomposition is the reverse of synthesis. The dance model for a decomposition reaction would be a couple that finishes a dance and separates, as shown in **Figure 2.**

decomposition reaction a reaction in which a single compound breaks down to form two or more simpler substances

single-displacement reaction a reaction in which one element or radical takes the place of another element or radical in a compound

Reading Check How is a decomposition reaction different from a synthesis reaction?

Single-Displacement Reactions

Sometimes, an element replaces another element that is a part of a compound. This type of reaction is called a **single-displacement reaction.** The products of single-displacement reactions are a new compound and a different element. The dance model for a single-displacement reaction would show a person cutting in on a couple who is dancing. A new couple is formed. And a different person is left alone, as shown in **Figure 3.**

Figure 3 *Zinc replaces the hydrogen in hydrochloric acid to form zinc chloride and hydrogen gas in this single-displacement reaction.*

$Zn + 2HCl \rightarrow ZnCl_2 + H_2$

Figure 4 Reactivity of Elements

$Cu + 2AgNO_3 \rightarrow 2Ag + Cu(NO_3)_2$
Copper is more reactive than silver.

$Ag + Cu(NO_3)_2 \rightarrow$ no reaction
Silver is less reactive than copper.

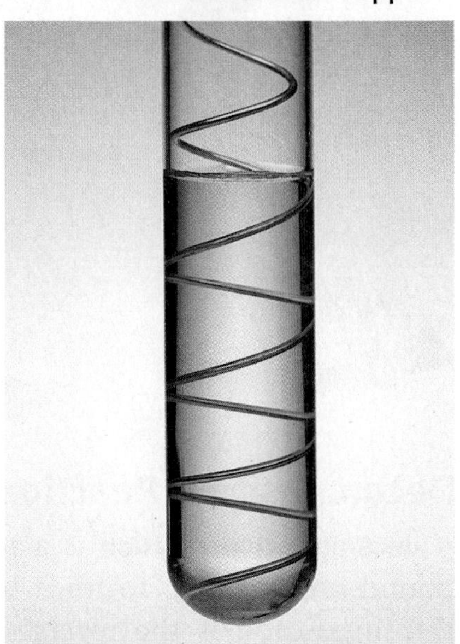

Reactivity of Elements

In a single-displacement reaction, a more reactive element can displace a less reactive element in a compound. For example, **Figure 4** shows that copper is more reactive than silver. Copper (Cu) can replace the silver (Ag) ion in the compound silver nitrate. But the opposite reaction does not occur, because silver is less reactive than copper.

The elements in Group 1 of the periodic table are the most reactive metals. Very few nonmetals are involved in single-displacement reactions. In fact, only Group 17 nonmetals participate in single-displacement reactions.

Reading Check **Why can one element sometimes replace another element in a single-displacement reaction?**

For another activity related to this chapter, go to **go.hrw.com** and type in the keyword **HP5REAW.**

Identifying Reactions

1. Study each of the following equations:
   $4Na + O_2 \rightarrow 2Na_2O$ $P_4 + 5O_2 \rightarrow 2P_2O_5$
   $2Ag_3N \rightarrow 6Ag + N_2$ $Zn + 2HCl \rightarrow ZnCl_2 + H_2$
2. Build models of each of these reactions using **colored clay.** Choose a different color of clay to represent each kind of atom.
3. Identify each type of reaction as a synthesis, decomposition, or single-displacement reaction.

Double-Displacement Reactions

A **double-displacement reaction** is a reaction in which ions from two compounds exchange places. One of the products of this type of reaction is often a gas or a precipitate. A dance model of a double-displacement reaction would be two couples dancing and then trading partners, as shown in **Figure 5.**

double-displacement reaction a reaction in which a gas, a solid precipitate, or a molecular compound forms from the exchange of ions between two compounds

Figure 5 *A double-displacement reaction occurs when sodium chloride reacts with silver fluoride to form sodium fluoride and silver chloride (a precipitate).*

SECTION Review

Summary

- A synthesis reaction is a reaction in which two or more substances combine to form a compound.
- A decomposition reaction is a reaction in which a compound breaks down to form two or more simpler substances.
- A single-displacement reaction is a reaction in which an element takes the place of another element that is part of a compound.
- A double-displacement reaction is a reaction in which ions in two compounds exchange places.

Using Key Terms

1. In your own words, write a definition for each of the following terms: *synthesis reaction* and *decomposition reaction.*

Understanding Key Ideas

2. What type of reaction does the following equation represent?

$FeS + 2HCl \longrightarrow FeCl_2 + H_2S$

a. synthesis reaction
b. double-displacement reaction
c. single-displacement reaction
d. decomposition reaction

3. Describe the difference between single- and double-displacement reactions.

Math Skills

4. Write the balanced equation in which potassium iodide, KI, reacts with chlorine to form potassium chloride, KCl, and iodine.

Critical Thinking

5. Analyzing Processes The first reaction below is a single-displacement reaction that could occur in a laboratory. Explain why the second single-displacement reaction could not occur.

$CuCl_2 + Fe \longrightarrow FeCl_2 + Cu$
$CaS + Al \longrightarrow$ no reaction

6. Making Inferences When two white compounds are mixed in a solution, a yellow solid forms. What kind of reaction has taken place? Explain your answer.

SCILINKS.
NSTA
Developed and maintained by the National Science Teachers Association
For a variety of links related to this chapter, go to www.scilinks.org
Topic: Reaction Types
SciLinks code: HSM1272

SECTION 4

Energy and Rates of Chemical Reactions

What You Will Learn

- Compare exothermic and endothermic reactions.
- Explain activation energy.
- Interpret an energy diagram.
- Describe five factors that affect the rate of a reaction.

Vocabulary

exothermic reaction
endothermic reaction
law of conservation of energy
activation energy
inhibitor
catalyst

READING STRATEGY

Paired Summarizing Read this section silently. In pairs, take turns summarizing the material. Stop to discuss ideas that seem confusing.

What is the difference between eating a meal and running a mile? You could say that a meal gives you energy, while running "uses up" energy.

Chemical reactions can be described in the same way. Some reactions release energy, and other reactions absorb energy.

Reactions and Energy

Chemical energy is part of all chemical reactions. Energy is needed to break chemical bonds in the reactants. As new bonds form in the products, energy is released. By comparing the chemical energy of the reactants with the chemical energy of the products, you can decide if energy is released or absorbed in the overall reaction.

Exothermic Reactions

A chemical reaction in which energy is released is called an **exothermic reaction.** *Exo* means "go out" or "exit." *Thermic* means "heat" or "energy." Exothermic reactions can give off energy in several forms, as shown in **Figure 1.** The energy released in an exothermic reaction is often written as a product in a chemical equation, as in this equation:

$$2Na + Cl_2 \rightarrow 2NaCl + \textit{energy}$$

Figure 1 Types of Energy Released in Exothermic Reactions

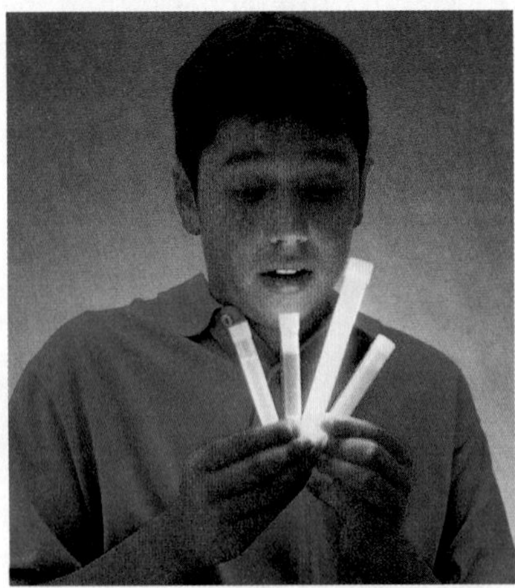

Light energy is released in the exothermic reaction that is taking place in these light sticks.

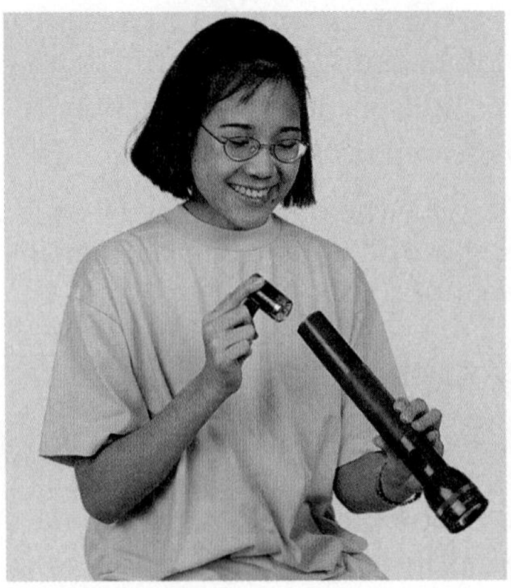

Electrical energy is released in the exothermic reaction that will take place in this battery.

Light and thermal energy are released in the exothermic reaction taking place in this campfire.

Endothermic Reactions

A chemical reaction in which energy is taken in is called an **endothermic reaction.** *Endo* means "go in." The energy that is taken in during an endothermic reaction is often written as a reactant in a chemical equation. Energy as a reactant is shown in the following equation:

exothermic reaction a chemical reaction in which heat is released to the surroundings

endothermic reaction a chemical reaction that requires heat

law of conservation of energy the law that states that energy cannot be created or destroyed but can be changed from one form to another

$$2H_2O + energy \rightarrow 2H_2 + O_2$$

An example of an endothermic process is photosynthesis. In photosynthesis, plants use light energy from the sun to produce glucose. Glucose is a simple sugar that is used for nutrition. The equation that describes photosynthesis is the following:

$$6CO_2 + 6H_2O + energy \rightarrow C_6H_{12}O_6 + 6O_2$$

Reading Check **What is an endothermic reaction?** (*See the Appendix for answers to Reading Checks.*)

The Law of Conservation of Energy

Neither mass nor energy can be created or destroyed in chemical reactions. The **law of conservation of energy** states that energy cannot be created or destroyed. However, energy can change forms. And energy can be transferred from one object to another in the same way that a baton is transferred from one runner to another runner, as shown in **Figure 2.**

The energy released in exothermic reactions was first stored in the chemical bonds in the reactants. And the energy taken in during endothermic reactions is stored in the products. If you could measure all the energy in a reaction, you would find that the total amount of energy (of all types) is the same before and after the reaction.

Figure 2 *Energy can be transferred from one object to another object in the same way that a baton is transferred from one runner to another runner in a relay race.*

Endo Alert

1. Fill a **plastic cup** half full with **calcium chloride solution.**
2. Measure the temperature of the solution by using a **thermometer.**
3. Carefully add **1 tsp of baking soda.**
4. Record your observations.
5. When the reaction has stopped, record the temperature of the solution.
6. What evidence that an endothermic reaction took place did you observe?

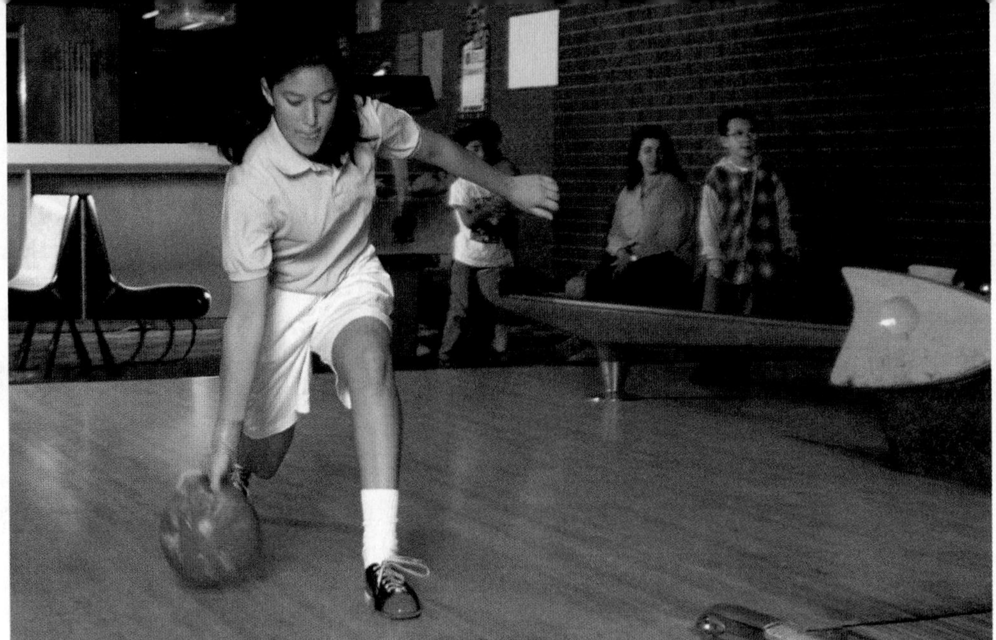

Figure 3 *Chemical reactions need energy to get started in the same way that a bowling ball needs a push to get rolling.*

Rates of Reactions

A reaction takes place only if the particles of reactants collide. But there must be enough energy to break the bonds that hold particles together in a molecule. The speed at which new particles form is called the *rate of a reaction.*

Activation Energy

Before the bowling ball in **Figure 3** can roll down the alley, the bowler must first put in some energy to start the ball rolling. A chemical reaction must also get a boost of energy before the reaction can start. This boost of energy is called activation energy. **Activation energy** is the smallest amount of energy that molecules need to react.

activation energy the minimum amount of energy required to start a chemical reaction

Another example of activation energy is striking a match. Before a match can be used to light a campfire, the match has to be lit! A strike-anywhere match has all the reactants it needs to burn. The chemicals on a match react and burn. But, the chemicals will not light by themselves. You must strike the match against a surface. The heat produced by this friction provides the activation energy needed to start the reaction.

WRITING SKILL **The Strike-Anywhere Match** Research the invention of the strike-anywhere match. Find out who invented it, who patented it, and when the match was introduced to the public. In your **science journal,** write a short report about what you learn from your research.

Reading Check **What is activation energy?**

Sources of Activation Energy

Friction is one source of activation energy. In the match example, friction provides the energy needed to break the bonds in the reactants and allow new bonds to form. An electric spark in a car's engine is another source of activation energy. This spark begins the burning of gasoline. Light can also be a source of activation energy for a reaction. **Figure 4** shows how activation energy relates to exothermic reactions and endothermic reactions.

Figure 4 Energy Diagrams

Exothermic Reaction Once an exothermic reaction starts, it can continue. The energy given off as the product forms continues to supply the activation energy needed for the substances to react.

Activation energy
Reactants
Energy
Energy given off
Products
Reaction progress

Endothermic Reaction An endothermic reaction continues to absorb energy. Energy must be used to provide the activation energy needed for the substances to react.

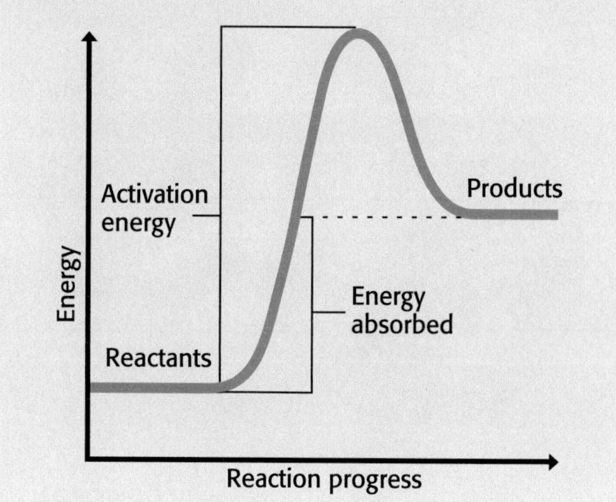

Factors Affecting Rates of Reactions

The rate of a reaction is a measure of how fast the reaction takes place. Recall that the rate of a reaction depends on how fast new particles form. There are four factors that affect the rate of a reaction. These factors are: temperature, concentration, surface area, and the presence of an inhibitor or catalyst.

Temperature

A higher temperature causes a faster rate of reaction, as shown in **Figure 5.** At high temperatures, particles of reactants move quickly. The rapid movement causes the particles to collide often and with a lot of energy. So, many particles have the activation energy to react. And many reactants can change into products in a short time.

Figure 5 *The light stick on the right glows brighter than the one on the left because the one on the right is warmer. The higher temperature causes the rate of the reaction to increase.*

Which Is Quicker?

1. Fill a **clear plastic cup** with **250 mL of warm water.** Fill a **second clear plastic cup** with **250 mL of cold water.**
2. Place **one-quarter of an effervescent tablet** in each of the two cups of water at the same time. Using a **stopwatch,** time each reaction.
3. Observe each reaction, and record your observations.
4. In which cup did the reaction occur at a faster rate?

Figure 6 Concentration of Solutions

▼ When the amount of copper sulfate crystals dissolved in water is **small,** the concentration of the copper sulfate solution is **low.**

▼ When the amount of copper sulfate crystals dissolved in water is **large,** the concentration of the copper sulfate solution is **high.**

Concentration

In general, a high concentration of reactants causes a fast rate of a reaction. *Concentration* is a measure of the amount of one substance dissolved in another substance, as shown in **Figure 6.** When the concentration is high, there are many reactant particles in a given volume. So, there is a small distance between particles. The particles run into each other often. Thus, the particles react faster.

Reading Check **How does a high concentration of reactants increase the rate of a reaction?**

CONNECTION TO Biology

Enzymes and Inhibitors Enzymes are proteins that speed up reactions in your body. Sometimes, chemicals called *inhibitors* stop the action of enzymes. Research how inhibitors are beneficial in reactions in the human body. Make a poster or a model that explains what you have learned, and present it to your class.

ACTIVITY

Surface Area

Surface area is the amount of exposed surface of a substance. Increasing the surface area of solid reactants increases the rate of a reaction. Grinding a solid into a powder makes a larger surface area. Greater surface area exposes more particles of the reactant to other reactant particles. This exposure to other particles causes the particles of the reactants to collide with each other more often. So, the rate of the reaction is increased.

Inhibitors

An **inhibitor** is a substance that slows down or stops a chemical reaction. Slowing down or stopping a reaction may sometimes be useful. For example, preservatives are added to foods to slow down the growth of bacteria and fungi. The preservatives prevent bacteria and fungi from producing substances that can spoil food. Some antibiotics are examples of inhibitors. For example, penicillin prevents certain kinds of bacteria from making a cell wall. So, the bacteria die.

inhibitor a substance that slows down or stops a chemical reaction

catalyst a substance that changes the rate of a chemical reaction without being used up or changed very much

Catalysts

Some chemical reactions would be too slow to be useful without a catalyst (KAT uh LIST). A **catalyst** is a substance that speeds up a reaction without being permanently changed. Because it is not changed, a catalyst is not a reactant. A catalyst lowers the activation energy of a reaction, which allows the reaction to happen more quickly. Catalysts called *enzymes* speed up most reactions in your body. Catalysts are even found in cars, as seen in **Figure 7.** The catalytic converter decreases air pollution. It does this by increasing the rate of reactions that involve the harmful products given off by cars.

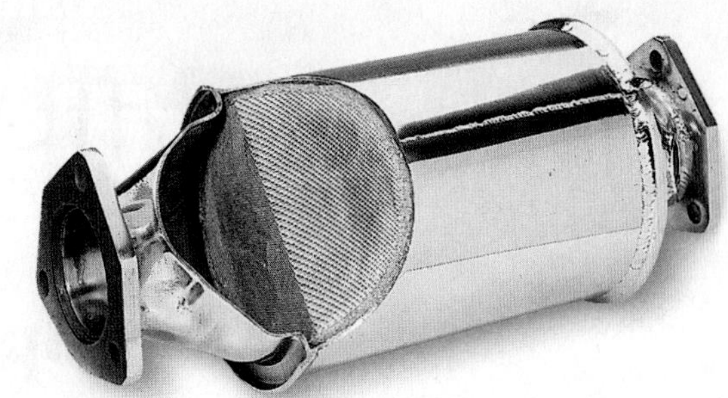

Figure 7 *This catalytic converter contains platinum and palladium. These two catalysts increase the rate of reactions that make the car's exhaust less harmful.*

SECTION Review

Summary

- Energy is given off in exothermic reactions.
- Energy is absorbed in an endothermic reaction.
- The law of conservation of energy states that energy is neither created nor destroyed.
- Activation energy is the energy needed for a reaction to occur.
- The rate of a chemical reaction is affected by temperature, concentration, surface area, and the presence of an inhibitor or catalyst.

Using Key Terms

The statements below are false. For each statement, replace the underlined term to make a true statement.

1. An <u>exothermic</u> reaction absorbs energy.
2. The rate of a reaction can be increased by adding <u>an inhibitor</u>.

Understanding Key Ideas

3. Which of the following will not increase the rate of a reaction?
   a. adding a catalyst
   b. increasing the temperature of the reaction
   c. decreasing the concentration of reactants
   d. grinding a solid into powder
4. How does the concentration of a solution affect the rate of reaction?

Critical Thinking

5. **Making Comparisons** Compare exothermic and endothermic reactions.
6. **Applying Concepts** Explain how chewing your food thoroughly can help your body digest food.

Interpreting Graphics

Use the diagram below to answer the questions that follow.

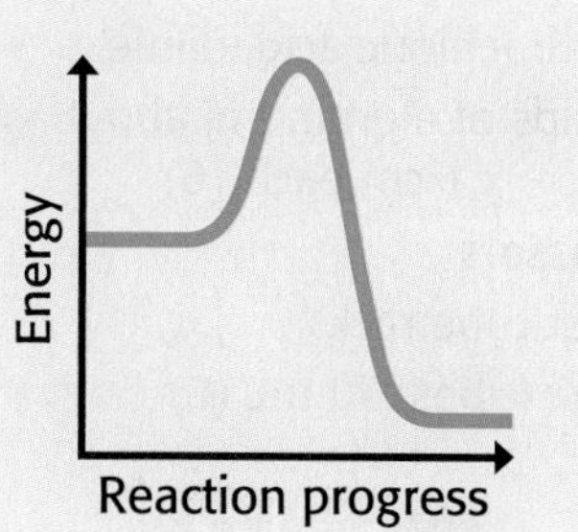

7. Does this energy diagram show an exothermic or an endothermic reaction? How can you tell?
8. A catalyst lowers the amount of activation energy needed to get a reaction started. What do you think the diagram would look like if a catalyst were added?

SCILINKS.
NSTA
Developed and maintained by the National Science Teachers Association
For a variety of links related to this chapter, go to www.scilinks.org
Topic: Exothermic and Endothermic Reactions
SciLinks code: HSM0555

Using Scientific Methods

Skills Practice Lab

Speed Control

OBJECTIVES

Describe how the surface area of a solid affects the rate of a reaction.

Explain how concentration of reactants will speed up or slow down a reaction.

MATERIALS

- funnels (2)
- graduated cylinders, 10 mL (2)
- hydrochloric acid, concentrated
- hydrochloric acid, dilute
- strips of aluminum, about 5 cm x 1 cm each (6)
- scissors
- test-tube rack
- test tubes, 30 mL (6)

SAFETY

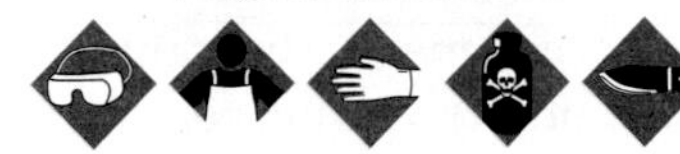

The reaction rate (how fast a chemical reaction happens) is an important factor to control. Sometimes, you want a reaction to take place rapidly, such as when you are removing tarnish from a metal surface. Other times, you want a reaction to happen very slowly, such as when you are depending on a battery as a source of electrical energy.

In this lab, you will discover how changing the surface area and concentration of the reactants affects reaction rate. In this lab, you can estimate the rate of reaction by observing how fast bubbles form.

Part A: Surface Area

Ask a Question

1. How does changing the surface area of a metal affect reaction rate?

Form a Hypothesis

2. Write a statement that answers the question above. Explain your reasoning.

Test the Hypothesis

3. Use three identical strips of aluminum. Put one strip into a test tube. Place the test tube in the test-tube rack. **Caution:** The strips of metal may have sharp edges.

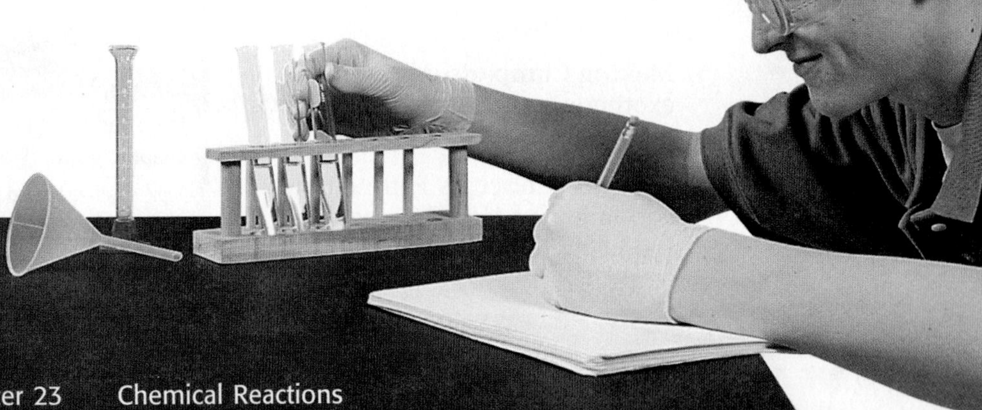

4. Carefully fold a second strip in half and then in half again. Use a textbook or other large object to flatten the folded strip as much as possible. Place the strip in a second test tube in the test-tube rack.
5. Use scissors to cut a third strip of aluminum into the smallest possible pieces. Place all of the pieces into a third test tube, and place the test tube in the test-tube rack.
6. Use a funnel and a graduated cylinder to pour 10 mL of concentrated hydrochloric acid into each of the three test tubes. **Caution:** Hydrochloric acid is corrosive. If any acid should spill on you, immediately flush the area with water and notify your teacher.
7. Observe the rate of bubble formation in each test tube. Record your observations.

Analyze the Results

1. **Organizing Data** Which form of aluminum had the greatest surface area? the smallest surface area?
2. **Analyzing Data** The amount of aluminum and the amount of acid were the same in all three test tubes. Which form of the aluminum seemed to react the fastest? Which form reacted the slowest? Explain your answers.
3. **Analyzing Results** Do your results support the hypothesis you made? Explain.

Draw Conclusions

4. **Making Predictions** Would powdered aluminum react faster or slower than the forms of aluminum you used? Explain your answer.

Part B: Concentration

Ask a Question

1. How does changing the concentration of acid affect the reaction rate?

Form a Hypothesis

2. Write a statement that answers the question above. Explain your reasoning.

Test the Hypothesis

3. Place one of the three remaining aluminum strips in each of the three clean test tubes. (Note: Do not alter the strips.) Place the test tubes in the test-tube rack.
4. Using the second funnel and graduated cylinder, pour 10 mL of water into one of the test tubes. Pour 10 mL of dilute acid into the second test tube. Pour 10 mL of concentrated acid into the third test tube.
5. Observe the rate of bubble formation in the three test tubes. Record your observations.

Analyze the Results

1. **Explaining Events** In this set of test tubes, the strips of aluminum were the same, but the concentration of the acid was different. Was there a difference between the test tube that contained water and the test tubes that contained acid? Which test tube formed bubbles the fastest? Explain.
2. **Analyzing Results** Do your results support the hypothesis you made? Explain.

Draw Conclusions

3. **Applying Conclusions** Why should spilled hydrochloric acid be diluted with water before it is wiped up?

Chapter Review

USING KEY TERMS

Complete each of the following sentences by choosing the correct term from the word bank.

subscript	exothermic reaction
inhibitor	synthesis reaction
product	reactant

1. Adding a(n) ___ will slow down a chemical reaction.

2. A chemical reaction that gives off heat is called a(n) ___.

3. A chemical reaction that forms one compound from two or more substances is called a(n) ___.

4. The 2 in the formula Ag_2S is a(n) ___.

UNDERSTANDING KEY IDEAS

Multiple Choice

5. Balancing a chemical equation so that the same number of atoms of each element is found in both the reactants and the products is an example of
   a. activation energy.
   b. the law of conservation of energy.
   c. the law of conservation of mass.
   d. a double-displacement reaction.

6. Which of the following is the correct chemical formula for dinitrogen tetroxide?
   a. N_4O_2
   b. NO_2
   c. N_2O_5
   d. N_2O_4

7. In which type of reaction do ions in two compounds switch places?
   a. a synthesis reaction
   b. a decomposition reaction
   c. a single-displacement reaction
   d. a double-displacement reaction

8. Which of the following actions is an example of the use of activation energy?
   a. plugging in an iron
   b. playing basketball
   c. holding a lit match to paper
   d. eating

9. Enzymes in your body act as catalysts. Thus, the role of enzymes is
   a. to increase the rate of chemical reactions.
   b. to decrease the rate of chemical reactions.
   c. to help you breathe.
   d. to inhibit chemical reactions.

Short Answer

10. Name the type of reaction that each of the following equations represents.
    a. $2Cu + O_2 \rightarrow 2CuO$
    b. $2Na + MgSO_4 \rightarrow Na_2SO_4 + Mg$
    c. $Ba(CN)_2 + H_2SO_4 \rightarrow BaSO_4 + 2HCN$

11. Describe what happens to chemical bonds during a chemical reaction.

12. Name four ways that you can change the rate of a chemical reaction.

13. Describe four clues that signal that a chemical reaction is taking place.

Math Skills

14 Write balanced equations for the following:

a. $Fe + O_2 \rightarrow Fe_2O_3$

b. $Al + CuSO_4 \rightarrow Al_2(SO_4)_3 + Cu$

c. $Mg(OH)_2 + HCl \rightarrow MgCl_2 + H_2O$

15 Calculate the number of atoms of each element shown in the formulas below:

a. $CaSO_4$

b. $4NaOCl$

c. $Fe(NO_3)_2$

d. $2Al_2(CO_3)_3$

CRITICAL THINKING

16 **Concept Mapping** Use the following terms to create a concept map: *products, chemical reaction, chemical equation, chemical formulas, reactants, coefficients,* and *subscripts.*

17 **Evaluating Assumptions** Your friend is very worried by rumors that he has heard about a substance called *dihydrogen monoxide* in the city's water system. What could you say to your friend to calm his fears? (Hint: Write the formula of the substance.)

18 **Analyzing Ideas** As long as proper safety precautions have been taken, why can explosives be transported long distances without exploding?

19 **Applying Concepts** You measured the mass of a steel pipe before leaving it outdoors. One month later, the pipe had rusted, and its mass had increased. Does this change violate the law of conservation of mass? Explain your answer.

20 **Applying Concepts** Acetic acid, a compound found in vinegar, reacts with baking soda to produce carbon dioxide, water, and sodium acetate. Without writing an equation, identify the reactants and the products of this reaction.

INTERPRETING GRAPHICS

Use the photo below to answer the questions that follow.

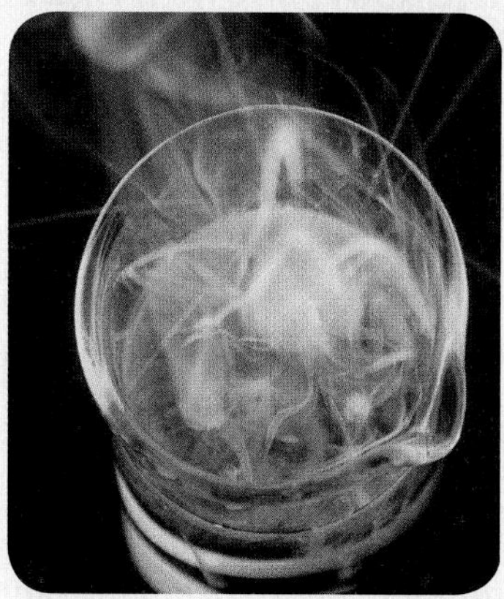

21 What evidence in the photo supports the claim that a chemical reaction is taking place?

22 Is this reaction an exothermic or endothermic reaction? Explain your answer.

23 Draw and label an energy diagram of both an exothermic and endothermic reaction. Identify the diagram that describes the reaction shown in the photo above.

Multiple Choice

Use the picture below to answer question 1.

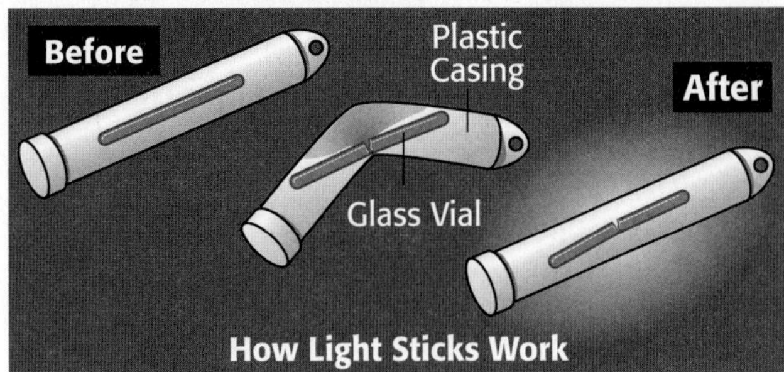

1. **The picture above shows a light stick. Light sticks begin to glow when the vial inside the stick is broken. Chemicals inside the vial mix with chemicals outside of the vial. Which of the following statements BEST supports the idea that a chemical reaction is occurring?**

   A. The vial is broken into smaller pieces.

   B. Energy is released in the form of light.

   C. Two different substances are combined.

   D. The substances are in a flexible container.

2. **Chemical reactions are used in many processes, such as cooking food, heating homes, and powering automobiles. In chemical reactions, energy is transferred from one molecule to another. How is this energy transferred?**

   A. by the gravitational attraction between molecules

   B. by the bumping of one molecule into another molecule

   C. by one molecule sending out electricity to another molecule

   D. by one molecule sending out heat waves to another molecule

3. **Some spoons are made with the element silver (Ag). Over time, these spoons will turn black if it is not cleaned with a special solution. Which of the following statements BEST explains why the element silver in the spoons turns black?**

   A. It absorbs energy when exposed to warm food.

   B. It breaks down into smaller and smaller particles.

   C. It reacts with substances in the air to form a new substance.

   D. It changes from one phase of matter into another phase of matter.

4. **Which of the following contains one oxygen atom?**

   A. H_2O

   B. CO_2

   C. $2N_2O$

   D. Co

5. **Which process causes substances to react to form one or more new substances?**

   A. chemical change

   B. physical change

   C. evaporation

   D. freezing

Use the graph below to answer question 6.

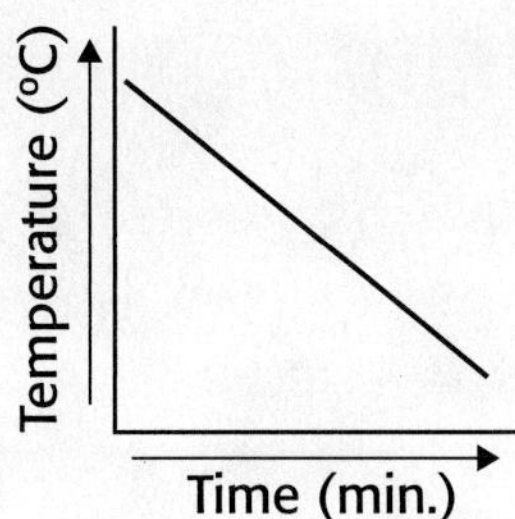

6. The graph above shows the change in temperature over time in a chemical reaction. According to the graph, how would this reaction be described?

A. endothermic

B. exothermic

C. unbalanced

D. combustion

7. Which chemical equation correctly shows the formation of water from hydrogen and oxygen?

A. $H_2 + O_2 = H_2O$

B. $2H_2 + O_2 = 2H_2O$

C. $H_2 + 2O = H_2O$

D. $H + O_2 = H_2O$

8. A scientist carries out a reaction in a test tube. After the bubbling stops, she notices that the test tube is very warm. What might she conclude about the reaction?

A. The reaction happened very quickly.

B. The reaction is endothermic.

C. The reaction is exothermic.

D. No reaction took place.

9. A substance that is used to speed up a chemical reaction is called

A. a reactant.

B. an inhibitor.

C. a precipitate.

D. a catalyst.

10. During a laboratory experiment, Tran applied the law of conservation of energy. Which of the following did he assume to be true?

A. Energy is not changed.

B. Energy is not created or destroyed.

C. The total energy of the reactants is greater than the total energy of the products.

D. The total energy of the reactants is less than the total mass of the products.

Open Response

11. What are three ways by which the rate of a chemical reaction can be increased?

12. Compare synthesis and decomposition reactions, and give an example of each.

Standardized Test Preparation

Science in Action

Science, Technology, and Society

Bringing Down the House!

Have you ever watched a building being demolished? It takes only minutes to demolish it, but a lot of time was spent planning the demolition. And it takes time to remove hazardous chemicals from the building. For example, asbestos, which is found in insulation, can cause lung cancer. Mercury found in thermostats can cause brain damage, birth defects, and death. It is important to remove these substances because most of the rubble is sent to a landfill. If hazardous chemicals are not removed, they could leak into the groundwater and enter the water supply.

Math Activity

A city produces 4 million tons of waste in 1 year. Of this waste, 82% is solid waste. If 38% of the solid waste comes from the construction and demolition of buildings, how many tons of waste does this represent?

Weird Science

Light Sticks

Have you ever seen light sticks at a concert? Your family may even keep them in the car for emergencies. But how do light sticks work? To activate the light stick, you have to bend it. Most light sticks are made of a plastic tube that contains a mixture of two chemicals. Also inside the tube is a thin glass vial, which contains hydrogen peroxide. As long as the glass vial is unbroken, the two chemicals are kept separate. But bending the ends of the tube breaks the glass vial. This action releases the hydrogen peroxide into the other chemicals and a chemical reaction occurs, which makes the light stick glow.

Social Studies Activity

Who invented light sticks? What was their original purpose? Research the answers to these questions. Make a poster that shows what you have learned.

Careers

Larry McKee

Arson Investigator Once a fire dies down, you might see an arson investigator like Lt. Larry McKee on the scene. "After the fire is out, I can investigate the fire scene to determine where the fire started and how it started," says McKee, who questions witnesses and firefighters about what they have seen. He knows that the color of the smoke can indicate certain chemicals. He also has help detecting chemicals from an accelerant-sniffing dog, Nikki. Nikki has been trained to detect about 11 different chemicals. If Nikki finds one of these chemicals, she begins to dig. McKee takes a sample of the suspicious material to the laboratory. He treats the sample so that any chemicals present will dissolve in a liquid. A sample of this liquid is placed into an instrument called a *gas chromatograph* and tested. The results of this test are printed out in a graph, from which the suspicious chemical is identified. Next, McKee begins to search for suspects. By combining detective work with scientific evidence, fire investigators can help find clues that can lead to the conviction of the arsonist.

Language Arts ACTIVITY

WRITING SKILL Write a one-page story about an arson investigator. Begin the story at the scene of a fire. Take the story through the different steps that you think an investigator would have to go through to solve the crime.

To learn more about these Science in Action topics, visit go.hrw.com and type in the keyword **HP5REAF**.

Current Science

Check out Current Science® articles related to this chapter by visiting go.hrw.com. Just type in the keyword HP5CS14.

24

Chemical Compounds

The Big Idea

Chemical compounds are classified into groups based on their bonds and on their properties.

SECTION

About the Photo

The bean weevil feeds on bean seeds, which are rich in chemical compounds such as proteins, carbohydrates, and lipids. The bean weevil begins life as a tiny grub that lives in the seed where it eats starch and protein. The adult then cuts holes in the seed coat and crawls out, as you can see in this photo.

PRE-READING ACTIVITY

FOLDNOTES **Layered Book** Before you read the chapter, create the FoldNote entitled "Layered Book" described in the **Study Skills** section of the Appendix. Label the tabs of the layered book with "Ionic and covalent compounds," "Acids and bases," "Solutions of acids and bases," and "Organic compounds." As you read the chapter, write information you learn about each category under the appropriate tab.

START-UP ACTIVITY

Sticking Together

In this activity, you will demonstrate the force that keeps particles together in some compounds.

Procedure

1. Rub **two balloons** with a **wool cloth.** Move the balloons near each other. Describe what you see.
2. Put one balloon against a wall. Record your observations.

Analysis

1. The balloons are charged by rubbing them with the wool cloth. Like charges repel each other. Opposite charges attract each other. Do the balloons have like or opposite charges? Explain.
2. If the balloon that was placed against the wall has a negative charge, what is the charge on the wall? Explain your answer.
3. The particles that make up compounds are attracted to each other in the same way that the balloon is attracted to the wall. What can you infer about the particles that make up such compounds?

SECTION 1

Ionic and Covalent Compounds

What You Will Learn

- Describe the properties of ionic and covalent compounds.
- Classify compounds as ionic or covalent based on their properties.

Vocabulary

chemical bond
ionic compound
covalent compound

READING STRATEGY

Reading Organizer As you read this section, create an outline of the section. Use the headings from the section in your outline.

When ions or molecules combine, they form compounds. Because there are millions of compounds, it is helpful to organize them into groups. But how can scientists tell the difference between compounds?

One way to group compounds is by the kind of chemical bond they have. A **chemical bond** is the combining of atoms to form molecules or compounds. Bonding can occur between valence electrons of different atoms. *Valence electrons* are electrons in the outermost energy level of an atom. The behavior of valence electrons determines if an ionic compound or a covalent compound is formed.

Ionic Compounds and Their Properties

The properties of ionic compounds are a result of strong attractive forces called ionic bonds. An *ionic bond* is an attraction between oppositely charged ions. Compounds that contain ionic bonds are called **ionic compounds.** Ionic compounds can be formed by the reaction of a metal with a nonmetal. Metal atoms become positively charged ions when electrons are transferred from the metal atoms to the nonmetal atoms. This transfer of electrons also causes the nonmetal atom to become a negatively charged ion. Sodium chloride, commonly known as *table salt,* is an ionic compound.

chemical bond the combining of atoms to form molecules or compounds

ionic compound a compound made of oppositely charged ions

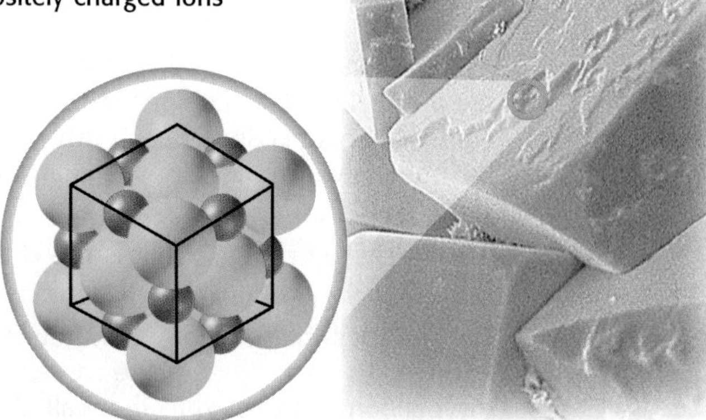

Figure 1 *The sodium ions, shown in purple, and the chloride ions, shown in green, are bonded in the crystal lattice structure of sodium chloride.*

Brittleness

Ionic compounds tend to be brittle solids at room temperature. So, they usually break apart when hit. This property is due to the arrangement of ions in a repeating three-dimensional pattern called a *crystal lattice,* shown in **Figure 1.** Each ion in a lattice is surrounded by ions of the opposite charge. And each ion is bonded to the ions around it. When an ionic compound is hit, the pattern of ions shifts. Ions that have the same charge line up and repel one another, which causes the crystal to break.

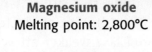

Figure 2 Melting Points of Some Ionic Compounds

Potassium dichromate
Melting point: 398°C

Magnesium oxide
Melting point: 2,800°C

Nickel(II) oxide
Melting point: 1,984°C

High Melting Points

Because of the strong ionic bonds that hold ions together, ionic compounds have high melting points. These high melting points are the reason that most ionic compounds are solids at room temperature. For example, solid sodium chloride must be heated to 801°C before it will melt. The melting points of three other ionic compounds are given in **Figure 2.**

Solubility and Electrical Conductivity

Many ionic compounds are highly soluble. So, they dissolve easily in water. Water molecules attract each of the ions of an ionic compound and pull the ions away from one another. The solution that forms when an ionic compound dissolves in water can conduct an electric current, as shown in **Figure 3.** The solution can conduct an electric current because the ions are charged and are able to move freely past one another. However, an undissolved crystal of an ionic compound does not conduct an electric current.

Reading Check **Why do solutions of ionic compounds dissolved in water conduct an electric current?** (*See the Appendix for answers to Reading Checks.*)

For another activity related to this chapter, go to **go.hrw.com** and type in the keyword **HP5CMPW.**

Figure 3 *The pure water does not conduct an electric current. However, the solution of salt water conducts an electric current, so the bulb lights up.*

covalent compound a chemical compound formed by the sharing of electrons

Covalent Compounds and Their Properties

Most compounds are covalent compounds. **Covalent compounds** are compounds that form when a group of atoms shares electrons. This sharing of electrons forms a covalent bond. A *covalent bond* is a weaker attractive force than an ionic bond is. The group of atoms that make up a covalent compound is called a molecule. A *molecule* is the smallest particle into which a covalently bonded compound can be divided and still be the same compound. Properties of covalent compounds are very different from the properties of ionic compounds.

Low Solubility

Many covalent compounds are not soluble in water, which means that they do not dissolve well in water. You may have noticed this if you have ever left off the top of a soda bottle. The carbon dioxide gas that gives the soda its fizz eventually escapes, and your soda pop goes "flat." The attraction between water molecules is much stronger than their attraction to the molecules of most other covalent compounds. So, water molecules stay together instead of mixing with the covalent compounds. If you have ever made salad dressing, you probably know that oil and water don't mix. Oils, such as the oil in the salad dressing in **Figure 4,** are made of covalent compounds.

Reading Check Why won't most covalent compounds dissolve in water?

CONNECTION TO Language Arts

WRITING SKILL **Electrolyte Solutions** Ionic compounds that conduct electricity when they are dissolved in water are called *electrolytes*. Some electrolytes play important roles in the functioning of living cells. Electrolytes can be lost by the body during intense physical activity or illness and must be replenished for cells to work properly. Research two electrolytes that your body cells need and the function that they serve. Present your findings in a one-page research paper.

Figure 4 *Olive oil, which is used in salad dressings, is made of very large covalent molecules that do not mix with water.*

Low Melting Points

The forces of attraction between molecules of covalent compounds are much weaker than the bonds holding ionic solids together. Less heat is needed to separate the molecules of covalent compounds, so these compounds have much lower melting and boiling points than ionic compounds do.

Electrical Conductivity

Although most covalent compounds don't dissolve in water, some do. Most of the covalent compounds that dissolve in water form solutions that have uncharged molecules. Sugar is a covalent compound that dissolves in water and that does not form ions. So, a solution of sugar and water does not conduct an electric current, as shown in **Figure 5.** However, some covalent compounds do form ions when they dissolve in water. Many acids, for example, form ions in water. These solutions, like ionic solutions, conduct an electric current.

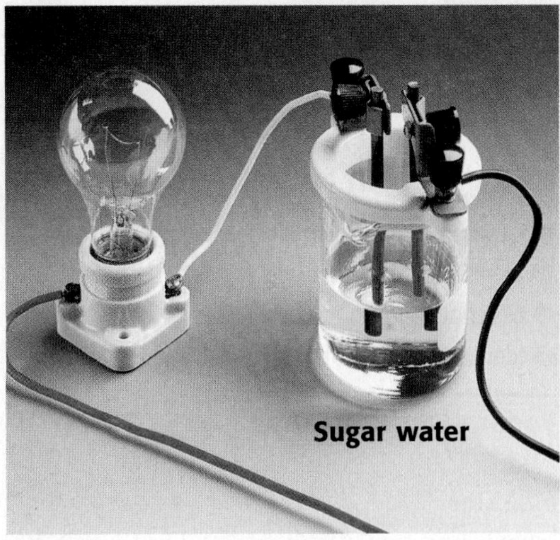
Sugar water

Figure 5 *This solution of sugar, a covalent compound, and water does not conduct an electric current because the molecules of sugar are not charged.*

SECTION Review

Summary

- Ionic compounds have ionic bonds between ions of opposite charges.
- Ionic compounds are usually brittle, have high melting points, dissolve in water, and often conduct an electric current.
- Covalent compounds have covalent bonds and consist of particles called molecules.
- Covalent compounds have low melting points, don't dissolve easily in water, and do not conduct an electric current.

Using Key Terms

1. Use each of the following terms in a separate sentence: *ionic compound, covalent compound,* and *chemical bond.*

Understanding Key Ideas

2. Which of the following describes an ionic compound?
   a. It has a low melting point.
   b. It consists of shared electrons.
   c. It conducts electric current in water solutions.
   d. It consists of two nonmetals.
3. List two properties of covalent compounds.

Math Skills

4. A compound contains 39.37% chromium, 38.10% oxygen, and potassium. What percentage of the compound is potassium?

Critical Thinking

5. **Making Inferences** Solid crystals of ionic compounds do not conduct an electric current. But when the crystals dissolve in water, the solution conducts an electric current. Explain.
6. **Applying Concepts** Some white solid crystals are dissolved in water. If the solution does not conduct an electric current, is the solid an ionic compound or a covalent compound? Explain.

SCILINKS.
NSTA
Developed and maintained by the National Science Teachers Association
For a variety of links related to this chapter, go to www.scilinks.org
Topic: Ionic Compounds; Covalent Compounds
SciLinks code: HSM0817; HSM0365

SECTION 2

Acids and Bases

Would you like a nice, refreshing glass of acid? This is just what you get when you have a glass of lemonade.

What You Will Learn

- Describe four properties of acids.
- Identify four uses of acids.
- Describe four properties of bases.
- Identify four uses of bases.

Vocabulary

acid
indicator
base

READING STRATEGY

Reading Organizer As you read this section, make a table comparing acids and bases.

Lemons contain a substance called an *acid*. One property of acids is a sour taste. In this section, you will learn about the properties of acids and bases.

Acids and Their Properties

A sour taste is not the only property of an acid. Have you noticed that when you squeeze lemon juice into tea, the color of the tea becomes lighter? This change happens because acids cause some substances to change color. An **acid** is any compound that increases the number of hydronium ions, H_3O^+, when dissolved in water. Hydronium ions form when a hydrogen ion, H^+, separates from the acid and bonds with a water molecule, H_2O, to form a hydronium ion, H_3O^+.

Reading Check **How is a hydronium ion formed?** (*See the Appendix for answers to Reading Checks.*)

acid any compound that increases the number of hydronium ions when dissolved in water

Acids Have a Sour Flavor

Have you ever taken a bite of a lemon or lime? If so, like the boy in **Figure 1,** you know the sour taste of an acid. The taste of lemons, limes, and other citrus fruits is a result of citric acid. However, taste, touch, or smell should NEVER be used to identify an unknown chemical. Many acids are *corrosive,* which means that they destroy body tissue, clothing, and many other things. Most acids are also poisonous.

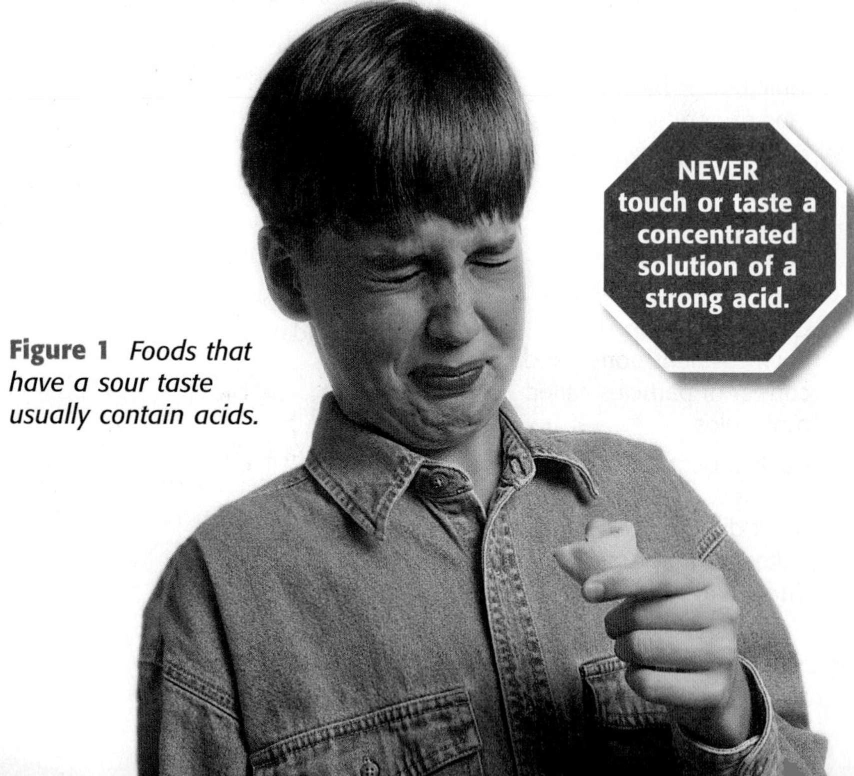

NEVER touch or taste a concentrated solution of a strong acid.

Figure 1 *Foods that have a sour taste usually contain acids.*

Figure 2 **Detecting Acids with Indicators**

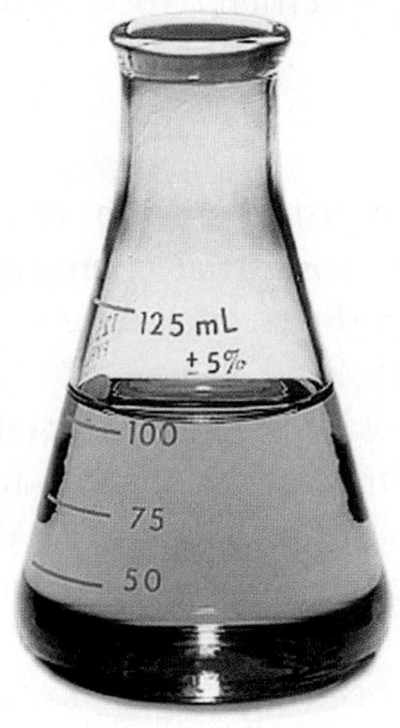

The indicator, bromthymol blue, is pale blue in water.

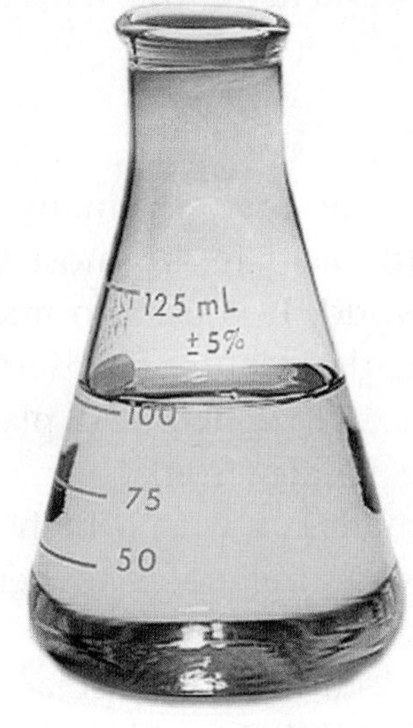

When acid is added, the color changes to yellow because of the presence of the indicator.

indicator a compound that can reversibly change color depending on conditions such as pH

Acids Change Colors in Indicators

A substance that changes color in the presence of an acid or base is an **indicator.** Look at **Figure 2.** The flask on the left contains water and an indicator called *bromthymol blue* (BROHM THIE MAWL BLOO). Acid has been added to the flask on the right. The color changes from pale blue to yellow because the indicator detects the presence of an acid.

Another indicator commonly used in the lab is litmus. Paper strips containing litmus are available in both blue and red. When an acid is added to blue litmus paper, the color of the litmus changes to red.

Acids React with Metals

Acids react with some metals to produce hydrogen gas. For example, hydrochloric acid reacts with zinc metal to produce hydrogen gas, as shown in **Figure 3.** The equation for the reaction is the following:

$$2HCl + Zn \longrightarrow H_2 + ZnCl_2$$

In this reaction, zinc displaces hydrogen in the compound, hydrochloric acid. This displacement happens because zinc is an active metal. But if the element silver were put into hydrochloric acid, nothing would happen. Silver is not an active metal, so no reaction would take place.

Figure 3 *Bubbles of hydrogen gas form when zinc metal reacts with hydrochloric acid.*

Acids Conduct Electric Current

When acids are dissolved in water, they break apart and form ions in the solution. The ions make it possible for the solution to conduct an electric current. A car battery is one example of how an acid can be used to produce an electric current. The sulfuric acid in the battery conducts electricity to help start the car's engine.

CONNECTION TO Biology

Acids Can Curl Your Hair! Permanents contain acids. Acids make hair curly by denaturing a certain amino acid in hair proteins. Research how acids are used in products that either curl or straighten hair. Then, make a poster that demonstrates this process. Present your poster to your classmates.

ACTIVITY

Uses of Acids

Acids are used in many areas of industry and in homes. Sulfuric acid is the most widely made industrial chemical in the world. It is used to make many products, including paper, paint, detergents, and fertilizers. Nitric acid is used to make fertilizers, rubber, and plastics. Hydrochloric acid is used to make metals from their ores by separating the metals from the materials with which they are combined. It is also used in swimming pools to help keep them free of algae. Hydrochloric acid is even found in your stomach, where it aids in digestion. Hydrofluoric acid is used to etch glass, as shown in **Figure 4.** Citric acid and ascorbic acid (Vitamin C) are found in orange juice. And carbonic acid and phosphoric acid help give a sharp taste to soft drinks.

Reading Check **What are three uses of acids?**

Figure 4 *The image of the swan was etched into the glass through the use of hydrofluoric acid.*

Figure 5 **Examples of Bases**

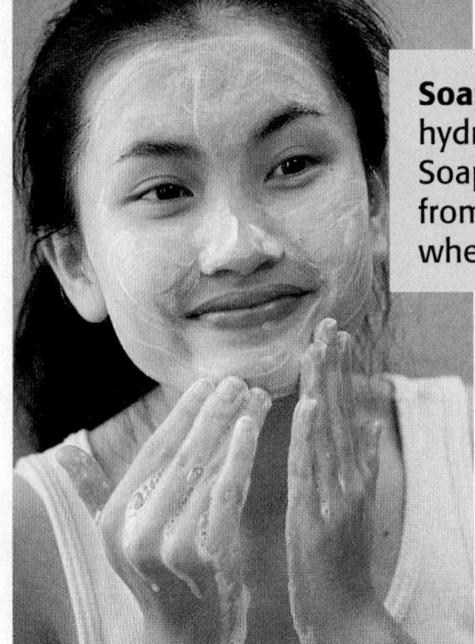

Soaps are made from sodium hydroxide, which is a base. Soaps remove dirt and oils from skin and feel slippery when you touch them.

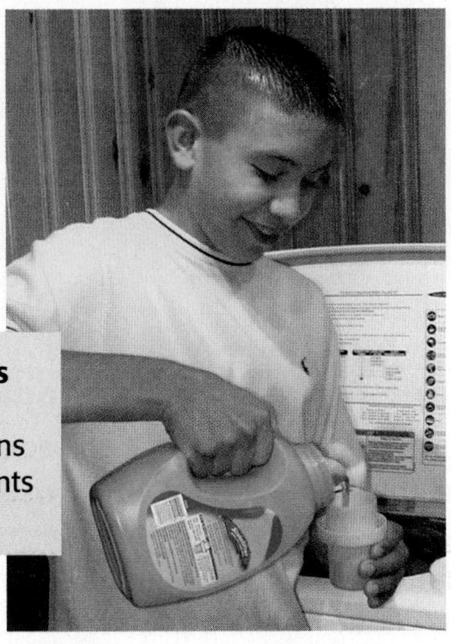

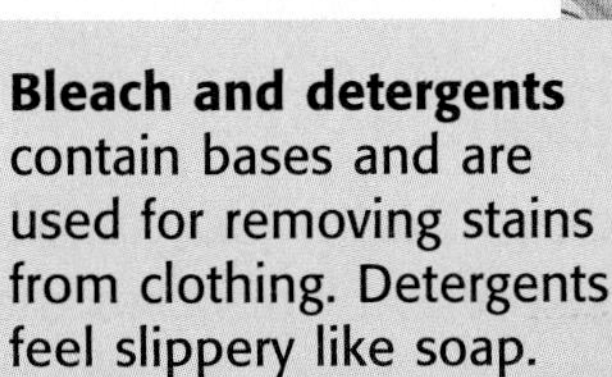

Bleach and detergents contain bases and are used for removing stains from clothing. Detergents feel slippery like soap.

Baking soda is a very mild base. It is used in toothpastes and mouthwashes to neutralize acids, which can produce unpleasant odors.

Bases and Their Properties

A **base** is any compound that increases the number of hydroxide ions, OH^-, when dissolved in water. For example, sodium hydroxide breaks apart to form sodium ions and hydroxide ions as shown below.

base any compound that increases the number of hydroxide ions when dissolved in water

$$NaOH \longrightarrow Na^+ + OH^-$$

Hydroxide ions give bases their properties. **Figure 5** shows examples of bases that you are probably familiar with.

Bases Have a Bitter Flavor and a Slippery Feel

The properties of a base solution include a bitter taste and a slippery feel. If you have ever accidentally tasted soap, you know the bitter taste of a base. Soap will also have the slippery feel of a base. However, taste, touch or smell should NEVER be used to identify an unknown chemical. Like acids, many bases are corrosive. If your fingers feel slippery when you are using a base in an experiment, you may have gotten the base on your hands. You should immediately rinse your hands with large amounts of water and tell your teacher.

NEVER touch or taste a concentrated solution of a strong base.

SCHOOL to HOME

Acids and Bases at Home

Ask an adult to join in a contest with you. The object is to find products at home that contain an acid or a base. Each person will write the name of the product and the name of the acid or base that it contains. The person who finds the most products containing an acid or base is the winner.

ACTIVITY

Figure 6 Detecting Bases with Indicators

The indicator, bromthymol blue, is pale blue in water.

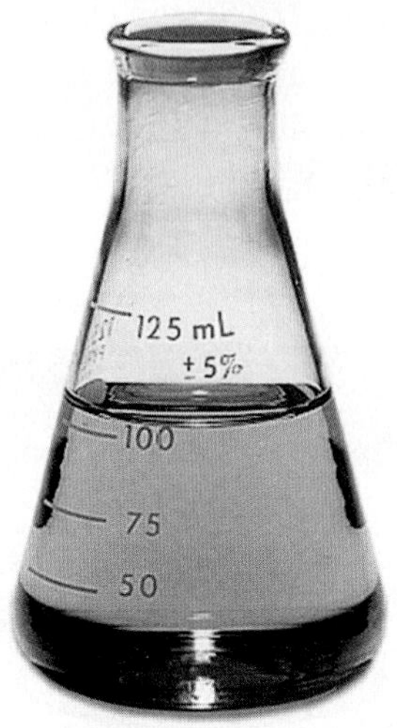

When a base is added to the indicator, the indicator turns dark blue.

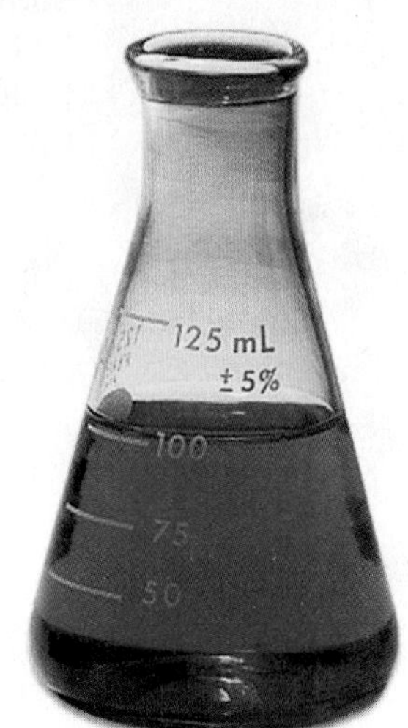

Bases Change Color in Indicators

Like acids, bases change the color of an indicator. Most indicators turn a different color in the presence of bases than they do in the presence of acids. For example, bases change the color of red litmus paper to blue. And the indicator, bromthymol blue, turns blue when a base is added to it, as shown in **Figure 6.**

Bases Conduct Electric Current

Solutions of bases conduct an electric current because bases increase the number of hydroxide ions, OH^-, in a solution. A hydroxide ion is actually a hydrogen atom and an oxygen atom bonded together. The extra electron gives the hydroxide ion a negative charge.

Blue to Red—Acid!

1. Pour about 5 mL of **test solution** into a **spot plate.** Test the solution using **red litmus paper** and **blue litmus paper** by dipping a **stirring rod** into it and then touching the rod to a piece of litmus paper.
2. Record any color changes. Clean the stirring rod.
3. Repeat the above steps with each solution. Use new pieces of litmus paper as needed.
4. Identify each solution as acidic or basic.

Uses of Bases

Like acids, bases have many uses. Sodium hydroxide is a base used to make soap and paper. It is also used in oven cleaners and in products that unclog drains. Calcium hydroxide, $Ca(OH)_2$, is used to make cement and plaster. Ammonia is found in many household cleaners and is used to make fertilizers. And magnesium hydroxide and aluminum hydroxide are used in antacids to treat heartburn. **Figure 7** shows some of the many products that contain bases. Carefully follow the safety instructions when using these products. Remember that bases can harm your skin.

Reading Check What three ways can bases be used at home?

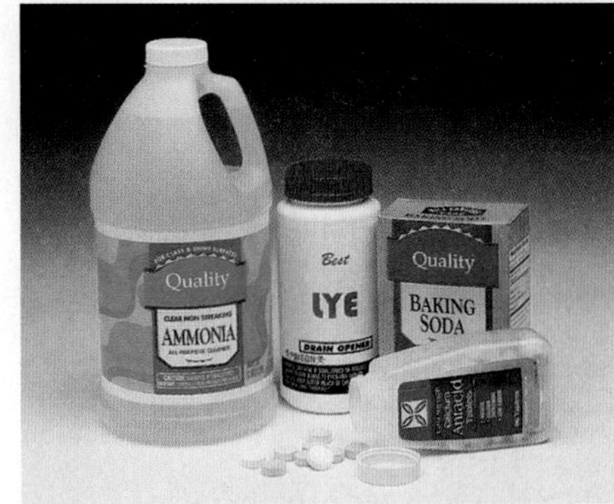

Figure 7 *Bases are common around the house. They are useful as cleaning agents, as cooking aids, and as medicines.*

SECTION Review

Summary

- An acid is a compound that increases the number of hydronium ions in solution.
- Acids taste sour, turn blue litmus paper red, react with metals to produce hydrogen gas, and may conduct an electric current when in solution.
- Acids are used for industrial purposes and in household products.
- A base is a compound that increases the number of hydroxide ions in solution.
- Bases taste bitter, feel slippery, and turn red litmus paper blue. Most solutions of bases conduct an electric current.
- Bases are used in cleaning products and acid neutralizers.

Using Key Terms

1. In your own words, write a definition for each of the following terms: *acid, base,* and *indicator*.

Understanding Key Ideas

2. A base is a substance that
   a. feels slippery.
   b. tastes sour.
   c. reacts with metals to produce hydrogen gas.
   d. turns blue litmus paper red.
3. Acids are important in
   a. making antacids.
   b. preparing detergents.
   c. keeping algae out of swimming pools.
   d. manufacturing cement.
4. What happens to red litmus paper when it touches a base?

Math Skills

5. A cake recipe calls for 472 mL of milk. You don't have a metric measuring cup at home, so you need to convert milliliters to cups. You know that 1 L equals 1.06 quarts and that there are 4 cups in 1 quart. How many cups of milk will you need to use?

Critical Thinking

6. **Making Comparisons** Compare the properties of acids and bases.
7. **Applying Concepts** Why would it be useful for a gardener or a vegetable farmer to use litmus paper to test soil samples?
8. **Analyzing Processes** Suppose that your teacher gives you a solution of an unknown chemical. The chemical is either an acid or a base. You know that touching or tasting acids and bases is not safe. What two tests could you perform on the chemical to determine whether it is an acid or a base? What results would help you decide if the chemical was an acid or a base?

SCILINKS.
NSTA
Developed and maintained by the National Science Teachers Association
For a variety of links related to this chapter, go to www.scilinks.org
Topic: Acids and Bases
SciLinks code: HSM0013

SECTION 3

Solutions of Acids and Bases

What You Will Learn

- Explain the difference between strong acids and bases and weak acids and bases.
- Identify acids and bases by using the pH scale.
- Describe the formation and uses of salts.

Vocabulary

neutralization reaction
pH
salt

READING STRATEGY

Discussion Read this section silently. Write down questions that you have about this section. Discuss your questions in a small group.

Suppose that at your friend's party, you ate several large pieces of pepperoni pizza followed by cake and ice cream. Now, you have a terrible case of indigestion.

If you have ever had an upset stomach, you may have felt very much like the boy in **Figure 1.** And you may have taken an antacid. But do you know how antacids work? An antacid is a weak base that neutralizes a strong acid in your stomach. In this section, you will learn about the strengths of acids and bases. You will also learn about reactions between acids and bases.

Strengths of Acids and Bases

Acids and bases can be strong or weak. The strength of an acid or a base is not the same as the concentration of an acid or a base. The concentration of an acid or a base is the amount of acid or base dissolved in water. But the strength of an acid or a base depends on the number of molecules that break apart when the acid or base is dissolved in water.

Strong Versus Weak Acids

As an acid dissolves in water, the acid's molecules break apart and produce hydrogen ions, H^+. If all of the molecules of an acid break apart, the acid is called a *strong acid*. Strong acids include sulfuric acid, nitric acid, and hydrochloric acid. If only a few molecules of an acid break apart, the acid is a weak acid. Weak acids include acetic (uh SEET ik) acid, citric acid, and carbonic acid.

Reading Check **What is the difference between a strong acid and a weak acid?** (*See the Appendix for answers to Reading Checks.*)

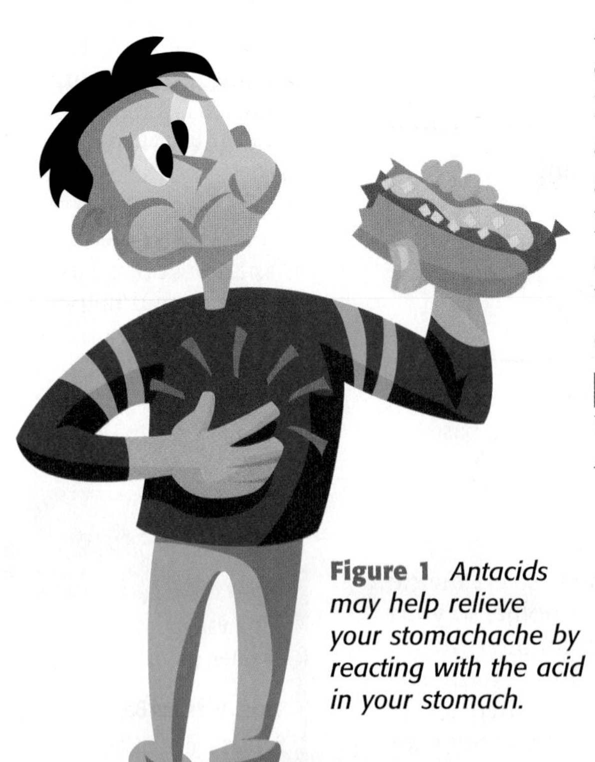

Figure 1 *Antacids may help relieve your stomachache by reacting with the acid in your stomach.*

Strong Versus Weak Bases

When all molecules of a base break apart in water to produce hydroxide ions, OH^-, the base is a strong base. Strong bases include sodium hydroxide, calcium hydroxide, and potassium hydroxide. When only a few molecules of a base break apart, the base is a weak base, such as ammonium hydroxide and aluminum hydroxide.

pHast Relief!

1. Pour **vinegar** into a **small plastic cup** until the cup is half full. Test the vinegar with **red and blue litmus paper.** Record your results.
2. Crush one **antacid tablet,** and mix it with the vinegar. Test the mixture with litmus paper. Record your results.
3. Compare the acidity of the solution before the antacid was added with the acidity of the solution after it was added.

Acids, Bases, and Neutralization

When the base in an antacid meets stomach acid, a reaction occurs. The reaction between acids and bases is a **neutralization reaction** (NOO truhl i ZA shuhn ree AK shuhn). Acids and bases neutralize one another because the hydrogen ions (H^+), which are present in an acid, and the hydroxide ions (OH^-), which are present in a base, react to form water, H_2O, which is neutral. Other ions from the acid and base dissolve in the water. If the water evaporates, these ions join to form a compound called a *salt*.

The pH Scale

An *indicator*, such as litmus, can identify whether a solution contains an acid or base. To describe how acidic or basic a solution is, the pH scale is used. The **pH** of a solution is a measure of the hydronium ion concentration in the solution. A solution that has a pH of 7 is neutral, which means that the solution is neither acidic nor basic. Pure water has a pH of 7. Basic solutions have a pH greater than 7. Acidic solutions have a pH less than 7. **Figure 2** shows the pH values for many common materials.

neutralization reaction the reaction of an acid and a base to form a neutral solution of water and a salt

pH a value that is used to express the acidity or basicity (alkalinity) of a system

Figure 2 pH Values of Common Materials

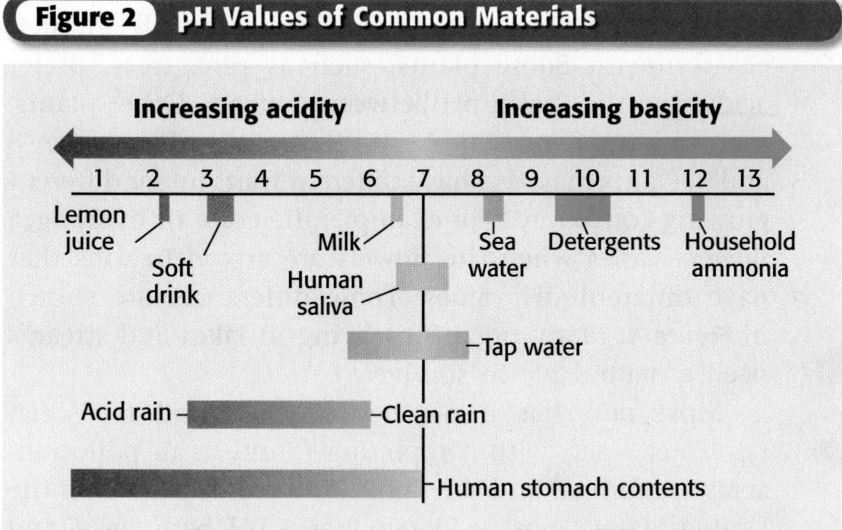

Figure 3 Using Indicators to Find pH

pH Indicator Scale

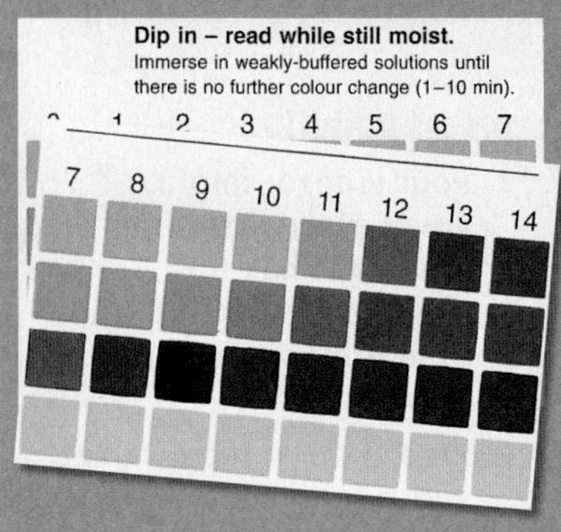

Dip in – read while still moist.
Immerse in weakly-buffered solutions until there is no further colour change (1–10 min).

pH 4

pH 10

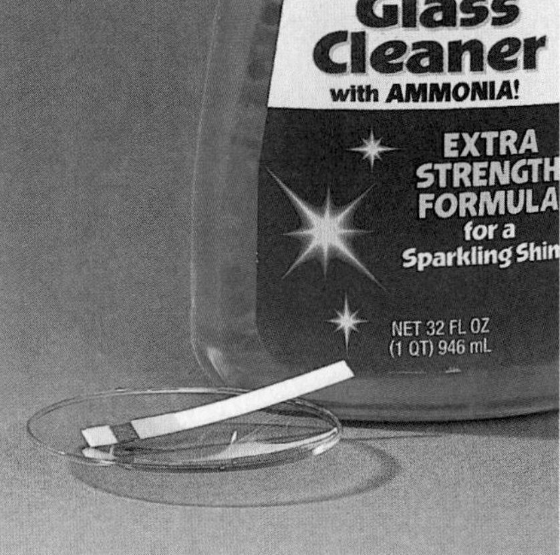

Glass
Cleaner
with AMMONIA!
EXTRA
STRENGTH
FORMULA
for a
Sparkling Shin
NET 32 FL OZ
(1 QT) 946 mL

Using Indicators to Determine pH

A combination of indicators can be used to find out how basic or how acidic a solution is. This can be done if the colors of the indicators are known at different pH values. **Figure 3** shows strips of pH paper, which contains several different indicators. These strips were dipped into two different solutions. The pH of each solution is found by comparing the colors on each strip with the colors on the indicator scale provided. This kind of indicator is often used to test the pH of water in pools and aquariums. Another way to find the pH of a solution is to use a pH meter. These meters can detect and measure hydronium ion concentration electronically.

Reading Check How can indicators determine pH?

CONNECTION TO Biology

WRITING SKILL **Blood and pH** Human blood has a pH between 7.38 and 7.42. If the blood pH is lower or higher, the body cannot function properly. Research what can cause the pH of blood to rise above or fall below normal ranges. Write a one-page paper that details your findings.

pH and the Environment

Living things depend on having a steady pH in their environment. Some plants, such as pine trees, prefer acidic soil that has a pH between 4 and 6. Other plants, such as lettuce, need basic soil that has a pH between 8 and 9. Plants may also have different traits under different growing conditions. For example, the color of hydrangea flowers varies when the flowers are grown in soils that have different pH values. These differences are shown in **Figure 4.** Many organisms living in lakes and streams need a neutral pH to survive.

Most rain has a pH between 5.5 and 6. When rainwater reacts with compounds found in air pollution, acids are formed and the rainwater's pH decreases. In the United States, most acid rain has a pH between 4 and 4.5, but some precipitation has a pH as low as 3.

Figure 4 *To grow blue flowers, plant hydrangeas in soil that has a low pH. To grow pink flowers, use soil that has a high pH.*

Salts

When an acid neutralizes a base, a salt and water are produced. A **salt** is an ionic compound formed from the positive ion of a base and the negative ion of an acid. When you hear the word *salt,* you probably think of the table salt you use to season your food. But the sodium chloride found in your salt shaker is only one example of a large group of compounds called *salts*.

Uses of Salts

Salts have many uses in industry and in homes. You already know that sodium chloride is used to season foods. It is also used to make other compounds, including lye (sodium hydroxide) and baking soda. Sodium nitrate is a salt that is used to preserve food. And calcium sulfate is used to make wallboard, which is used in construction. Another use of salt is shown in **Figure 5.**

Figure 5 *Salts help keep roads free of ice by decreasing the freezing point of water.*

salt an ionic compound that forms when a metal atom replaces the hydrogen of an acid

SECTION Review

Summary

- Every molecule of a strong acid or base breaks apart to form ions. Few molecules of weak acids and bases break apart to form ions.
- An acid and a base can neutralize one another to make salt and water.
- pH is a measure of hydronium ion concentration in a solution.
- A salt is an ionic compound formed in a neutralization reaction. Salts have many industrial and household uses.

Using Key Terms

1. Use the following terms in the same sentence: *neutralization reaction* and *salt.*

Understanding Key Ideas

2. A neutralization reaction
   a. includes an acid and a base.
   b. produces a salt.
   c. forms water.
   d. All of the above
3. Explain the difference between a strong acid and a weak acid.

Math Skills

4. For each point lower on the pH scale, the hydrogen ions in solution increase tenfold. For example, a solution of pH 3 is not twice as acidic as a solution of pH 6 but is 1,000 times as acidic. How many times more acidic is a solution of pH 2 than a solution of pH 4?

Critical Thinking

5. **Analyzing Processes** Predict what will happen to the hydrogen ion concentration and the pH of water if hydrochloric acid is added to the water.
6. **Analyzing Relationships** Would fish be healthy in a lake that has a low pH? Explain.
7. **Applying Concepts** Soap is made from a strong base and oil. Would you expect the pH of soap to be 4 or 9? Explain.

SCILINKS
NSTA
Developed and maintained by the National Science Teachers Association
For a variety of links related to this chapter, go to www.scilinks.org
Topic: pH scale; Salts
SciLinks code: HSM1130; HSM1347

SECTION 4

Organic Compounds

What You Will Learn

- Explain why there are so many organic compounds.
- Identify and describe saturated, unsaturated, and aromatic hydrocarbons.
- Describe the characteristics of carbohydrates, lipids, proteins, and nucleic acids and their functions in the body.

Vocabulary

organic compound
hydrocarbon
carbohydrate
lipid
protein
nucleic acid

READING STRATEGY

Paired Summarizing Read this section silently. In pairs, take turns summarizing the material. Stop to discuss ideas that seem confusing.

Can you believe that more than 90% of all compounds are members of a single group of compounds? It's true!

Most compounds are members of a group called organic compounds. **Organic compounds** are covalent compounds composed of carbon-based molecules. Fuel, rubbing alcohol, and sugar are organic compounds. Even cotton, paper, and plastic belong to this group. Why are there so many kinds of organic compounds? Learning about the carbon atom can help you understand why.

The Four Bonds of a Carbon Atom

All organic compounds contain carbon. Each carbon atom has four valence electrons. So, each carbon atom can make four bonds with four other atoms.

Carbon Backbones

The models in **Figure 1** are called *structural formulas.* They are used to show how atoms in a molecule are connected. Each line represents a pair of electrons that form a covalent bond. Many organic compounds are based on the types of carbon backbones shown in **Figure 1.** Some compounds have hundreds or thousands of carbon atoms as part of their backbone! Organic compounds may also contain hydrogen, oxygen, sulfur, nitrogen, and phosphorus.

Reading Check **What is the purpose of structural formulas?** *(See the Appendix for answers to Reading Checks.)*

Figure 1 **Three Models of Carbon Backbones**

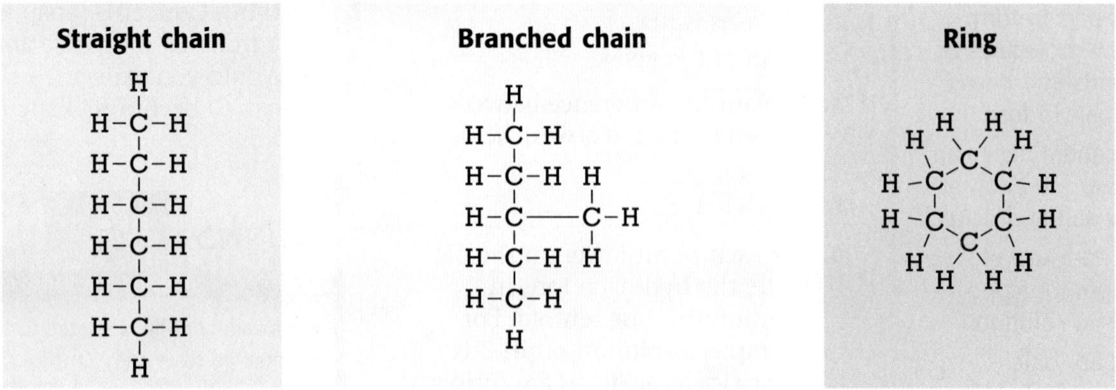

Straight chain

▲ All carbon atoms are connected in a straight line.

Branched chain

▲ The chain of carbon atoms branches into different directions when a carbon atom is bonded to more than one other carbon atom.

Ring

▲ The chain of carbon atoms forms a ring.

Figure 2 Three Types of Hydrocarbons

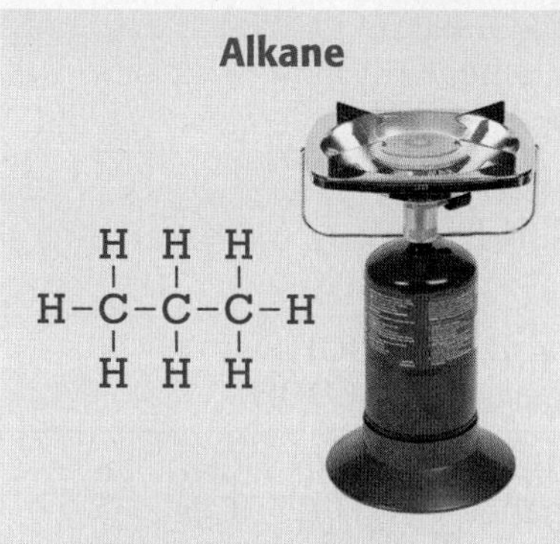

The **propane** in this camping stove is a saturated hydrocarbon.

Fruits make **ethene,** which is a compound that helps ripen the fruit.

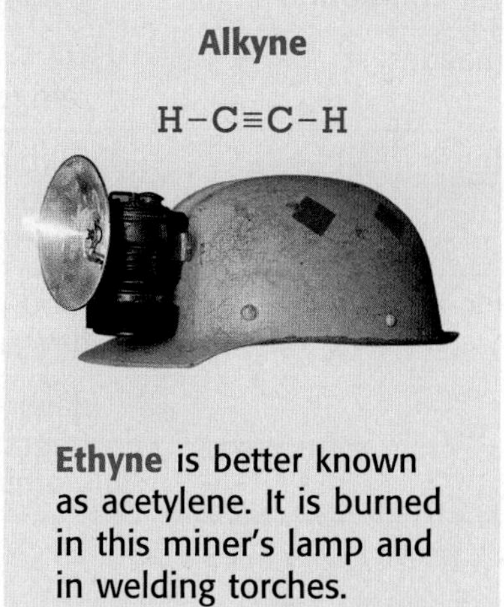

Ethyne is better known as acetylene. It is burned in this miner's lamp and in welding torches.

Hydrocarbons and Other Organic Compounds

Although many organic compounds contain several kinds of atoms, some contain only two. Organic compounds that contain only carbon and hydrogen are called **hydrocarbons.**

organic compound a covalently bonded compound that contains carbon

hydrocarbon an organic compound composed only of carbon and hydrogen

Saturated Hydrocarbons

The propane shown in **Figure 2** is a saturated hydrocarbon. A *saturated hydrocarbon,* or *alkane,* is a hydrocarbon in which each carbon atom in the molecule shares a single bond with each of four other atoms. A single bond is a covalent bond made up of one pair of shared electrons.

Unsaturated Hydrocarbons

An *unsaturated hydrocarbon,* such as ethene or ethyne shown in **Figure 2,** is a hydrocarbon in which at least one pair of carbon atoms shares a double bond or a triple bond. A double bond is a covalent bond made up of two pairs of shared electrons. A triple bond is a covalent bond made up of three pairs of shared electrons. Hydrocarbons that contain double or triple bonds are unsaturated because these bonds can be broken and more atoms can be added to the molecules.

Compounds that contain two carbon atoms connected by a double bond are called *alkenes.* Hydrocarbons that contain two carbon atoms connected by a triple bond are called *alkynes.*

Aromatic Hydrocarbons

Most aromatic (AR uh MAT ik) compounds are based on benzene. As shown in **Figure 3,** benzene has a ring of six carbons that have alternating double and single bonds. Aromatic hydrocarbons often have strong odors.

Figure 3 *Benzene is the starting material for manufacturing many products, including medicines.*

Table 1 Types and Uses of Organic Compounds

Type of compound	Uses	Examples
Alkyl halides	starting material for Teflon™ refrigerant (Freon™)	chloromethane, CH_3Cl bromoethane, C_2H_5Br
Alcohols	rubbing alcohol gasoline additive antifreeze	methanol, CH_3OH ethanol, C_2H_5OH
Organic acids	food preservatives flavorings	ethanoic acid, CH_3COOH propanoic acid, C_2H_5COOH
Esters	flavorings fragrances clothing (polyester)	methyl ethanoate, CH_3COOCH_3 ethyl propanoate, $C_2H_5COOC_2H_5$

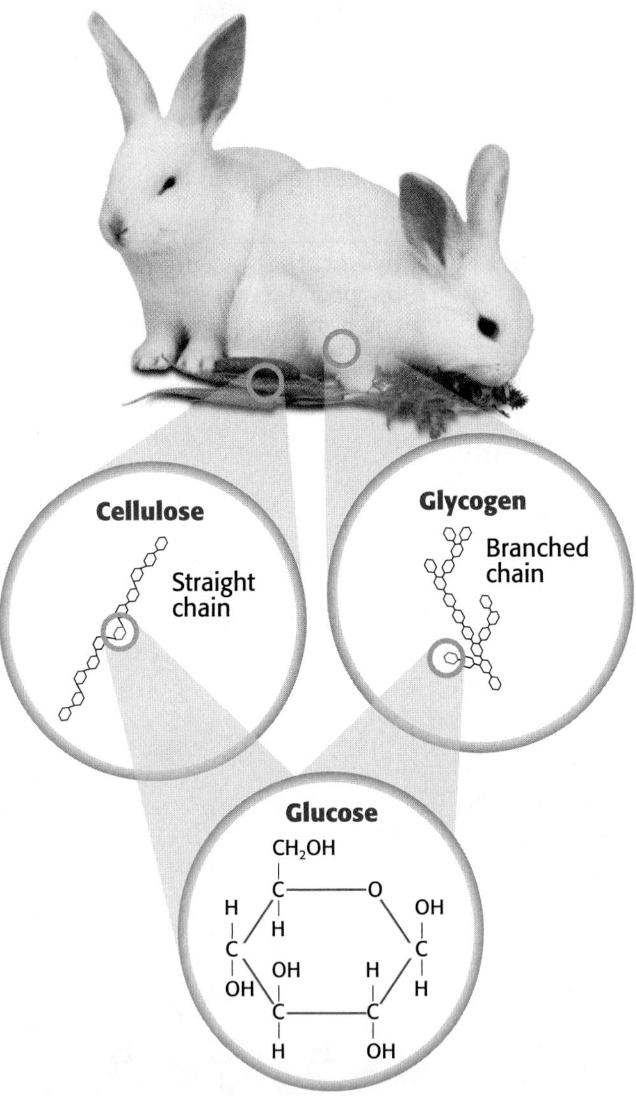

Figure 4 *Glucose molecules, represented by hexagons, can bond to form complex carbohydrates, such as cellulose and glycogen.*

Other Organic Compounds

There are many other kinds of organic compounds. Some have atoms of halogens, oxygen, sulfur, and phosphorus in their molecules. A few of these compounds and their uses are listed in **Table 1.**

Biochemicals: The Compounds of Life

Organic compounds that are made by living things are called *biochemicals*. Biochemicals are divided into four categories: carbohydrates, lipids, proteins, and nucleic acids (noo KLEE ik AS idz).

Carbohydrates

Carbohydrates are biochemicals that are composed of one or more simple sugar molecules bonded together. Carbohydrates are used as a source of energy. There are two kinds of carbohydrates: simple carbohydrates and complex carbohydrates.

Simple carbohydrates include simple sugars, such as glucose. **Figure 4** shows how glucose molecules can bond to form different complex carbohydrates. Complex carbohydrates may be made of hundreds or thousands of sugar molecules bonded together. *Cellulose* gives plant cell walls their rigid structure, and *glycogen* supplies energy to muscle cells.

Lipids

Lipids are biochemicals that do not dissolve in water. Fats, oils, and waxes are kinds of lipids. Lipids have many functions, including storing energy and making up cell membranes. Although too much fat in your diet can be unhealthy, some fat is important to good health. The foods in **Figure 5** are sources of lipids.

Lipids store excess energy in the body. Animals tend to store lipids as fats, while plants store lipids as oils. When an organism has used up most of its carbohydrates, it can obtain energy by breaking down lipids. Lipids are also used to store some vitamins.

carbohydrate a class of energy-giving nutrients that includes sugars, starches, and fiber; composed of one or more simple sugars bonded together

lipid a type of biochemical that does not dissolve in water; fats and steroids are lipids

protein a molecule that is made up of amino acids and that is needed to build and repair body structures and to regulate processes in the body

Proteins

Most of the biochemicals found in living things are proteins. In fact, after water, proteins are the most common molecules in your cells. **Proteins** are biochemicals that are composed of "building blocks" called *amino acids*.

Amino acids are small molecules made up of carbon, hydrogen, oxygen, and nitrogen atoms. Some amino acids also include sulfur atoms. Amino acids bond to form proteins of many shapes and sizes. The shape of a protein determines the function of the protein. If even a single amino acid is missing or out of place, the protein may not function correctly or at all. Proteins have many functions. They regulate chemical activities, transport and store materials, and provide structural support.

Reading Check What are proteins made of?

Food Facts

1. Select **four empty food packages.**
2. Without reading the Nutrition Facts labels, rank the items from most carbohydrate content to least carbohydrate content.
3. Rank the items from most fat content to least fat content.
4. Read the Nutrition Facts labels, and compare your rankings with the real rankings.
5. Why do you think your rankings were right, or why were they wrong? Explain your answers.

Figure 5 *Vegetable oil, meat, cheese, nuts, eggs, and milk are sources of lipids in your diet.*

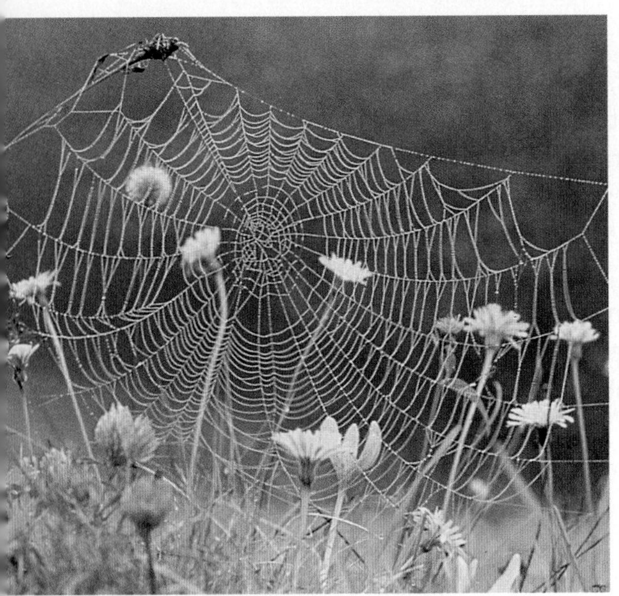

Figure 6 *Spider webs are made up of proteins that are shaped like long fibers.*

Examples of Proteins

Proteins have many roles in your body and in living things. Enzymes (EN ZIEMZ) are proteins that are catalysts. *Catalysts* regulate chemical reactions in the body by increasing the rate at which the reactions occur. Some hormones are proteins. For example, insulin is a protein hormone that helps regulate your blood-sugar level. Another kind of protein, called *hemoglobin,* is found in red blood cells and delivers oxygen throughout the body. There are also large proteins that extend through cell membranes. These proteins help control the transport of materials into and out of cells. Some proteins, such as those in your hair, provide structural support. The structural proteins of silk fibers make the spider web shown in **Figure 6** strong and lightweight.

Nucleic Acids

nucleic acid a molecule made up of subunits called *nucleotides*

The largest molecules made by living organisms are nucleic acids. **Nucleic acids** are biochemicals made up of *nucleotides* (NOO klee oh TIEDZ). Nucleotides are molecules made of carbon, hydrogen, oxygen, nitrogen, and phosphorus atoms. There are only five kinds of nucleotides. But nucleic acids may have millions of nucleotides bonded together. The only reason living things differ from each other is that each living thing has a different order of nucleotides.

Nucleic acids have several functions. One function of nucleic acids is to store genetic information. They also help build proteins and other nucleic acids. Nucleic acids are sometimes called *the blueprints of life,* because they contain all the information needed for a cell to make all of its proteins.

Reading Check **What are two functions of nucleic acids?**

CONNECTION TO Social Studies

DNA "Fingerprinting" and Crime-Scene Investigation The chemical structure of all human DNA is the same. The only difference between one person's DNA and another's is the order, or sequence, of the building blocks in the DNA. The number of ways these building blocks can be sequenced are countless.

DNA fingerprinting is new process. However, it has changed the way that criminal investigations are carried out. Research DNA fingerprinting. Find out when DNA fingerprinting was first used, who developed the process, and how DNA fingerprinting is used in crime-scene investigations. Present your findings in an oral presentation to your class. Include a model or a poster to help explain the process to your classmates.

DNA and RNA

There are two kinds of nucleic acids: DNA and RNA. A model of DNA (**d**eoxyribo**n**ucleic **a**cid) is shown in **Figure 7.** DNA is the genetic material of the cell. DNA molecules can store a huge amount of information because of their length. The DNA molecules in a single human cell have a length of about 2 m—which is more than 6 ft long! When a cell needs to make a certain protein, it copies a certain part of the DNA. The information copied from the DNA directs the order in which amino acids are bonded to make that protein. DNA also contains information used to build the second type of nucleic acid, RNA (**r**ibo**n**ucleic **a**cid). RNA is involved in the actual building of proteins.

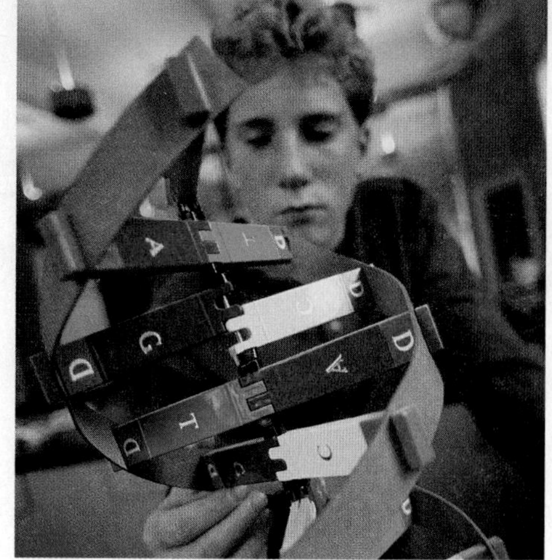

Figure 7 *Two strands of DNA are twisted in a spiral shape. Four different nucleotides make up the rungs of the DNA ladder.*

SECTION Review

Summary

- Organic compounds contain carbon, which can form four bonds.
- Hydrocarbons are composed of only carbon and hydrogen.
- Hydrocarbons may be saturated, unsaturated, or aromatic hydrocarbons.
- Carbohydrates are made of simple sugars.
- Lipids store energy and make up cell membranes.
- Proteins are composed of amino acids.
- Nucleic acids store genetic information and help cells make proteins.

Using Key Terms

1. Use the following terms in the same sentence: *organic compound, hydrocarbon,* and *biochemical.*
2. In your own words, write a definition for each of the following terms: *carbohydrate, lipid, protein,* and *nucleic acid.*

Understanding Key Ideas

3. A saturated hydrocarbon has
   - **a.** only single bonds.
   - **b.** double bonds.
   - **c.** triple bonds.
   - **d.** double and triple bonds.
4. List two functions of proteins.
5. What is an aromatic hydrocarbon?

Critical Thinking

6. **Identifying Relationships** Hemoglobin is a protein that is in blood and that transports oxygen to the tissues of the body. Information stored in nucleic acids tells a cell how to make proteins. What might happen if there is a mistake in the information needed to make hemoglobin?
7. **Making Comparisons** Compare saturated hydrocarbons with unsaturated hydrocarbons.

Interpreting Graphics

Use the structural formula of this organic compound to answer the questions that follow.

```
    H   H   H
    |   |   |
H - C - C - C - H
    |   |   |
    H   H   H
```

8. What type of bonds are present in this molecule?
9. Can you determine the shape of the molecule from this structural formula? Explain your answer.

SCILINKS
NSTA
Developed and maintained by the National Science Teachers Association
For a variety of links related to this chapter, go to www.scilinks.org
Topic: Aromatic Compounds; Organic Compounds
SciLinks code: HSM0095; HSM1078

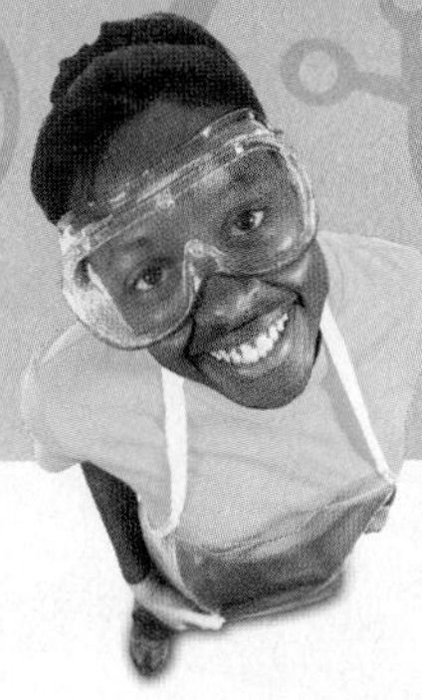

Skills Practice Lab

Cabbage Patch Indicators

Indicators are weak acids or bases that change color due to the pH of the substance to which they are added. Red cabbage contains a natural indicator. It turns specific colors at specific pHs. In this lab you will extract the indicator from red cabbage. Then, you will use it to determine the pH of several liquids.

OBJECTIVES

Make a natural acid-base indicator solution.

Determine the pH of various common substances.

MATERIALS

- beaker, 250 mL
- beaker tongs
- eyedropper
- hot plate
- litmus paper
- pot holder
- red cabbage leaf
- sample liquids provided by teacher
- tape, masking
- test tubes
- test-tube rack
- water, distilled

SAFETY

 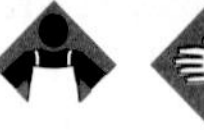   

Procedure

1. Copy the table below. Be sure to include one line for each sample liquid.

Data Collection Table			
Liquid	**Color with indicator**	**pH**	**Effect on litmus paper**
Control			

DO NOT WRITE IN BOOK

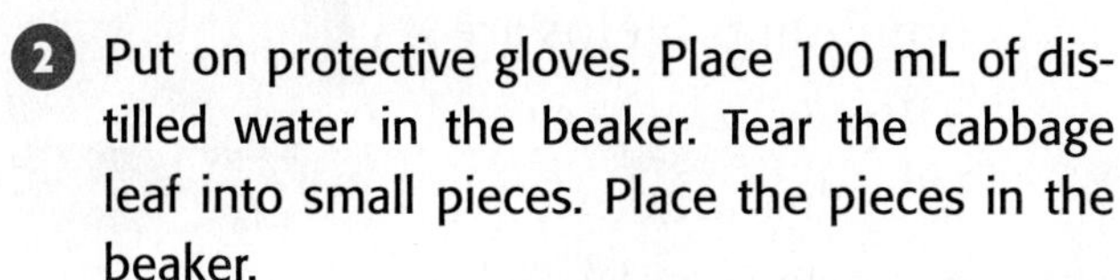

2. Put on protective gloves. Place 100 mL of distilled water in the beaker. Tear the cabbage leaf into small pieces. Place the pieces in the beaker.
3. Use the hot plate to heat the cabbage and water to boiling. Continue boiling until the water is deep blue. **Caution:** Use extreme care when working near a hot plate.
4. Use tongs to remove the beaker from the hot plate. Turn the hot plate off. Allow the solution to cool on a pot holder for 5 to 10 minutes.
5. While the solution is cooling, use masking tape and a pen to label the test tubes for each sample liquid. Label one test tube as the control. Place the tubes in the rack.
6. Use the eyedropper to place a small amount (about 5 mL) of the indicator (cabbage juice) in the test tube labeled as the control.
7. Pour a small amount (about 5 mL) of each sample liquid into the appropriate test tube.
8. Using the eyedropper, place several drops of the indicator into each test tube. Swirl gently. Record the color of each liquid in the table.
9. Use the chart below to the find the pH of each sample. Record the pH values in the table.
10. Litmus paper has an indicator that turns red in an acid and blue in a base. Test each liquid with a strip of litmus paper. Record the results.

Analyze the Results

1. **Analyzing Data** What purpose does the control serve? What is the pH of the control?
2. **Examining Data** What colors in your samples indicate the presence of an acid? What colors indicate the presence of a base?
3. **Analyzing Results** Why is red cabbage juice considered a good indicator?

Draw Conclusions

4. **Interpreting Information** Which do you think would be more useful to help identify an unknown liquid—litmus paper or red cabbage juice? Why?

Applying Your Data

Unlike distilled water, rainwater has some carbon dioxide dissolved in it. Is rainwater acidic, basic, or neutral? To find out, place a small amount of the cabbage juice indicator (which is water-based) in a clean test tube. Use a straw to gently blow bubbles in the indicator. Continue blowing bubbles until you see a color change. What can you conclude about the pH of your "rainwater?" What is the purpose of blowing bubbles in the cabbage juice?

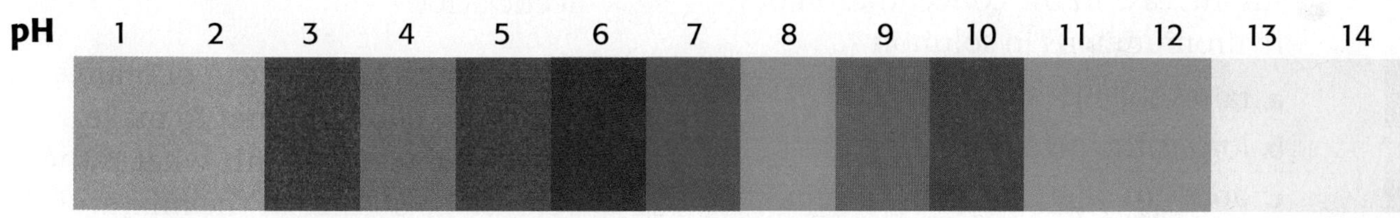

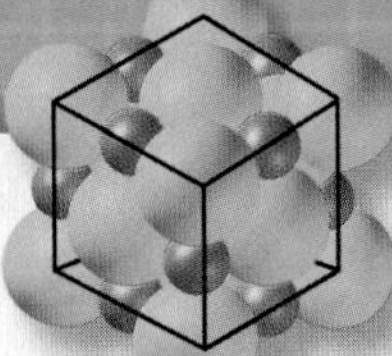

Chapter Review

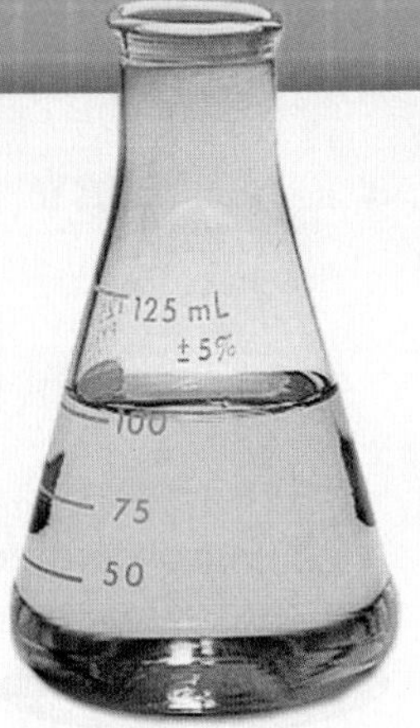

USING KEY TERMS

For each pair of terms, explain how the meanings of the terms differ.

1. *ionic compound* and *covalent compound*
2. *acid* and *base*
3. *pH* and *indicator*
4. *hydrocarbon* and *organic compound*
5. *carbohydrate* and *lipid*
6. *protein* and *nucleic acid*

UNDERSTANDING KEY IDEAS

Multiple Choice

7. Which of the following statements describes lipids?
   a. Lipids are used to store energy.
   b. Lipids do not dissolve in water.
   c. Lipids make up part of the cell membrane.
   d. All of the above

8. Ionic compounds
   a. have a low melting point.
   b. are often brittle.
   c. do not conduct electric current in water.
   d. do not dissolve easily in water.

9. An increase in the concentration of hydronium ions in solution
   a. raises the pH.
   b. lowers the pH.
   c. does not affect the pH.
   d. doubles the pH.

10. The compounds that store information for building proteins are
   a. lipids.
   b. hydrocarbons.
   c. nucleic acids.
   d. carbohydrates.

Short Answer

11. What type of compound would you use to neutralize a solution of potassium hydroxide?

12. Explain why the reaction of an acid with a base is called *neutralization.*

13. What characteristic of carbon atoms helps to explain the wide variety of organic compounds?

14. What kind of ions are produced when an acid is dissolved in water and when a base is dissolved in water?

Math Skills

15. Most of the vinegar used to make pickles is 5% acetic acid. So, in 100 mL of vinegar, 5 mL is acid diluted with 95 mL of water. If you bought a 473 mL bottle of 5% vinegar, how many milliliters of acetic acid would be in the bottle? How many milliliters of water were used to dilute the acetic acid?

16. If you dilute a 75 mL can of orange juice with enough water to make a total volume of 300 mL, what is the percentage of juice in the mixture?

CRITICAL THINKING

17. **Concept Mapping** Use the following terms to create a concept map: *acid, base, salt, neutral,* and *pH*.

18. **Applying Concepts** Fish give off the base, ammonia, NH_3, as waste. How does the release of ammonia affect the pH of the water in the aquarium? What can be done to correct the pH of the water?

19. **Analyzing Methods** Many insects, such as fire ants, inject formic acid, a weak acid, when they bite or sting. Describe the type of compound that should be used to treat the bite.

20. **Making Comparisons** Organic compounds are also covalent compounds. What properties would you expect organic compounds to have as a result?

21. **Applying Concepts** Farmers have been known to taste their soil to determine whether the soil has the correct acidity for their plants. How would taste help the farmer determine the acidity of the soil?

22. **Analyzing Ideas** A diet that includes a high level of lipids is unhealthy. Why is a diet containing no lipids also unhealthy?

INTERPRETING GRAPHICS

Use the structural formulas below to answer the questions that follow.

a.

H
H–C–H
H C H
C C
C C
H C H
H

b.

H
H–C–H
H–C–H H
H–C——C–H
H–C–H H
H–C–H
H

c.

H
H–C–H H
H–C——C–H
H–C–H H
H–C–H
H

d.

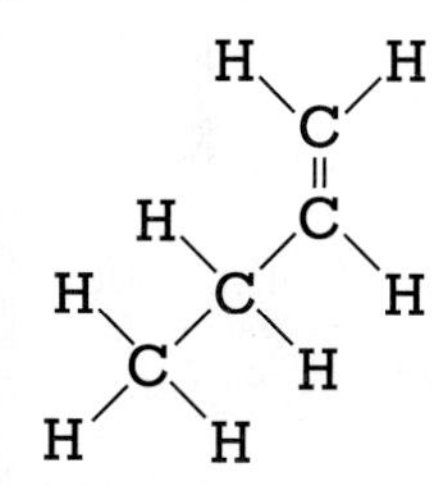

23. A saturated hydrocarbon is represented by which structural formula(s)?

24. An unsaturated hydrocarbon is represented by which structural formula(s)?

25. An aromatic hydrocarbon is represented by which structural formula(s)?

Multiple Choice

Use the table below to answer question 1.

Properties of Some Compounds			
Compound	Melting point	Solubility	Electrical conductivity in solution
A	801°C	high	yes
B	398°C	low	yes
C	20°C	low	no
D	1,200°C	high	yes

1. **Which of the compounds in the table above is most likely a covalent compound?**

   A. compound A

   B. compound B

   C. compound C

   D. compound D

2. **Akeem reads the following description of a substance: "clear liquid, boiling point of 78°C, flammable, soluble in water." Which of the properties listed is a chemical property?**

   A. clear liquid

   B. boiling point of 78°C

   C. flammable

   D. soluble in water

3. **A compound dissolved in water turns red litmus paper blue and changes the indicator bromthymol blue to dark blue. What kind of compound is it?**

   A. an acid

   B. water

   C. table salt

   D. a base

4. **What type of compound increases the number of hydronium ions (H^+) when dissolved in water?**

   A. an acid

   B. a base

   C. an indicator

   D. hydrogen gas

5. **Which of the following is a kind of biochemical that does not dissolve in water and that is found in cell walls, fats, oils, and waxes?**

   A. glycogen

   B. carbohydrate

   C. lipid

   D. cellulose

6. **Jacques is going to perform a laboratory experiment with organic compounds. He can conclude that all the organic compounds he will study must contain a certain element. What is that element?**

   A. hydrogen

   B. carbon

   C. oxygen

   D. nitrogen

Use the figure below to answer question 7.

7. The figure above shows the structural formula of a covalent compound. Which of the following statements is true about the compound?

A. The compound has ionic bonds.

B. The compound may be an organic compound.

C. The compound may be a salt.

D. The compound has metallic bonds.

8. During a laboratory experiment, Martin observes a substance with a high melting point. This substance also dissolves in water easily. Which of the following is a valid conclusion?

A. He is looking at a substance with a covalent bond.

B. He is looking at an acid.

C. He is looking at a substance with an ionic bond.

D. He is looking at a substance with a metallic bond.

9. The ions in an ionic compound are arranged in a repeating, three-dimensional pattern. What is this pattern called?

A. ionic solution

B. chemical bond

C. valence electron

D. crystal lattice

10. What factor does the pH scale measure?

A. the degree of neutralization between acids and bases

B. the concentration of hydroxide ions in a solution

C. the number of salt molecules present in a solution

D. the concentration of hydronium ions in a solution

Open Response

11. Acids and bases are two kinds of chemical compounds. Compare and contrast at least four chemical and physical properties of acids and bases.

12. Alexa is writing a report about biochemicals. Describe the four categories of biochemicals that Alexa should include in her report. Give an example of each kind of biochemical.

Science in Action

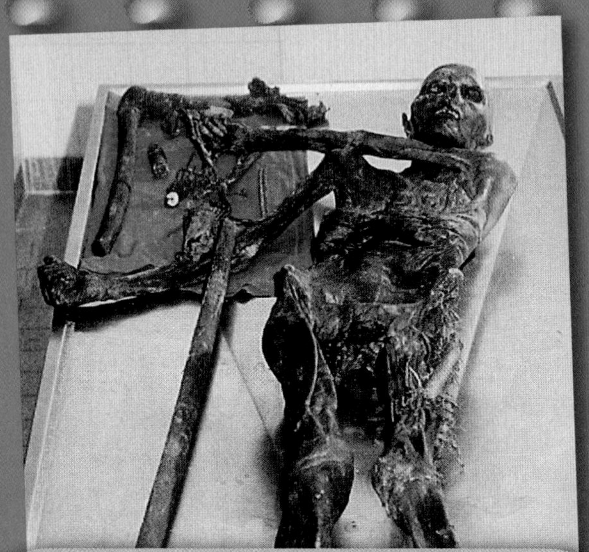

Science, Technology, and Society

Molecular Photocopying

To learn about our human ancestors, scientists can use DNA from mummies. Well-preserved DNA can be copied using a technique called polymerase chain reaction (PCR). PCR uses enzymes called *polymerases,* which make new strands of DNA using old strands as templates. Thus, PCR is called molecular photocopying. However, scientists have to be very careful when using this process. If just one of their own skin cells falls into the PCR mixture, it will contaminate the ancient DNA with their own DNA.

Social Studies ACTIVITY

WRITING SKILL DNA analysis of mummies is helping archeologists study human history. Write a research paper about what scientists have learned about human history through DNA analysis.

Weird Science

Silly Putty™

During World War II, the supply of natural rubber was very low. So, James Wright, at General Electric, tried to make a synthetic rubber. The putty he made could be molded, stretched, and bounced. But it did not work as a rubber substitute and was ignored. Then, Peter Hodgson, a consultant for a toy company, had a brilliant idea. He marketed the putty as a toy in 1949. It was an immediate success. Hodgson created the name Silly Putty™. Although Silly Putty™ was invented more than 50 years ago, it has not changed much. More than 300 million eggs of Silly Putty have been sold since 1950.

Math ACTIVITY

In 1949, Mr. Hodgson bought 9.5 kg of putty for $147. The putty was divided into balls, each having a mass of 14 g. What was his cost for one 14 g ball of putty?

Careers

Jeannie Eberhardt

Forensic Scientist Jeannie Eberhardt says that her job as a forensic scientist is not really as glamorous as it may seem on popular TV shows. "If they bring me a garbage bag from the crime scene, then my job is to dig through the trash and look for evidence," she laughs. Jeannie Eberhardt explains that her job is to "search for, collect, and analyze evidence from crime scenes." Eberhardt says that one of the most important qualities a forensic scientist can have is the ability to be unbiased. She says that she focuses on the evidence and not on any information she may have about the alleged crime or the suspect. Eberhardt advises students who think they might be interested in a career as a forensic scientist to talk to someone who works in the field. She also recommends that students develop a broad science background. And she advises students that most of these jobs require extensive background checks. "Your actions now could affect your ability to get a job later on," she points out.

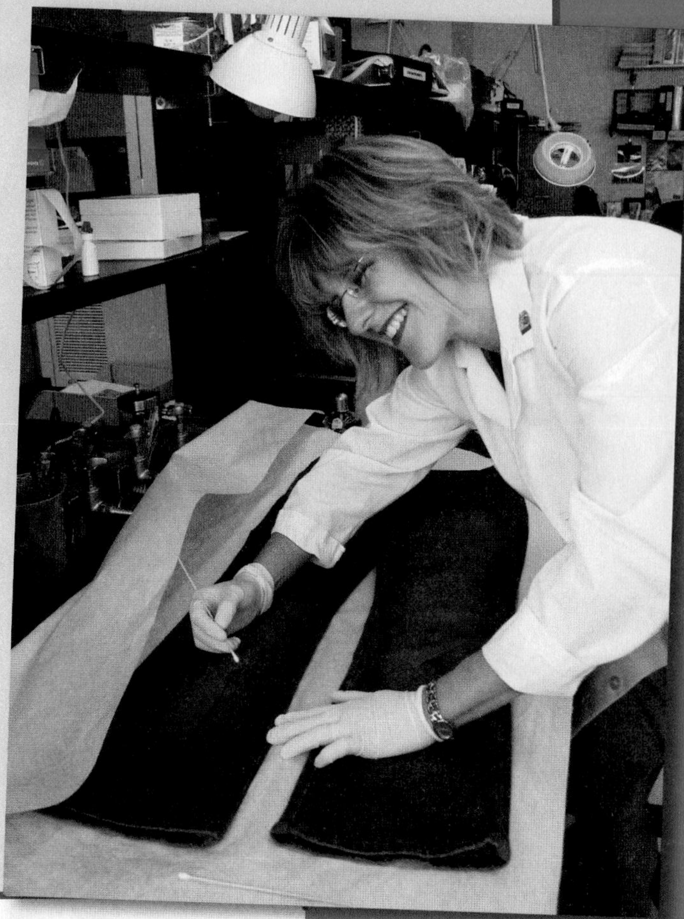

Language Arts ACTIVITY

WRITING SKILL Jeannie Eberhardt says that it is very important to be unbiased when analyzing a crime scene. Write a one-page essay explaining why it is necessary to focus on the evidence in a crime and not on personal feelings or news reports.

To learn more about these Science in Action topics, visit go.hrw.com and type in the keyword **HP5CMPF**

Current Science

Check out Current Science® articles related to this chapter by visiting go.hrw.com. Just type in the keyword HP5CS15

Atomic Energy

The Big Idea

Radioactive decay, nuclear fission, and nuclear fusion are changes that release energy from the nuclei of atoms.

SECTION

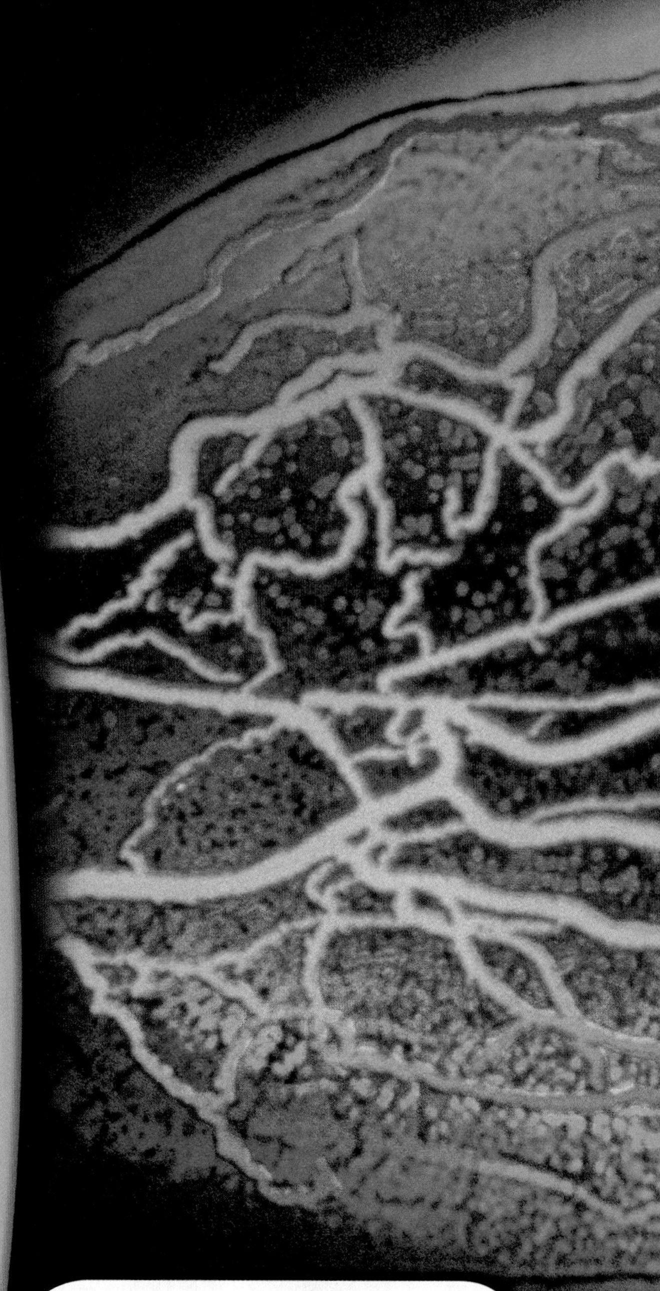

About the Photo

Look closely at the blood vessels that show up clearly in this image of a human hand. Doctors sometimes inject radioactive substances into a patient's body to help locate tumors and measure the activity of certain organs. Radioactive emissions from the substances are measured using a scanning device. Then, computers turn the data into an image.

PRE-READING ACTIVITY

Graphic Organizer

Spider Map Before you read the chapter, create the graphic organizer entitled "Spider Map" described in the **Study Skills** section of the Appendix. Label the circle "Radioactive Decay." Create a leg for each type of radioactive decay. As you read the chapter, fill in the map with details about each type of decay.

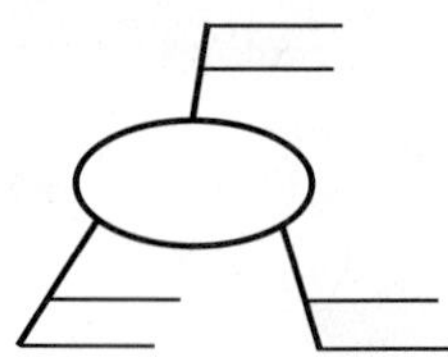

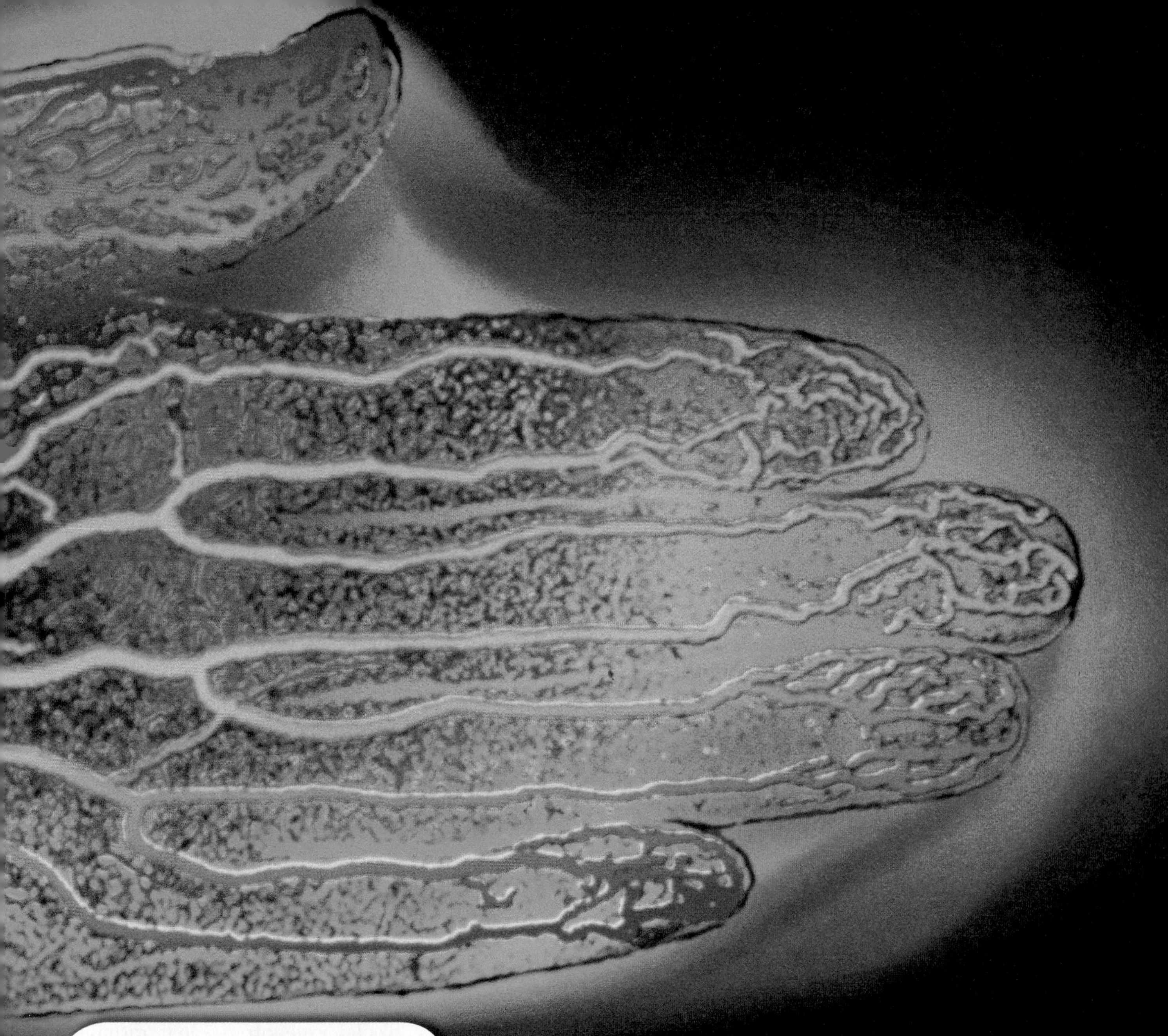

START-UP ACTIVITY

Watch Your Headsium!

In this activity, you will model the decay of unstable nuclei into stable nuclei.

Procedure

1. Place **100 pennies** with the heads' side up in a **box with a lid.** The pennies represent radioactive nuclei. Record 100 "headsium" nuclei as "Trial 0."
2. Close the box. Shake it up and down for 5 s.
3. Open the box. Remove the stable tails-up nuclei, or "tailsium" nuclei. Count the number of headsium nuclei remaining, and record it as "Trial 1."
4. Perform trials until you don't have any more pennies in the box or until you have finished five trials. Record your results.

Analysis

1. On a piece of **graph paper,** graph your data by plotting "Number of headsium nuclei" on the *y*-axis and "Trial number" on the *x*-axis. What trend do you see in the number of headsium nuclei?
2. Compare your graph with the graphs made by the other students in your class.

SECTION 1

Radioactivity

When scientists do experiments, they don't always find what they expect to find.

What You Will Learn

- Describe how radioactivity was discovered.
- Compare alpha, beta, and gamma decay.
- Describe the penetrating power of the three kinds of nuclear radiation.
- Calculate ages of objects using half-life.
- Identify uses of radioactive materials.

Vocabulary

radioactivity	isotope
mass number	half-life

READING STRATEGY

Reading Organizer As you read this section, create an outline of the section. Use the headings from the section in your outline.

In 1896, a French scientist named Henri Becquerel found much more than he expected. He found a new area of science.

Discovering Radioactivity

Becquerel's hypothesis was that fluorescent minerals give off X rays. (*Fluorescent* materials glow when light shines on them.) To test his idea, he put a fluorescent mineral on top of a photographic plate wrapped in paper. After putting his setup in bright sunlight, he developed the plate and saw the strong image of the mineral he expected, as shown in **Figure 1.**

An Unexpected Result

Becquerel tried to do the experiment again, but the weather was cloudy. So, he put his materials in a drawer. He developed the plate anyway a few days later. He was shocked to see a strong image. Even without light, the mineral gave off energy. The energy passed through the paper and made an image on the plate. After more tests, Becquerel concluded that this energy comes from uranium, an element in the mineral.

Naming the Unexpected

This energy is called *nuclear radiation,* high-energy particles and rays that are emitted by the nuclei of some atoms. Marie Curie, a scientist working with Becquerel, named the process by which some nuclei give off nuclear radiation. She named the process **radioactivity,** which is also called *radioactive decay*.

Figure 1 *Sunlight could not pass through the paper. So, the image on the plate must have been made by energy given off by the mineral.*

Figure 2 Alpha Decay of Radium-226

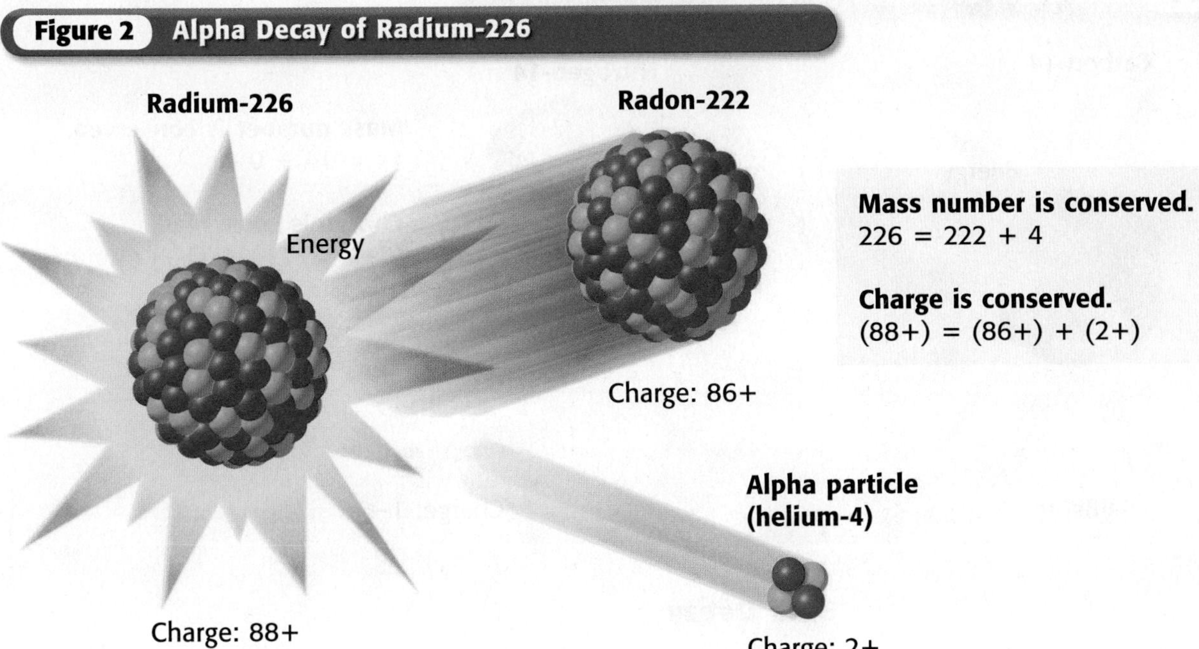

Kinds of Radioactive Decay

During *radioactive decay,* an unstable nucleus gives off particles and energy. Three kinds of radioactive decay are alpha decay, beta decay, and gamma decay.

radioactivity the process by which an unstable nucleus gives off nuclear radiation

mass number the sum of the numbers of protons and neutrons in the nucleus of an atom

Alpha Decay

The release of an alpha particle from a nucleus is called *alpha decay*. An *alpha particle* is made up of two protons and two neutrons. It has a mass number of 4 and a charge of 2+. The **mass number** is the sum of the numbers of protons and neutrons in the nucleus of an atom. An alpha particle is the same as the nucleus of a helium atom. Many large radioactive nuclei give off alpha particles and become nuclei of atoms of different elements. One example of a nucleus that gives off alpha particles is radium-226. (The number that follows the name of an element is the mass number of the atom.)

Conservation in Decay

Look at the model of alpha decay in **Figure 2.** This model shows two important things about radioactive decay. First, the mass number is conserved. The sum of the mass numbers of the starting materials is always equal to the sum of the mass numbers of the products. Second, charge is conserved. The sum of the charges of the starting materials is always equal to the sum of the charges of the products.

Reading Check **What two things are conserved in radioactive decay?** (*See the Appendix for answers to Reading Checks.*)

Figure 3 Beta Decay of Carbon-14

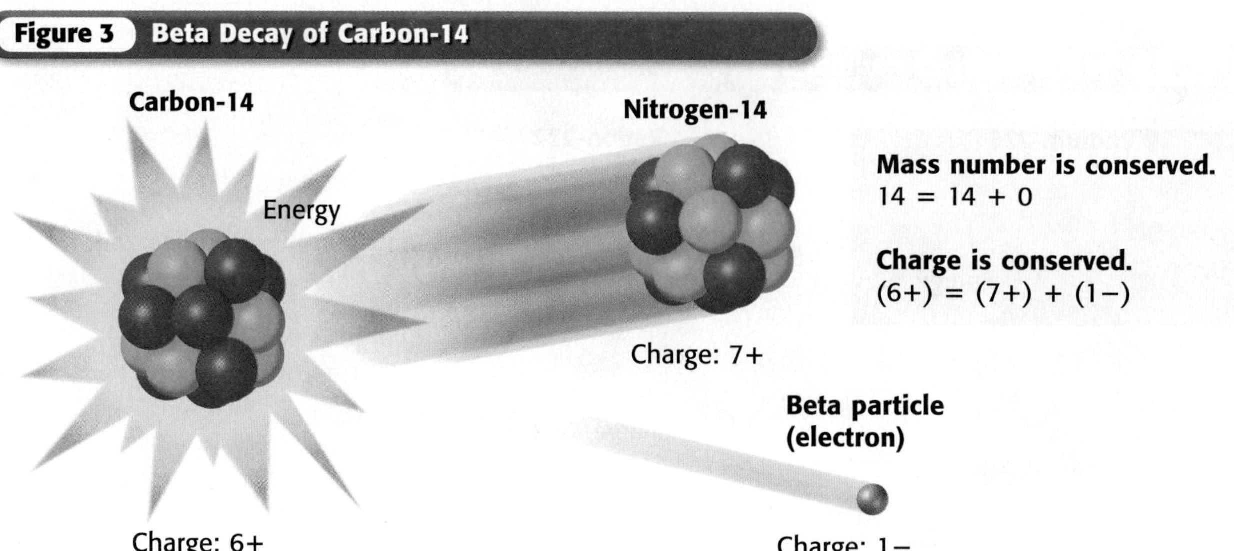

Beta Decay

The release of a beta particle from a nucleus is called *beta decay*. A *beta particle* can be an electron or a positron. An electron has a charge of 1−. A positron has a charge of 1+. But electrons and positrons have a mass of almost 0. The mass number of a beta particle is 0 because it has no protons or neutrons.

Two Types of Beta Decay

A carbon-14 nucleus undergoes beta decay, as shown in the model in **Figure 3.** During this kind of decay, a neutron breaks into a proton and an electron. Notice that the nucleus becomes a nucleus of a different element. And both mass number and charge are conserved.

Not all isotopes of an element decay in the same way. **Isotopes** are atoms that have the same number of protons as other atoms of the same element do but that have different numbers of neutrons. A carbon-11 nucleus undergoes beta decay when a proton breaks into a positron and a neutron. But during any beta decay, the nucleus changes into a nucleus of a different element. And both mass number and charge are conserved.

isotope an atom that has the same number of protons (or the same atomic number) as other atoms of the same element do but that has a different number of neutrons (and thus a different atomic mass)

Gamma Decay

Energy is also given off during alpha decay and beta decay. Some of this energy is in the form of light that has very high energy called *gamma rays*. The release of gamma rays from a nucleus is called *gamma decay*. This decay happens as the particles in the nucleus shift places. Gamma rays have no mass or charge. So, gamma decay alone does not cause one element to change into another element.

The Penetrating Power of Radiation

The three forms of nuclear radiation have different abilities to penetrate, or go through, matter. This difference is due to their mass and charge, as you can see in **Figure 4.**

Effects of Radiation on Matter

Atoms that are hit by nuclear radiation can give up electrons. Chemical bonds between atoms can break when hit by nuclear radiation. Both of these things can cause damage to living and nonliving matter.

Damage to Living Matter

When an organism absorbs radiation, its cells can be damaged. Radiation can cause burns like those caused by touching something that is hot. A single large exposure to radiation can lead to *radiation sickness*. Symptoms of this sickness include fatigue, loss of appetite, and hair loss. Destruction of blood cells and even death can result. Exposure to radiation can also increase the risk of cancer because of the damage done to cells. People who work near radioactive materials often wear a film badge. Radiation will make an image on the film to warn the person if the levels of radiation are too high.

Reading Check **Name three symptoms of radiation sickness.**

Figure 4 The Penetrating Abilities of Nuclear Radiation

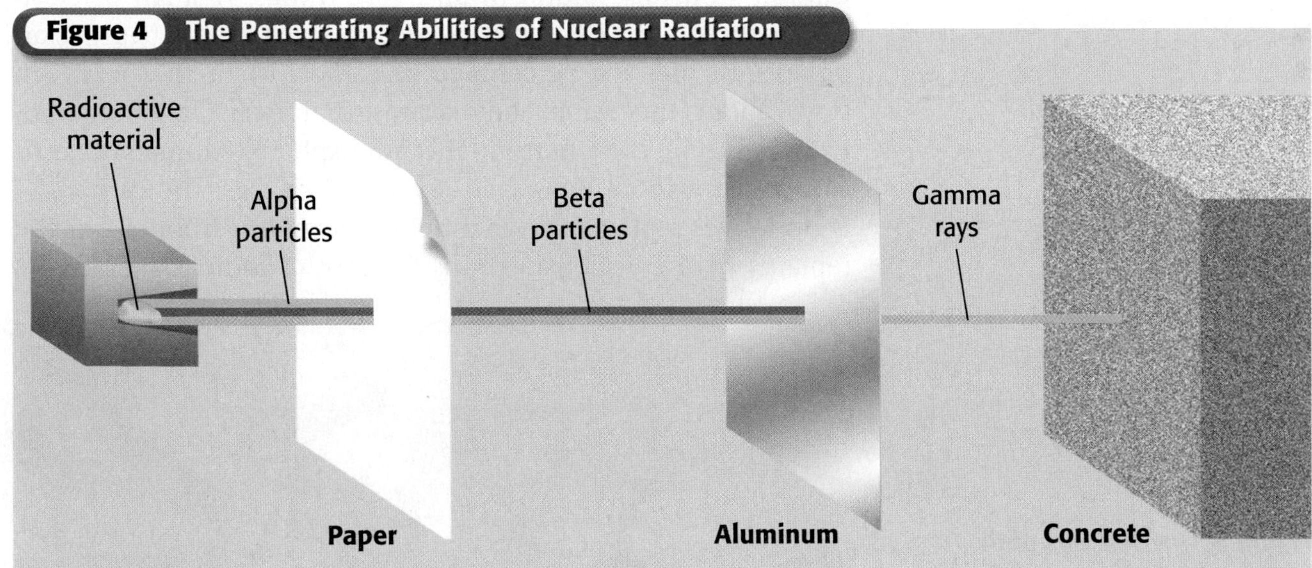

▲ **Alpha particles** have a greater charge and mass than beta particles and gamma rays do. Alpha particles travel about 7 cm through air and are stopped by paper or clothing.

▲ **Beta particles** have a 1− or 1+ charge and almost no mass. They are more penetrating than alpha particles. Beta particles travel about 1 m through air but are stopped by 3 mm of aluminum.

▲ **Gamma rays** have no charge or mass and are the most penetrating. They are blocked by very dense, thick materials, such as a few centimeters of lead or a few meters of concrete.

Damage to Nonliving Matter

Radiation can also damage nonliving matter. When metal atoms lose electrons, the metal is weakened. For example, radiation can cause the metal structures of buildings, such as nuclear power plants, to become unsafe. High levels of radiation from the sun can damage spacecraft.

CONNECTION TO Environmental Science

WRITING SKILL **Radon in the Home** Radioactive radon-222 forms from the radioactive decay of uranium found in soil and rocks. Because radon is a gas, it can enter buildings through gaps in the walls and floors. Research the hazards of radon. Identify methods used to detect it and to prevent exposure to it. Present your findings by writing a pamphlet in the form of a public service announcement.

Damage at Different Depths

Gamma rays go through matter easily. They can cause damage deep within matter. Beta particles cause damage closer to the surface. Alpha particles cause damage very near the surface. But alpha particles are larger and more massive than the particles of other kinds of radiation. So, if a source of alpha particles enters an organism, the particles can cause the most damage.

Finding a Date by Decay

Finding a date for someone can be tough—especially if the person is several thousand years old! Hikers in the Italian Alps found the remains of the Iceman, shown in **Figure 5,** in 1991. Scientists were able to estimate the time of death—about 5,300 years ago! How did the scientists do this? The decay of radioactive carbon was the key.

Carbon-14—It's in You!

Carbon atoms are found in all living things. A small percentage of these atoms is radioactive carbon-14 atoms. During an organism's life, the percentage of carbon-14 in the organism stays about the same. Any atoms that decay are replaced. Plants take in carbon from the atmosphere. Animals take in carbon from food. But when an organism dies, the carbon-14 is no longer replaced. Over time, the level of carbon-14 in the remains of the organism drops because of radioactive decay.

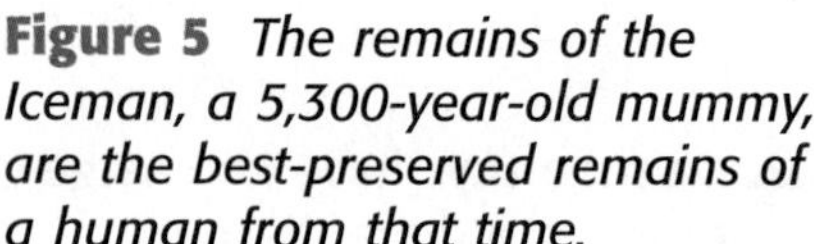

Figure 5 *The remains of the Iceman, a 5,300-year-old mummy, are the best-preserved remains of a human from that time.*

Figure 6 Radioactive Decay and Half-Life

The **original sample** contains a certain amount of radioactive isotope.

After **one half-life,** one-half of the original sample has decayed, and half is unchanged.

After **two half-lives,** one-fourth of the original sample remains unchanged.

After **three half-lives,** only one-eighth of the original sample remains unchanged.

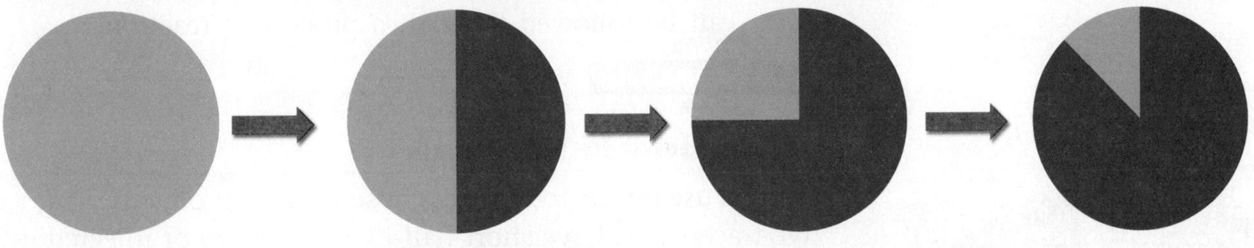

A Steady Rate of Decay

Scientists have found that every 5,730 years, half of the carbon-14 in a sample decays. The rate of decay is constant. The rate is not changed by other conditions, such as temperature or pressure. Each radioactive isotope has its own rate of decay, called half-life. A **half-life** is the amount of time it takes one-half of the nuclei of a radioactive isotope to decay. **Figure 6** is a model of this process. **Table 1** lists some isotopes that have a wide range of half-lives.

half-life the time needed for half of a sample of a radioactive substance to undergo radioactive decay

Reading Check **What is the half-life of carbon-14?**

Determining Age

Scientists measured the number of decays in the Iceman's body each minute. They found that a little less than half of the carbon-14 in the body had changed. In other words, not quite one half-life of carbon-14 (5,730 years) had passed since the Iceman died.

Carbon-14 can be used to find the age of objects up to 50,000 years old. To find the age of older things, other elements must be used. For example, potassium-40 has a half-life of 1.3 billion years. It is used to find the age of dinosaur fossils.

Table 1 **Examples of Half-Lives**

Isotope	Half-life	Isotope	Half-life
Uranium-238	4.5 billion years	Polonium-210	138 days
Oxygen-21	3.4 s	Nitrogen-13	10 min
Hydrogen-3	12.3 years	Calcium-36	0.1 s

How Old Is It?

One-fourth of the original carbon-14 of an antler is unchanged. As shown in **Figure 6,** two half-lives have passed. To determine the age of the antler, multiply the number of half-lives that have passed by the half-life of carbon-14. The antler's age is 2 times the half-life of carbon-14:

$$\text{age} = 2 \times 5{,}730 \text{ years}$$
$$\text{age} = 11{,}460 \text{ years}$$

Determine the age of a wooden spear that contains one-eighth of its original amount of carbon-14.

Uses of Radioactivity

You have learned how radioactive isotopes are used to determine the age of objects. But radioactivity is used in many areas for many things. The smoke detectors in your home might even use a small amount of radioactive material! Some isotopes can be used as tracers. *Tracers* are radioactive elements whose paths can be followed through a process or reaction.

Reading Check What is a tracer?

Radioactivity in Healthcare

Doctors use tracers to help diagnose medical problems. Radioactive tracers that have short half-lives are fed to or injected into a patient. Then, a detector is used to follow the tracer as it moves through the patient's body. The image in **Figure 7** shows an example of the results of a tracer study. Radioactive materials are also used to treat illnesses, including cancer. Radioactive materials can even help prevent illness. For example, many food and healthcare products are sterilized using radiation.

INTERNET ACTIVITY

For another activity related to this chapter, go to **go.hrw.com** and type in the keyword **HP5RADW.**

Radioactivity in Industry

Radioactive isotopes can also help detect defects in structures. For example, radiation is used to test the thickness of metal sheets as they are made. Another way radioactive isotopes are used to test structures is shown in **Figure 7.**

Some space probes have been powered by radioactive materials. The energy given off as nuclei decay is converted into electrical energy for the probe.

Figure 7 **Uses of Radioactivity in Healthcare and in Industry**

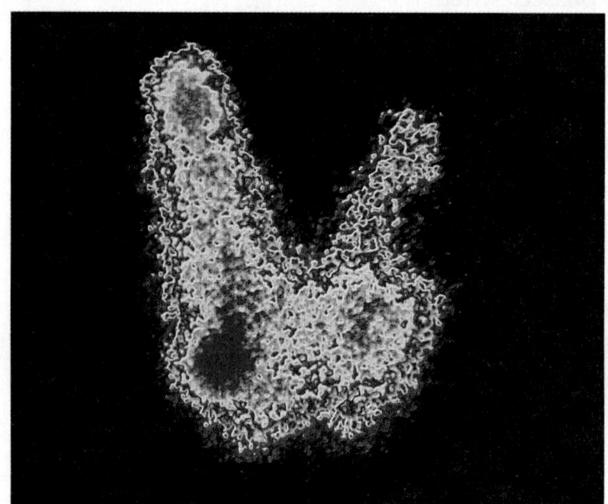

Radioactive iodine-131 was used to make this scan of a thyroid gland. The dark area shows the location of a tumor.

Tracers are used to find weak spots in materials and leaks in pipes. A Geiger counter is often used to detect the tracer.

SECTION Review

Summary

- Henri Becquerel discovered radioactivity while trying to study X rays. Radioactivity is the process by which a nucleus gives off nuclear radiation.
- An alpha particle is composed of two protons and two neutrons. A beta particle can be an electron or a positron. Gamma rays are a form of light with very high energy.
- Gamma rays penetrate matter better than alpha or beta particles do. Beta particles penetrate matter better than alpha particles do.
- Nuclear radiation can damage living and nonliving matter.
- Half-life is the amount of time it takes for one-half of the nuclei of a radioactive isotope to decay. The age of some objects can be determined using half-lives.
- Uses of radioactive materials include detecting defects in materials, sterilizing products, diagnosing illness, and generating electrical energy.

Using Key Terms

1. Use the following terms in the same sentence: *mass number* and *isotope*.

Understanding Key Ideas

2. Which of the following statements correctly describes the changes that happen in radioactive decay?
   - **a.** Alpha decay changes the atomic number and the mass number of a nucleus.
   - **b.** Gamma decay changes the atomic number but not the mass number of a nucleus.
   - **c.** Gamma decay changes the mass number but not the atomic number of a nucleus.
   - **d.** Beta decay changes the mass number but not the atomic number of a nucleus.
3. Describe the experiment that led to the discovery of radioactivity.
4. Give two examples of how radioactivity is useful and two examples of how it is harmful.

Math Skills

5. A rock contains one-fourth of its original amount of potassium-40. The half-life of potassium-40 is 1.3 billion years. Calculate the rock's age.
6. How many half-lives have passed if a sample contains one-sixteenth of its original amount of radioactive material?

Critical Thinking

7. **Making Comparisons** Compare the penetrating power of the following nuclear radiation: alpha particles, beta particles, and gamma rays.
8. **Making Inferences** Why would uranium-238 not be useful in determining the age of a spear that is thought to be 5,000 years old? Explain your reasoning.

Interpreting Graphics

9. Look at the figure below. Which nucleus could not undergo alpha decay? Explain your answer.

Beryllium-10

6 neutrons
4 protons

Hydrogen-3

2 neutrons
1 proton

For a variety of links related to this chapter, go to www.scilinks.org
Topic: Discovering Radioactivity; Radioactive Isotopes
SciLinks code: HSM0412; HSM1256

SECTION 2

Energy from the Nucleus

What You Will Learn

- Describe nuclear fission.
- Identify advantages and disadvantages of fission.
- Describe nuclear fusion.
- Identify advantages and disadvantages of fusion.

Vocabulary

nuclear fission
nuclear chain reaction
nuclear fusion

READING STRATEGY

Reading Organizer As you read this section, make a table comparing nuclear fission and nuclear fusion.

From an early age, you were probably told not to play with fire. But fire itself is neither good nor bad. It simply has benefits and hazards.

Likewise, getting energy from the nucleus of an atom has benefits and hazards. In this section, you will learn about two ways to get energy from the nucleus—fission (FISH uhn) and fusion (FYOO zhuhn). Gaining an understanding of the advantages and disadvantages of fission and fusion is important for people who will make decisions about the use of this energy—people like you!

Nuclear Fission

The nuclei of some atoms decay by breaking into two smaller, more stable nuclei. **Nuclear fission** is the process by which a large nucleus splits into two small nuclei and releases energy.

The nuclei of some uranium atoms, as well as the nuclei of other large atoms, can undergo nuclear fission naturally. Large atoms can also be forced to undergo fission by hitting the atoms with neutrons, as shown by the model in **Figure 1.**

Reading Check **What happens to a nucleus that undergoes nuclear fission?** *(See the Appendix for answers to Reading Checks.)*

Figure 1 **Fission of a Uranium-235 Nucleus**

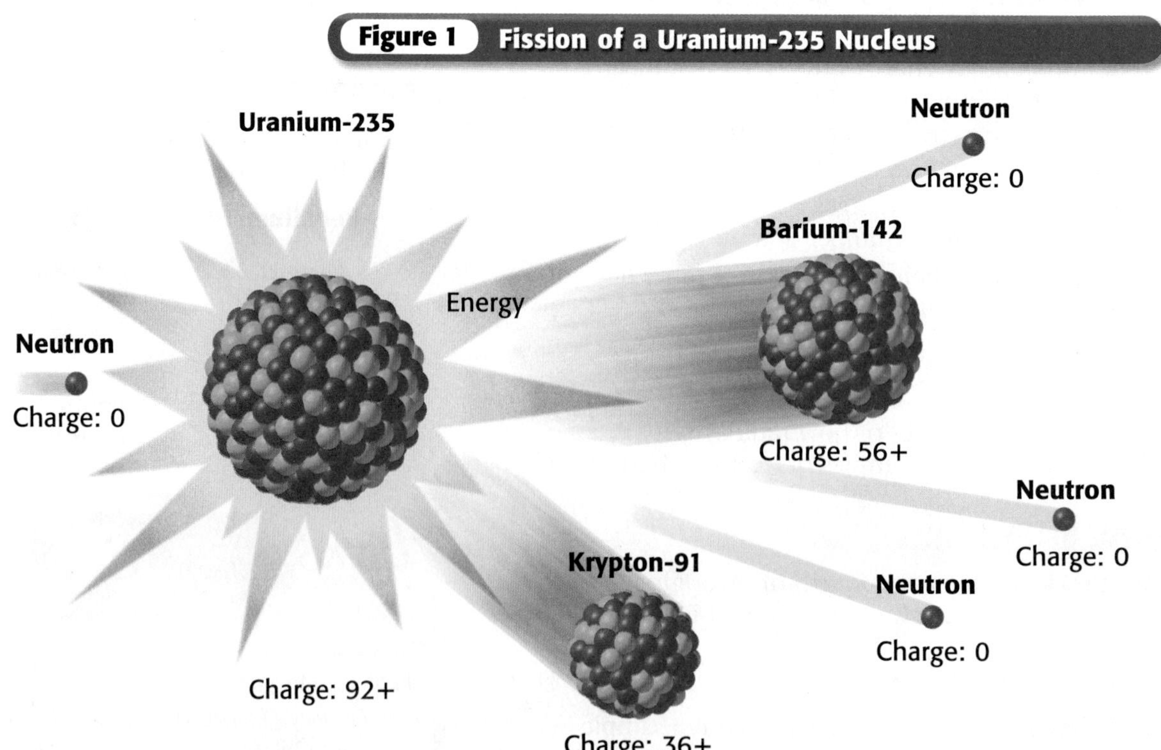

Energy from Matter

Did you know that matter can be changed into energy? It's true! If you could find the total mass of the products in **Figure 1** and compare it with the total mass of the reactants, you would find something strange. The total mass of the products is slightly less than the total mass of the reactants. Why are the masses different? Some of the matter was converted into energy.

The amount of energy given off when a single uranium nucleus splits is very small. But this energy comes from a very small amount of matter. The amount of matter converted into energy is only about one-fifth the mass of a hydrogen atom. And hydrogen is the smallest atom that exists! Look at **Figure 2.** The nuclear fission of the uranium nuclei in one fuel pellet releases as much energy as the chemical change of burning about 1,000 kg of coal.

Figure 2 *Each of these small fuel pellets can generate a large amount of energy through the process of nuclear fission.*

Nuclear Chain Reactions

Look at **Figure 1** again. Suppose that two or three of the neutrons produced split other uranium-235 nuclei. So, energy and more neutrons are given off. And then suppose that two or three of the neutrons that were given off split other nuclei and so on. This example is one type of **nuclear chain reaction,** a continuous series of nuclear fission reactions. A model of an uncontrolled chain reaction is shown in **Figure 3.**

nuclear fission the splitting of the nucleus of a large atom into two or more fragments; releases additional neutrons and energy

nuclear chain reaction a continuous series of nuclear fission reactions

Figure 3 An Uncontrolled Nuclear Chain Reaction

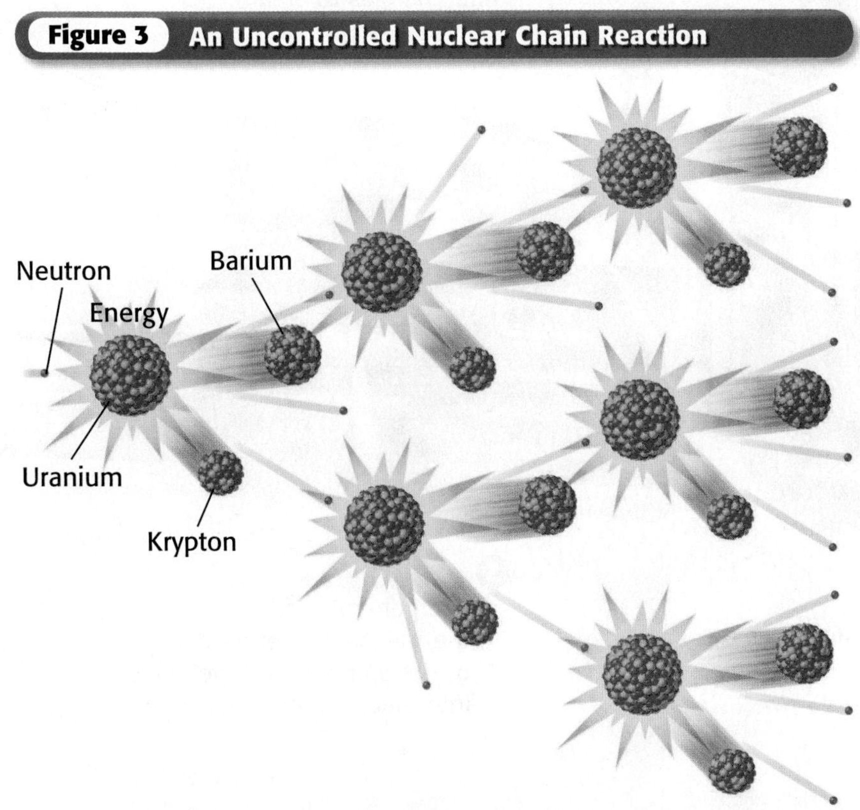

Energy from a Chain Reaction

In an *uncontrolled chain reaction,* huge amounts of energy are given off very quickly. For example, the tremendous energy of an atomic bomb is the result of an uncontrolled chain reaction. On the other hand, nuclear power plants use *controlled chain reactions*. The energy released from the nuclei in the uranium fuel within the nuclear power plants is used to generate electrical energy. **Figure 4** shows how a nuclear power plant works.

Advantages and Disadvantages of Fission

Every form of energy has advantages and disadvantages. To make informed decisions about energy use, you need to know both sides. For example, burning wood to keep warm on a cold night could save your life. But a spark from the fire could start a forest fire. Nuclear fission has advantages and disadvantages that you should think about.

Figure 4 How a Nuclear Power Plant Works

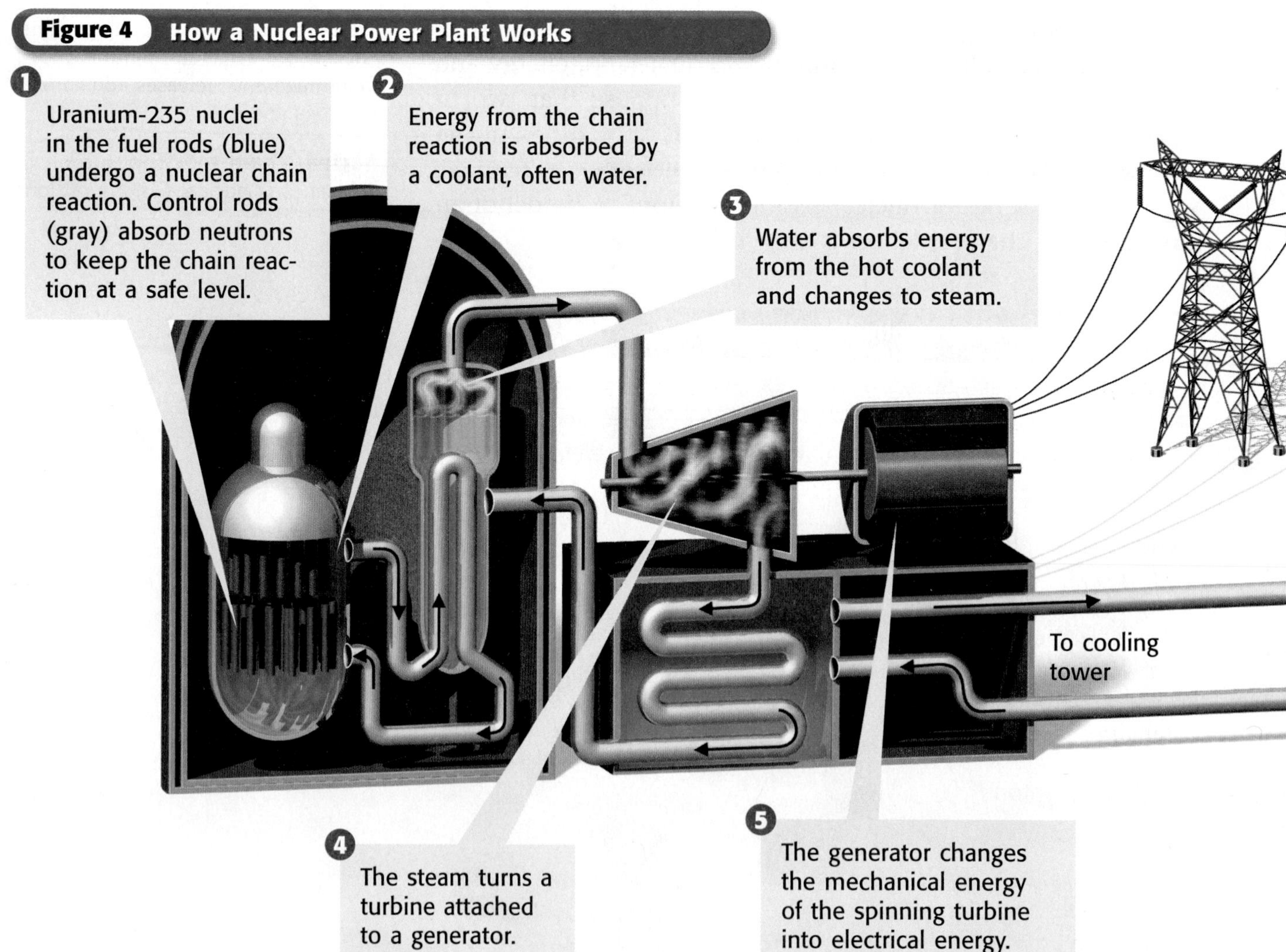

1 Uranium-235 nuclei in the fuel rods (blue) undergo a nuclear chain reaction. Control rods (gray) absorb neutrons to keep the chain reaction at a safe level.
2 Energy from the chain reaction is absorbed by a coolant, often water.
3 Water absorbs energy from the hot coolant and changes to steam.
To cooling tower
4 The steam turns a turbine attached to a generator.
5 The generator changes the mechanical energy of the spinning turbine into electrical energy.

Accidents

A concern that many people have about nuclear power is the risk of an accident. In Chernobyl, Ukraine, on April 26, 1986, an accident happened, as shown in **Figure 5.** An explosion put large amounts of radioactive uranium fuel and waste products into the atmosphere. The cloud of radioactive material spread over most of Europe and Asia. It reached as far as North America.

Figure 5 *During a test at the Chernobyl nuclear power plant, the emergency protection system was turned off. The reactor overheated, which resulted in an explosion.*

What Waste!

Another concern about nuclear power is nuclear waste. This waste includes used fuel rods, chemicals used to process uranium, and even shoe covers and overalls worn by workers. Controlled fission has been carried out for only about 50 years. But the waste will give off high levels of radiation for thousands of years. The rate of radioactive decay cannot be changed. So, the nuclear waste must be stored until it becomes less radioactive. Most of the used fuel rods are stored in huge pools of water. Some of the liquid wastes are stored in underground tanks. However, scientists continue to look for better ideas for long-term storage of nuclear waste.

WRITING SKILL **Storage Site** The government of the United States is required by law to build underground storage for nuclear waste. The waste must be stored for a very long time and cannot escape into the environment. In your **science journal,** write a one-page paper describing the characteristics of a good location for these underground storage sites.

Nuclear Versus Fossil Fuel

Nuclear power plants cost more to build than power plants that use fossil fuels. But nuclear power plants often cost less to run than plants that use fossil fuels because less fuel is needed. Also, nuclear power plants do not release gases, such as carbon dioxide, into the atmosphere. The use of fission allows our supply of fossil fuels to last longer. However, the supply of uranium is limited.

Reading Check **What are two advantages of using nuclear fission to generate electrical energy?**

Quick Lab

Gone Fission

1. Make two paper balls from a **sheet of paper.**
2. Stand in a group with your classmates. Make sure you are an arm's length from your other classmates.
3. Your teacher will gently toss a paper ball at the group. If you are touched by a ball, gently toss your paper balls at the group.
4. Explain how this activity is a model of a chain reaction. Be sure to explain what the students and the paper balls represent.

Figure 6 Nuclear Fusion of Hydrogen

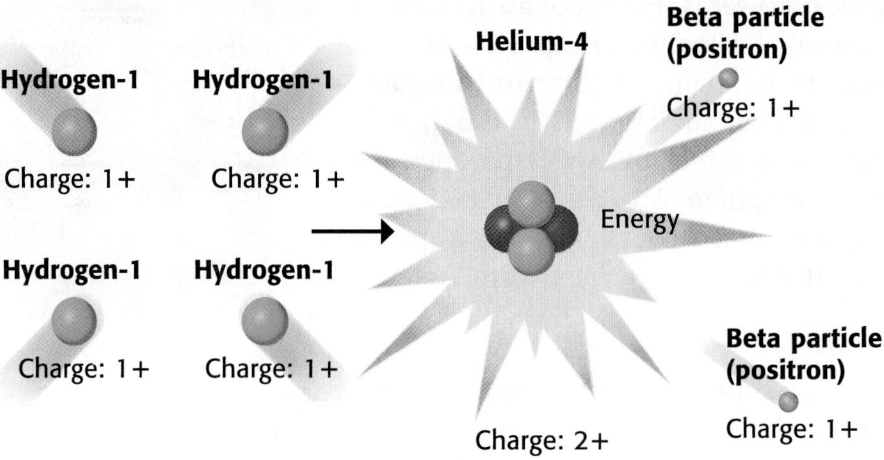

Nuclear Fusion

nuclear fusion the combination of the nuclei of small atoms to form a larger nucleus; releases energy

Fusion is another nuclear reaction in which matter is converted into energy. In **nuclear fusion,** two or more nuclei that have small masses combine, or fuse, to form a larger nucleus.

Plasma Needed

In order for fusion to happen, the repulsion between positively charged nuclei must be overcome. Very high temperatures are needed—more than 100,000,000°C! At these high temperatures, matter is a plasma. *Plasma* is the state of matter in which electrons have been removed from atoms. So, plasma is made up of ions and electrons. One place that has such temperatures is the sun. In the sun's core, hydrogen nuclei fuse to form a helium nucleus, as shown in the model in **Figure 6.**

Reading Check Describe the process of nuclear fusion.

CONNECTION TO Astronomy

Elements of the Stars Hydrogen is not the only fuel that stars use for fusion. Research other elements that stars can use as fuels and the fusion reactions that make these elements. Make a poster showing what you learn.

ACTIVITY

Advantages and Disadvantages of Fusion

Energy for your home cannot yet be generated using nuclear fusion. First, very high temperatures are needed. Second, more energy is needed to make and hold the plasma than is generated by fusion. But scientists predict that fusion will provide electrical energy in the future—maybe in your lifetime!

Less Accident Prone

The concern about an accident such as the one at Chernobyl is much lower for fusion reactors. If a fusion reactor exploded, very little radioactive material would be released. Fusion products are not radioactive. And the hydrogen-3 used for fuel in experimental fusion reactors is much less radioactive than the uranium used in fission reactors.

Oceans of Fuel

Scientists studying fusion use hydrogen-2 and hydrogen-3 in their work. Hydrogen-1 is much more common than these isotopes. But there is enough of them in Earth's waters to provide fuel for millions of years. Also, a fusion reaction releases more energy per gram of fuel than a fission reaction does. So, fusion saves more resources than fission does, as shown in **Figure 7.**

Figure 7 *Fusing the hydrogen-2 in 3.8 L of water would release about the same amount of energy as burning 1,140 L of gasoline!*

Less Waste

The products of fusion reactions are not radioactive. So, fusion is a "cleaner" source of energy than fission is. There would be much less radioactive waste. But to have the benefits of fusion, scientists need money to pay for research.

SECTION Review

Summary

- In nuclear fission, a massive nucleus breaks into two nuclei.
- In nuclear fusion, two or more nuclei combine to form a larger nucleus.
- Nuclear fission is used in power plants to generate electrical energy. A limited fuel supply and radioactive waste products are disadvantages of fission.
- Nuclear fusion cannot yet be used as an energy source, but plentiful fuel and little waste are advantages of fusion.

Using Key Terms

Complete each of the following sentences by choosing the correct term from the word bank.

nuclear fission
nuclear fusion
nuclear chain reaction

1. During ___, small nuclei combine.
2. During ___, nuclei split one after another.

Understanding Key Ideas

3. Which of the following is an advantage nuclear fission has over fossil fuels?
   a. unlimited supply of fuel
   b. less radioactive waste
   c. fewer building expenses
   d. less released carbon dioxide
4. Which kind of nuclear reaction is currently used to generate electrical energy?
5. Which kind of nuclear reaction is the source of the sun's energy?
6. What particle is needed to begin a nuclear chain reaction?
7. In both fission and fusion, what is converted into energy?

Math Skills

8. Imagine that a uranium nucleus splits and releases three neutrons and that each neutron splits another nucleus. If the first split occurs in stage 1, how many nuclei will split during stage 4?

Critical Thinking

9. **Making Comparisons** Compare nuclear fission with nuclear fusion.
10. **Analyzing Processes** The floor of a room is covered in mousetraps that each hold two table-tennis balls. One ball is dropped onto a trap. The trap snaps shut, and the balls on it fly into the air and fall on other traps. What nuclear process is modeled here? Explain your answer.

For a variety of links related to this chapter, go to www.scilinks.org

Topic: Nuclear Fission; Nuclear Fusion
SciLinks code: HSM1048; HSM1050

Model-Making Lab

Domino Chain Reactions

Fission of uranium-235 is a process that relies on neutrons. When a uranium-235 nucleus splits into two smaller nuclei, it releases two or three neutrons that can cause neighboring nuclei to undergo fission. This fission can result in a nuclear chain reaction. In this lab, you will build two models of nuclear chain reactions, using dominoes.

OBJECTIVES

Build models to represent controlled and uncontrolled nuclear chain reactions.

Compare models of controlled and uncontrolled nuclear chain reactions.

MATERIALS

- dominoes (15)
- stopwatch

Procedure

1. For the first model, set up the dominoes as shown below. When pushed over, each domino should hit two dominoes in the next row.

2. Measure the time it takes for all the dominoes to fall. To do this, start the stopwatch as you tip over the front domino. Stop the stopwatch when the last domino falls. Record this time.
3. If some of the dominoes do not fall, repeat steps 1 and 2. You may have to adjust the setup a few times.
4. For the second model, set up the dominoes as shown at left. The domino in the first row should hit both of the dominoes in the second row. Beginning with the second row, only one domino from each row should hit both of the dominoes in the next row.
5. Repeat step 2. Again, you may have to adjust the setup a few times to get all the dominoes to fall.

Analyze the Results

1. **Classifying** Which model represents an uncontrolled chain reaction? Which represents a controlled chain reaction? Explain your answers.

2. **Analyzing Results** Imagine that each domino releases a certain amount of energy as it falls. Compare the total amount of energy released in the two models.

3. **Analyzing Data** Compare the time needed to release the energy in the models. Which model took longer to release its energy?

Draw Conclusions

4. **Evaluating Models** In a nuclear power plant, a chain reaction is controlled by using a material that absorbs neutrons. Only enough neutrons to continue the chain reaction are allowed to continue splitting uranium-235 nuclei. Explain how your model of a controlled nuclear chain reaction modeled this process.

5. **Applying Conclusions** Why must uranium nuclei be close to each other in order for a nuclear chain reaction to happen? (Hint: What would happen in your model if the dominoes were too far apart?)

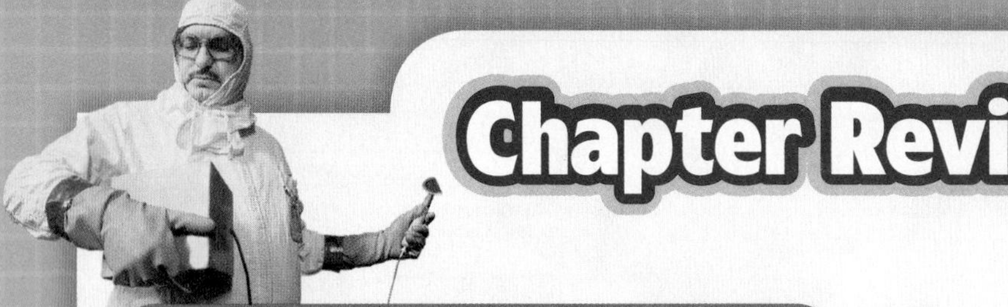

Chapter Review

USING KEY TERMS

The statements below are false. For each statement, replace the underlined term to make a true statement.

1. Nuclear fusion involves splitting a nucleus.

2. During one beta decay, half of a radioactive sample will decay.

3. Radioactivity involves the joining of nuclei.

4. Isotopes of an element have different atomic numbers.

UNDERSTANDING KEY IDEAS

Multiple Choice

5. Which of the following is a use of radioactive material?
   a. detecting smoke
   b. locating defects in materials
   c. generating electrical energy
   d. All of the above

6. Which particle both begins and is produced by a nuclear chain reaction?
   a. positron
   b. neutron
   c. alpha particle
   d. beta particle

7. Which nuclear radiation can be stopped by paper?
   a. alpha particles
   b. beta particles
   c. gamma rays
   d. None of the above

8. The half-life of a radioactive atom is 2 months. If you start with 1 g of the element, how much will remain after 6 months?
   a. One-half of a gram will remain.
   b. One-fourth of a gram will remain.
   c. One-eighth of a gram will remain.
   d. None of the sample will remain.

9. The waste products of nuclear fission
   a. are harmless.
   b. are safe after 20 years.
   c. can be destroyed by burning them.
   d. remain radioactive for thousands of years.

10. Which statement about nuclear fusion is false?
    a. Nuclear fusion happens in the sun.
    b. Nuclear fusion is the joining of the nuclei of atoms.
    c. Nuclear fusion is currently used to generate electrical energy.
    d. Nuclear fusion can use hydrogen as fuel.

Short Answer

11. What are two dangers associated with nuclear fission?

12. What are two of the problems that need to be solved in order to make nuclear fusion a usable energy source?

13. In fission, the products have less mass than the starting materials do. Explain why this happens.

Math Skills

14 A scientist used 10 g of phosphorus-32 in a test on plant growth but forgot to record the date. When measured some time later, only 2.5 g of phosphorus-32 remained. If phosphorus-32 has a half-life of 14 days, how many days ago did the experiment begin?

CRITICAL THINKING

15 **Concept Mapping** Use the following terms to create a concept map: *radioactive decay, alpha particle, beta particle, gamma ray,* and *nuclear radiation.*

16 **Expressing Opinions** Smoke detectors often use americium-243 to detect smoke particles in the air. Americium-243 undergoes alpha decay. Do you think that these smoke detectors are safe to have in your home if used properly? Explain. (Hint: Think about how penetrating alpha particles are.)

17 **Applying Concepts** How can radiation cause cancer?

18 **Analyzing Processes** Explain why nuclei of carbon, oxygen, and iron can be found in stars.

19 **Making Inferences** If you could block all radiation from sources outside your body, explain why you would still be exposed to some radiation.

INTERPRETING GRAPHICS

20 The image below was made in a manner similar to that of Becquerel's original experiment. What conclusions can be drawn from this image about the penetrating power of radiation?

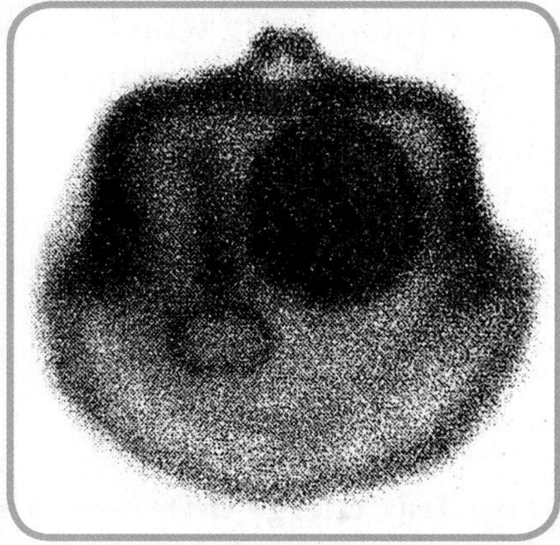

Use the graph below to answer the questions that follow.

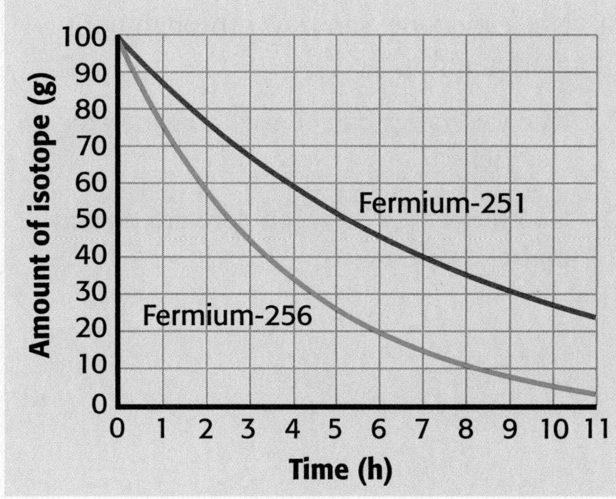

21 What is the half-life of fermium-256?

22 What is the half-life of fermium-251?

Multiple Choice

Use the image below to answer question 1.

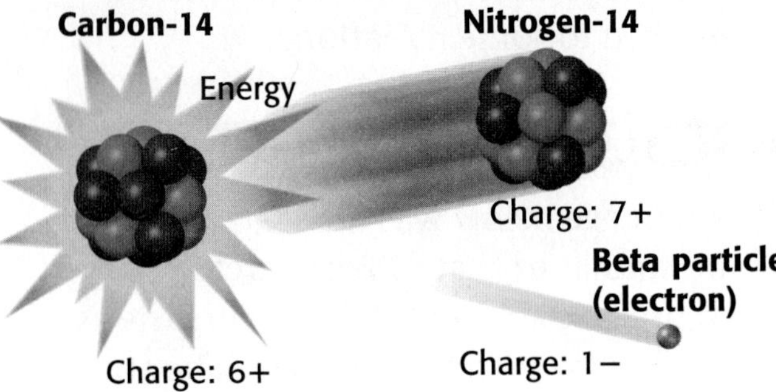

1. The image above shows the decay of a radioactive nucleus. By which nuclear process is this nucleus decaying?

A. alpha decay

B. beta decay

C. nuclear fission

D. nuclear fusion

2. How is nuclear energy different from other forms of energy?

A. Nuclear energy can be converted to other forms of energy.

B. Nuclear energy can travel through both matter and space.

C. Nuclear energy can be used to generate electricity.

D. Nuclear energy has been converted from matter.

3. In a nuclear power plant, energy from nuclear fission reactions is absorbed by a coolant that travels through pipes that are submerged in large tanks of water. The thermal energy of the coolant is transferred to the water. Through what method is the thermal energy primarily transferred to the water?

A. conduction

B. convection

C. conversion

D. radiation

4. Who is credited with discovering radioactivity?

A. Marie Curie

B. Pierre Curie

C. Henri Becquerel

D. Albert Einstein

5. What type of radioactive decay causes a radium-226 nucleus to change to a radon-222 nucleus?

A. alpha decay

B. beta decay giving off an electron

C. beta decay giving of a positron

D. gamma decay

6. **Ernesto wants to build a shield that he can stand behind that will block gamma rays. Which material should he use?**

   A. several sheets of paper

   B. doubled-up aluminum foil

   C. heavy leather pieces

   D. thick sheets of lead

Use the graph below to answer question 7.

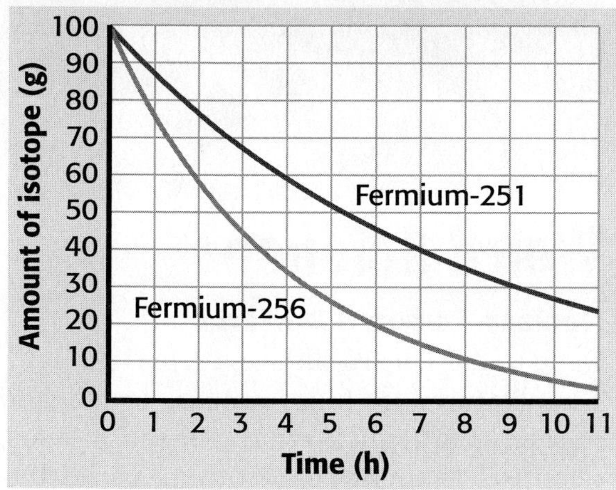

7. **The graph above shows the decay rates of two isotopes of fermium. What is the approximate half-life of fermium-256?**

   A. 2.5 h

   B. 5.3 h

   C. 5.5 h

   D. 11.0 h

8. **A nuclear chain reaction is a continuous series of nuclear fission reactions. Chain reactions in nuclear power plants are controlled by inserting control rods in the nuclear reactor. How do control rods work?**

   A. Control rods absorb excess uranium-235.

   B. Control rods absorb emitted barium-142.

   C. Control rods absorb excess energy.

   D. Control rods absorb emitted neutrons.

9. **The half-life of polonium-210 is 138 days. If a sample of polonium-210 has an initial mass of 64 g, how much polonium-210 will remain after 414 days?**

   A. 2.0 g

   B. 8.0 g

   C. 32 g

   D. 58 g

Open Response

10. **Shoes made from plant material worn by prehistoric people were found in caves in Missouri and Kentucky. Scientists used carbon-14 dating to determine the age of the shoes. Explain how carbon-14 dating works.**

11. **Jacob is arguing the disadvantages of radioactivity and Asha is defending the benefits of radioactivity. Describe two points that each student can make during the debate.**

Science in Action

Science, Technology, and Society

Irradiated Food

One way to help keep food fresh for longer periods of time is to irradiate it. Exposing food to radiation can kill organisms such as mold or bacteria that cause food to spoil. In addition, irradiated potatoes and onions can be stored for a longer time without sprouting. Radiation can even be used to control pests such as beetles that could cause a lot of damage to stored grains.

Social Studies ACTIVITY

WRITING SKILL Food preservation is an important development of history. Write a one-page report that compares methods that you use to keep food from spoiling with methods used in the late 1800s.

Weird Science

Nuclear-Powered Bacteria

Deep under Earth's surface, there is no light. Temperatures are high, water is scarce, and oxygen is difficult to find. For many years, scientists thought that nothing could live under these extreme conditions. But in 1989, a team of scientists found bacteria living in rocks that are 500 m below Earth's surface. Since then, bacteria have been found living in rocks that are as deep as 3.5 km below Earth's surface! Scientists wondered what these bacteria use for food. These bacteria seem to get their food from an unusual source—the radioactive decay of uranium. The idea that radioactive decay can be a food source is new to science and is changing the way that scientists think about life.

Math ACTIVITY

How deep is 3.5 km? To help you imagine this depth, calculate how many Statues of Liberty could be stacked in a hole that is 3.5 km deep. The Statue of Liberty in New York is about 46 m tall.

People in Science

Marie and Pierre Curie

A Great Team You may have heard the saying "Two heads are better than one." For scientific discoveries, this saying is quite true. The husband and wife team Pierre and Marie Curie put their heads together and discovered the elements radium and polonium. Their work also helped them describe radioactivity.

Working side by side for long hours under poor conditions, Marie and Pierre Curie studied the mysterious rays given off by the element uranium. They processed huge amounts of an ore called *pitchblende* to collect the uranium from it. Strangely, the leftover material was more active than uranium. They spent several more months working with the material and discovered an element that was 300 times more active than uranium. Marie called it *polonium* in honor of Poland, which was the country in which she was born. For their research on radiation, the Curies were awarded the Nobel Prize in physics in 1903.

Language Arts ACTIVITY

WRITING SKILL Think of a time that you and a friend solved a problem together that neither of you could solve alone. Write a one-page story about how you each helped solve the problem.

To learn more about these Science in Action topics, visit go.hrw.com and type in the keyword **HP5RADF.**

Current Science

Check out Current Science® articles related to this chapter by visiting go.hrw.com. Just type in the keyword HP5CS16.

LabBook

Contents

Skills Practice Lab

Stayin' Alive!

Every second of your life, your body's trillions of cells take in, use, and store energy. They repair themselves, reproduce, and get rid of waste. Together, these processes are called *metabolism.* Your cells use the food that you eat to provide the energy you need to stay alive.

Your Basal Metabolic Rate (BMR) is a measurement of the energy that your body needs to carry out all the basic life processes while you are at rest. These processes include breathing, keeping your heart beating, and keeping your body's temperature stable. Your BMR is influenced by your gender, your age, and many other things. Your BMR may be different from everyone else's, but it is normal for you. In this activity, you will find the amount of energy, measured in Calories, you need every day in order to stay alive.

MATERIALS

- bathroom scale
- tape measure

Procedure

1. Find your weight on a bathroom scale. If the scale measures in pounds, you must convert your weight in pounds to your mass in kilograms. To convert your weight in pounds (lb) to mass in kilograms (kg), multiply the number of pounds by 0.454.

Example: If Carlos weighs 125 lb, his mass in kilograms is:

$$\begin{array}{r} 125 \text{ lb} \\ \times \underline{0.454} \\ 56.75 \text{ kg} \end{array}$$

2. Use a tape measure to find your height. If the tape measures in inches, convert your height in inches to height in centimeters. To convert your height in inches (in.) to your height in centimeters (cm), multiply the number of inches by 2.54.

If Carlos is 62 in. tall, his height in centimeters is:

$$\begin{array}{r} 62 \text{ in.} \\ \times \underline{2.54} \\ 157.48 \text{ cm} \end{array}$$

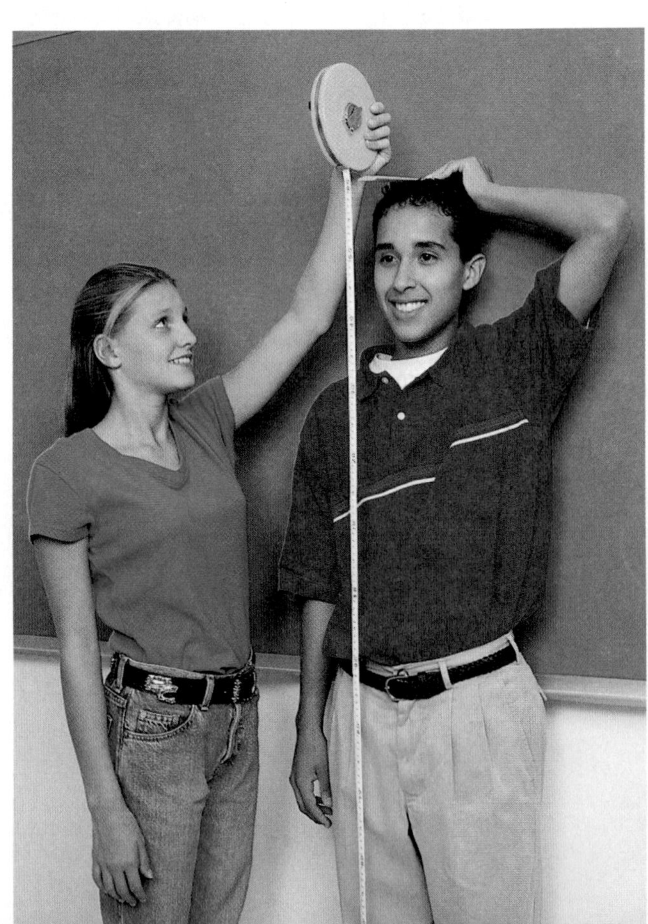

3. Now that you know your height and mass, use the appropriate formula below to get a close estimate of your BMR. Your answer will give you an estimate of the number of Calories your body needs each day just to stay alive.

Calculating Your BMR	
Females	**Males**
65 + (10 × your mass in kilograms)	66 + (13.5 × your mass in kilograms)
+ (1.8 × your height in centimeters)	+ (5 × your height in centimeters)
− (4.7 × your age in years)	− (6.8 × your age in years)

4. Your metabolism is also influenced by how active you are. Talking, walking, and playing games all take more energy than being at rest. To get an idea of how many Calories your body needs each day to stay healthy, select the lifestyle that best describes yours from the table at right. Then multiply your BMR by the activity factor.

Activity Factors	
Activity lifestyle	**Activity factor**
Moderately inactive (normal, everyday activities)	1.3
Moderately active (exercise 3 to 4 times a week)	1.4
Very active (exercise 4 to 6 times a week)	1.6
Extremely active (exercise 6 to 7 times a week)	1.8

Analyze the Results

1. In what way could you compare your whole body to a single cell? Explain.
2. Does an increase in activity increase your BMR? Does an increase in activity increase your need for Calories? Explain your answers.

Draw Conclusions

3. If you are moderately inactive, how many more Calories would you need if you began to exercise every day?

Applying Your Data

The best energy sources are those that supply the correct amount of Calories for your lifestyle and also provide the nutrients you need. Research in the library or on the Internet to find out which kinds of foods are the best energy sources for you. How does your list of best energy sources compare with your diet?

List everything you eat and drink in 1 day. Find out how many Calories are in each item, and find the total number of Calories you have consumed. How does this number of Calories compare with the number of Calories you need each day for all your activities?

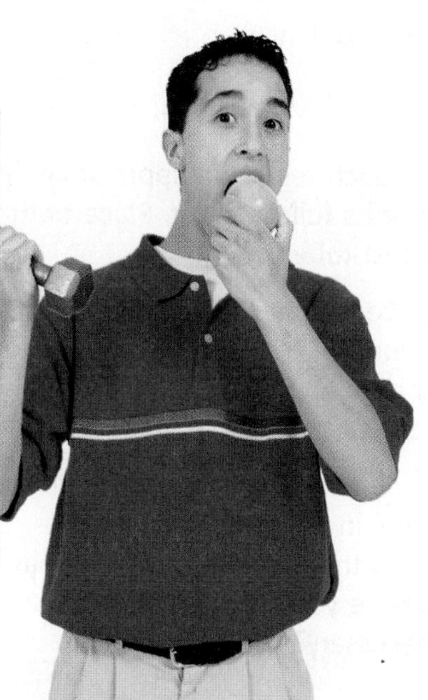

Skills Practice Lab

Weepy Weeds

You are trying to find a way to drain an area that is flooded with water polluted with fertilizer. You know that a plant releases water through the stomata in its leaves. As water evaporates from the leaves, more water is pulled up from the roots through the stem and into the leaves. By this process, called *transpiration,* water and nutrients are pulled into the plant from the soil. About 90% of the water a plant takes up through its roots is released into the atmosphere as water vapor through transpiration. Your idea is to add plants to the flooded area that will transpire the water and take up the fertilizer in their roots.

How much water can a plant take up and release in a certain period of time? In this activity, you will observe transpiration and determine one stem's rate of transpiration.

MATERIALS

- clock
- coleus or other plant stem cutting
- glass-marking pen
- metric ruler
- paper, graph
- test tube (2)
- test-tube rack
- water

SAFETY

Procedure

1. Make a data table similar to the one below for recording your measurements.

Height of Water in Test Tubes		
Time	**Test tube with plant**	**Test tube without plant**
Initial		
After 10 min		
After 20 min	DO NOT WRITE IN BOOK	
After 30 min		
After 40 min		
Overnight		

2. Fill each test tube approximately three-fourths full of water. Place both test tubes in a test-tube rack.

3. Place the plant stem so that it stands upright in one of the test tubes. Your test tubes should look like the ones in the photograph at right.

4. Use the glass-marking pen to mark the water level in each of the test tubes. Be sure you have the plant stem in place in its test tube before you mark the water level. Why is this necessary?

5. Measure the height of the water in each test tube. Be sure to hold the test tube level, and measure from the waterline to the bottom of the curve at the bottom of the test tube. Record these measurements on the row labeled "Initial."
6. Wait 10 min, and measure the height of the water in each test tube again. Record these measurements in your data table.
7. Repeat step 6 three more times. Record your measurements each time.
8. Wait 24 hours, and measure the height of the water in each test tube. Record these measurements in your data table.
9. Construct a graph similar to the one below. Plot the data from your data table. Draw a line for each test tube. Use a different color for each line, and make a key below your graph.
10. Calculate the rate of transpiration for your plant by using the following operations:

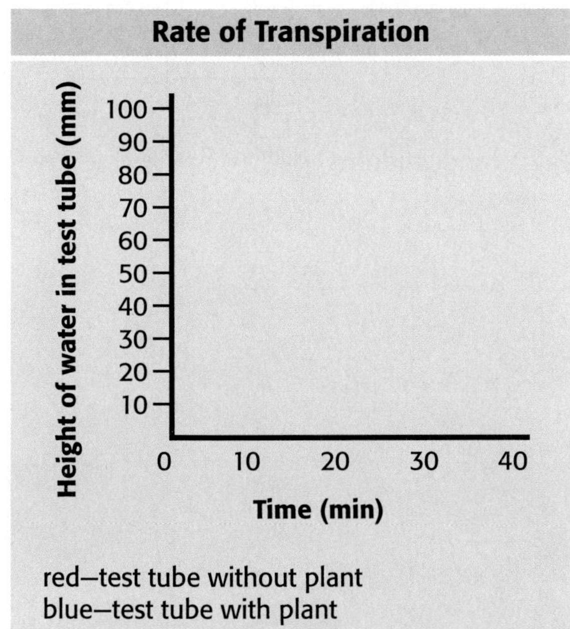

Test tube with plant:

Initial height
− Overnight height

Difference in height of water **(A)**

Test tube without plant:

Initial height
− Overnight height

Difference in height of water **(B)**

Water height difference due to transpiration:

Difference **A**
− Difference **B**

Water lost due to transpiration (in millimeters) in 24 hours

Analyze the Results

1. What was the purpose of the test tube that held only water?
2. What caused the water to go down in the test tube containing the plant stem? Did the same thing happen in the test tube with water only? Explain your answer.
3. What was the calculated rate of transpiration per day?
4. Using your graph, compare the rate of transpiration with the rate of evaporation alone.
5. Prepare a presentation of your experiment for your class. Use your data tables, graphs, and calculations as visual aids.

Applying Your Data

How many leaves did your plant sprigs have? Use this number to estimate what the rate of transpiration might be for a plant with 200 leaves. When you have your answer in millimeters of height in a test tube, pour this amount into a graduated cylinder to measure it in milliliters.

Inquiry Lab

Tracing Traits

Have you ever wondered about the traits you inherited from your parents? Do you have a trait that neither of your parents has? In this project, you will develop a family tree, or pedigree, similar to the one shown in the diagram below. You will trace an inherited trait through a family to determine how it has passed from generation to generation.

Procedure

1. The diagram at right shows a family history. On a separate piece of paper, draw a similar diagram of the family you have chosen. Include as many family members as possible, such as grandparents, parents, children, and grandchildren. Use circles to represent females and squares to represent males. You may include other information, such as the family member's name, birth date, or picture.

2. Draw a table similar to the one on the next page. Survey each of the family members shown in your family tree. Ask them if they have hair on the middle segment of their fingers. Write each person's name in the appropriate square. Explain to each person that it is normal to have either trait. The presence of hair on the middle segment is the dominant form of this trait.

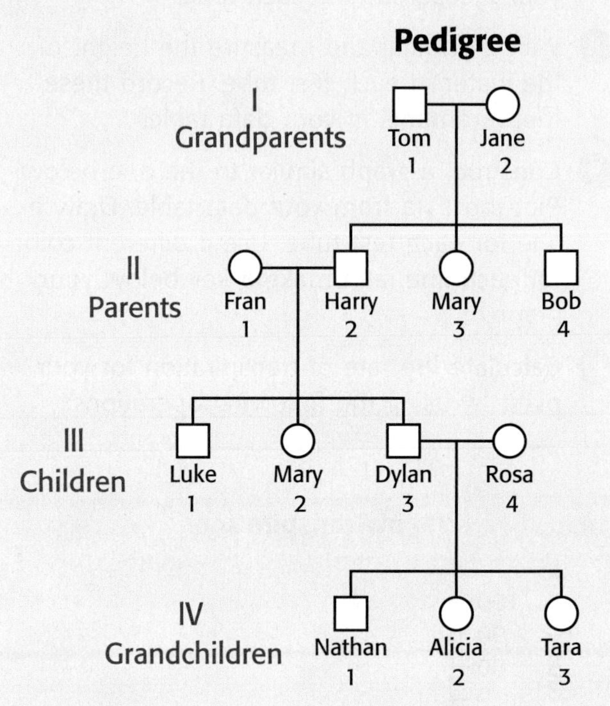

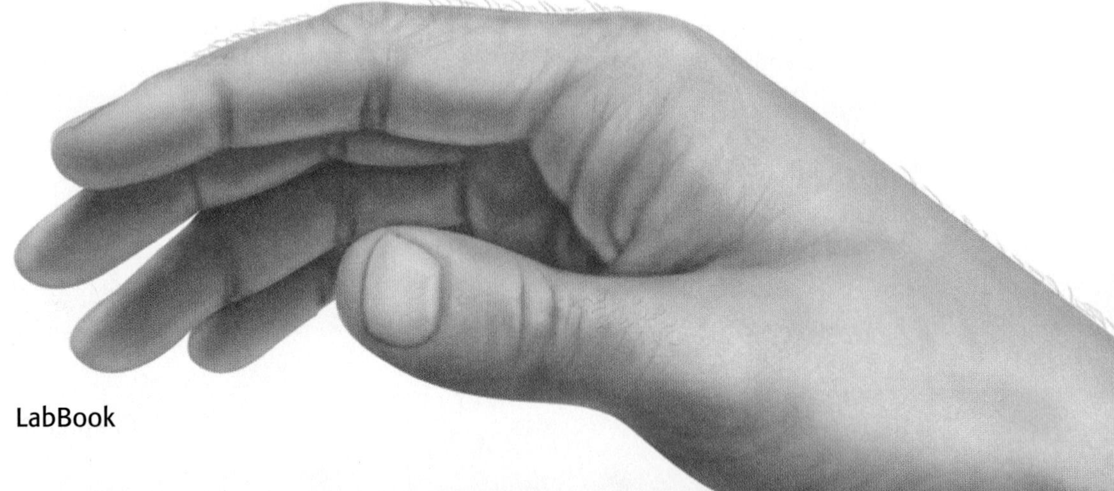

Dominant trait	Recessive trait	Family members with the dominant trait	Family members with the recessive trait
Hair present on the middle segment of fingers (H)	Hair absent on the middle segment of fingers (h)	DO NOT WRITE IN BOOK	

3. Trace this trait throughout the family tree you diagrammed in step 1. Shade or color the symbols of the family members who demonstrate the dominant form of this trait.

Analyze the Results

1. What percentage of the family members demonstrate the dominant form of the trait? Calculate this by counting the number of people who have the dominant trait and dividing this number by the total number of people you surveyed. Multiply your answer by 100. An example has been done at right.

Example: Calculating percentage

$$\frac{\text{10 people with trait}}{\text{20 people surveyed}} = \frac{1}{2}$$

$$\frac{1}{2} = 0.50 \times 100 = 50\%$$

2. What percentage of the family members demonstrate the recessive form of the trait? Why doesn't every family member have the dominant form of the trait?

3. Choose one of the family members who demonstrates the recessive form of the chosen trait. What is this person's genotype? What are the possible genotypes for the parents of this individual? Does this person have any brothers or sisters? Do they show the dominant or recessive trait?

Draw Conclusions

4. Draw a Punnett square like the one at right. Use this to determine the genotypes of the parents of the person you chose in step 3. Write this person's genotype in the bottom right-hand corner of your Punnett square. **Hint:** There may be more than one possible genotype for the parents. Don't forget to consider the genotypes of the person's brothers and sisters.

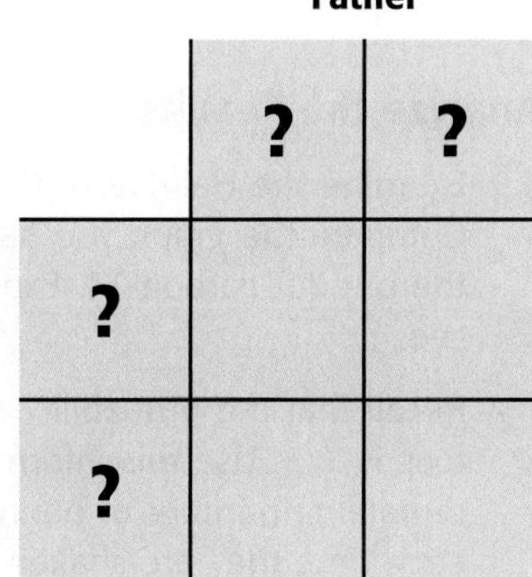

Skills Practice Lab

The Half-life of Pennies

Carbon-14 is a special unstable element used in the absolute dating of material that was once alive, such as fossil bones. Every 5,730 years, half of the carbon-14 in a fossil specimen decays or breaks down into a more stable element. In the following experiment you will see how pennies can show the same kind of "decay."

MATERIALS

- container with a cover, large
- pennies (100)

Procedure

1. Place 100 pennies in a large, covered container. Shake the container several times, and remove the cover. Carefully empty the container on a flat surface making sure the pennies don't roll away.
2. Remove all the coins that have the "head" side of the coin turned upward. Record the number of pennies removed and the number of pennies remaining in a data table similar to the one at right.

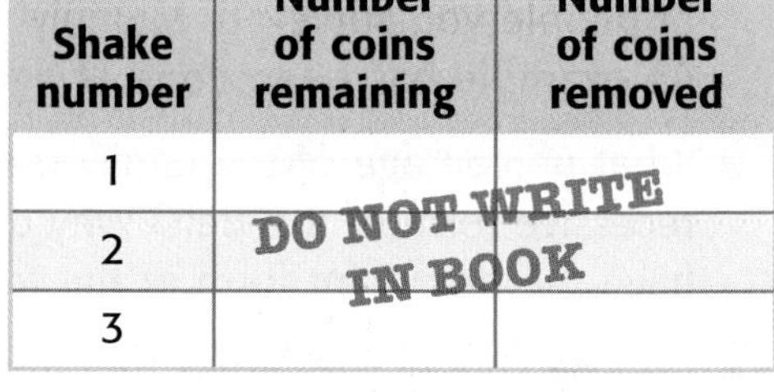

Shake number	Number of coins remaining	Number of coins removed
1		
2	DO NOT WRITE IN BOOK	
3		

3. Repeat the process until no pennies are left in the container. Remember to remove only the coins showing "heads."
4. Draw a graph similar to the one at right. Label the *x*-axis "Number of shakes," and label the *y*-axis "Pennies remaining." Using data from your data table, plot the number of coins remaining at each shake on your graph.

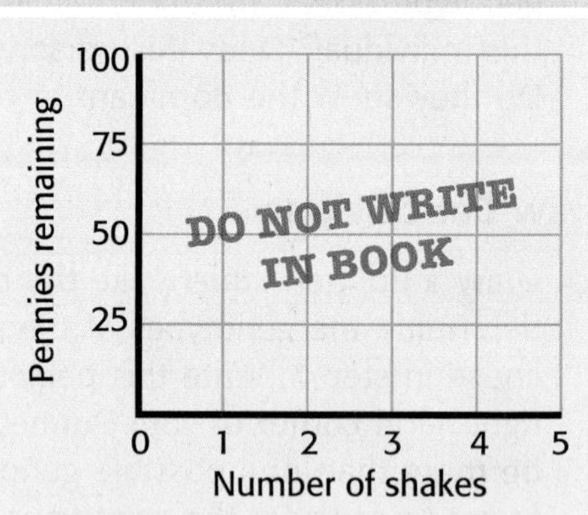

Analyze the Results

1. Examine the Half-life of Carbon-14 graph at right. Compare the graph you have made for pennies with the one for carbon-14. Explain any similarities that you see.
2. Recall that the probability of landing "heads" in a coin toss is 1/2. Use this information to explain why the remaining number of pennies is reduced by about half each time they are shaken and tossed.

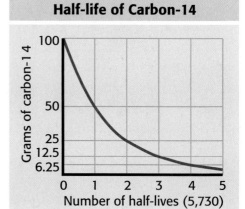

Half-life of Carbon-14

Grams of carbon-14: 100, 50, 25, 12.5, 6.25

0 1 2 3 4 5

Number of half-lives (5,730)

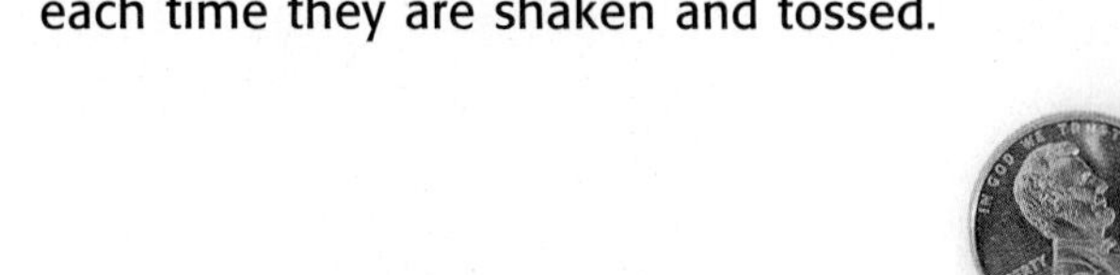

Inquiry Lab

Orient Yourself!

You have been invited to attend an orienteering event with your neighbors. In orienteering events, participants use maps and compasses to find their way along a course. There are several control points that each participant must reach. The object is to reach each control point and then the finish line. Orienteering events are often timed competitions. In order to find the fastest route through the course, the participants must read the map and use their compass correctly. Being the fastest runner does not necessarily guarantee finishing first. You also must choose the most direct route to follow.

Your neighbors participate in several orienteering events each year. They always come home raving about how much fun they had. You would like to join them, but you will need to learn how to use your compass first.

MATERIALS

- compass, magnetic
- course map
- pencils (or markers), colored (2)
- ruler

Procedure

1. Together as a class, go outside to the orienteering course your teacher has made.
2. Hold your compass flat in your hand. Turn the compass until the N is pointing straight in front of you. (The needle in your compass will always point north.) Turn your body until the needle lines up with the N on your compass. You are now facing north.
3. Regardless of which direction you want to face, you should always align the end of the needle with the N on your compass. If you are facing south, the needle will be pointing directly toward your body. When the N is aligned with the needle, the S will be directly in front of you, and you will be facing south.
4. Use your compass to face east. Align the needle with the N. Where is the E? Turn to face that direction. You are facing east when the needle and the N are aligned and the E is directly in front of you.
5. In an orienteering competition, you will need to know how to determine which direction you are traveling. Now, face any direction you choose.

6. Do not move, but rotate the compass to align the needle on your compass with the N. What direction are you facing? You are probably not facing directly north, south, east, or west. If you are facing between north and west, you are facing northwest. If you are facing between north and east, you are facing northeast.
7. Find a partner or partners to follow the course your teacher has made. Get a copy of the course map from your teacher. It will show several control points. You must stop at each one. You will need to follow this map to find your way through the course. Find and stand at the starting point.
8. Face the next control point on your map. Rotate your compass to align the needle on your compass with the N. What direction are you facing?
9. Use the ruler to draw a line on your map between the two control points. On your map, write the direction between the starting point and the next control point.
10. Walk toward the control point. Keep your eyes on the horizon, not on your compass. You might need to go around an obstacle, such as a fence or a building. Use the map to find the easiest way around.
11. Next to the control point symbol on your map, record the color or code word you find at the control point.
12. Repeat steps 8–11 for each control point. Follow the points in order as they are labeled. For example, determine the direction from control point 1 to control point 2. Be sure to include the direction between the final control point and the starting point.

Analyze the Results

1. The object of an orienteering competition is to arrive at the finish line first. The maps provided at these events do not instruct the participants to follow a specific path. In one form of orienteering, called *score orienteering,* competitors may find the control points in any order. Look at your map. If this course were used for a score-orienteering competition, would you change your route? Explain.

Draw Conclusions

2. If there is time, follow the map again. This time, use your own path to find the control points. Draw this path and the directions on your map in a different color. Do you believe this route was faster? Why?

Applying Your Data

Do some research to find out about orienteering events in your area. The Internet and local newspapers may be good sources for the information. Are there any events that you would like to attend?

Topographic Tuber

Imagine that you live on top of a tall mountain and often look down on the lake below. Every summer, an island appears. You call it Sometimes Island because it goes away again during heavy fall rains. This summer, you begin to wonder if you could make a topographic map of Sometimes Island. You don't have fancy equipment to make the map, but you have an idea. What if you place a meterstick with the 0 m mark at the water level in the summer? Then, as the expected fall rains come, you could draw the island from above as the water rises. Would this idea really work?

MATERIALS

- container, clear plastic storage, with transparent lid
- marker, transparency
- paper, tracing
- potato, cut in half
- ruler, metric
- water

Ask a Question

1. How do I make a topographic map?

Form a Hypothesis

2. Write a hypothesis that is a possible answer to the question above. Describe the method you would use.

Test the Hypothesis

3. Place a mark at the storage container's base. Label this mark "0 cm" with a transparency marker.
4. Measure and mark 1 cm increments up the side of the container until you reach the top of the container. Label these marks "1 cm," "2 cm," "3 cm," and so on.

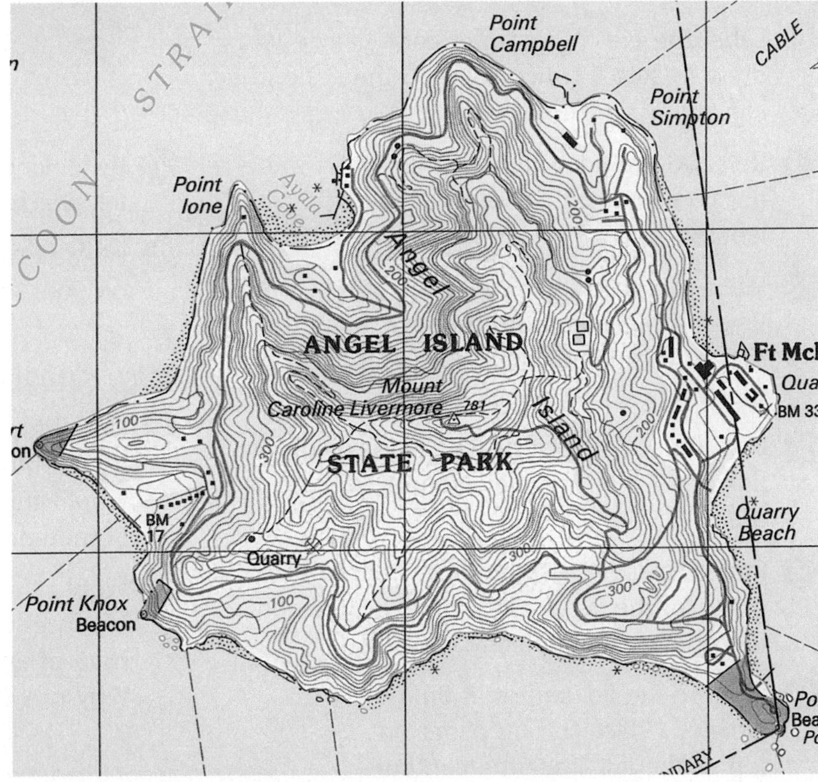

5. The scale for your map will be 1 cm = 10 m. Draw a line 2 cm long in the bottom right-hand corner of the lid. Place hash marks at 0 cm, 1 cm, and 2 cm. Label these marks "0 m," "10 m," and "20 m."
6. Place the potato, flat side down, in the center of the container.
7. Place the lid on the container, and seal it.

8. Viewing the potato from above, use the transparency marker to trace the outline of the potato where it rests on the bottom of the container. The floor of the container corresponds to the summer water level in the lake.
9. Label this contour "0 m." (For this activity, assume that the water level in the lake during the summer is the same as sea level.)
10. Pour water into the container until it reaches the line labeled "1 cm."
11. Again, place the lid on the container, and seal it. Part of the potato will be sticking out above the water. Viewing the potato from above, trace the part of the potato that touches the top of the water.
12. Label the elevation of the contour line you drew in step 11. According to the scale, the elevation is 10 m.
13. Remove the lid. Carefully pour water into the container until it reaches the line labeled "2 cm."
14. Place the lid on the container, and seal it. Viewing the potato from above, trace the part of the potato that touches the top of the water at this level.
15. Use the scale to calculate the elevation of this line. Label the elevation on your drawing.
16. Repeat steps 13–15, adding 1 cm to the depth of the water each time. Stop when the potato is completely covered.
17. Remove the lid, and set it on a tabletop. Place tracing paper on top of the lid. Trace the contours from the lid onto the paper. Label the elevation of each contour line. Congratulations! You have just made a topographic map!

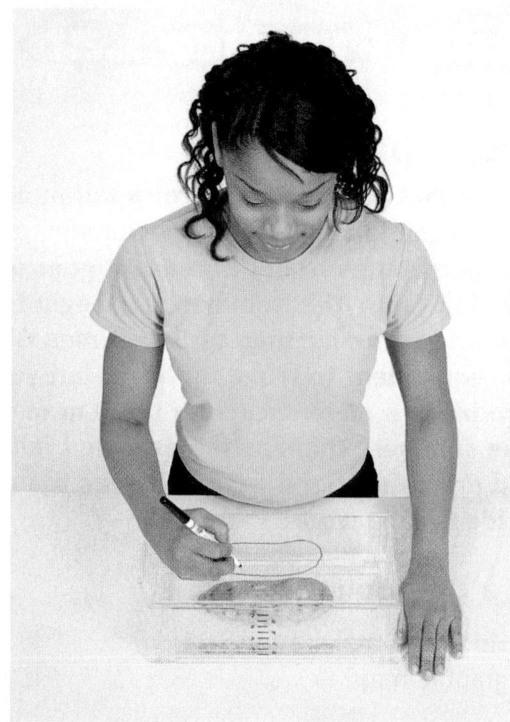

Analyze the Results

1. What is the contour interval of this topographic map?
2. By looking at the contour lines, how can you tell which parts of the potato are steeper?
3. What is the elevation of the highest point on your map?

Draw Conclusions

4. Do all topographic maps have a 0 m elevation contour line as a starting point? How would this affect a topographic map of Sometimes Island? Explain your answer.
5. Would this method of measuring elevation be an effective way to make a topographic map of an actual area on Earth's surface? Why or why not?

Applying Your Data

Place all of the potatoes on a table or desk at the front of the room. Your teacher will mix up the potatoes as you trade topographic maps with another group. By reading the topographic map you just received, can you pick out the matching potato?

LabBook

Skills Practice Lab

Mysterious Minerals

Imagine sitting on a rocky hilltop, gazing at the ground below you. You can see dozens of different types of rocks. How can scientists possibly identify the countless variations? It's a mystery!

In this activity, you'll use your powers of observation and a few simple tests to determine the identities of rocks and minerals. Take a look at the Mineral Identification Key on the next page. That key will help you use clues to discover the identity of several minerals.

MATERIALS

- gloves, protective
- iron filings
- minerals, samples
- slides, microscope, glass
- streak plate

SAFETY

Procedure

1. On a separate sheet of paper, create a data chart like the one below.
2. Choose one mineral sample, and locate its column in your data chart.
3. Follow the Mineral Identification Key to find the identity of your sample. When you are finished, record the mineral's name and primary characteristics in the appropriate column in your data chart. **Caution:** Put on your safety goggles and gloves when scratching the glass slide.
4. Select another mineral sample, and repeat steps 2 and 3 until your data table is complete.

Analyze the Results

1. Were some minerals easier to identify than others? Explain.
2. A streak test is a better indicator of a mineral's true color than visual observation is. Why isn't a streak test used to help identify every mineral?
3. On a separate sheet of paper, summarize what you learned about the various characteristics of each mineral sample you identified.

Mineral Summary Chart

Characteristics	1	2	3	4	5	6
Mineral name						
Luster						
Color						
Streak						
Hardness						
Cleavage						
Special properties						

DO NOT WRITE IN BOOK

Mineral Identification Key
1. **a.** If your mineral has a metallic luster, **GO TO STEP 2.** **b.** If your mineral has a nonmetallic luster, **GO TO STEP 3.**
2. **a.** If your mineral is black, **GO TO STEP 4.** **b.** If your mineral is yellow, it is **PYRITE.** **c.** If your mineral is silver, it is **GALENA.**
3. **a.** If your mineral is light in color, **GO TO STEP 5.** **b.** If your mineral is dark in color, **GO TO STEP 6.**
4. **a.** If your mineral leaves a red-brown line on the streak plate, it is **HEMATITE.** **b.** If your mineral leaves a black line on the streak plate, it is **MAGNETITE.** Test your sample for its magnetic properties by holding it near some iron filings.
5. **a.** If your mineral scratches the glass microscope slide, **GO TO STEP 7.** **b.** If your mineral does not scratch the glass microscope slide, **GO TO STEP 8.**
6. **a.** If your mineral scratches the glass slide, **GO TO STEP 9.** **b.** If your mineral does not scratch the glass slide, **GO TO STEP 10.**
7. **a.** If your mineral shows signs of cleavage, it is **ORTHOCLASE FELDSPAR.** **b.** If your mineral does not show signs of cleavage, it is **QUARTZ.**
8. **a.** If your mineral shows signs of cleavage, it is **MUSCOVITE.** Examine this sample for twin sheets. **b.** If your mineral does not show signs of cleavage, it is **GYPSUM.**
9. **a.** If your mineral shows signs of cleavage, it is **HORNBLENDE.** **b.** If your mineral does not show signs of cleavage, it is **GARNET.**
10. **a.** If your mineral shows signs of cleavage, it is **BIOTITE.** Examine your sample for twin sheets. **b.** If your mineral does not show signs of cleavage, it is **GRAPHITE.**

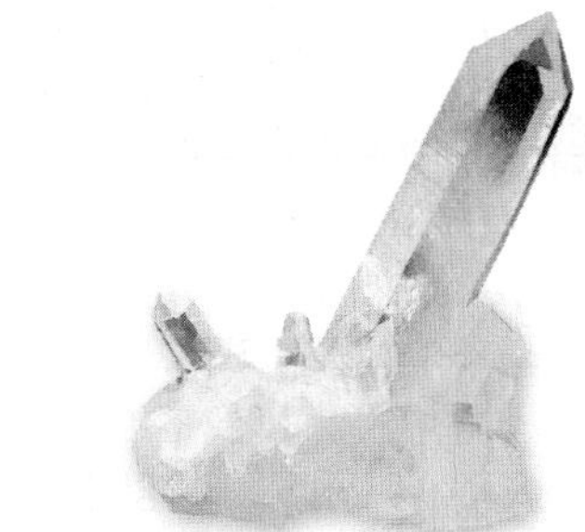

Applying Your Data

Using your textbook and other reference books, research other methods of identifying different types of minerals. Based on your findings, create a new identification key. Give the key and a few sample minerals to a friend, and see if your friend can unravel the mystery!

Using Scientific Methods

Skills Practice Lab

Crystal Growth

Magma forms deep below the Earth's surface at depths of 25 km to 160 km and at extremely high temperatures. Some magma reaches the surface and cools quickly. Other magma gets trapped in cracks or magma chambers beneath the surface and cools very slowly. When magma cools slowly, large, well-developed crystals form. But when magma erupts onto the surface, it cools more quickly. There is not enough time for large crystals to grow. The size of the crystals found in igneous rocks gives geologists clues about where and how the rocks formed.

In this experiment, you will demonstrate how the rate of cooling affects the size of crystals in igneous rocks by cooling crystals of magnesium sulfate at two different rates.

MATERIALS

- aluminum foil
- basalt
- beaker, 400 mL
- gloves, heat-resistant
- granite
- hot plate
- laboratory scoop, pointed
- magnesium sulfate ($MgSO_4$) (Epsom salts)
- magnifying lens
- marker, dark
- pumice
- tape, masking
- test tube, medium-sized
- thermometer, Celsius
- tongs, test-tube
- watch (or clock)
- water, distilled
- water, tap, 200 mL

SAFETY

Ask a Question

1. How does temperature affect the formation of crystals?

Form a Hypothesis

2. Suppose you have two solutions that are identical in every way except for temperature. How will the temperature of a solution affect the size of the crystals and the rate at which they form?

Test the Hypothesis

3. Put on your gloves, apron, and goggles.
4. Fill the beaker halfway with tap water. Place the beaker on the hot plate, and let it begin to warm. The temperature of the water should be between 40°C and 50°C. **Caution:** Make sure the hot plate is away from the edge of the lab table.
5. Examine two or three crystals of the magnesium sulfate with your magnifying lens. On a separate sheet of paper, describe the color, shape, luster, and other interesting features of the crystals.
6. On a separate sheet of paper, draw a sketch of the magnesium sulfate crystals.

7. Use the pointed laboratory scoop to fill the test tube about halfway with the magnesium sulfate. Add an equal amount of distilled water.
8. Hold the test tube in one hand, and use one finger from your other hand to tap the test tube gently. Observe the solution mixing as you continue to tap the test tube.
9. Place the test tube in the beaker of hot water, and heat it for approximately 3 min. **Caution:** Be sure to direct the opening of the test tube away from you and other students.
10. While the test tube is heating, shape your aluminum foil into two small boatlike containers by doubling the foil and turning up each edge.
11. If all the magnesium sulfate is not dissolved after 3 min, tap the test tube again, and heat it for 3 min longer. **Caution:** Use the test-tube tongs to handle the hot test tube.
12. With a marker and a piece of masking tape, label one of your aluminum boats "Sample 1," and place it on the hot plate. Turn the hot plate off.
13. Label the other aluminum boat "Sample 2," and place it on the lab table.
14. Using the test-tube tongs, remove the test tube from the beaker of water, and evenly distribute the contents to each of your foil boats. Carefully pour the hot water in the beaker down the drain. Do not move or disturb either of your foil boats.
15. Copy the table below onto a separate sheet of paper. Using the magnifying lens, carefully observe the foil boats. Record the time it takes for the first crystals to appear.

Crystal-Formation Table

Crystal formation	Time	Size and appearance of crystals	Sketch of crystals
Sample 1			
Sample 2			

16. If crystals have not formed in the boats before class is over, carefully place the boats in a safe place. You may then record the time in days instead of in minutes.
17. When crystals have formed in both boats, use your magnifying lens to examine the crystals carefully.

Analyze the Results

1. Was your prediction correct? Explain.
2. Compare the size and shape of the crystals in Samples 1 and 2 with the size and shape of the crystals you examined in step 5. How long do you think the formation of the original crystals must have taken?

Draw Conclusions

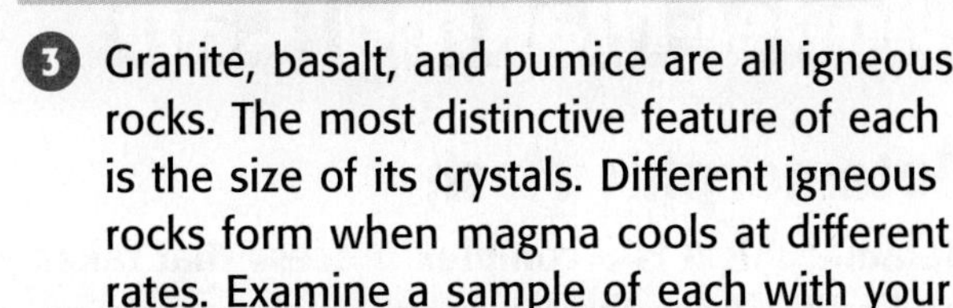

3. Granite, basalt, and pumice are all igneous rocks. The most distinctive feature of each is the size of its crystals. Different igneous rocks form when magma cools at different rates. Examine a sample of each with your magnifying lens.
4. Copy the table below onto a separate sheet of paper, and sketch each rock sample.
5. Use what you have learned in this activity to explain how each rock sample formed and how long it took for the crystals to form. Record your answers in your table.

Igneous Rock Observations			
	Granite	Basalt	Pumice
Sketch			
How did the rock sample form?			
Rate of cooling			

Communicating Your Data

Describe the size and shape of the crystals you would expect to find when a volcano erupts and sends material into the air and when magma oozes down the volcano's slope.

Model-Making Lab

Metamorphic Mash

Metamorphism is a complex process that takes place deep within the Earth, where the temperature and pressure would turn a human into a crispy pancake. The effects of this extreme temperature and pressure are obvious in some metamorphic rocks. One of these effects is the reorganization of mineral grains within the rock. In this activity, you will investigate the process of metamorphism without being charred, flattened, or buried.

MATERIALS

- cardboard (or plywood), very stiff, small pieces
- clay, modeling
- knife, plastic
- sequins (or other small flat objects)

SAFETY

Procedure

1. Flatten the clay into a layer about 1 cm thick. Sprinkle the surface with sequins.
2. Roll the corners of the clay toward the middle to form a neat ball.
3. Carefully use the plastic knife to cut the ball in half. On a separate sheet of paper, describe the position and location of the sequins inside the ball.
4. Put the ball back together, and use the sheets of cardboard or plywood to flatten the ball until it is about 2 cm thick.
5. Using the plastic knife, slice open the slab of clay in several places. Describe the position and location of the sequins in the slab.

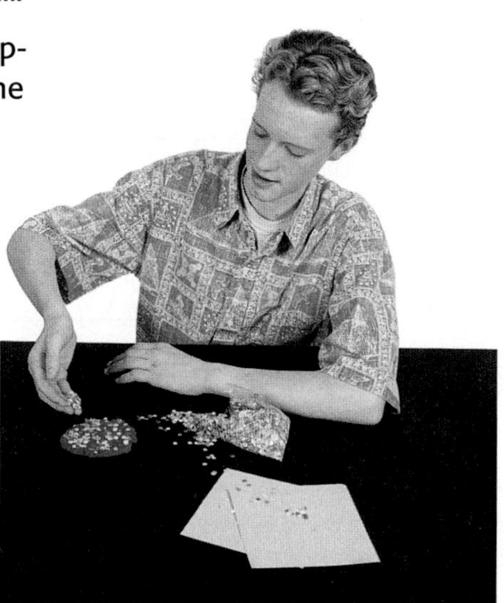

Analyze the Results

1. What physical process does flattening the ball represent?
2. Describe any changes in the position and location of the sequins that occurred as the clay ball was flattened into a slab.

Draw Conclusions

3. How are the sequins oriented in relation to the force you put on the ball to flatten it?
4. Do you think the orientation of the mineral grains in a foliated metamorphic rock tells you anything about the rock? Defend your answer.

Applying Your Data

Suppose you find a foliated metamorphic rock that has grains running in two distinct directions. Use what you have learned in this activity to offer a possible explanation for this observation.

Using Scientific Methods

Inquiry Lab

Life in the Desert

Organisms that live in the desert have some unusual methods for conserving water. Conserving water is a special challenge for animals that live in the desert. In this activity you will invent a water-conserving "adaptation" for a desert animal, represented by a piece of sponge. You will protect your wet desert sponge so it will dry out as little as possible over a 24 h period.

MATERIALS

- balance
- sponge, dry, 8 cm × 8 cm × 2 cm (2 pieces)
- water
- other materials as needed

Ask a Question

1. How can an animal conserve water in the desert?

Form a Hypothesis

2. Plan a method for keeping your "desert animal" from drying out. Your "animal" must be in the open for at least 4 h during the 24 h period. Real desert animals expose themselves to the dry desert heat to search for food. Write your plan and predictions about the outcome of your experiment.
3. Design and draw data tables, if necessary. Have your teacher approve your plan before you begin.

Test the Hypothesis

4. Soak two pieces of sponge in water until they begin to drip. Place each piece on a balance, and record its mass.
5. Immediately protect one sponge according to your plan. Place both pieces in an area where they will not be disturbed. You should take your protected "animal" out for feeding for a total of at least 4 h.
6. At the end of 24 h, place each piece of sponge on the balance again, and record its mass.

Analyze the Results

1. Describe the adaptation you used to help your "animal" survive. Was it effective? Explain.
2. What was the purpose of leaving one of the sponges unprotected? How did the water loss in each of your sponges compare?

Communicating Your Data

Conduct a class discussion about other adaptations and results. How can you relate these invented adaptations to adaptations for desert survival among real organisms?

Using Scientific Methods

Inquiry Lab

Discovering Mini-Ecosystems

In your study of ecosystems, you learned that a biome is a very large ecosystem that includes a set of smaller, related ecosystems. For example, a coniferous forest biome may include a river ecosystem, a wetland ecosystem, and a lake ecosystem. Each of those ecosystems may include several other smaller, related ecosystems. Even cities have mini-ecosystems! You may find a mini-ecosystem on a patch of sidewalk, in a puddle of rainwater, under a leaky faucet, in a shady area, or under a rock. In this activity, you will design a method for comparing two different mini-ecosystems found near your school.

MATERIALS

- items to be determined by the students and approved by the teacher

SAFETY

Ask a Question

1. Examine the grounds around your school, and select two different areas you wish to investigate. Decide what you want to learn about your mini-ecosystems. For example, you may want to know what kind of living things each area contains. Be sure to get your teacher's approval before you begin.

Form a Hypothesis

2. For each mini-ecosystem, make data tables for recording your observations.

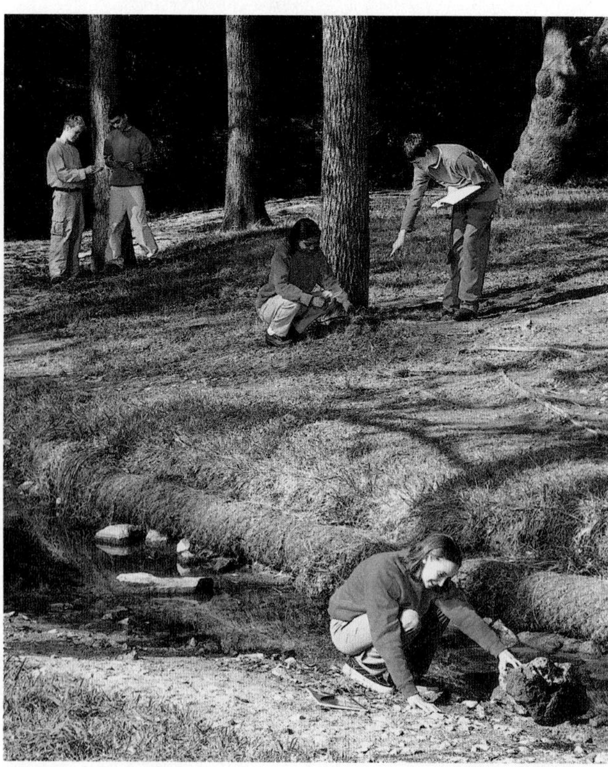

Test the Hypothesis

3. Observe your mini-ecosystem according to your plan at several different time points throughout the day. Record your observations.
4. Wait 24 h and observe your mini-ecosystem again at the same times that you observed it the day before. Record your observations.
5. Wait 1 week, and observe your mini-ecosystem again at the same times. Record your observations.

Analyze the Results

1. What factors determine the differences between your mini-ecosystems? Identify the factors that set each mini-ecosystem apart from its surrounding area.
2. How do the populations of your mini-ecosystems compare?
3. Identify some of the adaptations that the organisms living in your two mini-ecosystems have. Describe how the adaptations help the organisms survive in their environment.

Draw Conclusions

4. Write a report describing and comparing your mini-ecosystems with those of your classmates.

LabBook

Using Scientific Methods

Model-Making Lab

Oh, the Pressure!

When scientists want to understand natural processes, such as mountain formation, they often make models to help them. Models are useful in studying how rocks react to the forces of plate tectonics. A model can demonstrate in a short amount of time geological processes that take millions of years. Do the following activity to find out how folding and faulting occur in the Earth's crust.

MATERIALS

- can, soup (or rolling pin)
- clay, modeling, 4 colors
- knife, plastic
- newspaper
- pencils, colored
- poster board, 5 cm × 5 cm squares (2)
- poster board, 5 cm × 15 cm strip

SAFETY

Ask a Question

1. How do synclines, anticlines, and faults form?

Form a Hypothesis

2. On a separate piece of paper, write a hypothesis that is a possible answer to the question above. Explain your reasoning.

Test the Hypothesis

3. Use modeling clay of one color to form a long cylinder, and place the cylinder in the center of the glossy side of the poster-board strip.
4. Mold the clay to the strip. Try to make the clay layer the same thickness all along the strip; you can use the soup can or rolling pin to even it out. Pinch the sides of the clay so that the clay is the same width and length as the strip. Your strip should be at least 15 cm long and 5 cm wide.

5. Flip the strip over on the newspaper your teacher has placed across your desk. Carefully peel the strip from the modeling clay.
6. Repeat steps 3–5 with the other colors of modeling clay. Each person should have a turn molding the clay. Each time you flip the strip over, stack the new clay layer on top of the previous one. When you are finished, you should have a block of clay made of four layers.
7. Lift the block of clay, and hold it parallel to and just above the tabletop. Push gently on the block from opposite sides, as shown below.

8. Use the colored pencils to draw the results of step 6. Use the terms *syncline* and *anticline* to label your diagram. Draw arrows to show the direction that each edge of the clay was pushed.
9. Repeat steps 3–6 to form a second block of clay.
10. Cut the second block of clay in two at a 45° angle as seen from the side of the block.

LabBook

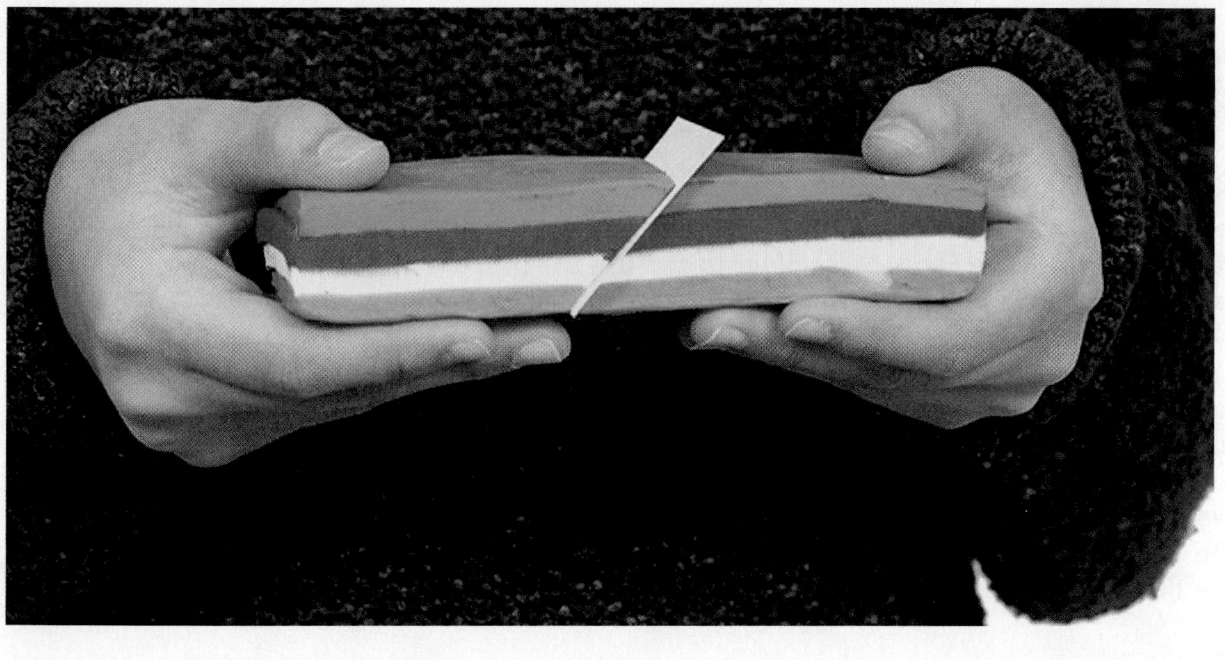

11 Press one poster-board square on the angled end of each of the block's two pieces. The poster board represents a fault. The two angled ends represent a hanging wall and a footwall. The model should resemble the one in the photograph above.

12 Keeping the angled edges together, lift the blocks, and hold them parallel to and just above the tabletop. Push gently on the two blocks until they move. Record your observations.

13 Now, hold the two pieces of the clay block in their original position, and slowly pull them apart, allowing the hanging wall to move downward. Record your observations.

Analyze the Results

1 What happened to the first block of clay in step 7? What kind of force did you apply to the block of clay?

2 What happened to the pieces of the second block of clay in step 12? What kind of force did you apply to them?

3 What happened to the pieces of the second block of clay in step 13? Describe the forces that acted on the block and the way the pieces of the block reacted.

Draw Conclusions

4 Summarize how the forces you applied to the blocks of clay relate to the way tectonic forces affect rock layers. Be sure to use the terms *fold, fault, anticline, syncline, hanging wall, footwall, tension,* and *compression* in your summary.

Skills Practice Lab

Earthquake Waves

The energy from an earthquake travels as seismic waves in all directions through the Earth. Seismologists can use the properties of certain types of seismic waves to find the epicenter of an earthquake.

P waves travel more quickly than S waves and are always detected first. The average speed of P waves in the Earth's crust is 6.1 km/s. The average speed of S waves in the Earth's crust is 4.1 km/s. The difference in arrival time between P waves and S waves is called *lag time.*

In this activity, you will use the S-P-time method to determine the location of an earthquake's epicenter.

MATERIALS

- calculator (optional)
- compass
- ruler, metric

SAFETY

Procedure

1. The illustration below shows seismographic records made in three cities following an earthquake. These traces begin at the left and show the arrival of P waves at time zero. The second set of waves on each record represents the arrival of S waves.

Seismographic Records

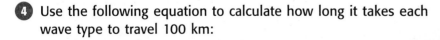

2. Copy the data table on the next page.
3. Use the time scale provided with the seismographic records to find the lag time between the P waves and the S waves for each city. Remember that the lag time is the time between the moment when the first P wave arrives and the moment when the first S wave arrives. Record this data in your table.
4. Use the following equation to calculate how long it takes each wave type to travel 100 km:

$$100 \text{ km} \div \textit{average speed of the wave} = \textit{time}$$

5. To find lag time for earthquake waves at 100 km, subtract the time it takes P waves to travel 100 km from the time it takes S waves to travel 100 km. Record the lag time.
6. Use the following formula to find the distance from each city to the epicenter:

$$distance = \frac{measured\ lag\ time\ (s) \times 100\ km}{lag\ time\ for\ 100\ km\ (s)}$$

In your data table, record the distance from each city to the epicenter.

Epicenter Data Table

City	Lag time (seconds)	Distance to the epicenter (km)
Austin, TX		
Bismarck, ND	DO NOT WRITE IN BOOK	
Portland, OR		

7. Trace the map below onto a separate sheet of paper.
8. Use the scale to adjust your compass so that the radius of a circle with Austin at the center is equal to the distance between Austin and the epicenter of the earthquake.

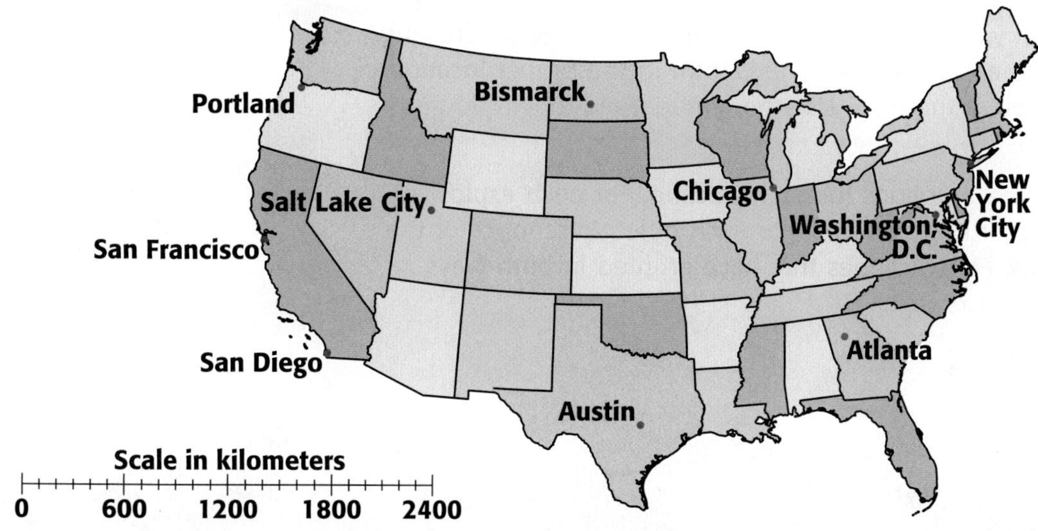

9. Put the point of your compass at Austin on your copy of the map, and draw a circle.
10. Repeat steps 8 and 9 for Bismarck and Portland. The epicenter of the earthquake is located near the point where the three circles meet.

Anayze the Results

1. Which city is closest to the epicenter?

Draw Conclusions

2. Why do seismologists need measurements from three different locations to find the epicenter of an earthquake?

Skills Practice Lab

Some Go "Pop," Some Do Not

Volcanic eruptions range from mild to violent. When volcanoes erupt, the materials left behind provide information to scientists studying the Earth's crust. Mild, or nonexplosive, eruptions produce thin, runny lava that is low in silica. During nonexplosive eruptions, lava simply flows down the side of the volcano. Explosive eruptions, on the other hand, do not produce much lava. Instead, the explosions hurl ash and debris into the air. The materials left behind are light in color and high in silica. These materials help geologists determine the composition of the crust underneath the volcanoes.

MATERIALS

- paper, graph (1 sheet)
- pencils (or markers), red, yellow, and orange
- ruler, metric

Procedure

1. Copy the map below onto graph paper. Take care to line the grid up properly.
2. Locate each volcano from the list on the next page by drawing a circle with a diameter of about 2 mm in the proper location on your copy of the map. Use the latitude and longitude grids to help you.
3. Review all the eruptions for each volcano. For each explosive eruption, color the circle red. For each quiet volcano, color the circle yellow. For volcanoes that have erupted in both ways, color the circle orange.

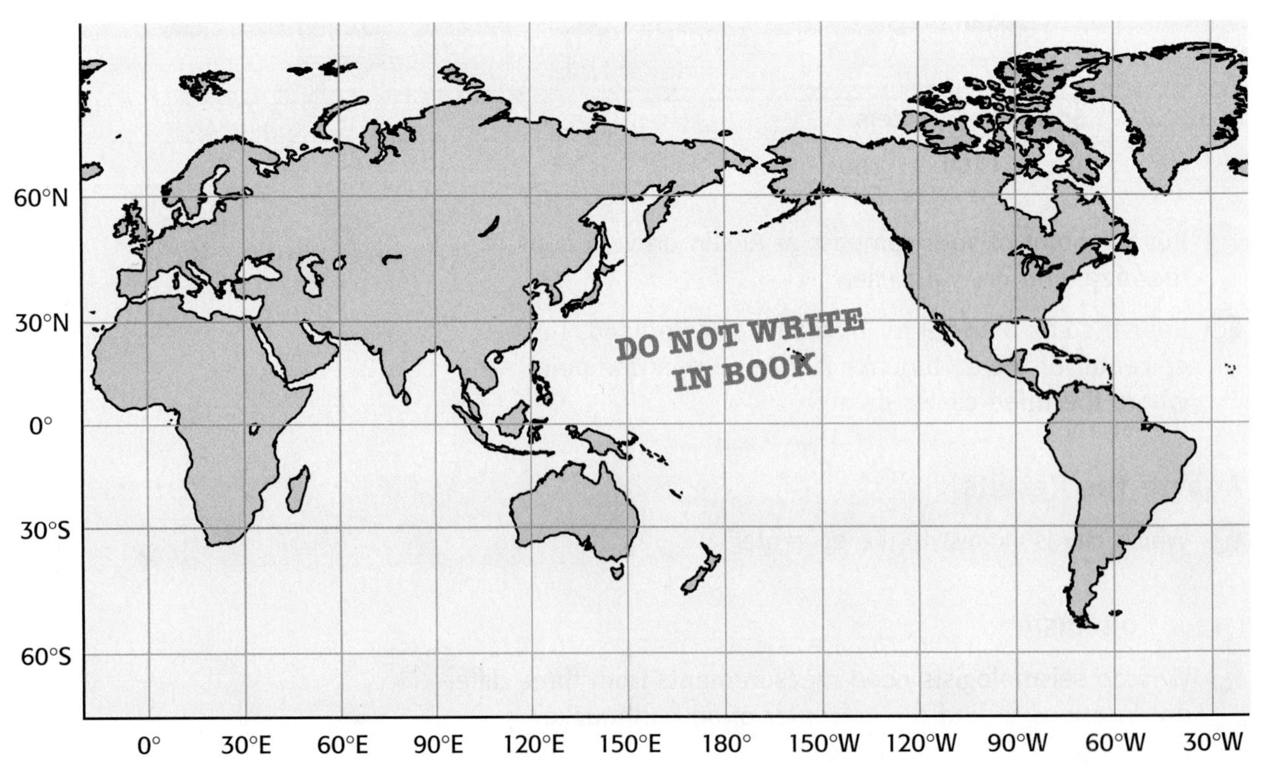

Volcanic Activity Chart		
Volcano name	**Location**	**Description**
Mount St. Helens	46°N 122°W	An explosive eruption blew the top off the mountain. Light-colored ash covered thousands of square kilometers. Another eruption sent a lava flow down the southeast side of the mountain.
Kilauea	19°N 155°W	One small eruption sent a lava flow along 12 km of highway.
Rabaul caldera	4°S 152°E	Explosive eruptions have caused tsunamis and have left 1–2 m of ash on nearby buildings.
Popocatépetl	19°N 98°W	During one explosion, Mexico City closed the airport for 14 hours because huge columns of ash made it too difficult for pilots to see. Eruptions from this volcano have also caused damaging avalanches.
Soufriere Hills	16°N 62°W	Small eruptions have sent lava flows down the hills. Other explosive eruptions have sent large columns of ash into the air.
Long Valley caldera	37°N 119°W	Explosive eruptions have sent ash into the air.
Okmok	53°N 168°W	Recently, there have been slow lava flows from this volcano. Twenty-five hundred years ago, ash and debris exploded from the top of this volcano.
Pavlof	55°N 161°W	Eruption clouds have been sent 200 m above the summit. Eruptions have sent ash columns 10 km into the air. Occasionally, small eruptions have caused lava flows.
Fernandina	42°N 12°E	Eruptions have ejected large blocks of rock from this volcano.
Mount Pinatubo	15°N 120°E	Ash and debris from an explosive eruption destroyed homes, crops, and roads within 52,000 km^2 around the volcano.

Analyze the Results

1. According to your map, where are volcanoes that always have nonexplosive eruptions located?
2. Where are volcanoes that always erupt explosively located?
3. Where are volcanoes that erupt in both ways located?
4. If volcanoes get their magma from the crust below them, what can you say about the silica content of Earth's crust under the oceans?
5. What is the composition of the crust under the continents? How do we know?

Draw Conclusions

6. What is the source of materials for volcanoes that erupt in both ways? How do you know?
7. Do the locations of volcanoes that erupt in both ways make sense, based on your answers to questions 4 and 5? Explain.

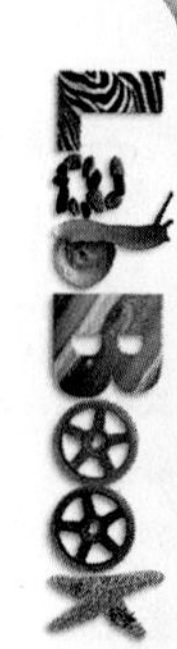

Applying Your Data

Volcanoes are present on other planets. If a planet had only nonexplosive volcanoes on its surface, what would we be able to infer about the planet? If a planet had volcanoes that ranged from nonexplosive to explosive, what might that tell us about the planet?

Skills Practice Lab

Volumania!

You have learned how to measure the volume of a solid object that has square or rectangular sides. But there are lots of objects in the world that have irregular shapes. In this lab activity, you'll learn some ways to find the volume of objects that have irregular shapes.

MATERIALS

Part A

- graduated cylinder
- water
- various small objects supplied by your teacher

Part B

- bottle, plastic (or similar container), 2L, bottom half
- funnel
- graduated cylinder
- pan, aluminum pie
- paper towels
- water

SAFETY

Part A: Finding the Volume of Small Objects

Procedure

1. Fill a graduated cylinder half full with water. Read and record the volume of the water. Be sure to look at the surface of the water at eye level and to read the volume at the bottom of the meniscus, as shown below.

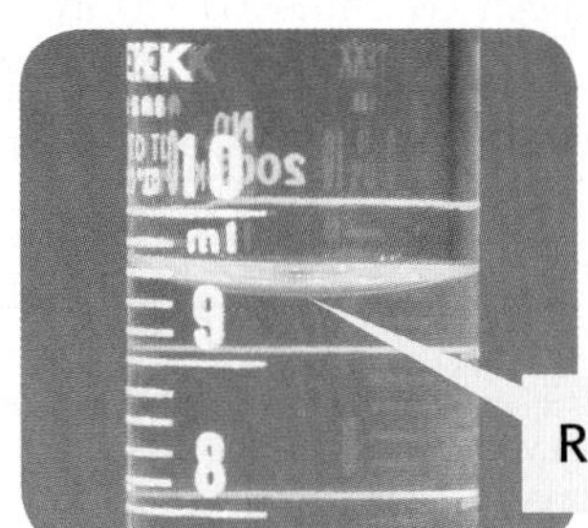

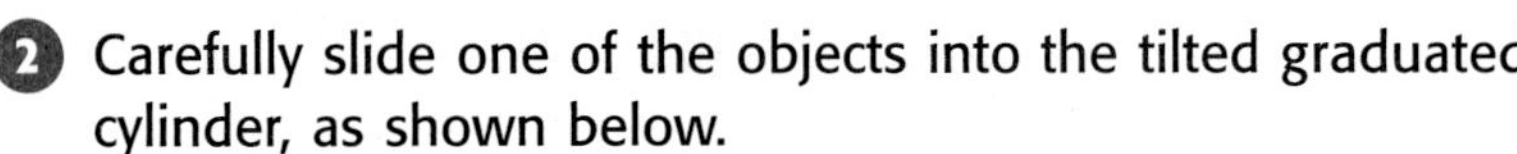

2. Carefully slide one of the objects into the tilted graduated cylinder, as shown below.
3. Read the new volume, and record it.
4. Subtract the old volume from the new volume. The resulting amount is equal to the volume of the solid object.
5. Use the same method to find the volume of the other objects. Record your results.

Analyze the Results

1. What changes do you have to make to the volumes you determine in order to express them correctly?
2. Do the heaviest objects always have the largest volumes? Why or why not?

Part B: Finding the Volume of Your Hand

Procedure

1. Completely fill the container with water. Put the container in the center of the pie pan. Be sure not to spill any of the water into the pie pan.
2. Make a fist, and put your hand into the container up to your wrist.
3. Remove your hand, and let the excess water drip into the container, not the pie pan. Dry your hand with a paper towel.
4. Use the funnel to pour the overflow water into the graduated cylinder. Measure the volume. This measurement is the volume of your hand. Record the volume. (Remember to use the correct unit of volume for a solid object.)
5. Repeat this procedure with your other hand.

Analyze the Results

1. Was the volume the same for both of your hands? If not, were you surprised? What might account for a person's hands having different volumes?
2. Would it have made a difference if you had placed your open hand into the container instead of your fist? Explain your reasoning.
3. Compare the volume of your right hand with the volume of your classmates' right hands. Create a class graph of right-hand volumes. What is the average right-hand volume for your class?

Applying Your Data

Design an experiment to determine the volume of a person's body. In your plans, be sure to include the materials needed for the experiment and the procedures that must be followed. Include a sketch that shows how your materials and methods would be used in this experiment.

Using an encyclopedia, the Internet, or other reference materials, find out how the volumes of very large samples of matter—such as an entire planet—are determined.

Skills Practice Lab

Determining Density

The density of an object is its mass divided by its volume. But how does the density of a small amount of a substance relate to the density of a larger amount of the same substance? In this lab, you will calculate the density of one marble and of a group of marbles. Then, you will confirm the relationship between the mass and volume of a substance.

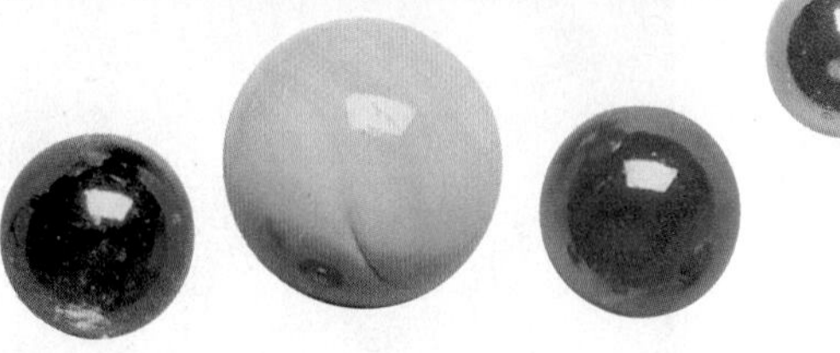

MATERIALS

- balance, metric
- graduated cylinder, 100 mL
- marbles, glass (8–10)
- paper, graph
- paper towels
- water

SAFETY

Procedure

1. Copy the table below. Include one row for each marble.

Mass of marble (g)	Total mass of marbles (g)	Total volume (mL)	Volume of marbles (mL) (total volume minus 50.0 mL)	Density of marbles (g/mL) (total mass divided by volume)
		DO NOT WRITE IN BOOK		

2. Fill the graduated cylinder with 50 mL of water. If you put in too much water, twist one of the paper towels, and use it to absorb excess water.
3. Measure the mass of a marble as accurately as you can (to at least .01 g). Record the mass in the table.
4. Carefully drop the marble in the tilted cylinder, and measure the total volume. Record the volume in the third column.
5. Measure and record the mass of another marble. Add the masses of the marbles together, and record this value in the second column of the table.
6. Carefully drop the second marble in the graduated cylinder. Complete the row of information in the table.
7. Repeat steps 5 and 6. Add one marble at a time. Stop when you run out of marbles, the water no longer completely covers the marbles, or the graduated cylinder is full.

Analyze the Results

1. Examine the data in your table. As the number of marbles increases, what happens to the total mass of the marbles? What happens to the volume of the marbles? What happens to the density of the marbles?
2. Graph the total mass of the marbles (y-axis) versus the volume of the marbles (x-axis). Is the graph a straight line?

Draw Conclusions

3. Does the density of a substance depend on the amount of substance present? Explain how your results support your answer.

Applying Your Data

Calculate the slope of the graph. How does the slope compare with the values in the column entitled "Density of marbles"? Explain.

Using Scientific Methods

Skills Practice Lab

Layering Liquids

You have learned that liquids form layers according to the densities of the liquids. In this lab, you'll discover whether it matters in which order you add the liquids.

MATERIALS

- beaker (or other small, clear container)
- funnel (3)
- graduated cylinder, 10 mL (3)
- liquid A
- liquid B
- liquid C

SAFETY

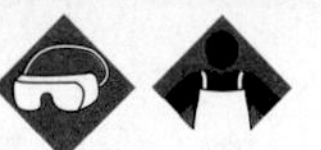

Ask a Question

1. Does the order in which you add liquids of different densities to a container affect the order of the layers formed by those liquids?

Form a Hypothesis

2. Write a possible answer to the question above.

Test the Hypothesis

3. Using the graduated cylinders, add 10 mL of each liquid to the clear container. Remember to read the volume at the bottom of the meniscus, as shown below. Record the order in which you added the liquids.
4. Observe the liquids in the container. Sketch what you see. Be sure to label the layers and the colors.
5. Add 10 mL more of liquid C. Observe what happens, and record your observations.
6. Add 20 mL more of liquid A. Observe what happens, and record your observations.

Analyze the Results

1. Which of the liquids has the greatest density? Which has the least density? How can you tell?
2. Did the layers change position when you added more of liquid C? Explain your answer.
3. Did the layers change position when you added more of liquid A? Explain your answer.
4. Find out in what order your classmates added the liquids to the container. Compare your results with those of a classmate who added the liquids in a different order. Were your results different? Explain why or why not.

Draw Conclusions

5. Based on your results, evaluate your hypothesis from step 2.

Using Scientific Methods

Skills Practice Lab

Full of Hot Air!

Why do hot-air balloons float gracefully above Earth, but balloons you blow up fall to the ground? The answer has to do with the density of the air inside the balloon. *Density* is mass per unit volume, and volume is affected by changes in temperature. In this experiment, you will investigate the relationship between the temperature of a gas and its volume. Then, you will be able to determine how the temperature of a gas affects its density.

MATERIALS

- balloon
- beaker, 250 mL
- gloves, heat-resistant
- hot plate
- ice water
- pan, aluminum (2)
- ruler, metric
- water

SAFETY

Ask a Question

1. How does an increase or decrease in temperature affect the volume of a balloon?

Form a Hypothesis

2. Write a hypothesis that answers the question above.

Test the Hypothesis

3. Fill an aluminum pan with water about 4 cm to 5 cm deep. Put the pan on the hot plate, and turn the hot plate on.
4. Fill the other pan 4 cm to 5 cm deep with ice water.
5. Blow up a balloon inside the 500 mL beaker, as shown. The balloon should fill the beaker but should not extend outside the beaker. Tie the balloon at its opening.

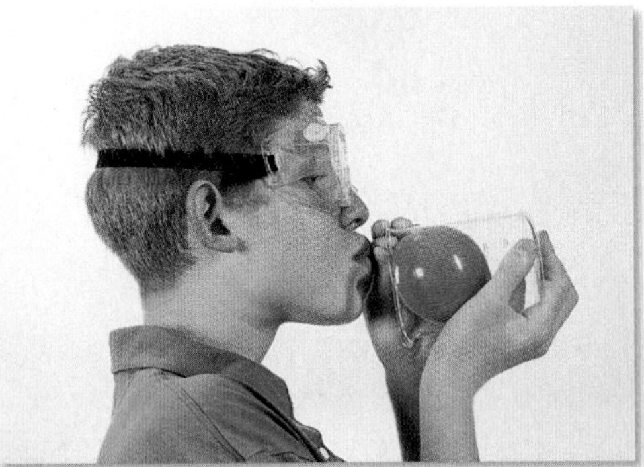

6. Place the beaker and balloon in the ice water. Observe what happens. Record your observations.
7. Remove the balloon and beaker from the ice water. Observe the balloon for several minutes. Record any changes.
8. Put on heat-resistant gloves. When the hot water begins to boil, put the beaker and balloon in the hot water. Observe the balloon for several minutes, and record your observations.
9. Turn off the hot plate. When the water has cooled, carefully pour it into a sink.

Analyze the Results

1. Summarize your observations of the balloon. Relate your observations to Charles's law.
2. Was your hypothesis from step 2 supported? If not, revise your hypothesis.

Draw Conclusions

3. Based on your observations, how is the density of a gas affected by an increase or decrease in temperature?

LabBook

Skills Practice Lab

Can Crusher

Condensation can occur when gas particles come near the surface of a liquid. The gas particles slow down because they are attracted to the liquid. This reduction in speed causes the gas particles to condense into a liquid. In this lab, you'll see that particles that have condensed into a liquid don't take up as much space and therefore don't exert as much pressure as they did in the gaseous state.

MATERIALS

- beaker, 1 L
- can, aluminum (2)
- gloves, heat-resistant
- hot plate
- tongs
- water

SAFETY

Procedure

1. Fill the beaker with room-temperature water.
2. Place just enough water in an aluminum can to slightly cover the bottom.
3. Put on heat-resistant gloves. Place the aluminum can on a hot plate turned to the highest temperature setting.
4. Heat the can until the water is boiling. Steam should be rising vigorously from the top of the can.
5. Using tongs, quickly pick up the can, and place the top 2 cm of the can upside down in the 1 L beaker filled with water.
6. Describe your observations.

Analyze the Results

1. The can was crushed because the atmospheric pressure outside the can became greater than the pressure inside the can. Explain what happened inside the can to cause the difference in pressure.

Draw Conclusions

2. Inside every popcorn kernel is a small amount of water. When you make popcorn, the water inside the kernels is heated until it becomes steam. Explain how the popping of the kernels is the opposite of what you saw in this lab. Be sure to address the effects of pressure in your explanation.

Applying Your Data

Try the experiment again, but use ice water instead of room-temperature water. Explain your results in terms of the effects of temperature.

Using Scientific Methods

Skills Practice Lab

A Sugar Cube Race!

If you drop a sugar cube into a glass of water, how long will it take to dissolve? What can you do to speed up the rate at which it dissolves? Should you change something about the water, the sugar cube, or the process? In other words, what variable should you change? Before reading further, make a list of variables that could be changed in this situation. Record your list.

MATERIALS

- beakers or other clear containers (2)
- clock or stopwatch
- graduated cylinder
- sugar cubes (2)
- water
- other materials approved by your teacher

SAFETY

Ask a Question

1. Write a question you can test about factors that affect the rate sugar dissolves.

Form a Hypothesis

2. Choose one variable to test. Record your choice, and predict how changing your variable will affect the rate of dissolving.

Test the Hypothesis

3. Pour 150 mL of water into one of the beakers. Add one sugar cube, and use the stopwatch to measure how long it takes for the sugar cube to dissolve. You must not disturb the sugar cube in any way! Record this time.

4. Be sure to get your teacher's approval before you begin. You may need additional equipment.

5. Prepare your materials to test the variable you have picked. When you are ready, start your procedure for speeding up the rate at which the sugar cube dissolves. Use the stopwatch to measure the time. Record this time.

Analyze the Results

1. Compare your results with the prediction you made in step 2. Was your prediction correct? Why or why not?

Draw Conclusions

2. Why was it necessary to observe the sugar cube dissolving on its own before you tested the variable?

3. Do you think changing more than one variable would speed up the rate of dissolving even more? Explain your reasoning.

4. Discuss your results with a group that tested a different variable. Which variable had a greater effect on the rate of dissolving?

Skills Practice Lab

Making Butter

A colloid is an interesting substance. It has properties of both solutions and suspensions. Colloidal particles are not heavy enough to settle out, so they remain evenly dispersed throughout the mixture. In this activity, you will make butter—a very familiar colloid—and observe the characteristics that classify butter as a colloid.

MATERIALS

- clock or stopwatch
- container with lid, small, clear
- heavy cream
- marble

SAFETY

Procedure

1. Place a marble inside the container, and fill the container with heavy cream. Put the lid tightly on the container.
2. Take turns shaking the container vigorously and constantly for 10 min. Record the time when you begin shaking. Every minute, stop shaking the container, and hold it up to the light. Record your observations.
3. Continue shaking the container, taking turns if necessary. When you see, hear, or feel any changes inside the container, note the time and change.
4. After 10 min of shaking, you should have a lump of "butter" surrounded by liquid inside the container. Describe both the butter and the liquid in detail.
5. Let the container sit for about 10 min. Observe the butter and liquid again, and record your observations.

Analyze the Results

1. When you noticed the change inside the container, what did you think was happening at that point?
2. Based on your observations, explain why butter is classified as a colloid.
3. What kind of mixture is the liquid that is left behind? Explain.

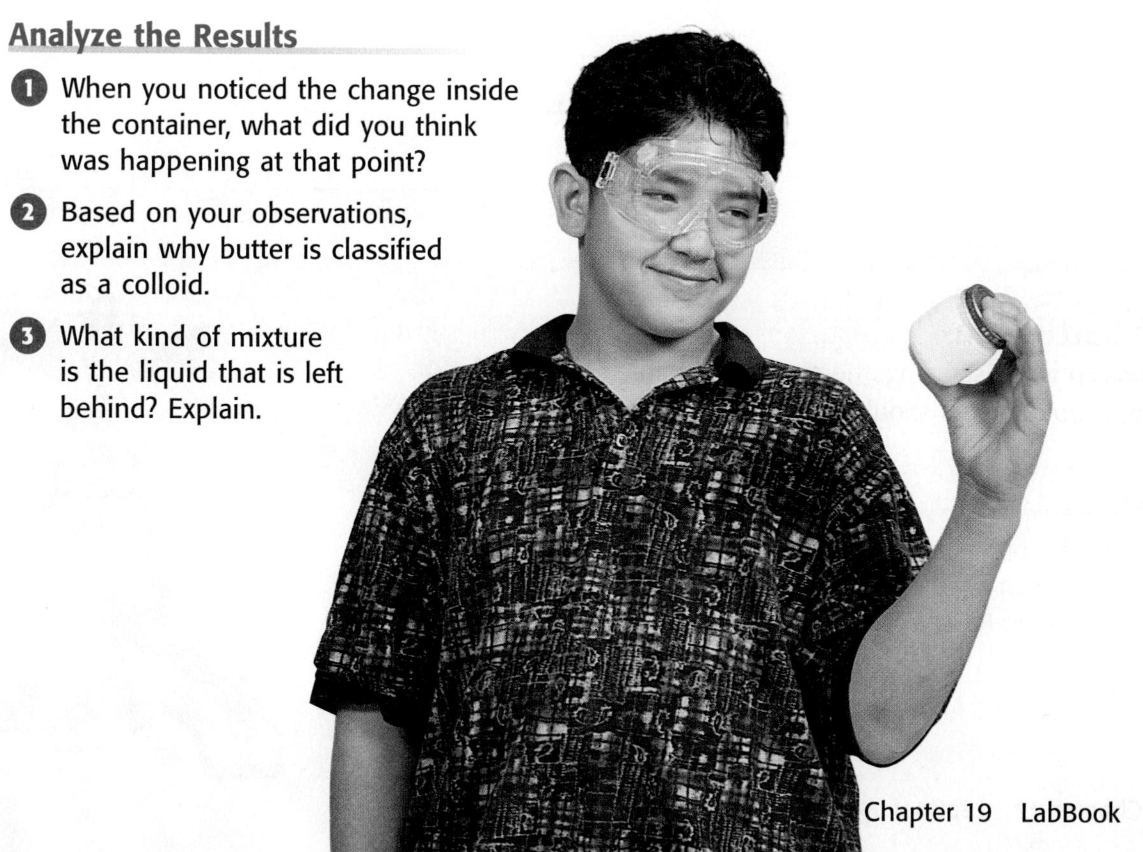

Model-Making Lab

Unpolluting Water

In many cities, the water supply comes from a river, lake, or reservoir. This water may include several mixtures, including suspensions (with suspended dirt, oil, or living organisms) and solutions (with dissolved chemicals). To make the water safe to drink, your city's water supplier must remove impurities. In this lab, you will model the procedures used in real water treatment plants.

MATERIALS

- beaker, 250 mL (4)
- charcoal, activated, washed
- cup, plastic-foam, 8 oz (2)
- graduated cylinder
- nail, small
- paper, filter (2 pieces)
- rubber band
- ruler, metric
- sand, fine, washed
- scissors
- spoon, plastic (2)
- water, "polluted"

SAFETY

Part A: Untreated Water

Procedure

1. Measure 100 mL of "polluted" water into a graduated cylinder. Be sure to shake the bottle of water before you pour so your sample will include all the impurities.
2. Pour the contents of the graduated cylinder into one of the beakers.
3. Copy the table below, and record your observations of the water in the "Before treatment" row.

Observations						
	Color	Clearness	Odor	Any layers?	Any solids?	Water volume
Before treatment						
After oil separation						
After sand filtration			DO NOT WRITE IN BOOK			
After charcoal						

Part B: Settling In

If a suspension is left standing, the suspended particles will settle to the top or bottom. You should see a layer of oil at the top.

Procedure

1. Separate the oil by carefully pouring the oil into another beaker. You can use a plastic spoon to get the last bit of oil from the water. Record your observations.

Part C: Filtration

Cloudy water can be a sign of small particles still in suspension. These particles can usually be removed by filtering. Water treatment plants use sand and gravel as filters.

Procedure

1. Make a filter as follows:
    a. Use the nail to poke 5 to 10 small holes in the bottom of one of the cups.
    b. Cut a circle of filter paper to fit inside the bottom of the cup. (This filter will keep the sand in the cup.)
    c. Fill the cup to 2 cm below the rim with wet sand. Pack the sand tightly.
    d. Set the cup inside an empty beaker.
2. Pour the polluted water on top of the sand, and let the water filter through. Do not pour any of the settled mud onto the sand. (Dispose of the mud as instructed by your teacher.) In your table, record your observations of the water collected in the beaker.

Part D: Separating Solutions

Something that has been dissolved in a solvent cannot be separated using filters. Water treatment plants use activated charcoal to absorb many dissolved chemicals.

Procedure

1. Place activated charcoal about 3 cm deep in the unused cup. Pour the water collected from the sand filtration into the cup, and stir with a spoon for 1 min.
2. Place a piece of filter paper over the top of the cup, and fasten it in place with a rubber band. With the paper securely in place, pour the water through the filter paper and back into a clean beaker. Record your observations in your table.

Analyze the Results

1. Is your unpolluted water safe to drink? Why or why not?
2. When you treat a sample of water, do you get out exactly the same amount of water that you put in? Explain your answer.
3. Some groups may still have cloudy water when they finish. Explain a possible cause for this.

Model-Making Lab

Finding a Balance

Usually, balancing a chemical equation involves just writing. But in this activity, you will use models to practice balancing chemical equations, as shown below. By following the rules, you will soon become an expert equation balancer!

MATERIALS

- envelopes, each labeled with an unbalanced equation

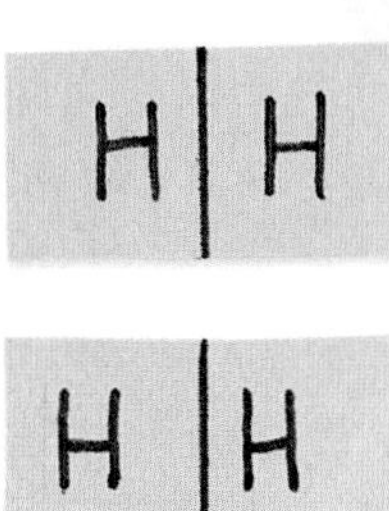

Example

$\_H_2 + \_O_2 \rightarrow \_H_2O$

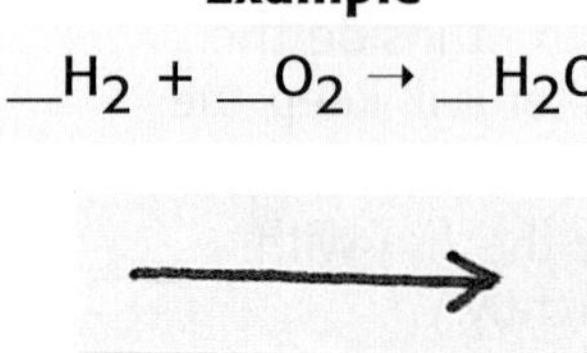

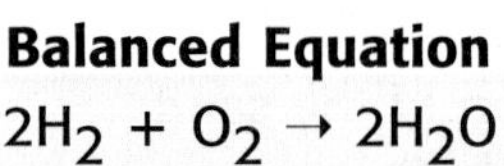

Balanced Equation

$2H_2 + O_2 \rightarrow 2H_2O$

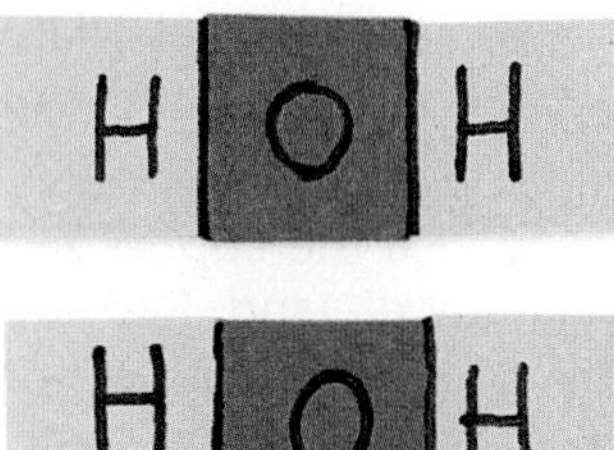

Procedure

1. The rules are as follows:
   - **a.** Reactant-molecule models may be placed only to the left of the arrow.
   - **b.** Product-molecule models may be placed only to the right of the arrow.
   - **c.** You may use only complete molecule models.
   - **d.** At least one of each of the reactant and product molecules shown in the equation must be included in the model when you are finished.
2. Select one of the labeled envelopes. Copy the unbalanced equation written on the envelope.
3. Open the envelope, and pull out the molecule models and the arrow. Place the arrow in the center of your work area.
4. Put one model of each molecule that is a reactant on the left side of the arrow and one model of each product on the right side.
5. Add one reactant-molecule or product-molecule model at a time until the number of each of the different-colored squares on each side of the arrow is the same. Remember to follow the rules.
6. When the equation is balanced, count the number of each of the molecule models you used. Write these numbers as coefficients, as shown in the balanced equation above.
7. Select another envelope, and repeat the steps until you have balanced all of the equations.

Analyze the Results

1. The rules specify that you are allowed to use only complete molecule models. How are these rules similar to what occurs in a real chemical reaction?
2. In chemical reactions, energy is either released or absorbed. Devise a way to improve the model to show energy being released or absorbed.

Using Scientific Methods

Skills Practice Lab

Cata-what? Catalyst!

Catalysts increase the rate of a chemical reaction without being changed during the reaction. In this experiment, hydrogen peroxide, H_2O_2, decomposes into oxygen, O_2, and water, H_2O. An enzyme present in liver cells acts as a catalyst for this reaction. You will investigate the relationship between the amount of the catalyst and the rate of the decomposition reaction.

MATERIALS

- beaker, 600 mL
- funnel
- graduated cylinder, 10 mL
- hydrogen peroxide, 3% solution
- liver cubes, small (2)
- mortar and pestle
- tape, masking
- test tubes, 10 mL (3)
- tweezers
- water, hot

SAFETY

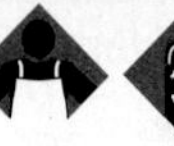

Ask a Question

1. How does the amount of a catalyst affect reaction rate?

Form a Hypothesis

2. Write a statement that answers the question above. Explain your reasoning.

Test the Hypothesis

3. Put a small piece of masking tape near the top of each test tube, and label the tubes "1," "2," and "3."
4. Create a hot-water bath by filling the beaker half full with hot water.
5. Using the funnel and graduated cylinder, measure 5 mL of the hydrogen peroxide solution into each test tube. Place the test tubes in the hot-water bath for 5 min.
6. While the test tubes warm up, grind one liver cube with the mortar and pestle.
7. After 5 min, use the tweezers to place the cube of liver in test tube 1. Place the ground liver in test tube 2. Leave test tube 3 alone.
8. Observe the reaction rate (the amount of bubbling) in all three test tubes, and record your observations.

Analyze the Results

1. Does liver appear to be a catalyst? Explain your answer.
2. Which type of liver (whole or ground) produced a faster reaction? Why?
3. What is the purpose of test tube 3?

Draw Conclusions

4. How do your results support or disprove your hypothesis?
5. Why was a hot-water bath used? (Hint: Look in your book for a definition of *activation energy.*)

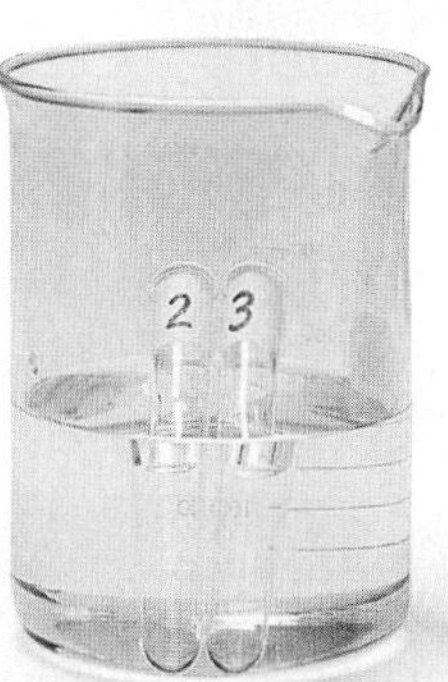

Skills Practice Lab

Putting Elements Together

A synthesis reaction is a reaction in which two or more substances combine to form a single compound. The resulting compound has different chemical and physical properties than the substances from which it is composed. In this activity, you will synthesize, or create, copper(II) oxide from the elements copper and oxygen.

MATERIALS

- balance, metric
- Bunsen burner (or portable burner)
- copper powder
- evaporating dish
- gauze, wire
- gloves, protective
- igniter
- paper, weighing
- ring stand and ring
- tongs

SAFETY

Procedure

1. Copy the table below.

Data Collection Table	
Object	**Mass (g)**
Evaporating dish	DO NOT WRITE IN BOOK
Copper powder	
Copper + evaporating dish after heating	
Copper(II) oxide	

2. Use the metric balance to measure the mass (to the nearest 0.1 g) of the empty evaporating dish. Record this mass in the table.
3. Place a piece of weighing paper on the metric balance, and measure approximately 10 g of copper powder. Record the mass (to the nearest 0.1 g) in the table. **Caution:** Wear protective gloves when working with copper powder.
4. Use the weighing paper to place the copper powder in the evaporating dish. Spread the powder over the bottom and up the sides as much as possible. Discard the weighing paper.

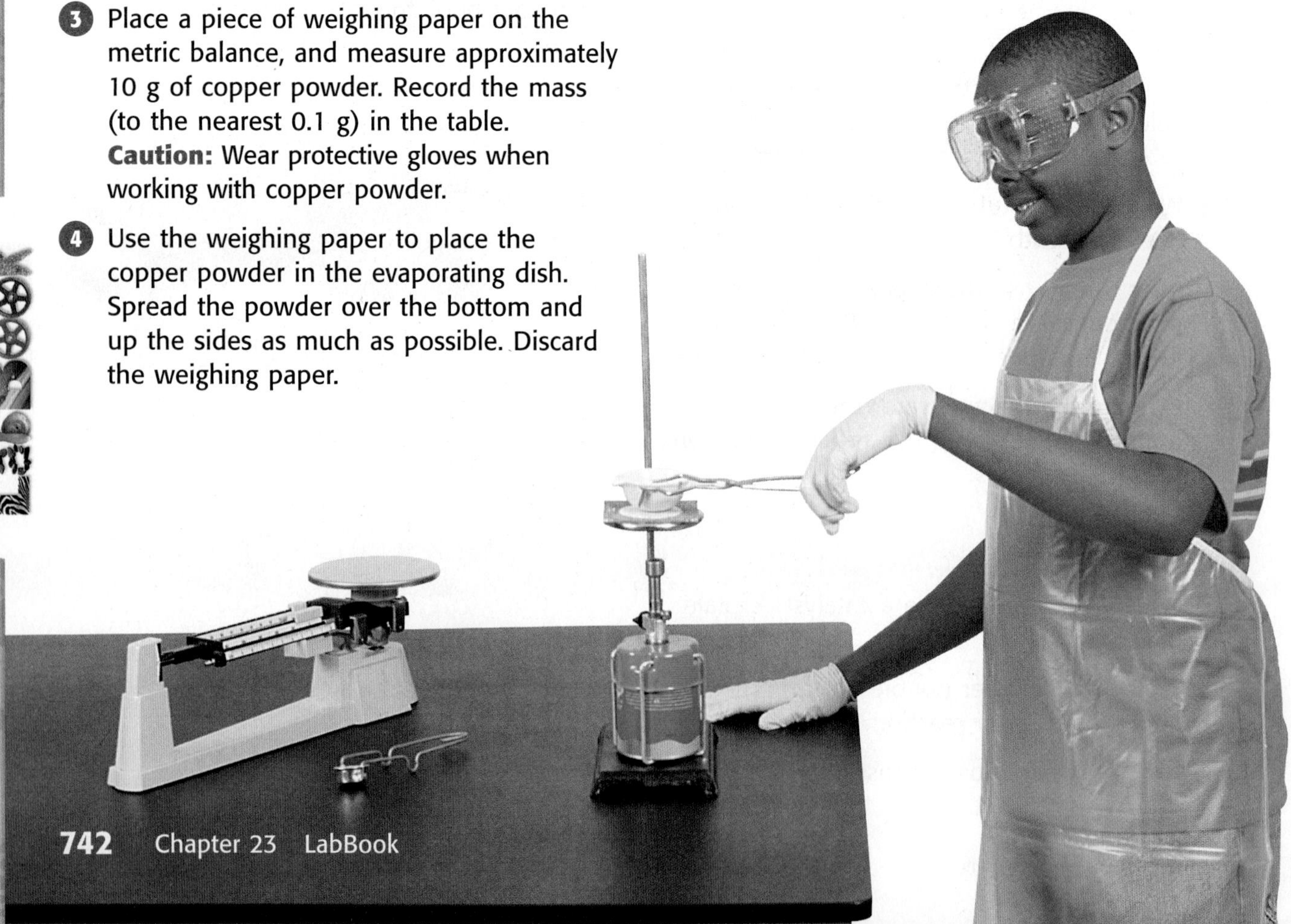

5. Set up the ring stand and ring. Place the wire gauze on top of the ring. Carefully place the evaporating dish on the wire gauze.
6. Place the Bunsen burner under the ring and wire gauze. Use the igniter to light the Bunsen burner. **Caution:** Use extreme care when working near an open flame.
7. Heat the evaporating dish for 10 min.
8. Turn off the burner, and allow the evaporating dish to cool for 10 min. Use tongs to remove the evaporating dish and to place it on the balance to determine the mass. Record the mass in the table.
9. Determine the mass of the reaction product—copper(II) oxide—by subtracting the mass of the evaporating dish from the mass of the evaporating dish and copper powder after heating. Record this mass in the table.

Analyze the Results

1. What evidence of a chemical reaction did you observe after the copper was heated?
2. Explain why there was a change in mass.
3. How does the change in mass support the idea that this reaction is a synthesis reaction?

Draw Conclusions

4. Why was powdered copper used rather than a small piece of copper? (Hint: How does surface area affect the rate of the reaction?)
5. Why was the copper heated? (Hint: Look in your book for the discussion of activation energy.)
6. The copper bottoms of cooking pots can turn black when used. How is that similar to the results you obtained in this lab?

Applying Your Data

Rust, shown below, is iron(III) oxide—the product of a synthesis reaction between iron and oxygen. How does painting a car help prevent this type of reaction?

Using Scientific Methods

Skills Practice Lab

Making Salt

A neutralization reaction between an acid and a base produces water and a salt. In this lab, you will react an acid with a base and then let the water evaporate. You will then examine what is left for properties that tell you that it is indeed a salt.

MATERIALS

- beaker, 100 mL
- eyedroppers (2)
- evaporating dish
- gloves, protective
- graduated cylinder, 100 mL
- hydrochloric acid
- magnifying lens
- phenolphthalein solution in a dropper bottle
- stirring rod, glass
- sodium hydroxide
- water, distilled

SAFETY

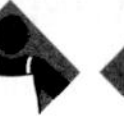

Ask a Question

1. Write a question about reactions between acids and bases.

Form a Hypothesis

2. Write a hypothesis that may answer the question you asked in the step above.

Test the Hypothesis

3. Put on protective gloves. Carefully measure 25 mL of hydrochloric acid in a graduated cylinder, and then pour it into the beaker. Carefully rinse the graduated cylinder with distilled water to clean out any leftover acid. **Caution:** Hydrochloric acid is corrosive. If any should spill on you, immediately flush the area with water, and notify your teacher.
4. Add 3 drops of phenolphthalein indicator to the acid in the beaker. You will not see anything happen yet because this indicator won't show its color unless too much base is present.
5. Measure 20 mL of sodium hydroxide (base) in the graduated cylinder, and add it slowly to the beaker with the acid. Use the stirring rod to mix the substances completely. **Caution:** Sodium hydroxide is also corrosive. If any should spill on you, immediately flush the area with water, and notify your teacher.
6. Use an eyedropper to add more base, a few drops at a time, to the acid-base mixture in the beaker. Be sure to stir the mixture after each few drops. Continue adding drops of base until the mixture remains colored after stirring.

7. Use another eyedropper to add acid to the beaker, 1 drop at a time, until the color just disappears after stirring.
8. Pour the mixture carefully into an evaporating dish, and place the dish where your teacher tells you to allow the water to evaporate overnight.
9. The next day, examine your evaporating dish, and with a magnifying lens, study the crystals that were left. Identify the color, shape, and other properties of the crystals.

Analyze the Results

1. The following equation is for the reaction that occurred in this experiment:

$$HCl + NaOH \longrightarrow H_2O + NaCl$$

NaCl is ordinary table salt and forms very regular cubic crystals that are white. Did you find white cubic crystals?

2. The phenolphthalein indicator changes color in the presence of a base. Why did you add more acid in step 7 until the color disappeared?

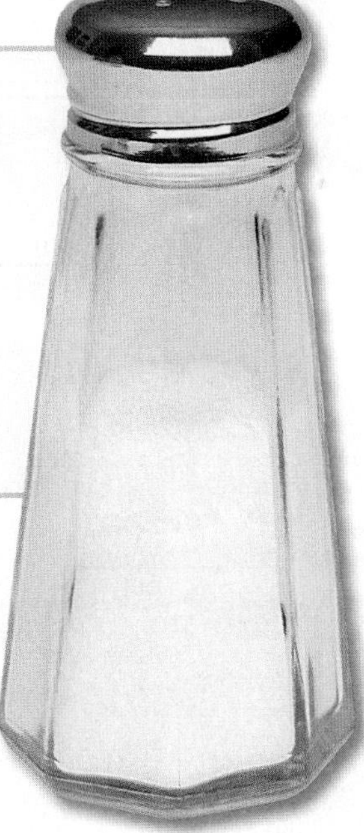

Applying Your Data

Another neutralization reaction occurs between hydrochloric acid and potassium hydroxide, KOH. The equation for this reaction is as follows:

$$HCl + KOH \longrightarrow H_2O + KCl$$

What are the products of this neutralization reaction? How do they compare with those you discovered in this experiment?

Contents

Inch
Yard
Fathom
Foot

Appendix

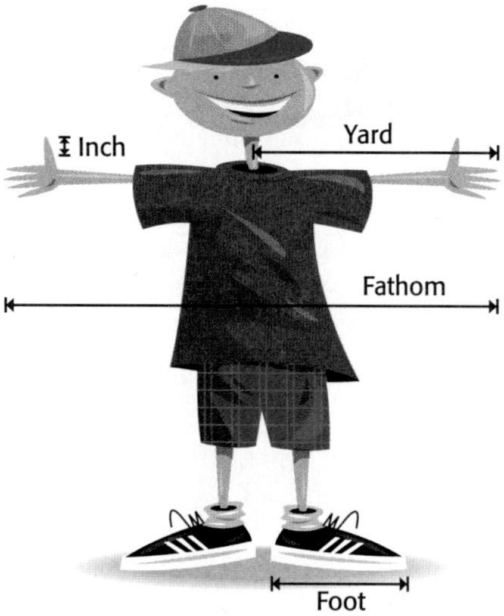

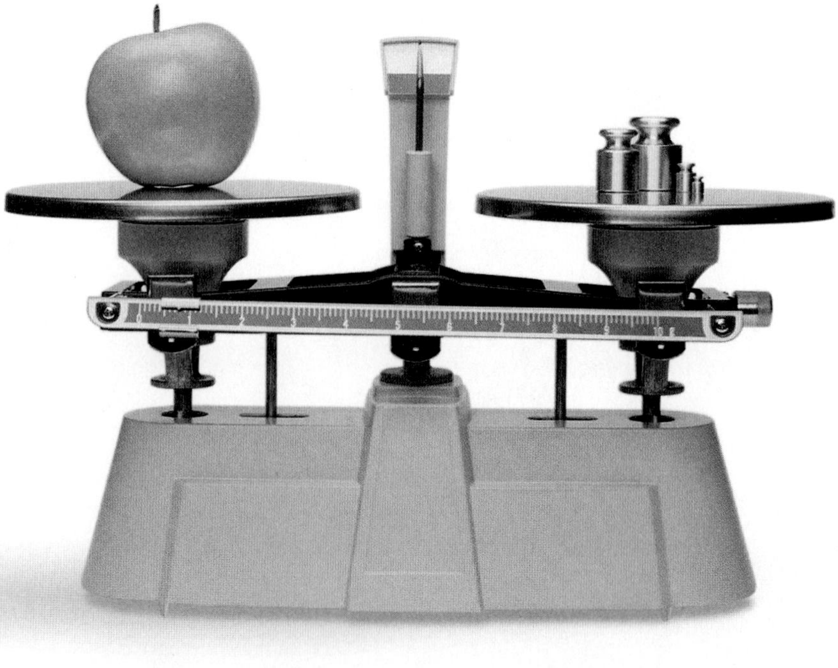

✓Reading Check Answers

Chapter 1 Science in Our World

Section 1

Page 4: Science is the knowledge obtained by observing natural events and conditions in order to discover facts and formulate laws or principles that can be verified or tested.

Page 7: Society can influence technology development by identifying important problems that need technological solutions.

Page 9: A volcanologist studies volcanoes and their products, such as lava and gases.

Section 2

Page 10: a series of steps used by scientists to solve problems

Page 12: A hypothesis is testable if an experiment can be designed to test the hypothesis.

Page 14: only one

Page 16: because the scientist has learned something

Section 3

Page 19: a mathematical model

Page 20: to explain a broad range of observations, facts, and tested hypotheses, to predict what might happen, and to organize scientific thinking

Section 4

Page 22: stopwatch, graduated cylinder, meterstick, spring scale, balance, and thermometer

Page 25: the kilogram

Page 27: Safety symbols alert you to particular safety concerns or specific dangers in a lab.

Chapter 2 The Cell in Action

Section 1

Page 41: Red blood cells would burst in pure water because water particles move from outside, where particles were dense, to inside the cell, where particles were less dense. This movement of water would cause red blood cells to fill up and burst.

Page 43: Exocytosis is the process by which a cell moves large particles to the outside of the cell.

Section 2

Page 45: Cellular respiration is a chemical process by which cells produce energy from food. Breathing supplies oxygen for cellular respiration and removes the carbon dioxide produced by cellular respiration.

Page 47: One kind of fermentation produces CO_2, and the other kind produces lactic acid.

Section 3

Page 49: No, the number of chromosomes is not always related to the complexity of organisms.

Page 50: During cytokinesis in plant cells, a cell plate is formed. During cytokinesis in animal cells, a cell plate does not form.

Chapter 3 Plant Processes

Section 1

Page 62: Sample answer: Chlorophyll reflects more wavelengths of green light than wavelengths of other colors of light. So, most plants look green.

Page 65: Sample answer: Photosynthesis provides the oxygen that organisms need for cellular respiration. Photosynthetic organisms form the base of nearly all food chains on Earth.

Section 2

Page 67: Sample answer: Animals may eat fruits and discard the seeds away from the parent plant. Other fruits, such as burrs, get caught in an animal's fur. Some fruits are carried by the wind.

Page 68: plantlets, tubers, and runners

Section 3

Page 70: Sample answer: The shoot tips will probably bend toward the light.

Page 71: Sample answer: Plants respond to the change in the length of day.

Page 72: Sample answer: Evergreen trees always have some leaves on them. Deciduous trees lose all of their leaves around the same time each year.

Chapter 4 Heredity

Section 1

Page 86: the passing of traits from parents to offspring

Page 89: During his second set of experiments, Mendel allowed the first-generation plants, which resulted from his first set of experiments, to self-pollinate.

Page 90: A ratio is a relationship between two different numbers that is often expressed as a fraction.

Section 2

Page 92: A gene contains the instructions for an inherited trait. The different versions of a gene are called *alleles*.

Page 94: Probability is the mathematical chance that something will happen.

Page 96: In incomplete dominance, one trait is not completely dominant over another.

Section 3

Page 99: 23 chromosomes

Page 100: During meiosis, one parent cell makes four new cells.

Chapter 5 Genes and DNA

Section 1

Page 117: Guanine and cytosine are always found in DNA in equal amounts, as are adenine and thymine.

Page 119: every time a cell divides

Section 2

Page 120: a string of nucleotides that give the cell information about how to make a specific trait

Page 123: They transfer amino acids to the ribosome.

Page 124: a physical or chemical agent that can cause a mutation in DNA

Page 125: Sickle cell disease is caused by a mutation in a single nucleotide of DNA, which then causes a different amino acid to be assembled in a protein used in blood cells.

Page 126: a near-identical copy of another organism, created with the original organism's genes

Chapter 6 The Evolution of Living Things

Section 1

Page 138: if they mate with each other and produce more of the same type of organism

Page 140: by their estimated ages and physical similarities

Page 142: a four-legged land mammal

Page 144: that they have common ancestry

Section 2

Page 147: 965 km (600 mi) west of Ecuador

Page 149: that Earth had been formed by natural processes over a long period of time

Page 150: Natural selection is the process by which organisms that are better adapted to their environment survive and reproduce more successfully than organisms that are less well adapted.

Section 3

Page 153: because they often produce many offspring and have short generation times

Page 154: Sample answer: A newly formed canyon, mountain range, or lake could divide the members of a population.

Chapter 7 The History of Life on Earth

Section 1

Page 167: absolute dating

Page 169: periods of sudden extinction of many species

Page 170: the idea that the Earth's continents once formed a single landmass surrounded by ocean

Section 2

Page 172: The early Earth was very different from today—there were violent events and a harsh atmosphere.

Page 175: a mass extinction

Page 176: "recent life"

Section 3

Page 179: the hominid family

Page 180: Africa

Page 183: Paleontologists will review their ideas about the evolution of hominids.

Chapter 8 Maps as Models of the Earth

Section 1

Page 197: A reference point is a fixed place on the Earth's surface from which direction and location can be described.

Page 198: True north is the direction to the geographic North Pole.

Page 200: lines of longitude

Section 2

Page 202: Distortions are inaccuracies produced when information is transferred from a curved surface to a flat surface.

Page 205: Azimuthal and conic projections are similar because they are both ways to represent the curved surface of the Earth on a flat map. Azimuthal projections show the surface of a globe transferred to a flat plane, whereas conic projections show the surface of a globe transferred to a cone.

Page 206: Every map should have a title, a compass rose, a scale, the date, and a legend.

Page 208: A GIS stores information in layers.

Section 3

Page 211: An index contour is a darker contour line that is usually every fifth line. Index contours make it easier to read a map.

Chapter 9 Minerals of the Earth's Crust

Section 1

Page 225: An element is a pure substance that cannot be broken down into simpler substances by ordinary chemical means. A compound is a substance made of two or more elements that have been chemically bonded.

Page 226: Answers may vary. Silicate minerals contain a combination of silicon and oxygen; nonsilicate minerals do not contain a combination of silicon and oxygen.

Section 2

Page 229: A mineral's streak is not affected by air or water, but a mineral's color may be affected by air or water.

Page 230: Scratch the mineral with a series of 10 reference minerals. If the reference mineral scratches the unidentified mineral, the reference mineral is harder than the unidentified mineral.

Section 3

Page 235: Surface mining is used to remove mineral deposits that are at or near the Earth's surface. Subsurface mining is used to remove mineral deposits that are too deep to be removed by surface mining.

Page 237: Sample answer: Gemstones are nonmetallic minerals that are valued for their beauty and rarity rather than for their usefulness.

Chapter 10 Rocks: Mineral Mixtures

Section 1

Page 248: Types of rocks that have been used by humans to construct buildings include granite, limestone, marble, sandstone, and slate.

Page 252: Rock within the Earth is affected by temperature and pressure.

Page 253: The minerals that a rock contains determine a rock's composition.

Page 254: Fine-grained rocks are made of small grains, such as silt or clay particles. Medium-grained rocks are made of medium-sized grains, such as sand. Coarse-grained rocks are made of large grains, such as pebbles.

Section 2

Page 257: Felsic rocks are light-colored igneous rocks rich in aluminum, potassium, silicon, and sodium. Mafic rocks are dark-colored igneous rocks rich in calcium, iron, and magnesium.

Page 259: New sea floor forms when lava that flows from fissures on the ocean floor cools and hardens.

Section 3

Page 261: Halite forms when sodium and chlorine ions in shallow bodies of water become so concentrated that halite crystallizes from solution.

Page 263: Ripple marks are the marks left by wind and water waves on lakes, seas, rivers, and sand dunes.

Section 4

Page 265: Regional metamorphism occurs when pressure builds up in rock that is buried deep below other rock formations or when large pieces of the Earth's crust collide. The increased pressure can cause thousands of square miles of rock to become deformed and chemically changed.

Page 266: An index mineral is a metamorphic mineral that forms only at certain temperatures and pressures and therefore can be used by scientists to estimate the temperature, pressure, and depth at which a rock undergoes metamorphosis.

Page 269: Deformation causes metamorphic structures, such as folds.

Chapter 11 The Rock and Fossil Record

Section 1

Page 281: Catastrophists believed that all geologic change occurs rapidly.

Page 282: A global catastrophe can cause the extinction of species.

Section 2

Page 285: Geologists use the geologic column to interpret rock sequences and to identify layers in puzzling rock sequences.

Page 287: An unconformity is a surface that represents a missing part of the geologic column.

Page 288: A disconformity is found where part of a sequence of parallel rock layers is missing. A nonconformity is found where horizontal sedimentary rock layers lie on top of an eroded surface of igneous or metamorphic rock. Angular unconformities are found between horizontal sedimentary rock layers and rock layers that have been tilted or folded.

Section 3

Page 291: A half-life is the time it takes one-half of a radioactive sample to decay.

Page 292: strontium-87

Section 4

Page 294: An organism is caught in soft, sticky tree sap, which hardens and preserves the organism.

Page 296: A mold is a cavity in rock where a plant or an animal was buried. A cast is an object created when sediment fills a mold and becomes rock.

Page 298: To fill in missing information about changes in organisms in the fossil record, paleontologists look for similarities between fossilized organisms or between fossilized organisms and their closest living relatives.

Page 299: *Phacops* can be used to establish the age of rock layers because *Phacops* lived during a relatively short, well-defined time span and is found in rock layers throughout the world.

Section 5

Page 301: approximately 2 billion years

Page 302: The geological time scale is a scale that divides Earth's 4.6 billion–year history into distinct intervals of time.

Page 304: The Mesozoic era is known as the *Age of Reptiles* because reptiles, including the dinosaurs, were the dominant organisms on land.

Chapter 12 The Earth's Ecosystems

Section 1

Page 319: Sample answer: *Deciduous* comes from a Latin word that means "to fall off." In temperate deciduous forests, the trees lose their leaves in the fall.

Page 320: evergreen trees; squirrels, insects, finches, chickadees, jays, porcupines, elk, and moose

Page 322: During the dry season, grasses on the savanna dry out and turn yellow. But their deep roots survive for many months without water.

Page 323: Sample answer: Desert plants grow far apart. Some plants have shallow, widespread roots to take up water after a storm. Some desert plants have fleshy stems and leaves to store water. They also have waxy coatings to prevent water loss.

Page 324: Sample answer: Alpine tundra is tundra found at the top of tall mountains, above the tree line.

Section 2

Page 326: Sample answer: Plankton are tiny organisms that float near the surface of the water. They form the base of the ocean's feeding relationships.

Page 327: Sample answer: Fishes that live near the poles have adaptations for the near-freezing water. Animals in coral reefs need warm water to live. Some animals migrate to warmer waters to reproduce. Water temperature affects whether some animals can eat.

Page 329: Sample answer: Some animals get food from material that sinks to the bottom from the surface. Other animals get energy from chemicals released by thermal vents.

Page 330: Sample answer: When corals die, they leave behind their skeletons. Other corals grow on these remains. Over time, the layers build up to form a coral reef.

Section 3

Page 333: Sample answer: The littoral zone is the zone closest to shore in which light reaches the lake bottom. The open zone extends from the littoral zone and goes as deep as sunlight can reach. The deep-water zone lies beneath the open-water zone.

Page 334: A swamp is a wetland ecosystem in which trees and vines grow.

Page 335: Sample answer: Many fishes will die as the pond fills in because bacteria that decompose material in the pond use up the oxygen in the water.

Chapter 13 Earth's Systems and Cycles

Section 1

Page 346: The geosphere is the rocky part of Earth that extends from Earth's core to its surface. The atmosphere is the mixture of gases that surrounds Earth. The hydrosphere contains all of Earth's water. The biosphere contains all of Earth's life.

Page 349: When tectonic plates move, rock is deformed and broken. Some of the energy that is generated as rock is broken and deformed is released as vibrations that travel through the ground. This shaking is an earthquake.

Page 350: Large volcanic eruptions can lower the average global temperature. This occurs as a result of a decrease in the amount of sunlight that reaches Earth's surface. This decrease is caused by volcanic ash and sulfur gases in the Earth's atmosphere, which block and reflect sunlight.

Section 2

Page 353: Answers may vary. Sample answer: All weather is restricted to the troposphere. The ozone layer is located in the stratosphere. The mesosphere is the coldest layer in the atmosphere. In the thermosphere, oxygen and nitrogen absorb harmful X-ray and gamma-ray radiation from space.

Page 354: Energy comes to Earth from the sun as electromagnetic waves. These waves include ultraviolet wavelengths, visible light, and infrared wavelengths.

Page 356: Greenhouse gases in Earth's atmosphere absorb reradiated infrared energy from Earth's surface and retain the energy in the atmosphere as thermal energy. This thermal energy is conducted and convected through the atmosphere, warming the atmosphere.

Section 3

Page 359: Surface currents and deep currents form the pattern known as the ocean conveyor belt because they transport warm and cold water for thousands of miles throughout the global ocean.

Page 360: The ocean can keep temperatures in coastal areas cooler during the summer and warmer during the winter.

Page 362: Animals depend on a continuous supply of energy from the sun in order to obtain the food they need.

Page 363: Decomposition is a process that recycles the matter and energy stored in the bodies of animals and plants which have died. Generally, when an animal or plant dies, organisms called decomposers consume the dead plant and animal matter. These decomposers use some of the stored matter and energy and release what is left into the environment.

Section 4

Page 365: Water moves from the ocean, to the atmosphere, to the land, and back to the ocean.

Page 366: The carbon cycle is important to Earth's organisms because carbon is one of the most common molecules in organisms.

Chapter 14 Plate Tectonics

Section 1

Page 379: The crust is the thin, outermost layer of the Earth. It is 5 km to 100 km thick and is mainly made up of the elements oxygen, silicon, and aluminum. The mantle is the layer between the crust and core. It is 2,900 km thick, is denser than the crust, and contains most of the Earth's mass. The core is the Earth's innermost layer. The core has a radius of 3,430 km and is made mostly of iron.

Page 380: The five physical layers of the Earth are the lithosphere, asthenosphere, mesosphere, outer core, and inner core.

Page 383: Although continental lithosphere is less dense than oceanic lithosphere is, continental lithosphere has a greater mass because of its greater thickness and will displace more asthenosphere than oceanic lithosphere.

Page 384: Answers may vary. A seismic wave traveling through a solid will go faster than a seismic wave traveling through a liquid.

Section 2

Page 386: Similar fossils were found on landmasses that are very far apart. The best explanation for this phenomenon is that the landmasses were once joined.

Page 389: The molten rock at mid-ocean ridges contains tiny grains of magnetic minerals. The minerals align with the Earth's magnetic field before the rock cools and hardens. When the Earth's magnetic field reverses, the orientation of the mineral grains in the rocks will also change.

Section 3

Page 391: A transform boundary forms when two tectonic plates slide past each other horizontally.

Page 392: The circulation of thermal energy causes changes in density in the asthenosphere. As rock is heated, it expands, becomes less dense, and rises. As rock cools, it contracts, becomes denser, and sinks.

Section 4

Page 394: Compression can cause rocks to be pushed into mountain ranges as tectonic plates collide at convergent boundaries. Tension can pull rocks apart as tectonic plates separate at divergent boundaries.

Page 396: In a normal fault, the hanging wall moves down. In a reverse fault, the hanging wall moves up.

Page 398: Folded mountains form when rock layers are squeezed together and pushed upward.

Chapter 15 Earthquakes

Section 1

Page 413: During elastic rebound, rock releases energy. Some of this energy travels as seismic waves that cause earthquakes.

Page 415: Earthquake zones are usually located along tectonic plate boundaries.

Page 417: Surface waves travel more slowly than body waves but are more destructive.

Section 2

Page 419: Seismologists determine an earthquake's start time by comparing seismograms and noting differences in arrival times of P and S waves.

Page 420: Each time the magnitude increases by 1 unit, the amount of ground motion increases by 10 times.

Section 3

Page 423: With a decrease of one unit in earthquake magnitude, the number of earthquakes occurring annually increases by about 10 times.

Page 424: Retrofitting is the process of making older structures more earthquake resistant.

Page 426: You should crouch or lie face down under a table or desk.

Chapter 16 Volcanoes

Section 1

Page 439: Nonexplosive eruptions are common, and they feature relatively calm flows of lava. Explosive eruptions are less common and produce large, explosive clouds of ash and gases.

Page 440: Because silica-rich magma has a high viscosity, it tends to trap gases and plug volcanic vents. This causes pressure to build up and can result in an explosive eruption.

Page 442: Volcanic bombs are large blobs of magma that harden in the air. Lapilli are small pieces of magma that harden in the air. Volcanic blocks are pieces of solid rock erupted from a volcano. Ash forms when gases in stiff magma expand rapidly and the walls of the gas bubbles shatter into tiny glasslike slivers.

Section 2

Page 444: Eruptions release large quantities of ash and gases, which can block sunlight and cause global temperatures to drop.

Page 446: Calderas form when a magma chamber partially empties and the roof overlying the chamber collapses.

Section 3

Page 449: Volcanic activity is common at tectonic plate boundaries because magma tends to form at plate boundaries.

Page 451: When a tectonic plate subducts, it becomes hotter and releases water. The water lowers the melting point of the rock above the plate, causing magma to form.

Page 452: According to one theory, a rising body of magma, called a mantle plume, causes a chain of volcanoes to form on a moving tectonic plate. According to another theory, a chain of volcanoes forms along cracks in the Earth's crust.

Chapter 17 The Properties of Matter

Section 1

Page 467: liters (L) and milliliters (mL)

Page 468: You could measure the volume of an apple by submerging the apple in a container of water and measuring the volume of the water that the apple displaces.

Page 470: kilograms (kg), grams (g), and milligrams (mg)

Section 2

Page 472: Some physical properties are color, shape, odor, weight, volume, texture, state, and density.

Page 474: If the object's density is less than the water's density, the object will float.

Page 477: A physical change is a change that occurs to a substance or object that does not change the identity of the substance.

Section 3

Page 478: Reactivity describes the ability of two or more substances to combine and form one or more new substances.

Page 480: Chemical changes occur when one or more substances are changed into entirely new substances that have different properties. A chemical property of a substance determines whether a chemical change will occur.

Chapter 18 States of Matter

Section 1

Page 495: The particles in a crystalline solid are arranged in a repeating pattern of rows that forms an orderly, three-dimensional arrangement.

Page 496: Viscosity is a liquid's resistance to flow.

Section 2

Page 499: There are more particles of gas in the basketball than there are in the beach ball. More particles hit the inside surface of the basketball, which causes increased force.

Page 500 Charles's law states that the volume of a gas in a closed container changes as the temperature of the gas changes. If the temperature increases, the volume increases. If the temperature decreases, the volume decreases.

Section 3

Page 502: A change of state is the change of a substance from one physical form to another.

Page 504: Evaporation is the change of a substance from a liquid to a gas.

Page 506: As a substance changes state, its temperature remains constant until the change of state is complete.

Chapter 19 Elements, Compounds, and Mixtures

Section 1

Page 518: An element is a pure substance because it contains only one type of particle.

Page 520: Metals are shiny, conduct heat energy, and conduct electric current.

Section 2

Page 523: Three physical properties used to identify compounds are melting point, density, and color.

Page 524: Compounds can be broken down into elements or simpler compounds.

Section 3

Page 526: Substances in a mixture keep their identities because no chemical change takes place when a mixture is made.

Page 529: An alloy is a solid solution of metal or nonmetal dissolved in another metal.

Page 531: As temperature increases, the solubility of a gas decreases.

Page 532: The particles of a suspension can be separated by passing the suspension through a filter.

Chapter 20 Introduction to Atoms

Section 1

Page 545: Dalton thought that elements are made of single atoms because elements always combine in specific proportions to form compounds.

Page 547: Rutherford could tell where the positively charged particles went because they hit a special coating that glowed where it was hit.

Page 548: Rutherford changed Thomson's model of the atom by proposing that the nucleus is a tiny, dense, positively charged area surrounded by electrons.

Section 2

Page 551: Protons and neutrons can be found in the nucleus.

Page 552: An atom becomes a positively charged ion when it loses an electron.

Page 554: Differences between isotopes are important when a certain isotope is radioactive.

Page 556: The four basic forces are the gravitational force, electromagnetic force, strong force, and weak force.

Chapter 21 The Periodic Table

Section 1

Page 568: Mendeleev had arranged elements based on increasing atomic mass.

Page 569: atomic number

Page 572: Most metals are solid at room temperature, ductile, malleable, and shiny. In addition, they are good conductors of electric current and thermal energy.

Page 574: Elements in a group often have similar chemical and physical properties.

Section 2

Page 577: It is easier for atoms of alkali metals to lose their outer electron than for atoms of transition metals to lose their outer electrons. Therefore, alkali metals are more reactive than transition metals.

Page 578: Yes, lanthanides and actinides are transition metals.

Page 579: silicon and germanium

Page 580: nitrogen and oxygen

Page 582: Atoms of noble gases have a full set of electrons in their outer level.

Chapter 22 Chemical Bonding

Section 1

Page 597: Most atoms form bonds only with their valence electrons.

Page 598: Atoms in Group 18 (the noble gases) rarely form chemical bonds.

Section 2

Page 599: Atoms are neutral because the number of protons in an atom always equals the number of electrons in the atom.

Page 601: Atoms in Group 17 give off the most energy when forming negative ions.

Section 3

Page 604: A covalent bond is a bond that forms when atoms share one or more pairs of electrons.

Page 606: There are two atoms in a diatomic molecule.

Page 608: Ductility is the ability to be drawn into wires.

Chapter 23 Chemical Reactions

Section 1

Page 621: A precipitate is a solid substance that is formed in a solution.

Page 622: In a chemical reaction, the chemical bonds in the starting substances break, and then new bonds form to make new substances.

Section 2

Page 625: Ionic compounds are made up of a metal and a nonmetal.

Page 626: Reactants are the starting substances in a chemical reaction, and products are the substances that are formed.

Page 628: 4

Section 3

Page 630: A synthesis reaction is a reaction in which two or more substances combine to form one new compound.

Page 631: In a decomposition reaction, a substance breaks down into simpler substances. In a synthesis reaction, two or more substances combine to form one new compound.

Page 632: In a single-displacement reaction, an element may replace another element if the replacing element is more reactive than the original element.

Section 4

Page 635: An endothermic reaction is a chemical reaction in which energy is taken in.

Page 636: Activation energy is the energy that is needed to start a chemical reaction.

Page 638: A high concentration of reactants allows the particles of the reactants to run into each other more often, so the reaction proceeds at a faster rate.

Chapter 24 Chemical Compounds

Section 1

Page 651: Ionic solutions conduct an electric current because the ions in the solution are charged and are able to move past each other easily.

Page 652: Most covalent compounds will not dissolve in water because the attraction of the water molecules to each other is much stronger than the attraction of the water molecules to the compound.

Section 2

Page 654: A hydronium ion forms when a hydrogen ion bonds to a water molecule in a water solution.

Page 656: Sulfuric acid is used in car batteries to conduct electric current. Hydrochloric acid is used as an algaecide in swimming pools. Nitric acid is used to make fertilizers.

Page 659: Bases can be used at home in the form of soap, oven cleaner, or antacid.

Section 3

Page 660: In a strong acid, all of the molecules of the acid break apart when the acid is dissolved in water. In a weak acid, only a few of the acid molecules break apart when the acid is dissolved in water.

Page 662: Indicators turn different colors at different pH levels. The color on the pH strip can be compared with the colors on the indicator scale to determine the pH of the solution being tested.

Section 4

Page 664: Structural formulas show how atoms in a molecule are connected.

Page 667: Proteins are made of building blocks called *amino acids.*

Page 668: Nucleic acids store genetic information and build proteins.

Chapter 25 Atomic Energy

Section 1

Page 681: mass number and charge

Page 683: fatigue, loss of appetite, and hair loss

Page 685: 5,730 years

Page 686: A tracer is a radioactive element whose path can be followed through a process or reaction.

Section 2

Page 688: A nucleus that undergoes nuclear fission splits into two smaller, more stable nuclei.

Page 691: Sample answer: Using nuclear fission to generate electrical energy can help our supply of fossil fuels last longer, can help protect the environment because gases such as carbon dioxide are not released during fission, and can save money because nuclear power plants often cost less to run than power plants that use fossil fuels.

Page 692: In nuclear fusion, two or more nuclei that have small masses combine to form a larger nucleus. During fusion, energy is released.

Study Skills

FoldNote Instructions

Have you ever tried to study for a test or quiz but didn't know where to start? Or have you read a chapter and found that you can remember only a few ideas? Well, FoldNotes are a fun and exciting way to help you learn and remember the ideas you encounter as you learn science!

FoldNotes are tools that you can use to organize concepts. By focusing on a few main concepts, FoldNotes help you learn and remember how the concepts fit together. They can help you see the "big picture." Below you will find instructions for building 10 different FoldNotes.

Pyramid

1. Place a sheet of paper in front of you. Fold the lower left-hand corner of the paper diagonally to the opposite edge of the paper.
2. Cut off the tab of paper created by the fold (at the top).
3. Open the paper so that it is a square. Fold the lower right-hand corner of the paper diagonally to the opposite corner to form a triangle.
4. Open the paper. The creases of the two folds will have created an X.
5. Using scissors, cut along one of the creases. Start from any corner, and stop at the center point to create two flaps. Use tape or glue to attach one of the flaps on top of the other flap.

Double Door

1. Fold a sheet of paper in half from the top to the bottom. Then, unfold the paper.
2. Fold the top and bottom edges of the paper to the crease.

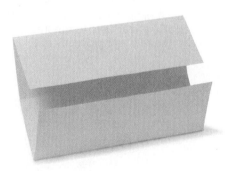

Booklet

1. Fold a sheet of paper in half from left to right. Then, unfold the paper.
2. Fold the sheet of paper in half again from the top to the bottom. Then, unfold the paper.
3. Refold the sheet of paper in half from left to right.
4. Fold the top and bottom edges to the center crease.
5. Completely unfold the paper.
6. Refold the paper from top to bottom.
7. Using scissors, cut a slit along the center crease of the sheet from the folded edge to the creases made in step 4. Do not cut the entire sheet in half.
8. Fold the sheet of paper in half from left to right. While holding the bottom and top edges of the paper, push the bottom and top edges together so that the center collapses at the center slit. Fold the four flaps to form a four-page book.

Layered Book

1. Lay one sheet of paper on top of another sheet. Slide the top sheet up so that 2 cm of the bottom sheet is showing.
2. Hold the two sheets together, fold down the top of the two sheets so that you see four 2 cm tabs along the bottom.
3. Using a stapler, staple the top of the FoldNote.

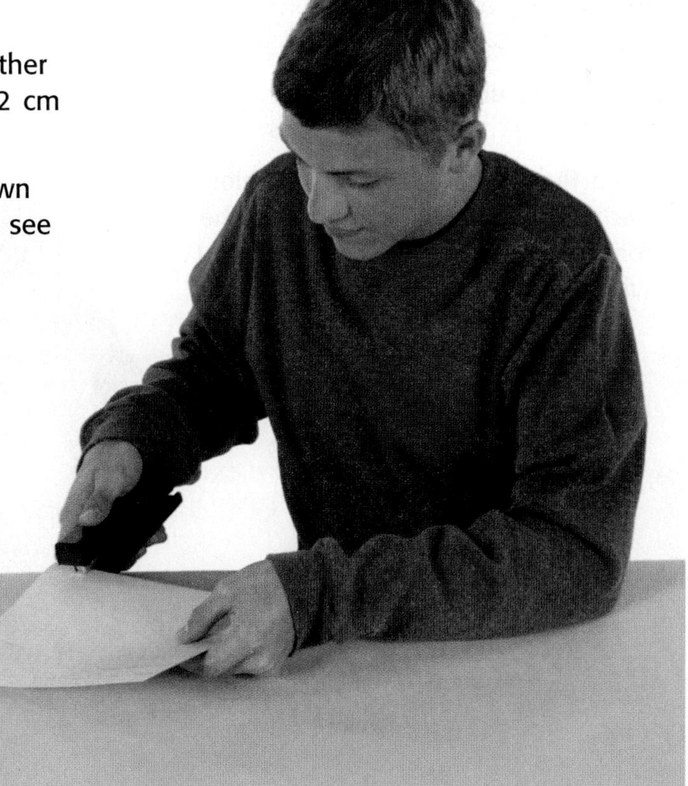

Key-Term Fold

1. Fold a sheet of lined notebook paper in half from left to right.
2. Using scissors, cut along every third line from the right edge of the paper to the center fold to make tabs.

Four-Corner Fold

1. Fold a sheet of paper in half from left to right. Then, unfold the paper.
2. Fold each side of the paper to the crease in the center of the paper.
3. Fold the paper in half from the top to the bottom. Then, unfold the paper.
4. Using scissors, cut the top flap creases made in step 3 to form four flaps.

Three-Panel Flip Chart

1. Fold a piece of paper in half from the top to the bottom.
2. Fold the paper in thirds from side to side. Then, unfold the paper so that you can see the three sections.
3. From the top of the paper, cut along each of the vertical fold lines to the fold in the middle of the paper. You will now have three flaps.

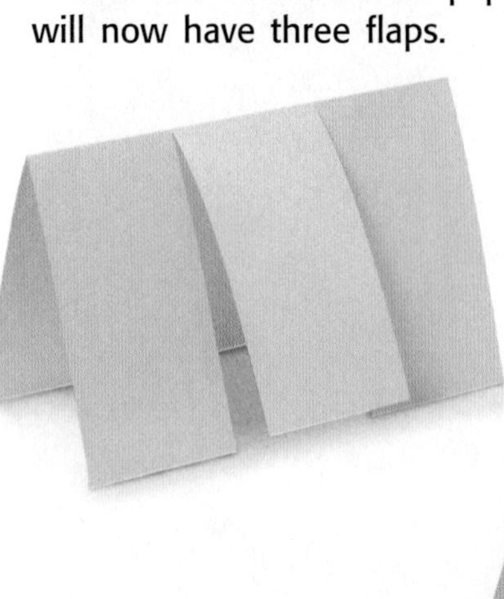

Table Fold

1. Fold a piece of paper in half from the top to the bottom. Then, fold the paper in half again.
2. Fold the paper in thirds from side to side.
3. Unfold the paper completely. Carefully trace the fold lines by using a pen or pencil.

Two-Panel Flip Chart

1. Fold a piece of paper in half from the top to the bottom.
2. Fold the paper in half from side to side. Then, unfold the paper so that you can see the two sections.
3. From the top of the paper, cut along the vertical fold line to the fold in the middle of the paper. You will now have two flaps.

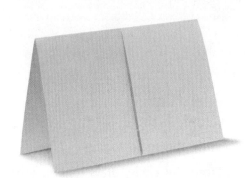

Tri-Fold

1. Fold a piece a paper in thirds from the top to the bottom.
2. Unfold the paper so that you can see the three sections. Then, turn the paper sideways so that the three sections form vertical columns.
3. Trace the fold lines by using a pen or pencil. Label the columns "Know," "Want," and "Learn."

Graphic Organizer Instructions

Have you ever wished that you could "draw out" the many concepts you learn in your science class? Sometimes, being able to *see* how concepts are related really helps you remember what you've learned. Graphic Organizers do just that! They give you a way to draw or map out concepts.

All you need to make a Graphic Organizer is a piece of paper and a pencil. Below you will find instructions for four different Graphic Organizers designed to help you organize the concepts you'll learn in this book.

Spider Map

1. Draw a diagram like the one shown. In the circle, write the main topic.
2. From the circle, draw legs to represent different categories of the main topic. You can have as many categories as you want.
3. From the category legs, draw horizontal lines. As you read the chapter, write details about each category on the horizontal lines.

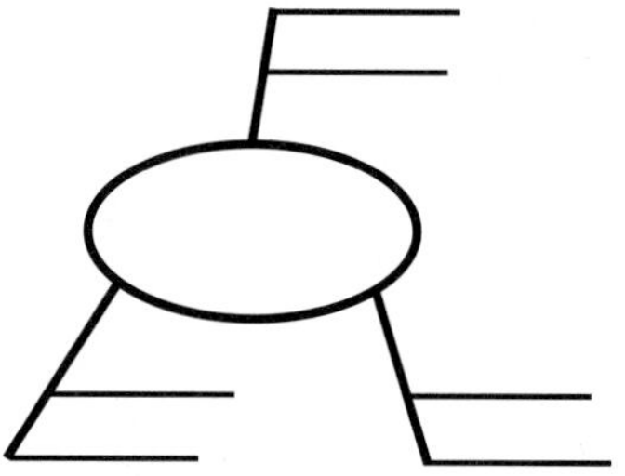

Comparison Table

1. Draw a chart like the one shown. Your chart can have as many columns and rows as you want.
2. In the top row, write the topics that you want to compare.
3. In the left column, write characteristics of the topics that you want to compare. As you read the chapter, fill in the characteristics for each topic in the appropriate boxes.

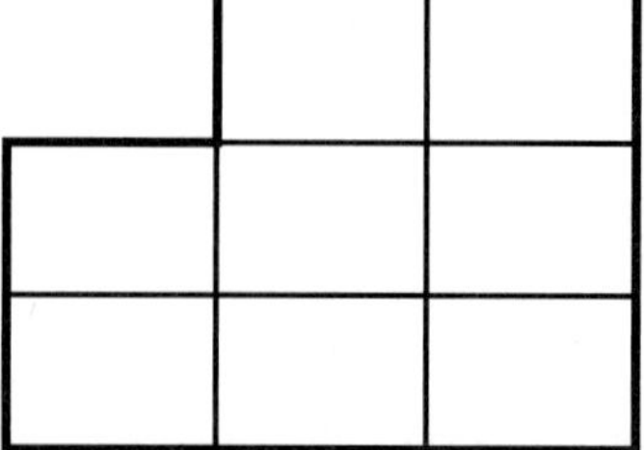

Chain-of-Events-Chart

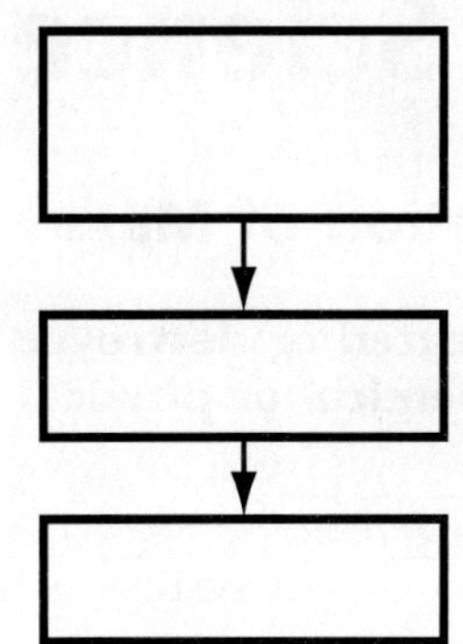

1. Draw a box. In the box, write the first step of a process or the first event of a timeline.
2. Under the box, draw another box, and use an arrow to connect the two boxes. In the second box, write the next step of the process or the next event in the timeline.
3. Continue adding boxes until the process or timeline is finished.

Concept Map

1. Draw a circle in the center of a piece of paper. Write the main idea of the chapter in the center of the circle.
2. From the circle, draw other circles. In those circles, write characteristics of the main idea. Draw arrows from the center circle to the circles that contain the characteristics.
3. From each circle that contains a characteristic, draw other circles. In those circles, write specific details about the characteristic. Draw arrows from each circle that contains a characteristic to the circles that contain specific details. You may draw as many circles as you want.

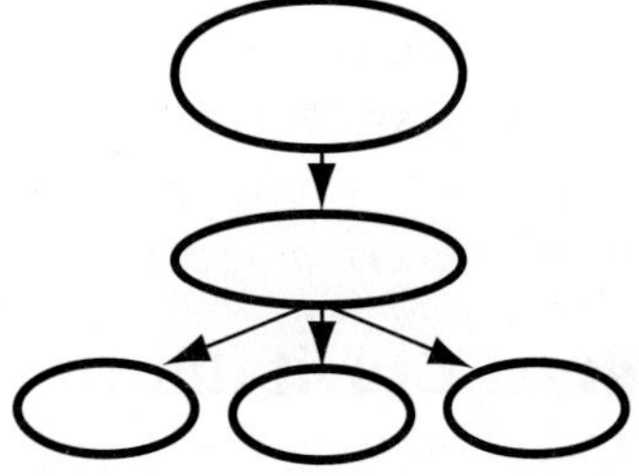

Physical Science Laws and Principles

Law of Conservation of Mass

Mass cannot be created or destroyed during ordinary chemical or physical changes.

The total mass in a closed system is always the same no matter how many physical changes or chemical reactions occur.

Law of Conservation of Energy

Energy can be neither created nor destroyed.

The total amount of energy in a closed system is always the same. Energy can be changed from one form to another, but all of the different forms of energy in a system always add up to the same total amount of energy no matter how many energy conversions occur.

Law of Universal Gravitation

All objects in the universe attract each other by a force called *gravity.* The size of the force depends on the masses of the objects and the distance between the objects.

The first part of the law explains why lifting a bowling ball is much harder than lifting a marble. Because the bowling ball has a much larger mass than the marble does, the amount of gravity between the Earth and the bowling ball is greater than the amount of gravity between the Earth and the marble.

The second part of the law explains why a satellite can remain in orbit around the Earth. The satellite is carefully placed at a distance great enough to prevent the Earth's gravity from immediately pulling the satellite down but small enough to prevent the satellite from completely escaping the Earth's gravity and wandering off into space.

Newton's Laws of Motion

Newton's first law of motion states that an object at rest remains at rest and an object in motion remains in motion at constant speed and in a straight line unless acted on by an unbalanced force.

The first part of the law explains why a football will remain on a tee until it is kicked off or until a gust of wind blows it off.

The second part of the law explains why a bike rider will continue moving forward after the bike comes to an abrupt stop. Gravity and the friction of the sidewalk will eventually stop the rider.

Newton's second law of motion states that the acceleration of an object depends on the mass of the object and the amount of force applied.

The first part of the law explains why the acceleration of a 4 kg bowling ball will be greater than the acceleration of a 6 kg bowling ball if the same force is applied to both balls.

The second part of the law explains why the acceleration of a bowling ball will be larger if a larger force is applied to the bowling ball.

The relationship of acceleration (a) to mass (m) and force (F) can be expressed mathematically by the following equation:

$$acceleration = \frac{force}{mass}, \text{ or } a = \frac{F}{m}$$

This equation is often rearranged to the form

$$force = mass \times acceleration, \text{ or } F = m \times a$$

Newton's third law of motion states that whenever one object exerts a force on a second object, the second object exerts an equal and opposite force on the first.

This law explains that a runner is able to move forward because of the equal and opposite force that the ground exerts on the runner's foot after each step.

Law of Reflection

The law of reflection states that the angle of incidence is equal to the angle of reflection. This law explains why light reflects off a surface at the same angle that the light strikes the surface.

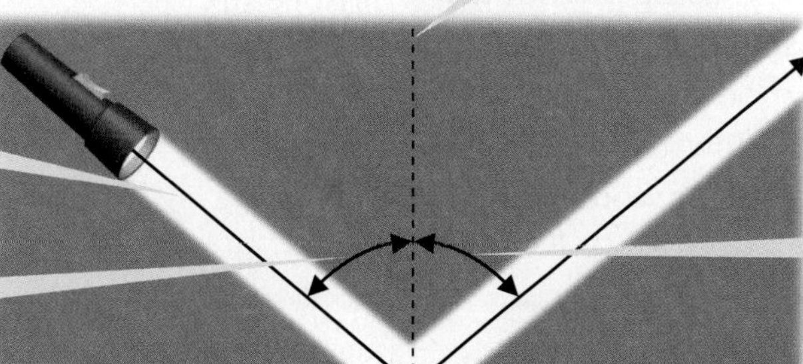
A line perpendicular to the mirror's surface is called the *normal.*
The beam of light reflected off the mirror is called the *reflected beam.*
The beam of light traveling toward the mirror is called the *incident beam.*
The angle between the incident beam and the normal is called the *angle of incidence.*
The angle between the reflected beam and the normal is called the *angle of reflection.*

Charles's Law

Charles's law states that for a fixed amount of gas at a constant pressure, the volume of the gas increases as the temperature of the gas increases. Likewise, the volume of the gas decreases as the temperature of the gas decreases.

If a basketball that was inflated indoors is left outside on a cold winter day, the air particles inside the ball will move more slowly. They will hit the sides of the basketball less often and with less force. The ball will get smaller as the volume of the air decreases.

Boyle's Law

Boyle's law states that for a fixed amount of gas at a constant temperature, the volume of a gas increases as the pressure of the gas decreases. Likewise, the volume of a gas decreases as its pressure increases.

If an inflated balloon is pulled down to the bottom of a swimming pool, the pressure of the water on the balloon increases. The pressure of the air particles inside the balloon must increase to match that of the water outside, so the volume of the air inside the balloon decreases.

Pascal's Principle

Pascal's principle states that a change in pressure at any point in an enclosed fluid will be transmitted equally to all parts of that fluid.

When a mechanic uses a hydraulic jack to raise an automobile off the ground, he or she increases the pressure on the fluid in the jack by pushing on the jack handle. The pressure is transmitted equally to all parts of the fluid-filled jacking system. As fluid presses the jack plate against the frame of the car, the car is lifed off the ground.

Archimedes' Principle

Archimedes' principle states that the buoyant force on an object in a fluid is equal to the weight of the volume of fluid that the object displaces.

A person floating in a swimming pool displaces 20 L of water. The weight of that volume of water is about 200 N. Therefore, the buoyant force on the person is 200 N.

Bernoulli's Principle

Bernoulli's principle states that as the speed of a moving fluid increases, the fluid's pressure decreases.

The lift on an airplane wing or on a Frisbee® can be explained in part by using Bernoulli's principle. Because of the shape of the Frisbee, the air moving over the top of the Frisbee must travel farther than the air below the Frisbee in the same amount of time. In other words, the air above the Frisbee is moving faster than the air below it. This faster-moving air above the Frisbee exerts less pressure than the slower-moving air below it does. The resulting increased pressure below exerts an upward force and pushes the Frisbee up.

Useful Equations

Average speed

$$\textit{average speed} = \frac{\textit{total distance}}{\textit{total time}}$$

Example: A bicycle messenger traveled a distance of 136 km in 8 h. What was the messenger's average speed?

$$\frac{136 \text{ km}}{8 \text{ h}} = 17 \text{ km/h}$$

The messenger's average speed was **17 km/h.**

Average acceleration

$$\textit{average acceleration} = \frac{\textit{final velocity} - \textit{starting velocity}}{\textit{time it takes to change velocity}}$$

Example: Calculate the average acceleration of an Olympic 100 m dash sprinter who reaches a velocity of 20 m/s south at the finish line. The race was in a straight line and lasted 10 s.

$$\frac{20 \text{ m/s} - 0 \text{ m/s}}{10\text{s}} = 2 \text{ m/s/s}$$

The sprinter's average acceleration is **2 m/s/s south.**

Net force

Forces in the Same Direction

When forces are in the same direction, add the forces together to determine the net force.

Example: Calculate the net force on a stalled car that is being pushed by two people. One person is pushing with a force of 13 N northwest, and the other person is pushing with a force of 8 N in the same direction.

$$13 \text{ N} + 8 \text{ N} = 21 \text{ N}$$

The net force is **21 N northwest.**

Forces in Opposite Directions

When forces are in opposite directions, subtract the smaller force from the larger force to determine the net force. The net force will be in the direction of the larger force.

Example: Calculate the net force on a rope that is being pulled on each end. One person is pulling on one end of the rope with a force of 12 N south. Another person is pulling on the opposite end of the rope with a force of 7 N north.

$$12 \text{ N} - 7 \text{ N} = 5 \text{ N}$$

The net force is **5 N south.**

Work

Work is done by exerting a force through a distance. Work has units of joules (J), which are equivalent to Newton-meters.

$$Work = F \times d$$

Example: Calculate the amount of work done by a man who lifts a 100 N toddler 1.5 m off the floor.

Work = 100 N × 1.5 m = 150 N•m = 150 J

The man did **150 J** of work.

Power

Power is the rate at which work is done. Power is measured in watts (W), which are equivalent to joules per second.

$$P = \frac{Work}{t}$$

Example: Calculate the power of a weightlifter who raises a 300 N barbell 2.1 m off the floor in 1.25 s.

Work = 300 N × 2.1 m = 630 N•m = 630 J

$$P = \frac{630\ J}{1.25\ s} = \frac{504\ J}{s} = 504\ W$$

The weightlifter has **504 W** of power.

Pressure

Pressure is the force exerted over a given area. The SI unit for pressure is the pascal (Pa).

$$pressure = \frac{force}{area}$$

Example: Calculate the pressure of the air in a soccer ball if the air exerts a force of 25,000 N over an area of 0.15 m^2.

$$pressure = \frac{25{,}000\ N}{0.15\ m^2} = \frac{167{,}000\ N}{m^2} = 167{,}000\ Pa$$

The pressure of the air inside the soccer ball is **167,000 Pa.**

Density

$$density = \frac{mass}{volume}$$

Example: Calculate the density of a sponge that has a mass of 10 g and a volume of 40 cm^3.

$$\frac{10\ g}{40\ cm^3} = \frac{0.25\ g}{cm^3}$$

The density of the sponge is $\mathbf{\frac{0.25\ g}{cm^3}}$.

Concentration

$$concentration = \frac{mass\ of\ solute}{volume\ of\ solvent}$$

Example: Calculate the concentration of a solution in which 10 g of sugar is dissolved in 125 mL of water.

$$\frac{10\ g\ of\ sugar}{125\ mL\ of\ water} = \frac{0.08\ g}{mL}$$

The concentration of this solution is $\mathbf{\frac{0.08\ g}{mL}}$.

Appendix

Math Refresher

Science requires an understanding of many math concepts. The following pages will help you review some important math skills.

Averages

An **average,** or **mean,** simplifies a set of numbers into a single number that *approximates* the value of the set.

Example: Find the average of the following set of numbers: 5, 4, 7, and 8.

Step 1: Find the sum.

$$5 + 4 + 7 + 8 = 24$$

Step 2: Divide the sum by the number of numbers in your set. Because there are four numbers in this example, divide the sum by 4.

$$\frac{24}{4} = 6$$

The average, or mean, is **6.**

Ratios

A **ratio** is a comparison between numbers, and it is usually written as a fraction.

Example: Find the ratio of thermometers to students if you have 36 thermometers and 48 students in your class.

Step 1: Make the ratio.

$$\frac{36 \text{ thermometers}}{48 \text{ students}}$$

Step 2: Reduce the fraction to its simplest form.

$$\frac{36}{48} = \frac{36 \div 12}{48 \div 12} = \frac{3}{4}$$

The ratio of thermometers to students is **3 to 4,** or $\frac{3}{4}$. The ratio may also be written in the form 3:4.

Proportions

A **proportion** is an equation that states that two ratios are equal.

$$\frac{3}{1} = \frac{12}{4}$$

To solve a proportion, first multiply across the equal sign. This is called *cross-multiplication*. If you know three of the quantities in a proportion, you can use cross-multiplication to find the fourth.

Example: Imagine that you are making a scale model of the solar system for your science project. The diameter of Jupiter is 11.2 times the diameter of the Earth. If you are using a plastic-foam ball that has a diameter of 2 cm to represent the Earth, what must the diameter of the ball representing Jupiter be?

$$\frac{11.2}{1} = \frac{x}{2 \text{ cm}}$$

Step 1: Cross-multiply.

$$\frac{11.2}{1} \times \frac{x}{2}$$

$$11.2 \times 2 = x \times 1$$

Step 2: Multiply.

$$22.4 = x \times 1$$

Step 3: Isolate the variable by dividing both sides by 1.

$$x = \frac{22.4}{1}$$

$$x = 22.4 \text{ cm}$$

You will need to use a ball that has a diameter of **22.4** cm to represent Jupiter.

Appendix

Percentages

A **percentage** is a ratio of a given number to 100.

Example: What is 85% of 40?

Step 1: Rewrite the percentage by moving the decimal point two places to the left.

0.85

Step 2: Multiply the decimal by the number that you are calculating the percentage of.

0.85 × 40 = 34

85% of 40 is **34.**

Decimals

To **add** or **subtract decimals,** line up the digits vertically so that the decimal points line up. Then, add or subtract the columns from right to left. Carry or borrow numbers as necessary.

Example: Add the following numbers: 3.1415 and 2.96.

Step 1: Line up the digits vertically so that the decimal points line up.

$$\begin{array}{r} 3.1415 \\ +\ 2.96 \\ \hline \end{array}$$

Step 2: Add the columns from right to left, and carry when necessary.

$$\begin{array}{r} {\scriptstyle 1\ 1} \\ 3.1415 \\ +\ 2.96 \\ \hline 6.1015 \end{array}$$

The sum is **6.1015.**

Fractions

Numbers tell you how many; **fractions** tell you *how much of a whole.*

Example: Your class has 24 plants. Your teacher instructs you to put 5 plants in a shady spot. What fraction of the plants in your class will you put in a shady spot?

Step 1: In the denominator, write the total number of parts in the whole.

$$\frac{?}{24}$$

Step 2: In the numerator, write the number of parts of the whole that are being considered.

$$\frac{5}{24}$$

So, $\mathbf{\frac{5}{24}}$ of the plants will be in the shade.

Reducing Fractions

It is usually best to express a fraction in its simplest form. Expressing a fraction in its simplest form is called *reducing* a fraction.

Example: Reduce the fraction $\frac{30}{45}$ to its simplest form.

Step 1: Find the largest whole number that will divide evenly into both the numerator and denominator. This number is called the *greatest common factor* (GCF).

Factors of the numerator 30:

1, 2, 3, 5, 6, 10, **15,** 30

Factors of the denominator 45:

1, 3, 5, 9, **15,** 45

Step 2: Divide both the numerator and the denominator by the GCF, which in this case is 15.

$$\frac{30}{45} = \frac{30 \div 15}{45 \div 15} = \frac{2}{3}$$

Thus, $\frac{30}{45}$ reduced to its simplest form is $\mathbf{\frac{2}{3}}$.

Appendix

Adding and Subtracting Fractions

To **add** or **subtract fractions** that have the **same denominator,** simply add or subtract the numerators.

Examples:

$$\frac{3}{5}+\frac{1}{5}=?\text{ and }\frac{3}{4}-\frac{1}{4}=?$$

Step 1: Add or subtract the numerators.

$$\frac{3}{5}+\frac{1}{5}=\frac{4}{}\text{ and }\frac{3}{4}-\frac{1}{4}=\frac{2}{}$$

Step 2: Write the sum or difference over the denominator.

$$\frac{3}{5}+\frac{1}{5}=\frac{4}{5}\text{ and }\frac{3}{4}-\frac{1}{4}=\frac{2}{4}$$

Step 3: If necessary, reduce the fraction to its simplest form.

$\mathbf{\frac{4}{5}}$ cannot be reduced, and $\frac{2}{4}=\mathbf{\frac{1}{2}}$.

To **add** or **subtract fractions** that have **different denominators,** first find the least common denominator (LCD).

Examples:

$$\frac{1}{2}+\frac{1}{6}=?\text{ and }\frac{3}{4}-\frac{2}{3}=?$$

Step 1: Write the equivalent fractions that have a common denominator.

$$\frac{3}{6}+\frac{1}{6}=?\text{ and }\frac{9}{12}-\frac{8}{12}=?$$

Step 2: Add or subtract the fractions.

$$\frac{3}{6}+\frac{1}{6}=\frac{4}{6}\text{ and }\frac{9}{12}-\frac{8}{12}=\frac{1}{12}$$

Step 3: If necessary, reduce the fraction to its simplest form.

The fraction $\frac{4}{6}=\mathbf{\frac{2}{3}}$, and $\mathbf{\frac{1}{12}}$ cannot be reduced.

Multiplying Fractions

To **multiply fractions,** multiply the numerators and the denominators together, and then reduce the fraction to its simplest form.

Example:

$$\frac{5}{9}\times\frac{7}{10}=?$$

Step 1: Multiply the numerators and denominators.

$$\frac{5}{9}\times\frac{7}{10}=\frac{5\times7}{9\times10}=\frac{35}{90}$$

Step 2: Reduce the fraction.

$$\frac{35}{90}=\frac{35\div5}{90\div5}=\mathbf{\frac{7}{18}}$$

Dividing Fractions

To **divide fractions,** first rewrite the divisor (the number you divide by) upside down. This number is called the *reciprocal* of the divisor. Then multiply and reduce if necessary.

Example:

$$\frac{5}{8}\div\frac{3}{2}=?$$

Step 1: Rewrite the divisor as its reciprocal.

$$\frac{3}{2}\rightarrow\frac{2}{3}$$

Step 2: Multiply the fractions.

$$\frac{5}{8}\times\frac{2}{3}=\frac{5\times2}{8\times3}=\frac{10}{24}$$

Step 3: Reduce the fraction.

$$\frac{10}{24}=\frac{10\div2}{24\div2}=\mathbf{\frac{5}{12}}$$

Appendix

Scientific Notation

Scientific notation is a short way of representing very large and very small numbers without writing all of the place-holding zeros.

Example: Write 653,000,000 in scientific notation.

Step 1: Write the number without the place-holding zeros.

653

Step 2: Place the decimal point after the first digit.

6.53

Step 3: Find the exponent by counting the number of places that you moved the decimal point.

6.53000000

The decimal point was moved eight places to the left. Therefore, the exponent of 10 is positive 8. If you had moved the decimal point to the right, the exponent would be negative.

Step 4: Write the number in scientific notation.

$\mathbf{6.53 \times 10^8}$

Area

Area is the number of square units needed to cover the surface of an object.

Formulas:

area of a square = side × side

area of a rectangle = length × width

area of a triangle $= \frac{1}{2} \times$ *base × height*

Examples: Find the areas.

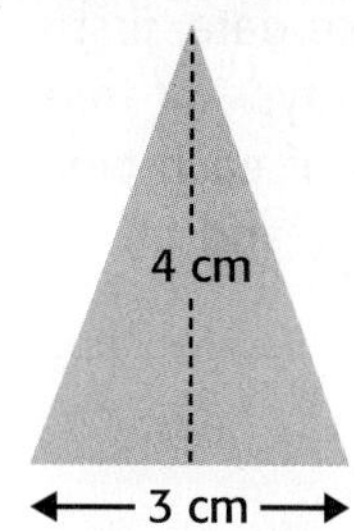

Triangle

area $= \frac{1}{2} \times$ *base × height*

area $= \frac{1}{2} \times 3 \text{ cm} \times 4 \text{ cm}$

area = $\mathbf{6\ cm^2}$

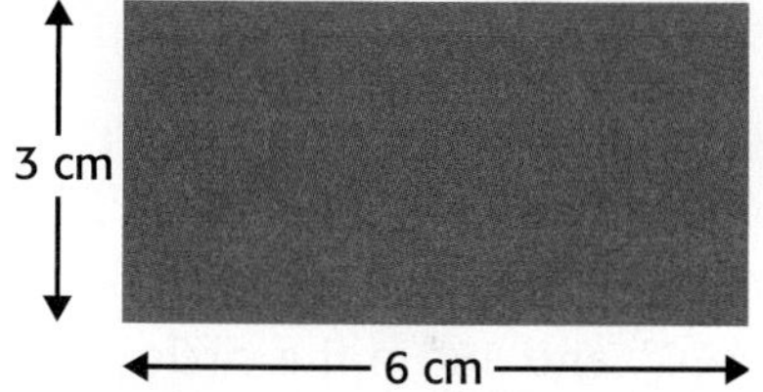

Rectangle

area = length × width

area = 6 cm × 3 cm

area = $\mathbf{18\ cm^2}$

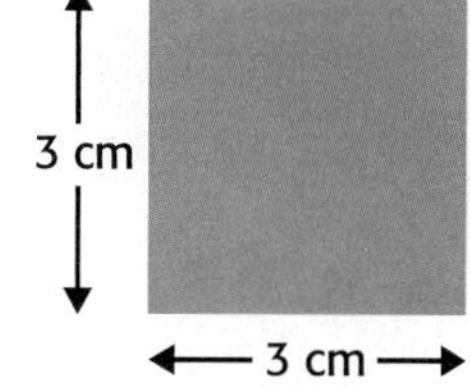

Square

area = side × side

area = 3 cm × 3 cm

area = $\mathbf{9\ cm^2}$

Volume

Volume is the amount of space that something occupies.

Formulas:

volume of a cube = side × side × side

volume of a prism = area of base × height

Examples:

Find the volume of the solids.

Cube

volume = side × side × side

volume = 4 cm × 4 cm × 4 cm

volume = $\mathbf{64\ cm^3}$

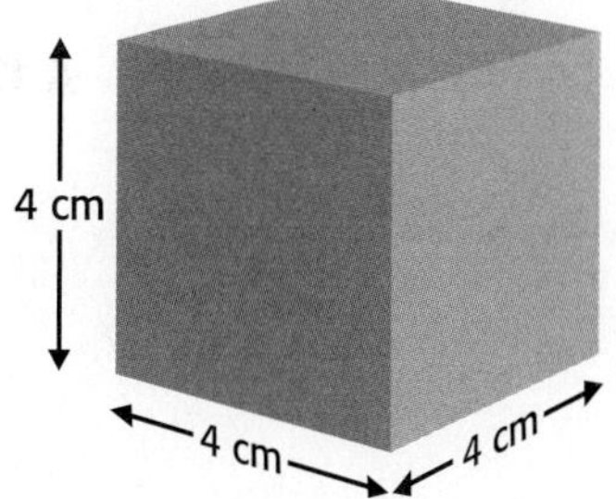

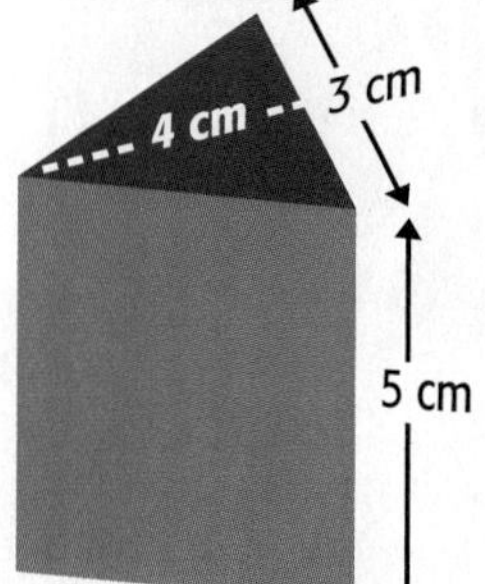

Prism

volume = area of base × height

volume = (area of triangle) × height

volume $= (\frac{1}{2} \times 3 \text{ cm} \times 4 \text{ cm}) \times 5 \text{ cm}$

volume $= 6 \text{ cm}^2 \times 5 \text{ cm}$

volume = $\mathbf{30\ cm^3}$

Appendix

Making Charts and Graphs

Pie Charts

A pie chart shows how each group of data relates to all of the data. Each part of the circle forming the chart represents a category of the data. The entire circle represents all of the data. For example, a biologist studying a hardwood forest in Wisconsin found that there were five different types of trees. The data table at right summarizes the biologist's findings.

Wisconsin Hardwood Trees	
Type of tree	**Number found**
Oak	600
Maple	750
Beech	300
Birch	1,200
Hickory	150
Total	3,000

How to Make a Pie Chart

1. To make a pie chart of these data, first find the percentage of each type of tree. Divide the number of trees of each type by the total number of trees, and multiply by 100.

$$\frac{600 \text{ oak}}{3{,}000 \text{ trees}} \times 100 = 20\%$$

$$\frac{750 \text{ maple}}{3{,}000 \text{ trees}} \times 100 = 25\%$$

$$\frac{300 \text{ beech}}{3{,}000 \text{ trees}} \times 100 = 10\%$$

$$\frac{1{,}200 \text{ birch}}{3{,}000 \text{ trees}} \times 100 = 40\%$$

$$\frac{150 \text{ hickory}}{3{,}000 \text{ trees}} \times 100 = 5\%$$

2. Now, determine the size of the wedges that make up the pie chart. Multiply each percentage by 360°. Remember that a circle contains 360°.

$20\% \times 360° = 72°$ $\quad 25\% \times 360° = 90°$

$10\% \times 360° = 36°$ $\quad 40\% \times 360° = 144°$

$5\% \times 360° = 18°$

3. Check that the sum of the percentages is 100 and the sum of the degrees is 360.

$20\% + 25\% + 10\% + 40\% + 5\% = 100\%$

$72° + 90° + 36° + 144° + 18° = 360°$

4. Use a compass to draw a circle and mark the center of the circle.
5. Then, use a protractor to draw angles of 72°, 90°, 36°, 144°, and 18° in the circle.
6. Finally, label each part of the chart, and choose an appropriate title.

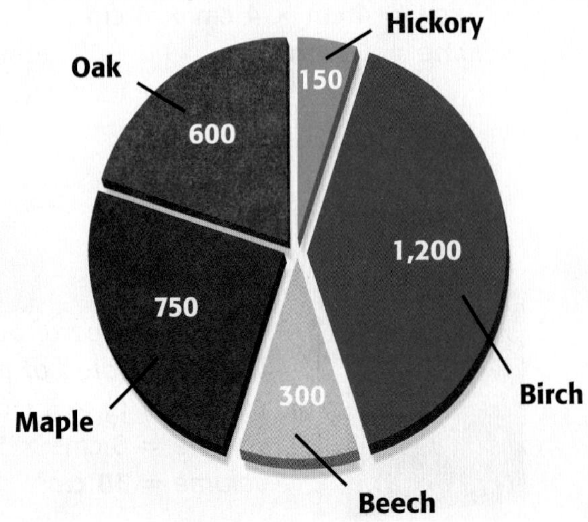

Line Graphs

Line graphs are most often used to demonstrate continuous change. For example, Mr. Smith's students analyzed the population records for their hometown, Appleton, between 1900 and 2000. Examine the data at right.

Because the year and the population change, they are the *variables*. The population is determined by, or dependent on, the year. Therefore, the population is called the **dependent variable,** and the year is called the **independent variable.** Each set of data is called a **data pair.** To prepare a line graph, you must first organize data pairs into a table like the one at right.

Population of Appleton, 1900–2000

Year	Population
1900	1,800
1920	2,500
1940	3,200
1960	3,900
1980	4,600
2000	5,300

How to Make a Line Graph

1. Place the independent variable along the horizontal (*x*) axis. Place the dependent variable along the vertical (*y*) axis.
2. Label the *x*-axis "Year" and the *y*-axis "Population." Look at your largest and smallest values for the population. For the *y*-axis, determine a scale that will provide enough space to show these values. You must use the same scale for the entire length of the axis. Next, find an appropriate scale for the *x*-axis.
3. Choose reasonable starting points for each axis.
4. Plot the data pairs as accurately as possible.
5. Choose a title that accurately represents the data.

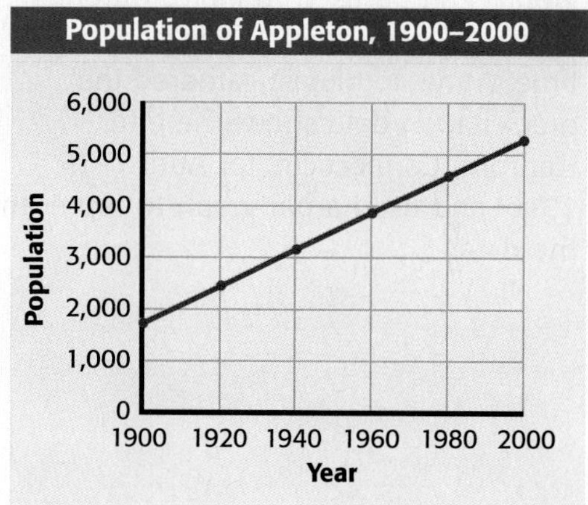

How to Determine Slope

Slope is the ratio of the change in the *y*-value to the change in the *x*-value, or "rise over run."

1. Choose two points on the line graph. For example, the population of Appleton in 2000 was 5,300 people. Therefore, you can define point *a* as (2000, 5,300). In 1900, the population was 1,800 people. You can define point *b* as (1900, 1,800).
2. Find the change in the *y*-value.
(*y* at point *a*) − (*y* at point *b*) =
5,300 people − 1,800 people =
3,500 people
3. Find the change in the *x*-value.
(*x* at point *a*) − (*x* at point *b*) =
2000 − 1900 = 100 years
4. Calculate the slope of the graph by dividing the change in *y* by the change in *x*.

$$slope = \frac{change\ in\ y}{change\ in\ x}$$

$$slope = \frac{3{,}500\ \text{people}}{100\ \text{years}}$$

$$slope = 35\ \text{people per year}$$

In this example, the population in Appleton increased by a fixed amount each year. The graph of these data is a straight line. Therefore, the relationship is **linear.** When the graph of a set of data is not a straight line, the relationship is **nonlinear.**

Using Algebra to Determine Slope

The equation in step 4 may also be arranged to be

$$y = kx$$

where y represents the change in the y-value, k represents the slope, and x represents the change in the x-value.

$$slope = \frac{change\ in\ y}{change\ in\ x}$$

$$k = \frac{y}{x}$$

$$k \times x = \frac{y \times x}{x}$$

$$kx = y$$

Bar Graphs

Bar graphs are used to demonstrate change that is not continuous. These graphs can be used to indicate trends when the data cover a long period of time. A meteorologist gathered the precipitation data shown here for Hartford, Connecticut, for April 1–15, 1996, and used a bar graph to represent the data.

Precipitation in Hartford, Connecticut April 1–15, 1996

Date	Precipitation (cm)	Date	Precipitation (cm)
April 1	0.5	April 9	0.25
April 2	1.25	April 10	0.0
April 3	0.0	April 11	1.0
April 4	0.0	April 12	0.0
April 5	0.0	April 13	0.25
April 6	0.0	April 14	0.0
April 7	0.0	April 15	6.50
April 8	1.75		

How to Make a Bar Graph

1. Use an appropriate scale and a reasonable starting point for each axis.
2. Label the axes, and plot the data.
3. Choose a title that accurately represents the data.

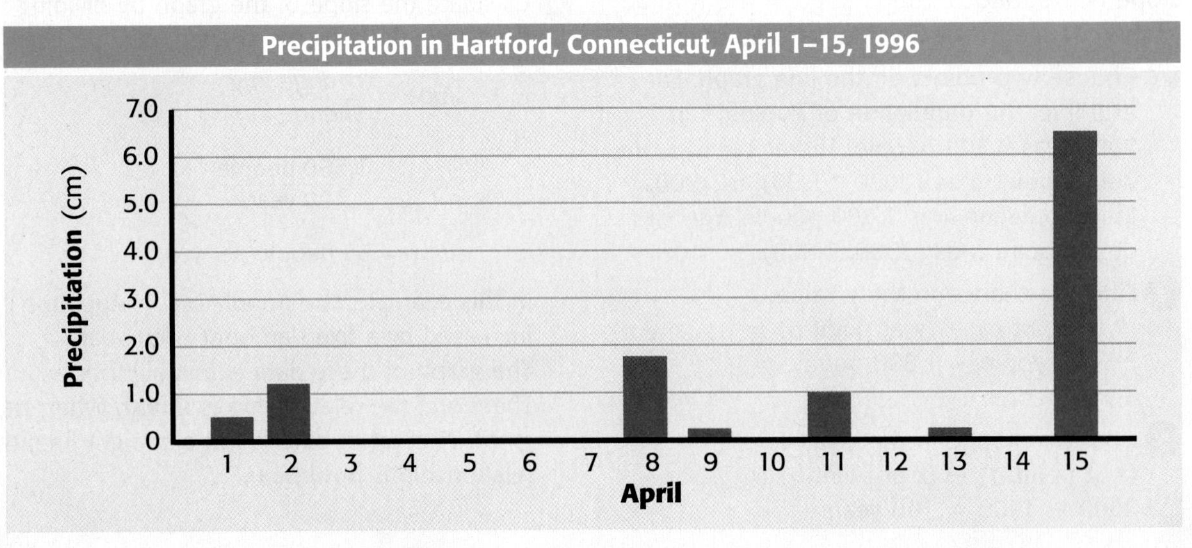

Measuring Skills

Using a Graduated Cylinder

When using a graduated cylinder to measure volume, keep the following procedures in mind:

1. Place the cylinder on a flat, level surface before measuring liquid.
2. Move your head so that your eye is level with the surface of the liquid.
3. Read the mark closest to the liquid level. On glass graduated cylinders, read the mark closest to the center of the curve in the liquid's surface.

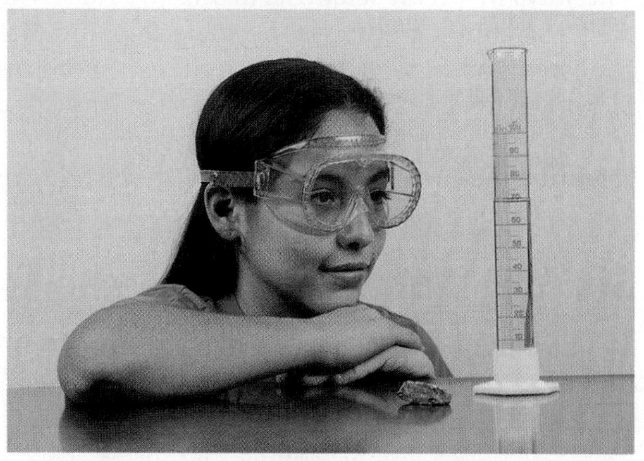

Using a Meterstick or Metric Ruler

When using a meterstick or metric ruler to measure length, keep the following procedures in mind:

1. Place the ruler firmly against the object that you are measuring.
2. Align one edge of the object exactly with the 0 end of the ruler.
3. Look at the other edge of the object to see which of the marks on the ruler is closest to that edge. (Note: Each small slash between the centimeters represents a millimeter, which is one-tenth of a centimeter.)

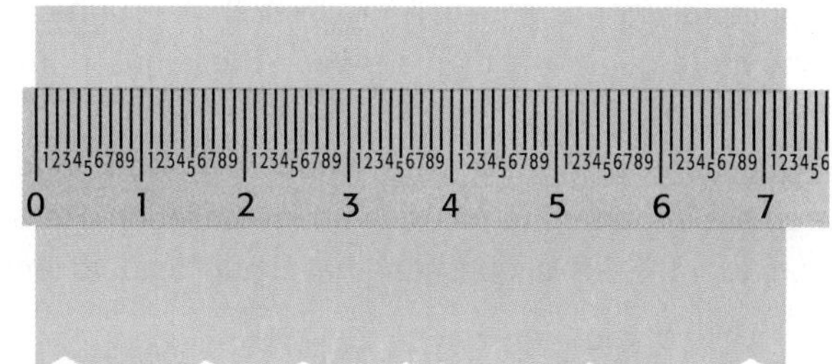

Using a Triple-Beam Balance

When using a triple-beam balance to measure mass, keep the following procedures in mind:

1. Make sure the balance is on a level surface.
2. Place all of the countermasses at 0. Adjust the balancing knob until the pointer rests at 0.
3. Place the object you wish to measure on the pan. **Caution:** Do not place hot objects or chemicals directly on the balance pan.
4. Move the largest countermass along the beam to the right until it is at the last notch that does not tip the balance. Follow the same procedure with the next-largest countermass. Then, move the smallest countermass until the pointer rests at 0.
5. Add the readings from the three beams together to determine the mass of the object.
6. When determining the mass of crystals or powders, first find the mass of a piece of filter paper. Then, add the crystals or powder to the paper, and remeasure. The actual mass of the crystals or powder is the total mass minus the mass of the paper. When finding the mass of liquids, first find the mass of the empty container. Then, find the combined mass of the liquid and container. The mass of the liquid is the total mass minus the mass of the container.

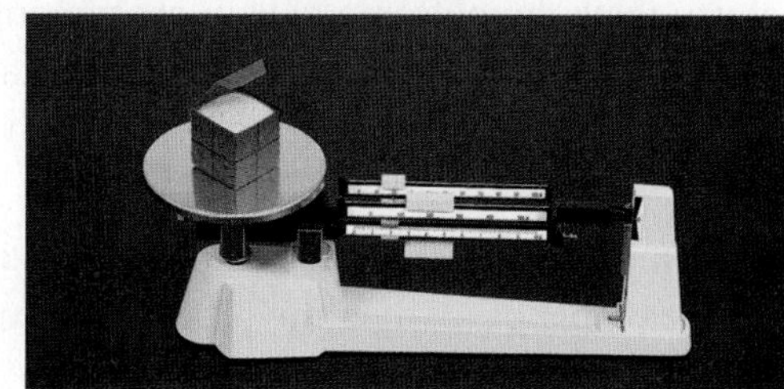

Scientific Methods

The ways in which scientists answer questions and solve problems are called **scientific methods.** The same steps are often used by scientists as they look for answers. However, there is more than one way to use these steps. Scientists may use all of the steps or just some of the steps during an investigation. They may even repeat some of the steps. The goal of using scientific methods is to come up with reliable answers and solutions.

Six Steps of Scientific Methods

Good questions come from careful **observations.** You make observations by using your senses to gather information. Sometimes, you may use instruments, such as microscopes and telescopes, to extend the range of your senses. As you observe the natural world, you will discover that you have many more questions than answers. These questions drive investigations.

Questions beginning with *what, why, how,* and *when* are important in focusing an investigation. Here is an example of a question that could lead to an investigation.

Question: How does acid rain affect plant growth?

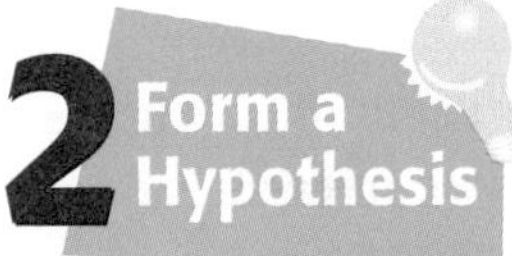

After you ask a question, you need to form a **hypothesis.** A hypothesis is a clear statement of what you expect the answer to your question to be. Your hypothesis will represent your best "educated guess" based on what you have observed and what you already know. A good hypothesis is testable. Otherwise, the investigation can go no further. Here is a hypothesis based on the question, "How does acid rain affect plant growth?"

Hypothesis: Acid rain slows plant growth.

The hypothesis can lead to predictions. A prediction is what you think the outcome of your experiment or data collection will be. Predictions are usually stated in an if-then format. Here is a sample prediction for the hypothesis that acid rain slows plant growth.

Prediction: If a plant is watered with only acid rain (which has a pH of 4), then the plant will grow at half its normal rate.

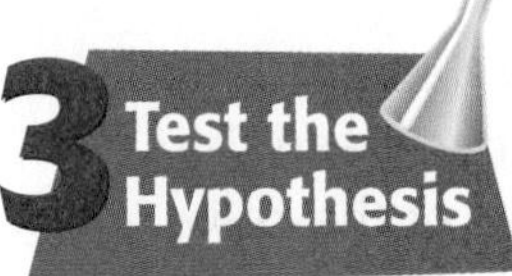

After you have formed a hypothesis and made a prediction, your hypothesis should be tested. One way to test a hypothesis is with a controlled experiment. A **controlled experiment** tests only one factor at a time. In an experiment to test the effect of acid rain on plant growth, the **control group** would be watered with normal rain water. The **experimental group** would be watered with acid rain. All of the plants should receive the same amount of sunlight and water each day. The air temperature should be the same for all groups. However, the acidity of the water will be a variable. In fact, any factor that is different from one group to another is a **variable.** If your hypothesis is correct, then the acidity of the water and plant growth are *dependant variables.* The amount a plant grows is dependent on the acidity of the water. However, the amount of water each plant receives and the amount of sunlight each plant receives are *independent variables.* Either of these factors could change without affecting the other factor.

Sometimes, the nature of an investigation makes a controlled experiment impossible. For example, the Earth's core is surrounded by thousands of meters of rock. Under such circumstances, a hypothesis may be tested by making detailed observations.

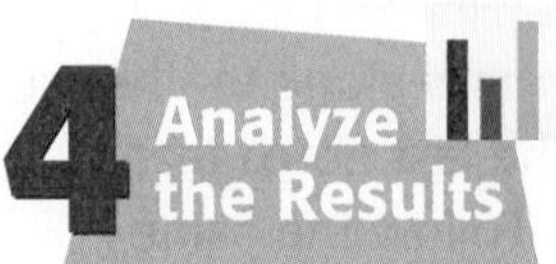

After you have completed your experiments, made your observations, and collected your data, you must analyze all the information you have gathered. Tables and graphs are often used in this step to organize the data.

Appendix

After analyzing your data, you can determine if your results support your hypothesis. If your hypothesis is supported, you (or others) might want to repeat the observations or experiments to verify your results. If your hypothesis is not supported by the data, you may have to check your procedure for errors. You may even have to reject your hypothesis and make a new one. If you cannot draw a conclusion from your results, you may have to try the investigation again or carry out further observations or experiments.

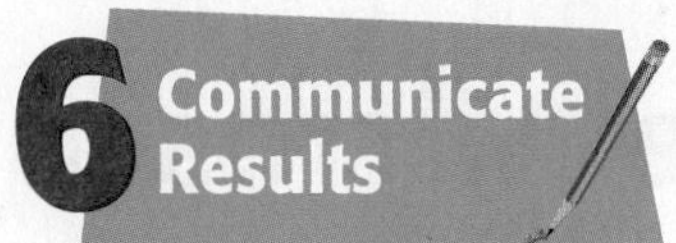

After any scientific investigation, you should report your results. By preparing a written or oral report, you let others know what you have learned. They may repeat your investigation to see if they get the same results. Your report may even lead to another question and then to another investigation.

Scientific Methods in Action

Scientific methods contain loops in which several steps may be repeated over and over again. In some cases, certain steps are unnecessary. Thus, there is not a "straight line" of steps. For example, sometimes scientists find that testing one hypothesis raises new questions and new hypotheses to be tested. And sometimes, testing the hypothesis leads directly to a conclusion. Furthermore, the steps in scientific methods are not always used in the same order. Follow the steps in the diagram, and see how many different directions scientific methods can take you.

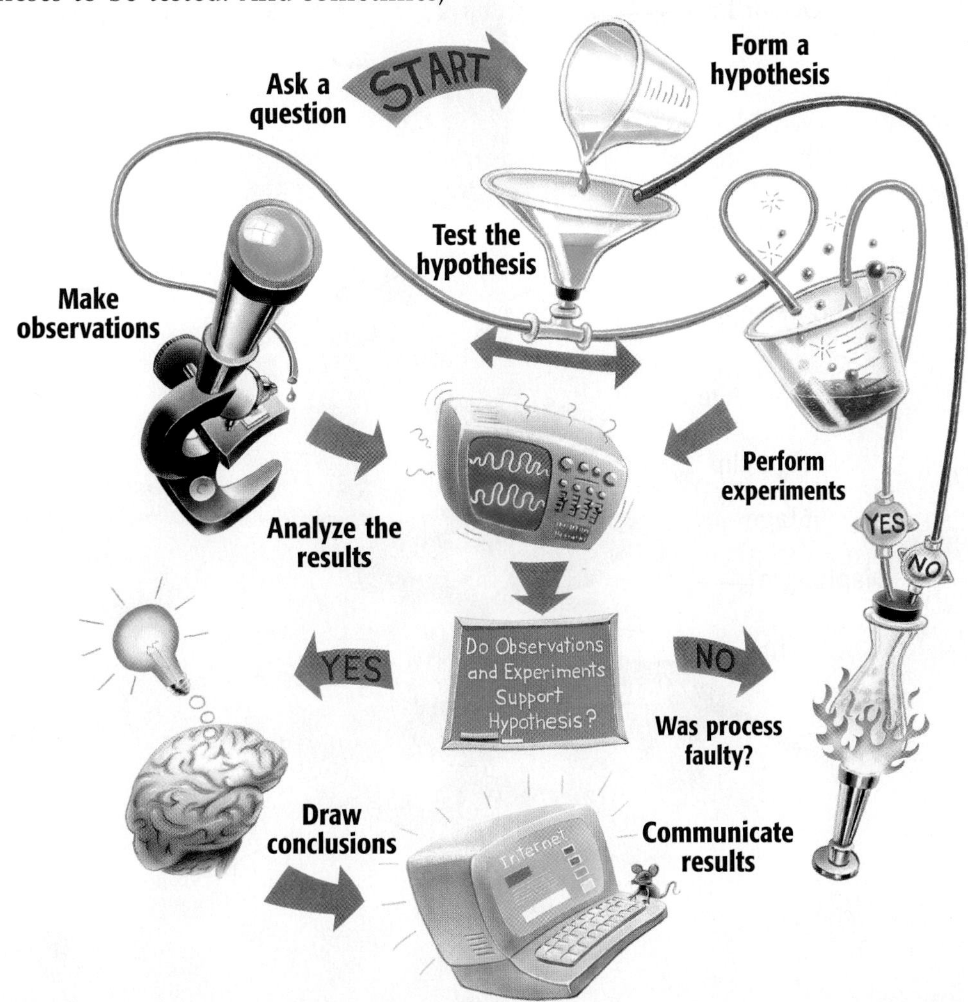

Appendix

Using the Microscope

Parts of the Compound Light Microscope

- The **ocular lens** magnifies the image 10×.
- The **low-power objective** magnifies the image 10×.
- The **high-power objective** magnifies the image either 40× or 43×.
- The **revolving nosepiece** holds the objectives and can be turned to change from one magnification to the other.
- The **body tube** maintains the correct distance between the ocular lens and objectives.
- The **coarse-adjustment knob** moves the body tube up and down to allow focusing of the image.
- The **fine-adjustment knob** moves the body tube slightly to bring the image into sharper focus. It is usually located in the center of the coarse-adjustment knob.
- The **stage** supports a slide.
- **Stage clips** hold the slide in place for viewing.
- The **diaphragm** controls the amount of light coming through the stage.
- The light source provides a **light** for viewing the slide.
- The **arm** supports the body tube.
- The **base** supports the microscope.

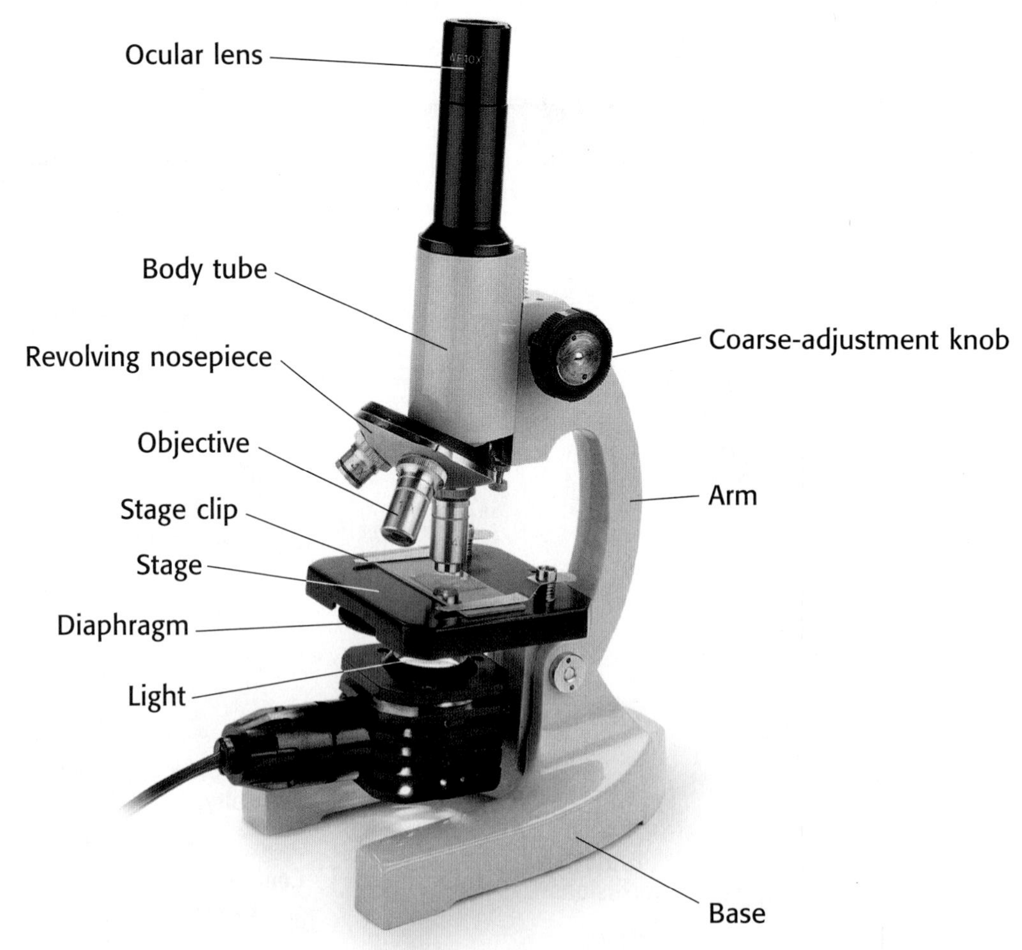

Appendix

Proper Use of the Compound Light Microscope

1. Use both hands to carry the microscope to your lab table. Place one hand beneath the base, and use the other hand to hold the arm of the microscope. Hold the microscope close to your body while carrying it to your lab table.
2. Place the microscope on the lab table at least 5 cm from the edge of the table.
3. Check to see what type of light source is used by your microscope. If the microscope has a lamp, plug it in and make sure that the cord is out of the way. If the microscope has a mirror, adjust the mirror to reflect light through the hole in the stage. **Caution:** If your microscope has a mirror, do not use direct sunlight as a light source. Direct sunlight can damage your eyes.
4. Always begin work with the low-power objective in line with the body tube. Adjust the revolving nosepiece.
5. Place a prepared slide over the hole in the stage. Secure the slide with the stage clips.
6. Look through the ocular lens. Move the diaphragm to adjust the amount of light coming through the stage.
7. Look at the stage from eye level. Slowly turn the coarse adjustment to lower the objective until the objective almost touches the slide. Do not allow the objective to touch the slide.
8. Look through the ocular lens. Turn the coarse adjustment to raise the low-power objective until the image is in focus. Always focus by raising the objective away from the slide. Never focus the objective downward. Use the fine adjustment to sharpen the focus. Keep both eyes open while viewing a slide.
9. Make sure that the image is exactly in the center of your field of vision. Then, switch to the high-power objective. Focus the image by using only the fine adjustment. Never use the coarse adjustment at high power.
10. When you are finished using the microscope, remove the slide. Clean the ocular lens and objectives with lens paper. Return the microscope to its storage area. Remember to use both hands when carrying the microscope.

Making a Wet Mount

1. Use lens paper to clean a glass slide and a coverslip.
2. Place the specimen that you wish to observe in the center of the slide.
3. Using a medicine dropper, place one drop of water on the specimen.
4. Hold the coverslip at the edge of the water and at a 45° angle to the slide. Make sure that the water runs along the edge of the coverslip.
5. Lower the coverslip slowly to avoid trapping air bubbles.
6. Water might evaporate from the slide as you work. Add more water to keep the specimen fresh. Place the tip of the medicine dropper next to the edge of the coverslip. Add a drop of water. (You can also use this method to add stain or solutions to a wet mount.) Remove excess water from the slide by using the corner of a paper towel as a blotter. Do not lift the coverslip to add or remove water.

SI Measurement

The International System of Units, or SI, is the standard system of measurement used by many scientists. Using the same standards of measurement makes it easier for scientists to communicate with one another.

SI works by combining prefixes and base units. Each base unit can be used with different prefixes to define smaller and larger quantities. The table below lists common SI prefixes.

SI Prefixes

Prefix	Symbol	Factor	Example
kilo-	k	1,000	kilogram, 1 kg = 1,000 g
hecto-	h	100	hectoliter, 1 hL = 100 L
deka-	da	10	dekameter, 1 dam = 10 m
		1	meter, liter, gram
deci-	d	0.1	decigram, 1 dg = 0.1 g
centi-	c	0.01	centimeter, 1 cm = 0.01 m
milli-	m	0.001	milliliter, 1 mL = 0.001 L
micro-	*μ*	0.000 001	micrometer, 1 *μ*m = 0.000 001 m

SI Conversion Table

SI units	From SI to English	From English to SI
Length		
kilometer (km) = 1,000 m	1 km = 0.621 mi	1 mi = 1.609 km
meter (m) = 100 cm	1 m = 3.281 ft	1 ft = 0.305 m
centimeter (cm) = 0.01 m	1 cm = 0.394 in.	1 in. = 2.540 cm
millimeter (mm) = 0.001 m	1 mm = 0.039 in.	
micrometer (*μ*m) = 0.000 001 m		
nanometer (nm) = 0.000 000 001 m		
Area		
square kilometer (km^2) = 100 hectares	1 km^2 = 0.386 mi^2	1 mi^2 = 2.590 km^2
hectare (ha) = 10,000 m^2	1 ha = 2.471 acres	1 acre = 0.405 ha
square meter (m^2) = 10,000 cm^2	1 m^2 = 10.764 ft^2	1 ft^2 = 0.093 m^2
square centimeter (cm^2) = 100 mm^2	1 cm^2 = 0.155 $in.^2$	1 $in.^2$ = 6.452 cm^2
Volume		
liter (L) = 1,000 mL = 1 dm^3	1 L = 1.057 fl qt	1 fl qt = 0.946 L
milliliter (mL) = 0.001 L = 1 cm^3	1 mL = 0.034 fl oz	1 fl oz = 29.574 mL
microliter (*μ*L) = 0.000 001 L		
Mass		*Equivalent weight at Earth's surface
kilogram (kg) = 1,000 g	1 kg = 2.205 lb*	1 lb* = 0.454 kg
gram (g) = 1,000 mg	1 g = 0.035 oz*	1 oz* = 28.350 g
milligram (mg) = 0.001 g		
microgram (*μ*g) = 0.000 001 g		

Temperature Scales

Temperature can be expressed by using three different scales: Fahrenheit, Celsius, and Kelvin. The SI unit for temperature is the kelvin (K).

Although 0 K is much colder than 0°C, a change of 1 K is equal to a change of 1°C.

Three Temperature Scales

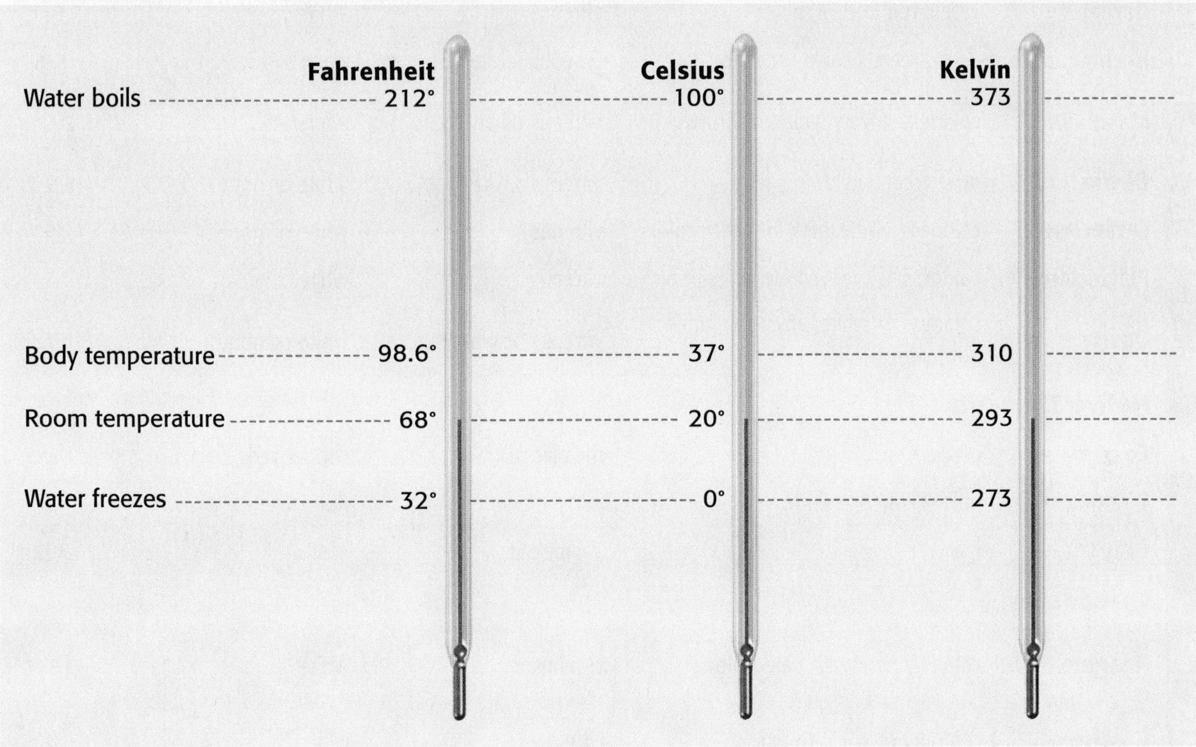

	Fahrenheit	Celsius	Kelvin
Water boils	212°	100°	373
Body temperature	98.6°	37°	310
Room temperature	68°	20°	293
Water freezes	32°	0°	273

Temperature Conversions Table

To convert	Use this equation:	Example
Celsius to Fahrenheit °C → °F	$°F = \left(\frac{9}{5} \times °C\right) + 32$	Convert 45°C to °F. $°F = \left(\frac{9}{5} \times 45°C\right) + 32 = 113°F$
Fahrenheit to Celsius °F → °C	$°C = \frac{5}{9} \times (°F - 32)$	Convert 68°F to °C. $°C = \frac{5}{9} \times (68°F - 32) = 20°C$
Celsius to Kelvin °C → K	$K = °C + 273$	Convert 45°C to K. $K = 45°C + 273 = 318\ K$
Kelvin to Celsius K → °C	$°C = K - 273$	Convert 32 K to °C. $°C = 32K - 273 = -241°C$

Appendix

Properties of Common Minerals

	Mineral	Color	Luster	Streak	Hardness
Silicate Minerals	**Beryl**	deep green, pink, white, bluish green, or yellow	vitreous	white	7.5–8
	Chlorite	green	vitreous to pearly	pale green	2–2.5
	Garnet	green, red, brown, black	vitreous	white	6.5–7.5
	Hornblende	dark green, brown, or black	vitreous	none	5–6
	Muscovite	colorless, silvery white, or brown	vitreous or pearly	white	2–2.5
	Olivine	olive green, yellow	vitreous	white or none	6.5–7
	Orthoclase	colorless, white, pink, or other colors	vitreous	white or none	6
	Plagioclase	colorless, white, yellow, pink, green	vitreous	white	6
	Quartz	colorless or white; any color when not pure	vitreous or waxy	white or none	7
Nonsilicate Minerals	**Native Elements**				
	Copper	copper-red	metallic	copper-red	2.5–3
	Diamond	pale yellow or colorless	adamantine	none	10
	Graphite	black to gray	submetallic	black	1–2
	Carbonates				
	Aragonite	colorless, white, or pale yellow	vitreous	white	3.5–4
	Calcite	colorless or white to tan	vitreous	white	3
	Halides				
	Fluorite	light green, yellow, purple, bluish green, or other colors	vitreous	none	4
	Halite	white	vitreous	white	2.0–2.5
	Oxides				
	Hematite	reddish brown to black	metallic to earthy	dark red to red-brown	5.6–6.5
	Magnetite	iron-black	metallic	black	5.5–6.5
	Sulfates				
	Anhydrite	colorless, bluish, or violet	vitreous to pearly	white	3–3.5
	Gypsum	white, pink, gray, or colorless	vitreous, pearly, or silky	white	2.0
	Sulfides				
	Galena	lead-gray	metallic	lead-gray to black	2.5–2.8
	Pyrite	brassy yellow	metallic	greenish, brownish, or black	6–6.5

Appendix

Density (g/cm^3)	Cleavage, Fracture, Special Properties	Common Uses
2.6–2.8	1 cleavage direction; irregular fracture; some varieties fluoresce in ultraviolet light	gemstones, ore of the metal beryllium
2.6–3.3	1 cleavage direction; irregular fracture	
4.2	no cleavage; conchoidal to splintery fracture	gemstones, abrasives
3.0–3.4	2 cleavage directions; hackly to splintery fracture	
2.7–3	1 cleavage direction; irregular fracture	electrical insulation, wallpaper, fireproofing material, lubricant
3.2–3.3	no cleavage; conchoidal fracture	gemstones, casting
2.6	2 cleavage directions; irregular fracture	porcelain
2.6–2.7	2 cleavage directions; irregular fracture	ceramics
2.6	no cleavage; conchoidal fracture	gemstones, concrete, glass, porcelain, sandpaper, lenses
8.9	no cleavage; hackly fracture	wiring, brass, bronze, coins
3.5	4 cleavage directions; irregular to conchoidal fracture	gemstones, drilling
2.3	1 cleavage direction; irregular fracture	pencils, paints, lubricants, batteries
2.95	2 cleavage directions; irregular fracture; reacts with hydrochloric acid	no important industrial uses
2.7	3 cleavage directions; irregular fracture; reacts with weak acid; double refraction	cements, soil conditioner, whitewash, construction materials
3.0–3.3	4 cleavage directions; irregular fracture; some varieties fluoresce	hydrofluoric acid, steel, glass, fiberglass, pottery, enamel
2.1–2.2	3 cleavage directions; splintery to conchoidal fracture; salty taste	tanning hides, salting icy roads, food preservation
5.2–5.3	no cleavage; splintery fracture; magnetic when heated	iron ore for steel, pigments
5.2	no cleavage; splintery fracture; magnetic	iron ore
3.0	3 cleavage directions; conchoidal to splintery fracture	soil conditioner, sulfuric acid
2.3	3 cleavage directions; conchoidal to splintery fracture	plaster of Paris, wallboard, soil conditioner
7.4–7.6	3 cleavage directions; irregular fracture	batteries, paints
5	no cleavage; conchoidal to splintery fracture	sulfuric acid

Sky Maps

Spring

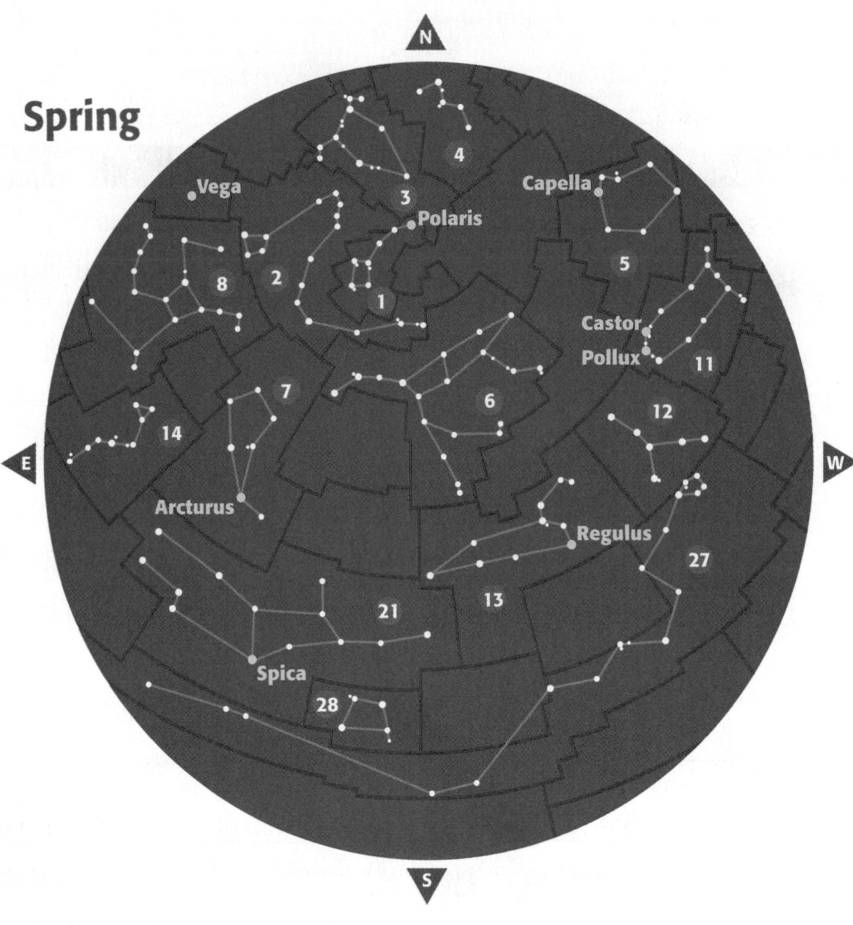

Summer

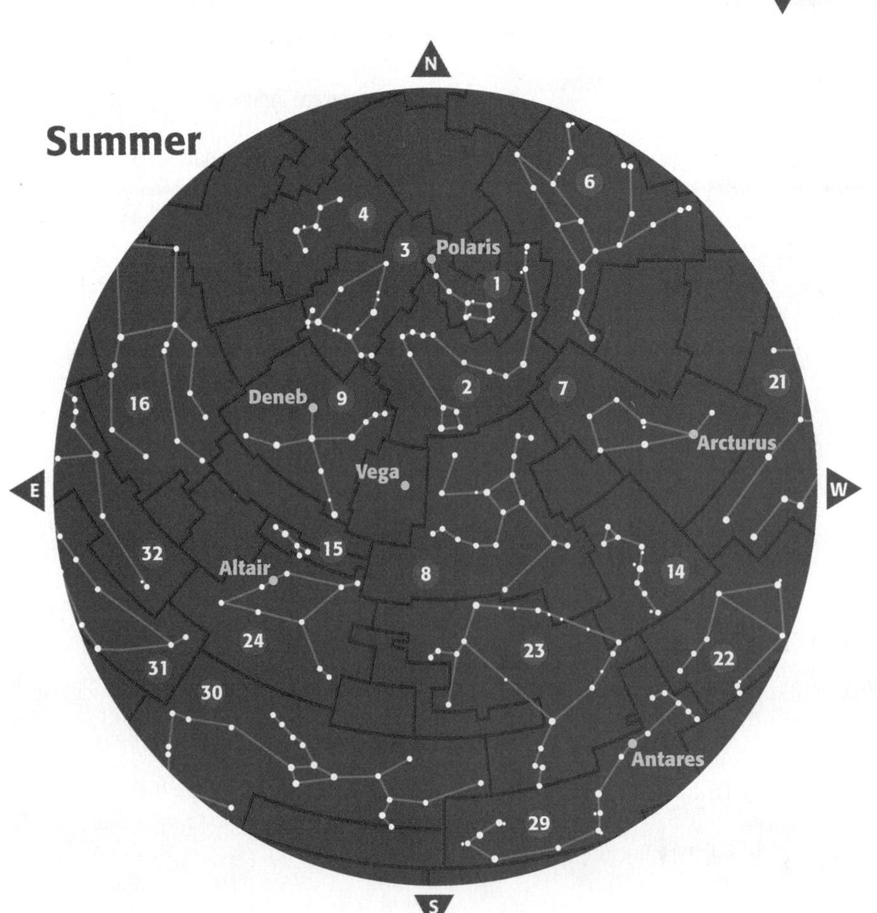

Constellations

1 Ursa Minor
2 Draco
3 Cepheus
4 Cassiopeia
5 Auriga
6 Ursa Major
7 Bootes
8 Hercules
9 Cygnus
10 Perseus
11 Gemini
12 Cancer
13 Leo
14 Serpens
15 Sagitta
16 Pegasus
17 Pisces

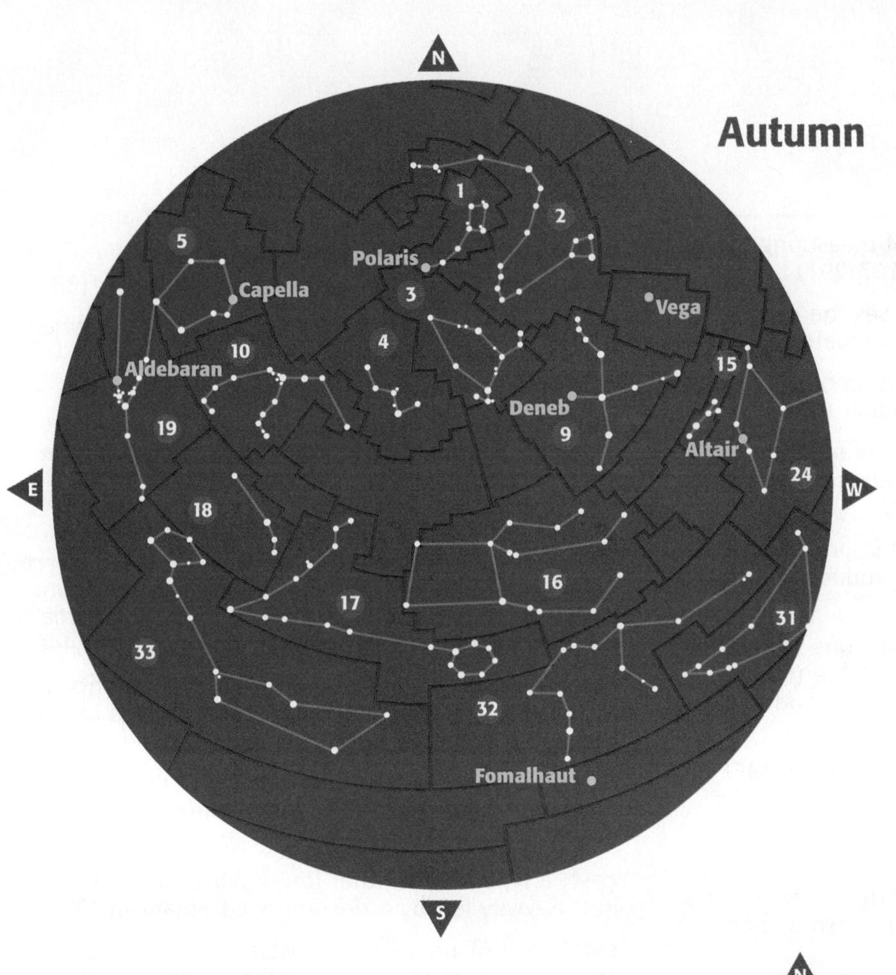

Constellations

18 Aries
19 Taurus
20 Orion
21 Virgo
22 Libra
23 Ophiuchus
24 Aquila
25 Lepus
26 Canis Major
27 Hydra
28 Corvus
29 Scorpius
30 Sagittarius
31 Capricornus
32 Aquarius
33 Cetus
34 Columba

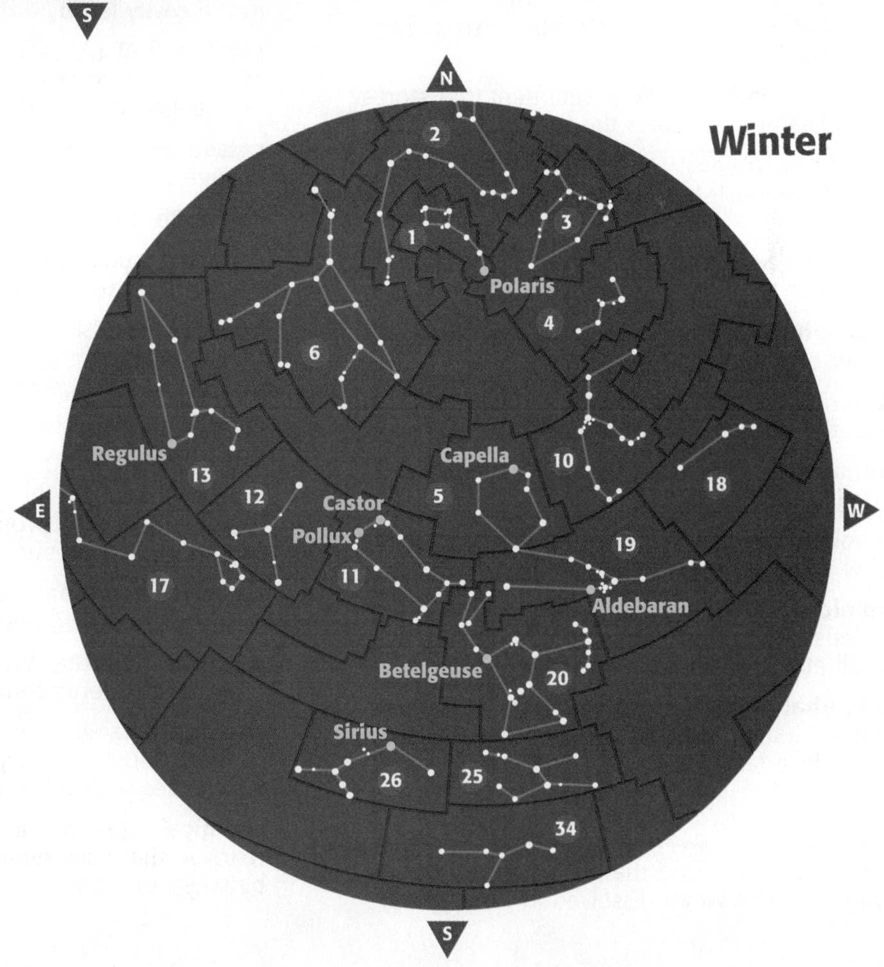

Glossary

A

absolute dating any method of measuring the age of an event or object in years (167, 291)

acid any compound that increases the number of hydronium ions when dissolved in water (654)

activation energy the minimum amount of energy required to start a chemical reaction (636)

active transport the movement of substances across the cell membrane that requires the cell to use energy (42)

adaptation a characteristic that improves an individual's ability to survive and reproduce in a particular environment (139)

alkali metal (AL kuh LIE MET uhl) one of the elements of Group 1 of the periodic table (lithium, sodium, potassium, rubidium, cesium, and francium) (577)

alkaline-earth metal (AL kuh LIEN UHRTH MET uhl) one of the elements of Group 2 of the periodic table (beryllium, magnesium, calcium, strontium, barium, and radium) (577)

allele (uh LEEL) one of the alternative forms of a gene that governs a characteristic, such as hair color (92)

aquifer a body of rock or sediment that stores groundwater and allows the flow of groundwater (361)

area a measure of the size of a surface or a region (24)

asthenosphere the soft layer of the mantle on which the tectonic plates move (381)

atmosphere a mixture of gases that surrounds a planet or moon (347)

atom the smallest unit of an element that maintains the properties of that element (545)

atomic mass the mass of an atom expressed in atomic mass units (555)

atomic mass unit a unit of mass that describes the mass of an atom or molecule (551)

atomic number the number of protons in the nucleus of an atom; the atomic number is the same for all atoms of an element (553)

azimuthal projection (az uh MYOOTH uhl proh JEK shuhn) a map projection that is made by moving the surface features of the globe onto a plane (205)

B

base any compound that increases the number of hydroxide ions when dissolved in water (657)

biome a large region characterized by a specific type of climate and certain types of plant and animal communities (318)

biosphere the part of Earth where life exists (347)

boiling the conversion of a liquid to a vapor when the vapor pressure of the liquid equals the atmospheric pressure (504)

Boyle's law the law that states that the volume of a gas is inversely proportional to the pressure of a gas when temperature is constant (500)

C

caldera a large, semicircular depression that forms when the magma chamber below a volcano partially empties and causes the ground above to sink (446)

carbohydrate a class of energy-giving nutrients that includes sugars, starches, and fiber; contains carbon, hydrogen, and oxygen (667)

carbon cycle the movement of carbon from the nonliving environment into living things and back (367)

cast a type of fossil that forms when sediments fill in the cavity left by a decomposed organism (296)

catalyst (KAT uh LIST) a substance that changes the rate of a chemical reaction without being used up or changed very much (638)

catastrophism a principle that states that geologic change occurs suddenly (281)

cell cycle the life cycle of a cell (48)

cellular respiration the process by which cells use oxygen to produce energy from food (45, 63)

Cenozoic era (SEN uh ZOH ik ER uh) the most recent geologic era, beginning 65 million years ago; also called the *Age of Mammals* (177)

change of state the change of a substance from one physical state to another (502)

Charles's law the law that states that the volume of a gas is directly proportional to the temperature of a gas when pressure is constant (500)

chemical bond an interaction that holds atoms or ions together (597, 650)

chemical bonding the combining of atoms to form molecules or ionic compounds (597)

chemical change a change that occurs when one or more substances change into entirely new substances with different properties (481)

chemical equation a representation of a chemical reaction that uses symbols to show the relationship between the reactants and the products (626)

chemical formula a combination of chemical symbols and numbers to represent a substance (624)

chemical property a property of matter that describes a substance's ability to participate in chemical reactions (478)

chemical reaction the process by which one or more substances change to produce one or more different substances (620)

chlorophyll (KLAWR uh FIL) a green pigment that captures light energy for photosynthesis (63)

chromosome in a eukaryotic cell, one of the structures in the nucleus that are made up of DNA and protein; in a prokaryotic cell, the main ring of DNA (48)

cleavage the splitting of a mineral along smooth, flat surfaces (229)

colloid (KAHL OYD) a mixture consisting of tiny particles that are intermediate in size between those in solutions and those in suspensions and that are suspended in a liquid, solid, or gas (532)

composition the chemical makeup of a rock; describes either the minerals or other materials in the rock (253)

compound a substance made up of atoms of two or more different elements joined by chemical bonds (225, 523)

compression stress that occurs when forces act to squeeze an object (395)

concentration the amount of a particular substance in a given quantity of a mixture, solution, or ore (530)

condensation the change of state from a gas to a liquid (505)

conduction the transfer of energy as heat through a material (355)

conic projection a map projection that is made by moving the surface features of the globe onto a cone (204)

continental drift the hypothesis that states that the continents once formed a single landmass, broke up, and drifted to their present locations (387)

contour interval the difference in elevation between one contour line and the next (211)

contour line a line that connects points of equal elevation (210)

controlled experiment an experiment that tests only one factor at a time by using a comparison of a control group with an experimental group (14)

convection the transfer of thermal energy by the circulation or movement of a liquid or gas (355)

convergent boundary the boundary formed by the collision of two lithospheric plates (391)

core the central part of the Earth below the mantle (347, 379)

covalent bond (koh VAY luhnt BAHND) a bond formed when atoms share one or more pairs of electrons (604)

covalent compound a chemical compound that is formed by the sharing of electrons (652)

crater a funnel-shaped pit near the top of the central vent of a volcano (446)

crust the thin and solid outermost layer of the Earth above the mantle (347, 379)

crystal a solid whose atoms, ions, or molecules are arranged in a definite pattern (225)

crystal lattice (KRIS tuhl LAT is) the regular pattern in which a crystal is arranged (603)

cylindrical projection (suh LIN dri kuhl proh JEK shuhn) a map projection that is made by moving the surface features of the globe onto a cylinder (203)

cytokinesis the division of the cytoplasm of a cell (50)

D

decomposition reaction a reaction in which a single compound breaks down to form two or more simpler substances (631)

deep current a streamlike movement of ocean water far below the surface (359)

deep-water zone the zone of a lake or pond below the open-water zone, where no light reaches (333)

deformation the bending, tilting, and breaking of the Earth's crust; the change in the shape of rock in response to stress (413)

density the ratio of the mass of a substance to the volume of the substance (26, 230, 473)

deoxyribonucleic acid (DNA), a molecule that is present in all living cells and that contains the information that determines the traits that a living thing inherits and needs to live (116)

deposition the process in which material is laid down (249)

desert an area that has little or no plant life, long periods without rain, and extreme temperatures; usually found in hot climates (323)

diamond is the hardest material known. It is used as a jewel and on cutting tools, such as saws, drills, and files (579)

diffusion (di FYOO zhuhn) the movement of particles from regions of higher density to regions of lower density (40)

divergent boundary the boundary between two tectonic plates that are moving away from each other (391)

dominant trait the trait observed in the first generation when parents that have different traits are bred (89)

dormant describes the inactive state of a seed or other plant part when conditions are unfavorable to growth (68)

double-displacement reaction a reaction in which a gas, a solid precipitate, or a molecular compound forms from the exchange of ions between two compounds (633)

E

elastic rebound the sudden return of elastically deformed rock to its undeformed shape (413)

electron a subatomic particle that has a negative charge (546)

electron cloud a region around the nucleus of an atom where electrons are likely to be found (548)

element a substance that cannot be separated or broken down into simpler substances by chemical means (225, 519)

elevation the height of an object above sea level (210)

endocytosis (EN doh sie TOH sis) the process by which a cell membrane surrounds a particle and encloses the particle in a vesicle to bring the particle into the cell (42)

endothermic reaction a chemical reaction that requires heat (635)

eon (EE AHN) the largest division of geologic time (303)

epicenter the point on Earth's surface directly above an earthquake's starting point, or focus (418)

epoch (EP uhk) a subdivision of a geologic period (303)

equator the imaginary circle halfway between the poles that divides the Earth into the Northern and Southern Hemispheres (199)

era a unit of geologic time that includes two or more periods (303)

erosion the process by which wind, water, ice, or gravity transports soil and sediment from one location to another (249, 350)

estuary (ES tyoo er ee) an area where fresh water from rivers mixes with salt water from the ocean (330)

evaporation (ee vap uh RAY shuhn) the change of a substance from a liquid to a gas (504)

evolution the process in which inherited characteristics within a population change over generations such that new species sometimes arise (139)

exocytosis (EK soh sie TOH sis) the process in which a cell releases a particle by enclosing the particle in a vesicle that then moves to the cell surface and fuses with the cell membrane (43)

exothermic reaction a chemical reaction in which heat is released to the surroundings (635)

extinct describes a species that has died out completely (169)

extinction the death of every member of a species (303)

extrusive igneous rock rock that forms as a result of volcanic activity at or near the Earth's surface (259)

F

fault a break in a body of rock along which one block slides relative to another (396)

fermentation the breakdown of food without the use of oxygen (45)

focus the point along a fault at which the first motion of an earthquake occurs (418)

folding the bending of rock layers due to stress (395)

foliated describes the texture of metamorphic rock in which the mineral grains are arranged in planes or bands (267)

fossil the trace or remains of an organism that lived long ago, most commonly preserved in sedimentary rock (140, 166, 295)

fossil record a historical sequence of life indicated by fossils found in layers of the Earth's crust (140)

fracture the manner in which a mineral breaks along either curved or irregular surfaces (229)

G

gap hypothesis a hypothesis that is based on the idea that a major earthquake is more likely to occur along the part of an active fault where no earthquakes have occurred for a certain period of time (423)

gas a form of matter that does not have a definite volume or shape (496)

gene one set of instructions for an inherited trait (92)

generation time the period between the birth of one generation and the birth of the next generation (153)

genotype the entire genetic makeup of an organism; also the combination of genes for one or more specific traits (93)

geologic column an arrangement of rock layers in which the oldest rocks are at the bottom (285)

geologic time scale the standard method used to divide the Earth's long natural history into manageable parts (169, 303)

geosphere the mostly solid, rocky part of the Earth; extends from the center of the core to the surface of the crust (347)

group a vertical column of elements in the periodic table; elements in a group share chemical properties (574)

H

half-life the time needed for half of a sample of a radioactive substance to undergo radioactive decay (291, 685)

halogen (HAL oh juhn) one of the elements of Group 17 of the periodic table (fluorine, chlorine, bromine, iodine, and statine); halogens combine with most metals to form salts (581)

hardness a measure of the ability of a mineral to resist scratching (230)

heredity the passing of genetic traits from parent to offspring (86)

hominid a type of primate characterized by bipedalism, relatively long lower limbs, and lack of a tail; examples include humans and their ancestors (179)

Homo sapiens (HOH moh SAY pee UHNZ) the species of hominids that includes modern humans and their closest ancestors and that first appeared about 100,000 to 150,000 years ago (182)

homologous chromosomes (hoh MAHL uh guhs KROH muh SOHMZ) chromosomes that have the same sequence of genes and the same structure (49, 98)

hot spot a volcanically active area of Earth's surface far from a tectonic plate boundary (452)

hydrocarbon an organic compound composed only of carbon and hydrogen (665)

hydrosphere (347)

hypothesis (hie PAHTH uh sis) an explanation that is based on prior scientific research or observations and that can be tested (12)

I

index contour on a map, a darker, heavier contour line that is usually every fifth line and that indicates a change in elevation (211)

index fossil a fossil that is found in the rock layers of only one geologic age and that is used to establish the age of the rock layers (298)

indicator a compound that can reversibly change color depending on conditions such as pH (655)

inertia (in UHR shuh) the tendency of an object to resist being moved or, if the object is moving, to resist a change in speed or direction until an outside force acts on the object (470)

inhibitor a substance that slows down or stops a chemical reaction (638)

intrusive igneous rock rock formed from the cooling and solidification of magma beneath the Earth's surface (258)

ion a charged particle that forms when an atom or group of atoms gains or loses one or more electrons (600)

ionic bond (ie AHN ik BAHND) a bond that forms when electrons are transferred from one atom to another, which results in a positive ion and a negative ion (600)

ionic compound a compound made of oppositely charged ions (650)

isotope (IE suh TOHP) an atom that has the same number of protons (or the same atomic number) as other atoms of the same element do but that has a different number of neutrons (and thus a different atomic mass) (291, 553, 682)

L

latitude the distance north or south from the equator; expressed in degrees (199)

lava plateau a wide, flat landform that results from repeated nonexplosive eruptions of lava that spread over a large area (447)

law a summary of many experimental results and observations; a law tells how things work (20)

law of conservation of energy the law that states that energy cannot be created or destroyed but can be changed from one form to another (635)

law of conservation of mass the law that states that mass cannot be created or destroyed in ordinary chemical and physical changes (627)

lipid a type of biochemical that does not dissolve in water; fats and steroids are lipids (667)

liquid the state of matter that has a definite volume but not a definite shape (496)

lithosphere the solid, outer layer of the Earth that consists of the crust and the rigid upper part of the mantle (381)

littoral zone (LIT uh ruhl ZOHN) the shallow zone of a lake or pond where light reaches the bottom and nurtures plants (333)

longitude the distance east and west from the prime meridian; expressed in degrees (200)

luster the way in which a mineral reflects light (228)

M

magma chamber the body of molten rock that feeds a volcano (440)

magnetic declination the difference between the magnetic north and the true north (198)

mantle the layer of rock between the Earth's crust and core (347, 379)

map a representation of the features of a physical body such as Earth (196)

marsh a treeless wetland ecosystem where plants such as grasses grow (334)

mass a measure of the amount of matter in an object (25, 469)

mass number the sum of the numbers of protons and neutrons in the nucleus of an atom (554, 681)

matter anything that has mass and takes up space (466)

meiosis (mie OH sis) a process in cell division during which the number of chromosomes decreases to half the original number by two divisions of the nucleus, which results in the production of sex cells (gametes or spores) (98)

melting the change of state in which a solid becomes a liquid by adding heat (503)

meniscus (muh NIS kuhs) the curve at a liquid's surface by which one measures the volume of the liquid (467)

mesosphere the strong, lower part of the mantle between the asthenosphere and the outer core (193); *also* the layer of the atmosphere between the stratosphere and the thermosphere and in which temperature decreases as altitude increases (381)

Mesozoic era (MES oh ZOH ik ER uh) the geologic era that lasted from 248 million to 65 million years ago; also called the *Age of Reptiles* (175)

metal an element that is shiny and that conducts heat and electricity well (520, 521)

metallic bond a bond formed by the attraction between positively charged metal ions and the electrons around them (607)

metalloid elements that have properties of both metals and nonmetals (520, 521)

meter the basic unit of length in the SI (symbol, m) (24)

mineral a class of nutrients that are chemical elements that are needed for certain body processes (225)

mitosis in eukaryotic cells, a process of cell division that forms two new nuclei, each of which has the same number of chromosomes (49)

mixture a combination of two or more substances that are not chemically combined (526)

model a pattern, plan, representation, or description designed to show the structure or workings of an object, system, or concept (18)

mold a mark or cavity made in a sedimentary surface by a shell or other body (296)

molecule (MAHL i KYOOL) the smallest unit of a substance that keeps all of the physical and chemical properties of that substance (605)

mutation a change in the nucleotide-base sequence of a gene or DNA molecule (124)

N

natural selection the process by which individuals that are better adapted to their environment survive and reproduce more successfully than less well adapted individuals do; a theory to explain the mechanism of evolution (150)

neutralization reaction (NOO truhl i ZA shuhn ree AK shuhn) the reaction of an acid and a base to form a neutral solution of water and a salt (661)

neutron a subatomic particle that has no charge and that is found in the nucleus of an atom (551)

nitrogen cycle the process in whichh nitrogen circulates among the air, soil, water, plants, and animals in an ecosystem (367)

noble gas one of the elements of Group 18 of the periodic table (helium, neon, argon, krypton, xenon, and radon); noble gases are unreactive (582)

nonfoliated describes the texture of metamorphic rock in which the mineral grains are not arranged in planes or bands (268)

nonmetal an element that conducts heat and electricity poorly (520, 521)

nonsilicate mineral a mineral that does not contain compounds of silicon and oxygen (226)

nuclear fission (NOO klee uhr FISH uhn) the splitting of the nucleus of a large atom into two or more fragments; releases additional neutrons and energy (689)

nuclear fusion (NOO klee uhr FYOO zhuhn) the combination of the nuclei of small atoms to form a larger nucleus; releases energy (692)

nucleic acid (noo KLEE ik AS id) a molecule made up of subunits called *nucleotides* (668)

nucleotide in a nucleic-acid chain, a subunit that consists of a sugar, a phosphate, and a nitrogenous base (116)

nucleus (NOO klee uhs) in physical science, an atom's central region, which is made up of protons and neutrons (548)

open-water zone the zone of a pond or lake that extends from the littoral zone and that is only as deep as light can reach (333)

ore a natural material whose concentration of economically valuable minerals is high enough for the material to be mined profitably (234)

organic compound a covalently bonded compound that contains carbon (665)

osmosis (ahs MOH sis) the diffusion of water through a semipermeable membrane (41)

P

paleontology the scientific study of fossils (283)

Paleozoic era (PAY lee OH ZOH ik ER uh) the geologic era that followed Precambrian time and that lasted from 543 million to 248 million years ago (174)

passive transport the movement of substances across a cell membrane without the use of energy by the cell (42)

pedigree a diagram that shows the occurrence of a genetic trait in several generations of a family (104)

period a unit of geologic time into which eras are divided (303)

period in chemistry, a horizontal row of elements in the periodic table (574)

periodic describes something that occurs or repeats at regular intervals (569)

periodic law the law that states that the repeating chemical and physical properties of elements change periodically with the atomic numbers of the elements (569)

pH a value that is used to express the acidity or basicity (alkalinity) of a system (661)

phenotype (FEE noh TIEP) an organism's appearance or other detectable characteristic (92)

photosynthesis (FOHT oh SIN thuh sis) the process by which plants, algae, and some bacteria use sunlight, carbon dioxide, and water to make food (44, 63)

physical change a change of matter from one form to another without a change in chemical properties (476)

physical property a characteristic of a substance that does not involve a chemical change, such as density, color, or hardness (473)

plankton the mass of mostly microscopic organisms that float or drift freely in freshwater and marine environments (326)

plate tectonics the theory that explains how large pieces of the Earth's outermost layer, called *tectonic plates*, move and change shape (170, 391)

Precambrian time (pree KAM bree uhn TIEM) the period in the geologic time scale from the formation of the Earth to the beginning of the Paleozoic era, from about 4.6 billion to 543 million years ago (172)

precipitate (pree SIP uh TAYT) a solid that is produced as a result of a chemical reaction in solution (621)

pressure the amount of force exerted per unit area of a surface (499)

primate a type of mammal characterized by opposable thumbs and binocular vision (178)

prime meridian the meridian, or line of longitude, that is designated as 0° longitude (200)

probability the likelihood that a possible future event will occur in any given instance of the event (94)

product a substance that forms in a chemical reaction (626)

protein a molecule that is made up of amino acids and that is needed to build and repair body structures and to regulate processes in the body (667)

proton a subatomic particle that has a positive charge and that is found in the nucleus of an atom (551)

pure substance a sample of matter, either a single element or a single compound, that has definite chemical and physical properties (519)

P wave a seismic wave that causes particles of rock to move in a back-and-forth direction (416)

R

radiation the transfer of energy as electromagnetic waves (355)

radioactive decay the process in which a radioactive isotope tends to break down into a stable isotope of the same element or another element (291)

radioactivity the process by which an unstable nucleus gives off nuclear radiation (681)

radiometric dating a method of determining the age of an object by estimating the relative percentages of a radioactive (parent) isotope and a stable (daughter) isotope (291)

reactant (ree AK tuhnt) a substance or molecule that participates in a chemical reaction (626)

recessive trait a trait that is apparent only when two recessive alleles for the same characteristic are inherited (89)

reclamation the process of returning land to its original condition after mining is completed (235)

relative dating any method of determining whether an event or object is older or younger than other events or objects (167, 285)

relief the variations in elevation of a land surface (211)

remote sensing the process of gathering and analyzing information about an object without physically being in touch with the object (207)

ribosome a cell organelle composed of RNA and protein; the site of protein synthesis (123)

rift zone an area of deep cracks that forms between two tectonic plates that are pulling away from each other (450)

ribonucleic acid (RNA), a molecule that is present in all living cells and that plays a role in protein production (122)

rock a naturally occurring solid mixture of one or more minerals or organic matter (249)

rock cycle the series of processes in which a rock forms, changes from one type to another, is destroyed, and forms again by geological processes (249, 365)

S

salt an ionic compound that forms when a metal atom replaces the hydrogen of an acid (663)

savanna a grassland that often has scattered trees and that is found in tropical and subtropical areas where seasonal rains, fires, and drought happen (322)

science the knowledge obtained by observing natural events and conditions in order to discover facts and formulate laws or principles that can be verified or tested (4)

scientific methods a series of steps followed to solve problems (10)

sea-floor spreading the process by which new oceanic lithosphere forms as magma rises toward the surface and solidifies (388)

seismic gap an area along a fault where relatively few earthquakes have occurred recently but where strong earthquakes have occurred in the past (423)

seismic wave a wave of energy that travels through the Earth and away from an earthquake in all directions (416)

seismogram a tracing of earthquake motion that is created by a seismograph (418)

seismograph an instrument that records vibrations in the ground and determines the location and strength of an earthquake (418)

seismology (siez MAHL uh jee) the study of earthquakes (413)

selective breeding the human practice of breeding animals or plants that have certain desired traits (148)

sex chromosome one of the pair of chromosomes that determine the sex of an individual (103)

silicate mineral a mineral that contains a combination of silicon, oxygen, and one or more metals (226)

single-displacement reaction a reaction in which one element takes the place of another element in a compound (631)

solid the state of matter in which the volume and shape of a substance are fixed (495)

solubility the ability of one substance to dissolve in another at a given temperature and pressure (530)

solute in a solution, the substance that dissolves in the solvent (528)

solution a homogeneous mixture of two or more substances uniformly dispersed throughout a single phase (528)

solvent in a solution, the substance in which the solute dissolves (528)

soot is formed from burning oil, coal, and wood and is used as a pigment in paints and crayons (579)

speciation (SPEE shee AY shuhn) the formation of new species as a result of evolution (154)

species a group of organisms that are closely related and can mate to produce fertile offspring (139)

states of matter the physical forms of matter, which include solid, liquid, and gas (495)

stoma one of many openings in a leaf or a stem of a plant that enable gas exchange to occur (plural, *stomata*) (64)

strata layers of rock (singular, *stratum*) (261)

stratification the process in which sedimentary rocks are arranged in layers (263)

streak the color of the powder of a mineral (229)

sublimation (SUHB luh MAY shuhn) the process in which a solid changes directly into a gas (506)

subsidence (suhb SIED'ns) the sinking of regions of the Earth's crust to lower elevations (400)

superposition a principle that states that younger rocks lie above older rocks if the layers have not been disturbed (285)

surface current a horizontal movement of ocean water that is caused by wind and that occurs at or near the ocean's surface (359)

surface tension the force that acts on the surface of a liquid and that tends to minimize the area of the surface (496)

suspension a mixture in which particles of a material are more or less evenly dispersed throughout a liquid or gas (532)

swamp a wetland ecosystem in which shrubs and trees grow (334)

S wave a seismic wave that causes particles of rock to move in a side-by-side direction (416)

synthesis reaction (SIN thuh sis ree AK shuhn) a reaction in which two or more substances combine to form a new compound (630)

T

tectonic plate a block of lithosphere that consists of the crust and the rigid, outermost part of the mantle (382)

temperature a measure of how hot (or cold) something is; specifically, a measure of the average kinetic energy of the particles in an object (26, 498)

tension stress that occurs when forces act to stretch an object (395)

texture the quality of a rock that is based on the sizes, shapes, and positions of the rock's grains (254)

theory an explanation that ties together many hypotheses and observations (20)

topographic map (TAHP uh GRAF ik MAP) a map that shows the surface features of Earth (210)

trace fossil a fossilized mark that is formed in soft sediment by the movement of an animal (296)

trait a genetically determined characteristic (148)

transform boundary the boundary between tectonic plates that are sliding past each other horizontally (391)

transpiration the process by which plants release water vapor into the air through stomata; *also* the release of water vapor into the air by other organisms (64)

tropism (TROH PIZ uhm) growth of all or part of an organism in response to an external stimulus, such as light (70)

true north the direction to the geographic North Pole (198)

tundra a treeless plain found in the Arctic, in the Antarctic, or on the tops of mountains that is characterized by very low winter temperatures and short, cool summers (324)

U

unconformity a break in the geologic record created when rock layers are eroded or when sediment is not deposited for a long period of time (287)

uniformitarianism a principle that states that geologic processes that occurred in the past can be explained by current geologic processes (281)

uplift the rising of regions of the Earth's crust to higher elevations (400)

V

valence electron (VAY luhns ee LEK TRAHN) an electron that is found in the outermost shell of an atom and that determines the atom's chemical properties (597)

variable a factor that changes in an experiment in order to test a hypothesis (14)

vent an opening at the surface of the Earth through which volcanic material passes (440)

viscosity the resistance of a gas or liquid to flow (496)

volcano a vent or fissure in the Earth's surface through which magma and gases are expelled (438)

volume a measure of the size of a body or region in three-dimensional space (25, 466, 499)

W

water cycle the continuous movement of water from the ocean to the atmosphere to the land and back to the ocean (365)

weight a measure of the gravitational force exerted on an object; its value can change with the location of the object in the universe (469)

wetland an area of land that is periodically underwater or whose soil contains a great deal of moisture (334)

Spanish Glossary

A

absolute dating/datación absoluta cualquier método que sirve para determinar la edad de un suceso u objeto en años (167, 291)

acid/ácido cualquier compuesto que aumenta el número de iones de hidrógeno cuando se disuelve en agua (654)

activation energy/energía de activación la cantidad mínima de energía que se requiere para iniciar una reacción química (636)

active transport/transporte activo el movimiento de substancias a través de la membrana celular que requiere que la célula gaste energía (42)

adaptation/adaptación una característica que mejora la capacidad de un individuo para sobrevivir y reproducirse en un determinado ambiente (139)

alkali metal/metal alcalino uno de los elementos del Grupo 1 de la tabla periódica (litio, sodio, potasio, rubidio, cesio y francio) (577)

alkaline-earth metal/metal alcalinotérreo uno de los elementos del Grupo 2 de la tabla periódica (berilio, magnesio, calcio, estroncio, bario y radio) (577)

allele/alelo una de las formas alternativas de un gene que rige un carácter, como por ejemplo, el color del cabello (92)

aquifer/acuífero un cuerpo rocoso o sedimento que almacena agua subterránea y permite que fluya (361)

area/área una medida del tamaño de una superficie o región (24)

asthenosphere/astenosfera la capa blanda del manto sobre la que se mueven las placas tectónicas (381)

atmosphere/atmósfera una mezcla de gases que rodea un planeta o una luna (347)

atom/átomo la unidad más pequeña de un elemento que conserva las propiedades de ese elemento (545)

atomic mass/masa atómica la masa de un átomo, expresada en unidades de masa atómica (555)

atomic mass unit/unidad de masa atómica una unidad de masa que describe la masa de un átomo o una molécula (551)

atomic number/número atómico el número de protones en el núcleo de un átomo; el número atómico es el mismo para todos los átomos de un elemento (553)

azimuthal projection/proyección azimutal una proyección cartográfica que se hace al transferir las características de la superficie del globo a un plano (205)

B

base/base cualquier compuesto que aumenta el número de iones de hidróxido cuando se disuelve en agua (657)

biome/bioma una región extensa caracterizada por un tipo de clima específico y ciertos tipos de comunidades de plantas y animales (318)

biosphere/biosfera la parte de la Tierra donde existe la vida (347)

boiling/ebullición la conversión de un líquido en vapor cuando la presión de vapor del líquido es igual a la presión atmosférica (504)

Boyle's law/ley de Boyle la ley que establece que el volumen de un gas es inversamente proporcional a su presión cuando la temperatura es constante (500)

C

caldera/caldera una depresión grande y semicircular que se forma cuando se vacía parcialmente la cámara de magma que hay debajo de un volcán, lo cual hace que el suelo se hunda (446)

carbohydrate/carbohidrato una clase de nutrientes que proporcionan energía; incluye los azúcares, los almidones y las fibras; contiene carbono, hidrógeno y oxígeno (667)

carbon cycle/ciclo del carbono el movimiento del carbono del ambiente sin vida a los seres vivos y de los seres vivos al ambiente (367)

cast/molde un tipo de fósil que se forma cuando un organismo descompuesto deja una cavidad que es llenada por sedimentos (296)

catalyst/catalizador una substancia que cambia la tasa de una reacción química sin consumirse ni cambiar demasiado (638)

catastrophism/catastrofismo un principio que establece que los cambios geológicos ocurren súbitamente (281)

cell cycle/ciclo celular el ciclo de vida de una célula (48)

cellular respiration/respiración celular el proceso por medio del cual las células utilizan oxígeno para producir energía a partir de los alimentos (45, 63)

Cenozoic era/era Cenozoica la era geológica más reciente, que comenzó hace 65 millones de años; también llamada *Edad de los Mamíferos* (177)

change of state/cambio de estado el cambio de una substancia de un estado físico a otro (502)

Charles's law/ley de Charles la ley que establece que el volumen de un gas es directamente proporcional a su temperatura cuando la presión es constante (500)

chemical bond/enlace químico una interacción que mantiene unidos los átomos o los iones (597, 650)

chemical bonding/formación de un enlace químico la combinación de átomos para formar moléculas o compuestos iónicos (597)

chemical change/cambio químico un cambio que ocurre cuando una o más substancias se transforman en substancias totalmente nuevas con propiedades diferentes (481)

chemical equation/ecuación química una representación de una reacción química que usa símbolos para mostrar la relación entre los reactivos y los productos (626)

chemical formula/fórmula química una combinación de símbolos químicos y números que se usan para representar una substancia (624)

chemical property/propiedad química una propiedad de la materia que describe la capacidad de una substancia de participar en reacciones químicas (478)

chemical reaction/reacción química el proceso por medio del cual una o más substancia cambian para producir una o más substancias distintas (620)

chlorophyll/clorofila un pigmento verde que capta la energía luminosa para la fotosíntesis (63)

chromosome/cromosoma en una célula eucariótica, una de las estructuras del núcleo que está hecha de ADN y proteína; en una célula procariótica, el anillo principal de ADN (48)

cleavage/exfoliación el agrietamiento de un mineral en sus superficies lisas y planas (229)

colloid/coloide una mezcla formada por partículas diminutas que son de tamaño intermedio entre las partículas de las soluciones y las de las suspensiones y que se encuentran suspendidas en un líquido, sólido o gas (532)

composition/composición la constitución química de una roca; describe los minerales u otros materiales presentes en ella (253)

compound/compuesto una substancia formada por átomos de dos o más elementos diferentes unidos por enlaces químicos (225, 523)

compression/compresión estrés que se produce cuando distintas fuerzas actúan para estrechar un objeto (395)

concentration/concentración la cantidad de una cierta substancia en una cantidad determinada de mezcla, solución o mena (530)

condensation/condensación el cambio de estado de gas a líquido (505)

conduction/conducción la transferencia de energía en forma de calor a través de un material (355)

conic projection/proyección cónica una proyección cartográfica que se hace al transferir las características de la superficie del globo a un cono (204)

continental drift/deriva continental la hipótesis que establece que alguna vez los continentes formaron una sola masa de tierra, se dividieron y se fueron a la deriva hasta terminar en sus ubicaciones actuales (387)

contour interval/distancia entre las curvas de nivel la diferencia en elevación entre una curva de nivel y la siguiente (211)

contour line/curva de nivel una línea que une puntos que tienen la misma elevación (210)

controlled experiment/experimento controlado un experimento que prueba sólo un factor a la vez, comparando un grupo de control con un grupo experimental (14)

convection/convección la transferencia de energía térmica mediante la circulación o el movimiento de un líquido o gas (355)

convergent boundary/límite convergente el límite que se forma debido al choque de dos placas de la litosfera (391)

core/núcleo la parte central de la Tierra, debajo del manto (347, 379)

covalent bond/enlace covalente un enlace formado cuando los átomos comparten uno más pares de electrones (604)

covalent compound/compuesto covalente un compuesto químico que se forma al compartir electrones (652)

crater/cráter una depresión con forma de embudo que se encuentra cerca de la parte superior de la chimenea central de un volcán (446)

crust/corteza la capa externa, delgada y sólida de la Tierra, que se encuentra sobre el manto (347, 379)

crystal/cristal un sólido cuyos átomos, iones o moléculas están ordenados en un patrón definido (225)

crystal lattice/red cristalina el patrón regular en el que un cristal está ordenado (603)

cylindrical projection/proyección cilíndrica una proyección cartográfica que se hace al transferir las características de la superficie del globo a un cilindro (203)

cytokinesis/citoquinesis la división del citoplasma de una célula (50)

D

decomposition reaction/reacción de descomposición una reacción en la que un solo compuesto se descompone para formar dos o más substancias más simples (631)

deep current/corriente profunda un movimiento del agua del océano que es similar a una corriente y ocurre debajo de la superficie (359)

deep-water zone/zona de aguas profundas la zona de un lago o laguna debajo de la zona de aguas abiertas, a donde no llega la luz (333)

deformation/deformación el proceso de doblar, inclinar y romper la corteza de la Tierra; el cambio en la forma de una roca en respuesta a la tensión (413)

density/densidad la relación entre la masa de una substancia y su volumen (26, 230, 473)

deoxyribonucleic acid DNA/ADN ácido desoxirribonucleico una molécula que está presente en todas las células vivas y que contiene la información que determina los caracteres que un ser vivo hereda y necesita para vivir (116)

deposition/deposición el proceso por medio del cual un material se deposita (249)

desert/desierto una región con poca vegetación o sin vegetación, largos períodos sin lluvia y temperaturas extremas; generalmente se ubica en climas calientes (323)

diamond/diamante una forma sólida, cristalina e incolora del carbono (579)

diffusion/difusión el movimiento de partículas de regiones de mayor densidad a regiones de menor densidad (40)

divergent boundary/límite divergente el límite entre dos placas tectónicas que se están separando una de la otra (391)

dominant trait/carácter dominante el carácter que se observa en la primera generación cuando se cruzan progenitores que tienen caracteres diferentes (89)

dormant/aletargado término que describe el estado inactivo de una semilla u otra parte de las plantas cuando las condiciones son desfavorables para el crecimiento (68)

double-displacement reaction/reacción de doble desplazamiento una reacción en la que se forma un gas, un precipitado sólido o un compuesto molecular a partir del intercambio de iones entre dos compuestos (633)

E

elastic rebound/rebote elástico ocurre cuando una roca deformada elásticamente vuelve súbitamente a su forma no deformada (413)

electron/electrón una partícula subatómica que tiene carga negativa (546)

electron cloud/nube de electrones una región que rodea al núcleo de un átomo en la cual es probable encontrar a los electrones (548)

element/elemento una substancia que no se puede separar o descomponer en substancias más simples por medio de métodos químicos (225, 519)

elevation/elevación la altura de un objeto sobre el nivel del mar (210)

endocytosis/endocitosis el proceso por medio del cual la membrana celular rodea una partícula y la encierra en una vesícula para llevarla al interior de la célula (42)

endothermic reaction/reacción endotérmica una reacción química que necesita calor (635)

eon/eón la mayor división del tiempo geológico (303)

epicenter/epicentro el punto de la superficie de la Tierra que queda justo arriba del punto de inicio, o foco, de un terremoto (418)

epoch/época una subdivisión de un período geológico (303)

equator/ecuador el círculo imaginario que se encuentra a la mitad entre los polos y divide a la Tierra en los hemisferios norte y sur (199)

era/era una unidad de tiempo geológico que incluye dos o más períodos (303)

erosion/erosión el proceso por medio del cual el viento, el agua, el hielo o la gravedad transporta tierra y sedimentos de un lugar a otro (249, 350)

estuary/estuario un área donde el agua dulce de los ríos se mezcla con el agua salada del océano (330)

evaporation/evaporación el cambio de una substancia de líquido a gas (504)

evolution/evolución el proceso por medio del cual las características heredadas dentro de una población cambian con el transcurso de las generaciones de manera tal que a veces surgen nuevas especies (139)

exocytosis/exocitosis el proceso por medio del cual una célula libera una partícula encerrándola en una vesícula que luego se traslada a la superficie de la célula y se fusiona con la membrana celular (43)

exothermic reaction/reacción exotérmica una reacción química en la que se libera calor a los alrededores (635)

extinct/extinto término que describe a una especie que ha desaparecido por completo (169)

extinction/extinción la muerte de todos los miembros de una especie (303)

extrusive igneous rock/roca ígnea extrusiva una roca que se forma como resultado de la actividad volcánica en la superficie de la Tierra o cerca de ella (259)

F

fault/falla una grieta en un cuerpo rocoso a lo largo de la cual un bloque se desliza respecto a otro (396)

fermentation/fermentación la descomposición de los alimentos sin utilizar oxígeno (45)

focus/foco el punto a lo largo de una falla donde ocurre el primer movimiento de un terremoto (418)

folding/plegamiento fenómeno que ocurre cuando las capas de roca se doblan debido a la compresión (395)

foliated/foliada término que describe la textura de una roca metamórfica en la que los granos de mineral están ordenados en planos o bandas (267)

fossil/fósil los indicios o los restos de un organismo que vivió hace mucho tiempo, comúnmente preservados en las rocas sedimentarias (140, 166, 295)

fossil record/registro fósil una secuencia histórica de la vida indicada por fósiles que se han encontrado en las capas de la corteza terrestre (140)

fracture/fractura la forma en la que se rompe un mineral a lo largo de superficies curvas o irregulares (229)

G

gap hypothesis/hipótesis del intervalo una hipótesis que se basa en la idea de que es más probable que ocurra un terremoto importante a lo largo de la parte de una falla activa donde no se han producido terremotos durante un determinado período de tiempo (423)

gas/gas un estado de la materia que no tiene volumen ni forma definidos (496)

gene/gene un conjunto de instrucciones para un carácter heredado (92)

generation time/tiempo de generación el período entre el nacimiento de una generación y el nacimiento de la siguiente generación (153)

genotype/genotipo la constitución genética completa de un organismo; *también* la combinación genes para uno o más caracteres específicos (93)

geologic column/columna geológica un arreglo de las capas de roca en el que las rocas más antiguas están al fondo (285)

geologic time scale/escala de tiempo geológico el método estándar que se usa para dividir la larga historia natural de la Tierra en partes razonables (169, 303)

geosphere/geosfera la capa de la Tierra que es principalmente sólida y rocosa; se extiende desde el centro del núcleo hasta la superficie de la corteza terrestre (347)

group/grupo una columna vertical de elementos de la tabla periódica; los elementos de un grupo comparten propiedades químicas (574)

H

half-life/vida media el tiempo que tarda la mitad de la muestra de una substancia radiactiva en desintegrarse por desintegración radiactiva (291, 685)

halogen/halógeno uno de los elementos del Grupo 17 de la tabla periódica (flúor, cloro, bromo, yodo y ástato); los halógenos se combinan con la mayoría de los metales para formar sales (581)

hardness/dureza una medida de la capacidad de un mineral de resistir ser rayado (230)

heredity/herencia la transmisión de caracteres genéticos de padres a hijos (86)

hominid/homínido un tipo de primate caracterizado por ser bípedo, tener extremidades inferiores relativamente largas y no tener cola; incluye a los seres humanos y sus ancestros (179)

Homo sapiens/Homo sapiens la especie de homínidos que incluye a los seres humanos modernos y a sus ancestros más cercanos; apareció hace entre 100,000 y 150,000 años (182)

homologous chromosomes/cromosomas homólogos cromosomas con la misma secuencia de genes y la misma estructura (49, 98)

hot spot/mancha caliente un área volcánicamente activa de la superficie de la Tierra que se encuentra lejos de un límite entre placas tectónicas (452)

hydrocarbon/hidrocarburo un compuesto orgánico compuesto únicamente por carbono e hidrogeno (665)

hydrosphere/hidrosfera la porción de la Tierra que es agua (347)

hypothesis/hipótesis una explicación que se basa en observaciones o investigaciones científicas previas y que se puede probar (12)

I

index contour/índice de las curvas de nivel en un mapa, la curva de nivel que es más gruesa y oscura, la cual normalmente se encuentra cada quinta línea e indica un cambio en la elevación (211)

index fossil/fósil guía un fósil que se encuentra en las capas de roca de una sola era geológica y que se usa para establecer la edad de las capas de roca (298)

indicator/indicador un compuesto que puede cambiar de color de forma reversible dependiendo de condiciones tales como el pH (655)

inertia/inercia la tendencia de un objeto a no moverse o, si el objeto se está moviendo, la tendencia a resistir un cambio en su rapidez o dirección hasta que una fuerza externa actúe en el objeto (470)

inhibitor/inhibidor una substancia que desacelera o detiene una reacción química (638)

intrusive igneous rock/roca ígnea intrusiva una roca formada a partir del enfriamiento y solidificación del magma debajo de la superficie terrestre (258)

ion/ion una partícula cargada que se forma cuando un átomo o grupo de átomos gana o pierde uno o más electrones (600)

ionic bond/enlace iónico un enlace que se forma cuando los electrones se transfieren de un átomo a otro, y que produce un ion positivo y uno negativo (600)

ionic compound/compuesto iónico un compuesto formado por iones con cargas opuestas (650)

isotope/isótopo un átomo que tiene el mismo número de protones (o el mismo número atómico) que otros átomos del mismo elemento, pero que tiene un número diferente de neutrones (y, por lo tanto, otra masa atómica) (291, 553, 682)

L

latitude/latitud la distancia hacia el norte o hacia el sur del ecuador; se expresa en grados (199)

lava plateau/meseta de lava un accidente geográfico amplio y plano que se forma debido a repetidas erupciones no explosivas de lava que se expanden por un área extensa (447)

law/ley un resumen de muchos resultados y observaciones experimentales; una ley dice cómo funcionan las cosas (20)

law of conservation of energy/ley de la conservación de la energía la ley que establece que la energía ni se crea ni se destruye, sólo se transforma de una forma a otra (635)

law of conservation of mass/ley de la conservación de la masa la ley que establece que la masa no se crea ni se destruye por cambios químicos o físicos comunes (627)

lipid/lípido un tipo de substancia bioquímica que no se disuelve en agua; las grasas y los esteroides son lípidos (667)

liquid/líquido el estado de la materia que tiene un volumen definido, pero no una forma definida (496)

lithosphere/litosfera la capa externa y sólida de la Tierra que está formada por la corteza y la parte superior y rígida del manto (381)

littoral zone/zona litoral la zona poco profunda de un lago o una laguna donde la luz llega al fondo y nutre a las plantas (333)

longitude/longitud la distancia hacia el este y hacia el oeste del primer meridiano; se expresa en grados (200)

luster/brillo la forma en que un mineral refleja la luz (228)

M

magma chamber/cámara de magma la masa de roca fundida que alimenta un volcán (440)

magnetic declination/declinación magnética la diferencia entre el norte magnético y el norte verdadero (198)

mantle/manto la capa de roca que se encuentra entre la corteza terrestre y el núcleo (347, 379)

map/mapa una representación de las características de un cuerpo físico, tal como la Tierra (196)

marsh/pantano un ecosistema pantanoso sin árboles, donde crecen plantas tales como el pasto (334)

mass/masa una medida de la cantidad de materia que tiene un objeto (25, 469)

mass number/número de masa la suma de los números de protones y neutrones que hay en el núcleo de un átomo (554, 681)

matter/materia cualquier cosa que tiene masa y ocupa un lugar en el espacio (466)

meiosis/meiosis un proceso de división celular durante el cual el número de cromosomas disminuye a la mitad del número original por medio de dos divisiones del núcleo, lo cual resulta en la producción de células sexuales (gametos o esporas) (98)

melting/fusión el cambio de estado en el que un sólido se convierte en líquido al añadirse calor (503)

meniscus/menisco la curva que se forma en la superficie de un líquido, la cual sirve para medir el volumen de un líquido (467)

mesosphere/mesosfera la parte fuerte e inferior del manto que se encuentra entre la astenosfera y el núcleo externo (193); *también*, la capa de la atmósfera que se encuentra entre la estratosfera y la termosfera, en la cual la temperatura disminuye al aumentar la altitud (381)

Mesozoic era/era Mesozoica la era geológica que comenzó hace 248 millones de años y terminó hace 65 millones de años; también llamada *Edad de los Reptiles* (175)

metal/metal un elemento que es brillante y conduce bien el calor y la electricidad (520, 521)

metallic bond/enlace metálico un enlace formado por la atracción entre iones metálicos cargados positivamente y los electrones que los rodean (607)

metalloid/metaloides elementos que tienen propiedades tanto de metales como de no metales (520, 521)

meter/metro la unidad fundamental de longitud en el sistema internacional de unidades (símbolo: m) (24)

mineral/mineral un sólido natural e inorgánico que tiene una estructura química definada (225)

mitosis/mitosis en las células eucarióticas, un proceso de división celular que forma dos núcleos nuevos, cada uno de los cuales posee el mismo número de cromosomas (49)

mixture/mezcla una combinación de dos o más substancias que no están combinadas químicamente (526)

model/modelo un diseño, plan, representación o descripción cuyo objetivo es mostrar la estructura o funcionamiento de un objeto, sistema o concepto (18)

mold/molde una marca o cavidad hecha en una superficie sedimentaria por una concha u otro cuerpo (296)

molecule/molécula la unidad más pequeña de una substancia que conserva todas las propiedades físicas y químicas de esa substancia (605)

mutation/mutación un cambio en la secuencia de la base de nucleótidos de un gene o de una molécula de ADN (124)

N

natural selection/selección natural el proceso por medio del cual los individuos que están mejor adaptados a su ambiente sobreviven y se reproducen con más éxito que los individuos menos adaptados; una teoría que explica el mecanismo de la evolución (150)

neutralization reaction/reacción de neutralización la reacción de un ácido y una base que forma una solución neutra de agua y una sal (661)

neutron/neutrón una partícula subatómica que no tiene carga y que se encuentra en el núcleo de un átomo (551)

nitrogen cycle/ciclo del nitrógeno el proceso por medio del cual el nitrógeno circula en el aire, el suelo, el agua, las plantas y los animales de un ecosistema (367)

noble gas/gas noble uno de los elementos del Grupo 18 de la tabla periódica (helio, neón, argón, criptón, xenón y radón); los gases nobles son no reactivos (582)

nonfoliated/no foliada término que describe la textura de una roca metamórfica en la que los granos de mineral no están ordenados en planos ni bandas (268)

nonmetal/no metal un elemento que es mal conductor del calor y la electricidad (520, 521)

nonsilicate mineral/mineral no-silicato un mineral que no contiene compuestos de sílice y oxígeno (226)

nuclear fission/fisión nuclear la partición del núcleo de un átomo grande en dos o más fragmentos; libera neutrones y energía adicionales (689)

nuclear fusion/fusión nuclear combinación de los núcleos de átomos pequeños para formar un núcleo más grande; libera energía (692)

nucleic acid/ácido nucleico una molécula formada por subunidades llamadas *nucleótidos* (668)

nucleotide/nucleótido en una cadena de ácidos nucleicos, una subunidad formada por un azúcar, un fosfato y una base nitrogenada (116)

nucleus/núcleo en ciencias físicas, la región central de un átomo, la cual está constituida por protones y neutrones (548)

O

open-water zone/zona de aguas superiores la zona de un lago o una laguna que se extiende desde la zona litoral y cuya profundidad sólo alcanza hasta donde penetra la luz (333)

ore/mena un material natural cuya concentración de minerales con valor económico es suficientemente alta como para que el material pueda ser explotado de manera rentable (234)

organic compound/compuesto orgánico un compuesto enlazado de manera covalente que contiene carbono (665)

osmosis/ósmosis la difusión del agua a través de una membrana semipermeable (41)

P

paleontology/paleontología el estudio científico de los fósiles (283)

Paleozoic era/era Paleozoica la era geológica que vino después del período Precámbrico; comenzó hace 543 millones de años y terminó hace 248 millones de años (174)

passive transport/transporte pasivo el movimiento de substancias a través de una membrana celular sin que la célula tenga que usar energía (42)

pedigree/pedigrí un diagrama que muestra la incidencia de un carácter genético en varias generaciones de una familia (104)

period/período una unidad de tiempo geológico en la que se dividen las eras (303)

period in chemistry/período en química una hilera horizontal de elementos en la tabla periódica (574)

periodic/periódico término que describe algo que ocurre o que se repite a intervalos regulares (569)

periodic law/ley periódica la ley que establece que las propiedades químicas y físicas repetitivas de un elemento cambian periódicamente en función del número atómico de los elementos (569)

pH/pH un valor que expresa la acidez o la basicidad (alcalinidad) de un sistema (661)

phenotype/fenotipo la apariencia de un organismo u otra característica perceptible (92)

photosynthesis/fotosíntesis el proceso por medio del cual las plantas, las algas y algunas bacterias utilizan la luz solar, el dióxido de carbono y el agua para producir alimento (44, 63)

physical change/cambio físico un cambio de materia de una forma a otra sin que ocurra un cambio en sus propiedades químicas (476)

physical property/propiedad física una característica de una substancia que no implica un cambio químico, tal como la densidad, el color o la dureza (473)

plankton/plancton la masa de organismos en su mayoría microscópicos que flotan o se encuentran a la deriva en ambientes de agua dulce o marina (326)

plate tectonics/tectónica de placas la teoría que explica cómo se mueven y cambian de forma las placas tectónicas, que son grandes porciones de la capa más externa de la Tierra (170, 391)

Precambrian time/tiempo Precámbrico el período en la escala de tiempo geológico que abarca desde la formación de la Tierra hasta el comienzo de la era Paleozoica; comenzó hace aproximadamente 4.6 mil millones de años y terminó hace 543 millones de años (172)

precipitate/precipitado un sólido que se produce como resultado de una reacción quimica en una solución (621)

pressure/presión la cantidad de fuerza ejercida en una superficie por unidad de área (499)

primate/primate un tipo de mamífero caracterizado por tener pulgares oponibles y visión binocular (178)

prime meridian/meridiano de Greenwich el meridiano, o línea de longitud, que se designa como longitud 0° (200)

probability/probabilidad la probabilidad de que ocurra un posible suceso futuro en cualquier caso dado del suceso (94)

product/producto una substancia que se forma en una reacción química (626)

protein/proteína una molécula formada por aminoácidos que es necesaria para construir y reparar estructuras corporales y para regular procesos del cuerpo (667)

proton/protón una partícula subatómica que tiene una carga positiva y que se encuentra en el núcleo de un átomo (551)

pure substance/substancia pura una muestra de materia, ya sea un solo elemento o un solo compuesto, que tiene propiedades químicas y físicas definidas (519)

P wave/onda P una onda sísmica que hace que las partículas de roca se muevan en una dirección de atrás hacia delante (416)

R

radiation/radiación la transferencia de energía en forma de ondas electromagnéticas (355)

radioactive decay/desintegración radiactiva el proceso por medio del cual un isótopo radiactivo tiende a desintegrarse y formar un isótopo estable del mismo elemento o de otro elemento (291)

radioactivity/radiactividad el proceso por medio del cual un núcleo inestable emite radiación nuclear (681)

radiometric dating/datación radiométrica un método para determinar la edad de un objeto estimando los porcentajes relativos de un isótopo radiactivo (precursor) y un isótopo estable (hijo) (291)

reactant/reactivo una substancia o molécula que participa en una reacción química (626)

recessive trait/carácter recesivo un carácter que se hace aparente sólo cuando se heredan dos alelos recesivos de la misma característica (89)

reclamation/restauración el proceso de hacer que la tierra vuelva a su condición original después de que se terminan las actividades de explotación minera (235)

relative dating/datación relativa cualquier método que se utiliza para determinar si un acontecimiento u objeto es más viejo o más joven que otros acontecimientos u objetos (167, 285)

relief/relieve las variaciones en elevación de una superficie de terreno (211)

remote sensing/teledetección el proceso de recopilar y analizar información acerca de un objeto sin estar en contacto físico con el objeto (207)

ribosome/ribosoma un organelo celular compuesto de ARN y proteína; el sitio donde ocurre la síntesis de proteínas (123)

rift zone/zona de rift un área de grietas profundas que se forma entre dos placas tectónicas que se están alejando una de la otra (450)

ribonucleic acid RNA/ARN ácido ribonucleico una molécula que está presente en todas las células vivas y que juega un papel en la producción de proteínas (122)

rock/roca una mezcla sólida de uno o más minerales o de materia orgánica que se produce de forma natural (249)

rock cycle/ciclo de las rocas la serie de procesos por medio de los cuales una roca se forma, cambia de un tipo a otro, se destruye y se forma nuevamente por procesos geológicos (249, 365)

S

salt/sal un compuesto iónico que se forma cuando un átomo de un metal reemplaza el hidrógeno de un ácido (663)

savanna/sabana una región de pastizales que, a menudo, tiene árboles dispersos; se encuentra en áreas tropicales y subtropicales donde se producen lluvias, incendios y sequías estacionales (322)

science/ciencia el conocimiento que se obtiene por medio de la observación natural de acontecimientos y condiciones con el fin de descubrir hechos y formular leyes o principios que puedan ser verificados o probados (4)

scientific methods/métodos científicos una serie de pasos que se siguen para solucionar problemas (10)

sea-floor spreading/expansión del suelo marino el proceso por medio del cual se forma nueva litosfera oceánica a medida que el magma se eleva hacia la superficie y se solidifica (388)

seismic gap/brecha sísmica un área a lo largo de una falla donde han ocurrido relativamente pocos terremotos recientemente, pero donde se han producido terremotos fuertes en el pasado (423)

seismic wave/onda sísmica una onda de energía que viaja a través de la Tierra y se aleja de un terremoto en todas direcciones (416)

seismogram/sismograma una gráfica del movimiento de un terremoto elaborada por un sismógrafo (418)

seismograph/sismógrafo un instrumento que registra las vibraciones en el suelo y determina la ubicación y la fuerza de un terremoto (418)

seismology/sismología el estudio de los terremotos (413)

selective breeding/reproducción selectiva la práctica humana de cruzar animales o plantas que tienen ciertas caracteres deseadas (148)

sex chromosome/cromosoma sexual uno de los dos cromosomas que determinan el sexo de un individuo (103)

silicate mineral/mineral silicato un mineral que contiene una combinación de sílice, oxígeno y uno o más metales (226)

single-displacement reaction/reacción de sustitución simple una reacción en la que un elemento toma el lugar de otro elemento en un compuesto (631)

solid/sólido el estado de la materia en el cual el volumen y la forma de una sustancia están fijos (495)

solubility/solubilidad la capacidad de una substancia de disolverse en otra a una temperatura y una presión dadas (530)

solute/soluto en una solución, la sustancia que se disuelve en el solvente (528)

solution/solución una mezcla homogénea de dos o más sustancias dispersas de manera uniforme en una sola fase (528)

solvent/solvente en una solución, la sustancia en la que se disuelve el soluto (528)

speciation/especiación la formación de especies nuevas como resultado de la evolución (154)

species/especie un grupo de organismos que tienen un parentesco cercano y que pueden aparearse para producir descendencia fértil (139)

states of matter/estados de la material las formas físicas de la materia, que son sólida, líquida y gaseosa (495)

stoma/estoma una de las muchas aberturas de una hoja o de un tallo de una planta, la cual permite que se lleve a cabo el intercambio de gases (64)

strata/estratos capas de roca (261)

stratification/estratificación el proceso por medio del cual las rocas sedimentarias se acomodan en capas (263)

streak/veta el color del polvo de un mineral (229)

sublimation/sublimación el proceso por medio del cual un sólido se transforma directamente en un gas (506)

subsidence/hundimiento del terreno el hundimiento de regiones de la corteza terrestre a elevaciones más bajas (400)

superposition/superposición un principio que establece que las rocas más jóvenes se encontrarán sobre las rocas más viejas si las capas no han sido alteradas (285)

surface current/corriente superficial un movimiento horizontal del agua del océano que es producido por el viento y que ocurre en la superficie del océano o cerca de ella (359)

surface tension/tensión superficial la fuerza que actúa en la superficie de un líquido y que tiende a minimizar el área de la superficie (496)

suspension/suspensión una mezcla en la que las partículas de un material se encuentran dispersas de manera más o menos uniforme a través de un líquido o de un gas (532)

swamp/ciénaga un ecosistema de pantano en el que crecen arbustos y árboles (334)

S wave/onda S una onda sísmica que hace que las partículas de roca se muevan en una dirección de lado a lado (416)

synthesis reaction/reacción de síntesis una reacción en la que dos o más sustancias se combinan para formar un compuesto nuevo (630)

T

tectonic plate/placa tectónica un bloque de litosfera formado por la corteza y la parte rígida y más externa del manto (382)

temperature/temperatura una medida de qué tan caliente (o frío) está algo; específicamente, una medida de la energía cinética promedio de las partículas de un objeto (26, 498)

tension/tensión estrés que se produce cuando distintas fuerzas actúan para estirar un objeto (395)

texture/textura la cualidad de una roca que se basa en el tamaño, la forma y la posición de los granos que la forman (254)

theory/teoría una explicación que relaciona muchas hipótesis y observaciones (20)

topographic map/mapa topográfico un mapa que muestra las características superficiales de la Tierra (210)

trace fossil/fósil traza una marca fosilizada que se forma en un sedimento blando debido al movimiento de un animal (296)

trait/carácter una característica determinada genéticamente (148)

transform boundary/límite de transformación el límite entre placas tectónicas que se están deslizando horizontalmente una sobre otra (391)

transpiration/transpiración el proceso por medio del cual las plantas liberan vapor de agua al aire por medio de los estomas; *también*, la liberación de vapor de agua al aire por otros organismos (64)

tropism/tropismo el crecimiento de un organismo o de una parte de él en respuesta a un estímulo externo, como por ejemplo, la luz (70)

true north/norte verdadero la dirección al Polo Norte geográfico (198)

tundra/tundra una llanura sin árboles situada en la región ártica o antártica o en la cumbre de las montañas; se caracteriza por temperaturas muy bajas en el invierno y veranos cortos y frescos (324)

U

unconformity/disconformidad una ruptura en el registro geológico, creada cuando las capas de roca se erosionan o cuando el sedimento no se deposita durante un largo período de tiempo (287)

uniformitarianism/uniformitarianismo un principio que establece que es posible explicar los procesos geológicos que ocurrieron en el pasado en función de los procesos geológicos actuales (281)

uplift/levantamiento la elevación de regiones de la corteza terrestre a elevaciones más altas (400)

V

valence electron/electrón de valencia un electrón que se encuentra en el orbital más externo de un átomo y que determina las propiedades químicas del átomo (597)

variable/variable un factor que se modifica en un experimento con el fin de probar una hipótesis (14)

vent/chimenea una abertura en la superficie de la Tierra a través de la cual pasa material volcánico (440)

viscosity/viscosidad la resistencia de un gas o un líquido a fluir (496)

volcano/volcán una chimenea o fisura en la superficie de la Tierra a través de la cual se expulsan magma y gases (438)

volume/volumen una medida del tamaño de un cuerpo o región en un espacio de tres dimensiones (25, 466, 499)

W

water cycle/ciclo del agua el movimiento continuo del agua: del océano a la atmósfera, de la atmósfera a la tierra y de la tierra al océano (365)

weight/peso una medida de la fuerza gravitacional ejercida sobre un objeto; su valor puede cambiar en función de la ubicación del objeto en el universo (469)

wetland/pantano un área de tierra que está periódicamente bajo el agua o cuyo suelo contiene una gran cantidad de humedad (334)

Index

Boldface page numbers refer to illustrative materials, such as figures, tables, margin elements, photographs, and illustrations

A

B

Index

D

E

Index

F

G

H

M

Index

P

T

U

V

W

X

Y

Z

Acknowledgments

continued from page ii

John Brockhaus, Ph.D.
Director of Geospatial Science Information Program
Department of Geography and Environmental Engineering
United States Military Academy
West Point, New York

Barbara Christopher
Science Writer and Editor
Austin, Texas

Joe W. Crim, Ph.D.
Professor and Head of Cellular Biology
Department of Cellular Biology
University of Georgia
Athens, Georgia

Roger J. Cuffey, Ph.D.
Professor of Paleontology
Department of Geosciences Pennsylvania State University
University Park, Pennsylvania

Scott Darveau, Ph.D.
Assistant Professor of Chemistry
Chemistry Department
University of Nebraska at Kearney
Kearney, Nebraska

Jim Denbow, Ph.D.
Associate Professor of Archaeology
Department of Anthropology and Archaeology
University of Texas at Austin
Austin, Texas

Cassandra Eagle, Ph.D.
Professor of Organic Chemistry
Chemistry Department
Appalachian State University
Boone, North Carolina

Turgay Ertekin, Ph.D.
Professor and Chairman of Petroleum and Natural Gas Engineering
Energy and Geo-Environmental Engineering
Pennsylvania State University
University Park, Pennsylvania

David Haig, Ph.D.
Professor of Biology
Department of Organismic and Evolutionary Biology
Harvard University
Cambridge, Massachusetts

P. Shiv Halasyamani, Ph.D.
Associate Professor of Chemistry
Department of Chemistry
University of Houston
Houston, Texas

David Hershey, Ph.D.
Education Consultant
Hyattsville, Maryland

Richard N. Hey, Ph.D.
Professor of Geophysics
Department of Geophysics & Planetology
University of Hawaii at Manoa
Honolulu, Hawaii

Ken Hon, Ph.D.
Associate Professor of Volcanology
Geology Department
University of Hawaii at Hilo
Hilo, Hawaii

Susan Hough, Ph.D.
United States Geological Survey (USGS)
Pasadena, California

Steven A. Jennings, Ph.D.
Associate Professor
Department of Geography and Environmental Studies
University of Colorado
Colorado Springs, Colorado

Mark N. Kobrak, Ph.D.
Assistant Professor of Chemistry
Chemistry Department
Brooklyn College of the City University of New York
Brooklyn, New York

Daniela Kohen, Ph.D.
Assistant Professor of Chemistry
Chemistry Department
Carleton College
Northfield, Minnesota

Joel S. Leventhal, Ph.D.
Emeritus Scientist, Geochemistry
U.S. Geological Survey
Lakewood, Colorado

Richard F. Niedziela, Ph.D.
Assistant Professor of Chemistry
Department of Chemistry
DePaul University
Chicago, Illinois

Eva Oberdoerster, Ph.D.
Lecturer
Department of Biology
Southern Methodist University
Dallas, Texas

Kenneth K. Peace
Manager of Transportation
WestArch Coal, Inc.
St. Louis, Missouri

Enrique Peacock-López, Ph.D.
Professor of Chemistry
Department of Chemistry
Williams College
Williamstown, Massachusetts

Kate Queeney, Ph.D.
Assistant Professor of Chemistry
Chemistry Department
Smith College
Northampton, Massachusetts

Michael H. Renfroe, Ph.D.
Professor of Biology
Department of Biology
James Madison University
Harrisonburg, Virginia

Kenneth H. Rubin, Ph.D.
Associate Professor
Department of Geology & Geophysics
University of Hawaii at Manoa
Honolulu, Hawaii

Laurie Santos, Ph.D.
Assistant Professor
Department of Psychology
Yale University
New Haven, Connecticut

Patrick K. Schoff, Ph.D.
Research Associate
Natural Resources Research Institute
University of Minnesota at Duluth
Duluth, Minnesota

Fred Seaman, Ph.D.
Retired Research Associate
College of Pharmacy
The University of Texas at Austin
Austin, Texas

Daniel Z. Sui, Ph.D.
Professor
Department of Geography
Texas A&M University
College Station, Texas

Colin D. Sumrall, Ph.D.
Lecturer of Paleontology
Earth and Planetary Sciences
The University of Tennessee
Knoxville, Tennessee

Richard S. Treptow, Ph.D.
Professor of Chemistry
Department of Chemistry and Physics
Chicago State University
Chicago, Illinois

Peter W. Weigand, Ph.D.
Professor Emeritus
Department of Geological Sciences
California State University
Northridge, California

Dale Wheeler
Associate Professor of Chemistry
A. R. Smith Department of Chemistry
Appalachian State University
Boone, North Carolina

Teacher Reviewers

Diedre S. Adams
Physical Science Instructor
West Vigo Middle School
West Terre Haute, Indiana

Barbara Gavin Akre
Teacher of Biology, Anatomy-Physiology, and Life Science
Duluth Independent School District
Duluth, Minnesota

Laura Buchanan
Science Teacher and Department Chair
Corkran Middle School
Glen Burnie, Maryland

Sarah Carver
Science Teacher
Jackson Creek Middle School
Bloomington, Indiana

Robin K. Clanton
Science Department Head
Berrien Middle School
Nashville, Georgia

Hilary Cochran
Science Teacher
Indian Crest Junior High School
Souderton, Pennsylvania

Karen Dietrich, S.S.J., Ph.D.
Principal and Biology Instructor
Mount Saint Joseph Academy
Flourtown, Pennsylvania

Randy Dye, M.S.
Science Department Head
Wood Middle School
Fort Leonard Wood, Missouri

Trisha Elliott
Science and Mathematics Teacher
Chain of Lakes Middle School
Orlando, Florida

Liza M. Guasp
Science Teacher
Celebration K–8 School
Celebration, Florida

Meredith Hanson
Science Teacher
Westside Middle School
Rocky Face, Georgia

Denise Hulette
Science Teacher
Conway Middle School
Orlando, Florida

James Kerr
Oklahoma Teacher of the Year 2002–2003
Union Public Schools
Tulsa, Oklahoma

Laura Kitselman
Science Teacher and Coordinator
Loudoun Country Day School
Leesburg, Virginia

Debra S. Kogelman, MAed.
Science Teacher
University of Chicago Laboratory Schools
Chicago, Illinois

Tiffany Kracht
Science Teacher
Chain of Lakes Middle School
Orlando, Florida

Deborah L. Kronsteiner
Science Teacher
Spring Grove Area Middle School
Spring Grove, Pennsylvania

Jennifer L. Lamkie
Science Teacher
Thomas Jefferson Middle School
Edison, New Jersey

Bill Martin
Science Teacher
Southeast Middle School
Kernersville, North Carolina

Maureen Martin
Green Team Science Teacher
Jackson Creek Middle School
Bloomington, Indiana

Thomas Lee Reed
Science Teacher
Rising Starr Middle School
Fayetteville, Georgia

Shannon Ripple
Science Teacher
Canyon Vista Middle School
Round Rock, Texas

Susan H. Robinson
Science Teacher
Oglethorpe County Middle School
Lexington, Georgia

Cary B. Rosillo
Science Teacher
Independence Middle School
Jupiter, Florida

Elizabeth J. Rustad
Science Department Chair
Coronado Elementary
Gilbert, Arizona

Helen P. Schiller
Instructional Coach
The School District of Greenville County
Greenville, South Carolina

Mark Schnably
Science Instructor
Thomas Jefferson Middle School
Winston-Salem, North Carolina

Stephanie Snowden
Science Teacher
Canyon Vista Middle School
Austin, Texas

Marci L. Stadiem
Science Department Chair
Cascade Middle School
Seattle, Washington

Martha Tedrow
Science Teacher
Thomas Jefferson Middle School
Winston-Salem, North Carolina

Sherrye Valenti
Curriculum Leader
Science Department
Wildwood Middle School
Wildwood, Missouri

ZoEllen Warren
Science Teacher
Oakville Middle School
Archer, Florida

Angie Williams
Teacher
Riversprings Middle School
Crawfordville, Florida

Lab Testing

Barry Bishop
Science Teacher
San Rafael Junior High School
Ferron, Utah

Paul Boyle
Science Teacher
Perry Heights Middle School
Evansville, Indiana

Daniel Bugenhagen
Science Teacher
Yutan Junior-Senior High School
Yutan, Nebraska

James Chin
Science Teacher
Frank A. Day Middle School
Newtonville, Maryland

Rebecca Ferguson
Science Teacher
North Ridge Middle School
North Richland Hills, Texas

Laura Fleet
Science Teacher
Alice B. Landrum Middle School
Ponte Vedra Beach, Florida

Susan Gorman
Science Teacher
North Ridge Middle School
North Ridge, Texas

C. John Graves
Science Teacher
Monforton Middle School
Bozeman, Montana

Janel Guse
Science Teacher
West Central Middle School
Hartford, South Dakota

Dennis Hanson
Science Teacher
Big Bear Middle School
Big Bear Lake, California

Norman Holcomb
Science Teacher
Marion Elementary School
Maria Stein, Ohio

Kenneth J. Horn
Science Teacher
Fallston Middle School
Fallston, Maryland

Karma Houston-Hughes
Science Mentor
Kyrene Middle School
Tempe, Arizona

Tracy Jahn
Science Teacher
Berkshire Junior-Senior High School
Canaan, New York

Kerry Johnson
Science Teacher
Isbell Middle School
Santa Paula, California

David Jones
Science Teacher
Andrew Jackson Middle School
Cross Lanes, West Virginia

Michael E. Krai
Science Teacher
West Hardin Middle School
Cecilia, Kentucky

Kathy LaRoe
Science Teacher
East Valley Middle School
East Helena, Montana

Maurine Marchani
Science Teacher
Raymond Park Middle School
Indianapolis, Indiana

Jason P. Marsh
Biology Teacher
Montevideo High School and Montevideo Country School
Montevideo, Minnesota

Kevin McCurdy
Science Teacher
Elmwood Junior High School
Rogers, Arkansas

Alyson Mike
Science Teacher
Radley Middle School
East Helena, Montana

Dwight Patton
Science Teacher
Carrol T. Welch Middle School
Horizon City, Texas

Joseph Price
Science Teacher
H.M. Browne Junior High School
Washington, D.C.

Terry Rakes
Science Teacher
Elmwood Junior High School
Rogers, Arkansas

Debra Sampson
Science Teacher
Booker T. Washington Middle School
Elgin, Texas

Rodney A. Sandefur
Science Teacher
Naturita Middle School
Naturita, Colorado

Helen Schiller
Science Teacher
Northwood Middle School
Taylors, South Carolina

David Sparks
Science Teacher
Redwater Junior High School
Redwater, Texas

Larry Tackett
Science Teacher
Andrew Jackson Middle School
Cross Lanes, West Virginia

Sharon L. Woolf
Science Teacher
Langston Hughes Middle School
Reston, Virginia

Lee Yassinski
Science Teacher
Sun Valley Middle School
Sun Valley, California

Gordon Zibelman
Science Teacher
Drexel Hill Middle School
Drexel Hill, Pennsylvania

Answer Checking

Hatim Belyamani
Austin, Texas

John A. Benner
Austin, Texas

Catherine Podeszwa
Duluth, Minnesota

Credits

PHOTOGRAPHY

Abbreviations used: (t) top, (c) center, (b) bottom, (l) left, (r) right, (bkgd) background

Front Cover (tl) Mike Powell/Getty images; (r) Andrew Syred/Getty Images; (bl) Daryl Benson/Masterfile; (DNA strand) David Mack/Photo Researchers, Inc.

Skills Practice Lab Teens Sam Dudgeon/HRW

Connection to Astronomy Corbis Images; **Connection to Biology** David M. Phillips/ Visuals Unlimited; **Connection to Chemistry** Digital Image copyright © 2005 PhotoDisc; **Connection to Environment** Digital Image copyright © 2005 PhotoDisc; **Connection to Geology** Letraset Phototone; **Connection to Language Arts** Digital Image copyright © 2005 PhotoDisc; **Connection to Meteorology** Digital Image copyright © 2005 PhotoDisc; **Connection to Oceanography** © ICONOTEC; **Connection to Physics** Digital Image copyright © 2005 PhotoDisc

Table of Contents iii (tr), Peter Van Steen/HRW; iii (br), Uniphoto/ImageState; iv (tl) © Chip Simons Photography; v (tl), Breck P. Kent/Animals Animals/Earth Scenes; v (bl), © National Geographic Image Collection/Ned M. Seidler; vi (tl), Sam Dudgeon/ HRW; vi (bl), James Beveridge/Visuals Unlimited; vi (br), © Gail Shumway/Getty Images; vii (bl), Tom Pantages Photography; viii (tl) E. R. Degginger/Color-Pic, Inc.; viii (cl), Mark A. Schneider/Photo Researchers, Inc.; viii (bl), Dr. E.R. Degginger/Bruce Coleman Inc.; viii (b), © Royalty Free/CORBIS; ix (tl), The G.R. "Dick" Roberts Photo Library; ix (bl), © Jeff Hunter/Getty Images/The Image Bank; x (tl), Randy Wells/ Stone/Getty Images; xi (bl), © National Geographic Image Collection/Robert W. Madden; xii (tl), Richard Megna/Fundamental Photographs; xii (bl), © Royalty-free/ CORBIS; xiii (tl), Victoria Smith/HRW; xiii (b), John Zoiner; xiii (b, inset), Mavournea Hay/HRW; xiv (tl), Victoria Smith/HRW; xiv (bl), © Konrad Wothe/Minden Pictures; xv (tl), Victoria Smith/HRW; xv (bl), Bob Thomason; xvii (tr), Sam Dudgeon/HRW; xviii (tr), Sam Dudgeon/HRW; xix (tr), Victoria Smith/HRW; xxi (tr), Victoria Smith/HRW; xxii (tr), Victoria Smith/HRW; xxiii (tr), Victoria Smith/HRW Photo; xxiv (bl), Victoria Smith/HRW

Safety First! xxviii, Sam Dudgeon/HRW; xxix(t), John Langford/HRW; xxix(bc), xxx(br) & xxx(tl), Sam Dudgeon/HRW xxx(bl), Stephanie Morris/HRW; xxxi(tl), Sam Dudgeon/ HRW xxxi(tr), Jana Birchum/HRW; xxxi(b), Sam Dudgeon/HRW

Chapter One 2-3 Craig Line/AP/Wide World Photos; 4 Peter Van Steen/HRW Photo; 5 (t) Peter Van Steen/HRW Photo; 5 (b) Sam Dudgeon/HRW Photo; 6 (b) Peter Van Steen/HRW Photo; 6 (t) Hank Morgan/Photo Researchers, Inc.; 7 Dale Miquelle/ National Geographic Society Image Collection; 8 (b) John Langford/HRW Photo; 8 (t) NC: Science VU/PNNL/Visuals Unlimited; 9 Jeremy Bishop/Science Photo Library/ Photo Researchers, Inc.; 11 (t) Peter Van Steen/HRW Photo; 12 Sam Dudgeon/HRW Photo; 14 John Mitchell/Photo Researchers; 16 Sam Dudgeon/HRW Photo; 17 (t) John Mitchell/Photo Researchers; 18 (l) © Fujifotos/The Image Works; 18 (r) © Fujifotos/The Image Works; 20 Art by Christopher Sloan/Photograph by Mark Thiessen both National Geographic_Image Collection/© National Geographic Image Collection; 24 David Austen/Publishers Network, Inc.; 25 (l) Peter Van Steen/HRW Photo; 25 (r) Peter Van Steen/HRW Photo; 26 (tl) Tony Freeman/PhotoEdit; 26 (tr) Victoria Smith/HRW; 26 (bl) Corbis Images; 34 (l), Craig Fugii/©1988 The Seattle Times; 35 (r), Bettman/CORBIS; 35 (bl), Layne Kennedy/CORBIS

Unit One 36 (tl), O.S.F./Animals Animals; 36 (cl), Hulton Archive/Getty Images; 36 (bl), Digital Image copyright © 2005 PhotoDisc; 36-37 (br & bl), Peter Veit/DRK Photo; 37 (cl), University of Pennsylvania/Hulton Getty; 37 (t), National Portrait Gallery, Smithsonian Institution/Art Resource; 37 (br), © National Geographic Image Collection/O. Louis Mazzatenta; 37 (cr), Digital Image copyright © 2005 PhotoDisc

Chapter Two 38-39 © Michael & Patricia Fogden/CORBIS; 40 Sam Dudgeon/HRW; 42 (br), Photo Researchers; 43 (tr), Birgit H. Satir, Ph.D., Professor, Albert Einstein College of Medicine, Bronx, NY 10461; 44 (l), Runk/Schoenberger/Grant Heilman; 45 (r), John Langford/HRW Photo; 47 Corbis Images; 48 CNRI/Science Photo Library/ Photo Researchers, Inc.; 49 (t), L. Willatt, East Anglian Regional Genetics Service/ Science Photo Library/Photo Researchers, Inc.; 49 (b), Biophoto Associates/Photo Researchers; 50 (b), Visuals Unlimited/R. Calentine; 50 (cl), Ed Reschke/Peter Arnold, Inc.; 50 (c), Ed Reschke/Peter Arnold, Inc.; 50 (cr), Ed Reschke/Peter Arnold, Inc.; 51 (cl), Ed Reschke/Peter Arnold, Inc.; 51 (c), Biology Media/Photo Researchers, Inc.; 51 (cr), Biology Media/Photo Researchers, Inc.; 52 Sam Dudgeon/HRW; 53 Sam Dudgeon/HRW; 54 (l), Runk/Schoenberger/Grant Heilman; 55 (cl), Biophoto Associates/Science Source/Photo Researchers; 55 (cr), Biophoto Associates/Science Source/Photo Researchers; 55 (br), John Langford/HRW Photo; 58 (l), Lee D. Simons/Science Souce/Photo Researchers; 59 (tr), Courtesy Dr. Jarrel Yakel; 59 (tr), David McCarthy/SPL/Photo Researchers, Inc.

Chapter Three 60-61 Breck P. Kent/Animals Animals/Earth Scenes; 64 (l), Dr. Jeremy Burgess/Science Photo Library/Photo Researchers; 67 (b), Visuals Unlimited/W. Ormerod; 69 (c), Paul Hein/Unicorn; 69 (l), Jerome Wexler/Photo Researchers; 69 (r), George Bernard/Earth Scenes; 70 (b), © Cathlyn Melloan/Getty Images/Stone; 71 (l), R. F. Evert; 71 (r), R. F. Evert; 72 (l), Dick Keen/Unicorn; 72 (r), Visuals Unlimited/ E. Webber; 73 (l), Visuals Unlimited/Bill Beatty; 73 (r), Visuals Unlimited/Bill Beatty; 74 Sam Dudgeon/HRW; 76 Jerome Wexler/Photo Researchers; 77 (t), Dr. Jeremy Burgess/Science Photo Library/Photo Researchers; 80 (l), © AFP/CORBIS; 80 (r), © Robert Landau/CORBIS; 81 (r), International Canopy Network/Evergreen State College; 81 (l), International Canopy Network/Evergreen State College

Unit Two 82 (t), Library of Congress/Corbis; 82 (c), MBL/WHOI Library; 82 (b), NASA; 83 (cr), John Reader/Science Photo Library/Photo Researchers, Inc.; 83 (bl), John Reader/Science Photo Library/Photo Researchers, Inc.; 83 (br), Ted Thai/Time Magazine; 83 (cl), © Ken Eward/Bio Grafx/Photo Researchers, Inc.; 83 (tl), © John Conrad/CORBIS

Chapter Four 84-85 © Maximilian Weinzierl/Alamy Photos; 86 Ned M. Seidler/ National Geographic Society Image Collection; 91 © Andrew Brookes/CORBIS; 92 © Joe McDonald/Visuals Unlimited; 93 (b), Sam Dudgeon/HRW; 95 Digital Image copyright © 2005 PhotoDisc; 96 (b), © Mervyn Rees/Alamy Photos; 97 (b), Image Copyright ©2001 Photodisc, Inc.; 97 (tl), Sam Dudgeon/HRW; 97 (tr), Sam Dudgeon/ HRW; 98 (br), Biophoto Associates/Photo Researchers, Inc.; 98 (b), Phototake/CNRI/ Phototake NYC; 103 (b), © Rob vanNostrand; 104 (b), © ImageState; 105 Biophoto Associates/Photo Researchers, Inc.; 106 (b), Sam Dudgeon/HRW; 107 (b), Sam Dudgeon/HRW; 109 (r), © Mervyn Rees/Alamy Photos; 109 (l), © Rob vanNostrand; 112 (c), Dr. F. R. Turner, Biology Dept., Indiana University; 112 (r), Dr. F. R. Turner, Biology Dept., Indiana University; 112 (l), Hank Morgan/Rainbow; 113, Courtesy of Stacey Wong

Chapter Five 114-115 US Department of Energy/Science Photo Library/Photo Researchers, Inc.; 117 (r), Science Photo Library/Photo Researchers M. Phillips/Visuals Unlimited; 121 (cl), J.R. Paulson & U.K. Laemmli/University of Geneva; 125 (br), Jackie Lewin/Royal Free Hospital/Science Photo Library/Photo Researchers, Inc.; 125 (tr), Jackie Lewin/Royal Free Hospital/Science Photo Library/Photo Researchers, Inc.; 126 (t), Visuals Unlimited/Science Visuals Unlimited/Keith Wood; 126 (b), Volker Steger/Peter Arnold; 127 Sam Dudgeon/HRW; 129 Victoria Smith/HRW; 134 (l), Robert Brook/Science Photo Library/Photo Researchers, Inc.; 135 (r), Photo courtesy of the Whitehead Institute for Biomedical Research at MIT; 135 (l), Garry Watson/ Science Photo Library/Photo Researchers, Inc.

Chapter Six 136-137 (t), © Stuart Westmoreland/CORBIS; 138 (bl), James Beveridge/ Visuals Unlimited; 138 (tc), © Gail Shumway/Getty Images/FPG International; 138 (br), Doug Wechsler/Animals Animals; 140 (l), Ken Lucas; 140 (r), John Cancalosi/ Tom Stack & Associates; 141 (cl), © SuperStock; 141 (bl), © Martin Ruegner/Alamy Photos; 141 (br), © James D. Watt/Stephen Frink Collection/Alamy Photos; 141 (tl), © Ron Kimball/Ron Kimball Stock; 141 (tr), © Carl & Ann Purcell/CORBIS; 141 (cr), © Martin B. Withers; Frank Lane Picture Agency/CORBIS; 142 (tr), Illustration by Carl Buell, and taken from http://www.neoucom.edu/Depts/Anat/Pakicetid.html.; 142 (tl, b), Courtesy of Research Casting International and Dr. J. G. M. Thewissen; 143 (t), © 1998 Philip Gingerich/Courtesy of the Museum of Paleontology, The University of Michigan; 143 (c), Courtesy of Betsy Webb, Pratt Museum, Homer, Alaska; 143 (b), Courtesy of Betsy Webb, Pratt Museum, Homer, Alaska; 145 (b), Visuals Unlimited/ H.W. Robison; 145 (t), James Beveridge/Visuals Unlimited; 146 (l), Christopher Ralling; 146 (r), © William E. Ferguson; 148 (b), Carolyn A. McKeone/Photo Researchers, Inc.; 152 (b), Getty Images/Stone; 155 (r), Zig Leszczynski/Animals Animals/Earth Scenes; 155 (l), Gary Mezaros/Visuals Unlimited; 157 Victoria Smith/ HRW; 158 (t), James Beveridge/Visuals Unlimited; 159 Courtesy of Betsy Webb, Pratt Museum, Homer, Alaska; 162 (l), Doug Wilson/Westlight; 163 (r), Wally Emerson/ Courtesy of Raymond Pierotti; 163 (l), George D. Lepp/Photo Researchers, Inc.

Chapter Seven 164-165 © Reuters NewMedia Inc./CORBIS; 178 (r), © Daniel J. Cox/Getty Images/Stone; 180 (b), John Reader/Science Photo Library/Photo Researchers; 180 (t), © Partick Robert/CORBIS; 181 John Gurche; 182 (tr), John Reader/Science Photo Library/Photo Researchers; 182 (tl & tc), E.R. Degginger/Bruce Coleman; 182 (bl), Neanderthal Museum; 182 (br), Volker Steger/Nordstar-4 Million Years of Man/Science Photo Library/Photo Researchers, Inc.; 190 (r), Rikki Larma/AP/ Wide World Photos; 190 (l), Copyright M. Ponce de León and Christoph Zollikofer, Zurich; 191 (r), © Robert Campbell/CORBIS; 191 (l), John Reader/Science Photo Library/Photo Researchers, Inc.

Unit Three 192 (tl), Science Photo Library/Photo Researchers, Inc; 192 (c), Francois Gohier; 192 (bl), © UPI/ Bettmann/CORBIS; 192 (br), Thomas Laird/Peter Arnold, Inc; 193 (tl), Science VU/Visuals Unlimited; 193 (tr), SuperStock; 193 (cl), AP/Wide World Photos; 193 (cr), NASA/Image State; 193 (br), File/AP/Wide World Photos

Chapter Eight 194-195, JPL/NASA; 196, Royal Geographical Society, London, UK/The Bridgeman Art Library; 197 (t), Sam Dudgeon/HRW; 197 (b), Tom Pantages Photography; 198, Sam Dudgeon/HRW; 202 (bl, br), Andy Christiansen/HRW; 206, Texas Department of Transportation; 207, Spaceimaging.com/Getty Images/NewsCom; 208 (bl, bc, br), Strategic Planning Office, City of Seattle; 208 (tl), Getty/NewsCom; 209, Andy Christiansen/HRW; 210, USGS; 211 (tl), USGS; 211 (tr), USGS; 212, USGS; 215, Sam Dudgeon/HRW; 217, USGS; 217 (br), Strategic Planning Office, City of Seattle; 220 (r), JPL/NASA; 220 (l), Victoria Smith/HRW; 221 (r), Bettman/CORBIS; 221 (bl), Layne Kennedy/CORBIS

Chapter Nine 222-223, Terry Wilson; 224, Sam Dudgeon/HRW; 225 (br), © Wendell E. Wilson; 226 (tr), Victoria Smith/HRW; 226 (bc), Sam Dudgeon/HRW; 226 (tl), Sam Dudgeon/HRW; 227, (copper), E. R. Degginger/Color-Pic, Inc.; 227, (calcite), E. R. Degginger/Color-Pic, Inc.; 227, (fluorite), E. R. Degginger/Color-Pic, Inc.; 227, (corundum), E. R. Degginger/Color-Pic, Inc.; 227, (gypsum), SuperStock; 227, (galena), Visuals Unlimited/Ken Lucas; 228, (vitreous), Biophoto Associates/Photo Researchers, Inc.; 228, (waxy), Biophoto Associates/Photo Researchers, Inc.; 228, (silky), Dr. E.R. Degginger/Bruce Coleman Inc.; 228, (submetallic), John Cancalosi 1989/DRK Photo; 228 (bl), Komatsu Mining Systems; 228, (resinous), Charles D. Winters/Photo Researchers, Inc.; 228, (pearly), Victoria Smith/HRW; 228, (metallic), Victoria Smith/HRW; 228, (earthy), Sam Dudgeon/HRW; 229 (tr, c, bl), Sam Dudgeon/HRW; 229, Tom Pantages; 230, (1), Visuals Unlimited/Ken Lucas; 230, (3), Visuals Unlimited/Dane S. Johnson; 230, (7), Carlyn Iverson/Absolute Science Illustration and Photography; 230, (8), Mark A. Schneider/Visuals Unlimited; 230, (9), Charles D. Winters/Photo Researchers, Inc.; 230, (10), Bard Wrisley; 230, (5), Biophoto Associates/Photo Researchers, Inc.; 230, (6), Victoria Smith/HRW; 230, (4), Mark A. Schneider/Photo Researchers, Inc.; 230, (2), Sam Dudgeon/HRW; 231 (tc), Sam Dudgeon/HRW; 231 (tr), Sam Dudgeon/HRW, Courtesy Science Stuff, Austin, TX; 231 (br), Tom Pantages Photography; 231 (bc), Sam Dudgeon/HRW; 231 (tl), Mark A. Schneider/Photo Researchers, Inc.; 231 (tl), Mark A. Schneider/Photo Researchers, Inc.; 231 (bl), 232 (t), Sam Dudgeon/HRW; 232 (bl), Victoria Smith/HRW Photo, Courtesy Science Stuff, Austin, TX; 232 (c), Breck P. Kent; 233 (br), Sam Dudgeon/HRW; 233 (c), Breck P. Kent; 233 (t), Visuals Unlimited/Ken Lucas; 234 (bl), © Lester Lefkowitz/CORBIS; 234 (br), Wernher Krutein; 235, Stewart Cohen/Index Stock Photography, Inc.; 236, Digital Image copyright © 2005 PhotoDisc; 237 (tr) © SuperStock; 238 (c), Russell Dian/HRW; 238 (b), 239 (tr), Sam Dudgeon/HRW; 240, Digital Image copyright © 2005 PhotoDisc; 241 (b), E. R. Degginger/Color-Pic, Inc.; 244 (tr), Esch Thierry/Paris Match/Gamma; 245 (t), Will & Dennie McIntyre/McIntyre Photography; 245 (b), Mark Schneider/Visuals Unlimited

Chapter Ten 246-247, Tom Till; 248 (bl), Michael Melford/Getty Images/The Image Bank; 248 (br), Joseph Sohm; Visions of America/CORBIS; 249, CORBIS Images/HRW; 252 (t), Joyce Photographics/Photo Researchers, Inc.; 252 (l), Pat Lanza/Bruce Coleman Inc.; 252 (r), Sam Dudgeon/HRW; 252 (b), James Watt/Animals Animals/Earth Scenes; 252 (l), Pat Lanza/Bruce Coleman Inc.; 253, (granite), Pat Lanza/Bruce Coleman Inc.; 253, (mica), E. R. Degginger/Color-Pic, Inc.; 253, (aragonite), Breck P. Kent; 253, (limestone), Breck P. Kent; 253, (calcite), Mark Schneider/Visuals Unlimited; 253, (feldspar), Mark Schneider/Visuals Unlimited; 253, (quartz), Digital Image copyright © 2005 PhotoDisc; 254 (tl), Sam Dudgeon/HRW; 254 (tc), Dorling Kindersley; 254 (tr, br), Breck P. Kent; 254 (bl), E. R. Degginger/Color-Pic, Inc.; 255, Joseph Sohm; Visions of America/CORBIS; 256 (l), E. R. Degginger/Color-Pic, Inc.; 257 (tr, tl, bl), Breck P. Kent; 257 (br), Victoria Smith/HRW; 259, J.D. Griggs/USGS; 260, CORBIS Images/HRW; 261, (conglomerate), Breck P. Kent; 261, (siltstone), Sam Dudgeon/HRW; 261, (sandstone), Joyce Photographics/Photo Researchers, Inc.; 261, (shale), Sam Dudgeon/HRW; 262 (tl), Stephen Frink/Corbis; 262 (br), Breck P. Kent; 262 (bc), David Muench/CORBIS; 263, Franklin P. OSF/Animals Animals/Earth Scenes; 264, George Wuerthner; 266, (calcite), Dane S. Johnson/Visuals Unlimited; 266, (quartz), Carlyn Iverson/Absolute Science Illustration and Photography; 266, (hematite), Breck P. Kent; 266, (garnet), Breck P. Kent/Animals Animals/Earth Scenes; 266, (chlorite), Sam Dudgeon/HRW; 266, (mica), Tom Pantages; 267, (shale), Ken Karp/HRW; 267, (slate), Sam Dudgeon/HRW; 267, (phyllite), Sam Dudgeon/HRW; 267, (gneiss), Breck P. Kent; 267, (schist), Sam Dudgeon/HRW; 268 (tl), E. R. Degginger/Color-Pic, Inc.; 268 (bl), Ray Simmons/Photo Researchers, Inc; 268 (tr), Andy Christiansen/HRW; 268 (br), Breck P. Kent; 269, Jim Wark/Airphoto; 271 (t), Sam Dudgeon/HRW; 271 (b), James Tallon; 276 (l), Wolfgang Kaehler/CORBIS; 276 (tr), Dr. David Kring/Science Photo Library/Photo Researchers, Inc.; 277 (r), James Miller/Courtesy Robert Folk, Department of Geological Sciences, University of Texas at Austin; 277 (l), Dr. Philppa Uwins, Whistler Research PTY/SPL/Photo Researchers, Inc.

Chapter Eleven 278, National Geographic Image Collection/Jonathan Blair, Courtesy Hessian Regional Museum, Darmstadt, Germany; 281, Dr. Clifford E. Ford; 283, Courtesy of Museum of Northern Arizona Photo Archives; 284 (l), Sam Dudgeon/HRW; 284 (r), Andy Christiansen/HRW; 286 (tl), Fletcher & Baylis/Photo Researchers, Inc.; 286 (tr), Ken M. Johns/Photo Researchers, Inc.; 286 (bl), Glenn M. Oliver/Visuals Unlimited; 286 (br), Francois Gohier/Photo Researchers, Inc.; 291, Sam Dudgeon/HRW; 292, Tom Till/DRK Photo; 293, Courtesy Charles S. Tucek/University of Arizona at Tucson; 294, Howard Grey/Getty Images/Stone; 295, Francis Latreille/Nova Productions/AP/Wide World Photos; 296 (b), The G.R. "Dick" Roberts Photo Library; 296 (t), © Louie Psihoyos/psihoyos.com; 297 (l), Brian Exton; 297 (r), Chip Clark/Smithsonian; 299, Thomas R. Taylor/Photo Researchers, Inc.; 300, James L. Amos/CORBIS; 301 (tl), Tom Till Photography; 301 (fish), Tom Bean/CORBIS; 301 (leaf), James L. Amos/CORBIS; 301 (turtle), Layne Kennedy/CORBIS; 301 (fly), Ken Lucas/Visuals Unlimited; 303, Chip Clark/Smithsonian; 304 (t), Neg. no. 5793 Courtesy Dept. of Library Services, American Museum of Natural History; 304 (b), Neg. no. 5799 Courtesy Department of Library Services, American Museum of Natural History; 305, Neg. no. 5801 Courtesy Department of Library Services, American Museum of Natural History; 306, Jonathan Blair/CORBIS; 308 (b), The G.R. "Dick" Roberts Photo Library; 309 (fly), Ken Lucas/Visuals Unlimited; 312 (tl), Beth A. Keiser/AP/Wide World Photos; 312 (tr), Jonathan Blair/CORBIS; 313, Courtesy Kevin C. May

Unit Four 314 (tl), Charles Scribner's Sons NY, 1906; 314 (bl), USGS/NASA/Science Source/Photo Researchers, Inc.; 315 (tl), © Bettmann/CORBIS; 315 (tr), © Bettmann/CORBIS; 315 (c), Lambert/Hulton Archive/Getty Images; 315 (cr), Steve Winter/National Geographic Society; 315 (cl), Randy Duchaine/Corbis Stock Market; 315 (b), Robotics Institute Carnegie Mellon University

Chapter Twelve 316-317 © Studio Carlo Dani/Animals Animals/Earth Scenes; 322 (t), Grant Heilman; 322 (b), Tom Brakefield/Bruce Coleman; 324 (t), © Kathy Bushue/Getty Images/Stone; 326-327 (b), Stuart Westmoreland/Getty Images/Stone; 326 (inset), Manfred Kage/Peter Arnold; 330 (b), © Jeff Hunter/Getty Images/The Image Bank; 334 (t), Dwight Kuhn; 334 (b), Hardie Truesdale/International Stock; 337 Sam Dudgeon/HRW; 342 (r), Dr. Verena Tunnicliffe; 342 (l), © Raymond Gehman/CORBIS; 343 (t), Lincoln P. Brower, Sweet Briar College; 343 (b), © Royalty-Free/CORBIS

Chapter Thirteen 344-345, Jeff Schmaltz, MODIS Rapid Response Team, NASA/GSFC; 348 (t), "World Ocean Map", Bruce C. Heezen and Marie Tharp, 1977, © Marie Tharp 1977. Reproduced by permission of Marie Tharp, 1 Washington Avenue, South Nyack, NY 10960; 349 (b), © Patrick Robert/Sygma/CORBIS; 351, Steve Satushek/Brand X Pictures/gettyimages; 358, CORBIS; 360, Rosenstiel School of Marine and Atmospheric Science, University of Miami; 361, Randy Wells/Stone/Getty Images; 362, Provided by the SeaWiFS Project, NASA/Goddard Space Flight Center and ORBIMAGE/NASA/Seawifs; 364 (t), Joyce Photographics/Photo Researchers, Inc.; 364 (l), Pat Lanza/Bruce Coleman Inc.; 364 (r), Sam Dudgeon/HRW; 364 (b), James Watt/Animals Animals/Earth Scenes; 367, © Joseph Sohm; Visions of America/CORBIS; 369 (t), Sam Dudgeon/HRW; 369 (b), Sam Dudgeon/HRW; 374 (t), Courtesy Stephen H. Hickman, USGS; 375 (t), Dr. Ashanti Pyrtle, College of Marine Science, University of South Florida; 375 (b), Dr. Ashanti Pyrtle, College of Marine Science, University of South Florida

Chapter Fourteen 376-377, James Balog/Getty Images/Stone; 379 (t), James Wall/Animals Animals/Earth Scenes; 382, Bruce C. Heezen and Marie Tharp; 393 (tc), ESA/CE/Eurocontrol/Science Photo Library/Photo Researchers, Inc.; 393 (tr), NASA; 394 (bl, br), Peter Van Steen/HRW; 395 (bc), Visuals Unlimited/SylvesterAllred; 395 (br), G.R. Roberts Photo Library; 397 (tl), Tom Bean; 397 (tr), Landform Slides; 398, Jay Dickman/CORBIS; 399 (b), Michele & Tom Grimm Photography; 400, Y. Arthus-B./Peter Arnold, Inc.; 401, Peter Van Steen/HRW; 403, Sam Dudgeon/HRW; 408 (bl), NASA/Science Photo Library/Photo Researchers, Inc.; 408 (c), Painting © Fran Seigel; 408 (tr), Photo by S. Thorarinsson/Solar-Filma/Sun Film-15/3/courtesy of Edward T. Baker, Pacific Marine Environmental Laboratory, NOAA; 409 (r), Bettman/CORBIS

Chapter Fifteen 410-411, Robert Patrick/Sygma/CORBIS; 413, Roger Ressmeyer/CORBIS; 419, Earth Images/Getty Images/Stone; 421, Bettmann/CORBIS; 424, Michael S. Yamashita/CORBIS; 426, Paul Chesley/Getty Images/Stone; 428, NOAA/NGDC; 429, Sam Dudgeon/HRW; 431, Bettmann/CORBIS; 434, Sam Dudgeon/HRW; 434 (t), Courtesy Stephen H. Hickman, USGS; 435 (t), Todd Bigelow/HRW; 435 (b), Corbis Images

Chapter Sixteen 436-437, Carl Shaneff/Pacific Stock; 438 (bl), National Geographic Image Collection/Robert W. Madden; 438 (br), Ken Sakamoto/Black Star; 439 (b), Breck P. Kent/Animals Animals/Earth Scenes; 439, Joyce Warren/USGS Photo Library; 441 (tl), Tui De Roy/Minden Pictures; 441 (bl), B. Murton/Southampton Oceanography Centre/Science Photo Library/Photo Researchers, Inc.; 441 (tr), Visuals Unlimited/Martin Miller; 441 (br), Buddy Mays/CORBIS; 442 (tr), Tom Bean/DRK Photo; 442 (tl), Francois Gohier/Photo Researchers, Inc.; 442, (tlc), Visuals Unlimited Inc./Glenn Oliver; 442, (tlb), E. R. Degginger/Color-Pic, Inc.; 443 (tr), Alberto Garcia/SABA/CORBIS; 443, Robert W. Madden/National Geographic Society; 444, Images & Volcans/Photo Researchers, Inc.; 445 (br), SuperStock; 445 (cr), SuperStock; 445 (tr), Roger Ressmeyer/CORBIS; 446 (tl), Yann Arthus-Bertrand/CORBIS; 447, Joseph Sohm; ChromoSohm Inc./CORBIS; 452 (bl), Robert McGimsey/USGS Alaska Volcano Observatory; 456 (tr), Alberto Garcia/SABA/CORBIS; 460 (bl), CORBIS; 460 (tr), © Bettmann/CORBIS; 460 (tc), © Sigurgeir Jonasson; Frank Lane Picture Agency/CORBIS; 461 (bl), Courtesy Christina Neal; 461 (r), Courtesy Alaska Volcano Observatory

Unit Five 462 (t), Corbis-Bettmann; 462 (bl), Enrico Tedeschi; 462 (c), UPI/CORBIS/Bettman; 463 (cr), REUTERS/William Philpott/NewsCom; 463 (cl), Sam Dudgeon/HRW; 463 (tr), Brown Brothers/HRW Photo Library; 463 (bl), ©Natalie Fobes/Getty Images; 463 (br), REUTERS/Charles W. Luzier/NewsCom

Chapter Seventeen 464-465 (all), Mark Renders/Getty Images; 466 (b), Sam Dudgeon/HRW; 466 (bc), Digital Image copyright © 2005 PhotoDisc; 467 (cr), Sam Dudgeon/HRW; 468 (cl), Sam Dudgeon/HRW; 468 (cl), Victoria Smith/HRW; 469 (all), Sam Dudgeon/HRW; 470 (tl), John Langford/HRW; 470 (br), Corbis Images; 472 (b), Sam Dudgeon/HRW; 473 (tl), Victoria Smith/HRW; 473 (tr, tc, c), Sam Dudgeon/HRW; 473 (cl), Peter Van Steen/HRW; 473 (cr, bl), John Morrison/Morrison Photography; 474 (tl), Richard Megna/Fundamental Photographs; 474 (bl), Victoria Smith/HRW; 476 (tr), Lance Schriner/HRW; 476 (tl), John Langford/HRW; 477 (tr), Victoria Smith/HRW; 477 (inset), Sam Dudgeon/HRW; 478 (br), Rob Boudreau/Getty Images; 479 (cl, cr), Charlie Winters/HRW; 479 (tl, tr), Sam Dudgeon/HRW; 480 (c, cr), Morrison Photography; 480 (bl), Joseph Drivas/Getty Images; 480 (br), © SuperStock; 481 (all), Sam Dudgeon/HRW; 482 (all), Charlie Winters/HRW; 483 (tr), CORBIS Images/HRW; 484 (b), Sam Dudgeon/HRW; 486 (bc), Richard Megna/Fundamental Photographs; 487 (cr), Lance Schriner/HRW; 490 (tl), © David Young-Wolff/PhotoEdit; 491 (cr), Courtesy Mimi So; 491 (b), Steve Cole/PhotoDisc/PictureQuest

Chapter Eighteen 492-493 (all), Teresa Nouri Rishel/Dale Chihuly Studio; 495 (bl), Digital Image copyright © 2005 PhotoDisc; 495 (br), Susumu Nishinaga/Science Photo Library/Photo Researchers, Inc.; 496 (tr), Victoria Smith/HRW; 496 (bl), © Dr Jeremy Burgess/Photo Researchers, Inc.; 497 (tr), Scott Van Osdol/HRW; 498 (br), AP Photo/Beth Keiser; 499 (bl), Corbis Images; 499 (br), Victoria Smith/HRW; 503 (bc), Scott Van Osdol/HRW; 503 (tr), Richard Megna/Fundamental Photographs; 505 (bl), Ed Reschke/Peter Arnold, Inc.; 506 (tl), Omni Photo Communications, Inc./Index Stock Imagery, Inc.; 508 (br), Victoria Smith/HRW; 509 (br), Sam Dudgeon/HRW; 510 (bc), Sam Dudgeon/HRW; 511 (bl), Charles D. Winters/Photo Researchers, Inc.; 514 (tr), CORBIS Images/HRW; 514 (tl), Scoones/SIPA Press; 515 (cr), Susanna Frohman/San Jose Mercury News/NewsCom; 515 (bl), Andrew Goldsworthy

Chapter Nineteen 516-517 (all), Scott Van Osdol/HRW; 518 (br), Jonathan Blair/Woodfin Camp & Associates, Inc.; 518 (bl), Victoria Smith/HRW; 519 (br), Russ Lappa/Photo Researchers, Inc.; 519 (bl, bc), Charles D. Winters/Photo Researchers, Inc.; 520 (tl), © Zack Burris/Zack Burris, Inc.; 520 (tcl), Yann Arthus-Bertrand/CORBIS; 520 (tcr, tr), Walter Chandoha; 521 (lead), Victoria Smith/HRW; 521 (copper, tin, sulfur), Sam Dudgeon/HRW; 521 (neon), Runk/Shoenberger/Grant Heilman Photography Inc.; 521 (silicon), Joyce Photographics/Photo Researchers, Inc.; 521 (boron), Russ Lappa/Photo Researchers, Inc.; 521 (antimony), Charles D. Winters/Photo Researchers, Inc.; 521 (iodine), Larry Stepanowicz; 522 (bl), Runk/Schoenberger/Grant Heilman Photography Inc.; 523 (bl), Runk/Shoenberger/Grant Heilman Photography; 523 (bc), Richard Megna/Fundamental Photographs; 523 (br), Sam Dudgeon/HRW; 524 (tl), Richard Megna/Fundamental Photographs; 525 (tr), John Kaprielian/Photo Researchers, Inc.; 526 (br), Sam Dudgeon/HRW; 527 (tl), Charles D. Winters; 527 (cl), Sam Dudgeon/HRW; 527 (bc), Charles D. Winters/Photo Researchers, Inc.; 527 (bl), Klaus Guldbrandsen/Science Photo Library/Photo Researchers, Inc.; 527 (tr, cr, br), John Langford/HRW; 528 (tl), Sam Dudgeon/HRW; 529 (bl), Richard Haynes/HRW; 530 (tr), Sam Dudgeon/HRW; 531 (all), John Langford/HRW; 532 (bl), HRW; 532 (br), Lance Schriner/HRW; 533 (tr), Sam Dudgeon/HRW; 534 (bl), © Stuart Westmoreland/Getty Images; 535 (b), Sam Dudgeon/HRW; 536 (tr), Sam Dudgeon/HRW; 536 (tl), Walter Chandoha; 537 (tr), Sam Dudgeon/HRW; 540 (tl), Peter Van Steen/HRW; 541 (tr), Courtesy of Aundra Nix; 541 (cr), Astrid & Hans-Frieder Michler/SPL/Photo Researchers, Inc.

Chapter Twenty 542-543 (all), P. Loiez Cern/Science Photo Library/Photo Researchers, Inc.; 544 (bl), Victoria Smith/HRW; 544 (bc), Courtesy JEOL; 545 (b), Corbis-Bettmann; 548 (br), John Zoiner; 548 (bc), Mavournea Hay/HRW; 550 (b), Sam Dudgeon/HRW; 555 (tr), Corbis Images; 557 (b), Sam Dudgeon/HRW; 558 (br), Victoria Smith/HRW; 559 (br), Sam Dudgeon/HRW; 560 (bl), Corbis-Bettmann; 561 (bl), Fermilab; 564 (tr), NASA; 564 (tl), Giraudon/Art Resource, NY; 565 (br), Fermi National Accelerator Laboratory/CORBIS; 565 (tr), Stephen Maclone

Chapter Twenty One 566-567 (all), Gerard Perrone/Courtesy of Eric Ehlenberger; 569 (tr), Sam Dudgeon/HRW; 572 (all), Sam Dudgeon/HRW; 573 (tr), Sam Dudgeon/HRW; 573 (tc), Richard Megna/Fundamental Photographs; 573 (bl), Russ Lappa/Photo Researchers, Inc.; 573 (bc), Lester V. Bergman/Corbis-Bettmann; 573 (tl), Sally Anderson-Bruce/HRW; 574 (bc, br), Richard Megna/Fundamental Photographs; 574 (bl), Tom Pantages Photography; 575 (br), HRW; 575 (tr), Sam Dudgeon/HRW; 576 (bl), Charles D. Winters/Photo Researchers, Inc.; 576 (bc, br), Richard Megna/Fundamental Photographs; 577 (tr), Sam Dudgeon/HRW; 578 (tl, cl), Sam Dudgeon/HRW; 578 (tr), ©1990 P. Petersen/Custom Medical Stock Photo; 578 (tc, bl), Victoria Smith/HRW; 579 (cr), Phillip Hayson/Photo Researchers, Inc.; 579 (br), Sam Dudgeon/HRW; 580 (tl), Sam Dudgeon/HRW; 580 (b), CORBIS Images/HRW; 581 (tl, tc), Richard Megna/Fundamental Photographs; 581 (tr), Charlie Winters/HRW; 582 (bl), NASA; 582 (tl), © Jeff Greenberg/Visuals Unlimited; 583 (tr), Sam Dudgeon/HRW; 584 (b), Sam Dudgeon/HRW; 585 (br), John Langford/HRW; 586 (tl), Sam Dudgeon/HRW; 590 (tr), CORBIS Images/HRW; 591 (cr), © Lawrence Berkeley National Laboratory/Photo Researchers, Inc.; 591 (cl), © Bettmann/CORBIS

Unit Six 592 (c), Argonne National Laboratory/Corbis-Bettmann; 592 (b), Wally McNamee/Corbis; 593 (tr), Sygma; 593 (bl), Reuters/Nasa/Hulton Archive/Getty Images; 593 (c), Archive France/Hulton Archive/Getty Images; 593 (br), General Motors Corporation. Used with permission, GM Media Archives.

Chapter Twenty Two 594-595 (all), © Doug Struthers/Getty Images; 596 (bl), © Charles Gupton/CORBIS; 600 (br), © Konrad Wothe/Minden Pictures; 603 (cl), Paul Silverman/Fundamental Photographs; 606 (tr), Sam Dudgeon/HRW; 607 (tc), Sam Dudgeon/HRW; 607 (bl), © Jonathan Blair/CORBIS; 608 (tr), Victoria Smith/HRW; 609 (tr), John Langford/HRW; 611 (b), Sam Dudgeon/HRW; 612 (br), Victoria Smith/HRW; 613 (cr, br), Sam Dudgeon/HRW; 613 (tc), © Konrad Wothe/Minden Pictures; 616 (tr), Peter Oxford/Nature Picture Library; 616 (tl), Diaphor Agency/Index Stock Imagery, Inc.; 617 (cr), Steve Fischbach/HRW; 617 (bl), W. & D. McIntyre/Photo Researchers, Inc.

Chapter Twenty Three 618-619 (all), Corbis Images; 620 (bl), Rob Matheson/The Stock Market; 620 (br), Sam Dudgeon/HRW; 621 (cl, cr), Richard Megna/Fundamental Photographs, New York; 621 (br), Scott Van Osdol/HRW; 621 (bl), J.T. Wright/Bruce Coleman Inc./Picture Quest; 622 (all), Charlie Winters; 623 (br), Charlie Winters/HRW; 626 (tl), John Langford/HRW; 626 (bl), Richard Haynes/HRW; 627 (tr), Charles D. Winters/Photo Researchers, Inc.; 627 (tc), John Langford/HRW; 627 (tl), © Ingram Publishing; 632 (tl), Peticolas/Megna/Fundamental Photographs; 632 (tr), Richard Megna/Fundamental Photographs; 634 (bl), Victoria Smith/HRW; 634 (bc), Peter Van Steen/HRW; 634 (br), © Tom Stewart/The Stock Market; 635 (br), © David Stoecklein/CORBIS; 636 (t), Michael Newman/PhotoEdit; 637 (cr), Richard Megna/Fundamental Photographs; 638 (t), Sam Dudgeon/HRW; 639 (tr), Dorling Kindersley Limited courtesy of the Science Museum, London/CORBIS; 639 (bl), Victoria Smith/HRW; 640 (b), Victoria Smith/HRW; 642 (tr), Richard Megna/Fundamental Photographs; 643 (cr), Richard Megna/Fundamental Photographs; 643 (br), Rob Matheson/The Stock Market; 646 (tr), Tony Freeman/PhotoEdit; 646 (tl), Henry Bargas/Amarillo Globe-News/AP/Wide World Photos; 647 (all), Bob Parker/Austin Fire Investigation

Chapter Twenty Four 648-649 (all), © Dr. Dennis Kunkel/Visuals Unlimited; 650 (bl), © Andrew Syred/Microscopix Photolibrary; 651 (all), Richard Megna/Fundamental Photographs; 652 (b), Victoria Smith/HRW; 653 (tr), Richard Megna/Fundamental Photographs; 654 (br), Jack Newkirk/HRW; 655 (br), Charles D. Winters/Timeframe Photography, Inc.; 655 (tl, tr), Peter Van Steen/HRW; 656 (br), Tom Tracy/The Stock Shop/Medichrome; 657 (tc), Victoria Smith/HRW; 657 (tr), © Peter Cade/Getty Images; 657 (tl), © Bob Thomason/Getty Images; 658 (all), Peter Van Steen/HRW; 659 (tr), Peter Van Steen/HRW; 662 (bl), Digital Image copyright © 2005 PhotoDisc; 662 (tl), Victoria Smith/HRW; 662 (tc, tr), Scott Van Osdol/HRW; 663 (tr), Miro Vinton/Stock Boston/PictureQuest; 665 (tl), Sam Dudgeon/HRW; 665 (tc), John Langford/HRW; 665 (tr), Charles D. Winters/Timeframe Photography, Inc.; 666 (tc), Digital Image copyright © 2005 PhotoDisc; 667 (bl), Sam Dudgeon/HRW; 668 (tl), Hans Reinhard/Bruce Coleman, Inc.; 669 (tr), CORBIS Images/HRW; 670 (b), Sam Dudgeon/HRW; 672 (tr), Peter Van Steen/HRW; 673 (all), Digital Image copyright © 2005 PhotoDisc; 676 (tr), Dan Loh/AP/Wide World Photos; 676 (tl), Sygma; 677 (tr), Nicole Guglielmo; 677 (bl), Corbis Images

Chapter Twenty Five 678-679 (all), GJLP/CNRI/PhotoTake; 680 (br), Henri Becquerel/The Granger Collection; 680 (bl), Roberto De Gugliemo/Science Photo Library/Photo Researchers, Inc.; 681 (tr), Digital Image copyright © 2005 PhotoDisc; 684 (br), Sygma; 686 (br), Tim Wright/CORBIS; 686 (bl), Custom Medical Stock Photo; 687 (tr), Roberto De Gugliemo/Science Photo Library/Photo Researchers, Inc.; 689 (tr), Emory Kristof/National Geographic Society Image Collection; 691 (tr), © Shone/Gamma; 693 (tc), Sam Dudgeon/HRW; 693 (tr), John Langford/HRW; 694 (all), Sam Dudgeon/HRW; 695 (b), Sam Dudgeon/HRW; 696 (tl), Tim Wright/CORBIS; 697 (bl), John Langford/HRW; 697 (cr), Science Photo Library/Photo Researchers, Inc.; 700 (tl), Courtesy USDA; 700 (tr), SABA Press Photos, Inc.; 701 (cr), © Underwood & Underwood/CORBIS; 701 (bl), © The Nobel Foundation

STAFF CREDITS

The people who contributed to *Holt Science & Technology* are listed below. They represent editorial, design, production, eMedia, permissions, and marketing.

Chris Allison, Melanie Baccus, Wesley M. Bain, Juan Baquera, Angela Beckmann, Ed Blake, Sara Buller, Marc Burgamy, Rebecca Calhoun, Kimberly Cammerata, Soojinn Choi, Eddie Dawson, Julie Dervin, Michelle Dike, Lydia Doty, Jen Driscoll, Leigh Ann García, Catherine Gnader, Diana Goetting, Tim Hovde, Wilonda Ieans, Jevara Jackson, Simon Key, Jane A. Kirschman, Cathy Kuhles, Laura Likon, Denise Mahoney, Michael Mazza, Kristen McCardel, Richard Metzger, Micah Newman, Janice Noske, Joeleen Ornt, Cathy Paré, Jenny Patton, Laura Prescott, Bill Rader, Peter D. Reid, Curtis Riker, Michael Rinella, Jeff Robinson, Audrey Rozsypal, Beth Sample, Margaret Sanchez, Kay Selke, Elizabeth Simmons, Chris Smith, Dawn Marie Spinozza, Sherry Sprague, Jeff Streber, JoAnn Stringer, Roshan Strong, Jeannie Taylor , Bob Tucek, Tam Voynick, Clay Walton, Kira J. Watkins, Ken Whiteside, Holly Whittaker, David Wisnieski, Monica Yudron, Patty Zepeda